= Author's Trips

Scale

MILES

0 50 100   200   300   400   500

Books by JOHN GUNTHER

INSIDE U. S. A.

INSIDE LATIN AMERICA

INSIDE ASIA

INSIDE EUROPE

D DAY

THE TROUBLED MIDNIGHT

THE HIGH COST OF HITLER

INSIDE
U. S. A.

By JOHN GUNTHER
Author of INSIDE EUROPE, INSIDE ASIA,
INSIDE LATIN AMERICA

HARPER & BROTHERS

NEW YORK AND LONDON 1947

INSIDE U. S. A.

PRINTED IN THE UNITED STATES OF AMERICA BY
KINGSPORT PRESS, INC., KINGSPORT, TENNESSEE

TABLE OF CONTENTS

Foreword—ix

Chapter

1. California the Golden—1
2. A Bouquet of Californians—18
3. More About California, Its How and Why—42
4. Life and Works of Henry Kaiser—64
5. Ghosts and Silver in Nevada—76
6. Pacific Northwest Coming Up—85
7. Two Freshmen from the Mountain Slopes—102
8. Highways in the Sky—118
9. Staff and Stuff of Life, Plus Timber—134
10. Invitation to the West—144
11. The Montana Frontier—155
12. MVA vs. Behemoth River—183
13. Utah and the Mormons: Profile of a Community—190
14. —But Scenery Is Not Enough—213
15. "Stop Roaming, Try Wyoming"—227
16. The Miraculous Dakotas—237
17. On the Extreme Particularity of Kansas—256
18. Mind of the Middle West—270
19. Stassen: Young Man Going Somewhere—293
20. More About Minnesota, Plus Wisconsin—309
21. Iowa, Corn and Pigs—328
22. Notes for a Portrait of Missouri—341
23. Chicago Tribune, Illinois, and Indiana—359
24. A Talk with Vandenberg—391
25. World on Wheels: Ford Dynasty & UAW—398
26. Men and Politics in Ohio—422
27. —And More from the Ohio Mill—441
28. Inside New England I—456
29. Saltonstall—475
30. Inside New England II—485
31. Natural History in Massachusetts—507
32. New York: Dewey and the State—523
33. New York: Sketch of Megalopolis, with a Word on Wall Street—549
34. The Not-So-Little Flower—578
35. Hague Machine and New Jersey—589

v

36. The Great State of Pennsylvania—600
37. Pennsylvania: Steel and Pittsburgh—615
38. Atlantic Seaboard—630
39. Romance and Reality in Kentucky—640
40. The South: Problem Child of the Nation—653
41. Negro in the Woodpile—679
42. The Southeastern Marches—705
43. Model TVA—731
44. More About Tennessee, Plus Arkansas—749
45. Arnall, Talmadge, and the State of Georgia—767
46. Cotton, No Longer King, and the Former Realm of Huey Long—790
47. The Giant World of Texas—814
48. Who and Why in Texas Politics—839
49. University, God, and Beef—855
50. Oklahoma and the Indians—869
51. Last Stop: the New States of the Southwest—886
52. Finale—907
    Acknowledgments; List of Names—921
    Bibliography; Sources—935
    Index—947
                    List of Maps
    Chart—viii
    California and Nevada—2
    The Northwest—86
    Rocky Mountains and Great Plains—146
    Middle West—272
    The New England States—458
    New York and Pennsylvania—524
    The Southeastern States—654
    Mississippi Valley South—750
    Texas and Oklahoma—816
    West and Southwest—888

I hear America singing, the varied carols I hear.

—WALT WHITMAN

France was a land, England was a people, but America, having
about it still the quality of the idea, was harder to utter—
it was the graves at Shiloh, and the tired, drawn, nervous
faces of its great men, and the country boys dying in the
Argonne for a phrase that was empty before their bodies
withered. It was a willingness of the heart . . .

—F. SCOTT FITZGERALD

I like Americans.

—EDNA ST. VINCENT MILLAY

Now the dark waters at the bow
fold back, like earth against the plow;
foam brightens like the dogwood now
    at home, in my own country.

—MALCOLM COWLEY

Foreword

〜〜

This book follows its companion volumes *Inside Europe, Inside Asia,* and *Inside Latin America* as a reporter's attempt to chart another continental segment of the known political world of today. *Inside Europe* was in part a study of nationalism, *Inside Asia* of imperialism, *Inside Latin America* of colonial politics and economy; this book is a study of democracy in action. Its central spine and substance is an effort—in all diffidence—to show this most fabulous and least known of countries, the United States of America, to itself.

We begin with California—its crackpotism, its climate intellectual and otherwise, its social and political topography—and proceed slowly up the Pacific coast. We inspect the Northwestern states, foaming with social energy, and continue in a broad eccentric circle through the giant West. We swing down the massive cordillera of the Rockies, emerge into the Great Plains, and penetrate to the vastness of the middle western states and their profuse galaxy of trends, issues, problems. We make an upward detour through what used to be the mother and father of us all, New England, and then reach the detonating and labyrinthine complex of New York, with its get-rich-quickism, its social and political contrasts without end, and its culture-on-the-make. We circle around the formidable pivot of Pennsylvania, proceed slowly down the Atlantic seaboard, inspect the unpredictable border states, and break into the pregnable, fast-changing world of the South, where we see everything from the Negro problem to the miracles established by the Tennessee Valley Authority. Finally, we come to a kind of geographical climax in the prodigious entity of Texas, and conclude at last in the new states of the Southwest which are still a veritable frontier.

Here, then, is this enormous abstract something known as "the United States," spread before us. Here, in the first gaunt years of the Atomic Age, lies a country, a continental mass, more favored by man and nature than any other in history, now for the first time attempting with somewhat faltering steps to justify its new station as a mature world power. Here, beyond anything else on the whole earth, is a country blessed by an ideal geography and almost perfect natural frontiers, by incalculable bulk and wealth and variety and vitality, by a unique and indeed unexampled heritage in democratic ideas and principles—and a country deliberately founded on a good idea.

What are we doing with it?

Where are we all going, and how fast, and to what end?

What are its forces, problems, influences?

Who runs it, and how well?

Of course this book is written primarily for Americans. But also I have tried, I am afraid with only intermittent success, to maintain another point of view, that of thinking in terms of a man from Mars or the moon. I have tried to keep in mind what a literate but ill-informed man or woman in Zanzibar, Shanghai, Moscow, or Birmingham might like or need to know about the United States. The ignorance abroad of things American is truly astonishing. And I dared to hope that the man or woman in Moscow (Idaho) might be as interested in what I found as the man from Moscow (USSR); that Birmingham (Alabama) will read with as open eyes as Birmingham (England). It is a most extraordinary thing that no guidebook to the United States exists. There have been political surveys aplenty (but none really good since Bryce) and volumes of philosophical impression since de Tocqueville more than a hundred years ago as well as all manner of brilliant essays, but no guidebook. The last I know is the Baedeker published in 1893. I hasten to add that I am not trying to be a de Tocqueville, Bryce or Baedeker. The niche I am trying to fill is very much more contemporaneous and specialized. This is a political guidebook if a guidebook at all and certainly it is no work of philosophy. What I have been trying to do is to discover the forces that make this incomparable Golconda of a country move. My book is a search for facts and issues, and an attempt to survey —without prejudice or pretension—those that may be found.

Man from Mars, or Moscow, look at some preliminary figures. This book, for reasons which will become clear later, contains no "general" chapter on the United States as a whole. You can procure the over-all master statistics—area, population, and so on—from any almanac. For the moment, consider simply some of the American superlatives. The United States is the first nation in the world in production of coal, petroleum, steel, electric energy, copper, cotton, lumber, and multitudinous other industrial and agricultural materials; but its political stamina and wit leave something to be desired. It contains four-fifths of the world's automobiles and one-half its telephones; but not quite so overwhelming a proportion of its moral character or most interesting ideas. This country sells 700 million dollars' worth of cosmetics in a normal year, and kills forty thousand people in automobile accidents. It contains 155,116 separate and distinct governmental units, and a baby is born every eleven and one half seconds. The United States consumed 1,115,-000,000 quarts of ice cream last year, and 660,000,000 doughnuts. Ninety-five million Americans go to the movies every week, and 55 million copies of pulp magazines are sold each month. There are 71,000,000 holders of life insurance in the United States, 40,000,000 gamblers, 20,000,000 amateur photographers, 5,000,000 stamp collectors,

2,800,000 vegetarians, 60,000 amateur radio operators, and 25,000 practicing astrologers.

The Declaration of Independence does not include the word "republic," nor does the Constitution contain the word "democracy" or even the word "nation." Yet the United States is, we like to think, the greatest republic, the greatest democracy, and the greatest nation in the world. It is also one of the few great nations with no national planning agency. The United States is statistically the richest country in the world. It is also a country with no national unemployment or health insurance. Nothing, in fact, could be easier than to list some of our more preposterous and flamboyant contradictions:

In 1945, Americans spent $1,306,514,314 on race tracks operating under pari-mutuel betting. In 1946 a bill to appropriate 100 million dollars for cancer research was defeated in the House of Representatives.

The national income last reported was 158 billion dollars, a sum as big as the Andromeda Nebulae. But only one American family in thirty-four had an income of $7,500 per year or more, only one in ten had $4,000, and more than 50 per cent had less than $122.00 per month.

This nation is supposed to have the finest standards of public health in the world. But 40 per cent of all draftees in World War II were rejected as physically unfit for military service; not less than 12 per cent were mental or psychoneurotic cases. Of the troops still in Germany in 1946, one out of every four men had venereal disease.

This nation is supposed to have the finest standards of public education in the world. But 13.9 per cent of draftees were found to be illiterate in 1943, and something like three million adult Americans have never gone to school at all.

In 1945, Americans spent $1,200,000,000 on jewelry. At a public dinner in New York, for a worthy charitable purpose, the first prize in a quiz show was a 109-carat diamond or $50,000 cash. Women's shoes in 1946 were obtainable in 160 different sizes. But 40 per cent of all American homes have no bathtub or shower, 35 per cent have no indoor toilet, and 30 per cent have no running water.

This nation derives much of its strength from the puritan tradition, and in America there are 24,402,124 Roman Catholics. But for every three marriages in 1946, there was one divorce.

This nation has always had a strong prohibitionist tendency, and one-fifth of it is dry. But in 1945 it consumed 190,000,000 gallons of hard liquor, which cost just under seven billion dollars.

The United States is generally supposed to maintain efficient means of educating and enlightening public opinion, especially in wartime. A poll in early 1946 showed that 19 per cent of GI's in a

German area thought that Germany was justified in starting the war, 22 per cent believed that the Germans were justified in persecuting the Jews, and 51 per cent that Hitler had done Germany "a lot of good" between 1933 and 1939.

This is commonly supposed to be a country with decent and generous humanitarian instincts. Thirty-three companies and thirty individuals were convicted in May, 1946, for "conspiracy to fix prices and block improvement on artificial limbs for war veterans."

This is a country supposed to worship consolidation and rationalization above all. But Washington, D.C. has five different police forces, and no resident of the District of Columbia is allowed to vote.

Or look at things in a perspective somewhat broader. During wartime the United States was capable of feats of constructive energy almost beyond compass; history scarcely knows a more impressive record of co-ordinated elevation and intensity of national enterprise, to say nothing of sacrifice. Yet, once the war is over, its backwash smears over us, and the nation succumbs to greed, fear, ineptitude, fumbling of the morning hopes, shoddy dispersal of the evening dreams. That, in late 1946, the two most painful and pressing shortages in the land should be of the two most primitive necessities of life, food and housing, is evidence enough of disintegration, no matter how temporary these shortages may turn out to be. The United States produced the most titanic harvest in its history—and could not feed its own people. It performed magnificent and inordinate miracles of production during the war—and cannot build homes for its own citizens.

What this shows above all is lack of national plan, lack of clarity and long-range vision. It shows that there are, on an over-all national basis, cogs and brain power wanting. Does it also concurrently show that, to become efficient, this country needs the stimulus of war? Does it mean that 295,000 Americans have to be killed in order to give us true effectiveness as a nation? Were the dead no more than bait? We hear much phraseology these days to the effect that the United States "is the last bulwark of human freedom," "the last frontier of western civilization against barbarism," and the like. These phrases may be perfectly sincere and valid in intent but they can carry little responsible or permanent weight until the country learns better to manage its own peacetime affairs.

All this being said by way of introduction, there is also something else to be said—with equal or greater emphasis. The United States makes blunders and mistakes. But it is also, today and tomorrow and every day, backwash of war or no backwash of war, capable of the most immense and formidable achievements. There are American national vices. There are also virtues. Never forget, man from Zanzibar, Birmingham, Moon, or Mars, that this nation is at once bull shouldered and quick as a ballet dancer on its feet. It is supple and full of nerves and fiber. It is a country capable of spawning 100 thousand airplanes overnight, and that in fifty years or so produced Jack Dempsey, Edna St. Vincent Millay, the Brothers Mayo, both Roosevelts and Woodrow Wilson and Wendell Willkie, Ernest Hemingway, Ford and Rockefeller and Edison, Mr. Justice Holmes and Mr. Justice Brandeis, Clarence Darrow and Thorstein Veblen, Frank Lloyd Wright, Booker T. Washington, George Washington Carver and Dr. J. Robert Oppenheimer, who made the atomic bomb go off just where he wanted it, how, and when.

Personal: A Word on Method

This book has been a considerable time in the making. I began to think about it as long ago as 1936, and I did intermittent research from 1940 on. I started systematic work in the summer of 1944, and in November of that year entered on a series of trips and expeditions of discovery that took thirteen months. I began the actual writing in January, 1946, and have been at it ever since.

I visited all forty-eight states of course, and of cities in the country greater than two hundred thousand in population, of which there are forty-three, I saw all but five. Also I visited a great many smaller communities. Most of these I had never seen before; it often occurred to me that the only virtue I brought to the job, aside from curiosity, was ignorance. Until my trip (1944-46), I had never in my life been in Denver, New Orleans, Rochester, Atlanta, Memphis, Salt Lake City, Portland, Oregon or Portland, Maine; except to pass through on a train or fly over, I had never seen Arkansas, Oklahoma, Kentucky, Delaware, Mississippi, the Dakotas, or Montana. All this did, at least, serve to give me the advantage of a fresh eye and an unprejudiced approach. Not only was I writing for the man from Mars; I was one.

I did a good deal of homework before and during my trip. For instance I wrote to all forty-eight governors—and got forty-seven replies. I talked to Mr. Roosevelt, Mr. Truman, several cabinet ministers and Supreme Court justices, senators by the covey and congressmen by the shoal. I went to men prominent in labor, or agriculture, or journalism, or the world of Negroes, or the mechanics of government and politics, in New York and Washington, and asked them to tell me of key people to see in various states and cities. Friends by the score passed me on to other friends. Altogether I have notes of talks with some nine hundred people—over a million words of notes in all, I should imagine. I list the names of some who shared their wisdom with me so generously in Acknowledgments at the end of this book. I have not checked through this list to break down its complexion. I think it will show a fairly even balance between Republicans and Democrats, East and West and North and South, Russia haters and Russia lovers, Britain haters and Britain lovers, industrialists and labor leaders, conservatives and progressives. I tried to see everybody who was honest and who had a point of view. I cared nothing about what camp a man was in if he had integrity and knew something. My ideal day was to spend the morning with the First National Bank and the afternoon with the CIO, or to have lunch with the Republican state chairman and dinner with the Democratic national committeeman.

About halfway through the job I discovered, to my apprehension and embarrassment, that one volume would not hold the fantastically copious amount of material I was assembling. This book is, I hope, a completely integrated unit by itself. But I must follow it with another book. As a result of considerations at once implacable and convenient I found it necessary to divide myself like an amoeba, and split this work into two halves. This volume, *Inside U.S.A.*, deals with the United States as a whole on a broad regional and national basis. It deliberately excludes Washington, D.C. That will be the second book. The friendly reader need not be alarmed; there is plenty of material in this present volume— though easily I could have made it twice as long—and there is plenty remaining for the next.

I have subdivided my subject matter in a way that may seem arbitrary, but that follows a natural logic of its own. Whenever a person, an issue, a theme, a subject, seemed better fitted to treatment from the point of view of government in Washington, I have put him or it on ice. Thus, in this volume, there is nothing but incidental mention of Truman, Wallace, most cabinet ministers, and such men as General Eisenhower, John L. Lewis, and General Marshall, who seemed naturally to fit in a volume less hinged on regional geography than this. Similarly I have reserved until later all discussion on a national scale of labor, agriculture, journalism, religion and the position of the Roman Catholic church, the role of women, big business, the Washington bureaucracy, education, and the foreign born—though the reader will find all these subjects multifariously mentioned in the pages that follow where they impinge on a local scene. As to senators I have included in this book sketches of a round dozen because it was impossible to deal with their states without them. More senators will come later. Congressmen I have, except for passing mention, rigorously excluded from the present volume, because it seems so much more reasonable to handle them in a chapter on Congress in the second book.

Likewise I have not in this book dealt with either Fascism or Communism from a general point of view, although there are plenty of passing references to both Communists and Fascists. The subject as a whole I am saving up. Anyway the Communists, no matter how they are belabored by right-wing fanatics, represent no authentic indigenous

American force, and the Fascists, though inextricably involved with enemies of the United States, are a minor irritating scum at best. The fate of this country, is, I believe as of the moment, no more dependent on the one than on the other; Union Square counts for as little nationally as the yelpings of such scavengers in the bankrupt as Father Coughlin or Gerald L. K. Smith.

The reader may be puzzled why I have stratified this volume by states. Mainly this was a matter of convenience; moreover, as we shall see, every state has its own particular and special flavor. Also, since most Americans are very house proud, with highly developed local chauvinisms, I will be asked why, for instance, I give three long chapters to California and only a page or two to Idaho or West Virginia. The reason is of course obvious. I don't mean to slight anybody. But I had to draw the line somewhere or I would have been writing forty-eight separate books, which would have annoyed my publisher. Generally I sought to give most space to those states that best expressed an issue; I tried to find a theme, a "story," on which to hang geographical subdivisions, and California had to be long anyway in order to establish certain of the subthemes that run through the whole book. Also I felt a natural temptation to give more space to states little known than to those well known. It seemed to me logical to write at greater length about Utah and Montana, the wonders of which are practically unknown in the East, than about Wisconsin or New Jersey, whose character and problems are, in general, much more familiar.

Everywhere I went I asked two or three main questions: What makes your state (or city, or community) distinctive? If you had five minutes at the bar of heaven to describe the difference between Connecticut and Massachusetts, or Georgia and Alabama, what would you say? What does your state (or city, or community, or agricultural area) contribute to the life of the nation as a whole? What is it *like*? Above all, who runs it? What are the basic and irreversible sources of *power*—social power, economic power, political power? The astonishing thing was the luxuriant variety of answers. An enormous number of things run this country! No single person, principle, ideal, commodity, abstraction, or vested interest runs it, though, as we shall see, there are several overriding strains that duplicate themselves almost everywhere. Man from Mars, you will find this country enormously conglomerate—and also interlocked.

Then, as a general rule, talking to people about themselves as individuals, I would ask a simple personal question—"What do you believe in most?" In this category too the variety of answers was remarkably profuse. I got a bouncing superabundance of replies—"people" mostly, then "the" people, then "the people if you give them an even break," and also God, Santa Claus, work, children, Thomas Jefferson, the golden

rule, the Pythagorean theorem, a high tariff, a low tariff, better agricultural prices, happiness, public power, private power, good roads, bad
roads—I could continue almost without end.

Later it occurred to me, under the stimulus of wise and benevolent talk
in Washington, that this was a sound and splendid thing. That a whole
lot of phenomena run this country, and that people still believe in a whole
lot of phenomena—even granting a good deal of resultant peripheral confusion—is a healthy index of democracy. Because democracy, if healthy,
can feed on its own defects, and take succor and sustenance from its own
variety.

But enough by way of introduction. So now with California we begin
this long circumnavigation of the greatest, craziest, most dangerous,
least stable, most spectacular, least grown-up, and most powerful and
magnificent nation ever known.

INSIDE U. S. A.

Chapter 1

California the Golden

wwwwwwwwwwwwwwwwwwwwwwwwwwwwwwwwwwwwwwwwwwwwwwwwwwwwwwwwwwwwwwwwwwwwwwwwwwwwwww

Give me men to match my mountains.
—Inscription in State Capitol, Sacramento

CALIFORNIA, the most spectacular and most diversified American state, California so ripe, golden, yeasty, churning in flux, is a world of its own in this trip we are beginning. It contains both the most sophisticated and the most bigoted community in America; it is a bursting cornucopia of peoples as well as of fruit, glaciers, sunshine, desert, and petroleum. There are several Californias, and the state is at once demented and very sane, adolescent and mature, depending on the point of view. Also, it is blessed by supernal wonders in the realm of climate, and a major item controlling its political behavior is the Pacific Ocean.

The story of California is the story of migrations—migrations both into and within the state. The intense fluidity of America, its nomadism, is a factor never to be discounted. But first, a quick introductory runover which, I hope, will serve to indicate the general pattern of this book.

California and the Nation

A very good case may be made that California, next to New York, is the most important state in the union; which is one reason why I begin with it. It is, for instance, the one above all others that could best exist alone; several other states claim this honor (Missouri for example), but in actual fact California is unique in self-supporting attributes; it has everything—industry, agriculture, commerce, and the vital asset of a 1,054-mile coastline.

California, with twenty-five electoral votes now (more than any state except New York, Illinois, and Pennsylvania), and more to come after 1950, likewise plays a cogent political role in national affairs; its impact is never to be ignored. Historically this can be proved again and again, as witness—

Item: California decided the Wilson-Hughes election in 1916. Had not California gone for Wilson, by a dramatic and scant plurality (3,806 votes), the United States might conceivably have stayed out of World War I.

Item: It was a series of delicate and intricate maneuvers within the

I

California delegation that enabled Franklin D. Roosevelt to win the Democratic nomination for president in 1932.

Beyond this is the fact that California holds in microcosm the funda-mentals of almost all American problems from race relationships to reconversion, from the balance between pressure groups and the demo-cratic process to the balance between factory and farm. If either Fascism or Communism should ever smite this country, it is more likely to rise first in California than in any other state.

Also consider the immutable factor of topography. The world is still Mercator-minded; but a glance at any of the new order of maps will show that California is the seaboard, or perhaps one should say air-board, of the future, not merely to the Orient as is obvious but to much else. Put an airplane at the North Pole; it will reach San Francisco, say, Chicago, or New York, in approximately the same time. Frederick J. Turner, the historian of the frontier, wrote in 1914 that "the age of the Pacific Ocean begins, mysterious and unfathomable in its meaning to our own future."[1] California was, as we all know, the jumping-off place for the war against Japan, and it might well be the same thing— if Jingo blatherskites on either side commit treason against the human race—in a war against the Soviet Union. Meantime, with Europe seem-ingly crumbling and exhausted, the Golden State is the gateway to an Asia that may have much peaceful meaning for the United States. Con-sider merely the matter of Pacific trade. With modern air techniques, the great worlds of China, Japan, Australasia, India are only a jump away.

California, Its Beam and Bulk

California, the thirty-first state to enter the union, is the second state in area (158,693 square miles), and the third in population (somewhere around eight and a half million). It contains the highest point in the United States (Mount Whitney, just under 15,000 feet) and not more than eighty miles away is the lowest point, Death Valley, 276 feet below sea level. California is the first state in value of agricultural products, airplane manufacture, gold mining, and number of university graduates; it is second in oil, eggs, wool, and production of electricity. Thus one glimpses again its astonishing diversification; to be first in *both* agricul-ture and airplanes is really something. It has the highest living standard in the country, and the third highest per capita income of any state[2]— $1,480 as against $1,150 for the nation as a whole. It contains the single

[1] As quoted by Carey McWilliams, *Brothers Under the Skin*, p. 16. All the McWilliams books, aside from being fascinating reading, are indispensable to the study of California, particularly *Southern California Country*.

[2] California, New York, and Connecticut always run neck to neck in these figures. Those above are for 1945. California led in 1944.

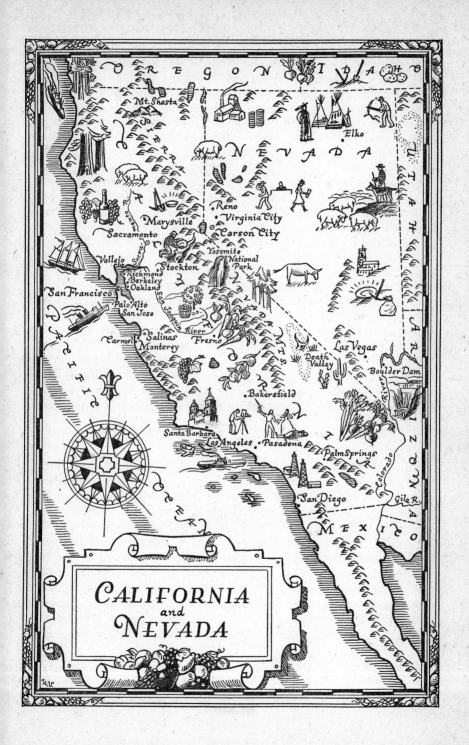

CALIFORNIA
and
NEVADA

richest American county (Los Angeles with its citrus crop) and the biggest county, San Bernardino.

Superimpose a map of California on a map of Europe; it will stretch from Amsterdam to Rome. Turn it sideways, and it will nearly cover the distance between Berne and Bucharest. Or, shift California to right angles and lay it across the United States; if you put the northern boundary at Chicago, it will stretch almost to the Atlantic; if you put Mount Shasta at Des Moines, the southern tip will touch Atlanta. Exercises like this quite aside, study of a normal map of California will surprise many people. For instance San Diego lies well to the *east* (not west) of Reno.

Fifty years ago James Bryce said in *The American Commonwealth,* one of the greatest books of political science ever written, "Of the States subsequent to the original thirteen, California is the only one with a genuine natural boundary." The forests of Oregon bound it on the north, and the Colorado River and the Mexican desert on the south; to the west is the broad iridescence of the Pacific, to the east the massive spiked barrier of the Sierra Nevada. There are no fewer than forty-one peaks higher than 10,000 feet in the state, and the Sierra Nevada is but one of two great ranges; the Coastal range stretches the whole length of the ocean side like the Nevada's smaller brother. In between, 350 miles by 50, is the wonderful glowing bowl known as Central Valley, the chief repository of California's agricultural wealth.

Look at any sizable road map. Only five major highways cross the state from east to west. And they have hard work crossing it. Literally, these are Alps that they twist through and climb. But observe roads like US 101 and US 395, and especially US 99; these are the great north-south roads, cutting down like clean-edged rivers. There is scarcely a turn in 99 (as seen on the map) all the way from Sacramento through Stockton and Fresno to Bakersfield; the road slices through Central Valley like a long knife splitting an oval melon. Railroad maps are instructive too. There are hundreds of square miles in California, districts comprising whole counties, that have no railways at all. Not a single line crosses the state between Truckee, north of San Francisco, and Death Valley, some 250 miles. The western slope of the Sierra Nevada is taken up almost wholly by national forests and national parks, of which the most famous are of course Yosemite (which name means Grizzly Bear in the original Indian) and Sequoia, where the trees are the biggest and oldest living things on earth. If your map shows national forests in green, there will be a broad green belt stretching almost without interruption from the Oregon frontier to the outskirts of Los Angeles, and almost totally enclosing Central Valley, with its twelve million fertile acres.

California is, it is often said, two states; the dividing line is the

Tehachapi, one of the few semilateral mountain ranges in the United States.[3] Suppose the Sierra Nevada to be an enormous dinosaur; the Tehachapi is the last flick of its bony tail, whipping over to the sea. But more than just this spine of mountain divides northern California from the south. The chief criterion of demarcation is water. Above the Tehachapi, speaking roughly, water is abundant; below, it is scant and precious. As interesting as any line drawn by river or rail is the right of way of the Los Angeles Aqueduct; Los Angeles is below the Tehachapi, but part of the water supply of a community of three million people lies above. Water aside, the fact that the state is two states causes other problems, for instance the matter of duplication in institutions and the like. There is a state capitol in Los Angeles as well as Sacramento; there are three penitentiaries; the university is split in two, with separate campuses—virtually autonomous—at Los Angeles and Berkeley.[4]

Northern California is itself so variegated—and its characteristics are in general so well known—that to describe it in a paragraph, no matter how tentatively, is neither possible nor necessary. Here are the Golden Gate and the wonderful complex of communities around San Francisco; here are Mount Shasta, Lake Tahoe, and the only active volcano in the United States (Mount Lassen); here is the upper Sonora, of which John Muir wrote, "For a distance of 400 miles, your foot crushed a hundred flowers at every step"; here are those fascinating communities Carmel, Monterey, and Salinas. The whole gamut of California history may be traversed in twenty miles in this region, from Monterey which as everyone knows was the old Spanish capital, to Salinas which was a mecca of the Okies.

Southern California, the third of the state below the Tehachapi, is something else again; it has a mood and character absolutely different from the north, so much so that it is practically a different commonwealth. This is the California of petroleum, crazy religious cults, the citrus industry, towns based on rich *rentiers* like Santa Barbara and Pasadena, the movies, the weirdest architecture in the United States, refugees from Iowa, a steeply growing Negro population, and devotees of funny money. It is, above all, the world where climate is worshipped as a god. "The most valuable ingredient of the California way of life, sunshine, is free," as *Life* once wrote. Yet all southern California would shrivel and disappear—almost overnight—if it were not for *imported* water. Everything depends on irrigation i.e. artificial rain. The "rain" comes by pipe and canal.

I began this section by saying that the population of California was "around" eight and a half million. There is a reason for this lapse into

[3] The only actual east-west range I can think of is the Uinta in Utah.
[4] Several of these facts and figures come from *California*, a Guide to the Golden State, in the American Guide Series. Another invaluable source is the West Coast issue of *Fortune*, February, 1945.

the *à peu près*, namely, that no one knows what the exact figure is. In 1940 it was 6,907,387. But with the war—as we all know—came a tremendous influx not merely of military personnel but of defense workers and their families. By 1943 the population was estimated at 8,373,800 and by 1944 at 8,842,700; today it is probably about the same, though some estimates go as high as 9,200,000. Conservatively, it is agreed by all authorities that in five years the state has gained at least 1,500,000 people, an increase of 22.4 per cent.

Some astonishing details are released if we break these figures down. For instance San Diego jumped from a population of 203,341 in 1940 to an estimated 362,658 in 1946—a rise of not less than 78 per cent. The San Francisco area rose from 1,461,800 to 1,840,500 (26 per cent), and Los Angeles County from 2,916,400 to 3,357,000 (15 per cent). Los Angeles is today the fourth largest city in the country. Some single counties—particularly in the Bay region—more than doubled their population in the war period; they rose 100 per cent or more. This prodigious increase came, moreover, atop other increases; for instance, the population of the state rose 65 per cent in the years from 1920 to 1930, and it is entirely possible, even probable, that within the next few decades it will surpass New York and Pennsylvania to become the most populous in the union.

The median age in California is, incidentally, thirty-three. This compares to twenty-nine for the United States as a whole and twenty-three in the "youngest" state, New Mexico. The reason for this is of course the great number of old folks who have poured in from the Middle West; most Californians today are not, as is well known, California born. Another population figure is that about one-ninth of the people of the state are foreign born. To an outsider, this figure may seem high and striking; actually—as we shall presently see in connection with other states—it is comparatively low.

Most of the war workers who entered California from 1940 to 1945 went into two extremely volatile industries, aircraft and shipbuilding; hence the issue of reconversion was more than normally acute. Beyond this, the influx produced other problems, for instance the fact that no one can guess how California will vote next time. Again, shall the state attempt to get rid of the new "in-migrants," as some people wish, and if so, how; if not, how will it possibly find jobs and residence for them all? The housing problem in the state is, as everywhere, anguishing. Most responsible Californians hope that the new arrivals will stay and find jobs and a place to live; out of a new melting pot they hope to absorb new strength; the motto is, "Don't talk reconversion, but *convert* instead."

California is so celebrated for Central Valley and its agriculture—avocados, melons, spinach, asparagus, grapefruit, olives, what not—that one is tempted to think of it as predominantly rural. This is not true

from the population point of view, even though agriculture (and associated industries like canning) supports more people than any other industry. But California is an urban state, not rural; even Los Angeles
County is an urban area. The simplest of statistics tells the story. About
80 per cent of the total population lives in cities and metropolitan areas;
not less than 5,200,000, over *half* the total number of people in the state,
are clustered around Los Angeles and San Francisco alone.

California and Texas

These two great states are often compared and this comparison is
worth exploring for a paragraph or two. Suppose we outline some
similarities first. Both states are giants; both have a martial history
and tradition; each was an independent republic for a time, under its
own flag, something that can be said of no other American state except
Vermont.[5] But whereas Texas was independent, legitimately and actually
independent for ten close-packed, stormy years, the California "republic"
lasted only a few weeks. The fact that Texas *was* an independent state,
albeit briefly, is an inescapable reality to most Texans; it is the cause
of what we will later describe as "Texan nationalism"; a visitor to
Texas is reminded of it ceaselessly. No such spirit exists comparably in
California. In dozens of visits to the state, in conversation and inquiry
with a hundred Californians, I only heard its former independence
mentioned once.

Both Texas and California are empires in a manner of speaking; both
have what might be called—not too literally—strong imperialist tendencies. For twenty years California and Arizona have been squabbling
(largely over questions of water and irrigation); I heard one Californian
say in mild disgust, "If we came out against smallpox, Arizona would
be for it." Also, Californians are apt to think of Nevada as a kind of
satrapy and its Senator McCarran is often described by Californians
as their "third" senator.

Texas is, in a way, more raucous than California; California is more
romantic. On most political issues, California is more sophisticated; in
things religious, it is more eccentric. Californians, like Texans, love to
tell tall tales, but theirs don't have quite the folklore quality of Texas
tales. Californians are, by and large, less self-conscious about their
glories. During the butter shortage I saw a waitress at the Mark Hopkins
Hotel in San Francisco point to a pat of prune jelly. "California butter!"
she exclaimed briefly. I had the feeling that no Texan would have spoken
about anything in his state in quite this humorously contemptuous way.

[5] But both Rhode Island and North Carolina had a brief period of "autonomous"
status after 1789, since they refused for a time to enter the union although the
Articles of Confederation no longer bound them. See Bryce, Vol. I, p. 422.

Finally, take the world of culture. Here California compares to Texas as Paris, say, compares to Albania. California is (New York alone excepted) the most "European" of all American commonwealths; Texas is a kind of vacuum. In the whole history of Texas, there are not a dozen poets, sculptors, scientists, musicians, whose names can even be recalled; an artist in Texas is as rare as an icicle in the Sahara; in the entire expanse of the state today, with its population of 6,400,000, there is only one writer of any consequence. But consider California; California swarms with poets, artists, men of science. There is no opulence in America to surpass it, even in New England. Think of the procession that begins with Bret Harte and Ambrose Bierce and continues today with Robinson Jeffers and John Steinbeck. In between consider Isadora Duncan, David Starr Jordan, Jack London, Frank Norris, Lincoln Steffens, Upton Sinclair, Gertrude Atherton, Henry George, Luther Burbank, William Saroyan, Donald Culross Peattie. All these were either California born or for definite reasons of literary association and residence are California marked. Or take, in an adjacent field, American Nobel Prize winners. There have been thirty-one so far. Not one is Texan. But six were either born in California or live there today. Such a fracas over academic freedom as occurred at the University of Texas would be inconceivable in California; its university is by most standards one of the six or eight best in the country; it has no regent trouble.

Sometimes people compare California to Florida, but from an intellectual point of view there is no comparison. Think of the European migration that has little by little converted the lovely balcony of hills near Santa Monica into a kind of Salzburg, a kind of Florence. Stravinsky, Montemezzi, Aldous Huxley, Isherwood, Artur Rubinstein, Emil Ludwig, Heifetz, Remarque, Franz Werfel, Thomas Mann—none of them went to Florida.[6] All of them chose the land between Los Angeles and the radiant California sea. Why? Because climate can be intellectual as well as physical.

History of California: Five-Minute Glimpse

> Then ho, brother, ho,
> To California go;
> There's plenty of gold in the world we're told,
> On the banks of the Sacramento.
>
> —Jesse Hutchinson, Jr.

The story of California is, I have said, the story of migrations; there have been at least six clearly defined waves of immigration within the past one hundred years.

[6] Could one possibly imagine such an institution as San Francisco's Bohemian Club existing in Miami?

First came the traders and frontiersmen, followed by early settlers like members of the Donner party who, caught in the mountains by winter snow, ate each other when food gave out. Second, the violent influx caused by the Gold Rush of 1849. Third, the tide brought in by the railroads, after the first transcontinental line was built in 1869. Fourth, the immense movement to southern California from the Middle West that began in the early 1920's and was, as Carey McWilliams says, "the first great migration of the automobile age." Fifth, the flight to California of the Okies and other agrarian refugees from the Dust Bowl and elsewhere. Sixth, the influx of war workers from 1940 to 1945. This last was nothing more or less than the Gold Rush all over again in a different dimension, a gold rush in aviation, the result of which was to make Los Angeles the "Detroit of airplanes."

Of course California history begins long before the age of American migrations with the Indians and Spaniards. In 1535 the most tremendous of the conquistadores, Cortes, looking for the seven golden cities, worked far enough north to reach what is now Lower California, and gave the region its name. The first white man of importance actually to set foot on what is now our California was a Portuguese, Juan Rodriguez Cabrillo, who discovered San Diego Bay in 1542. There followed three centuries of chaotic and inept Spanish and/or Mexican rule, tempered by the proselytizing of the Franciscans; and let it not be forgotten that Sir Francis Drake anchored his *Golden Hinde* a few miles north of San Francisco Bay in 1579. In 1821 Mexico freed itself from Spain, and in 1825 California became a territory of the Mexican republic; in 1836 came a short-lived "Free and Sovereign State of Alta California," organized by Mexican secessionists. But meantime, western pressure by North American traders, trappers, whalers, pioneers was steadily and inexorably increasing.

I cannot in this space describe except in boniest outline the highly multicolored events that brought California into the union. The story is magnificently told, as is much else, in Bernard DeVoto's *The Year of Decision, 1846*. For everybody to ponder is the degree and the extent of American imperialism in the period. We never formally invaded California. We offered once to buy it. There were no shenanigans like those in Texas. But President Polk made no bones about his intention of acquiring California, by force if necessary; and its actual inclusion into the United States came, as everyone knows, as a result of one of the most vulgarly cold-blooded wars in history, that against Mexico in 1846. Still, the point should be made that California was, and inevitably had to be, ours; the westward swell of migration was bound to reach the Pacific; the United States without California would have been as ridiculous as France without Brittany or England without Kent;

politically, geographically, humanly, the impulse to fill the great bowl of the West was unavoidable and irresistible.

Two men, one very widely known, one known not at all but from a contemporary point of view almost equally remarkable, were major actors. The first was Frémont, as gallant a figure as ever left sparklets of glamor across the pages of history. The other was the United States consul at Monterey, Thomas O. Larkin. This Larkin was a man of resource. He was a newspaperman, a trade agent, and a spy. Behind his immunity as a representative of the State Department he maneuvered to get California into the United States or, failing that, to establish its independence, in almost precisely the manner that von Papen maneuvered to make pre-Anschluss Austria part of Germany. The whole history of California in this period is like that of the Sudetenland in the 1930's. The British were of course active in California too. There was a considerable movement among Californians to seek a protectorate under Great Britain (Texas similarly flirted with the British in order to strengthen its hand vis-à-vis Washington), and the British encouraged this because it gave them a card in their territorial dispute with the United States over Oregon. The British agent at Monterey, J. A. Forbes, was beaten by Frémont and Larkin, but he (and also the Hudson's Bay Company) played a role that seems fascinating today.

Russian traders were active in California too. A shipload of them landed in 1812 above San Francisco; they were strong enough to build a fort, flout Mexican authority, and maintain their own territorial enclave for almost a generation. One of their best customers was a Swiss, John Augustus Sutter, who created for himself a kind of principality called New Helvetia in what is now the Sacramento area. The Russians withdrew from California in 1841, peaceably and of their own volition.

The first American immigrant train arrived in California the same year. "Incidents" began to happen—which startlingly resemble the modern variety of "incidents" like those at Mukden and Wal Wal—and Frémont and the others took quick and vigorous advantage of them. There was very little bloodshed. One group of Americans set up the "California Republic" on June 14, 1846; it only lasted, under its own flag decorated with grizzly bear and star, until July 7, because it wasn't necessary for it to last longer, since the United States had declared war on Mexico. Frémont accepted the Mexican surrender in January, 1847, on a mountain pass near Los Angeles, and Mexico formally gave up all claims to California (and much else) in the next year. The American victors set up a legislature and wrote and ratified a constitution, and in 1850 California was admitted to the union. Alone among western states, it came to statehood full-fledged; there was no probationary period of being a territory.

Vigilantes, Southern Pacific, and Hiram Johnson

Of the Gold Rush, which began in 1848 with the discovery of gold on the property of the Swiss–Mexican–American John Sutter, and which became, in the words of one authority, "the greatest mass movement of people since the Crusades," I can write little. Gold brought wealth to California (and to the nation) ; it brought romance ; and it brought violence. Of the Gold Rush mining towns few survive today, except in ghost form. But some of their names carry a reminiscent flash : it is not hard to guess the kind of men and women who lived in Brandy Gulch, Hangtown, Piety Hill, Hell's Delight, Puke Ravine, Petticoat Slide, Gouge Eye, Swell-Head Diggings, and Poker Flat.[7]

Between the forty-niners and the present century the history of California is largely that of a railroad, but one must pause briefly to mention two other phenomena, vigilantism and the "Sand-Lot" demagoguery of a nearly forgotten worthy named Dennis Kearney. The vigilantes were not, as we understand the term, "Fascists," nor were the Sand Lotters "Communists," but the roots of much of the extremism of California today can be traced back to these early exemplars.

San Francisco in the 50's was the most rambunctious, gaudy and vociferous town on earth. There were, according to the *California* Guide, more than a thousand murders between 1849 and 1856, with only one conviction. Corruption of the city administration was complete ; the law was a motley joke ; a gang known as "the Hounds" ran wild. So the citizenry rose in wrath in 1851, constituted a vigilance committee, and set up its own police—with artillery ! The first committee sentenced only four men to be hanged (out of ninety-one arrested) ; the executions were public, and held to the tune of tolling bells. The Hounds organization was broken. But more violence came later. The chief crooks and racketeers had the protection of big businessmen and big politicians, exactly as in the Capone days seventy years later in Chicago. Against the ring rose the voice of a solitary editor, James King of William. As a result, King himself was shot. The murderer was a politician named Casey whom he had attacked in print. Again a vigilance committee was organized, this time with eight thousand outraged members. It sat for four months, overruled the courts and other authorities, hanged Casey as the bells tolled again, and "exiled" twenty-five other gangsters and racketeers. This broke the back of San Francisco terrorism.

In the 1870's came the rise of Dennis Kearney's "Workingman's Party of California," one of the first authentically radical parties in American history. Kearney, an Irishman, was scarcely literate. Also he was some-

[7] *California, an Intimate History,* by Gertrude Atherton, p. 127.

thing of a genius. His followers became known as the Sand-Lot party because he addressed them in vacant lots. He was both an unmitigated demagogue and a responsible politician with some highly contemporary ideas. Kearney could be the mouthpiece of the *New Republic*; every plank he had—except one—fits in the structure of modern liberalism. The exception is that he was virulently anti-Chinese, because of the dangers he thought cheap Chinese labor represented to the rest of the community, whereas today most radicals approve of and encourage equal status for alien or quasi-alien groups. As for the rest, Kearney wanted "to wrest the government from the hands of the rich and place it in those of the people . . . to destroy the great money power of the rich . . . to destroy land monopoly in our state by a system of taxation that will make great wealth impossible in the future." Kearney, like most Californians of the period, was a violent character, and his words were strong. He talked about "a little judicious hanging of capitalists," and he once spoke as follows:

The Central Pacific men are thieves, and will soon feel the power of the workingmen. When I have thoroughly organized my party we will march through the city and compel the thieves to give up their plunder. I will lead you to the city hall, clear out the police force, hang the prosecuting attorney, burn every book that has a particle of law in it, and then enact new laws for the workingmen.
                    —R. G. Cleland, *From Wilderness to Empire*, p. 342

Actually Kearney did not have to resort to violence. His party, drawing strength not only from the underpossessed but from small farmers and businessmen, grew so powerful by 1878 that it was able to force a change in the organic law of the state. A constitutional convention was called, in which the Sand Lotters had a third of the vote, and a new constitution was written and ratified (1879) which is still in force today. This was by all odds the most progressive constitution ever adopted by an American state up to that date. It cut the powers of special privilege; it established the eight-hour day; it provided for regulation of railways and utilities; it even made "improper" lobbying a felony.

We must now allude briefly to the tremendous story of the railroads, with a later acrid word on Hiram Johnson. On May 10, 1869—one of the great dates in American history—the Central Pacific (later called the Southern Pacific) met the Union Pacific at a point in Utah, and for the first time the American continent was crossed and linked by rail. A second transcontinental line was completed in 1881, and a third in 1885. Now in those days a railroad was more than just a railroad. The great early roads were direct and primary agents in penetrating, bursting open, fertilizing, and exploiting the whole of the American West. They were laws unto themselves; or else they made the laws. Leland Stanford, one of the formidable four who built the Central Pacific, was at one time or other president of the railway, governor of the state, and federal senator; his Senate seat is supposed to have cost him a 100 thousand dollars. The economic power of the companies depended on more than mere transportation, though in the field of transportation they could do anything they wished; this was long before the days of the Interstate Commerce Commission; for instance a rate war between the Southern Pacific and the Santa Fe once brought the passenger fare from St. Louis to Los Angeles to one dollar!

But much more important than transportation per se was the factor of land. To encourage railway building and to get the public domain into useful private ownership as quickly as possible, the federal government gave the various lines enormous grants of land along their right of ways, usually every other section, free. The total amount so distributed was not less than 130,000,000 acres. This, as every school child knows, is a root element in our history; a dozen times we shall have recourse to mention it—in the story of the development of Minnesota, or Montana, of the great Southwest.[8] What did the railroads do with their agglutinations of property? The answer could not be simpler: they either sold it or held onto it. By offering parcels and subdivisions at great profit to pioneers they of course killed two birds with one stone; first, made money, second, built up a "colonial" population adjacent to the line and utterly dependent on it. But in many cases they did not sell; for instance, today, Southern Pacific is still the largest private landowner in California. That the railways should begin to play politics was of course inevitable. They had serious interests to protect. They had to be assured of "loyalty" on the part of governors and legislators. They became inextricably involved in public policy. They did not always live up to their responsibilities. Some were as devoid of civic spirit as a stoat. Ambrose Bierce liked to print Leland Stanford as £eland $tanford, and even Bryce, writing in 1888, says

> California was for many years practically at the mercy of the Central Pacific Railway, then her only road to the Mississippi Valley and the Atlantic. . . . What made the position more singular was that although these railroads had been built under statutes passed by the states they traversed . . . they were built with Eastern capital, and were owned by a number of rich men living in New York, Boston, or Philadelphia, unamenable to local influences, and caring no more about the wishes and feelings of the State whence their profits came than an English bondholder cares about the feelings of Chile.

[8] Texas, by terms of its peculiar treaty, was the only state in which the railways were *not* given federal land; this was a considerable factor in giving Texas a different development.

Until the governorship of Hiram Johnson which began in 1910, California was almost completely dominated by the railroads, and no understanding of the politics of the state is possible without this background. Corruption was widely prevalent and few people seemed to object. Aggregate bribes (to state senators) by the railroads reached astronomical sums; to individual newspapers, they descended to stipends of $250 per month. By controlling the legislature Southern Pacific also elected its own U. S. senators, like Stanford; it could virtually make or break any business, by favoritism in freight rates; it even maintained what it called a "Political Bureau"—shades of the Kremlin a generation later! On the other hand, it is important to mention the indisputably great contribution that Southern Pacific made in these years to the development of California and the entire West, and its brilliant achievements in transportation *per se* as well as in creating wealth and opportunity.

This is of course old stuff; almost everybody knows the story. The point to make is that the history of California until 1910 or thereabouts was largely one of revolt against Southern Pacific domination—a revolt that succeeded. The instrument that Johnson used was of the simplest, that of political reform and then political control through the direct primary. Once the machines could not control votes wholesale, and the direct primary made such control impossible, the railway and its allies were beaten. Once a tough governor like Johnson, with the people behind him, ousted the bosses in the legislature and could count on honest elections, the fight was mostly won.

Hiram W. Johnson, who died in the summer of 1945 at the age of seventy-nine, was, it is extraordinary to tell, son of a father—Grove L. Johnson—who was Southern Pacific's own chief lobbyist! The struggle was not only between the public and a vested interest, nor even between a lone crusader and a corporation; it was between a son and a father. Grove had once served a penitentiary sentence, and for many years he and Hiram, stubborn men both, never spoke. Once they campaigned against one another, and Grove told his audience that Hiram and another son might be found addressing a rival crowd down the street. "And who are those men?" Grove bellowed. "One is full of booze—the other of conceit! Who are they? My sons!"

Hiram first became conspicuous in San Francisco in 1908 or thereabouts, when a crook named Ruef ran the city and Grove was a creature of the local machine. Exactly as in the vigilante days the respectable community finally rose in anger and sought—by legal means this time—to turn the gang out. A special prosecutor, Francis J. Heney, succeeded in getting indictments against Ruef and members of the Ruef crowd. Then Heney was shot in the courtroom. And by a talesman earlier released from jury service! But public indignation climbed higher and a new special prosecutor was appointed to take the case over. This new special prosecutor was, of all men, the son hated by his father and the father's direct antagonist—Hiram Johnson.

Partly because of his success at the trial—Ruef was sentenced to fourteen years—Hiram ran for governor (as a Republican) in 1910 and was elected. He was re-elected in 1914 (as a Progressive), and was the only governor in California history, until Earl Warren, ever to be re-elected to a four-year term.[9] Before this, he had run for vice president of the United States with Theodore Roosevelt on the Bull Moose ticket. Hiram moved on to the Senate in 1917, and stayed there until his death, elected time after time by overwhelming votes, and on whatever program he happened to feel like choosing. He was, as everyone knows, an implacable isolationist in both 1917 and 1941; but except for the most trifling of historical accidents he would have been president of the United States in 1923. At the Republican convention in 1920 he was offered the vice presidential nomination under Harding; he refused, largely out of vanity, and when Harding died it was a man named Calvin Coolidge, not Hiram Johnson, who acceded to the presidency.

The following is an example of Hiram's prose style. He was attacking a man named Otis, who for many years was publisher of the Los Angeles *Times*:

> In the City of San Francisco we have drunk to the very dregs of infamy; we have had vile officials; we have had rotten newspapers. But we have nothing so vile, nothing so low, nothing so debased, nothing so infamous in San Francisco as Harrison Grey Otis. He sits there in senile dementia with a gangrene heart and rotting brain, grimacing at every reform, chattering impotently at all things that are decent, frothing, fuming, violently gibbering, going down to his grave in snarling infamy . . . disgraceful, depraved . . . and putrescent.
> —From *Southern California County*, Carey McWilliams, p. 275

But some of these words might well have been used by political enemies about Hiram himself, because during his last years in the Senate he too suffered from what was close to senile dementia. In those years it was the habit in California to say that the state had only one senator. And before his death I heard colloquies like this, "Why is Hiram Johnson still alive?—Because he's too mean to die!"

Be that as it may, Johnson was probably the greatest governor California ever had; he was attractive and skilled, with a wonderfully quick mind and all the guts in the world. After Johnson's first legislature Theodore Roosevelt said, "This session has passed the most comprehensive program of constructive legislation ever passed at a single

---

[9] In the 1850's a man named Bigler served two two-year terms.

session of an American legislature." Strangely enough, great pressure had to be put on Johnson to enter politics in the first place. He was a poor man; he liked his career at law; his wife hated the hurly-burly of the political arena. Also, he told friends at the beginning that he could not possibly run for office, because of his father. "Do you know the place my paternal ancestor [he would seldom use the word "father" of Grove] has in the politics of this state?" he would say. Or, "If I run for governor, people will fling at me the one thing on which I cannot defend myself—Grove L. Johnson." Largely Hiram was persuaded to run through the intermediation of Chester H. Rowell, for many years editor of the Fresno *Republican* and later of the San Francisco *Chronicle.* Rowell had helped create an early reform movement called the "Lincoln-Roosevelt League," and Johnson was the beneficiary of much of his hard work. There is, incidentally, no good biography of Hiram Johnson, by all odds one of the most striking Americans of recent times. It will be a wonderful book for someone to write some day, and I hope that valiant old Rowell can be talked into doing it.

As a senator Johnson's record was, as we know, mixed. On foreign policy he was hopelessly obtuse. One clue to his grumpiness, his dislike of most of his colleagues, and above all his pathological hatred of both Wilson and Roosevelt was his enormous vanity.[10] It didn't matter *who* was president; what Hiram resented was that there *was* a president, and that he himself wasn't it. He had to be No. 1. And the easiest way for him to be No. 1 in the Senate was to be the king insurgent. Which in due time he became.

I heard another estimate of Johnson which is at least brief: "Hiram always despised the only two things he didn't have—money and *sound* knowledge."

Some Characteristics of the Californians

William Blake once said, "To generalize is to be an idiot," and any attempt to clinch what I have already said in this chapter about California "character" is, and must necessarily be, absurd, if only because the state is too replete with conflicting types, too various. But a few more words may be in order.

1. California has, I should say on the whole, more authentic exuberance and color than any other state.

2. It was built by adventurers, by individualists, in a mood of what Professor D. W. Brogan calls "masculine, anarchical barbarism." I asked the contemporary labor leader, Harry Bridges, what he considered to be

---

[10] Charles Evans Hughes made the grievous error of not calling on Hiram when campaigning in California in 1916; as a direct result, he lost the state and the presidency, because Johnson, angry at the rebuff, threw his influence against him. At least this is a story often told. Some authorities deny it.

the state's chief distinction, and he replied at once, "The pioneer spirit." Almost all Californians today consider themselves the survivors of a great adventure. Only the most enterprising of Americans took the long route around Cape Horn or tramped across the Panamanian isthmus in the Gold Rush days, and only the strongest or the luckiest survived.

3. It is a state that moves fast and changes quickly. No one can easily put salt on its tail.

4. Most Californians have great state pride, whether they were born in California or not. But there is a subtle distinction between authentic native sons, Californians, and the non-natives or Californiacs.

5. Another distinction is diversity within diversification. It is not enough to say that California has great wealth in "both" mining and agriculture; what really counts is the number of specialties within each category. For instance sixty different minerals of economic value are to be found in the state, and as to agriculture, a farmer's crop may range from subtropical fruits to wheat.

6. California is the outside fringe, a long way from Washington, and bound to itself by desert, mountains, and the sea.

7. Belief in miracles. The worshiper at the Aimee Semple McPherson temple, the radical unemployed with his Ham & Eggs, both express the same kind of emotional yearning.

8. Finally, a zest for direct action and a tradition of going to extremes.

An American Paradox

As a postscript to this chapter, let us once again mention Hiram Johnson. The phenomenon is at first sight puzzling—how it should have come about that Johnson, a slashingly vigorous liberal in domestic affairs, should at the same time have been a blind reactionary on international affairs. Actually this paradox is a familiar American characteristic; we find it not only in Hiram but in other giants of his generation like George Norris and Bob LaFollette, and today in much lesser men like Nye and Wheeler. As a general rule, western senators of the old school are, or were, fervent isolationists. There would appear to be four main reasons. First, they disliked the East, and were suspicious and jealous of the Atlantic seaboard which was generally interventionist. Second, they hated gold, finance, capital, and especially J. P. Morgan. They thought that Morgan and the British empire were practically synonymous; they were anti-British, and they opposed American participation in World Wars I and II, partly because they hated eastern finance which was tied to British strings. Third, they felt a duty to devote their reformist energies, visions, talents, exclusively to the American scene; anything to do with Europe was an extravagance or an inadvertence; it was off the **main** beam; they wanted to expend everything they had, to the last ounce and inch, on the enormously pressing *domestic* problems that were crying for solution. Fourth, they were as a rule untraveled, politically under-developed, and "provincial" in both the best and worst senses of that term.

This familiar paradox also exists in reverse. For instance there are eastern senators today who are violently reactionary as regards internal American policy, and yet fervent "liberals," i.e. interventionists, in relation to things abroad.

Chapter 2
A Bouquet of Californians

~~~~~~

> Remember that the men who stocked California in the 50's were
> physically, and as far as regards certain tough virtues, the pick
> of the earth . . . It needs no little golden badge . . . to mark the
> native son of the Golden West. Him I love because he is devoid
> of fear, carries himself like a man, and has a heart as big as
> his boots.
>
> —Rudyard Kipling

EARL WARREN, running as a nonpartisan and permitted by the
anarchic California electoral system to file on both Republican and
Democratic tickets, defeated Robert W. Kenny in the 1946 primaries
and thus became the first governor in the history of the state to win
both party nominations, and the only one except Hiram Johnson ever
to win two four-year terms. The general election in November was no
more than a formality confirming Warren's spectacular and unprecedented triumph. Immediately he began to be talked about as an obvious
and weighty candidate for the Republican nomination for the presidency
in 1948. What manner of man is Warren—how shall we add him up?

Earl Warren is honest, likable, and clean; he will never set the world
on fire or even make it smoke; he has the limitations of all Americans
of his type with little intellectual background, little genuine depth or
coherent political philosophy; a man who has probably never bothered
with abstract thought twice in his life; a kindly man, with the best of
social instincts, stable, and well balanced; a man splendidly devoted
to his handsome wife and six healthy children; not greedy, not a
politician of the raucous, grasping kind that has despoiled so much in
the United States; a "typical" American in his bluffness, heartiness,
healthy apple-pie atmosphere and love for joining things; a man glad
to carry a bundle for his missus in the neighborhood supermarket and
have an evening out with the boys once in awhile; a man with nothing
of a "grand line" and little inner force, to throw out centrifugal or
illuminating sparks; a friendly, pleasant, average Californian; no more
a statesman in the European sense than Typhoid Mary is Einstein;
and a man who, quite possibly and with luck, could make a tolerable
president of the United States.

Warren is nowhere near so colorful as Kenny, about whom more
hereunder. He is much more sober stuff. He beat Kenny (roughly by

590,000 votes to 520,000) for a variety of cogent reasons. Incidentally—and this represents a striking but not unusual feature of American political life—the two contestants were, and are, good friends; Kenny was Warren's attorney general and they worked together closely for four years, though Warren is, of course, a Republican, and Kenny a Democrat; Warren was—another point in their close association—Kenny's predecessor as attorney general. Reasons for Warren's victory: (*a*) a good record, which was liberal enough to bring him a substantial liberal vote; (*b*) at the same time unanimous support by all conservative forces and Republicans; (*c*) the death of Roosevelt, and the subsequent breakdown of the broad dykes channeling the Roosevelt coalition; (*d*) a fierce intramural quarrel in the Democratic camp, between leftists and superleftists, which left Kenny bouncing in thin air. He was unable to lead a unified ticket, because of the murderous fight between Will Rogers Jr. and Ellis Patterson for nomination to the senate, a fight so mixed up with splinter leftism that any independent liberal needed a slide rule and a protractor to find where the lines met, interlocked, and parted.

Warren won—another striking point—even though Democratic registration in the state far exceeds Republican. But I have already mentioned the great influx of war migrants that not only added vastly to the electorate; it steadily caused shifts of population within the state, which means that registration doesn't always mean what it ought to mean. California was for years overwhelmingly Republican. Under Roosevelt it was as overwhelmingly Democratic; FDR carried it all four times he ran. Many times in this book we shall allude to this phenomenon, that in state after state the enormous magnetic, polarizing force of Roosevelt caused a complete political switch around, in 1932, 1936, 1940, and 1944. Meantime we know well what happened in November, 1946. All over the country the midterm elections swept the Democrats and Rooseveltians out, and Republicans like Warren—all breeds and counterbreeds of Republicans—triumphantly in. The Roosevelt era ended; what was left of the New Deal slipped back into history; the post-Roosevelt epoch, with all that it may portend, with all its tentative feelings toward a new equilibrium still to be fixed, began.

Warren was born in Los Angeles in 1891. He worked at every kind of job as a young man, from selling papers to playing the clarinet. His father, a railway mechanic, was murdered some years ago—in a crime that had no political significance but which is another indication that California's tradition of frontier violence is not so far away. Warren entered political life as a committee clerk in Sacramento after a brief period of law practice, and rose slowly. He was district attorney for Alameda County (which includes Oakland and Berkeley) from 1925 to 1938, and then attorney general of the state. Little is remembered for or against him in those jobs except the *Point Lobos* case, which is too complex for treatment here. A ship's engineer was murdered in 1936 on the freighter *Point Lobos*; three men went to the penitentiary for "conspiracy" to commit this crime, on highly dubious evidence; later they were pardoned. All three were labor leaders whom the conservative community wanted to "get" and the man murdered was a labor spy. Warren, as district attorney, was hotly accused of bias and the case as a whole was called an antilabor frame-up; but there is no evidence that he himself did anything improper.

In 1942 Warren ran for governor; he won largely because California was so fed up with his Democratic predecessor, Culbert Levy Olson. Also, he was running in a nonpresidential year, and hence did not have a Roosevelt ticket to oppose. Technically he stood as a nonpartisan and he won handsomely. By 1944 he was a national figure, and he was offered the Republican vice presidential nomination under Dewey; he turned it down. There were two reasons for this: first, he has no private fortune, and with a large family to support and his children at the most expensive age, he could not afford the office; second, he shrewdly sensed that Roosevelt could not be beaten and that if FDR carried California it would be quite a black eye for Mr. Warren. His caution did not endear him to the Republican hierarchy, and during the campaign he was accused (*a*) of being too lukewarm to Dewey and (*b*) too friendly. People said that as a nonpartisan he should not have played politics at all. Meantime, he lost the Republican left too, as a result of some obscure finagling over Willkie. Willkie had wanted to run in the California primaries, and only chose Wisconsin instead (where he was so disastrously beaten) out of consideration for Warren; the Willkieites then claimed that Warren "let Willkie down."

During his first term Warren was fairminded, conscientious, tolerant, and uninspired. He lifted old age pensions from forty to fifty dollars a month; he tried to push through a compulsory health insurance bill, which the lobbies beat; he set about a program of prison reform; hedging against postwar unemployment, he greatly improved the governmental machinery of the state, and created a Reconstruction and Re-employment Commission that has done admirable work. He played hard for AF of L support (which he now has); hence, he tended as a rule to support everything the AF of L asked for. Finally, he "reduced taxes." But beware of this cliché. It can be said of a dozen governors in a dozen states that, to their credit, they "reduced taxes." But to "reduce taxes" is the simplest thing in the world in years when tax receipts, owing to war industry, have been greater than ever before in history; most states have enormous surpluses today, not deficits. The real point is why taxes were not reduced more.

Warren's dominant note is, to sum up, decency, stability, sincerity, and lack of genuine intellectual distinction. But how many American governors have genuine intellectual distinction?

A Word About Bob Kenny

Robert W. Kenny, whom Warren beat for governor in the 1946 primaries, is one of the most engaging men in America. His effervescent courage and liberalism are both incontestable; he is also an almost too-shrewd politician with caressing eyes upon the future political career of Bob Kenny. If I should be asked what his chief personal quality is, I would answer with some such word as "disarmingness," in that he is one of the most unconventional men I ever met. No one but Bob Kenny could squat on the ledge of a skyscraper to be photographed watching a parade; no one can play better the role of a San Francisco *bon vivant* without sacrificing dignity; no one can so brashly defy all political conventions and so debonairly get away with it—almost. This does not mean that Kenny is not serious. He is serious. But also he is an imp. Moreover, he is an imp who weighs two hundred pounds. He greets you, asks you to a cocktail party in his office, becomes a friend, takes you for a week-end drive to Nevada, loves to gamble and is very good at it, and is unquenchably alive with wit and candor all the time. He has friends, intimate friends, in every camp. The first time I met him he was drinking amiably with two companions; one was a Jesuit priest, the other was Harry Bridges.

Kenny's humor, vivacity, sense of phrase, bright brains, and outrageousnesses are a joy. I asked him once where a certain former governor was living. He replied, "East Oblivion." He told me of one colleague, "He has a mind like a miller bug—it just skates on the surface." Once he said of himself, "I was ashamed of being a Republican and afraid of being a Democrat." After a stupendous lunch that lasted three hours, in a restaurant that wasn't supposed to serve lunch, I asked him if he could give me some kind of biographical handout. Most politicians deny coyly that they have any such prepared document; Kenny boomed with laughter and said, "Of course—I'm a politician!"

When Mr. Truman visited San Francisco in July, 1945, the newspapers reported a small colloquy:

> Truman: "Why don't you run for governor, Bob?"
> Kenny: "I don't want to run for office. I want to run away from it."
> Truman: "I've been doing that all my life, Bob, and look where I am now."
> Kenny: "Yes, and what you have now is a job without a future."

Kenny, a three-generation Californian, was born in Los Angeles in 1901, but his family is San Franciscan; thus he spans both ends of the state. His grandfather and Bancroft, the historian, were partners; the original Kenny home still stands intact at 1067 Green Street, San Francisco. He has private means; yet he has always been on the side of the underpossessed. (By contrast—and this is the kind of American paradox that causes foreign visitors, bred on dogma, to hold their heads—Warren, though a poor boy who had to struggle for a living, is a conservative.)

Kenny worked all over the lot, though he didn't have to. He was a banker, lawyer, newspaperman; he was bureau manager for the United Press in Los Angeles for awhile, and once worked briefly for the Chicago *Tribune* in Paris. He was No. 1 in passing the state civil service examination as a youngster, and at twenty-eight was appointed to a judgeship in Los Angeles (to fill a vacancy—normally in California judges are elected); after serving in both municipal and superior courts he ran for the state senate against a Ham & Eggs candidate, and won by a thundering majority though he spent no money and made no speeches. On his first day in the senate he rocked the state by introducing fifty bills! Then after four years as senator he was elected attorney general. This was in 1942, the year of a Republican clean sweep. He was the only Democrat to get through.

Kenny did not particularly want to run for governor in 1946. He likes being attorney general, he set up a splendid record in the job, and he could probably have been re-elected to the end of time. On finally accepting the nomination, he declared, "I guess I should accept congratulations in about the way that a pregnant woman does. She didn't want to get in that condition, but as long as she is—"[1] Then he slipped over to Europe to see the Nuremberg trials. His explanation: "The first month of a campaign is when things go wrong and all the silly little decisions have to be made. . . . I'll be away."

What beat him when he returned was not his wisecracking or insouciance but Warren's unassailable popularity and the fact that he himself was pushed into a position where he had to carry water on both shoulders. The Democratic party is a crazy hodgepodge in California; he had to hold the balance on both wings. Also the tidelands issue hurt him. In Chicago in 1944, where he was leader of the California delegation, he backed Truman against Wallace; in 1946, despite this, he got CIO benediction but by trying to satisfy everybody in all camps he alienated what should have been his most solid liberal support. He told me once that his technique was, in general, to try to nail down the right, then cultivate the left. "If you see anybody more extreme than you are, you have to run over there and rub him out—never get

<hr>

[1] *Time,* March 18, 1946.

caught in the middle of a field with a loose ball." This sounds very pretty, but it didn't quite work out. Kenny got caught with two or three loose balls—and was kicked all over the place.

No one, however, should think that his political career is over. He is one of the ablest liberals in California, and still something of a white hope for the entire West.

Mayor of San Francisco

Roger D. Lapham is an attractive white-haired, vigorous man in his early sixties who gets to work at 7 A.M. and who keeps a curious calendar in his office, set each morning, that tells how much longer he will be mayor. The day I saw him it read, "Days Gone—541; Days to Go—920."

Transportation is a headache in every American city, and in San Francisco more so than usual. Every visitor will observe that there are four different lines of track on Market Street because until 1944 there were two competing streetcar systems. Five times efforts were made to merge the Market Street Railway, privately owned, with the municipal company; each failed when put to public vote, and the lunatic anomaly persisted that San Franciscans paid a 5¢ fare on the municipal railway, 6¢ on the cable cars, and 7¢ on the Market Street system. Shortly after his election to the mayoralty Lapham got busy. One of his techniques was to open the phone book at random early in the morning, and call up a dozen people, saying, "This is Roger Lapham. Will you help me straighten out the transportation tangle?" In the end the merger went through, and San Francisco is on the way to having one fare and a universal transfer.

Lapham is a millionaire shipping magnate; yet he owes his career in part to Harry Bridges. San Francisco is, as everyone knows, one of the strongest labor towns in the country, and during the 30's it suffered acute and prolonged labor trouble; there was a general strike in 1934, the second general strike in American history, and in November, 1936, the famous "hundred days" strike of the longshoremen tied up the waterfront completely. Lapham organized an Employers' Council to fight the strike. But his mood and methods were conciliatory. "We had to organize too, to stand on equal terms," he explains today. Up to December, 1936, he had never taken part in public affairs; then, before eleven thousand people, most of whom were union members, he engaged in debate with Bridges at the Civic Auditorium. Lapham thought that he would be hissed off the stage, but the crowd heard him in perfect order, and the fair-minded speech he made turned him into a public figure. Nowadays when he meets Bridges he is apt to say, "Harry, if it hadn't been for that debate, I wouldn't be mayor."

Lapham is New York born; he went to Harvard, and then entered his uncle's shipping business; for many years he was president and then chairman of the board of the American-Hawaiian Steamship Company. He first saw San Francisco in 1901, after a voyage around the Cape; he has lived in it and loved it since 1915. In December, 1941, Frances Perkins called him to Washington, asking him to be one of the original members of the War Mediation Board; then he joined the War Labor Board as one of the four employer members and stayed with it eighteen months. In 1943 friends persuaded him to run for mayor of San Francisco. He is a registered Republican (though he voted for FDR in 1932); yet he got the support of the Democratic machine. He won in a walk, and has turned out to be the best mayor the city ever had.

Lapham has several eccentricities; for instance he likes to wear blindingly gaudy neckties and he plays a wonderful game of bridge that bewilders opponents, because he bids without looking at the cards. But details like this do not matter. What does matter is that he is a man of integrity and public spirit who was willing to enter political life and give everything he has to it at a time when most men would be thinking of comfortable retirement. He was born with a gold spoon in his mouth; yet his only interest now is public service. His education is, as it were, beginning; as a friend put it to me, "Roger Lapham learned more in the sixth decade of his life than most people forget in a lifetime."

Late in 1945 a group of municipal employees threatened to strike in protest at the hiring of a Nisei named Miyama, who had been interned at the Tule Lake Relocation center. Miyama had duly passed a civil service examination, and was properly certified to work. Lapham issued an ultimatum: "This man is going to work here if the whole city walks out tomorrow." The city did not walk out, and Mr. Miyama got his job.

In midsummer 1946 came a curious episode. Lapham was accused of being "dictatorial" and "negligent," the last two adjectives that one would normally associate with him, and a group of citizens—pretty much on the outside fringes—got up a petition to demand his recall. The chief motivation was resentment at high taxes and the transportation merger, which had made necessary a raise in local fares. Lapham himself then signed one of the recall petitions demanding his own ouster and asked that all good citizens do likewise, so that the matter could promptly come to public vote. A special election was held, and he won by a comfortable majority.

Glimpse of Bridges

The person Harry Renton Bridges most reminded me of was Jimmy Walker, strange as that may seem. Lean, boyish, alert, with a hawklike

humor and a touch of the dapper—also a good solid touch of city
streets—Bridges resembles in several respects the former mayor of
New York. He is, however, not a playboy. He hasn't the time. Not only
is Bridges president of the International Longshoremen's and Warehousemen's Union and head of the California CIO; he was for seven
years "the most hounded, searched, spied, snooped, shadowed, and
wiretapped man in the whole American labor movement." This period
is now presumably over, and the "Bridges case" concluded. In June,
1945, the Supreme Court invalidated a long-standing order to deport
him as an undesirable alien, and in September he became an American
citizen.

Bridges was born of a middle-class family in Australia. At seventeen
he ran away to sea. As a merchant sailor he worked all over the world,
and in 1920, aboard a schooner, arrived in San Francisco; he has
stayed in the United States ever since. He became a longshoreman and
organized the longshoremen into what was then an AF of L union; a
lively scrapper, he made this quickly into an effective militant force.
After the bloody strikes of the 1930's he worked out a series of agreements with the shipowners—it was at this time that he first met Lapham
—which by and large have been respected ever since.

The story of the deportation proceedings is too well known and
abstruse for treatment here. The labor haters recognized Bridges as
the dominant workers' leader on the West Coast, and they set out to
break him, get rid of him, by fair means or foul. After preliminary
skirmishing he was brought to trial in 1939 on the charge that he was
(a) an alien and (b) a member of the Communist party and therefore
deportable. The evidence of formal Communist affiliation was flimsy;
mostly it was based on the testimony of two rivals who hated him. Dean
James M. Landis heard the first case and dismissed it. Then, by change
in statute, the position was altered so that Bridges would be deportable
even if he were not a Communist at the time, if it could be proved that
he ever *had* been a Communist. After four years of the most convoluted
legal procedure, Attorney General Biddle ordered that Bridges be de-
ported. This was in 1942. Then came a series of appeals to the federal
courts, and after three more years the Supreme Court canceled the
deportation order.

Lapham's attitude on all this was double. What did it matter if
Bridges was or wasn't a Communist, since he took the party line
anyway? But why deport him, which would simply mean his martyriza-
tion?

Actually Bridges keeps aloof from party politics as such, and is on
record (*Fortune,* February, 1945) as stating that he "wants American
free enterprise, American capitalism, to work." When war came in
1941 he took the line that "there is a difference between the right to
strike and the exercise of the right to strike," and actively sponsored

and pushed through a no-strike pledge by all CIO unions on the West Coast. His relations with Lapham's Employers' Council grew more cordial; all he asked was that, in return for the no-strike pledge, there should be no union busting. "We won our fight for union security," he told *Fortune,* "and there's no point in fighting when the battle is over." As a result San Francisco, so often strike paralyzed, went through the whole period of the war without a single labor dispute of consequence. But after the war, as everybody knows, accumulated pressures blew the lid off, and nationwide maritime strikes took place.

In June, 1946, Bridges helped form a national Committee of Maritime Unions embracing six CIO waterfront and seagoing unions, among them the immensely powerful National Maritime Union bossed by Joe Curran of New York, plus one independent. This committee proceeded to call a strike for June 15. At the last minute of the eleventh hour, a settlement was reached by intervention of the federal government. An uneasy truce supervened till September. Then came more and hotter fireworks, when a strike was called by Harry Lundeberg, head of the Sailors' Union of the Pacific and the Seamen's International Union, which are AF of L affiliates. Lundeberg, next to Bridges, is the most colorful, aggressive and dramatic of west coast labor leaders. He is a Norwegian by birth and an extremist and direct actionist; he once belonged to a Spanish syndicalist union, and he and Bridges are bitter enemies.[2] This situation reached a climax just as these chapters of this book go to press. The AF of L strike was called off after nine days, when a CIO strike was scheduled to begin.

Before this Bridges and Philip Murray, head of the CIO, had had a healthy tiff. Murray announced in July that the CIO territory in California would be split into two administrative units, north and south, with Bridges remaining in charge in the north, but with Los Angeles taken away from him. This of course reflected the growing split in the CIO between right and left wings; even if Bridges is not a Communist, it was a move by Murray to check radical aggressiveness. Bridges' San Francisco office immediately announced that Bridges had resigned as California regional director. Murray meanwhile stated that his order "did not reflect on Mr. Bridges' integrity." A few hours later it was announced that Bridges had not resigned. For a time it was not clear whether the Bridges bailiwick had been cut in half or not, or what were the precise limits of his frontier.

There is no thuggery, no goon squadism, in Bridges' union. It is no easy thing to run a union honestly, but he manages to do so. It is instructive to watch him in the chair. He welcomes big meetings (whereas a good many unions try to keep attendance at a minimum); he encourages the freest and most acrimonious discussion; everything

² Cf. Victor Riesel in the New York *Post,* September 6, 1946.

is decided by open vote, down to the most minor issues; yet he is an absolute dictator who runs the whole thing with the precision of a jeweler fixing a watch.

Outside his office he likes to point proudly to a scroll:

IN APPRECIATION PRESENTED TO THE
INTERNATIONAL LONGSHOREMEN'S AND WAREHOUSEMEN'S UNION
FOR UPHOLDING THE PRINCIPLES OF RIGHTEOUS-
NESS IN REFUSING TO LOAD SCRAAP [sic] METAL FOR
JAPAN IN DECEMBER 1938, AS A PROTEST AGAINST
JAPAN'S UNDECLARED AGGRESSIVE WAR IN CHINA.
THE CHINESE PEOPLE OF SAN FRANCISCO
JUNE 8, 1945

Bridges has a pointed wit. Once a rich conservative tried to squirm into his good graces by saying effusively that he read *PM*. "That reactionary sheet?" was his reply.

"Big Wop"

Amadeo P. Giannini, a heavy lonely man now aged seventy-six, is chairman of the board of Bank of America, the biggest private bank in California, the United States, and the world. It has more than three million depositors and it blankets California with something like five hundred branches. For a long time it ran nip and tuck with Chase National of New York to be the world's largest bank, but early in 1946 it passed Chase with total deposits of more than $5,200,000,000.

Giannini is a somewhat rare phenomenon in the United States: a banker from the wrong side of the tracks and proud of it. To people like the Crockers he was an upstart and an outsider; but he beat them at their own game. He was born in San Jose, near San Francisco, and started life as a vegetable peddler; he went into banking after being rebuffed by a small bank he wanted to buy. His was the only bank open (it was known then as Bank of Italy) after the fire-*cum*-earthquake of 1906; he spread out everywhere by getting the absolute confidence of small depositors and debtors (for instance any person regularly employed may borrow three hundred dollars merely on his signature); he cares very little for money personally, and is not a very rich man by millionaire standards; but he is prouder of his bank than a Neapolitan of Vesuvius.

Giannini—there has been considerable illness in his family—is almost a recluse; he does not even belong to the California Bankers Association. Society does not discriminate against him; it is he who discriminates against society. He belongs to no clubs, not even the Bohemian; the only post he holds is that of a regent at the university, to which he has made large gifts. In December, 1944, a group of local businessmen gave a public dinner to Paul C. Smith, the editor of the San Francisco *Chronicle*. Giannini came. It was his first public appearance in fifteen years. Some years before he had been ferociously pro-Mussolini, but at the time of the Abyssinian war Smith told him some of the facts of life. Not only was Giannini impressed; he changed the name of his bank from Bank of Italy to Bank of America National Trust and Savings Association.

Giannini's financial role in the community is of necessity enormous; he helps to finance Hollywood, and he played with Henry Kaiser from the beginning, when all the Anglo-Saxon professionals thought that Kaiser was slightly cracked. As to politics he has only intervened once. This was in the mid 1920's when he felt that a governor was unfairly blocking his extension into branch banking. He got both angry and busy, and helped elect another governor.

Giannini, whose history is almost inextricably conjoined with that of modern California, snubs his home state every winter by taking a long holiday—in Florida!

States and Governors

What is a state? What is a governor? Again, let me point out that this book is neither a work of history nor a civics text, but it may be useful to define these terms very briefly. Perhaps the man from Mars doesn't understand them as well as we do.

The United States is a federal government—"a commonwealth of commonwealths"—but the *state* is the nucleus of the American political system. For instance the right of a citizen to vote derives not from the federal government but from the state—which is the chief reason residents of the District of Columbia cannot vote. Also, in theory at least, the president of the United States is elected, through the mechanism of the electoral college, not by the "nation" but by the states. Not only in theory. Two American presidents—Benjamin Harrison and Rutherford Hayes—reached the White House even though they received a minority of the popular vote, because arrangement of the figures by state totals gave them the majority required. Each state makes its own constitution, out of its own authority,[3] and its own laws, which are, as everybody knows, indescribably various. Above all a state rules its cities; we have the spectacle of a largely rural legislature in Albany having the final decision on New York City's subway fare.

All this being true the "sovereignty" of the states today is largely artificial; the old doctrine of states' rights has been pretty well thinned

[3] But Congress can influence the kind of constitution a state may adopt. For instance Utah was not admitted to the union until it promised to abolish polygamy.

down, and most states—except in atmosphere—are little more than a
superior type of county. The tremendous federal bureaucracy of the
New Deal; such interstate conceptions as that expressed by the TVA;
incessant movements of population from one state to another; "com-
pacts" between states such as those that regulate the harbor and water
supply of New York City; federal grants as for highways; the water
treaty between western states over the usage of the Colorado River—
these and a hundred similar considerations have tended to reduce the
practical consequence of state authority.

Of course what are commonly thought of as special characteristics of
the states have become confused, and many careers of energetic
Americans completely transcend state lines. For instance Professor
Kenneth B. Murdock of Harvard said once, "I've seen Kentuckians
who hated whisky, Virginians who weren't descended from Pocahontas,
Indianans who hadn't written a novel . . . spendthrift Yankees, cold-
blooded Southerners, narrow-minded Westerners."[4] That estimable
political philosopher and seer Walter Winchell once pointed out (New
York *Daily Mirror,* February 25, 1946), that Mr. Justice Douglas of
the Supreme Court, one of the most useful of all living Americans,
was born in a town called Maine in Minnesota, raised in Yakima,
Washington, went to school in Walla Walla, Washington, studied and
taught at schools in both New York and Connecticut, lives in Maryland,
works in Washington, D. C., and is yet a "citizen" of Oregon where he
has a ranch.

Nevertheless the states are not to be ignored, as geographical entities
or otherwise. Not only are they a convenience in the over-all organization
of a book like this; they are still capable of exerting considerable
political power, power that is sometimes annoying in the extreme to the
federal government. For instance it was found impossible in the spring
of 1946 to extend the life of the United States Employment Service,
useful as this might well have been. The states (through their congressmen) insisted on a return to the former system of state control. States'
rights may have been thinned down as a doctrine, but they make lively
local issues everywhere. Hardly a month passes without vigorous
controversy arising on some subject—from tideland oil to the geographic
distribution of federal appointments—having to do with the "autonomy"
of states and the basic relationship between state and nation.

Almost every European student, visiting America for the first time,
asks two questions. First, why is the capital of an American state
likely to be so inconspicuous a town? Consider Springfield (as against
Chicago), Salem (as against Portland), Frankfort (as against Louisville), Olympia (as against Seattle), Dover (as against Wilmington),

[4] In a speech before the New England Society of Cleveland and the Western
Reserve, 1928.

and any of a dozen others. Second, why are so few political parties organized on a state basis? None exists, since the death of the Wisconsin Progressives in 1946.

The reason why the early constitution makers chose a small town as capital, usually one near the center of the state, was in most cases double. First, rural fear of the big city vote and urban influence generally. Second, transportation. Before the railways (and automobiles) it was essential that the capital be equally accessible to all. As to political parties on state lines they have never developed seriously because no "Illinois" party set against, say, a "Minnesota" party could possibly get anywhere on the national level. The organization of the union by states grew up, in a way, out of fear that the country *would* become a real nation. But it has worked out just the other way.

Turn now to the institution of governor. He is, of course, the chief executive of the state, ruling by virtue of a constitution and with his prerogatives checked by a legislature and a judiciary; he is commander-in-chief of the state guard which is his own armed force, so to speak, and which is not subject (except by agreement) to federal commands; in most states he has a veto power; in other words his functions are, in miniature, almost exactly those of the president in Washington. There are, however, some differences. Governors are elected directly, not by an electoral college. And, a strange phenomenon that causes much confusion in state administration, they do not as a rule choose their own cabinets. Take California. Warren and Kenny are of course of different parties; yet they were elected together in 1942 and had to serve and work together. This is as if, while FDR was president, his attorney general—elected independently—should have been John Bricker. The structure of state government is almost farcically haphazard, in that no constitutional office is dependent on any other. Governor, lieutenant governor, attorney general, treasurer, secretary of state, are all elected independently, and the victors may be deadly rivals. Even when they are all of the same party, there may be no slate, no common platform, no embracing unity. Of course every governor does have the power of appointment to certain nonelective offices. Otherwise he couldn't function. Finally, as is known to everyone, governors are so important because the governorship of a great state is such a familiar steppingstone to the presidency. Consider Cleveland, Wilson, Coolidge, and the two Roosevelts.

Twenty-five of the forty-eight American governors serve four-year terms, twenty-two serve two-year terms. The term of one (New Jersey) is three years. In most states, particularly those in the South, no governor may succeed himself except after the lapse of another term; this, the "eunuch rule," was written into the early constitutions to prevent a strong governor from building up a permanent machine. In states with two-year terms where the governor may run for re-election, he is apt to start campaigning for a second term the minute he is installed in the first. About all this we shall make mention later.

A peculiar office is that of lieutenant governor. Some few states have abolished this office; because, except to preside over the state senate, the incumbent (particularly if he is of a different party from the governor) has very little to do. As a result an energetic lieutenant governor, in order to get away from the essential triviality of his job, is apt to make a nuisance of himself simply because he wants to do *something*, and in many states governor and lieutenant governor are rivals and antagonists. Talk about American "rationality"!

Finally, the legislatures. These are, in every state except Nebraska, bicameral; roughly, the pattern of the federal Congress is followed, with a division of authority between senate and assembly. Only five legislatures meet annually (New York, Rhode Island, New Jersey, Massachusetts, South Carolina); sessions of the other 43 are biennial, because there isn't enough business to justify calling a session every year. Moreover, even the biennial sessions are apt to be pretty brief, which leads to the important point that, with the exception of a few rich men, all state legislators in the United States must have *other* jobs. They are merchants or farmers or, in large part, lawyers. Making the laws of the state is not their profession. Making money is their profession. Making the laws is what they do in their spare time.[5]

A basic issue in almost every state legislature—and indeed in the politics at large of almost every state—is the conflict between town and country. The distrust of big cities by rural areas is a factor in American history almost as old as the history itself. The population shifts; but reapportionment of legislative seats does not shift correspondingly. For instance San Francisco and Los Angeles between them, with an overwhelming preponderance of the wealth, intellectual attainment, and political experience of the state, as well as more than half the total population, have only two senators out of forty. The "cow counties" (this, we shall see, happens in many other states besides California) have an altogether unfair preponderance over the towns. Among other things this serves to check political expression by urban labor.

What is the "ideal" California legislator? The most ironic definition I heard came from a member of Warren's staff: "A man who votes for all appropriations, and against all taxes."

[5] Some occupations of California assemblymen are funeral director, "rancher and machinery," industrial relations director, production engineer, real estate, accountant, jobber, teacher, machinist, insurance broker, master mechanic, tax statistician, service station operator, retired railway conductor, painter, trucking contractor, editor, cattleman, poultry dealer, pharmacist, labor leader, "land and water development," advertising executive, and law student. Of the forty senators thirteen are lawyers.

Line on Lobbies

These exist in every state, exactly as they exist in and around the national government. There is nothing inherently wrong with lobbying in itself; the phenomenon is inevitable in any democracy so varied and diffuse as ours. There is nothing evil in the concept of power, or in the guidance of public and legislative opinion toward a political objective; what may be evil is the evil use of power. Thus there exist, depending on the point of view, "good" and "bad" lobbies. The Political Action Committee will call the National Association of Manufacturers pernicious; and vice versa. The State Department helped build one of the most powerful lobbies in the country to explain the issues behind Dumbarton Oaks and the San Francisco Charter; but no one could claim that this procedure was improper or incorrect. The United States is an enormously diversified nation, and a *legitimate* lobby can usefully fill a special role, that of representing groups which otherwise have no special representation. A shrewd legislator put it to me this way in Sacramento: "The lobby is the American substitute for the one good thing that distinguished the corporative state. The Farm Bureau and Farmers Union are, for instance, Deputies for Wheat."

But let us point out promptly that, as operated in practice, lobbying in many legislatures viciously abuses its prerogatives. The "pressure boys" use every kind of weapon to thwart and defeat the public, out of the most grasping kind of greed and selfishness. A point to mention is that, in many states, accredited lobbyists are actually permitted to sit in the senate or assembly hall. They cannot, of course, vote; but they can tell legislators what to vote for. How is a legislator influenced? The days of slipping thousand dollar bills into his pocket are, at least in California, over; direct bribery is considered clumsy, and even dangerous. But suppose a legislator is an insurance man in a county seat, or a lawyer hungering for clients. It will be the easiest thing in the world for the lobbyist of a big corporation to throw business his way—or threaten to withhold it.

California was so abused by the agents of special privilege that, as noted in Chapter 1, improper lobbying was made a felony. So today a lobbyist must be registered; he is known as a "certified advocate." I have mentioned the early days of Southern Pacific. Today, this great railroad plays no direct role in politics and performs no such antics as distinguished it fifty years ago; yet it is a suggestive illustration of its prestige that when Walter Little resigned recently as Speaker—no less—of the California assembly to become legislative representative of the four major railways in the state, people in Sacramento thought that he was coming up in the world! And the railways still wield great—but quite normal and natural—financial power. For instance testimony before the Interstate Commerce Committee of the U.S. Senate in 1941 showed these recent contributions:[6]

San Francisco Chamber of Commerce	$15,300
Los Angeles Chamber of Commerce	35,625
California State Chamber of Commerce	50,000
Industrial Association of San Francisco	30,175
All Year Club of Southern California	35,250
California Tax Payers Association	53,750
Californians, Inc.	96,000

Let us now pose a naïve question. How does a lobbyist or legislative agent or "certified advocate" work vis-à-vis his employers? Simple. Suppose some special interests want to push a dubious measure through. They hire Lobbyist X. Then Lobbyist X, if unscrupulous, may exaggerate—or even invent—opposition to the bill, in order that his own services will seem more valuable. Or, a perfectly innocent measure may come up, supported by some quite legitimate group. But it is feared that it may not pass, so the group advocating it may pay Lobbyist Y a thumping fee when all that was really necessary would be the normal expense of postage, telephoning, and the like. There may be nothing whatever "wrong" with a bill; just the same, a lobbyist (and a lot of them simply love to do things the crooked way) will do his best to make it seem as difficult to pass as possible. The legislature as a whole knows these facts well; in 1946, in fact, an effort was made in California to force a legislative investigation of the whole subject of lobbying, but it was beaten. Seventeen American states, it was pointed out in the debate, require all lobbyists to file a statement of their expenses—and where the money went—at the end of each session; but California does not.

"Politics Fill Me with Doubt and Dizziness"

We proceed now to examine cursorily some of the special particularities of politics in California, some idiosyncrasies that make it notable. For one thing, though this is true elsewhere too, practically all state jobs are under civil service. There is no such condition as that in some southern states, where even the police are not civil servants, and where a new governor can, if he wants, make a totally new police force out of political appointees. This would be impossible in California. There is no mechanism for building up a state machine through political patronage; precinct captains can't grab off the loot. For another thing, all municipal, county, and particularly judicial jobs are nonpartisan. In Illinois, let us say, judges—and also mayors, county commissioners, sheriffs, and so on—run as Democrats or Republicans. In California, as in several western states, this is forbidden. The mayor of San Francisco happens to be

[6] As quoted by *PM*, March 22, 1946.

a Republican, privately; the mayor of San Diego happens to be a Democrat. But this plays no role in the campaign; party affiliations are *not*
printed on the general election ballot. Of course, as the thing works out,
people in general know the sympathies of candidates, but there is
extremely little partisan spirit—about judgeships in particular. This
applies, let me repeat, to municipal, county, and judicial offices; it does
not apply, as we know, to state offices such as governor. In practice, most
judges are Republican, but this is because, by and large, most lawyers
are Republican, and judges of course rise out of the lawyer class.

And now another important factor, the open primary. As Bob Kenny
once said to an interviewer, "Here we have something political scientists have dreamed of—no bosses, a completely free-wheeling political
setup. Politically, we're about the purest state in the union." And Harry
Bridges told me once, "This *is* a nonpartisan state, and no kidding!" The
institution of the open primary has, in fact, made chaos of normal political procedure. The professional politicians still hold up their hands in
horror; they say "the party system has been destroyed." Anybody can
run for office. All it takes is a ten-dollar fee. Hence it is extremely difficult
for the professionals to practice infanticide on a budding politician. Moreover candidates for state (or federal) office are—like Warren—apt to
run in both party primaries. Anybody accustomed to the politics of
Pennsylvania or New Jersey will find his mind reeling if he looks at the
California method. Here, chosen quite at random, are some returns in the
1944 primary race for state senator:

Second Senatorial District

Randolph Collier (Dem)	4,290 votes
Randolph Collier (Rep)	3,258

Eleventh Senatorial District

Frank L. Gordon (Rep)	5,292
Frank L. Gordon (Dem)	5,818

Or, just to make it livelier:

Fifteenth Senatorial District

Frank H. Fowles (Rep)	1,343
Thomas McCormack (Rep)	4,137
Frank H. Fowles (Dem)	2,495
Thomas McCormack (Dem)	7,483

A candidate for state or federal office may, in other words, file in both
camps and run against himself. If he gets a majority in both primaries,
then he is of course the sole nominee in the general election (unless a
totally new candidate pops up), and the general election becomes a mere
formality. But, a point in qualification, a candidate must get the nomination of his *own* party to keep in the race; a Democrat cannot

qualify as a Republican too, unless he wins the Democratic primary. This sometimes causes mix-ups that would befuddle an atomic physicist. For instance a man named Costello (who incidentally had been a member of the Dies Committee) ran for re-election to Congress from Los Angeles in 1944. The CIO set out to beat him, and did. Costello was, and is, a Democrat. But whereas he lost the Democratic primary, he won the Republican! This meant that he could not run in the general election at all!

This was "explained" to me by a friend in Hollywood, who concluded, "It adds up to the fact that Brer Rabbit could be the next governor of California, or Mike Romanoff."

Finally, and most important, there is the fact that California (like most western states) has the initiative, the referendum, and the recall. I have before me a pamphlet entitled:

PROPOSED AMENDMENTS
TO CONSTITUTION

PROPOSITIONS AND PROPOSED LAWS
TOGETHER WITH ARGUMENTS

TO BE SUBMITTED TO THE ELECTORS
OF THE STATE OF CALIFORNIA AT THE

GENERAL ELECTION

The text includes (with neutrally prepared arguments for and against) a series of proposals for new legislation, on which the people vote directly yes or no. Any kind of bill may thus become law in California, by simple vote of the people, if enough petitioners endorse it. If someone got up a petition stating "All Jews in California Are to Be Shot on May First" it could in theory get on the ballot if enough people signed it. In practice it doesn't work out quite so simply; something like one hundred thousand bona fide names of voters are necessary to make a petition valid, and it must be certified as "not deceptive" by the secretary of state; it takes a good deal of organization to work a petition up, and the cost is estimated at about ten cents a signature. A semieccentric petition that got on the ballot recently asked that a copy of the Bible be put in every schoolroom in the state, and studied daily; it was defeated by 571,000 votes to 439,000.

Consider now the tensions, conflicts, and alliances within the parties. Generally speaking the Republican party in California is run by something called the Cameron-Chandler-Knowland Axis, named for three newspaper publishers—George T. Cameron of the San Francisco *Chronicle*, Harry Chandler of the Los Angeles *Times*, and Joseph R. Knowland of the Oakland *Tribune*. But it would be a gruesome exag-

geration to assume that this axis is a solid, single bloc; for instance
Cameron took a strong Willkie line, whereas Knowland was hot for
Dewey. Governor Warren is the chief present-day axis favorite. But he
is closer to Knowland than to Cameron or Chandler. When Warren
first ran for governor, it was the Knowland colors he was carrying,
and subsequently Warren named his son, Major William F. Knowland,
aged thirty-seven, to the Senate when Hiram Johnson died. Sometimes
one is asked about the influence in local affairs of another Californian,
Herbert Hoover. The answer is politically nil and intellectually considerable.

As to the Democrats the situation is much more complex. Their leader,
after a long process of ambushes and annihilations, was for a time Bob
Kenny; at present the state chairman is Colonel James Roosevelt, eldest
son of the late president, who resigned as chairman of the Hollywood
Independent Citizens' Committee for the Arts, Sciences and Professions
to take the job. Until 1932 the Democratic party had many ups and
downs in California; then FDR carried the state—partly because he
stood for repeal of prohibition, which was a tremendous California issue
—and, under his blanket coverage, all sorts of splinter groups emerged.
On one side was William Gibbs McAdoo, who, as I heard it put, "was
elected senator before he even opened his carpetbag." On the other was
Upton Sinclair who, during the depression, really stood for something.
Then arose a would-be redeemer in the person of Culbert L. Olson who
in 1939, after a fratricidal struggle in which the McAdoo forces were
finally beaten, became the first Democratic governor the state had had in
forty years. But Olson's men were more preoccupied by interparty
troubles than anything else, and his record as governor was disappoint-
ing; hence, Warren succeeded him in 1943. Olson's influence has now
disappeared. Then entered another actor—Ed Pauley. He is not, and
never has been, a boss on the *state* level; however, as treasurer of the
Democratic National Committee he was the channel to Hannegan and
national affairs. But—to reiterate the point—there is little state patronage
in California, and so Pauley never had much to offer locally. Pauley,
until the Ickes quarrel, was in a position to ask for almost anything in
Washington; but he had few jobs to bestow in California.[7] And local
politics in the United States depend absolutely on the power to give jobs.
Finally, after 1944, Kenny began to pick up the pieces; his defeat in 1946
opened the field again, and at the moment the Democratic machine is run
by an uneasy Jimmy Roosevelt-Will Rogers Jr. coalition. Just before
the November, 1946, election Roosevelt got into trouble by announcing
that he would vote for Warren, inasmuch as Warren, by winning the

[7] But of course the oil companies and oil men often play politics. See testimony
before the Senate Naval Affairs Committee in February, 1946.

Democratic as well as the Republican nomination, *was* the Democratic candidate (although a Republican), and since he, Roosevelt, could not support either the Communist or prohibitionist who were Warren's only opponents. For this Roosevelt was soundly denounced by the PAC, his own presumptive partner. Man from Mars, blink!

In Washington, California has some interesting people. The senior senator, Sheridan Downey, has a Ham & Eggs past, but he is a generous and useful citizen. The big-money interests are said to have spent almost a million dollars to defeat him in 1938, but he won, because he represented something paramount and permanent in California affairs, the forces of *dis*content. Downey did not come up in 1946. The midterm elections might well have unhorsed him, as they unhorsed almost everybody else of his type, not merely in California but—as we know—nearly everywhere in the nation. The Republican clean sweep really did sweep clean in California. Knowland beat Rogers, and bright and educated spirits in the congressional delegation like Jerry Voorhis and George E. Outland lost their jobs. Helen Gahagan Douglas was the only conspicuous New Dealer to survive the holocaust.

Wendell Willkie once told me that the first thing to find out about a state was the size and temper of its middle vote, its independents. For instance in Massachusetts, let us say, about 45 per cent of the vote will always be Republican, and about 40 per cent will always be Democratic; the way the other 15 per cent goes will tell the story. In some states this independent vote is smaller, and lines can be drawn even more acutely. But in California the bulge in the middle is enormous—which is a final reason why it is so unpredictable politically. Only about a third of the people can be counted upon as being certain on either side; the center is almost as wide as either wing, and almost as variable as the wings are fixed.

Who and What Run California?

Having now cursorily inspected men and politics in California, we proceed to look at corollary forces. But this is a convenient point for mentioning first how remarkably the five men I have talked about in this chapter—Warren, Kenny, Lapham, Bridges, Giannini—represent ideas and trends and issues that, time and time again, will crop out in this book implicitly if not explicitly. The topsy-turviness of the American political system and the decline of party politics as such; the importance of personality; the independence of so many voters; the way so very many Americans are self-made; the melting pot and how well it melts; the tendency of some representatives of the propertied class to go into public service; the powerful growth of labor as a political force; the basic and germinal problem that is probably the most important in

America, how to reconcile political liberty with economic security—all this is demonstrated even in such a brief account as this of five men picked almost at random.

As to general forces in California, aside from those already named, let us take the conservative side to begin with.

First, agriculture. This is, of course, big business in California, and the most conspicuous pressure group in agriculture is something known as Associated Farmers which is not in fact a farmers' organization exclusively but a kind of lobby including railroad men, canners, shippers and the like. Its line is reactionary in the extreme. Most observers think that its influence is diminishing. But until recently at least, it played a fairly strong political role in the state, both by campaign contributions to the parties and by attempting to prevent the organization of farm labor. Associated Farmers actively promoted vigilantism, antipicketing drives and so on in the 1930's, to break the great agrarian strikes—like the lettuce strike near Salinas—then in progress. Hundreds of pages could be written about this; the LaFollette Committee of the U.S. Senate, investigating infringement of civil liberties, took thousands of words of testimony. Carey McWilliams (*Ill Fares the Land,* p. 25) says that in one four-year period Associated Farmers got $178,542 in contributions; most were from such corporations as Southern Pacific, Pacific Gas and Electric, and Santa Fe; one packing company alone contributed $74,161.09. Two per cent of California landowners "control one-fourth of the acreage and nearly one-third of the crop value of the state," so it is not surprising that the big-money farmers are closely interlocked with other business interests. In a somewhat different category, but well worth mention, are the great marketing co-operatives, like the California Fruit Growers Exchange, which invented the Sunkist trademark and which is the biggest enterprise of its kind in the world.

Second, the great corporations, particularly Standard Oil, which can exert influence in several ways. Also in this rubric are the Pacific Gas and Electric Company (the dominant power company in the state), the Spreckels interests in San Diego, the chain stores, various cement, shipping and life insurance companies, the big canneries, Giannini's Bank of America, and of course the railroads.

Third, the Merchants and Manufacturers Association, which is the California equivalent of the NAM. It is of course a force strongly on the conservative side, but whether or not it affects a great number of actual votes is doubtful. It may, however, influence politics by putting up candidates, and by attempts to get antilabor bills on the ballot; it is violently antiunion. In general, M & M works closely with Associated Farmers. Its president is a former president of Southern Pacific, and its bailiwick is Los Angeles. Some small businessmen, who claim that they don't like M & M, may nevertheless be persuaded into becoming members; or a

small contractor may join up, even if he disapproves, because membership may help throw business his way. This is the country where contacts
equal contracts.

Fourth, the Los Angeles Chamber of Commerce; and never should it
be forgotten that Los Angeles County possesses about 40 per cent of the
wealth of California, and 42 per cent of the vote. It is, like most chambers
of commerce in the United States, very conservative except in booster
statistics. The Los Angeles Chamber should be carefully differentiated
from the *state* Chamber of Commerce, which is much more liberal.

Fifth, the American Legion, which maintains a powerful lobby in California. It is usually a factor behind the bogus "red scares";[8] it took the
lead in agitation against the dispossessed Japanese.

Sixth, real estate interests generally. These are particularly important
because so many Californians move about constantly.

Turn now to liberal forces. The chief among them is of course labor.
Just as the CIO is apt to say indignantly that Associated Farmers and
the M & M "run the state," so the Associated Farmers and the M & M
say indignantly that "labor runs the state." Both are wrong; neither side
comes anywhere near to running California exclusively. But certainly
labor has been a sharply rising influence. The AF of L has about a
million members; it is in the main strongly anti-Communist; it works
fairly well with the CIO when both have a common political aim, for
instance the recent defeat of Proposition Number 12 which threatened
to prohibit the closed shop in the state. This measure was introduced and
sponsored by the M & M. Yet, interestingly enough, among the organizations which lined up *with* the AF of L and the CIO against it were the
California, San Francisco, and Sacramento (but not Los Angeles)
chambers of commerce, the city councils of San Diego and Richmond,
the Los Angeles Church Federation, and the California Farm Bureau.
Presumably all these organizations were willing to concede that the days
of the open shop were no more, at least in California as of that time.

The AF of L is strongest in the building trades, and among nurses,
teachers, clerks, and culinary workers; the main CIO strength is in aircraft and on the waterfront. The CIO, with a much smaller membership,
is divided more or less down the middle, between those who would like
to kick the Communists out, but don't dare, and those who are apt to say,
"Oh well, let them stay!" The state CIO leader is, as everyone knows,
the redoubtable Bridges, but as we know his position has not been too
secure lately; the Communists are real specimens, not Dies Committee
ghosts or red herrings. The Political Action Committee of the CIO has
had great strength in California; it did a spectacular job in the 1944
elections as a kind of twentieth century Tammany Hall, turning out the

[8] Upton Sinclair was once arrested while reading the Declaration of Independence
aloud in public, during the worst days of Los Angeles red hunting.

vote; one of its chief foci of power has been Hollywood. Whether its massive defeat in 1946 represents a permanent or only a temporary setback is something that, at the moment, no man can easily know.

Another word on labor. It should, of course, always be kept in mind that California has a savagely brutal tradition of antilabor extremism and conspiracy. Next to the Sacco-Vanzetti case, what are probably the two greatest *causes célèbres* in American labor history are Californian, the dynamiting of the Los Angeles *Times* and the consequent trial of the McNamaras in 1911, and the Mooney frame-up in San Francisco in 1916.

Second—among forces more or less liberal—is the immense bloc of old folks, the "senior citizens" and radically inclined pensionnaires. These I discuss in the chapter following.

Among forces mixed up in themselves and hence more difficult to classify are Hollywood (also to be discussed later), the splendid civil service, the liquor interests, which play a role in the politics of almost every American state, and the schoolteachers. These latter and their "education lobby" are also factors almost everywhere in America; time and time again we shall mention them. The pattern is the same all over the country, and the objective highly commendable—to get more money for the schools. But this means higher taxes, and so business interests as a rule, which want taxes down, fight the education people as much as they dare.

As to newspapers—still another, nonhomogeneous force that we shall find in every state—they are a mixed bag in California. The Los Angeles *Times*, bitterly anti-New Deal and antilabor, is a heavy standpat force; the Los Angeles *News*, edited by Manchester Boddy, is eloquent and liberal, but it seems to be more an anthology of columns than a newspaper. The other two Los Angeles papers belong to Hearst. The best paper in the state, by far, is the *Chronicle* of San Francisco, which has a wonderfully picturesque history and which under George T. Cameron and Paul C. Smith, one of the most brilliant editors in the United States, maintains its tradition vigorously.

That preposterous old aurochs, Hearst, is of course a Californian, and the San Francisco *Examiner* is the "home" paper of the whole Hearst herd, but the old man himself has little specifically California influence nowadays. Only seldom does he promote individual candidates of his own—though his papers have warmly supported Warren; rather, he tries to knock off opponents by shouting "Red." Nevertheless, late in 1946, he sent a telegram to all Hearst editors in the country, urging "support of the whole Republican ticket during the last days of the campaign," under the slogan, "Vote against New Deal Communism, Vote Republican, Vote American." Hearst still lives like a shogun, a nabob, from an antique world. To describe his adventures in national politics would take a chapter.

Finally, consider federal pay rolls and federal credit, a factor of extreme importance in the immediate postwar period. There are, for instance, more federal job holders in California (313,400) than in any other state (even New York), and, incredible as the fact may seem, more than in Washington, D.C. The great airplane companies in the Los Angeles area could not, during the war, have ever met their bills if the U.S. Army, i.e. the federal government, had not been purchasing their airplanes; and of course the plants themselves could not have been expanded to their war capacity without federal help.

Also—to conclude—there are some remarkable and distinctively Californian minor lobbies. The chiropractors have one, so do the osteopaths, and so does a celebrated Los Angeles cemetery.

Chapter 3

More About California, Its How and Why

∿∿∿

> California, more than any other part of the Union, is a country by itself, and San Francisco a capital.
>
> —James Bryce

> East is East, and West is San Francisco . . . Californians are a race of people; they are not merely inhabitants of a state.
>
> —O. Henry

> Los Angeles is fertile soil for every kind of impostor that the face of the earth has been cursed by. The suckers all come sooner or later and the whole twelve months is open season.
>
> —H. L. Mencken quoting a local patriot

> Thought is barred in this city of Dreadful Joy [Los Angeles] and conversation is unknown.
>
> —Aldous Huxley in 1926

MOST Americans take the highly divergent characteristics of San Francisco and Los Angeles for granted; we know all about their special qualities. But suppose the man from Mars—or Moscow—should suddenly arrive in the United States, and ask that these two great cities be exposed to him.

San Francisco is, as every American knows, brilliant, polyglot, sophisticated, with some of the best hotels and restaurants in the world, and views of incomparable beauty and distinction. Los Angeles has beautiful views too, and some fine places to eat and drink in, but it is no rival to San Francisco in these respects. San Francisco fronts the sea, and you can sniff the spices of Cathay; it is a Bagdad of the West. But no fewer than 400,000 southern Californians are Iowa born; Los Angeles is Iowa with palms.

San Francisco is a community (like New York) built high, I heard it said; Los Angeles is a community built wide. San Francisco's brightly corrugated hills are stitched in by bay and ocean, but Los Angeles spreads out all over the place; it covers not less than 451 square miles, and is the largest city on earth in area; to cross it by motorcar may mean a trip of fifty miles. San Francisco doesn't care much whether it is big or small; it is, as Bret Harte once wrote, "serene and indifferent to fate." But the Angelenos are very proud of their monstrous size, and as far away as Butte, Montana, a prankster may erect a sign, LOS ANGELES —CITY LIMITS.

San Francisco has, as we know, a robust and chromatic history; its roots go deep. Los Angeles too has some interesting·history; but try to think of any Angeleno family that could fairly be called "old." San Francisco was built by gold, railways, and the port; Los Angeles by oil, climate, and real estate. In San Francisco people will tolerate everything, including the intolerable; but Los Angeles (the coruscating enclave of Hollywood excepted) takes a middle-aged and middle-western conception of manners and morals. Another point is that San Francisco has more native Californians, and a younger population; if an Angeleno says he was born in Los Angeles, people almost expect him to be an aborigine with a ring in his nose. By contrast, it took Paul C. Smith a long time to live down the fact that he was not San Francisco born. San Francisco pays little attention to its sister city but Los Angeles, though three times bigger, is apt to be pretty jealous. When Los Angeles had its zoot suit riots, San Francisco made small note of the fact; when, on V-J Day, San Francisco went wild and Market Street saw three fine days of hurly-burly with a lot of window smashing and some amiable rape, Los Angeles held its head in horror and talked smugly about "regrettable misconduct in the north."

To sum up, San Francisco (which incidentally was once called Yerba Buena) is tranquil and mature, whereas Los Angeles is the home par excellence of the dissatisfied; with its wonderful "imperial position" San Francisco has more authentic *joie de vivre* than any other American city I know; finally, it possesses the incomparable quality of charm. What other American city has flowers at every other street corner, like prewar Riga or Vienna? What other city has small shops, even the pharmacies, so meticulously chic? In what other city is it a heat wave if the temperature reaches seventy-eight in August, and where you can start crossing the bridge in smiling sunshine and emerge in fog? Even the telephone exchanges are romantically named in San Francisco—to wit China, Klondike, Seabright, Skyline, Evergreen.

Los Angeles has of course been called every name in the book, from "nineteen suburbs in search of a metropolis" to a "circus without a tent" to "less a city than a perpetual convention." Frank Lloyd Wright, the architect, is supposed to have said once, "If you tilt the whole country sideways, Los Angeles is the place where everything loose will fall." And listen to Westbrook Pegler: "It is hereby earnestly proposed that the U.S.A. would be much better off if that big, sprawling, incoherent, shapeless, slobbering civic idiot in the family of American communities, the City of Los Angeles, could be declared incompetent and placed in charge of a guardian like any individual mental defective."[1]

Everything goes in Los Angeles, so it may be thought; but here are some things forbidden by city ordinance, as itemized by H. L. Mencken in *Americana*:

Shooting rabbits from streetcars.
Throwing snuff, or giving it to a child under 16.
Bathing two babies in a single bathtub at one time.
Making pickles in any downtown district.
Selling snakes on the streets.

Freakishness, however, is not the characteristic that makes the town most interesting. What distinguishes it more is (*a*) its octopuslike growth, and (*b*) the way it lives on climate, mobility, and water.

Not only the Chamber of Commerce and the real estate interests made Los Angeles stretch and spread. What happened was that the suburbs could not afford to go two hundred or more miles for their own water. Beverly Hills, Glendale, and Pasadena are "independent," because (though they do belong to the Metropolitan Water District) they have their own water supply; the other communities do not, and hence are forced to incorporate with Los Angeles, which has superior taxing power, to get water in. This has produced some geographical anomalies. For instance the community of Tujunga is part of the city of Los Angeles, but it is altogether separated from the municipality proper by non-Los Angeles territory, as East Prussia was once separated from West by the Polish Corridor. Hollywood is part of Los Angeles. But Beverly Hills is not. In general what is going on is a spreading out of the *city* of Los Angeles to a point where it will someday be coterminous with the county.

Since the entire life of the area depends on imported water, a political conflict between the people and the public utilities that provided water (and power out of water) was inevitable. This was resolved in Los Angeles by the creation of a municipal authority; the city owns its own water and power systems, which are the biggest in the country. (San Francisco has municipal water, by contrast, but not power.) Another point: water means electricity and this in turn means clean industry—the great Douglas and Lockheed factories are smokeless—which in turn means clean towns. Finally, to call the civilization of Los Angeles "artificial" is to beg the question, since the whole giant community has been artificially created out of desert by irrigation.

The chief reason for the prodigious flow of people into California is that the old rheumatism doesn't twitch there any more, and the climate

[1] New York *World-Telegram*, November 22, 1938. Mr. Pegler was being annoyed at Upton Sinclair and the Townsendites.

helps to produce tall and healthy folk who can live most of their lives out
of doors. Children get quarts of orange juice from the time they are
born; the sun almost always shines and when it does rain—there can be
berserk storms as everybody knows—the Angelenos dismiss such crimes
of nature as "seasonal dew." Then consider the factor of the automobile.
The population of southern California is by all odds the most automobile
conscious in the world; most people, if they had to choose between a
house and a car, would probably choose the car, though the proportion
of home owners is the biggest in the United States; this has had one
interesting social consequence among others. The growth of the community came to depend on *public* highways, not on the private right of
ways of railroads; so part of the population at least became planning
conscious and social minded.

Los Angeles is, heaven knows, full of crackpots; yet it is a smart town
politically. Nobody bosses it, and the tensions are more than normally
acute, since it is the seat of both the most extreme conservatism in the
state and the most outspoken radicalism. The cleavages are much
sharper than in San Francisco. And people can act quickly, if aroused. A
councilman named McClanahan came out for Gerald L. K. Smith in
1945. Promptly the issue was put to public vote and he was recalled.

I have said that San Francisco is polyglot. So as a matter of fact is
Los Angeles, which is the second largest Mexican city in the world with
250,000 Mexicans; also it has about 135,000 Negroes, a big Filipino
colony, and a smattering of Chinese and Japanese.

Chinese and Japanese

San Francisco's Chinatown is unique if only because it is so conspicuous—a solid bloc of twenty thousand directly in the center of the
town. It is the biggest Chinese community, outside China, in the world,
except that of Singapore. Its origin, like much else in California, is the
old Central Pacific and the mines, which imported the first Chinese for
coolie labor.

What makes Chinatown additionally remarkable is its self-contained-
ness; it is a complete city within a city, with its own hospital, its own
telegraph equipped to handle messages in Chinese (even the Western
Union clock has Chinese characters), its own branch post office built in
the Chinese manner, its own pharmacies and food shops, a radio station
run by a bright young man named Tommy Tong, two theaters, five daily
newspapers, and above all the telephone exchange. The girls who run this
are of the third generation at the job. The first operators were men; they
taught their daughters, and the granddaughters took over in turn. The
girls have to know six Chinese dialects, and must memorize about 2,300
names and numbers. A telephone directory in Chinese exists, but few

subscribers use it; names have to be indexed by street instead of alphabetically (since there is no such thing as a Chinese alphabet) and most people simply rely on the operator's memory.

Chinatown is run by an organization known as the Six Companies, which represents the major clans; the Six are really a single board of governors or fathers. It raises special funds, gives advice, and serves as a kind of government within a government. The president changes every year; when I was in San Francisco he was Albert Chow, the first American-born Chinese ever to hold the job. Chow, when asked to describe himself, once replied that he was a "well-known notary public and *bon vivant*." About two-thirds of his compatriots are now U.S. born; hence they are citizens and may vote. Until fairly recently, the vote was almost unanimously Republican, for historical reasons dating back to John Hay and the Open Door; today it is almost as solidly Democratic. No one knows how long this will last.

There are some remarkable human beings in Chinatown. Take Dr. Margaret J. Chung, who, one of eleven children, worked her way through the University of California as a waitress; she is now one of the best-known surgeons on the West Coast, and a famous patroness of American servicemen during the war. Ninety per cent of her medical clientele is white. Or take Frank Fatt, the amiable restaurateur, or Joe Shoong, who once worked for thirty dollars a month in a shirt factory, and who today, the owner of the National Dollar Stores, is one of the richest Chinese in the United States. Or take Charlie Low. His father had a general store in Nevada. The family, miserably poor, migrated to San Francisco, intending to return to China. Low walked into the Bank of America on Powell Street, and saw that one of the cashiers was Chinese. This convinced him anew that America was a wonderful land of opportunity, and he decided to stay on. Today he has three professions; first, master of ceremonies at a celebrated night club, the Forbidden City; second, proprietor of the most modern apartment house in Chinatown; third, a crack polo player and the owner of a string of horses.

. . . .

During the war and for a time thereafter a prime issue perplexing California and the West was the displaced Japanese. These were of two categories, the Issei or foreign born, and the Nisei, those American born but of Japanese descent. Of the first, who were aliens, there were about 45,000; of the latter, who had American citizenship, about 80,000. All, by terms of a military order early in 1942, were uprooted, expelled from their homes, transferred to various concentration camps and relocation centers, and put under lock and key presumably for the duration.

Now, this was purely a West Coast phenomenon. Most Japanese-Americans elsewhere in the country were not molested, and enemy aliens on the Atlantic seaboard were not interned except for cause. To many, the forcible evacuation of the frugal, industrious, and in general quite patriotic Nisei seemed an outrage. The ancient principle that a citizen has individual rights, and should not be punishable by group indictment, was clearly violated; a distinguished professor of law at Yale University,[2] pointing out that "one hundred thousand persons were sent to concentration camps on a record which wouldn't support a conviction for stealing a dog," called the episode our worst wartime mistake, a threat to society, and a violation of law that denied every value of democracy.

In 1944 the army reversed itself, and decided as from January 3, 1945, to release all evacuees except a small minority who, when first arrested, had expressed allegiance to Japan, or who were for other reasons considered incorrigibly disloyal. These—only about four thousand five hundred in all—were eventually repatriated to Japan. All the rest—many of whom had sons in the American services with excellent war records—were free to return to their homes. But about half, though they had lived in California or the West all their lives, decided to settle elsewhere. This was because they had found other parts of the United States more agreeable and because a lot of Californians had gone in for a reckless and inflammatory campaign to keep them out, though their loyalty had been proved by exhaustive Army screening, and their right as American citizens to return to California was incontestable.

About forty thousand Nisei did return. They had a hard time for awhile. They were discriminated against vigorously; threats, vandalism, arson, and minor outrages occurred, and something called the Japanese Exclusion League fed the fires of anti-Nisei propaganda. But, it is only fair to add, most of the excesses took place in isolated interior counties, and no violence took place on a serious or widespread scale. The focus of resistance to the Japanese was in almost every case the same, that of the white horticulturists, vegetable growers and the like who hated them as competitors. The exclusionists were motivated more by economic than by racial bias. In some cases feeling against a Japanese farmer was deliberately whipped up by whites who had grabbed his land while he was interned.

One result of all this became manifest to the housewife at least. No class of people has ever rivaled the California Japanese in the subtleties of specialized farming. A lady told me in Monterey, "We haven't had a good vegetable here since the Nisei were kicked out."

Politics of the Movie Industry

> The only way to avoid Hollywood is to live there.
> —Igor Stravinsky

I would like nothing better than to describe Hollywood at length—that fabulous world of profit hunger, agents, ulcers, all the power

[2] Eugene V. Rostow in *Harper's Magazine*, September, 1945.

and vitality and talent and craftsmanship with so little genius, options, dynastic confusions, goona-goona, the vulgarization of most personal relationships, and 8,000 man hours spent on a sequence that takes three minutes. There might well be a line or two on any of several salient characteristics, for instance that Hollywood is a place above all others where creation is a composite phenomenon, not individual.[3] Or on its femininity (I don't mean effeminateness)—the preoccupation with gossip, personality, dramatic nuances, "entrances"—and its Jewishness. Or on the quasi-theological aspects of the star system, what Rebecca West many years ago described as "a new secular form of old religious ideas." Or the fact that the movie industry is the only one I know which supports its own blackmail, in the form of trade journals and the like.

And of course the temptation to include auxiliary gems is almost irresistible. For instance this paragraph from Leonard Lyons:

MARRIAGE. Nunnally Johnson gave a dinner party for eight in Hollywood. During a discussion of an impending wedding of a screenstar, one of the guests started musing about the length of Hollywood marriages. When he went home later, he tabulated the number of marriages represented at that dinner party for eight. They totalled 26.

Or this remark by Maureen O'Hara as quoted by Hedda Hopper:

I guess Hollywood won't consider me anything except a cold hunk of potato until I divorce my husband, give my baby away, and get my name and photograph in all the newspapers.

Or the following tidbit from the *New Republic* (November 5, 1945):

Lizabeth Scott, heroine of "You Came Along" . . . was Elizabeth Scott in 1941. During the war she patriotically dropped the "E" to conserve newsprint.

Two fundamental things, it seems, underlie most of the politico-economic-social stresses of the community. The first is that a great many people in the top income brackets—and a fantastic number of people earn fantastic salaries—only reached these brackets at the time that taxation first became really intense. This made them loathe and detest Roosevelt and the New Deal; it gave them a grudge against society as represented by government, and, as they made more and more money, they became more and more reactionary. The other thing is that a good many talented folk—writers and so on as well as executives—who are not on the supreme level of Louis B. Mayer but who never-

---

[3] The word "Hollywood" is of course an abstraction. Most of the chief studios are not located in Hollywood at all, but in neighboring communities, and most stars, directors, and so on live not in Hollywood itself but in Beverly Hills or near the ocean.

theless get tidy salaries like a thousand dollars a week, feel a sense of subconscious guilt at earning so much money. Hence they tend to submerge or deflect their bad conscience by generosity to all kinds of leftist "causes" and escape-valve politics.

That the movie world is highly self-conscious politically is well known; the activity is violent on both the Washington and local level. But normally the Hollywood moguls pay little attention to Sacramento, since the major companies are controlled by eastern capital and are in reality based in New York; they do their main lobbying in Washington and the East. But when Upton Sinclair ran for governor, they naturally woke up and had catfits; some even threatened to leave the state if he got in, and they spent dazzling sums supporting his opponent. The arch-Republican, arch-conservative studio is the fat king M-G-M. Warners, on the other hand, is Democratic. Darryl Zanuck of 20th Century-Fox, who produced "Wilson," was an orthodox (but liberal) Republican, then a Willkieite, then a strong Roosevelt man. Frank Freeman of Paramount is a middle roader; the studio was very proud of itself for producing "For Whom the Bell Tolls," even though the Hemingway story was drastically denatured. David Selznick is a tenaciously extreme Republican. Sam Goldwyn voted for Roosevelt for the first time in his life in 1944. In fact a Goldwyn committee raised $51,684 of the total of $137,998 that the Democrats collected for the state campaign in that year; among substantial contributors were Spencer Tracy, Jack Benny, and James Cagney. The Republicans on their side collected a much larger sum—$1,040,884, with Cecil B. de Mille, Ginger Rogers, Bing Crosby, and Walter Pidgeon among contributors.

Behind the two wings, which cut across all the studios, are two groups, the Motion Picture Alliance for the Preservation of American Ideals, on the right, and the Hollywood Independent Citizens Committee of Arts, Sciences and Professions on the left. The MPA has its share of witch hunters, red-scare artists, and embittered ex-liberals; it was organized to "correct the growing impression that this industry is made up of and dominated by Communists, radicals, and crackpots"; among its members are Sam Wood, Gary Cooper, Walt Disney, Rupert Hughes, and a brace of M-G-M retainers. The Hollywood Committee, founded in 1943, has a considerably more distinguished list of members, including—to pick at random—Marc Connelly, Orson Welles, Olivia de Havilland, Thomas Mann, Artur Rubinstein, Norman Corwin, Charles Boyer, Humphrey Bogart, Paulette Goddard, Lewis Milestone, Gregory Peck. These were among the "crackpots" that the MPA went after. Another element in the scene is the Hollywood Free World Association, the leading spirits of which have been Dudley Nichols, Arthur Hornblow, and Walter Wanger. This is not, like the Hollywood Committee, an overtly political organization, but it too has been attacked by MPA. In fact, a Free World dinner for Henry Wallace early in 1944 was what set the fireworks off, and the Free Worlders automatically became what the Coughlin-Gerald L. K. Smith axis calls the "red opposition." I asked one Hollywood friend who was the "brains" of MPA. Answer: "the College of Cardinals in M-G-M."

One assertion to make is that, even with such internecine tussles going on, writers and producers and actors continue to work together amicably. Sam Wood, boss of the MPA, directed "For Whom the Bell Tolls." But Dudley Nichols, the spearhead for the other side, wrote the script! Even in the most reactionary studio, nobody will be quicker than an MPA sympathizer to grab off a Russian director, say, or a best-selling novel by a leading antifascist, if the prospect is lucrative enough, since the profit motive is the final arbiter in Hollywood, the ultimate and unanswerable determinant of all behavior.

Involved in all this is an extremely difficult and sinuous labor situation. All the big studios are antilabor, even those most "liberal." The first of the important guilds, and still one of the strongest and best run, is the Screen Writers Guild, of which Dudley Nichols was president for two stormy years. The producers tried to break it with a company union called the Screen Playwrights; this perished after a vote under the Wagner Act. Actors also have a powerful guild, as do the cameramen and technicians; directors have a guild too, but it is weak, largely because they do not need as much protection as actors and so pay less attention to their own organization. Beyond all this is the celebrated International Alliance of Theatrical and Stage Employees (IATSE), an AF of L union which has had a highly disagreeable past to say the least. That for a long interval it fell into the hands of crooks like George E. Browne and Willie Bioff is, of course, scandalous and disgusting. Browne was sentenced to eight years and Bioff to ten, and each fined twenty thousand dollars, on conviction in 1941 for extortion and conspiracy. In 1945 came a Hollywood strike that lasted 238 days, and made national news as workers stormed picket lines outside the studios. This was a purely jurisdictional struggle between IATSE and a rival AF of L union, the radical and up-and-coming CSU (Conference of Studio Unions) led by Herbert Sorrell. A second big strike followed in 1946. IATSE is enormous and conservative, an old-type union organized vertically; CSU is a smaller craft union including carpenters, painters, electricians, and folk who do minor but strategically important specialized jobs; also, the reactionaries charge, it is packed with Communists. CSU stuck in IATSE's side like a burr; and the whole issue became interpreted as one between the "stanch old

AF of L" and Communism. The producers are, of course, almost helpless in a dispute of this kind, though naturally they like IATSE, much as they hated it before, better than they like CSU.

A word, finally, on the Hays office. Actually there are now two. Warners withdrew from the old Hays office (Motion Picture Producers and Distributors Association) last year, which weakened it considerably; then Eric Johnston, as bright a young man as this country has produced these many years, was imported to take it over, give it a thorough over-hauling, and bring it up to date. But meantime a rival organization under Donald Nelson, the former head of war production, was formed by some of the "independents"—Disney, Selznick, Wanger, Goldwyn (who also belonged to Hays)—called the Society of Independent Producers. I asked an expert if Nelson got the job because of his spectacular record in Washington. Reply: "Not at all. We picked him up because he went to China and hence knows all about civil wars."

The federal Department of Justice brought suit against the big movie companies, alleging monopoly in distribution and exhibition, back in 1938 under the antitrust law. The case is still *sub judice*. If the government wins, the industry will have to sell some sixty million dollars worth of theaters. The key to practically everything in Hollywood is that the great studios control the theaters where their products show. Paramount owns 1,376 theaters, Warners 509, and 20th Century-Fox 546.

Cults of the Spectacular

No discussion of California can possibly be complete without at least brief reference to what might be called cultism. Nothing in the world quite rivals the cults of California; the state has drawn the cream of believers in utopia from everywhere in the union. The phenomenon is, it would seem, severally based. I have already mentioned the geographical factor, viz., that the Pacific coast is the end of the line in the westward trek across the continent. The hills around Ventura, let us say, are the last stop; California is stuck with so many crackpots if only because they can't go any farther.

Most of the migrants who settle in California from Iowa and Kansas have quite special characteristics. First, they are old. But no official in the state ever dreams of using phrases like "elderly pauper"; they are called "senior citizens." Second, most of them are not, as a matter of fact, paupers at all; a good many have half-acre chicken or rabbit farms; many have a *little* money, and come to California to retire on the income from their savings, which may amount to forty or fifty dollars a month. Third, most have leisure. They don't have to work. Yet most are also people of more than average intelligence; so, having plenty of time to think, they developed the idea that if they could get

forty or fifty dollars per month *more* from the state, through some
pension scheme, they would be doubly better off. Thus the unique
phenomenon of a *radical* rentier class arose.

My friend Walter Duranty suggests a point here. It is the effect of
excessive sunlight on northerners. "Iowa gets here," he put it, "and
goes crazy." Something of the same characteristic may be observed in
the south of France. The Provençal natives don't become eccentric, but
the invading British do. Even Aldous Huxley became a mystic when
exposed to the California sun long enough. The religious factor is,
indeed, closely associated with all the movements of the discontented,
particularly in the south. The radical rentiers look for salvation in
lunatic manifestations of God as well as in lunatic manifestations of
medicine and economics. They were folk who were "somebody" back
home; they think they know the answers; they like certainty; hence,
in every field, they seek dogma.

Pick up any copy of a Los Angeles newspaper, and read the "religious"
advertisements. They are unique; this is theology *in extremis*. I cannot
go into details; merely to list the most bizarre organizations would
take a page. But the fabulous *economic* power of the chief crackpot
groups is not always appreciated. The size of their congregations, the
amount of real estate they accumulate, the number of contributors on
whom they call, can become staggering. Take the case of Arthur Lowler
Osborn Fountaine Bell and his Mankind United organization. His
new church has, according to *Time* (May 21, 1945), $3,400,000 in
assets, including "two laundries, six hotels, five restaurants, two
canneries, two lumber mills . . . a cheese factory, and 10,000 acres."
What does Mr. Bell believe in? That "he has seven doubles all capable
of thinking as one," and that he "can transport himself anywhere in
an instant by an act of his own will." Mr. Bell's agility was not,
however, sufficient to keep him from being indicted for sedition after
Pearl Harbor. He was convicted in a Federal court; at the moment of
writing, the case is on appeal. Most of the extreme cultists have, or had,
strong Fascist leanings, since they believe in salvation through "energy
and power." Or consider the "I Am" organization which, according to
Carey McWilliams, had at one time over three million dollars in assets,
mostly from sales of its revelations in pamphlet form, small individual
contributions from believers, and "love offerings." For the "I Am" crowd
had strong sexual as well as revivalist overtones, as did the McPherson
movement. And it, too, was explored and cultivated by would-be Fascists.

There is, finally, another factor. It rises, as Raymond Swing once
pointed out in an acute essay on Dr. Townsend, straight out of traditional
western leanings toward cheap money, "inconsequent radicalism," and
the belief that you can beat the law of supply and demand by inflation. A
good deal of California radicalism is simply free silver up-to-date.

As to serious or quasi-serious examples of direct political power in this field, we may allude to three. (But one should not forget that Henry George, a Californian, started Single Tax as far back as 1871.) All three were, of course, given great impetus by the smothering depression of the 30's, which ruined thousands of little people living on fixed incomes; all three substantially declined when good times came again. Let a new depression come, and the cults and crackpots will rise like weeds; the worse conditions get, the wilder will be the efforts to ameliorate them.

1. Upton Sinclair and EPIC. Sinclair is not a crackpot. He is an extremely honest man, a crusader and reformer, a good novelist, absolutely without humor and wonderfully stuffed with ego. I cannot in this space describe details of his plan, End Poverty in California. Much in it is probably sound if you believe in production for use, not profit. Sinclair stood for the establishment of land colonies, the creation of various state authorities like CAP (California Authority for Production), a stiff tax on unimproved land, and fifty dollars per month pensions for all needy persons over sixty. Sinclair's great days were in the middle 30's. He ran for governor in 1934, and despite fierce Roosevelt-Farley opposition won the Democratic nomination handily and was only narrowly beaten in the run-off. Sinclair got almost nine hundred thousand votes. His opponent, a sixty-nine-year-old former Iowa conservative named Merriam, added very little positive to the campaign; one slogan was, "Hold your nose and vote for Merriam." What defeated Sinclair was not Merriam but, in short, big business. "No politician since William Jennings Bryan has so horrified and outraged the Vested Interests," wrote *Time*, and the Merriam forces had to spend several million dollars to win. And though they beat Sinclair himself, no fewer than thirty-seven EPIC candidates were elected to the legislature.

2. The Townsend plan. This movement, proposing old age revolving pensions, reached its greatest growth in about 1936, under the leadership of Dr. Francis E. Townsend of Long Beach. It spread all over the country; it held a well-attended national convention in Cleveland; it is still a force in a great many American communities. Townsend supported Lemke for president in 1936 and, although a decent old man himself, let Father Coughlin speak on his platform. It is fascinating today to glance at the comments of serious economists and political writers, like Walter Lippmann, when they first investigated Townsend ten years ago. He scared them stiff. And with reason. Townsend's economic aims were preposterously impossible of fulfillment; at the beginning, he suggested pensions of not less than two hundred dollars a month for all men and women in the nation over sixty, if unemployed. He hoped to pay for this by a national sales tax, which would have cost the country 70 per cent of the total national income.

3. Ham & Eggs. Politically, this was the most serious business of the

three, and it attracted some quite respectable adherents, like Senator Downey whom it helped elect. The Communists supported it for awhile, and it was endorsed by both AF of L and CIO. Ham & Eggs began with a man named Robert Noble. He picked up contributions for a radio program in Los Angeles, and spoke for a pension plan to pay everybody over sixty the sum of twenty-five dollars every Monday. This made one hundred dollars a month as against Townsend's two hundred dollars, and hence seemed more realizable. Noble was an old Huey Long adherent. He lost control of Ham & Eggs when two young advertising men, Willis and Lawrence Allen, moved in on it. They increased the pension proposal to thirty dollars a week (to be paid on Thursday instead of Monday) and dropped the age from Townsend's sixty to fifty, which got more voters in. Quickly they became a powerful force, which has been described in fact as "the strongest political bloc ever created in California."[4] At *one* mass meeting in Los Angeles, sixty-four thousand people paid fifty cents each to get in; in 1938 its proposition was put on the ballot for the first time. Ham & Eggs got 1,143,670 votes, but it was beaten by a narrow margin. The movement kept on going, and in 1939 forced Olson (who was frightened of it by this time though it had contributed substantially to his election) to submit to the electorate a twelve thousand word constitutional amendment; if this had passed, not only would it have automatically become the law of the state, but also it would have transformed California into a Ham & Eggs dictatorship. "The issue was not," Lippmann wrote, "whether retired citizens over fifty should be given $30 of doubtful money every Thursday; it was whether the people could be bamboozled into surrendering sovereignty of the state." The proposal was beaten, but Ham & Eggs was still capable of getting about a million votes. Then came the war, and gradually the movement lost grip and influence. Its leaders tried to get on the ballot again in 1942, but without success; in 1944 they were on it again with another scheme, but were badly defeated.

California has, by the way, its own "Little Dies" committee, led by a state senator from Los Angeles, Jack B. Tenney. He was once president of Local 47, AF of L, the musicians' union in Los Angeles; he once wrote a song called "Mexicali Rose"; a disgruntled radical who became violently antiradical, he is a typical enough American phenomenon. The committee has, however, done some useful work in exploring the background of such organizations as Mankind United and the National Copperheads.

The Pleasant Town of San Diego

We turn now to something a bit more placid—though placidity was certainly not the word for San Diego when I visited it during the apex of

[4] *New Republic*, October 25, 1939.

its activity as a naval base. At that time it was easily the most crowded city in the United States; a single factory, Consolidated Vultee, employed 48,000 workers, and a transient body of 125,000 soldiers, sailors, and marines was jammed into the community on top of its violently expanding civilian population.

San Diego is a shining plaque of a city, built around a great park with glorious views of hill and harbor; it has the "shortest thermometer" in the United States, with an average summer temperature of sixty-eight and winter of fifty-five. But the diversity of the area is tremendous; you can pick oranges in the morning, ski at noon, and swim at dusk. San Diego is, next to Phoenix, Arizona, the cleanest city I have ever seen; it has only a handful of smokestacks, even with its aircraft industry. And this brings up what has traditionally been its chief problem. The San Diegans are divided between the "geranium" and "smokestack" classes. The smokestackers want to bring in more industry, and the geranium folk resist this at all costs. They say, "Let San Diego live as it always did, on tourists, on retired Navy pensionnaires, on celery, asparagus, and climate." To date the geranium people have won hands down, despite the war. I have seldom visited a place where the citizenry is so beauty conscious. They may be completely apathetic over a political upheaval; but let an acacia be blown down in Balboa Park, and a storm will rise. Some of the tall old palms in the central plaza are termite ridden; fronds fall off, and pedestrians have been injured. The Park Commission wanted to take the palms down. But the proposal was beaten by public vote.

San Diego covers 105.8 square miles, which means expensive problems in fire and police protection; it has spread out enormously, like Los Angeles, and for the same good reason—water; the adjacent villages cannot afford water on their own and have to be annexed. San Diego uses water about 100 per cent faster than it can be stored, and the supply on hand will, it is estimated, be seriously deficient in case of drought; hence, a $17,500,000 aqueduct has been authorized to bring more water all the way from the Colorado, though local citizens with "water-bearing" land, that is, property from which rain drains down, bitterly opposed the project. This, minor perhaps, is one example of many we shall find in this book of opposition by special interests to the interests of the community as a whole.

I write about San Diego for another reason: to mention briefly its mayor, Harley Knox. He is, like Lapham in San Francisco, an admirable example of the good citizen in politics. Knox was born in Nebraska. He left it as a boy of twelve, when the temperature was forty below; he has never been back since. He could not afford to go either to high school or college. Also, it happens, he is one of the best-educated Americans I know. Knox built up a successful dairy business, and the thought of politics never entered his head until 1939, when he was drafted by the business community to serve in the city council. He had always been deeply interested in juvenile welfare work. In 1943 he ran for mayor. One of his opponents in the primary (which is of course nonpartisan) boasted that he had a thirty thousand dollar campaign fund, and that Knox didn't have a chance. Knox replied, "If it was worth all that money for someone to make you mayor, I don't think they were preparing to buy good government." Knox won by a 2½-1 majority. I talked with him one evening, and we ended up in the roof garden of a hilltop hotel. A modest man, nobody there knew that he was mayor. He kept looking at the glimmering, beckoning lights along the harbor with an intense, happy, glowing pride; as well as anything I found in forty-eight states, he showed what a city can mean to its first citizen.

Knox, as mayor, holds a position that is mostly ceremonial, though his power of appointment is considerable and his personality is an essential clue to the community's civic mindedness. The San Diego government was reconstituted in 1932, with a reform government that "took." There is no graft, no spoils system. Administratively the city is run by an appointed manager, one of the 363 city managers in the United States.

Central Valley and Its Project

The heart of California, its most vital area, is not San Francisco or Los Angeles or San Diego; it is Central Valley. Nothing in the world is so fertile as Central Valley except perhaps the Valley of the Nile—or another valley in California itself, Imperial Valley in the extreme south of the state, which has also been made fantastically rich by irrigation. Central Valley is in fact two valleys. The Sacramento River in the north, the San Joaquin in the south, both help to make it; the combined rivers pour into San Francisco Bay.

"Agriculture in Central Valley," says *Fortune* (February, 1945), "is not so much a farm chore as an industrial operation." Nothing is left to chance; the fertility is "unbelievable," and the harvest moves with mathematical precision. This is made possible, of course, by irrigation. The trouble with most farming is that rain and weather are unpredictable. But in Central Valley all such vagaries as not knowing when it is going to rain are done away with. The "rainfall" is provided by the artifice of man; the controls are as precise as those of a laboratory, and the water can be turned on or off at will.

Central Valley also provides what is today one of the overriding political issues in the state, the future of the Central Valley Project, which, if it is completed, will open up new thousands of arid acres to fertility. The annual runoff of the two rivers at San Francisco Bay is about thirty-two million acre feet, which is about twice that of the Colorado; yet the Colorado drains seven states, whereas Central Valley exists in only one. We hear a great deal these days about the splendid work in another valley of the TVA; California has been grappling with the same problem, but as a one-state enterprise, for forty years. One reason why the TVA is a dazzling success whereas the Central Valley Project is still incomplete and in a violently controversial stage is that TVA, by terms of its authority, can do things that a single state cannot do. One major point is that the northern part of Central Valley, in the Sacramento basin, gets too much rainfall; the southern part, in the San Joaquin area, gets too little. So the problem has been—if I may oversimplify—to transfer surplus water from north to south, thus furthering flood control and irrigation both. The federal government has had a part in this development since 1937, when Shasta Dam, one of the greatest in the world, was built, and private power interests have fought completion of the project with continuing tenacity. Questions of land tenure are also importantly involved, since no water from a federal installation, may, by federal law, be given to farmers who own more than 160 acres. So all the big landowners (like the Kern County Land Company, which has more than 354,000 acres) have become involved in the issue. No one can deny the immediate necessity of over-all planning for the whole area, if it is not some day to revert to desert. Finally, there is the issue of "salinity." Water, even in California, isn't always well behaved; noisy rivers like the Sacramento sometimes burst their banks, and when this happens millions of gallons of irrigation may be lost; what is more, salt water from San Francisco Bay then leaks back into the valley, and ruins the soil.

Of matters like this we shall soon hear a great deal more, when we reach Oregon and Washington.

Oil on Troubled Waters

To ask the question "What is oil?" is almost like asking "What is love?" Oil is at once a tantalizingly complex mixture of hydrocarbons; the net result of millions of years of decay in animal and vegetable matter washed into the sea and then compacted in rock under the land; a devouring monster; life blood to nations and a prime source of martial strength; the "black Golconda"; the basis of the wealth of such an admirable institution as the Rockefeller Foundation; the direct cause of one recent war and more than one great international crisis; a mirage beckoning the adventurous; and an American industry worth fourteen billion dollars.

I looked at the refineries near Long Beach, and smelled them, and drove through the thickets and hedges of derricks planted like trees. California accounts for about 20 per cent of total U.S. petroleum production, 1,213,254,000 barrels; it has about 20,000 wells in 112 separate fields owned by 1,060 different people or companies, including "concubine subsidiaries." Its oil will last, according to some present estimates and not including potential tidewater production, not more than fifteen years or so more. The state does not belong to the Federal Oil Compact, which establishes over-all production quotas; it tries to keep production stable by agreement among the companies, who have an "oil umpire." But what is known as the "rule of capture" makes conservation difficult. This rule has governed much of the industry ever since oil was first drilled in Pennsylvania in 1859, and means simply that, inasmuch as the surface owner also owns subsoil rights, he can drain off his neighbor's pool as well as his own if the configuration of the subsurface lies that way, unless his neighbor drains *his* first. "Thus, fields were over-drilled and produced too rapidly, without regard to good engineering practice or to whether the oil was needed at the time."[5]

A forty-two-gallon barrel of crude oil, as produced in California or elsewhere, will according to *Life* (May 18, 1942), produce half a gallon of high octane aviation gasoline, capable of driving a P-40 for twenty seconds; 18.4 gallons of regular gasoline, which will drive an automobile 9¼ hours at 30 miles an hour; 10.2 gallons of residual fuel, which will drive the *Queen Mary* 105 feet; 6 gallons of distillate fuel which will drive a Diesel truck for 6 hours; 2.4 gallons of kerosene, which will drive a farm tractor for 2½ hours; 1.2 gallons of lubricating oil which could be used in all the above; and a residuum of hydrocarbon gases, asphalt, wax, and petroleum coke, which can be used for practically anything, down to a salve for chapped lips. The barrel of crude oil sells originally for about one dollar. No wonder the oil business makes money. And no wonder that, more than any other industry in the United States, it has attracted the piratical.

The essence of the California tidelands dispute can be told in a paragraph or two. (1) Oil is not only indispensable to the national economy; it is indispensable to national defense. (2) The proved United States reserves are about twenty billion barrels. (3) More than six billion barrels were used in World War II, and it is competently estimated that the entire national supply may only last another twenty years.

Now, for reasons of geology which are fairly obvious, oil lies under the sea as well as land, and if the sea is reasonably shallow, it is not too hard to get at. Oil can, it is thought, be profitably drilled at an ocean depth of about six hundred feet and there may be as many as twenty-two billion barrels available under water along the whole length of the Gulf and Pacific coasts. Not all of this is, strictly speaking, tidelands oil, since tideland means only the strip between low tide and the three-mile limit; it may be entirely feasible to drill for oil beyond the three-mile

[5] *Encyclopaedia Britannica*, Vol. XVII, p. 667.

limit in many areas; in fact Mr. Ickes urged President Roosevelt several years ago to extend our oil frontier to include the entire continental shelf, the belt of subaqueous land ranging from five to one hundred miles broad, all around the country.

But the question of property rights in submerged land is abstruse in the extreme. It is like the question of air rights over a railroad track— on which skyscrapers may be built—in reverse. Both the federal government and the states claim the subaqueous or tidewater properties. For many years federal right to the tidelands was taken almost for granted; that the national government should have something to say about what, elementally, is its own boundary, seemed only logical. But the question of oil reserves became pressing, and some very special interests got to work. Late in 1945 the House of Representatives, by a vote of 108 to 11, after only half a day of debate and without hearing any experts from Army, Navy, or the Department of Interior, passed one of the most sensational laws in the history of American legislation, providing that the United States of America should renounce and disclaim any right or interest in all lands "beneath tidewaters and navigable waters within the boundaries of the respective states." A neater job of lobbying has never been put over. But the very outrageousness of the proceeding was a boomerang. National interest began to be aroused—especially after the St. Louis *Post-Dispatch* forced the story open for which feat one of its reporters, Edward A. Harris, later won a Pulitzer prize. Meantime the federal government got busy too. Attorney General Clark brought a test suit before the Supreme Court, to explore the validity of the state claims and to obtain federal title if possible. Then the states went into action in turn. Forty-four attorneys general (including Bob Kenny) met together and protested that their rights were being contravened. They—and the private oil operators—want at all costs to keep the federal government out.[6]

"The stake of the oil companies, and of the states of California and Texas, is a mammoth one," wrote Alan Barth in *The Nation* (November 3, 1945). "Private operators have leased the tidelands from the states and have paid royalties to state treasuries on the oil they extracted. The arrangement has, of course, been mutually profitable; but it has not resulted in any conservation of oil for national defense purposes. This happy partnership might have continued without a care had it not been for a notion which formed in the back of Harold Ickes' curmudgeonish head that perhaps California and Texas were leasing lands which really belonged to the nation."

Explosion came finally when the Senate Naval Affairs Committee

[6] The bill was successfully squeezed through the Senate largely through the efforts of Pat McCarran, but President Truman promptly vetoed it, and the House sustained the veto, August 2, 1946.

investigated the nomination of Edwin W. Pauley, California oil man, to be undersecretary of the Navy. Pauley had been a main progenitor of the tidelands bill. On February 4, 1946, testifying under oath, Ickes stated that "Pauley said he could raise $300,000" [as contribution to Democratic party funds] "from oil men in California who have interests in offshore oil if they could be assured that the federal government would not try to assert title to these oil lands. . . . This is the rawest proposition that has ever been made to me." What happened then is known to everyone. But some details may have escaped notice. One is that Pauley's oil company, Petrol Corporation of California, which according to Mr. Harris of the *Post-Dispatch* has a "heavy stake in oil-rich tidelands," conveniently kept a telephone under its own name in the offices of the Democratic National Committee. Pauley was, as everybody knows, the committee's treasurer. Another is that a Los Angeles advertising agency hired two distinguished and obliging members of the California legislature, no less, at two hundred dollars a month to work for Pauley's Petrol Corporation.

In raising money for the Democratic National Committee Pauley did nothing that plenty of other people haven't done. But the case had much wider implications—whether the nation itself shall have the right to conserve its most precious natural resource, oil, and whether it is right and fitting that *any* oil man should be a presumptive secretary of the Navy. Also the point was well made that the democratic free-enterprise system takes hard knocks these days, and the case of Mr. Pauley does not enhance democratic prestige, whether you spell democratic with a big or little D.

Negroes in California

Now for the first time in this book we allude to a dominant and supremely difficult American problem, that of the Negro. I hope later, in a chapter on the Negro in the South, to discuss this in general terms and with specific reference to southern conditions, under which it is met in its most exacerbated form. As to Negroes elsewhere, particularly in the North, I propose to include a few brief passages in appropriate chapters, which will deal with the issue as seen locally, for instance in Chicago, Detroit, New York, and Pittsburgh. Almost everywhere the same underlying characteristics are manifest. From the Negro point of view the great subproblem is that of segregation; from the point of view of the community as a whole it is usually housing. On a national level we cannot ignore basic political considerations; for instance the Negro vote can be the balance of power in a good many highly important states.

In California the Negro problem is, like most problems, double; it exists in quite different dimensions as between the Los Angeles region and San Francisco. The war brought a tremendous influx of Negroes to

the state. There are no accurate figures; the best guess is that the total
Negro population is around 400,000. Los Angeles jumped from 50,000
Negroes to, let us say, 135,000; San Francisco from 4,070 to something
like 32,000. The rise in San Diego was 75 per cent. Toward the end of
1945, Negroes were still entering California at the rate of about 1,000
per week.

First, consider the issue on a statewide basis. Technically there is no
legal discrimination against Negroes in California; there is no Jim
Crowism in transportation or the schools. Some towns in the south,
however, like El Centro, do in effect have segregated schools. San
Francisco has no restrictions; towns like Fresno and Bakersfield, midway between north and south, have restrictions. Several Negroes have
risen to important positions in the political life of the state, like Augustus
F. Hawkins, who has been an assemblyman from Los Angeles for six
consecutive terms. Recently Governor Warren appointed as chairman
of the Adult Probation Authority, an important post, a Negro named
Walter Gordon, a former all-American football player who was a coach
at Berkeley. As to the Negro vote in California, since Roosevelt it has
been almost solidly Democratic. We shall find this pattern in almost
every Negro community in the country.

Now take Los Angeles. This is the main port of entry to the state for
the southern Negro, and most of those who arrive have never experienced nonsegregation before. So there has been a certain amount of
friskiness, throwing weight around, and crime. The majority of newcomers tend to cling together, and at least two large and fast-growing
Negro districts have become solidly established, one on the east side,
one on the west. One high school, Jefferson, is like high schools in
Harlem almost exclusively Negro. The city is not yet covenanted, and
good homes in permanent locations are open to those Negroes who can
afford them. Moreover it is important to remember that the migrants
into Los Angeles have been able to affix themselves to what was already
a well-integrated Negro community. Plenty of Los Angeles Negroes are
well off; there is a large independent Negro church and an excellent
newspaper; Negroes by and large know all about their constitutional
rights, organize "Negro Improvement Associations," and are not afraid
of going into court to protect themselves. On the other hand, anti-Negro
prejudice is steeply rising.

San Francisco is something else again. It is much more tolerant on
the whole; yet the Negro newcomer is apt to have a harder time. On
the day that Truman attended the San Francisco Conference, indication
of the city's tolerance came with nice emphasis—the traffic cop controlling the whole movement of the parade from its most important
pivot, the intersection between the Fairmont and Mark Hopkins hotels,
was a Negro officer, and thousands of people saw him direct the presi-

dential cavalcade. A minor item in relation to tolerance is that a Negro visiting San Francisco can't always predict whether a hotel will take him in. Two of the city's first-class hotels accept Negroes without question; a third does so on some occasions, not on others. The procedure seems to vary week by week. And most Negro visitors would prefer to be excluded rather than to be kept on tenterhooks. (Los Angeles hotels and restaurants are much less tolerant, of course; it would be hard to imagine a Negro feeling comfortable in any of its good hotels, even granting that he would be admitted.)

Until the war San Francisco had so few Negroes—fewer by proportion than any other city in the country—that the problem scarcely existed; indeed, Negroes had a certain local prestige. Since the war, the main trouble has been housing. San Francisco is as we know a peninsula, and can't bulge out like Los Angeles; with housing terribly short anyway, the Negro got badly pushed around. The municipality sent experts to St. Louis to find out how that city established its restrictive covenants, but the Negro community says that these were then affixed unfairly and without consultation. A good many landlords sucked the Negroes in wholesale to fill places vacated by the Japanese; then they howled plaintively about the terrible harvest they reaped. As a result there are in San Francisco few solid or semisolid Negro blocks like those in Chicago or Los Angeles; the Negroes are interspersed everywhere in the town, mixed up street by street. Some have been forced to live in old tenements condemned by the health authorities years before; the rules had to be relaxed, if only to keep people from sleeping on the streets. Some 1,300 Negroes work, incidentally, in the municipal transportation system; there is no serious discrimination in employment. A final point is that the CIO encourages Negro membership much more than the AF of L (and San Francisco is a tremendously strong AF of L town). To sum up, the Negro situation hasn't crystallized as yet in San Francisco; it may be a long time before it does.

State of Jefferson

Hawaii may, before very long, be the forty-ninth American state; before 1941 there was an attempt to make another. Four of California's extreme northern counties, including Del Norte and Siskiyou, joined with one of the southernmost Oregon counties, Curry, and attempted to promote a union. These counties are remote, isolated, and somewhat neglected by their mother states; moreover they form a natural bloc. The man largely responsible for suggesting the idea—he wanted to call the new state Jefferson—died however of a heart attack, and when Pearl Harbor came the campaign was dropped. A reporter for the San

Francisco *Chronicle*, Stanton Delaplane, won a Pulitzer prize for his description of the episode.

This was, so far as I know, the most serious unsuccessful attempt to create a new state from existing states since 1788, when a fragment which called itself the "State of Franklin" split off from North Carolina and in fact had a life of its own for a brief period. One of the provisions of Franklin's "constitution" was that doctors, preachers, and lawyers were forbidden to be members of its legislature. Its annals are still famous in Tennessee and Carolina folklore.

California Miscellany

California is the state par excellence of athletes and especially tennis players; of mink farms and camellia "ranches"; of the world's largest man-made harbor (at San Pedro), and of the Santa Anita race track which has taken in as much as eight hundred thousand dollars in a day. It contains the biggest city in the country (Long Beach) not served by a steam railroad; its university is the largest in America, and its state budget is bigger than any except New York's.

California has some of the oldest jalopies in the nation, and towns called Igo and Ono. It is the state where high-school teachers have to be college graduates with a master's degree, and where some counties operate under a city manager plan. It has the harshest criminal syndicalism law in the country, and it is one of eight states with a community property law, derived from Spain.

California is the state where your automobile may contain an altimeter, where fifteen thousand people may go to a barn dance on a pier that will last from Friday evening to dawn of Monday, and where crude cardboard signs, CHECKS CASHED HERE, can be seen almost everywhere.

It is the state where the senate judiciary committee recently killed a bill to allow unfaithful wives of servicemen to give their illegitimate children away for adoption without informing their husbands, where the Los Angeles courts bestow more divorces than those of Reno, and where there are more traffic accidents than anywhere on earth.

Chapter 4

Life and Works of Henry Kaiser

~~~~~~

Building is my business.
—Henry J. Kaiser

IN A curious way Kaiser is an anachronism. His is not so much the voice of the future, one might say, as that of an early American pioneer. It is impossible to understand Kaiser without realizing that he is remarkably like some of the early railway corsairs; he too is a builder and contractor, tough, creative, packed with ideas and energy, above all a man who likes to *make* things. As I heard it said in San Francisco, "People look at Kaiser, and think he is something new—a radical. But he's their grandfather."

You cannot convince Kaiser that a thing can*not* be done, no matter how grandiose, any more than you could have convinced Huntington or Stanford that it was impossible to push the Central Pacific over the Sierras. This is a paramount secret of his power and success.

But there are, of course, differences between Kaiser and his semi-prototypes. The latter found their opportunity and moneybags in the richness of the earth and the necessity to conquer distance; Kaiser found his—during the war at least—partly in something much more prosaic, federal credit. Which leads to the observation that whereas the railroad and mining kings worked with and enormously served to encourage "free" enterprise, Kaiser on the contrary has been a kind of link to enterprise by government, since government was on his side.[1]

Another important difference is that the men of the 70's were, by and large, marauders who cried, "Let the people be damned!" But Kaiser has great social consciousness and conscience. The welfare of the people as a whole is, he thinks, the basic desideratum in any enter-prise; he believes in "public" welfare literally, and cares very little about money for money's sake.

Hence, many "orthodox" tycoons today think that Kaiser is lunatic and dangerous. The Hearst papers call him a "coddled New Deal pet"— though he is a registered Republican and was once mentioned as a Republican candidate for the presidency—and he is perpetually being denounced as a kind of economic anti-Christ. I even heard a friend say

[1] But only, he says, because his companies were the lowest bidders on projects or because he performed prodigies of building beyond the capacity of anybody else.

fervently, "I'm a left winger, but by God Henry Kaiser scares *me*!"

Kaiser did indubitably operate during the war on government money in part; for instance the RFC lent him $110,000,000 for the steel plant at Fontana, near Los Angeles, and the great shipyards at Richmond and Vancouver were of course run by Kaiser for the government. Yet to say that he is merely a "subsidized guy" is grossly to miss the point. He was, and is, a genuine builder, as a glance at the record will prove beyond doubt.

Career on Thumbnail

When Henry John Kaiser was twenty-three years old he was already owner of a small photographic shop in Lake Placid, New York. A young lady named Bessie Fosburgh, whose father was a comparatively wealthy Virginia lumberman, came in to buy some film. Henry became interested in Bess, and Bess became interested in Henry when she saw that other girls, among the summer visitors to Lake Placid, liked him too. They fell in love, and Henry forthwith proposed marriage. Mr. Fosburgh did not, however, think much of the eligibility of the young man who seemed to be little more than a small town salesman without a future. So he forbade the marriage unless Henry, within a year, fulfilled three conditions: first, own a house; second, have a bank account with a balance of $1,000; third, be earning $125 a month. That, thought Papa Fosburgh, would finish Henry. Whereupon Henry packed up and left Lake Placid, went out to Spokane, and returned 365 days later with all three conditions duly fulfilled.

The Kaisers have been a wonderfully happy family ever since. They call each other "Mother" and "Father" and in public are as comfortable together as good old shoes. They have two sons, Henry Jr. and Edgar, both of whom hold high office in the Kaiser domain, and both parents adore them. I have seldom seen a more affectionate family. Mrs. Kaiser told me once, "We just have fun all the time." Saying good-by to his boys in the office, Mr. Kaiser embraces them.

Kaiser was born on May 9, 1882, at Sprout Brook, New York, one of four children of a German settler who came over after '48. Everybody in the family had to work hard for a living, and Henry's schooling stopped just before eighth grade at the age of thirteen. From that date to this he has never stopped working. For three weeks, aged thirteen, he walked the streets of Utica, New York, looking for a job, any job that would pay enough to eat on. He told me that the deepest emotion of his life—the joy of achievement—was rooted in this childhood experience. "I'm doing now all the things I swore I'd do when I was thirteen." And he has thought ever since that all young people are entitled to better opportunities. Also his intense interest in such things as modern medical care dates from this period. His mother died at the age of forty-nine, and he has never stopped thinking that good medical facilities could have prolonged her life twenty years. What she didn't get, he wants to give to others. Hence the elaborate prepayment plan for medical services he set up for workers and employees, one of the most notable experiments in group medicine ever launched in this country. It was, of course, fought with bitter tenacity by the medical vested interests. Kaiser's reply was to extend the project outside his own companies to near-by communities at large.

The "joy in achievement" motif runs straight through his life. He showed me a watch Edgar gave him in 1943, with the inscription, "The Understanding of the Joy of Achievement is Your Priceless Gift to Your Boys."

Kaiser's first "real" job came at sixteen, as a cash boy in a Utica department store; later he became a salesman. He got into the photographic business, as a shipping and billing clerk, and bought the Lake Placid photo shop. On the west coast, setting out to meet the Fosburgh conditions, he was first a clerk in a hardware company, then a gravel and cement dealer, then a paving contractor. By 1914 he had his own company, Henry J. Kaiser Co., Ltd., with a $325,000 contract for road paving in British Columbia. By 1916, when he was thirty-four, the company had million dollar contracts in Washington and California, and Kaiser was in the big-time at last.

A full list of joint venture contracts undertaken by Kaiser and various associates has never, I believe, been printed; it has been made available to me but it occupies seven closely typed pages, and I cannot possibly include it all. Note that Kaiser helped build *both* Bonneville and Boulder dams—as well as Grand Coulee!

PROJECT	CONTRACTOR	SPONSOR	APPROX. VOLUME
Boulder Dam (1931-36)	Six Cos. Inc.	Six Cos. Inc.	$54,861,316
East Bay Substructure Oakland–San Francisco Bay Bridge (1933-34)	Bridge Builders, Inc.	Bridge Builders, Inc.	4,582,721
Bonneville Dam & Lock Approach Canal near Bonneville, Oregon (1934-38)	Columbia Const. Co.	Henry J. Kaiser Co.	16,846,114
Gray's Harbor Jetties, Gray's Harbor, Wash. Three separate projects (1935-42)	Columbia Const. Co.	Henry J. Kaiser Co.	7,724,724
Columbia River Rock Jetty near Illwaco, Wash. (1937-39)	Columbia Const. Co.	Henry J. Kaiser Co.	1,188,387

PROJECT	CONTRACTOR	SPONSOR	APPROX. VOLUME
Grand Coulee Dam west of Spokane, Wash. (1939-42)	Consolidated Builders, Inc.	Henry J. Kaiser Co.	$40,821,667
Shasta Aggregates near Redding, Calif. (1939-44)	Columbia Const. Co., Inc.	Henry J. Kaiser Co.	7,732,048
Shore Facilities, Mare Island, Calif. (1940-43)	The Kaiser Company	The Kaiser Company	10,057,527
Long Beach and Los Angeles Breakwater, Long Beach and Los Angeles, Calif. (1941-42)	Columbia Const. Co.	Henry J. Kaiser Co.	8,700,000
Mare Island Shipyard Construction near Vallejo, Calif. (1941-43)	The Kaiser Co.	The Kaiser Co.	7,366,144
Drydock, Vancouver, Wash. (1944-45)	Columbia Const. Co.	Columbia Const. Co.	3,276,400

To say nothing of a billion dollars' worth of other installations all over the country, in which he participated with others.

But this was all secondary in a way, for Kaiser also created industrial operations all his own. Of these the most important was the Permanente Cement Company, near San Francisco; until the war, this was one of the biggest segments of the empire, though the core and "capitol" remained the sand and gravel plant at Radum, California. Permanente broke what had been a West Coast cement monopoly. Kaiser forced the price way down. Came the war. Kaiser was still comparatively unknown outside California business circles. He started making ships and steel—for him two utterly new fields—and became a national figure overnight. His Permanente Metals Corporation developed "goop" out of magnesium—this was the incendiary material that helped finish off the war with Japan—and he made shells in Colorado and aircraft in the East, while becoming the biggest shipbuilder in history.

Today Kaiser runs eighteen or twenty different companies covering twenty-six or twenty-seven industries. His interests include gypsum, helicopters, ferrosilicon, housing projects, insurance, and busses made of magnesium. Because he found steel hard to get, he has very recently made prodigious inroads into aluminum. And, as everybody knows, he is tilting at that most dangerous and dramatic of all American super-windmills—the automobile.

Kaiser: Attributes and Characteristics

Henry Kaiser is a very large heavy man with a fringe of gray hair at
the back of a big, bald, squarish skull. He has a heavy thick nose, a
heavy thick jaw, and dark benevolent eyes behind shining rimless spectacles. He eats everything, drinks moderately, and likes to work fourteen
hours a day. He loves to tinker with things, and has amazing mechanical
aptitudes. Once he took five minutes' instruction in an autogyro, and
then took off and flew it, though he weighs close to 260 pounds and
had never been aloft alone before.

Nowadays he flies practically not at all, though his associates are
crossing and recrossing the country by plane all the time. This is because
his wife hates to have him fly. His only hobby now, outside work, is
experimenting with speedboats on Lake Tahoe, where he has a summer
home. Every summer he tries out new combinations of engines and hulls.

Kaiser has his headquarters in Oakland but he spends considerable
time traveling. His offices in New York are in Rockefeller Center. The
telephone is, however, unlisted, and there is no name on the door. The
location of the eastern headquarters of the man who is probably the
most important industrialist in the United States is, in other words, a
secret; the Kaiser offices are a hideout. Perhaps allied to this strange
point is the fact that until he went into automobiles Kaiser never did
any direct advertising. He bought no radio time, and there were no
Kaiser ads of any kind in newspapers or national magazines.

Inside the New York offices, which are luxuriously crisp and modern,
Kaiser sits in a moderately large room behind an empty table. If the
phone rings, he gets up, begs his visitor's pardon, and takes the call in
an adjoining office. His assistants move in and out of his own room all
the time. He pays attention or not as he chooses, while his courtesy to
the visitor remains fixed. It is all like a madhouse with a velvet lining,
a madhouse run on greased ball bearings.

If interrupted, even if he has been out of the room for several moments,
he will return to pick up a sentence at the exact word where it was
dropped. Almost all intelligent executives have this trait, but in Kaiser
it is very pronounced. "I've always contended that you can and should
be able to keep two things in mind at once," he told me.

Most sketches of Kaiser make him seem somewhat ponderous and
forbidding, and people tell me that when he loses his temper it is a
sight to see; but most of the time his mood is comparatively benign.
Friendship means a great deal to him, he loves people, and he is excellent
company in any kind of gathering. Sometimes he startles new acquaintances by quoting Longfellow by heart and at considerable length.

He runs everything with the minimum of paper work; he practically
never writes a letter, and nowadays reads very little but the newspapers.

But it is an impressive sight to see Henry Kaiser read a newspaper. He is a chain reader. He holds it with hands outspread, at arm's length, with his elbows on his knees, and shells it like a walnut.

Mostly Kaiser relaxes by plunging out of one enterprise into another; he replenishes energy by variety of occupation. He never goes back to a job, he told me; he has never even seen Boulder Dam or Grand Coulee since their completion. He does have to look at the San Francisco-Oakland Bridge, which he helped to build, but he calls it a superhighway, not a bridge at all. "I have no interest in a thing once it's done." He corrected himself. "I've always thought a job *was* done when it was half done."

I asked him once what the turning point in his life was and he answered, "Cuba." He went there in 1927 to build some two hundred miles of road in the province of Camaguey; the contract amounted to $17,702,286, a sum phenomenal for those days. "It was a great adventure. We had to create all our own materials, except cement. People used oxen and wheelbarrows. We had to start from the beginning," Kaiser recounts. What Cuba taught him was the necessity for team work, group work, which in turn depended on personal relationships. This principle he soon applied elsewhere by promoting partnerships and associations among fellow contractors who then worked on a project together; hence arose the famous "Six Companies" (not to be confused with the Six Companies of Chinatown!) and their co-operative bidding on various jobs. People said that the partners wouldn't stick together long enough to make a bid, let alone do any building. People got fooled.

His closest associates are almost fanatically devoted. They are like movie people; they work a murderously long day, Sundays included, and after hours they still keep on working, in that all their talk is shoptalk. "Kaiser Industries is a family outfit," I heard it said, "and it operates exactly like a family. Once you're in, you're in for life. But you don't *get* in by sitting on your tail." Closest in the circle are, of course, the two sons. Henry Jr. ran the ordnance plants at Denver and Fontana during the war; Edgar ran the Oregon shipyards and is now general manager of Willow Run. Also very close are Edna Knuth, the confidential secretary, and E. E. Trefethen Jr. who as "principal assistant" is vice president of most Kaiser companies. He is only about thirty-five. A chum of Edgar's, he once took a week's job running a steam locomotive at Livermore, California; he caught the old man's fancy and, moving up fast, has been close ever since. The oldest of the senior executives in point of service is A. B. Ordway, who was administrative manager at Richmond and for a time was general manager of the insurance company which Kaiser helped organize and which is the second largest industrial insurance company in the West; Ordway now heads the iron and steel operation at Fontana. The light metals boss is D. A. Rhoades, another veteran who led the

Kaiser entry into aluminum. S. D. Hackley at Bristol, Pennsylvania, is in charge of airplanes and appliance manufacture. One of the big bosses at Fontana is Chad F. Calhoun. An indispensable executive in many industrial operations is Clay P. Bedford, vice president in charge of manufacturing at Willow Run. Twenty years ago Bedford was shoveling sand for a living in one of the first construction jobs Kaiser ever undertook. Incidentally, "Totem" James A. Shaw, the oldest employee in service, is a Negro.

What does Henry Kaiser believe in most? Work—more work—people —himself. What interests him most? "The power that is in the souls of men, and how to reach it," he told me. Then, above all, how to improve things. He went on, "The most wonderful thing about life is that it isn't perfect." When he goes into a project he asks himself two things. First, is it financially practicable? Second, is it a contribution—will it make something available to more and more people at a better price?

He doesn't talk much about politics, per se; it is the bent of his mind to think more in terms of kilowatt energy than votes. He believes in democracy, in competition, in open team play. "Sometimes Washington goes crazy," he says, "but then a democracy ought to fumble and flounder every once in awhile—that's what democracy is." He does not, he told me, believe in "power." He explained, "Power corrupts. You use it, abuse it, then lose it." It is the "immensity of resource" of the United States that moves him most. He hates monopoly, no matter how it is disguised, and he wants industrial decentralization above all. He thinks that "devotion of the United States to its own ideals is what will keep it going."

As to labor Kaiser's friendly relations are well known. He wants to be able to calculate his costs to the last inch, and he never budges without a labor contract. In January, 1946, he signed up with the CIO for an 18½¢ increase at Fontana, while Big Steel kept hesitating in the East; he told me that this boost increased the plant's efficiency by 15 per cent and thus saved money, instead of costing anything. Similarly, during the General Motors strike, he offered Kaiser-Frazer workers a scale based on the highest wages ever paid by Ford, plus whatever General Motors workers would get, plus a five dollar bonus for each completed car. Production depends in the last analysis on the will of labor to produce, he feels; you can't have healthy and viable industry without, first, a healthy labor movement, and second, social insurance, community health, hospitalization plans and decent housing. "To break a union is to break yourself," is one aspect of the Kaiser credo.

Richmond and Fontana

We went out to Richmond, across the bay from San Francisco, on the day that Kaiser's 732nd ship was launched. The first thing I noticed: a chain of cars from the old Sixth Avenue El in New York, which Kaiser used to help move his workers to where they slept and back.

Richmond consists of four yards, built by Kaiser for the U.S. Maritime Commission, on a fee basis in conjunction with other companies. Yards No. 1 and No. 2 were operated by the Permanente Metals Corporation, No. 3 by Kaiser Co., Inc., No. 4 by Kaiser Cargo Co., Inc. For the four together, the peak of wartime employment was 91,000. As of V-J Day the yards had built $1,800,000,000 worth of ships, mostly Liberties and Victories, amounting to about 7,000,000 tons which is 20 per cent of the entire American production of merchant shipping during the war. One-fifth of the American merchant navy was, in other words, built by Kaiser in this single area. Count in the Oregon yards, and the proportion goes up to one-third.

Kaiser turned out combat ships too; in fact his Vancouver, Washington, yards built fifty baby flattops, small aircraft carriers, in eighteen months. Not only did the Navy say that this could not be done; it fought the project with embittered stubbornness, holding that ships built so fast could not be seaworthy; Kaiser got the program started only by going to Roosevelt over the heads of both admirals and Navy Department. For a time he was delivering carriers at the unprecedented and seemingly impossible rate of one a week.

The Liberties rolled off at Richmond even faster. At peak, a ship could be built in four and one-half days, that is the various prefabricated parts and sections were put together in that time, and launchings once reached a rate of thirty-two per month, or one million-dollar ship a day. We visited yard No. 2, and I began dimly to see how the job was done. Part of the secret lay in prefabrication, part in the astute application of new techniques. Take deck houses. These were the toughest problem to solve, because they are the soul and brain of the ship and complex to make. In World War I it took 180 days to build a ship; most of the delay came from deck houses. So a method was contrived to build them in sections—upside down! They proceed down a monstrously large assembly line just like an automobile; then, when finished, they are cut into four huge parts, and each part is carted to the ship on an enormous specially-built eighty-five-ton trailer; finally the deck house is welded together again on the ship itself.

Richmond trained something like three hundred thousand welders out of soda clerks and housewives. Normally it takes two to three months to make a tolerable welder. The Kaiser technique turned them out in ten days, because they were only taught "down-hand" welding, which means welding below the waist, so that the weld itself flows by gravity. To make a good weld overhead takes skill, but practically anybody can do it on the lower level. So forepeaks were built sideways, and the actual sides of ships, cut, shaped and welded to predetermined patterns, were built flat, rather than inside a tall and costly scaffolding. The Kaiser principle was to fit the job to the man, instead of vice versa.

Richmond expanded so fast that a near-by mountain once got in the way. So three million cubic feet of it were moved.

A fancy explosion came in 1946 when Congress began an investigation of huge wartime profits by the shipbuilding industry in general. Nineteen firms, it was charged, had made $365,000,000 profit on a capital investment of $22,979,275. Six Kaiser companies were cited in the complaint drawn up by the General Accounting Office; this asserted that Kaiser and his associates, on an investment of only $2,510,000, had realized profits of more than $190,000,000. The sight—and sound—of Kaiser on the witness stand was stimulating. His rebuttal stated that his firms' combined net profits amounted to only one-tenth of 1 per cent on dollar volume (New York *Herald Tribune*, September 24, 1946).

. . . .

Fontana, built on 1,300 acres of walnut groves and vineyards about sixty miles inland from Los Angeles, is Kaiser's great adventure in steel, and a de luxe war baby. It looks like no other steel plant on earth; to see a blast furnace out among the oranges seems incongruous. Kaiser built it from scratch—assisted by some borrowed steel experts—in record time; the ground was cleared in April, 1942, and the first furnace blew in nine months later. This feat was, moreover, performed when all labor and materials were jacket tight.

The idea behind Fontana was, of course, to provide the West coast with a plant capable of making steel plate for Navy and Maritime Commission building. Suppose the Japanese had cut the Panama Canal. The West had no steel industry of any size, and it was imperatively necessary to set one up. The Army, afraid of a Japanese invasion, insisted on an inland site, instead of tidewater. Fontana has to go something like 175 miles for its ore,[2] and 800 for coal; but limestone is near by, and—a valuable item—Los Angeles is a first-rate source for scrap. So Fontana blossomed in the sun, and California for the first time had something it had always craved, a steel industry of its own.

Fontana's future is, at the moment, tied up in a titanic struggle with eastern steel. Kaiser built it with a $110,000,000 loan from the RFC, which must be refinanced. He does not think it fair or just that this whole sum should have to be repaid, since Fontana was built as a war measure at emergency speed and almost without regard to cost. He points out that the plant was built for plate, and that to reconvert it to peacetime steel for automobiles and countless other products useful to the

[2] This distance was lately cut to 130 miles when the Kaiser interests acquired Eagle Mountain, which is supposed to contain a hundred million tons of ore, in San Bernardino County.

West is an expensive proposition. What he hopes, of course, is that Fontana will not only help take up the slack in California reconversion but will be the pivot of future industrialization in the state by providing an integrated steel supply. But eastern steel has always bitterly opposed this kind of development. It fought Fontana because it wants to sell its own steel to California, at its own handsome price. In fact Kaiser asserts now that former bosses in the RFC opposed the construction of Fontana in the first place, and did their best to impede its operation, even during the war, to protect the interests of Big Steel in the East, which was warily watching the evolution of this formidable competitor. He says (New York *Times*, August 8, 1946) that he has sworn evidence that a special consultant to Jesse Jones, then head of the Defense Plant Corporation, told him, "I will never recommend spending government money on a steel plant in California to be operated by you. We prefer to have the United States Steel Corporation . . . in Utah." But Kaiser got the money, and went ahead. His most recent step in this campaign was a demand for a Senate investigation of Big Steel. Meantime the eastern steel companies are doing everything they can to freeze him out of the steel and other commodities he needs desperately for his new venture in automobiles.

Deeply involved in all this is the question of freight rates, to be discussed later in this book. The greatest single barrier to national productiveness, Kaiser feels, is the burden imposed on the nation by regional freight differences. For a generation steel has cost between six and twenty dollars a ton more in the West than the East, because of shipping charges, which Kaiser and most Californians think is an outrage, and want to change. And Fontana could not operate at all—much less create a great all-West steel industry—if it were not protected by a temporary differential.

Kaiser-Frazer Invasion of Detroit

Americans are crazy about names, they're crazy about gambling, and they're crazy about automobiles. Perhaps this as much as anything explains the bizarre events attending the birth of Kaiser-Frazer.

Kaiser had been thinking in terms of automobiles for a long time. But his closest advisers kept telling him, "Listen, a dam or a shipyard is O.K., but automobiles—my God, lay off!" He maintains, however, a kind of experimental laboratory at Emeryville, near Oakland, where he could not resist fussing with ideas for new types of cars; for instance as far back as 1942 he built a model with a detachable engine that fit in either front or back.[3] The people, he felt, wanted two things above all in an auto-

---

[3] This Emeryville laboratory is a fascinating place. Here the Kaiser staff has tinkered with any number of new ideas in housing, roofing, plastics, glass furniture, speedboats, small scooter-type cars, awnings, and kitchen gadgets.

mobile, comfort and safety. To satisfy the first wish, he experimented toward more room; for the second, wider vision.

Two men are major actors in the early history of Kaiser-Frazer. One was R. J. Thomas, head of the United Automobile Workers, CIO. As soon as he learned that Ford was going to close down Willow Run after the war he went to Kaiser, urging him to buy it. His motive was, of course, to get the Californian into the automobile business and thus help keep employment up in the Detroit area. Kaiser was impressed by Thomas, and they talked it over. Next, Joseph W. Frazer happened to call at about the same time on A. P. Giannini. Frazer, an old hand in the automobile business, former head of Willys-Overland, and president of Graham-Paige, wanted help in financing a new venture. Old Giannini said, "You ought to get in touch with Henry Kaiser." A meeting was arranged, Kaiser and Frazer liked one another at once, and the new company was in effect born that minute.

Oddly enough Kaiser and Frazer had had contact before, but it was indirect and not exactly smooth. Kaiser has never joined the National Association of Manufacturers. Nevertheless, after considerable persuasion, he consented to address an NAM convention and in the course of his speech urged the automobile tycoons to come out with new models even though the war was in progress. Frazer heard the speech—he was building jeeps at the time—and was so outraged that he denounced Kaiser publicly. So when Giannini suggested that he and Kaiser meet, he feared that Kaiser would be unfriendly. But the partnership has been as smooth as ice cream since the first meeting. "We fell into the same groove right away," Kaiser explains.

The early days of Kaiser-Frazer are too well known to need recountal here. Detroit was both skeptical and then impressed—especially when Kaiser began to pick up dealers by the hundred—and the big manufacturers concertedly sought to prevent his buying tools and parts. Then things happened. "The U.S. public, with stars in its eyes, subscribed $53,450,000 worth of stock . . . for a car in which no one has ever ridden," as *Fortune* put it. When two hand-built mock-up cars were displayed in New York in January, 1946—the only two Kaiser-Frazers then in existence—people fought through police lines at the Waldorf to put in almost ten million dollars' worth of orders. Kaiser's own explanation of this is that "the masses of the people are hungry to participate in an enterprise in which they have faith." But as of the moment of writing Kaiser-Frazers are only just beginning—very, very slowly—to come off the assembly line. The automobile business is not a picnic for anybody these harried days.

More than fifty million dollars behind a car before it ran! This is the sort of thing—we shall find others before this long book is done—which, as the saying is, could only happen in the U.S.A.

What Next for Kaiser?

Henry Kaiser showed me two things while we talked. One was a booklet describing the five-passenger Kaiser-Hammond airplane, 140-mile-per-hour, spin proof, stall proof. He is hoping to produce it in a year or so, provided he isn't too busy building what he thinks is more imperative—a couple of thousand new air*ports*. The other was a kind of aluminum basin on the floor beside his desk, the Kaiser "Jet-Propelled Dishwasher." Of these he plans confidently to sell a million at a modest price. The dishwasher does not need electric current; it fits on any tap, and gets free power from the running water. From airplanes to a household gadget—that seems to be the Kaiser gamut. No wonder American men of affairs are by and large more interesting than the politicians.

.   .   .   .   .   .

So now we conclude with California. Let us look briefly at the curious state of Nevada next, and then proceed upward to the virile area of the great Northwest.

Chapter 5

Ghosts and Silver in Nevada

wwwwwwwwwwwwwwwwwwwwwwwwwwwwwwwwwwwwwwwwwwwwwwwwwwwwwwwwwwwwwwwwwwwwwwwwwwwwwww

NEVADA, the sixth largest state in size and the smallest in number of people, covers 110,540 square miles, and is the only state whose population, 110,247 by the last census, is almost exactly equivalent to the area; there is one Nevadan for each square mile. It is thus the least densely populated state, and its capital, Carson City (population 2,478), is the smallest.[1] Nevada is mostly desert, mountains, and fabulous natural resources. It is one of the friendliest states I know, and it lives on four things, mining, livestock, the divorce trade, and gambling.

First a word on why I include this particular chapter at this juncture. Mainly it is that though Nevada of course belongs to the West, it is in blunt fact a kind of hinterland to California. In Chapter 2, I mentioned —all too briefly—some characteristics of the states. Experts vary in how to classify them geographically. The *Handbook of the United States* published by the OWI during the war as a guide for American officials abroad includes Nevada in a special region "of rugged mountain ranges, enclosed basins of interior drainage, and wide desert plains," that also comprises the California desert, western Utah, and parts of Idaho and Oregon. Professor Brogan in his *U.S.A.* separates Nevada from California and includes it in the "Mountain and Great Plains" states though he gives Idaho to the "Pacific Northwest." The admirable U.S.A. number of *Fortune* (February, 1940) simply lumps California and Nevada together as a single block called "Far West."[2]

Visitors from abroad who look closely at a map of the United States for the first time are often struck by the straight lines of most state frontiers, especially in the West. They are apt to deduce from this, erroneously, that such frontiers—since they do not follow mountain ranges or river lines—must of necessity be artificial. But this is not really the case. I mentioned above that states' rights have been thinned down. But not state identities or lines! Indeed these are still astonishingly distinctive. Look at Utah and Nevada from an airplane. They are indistinguishable.

---

[1] Runners-up: Pierre (4,332), Dover (5,517), Montpelier (8,006), Frankfort (11,492).

[2] On an over-all basis the confusions are just as great. Regionalism and sectionalism conflict. For instance the Federal Reserve System divides the country into twelve areas; the federal judicial system recognizes ten; the *Statistical Abstract of the United States* normally breaks down its figures into eight.

You could not possibly tell where one stops and the other begins. Yet the two states differ so enormously that they might belong to different worlds. Utah is a creature of the Mormon church; it was settled mostly from the Middle West, by burghers with a remarkable religious fixation; Nevada was settled in reverse, so to speak, by miners and prospectors and gamblers who found California too tame. Utah is the most staid and respectable of states; Nevada is, by common convention at least, the naughtiest.

Nevada entered the union in 1864, only fourteen years after its first settlement; it was the first of the intermountain states to be admitted. This was largely because Abraham Lincoln needed votes with which to push through the 13th amendment, that which abolished slavery. The matter was of such urgency that Nevada's brand new constitution was telegraphed *in ioto* to Washington—at a cost of $3,416.77—so that the Nevada representative might vote in time.[3]

It is of course quick and easy divorce that has made Nevada famous everywhere. As far back as 1861, when the state was still a territory, the Nevadans made six months the term of residence necessary for divorce. Partly this was the result of general western breeziness; the attitude was that if two people no longer wanted to live together, it was very well their own affair. Also there were no settled agricultural or industrial communities, and the miners wandered among California, Utah and Arizona camps, seldom living in Nevada longer than six months. Not until about 1906 did Easterners begin to take advantage of the Nevada divorce laws. Then the easy Reno system brought in a lot of business. Even so, the local reform element succeeded in passing a law requiring a one-year's residential period beginning in 1914; but the business and professional men suffered so much that the legislature in 1916 restored the six months' law. In the 1920's and the early 1930's, other states, like Florida, Arkansas and Idaho pulled down their own residential periods for divorce. Nevada, to keep ahead, then did likewise, first reducing the time to three months and finally to the present term of six weeks.

Nevadans themselves—despite their free-and-easiness and the instant availability of the courts—don't exceed the national average in number of divorces; the overwhelming bulk of the trade comes from outside. A strange paradox that may account for Nevada's own moderation is the strong local influence of the Roman Catholic church. Both senators, Pat McCarran and E. P. Carville (formerly the governor),[4] are Catholic; so is the attorney general, and the archbishop of Reno—a well-known Catholic on the liberal side—has very considerable prestige and power.

Nevada's two chief cities, Reno and Las Vegas, compete vigorously in

[3] See *Rocky Mountain Politics,* edited by Thomas C. Donnelly, p. 89.
[4] Carville was defeated in 1946. His successor is a Republican, George W. Malone.

divorce traffic; Reno is still far ahead (with 7,076 divorces last year as against 2,944 in Las Vegas), but Las Vegas, in the southern part of the state, is a lively and fast-growing rival. Reno accuses it of muscling in. These two cities, with their savory mixture of wild-West and urban sophistication, their fluorescent neon-lighted gambling dens and fashionable ranches on the outskirts, are among the most picturesque in the United States. Reno compares to Las Vegas as San Francisco, one might say, compares to Los Angeles. Las Vegas is in fact part of the Los Angeles orbit; it is very show-offish, loaded with California money, and possessed of one of the most attractive hotels on earth. One small item about Reno, possibly apocryphal: during the curfew in World War II, it was hard if not impossible to close up places that violated the law, for the simple reason that most doors in this easy-going city have no locks!

Nevada likes to call itself "the one sound state," and postcards are available pointing out that it has no retail sales tax, no corporation tax, no state income tax, no inheritance tax—"and no thumb tax" on the roads. But the inadequacy of the schools and hospitals makes this boast a mockery. What, then, is the basis of public finance? First, the property tax, which is paid mostly by the railways, mines, and big stock-raising interests. Eighty-seven per cent of the land of Nevada is, however, still public land. Second, gambling.

This is by far the hottest issue in the state. Nevadans are not hypocrites and gambling was legalized from statehood on; in 1910, however, a reform group changed the law, and gambling was "prohibited." Of course it flourished anyway; to clean up gambling in any mining area is like trying to mop up the Mississippi with a dishrag. Also, being "illegal," it flourished to the accompaniment of vast corruption; the authorities had to be paid off. This state of affairs became a nuisance, and in 1931 gambling was legalized again; Nevada is today the only wide-open state—legally speaking—in the union. But the 1931 law did not *tax* gambling, except in the form of local license fees.

So far so good. Gambling proliferated, and so did Nevada—in a manner of speaking. Practically every delicatessen, railway waiting room, and drug store had its slot machines; and the big houses or clubs had faro, roulette, poker, craps, what you will. But the state continued to need money. It was "sound"—but very hard up. So a movement began to tax gambling. One of its leaders was State Senator Kenneth Johnson, himself the proprietor of a gambling house.[5] His point of view was that if gambling was to last, the rank and file of the people must share in the proceeds somehow. The financial stringency became worse; Nevada could hardly pay its schoolteachers. The salary of the secretary of state was only $3,600 a year, which put a ceiling on salaries for all other

[5] His wife is a linotype operator, by the way; thus in America do the professions mix.

public officials; some fifty thousand dollars was urgently needed to clean out the coyotes preying on the sheep herds, but the money wasn't there. Yet, day by day, armored cars rolled and rollicked out of Las Vegas for Los Angeles, carrying cash away. One establishment in Las Vegas was estimated to gross $120,000 per month; one in Reno did even better. But there were two important sources of opposition to a gambling tax. One came naturally from most gamblers, who didn't like to see their profits chewed into, the other from officials who feared that, if gambling were taxed, if it were allowed to contribute directly to the public welfare, the gambling interests would come to boss the state. The upshot was that a bill for a 10 per cent tax on gross gambling receipts was passed by the senate, but cut down to 1 per cent by the house. This 1 per cent tax is now in force. It only became operative in the summer of 1945, and no one knew then quite what revenue would accrue. Figures of gambling proceeds have always been a tightly guarded secret. One estimate is that the gross may reach forty million dollars per year, which would bring the state four hundred thousand dollars or almost half its budget.

Is gambling honest in Nevada? Yes—with your fingers crossed. The business is so lucrative anyway that, except in minor fly-by-night places, there is no real incentive to running a crooked game. An interesting point is that most of the big clubs have very little discernible police protection, though a hundred thousand dollars may be lying on the tables. But much of this is in silver cartwheels which, it is argued, are too bulky to make big-scale theft practicable; also, since all the roads lead into the desert, there is no place for a thief to go. Croupiers and dealers are, incidentally, paid very high wages—as much as twenty-five dollars a day. This is to discourage "leakage."

Politics is, in Nevada, inveterately personal. I talked to one official who said that, to get elected, he had to "shake every hand" in the state; another, a publican by trade, explained that he had won an election because "Everybody knows I'm the only man in Nevada who serves a full ounce." For a long time both the Republican and Democratic national committeemen had the same telephone number—Reno 3111—which was that of a famous old-timer in state politics, George Wingfield. And Nevada politics are full of tricks. In one recent election Kenneth Johnson found himself running against Kenneth Johnson. His opponents had found a man of the same name, and put him on the ballot in an attempt to split the vote.

Nevada was consistently Republican from 1916 to Roosevelt; during Roosevelt it was consistently Democratic, though the Republicans at present control the senate. It has, like most western states, the direct primary, initiative, referendum and recall; hence the democratic process is very "pure." One point worth mention is the power of the newspapers, although most are absentee owned; they are very prosperous partly because of high rates for legal advertising, and several have what are jokingly called "permanently reserved seats" in the legislature. As to financial power, it devolves mostly on California; the chief banks are dependent on Giannini.

Another point is the Nevada tradition of always having a "strong" senator in Washington. This was William M. Stewart for many years, and then the veteran Key Pittman, who was Tom Connally's predecessor as chairman of the Foreign Relations Committee. The "strong" senator today is of course Pat McCarran, "easy-going, old-shoe Pat," who has been God's own gift not only to the people of Nevada but to various interests outside the state.

Why should Nevada, the least populous American state, always have a "strong" senator? First, because as everybody knows, Nevada, with 110,000 people,[6] has precisely the same senatorial representation as, say, New York. Second, a strong man in Congress usually derives from a strong issue, and Nevada has had that from the beginning—silver.

Visit to a Ghost

Virginia City, the home of the Comstock Lode, is the first ghost town I ever saw. Bob Kenny of California took me there. We drove out one sunny summer morning from Reno, along twenty-three miles of glossy roads that led curvingly across the sagebrush to the violet and amber mountains.

Up to 1939, the Comstock Lode, probably the richest single mining property ever discovered, produced about six hundred million dollars in gold, about five hundred million dollars in silver. It has 750 miles of tunnels, shafts, drifts, inclines, and underground workings, and it helped finance the Civil War. It was the basis of such fortunes as that of the Mackays who created Postal Telegraph, and it was the undisputed dictator of Nevada politics for a generation. It was discovered in 1859, and for forty-odd years it made Virginia City one of the saltiest, most obstreperous towns on earth.

But not today. Virginia City looks like a lavender flower pressed in a book. Pick it up; it will crumble into dust. We passed the Bowers mansion, which once had solid silver doorknobs; we passed over the entrance to the Sutro tunnels, which with their laterals are nine miles long; we saw some "glory holing." Nevada prospectors, with gold in their veins, still look for it in veins of earth. Anybody can get out and dig, and a glory hole is simply an attempt to find ore by digging from the surface. Most mining had, however, stopped when I was in Nevada, following Directive L 208 of the War Production Board, which shut down on

---

[6] By the end of 1946, this figure had risen to 135,000, it is believed.

gold and silver so that skilled miners could work on more strategic minerals, like copper.

We saw the Miners Union Hall, that resembles nothing so much as a man with a hangover; it is the oldest building of this type in the world. We saw the skeleton of the Hotel International, which burned down in 1914; it was once the biggest hotel in the West, and the first one with an elevator. We saw a deserted newspaper office, with its windows shored up by ironing boards. A plaque says:

MARK TWAIN
WHO GREATLY ENRICHED THE LITERATURE OF THE WEST
STARTED HIS CAREER AS A WRITER IN
THIS BUILDING IN 1862 ON THE EDITORIAL
STAFF OF THE TERRITORIAL ENTERPRISE

Further on is the rickety, worm-eaten shell of what was once a famous opera house. A sign on the wall says:

VINI VIDI VICI
THE OLD MEXICAN LINIMENT
GOOD FOR MAN OR BEAST
PENETRATES TO THE ROOT OF THE DIFFICULTY

Virginia City is, then, a fragrant tomb. The population was forty thousand in its heyday; today, two thousand. Never have I seen such deadness. Not a cat walks. The shops are mostly boarded up, the windows black and cracked; the frame buildings are scalloped, bulging, splintered; C Street droops like a cripple, and the sidewalks are still wooden planks; the telephone exchange, located in a stationery shop, is operated by a blind lady who had read my books in Braille.

But also in Virginia City is the Crystal Bar, its most palatable relic. Bill Marks, the barman who has been there for a generation, mixed us a bonanza fizz, and showed us his ancient treasures—a gas-lit chandelier quivering with colored lights; pictures of the Corbett-Fitzsimmons fight in 1897; crystal glasses that boom with sound; an old timetable of the Virginia & Truckee Railway, and a visitors' register going back to 1875, with the signatures of General Grant, Jim Fair and the other bonanza kings, and of Thomas A. Edison, this latter like an etching on copper plate. We saw old metal-plate phonographs that still work, a clock painted on a glass mirror which, if you spin the hands, adjusts itself automatically to the correct time, and the 1880 predecessors of modern pinball games.

"Hi Ho Silver!"

Silver is not like wheat or even lumber. You can't grow it back, and a silver mine is a strictly expendable proposition, as the Comstock Lode well proves. But the main reason why silver is such a permanent and lively issue in Nevada is that it doesn't pay, according to the Nevadans. In the great days of Virginia City silver was worth $1.24 an ounce; at one time during the 30's it dropped to 27¢; now it has been stepped up to about 70¢. To many folk in the East, this seems far too high—for instance to silversmiths in Connecticut; to the West it seems too low. The Nevadans could, they say, produce "marginal" silver in great quantities, if the price went up, and thus ameliorate the state's great economic difficulties—though this would mean of course that the rest of the nation would be paying Nevada an even greater levy than at present for its silver crop.

Silver has dominated Nevada politics from the beginning; nobody not acceptable to the great mining interests could possibly have been elected to anything. Voters were simply lined up in any convenient bar and led to the polls by the nose; they would get as much as ten dollars each for their trouble. This was of course long ago. An actual "Silver party" existed for awhile, and the House of Representatives once had a "Silver member." Then William Jennings Bryan came out for the free (and unlimited) coinage of silver in his celebrated Cross of Gold speech in 1896, and the silverites became Democratic. Nowadays practically all citizens of Nevada take the same prosilver line, but the Republicans are more outspoken, since they blame the New Deal for keeping silver down, though actually the price has risen. This in turn means that Nevada is one of the few states where the Republican party is inflationary, that is, it wants a higher price for silver.

Behind all this is, of course, a national situation which is hardly within the province of this chapter. Both gold and silver were legal tender in the United States, at a ratio whereby the value of gold was fixed at sixteen times that of silver, until 1873. The silver people have been fighting with unremitting pertinacity to restore silver to its former position ever since, or, at the very least, to increase its price. The issue was a hardy perennial for fifty years. Finally in 1934 a new Silver Purchase Act was passed by Congress, whereby the Treasury promised to support an artificial price of $1.29 an ounce, which to most people seemed an outrageously high figure. The Treasury accumulated a fantastic silver surplus, but it was only permitted to sell this for industrial use at a price around seventy cents, a price set by the silver bloc. This was not enough for the silver senators. They proposed new legislation in 1946 to lift the price still higher. Almost every reputable economist, commentator, and newspaperman in the East joined to call this one of the most blatant hold-up attempts in the whole history of the silver gouge. Consider for instance these excerpts from a letter to the New York *Times* (May 20, 1946), signed by fifty-odd members of the Economists National Committee on Monetary Policy:

There is no more validity in the argument of the silver bloc that silver should be bought and sold at its nominal monetary valuation of $1.29 per fine ounce, or at any price above the open-competitive market price, than there would be in an argument that the paper used to make paper currency should be bought and sold in the market at the nominal monetary value of the piece of currency manufactured from this paper.

Congress and the people of this country might do well to remind themselves that it was this same pro-silver bloc which revealed it was not only willing but determined, *even in time of war*, to protect its subsidy regardless of any adverse effects on the general welfare. *It was this bloc that forced the Treasury to withhold much-needed silver from war industries for many months after we entered the war.* [Author's italics.]

The attitude of the silver bloc in respect to the public welfare, where silver is involved, appears to be no better today than it was during the late war, especially in 1942.

It is the duty of Congress and the President to see to it that the general welfare, rather than the desires of the silver bloc, is served when silver legislation is undertaken.

But the silver bloc is one of the most efficient, sophisticated, and ruthless in the nation—though hardly more to be singled out than the beet sugar bloc or cattle bloc. It comprises only fourteen senators, who represent seven states, with an aggregate population of about 3,600,000. These are exactly equal in power, however, to fourteen eastern senators who may represent 51,900,000 people. Such is the working out of one of the most conspicuous of all vagaries in the federal Constitution, and the silver bloc knows well—by trading votes and favors—how to take advantage of it for its own highly self-conscious aims.

What happened? After two months of debate—during which time eastern silversmiths had to melt silver dollars to keep in business, while at West Point, New York, the greatest silver hoard ever known to man lay inert and useless—Congress finally raised the price to 90.5¢ per ounce. The silver senators, to force the vote that brought this victory, even held up an appropriations bill that delayed payment of salaries to post office and treasury employees of the U.S. government. Another factor is that the new price will "complete the demoralization of currencies in many countries (Mexico, India, China) which the Silver Bloc's grab started."[7] Now the silverites are hell-bent to lift the price again to $1.29. The taxpayers as a whole will of course foot the bill—to keep alive fewer than three thousand western mines. Final note: the entire mining industry in eleven western states supports only 3,700,000 people. Superfinal note: the total value of silver production in the United States is about one-half that of peanuts.

[7] *Time,* July 29, 1946.

McCarran is a fascinating character. A man who served with him in the Senate for some years, and who has since been elevated to a very superior position, once told me that "the trouble with McCarran is that he can't get along with himself." This may account for his sudden changes of mind and cantankerousness. McCarran was swept into office on Roosevelt's coattails in 1932, and then turned violently against him. FDR tried to get him "purged," but failed. A dominant note in McCarran is his extreme Irishness. Oddly enough, though silver is of course his main pivot and preoccupation, he resembles more another Nevada metal —gold—in that he is soft, heavy, and not a good conductor.

Chapter 6

Pacific Northwest Coming Up

wwwwwwwwwwwwwwwwwwwwwwwwwwwwwwwwwwwwwwwwwwwwwwwwwwwwwwwwwwwwwwwwwwwwwwwwwwwww

> Kentucky is said to be the land of fair women and fast horses;
> Oregon is the land of man-sized men and happy homes. It is
> the absolute truth that I have never heard an Oregonian speak
> evil of another Oregonian. . . . The Oregonians are typical
> aristocrats. . . . No Oregonian is a snob because no Oregonian
> imagines for a minute that anyone could look down on him.
> —John Leader, *Oregon Through Alien Eyes*
>
> Or lose thyself in the continuous woods
> Where rolls the Oregon, and hears no sound
> Save its own dashings.
> —William Cullen Bryant

OREGON and Washington are twins except as to character; they fit
together like chunks of a well-constructed jigsaw puzzle. They
form an almost perfectly integrated natural unit, and their history,
geography, climate, natural resources, problems, are closely similar.
This—with Idaho as a sort of pendant—is the splendid open world of
the Northwest, which means the world of the Columbia River basin.
Roses at Christmas, salmon that climb ladders, the greatest timber
stands in the nation, personalities like Wayne Morse and Dave Beck,
the tall tales of Paul Bunyan, spacious and maximal issues like public
power, wheat fields that look painted by Van Gogh, and more social
energy, more social vision than in any comparable region in the country
—these are some distinguishing characteristics of Oregon and Washington.

Also, mostly on account of the variegated weather, the Northwest is
an area of violent contrasts within the whole. The town of Port Angeles,
Washington, has the heaviest rainfall in the U.S.A., 141 inches per year.
Across the mountains, not more than a metaphorical stone's throw away,
is Grand Coulee, the greatest irrigation project ever built by man.

History of the region—and this too is vital and diversified—begins
with the early fur traders, like John Jacob Astor who established a post
at Astoria in 1811, explorers like Lewis and Clark and, of course, the
Indians. Whereas in California, as an example, the Indians were largely
passive, almost totally backward and without culture, those of the Northwest were so picturesque and well developed that the whole area is still
vividly underlaid with an Indian tradition. Both Washington and Oregon

were, as is well known, originally part of the same Oregon Territory, as were Idaho and parts of Montana and Wyoming. British influence was very strong in the early days, and in fact the territory was ruled jointly by the United States and Great Britain for twenty-eight years, something which can be said of no other region in the U.S. "Had the question of ownership been decided on the respective merits of the rival nations' claims," says the Washington State Guide pertly, "no reasonable doubt exists that England would hold the Oregon country today." The United States neither fought for Oregon nor purchased it; the huge territory fell into our lap—with some assistance from the power politics of President James K. Polk. But just as Washington and Oregon might well be British today, had not the irresistible pressure of American westward expansion intervened at a time when the British were anxious to avoid a quarrel, so might British Columbia be American today, had we not receded from our original claim to the celebrated "54-40 or Fight" frontier.

One colorful item in the Oregon story is that Dr. John McLoughlin, chief factor of the Hudson's Bay Company west of the Rockies, ruled it almost singlehanded for more than twenty years from his citadel at Fort Vancouver. Another is that Daniel Webster dismissed the whole area as perfectly useless, saying on one occasion, "What can we do with the western coast, a coast of 3,000 miles, rockbound, cheerless, uninviting, and not a harbor on it? What use have we for such a country? I will never vote one cent from the public treasury to place the Pacific Ocean one inch nearer Boston than it is now!" Still another is that when the bill creating Oregon Territory became law, the governorship was first offered to a comparatively unknown young politician from Illinois—Abe Lincoln.

Both Oregon and Washington are split straight down the middle by the Cascades. Also the Cascades cut the weather in half, so to speak. Humid air rises from the Pacific, which is fed here by the warmish Japan Current, and drops as rainfall when it bumps into the Cascades. So the western or coastal slope of both states is temperate, moist, hazy; the eastern half is hot, high, semiarid. So, in turn, the western slope is largely industrial, with great ports and towns like Portland and Seattle; the east is agricultural—wheat and cattle country. The west is thickly populated but in the east—especially in Oregon which contains one of the loneliest and least-known regions in America—you can travel 150 miles between communities. Even the elemental timber is absolutely different. The line of the Cascades cuts down like a sharp welt. On the west side, the forests are mostly Douglas fir with hardly a single ponderosa pine; on the east, they are solidly ponderosa pine, with hardly a single Douglas fir.

Plenty of people have suggested that Oregon and Washington be split up and put together a different way, with the Cascades as a north-south boundary. But then the new state on the east would be nothing more than an agricultural hinterland to the industrial west. Each new state would be almost perfectly homogeneous, but correspondingly it would lack balance and variety.

So much for general background—and for the all-of-a-piece physical similarities. I said in Chapter 5 that no traveler, flying across Utah and Nevada, could possibly tell the difference between them. The same thing is even more strikingly true of Oregon and Washington. They look as much alike as twin peas or marbles. But—and this "but" is the heart of the Northwest story—there is a tremendous difference between the two states otherwise. Nowhere else in the country can the extraordinary tenacity of state characteristics be better observed, the deep-rooted instinct of a state to grow its own way without regard to its neighbor. Oregon and Washington are, except in physiognomy, almost as different as Maine and Florida. Let us explore.

Oregon was settled by New Englanders in the first instance, and has a native primness, a conservatism, much like that of New Hampshire or Vermont. It is, indeed, one of the most astonishing things in America that Portland, Oregon, should be almost indistinguishable from Portland, Maine. But Washington—in acute contrast—is a gold-rush state, explosive, articulate, intractable. Jim Farley is supposed to have said once that "there are 47 American states—and the Soviet of Washington."

Oregon is one of the most consistently Republican states on the local level; Washington, with a tradition of Populism and Progressivism, has been as consistently Democratic. Labor is weak and diffuse in Oregon, whereas in Washington it is strong and getting stronger. Oregon is very conservative socially and financially; Washington has a more come-easy go-easy atmosphere. In social legislation, Washington is probably the most progressive state in the country; Oregon is one of the least though it inaugurated many reforms that its neighbors promptly picked up. That all this should be so, in two states not only adjacent but geographically indistinguishable, is one of the strangest paradoxes in the United States.

Washington points out proudly that it has had the direct primary since 1907, woman suffrage since 1909, and the initiative and referendum since 1911. Its unemployment compensation rates are the highest in the country, twenty-five dollars per week for twenty-six weeks (the scale that President Truman sought unsuccessfully to extend to the nation as a whole in 1946), and it pays fifty dollars a month old age pensions to everybody over sixty-five. This pension scheme—probably the most advanced in the United States—has, moreover, been in effect ever since

1933, though the rates were lower then. Washington spends seventy-two million dollars a year (almost 20 per cent of the total budget) on state aid to schools, and it has an admirable record in such things as nursery schools, otological clinics, aid to the blind and to needy children, coal mining safety laws, equal pay for women, expansion of bus services, anti-tuberculosis legislation, and the like. It pays the highest wages in the nation, next to Detroit, and went through the war without a single strike. It has more bathrooms per capita than any other state, and more electric light.

By contrast look at Oregon. It is one of the lowest states in financial aid to schools. It was the first state in the West to pass an enabling act under the Federal Housing Authority but the last actually to create such an authority. Nevertheless it has to hand plenty of the mechanism for progressive social legislation. It was here, following the reforms of William S. U'Ren at the turn of the century, that the recall, initiative, and referendum were, in fact, first invented; the whole system was called the "Oregon system" in the beginning. Oregon has, indeed, as good a setup for liberal government as any state—but it makes comparatively little use of it. The promise was superb, and the performance relatively indifferent.[1]

Washington is extremely liberal in regard to civil liberties; Oregon is less so. In the early 20's—largely because so many Southerners had moved in—Oregon was, in fact, strange as it may seem, the strongest Ku-Klux Klan state in the union outside the solid South, and hangovers of this still show. Agitation against the Nisei was fiercer in Oregon than anywhere else in the West; the Portland police department for years maintained a "red squad" like that in Los Angeles; Portland was considered one of the main Nazi centers in the country by the FBI, and I heard more and more bitter anti-Negro talk there than in any other northern city. I even heard people speak with indignation about Jack Reed, a Portland boy, who has been dead and interred in the Kremlin wall these many years. His father was a U.S. marshal, and the feeling is that "he let the community down" by siring a famous radical.

But—let us be scrupulously careful to inspect both sides and not generalize too much in one direction—Oregon was one of the first states to have a Jewish governor, and Wayne Morse, its junior senator, is one of the two or three most vigorously outspoken liberals in the Senate

[1] An important point in qualification of the above is that Oregon has no sales tax, whereas Washington has a comparatively heavy one. Yet, by general definition, a sales tax is a kind of poor man's income tax, since a man earning fifty dollars a month has to pay the same tax on commodities as a millionaire. But Oregon has four times voted *against* a sales tax, on the ground that it is unjust to the poor. It has an income tax instead. The situation in Washington is the reverse. Mostly this is the result of pressure by the Washington State Taxpayers League, a powerful group dominated by the lumber interests, which wants to keep all taxes but the sales tax down.

today. Late in 1946 the radical Townsendites succeeded in getting on the ballot, for subsequent decision, a "Little Townsend Plan" which, if it becomes law, will pay one hundred dollars a month to everybody in the state over sixty-five, to be financed by a tax on all gross incomes. Finally, Reed College, Portland, is one of the most progressive schools in the country, and Oregon like Washington has a splendid record in the development and use of public power.

An Attempt to Explain These Differences

First, settlement. Oregon was, I have noted, first settled in the main by New Englanders. The place names—not merely Portland and Salem, the capital—are New Englandish all over the state; consider Pendleton, Medford, and so on. (In Washington, by contrast, most conspicuous place names are Indian, like Yakima, Tacoma, Spokane, Walla Walla.) The second wave of immigration came largely from the middle South— the Ozark country and Arkansas—and consisted of folk who didn't care much about the Gold Rush in either Alaska or California, of middle-aged people who wanted to settle down. Washington, on the other hand, got proportionately a more adventurous and vital stock, though Oregonians will assassinate me for saying so. Also to Washington came a tremendous influx of Scandinavians, which strongly contributed to its progressivism. A Scandinavian name—like Wallgren, Magnuson, and so on—is almost as useful a political asset in Washington as in Minnesota, and it is proverbial that farmers of Scandinavian descent, moving westward out of the Dakotas, are radically inclined.

British influence is, incidentally, still strong in parts of Oregon, particularly Portland. British traders, wheat exporters, cattlemen, came in after the Hudson's Bay days; mortgage loan companies, owned in Britain, flourished and were manned by young Englishmen. This had a marked effect on recreation, among other things. Portland is, I should imagine, the only American city (except Philadelphia) where cricket has been regularly played, and it was the first city on the West coast to have a golf links. Thirty years ago there were not less than twenty-seven golf courses in the town.

Second, railways. Oregon had its famous Trail, but the railways that came later cut across Washington instead; today Washington has three transcontinental lines and Oregon only one—moreover this one only touches a small corner of the state. Hence, the Oregon interior has never been fully opened up; it has been less accessible to the irrigation of new influences and ideas.

Third, religious factors. The Roman Catholic church is stronger in Oregon than Washington, which tends to make the former more conservative. Washington is mostly Lutheran and freethinking.

Fourth, land tenure. The lumber barons, who were the most flagrant of all American despoilers, grabbed off considerably more land in Oregon than Washington. Hence Oregon has less state land to provide income for schools and public services.

Fifth, the labor movement, which as mentioned above has always been strong in Washington, and in Oregon comparatively weak.

Beyond all this there are, one might add, elements mysterious and unknown. No listing of simple facts can wholly or satisfactorily explain why communities differ, or why their specialized characteristics may be unique. Why, for instance, to jump far afield, should Texas have what seem to be the prettiest girls in the world? This phenomenon can hardly be explained purely on grounds of climate, sunshine or outdoor life; Arizona has more sunshine, and California is probably healthier. But walk across the campus at Austin, or roam the downtown streets of Dallas; there are more Miss Americas per square yard than anywhere else in the country per square mile. A manifestation like this must, it would seem, derive from some kind of spiritual or irrational salt-and-pepper that no itemization of other factors can altogether account for. And so it is with the progressivism of Washington, the conservatism of Oregon.

Finally, a word of one striking similarity between the two states. Each has a peculiarly complex system of liquor regulation, or semiprohibition, which may cause acute anguish to the uninformed or unwary traveler.

Portland and Seattle

Nothing could better illustrate the differences between Oregon and Washington than their two chief cities, which are as unlike as tea and gin. Many years ago a magazine writer called Portland a "spinster city," and except that in recent years it has been a spinster city with a war baby, the description still holds good. The baby grew hard and fast; Portland rose in population from 305,394 to 660,600 in less than a decade, and just to the north a completely new town, Vanport, was built from scratch to a population of 32,400 almost overnight. The conservative Portland citizenry did not altogether like this influx; I heard a hotel clerk say, with an elegant wrinkle of the nose, "The only streetcar left that you can ride on without getting grease spots is to Council Crest," Council Crest being the most fashionable section of the city.

Yankee traders who went around the Horn founded Portland in 1845. Francis W. Pettygrove of Portland, Maine, and Amos L. Lovejoy of Boston, Massachusetts, each wanted to name it for his own home town, and Pettygrove won by tossing a coin. Otherwise, we should be talking today of "Boston, Oregon." The Puritan atmosphere persists heavily. The streets bear names like Everett and Hawthorne; it is a city of homes and the chief bookstore is admirable; on the main street is a large illuminated sign JESUS LIGHT OF THE WORLD.

Portland was, during the war, the port for Russian lend lease, just as it was Russia's chief port in America during the days of Catherine the Great. The Russian sailors, sometimes under the command of women captains stout as barrels, behaved well, did not fraternize, and seemed to spend most of their time at the big department stores buying cheap consumers' goods like bolts of cloth.

Portland has no symphony orchestra. It has no civic center. Everybody wants one, in theory, but Portlanders don't spend money easily, and the community has a horror of a white elephant; so the proposal to create a civic center like that in San Francisco was brutally voted down. Portland, despite its respectability, has the second highest rate of incidence of venereal disease in the nation, and its city jail, with a "drunk tank" in which prisoners were sometimes found dead from beatings, has been a major source of scandal. Its biggest department store, Meier and Frank, is Jewish owned, and Aaron Frank is probably the richest man in the city (though some of the timber fortunes are still very big); its chief club, of the same superior category as the Hope in Providence or the Pendennis in Louisville, is the Arlington; its most distinguished citizen is a liberal banker, E. B. MacNaughton, president of the First National. One striking thing about Portland is the number of four-tap water fountains all over the city. These were built by a lumber tycoon named Simon Benson, a virulent prohibitionist; he thought that his lumbermen might be weaned from hard liquor by a copious availability of fresh water, and the fountains are still there— together with still-tippling lumbermen.

What liberalism there is in Portland—and its good spirit of *noblesse oblige*—was well symbolized by Charles Erskine Scott Wood. His corporate clients were the city's leading bankers, steamship operators and railroad magnates. But Wood had two offices. At the other he conferred with Emma Goldman, Eugene Debs and IWW organizers. He called himself a "philosophical anarchist," and addressed wobbly meetings wearing the old U.S. Army campaign hat he wore as a young lieutenant with the 21st Infantry when he was pursuing Joseph, the Nez Percé chieftain. Wood died in February of 1944, the oldest living graduate of West Point. To the end he flailed out at the Dies Committee, supported FDR, and denounced the "wicked" utility corporations.

Mount Hood, the exquisitely beautiful peak just behind the city, startlingly resembles Mont Blanc. But it is almost as difficult to see Mount Hood from Portland as Mont Blanc from Geneva, because of the semiperpetual drizzling mist. Just the same Portland loves it. Hundreds of citizens from legless newsboys to seventy-year-old widows attempt to climb it day in and day out, and many do. Lately a proposal was heard to build a cog railway or aerial tramway to the summit. It was howled down by indignant Portlanders who insist on keeping their precious mountain unspoiled.

Portland was a healthy young metropolis while Seattle, founded in 1852, was still a remote village. The population of Seattle only numbered 3,533 as recently as 1880. Then it streaked out like a skyrocket and, a fast tough town, has been streaking out ever since. The two cities do not, however, have anything of the rivalry of, say, San Francisco and Los Angeles. Portland is too superior to worry much, and Seattle too chaotic. I did, however, hear one Portlander complain, "Seattle just figures to get the best of everything," in a wan and decrepit voice.

No city in America, not even San Francisco, has quite the spectacular beauty of Seattle; and no city has so few hours of what the health authorities call "effective sunlight." Mount Rainier (which is still stubbornly called Mount Tacoma by Seattle's rival city, Tacoma) is—when you can see it—an incomparably beautiful sentinel, and resembles the Jungfrau much as Mount Hood resembles Mont Blanc; the town as a whole, built on seven hills between Puget Sound and the glistening cobalt mirror of Lake Washington, has not less than two hundred miles of waterfront. Its streets are so steep, like those of San Francisco, that you practically need spikes in your shoes, and its politics are almost as spectacular as the scenery; this is a town where mayors have been twice recalled in recent years, where fabulous characters like Victor Aloysius ("Just Call Me Vic") Meyers[2] leap straight out of night clubs into public office, and where the Boettigers worked for Hearst. Seattle has the highest suicide rate of any American city (people blame the weather); it is the city where your car is dragged off instantly and impounded if you park it incorrectly and where jaywalkers are incontinently arrested; where chunks of smoked salmon are called "squaw candy" and where a rough frontier civilization has not quite jelled.

The story of Seattle is, in a way, an Alaskan story. It is the great gateway to Alaska, being two days nearer by sea than San Francisco, and the totem poles in public squares still give you a sniff of the Klondike air. Seattle's position vis-à-vis Alaska may be appreciated if you realize that it is not merely the jumping-off place to Juneau, but also to New York; Seattle lies almost halfway between the extreme western tip of the Aleutians and Montauk Point. Gold made Alaska, and Alaska made

---

[2] Meyers, lieutenant governor of the state, is really something. For years he was master of ceremonies and a band leader at his own *boite de nuit*, the Club Victor. During his last campaign one of his slogans was "I don't believe in daylight saving time. Seattle should have two-four time, allegro." Another was, "Habitually I go without a vest so that I can't be accused of standing for the vested interests," and another, "There's going to be no cheap chiseling at the City Hall; I intend to take it all myself." His slogan in 1944 was "Me and Roosevelt will win in a walk." In plain fact he did win by some 430,000 votes to 190,000. The details above are from Richard L. Neuberger's *Our Promised Land*, pp. 272-290.

Seattle. In 1897 the Klondike mines came in, and a boom started that has gone on practically without interruption ever since. Nowadays gold is not so important. But Seattle lives on Alaskan timber and Alaskan fish. An acute issue at the moment is airline communications with Alaska. Seattle thinks of itself as the natural and inevitable jumping-off place for Alaskan traffic, but the Civil Aeronautics Board, working out an over-all route to the Orient, chose Minneapolis instead. The route will be Chicago-Minneapolis-Edmonton-Anchorage-Tokyo, as at present planned, leaving Seattle out and wounding its feelings badly.

Alaska itself is not part of this book, but one should at least mention that the Alaskans are rebelling at what they consider "domination" by Seattle. They point out that virtually everything of value in the territory —canneries, steamship lines, gold mines, trading companies—is owned in Seattle. Of the proceeds of the 59 million dollar salmon industry, less than six million dollars stays in Alaska where the fish are caught. Alaskans have, indeed, rejoiced lately at the fact that the Alcan Highway as well as the new air route will apparently go through Edmonton and Minneapolis instead of Seattle; they say that this will help release them from their "bondage."

Seattle is very proud of its rambunctious origins; it has learned a lot through growth and struggle. People believe in merit in this hard-boiled town; there are few fictitious values, either among rich or poor. Most of the big money, made out of western resources, flowed east; this is still bitterly resented. What happened first was that Seattle had to fight hard to get a railway, during the brawl and bluff days of Hill and Harriman. The Northern Pacific wanted its western terminus at Tacoma, its own company town, even though this meant strangling Seattle just as it was beginning to bud nicely. In retaliation Seattle set out to make a railway of its own, and—literally—the town folk started to build one with their own bare hands. This was a heroic gesture, but it didn't quite work. Finally in 1890 the Northern Pacific came in and Jim Hill's Great Northern followed three years later.

Everybody knows the story of the Mercer girls, a yarn nicely expressive of the Seattle spirit. In the 60's the new community had, as was natural, a great woman shortage. So a venturesome citizen named Asa Mercer, who was also president of the university, traveled east to the Atlantic seaboard and came back with a covey of virgins who were willing to marry, sight unseen, the lonely but stalwart pioneers. There were eleven girls in the first Mercer shipment. When they arrived, "the single men of the town turned out looking like grizzlies in store clothes and with their hair slicked down like sea otters."[3] In 1866, Mercer went east again, and brought back forty-six more women; some of these were Civil War widows, and, as if to prove the virtue of his wares, he

[3] *Washington,* in the American Guide Series, p. 216.

married one himself. The Mercer family had a real colonizing zest. A brother was the first man to bring horses into Seattle.

We should have one word at least for the pleasant city of Spokane. It lies in eastern Washington, and is the "capital" of an area that includes the Idaho panhandle and parts of Montana and Oregon; this region—largely pivoted on wheat production—is sometimes known as the Inland Empire, and once a semiserious agitation began to make it a separate state, to be known as Lincoln. Spokane is the largest inland city in the West except Denver; it is the old home town of Eric Johnston and Lewis Schwellenbach; its leading newspaper is one of the most rigorously conservative in the United States; it has considerable charm and pictorial distinction; and it contains one of the best hotels in the country, the Davenport, where every coin is washed before being given in change.

Politics in Oregon, Plus Snell

Fifty years ago if you should have asked "Who runs Oregon?" the answer would have been triple: (1) the Portland *Oregonian*, (2) the Southern Pacific, (3) the lumber kings. Nowadays all three have lost most of their direct influence, though the *Oregonian* is still a force. Twenty years ago the answer might have been "the McNary machine," but Senator Charles L. McNary is dead—and even when he was vice presidential candidate under Willkie, Roosevelt carried the state.

The governor of Oregon, Earl Snell, has done his best to build up a machine similar to McNary's, but it creaks at the joints, and no one knows how long it will last. Snell is an interesting enough man, but Oregon does not go in for strong governors; usually the governor, treasurer, and secretary of state form a kind of triumvirate.[4] Snell's chief political characteristic is, it would seem, an ability to get along with everybody. He is genial, mediocre, and perpetually on the fence. He owns a garage and filling station in Arlington, and spends a good deal of time there. He was secretary of state for some years, and as such did favors for practically everybody; his name appeared on all such routine documents as applications for automobile licenses and the like, and he became widely known and popular. Snell is one of the world's greatest joiners. He belongs to everything. He was an active Townsendite. He is a pillar of the American Legion, and the Legion is in turn a central pillar of his machine.

He never makes any kind of move until he is sure that it will be greeted favorably; he works hard to please the farmers and, if labor puts on enough pressure, he will sign prolabor bills; thus his labor record is fairly good. He is not a student; toss him into a controversy, and he will blow up. He can make three speeches a day and say nothing whatsoever;

[4] Oregon is one of the few American states with no office of lieutenant governor.

he can be black and white at the same time. That a man like Snell, who
has no discernible principles, can at the same time be a quite good governor with a quite good program, is both a characteristic and a somewhat
baffling American phenomenon. He carries water on both shoulders; yet
the upshot is that he gives most people what they want. Certainly Snell
is one of the most triumphant vote getters in the history of the state. In
the 1946 primaries he beat his opponent, a Portland house painter, by
five to one, and in the November run-off coasted through to an easy
victory.

Snell aside, the two most interesting political personalities in Oregon
are Charles Sprague, a former governor who is editor of the Salem
Statesman, and the present state treasurer, Leslie Scott. Sprague, a firm
civil liberties advocate and a fine type of western liberal Republican, cannot be budged on a principle, and as a result has often made himself unpopular. Scott, a wealthy man with varied interests, is earthy, cautious,
suspicious, conservative in the extreme, and without a dishonest hair.

Oregon, on the state level is overwhelmingly Republican; within
this circumscription the main power factors might be outlined as follows:
First, the Townsendites. But these are a steadily declining force if
only because most are old, and are progressively dying off. *Second,* the
Legion. *Third,* in a less reputable rubric, leftovers from the Ku-Klux
and the Bund. *Fourth,* the farmers, with the Grange as the dominant
agriculture group, followed closely by the Farmers Union. Perhaps
it is another Oregon paradox, but the farmers in this conservative state
are for the most part liberal. This is because they want public power and
rural electrification; hence they tend to oppose the private utility interests. Most Oregon farmers detest labor, on the other hand. They want
cheap utilities and cheap labor both. *Fifth,* women. Oregon was one of
the earliest woman suffrage states, and the Parent Teachers Association, the Federation of Women's Clubs, the League of Women Voters
are all conspicuous and forceful. *Sixth,* the churches and denominational
schools. Describing Oregon twenty years ago, Charles H. Chapman tells
how every settler's camp had its school—"the Methodists at Salem, the
Congregationalists at Forest Grove, the Presbyterians at Albany, the
Baptists at McMinnville, the Wesleyan Methodists at Corvallis, the
Quakers at Newberg, the Campbellites at Monmouth."[5] Finally, as in
New England, Unitarian influence is very strong, especially in "upper"
circles.

Turn now to labor. The AF of L outnumbers the CIO in a ratio of
about seven to one, and the two organizations—in great contrast to
Washington where a sort of Popular Front is in operation—don't even
walk the same side of the street; more than anywhere else in the West,
they dislike and distrust one another. Of course, conservative elements,

[5] *These United States,* Vol. I, p. 283.

which naturally profit by this split, try to widen and extend it. Even the AF of L is thought to be pretty "red" in Oregon; the CIO is considered positively insurrectionary. But, a nice point, as the CIO goes further left, there is a tendency to think of the AF of L as being more respectable.

A major political issue in Oregon is—as in so many American states—redistricting. The state has not been redistricted for something like twenty-five years; yet in these years there have been important population shifts, like that of labor coming in to the towns. This is one reason why labor has been at such a disadvantage politically. Portland, the focus of labor strength, has only thirteen seats in the state legislature; it should have, by basis of *present* population, at least twenty-one. I talked to one state senator who, representing three counties with a population of well over half a million, has exactly the same vote as a colleague from a single county of twenty thousand. This is the rotten borough system *in excelsis*; what it amounts to is a not-so-subtle form of disfranchisement.

Richard L. Neuberger, America's best informed journalist on Northwest affairs, wrote recently in *The Progressive*:

> As a member of the Oregon Legislature in 1941, I remember attempting to raise the salaries paid our schoolteachers. . . . The average salary for teachers in California is $2,201, in Washington $1,746, and in Oregon only $1,286. . . . Our bill to reserve new educational funds for the pay of classroom teachers . . . was defeated by a vote of 33 to 27. The votes of the over-represented sagebrush areas defeated it. . . . But if the various counties had been represented in the legislature as the state founders intended, the bill would have passed approximately 42 to 18.

Oregon has one unusual political characteristic; it permits slogans, not to exceed twelve words in length, on the ballot. McNary ran in 1930 with the slogan, "Present United States Senator; Oregon development; improved agriculture; law enforcement." Snell won the governorship in 1942 with "Leadership for Oregon's war effort and tax problems—Snell gets things done." Wayne Morse ran in 1944 with "Aggressive, experienced, respected. Protect America by forceful leadership in the Senate."

Washington Politicians: Gallery in Miniature

MON C. WALLGREN. Congressman 1932-40, senator 1940-44, and now governor of the state—one of the few senators ever to quit Washington, D.C., for a governorship. Able, close to Truman, not a rabble rouser, strongly prolabor. Elected governor in 1944 mostly on the Roosevelt wave. Was a watchmaker by trade, worked as a boy in his father's jewelry shop in Everett, a lumber town north of Seattle. One of the best three-cushion billiard players in America; was once a runner-up to Hoppe in straight billiards, and a semi-pro champion in 18.2 balkline. When I asked a Washington worthy once what Wallgren "had," the answer was (a) amiability, (b) a Scandinavian name. But Mon Wallgren has more than just that. Nobody pushes him around, and his record has been first rate.

WARREN G. MAGNUSON, U. S. senator. The best-looking man in the Senate, one of the most forward looking, and at forty-one the second youngest. Blond, husky, squarely built. Born in Minnesota, orphaned in childhood, followed the harvests west as a farmhand, peddled ice for Dave Beck's teamsters, worked his way through the University of Washington law school. A Lutheran. A good football player, and his football record helped him considerably when he went into politics. Minor posts on the state level until 1936, then four times Congressman—he campaigned in the beginning by personal house-to-house canvassing—and senator in 1944. Three days younger than Bill Fulbright of Arkansas, and hence the youngest man in the Senate until Hugh Mitchell, also from Washington, a state which certainly picks men young, got there. Magnuson is a great one for being concentratedly busy, for making friends, for being unaware of time. At 4:30 P.M. he will be apt to say, "Have I had lunch yet?" He and Wallgren were Congressmen at the same time, and are close friends; Magnuson carries the ball in Washington, D.C., so to speak, and Wallgren in the state. Believes in tolerance, hard work, social service. Highly ambitious. Has a good liberal record in the Senate, and thinks that his state has the greatest potential future of any in the union.

HUGH B. MITCHELL. Aged 39. For some years Wallgren's secretary, and was appointed by him to fill out his unexpired term; he is the third member of the Wallgren-Magnuson-Mitchell triumvirate, and possibly the ablest of the three. An emphatic progressive—yet the New York *Daily News* warmly praised him recently. Mitchell is a student, somewhat lacking in color, a former newspaper reporter, and the son of Harry B. Mitchell, the president of the Civil Service Commission. Had an outstanding Senate record—though the real estate lobby and such agglomerations of monopoly as the Aluminum Company of America didn't like him much. He fought hard for the OPA and for cheap housing for veterans. Chief sponsor of the bill to create a Columbia Valley Authority like the TVA. Defeated in the Republican landslide of 1946.[6]

[6] Mitchell's successor is the 40-year-old war veteran and former nonpartisan mayor of Tacoma, Harry B. Cain. He is a former Democrat who turned Republican (*cf.* Thomas L. Stokes, New York *World-Telegram*, Oct. 5, 1946) in 1944, and has a distinct liberal record though he is not so liberal as Mitchell. He is Washington's first Republican senator since 1932. So again we see the Roosevelt era ending.

Pressure Groups Fore and Aft

Neither political party has a real machine in Washington. The chief pressure groups might be listed as the following, cutting across both parties:

1. The railways, which are perforce involved in land and lumber interests, both as carriers and because of their original land grants.

2. The pensioners, who in Washington have an organization of their own, the Old Age Pension Union.

3. The Grange, which takes a fairly strong liberal line, and the other agricultural organizations.

4. The public power interests, of which more hereunder.

5. The Swedish population and the Lutheran church and other religious groups.

6. Above all, labor, and the powerful leftist coalition that labor controls.

These disparate groups function better together in Washington than in any other state. Consider for instance the Advisory Commission to the Department of Conservation and Development, which represents an attempt at democratic planning at its best. Wallgren set this up— the first organization of its kind in the United States—as a nonpartisan experts' group to deal with problems bound to afflict Washington after the war; the fifteen members could not possibly represent more divergent special interests, but all have worked together well and amicably. The chairman is Henry Cartensen, master of the Washington State Grange; the executive secretary is Howard G. Costigan, a pronounced left winger; others are Nicholas Bez, the chief representative of the Slovene community and a celebrated salmon-fishing magnate who has also lately acquired important king-crab interests in the Bering Sea; both Roy Atkinson, the regional director of the CIO, and Dave Beck of the AF of L; Claire Egtvedt, chairman of the board of the Boeing Aircraft Company; Colonel W. B. Greeley, representing the big lumber interests; and on the extreme left Karly Larsen, president of the International Woodworkers of America, who was once a member of the IWW.

Finally, a word on a remarkable organization known as the Washington Commonwealth Federation. This, dormant now, was a considerable force in the 1930's; it was, in essence, the first effective popular front in America. What broke it up, largely, was Communist infiltration and the bewildering twists and turns after 1939 in the Communist party line —though the Communists never numbered more than five thousand out of roughly two hundred thousand members—and then a fraying out and a frittering away as a result of the splintering that curses almost all leftist movements. Also much of its vitality arose out of hard times, and with the war boom everybody had jobs and the times turned soft.

The WCF—its story is worth a brief line—derived chiefly from an Unemployed Citizens League that sprang up in the Northwest in 1932-33; then too it was strongly influenced by the Commonwealth Federation in Canada.[7] During the depression, relief in Washington was largely a matter of self-help at first. People had the old western spirit; they banded together to cut wood and make shoes. Fifty per cent of Kings County was at one time on local relief; in some lumber areas, like Gray's Harbor, the figure rose to 80 per cent. Then came FDR and federal relief. The local organizations did not shrivel up, however; they turned their energy to politics. First came something called the "Commonwealth Builders," which launched a production-for-use program closely paralleling the EPIC movement in California; it elected no fewer than forty-one members out of a legislature of ninety-nine in 1934; it was the rock bottom basis of the careers of almost all Washington liberals, like Magnuson, former senator Homer T. Bone, Lewis Schwellenbach (now secretary of labor), and the remarkable congressman who died a suicide, Marion A. Zioncheck. Schwellenbach and Howard Costigan called a convention in Tacoma representing all leftist groups in 1936, and the WCF was born. But splinter feuds began almost at once; for instance an attempt was made to "recall" Schwellenbach because he wasn't radical enough. Nevertheless the state has an extremely effective leftist movement. AF of L, CIO, and the railway brotherhoods have combined to maintain a "joint labor lobby" at Olympia, the only one of its kind in America, with forty-nine representatives who meet every morning, plan concerted action, and see legislation through. They work in close harmony with the pension groups, Negro groups, and the Farmers Union. Operating in 1944, this coalition elected Wallgren, Magnuson, four out of six congressmen, and every state official.

Came a pungent episode in 1946. Costigan and thirty-six-year-old Representative Hugh DeLacy, an active left winger, ran against one another in the primary race for Congress. Both had been former presidents of the Commonwealth Federation. Costigan accused DeLacy of complete subservience to the Communists; DeLacy accused Costigan of various sins. The real issue was Communism. In the 1939-41 period DeLacy, taking the straight party line, had called the war an imperialist adventure; later of course he reneged. This fracas aroused more than local interest, because members of the Roosevelt family became involved. Colonel Jimmy Roosevelt warmly endorsed DeLacy, and Anna Roosevelt Boettiger (whose husband had been publisher of the Seattle *Post-Intelligencer* for some years) supported Costigan. DeLacy won the primary, but was badly beaten in the general election in November. Communism beat him.

Also in 1946 came a development highly embarrassing to another

[7] A similar federation also existed in Oregon for a time.

Washington congressman, and one with a strong liberal record, John M. Coffee, who also lost his seat in the November debacle. It was discovered as an offshoot of the Garsson investigation that Coffee had, in 1941, accepted a check for $2,500 from a Tacoma contractor, which he failed to list among his "campaign contributions." Coffee promised never again to accept any more such gifts, and after a minor furor the case was dropped.

What's happened to the IWW? No one can easily visit the Northwest without asking this question. The organization still exists—it publishes a paper in Chicago and maintains a hall in Seattle—but it has little but academic importance nowadays. Shades of Centralia and Big Bill Haywood! Some of the old wobblies are now Communists, like Elizabeth Gurley Flynn; some, like one Tacoma editor, are now fanatic Commy baiters; some, like Larsen, are in the CIO. The loggers are organized now into Larsen's union, conditions of work are much better (for which the IWW should get some credit). What killed the IWW was of course the growth of political training in the labor movement. Gradually its remnants were integrated into the CIO.

Back to Beck

Dave Beck, international vice president of the Teamsters Union, has a pink moon face and icy blue eyes that look like an albino's; he is the most powerful labor leader in the Northwest, and one of the most important in the country. Seattle is 90 per cent unionized, the AF of L overwhelmingly dominates the labor field, and Beck's Teamsters dominate the AF of L.

Beck was born in Stockton, California, in 1896 and moved to Seattle at the age of four. He left high school at sixteen to go to work driving a laundry wagon and he has been driving them, figuratively, ever since.

He went into Navy aviation in World War I and became what was then called a "flying engineer." He chased Zeppelins and took part in bombing raids on Helgoland. If the weather was bad, the planes had to go back for want of gas; he smiles now when he remembers this, thinking of the range of modern bombers.

In his first labor election in 1925, Beck became secretary of the Laundry Dye and Drivers Union in Seattle, one of the outstanding locals in the country. In the same year, at the national convention of the Teamsters in Seattle, he met his boss Dan Tobin for the first time. Tobin asked him to join the national pay roll, and presently he was in charge of the Teamsters in eleven western states, which he still is.

Beck has been called the businessman's business agent in the labor movement. He is probably the most ardent exponent of the capitalist system in the Northwest, and his speeches are almost indistinguishable from what might come from the NAM. His basic belief is that private enterprise must be supported at all costs, since business cannot pay good wages unless it makes a profit.

He believes, however, that government regulation of business may be necessary. "But," he told me, "don't put the government in as a competitor!" He loathes anything that smacks of socialism.

On the federal level he was a Roosevelt New Dealer; on the state level he takes a much more conservative line; he is probably the only Washington laborite of consequence who believes in private as opposed to public power. One reason for this is his fear that public power may frighten capital away.

He thinks that the lumber industry is hopelessly reactionary, and that the lumber barons brought the old violence of the IWW on themselves, by a totally parochial labor policy.

He is enormously proud of the Teamsters' record during the war. There are 175,000 teamsters in the western states; as of the date we talked, late in 1945, there had not been a single strike since Pearl Harbor, without an iota of sacrifice in wages, hours, or conditions.

His relations with the CIO are peculiar. The CIO still has the waterfront, which Beck severely lets alone. He cordially hates Bridges in San Francisco, and Bridges hates him back.

His relations with his own AF of L are also in a way peculiar. The Teamsters withdrew from the State Federation of Labor some years ago following a complex three-way split.

Recently Governor Wallgren appointed Beck to the Board of Regents of the University of Washington. The Seattle press greeted this with sobriety, and pointed out that although Beck was not an alumnus (of the University of Washington or any other) he had once taken some extension courses.

Politically Beck has great power, through his Teamsters Promotion League which helps get out the vote, and by financial support of candidates he likes.

Beck is a competent and capable executive, and has had several offers to go into business, with companies like Boeing; he has always turned them down out of fidelity to the labor movement.

There are few fixed patterns in American life and Beck, to sum up, is a wonderful example of the chaotic individualism of much of the United States. He is a labor boss who devoutly believes in capitalism; a strict and firm conservative who strongly supported FDR; and an employer of brawn and muscle who is listened to with extreme respect by any chamber of commerce he chooses to address.

Chapter 7

Two Freshmen from the Mountain Slopes

vvvvvvvvvvvvvvvvvvvvvvvvvvvvvvvvvvvvvvvvvvvvvvvvvvvvvvvvvvvvvvvvvvvvvvvvvvvvvvvvvvvvvvvvvvvvvvvvv

> I will not wear another man's collar.
> —Wayne L. Morse

WAYNE LYMAN MORSE, Republican senator from Oregon, whom his opponents call a "secret New Dealer" and a "labor stooge," is a tall lean man with a sharp nose and sharp dark mustache, tough, talented and emphatic. When making his first campaign in 1944, he found that he was getting nowhere in the conservative ranch country in the eastern part of the state. Morse had an idea. His whole career has been that of an intellectual, but he decided to ride with the boys. He was a professor of law, but he knew quite a lot about good horse flesh. So he visited Pendleton during its famous roundup, and though this was the home town of his opponent, he made no speeches. He simply spent three days riding. His horse, which he raised himself, is a prize-winning stallion named Spice of Life. Then Morse—and horse—made a little tour of the ranch country. One of his hosts, a feudal baron to whom he had been anathema, finally burst out, "Any guy who can raise a horse like that and ride like that can't be the son of a ——— I always thought he was!"

This story went all over the state, and helped the young professor of law considerably in what turned out to be an easy victory. Morse carried every county in Oregon, something that had never happened in its history.

Spice of Life is still with Morse in Washington, D.C. So is another prize winner, Oreganna Bourbon. Morse came east by Ford and trailer, taking with him both horses, his wife, and three baby girls. Spice of Life is an impressive animal, and has won all sorts of prizes in the East, including the grand championship at Green Meadows, Maryland.

The senator comes by his horsiness honestly. He was born on a three hundred acre homestead farm near Madison, Wisconsin, forty-six years ago, in 1900. The family is of old Yankee stock, and one forebear was Samuel F. B. Morse; several of his ancestors fought in 1776, and he carefully keeps up his membership in the Sons of the American Revolution. Both his grandfather and father were practical farmers, specialists in livestock and horse and sheep breeders. From the earliest days, young Wayne was taught to get along with animals and especially to raise poultry; while still in high school, he exhibited prize birds at county fairs. Above all, his father kept him interested in horses. Wayne never forgot, and still likes to quote to this day, something his father told him when he was only knee high, "The outside of a horse is good for the inside of a boy."

But it is more than merely horses that brought Wayne Morse to Washington, and made him one of the most outspoken and conscientious legislators in the country.

. . . .

Morse's dominant characteristic, outside his obvious brain power and wire-taut nervous energy, is courage. He told me once, "You know, people like a scrapper. I always try to be good natured, but I certainly punch hell out of a lot of people."

Morse practically never equivocates or straddles. He speaks out for what he thinks is right, and lets the chips fall where they may. For instance he fought Harry Bridges to a standstill in an arbitration case, and then appeared as a character witness *for* him in one of the Bridges trials. He tries to decide every issue on its merit, without regard to party label. He never takes the "blanket view" of a man like Bushfield. For instance he once told the Senate that the OPA "needed a house-cleaning from top to bottom and I would start with Chester Bowles and send him back to the advertising business." But at about the same time he voted *for* the confirmation of Henry Wallace as secretary of commerce and Aubrey Williams as REA administrator. Only two other Republican senators voted for Williams: Aiken (Vermont) and Langer (North Dakota).

In January, 1946, Morse vigorously attacked Senator Taft of Ohio as a survivor of the old Ohio gang that had destroyed the traditional liberalism of the Republican party, and then in April he let loose a blast heard around the country, following the choice of Taft's candidate, B. Carroll Reece, as new chairman of the Republican National Committee:

> The meeting of the Republican National Committee at the Statler Hotel last night was a grand flop. If [this] program is to constitute Republican policy during the next two years, the Republican National Committee will re-elect Harry Truman in spite of everything he is doing to defeat himself.
> We listened to the same old clichés and reactionary nostrums *ad nauseam* which have produced Republican defeats since 1932.

A little later he snapped hard and briskly at Mr. Truman, saying that the president's speech to Congress on May 25 about the railway strike was "one of the cheapest exhibitions of ham acting" ever known. Morse's allegation was that Truman knew that the railroad workers had already promised to go back to work when he spoke. Later—when Wallace resigned in September, 1946—Morse again attacked Truman with tart sarcasm: "If the president, too, will only remain silent . . . then I'm sure the country will be able to struggle through."

Morse voted for Bretton Woods and the United Nations charter and, like Stassen whom he closely resembles in some respects,[1] he thinks that the United States, as well as other nations, must be prepared to yield some measure of sovereignty if the UN is going to work. He was a prime mover in trying to keep the Kilgore subcommittee (investigating interrelations between American and German industry) alive and—like Henry Luce and many other good Republicans—he conspicuously joined the committee for aid to the families of General Motors strikers, early in 1946. He voted for the Full Employment bill, and refused to support a compromise that weakened FEPC; in fact, a Peck's bad boy of the Senate as Marquis W. Childs once called him, he caused angry consternation on the right in July, 1946, when he forced a vote on FEPC by getting it attached as a rider to the tidelands bill.

On the other hand—progressives say—Morse voted to take controls off dairy and meat products; his attitude in the fight on public vs. private power is uncertain and he has never taken a strong line on lumber conservation; he is the only Northwest senator not committed to the idea of a Columbia Valley Authority, and in 1946 he disconcerted his liberal friends by campaigning for a lot of Republican deadwood in the area.

· · · · · · ·

The outline of Morse's career is simple. He went to the Madison public schools and then the University of Wisconsin, which was at that time the most progressive university in the country. He got his bachelor of arts degree in 1923 and became a master of arts a year later. A good student, he worked hard on the debating team and also found time to get a commission in the Field Artillery Reserve, U.S. Army, after four years of military training. He decided to be a teacher, and went to the University of Minnesota where he was instructor in argumentation and coach to the debating team; here he received a law degree in 1928. He went on to Columbia with a $1,500 teaching scholarship, and his doctor's thesis at Columbia, on the American grand jury system, is still talked about as something of a classic.

Meantime, in 1924, he married Miss Mildred Downie who had been a classmate at Wisconsin. Mrs. Morse was a crack student in home economics; and while her husband was studying law, she taught home economics in a Minneapolis high school. This too is part of a familiar

[1] And who was once one of his students at the University of Minnesota.

American pattern, that of the brilliant-but-poor young student ably assisted by a young woman with her own job as well as the job of raising a family and washing dishes. Incidentally, when Morse became senator and although he needed the money badly, he refused to put her on his pay roll, though senators from Truman up and down have long sanctified this practice. Morse is a stickler on such financial matters.

The Morses went out to Oregon in 1929. He had never seen the state before, and his antagonists sometimes call him a carpetbagger, since he has only been an Oregon resident a mere seventeen years. First he was assistant professor of law at the University of Oregon in Eugene. Two years later, at the age of thirty-one, he became professor of law and dean of the law school, one of the youngest law deans in the country. He held this post until he resigned to run for the Senate—the first time he ever ran for anything—in 1944.

But Morse had steadily been weaving himself into the fabric of public affairs. He became a member of the Oregon Crime Commission and a consultant to the legislature. His specialty was criminal law, and he was for a time chairman of the American Bar Association's committee on prisons, probations, and paroles; he worked with the Department of Justice for years as director of a national research project on these topics. He helped write an Oregon crime survey in 1934 and was chiefly responsible for a five-volume study of national scope, *The Attorney General's Survey of Release Procedure*. As legislative consultant in Oregon, he helped draft bills in his field, and, in the words of a campaign biography, "many reforms relating to parole, probation, and prison administration, as well as labor law, were based on Wayne Morse's writings and decisions."

Then came something bigger. In 1935 he was invited to arbitrate in a dispute between a lumber operator in the Willamette Valley and labor. He did a neat job, and other jobs like it began falling his way. He was fair; he was impartial; and he never confused the principle of arbitration with mere compromise. What he sought was the essential right in any dispute. Then in 1938, Secretary of Labor Perkins appointed him Pacific Coast arbitrator for all maritime disputes between waterfront employers and longshore unions—although he was a stanch Republican. Both labor and management specifically asked Miss Perkins to appoint him. Between 1938 and 1942 he settled about a hundred cases, and saved industry in the Northwest millions upon millions of dollars and thousands of strike hours.

In January, 1942, Roosevelt made him a public member of the National War Labor Board, which post he held until February, 1944. During these twenty-five months he wrote more than half of all the opinions the board made. He quit in disgust because of a complex quarrel over coal involving Ickes, John L. Lewis, and the president.

He thought that the president should have been willing to meet Lewis head-on, instead of giving way to him. Before this he had had a vivid fight with Byrnes, who was then head of the Office of Emergency Management, when he charged that OEM was trying to tell the WLB what its decisions should be before it had completed its investigation. Cases that should have been decided on principle were, Morse felt, being prejudged. Roosevelt, as reward for his work on the WLB, had promised him a judgeship in the circuit court of appeals. Morse is a poor man, and this would have meant a good job for life. But when he refused to kowtow to Byrnes and Ickes, the president reneged on the appointment, and he never got the job.

.   .   .   .

Early in 1944, Morse met the able and persuasive E. Palmer ("Ep") Hoyt, who was then editor of the *Oregonian*.[2]

"You ought to run for senator," Hoyt said.

"Ridiculous," Morse replied. "I've never run for office in my life."

"We all think you ought to run," Hoyt said.

"Who's we?" Morse asked.

"We" meant the progressive Republicans of the community—especially those who loathed the incumbent senator, Rufus C. Holman. Holman was a pronounced isolationist who voted against practically every major national defense measure. So Morse had two fights on his hands—the Republican primaries against Holman, then the general election against a Democrat, Edgar Smith. He won both handily, this too although Roosevelt carried the state. The situation had elements of the picturesque. Morse, a former Roosevelt appointee, was fighting against FDR who however was being backed by almost all those backing Morse.

There was some very careful skating over thin ice to be done. The Republicans thought Morse a New Dealer, and the Democrats thought him a Republican, which he was. Everything seemed to be against him. He was a professor, and hence cursed; he had spent most of the war years in Washington and was unknown to the state at large; he might be either fish, fowl, or good pinko herring. Also, Holman had a certain popularity. Morse's technique was triple, and extremely clever. He (*a*) sought to satisfy the conservatives that he wasn't "dangerous"; (*b*) explained to the liberals *sotto voce* that he couldn't talk much, out loud, but that they could count on it that he would be sound on such issues as civil liberties and labor; (*c*) told labor that, after all, it should be glad to have a liberal Republican in office, especially if a Republican administration took over the country.

[2] Hoyt has now moved on to Denver where he has stirred up the entire population as publisher of the Denver *Post*.

Morse has never had any money but his modest salary. His campaign cost plenty, but he kept turning campaign contributions down. He refused to be beholden to anybody. He told all comers that, if elected, he would vote as he pleased, with no debts at all to any special interests. He rejected one offer of $3,500 from the liquor interests, and $4,100 from the CIO. In mid-1946 he introduced a Senate resolution which, if it passes, will bring a long-needed reform, to require senators publicly to report all their income every year, regardless of source.

He won because: (*a*) Oregon has been a basically Republican state for thirty years. It is the only western state that never once elected a Democrat to the Senate in all of Roosevelt's years in office. (*b*) Morse put on the best campaign in local history. He made 203 speeches in nine weeks, an all-time record, and after each one invited give-and-take questions from the floor. (*c*) In the primary, liberals could not possibly come out for Holman. (*d*) In the general election, many Democrats thought that Morse was better than their own man, who was anti-FDR; also the Democratic leadership was weak and vacillating.

The *New Yorker*, in the person of Howard Brubaker, ticked off Holman neatly after Morse beat him: "Senator Rufus Holman, of Oregon, accused of being an isolationist, was defeated. The homestate Republicans took the commendable position that any man who really wants isolation should have it."

So Wayne Morse got to Washington. Nobody has greater promise of being a first-rate public servant. Here is an honest man, with a good mind, good will, and guts.

Senator Glen H. Taylor

Wayne Morse came to the Senate on a horse; so did his freshman colleague from Idaho, Glen Taylor. But Taylor brought with him more than just a dapple gray—he brought show business and a banjo. Taylor is the first professional actor ever to sit in the halls of Congress.

When he arrived in Washington in January, 1945, he sat on the Capitol steps, and with the newsreel boys taking it all in, crooned a little song:

> Oh, give us a home
> Near the Capitol dome
> With a yard where the children can play—
> Just one room or two,
> Any old thing will do,
> We can't find a pla-a-ace to stay.

Later the veteran Senator Wagner of New York asked him about his qualifications for membership in the Banking and Currency Committee, for which he had applied. The Idaho freshman replied that he knew all about banking and its functions.

"What's your experience?" Wagner asked.

"I've had an important personal relationship with several banks," Taylor replied.

"Were you a vice president, perhaps?"

"No."

"A cashier?"

"No."

"A teller or a clerk?"

"No."

"What, then?" finally asked the puzzled Wagner.

"I was a depositor," Taylor replied.

He got the appointment.

Glen Taylor, no matter what people in Boise or Pocatello, Idaho, may tell you, is not a clown, not a hillbilly, not a buffoon. On the contrary he is an extremely serious man. He has a nice dry wit, abundant common sense, fertility of mind, and a modest enough sense of showmanship. Above all his character shows pertinacity of almost incredible dimensions. Bilbo sneered at him once that he might make a senator in "about five years," but he has already proved himself one of the most useful senators the country has.

Taylor's career is picaresque to say the least. He was born in Portland, Oregon, in 1904, and brought up in the hamlet of Kooksia, Idaho, one of the eight children of a retired Texas ranger who was also a minister. He quit school when he was twelve, and has never had any formal education since. The contrast to his friend Wayne Morse, an intellectual by profession, is immense. Taylor got into show business while still in his teens. The family was hard up and full of acting talent, and several of the brothers joined to make a troupe that went all over the West, playing repertory in a casual sort of way. Taylor met a young actress named Dora Pike while with a musical comedy company in Montana, and married her. They set up an organization known as the Glendora Players, and went right on barnstorming. Taylor played every kind of role, from romantic lead to comedian.

Then two things happened: the talkies and the depression. Between them they practically put Glendora out of business. The company shriveled from twenty to four and, in the end, to compete with the talkies, Taylor had to try to pack more and more thrills into an evening. One triumph imposed by bitter circumstance was a production of *Ten Nights in a Barroom*, rewritten for a cast of four.

"And during all this time I began to see all the misery," Taylor told me when I called on him in Washington. "It was in the early 30's. Kids didn't have proper clothes in winter. People came up to us, half starving and miserable, and offered us chickens in exchange for tickets. We still had a truck, and we kept moving from town to town every day, provided we took in enough at the box office to buy gas for each move. . . . Finally we went bust. And when folks were sick with hunger in the towns, we saw either fields still producing food or potatoes lying out to rot. I began to brood over how things could be so wrong. I found a book by Stuart Chase and it set me to thinking. I began to feel that all this misery was silly and unnecessary and that a man ought to do something to straighten out the confusion."

The Glendora troupe miraculously revived, and by the fall of 1937 Taylor had a truckload of scenery and spotlights and a company of seven, with Mrs. Taylor still the indispensable leading lady. Then another menace hit them—radio. A rival company in Great Falls was pushing them hard, because all its members could play some kind of musical instrument, and so could advertise their performances by musical spots on local radio programs. These rivals didn't even have scenery. Taylor, a real trouper, was outraged. Amateurs! But they did have music. Taylor says, "I was never one to see things go off and beat me." So he hired a band. It walked out. Glen and Dora put their heads together. This was a crisis indeed; this was make or break. So Taylor, who had been able to play the mouth organ and ukelele in an extremely primitive way, taught himself to handle a banjo and guitar, and Mrs. Taylor took piano lessons—by mail! Taylor bought one of his brothers, who was still a faithful member of the troupe, a trombone, which was also mastered by correspondence, and then Dora graduated to the saxophone. The Taylors were now their own band as well as theatrical company, and they set out once more on their route of ramshackle one-night stands in the Montana and Idaho hinterland.

In 1938, Taylor decided to run for Congress from the Pocatello district. It took four hard campaigns and six grinding years before he became senator, not congressman, and reached Washington. Until his election he had never in his life been east of Chicago.

The first campaign was a dashing and militant affair. The Taylor troupe, mounted on trucks, thundered into each community. A kind of stage was set up at any convenient spot, a loud speaker blared forth, and the entire company put on a show, playing and singing till the crowd was big and curious enough, whereupon Taylor emerged grim and taut to deliver a slashing political speech, assaulting all the politicians, pleading for the common man and flaying the plutocracy.

This was the Pappy O'Daniel technique, one might say. Not at all. First, Taylor was, and is, violently sincere. Second, he wasn't selling flour. He wasn't selling anything, in fact, except himself.

He was beaten of course. He ran fourth in a primary field of nine.

But he learned a lot, and people—even though they laughed at the "cowboy maestro"—liked him.

In 1940, Senator Borah, the ponderous and inexplicable negativist who for a generation had been synonymous with Idaho in the national mind, died. Taylor—it should be clear by this time that nothing whatever daunts him—decided to run for the succession. This was as if a water boy set out to succeed Jack Dempsey. The party wheel horses stormed and gaped. From Democrat headquarters Taylor, an obvious outlaw, got no support at all. He had practically no money. With what money he did have he did not buy radio time or advertising space in the newspapers—he bought a horse. And on this horse he campaigned for four hundred miles. He would go up to a lonely farmhouse, dismount, introduce himself, ask for a vote, and ride off again. The horse was named Ranger—of all names. The miraculous thing is that though Taylor was beaten in the general election (but by a fairly close margin) he won the primary. In other words he beat the Democratic machine, and the party, whether it liked it or not, had to take note of him.

Came the war, and Taylor was flat broke. He went to an Idaho defense plant and asked for a job as a truck driver. "Why, you're the guy who ran for senator!" he was told. "We ain't got no jobs for any guy like you!" So he had to flee the state and look for work where the lethal secret of his political past was unknown. He did get a job in San Francisco, earned good money as a painter's assistant, and didn't save a nickel. Why not? "You can't buy publicity without money," he told me sagely, "but politics is like show business and publicity is the one thing you ought to have, if it's the right kind." So he spent his earnings on maintaining contacts in Idaho. He wrote three thousand letters—longhand!—to people in his district.

Came the 1942 elections. He returned to Pocatello, filed again, ran again, and was licked again. He went back to California, got a job as a sheet metal worker, stayed with it for sixteen months, watched affairs in Idaho with the eye of a hungrily expectant falcon, and returned to run once more in 1944. This time he had sixty dollars saved. He spent it on buying a business suit—he had decided to give up both trouping and the horse—and a few pamphlets. Nothing could keep him down. The Democratic machine even tried to split the ticket in order to sabotage Taylor's vote. But by this time the people—or just enough people, to be precise—were behind him. He won the primary by exactly 216 votes, against the incumbent senator, D. Worth Clark (who is now a partner of Tommy Corcoran in Washington, D.C.), and romped home in the runoff against the governor, Clarence A. Bottolfsen, by 105,000 votes to 98,918.

Taylor looks back to all this now as a kind of crazy six-year dream. Sometimes he misses Idaho, its friendliness, its high and open skies.

"It's a free man's country," he told me. "A guy who has something, he'll get somewhere." But he's having a wonderful time in Washington, and not until 1949 does he have to face a new campaign.

His maiden speech was in support of Henry Wallace. He voted for the Reciprocal Trade Agreements, for Bretton Woods, and for the United Nations charter. He voted for the British loan, then turned against it, because he thought that British policy might involve us in war with Russia. He is a firm believer in international good will and amity, and on October 24, 1945, he rose and addressed the Senate with the following unexpected words:

> *Mr. Taylor.* Mr. President, I ask unanimous consent, out of order, to submit a resolution at this time.
> *The President pro tempore.* Without objection, the resolution may be submitted.
> *Mr. Taylor.* Mr. President, I should like to make a brief statement in connection with the resolution. I dislike very much to interrupt consideration of the tax bill. On the other hand, it may be a welcome respite for Senators to hear of something besides taxes for a few moments.
> Mr. President, this is a rather momentous occasion in my experience in the Senate. This is the first resolution I have ever introduced. Furthermore, it is a resolution which may be rather startling to some, and, to say the least, controversial.
> My proposal in the resolution is that the Senate go on record as favoring the creation of a world republic.

A few days later Taylor told a newspaper columnist that the American press truly perplexed him. When he sang a ditty on the Capitol steps, he pointed out, it made the front pages all over the country. When he delivered a long, cogent, and perfectly serious argument for the formation of a world republic, it made page 16 in exactly one newspaper.[3]

Taylor's style in the Senate is exactly what one would not expect. The man is undoubtedly an actor, but he doesn't talk like one. His manner is quiet, his language excellent, his approach candid, his mood beguiling. There can be few men who speak with a more subtle combination of formality and charm. Listen again to the *Congressional Record*:

> *Mr. Taylor.* I should like to make my position clear to the Senator from Colorado and to other Members of the Senate. I hold no brief for Mr. Petrillo. . . . This bill would, I believe, work great hardship on the whole theatrical profession, that is, insofar as it is connected with radio. I have great numbers of telegrams from members of the radio profession, singers, actors, writers, directors, and I am put in a rather unusual position. If there were only one lawyer in the United States Senate and a bill came up in the Senate which

[3] Leonard Lyons, New York *Post*, December 13, 1945.

all the lawyers of the country thought was going to be very detri-
mental to their best interest, they would probably get in touch with
the one lawyer in the United States Senate to present their case
for them. That is what has happened to me. It happens, I believe,
that I am the only man with a theatrical background here, so people
in the entertainment field have picked on me to try and help them
in their extremity.

Taylor is always modest and homely, seldom brilliant, absolutely
honest, and colloquial when the occasion fits. As witness:

> I've never been rich. But the most debt I ever incurred at one time
> was $2,500 before I came to the Senate. I'm in debt $14,000 now.
> So help me, I ran for the Senate three times before I made the grade,
> and two of those times I didn't know what the salary was.
> When I came here I wanted a two-bedroom apartment. I could
> have got that kind for $250 a month, only I had children. So I
> decided to buy. . . . I found a row house in a dark neighborhood
> for $10,000. When I offered to buy it, they raised it to $12,000.
> . . . So I put my wife on my office payroll. Whether on the payroll
> or not, she would have spent a lot of time in the office, because we
> enjoy each other's company.

It was in this connection that he mentioned that Louis B. Mayer of
Metro-Goldwyn had earned nine hundred thousand dollars the year
before; he added mildly, "Maybe he's worth more than we are." Once
he had a nice brush with Pappy O'Daniel of Texas, denying a statement
by O'Daniel to the effect that all that senators cared about was votes;
he said, "I will not compromise with the things I believe in, for the sake
of votes." On another occasion, after talking about how he loved his
job, he concluded, "But I'm going to vote in the Senate as if I never
expected to come back." This statement is worth pointing an emphatic
finger at; not many senators—or any other officeholders in America—
would care or dare to say the same.

In 1946, Taylor made a fine little commotion by saying that he did
not know whether he could go on accepting his salary because, like all his
colleagues he had just been circularized by the financial clerk of the
Senate asking him to swear that he was not a member of any organization asserting the right to strike against the government. Taylor put
in a couple of days of research, and found that he could not absolutely
affirm that this right was not upheld by rules of the Sheet Metal
Workers International Association (AF of L) in which he retains
proud but inactive membership. He concluded by refusing to sign the
circular. "There," he said, "the matter rests. It is up to the financial
clerk to make the next move, and we will see whether or not I am
eligible to be paid." (*Congressional Record*, July 11, 1946.) A few
weeks later Taylor came out with another bombshell, suggesting—"in

his verdant ignorance" as he put it—that Congress, at the end of each session, "should publish the voting records of its members."[4] Incredibly enough—for a country supposed to be rational minded—this has never been done.

For a man who had to leave school at eighth grade Taylor has a considerably developed dialectical skill. A Washington reporter recently quoted him explaining how he could often vote against the administration, yet be for it:

> I do not feel that I am against the Administration. If my brother were doing something which I felt in my heart was wrong and I tried to dissuade him, I do not believe it could honestly be said that I was against him. I would be for him. I am for the Administration. I want to keep the record clear.

Taylor is a tall man, good looking, spare, with the mobile mouth of an actor and a craggy nose. The Taylors have two sons. One, aged nine, is named Arod (his mother's name spelled backward); the other, three, is P. J. He was named for Taylor's father, whose name was Pleasant John.

Footnote on Idaho

Like all pioneers, Idahoans are materialists.
—M. R. Stone

Idaho is split across the middle by the mountains, and the northern panhandle differs so drastically from the south that it is virtually two states. It measures almost seven hundred miles from top to toe. There is no direct north-south railway, and to get from Moscow, the university town in the north, to Boise, the capital, by rail is quite a job; the journey takes twenty-three hours, and you have to go by way of both Washington and Oregon. Idaho is not a widely known state, and it has never exploited its own past, which in truth is romantic enough, as has California, say, or New Mexico. Idaho is torn, above all, between two other states; between the pull of Washington in the north, that of Utah in the south. Half of Idaho belongs to Spokane, I heard it said, and the other half to the Mormon church.

North Idaho is indeed part of the "inland empire," with Spokane its natural citadel and market. It is largely wheat, timber, and mining country, and the leading newspaper is not the Boise *Statesman*, which is read by few northerners, but the Spokane *Spokesman Review*. Its great stand of virgin white pine is the last of such size left in the world, and it mines enough silver to make it the biggest silver-producing state. South (not "southern") Idaho, with some of the wildest and least known

---

[4] New York *Post*, August 16, 1946.

territory on the continent outside Alaska, is irrigated in part by the Snake River with its "thousand miles of rainfall"; this is also a region dominated by agriculture—including the celebrated potato crop—and such examples of leftover war industry as the gun relining plant at Pocatello. Incidentally it is curious that Idaho, such a landlocked state, should possess the second largest Naval training station in the country, on Lake Pend Oreille.

I asked an Idaho patriot why the potatoes were so big. Answer: "We fertilize 'em with cornmeal, and irrigate with milk."

Practically all local issues are focussed on the north-south split. The north is outnumbered by the south two to one, and hence is at a grave political disadvantage, which it tries to surmount by bargaining in the legislature; it fears being run by the richer south, and wants to be let alone. It cares very little for the politicians in Boise; it wants the same kind of development—particularly in things like public power—that Washington has. One standing quarrel has to do with the university.[5] The old joke is that Moscow, in the north, got this institution as part of a deal in which the state penitentiary went to the south. Pocatello has a junior college called the Southern Branch of the University of Idaho and the south wants to expand this into a full-fledged four-year school. The north resists, saying that Idaho can't afford two state universities, and that it's better to have one strong school—no matter how inconveniently placed—than two weak ones. But as a result, most students in the south drain off to Utah.

Moscow, a charming town, gets its curious name not from anything Russian, but from an Indian tribe called originally "Masco." The state has some picturesque place names. Two towns closely adjacent are named Desnet and Tensed. Desnet was named for a missionary, and the next community, unable to think of another name, simply inverted it.

Also Moscow (population 6,014) contains, in addition to the university, one of the most astonishing evangelists in the United States, a worthy named Frank B. ("Doc") Robinson who preaches by mail. He gives correspondence courses in something called "Psychiana, the world's fastest-growing religion," and his mail is so big that the local post office bulges at the beams. Robinson is a wealthy man, a prominent civic leader, and the publisher of the town's secular newspaper, the daily *Idahoan*. Sample of his ecclesiastical style:

> I TALKED WITH GOD (Yes I did—Actually and Literally) and as a result of that little talk with God, a strange Power came into my life. . . . It's fascinating to talk with God, and it can be done very easily, once you learn the secret. And when you do—well—there will come into your life the same dynamic Power that came into mine. The shackles of defeat which bound me for years went

[5] Of the three regents of this school one is a housewife, the other two are farmers.

a-shimmering—and now?—well, I am President of the News Review Publishing Company, which corporation publishes the largest circulating afternoon daily in North Idaho. I own the largest office building in our City, I drive a beautiful Cadillac limousine. I own my own home, which has a lovely pipe organ in it [*sic!*] . . . And all this has been made possible because one day, ten years ago, I actually and literally talked with God.

You, too, may experience that strange mystical Power . . . and when you do, if there is poverty, unrest, unhappiness, or ill-health in your life—well, this same God-Power is able to do for you what it did for me! . . . For this is not a human Power. It's a God-Power. . . . Well, just write a letter or postcard to Dr. Frank B. Robinson, Dept. 97, Moscow Idaho, and full particulars of this strange Teaching will be sent to you free of charge. But write now—while you are in the mood. It only costs one cent!

Idaho is a borderline state politically, and as Taylor's campaigns show, most contests are very close. Bottolfsen and another governor, Clark, once alternated in the governorship by winning successive races by only a few hundred votes, and a recent governor and senator, Charles C. Gossett, once carried an important county by a majority of one. Taylor, by the way, invaded the state lustily in the summer of 1946 to attack and beat Gossett, who represents the conservative Democrats and who had once beaten him. The best organized political machine, until Taylor came along, was that of the Clark family. Idaho had a "Clark party"; people talked of the "Clark forces." One Clark was a senator, and another was governor and is still a federal judge.

Without mention of the factors that, *mutatis mutandis*, are present in almost all American states—the party organizations, the women's vote, the farmers, the liquor interests—one might summarize political forces in Idaho as follows. First, the great mining companies, like Bunker Hill & Sullivan (at Kellogg—zinc and lead) and the Sunshine Mining Company near Coeur d'Alene, which has the world's biggest silver mine. Working closely with the mining interests are the big lumber companies, like the Clearwater Timber Company and the local Weyerhaeuser interests, and the Idaho Power Company which is active all over the state. This was once part of Electric Bond and Share. The biggest lobby in the legislature is a combination of mines, lumber, and utilities. Yet Idaho is not nearly so business dominated and exploited as, say, Montana or Colorado. There is no single corporation that has anything like the power of Anaconda in Montana. Idaho is not a colony.

Second, the Mormon church, which is the biggest religious denomination in the state. "Eighty per cent of the Idaho vote," runs a local truism, "is agricultural, and 40 per cent is Mormon." There are some communities in the irrigated southeastern areas that are 70 per cent Mormon or more, and the putative influence of the church was considered so strong that, when Idaho became a state back in 1890, the constitution went out of its way specifically to outlaw polygamy. The Mormons "take their orders from Utah"—so Idahoans are apt to say. As we shall discover when we come to Utah, the Mormon community is a very conservative force politically, and also a powerful influence for sobriety, good citizenship, and admirable social values. As part of the complex north-south balance of power in Idaho, it is a tradition that no Mormon may be governor of the state.

Third—and uniquely in the nation—the Basques.[6] These are mostly shepherds. They form the largest Basque colony this side of the Pyrenees. They are almost as radical as the Mormons are conservative, and they played a considerable role in the 1944 elections; in fact, they swung the balance. This was partly the result of an invasion of the state by the CIO. Labor is extremely weak in Idaho, and until recently had no political voice at all. Then Roy Atkinson, the regional director of the PAC in Seattle, got busy. He won the support of a Basque leader named Pete Leguenecahe, organized the Basque vote, and put it behind the Democrats, like Taylor, who were fighting the conservative machine.

Fourth, a minor point but worth mention, Idaho has received in recent years a fair quota of dust-bowl immigrants and migrants from the Dakotas. These—perhaps only temporarily—have added to the dissident vote in the state.

Fifth—and this is true in all western states—the education lobby. Idaho has very little to spend on social services, say $2,250,000 per year, but it does its best to keep up the schools. Uniquely in the country, the Board of Education is considered to be a fourth equal partner in the state government along with the executive, legislature, and judiciary.

Finally, the Idaho *Statesman*, which has a prestige and position all its own despite journalistic depredations from outside. The *Statesman* consists, in a word, of a remarkable blue-blooded lady named Margaret Cobb Ailshie, who is editor, owner, publisher, and dominator. She owns the other Boise paper too, and the town is thus one of the very many in America in which a single person or family has a complete monopoly in journalism. Mrs. Ailshie, who inherited the *Statesman* from her equally remarkable father, is an extreme reactionary—something to the right of Louis XIV or Boies Penrose say—and a genuine patrician.

It is an interesting commentary on the slipperiness of the American attitude to institutions and a kind of national short-mindedness that Borah, incontestably the best-known citizen that Idaho ever produced, left no political family of any kind, no tradition or inheritance, no machine. His following was, of course, supraparty. But one can travel the length and breadth of the state nowadays and scarcely hear his name. Of course Borah never paid much attention to Idaho per se. For in-

[6] But Oregon also has a Basque community.

stance he never owned a house in Boise, but simply kept a few rooms in the Hotel Owyhee. His widow—though her father was a former governor—has never come back to the state.

Idaho has much else that might be mentioned—the last "white" (=fast) water of the great log drives, a colorful congressman in the person of Compton White, the attractive railway-tourist development known as Sun Valley, and a remarkable novelist in the person of Vardis Fisher. To conclude, it is fond of a little joke—that it would be the biggest state in the union if ironed out flat.

Chapter 8

Highways in the Sky

〰〰〰

> Indebtedness to oxygen
> The chemist may repay,
> But not the obligation
> To electricity.
>
> —Emily Dickinson

A DOMINANT issue all over the Northwest is power—its production, control, and use. First I went to Bonneville, to get some glimpse of what public power means, and then to Grand Coulee, the biggest structure ever built by man.

The Columbia River drops 1,290 feet in its swift, heavy, six hundred mile flow through the state of Washington. Its stupendous weight of water, controlled by dams, is the greatest single source of power in the United States and probably the world. Not less than 42 per cent of the total potential hydroelectric energy of the entire country is contained in the Pacific Northwest, and its potential annual output is not less than 120 billion kilowatt hours. This means that it can produce considerably more electricity than the whole United States consumed in the year 1929.

The Columbia rises in the Canadian Rockies, and flows 1,214 miles; at the point known as the Dalles its mean flow is 195,000 second-feet, which is double that of the Nile at Assuan. It is full of anarchical bends, twists, troughs, and gorges, and it is fed by astonishing tributaries like the Snake. One canyon bitten out by the Snake, which is itself 1,038 miles long, is deeper than the Grand Canyon of the Colorado by a thousand feet.

Two great federal dams, built like beautifully articulated plugs, block the fruitful torrent of the Columbia. The first of these, Bonneville, named for an early explorer, lies forty miles east of Portland, on the Oregon-Washington frontier; the second, Grand Coulee, is 380 miles further up, near Spokane in the heart of northeast Washington.

These dams are what make the power; they make much else, too, including some fancy politics. Power—electricity—flows out from Bonneville and Grand Coulee in a ductile stream almost as tremendous as the river itself. It loops complexly into a power transmission grid system of more than 2,800 circuit miles of line, most of which operates at a rated capacity of 230,000 volts; it lights cities in four great states, manufactures metals, irrigates farms, and keeps your toaster going. Across the gray-blond mountains and the copper-colored wheat fields, the steel towers carrying this power look like huge Meccano toys, or the dancing men of Sherlock Holmes. The transmission lines are a kind of sky highway—a taut and almost invisible network of highways giving life to industry, water to dry fields, health to man.

The present installed capacity of Columbia River power is about 1,226,400 kilowatts, and it will eventually reach 20,000,000 kilowatts, the experts say. Where does all this come from? The answer is both simple and, when you come to think about it, astonishing. It comes from ice, rain, and melting snow in the Rockies. Another point is that Columbia power is not only abundant; it is cheap, and Bonneville's rate for electricity—$17.50 per kilowatt year—is the lowest in the country. Still another is the newness of the whole development; both Bonneville and Coulee date from the middle 30's. New? A booster pamphlet on the region bids us remember that "Electricity itself is only 62 years old in the Pacific Northwest—less than one man's lifetime."

Columbia power not only made possible the production of the Kaiser shipyards at Vancouver and the Boeing plants at Renton and Seattle; it helped create overnight a new light metals industry in the West which in turn produced some thirty thousand combat planes, one-third of total United States production during the war; above all, it played an indispensable role in making the atomic bomb. The bomb is, in truth, a kind of apocalyptic, demonic child of the Columbia. The army selected Hanford, Washington, near Pasco, as the site for its great plutonium plant because of the availability of Columbia power in illimitable quantities. Here the stuff that went into the bomb was actually made, in a witch's pot that cost 350 million dollars.

The activities of this Hanford plant were secret in the extreme— naturally. The most extraordinary and sensitive precautions were taken, but nobody could altogether hide an operation of such size. Plenty of people knew that unprecedented amounts of energy were being used; few could have realized that the temperature of the entire river rose, so enormous was this amount. I began to hear tidbits of gossip from the time I reached Seattle, just as in New Mexico I had heard bizarre rumors about Los Alamos. One of the most prescient men I ever met—who had absolutely no connection with the project and who had no secret information of any kind—suggested at lunch in Seattle three weeks before the first bomb was detonated, that one part of the "thing" (whatever it was) was being made in New Mexico, another in Washington, and that it would be assembled somewhere else. This was pretty good guessing, though wrong in one particular. Most people in the area thought that the Hanford project had to do with a kind of poison gas—which indeed the atom bomb does produce in effect—inasmuch as du Pont people ran the plant.

But today the Northwest prefers to think of the Columbia area in terms of peace, not war. The region has an industrial and social future without parallel in the nation. Reason: public power from the Columbia.

Trip to Bonneville

Energy is eternal delight.
—William Blake

We drove out to Bonneville from Portland on a hot, cloud-heavy summer day, along a crest of road—the route of the old Oregon Trail—winding parallel with the Columbia. Waterfalls are set back in piney clefts, and fling their silver out like jabots. We crossed the Sandy River, where the smelt run comes once a year. The little fish, sucked in from the Pacific, are thick enough to walk on; people come from miles around and scoop them out in everything from bird cages to butterfly nets to their bare hands; anybody is allowed fifty pounds per day. We paused a moment at Crown Point, where the river bends like a broad curved sword, and passed Multnomah Falls, a lovely sight. And we were careful not to smoke. Summer is a time of year famous for big "burns"—forest fires.

The Bonneville power house, with its ten forty-eight foot generators, is a high narrow hall a thousand feet long that reminded me of a cathedral; there is no noise but the slightest hum. What this is is an electricity factory. Generators Nos. 1 and 2 have a name-plate capacity of 43,200 kilowatts; Nos. 3 to 10 have 54,000 each; during the war they were pressed to produce much more. The juice—electricity—flows out as smooth as milk; and it has power enough to tear Mars apart. Deep below are the turbines, which eat up 14,000 cubic feet of water per second. The fall of water on the blades does all the work; no fuel of any kind is necessary. Even a log, sucked into these giant turbines, wouldn't make a dent. The whole establishment is run by exactly eleven quiet engineers. I was amused by the small printed sign under Alternating Current Generator No. 1, a machine as big as a house: "13,800 volts. 48,000 KW. Caution: Before Operating Read Instructions."

Bonneville and Coulee are part of the same system, and both are operated by the federal government, but there are important differences between them. Bonneville is a project not only designed for power but for navigation—hence the locks; Coulee is made for irrigation and reclamation as well as power. Bonneville was built by the Engineers Corps, U.S. Army, and is operated by the Army; Coulee was built and is operated by the Bureau of Reclamation of the Department of the Interior. A third entity known as the Bonneville Power Administration, also an agency of the federal government under the Department of the Interior, markets power from *both* Bonneville and Coulee; it is the jobber, so to speak. Both the great dams produce power; the BPA alone transmits it. It "transmits" power—yes—but it does not "distribute" power. The BPA is not in the retail power business. It takes the electricity over at the bus bar atop the Bonneville power house and from the switching station on the bluff above Coulee and then sells to both private companies and public agencies, also of course to industry. It supplied roughly 50 per cent of the entire power load of both Oregon and Washington in 1944.

The Bonneville project has a mixed parentage—Army engineers, Senator McNary, the ghost of George Norris, the early New Deal, Roosevelt's deep personal interest; it was authorized in 1935, and to date has cost about $80,000,000. The act creating the Power Administration was passed by Congress two years later and is one of the most striking pieces of social legislation in the history of the United States, in that it specifically requires the administrator "to encourage the widest possible use of all electric energy that can be generated," and, on selling it, at all times to "give preference and priority to public bodies and cooperatives." The private utility companies come second.

The Bonneville administrator is Paul J. Raver, an engineer by profession. For a time he was professor of public utilities at Northwestern University, then a member of the Illinois State Rural Electrification Committee, and finally chairman of the Illinois Commerce Commission. Ickes gave him the Bonneville job in 1939. They had never met, and Ickes asked him just one question, "Do you believe in public power?" Raver did—and has been working on BPA ever since.

The great power house at Bonneville is well worth visiting, and electricity is not the only thing to look at. In fact, the really star attraction is the fish.

Fish Story

Let us explore. The Pacific coast Chinook salmon is a very remarkable fish indeed. It will perpetuate itself only at the place where it was born —something unique in nature—and it dies immediately after the act of procreation.

The cycle goes like this. The mature fish, about four years old, swims in from the Pacific; this is when he is best to eat, and twice a year millions of pounds of fish are caught in the great salmon runs and are processed and canned and sold as food all over the earth. The Northwest's fishing industry is worth 100 million dollars per year. But for this to be maintained, fish must also be maintained; they must be given opportunity to reproduce themselves. The Chinook goes about this in a very peculiar way. He cannot or will not spawn in the sea. So with his female counterpart he swims up the Columbia toward fresh water. Then, by a marvelously developed instinct, he looks for the exact fresh water stream where he himself was spawned four years before. During the tremendously fatiguing swim upstream—against a heavy current for hundreds of miles—the salmon eats little, because the stomach starts to atrophy when he hits fresh water; he lives off his fat, and saves every bit of surplus energy for spawning.

The fish pair off in the correct fresh water stream when they find it, and the female, making a nest with her tail, lays her eggs on a bank below the surface; this nest may be as big as three feet across and several feet deep, and the female can lay as many as five thousand eggs in a day or so. The male then swims alongside and, floating closely over the female, deposits his milt; the water will kill the live milt in less than a minute, and the operation is carried on with extreme efficiency and dispatch. Their job done, both male and female die. This is the first and only time they have conjunction, and the act kills them. They themselves do not survive the giving of new life; the flesh sloughs off afterward, and the corpses rot and disappear. Meantime the new life cycle has begun. The baby salmon, called fingerlings, are big enough to start the long voyage downstream after five to eight months. They reach the ocean, grow to maturity and, then, duplicating the pattern of their parents, fight their way up the river, seek their birthplace, pair off, spawn, and die in turn.

Bonneville enters this story because—so a lot of people feared—the salmon obviously would not be able to get over the dam, hence they could not spawn, and hence the Columbia fishing industry was doomed. In particular the private power interests, who at the beginning fought Bonneville with vehement intensity, predicted this disaster. But nowadays a dam is much more than merely a dam, more than just a beam of concrete across a river. Bonneville learned well from the example of TVA. The engineers looked at their job in the widest possible perspective, knowing, in the words of a Department of Interior booklet, that "what happens to a river, what happens to the land—forests, minerals, farms—is all part of one indivisible process," that river development means not only electricity and navigation and flood control, but saving the topsoil on hillsides, reforestation, techniques in restoring fertility to barren or exhausted land, and industrial development. So it is not surprising that the Bonneville builders kept the fish in mind. What they did was to build ladders for the fish to climb, around the edges of the dam.

These ladders are among the most ingenious things I have ever seen, and to watch the salmon climb them is a unique experience. "All we have to do," smiled my guide, "is lure 'em upstairs. The dam blocks 'em off, so the job is to try and sneak 'em over." The salmon is a smart fish. But a clever manipulation of currents sets him in a sidestream, where a series of shallow steps acts as a challenge to his gameness, his fighting blood. Yet, the current must not actually help him along, because then the salmon won't swim at all. The north fishway is about a mile long, with a series of crossbeams and steps in a twenty-foot canal, with traps where the fish are guided upstream by the force of the current. The water is eight feet deep, and there are submerged orifices on alternate sides, to make the flow eccentric and fool the fish into jumping farther. It takes a lively salmon about three hours to make the trip. The fence along the ladder is twelve feet high, to keep the big ones from jumping out.

These Bonneville fish ladders have for the first time produced an accurate census of the Columbia's river life. A white board is set under the first trap; here a girl sits with a counting device, checking off each fish. On the day I visited it, 471 Chinooks went over the dam, 38 "jacks" (immature salmon), 192 steelhead trout, 379 blueback salmon, 487 whitefish, 4,015 shad, 72 carp, and a great variety of others. Also there were lampreys, fascinating to watch; they slide themselves along by hanging to the concrete sides. This total of 471 Chinooks is as nothing. In the great "fall run," as many as 30,000 may climb the ladders in a day, and sometimes the traffic is so crowded that salmon sleep at the bottom all night, awaiting their turn to get through. The fingerlings, downstream travelers, are also helped along, in the opposite direction; 314 went down the day I was there.

A word finally on what Bonneville has done for navigation. The river was unnavigable beyond this point before, except for low-draft boats. When the dredging project is complete, deep draft ships will be able to pass through the locks and proceed upriver as far as the Dalles, 175 miles from the ocean, and barges will get through all the way to Pasco (300 miles) at the confluence of the Columbia and Snake. Lumber and wheat will go downstream, and petroleum will go up. The "inland empire," much of it inaccessible to railroads, is being tapped at last.

Largest Single Structure Built by Man

The water breaks over in a smooth green moving wall, and then bursts into a churning foam of white. The green water sliding down is solid and smooth like a broad conveyor belt. Eleven blindingly white waterfalls intersect the swelling bulge and, propelled forward as if by giant hoses, spill out and down. The white curtain of spray is 30 feet thick, and the roar of the mixing waters can be heard for miles.

Frank E. Banks, the supervising engineer, Grand Coulee Dam, who saw the project through its construction stages, told us about the mammoth job, and Major S. E. Hutton, his assistant, took us around. Major Hutton is a character, a small peppery man with a small peppery beard who is the kind of public servant America should be proud of. He is a builder, full of vision and ideals. And he loves the Brobdingnagian dam as a father loves a growing child.

Let us stagger through some superlatives first. Grand Coulee dam is 4,300 feet long at the crest, the height above bedrock is 550 feet, and the drop of water about 330, which is twice that of Niagara. It cost about 200 million dollars to build and required more than 10,000,000 cubic yards of concrete, 20,000,000 cubic yards of excavation. One can have fun with figures like these. A writer in *Fortune* has calculated that this amount of concrete would build a highway completely encircling the United States; Stuart Chase points out that the structure weighs 23,000,000 tons, three times as much as the Pyramid of Cheops; Bruce Bliven mentions in a recent *New Republic* that the whole population of the United States would fit into the space of the dam, that the irrigation pumps could suck up "the entire flow of any American river except the Mississippi," and that "the poured concrete would put a floor over three states as big as Pennsylvania."

Behind Coulee is the artificial lake it made, the storage reservoir known now as Roosevelt Lake. This is 151 miles long, and it holds 436,000,000,000 cubic feet of water. The drainage area is 74,000 square miles, which is almost as big as Nebraska and three times the size of Ireland. In prewar times the Dnieper installations in Russia were generally considered the most powerful of their kind on earth; Dnieperstroi generated about 500,000 kilowatts. Grand Coulee has a capacity of 648,000 kilowatts, which equals 868,600 horsepower. When all fifteen of its generating units are finally installed, this will give an ultimate name plate capacity of 1,620,000 kilowatts. This is more than that of Boulder Dam and almost as much as all of TVA.

The dam was completed on June 2, 1942, when the first spill of water came down like a strictly harnessed ocean; but concrete in its middle is still cooling, and won't be finally cold for seventy-five more years. Once during the construction the engineers had to "freeze" part of a mountain, in order to secure one end of the dam into soft rock. This was done by running actual refrigeration apparatus under the surface. The Grand Coulee approach was, as Major Hutton says, "If a hard mountain gets in your way, move it. If it's just a soft mountain, freeze the darned thing, forget it, and keep on going."

At the bottom of what seemed to be a kind of quarry, we saw work beginning on the future pumping station. Each pump will be big enough to provide the entire water needs of New York City. There will be ten such pumps at Grand Coulee. Crossing the dam top—where thousands of sheep may placidly walk—we encountered an eighty-foot crane, painted pale green, that weighs I don't know how many tons. It was used to hoist the 115-ton penstock gates. It started to move. It ap-

proached us slowly but with determination. It is the largest single thing
I ever saw move, except the *Queen Mary*.

Coulee is the creation of (*a*) three men, and (*b*) the idea of planned
economy. The three men were, and are, William Clapp, a lawyer in
Ephrata, Washington, James O'Sullivan, an engineer on the Columbia
Basin Commission, and Rufus Woods, the pertinacious publisher of the
Wenatchee *World*.[1] In about 1918, Clapp brought forward a new notion to Woods, that a dam at Grand Coulee would not only create power
but could irrigate thousands of near-by acres dying for lack of water.
Woods promptly wrote a story launching the idea. Everybody, or almost
everybody, laughed at him scornfully, but he became further stirred and
stimulated, and for fifteen years never let the project drop. Gradually
the idea took formal shape; there was great dispute, however, as to the
exact site. The Army engineers and the Bureau of Reclamation became
interested and, in 1920, O'Sullivan met Franklin Roosevelt in Spokane.
He told him about the idea, and FDR—who was then campaigning for
vice president—mentioned it in a speech at once and never forgot it.
Work finally began in the autumn of 1933.

"Our philosophy comes out of our experience," Major Hutton told
me. Anybody can dig for coal. But a river system is too big for private
exploitation. Only the government—working harmoniously with private
contractors and the like—can handle a project so enormous on so many
levels. Stuart Chase wrote in the *Atlantic Monthly* in 1938, "The big
dams . . . are not primarily power projects, but something more fundamental. In the last hundred years, man has all but wrecked the balance of
nature in the North American continent. Flood, drought, dust storms,
erosion, the destruction of forest and grass cover, are making hideous
inroads on the organic stability of the United States. Some 10,000,000
Americans have already lost their living from natural resources. The
chief purpose of the great dams is to restore the equilibrium."

Aside from generation of power the main purpose of Grand Coulee
is irrigation. The Columbia Basin Reclamation project will, it is hoped,
reclaim about 1,200,000 acres of land—most of it south and east of the
Big Bend—in the next twenty-five years, on which some forty thousand
families can be settled, at an estimated cost of $280,000,000. There will
be four thousand miles of canal, the pumping station, and enough water
to make this whole arid hinterland blossom. The land, which grows
very little now, is expected under irrigation to produce as much as forty-
five million dollars worth of crops per year, and each farmer will have
forty years to pay off his share of the construction costs (eighty-five

---

[1] The motto of this paper is "Published in the Apple Capital of the World and in
the Buckle of the Power Belt of the Great Northwest," and it calls itself the
"greatest daily in the world for cities under 15,000." In June of last year, it
temporarily ran out of paper. Mr. Woods rounded up members of his staff, went out
into the woods, and cut logs that made forty tons of newsprint.

dollars per acre) without interest, atop a maintenance fee which is estimated at only $2.60 per year for 160 acres. All the holdings will be small, to encourage newcomers. What a paradise this could be for returned veterans, say, caught in the merciless housing shortages of the towns! The first vote on putting the project into effect took place in August 1945, when landowners voted for irrigation according to the government's plan by 2,342 to 52.

One thing Coulee could not do. Nobody, no matter how ingenious, could devise a fish stairway that would let salmon climb 330 feet. Not even Chinooks can cross anything that high. So a remarkable experiment in artificial semination has begun under auspices of the Fish and Wildlife Service. The salmon that might spawn beyond Coulee are collected, kept alive with oxygen and dry ice, sent to a fertilization station, and there propagated artificially.[2] The fingerlings are then developed in a hatchery, and eventually discharged downstream. Moreover—believe it or not—these fingerlings are so conditioned that, when they grow up and return upriver to spawn, they are content to do this in the substitute hatcheries, and so do not attempt to cross the Coulee barrier.

Public versus Private Power

> Power, like a desolating pestilence,
> Pollutes whate'er it touches.
>
> —Shelley, *Queen Mab*

This chapter is hardly the place for any extended discussion of the question of public vs. private power on a national scale. Let us merely touch on a few details with particular reference to the Northwest.

Privately owned utilities are a thirteen billion dollar business in the U.S.A. The industry has taken a severe beating in the past twenty years, and in part this was its own fault; no one is likely to forget the depredations of Mr. Insull. In 1935 came the Public Utility Holding Company Act, and since that time the Securities and Exchange Commission has torn no fewer than 344 subsidiary companies (with assets of more than four billion dollars) away from their parent combines. Company after company was found grossly overcapitalized, with consequent inflated rates. Squeezing the water out of all these corporations was a long, thankless, and useful job.

In 1929 seventeen great holding companies controlled 85.76 per cent of the nation's power. Electric Bond & Share alone held 15.26 per cent, Insull 10.40 per cent. Since that time the winds have stringently changed. Over the country as a whole far more power is still generated and sold by private companies than by public agencies, but the gap is not so big.

[2] Cf. "The Great Salmon Experiment," by Richard L. Neuberger, *Harper's*, February, 1945.

Today, of the total central station capacity of the nation, about forty million kilowatts are private, about ten million public.

The growth of public power—both as a social concept and a business operation—has been more notable in the Pacific Northwest than anywhere in America except the valley of the Tennessee. Public power projects in Washington and Oregon increased their total kilowatt capacity from 313,813 to 1,715,000 between 1935 and 1943, an increase of more than 400 per cent. Private power meantime fell from 917,649 kilowatts to 881,553. Politically this became an extremely important issue. All four contenders in the Oregon senatorial race in 1944 were invited by the state Grange to answer the question: Should the government own and operate transmission lines to bring power from the point of origin to market? All four said yes. Why? They wanted votes. And the voter —the consumer—knew on which side his electricity was buttered. According to the Department of Public Services at Olympia, the average cost last year to the Washington consumer of private power was 1.1 cent per kilowatt hour, that of public power about half a cent. In other words the consumer could get twice as much public power as private for roughly the same cost. Of course the private power people will point out in justification of their price levels that they had to pay stiff taxes, whereas public power did not. Public power sold, in 1943, three billion more kilowatt hours than private, and charged six million dollars less. Think that over, ghost of Insull.

There are five large private utility companies at present operating in the Northwest. They are:

1. The Portland General Electric Co., an independent local concern.
2. Puget Sound Power and Light Co. Recently reorganized. It furnishes power to Seattle, Tacoma, and so on in competition with the municipal systems, as we shall see.
3. Washington Water Power Co., Spokane. Subsidiary of Electric Bond & Share.
4. Pacific Power and Light Co. Operates in Central Washington and Oregon. Subsidiary of Electric Bond & Share.
5. Northwestern Electric Co. Operates in Portland and southern Washington. Subsidiary of Electric Bond & Share.

Electric Bond & Share spreads over into several states, and each independent unit and subsidiary has its own marked-out domain; they own their own dams and hydroelectric plants or steam generators; they sell direct to the consumer, and the consumer—except in certain exceptional communities—has no choice but to buy at the rate set.

What Bonneville did when it entered the picture was of course to force rates down. The private utilities had to buy from BPA or do without, since the whole area—especially during the war—was power short and power hungry. And inasmuch as BPA rates were low, they had to keep theirs low too, even if this meant cutting profits, and in spite of taxes. The cumulative total of private utility rate reductions in Oregon and Washington was nearly $45,000,000 between 1938 and 1945. Consider however some other figures that apply to the rest of the country. Seattle and Portland both pay $5.70 for 500 kilowatt hours of electric service. Chicago pays $9.15, and New York $13.46.[3]

Also Bonneville served to increase consumption. The Alcoa plant at Vancouver, Washington, for instance, bought more power in 1944 than did the entire city of Portland (and incidentally produced more aluminum than the entire United States before the war), even though Portland's own consumption increased considerably.

Most of the private power executives I met, not only in the Northwest but elsewhere in the country, wore a somewhat apologetic mood, and were inclined to be on the defensive. When, however, they state their case, they invariably raise two main points. First, taxes. Their properties are, they point out, taxed, but a federal project like Bonneville is not. They are, therefore, at a serious disadvantage in financial competition. The tax issue is enormously complex; merely to lay out the main lines of dispute would take a page. Public power adherents answer the tax argument by making the point—among others—that Bonneville is, in effect, owned by the people and therefore should no more be taxed than the federal post office—or a road or river.[4] Second, advocates of private power say that the fact that their companies are "regulated" prevents abuses. Not only do all utility companies live under the coldly scrutinizing eye of the Federal Power Commission and the SEC, which carefully regulate their profits and behavior; almost every state has its own state power commission. Budgets of utility companies must as a rule be filed with the state authorities, and profits and dividends are generally limited to a fair return. On the other hand, in some states the power commissions are weak and venal, and under the control of the companies' own lobbyists. It is the life blood of a private utility to have a favorably inclined state power commission.

Private power hates public power for two overriding reasons. (1) Greed. Public power—or the possibility of public power—keeps profits down, by adducing the threat of cheaper rates. And if a private utility

---

[3] Some other cities rank as follows:

Los Angeles	$6.74	Detroit	$ 9.00
Memphis	7.90	Denver	9.30
San Francisco	7.92	St. Paul	9.63
Cincinnati	8.05	Dallas	9.95
Atlanta	8.62	Baltimore	10.68
Washington, D.C.	8.62	Boston	12.40

Figures from the Federal Power Commission, as printed in *PM*, June 5, 1946.

[4] Also Bonneville does make payments "in lieu of taxes." For a discussion of the same situation in regard to TVA, see Chapter 43 below.

cannot meet public rates, it is doomed. (2) Fear of government. Private power thinks it is being swallowed up by a federal bureaucracy.

The case for public power, on its side, has been amply and eloquently stated many times, and rests on three foundations.

(1) The tremendous hydroelectric potential in American river valleys, an essential national resource, belongs as of right to the people as a whole, not to any vested interest. A power line, like a highway, is a means of transporting a common necessity; nobody should have the right to monopolize a necessity so universal. Electricity is like water. It should be available to all for a modest service fee. Scarcely any municipality in the country has "private water" any longer,[5] and private power is almost as crying an anachronism.

(2) As noted above, no private company can possibly be big enough or inclusive enough to undertake the overall development of a whole river, involving huge multiple-purpose projects and crossing state lines and various economic frontiers.

(3) In the immediately practical realm, public power is cheaper. This is more than just a matter for housewives. A difference of one mill in the kilowatt rate can make a difference of millions in the cost of industry, and can immensely promote or impede the general prosperity of a community.

Above and beyond all this is something else and bigger; what really lies at the heart of the public-private power controversy is the major question: What kind of society is to be built in the United States? Private power, say the public power adherents, serves to confirm or resurrect trends toward monopoly, exploitation, and abuses of the system of free enterprise. Public power, say the private power adherents, means a trend toward socialization, bureaucracy and planned economy.

Some of the utility magnates may seem worried and defensive, but they represent what is probably the most keen-witted, ruthless, and effective lobby in the United States. There is no other lobby that one meets at every level—city, county, township, state. Fifty or sixty years ago one of the greatest struggles in American life was, as we know, that between the people and the railroads, between grossly overcapitalized agglomerations of railway power and individual human beings. Something of the same kind of struggle is going on now, between the people and the utility companies, though the utilities can no longer go berserk as the railways did.

J. D. Ross and City Light

Public power is an old story in Seattle, and Seattle is one of the few cities in the country with public and private power both—City Light,

---

[5] Butte, Montana, is the most conspicuous of those that do.

as the municipally-owned system is called, and the Puget Sound Power and Light Company, the private company. They push each other hard. Let a newcomer move into a Seattle house, and importuning salesmen from each will be on the doorstep the next minute. After forty years of lively and acute competition City Light today has 71.2 per cent of the city's total electric business. Here is an instance of public power and private power fighting it out openly and above board with public power the overwhelming winner. Such a fight is of course an excellent thing for the consumer, whether household or industrial. Seattle's rates for electric energy are, we have seen, the lowest in the United States.

The story behind City Light is the story of J. D. Ross. This was a remarkable man. Briefly he served on the Securities Exchange Commission and he was Bonneville's first administrator, but practically nothing was known of him nationally. Yet twentieth century America has produced few more interesting careers. Ross, who died in 1939, was born in Canada. As a young man he got a job as an electrician with the Seattle municipality which was then building its first power plant. This was in 1902. For nearly forty years thereafter the lives of J. D. Ross and City Light were synonymous. He was the first great pioneer of the public power idea; he was marketing power years before TVA and Grand Coulee were dreamed of. When City Light started operations the citizens of Seattle paid twenty-three cents per kilowatt hour for electricity! Year by year, Ross—whose title was simply superintendent of the lighting department of City Light—managed to produce and sell electricity more and more cheaply, and year by year he forced down competing rates. He was a Republican and a Presbyterian, whose "love for mankind expressed itself in kilowatts," it has been said.[6] He was a first-class mathematician, a whipsaw of a businessman, and an old-style western evangelist all in one. City Light is today one of the most successful businesses in the country, worth $71,000,000, but Ross's own salary was never bigger than $7,500 a year. The private power people did everything possible to get rid of him, and once did so. A forgotten mayor, Edwards by name, discharged "Jaydee" in 1931. A few weeks later the issue was put to the polls and Edwards was recalled by the massive vote of 125,000 to 15,000. Like most great men, Ross was full of quirks and oddities. Not only did he build a dam and power plant at Skagit, a hundred miles north of Seattle, as a source of energy for his precious City Light; he made it a municipal camping ground on a nonprofit basis. Not only did he build parks and ornamental gardens; he installed hidden loud-speakers in the woods to play bird songs, in case the birds themselves didn't feel like singing.

Ross's great contribution is, however, something else. Quite inde-

[6] See "J. D. Ross, Public Power Magnate," *Harper's Magazine,* June, 1940, by Carl Dreher, a full and admirable sketch.

pendently, he discovered what Henry Ford discovered, that the cheaper you make a good commodity, the richer will be your returns. He made power cheap, and so more people were able to buy more of it. This produced a pleasantly nonvicious circle, in that the more power you continued to sell, the more you could afford to reduce rates further. The most impressive of all Seattle statistics is not the relative cheapness of its power, but how much it uses. It is that Seattle consumes an average of 3,012 kilowatt hours per customer per year as against a national average (residential consumption) of 1,056.

Rural Electrification and the PUD's

There must be brief word on the PUD's. These are the Public Utility Districts in Washington, Peoples' Utility Districts in Oregon. The PUD's are, in a word, "the rural equivalents of a municipal power authority."

This serves to bring up a question as important—and controversially abstruse—as any in the United States, that of rural electrification. Not one American urban dweller in ten thousand realizes it, but 63 per cent of all farms in the United States are still without electricity. The very pigpens in Denmark and Sweden, I have heard it said, have more access to electric power than all but a minority of American farms. Consider some consequences of this. The farmer has no telephone, no electric light, no washing machine, no power with which to operate pump or well or provide hot water, no energy with which to put to use everything from a churn to the fixtures of a modern chicken coop. Something like four *million* American farms have no electric service of any kind.

No one can say that this is entirely the fault of the power companies. Yet for years the private utilities were extremely reluctant to build lines out into the countryside; when they were willing to do so, the cost was likely to be prohibitive and the rates exorbitant. This is of course because country traffic is not, as a rule, lucrative. The "country load" does not pay anything like the "city load." The work of the Department of Agriculture, through the Rural Electrification Administration, to improve this situation and bring power into farming areas, has been one of the most stimulatingly successful adventures in social progress made in this country in many years. The PUD's are, however, something different.

In about 1930 citizens of various Washington and Oregon communities began to get together, and by initiative to the legislature established their right, if the majority of people so decided, to create their own power systems. Today twenty-nine out of the thirty-nine counties of Washington have strong, flourishing PUD's. They buy power from Bonneville or elsewhere, and distribute it co-operatively, under a completely democratic procedure; each PUD is autonomous, and its commissioners are elected by the people. The PUD's have become big business; they serve some forty thousand customers and two hundred thousand people in various areas of the state, and operate about twenty million dollars worth of property. Moreover they have stayed above water financially, proving the Ross dictum that electricity will always pay if you can use enough of it. The PUD's are so strong, in fact, that fourteen of them banded together in 1945 to attempt to buy out that goliath of private power, Puget Sound Power and Light. The private companies have of course fought them bitterly. For example there was Referendum No. 25 in 1945, which proposed extension of PUD activities. As the law is written at present, no PUD may operate outside its own county limits. Yet there are several districts where, if they could link up, there would be a considerable saving. "Operating separately," says a recent PUD publication, "each district carries on its own negotiations for the portion of a utility system which happens to fall within its boundaries. Naturally a big company is unwilling to lop off pieces of its system, one here and one there. As a consequence, it asks large sums as compensation. Referendum No. 25 would make the whole process more rational. It would save the public millions of dollars in separate suits, severance damages, and interest charges." But Referendum No. 25 was beaten by a narrow vote. The private utilities spent large sums to knock it out.[7]

Columbia Valley Authority

When Paul J. Raver, the BPA administrator, visits the Bonneville installations, he is a guest of the U.S. Army engineers; when he visits Grand Coulee, he is a guest of the Bureau of Reclamation. At least twenty different federal agencies have various overlapping functions in the Columbia valley, under three great government departments, Army, Interior (Bureau of Mines), and Agriculture (including the Forest Service). Yet a river does not recognize bureaucratic frontiers—any more than it recognizes state lines. Above all, the region as a whole needs systematic research, over-all research co-ordinated with a plan which can in turn be converted into a co-ordinated program under a single budget. But this is almost impossible under the present arrangement, with its duplication of authority and lack of integrated leadership. Each federal agency reports individually and separately to Washington, and the result is crippling. No one knows what is going on in the other agencies, and no one wants to intrude. The single step so far taken toward a solution of this problem has been the voluntary institution of the Columbia Basin Inter-Agency Committee, which includes representatives of Agriculture, Interior, Army, the Federal Power Commission, and the BPA. But this

[7] In November, 1946, however, Initiative No. 166, which would have severely hurt the PUD's, and which the power companies supported, was likewise beaten.

functions without Congressional sanction and with neither specific responsibility nor authority.

Perhaps all this is to overstate the picture. The fact remains that a strong movement has begun for creation of a Columbia Valley Authority, modelled in part on TVA, to take over development of the region as a whole—279,000 square miles—under a single administration and a single long-range plan. We shall see the same thing later in connection with MVA and the Missouri.

But powerful forces are arrayed against the CVA idea, including the privately owned utilities in particular. Also the Army engineers—a very conservative and tight-knit group who have been working in this area on their own for forty years—don't want to be squeezed out, and the Department of the Interior holds jealously to its prerogatives. (CVA adherents say, in rebuttal, that none of the existing federal agencies would have to be displaced; they would simply be co-ordinated better.) Private interests fear socialism and "regimentation," and everybody who hates Washington says that states' rights will be infringed and local authority destroyed—though the example of TVA is to prove the exact contrary. One of the great things about TVA is the decentralization it insists on and promotes. Some opponents of CVA also claim that there is such a thing as an agency being *too* big, though here again the TVA example indicates the opposite. Finally, almost everybody who sees Communism, New Dealism, and the bogey of planned economy under every bed looks at the idea of a CVA in horror not unmixed with trepidation.

Three separate bills to create a CVA were before Congress in 1946. The most important was that sponsored by Senator Hugh Mitchell. It died with the adjournment of the seventy-ninth Congress, and Mitchell himself was beaten.

Men like Raver—the real kilowatt zealots—go beyond the idea of CVA. They show you maps which, in their potentialities, are indeed novel and thrilling—maps which show neither roads nor states nor railways, but only the power lines and their network in the sky, power lines that can be increased multitudinously and that could knit the entire West into a single enormous circuit, giving useful energy to everybody.

Be that as it may be, the basic issue presented by CVA remains— whether or not a river valley should belong fully to its people.

Chapter 9

Staff and Stuff of Life, Plus Timber

wwwwwwwwwwwwwwwwwwwwwwwwwwwwwwwwwwwwwwwwwwwwwwwwwwwwwwwwwwwwwwwwwwwwwwwwwww

Wheat is civilization.,
—Jay Franklin

I FELL asleep in the plane from Seattle to Spokane, and woke up thinking that I must be dreaming. I could not believe what I saw; it was the most beautiful thing I have ever seen in nature. Below us throbbed the wheat. This is undulating country, and the wheat, planted along the hills in eccentric rings and ovals, climbs up one slope and down another. We were flying very low, and the tops of the wheat were intermittently touched by wind; it looked as if somebody were running a gentle invisible thumb over orange plush.

And the colors! The whole rippling blanket underneath might have been the palette of an artist painting sunsets. The colors are fantastically variegated because the wheat, planted at different times, is ripening at different stages of growth; they run from a deep red-copper through a buttery chrome to gamboge to fawn. Some fields looked like maple leaves and some like richly scrambled eggs. Think of all the red-headed girls you ever met; they are all down there in the wheat—auburn, russet, titian, chestnut, sandy. Then throw in the blondes.

But these are not the only colors. Look at the browns and greens. The deep sienna brown is just earth. This is because half the acreage must be left fallow each year in this dry part of the world. The green stripes and pools may be mustard, tumbleweed, or thistle. One convoluted pasture, with the green curling through the yellow in fine twisting lines, resembled nothing so much as an *omelette aux fines herbes*.

I arrived in Spokane—wide awake—and wanted badly to see what this wheat looked like on the ground. Nelson Hazletine of the Bonneville Power Administration drove me 110 miles through the wheat to the town of Hooper, where the MacGregor family has a ranch.

This Big Bend country between Spokane and Yakima—also the Palouse area nearby—is probably the most prolific wheat region in the world. If you own enough land and have four successive good years, you can retire a millionaire. The Big Bend has now had several years in a row of superbumper crops, with yields like forty bushels and up per acre.

Four factors, it seems, make this Washington area so prodigal. First, it has a good and consistent snow cover during the winter, while the wheat is growing, and yet isn't cold enough for winterkill. Second, the sunlight is unspoiled during late spring, with comfortable warmth but no great destroying heat. Third, hail—a savage enemy to wheat—is rare, and very heavy rains just before the harvest, which can do great damage, are unusual. Fourth, the hilly terrain makes the wheat less vulnerable to fire. A whole county planted in wheat can burn out, seemingly in an hour or so; one county, Whitman, did so four years ago when a number of lightning fires struck simultaneously. Wheat burns like cellulose. It makes one of the hottest and most avid of all fires.

We drove out to look, through solid seas of wheat, green on one side of a hill, and mushroom-colored beige on the other, rolling and twisting like desert sand. In some places there are acid spots—perhaps the site of an old fence line or haystack that has poisoned the soil—where wheat won't grow. We passed pools of platinum—oats and barley. We passed pools of emerald—alfalfa planted in the gullies to hold the topsoil down, to check wind erosion. We passed some bad burns in wheat the color of yellow cabs, and saw the long green firebreaks and the side strips where the combines need room for turning. It seems unbelievable that a combine can climb hills as steep as some of these. Above all, we saw the fallow pools, dead brown except for green weeds and "trash," which are the key to everything. Precipitation in this part of Washington is only about twelve inches; it is definitely a semiarid area, though the top soil—literally—may be eighty feet thick or thicker. Because of the lack of rain each farmer sows only half his land; the fallow sections are resting, absorbing moisture, sucking it in, waiting to be put to work next year.

There were other things besides wheat. This is all lava country, and we saw the basalt buttes and outcroppings of scab rock. A twister—dust storm—followed us for half an hour, moving right along in the shape of a spinning top, and porcupines and ground hogs crossed the road. The squat shining towers carrying electricity to the farms still strode along our route. Every once in awhile came a house, which forms a kind of self-contained island in the ocean of wheat—a pool of dark green, cottonwoods and poplars, a windmill, the house always painted white, the barn always painted red.[1] We passed wild-West villages like Colfax where horse thieves were hanged not so many years ago, and Ritzville which is settled by, of all things, Volga Germans. The main streets of the towns are identical, with silly square false fronts on the houses to conceal their perfectly legitimate peaked roofs.

A word now on wheat in general. The main thing to say is that it

[1] Traditionally because red is the cheapest paint.

gives energy to all mankind; without it, man could not easily live, which
cannot be said of any other commodity except air and water. Nobody
knows who discovered wheat; probably it was known to nomadic
tribesmen in Central Asia ten thousand years ago as a sort of wild
grass, and certainly the use of bread is as old as recorded history. Wheat
is not indigenous to North America; the Spaniards brought it in, and
then British settlers planted it in Virginia as early as 1618. Oddly enough
corn, on its side, is not indigenous to Europe; Europe gave us wheat,
and we gave Europe corn in exchange. Wheat is still the world's premier
crop, the essential barometer of its agricultural well-being; it is not,
however, the biggest crop in the United States—corn is—though one-
third of all American farmers plant wheat, and it covers something like
59,000,000 acres. On the price of wheat the fate of continents may
depend. When wheat hit an all-time low of 37¢ a bushel in 1932, this
country was sagging under the worst depression ever known; when
wheat sells at better than $1.50, as of the moment, life takes on a bonanza
glow.

One ton of wheat, in the form of bread flour, makes 1,932 one-pound
loaves, or 2,400,000 calories; fed to livestock, it is the equivalent of 249
dozen eggs, 841 quarts of milk, and 207 pounds of beef.[2] More time,
effort, and expert skill have gone into research on wheat than any other
comparable substance in the world. Agricultural scientists spend their
lives crossing its varieties, and in the United States alone there are at
least five hundred wheat breeding stations. Wheats are named almost
as remarkably as race horses. Among the hard red spring wheats are
Red Fife, Sea Island, Montana King; among the durums (used in macaroni and the like) Kubanka, Mindum, Monad; among the hard red
winters, Eagle Chief and Early Blackhull; among the soft red winters,
Harvest Queen, Red Rock, Climax, Imperial Amber, and Prosperity;
among the whites (the type mainly grown in the Northwest), Goldcoin,
Hard Longberry No. 1, Oregon Zimmerman, Little Club, Wilhelmina,
and Surprise.

Wheat has diseases, as everybody knows, just as has man. An epidemic
of rust in 1935 cost one hundred million dollars in North Dakota alone.
One wheat illness has the fine aromatic name of bunt or stinking smut.

Fall, winter, and spring wheat are, of course, named for the time
of planting; all are harvested in midsummer and the harvest lasts about
six weeks. About three-quarters of American wheat is winter wheat.
Spring wheat is much more vulnerable, both to winter frosts and to hot
winds in summer. What the breeders do is try to develop strains with a
quick life cycle—for instance a celebrated type called Marquis matures
in 110 days as against 140 for other varieties—and that will resist bad

[2] *Fortune,* May, 1946.

weather. The Russians, much to the admiration of our own Department of Agriculture, have done some astonishing work in this field. They have for example developed a chemical treatment of winter wheat whereby they can plant it in spring, thus avoiding any hazard of winter-kill, and harvest it in August exactly as if it had been planted the previous fall. Also they are trying hard to breed a variety that will grow, mature, and grow again after harvest, like grass, so that no plowing or seeding will be necessary.

Wheat is a ponderous operation in the Northwest. It has to be, since only half the land is used each year. Five thousand acres are scarcely enough room to move around in. "We no longer raise wheat here," Carey McWilliams quotes a Washington farmer as saying, "we manufacture it."[3] This process reaches its apogee, as we shall see, in such mastodonic farms as that of Colonel Tom Campbell in Montana.

The MacGregor ranch at Hooper, where I had the pleasure of delving into these mysteries, is operated by the MacGregor Land & Livestock Company, which was founded by four brothers of Scottish descent. The family came originally from the Isle of Mull. My hosts were Alexander Campbell MacGregor—who was once a schoolteacher and a druggist in Chicago—and his nephew John M. MacGregor. The ranch covers 33,000 acres, as big as a township in Connecticut. The rainfall averages only twelve inches (in 1944 only nine and a half); yet the MacGregor property grows forty bushels to the acre or more. Everything is pretty much mechanized, and three tractors do what two hundred horses did twenty years ago; six "cat skinners," four combine operators (wages eighteen to twenty-five dollars per day), six truck drivers, and a "roust-about" replace a staff that once numbered sixty-four. Among the wheats produced are Rex, with a huge kernel like an acorn, and Orofed, a new cross between Turkey Red and Federation. The harvest, when it comes, is a twenty-four-hour business; the combines chew up and down the hills day and night.

I saw a hillside of pale luminous green; it was mustard. This is a curious "contract" crop. Two or three companies control all the mustard seed in the United States, and they let it out to individual farmers by a kind of lease arrangement.

Also I saw the sheep. These are a good stock to keep in this part of the world, because they eat wheat stubble. The MacGregors have eight thousand head. The trouble with sheep, I heard it said, is that they are a frontier industry, and the Northwest is no longer a frontier. Sheep need more handling than cattle, because they are not "run under fence"; they have to be "migrated" each year, and this costs money. The sheep stay on the ranges in winter and spring, and then travel in escorted "bands" (not flocks) of about 1,200 to 2,000 to the mountains

[3] *Ill Fares the Land*, p. 301.

every summer—a kind of holiday. The men who take them are, incidentally, not called shepherds, but herders. The sheep business could
not, I heard, survive except for the duty on imported wool (thirty-four
cents a "clean" pound) and the domestic bounty fixed by the Commodity
Credit Corporation, twenty cents. The result of both is that the American
wool grower gets about ten cents a pound more than the "normal" world
price. Some ranchers in the Northwest are liquidating their sheep these
days in favor of cattle, since the latter are more lucrative. Not only
in the Northwest but all over the United States this trend to cattle—
and consequent shift in the livestock population—is going on.

When I visited Hooper, wheat, the peg on which everything in the
whole region hangs, was worth about $1.35 a bushel.[4] The government's
price—established by the nightmare-complex institution known as
parity—was $1.30. The technique of selling wheat was—and is—roughly
as follows. The farmer delivers his harvest to the elevators and the
Commodity Credit Corporation, through the local bank, lends him its
value calculated at $1.30. Or it will pay this in cash if the farmer wants
to sell outright. On a designated day the following spring the farmer,
if he has taken his proceeds in the shape of the loan, can cash the loan,
and the government takes title to the wheat. Or, if the open market
price is higher, say $1.35, the farmer can sell for this, repay his loan,
and keep the margin as a tidy profit. This procedure, which was developed
during the New Deal, has been bitterly attacked by farmers, and as
bitterly defended. But it cannot be denied that it gives the wheat grower
a guaranteed price. He is never at the mercy of a falling market, unless
the government should withdraw its support. The biggest hazard in
wheat has not been frost, winds, or grasshoppers; it has been price. And
farmers today have more security in price than ever before in the history
of the nation.

In 1945 the total U. S. wheat harvest hit an all-time high, 1,123,000,000
bushels. Of the 1946 crop—final figures for which are not yet available—
one-quarter, which will probably amount to more than 250,000,000
bushels, was under requisition order by the government, earmarked for
famine relief abroad. There was shocking delay, muddleheadedness, and
plain selfishness and cowardice in putting this program into action. A
major difficulty was lack of storage space and box cars; in September,
not less than three million bushels were lying roofless in the Spokane
area. But it did finally get under way and the American citizen in 1946
began to eat and drink less wheat and other grains, whether in the form
of bread, cake, beer, whisky, or odd things like breakfast cereals.

[4] Late in 1946 it reached $1.85.

Words on Wood

The forests of America, however slighted by man, must have
been a great delight to God, because they were the best He
ever planted.

—John Muir

Chop your own wood and it will warm you twice.

—Henry Ford

We sat on a terrace in Seattle, and looked across the dancing blue
saucer of Lake Washington; on the far shore were banks of trees, and
I began to learn a new vocabulary. Halfway down the slope the tree
line stops, and patches in the forest are bare, like bald spots, but with
a few trees left standing—"seed blocks" as they are called. Then I heard
two phrases, *sustained yield* and *selective logging,* the keys to the future
of the lumber industry in the United States, a future uncertain in the
extreme.

Selective logging means simply that a "stand" of timber should not be
cut down in sections willy-nilly, but that only mature trees should be
chosen, and that enough growing trees should remain to bear seed and
produce, in time, their successors. Such a process will, in the end,
make for sustained yield, which means just what it says. It will keep
the forests going, instead of destroying them; it will preserve this
precious and indispensable natural resource, instead of throwing it away.

The timber tycoons had a slogan once—"trees are a crop." As a
matter of fact they are not. The only authentic crop from a tree is the
cone. It takes a minimum of 80 years for a Douglas fir to reach saw-
log size, from 140 to 180 for a ponderosa pine. So, in a sense, these
trees do make a crop—every 80 to 180 years. But the lumber industry
was based for a couple of generations on the philosophy of harvesting a
"crop" that was not renewed.

Timber was the first of the great beneficent American heritages. This
country is unique—it still has virgin "old growth" timber that was here
when the white man came. Almost everywhere else in the world, the
virgin timber had disappeared by the time people got around to trying
to manage it. We in the United States have actually been able to put
virgin stands under management, but we have been very late to do so.
The United States still has virgin timber left—but not so much. In the
thirty years prior to 1938, according to the Forest Service, the "total
volume of standing saw timber was reduced almost 40 per cent." Virgin
forests were cut from an original acreage of 820,000,000 to about
100,000,000. Since 1938—what with enormous military demands for
timber during the war—the loss has been even more acute. From 1941
to 1945 the country as a whole cut about 16 billion cubic feet of timber

per year, whereas new growth only amounted to 11 billion cubic feet; in the Northwest, the drain was even worse, amounting to about three times the growth. At the moment of writing—when timber is very scarce and desperately needed for such projects as housing—the United States is still consuming, i.e. destroying, half again as much as it grows. This fact is shocking enough to be worth repeating. "Timber cut or destroyed is 50 per cent more than total growth."

The lumber tetrarchs came in with the railroads, and their holdings in the Northwest grew enormously; in those days timber did indeed seem inexhaustible and one private property was once as big as Delaware. In theory the owners, to keep their business going on in perpetuity, should have harvested each year a maximum of one-eightieth of the "crop," since it takes a Douglas fir eighty years to become mature. Of course they did nothing of the kind. Some companies simply cut and ran. They calculated that their mills would last thirty-five years or so; they ripped the land clean in that time, and then moved out. Also there were —and are—the "gypo-loggers," the real hit-and-run cutters, men with "teapot mills" in deserted stump land, who had no more regard for conservation than a hyena. For many years the timber business was a race between the timber cutter and the tax assessor. A company would log off its land, then abandon it, since this saved them taxes. The faster taxes were raised on timbered land, the faster the cutters cut.

Tying in with this is a seemingly foreign and anomalous factor, the public schools. The schools possess a great deal of forest land in Washington and Oregon, out of which they naturally want as much revenue as they can get. So a kind of alliance exists between the big timber interests and the parent teachers association. Consider the strange business of Referendum No. 27. The state's timber resources—and 62 per cent of Washington's total income derives from lumber, directly or indirectly, in normal times—were formerly controlled by seven different agencies, among them the regents of the university, the State Land Board, the Department of Conservation, and the like. A law was passed in 1945 unifying all this into a Timber Resources Board and setting forth a conservation program that gave the state additional authority over private logging. This law was challenged the next year by a referendum, and the state's whole forestry program imperilled because of political pressure from big timber interests and the schools.

Another factor is the gradual absorption of small timber properties by big. Suppose a retired merchant or doctor, say, owns a few thousand acres of Douglas fir. His taxes are going up and he has no incentive to think in terms of long-range reforestation, nor has he the resources to log the land himself. So a big company buys him out, and proceeds to cut.

The lumber companies may pay lip service to the principle of sustained yield—usually after having logged a property off—and they may profess a conscientious interest in conservation, but not many think in terms of maintaining a whole forest as a living entity in perpetuity. The Forest Service says flatly, "Some *eighty per cent* [italics mine] of the cutting in private lands is still done without conscious regard to future crops."

Another complaint against big-money lumber is about right of way. The lumber companies, with millions of bare acres behind them, continue to hold this "logged-off" land and to buy new land particularly along the highways in order to block access to unlogged land that lies beyond. Or a company will buy *around* a stand of state-owned timber, so that nobody else can easily get access. One more complaint has to do with minerals. The timber owners control subsurface rights, and what may be mineral resources of unprecedented value has never been explored or made useful to the state or the people as a whole.

More than 10 per cent of every milled log is sawdust, and a tremendous development has taken place recently in timber by-products. You can make everything from molasses to aspirin tablets out of sawdust. But the new pulp factories have created new and pressing problems. For one thing the discharge of waste products from the riverside plants kills the fish, and as a result a fine local war is that between the timber industry and the fisheries. Of course the chemical and pulp and plastics industries will have to shut up shop if the millers continue indefinitely to saw up everything they can lay hands on. For, again in the words of the Forest Service, "Half the sawmills, pulp, shingle, veneer, and other log-using plants in Oregon and Washington have private timber in sight for not more than five years."[5]

Four companies control about 95 per cent of Northwest lumber. These are Long-Bell, Blowdell-Donovan, the Crown Zellerbach Pulp and Paper Company, and the Weyerhaeusers, who are of course the biggest single force in the industry. Their sales in 1943 amounted to $77,775,195, and their net profits $8,360,797.[6] The Weyerhaeusers—a fascinating family about which a whole chapter might be written—derive from Minnesota, and though the company headquarters are in Tacoma, most surviving members still live in St. Paul. The company saws not less than 4 per cent of *all* the lumber in America. It has, after a buccaneer past, had vision enough lately to think very seriously about conservation, and it has built and maintains immense tree farms to encourage sustained yield.

[5] This quotation is from a useful little pamphlet, *A Forest Conservation Program,* p. 5. Of course forest wastage is not confined to the Northwest. For instance in 1943 the entire town of Weirgate, Texas, "was sold to a wrecking company after a life of only 25 years in which some 100,000 acres of virgin long-leaf pine were stripped." Similarly, lack of timber "forced the closing of the last big sawmill in Rhinelander, Wis., at the very time when the nation's need for lumber was most acute."

[6] *Fortune,* West Coast number, February, 1945.

We have talked much of public power. There is also—perhaps the reader should brace himself—such a thing as public timber. Most distinctly the United States government is in the lumber business. The origin of this goes back to Grover Cleveland, Theodore Roosevelt, and the early conservationists. The national forests and national parks were established, and the Forest Service began its admirable work. Of the total American forest lands, about one-third are national today and under scientific management; the government cut and sold about $1,500,000,000 worth of timber in 1944.

Public timber has been dominated by the concept of sustained yield from the beginning. What the government cuts, it cuts selectively. And the Forest Service believes firmly that there should also be public regulation of private forest land.

Silver Wings at Renton

Having seen where electricity was made, at Bonneville and Grand Coulee, I wanted also to see how it was used; having seen ships mass-produced by Kaiser at Richmond, I wanted to see airplanes mass-produced too. So I visited the Boeing headquarters at Seattle and its great B-29 assembly plant at Renton, seven miles away on the glistening waters of Lake Washington.

The dominant impression is silveriness; I kept thinking of Walter de la Mare's lovely poem called "Silver." The wings, the fuselages, slowly moving into place on the assembly lines, shine and shimmer like silver foil. In most factories you see grease and waste, oil stains on the floor, and grubby, funguslike walls and corridors; you hear metallic clamor. But Renton is silent, graceful, and sleekly caparisoned in aluminum.

Renton itself fabricates nothing but spar chords, which are the biggest aluminum products ever extruded; the aluminum is squeezed out like tooth paste or spaghetti. Renton gets its bomb bays from Vancouver, its nacelles from Fisher Body in Detroit, its wing tips from Cleveland, its landing gear from Milwaukee, and its engines from the prodigious Dodge factory in Chicago which was especially built to make power plants just for the B-29.

What we watched was the process whereby these various parts—and a thousand others, including eleven miles of wire and 147 different electric motors—become an airplane. The plant was, when I was there, turning out six B-29's a day; each takes about five days to make and Renton has produced 6,983 in all. There are two assembly lines in each of two massive bays. We saw a "raw" wing, just arrived from Seattle, slide into place on a powered track; it comes in sideways, riding on a dolly. Ahead of us, neatly in line, each waiting its turn, were twenty-eight other similar wings, ready for assembly. The wiring of each wing is already complete—all you have to do is turn a button—and the landing gear and motors are bolted on. The wing is "energized," and the landing gear tested in a pit under the assembly. Each motor weighs three thousand pounds, but it is fixed to the ship by only six half-inch bolts. We moved on to see each "station" in the assembly. At position No. 1 the fuselage is a carapace of metal, bare and naked. But at position No. 4, only a few yards and a few man-minutes farther on, the body is finished except for the tail; and at No. 6 it is a complete airplane, and could fly, except that the propellers have not been fitted to the motors. The last detail is paint. The B-29's I saw took three hundred pounds of black paint each—for the underwings—and this takes three hours to dry. The plane then comes out on the apron on the lake front, stretches its muscles in a little jaunt around a circle, and is ready to take off.

At peak Boeing employed 55,000 workers—of whom 46 per cent were women—hired in twenty-three states. The average wage was $1.07 per hour. The shop is 100 per cent AF of L. This huge labor pool was, I heard, of a "very peculiar and unstable class." At one period not less than 12 per cent of all workers had criminal records of one kind or another—an interesting commentary on the state of civilization in the United States. But Boeing kept them on, and was glad to have them. During the height of the B-29 program, an official told me, "We hired anybody who had a warm body and could walk inside the gate."

After Renton, I was allowed in Seattle to see something very special—the life-size mock-up (i.e. model) of a plane then known as the XC 97, and also the plane itself, one of the three in existence at that time. This plane, the Boeing Stratocruiser, is the civilian variant of the B-29. It looks like a Zeppelin with a razor back, and it can hold seven jeeps, four ambulances, two ton-and-a-half trucks, or two baby tanks. It will carry 120 passengers, and it has a cocktail lounge—as all assiduous readers of Boeing advertisements know. The thing is so big that I asked irreverently where the bowling alley was. The cruising speed of this monster is 340 miles an hour, and on January 9, 1945, it broke the world's speed record for coast-to-coast flight, covering the 2,323 miles between Seattle and Washington in 6 hours 3 minutes 50 seconds, which cut 54 minutes from the record previously held by the Lockheed Constellation. It flew at 30,000 feet, and to land at Washington it had to start letting down at Pittsburgh. Incidentally it made Pittsburgh-Washington in twenty minutes. So the war has, it would seem, produced at least one thing useful to mankind and its uncertain future, if mankind wants to fly securely from New York, say, to London in 11 hours.

.   .   .   .

We conclude now with the Pacific coast. No section of the country has a more intense vitality or a greater promise than this Western rim.

Chapter 10

Invitation to the West

〰〰〰

The West, at bottom, is a form of society, rather than an area.
—Frederick Jackson Turner

I have fallen in love with American names,
The sharp names that never get fat,
The snakeskin-titles of mining claims,
The plumed war-bonnet of Medicine Hat,
Tucson and Deadwood and Lost Mule Flat.
—Stephen Vincent Benét, *American Names**

FIRST to define terms. It would seem that we have been in western regions a long time already, but actually in one sense California, Oregon, and Washington are not "the West" at all. In Portland I actually heard a lady say that she was "going West" on a brief trip—and she meant Utah! People on the Pacific Coast think of themselves as belonging to the "coast"; the "West" is quite something else again. Let us, however, be more inclusive. Of course the West comprises all the eleven states that lie wholly or in part west of the Continental Divide from any national point of view. But of these the three fronting the Pacific are a special case, and so, as we shall see at the very end of this book, are the Southwestern states of Arizona and New Mexico. Normally, when saying "West" with any discrimination, we mean the eight Rocky Mountain states—Montana, Idaho, Nevada, Utah, Colorado, Wyoming, New Mexico, and Arizona. Of these eight, I am considering only four in the chapters that follow—Montana, Utah, Wyoming, and the high king of them all, Colorado—though we shall spill over the edges a good deal in this introduction.

There are other definitions. For instance Wendell Berge, assistant attorney general of the United States in charge of antitrust affairs, calls fifteen states "western" in his book *Economic Freedom for the West*. He includes Kansas, Nebraska, and both Dakotas. Then, by another accepted classification, there are ten "Missouri River" states—the obvious ones plus Kansas, Iowa, and a small part of Minnesota—which Great Muddy drains.

If we forget state lines, demarcation of the West is much easier—almost too easy. It is simply that third of the continent west of what is probably the most singular of all American frontiers, the line of the

* Copyright, 1931, by Stephen Vincent Benét.

144

98th meridian. Some authorities choose the 100th meridian, not the 98th, but the greatest authority of all, Professor Walter Prescott Webb, author of *The Great Plains*, says the 98th, and so the 98th it shall be. This fascinatingly sharp line, this altogether knifelike meridian, marks the division between country that has more than twenty inches of rainfall per year, and country that has less. The West is short-grass country, and (with the exception of a limited enclave in Washington and Oregon) it has the primitive and overwhelming problem of lack of water.

Americans are apt to take the West for granted. We learned about Buffalo Bill in childhood; we go to the circus and to "westerns." But suppose the man from Mars, "that well known alien" as Clare Boothe Luce once called him, should never once have heard the word "West," and could not perform the instinctive and automatic associations to it that are native to almost every American. Suppose one had to explain as to a child, and account for, the aroma of such names and phrases as Fort Laramie, the Pony Express, Custer's last stand, the Pawnee Fork, Jim Bridger, the covered wagon, Kit Carson, Cripple Creek, Sitting Bull, the "wild" West itself.

Two things made the West more than any other—the transcontinental railroads and the Homestead Act of 1862. And long before the Homestead Act, under which something like one hundred million acres were distributed, was the Northwest Ordinance of 1787, which assured democratic institutions and local self-rule to the frontiersmen, and set the pattern for a century of development. As every school child knows, the Homestead Act made land free to settlers,[1] except for a purely nominal charge. Nothing quite like this ever happened in history before. The immense westward migrations that created the United States, which were themselves of unprecedented and unique caliber, were based on the promise of *free* land in the public domain. Homesteading still exists, although the Taylor Grazing Act of 1934 withdrew much of the acreage remaining and established co-operative grazing districts, on the ground that it was range land, not fit for farming. This was necessary because so many million acres had been destroyed by wanton overuse, by stupid and greedy agricultural techniques.

The spine of the whole mountain area is, of course, the Rockies, and a curious south-north current, if that is the proper word, pulls it together and gives it the homogeneity of a true region. There are people alive today who can remember when there was not a fence between the Mexican border and Canada. Draw a line Santa Fe–Pueblo–Denver–Laramie–Butte–Great Falls; this line, following the shadow of the continental divide, is the West's heart line. Here is the great preponderance of both wealth and population. Literally 85 per cent of the people of

---

[1] Also it served to make the whole West "a creature of the national government." Cf. James Truslow Adams, *The Epic of America,* p. 166.

Colorado live within a fifteen-mile strip along the divide. Of course—roughly speaking—this was also the route of the old cattle trails; it is the route today of cheap Mexican labor, migrating north each year to work the beet fields, and of expensive mechanized combine teams, that follow the same direction southward, harvesting the wheat. Eighty per cent of the river water of the United States rises in this region—yet agriculture is all but impossible without irrigation.

Daniel Webster, that doughty New Englander, made some remarkably wrong guesses in his day, as we already know. Here is what he said once about the mountain area: "Not worth a cent. . . . A region of savages, wild beasts, shifting sands, whirlwinds of dust, cactus, and prairie dogs."

East of West, sloping down from the titanic, Jovian Rockies, are the Great Plains. "The distinguishing climatic characteristic of the Great Plains environment from the 98th meridian to the Pacific Slope is a deficiency in the most essential climatic element—water," says Professor Webb. One more word about this magical meridian. It cuts straight through six states, bisecting them as by a cleaver—the Dakotas, Nebraska, Kansas, Oklahoma, Texas. It is the eastern frontier of the West. Not only does it mark, with certain oscillations, the violently important twenty-inch rainfall line; it marks a dividing line for hail, prairie, windmills, jack rabbits. The western side, limited in rainfall, is cattle country; on the other, we touch the edge of corn. On the west the grass (short) is buffalo and grama; on the other (longer) it is bluestem-sod, bluestem bunch, wheat grass, and needle. To the one side, we are still in the West; on the other, we verge toward the Middle West and the Mississippi Basin.

But it will be quite some time before this book reaches so far. We still have a great deal of undiluted West to deal with.

Some Generalizations About the West

The West may be called the most distinctively American part of America, because the points in which it differs from the East are the points in which America as a whole differs from Europe.
　　　　　　　　　　　　　　　　　　—Lord Bryce

Throughout our whole history the United States has been facing westward.
　　　　　　　　　　　　　　　　　　—James Truslow Adams

(1) West means frontier. The word has more than mere geographical significance. For instance Amarillo, Texas, a thousand miles east of Santa Barbara, California, is at least a thousand times more "western." And the West still carries the stigmata of a frontier civilization—it is the newest part of the nation, the most sparsely settled, the most individualistic, the friendliest. This is all shirt-sleeve country, he-man country,

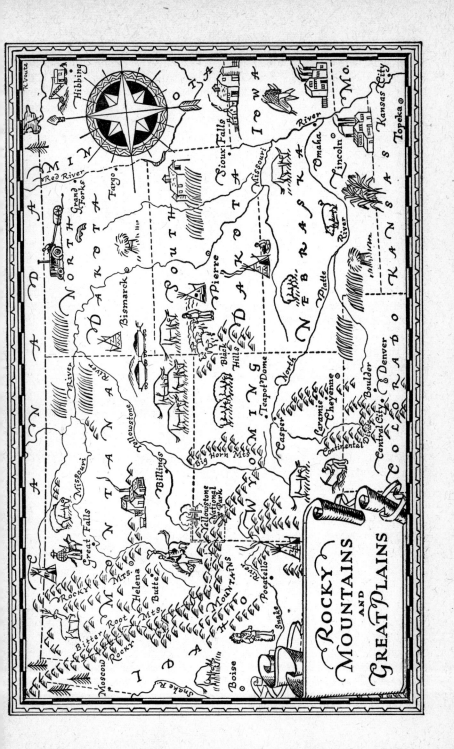

where the beds are usually double and where you drink beer straight from the bottle.

The frontier is, moreover, still a quite living reality to most Westerners. Custer seems almost as contemporaneous as Eisenhower. Indeed, only a little more than a generation separates today from the gaudiest events of western history. The newspapers reported in August, 1946, the death, at ninety-six, of a man who helped bury those killed by Sitting Bull at Little Big Horn. No one should ever forget how new this prodigious world of the West is, to say nothing of its prodigious pace of development.

In the early days the basis of all economy was the ownership of land. And having acquired property very quickly, the owners were more eager to hold onto what they had; hence the West's retentive individualism. A derivative point is that, by and large, frontiersmen have an extremely personal outlook on life and politics. In urban areas, roughly speaking, a man depends on society for a livelihood; on the land (until the catastrophes of the 30's at least) he depends largely on himself.

One point seldom made is that, whereas legend has bestowed on the frontiersmen all the furbelows of heroism and romance, in actual fact many who carved out the frontier were riffraff. It was not only the strong who went West but the weak too. The failures, those who could not earn livings in Tennessee or Missouri, the younger sons and the wastrels, all joined the westward trek. Many came, not because they were enterprising and courageous, but because they got squeezed out. Many frontiersmen were the nineteenth century equivalents of the Arkies and Oakies of today.

(2) An instinct toward nullification of statutes, contempt of authority, and lawlessness. Butte, for instance, like Reno as we know, never paid the slightest attention to prohibition, even *pro forma*. A tendency to direct action, if necessary to violence, lies very close to the surface of American character. Consider the Indian Wars. It is indeed an astonishing thing, as Professor Brogan has pointed out, that Canada which pursued roughly the same development as the United States never had any Indian wars at all.

(3) Nomadism. Americans are inveterate wanderers; no other nation on earth, especially since the advent of the automobile, has so many nomads; and the West is particularly nomadic. Also the automobile, by reducing distances and wiping out many small communities, helped kill the old frontier. The West's dependence on the automobile is of course enormous. For instance Wyoming, though very poor, has more cars per capita than any other state.

(4) Economically the West lives mostly by the production of prime resources and raw materials—copper, other minerals, petroleum, cattle, wheat—and its reserves of coal and oil shale are so enormous as to be

incalculable. West of the 98th meridian is 39.5 per cent of the total land of the United States, but only 9.5 per cent of the total farmed area. The West, despite irrigation, cannot feed itself; to live it must import not merely industrial products from the East, but also food. So its economy is of necessity a raw material economy. Berge,[2] calculating on the basis of fifteen states, points out that the West provides 33.6 per cent of the nation's cattle, 58.8 per cent of its sheep, 72.1 per cent of its sugar beets, 94.7 per cent of its copper, 90.5 per cent of its gold, 99.2 per cent of its silver, 28.3 per cent of its petroleum, 92.1 per cent of its mercury, 60.4 per cent of its zinc. On the other hand these fifteen states account for something less than 10 per cent of all American manufacturing, and something under 17 per cent of the total national income.

(5) Politics. Here we have several paradoxes to explore. This is the region par excellence of Jeffersonians in the literal sense, i.e. haters of too much government. Here, among these self-made men in the open spaces, a kind of direct personal democracy, with hatred of regimentation, has always flourished. One would thus expect that the whole area would have been stanchly anti-Roosevelt. But—though there were and are plenty of Roosevelt haters—FDR won not less than forty-one times out of forty-four western tries, counting the West as the eleven states behind the divide. He lost Wyoming once, and Colorado twice; these three defeats aside, he carried every Western state every time he ran.[3]

One reason for this is that the New Deal—and Roosevelt personally— did a lot for the West, for instance in hydroelectric development and irrigation. Another is that the great depression struck the whole West with savage fury; at one time, to cite a single example, 25 per cent of the population of Montana was on relief. Behind this was the deep general tradition of western liberalism; the direct primary, popular election of senators, the initiative, referendum, and recall were all western born as we know. Still another factor is that the West has always hated the "big money" power of the East—we shall talk about absentee ownership in a moment—and has usually stood for cheap money. Hence it approved the multifarious measures of the New Deal that favored debtor as against creditor, and tended to produce inflation.

One should not, however, exaggerate the western disposition to liberalism or radicalism. There are tories in Salt Lake City and Denver who make Hoover seem like an anarchist, and men like Millikin (Colorado) and Cordon (Oregon) are among the most extreme reactionaries in the Senate. Still, look at Wayne Morse and Glen Taylor, Murray of Montana, practically everybody from Washington as we have seen, both

---

[2] *Op. cit.,* pp. 151 and 154.

[3] Incidentally only two American presidents have been born west of the Mississippi River: Herbert Hoover and Harry Truman.

the Utah senators, both the New Mexico senators, and (in a kind of special category) O'Mahoney of Wyoming.

The western senators (and representatives) do not as a rule vote as a bloc. There is no united front like that of the solid South. What does happen is that there are blocs within blocs, representing silver and other such special interests, who trade votes among themselves. But recently western senators took a unanimous stand against, of all things, the Reciprocal Trade Treaties. Of the total of thirty-three negative votes on this question fourteen were western. Yet the West is supposed to be pro-New Deal and liberal! Once again, there are no generalizations in American politics that vested selfishnesses cannot cut through. Both senators from Montana, Colorado and Wyoming, whether Republican or Democratic, together with those from the Dakotas, Kansas, and Nebraska voted to knock out the Hull program for tariff reduction. Reason? Wheat, sugar, beef carry great weight in these areas.

A point not without interest is that the eight mountain states had exactly 3.6 per cent of the national vote in 1940. Yet the sixteen senators of the region had a voting power equivalent to those of eight eastern states representing 50.5 per cent of the national vote.

The West has not, any more than any other section of the country, come to grips as yet with a problem that may well become the central problem of our times. It is that good Jeffersonians seek, as an ideal, to get along with as little government as possible. But what about the bomb? What kind of politics is the West going to have in the atomic era which makes the entire population infinitely more dependent on centralized authority than ever before in history?

All over the West, with its splendid individualism, its direct democratic procedures and its genuine interest in and regard for the community, I heard the phrase, "I've never voted a straight ticket in my life." All over the West I found that a familiar cliché of the politicians, "that people vote to reject, not to approve," was just as wrong as the clichés of professional politicians usually turn out to be.

A last detail in this field: most excitement in local elections in the West attends, not the race for governor, but that for sheriff. The sheriff is the chief law enforcement officer, and the job can be very lucrative.

(6) Cattle. There should be a special rubric for this, because almost the whole of the less-than-twenty-inch-rainfall area is cattle (and sheep) country. Look at any map adequate in such details: the cattle line, rainfall line, short-grass line, are coterminous, almost to the inch. But let us save discussion of cattle in general until we reach Texas, which is by far the greatest cattle state. In passing, however, it is impossible not to mention that the struggle between farmer and cattleman, for instance over fencing, is at the bottom of western political development almost everywhere. Again in passing, think what words and phrases cattle culture has given

to the language—outfit, take the hide off, panhandler, riding herd, hog-tied, cowed.[4]

(7) Women, who have always played a particularly active role in western politics. The woman suffrage movement had its first impetus in the West—Wyoming had votes for women as early as 1869; Montana was the first state to have a woman representative (Jeannette Rankin), and Wyoming was the first with a woman governor. Equality for women of course derives straight out of the circumstances of frontier life.

(8) The weather. This plays a role in western life almost impossible for an Easterner to appreciate. The implacable violence of western weather, its changeableness, the irreversible impact of what may be its sudden attack, is a preoccupation never far away; here indeed man does face nature. While I was in Colorado 6.31 inches of rain fell in ninety minutes in the Eleven Mile Canyon area; this was the fiercest storm on record in the state. In Montana, there are records of snow in July, and Butte in one year registered forty degrees below zero on one day, forty above a few days later. In 1916 central Montana had subzero weather for thirty-two days in a row, and what is believed to be the lowest temperature ever recorded in the western hemisphere is the sixty-three below of one Montana town. Another, not far away, once registered 117 degrees above. Flash floods, blizzards, prolonged drought—these are a few among the perils of western weather. And behind everything is the question of rainfall. Water equals life.

(9) I mentioned above that prohibition was never enforced in several western towns; nevertheless prohibition was, and is, a substantial issue. Considerable areas of several western states are dry under local option, and several cities are "charter dry." Why should the reckless, come-easy go-easy West, where a saloon is almost as conventional an attribute to a landscape as a church in New England, have this impulse? First, the early Populists were mostly dry, and several of the historic western liberals, like Bryan and Norris, were fanatic drys. Second, the economic influence of women, who strenuously resented and opposed the transmutation of wages into alcohol. Third, a general reformist tendency—the same influence, in a different dimension, that brought direct primaries and state-supported schools—especially among the Scandinavians who were prominent early settlers.

(10) Catholic influence is, except in largely Irish towns like Butte and of course excepting the Southwest and the southern (Spanish-American) counties in Colorado, comparatively minor on the whole. Similarly there is less Jewish influence in the West than anywhere else in the United States.

(11) Except in war-boom cities the Negro problem, that most Laocoönlike and unruly of all American problems, hardly exists in the West.

[4] The other great western industry, mining, has also produced phrases, for instance "to pan out" and "pay dirt."

As of 1940, the total Negro population of Wyoming for instance was only 956, of Idaho 595. But the few Negroes who do live in the West live, by and large, fairly well; for instance the proportion of Negroes owning their own homes in Denver is the highest of any American city.

(12) Exodus. A great and disconcerting issue is the flow outward of brains, youth, and talent. The bright youngsters in education or law or finance, finding opportunities to be far greater in the East, move out. The western universities find it almost impossible to keep their best professors. So the area becomes arid intellectually as well as otherwise; the hinterland is impoverished in brains as well as capital; and it is easier for the older generation to maintain a standpat attitude, since the leaven of youth is largely gone.

Freight Rates and "Colonial" Economy

This weighty topic is full of thorns and pitfalls. Expressed in a sentence it is that the West, like the South, considers itself seriously discriminated against by the industrial East, through such factors as unfair freight rates and absentee ownership.

A small anecdote is to the point. I heard it first in Georgia, but it applies equally to Utah or New Mexico. A man dies and is buried, an archetypically local citizen. Then it is found that his shoes came from New England, his shirt and underclothes from upper New York state, his eyeglasses from New Jersey, and his false teeth from Pittsburgh. The casket was made of Michigan pine, and its nails came from Hartford, Connecticut. The car leading him to the grave was manufactured in Detroit, and the pastor read the last services from a Bible printed in New York from paper made in Maine. All that the "typical" citizen contributed to his own funeral was his corpse; all that the community contributed was the hole in the ground.

Why, however, should the West want to become industrialized? The answer Westerners themselves give is simple enough—Why not? They see no reason for remaining indefinitely at the exorbitant mercy of the East for everything from dynamos to gloves to can openers. The West disclaims any desire to create any unreasonably ambitious or competitive autarchy. All it wants is fairer treatment, and a little more to say about its own price levels. During the war twenty-one billion dollars worth of industry was planted in the West (including the Pacific coast), mostly by the giant fingers of the government. Westerners saw the beckoning mirage of their own integrated steel industry, out of a combination of Kaiser at Fontana, the Geneva plant in Utah, and the iron works in Colorado. They proved that they could make aluminum for 11.3 cents a pound, as against 15½ in the East, largely because public power is cheap. They saw a chance to raise the standards of living, to absorb postwar unemployment, to reverse population trends. The West was, in C. Hart-

ley Grattan's phrase, "hell bent for industrialization," but except in
California—as of the moment of writing—it has been pretty well beaten
down.

Freight rates make a savage little story. By arrangements made in the
first instance by the railways themselves, but approved by the Interstate
Commerce Commission, one of the most powerful public bodies in the
country, the United States is divided into five freight territories. Take
the class rate for shipment of goods in the eastern or "official" territory
as 100. Then the rate in Southern Territory is 139, Western Trunk Line
Territory 147, Southwestern Territory 175, and Mountain-Pacific Territory 171. Consider what this means in practice to the consumer, to you
and me if we happen to live in the less-favored regions. Everybody has
seen the words "F.O.B.", Free on Board, in advertisements of multifarious types of goods. What these three letters mean is that an electric
refrigerator, say, in Ogden, Utah, may cost you 20 per cent more than
the same refrigerator in Indianapolis, because the manufacturer only
pays the transportation costs from his plant to the railroad—the freight
proper is paid by the purchaser. Consider some examples. Colorado itself
refines plenty of gasoline; yet it has to pay for gasoline the price set in
Oklahoma and *also* the theoretical cost of shipping it from Tulsa to
Denver ("Tulsa plus"), even though it could be bought in Denver with
no freight charges entering into the transaction at all. It is cheaper to
send a piano, say, from Chicago to Seattle, on a train that must pass
through the railway station at Helena, Montana, than from Chicago to
Helena. There is a kind of craziness about this. Suppose you are a shop-
keeper in Cheyenne, and you order a candy shipment from St. Louis.
The freight will cost you more in Cheyenne than it would cost a retailer
a thousand miles further west, in Portland and Seattle.

Here are some more general figures from Wendell Berge. "The rate
on work clothing in carload lots from Macon, Georgia to Chicago, a distance of 817 miles, is $15.60 per thousand pounds as compared with a
rate of only $11.20 from Philadelphia to Chicago, a haul of 814 miles.
From Omaha, Nebraska, to Columbus, Ohio, a distance of 748 miles,
the comparable rate is $18.70 per thousand pounds while the rate is
$15.20 from Fitchburg, Mass., to Columbus, a distance of 743 miles. . . .
Examples of such disparities among the principal rate territories could
be multiplied almost endlessly."

The reasons for these discriminatory rates, by which the West (also
the South) think they are being unmercifully cheated, go back a long
way. For many years the West had no industry of its own to speak of
and hence, the railways say, it didn't "deserve" cheap rates. It was
"colonial" territory to be milked at will. The conflict is basic as between
the railroads, who want freight rates to be as high and lucrative as possible, and industry and the consumer who want them low, and thus
reflects one of the oldest of American issues, the rivalry between industry

and agriculture. More specifically the rivalry today is between eastern industry which wishes to preserve its western markets in all their volume, and western agriculture which would like to process its raw materials nearer home. The western railways themselves assist in opposing industrialization of the West. Of course several western roads are eastern owned.

The whole freight rates story was first broken open in the South, by former Governor Ellis Arnall of Georgia who recently brought suit in the Supreme Court charging a group of railroads with conspiracy to maintain discriminatory rates. It may be years before the case is finally adjudicated. The South, as we shall presently see, backed Arnall almost to a man. The West did not respond with any such unanimity when an attempt was made, in the summer of 1946, to create a common front between southern *and* western governors at a meeting in Denver. The governor of Colorado, an extreme conservative, imported the redoubtable William M. Jeffers, president of Union Pacific, to address the conference, whereupon Jeffers persuaded the western governors to lie low. In May, 1945, however, came what may turn out to be an important amelioration. Largely because of the fuss and public airing provoked by Arnall's suit, which was made in the name of the state of Georgia, the Interstate Commerce Commission ordered a 10 per cent reduction in what are known as "class rates" in the South and West. Also the commission prescribed a uniform system of freight classification for the nation, including the West, something unknown before. Until this happened, a sewing machine could be classified as a sewing machine in one part of the country, but as quite something else in another, with different rates applying. This in a country as businesswise as the U.S.A.!

The other great western grievance is absentee ownership. The West produces raw materials in illimitable profusion; but it doesn't get a fair share of the return by any means. Most of the giant western producers—Climax Molybdenum, Colorado Fuel and Iron, the three great copper companies (Kennecott, Anaconda, Phelps Dodge) that produce 84.5 per cent of the nation's copper, and United States Potash, are all owned in the East, as are most of the oil concerns and utilities. This means, first, that the great preponderance of profits and dividends are sucked out of the West, though produced on the West's own territory out of western resources. Professor Morris E. Garnsey of the University of Colorado wrote recently,[5] "Such remote control clearly has the tendency to intensify the traditional business policy of emphasis on short-run profits. 'Get control of the raw material, get it out as cheaply as possible, and haul it away as fast as possible. We're here today and gone tomorrow. Never mind what we leave behind!' Such is the common policy of absenteeism. . . . The interests of the local area are a secondary consideration. The region becomes a colonial dependency of an industrial empire."

[5] "The Future of the Mountain States," *Harper's Magazine*, October, 1945.

Finally, one should note carefully that the federal government is also a very large absentee owner. The United States itself is by far the greatest landowner in the nation; in the mountain states alone, it owns almost one *half* the total area. This can produce irritating problems. Officials in Washington who have never been West of the Mississippi make policy for a region of which they know nothing. Moreover this vast area is mostly exempt from taxes, and so contributes little to local revenue.

Footnote to the Past

One of the most prescient travelers who ever lived, Alexis de Tocqueville, wrote in 1835, more than a century ago, a passage which contains such overtones that I beg leave to quote it.[6] The pace of history, always fast in the West, has never been faster than today. We may see from de Tocqueville's calm wisdom not only how far we have come, but also where we may go.

> Sometimes the progress of man is so rapid that the desert reappears behind him. The woods stoop to give him a passage, and spring up again when he is past. It is not uncommon, in crossing the new states of the West, to meet with deserted dwellings in the midst of the wilds; the traveller frequently discovers the vestiges of a log house in the most solitary retreat, which bear witness to the power, and no less to the inconstancy, of man . . .
> I remember that in crossing one of the woodland districts that still cover the state of New York [*sic*], I reached the shores of a lake which was embosomed in forests coeval with the world.

Tocqueville proceeds at some length to describe the extraordinarily virgin quality and solitude of a tiny islet. Then—

> I was far from supposing that this spot had ever been inhabited, so completely did Nature seem to be left to herself; but when I reached the center of the isle, I thought that I discovered some traces of man. I then proceeded to examine the surrounding objects with care, and I soon perceived that a European had undoubtedly been led to seek a refuge in this place . . . The logs which he had hastily hewn . . . had sprouted afresh; the very props were intertwined with living verdure . . . I stood for some time in silent admiration for the resources of Nature and the littleness of Man; and when I was obliged to leave that enchanting solitude, I exclaimed with sadness, "Are ruins, then, already here?"

M. de Tocqueville knew a lot. The history of the West has been in large part a race between man and the ruins he himself has made.

[6] Reprinted from *Democracy in America*, by Alexis de Tocqueville, translated by Phillips Bradley. Volume I, p. 295. By permission of Alfred A. Knopf, Inc. Copyright, 1945, by Alfred A. Knopf, Inc.

Chapter 11

The Montana Frontier

Hot afternoons have been in Montana.

—Eli Siegel

Montana's real trouble . . . is that her graveyards aren't big
enough.

—Arthur Fisher

TO SAY that the story of Montana is the story of a struggle between
the people and a corporation, the Anaconda Copper Mining Company,
would be to oversimplify. Or to say that Montana is, or was, pre-eminently the state of a man now passed over and broken, Burton K.
Wheeler, would be a grave error in proportion. Anaconda, a company
aptly named, certainly has a constrictorlike grip on much that goes on,
and Montana is the nearest to a "colony" of any American state, Delaware
alone possibly excepted; this extraordinary story deserves copious telling, and we shall tell it. But first it is only fitting and proper to have
some words about Montana in general, Montana as a whole—to describe
the kind of place it was and is and will be long after Anacondas and
Wheelers are forgotten.

This is a splendid, various, and exciting state. It illustrates, once
again, the stupefying vastness and variety of the United States, its overwhelming sense of power, spaciousness, uncurbable vitality, wealth and
youth beyond computation—and also rawness, greed, lack of over-all
clarity and plan, lack of any sense of historical continuity, instinct to
waste, and unpredictably errant political behavior.

Montana is as big as Illinois, Michigan, and Indiana. It is bigger than
Italy or Japan. To say that it is the third American state in size does
not, perhaps, make its enormousness tangible; say instead that one out
of every twenty-five American square miles is Montanan. Yet this
mastodonic territory contains only about 500,000 people, approximately
the population of New Orleans or Minneapolis. Montana is three times
bigger than New York state; its population is less than one-fifteenth
that of New York City.

A point of great moment to Montanans—and something very foreign
to the United States as a whole, which boosters don't like and prefer
not to talk about—is that the population is going down, not up. By the

census of 1940 the population was 559,456. An estimate for 1943, carefully based on war ration cards, was 470,033. As of today (late 1946) the figure is believed to be somewhat more; even so the state has probably lost about eighty thousand people, or almost 15 per cent of its 1940 total, in six years. Many of these emigrants went to find war jobs in Seattle and elsewhere on the West Coast; some have of course returned, but as yet there has been no decisive trend that way, if only because Montana itself hasn't many jobs to offer except in the mines. Anaconda, as we shall see, plays a large black role in this. Strangely enough this tendency toward decline is nothing new; Montana is the only state that has lost population for fifty years.[1] I found frightened remarks about this in pamphlets published as far back as 1920; the phenomenon is unique, and has been carefully studied. The chief reasons are lack of industry, inadequate facilities for adult education, a tremendous epidemic of bank failures in the early 1920's (not 1930's) when one-third of all banks in the state died, loss of topsoil caused by erosion, concentration of small farms into big, backwardness in rural electrification, and of course the fact that, during the war, miners saw no point in dangerous work underground, for an average daily wage of $7.75, when they could get $14.00 in aluminum and airplane plants a few hundred miles further west, above ground and in sparkling sunshine.[2]

Not only has the population diminished; it has changed considerably in character. For one thing most out-migrants were young people, which has lifted the average age of the state; for another, most were workers, which has meant a decline in the labor vote. Depopulation almost always tends to make a community conservative.

While I was in Helena I saw an inch-long item in the local newspaper, noting the "abandonment of the Armington-Neihart branch line of the Great Northern Railway . . . after more than 50 years of operation." The line was simply discontinued and its right of way will become wilderness, because "the railway claimed that further operation would be financially unprofitable." But the local communities involved bitterly resent being deprived of rail transportation.

H. Lowndes Maury, one of the grand old men of Montana, who has tried more suits before the state supreme court than any man living or dead (he appears in 92 of the 114 volumes of records), a liberal who is a constant irritating burr in the side of the "Company," has four sons and two daughters. That all six should have left Montana and chosen to pursue careers elsewhere—brilliant and remarkable careers—is a small but relevant item showing how, in Montana as elsewhere in the Rocky

[1] But the rate of decline recently has been steeper, 18 per cent, in one other state, North Dakota.

[2] A postwar development is that wages in the mines have gone up to something over $9.00.

Mountain states, the tendency of the bright youngsters is to get out.[3]

One great change in the character of the population began, in 1910 or thereabouts, with the advent of "dry farming." This annoying word, as everybody should know, really means wet farming; it is farming dependent upon rain instead of irrigation. When the big farmers began to plow up ranch land for wheat, it meant the end of the open range; also it meant ruin and devastation when the topsoil began to blow off years later. The first Montanans were extremely progressive folk. They had to be. They fought for a living and a career was a perilous adventure. Schoolteachers came out from Minnesota to marry gold miners and stock growers. But now, the old Montana hands told me, the "pioneer spirit" is largely dissipated. This declension in character was shaped by changes in the towns too. For instance the chain stores squeezed out the old type of highly individualistic and idiosyncratic merchants. In both rural districts and the towns, the atmosphere was standardized and cheapened; the inhabitants became less picturesque.

Finally, in regard to population, we reach in Montana for the first time in this book a big and varied blanketing of foreign born. Forty-five and .2 per cent of all Montanans are foreign born or of foreign or mixed parentage. Moreover they are not predominantly of one racial group, like the Mexicans in Los Angeles or Scandinavians in Washington. Montana has Canadians, Swedes, Poles, Italians, Cornishmen, Jugoslavs, Finns, and vast quantities of Irish; in the mines of Butte not less than forty different foreign stocks are represented.

Montana, a noble area, is monumentally ridged on its left side by the continental divide. The backbone of the continent passes through this state. But one cannot so simply divide Montana into two separate spheres as one can divide Oregon, say, or Colorado. The western part is largely a mountain area, dominated by Butte and with its economy and politics based on minerals; Butte is Democratic by and large, with strong Irish and Catholic influences. The east is predominantly wheat and livestock country, part of the Great Plains, and much of it is Republican, Scandinavian, and conservative. Lumbering and smaller-scale agriculture, for instance sugar beets and fruit, are major pursuits in the western valleys. A third Montana world, little known, is that of the Bad Lands; the word "bad" does not, of course, mean wicked but merely a geological formation of scarred and forlorn rock twisted into macabre shapes. Also much of Montana is cattle country. Wheat is a very up-and-down proposition, in which you can make a killing or lose your shirt every other year; so some people keep cattle too, if only for their stabilizing quality. Finally, Montana is the only state in the union with great districts set apart by the federal Forest Service as "primitive

[3] One of Maury's sons, Reuben, is chief editorial writer of the New York *Daily News*. One of his nephews is Maury Maverick of Texas.

areas," where even roads are not allowed so that these mountain and forested paradises will remain unspoiled.

For forty years Montana, which in its history has belonged to six other states or territories (for a long time it was part of Idaho), lived mainly on furs. The trappers came up from St. Louis or down from Montreal. Then fashions changed about 1850 and men no longer wore beaver hats. This killed the fur trade, more or less. The gold rush started in the 60's, and a mining camp named Virginia City (no relation to Nevada's Virginia City) became the temporary capital. Gold brought in people, which meant ineluctably that agriculture and stock raising had to come. But eastern Montana wasn't really opened up till Custer's death in 1876, and buffalo were still roaming in the 1880's. Meantime the long-horns had pushed up from Texas, and the pirates who created Anaconda arrived from Ireland and New York.

Montana place names have a healthy nostalgic tang. One range of hills is the Scratch Gravel Mountains and one mine is called Molly Muck-a-Chuck-New York; a town was once called Copperopolis. Among gulches there are Seven Up Pete, Buttermilk Jim (near the interesting town of Boulder), Ready Cash, and Never Sweat; among creeks are Fool Hen, Keep Cool, Nary Time, and Try Again.[4]

You can drag choice Americana out of the state by the carload. For instance Alvin Johnson in the *Yale Review* (Autumn, 1944) tells this anecdote about trying to make conversation with a rancher's wife, without success. "Listen, friend," said Mr. Johnson's host, "it ain't no use for you to try to talk to my wife. She won't say a word. She thinks she's crazy, though she ain't. She thinks if she says anything, she'd show it. She ain't said a word to me for two years. But she's a mighty fine woman, and you can see for yourself, she's a hell of a fine cook."

Helena to Billings: Past to Present

Helena, the capital of Montana, is a mountain village 4,124 feet high, containing about twelve thousand people. Nowhere have I come across more bizarre or typical American contradictions. The civic center is in the form of a Mohammedan shrine, complete with tall minaret; the main street winds through the town like a shallow letter S, because it follows the route of Last Chance Gulch, where gold was found in 1864; Helena, a backwater, contains one of the most brilliantly satisfying restaurants in the whole country; the building of its leading hotel was partially financed by gold found in digging its own foundations.[5]

[4] For these names I am indebted to Howard A. Johnson, formerly chief justice of the state supreme court.

[5] The town was named by a miner from Minnesota for his own home town, after the first choice, "Last Chance," was given up as too undignified. Originally the

Two amiable friends took me for a drive a short distance from the center of town, and for the first time in my life I saw a gold mine. It is actually within the city limits. A big ugly gray dredge, that cost six hundred thousand dollars and weighs six hundred tons, squats in a dirty pool of its own creation; the dredge eats out the earth to the waterline and then floats on the scum it makes. An endless chain of clanking buckets picks up the mud, to a depth of 58 feet under water; "placer dirt" comes out, which is washed, treated with mercury, and separated on the "riffles," a long trough like a laundry board. The dredge which performs this operation and thus produces gold—also sapphires— is itself capable of motion. Having exhausted one cut in a hill, having gouged out one lopsided muddy hole, it grunts across country to a new likely spot, and starts over. The dredge I saw is stalled, however, because to get to the next favorable place it would have to grind through a natural gas line, the owners of which demand thirty thousand dollars as a price for getting out. Helena has a nine-hole golf course, where one may play the only "gold-plated golf" in the world. The dredge people think that gold is there, and they want to buy it. But when they offered twenty thousand dollars, the town golfers held out for two hundred thousand dollars because, they told me, a mining company seldom offers more than 10 per cent of what they think a property is worth. Meantime, you can play golf and slice balls into the noisy buckets moving up and down along the dredge.

The trails of these dredges may be seen in several places near Helena. They leave the kind of furrow that an enormous, obscene, un-housebroken worm might leave—an encrusted seam of broken earth, with mud and rocks lying across a winding trail like excrement. Nobody ever bothers to clean up afterward. In this part of Montana almost everybody owns a mining claim or two; the owners hold onto the property hoping some day to make a deal with the dredgers, who will then send in their megalosaurians.

From Helena I drove up to Great Falls. Talk about variety of spectacle! Hawks on fence posts, that only become frightened and fly away when you stop; Frenchy's Air Conditioned Cafe, with pretty girls lying about in hammocks; dead rattlesnakes; signs GAME CROSSING 1000 FEET AHEAD and an electric eye to count what crosses; girls in pigtails and bright habits riding out from the dude ranches; the house where Gary Cooper was born; "snow fences" to keep the road clear in winter, though it was 91 degrees in the shade—we saw all this among much else. Several times we crossed the winding Missouri (about which more anon), which up here near the source is a placid, almost stagnant stream,

---

pronunciation rhymed with Lena. But the boisterous community of the day wanted to get the sound "hell" in somehow, and so Hel'-ena it became. My source for this is a local pamphlet.

dark green between defiles of light green hills, wandering among fields of yellow mustard, purple-topped alfalfa, and fawn-colored timothy. Above all I watched the wheat, so different from Washington wheat. Half of each acreage is left fallow, as in Washington, but the fallow is plowed in symmetrical narrow strips to check wind erosion, not contoured over the hills; the Montana fields look like striped wallpaper laid flat. We came into Great Falls, which appears to be built on a series of vast bluffs, and I saw something that I never saw elsewhere in America or abroad—female MP's. They were on duty at the entrance to the airport; they sat with their feet on desks and spat tobacco and were reputed to be the toughest Amazons ever known this side of Scythia.

Great Falls itself is dominated by two things, (*a*) the huge smokestack of Anaconda's copper reduction plant, and (*b*) O. S. Warden. The smokestack, 512 feet high, was built by the old Amalgamated Copper Company; when dedicated in the 1890's a fifty-foot-square platform was set on top, and a community dance held thereon.[6] Mr. Warden, who was born in New Hampshire, is publisher of the Great Falls *Tribune* and *Leader*, which with the Lewistown *Democrat-News*, are among the very few papers in the state not controlled bag and barrel by Anaconda. Mr. Warden is eighty-two years old, and the first vote he ever cast was for Benjamin Harrison. Last year he attended his fifty-fifth reunion at Dartmouth, and enrolled as a future student there—his three-year-old son! More about Mr. Warden later.

I flew back to Helena, on what was very nearly the roughest trip I ever made in an airplane, and then Judge Johnson drove me down to Butte. The road follows the very lip of the divide; we were crawling right down the vertebrae of America. We passed an old mining town called Basin, and another town that has thirteen lawyers and fourteen saloons, and a pleasant ranch fed by hot springs in Boulder. We looked at a horse farm that produces dog meat, Korean lettuce growers, and a house about four feet by six or so it seems, where an Italo-Swiss family has nineteen children. Once or twice we stopped to inspect the historical markers, and I copied the text of several. These are located all over the state, and are uniquely flavorsome. Robert H. Fletcher, formerly of the state highway department, now of the Montana Power Company, did the writing. Here is No. 64, a little south of Helena:

> Time was when ox and mule teams used to freight along this route. A 5-ton truck doesn't look as picturesque but there hasn't been much change in the language of the drivers.

[6] Another famous Montana smokestack, also an Anaconda property, is in the town of Anaconda. I was told that the Washington Monument would fit inside it. I am not sure I believe this. It was built so high in order to carry poisonous fumes out of the immediate vicinity. The scheme did not work as well as expected and much vegetation in the area was killed.

Jerk line skinners were plumb fluent when addressing their teams. They got right earnest and personal. It was spontaneous—no effort about it. When they got strung out they were worth going a long way to hear. As a matter of fact you didn't have to go a long way, provided your hearing was normal. . . .

Those times have gone forever.

Perhaps I may quote a few more passages from Mr. Fletcher:[7] From Marker No. 7 on US 2:

Kid Curry's stomping ground in the '80's was the Little Rockies country about forty miles southwest of here. July 3rd, 1901, he pulled off a premature Independence Day celebration by holding up the Great Northern No. 3 passenger train and blowing the express car safe near this point. His departure was plumb hasty. The Great Northern would still probably like to know where he is holed up.

From No. 9 at Chinook, called The Battle of the Bear's Paw:

This battle was fought in October, 1877 on Snake Creek about 20 miles south of here near the Bear's Paw mountains, where after a three days' siege Chief Joseph, leader of the Nez Percé Indians, surrendered to Col. Nelson A. Miles of the U.S. Army.

This greatest of Indian generals fought against fearful odds. He and his warriors could have escaped by abandoning their women, children and wounded. They refused to do this.

His courage and fairness were admired by Col. Miles who promised him safe return to Idaho. One of the blackest records in our dealings with the Indians was the Government's repudiation of this promise and the subsequent treatment accorded Joseph and his followers.

From No. 11 on US 2 west of Chester:

You can see the Sweet Grass Hills or the Three Buttes to the north of here on a reasonably clear day. Things sure grow in this country. Some old timers claim that when they arrived those buttes weren't much bigger than prairie dog mounds. . . .

The pay dirt has been pretty well worked out and the glamour of boom days is gone, but a few old timers still prospect the gulches, hoping some day to find that elusive pot of gold at the rainbow's end, called the Mother Lode.

From No. 25 at Pompey's Pillar:

Captain Wm. Clark, of the Lewis and Clark Expedition, stopped here July 5, 1806 on his way down the Yellowstone. He wrote in his journal that the rock was . . . "200 feet high and 400 paces in secumpherance and only axcessable on one side. . . . The natives have ingraved on the face of this rock the figures of animals, etc."

[7] The complete set has been printed, *Montana Highway Historical Markers,* by Bob Fletcher, Helena, 1938. Used here by Mr. Fletcher's kind permission.

The signature is still there. Only fools destroy, but it had to be protected from vandals by a steel screen erected by the Northern Pacific Railway Co.

From No. 31 at Gallatin Valley:

. . . In the early '60's John Bozeman, young adventurer, and Jim Bridger, grand old man of the mountains, guided rival wagon trains of emigrants and gold seekers through here over the variously called Bonanza Trail, Bridger Cut-off, or Bozeman Road, from Fort Laramie, Wyoming, to Virginia City, Montana. The trail crossed Indian country in direct violation of treaty and was a "cut-off" used by impatient pioneers who considered the time saving worth the danger.

Traffic was not congested.

From No. 59 at Bannack:

. . . Henry Plummer, sheriff and secret chief of the road agents, was hanged at Bannack in '64 by the Vigilantes. It tamed him down considerably.

After this I don't quite know how to bring Montana up to date except by quoting from something very different. Visitors from abroad may not realize it, but an American characteristic never to be ignored is the capacity of medium-sized towns to flaunt their glories, and in particular to choose glories that would puzzle citizens of Rouen, say, Perugia, or Innsbruck. The chief ammunition is statistics. These are taken with deadly earnestness. They are no laughing matter. Consider the Montana town of Billings. Here is some material from a brochure put out by its Commercial Club. I am quoting not more than a fiftieth of what it contains, and my only excuse for using even this much is that it is so typical of a thousand other American communities, their habit of mind and approach to the world outside:

Climate: Billings climate is marked by an abundance of sunshine. Tornadoes are unknown. Frost-free period is 131 days.

Churches: Eighteen denominations maintain twenty-eight churches in Billings.

Golf courses: four.

Homes: More than 450 commercial travellers make Billings their home.

Children under 21 years: 10,105.

Electric meters (resident): 7,280. Residential rate: 1st 12 kw— 7.5¢; next 48 kw—4.5¢; next 90 kw—3¢; next 100 kw—2¢.

Water meters: 6,078.

Postal receipts: $302,694.50.

Bank deposits (3 banks): $16,098,635.46.

Taxes: The property tax of 92.60 mills is based on one-third of true valuation.

Value livestock: $10,414,394.00.

Field crops produced annually in Billings trade area—Wheat: 7,809,230 bushels.

Wholesale trade—75 establishments, 839 employes, total annual payroll $1,312,000, population served in primary area, 167,721.

A far cry from Bozeman, Bridger, and Sitting Bull!

"Butte Is the Black Heart of Montana"

This is the toughest, bawdiest town in America, with the possible exception of Amarillo, Texas. Also it is something that Amarillo is not, and something so singular that the shock persists long after a visit—a town almost literally dying on its feet.

Butte, "a mile high, a mile deep," built on the "richest hill on earth," and generally described as the greatest mining camp ever known, lies in a ragged and bleached cup of hills on a spur of the divide. By night it has a certain infernolike magnificence, with lights appropriately copper colored—I heard it called "the only electric-lit cemetery in the United States." By day it is one of the ugliest places I have ever seen. The mine dumps, heaps of slag that nobody removes, line the hills; there is hardly any vegetation, since fumes from open hearth smelting in the old days seared and poisoned the living green; the frowsy streets are faced with slovenly and dilapidated ancient tenements. Butte is of course the central pivot of Anaconda. The gallows frames show where the mines are, and underneath are not less than 2,700 miles of winzes, shafts, and tunnels; the town sits crazily on a shaky and sagging crust of ore; underground practically every other cubic inch is metal.

For the romance of Butte, for its extraordinarily naked and colorful history—if you like your colors raw—I can only recommend *Copper Camp*, a book compiled by writers of the Works Projects Administration and sponsored by the Montana State Department of Agriculture, Labor, and Industry.[8] This is riproaring folklore at its best; I know few books with such a concentration of lusty anecdote. It will tell you of such "sporting" events as fights between bull and bear, and between dog and wolf; of fantastic feats in hard drinking and gambling and of the girls in the prostitutes' line with the silver dollars so heavy in their stockings that the metal would spill out into the street; of suburbs called Seldom Seen and saloons named Graveyard, Frozen In, and Cesspool; of a judge nicknamed "Long Distance Mike" because of his severe sentences, and a Jewish expressman who called his horse Jesus Christ; of Cornish pie for breakfast and one splendid barman who, when a guileless and upright visitor asked for a glass of milk, replied, "Do you see any room in here for a ——— cow?"

[8] Hastings House, New York, 1943.

The Butte of today demands a different kind of attention. It is one of the few cities in the country with no housing shortage. As of 1946 there were 3,400 houses, apartments, and offices absolutely empty. That gallant veteran, Lowndes Maury, took me for a walk. I looked at a gaunt empty structure in the middle of town started thirty years ago, and never finished. Next door is a building, once a hotel, with half the windows out and swarming with pigeons. Judge Maury suggested that the owner might at least knock out the rest of the windows and let the pigeons all the way in. I walked down Main Street, and in two blocks counted fourteen places of business shut. Whole neighborhoods are mouldy, whole streets are rotten and decaying. Anaconda a few years ago employed about seven thousand men underground; the figure now is 2,400. Then, along dingy streets, with broken curbs and half the houses cracked and tottering, Mr. Maury showed me the phenomenon known as a "step crack." This is the crooked line in a wall, following the bricks, that bulges open as the houses begin to decompose; the cracks grow as a building slowly subsides, having been undermined by the tunnels and mine shafts below. I looked at streets sagging and buckled in the center, at abandoned tenements where the windows had caved in as a result of pressure from the bending walls. One strip in the southwestern part of Butte, 600 feet wide and a mile long, has been so solidly undermined that the whole area is in danger of collapsing. Occasionally some luckless house owner, as he sees his home begin to disintegrate, dares to sue the "Company." Judge Maury likes to take on these suits, and generally a settlement is reached, because the defendants know he will fight to the end—though I also heard from another source that no jury in Silver Bow County in forty years has ever dared to return a verdict against the mines.

Butte has a long history as a labor town; the Butte Miners Union, organized in 1881, is one of the historic unions of the country; it was for many years Local No. 1 of the Western Federation of Miners under Big Bill Haywood; it is still Local No. 1 of the International Union of Mine, Mill, and Smelter Workers, CIO. The miners today, called "muckers," take pride in trying to keep their homes clean, educating their children decently, and playing a progressive role in the community. They have a good many complaints. They work underground for eight and a half hours a day, without a hot lunch; there is no central hiring hall though all the mines belong to or are operated under lease by the same company—a man out of work has to "rustle" from mine to mine; the work is hot, arduous, and dangerous; accidents are common, and equitable compensation hard to get. The union headquarters is a remarkably picturesque old building, once the property of the Silver Bow Club, a haunt of millionaires. In April, 1946, after going through the war years without a single strike, Butte exploded in a much-pub-

licized riot, the origins of which are obscure in the extreme. Two
thousand miners struck; mobs ostensibly led by infuriated workers
attacked the homes of a handful of company salaried employees who
were working as maintenance men. But the Miners Union disavowed
responsibility for the violence, and supplied deputies to the sheriff.
Within three days the trouble had blown over.

Butte has the craziest frontiers of any American city. "The city
limits," Joseph Kinsey Howard recounts in *Montana, High, Wide, and
Handsome*,[9] one of the best books about an American state ever written,
"defy every rule of logic or elementary draftsmanship because they dodge
nearly all the mines; the boundary will run straight as a die to a mine
fence, then swerve neatly around it, leaving the mine property happily
exempt from city taxation." One important street is, believe it or not,
technically part of Butte on one side but not on the other—so that some
railway property is tax exempt. The mines beneath Butte have yielded
more than two and one-half billion dollars worth of ore so far. But it is
the only American city I have ever seen with no decent park or playground. The population today is estimated at 31,000. But there are
40,000 cadavers in the cemeteries, making it one of the few towns on
earth with more people dead than alive.

No word on Butte, no matter how brief, can be complete without
mention of its more flamboyant side. It is not quite so wide open as
Reno or Las Vegas but almost. It still has a prostitutes' "line"; Mercury
Street—of all odd names!—is where the cribs are. But so many pretty
and businesslike maidens deserted Butte to become riveters in Seattle
that, when I was there, citizens complained bitterly about the "girl
power shortage." The bars are preposterous and prodigious. I saw
grandmothers teaching six-year-old kids to play slot machines. And—if
only to prove once more that America is a capriciously variegated country—two miles from Butte, in the suburb of Meaderville, is one of the
best restaurants in the United States. Here, under the very shadow of
the gallows frames and with the dollar slot machines making a splendid
clink, coatless miners buy Lucullan meals. I don't mean to sound un-
gracious, however. I will never forget Mr. Teddy Traparish and his
Rocky Mountain Cafe. The steaks are seven inches thick, and cover
half an acre.

I thought I had an interesting and moderately original idea when
visiting Butte, that of the seemingly inextricable connection between
mining as a trade with gambling and high-life generally. But I found
that that canny Scot, James Bryce, had evolved a theory about this
fifty years ago. His language is, as always, a wonderful exercise in the
staid:

[9] Yale University Press, 1943, p. 96. Reprinted by permission.

The wildness of that time passed into the blood of the people, and has left them more tolerant of violent deeds, more prone to interferences with, or supersessions of, regular law, than are the people in most parts of the Union. . . . The chief occupation was mining, an industry which is like gambling in its influence on the character, with its sudden alterations of wealth and poverty, its long hours of painful toil relieved by bouts of drinking and merriment, its life in a crowd of men who have come together from the four winds of heaven, and will scatter again as soon as some are enriched and others ruined, or the gold in the gulch is exhausted.

The American Commonwealth, II, pp. 425-6

A more modern explanation is, of course, that mining is dangerous and ill-paid work, and to keep any men underground at all, the companies deliberately encourage escapism in the form of good liquor, pretty girls, and gambling. Also, if means are provided whereby a man's wages are quickly snapped away, it won't be so easy for him to quit and get a better job.

I found two eye-opening drinks in Montana that I had never seen before. A Black Spider is a combination of rum, Coca-Cola, and creme de menthe. A Presbyterian is bourbon, gingerale and dry soda. Nor had I ever heard a short Scotch described as a Gazooni, or bourbon and water as a Ditch High.

Attached to all this is the familiar American hypocrisy about prohibition, gambling, and the like. In theory gambling is "illegal" in Montana, except for penny-ante card games and licensed slot machines operated by fraternal organizations. But here is an advertisement I ran across in a local paper:

DOING BEST BUSINESS IN TOWN, BAR and cafe, good beer stock, fair stock of whisky. Includes roulette wheel, crap, twenty-one and poker tables, also five, ten, twenty-five cent slots. $5,000. Box F-79, Standard.

But now we must turn to something else, a massive factor in the politics and economy of Montana, the Anaconda Copper Mining Company or ACM or just the "Company" for short.

The Sixth Floor

Rocks rich in gems, and mountains big with mines,
Whence many a bursting stream auriferous plays.
—James Thomson, *The Seasons*

The *Encyclopaedia Britannica* puts it quite succinctly:

ANACONDA COPPER MINING COMPANY . . . the world's premier company in the non-ferrous metal industry . . . controls the annual production of more than 1,000,000,000 lbs. of copper, 500,000,000 lbs. of zinc, 150,000,000 lbs. of lead, and more than 5 per cent of the world production of silver. In addition to almost the entire ownership of the Butte (Montana) mining district, it has large investments in fifteen other American states, as well as in Canada, Mexico, and Chile. It is also a large producer of lumber, coal, gold, arsenic, sulphuric acid, superphosphate, zinc oxide, and white lead, and has a large custom smelting and refining business, with plants at Anaconda and Great Falls, Montana; Tooele, Utah; Miami, Arizona; East Chicago, Indiana; and Perth Amboy, N. J. Through its ownership of the American Brass Company and its equity in Anaconda Wire and Cable Company, it is the world's largest user of copper and manufacturer of copper and brass products, with plants located in California, Connecticut, Illinois, Michigan, Montana, New York, Rhode Island, and Toronto, Canada.

Among the principal subsidiary and associated companies of Anaconda Copper Mining Co. are: American Brass Company and subsidiaries; Andes Copper Mining Company; Arizona Oil Company; Butte, Anaconda, and Pacific Railway Company; Butte Water Company; Chile Copper Co. and subsidiary companies; International Smelting and Refining Company . . . [Nine other subsidiaries are named.] In 1939 the outstanding capital stock was $443,716,900, and the total assets $587,932,841. The net income was $20,236,552, and the surplus for the year, $7,518,600.

All that the *Britannica* does not say is that for many years Anaconda also ran Montana. So now for the first time in these pages we confront one of the most typical of all American phenomena, one that differentiates this country in degree if not kind from any other—the giant agglutinative corporation.

Anaconda has several distinctions aside from size. It is probably the most secretive of great American corporations, and, as may be discerned from the quotation above, it is one of the few that, like some peculiar creatures in zoology, competes with itself—it mines raw copper, smelts and refines it, fabricates it, sells it; Anaconda is both one of the largest producers of copper in the world and one of the largest consumers; it uses more than it can mine itself; it drinks in copper from everywhere, and sweats it out like some monstrous fountain.

Its history, being inextricably commingled with that of Butte, is studded and spangled with violence and robust color. Everybody has heard something of the "War of the Copper Kings." First came William A. Clark, of Scots origin, and a savage and magnetic Irishman named Marcus Daly; at that time, in the 1880's, the Butte gulches were supposed to contain only gold and silver, which gave out, whereupon Daly struck deeper and found copper; Clark, one of the most tidily ruthless men who ever lived, busied himself bribing his way to the federal Senate, and Daly created Anaconda. One of his partners was the father of William Randolph Hearst. Then money from the East came in, in part from the Rockefellers, and a new corporation called Amalgamated was formed. Clark and Daly became fantastically bitter enemies. Money came from abroad too; one of the largest single stockholders in Anaconda to this day is a Dutch consortium of which Queen Wilhelmina is supposed to be a member. Wealth incalculable depended on conflicting mine sites, and something known as the "law of apex" came to be adopted; this meant, in brief, that whoever owned the apex of a vein owned all the rest of the vein, no matter where it led underground. (A similar principle, as we know, exists in the petroleum industry.) Inevitably the murderous fight for copper involved everything else in Montana since, first, rival magnates sought to control the courts (Butte for a time had more lawyers than any other city of its size in the world), and then the legislature. At the turn of the century a brilliant and dashing young engineer, F. Augustus Heinze, of partly German blood, "hijacked" both Clark and Daly. He bought judges right and left, harangued vast crowds from the steps of the courthouse, howled against the absentee "kerosene interests" (Standard Oil), sued Amalgamated for 100 million dollars worth of claims, and left Montana in 1906 with a fortune estimated at 50 million dollars. Seldom has financial history known a more muscular and successful raid. Heinze became the miners' hero; once when he returned to Butte briefly a crowd of twenty thousand people met him at the station. Meantime Daly died and Clark sold out his interests. The interrelations between these grotesque potentates is as complex as that of the Holy Roman emperors after Diocletian. Presently Amalgamated, which had swallowed Anaconda, was in turn swallowed by Anaconda which revived. Then an Irishman who had been a department store clerk, John D. Ryan, succeeded Daly, and ran Anaconda singlehanded until his own death in 1933. Ryan may be judged from the fact that he once bought a power site for $950,000 from the Chicago, Milwaukee, and St. Paul Railroad, and sold it three months later to the Montana Power Company for $5,000,000—while he was a director of both companies![10]

Anaconda today is headed by Cornelius F. Kelley, a seventy-one-year-old Nevadan who was Ryan's lawyer and associate for many years. Kelley is plump, cold, and able. His salary is believed to be around $175,000 a year, a janitor's wage by Hollywood standards, but still a tidy sum. The only Anaconda man I talked to was one of his underlings, a man so smooth, so glossily defensive, that he resembled soap. One remarkable thing is that the "Company" has no building of its own in Butte; instead, it hires the upper reaches of a department store

[10] Cf. "The Montana Twins in Trouble," by Joseph Kinsey Howard, *Harper's Magazine*, September, 1944.

called Hennessey's. Thus a familiar euphemism for the company—the "Sixth Floor."

Anaconda has a number of large black automobiles, with low-numbered license plates; bystanders say "The Company's out!" much as they might say "The elephants are loose!" when these leave the Hennessey building for unknown destinations. When the legislature meets, "somebody"—though it isn't always easy to define just who the "somebody" is—takes a floor in a Helena hotel, and fills it with amiable opportunities for diversion. The days of "coming in through the transom" are no more, i.e., the habit of dropping bills "surreptitiously" into a hotel room; but bribery knows other means. One Montana lobbyist boasted recently, "Give me a case of Scotch, a case of gin, one blonde, and one brunette, and I can take any liberal!" Labor folk, fearful of the effect of such Babylonian temptation on human nature, sometimes hire agents to keep an eye on their own men; once they get seduced into going upstairs, they're lost.

Generally, on the Montana level, the company is criticized on a number of scores. *First,* incomparable and monumental stinginess. Aside from one threadbare little park (which it acquired from Clark), it has never given the city of Butte, from which it has extracted a roaring Golconda of wealth, anything.

Second, politics. For years the company dominated both parties, and controlled almost all elections, if necessary by dragging in the "cemetery vote," and a common saying is that it "has only lost one governorship since statehood"; a good Republican named Dixon was elected in 1920 (against Wheeler) but he was duly defeated the next time he ran. Above all, the company wants to be sure of what a new governor will veto—in case some undisciplined legislators break loose with legislation it doesn't like. Even today, there is no secret in the legislature as to who are "Company men." They maneuver first to elect the speaker, then to control membership of the committees, especially those that have to do with public development, hydroelectric power, and taxes.

Third, an extreme vindictiveness, extending from the highest categories to the lowest. Anaconda, so they say, stops at nothing. For instance a distinguished justice of the state supreme court, initially viewed by the company without disfavor, was unmercifully smeared later and all but driven from the bench, purely because he had once had an accidental association with Leif Erickson, a political candidate whom the company loathed; the better to try to "get" Erickson, the company sacrificed the judge. Or take Lowndes Maury whom I have mentioned above. Thirty-five years ago he was a lawyer for the Montana Power Company. Maury today is a stanch proponent of MVA (Missouri Valley Authority) which the Sixth Floor bitterly opposes. So a whispering campaign began to the effect that Maury, in his advocacy of MVA, must be "insincere," because he was once an official of the power concern! Or drop to lower echelons. A miner succeeded recently in getting compensation for an injury after a long legal fight; he then got a job on one of the local railroads; after three months, the arm of the company reached out, and the railroad was asked to get rid of him. Two years ago the subsurface tunnels undermined a schoolhouse in Butte. The building began to break apart and had to be abandoned, after condemnation by the authorities. The company sought to get release from damages, and then offered new land in exchange for the old site—whereupon the new site was discovered to be as dangerously undermined as the other. Finally a cash settlement was made.

Fourth, a defeatist atmosphere. For several ills in Montana, Anaconda is not to blame; yet its hand has lain so heavily on the state for so long that, if a cat sneezes, it gets the blame. So there is a general stultification, even if the ACM itself is not responsible. Progressive people do not do things they might easily succeed in doing, out of fear of the company, though its permission is no longer necessary. Also suspicion and apprehension make for a general deterioration of personal relationships; not only is everybody afraid of the company, but the company is afraid too. Sometimes the euphemisms it encourages are a boomerang. An extremely reputable eastern newspaper did an article recently on labor relations in Montana without ever mentioning Anaconda by name; it referred merely to "Butte management," which is a really signal triumph in evasion. But the net result was to make everybody in Montana laugh with the kind of laughter that burps at the edge. Some youngsters in Butte, including several in "Company" employ, let off steam by a happy derisiveness. "Well, well," they will say, "our company got licked in the last election. It is one of the worst insults ever known to have been suffered by our company."

To all this Anaconda officials themselves reply that they want to be fair, that they don't "play politics," and that they are obliged to do a lot of things they don't like in self-protection against the "radicals."

Fifth, the company is blamed in part for depopulizing the state, because it keeps new industry out. Anaconda wants no rivals in the labor market; it wants a pool of cheap labor all its own, with itself the only hiring agency. It opposes power developments on the rivers, partly out of fear that some such company as Alcoa might come in with aluminum plants. One great airplane concern thought briefly of starting a factory in Montana, according to local report; it took one look on the spot, and then got out, because of the "legislative pressure" that might work against it. Then, too, by controlling the smelters and manpower distribution, Anaconda can throttle any independent miners; also virgin territory that might yield great mineral wealth, much of it owned by ACM but not worked, remains untapped. Also in this general economic field, so obviously that it scarcely needs mention, is the fact that Anaconda takes out of Montana enormously more wealth than it puts in.

Sixth, the newspapers. The situation is unique in America. Of the fourteen dailies in the state seven are company owned or controlled; in four of the five chief cities, the company dailies are the only papers. Why the company thinks that such an antediluvian tactic as ownership of its own newspapers is a good idea remains a mystery to most experts in public opinion; it derives straight from the Daly-Ryan tradition of holding close to the chest everything they could get; but Ryan himself once told an independent editor, "You know, it's a kind of advantage that you're not on our pay roll, after all, because if *you* print something good about us, people believe it!" As to circulation the company papers run behind; for instance Mr. Warden's independent Great Falls *Tribune* has 27,000 in a town of 35,000; the company paper in Butte, the *Montana Standard*, has 16,000 in a town of 31,000. The Warden policy is quite simple. He rarely opposes the company directly; he prints the news. Anaconda knows that he cannot be bullied, bought, or frightened off; it also knows that he will oppose equally anything unjust to Anaconda, and anything unjust that Anaconda does. The company could ruin Warden and drive him out of the state, but it would cost a tremendous amount of money and no end of scandal—and he has told them so. As to the company press itself it does its best to appear "unslanted." But nobody is fooled. One company paper refused in the 1944 campaign to accept a paid advertisement for Erickson which said simply that Erickson was not a "Communist" and, far from being a newcomer as had been charged, had lived in Montana for twenty years. Another recently devoted its whole front page to an attack against the Columbia Valley Authority, which until then most local people had never heard of. The *Independent-Record* in Helena ordinarily uses the appellation "Mr." before the name of only one American—Cornelius F. Kelley. Its staff thinks, however, that a prevailing situation should be equalized by using "Mr." in front of God too, when God is mentioned.

Of course there is plenty that the company press does its best not to print. For instance in New York early in 1946 the Anaconda Wire and Cable Company settled for $1,626,000 a claim of the United States government for damages "based on charges that three Anaconda plants shipped untested wire and cable to American and British armed forces." (New York *Herald Tribune*, March 1, 1946.) Previously, officials and employees in Anaconda Wire and Cable factories in Marion, Indiana, and Pawtucket, Rhode Island, had been tried and convicted on criminal charges "for conspiring to defraud the government" and of delivering inferior wire. Both plants were fined ten thousand dollars; five employees at Marion got suspended sentences, and four Pawtucket officials went to jail. On this wire, American soldiers in the field depended for their lives.

But Anaconda Wire and Cable underlings used the most elaborate and intricate methods to deceive government inspectors as to its quality, even installing checking machines that were themselves fraudulent. The judge hearing one case said that "the company perpetrated these frauds with intent to increase their profits without regard to the lives of American boys." All this is a matter of public record: former Senator Bone of Washington made a speech in Congress saying that "the men who did this dreadful thing would be lined up before a firing squad if they were in Germany or Russia." But you will not find much about it in most papers published in Montana.

Montana has four lively weeklies that do dare oppose the company. Their circulation and influence is, however, very limited. They are the *People's Voice* (Helena), the *Western News* (Hamilton), the *Yellowstone* (Billings), and the *Montana Labor News* (Butte).

Seventh, education. Like most corporations, the ACM works hard to keep taxes down; this of course means that less money is available for the schools; the pattern is familiar everywhere, and is not peculiar to Anaconda or Montana. But another aspect merits attention, the curious fact that the University of Montana exists in six units in six different localities, though it is all the same organism and institution. The state university (with a justly famous school of journalism) is at Missoula, the state college is at Bozeman, the school of mines is at Butte, the state normal college is at Dillon, the Eastern Montana Normal is at Billings, and Northern Montana College is at Havre. All these have separate budgets and separate legislative appropriations, and the students and faculty are not interchangeable. Dr. E. O. Melby, the former chancellor of the university as a whole, thought that such chaotic irrationality might be modified, and suggested in 1945 that at least the six budgets be consolidated. One anomaly was that Dillon had exactly twenty-two students while the rest of the state was crying for teachers. But Melby was defeated; he resigned (and is now dean of the school of education at New York University) together with several of his professors. The legislature insisted on retaining the old six-way system, in part because a university in six parts makes for good lobbying. A lobbyist could always go to a legislator from Dillon, say, and promise some improvement to that particular community, in exchange for support of a company bill that might be coming up.

We must mention now the Montana Power Company, the great utility closely tied up with Anaconda—so closely that the term "Company" is often used to embrace the two together. Montana Power was founded by John D. Ryan, and for many years he was president of both; now, however, though allied, the two corporations are separate entities. But one Montana Power director recently became counsel for Anaconda, and until recently when Bob Fletcher took the job, the same man, by name Charles Towne, was press agent for both companies. Also Anaconda is Montana Power's biggest customer by far; the two have an inevitable community of interest. As the association has worked out, Montana Power—with officials and employees in scores of towns and villages—has become a kind of eyes and ears for the ACM. It maintains the listening posts out in the hinterland. And it reads every bill to come before the legislature with its own and Anaconda's interests intimately in mind—naturally. The history of Montana Power, one of the most formidable utility companies in the United States, cannot be dealt with in this space. The story is well told in the *Harper's* article cited above, "The Montana Twins in Trouble." That, for instance, Montana Power was forced recently by the SEC to divest itself of a hotel in Great Falls, owned by a subsidiary, is a detail almost microscopically small—but typical of its wide range of interests. When I was in Montana it was busy publishing advertisements in a dozen country weeklies, all with the same point—to make the idea of an MVA ridiculous by attacks on TVA. Then too, but this is on a minor level and I'm not sure but what company haters may not have been overusing their imaginations, I heard about the connection between Montana Power and, of all things, Lewis and Clark! The one hundred and fortieth anniversary of the Lewis and Clark expedition was being celebrated by a relay of Boy Scouts carrying a pouch along their trail; the American Pioneer Trails Association in New York, of which Cornelius F. Kelley (no less) is a director, was a prime mover in the celebration, and Anaconda men toured the state to help mark the route. This was interpreted widely as a company "plot" to build political fences, win good will, and incidentally spread propaganda against MVA. Anyway the episode produced a joke. People were baffled by ACM's sudden interest in the two explorers, and it was said that at last Anaconda had got around to organizing Montana on a "Lewis and Clark basis."

A matter much more serious is rural electrification. Montana boils with streams; the power company has been there since 1912; but in 1935 only 5.5 per cent of farms in the state had central station electric service. The figure is up to 27.8 per cent now, but this is largely because the Rural Electrification Administration has financed a number of co-operatives roughly like the Public Utility Districts in Washington. Before the REA came in, farmers in isolated areas were helpless, because the charges to bring private power in were inordinately prohibitive. Let us point out, however, that this kind of exorbitance is not peculiar to Montana. I have friends in that small superstate Vermont, who although only a few miles from sizable towns had to build and pay for their own power lines because the local utilities refused to do so except at fantastic cost.

Finally we should at least barely mention two other great economic factors in the life of Montana, which in general follow the same line as the company. First, the livestock men. They are the biggest source of revenue the state has; they are even more conspicuous in the legislature than Anaconda. Second, the railroads. The Northern Pacific got from Congress in 1864—free!—every other section of land along its line for seven hundred miles in Montana; this amounted to some twenty-three thousand square miles (an area three times bigger than New Jersey); and naturally the railroad laid its route to tap as much valuable land as possible. The Great Northern, by contrast, is not and never was a land grant railroad; it was built by Jim Hill without public aid and Hill is almost as legendary a hero in Montana as in Minnesota and the Dakotas. The Milwaukee Road came later. It was deeply involved in the later stages of the copper wars and, once, on the steps of the Butte railway station, was sold at auction in half an hour for 140 million dollars. The Milwaukee is electrified for four hundred miles of its Montana run, and hence is a very substantial customer of Montana Power.

Now to conclude this section. No one can possibly underestimate the importance of Anaconda in Montana affairs, yet it would be a gross error to think that the company is unopposed. From a paper called the *Montana Builder* I take the following: "Mr. Cornelius Kelley, members of the board of A.C.M., the handwriting is on the wall. Get rid of these cheap gangsters who befoul the halls of our state capitol." And much else appears in similar overt vein. Nor should it be forgotten that, in the last analysis, the bulk and rank and file of *people* in the United States count as well as corporations. Anaconda and Montana Power are important in Montana—yes. Nevertheless a progressive like Thomas J. Walsh was a Montana senator for years; at present the Montana delegation in Washington includes such authentic and vivid liberals as Senator James E. Murray and Representative Mike Mansfield; and in the summer of 1946, Leif Erickson beat Wheeler for nomination to the Senate, though he was himself beaten in the general election following.

On Certain Confusions in the Life of
Burton K. Wheeler

I don't mean to claim wisdom after the event, but I thought that Wheeler was a spent force considerably before his defeat for renomination to the Senate. In Washington earlier in the year he seemed to have lost grip—always garrulous, with his big cruel mouth chewing at a thin cigar, he was talkative to the point where his conversation became interminable anecdotage; he seemed to have descended to a level where it was almost inconceivable that he could ever have had a coherent intellectual background or philosophy.

There is nothing morally wrong about being an isolationist. Thousands of good Americans—normally intelligent and sincere Americans—are isolationists. Isolationists may have been witless, or improperly tuned to the march of events and the shrinkage of the hemispheres, or victims of laziness or wishful thinking, but they were not criminals. They represented one wing of a perfectly authentic American tradition (as we shall see later on when we come to the Middle West) and there are, even now, a great many earnest and peace-loving Americans with full internationalist sympathies who would be delighted to be isolationists— if the world would only let this be possible. The trouble with Wheeler was that he was the serf, the helpless victim of obsession. He saw an "international banker" under every cot; he thought that England was Sodom and Gomorrah, and he hated one man, Franklin D. Roosevelt, with a fierce, fixed, vituperative and vindictive passion.

I am not even sure how Wheeler came to his isolationism. He was, and is, a politician first and last. Perhaps subconsciously, he was grasping for an issue. In the autumn of 1939, Roosevelt appealed for modification of the Neutrality Act to permit the sale of arms to the allies on a cash-and-carry basis. FDR's speech was muddled and specious but nobody in the Senate had ability enough to oppose him, Wheeler alone excepted. Borah was ill and tired, Hiram Johnson had galloping senility, and Nye simply lacked the stature necessary. Wheeler had tasted the sweet blood of leadership when he fought Roosevelt—and beat him to a standstill—in the Court Packing bill two years before. So he took charge of the isolationist "crusade," and from then on events continually and progressively boxed him into more uncomfortable and tighter corners. I think also that a second point contributed early in the war to Wheeler's isolationism, namely that he thought, like Lindbergh, that Germany would win and he wanted to play the winning side. Third, he was profoundly influenced by his wife, who hates the British empire even more than he does.

Thus arose some of the dreadful intellectual confusions. In the 20's Wheeler pleaded earnestly for recognition of Russia by the U.S.[11] In the 40's he was a passionate Russia hater. In 1939 he thought that the German invasion of Poland couldn't be helped, and urged that Poland should give up Silesia and the Corridor to avoid a fight. In 1945 he was one of the loudest to urge that Poland should be encouraged to resist Russian aggression at all costs. He fought Lend Lease—saying that "it would plow under every fourth American boy"—and voted against almost every measure that might have strengthened the United States, and then, immediately after the war was over, attacked American policy for its "weakness." No matter how he slid and slithered, he came to the

[11] President Coolidge asked him on his return from a trip to Moscow, "Is it true that the Russians haven't got religion?" Wheeler replied, "For a long time they had too much of the wrong kind."

fate that sooner or later overtook almost all isolationists; willy-nilly he was forced into a position of seeming to be pro-German.

Consider too the bad company he got in. Stacks of America First mail, franked with his stamp, were found in George Sylvester Viereck's office. Every Fascist and sub-Fascist sheet in the country called him a hero from Father Coughlin's *Social Justice* to the *Weekly Roll Call* of William D. Pelley, the Silver Shirt leader who later went to jail for sedition; from Gerald B. Winrod's *Defender* to Gerald L. K. Smith's *Cross and Flag* to official organs of the Nazi Bund. In order to beat a left-wing Montana congressman, Jerry O'Connell, Wheeler once supported and helped elect a man named Thorkelson, now dead, who was the most outspoken and poisonous anti-Semite ever to sit in the halls of Congress.

In his own defense Wheeler points out that it is unfair to call him "reactionary" or "anti-Semitic" just because he wanted to keep out of war. He told me that he was denouncing Hitler while "Lord Halifax was out shooting with him." He says that he can't help it if Gerald L. K. Smith quotes him; he claims to have nothing but contempt for Coughlin, Smith, and their rabble. Wheeler voted for ratification of the San Francisco charter—and at the same time publicly boasted that he would do everything in his power to water it down. In 1946 he demanded "that the United States quit appeasing Russia and let her know once and for all that we did not fight this war to let her enslave Europe." Well and good. But it is difficult not to rejoin, as did one newspaper, "Well, well, look who's talking!" For years Wheeler had put himself into the category of seeming to be a friend to enemies of the nation; his speeches during the war frankly encouraged the breakup of the allied coalition. That he should, with the war won, oppose appeasement of Russia is perfectly legitimate and reasonable. But it would come with better grace if he had not been the boss appeaser to both Germany and Japan in and after 1939.

Wheeler, the tenth child of a Quaker shoemaker, was born in Massachusetts in 1882. He went to the University of Michigan and then pushed further west to carve out a career as a lawyer. Legend is that he was passing through Butte, en route to Seattle, when he was stripped of every cent in a crooked poker game. He stayed in Butte of necessity, got a job in a law office, and has been a Montanan ever since. Now let there be no doubt of Wheeler's good liberal record in the early days. He was an agrarian progressive of the Norris-LaFollette type, and it seemed that he would rival them in good works and stature. He served in the state legislature for a time as a reform candidate and, then, through the influence of Senator Walsh, whose protégé he was, he became United States attorney. He kept his head during the witch-hunt days after World War I, and in 1920 ran for governor. Feeling against him ran so high that he was once threatened with tar-and-feathering, and once he was physically run out of a town. He was soundly beaten in this race for governor. Then in 1922 he ran for senator, and was elected—just as soundly.

This brings up the moot question of Wheeler's relations with the "Company." I do not think he has ever, as is often charged, been an Anaconda tool or puppet, though the company has certainly supported him on occasion. In 1920, however, it feared and hated him as a progressive and was in large measure responsible for his defeat. How, then, could he have won so handsomely just two years later? One factor was the hard times suddenly prevalent. Another, most Montanans say, is that the company recognized him as such an able and dangerous antagonist that it let him win the senatorship in order to push him out of the state. Then for years the two most conspicuous of Montana institutions watched each other warily. I do not think that the remark was printed at the time but Wheeler, campaigning in 1922, is supposed to have made a pledge, "If you ever see a picture of me on the front page of any company paper you will know I have sold out." Wheeler's own description to me of his position vis-à-vis Anaconda is that it had tried to "influence" him without success, that it always opposed him till 1934, and "then gave up because they knew it wouldn't do any good." He agreed, however, that for many years "nobody could be elected dog catcher in Montana without Sixth Floor support." His explanation, incidentally, of the remark about the picture in the paper is that he was referring, not to the company press, but to the Butte *Miner* which was then controlled by Senator W. A. Clark. Wheeler's actual words were, he says, "If I ever hear a good word about me from Clark, I'll search my own pockets to see what I've stolen."

Wheeler, company or no company, has always played a hard, close role in Montana politics. He has substantial business and real estate interests in the state, and he is believed to be part owner of the Z Bar Network, comprising radio stations in Helena, Butte, and Bozeman, and linked up with KFPY in Spokane. He sought to run both parties locally; he tried always to get both the conservative and liberal vote. He is, of course, a Democrat and the present governor, Sam C. Ford, is a Republican, but Ford is a good friend of Wheeler's and several key posts are held by Wheeler associates, like J. Burke Clements, chairman of the Industrial Accident Board, who was Wheeler's campaign manager for the 1940 presidential nomination, and Barclay Craighead, head of Unemployment Compensation, who was one of his Senate secretaries. Incidentally Clements is also a political commentator on Wheeler's Helena radio station, which is managed by another crony, Ed Craney who is a distinct power in state and municipal affairs.

In Washington, Wheeler started his senatorship with high promise.[12]

[12] By interesting coincidence Wheeler entered the Senate on the same day as Henrik Shipstead of Minnesota, and both were beaten at the same time twenty-three years later.

He led the fight to open up the Teapot Dome scandals, which got him into a peck of trouble. Harry M. Daugherty, Harding's attorney general, had him indicted before a federal court for allegedly using improper influence in arguing an oil lease case before the Department of the Interior; this was pure vindictive retaliation, a frameup. Wheeler was acquitted after the jury had been out ten minutes. His wife was about to have a baby; she said if necessary she would have it in the courtroom. In 1924, as everyone knows, Wheeler ran for vice president as a Progressive under old Bob LaFollette,[13] but he switched back from Progressive to Democrat and was handsomely re-elected senator in 1928. In the early Roosevelt days Wheeler was the administration's chief wheel horse in putting through the Holding Company Act regulating utilities, and he had a good deal to do with railroad and labor legislation. What caused his violent enmity to Roosevelt later? First, the fact that Wheeler, a desperately vain man, considered himself slighted by Roosevelt on Montana patronage; also, he had hoped to succeed Walsh as attorney general, but FDR passed him over for Homer Cummings of Connecticut. Second, the fight over packing the Supreme Court. But despite the fierceness of his enmity, Wheeler says that he "could have had the vice presidential nomination in 1940 if he had wanted it"; he even told me that, Roosevelt or no Roosevelt, he could, if he had wished, been vice president in 1944—which means that he would be president today.

In the summer of 1946 came catastrophe. Wheeler, like Shipstead and Nye, was knocked out in the most humiliating kind of political defeat, a primary race. The isolationist taint, plus much else, was too much to overcome. I have several times mentioned in this chapter the man who beat him for the nomination, Leif Erickson. Erickson was a former justice of the state supreme court, the president of the MVA Association, and a young, attractive, uncompromising liberal. Wheeler's enmity to MVA had something to do with the result, because it alienated the powerful Farmers Union; and Erickson had the prime asset so important everywhere in the Northwest of a Scandinavian name. Wheeler at first thought to split Erickson's vote by prevailing on some third candidate to run, but he couldn't find anybody. He blames his defeat on the Political Action Committee and the New York newspaper *PM*. But the PAC as such did not enter the campaign at all, and *PM* has a circulation in Montana of exactly forty-two! Wheeler lamented to me, "The Jewish press always kicks the — out of me." *PM* is of course owned and edited by such Jews as Marshall Field and Ralph McAllister Ingersoll. What did beat Wheeler was labor.[14] The Butte labor community

[13] While, as the *New Republic* once pointed out, FDR was supporting an extremely conservative Wall Street lawyer, John W. Davis.
[14] But it is quite true that a few eastern liberals contributed money—in small amounts—to Erickson's campaign.

turned against him almost to a man, and so—despite Truman's personal intervention—did the railway brotherhoods, which are extremely important in Montana, a state crossed by three great transcontinental lines.

Giant of Wheat

I met him in Washington, D.C., not on his own mammoth property at Hardin, Montana; he is one of the most interesting of all Montanans—Thomas C. Campbell, the greatest wheat farmer in the world.

Twice in his life Tom Campbell has had singular confrontations with singular men, the late J. P. Morgan and Joseph Stalin. He went to see Morgan, uninvited, during World War I when the Germans were making their great offensives in April, 1918; it was anticipated that the war would go through another winter, at least, and wheat was desperately short. Franklin K. Lane, then secretary of the Interior, sent Campbell out to Montana to see what he could do. He looked at millions of acres of land, some of it government property on Indian reservations, that might be made to grow wheat in spite of its aridity. But he needed money, which Washington wouldn't give him, to finance leases. So, without introduction and on his own hook, he called on Morgan. The interview lasted seven minutes, during which Morgan asked five questions: (*a*) How old are you? (*b*) Have you a university degree? (*c*) Have you had any experience in wheat production? (*d*) Do you intend to run the job yourself? (*e*) How much money do you need? The sum was two million dollars and Campbell got it the next day. He went back west, and organized the Montana Farming Corporation.

(Morgan never got the money back. Wheat dropped from $2.75 in 1919 to $1.05 in 1921, and Campbell had a hard time with his property. The younger Morgan partners wanted to get out of agriculture and some years later simply wrote the two million dollars off. Campbell himself was then able to buy back the same holdings, under the name Campbell Farming Corporation, for $100,000 cash and $500,000 worth of notes.)

Campbell met Stalin during the first Five Year Plan; he was the first American citizen, he says, whom Stalin ever received. The Russians had approached Campbell asking him to teach them how to make a mechanized farm work. At that time he thought that Bolsheviks ate babies for breakfast, and his friends were horrified that he should even consider accepting the invitation. But, fingers crossed, he went to Moscow and became a consulting engineer to the Soviet agricultural authorities; presently he was helping to build Gigant, the million-acre mechanized farm that was one of the chief Soviet showpieces before World War II. At first the Russians wanted to mechanize everything hand over fist, without pause or preparation; they wanted a tractor for every acre. Campbell persuaded them to go more slowly. He found that 90 per cent of the crops of the U.S.S.R. were planted and harvested with implements the Pharaohs might have used; there were 90 million horses in the country. Campbell said, "Let's use the horses for awhile, with modern *horse* machinery." But the Russians, eager folk, were disappointed by his caution. Stalin listened to the argument most of an evening, and then said, "Since we have hired this man, let us accept his advice." That decided it. Campbell was allowed to convert Russian agriculture to mechanization by easy stages, prudently. Later the tractors and combines duly began to pour in. Campbell likes to think now that this was a contribution to winning the war. The Russians, he told me, could not possibly have withstood the impact of the German invasion had they not had a dozen years of precious experience with agricultural machines. This gave them the background and mechanical know-how for handling tanks and military vehicles. His tractors near Odessa became, as it were, the tanks and armored cars of Stalingrad. What won the war was, in a word, mechanization of the peasantry.

Tom Campbell, a vigorous and friendly white-haired man of sixty-five, is of Scots and Canadian stock. His father, a lumberman living in Ontario, wanted to go west. This was before the railways, and the family went out in a wagon. They came up the Red River Valley, where the grass grew to the hub wheels, and Campbell's mother said, "This is fine soil, fine grass; let's stay right here." So, at a point near what is now Grand Forks, North Dakota, the group took root. Tom says today that his earliest memories are of resentment at the murderously hard physical labor his father and mother had to perform and at the age of eight, so he swears, his ambition was already set—to be the biggest wheat farmer in the country. Campbell was the first graduate of the mechanical engineering department of the University of North Dakota; then he went to Cornell for graduate work in engineering. He had a natural bent for mechanics, which it seemed logical to apply to agriculture. So he began to experiment with mechanization. Came World War I, and he moved from North Dakota to Hardin, Montana, about sixty miles from Billings, where he still is.

The Campbell properties today cover 95,000 acres; there is nothing more dramatic in the West than the manner of the cultivation, the method of the harvest. On soil that averages less than sixteen inches of rainfall per year, Campbell gets thirty-five bushels of wheat per acre. First, like all modern wheat farmers in this area, he conserves half his soil each year by planting in alternate strips and leaving the rest fallow. Second, by proper tillage and the use of an ingenious tool known as the rod-weeder, he keeps weeds down to a minimum, so that the soil, hoarding up precious moisture, has complete rest during its year's holiday.

Third, he seeds at a special "angle of repose," in rows far apart, as a precaution against wind erosion and winter freeze. One tractor carries an 84-foot-wide series of drills, which moving at three miles an hour can seed five hundred acres in a day—as against the half an acre a day which is the best hand labor can do. Seeding, of course, goes on by night as well as by day, just as do the harvests. August at Hardin, when the combine teams work all night, is almost as astonishing an example of American "industrialization" as, say, the mills near Pittsburgh. Campbell harvests an acre of wheat in fourteen man-minutes. He can run his whole immense establishment with a staff of twenty-five men. Even during the harvest he needs no more than 150.

One of Campbell's 120 horse power tractors can pull twelve fourteen-inch plows, which means that two men can plow seventy-five to eighty acres in twelve hours. Tell that to any grandfather who grew up in Iowa! This is, of course, agricultural mass production *in excelsis*. The earth itself becomes the assembly line.

Plenty of people dislike Campbell and his methods. He was accused in the 1930's of having caused the loss of millions of tons of topsoil, because he planted too much and too deep. The Farmers Union resents him sharply; he "works men two months a year, then drops them"; his method is "antisocial" and the concentration of many small farms into one big farm is "Fascistic"; he builds no schools, no communities. But Campbell himself is on several counts distinctly on the liberal side; of such confusions is American life full. I have no idea whether he is a Republican or a Democrat, but he says that the government has always been his best partner, and always will be; that the Department of Agriculture knows more about its subject and teaches it better than any university in the world; that Stalin was smart enough to have inaugurated a tolerable agriculture from the beginning, whereas we didn't get started right until the New Deal; and that every American depression has come because industry sought to buy agricultural produce as cheaply as possible with the result that the farmers who produced this had no money to buy the industrial stuff without the sale of which industry itself couldn't live.

Montana Miscellany

Montana is a great state for wild flowers (claiming more varieties than any other) and for prize fighters (Stanley Ketchell, Battling Nelson, Kid McCoy) and movie stars (Myrna Loy, Gary Cooper). It contains Glacier National Park, and the newspapers are full of advertisements of such commodities as LARIAT ROPE—TOP GRADE MANILA—6½¢ A FOOT. Though by no means rich it led the nation five times in five consecutive bond drives, as the first state to exceed its quota; and it is the chief state aside from California with a strong Vigilante past. Only fourteen out of its fifty-six counties have made soil surveys, and only 18 per cent of its land is owned by the farmers tilling it. Montana is the state where Indians call a divorce "splitting the blanket," where hogs once ate the automobile license plates which were made of ersatz material, and where fur-bearing fish have been photographed. Finally, it is the American state that, by far, has the greatest number of earthquakes. The Chamber of Commerce will not thank me for saying this, but there have been three thousand since 1935.

Chapter 12

MVA Versus Behemoth River

wwwwwwwwwwwwwwwwwwwwwwwwwwwwwwwwwwwwwwwwwwwwwwwwwwwwwwwwwwwwwwwwwww

> Creation of a Missouri Valley Authority and its operation would
> constitute the greatest peacetime public undertaking in Ameri-
> can history, both by virtue of the diversity of its functions and
> the size of its expenditure.
>
> —Joseph Kinsey Howard

A GREAT and embracing western issue is MVA. The pressures
involved are the same as those noted above in discussion of the
Columbia Valley Authority, but on an enormously broader scale; the end
in view is constitution of an authority for the berserk Missouri, America's longest river, much like the one operating now in the valley of the
Tennessee. In a sentence, the story of MVA is that of an attempt to yoke
one of the great rivers of the world and put it to man's use on a regional
basis—"to make the Missouri blue again," as I heard it put. The issue,
again in a sentence, simmers down to the question of who and what
should own a river, if not the people as a whole.

I hope this does not sound dull. Certainly the Missouri itself is far
from dull. This outlaw hippopotamus, this mud-foaming behemoth of
rivers, rises in southwestern Montana and finally meets the Mississippi,
near St. Louis, 2,470 miles away. Describing it has provoked some fine
and fancy language; it has been called "the hungriest river ever created
. . . eating yellow clay banks and cornfields, eighty acres at a mouthful,
winding up its banquet with a truck garden and picking its teeth with
the timbers of a big red barn."[1] Feeding it are tributaries almost as
truculent as itself, like the Yellowstone, the Big Horn, the Cheyenne, the
Platte; the last has been described as "a mile wide, an inch deep, stand
it on end and it will reach to heaven, so muddy that the catfish have to
come up to sneeze." The Missouri drains something like 516,000 square
miles, or roughly one-sixth of the entire U.S.A.; it carves its variable
and refractory way through seven states, and drains ten, with a total
population of thirteen million (the population of the basin itself is about
6,800,000); on its banks are three state capitals (Bismarck, Pierre,
Jefferson City), to say nothing of towns like Great Falls and Sioux City,
and metropolises like Kansas City and Omaha, Nebraska.

What makes the Missouri most notable and frightening is, however,

Stanley Vestal, *The Missouri*, in the Rivers of America series.

183

not its size but its voracity. It wanders obstinately all over the place—one remark is that the Missouri River and a woman's heart are the two most inconstant things in nature—and eats anything. In the three years from 1942 to 1944 it caused flood damage of more than 150 million dollars; the figure is almost impossible to believe, but it carries with it 550 *million* tons of irreplaceable silt, gravel, sand, and soil annually. Another calculation puts the loss at one ton of soil per acre per year; several million tons of actual farms are washed into the Mississippi every year. What is soil? It is what makes America live—in the shape of grass, grains, milk, meat.[2]

Efforts to control the Missouri and modify its appetite have gone on for many years—without much success as the foregoing figures would seem to indicate—and the complicated snarl today between the Pick-Sloan plan and the proposal for an MVA is merely the last, up-to-the-minute chapter in an involved history.

A valley authority on a TVA basis would, its advocates claim—even though an MVA would have to be very much larger than TVA—put the Missouri in order on all sorts of counts. Three separate main problems attend a turbulent river as a rule, irrigation at the source, navigation in the middle, flood control at the bottom. As to irrigation an MVA would probably bring under cultivation something like 4,700,000 additional acres, virtually doubling the present irrigated area. As to navigation it would make practicable a deep-water channel; as to floods these would, in theory, be totally eliminated by an over-all plan for controlling the river far enough up. Aside from this—though this is plenty—there are several other factors, for instance power. An MVA would, it is calculated, provide more than ten billion kilowatt hours annually of electric energy, enough to transform the entire region, by bringing in industry and raising living standards. Or take such a comparatively small matter as fertilizer. TVA, working with less than 5 per cent of the phosphate deposits in the country, has developed a fertilizer industry incalculably useful to American agriculture everywhere. The West has more than 80 per cent of the nation's natural phosphate, but no fertilizer industry at all with the exception of one plant. Or consider the matter of recreation. Very little has been done to encourage boating, fishing, and the like on the Missouri reservoirs existing at present; they could easily be made into healthful vacation spots. But far outweighing all this is something else—the fundamental concept of valley development as a whole, that of a single authority located within the region as worked out by TVA. Neither God, nature, the Missouri nor the Tennessee recognizes state frontiers. A river cannot be broken into fragments or harnessed piece by piece. Horizontally, vertically, the problem should be tackled as a unit, the river dealt with as an entity from source to mouth, and from the

[2] For further word about soil see Chapter 43 below.

viewpoint of its future potentialities, through control of erosion, conservation, and building up of natural resources.

Another word on electric power and its relation to the health and progress of a community as a whole. Some startling figures are available:

STATE	WHAT ITS PEOPLE PAID FOR CURRENT 1943	WHAT THEY WOULD HAVE PAID UNDER TVA RATES	TVA RATE SAVINGS
Colorado	$23,217,300	$12,585,644	$10,631,656
Iowa	48,396,200	26,763,942	21,632,258
Kansas	33,468,300	18,583,310	14,884,990
Missouri	76,496,800	46,920,231	29,576,569
Montana	16,300,200	11,189,044	5,111,156
Nebraska	20,921,900	11,975,738	8,946,162
North Dakota	7,154,000	3,296,694	3,857,306
South Dakota	8,043,800	3,754,742	4,289,058
Wyoming	4,471,700	2,142,380	2,329,320

In Montana, only 27.8 per cent of rural homes have electric light, only 14.7 per cent have running water, only 9 per cent have a bathtub or shower. The same figures for North Dakota are 15.5, 6.0, and 4.7; for Colorado 34.6, 21.3, and 12.4; for Missouri 15.9, 6.3, and 4.7. Gentle citizens of Missouri, glance at these figures again; of your farmers, only sixteen out of a hundred can turn on an electric light, only five out of a hundred can take a bath.

I noted in Chapter 11 the decline of population in Montana, and this same problem exists in Nebraska and the Dakotas; these four states have lost 232,000 people in ten years. Montana has sixteen thousand fewer farms than it had twenty years ago, and in some counties the population loss runs to 20 per cent. Remedies? Soil control, irrigation, industry—all the things that an MVA might bring, including fifty thousand jobs. But, says Joseph Kinsey Howard, there has been "a definite conspiracy in Montana to keep industry out of the state."[3] The big companies already there, chiefly Anaconda Copper, don't want rivals; above all they don't want competing labor. The forces that tend to prevent industrialization in Montana, and elsewhere in the West, are of course the same forces that opposed public power in Oregon and Washington and that now fight MVA. Again to quote Mr. Howard: "What chances have Montanans who want public power development when they have a state public service commission which decides the private power company is overcapitalized only by 19 million dollars, in the face of a Federal Power Commission order to the company to squeeze 51 million dollars of 'water' out of its accounts?"

The Missouri River today is in the joint charge of the Army engineers and the Bureau of Reclamation, both of which are of course federal

[3] In a statement to a U. S. Senate subcommittee, September 22, 1945. Mr. Howard is the author of *Montana, High, Wide, and Handsome*, cited above.

agencies. This cuts some ground from under opponents of MVA who set up wolf cries of totalitarianism and say that more federal authority would be leftist and dangerous. Actually, if things should work out as they did in Tennessee, a valley authority on the spot but under control of Congress might very well prove to be more decentralized, more democratic, and less bureaucratic than the present system which is topheavy with confusions.

The major objection to the MVA idea is fear of socialism. But in all fairness let us outline other items: (1) States' rights. It is asserted that these might be infringed, but TVA did not do so; in any case it is the federal government, by repeated interpretations of the Constitution, that has final authority over navigable rivers. (2) Taxes. But federal projects built by Army engineers and/or Bureau of Reclamation would also be tax free, and MVA, by terms of the Murray bill, would make substantial payments to local authorities in lieu of taxes and out of revenue from the sale of power and water. (3) The Pick-Sloan plan can do the job. But engineers and Reclamation have been in the area for fifty years; and look at it. (4) MVA might mean patronage, spoils politics, and bureaucracy. This argument is not particularly strong; the great thing about TVA is that it has always kept politics rigorously out. (5) The cost will not be worth it. Again one must turn to TVA, which is nicely paying for itself year by year, and which has to a fantastic degree increased the real wealth of an entire region, of course on a tax-free basis to an extent.

But to proceed now to what is actually happening. For years, there have been rival schools of thought about the Missouri. The Bureau of Reclamation is primarily interested in irrigation, and it worked mostly upriver where this is the biggest problem. The Army engineers, on the contrary, are primarily interested in navigation and flood control; hence for the most part they worked downriver. The engineers did, however, build at Fort Peck in Montana the largest earth-filled dam in the world, and this is upriver; so are other projects that the Army plans. But the two agencies did not, on the whole, co-operate or work very well together; a rivalry developed, and experts for each denounced the plans of the other; the river was in effect cut in half, divided between the two. Eventually two competing plans for development of the Missouri were produced. One was the work of a remarkably able officer, Colonel Lewis A. Pick, who is a general now; during the war he built the Ledo Road in China. The Pick plan outlined projects to cost $650,000,000 (almost two and a half times the cost of Grand Coulee) and to include vast levees, multiple-purpose dams, and reservoirs. But—the details are far too technical for inclusion here—it happened that another Army scheme aroused fierce opposition by upriver people at about this time. This latter scheme outlined a nine-foot navigation channel from Sioux City to the Mississippi, which, according to upriver calculations, would drain out so

.. *Reprinted from the May Book-of-the-Month Club News* ...

INSIDE U. S. A.

By JOHN GUNTHER

THAT peripatetic digester of continents, John Gunther, has at last come home. This latest and longest of his famous series, *Inside U. S. A.*, is to my mind the most ambitious and the best. In these half million words the hardest-working of contemporary American reporters attempts the impossible task of transnavigating the forty-eight states and 140,000,000 people that make up "the greatest, craziest, most dangerous, least stable, most spectacular, least grown-up, and most powerful and magnificent nation ever known." That he has succeeded as well as he has is a consequence of his possession of a clear eye, a warm and convivial manner (without which he could never have persuaded over nine hundred people to talk frankly with him), a reliable sense of proportion, and a dogged energy that has enabled him to impose some sort of order on a refractory wilderness of facts. If any single book can tell us what it means to be an American citizen, in concrete and current detail, *Inside U. S. A.* is it.

In the course of thirteen months of almost continuous travel, John Gunther visited all of the forty-eight states — including the forty-ninth, New York City. Through a clear and powerful lens he examined thirty-eight out of the forty-three cities over 200,000 in population. (He omits Washington whose complexities will form the subject of another book).

Everywhere, whether he talked with the local diehard or the local radical, the state's governor or the hotel's bellhop, he searched the civic soul with a brace of questions: What makes your community distinctive? Who *really* runs it? The answers to these queries, properly organized, permit him to call his book "a study of democracy in action." Do not misunderstand: Mr. Gunther is no Lord Bryce, no Tocqueville, though he has intelligently absorbed what these great philosophers of government have written about us. His study is empirical, not profound, aspiring to make up in liveliness, dash and clarity what it is bound to lack in analytical rigor. Whatever its shortcomings (and of these the author is fully and ruefully aware) it does manage to give us a living sense of our diversity in unity and at the same time to locate, wherever their effects can be felt, the levers of power.

However, to call *Inside U. S. A.* "a study of democracy in action" seems overabstract. Actually it is a complex and at times bewildering mixture of geography, topography, history, reportage, political and social analysis, character-portraiture, biography, speculation, gossip and wisecracks. It is full of homely illustrations drawn from our folkways; yet at no time does Mr. Gunther fail to see America for the Americana. Its emotional tone is varied, ranging from admiration for the peaks of our physical achievement (Bonneville, TVA) to cool condemnation of our incredible wastes and follies. But through the entire book—and this is what gives it its special quality—runs an exultant but not in the least chauvinist note of faith in our capacities, faith in the country which, whatever its truancies, whatever its "preposterous and flamboyant contradic-

tions," is unique in history in that it was "deliberately founded on a good idea."

Fifty-two chapters make up *Inside U. S. A.*—and, to draw the meat out of the book, you needn't read every one. Some of these chapters handle whole regions—the Pacific Northwest or the Middle West, called by Mr. Gunther "the central pivot and umbilicus of the nation." Others estimate separate states: Nevada, resting on livestock, mining, gambling and divorce; Kansas, with its abnormal pride in its averageness; Pennsylvania, with its inner-circle Philadelphians who consider "Mr." Franklin "to have been of a somewhat shady family." A few concentrate on cities — the chapter on New York, for example, is one of the sharpest, even though no treatment of Megalopolis can ever be anything but tentative and incomplete. A few chapters, in headlong disregard of conventional canons of proportion, give full treatment to a few personalities. There is, for example, a glowing sketch of Henry Kaiser, concluding with Mr. Gunther's discovery that "American men of affairs are by and large more interesting than the politicians." (I consider this faint praise indeed of our men of affairs.) Among the dozens of outstanding personalities discussed in greater or less detail are: Wayne Morse and Wilson Wyatt (I bracket them to give you an idea of the kind of American Mr. Gunther admires); Taft and Dewey ("as devoid of charm as a rivet," says Mr. Gunther of Mr. Dewey); LaGuardia, with whom Mr. Gunther spent an entire exhausting day — exhausting for Mr. Gunther; Bricker—"a vast vacuum occasionally crossed by homeless, wandering clichés"; Arnall, Glen Taylor, Stassen, Vandenberg, Saltonstall.

Some chapters—and these are perhaps the most penetrating — deal freshly and concretely with great social experiments such as Bonneville, Grand Coulee, TVA, and the much disputed potential Missouri Valley Authority. Others concentrate on institutions, such as Mormonism in Utah, Anaconda Copperism in Montana, Hagueism in New Jersey. Steel is the key to the Keystone State, as the Homestake gold mine (and pheasants) are to South Dakota. The South is considered with what seems to this damyankee extraordinary fairness and sympathy. Mr. Gunther rests his examination of "the problem child of the nation" on two basic propositions: the South's standard of living must be raised; the "Negro problem" must be solved. As to this latter, he knows that it is a problem of national, not regional,

importance. As he says gravely, truly, and finally, "A cancer will destroy a body, unless cured."

It is hard not to get from Mr. Gunther's round-up the impression of a tremendous disproportion between our physical and mental resources, or, to define the matter more closely, between the amount of education in the country and the number of educated men. Our political leaders often seem inferior to the average decent American. We are provincial, money-conscious, wasteful, woman-dominated, says Mr. Gunther. And yet, one feels him saying in every line, we are potentially a conglomeration of people intended by accident or fate to be a force for overwhelming good in the world. Our very mixed-up-ness is our salvation, as is our refusal to stay put in any one pattern.

I cannot summarize the author's own view better — and it is one I think my readers will share — than by quoting one sentence of his: "This country is, I once heard it put, absolutely 'lousy with greatness'—with not only the greatest responsibilities but with the greatest opportunities ever known to man."

CLIFTON FADIMAN

In accordance with a suggestion made by a number of our subscribers, this monthly reprint from the Book-of-the-Month Club *News* is printed in this format so that it can be pasted, if desired, to the flyleaf of the book.

much flow that northerly irrigation would be killed; hence violent protests arose to both the Army projects. The upriver people shouted, "You're trying to steal our river!" The downriver people shouted, "Control the river, or you'll drown us out!"

The second Missouri plan, more ambitious and studied and the result of careful work over a long period—the brilliant Pick had produced his plan in three months—was largely the work of W. G. Sloan of the Bureau of Reclamation. It called for no fewer than ninety dams in seven states, with the cost estimated at $1,200,000,000, which is about half the price of the atomic bomb.

Then came an interesting development. That splendid crusading newspaper the St. Louis *Post-Dispatch* broke open the whole issue by appealing for an MVA to replace *both* the Pick and Sloan plans. It appealed for a "One River One Problem" policy. This is one of the comparatively rare cases in recent American history where a newspaper, singlehanded, provoked a considerable national struggle. Senator James E. Murray of Montana introduced a bill for MVA in Congress on August 18, 1944, and President Roosevelt—also a senator named Truman—gave his blessing to the idea.

Now the fight got really hot. An MVA bill, if passed, would have eliminated from the area both Bureau of Reclamation and Army engineers, or at least greatly cut down their functions. Both agencies are extremely sensitive and jealous of their prerogatives in the region, as we know from the history of Bonneville and Grand Coulee, and they joined forces to squeeze the interloper out. Two rival bodies of the federal government combined, in a word, to prevent formation of a third. Their proposal—to forestall MVA—is known as the joint "Pick-Sloan Plan"; it was a compromise, patched up in a hurry with nobody in supreme responsibility, and its critics say that it does not envisage the best possible development of the river as a whole; for instance it includes projects to cost $267,000,000, which each of the partners had previously rejected! This, however, was the price of agreement. Jim Patton, president of the National Farmers Union, called the combined plan a "shameless, loveless shotgun marriage"; the St. Louis *Post Dispatch* termed it "the second Missouri Compromise."

Congress, however, delayed action on the Murray bill, and in December, 1944, approved the Pick-Sloan plan, but without appropriations. Then President Roosevelt signed it on the explicit understanding that future development of a true valley authority should not be prejudiced. Opposition to Pick-Sloan grew in the river basin, and Senator Murray reintroduced his bill for MVA, with trimmings, early in 1945. Fierce partisanship was aroused by now; a public petition for MVA with a million signatures was promoted; and enemies of the project, on their side, went into serious action. The new Murray bill was turned over not to one but to three Senate committees, commerce, irrigation, and agriculture, and was finally abandoned for the session without coming to a vote. The man chiefly responsible for burying it was Senator Overton of Louisiana, a strong "private water" man and a relentless enemy of the whole valley authority idea; by strange coincidence he was chairman not only of the Commerce Committee that first held hearings on the bill (though normally it might have been expected to go to Agriculture where it would have had friendlier treatment) but also of the subcommittee of Irrigation that continued the long hearings. The Murray bill is, of the moment, comatose. But operations under the Pick-Sloan scheme have not yet begun on any scale, and Big Muddy is still running across 2,470 miles of land, licking her fine chops.

The MVA fight produced some notably tricky politics, and lobbying on a scale unknown since the days of Antony and Cleopatra. The most seasoned of professionals got to work. One device that confused the issue was creation of something called the Missouri Valley Development Association, with initials MVDA. Regional committees for MVA itself were formed in each appropriate state, and met vehement opposition. Very powerful groups like the Mississippi Valley Association, the National Reclamation Association and a Ten States Committee took sides against MVA, and an imposing list of clubs and such—some thirty in all including such apparently remote entities as the Propeller Club of the United States, the Pittsburgh Coal Exchange, and the Upper Potomac River Board—all joined in. Above all the great power companies came out of holes where they had been hiding since Insull, and began to shout. Not less than 167 different electric and utility companies joined in a national advertising program, with full pages in the weeklies saying LET'S CROSS THESE RIVERS BEFORE WE COME TO 'EM, and calling out that government in any business endangered *all* business. (As if Pick-Sloan were not the government!) One big advertising agency sent "investigators" all over the valley, and the *Post-Dispatch* protested that money for this campaign "is said to come . . . from kickbacks and rebates concealed in the prices that manufacturers . . . charge the utility companies for materials and equipment."

The country as a whole—that small minority that was interested at least—was not bowled over by the power companies. The *Saturday Evening Post*, *Collier's*, and *Life* all printed extremely fair presentations of the issue, which on the whole favored MVA. The *Post* article in particular, which the *Reader's Digest* reprinted, blew some of the froth away and gave the authority idea considerable sympathy. Incidentally one of the most consistent and aggressive supporters of MVA is, of all sheets in the world, the New York *Daily News*, which printed at least four full column editorials warmly advocating it during the winter of discussion. The valley concept is so big, in fact, that it cuts across most categories.

For instance such an inveterate opponent of New Dealism, socialism, and Washington bureaucracy as Louis Bromfield is a fanatic partisan for TVA; so is a man who on every other count would be judged an extreme reactionary, Congressman John E. Rankin.

To sum up, supporters of MVA, dormant but still kicking, may take comfort in the odd irony that it was they who served to bring Pick and Sloan together. And all good Americans, keeping their fingers crossed, must hope vigorously that the Pick-Sloan scheme will work well, if indeed MVA should ever be buried beyond resuscitation.

Chapter 13

Utah and the Mormons: Profile of a Community

~~~~~~

> For the strength of the hills we bless Thee, Our God, our
> Fathers' God.
> > —Mormon hymn

> Give me ten years, and I shall ask no odds of the United States.
> > —Brigham Young in 1847

THE uniqueness of Utah among American states is utter and absolute, because its salient characteristics depend on a complex struggle for power, first between the Mormon church and the rest of the community, second within the Mormon church itself. Who runs Utah? What is Utah like? No one can begin to answer these questions—or even to describe the state, its vastness of horizon, its wide aridity, its dinosaurlike bony mountains—without reference to that extraordinary combination of theocracy, do-goodism, industriousness, and flint-hard belief in the virtue of a living God, the Church of Jesus Christ of Latter Day Saints.

The Mormons comprise roughly 60 per cent of the people of Utah, with their strength focused both in rural districts and in the capital, Salt Lake City. But the political and economic power of the church far out-reaches the population ratio. The governor of Utah, Herbert B. Maw, is a Mormon, and a first-rate governor he is. Both of the state's senators are Mormons, and so are both its congressmen (for the first time in history). Eighteen out of twenty-three state senators are Mormon, and thirty-six out of a legislature numbering sixty.

Few individual Mormons are exaggeratedly wealthy, but the church itself is immensely rich. In the Salt Lake City area alone it owns wholly or in part:

The ZCMI (Zion's Co-operative Mercantile Institution), one of the first co-operative retail stores established in the United States, and today one of the biggest and most prosperous.

The Hotel Utah (which is to Salt Lake City what the Waldorf is to New York).

Temple Square Hotel.

Deseret News (leading newspaper).
KSL (radio station).
Utah-Idaho Sugar Company.
Utah State National Bank.
Zion Savings Bank & Trust Company.
Beneficial Life Insurance Company.
Great quantities of real estate.

And the church is commonly believed to be a very substantial stock-holder in the Union Pacific Railroad, which is Utah's life line.

The late president of the church, Heber J. Grant, was a director of Union Pacific for almost twenty years. He had to give up this job, however, when Congress passed the Clayton Act, by terms of which no director of a company selling any considerable volume of goods to a railway could remain a director of the railway. And Grant was president of ZCMI (as well as of the church itself), of which Union Pacific was a heavy customer.

Grant's successor, the venerable George Albert Smith, was at the time of his accession president of the Utah State National Bank, the Zion Savings Bank, the Beneficial Life Insurance Company, and the Utah-Idaho Sugar Company, as well as vice president of the Utah Savings & Trust Company, and a director of Western Air Lines, the Libbey Investment Company, a creamery, and Heber J. Grant & Co. Mormons believe in concentration of economic as well as ecclesiastical power—to put it mildly.

Social Attributes of the LDS

Good Mormons do not smoke, nor do they drink alcohol, tea, or coffee. The legend that spices, mustard, pepper, and similar stimulants are also barred is, however, groundless. A borderline case is Coca-Cola. This beverage is reputed to contain caffein, a drug, and is therefore condemned, but the condemnation is by "word of wisdom," not by specific commandment, and some Mormons drink it. The church is adamant, however, on alcohol and particularly tobacco. *The Improvement Era,* an unofficial publication, carries a feature called the No-Liquor-Tobacco Column; one issue denies that there are any vitamins in beer, and another argues that overuse of cigarettes killed Wendell Willkie.

Here is a recent mention of tobacco:

Tobacco companies, through clever advertising, have made the approach to smoking simple, yet deadly effective—playing to the emotions and dealing with that all-important human urge—social popularity. The tobacco situation can be changed and reversed by the same approach . . . through an emotional appeal dealing with social unpopularity. Tobacco stinks. It does not make any

difference who smokes it, or the form, or the brand, it always stinks
. . . A slang phrase of youth today is "It stinks" for anything
they don't approve. Tobacco can soon be placed in this realm if
proper leadership is given. When the idea, *"It Stinks,"* is thoroughly associated with tobacco . . . a big part of the battle will have
been won.

The first presidency of the church, its ruling body, sounded this note
on alcohol in October, 1942:

Over the earth, and it seems, particularly in America, the demon
drink is in control. Drunken with strong drink [*sic*] men have lost
their reason; their counsel has been destroyed; their judgment
and vision are fled; they reel forward to destruction.

As to coffee, I have lunched with Mormons and non-Mormons at
the same table; the Mormons simply turned their cups down when coffee
was being served. I was told that some believers, very heterodox,[1]
sometimes put a drop or two of coffee in a cup of hot water, and thus
compromise with faith, but I never saw this happen.

There is a perfectly good historical and theological reason for Mormon
abstinences. The prophet Joseph Smith, founder of the sect, believed that
the use of drugs shortened life. And Mormons, who are astonishingly
long-lived anyway, want to keep on living just as long as possible;
moreover when they enter the life after "death" (Mormons don't "die"),
they spend eternity in the same body they wore on earth. Thus, it is
simple prudence to take care of it. As I heard it irreverently put, the
analogy might be that of a man who knows that he is going to have
only one automobile all his life, to say nothing of a million years in
the hereafter. If he has sense he will keep that automobile well oiled
and greased and will watch it carefully for defects and avoid abusing it.

Mormons seldom call themselves Mormons; the phrase Latter Day
Saints is much more common. Sometimes this may be shortened to the
initials; I have heard a Gentile ask of someone, "Is he LDS or not?"
Mormons and Gentiles mix with perfect freedom in business affairs, and
to an extent socially. Intermarriage is still comparatively rare, but a
Mormon boy may freely "go with" a Gentile girl, or vice versa. I have
heard Utah people say, "Some of my best friends are Mormons," almost
as uncultivated people in New York might say, "Some of my best
friends are Jews." (Incidentally Jews in Utah, being non-Mormon, are
theoretically subject to classification as Gentiles, which gave rise to the
well-known remark that "Utah is the only place in the world where
Jews are Gentiles.")

---

[1] There are plenty of backsliding Mormons, those born in the church but who
nowadays take a drink or do not worship. These are called Jack-Mormons. Non-
Mormons are known as "Gentiles."

The Mormons called Utah "Zion," but what might be termed their territory goes considerably beyond Utah itself; powerful communities exist in Arizona, Wyoming, and Idaho as we know. Another favorite word is "Deseret," which does not mean "desert," as is commonly believed, but "honey-bee"; it connotes that characteristic trait of the faith, industriousness.

Until Pearl Harbor the headship of the organization was fiercely isolationist, but many individual LDS's, especially those in medium positions, have a distinct world sense. This is partly because so many of them served as missionaries abroad; the church has proselytized with great skill, pertinacity, and vigor in the British Isles, Scandinavia, Hawaii, and elsewhere. Mormon missionaries, of whom there are about two thousand, are not paid; they have to support themselves, either by remittances from home if the family has a little money, or by other work (and frequently their wives do all but take in washing). It is a proud boast that Mormons have often converted rival missionaries in the field, but that no Mormon missionary has ever become a convert to another faith.

Mormons are great proselytizers not merely abroad, but right here at home, in fact. Many members of the church are priests and most are well trained in dialectics, so it is well to avoid heckling one about his creed, unless you are an expert. The church welcomes newcomers, and Mormonism is one of the simplest of all religions to enter. To get in, you need only convince your sponsor of your sincerity; there is no novitiate, and baptism can be immediate. All sins are washed away; you start with a clean sheet.

To members of all other faiths—Jews, Catholics,[2] what not—the Latter Day Saints are friendly, but possibly because Mormonism borrowed so much from Masonry (Masonic symbols like the beehive may be seen all over Utah), there is a tendency to dislike Freemasons. The Mormons will, however, often accept a converted Mason, whereas Masons are more hesitant to take in an LDS as a general rule.

Anybody may visit the Mormon tabernacle in Salt Lake City, with its celebrated organ and even more celebrated acoustics, and thousands of tourists have, but no Gentile may enter the Temple next door; in fact, only certain categories of Mormons themselves, those who have been "endowed," or are about to be, may do so. The Mormon church is thus the only one in the world in which worshipers, unless of a special class, may not enter the chief cathedral of the faith. I have heard this explained by the analogy that, after all, very few Catholics ever see the Pope. There are, by the way, only eight temples in the world—at Salt Lake

[2] But in Salt Lake City the large LDS and the small Roman Catholic communities vigorously proselytize each other.

City, St. George, Logan, and Manti, Utah; Mesa, Arizona; Idaho Falls, Idaho; Hilo, Hawaii; and Cardston, Alberta.

Sinclair Lewis and Lewis Browne, on a lecture tour last year, spent a stimulating day with David O. McKay, one of the three members of the first presidency of the church. They gazed upon the outer portals of the Temple, and Browne murmured his regret at not being able to see the interior.

"Couldn't it be arranged?" Lewis interjected.

"Certainly," replied McKay.

"How?" asked Browne eagerly.

"All you will have to do is adhere to the faith, give up alcohol and tobacco, and donate to the church one-tenth of your income in perpetuity."

The LDS organization is, as a matter of fact, supported by the tithe; every member is supposed to give 10 per cent of his income to the church. An astonishing fact is that this money, a very substantial sum, is never accounted for in detail. At church conferences the leadership submits a general statement of disbursements—how much of the annual budget went for education, how much for new churches, and so on—but no balance sheet is published. A member, to find out the extent of his own contributions through the years (in the event that he did not keep accurate details himself) may consult his own record, but under no circumstances is he allowed to see that of others. LDS officials are themselves very modestly paid. The allotments (the word "salary" is not used) are secret, but it is believed that the president gets something like $10,000 per year, and the twelve apostles $350 a month each. Nor is there any accounting of the vast revenues of the church from its investments.

Mormons pay great attention to education, and have always been justifiably proud of their literacy record. Indeed their accomplishments in this field are superlatively good, and as a result the state of Utah can offer statistics as impressive as any in the union. For instance:

In per cent of total population enrolled in public elementary and secondary schools, Utah (with 28.4%) is the highest in the country. (Lowest: New Hampshire)

In per cent of total population enrolled in high schools, Utah (31.6%) is third. (First, Orgeon; second, New York)

In per cent of state income spent on elementary and secondary education, Utah is third. First, South Dakota; second, New Mexico)

In per cent of population of high school age actually in high school, Utah is first, with 95.6%. (Lowest: Alabama with 28%)

Dr. E. L. Thorndike checked *Who's Who, Leaders in Education,* and *American Men of Science* to determine the place of birth of outstanding Americans. Using the decade 1890-1900 (thus to include men and women now at full maturity), and checking all three books, he found that Utah led the nation; its rate was 857 per million white inhabitants. Some other states:

Massachusetts	697
Connecticut	653
Colorado	600
Idaho	590
Vermont	586
New Hampshire	566
New York	445
California	437
Mississippi	153
Arkansas	148
Georgia	144
Louisiana	131

Similarly Mormons pay much attention to such matters as public health. And Utah is proud of having the second lowest syphilis rate in the nation, according to selective service records. (Wisconsin 6.4 draftees rejected per 1,000; Utah 7.3 per cent.)

Members of the church marry early as a rule, and their sexual standards are strict. Their birthrate is very high, and the death rate low.[3] Women are highly regarded, but it is almost impossible for a woman to become a leader in the hierarchy. The church is, as everyone knows, organized with extreme efficiency, down to the youngest child; Mark Twain is reputed to have said once that the only thing resembling it was the Prussian Army. Yet to emphasize this point unduly gives a slightly offside picture. The Mormon community in Utah is certainly God-fearing, but it is not, by and large, as "stern" or "forbidding" as the newcomer may think. Most Mormons are quite cheerful. They don't smoke or drink and "By hell" is a terrific oath, but dancing is allowed in meeting houses, and most members are anything but dour. The way a Mormon will greet a stranger on the street with a friendly "Good morning, sir" is refreshing and not easily forgotten. And the community as a whole is distinguished by pride, serenity, and an amazing amount of social vigor.

Of course the outstanding characteristic of the church in former days, what distinguished it from everything else in the public mind, was polygamy. But first a word on general background.

The Theocratic Structure

About the history of Mormonism I can write little; the vivid, nutritious story has been too often told. Suffice it to say that a farm boy named

[3] The ratio of births to deaths in Utah is 3.458 to 1, the highest in the country. A standard joke is that the chief means of transportation is baby carriages.

Joseph Smith grew up in the 1820's in western New York state, during a period of intense religious revivalism, and at the age of fourteen he saw God the Father and God the Son, as living persons; that in 1830 he completed a "translation" of the Book of Mormon and with six followers founded a church that, in the words of Bernard DeVoto, became "a cooperative society ruled by an ecclesiastical oligarchy"; that Smith married many wives, fled with his flock successively to Ohio, Missouri, and Nauvoo, Illinois, suffered the most barbarous persecutions, announced his candidacy for president of the United States, and was murdered by a mob in 1844; that after a period of schism and confusion Brigham Young, one of the most formidable characters in American history and a colonizer of the rank of Lyautey and Cecil Rhodes, succeeded Smith and led his following to refuge after a murderously difficult trek across the country; and that in Utah (which he called Deseret) he founded Salt Lake City, set on the community the stamp that it bears today, fought an Indian war, organized agriculture, introduced irrigation, and ruled for thirty years with a grip of iron, marrying the while a great number of wives and begetting many children.

That Mormonism should have arisen in the East—with remote and indirect origins that go to the root of New England—and should have become established finally in the West after traversing two-thirds of the continent, is suggestive. There are many divers-colored threads that help bind the United States together.

The following personal report shows with some vividness what life was like in Utah in frontier days:

> A few days after the last battle with the indians a government surgeon wanted James Or and me to take a sley cross over on the ice and secure the indians heads for he wanted to send them to Washington to a medical institution. hired a sley crost over on the ice the weather was bitter cold. the surgeon tok out his box of instruments and comenced it took him a quarter of an hour to cut of one head. the sun was getting low and frezing cold Jim and me took the job in our own hands we wear not going to wait on the surgeons slow motion jerked our knives out and had them all of in a few minutes.
>
> they wear frozen and come of easy in our fassion the surgeon stood back and watched us finish the job the surgeon shot some ducks ten or twelve boxed them up guts feathers and all. and told me to bring them down with the indian heads in a week or two to Salt Lake City. took them down according to agreement the weather turned warm and the ducks wear green with rot. the indian heads smelt loud drove to his office, and told him the ducks wear spoilt he opened the box pulled out a wing smelt it and says they are just right.

—Provo, Pioneer Mormon City, p. 59

Some good Mormons believe that Independence, Missouri, will be the seat of the Resurrection, and many believe that the New Kingdom may come at any time. For instance, consider the following from a newspaper called *Progressive Opinion*, which was given me in all seriousness by the present postmaster of Salt Lake City:

U.S. Government Preceding Kingdom Government

President Truman is making his summer White House at Independence, Mo., and that will be the seat of the government for the summer months. Thus the U.S. government at this place precedes the coming Kingdom government which will be established there . . . And verily, this may come about during Mr. Truman's term of office.

The central core of Mormon faith is, as noted above, the conviction that God is a *living* person, and that all members of the church are, literally, children of God and hence prophets, with life eternal. Mormons are apt to say, with a strange admixture of pride and sadness, "We are a peculiar people." Derivative assumptions go far afield. I have met members of the cult who devoutly believe that the United States had a great civilization, with teeming cities, long before the Indians (Kansas City, Missouri, was the "capital") ; that two tribes fought a terrific civil war in upper New York state in or around A.D. 500 (in punishment the Indians were afflicted with their red skins) ; that the heavens have been sealed for about 1,800 years, and that there were no prophets between Moroni, the son of Mormon, and Joseph Smith; and that all this and much else is clearly indicated in the present Hebrew Bible.

The Mormon manner of worship has, on the other hand, the bare minimum of fuss or pageantry. The cross is not used in or on meeting houses, nor is there any altar in the accepted sense, nor any pews, Mass, or pastor. Each member of the flock has equal standing. There are about seventy meeting houses in Salt Lake City; several represent an investment of as much as $150,000.[4] Except for ceremonies in the temple (which, a curious point, is closed on Sundays), the ceremonies of the LDS are vigorously practical. But the temple is something else again, and as noted above only the particularly devout may enter. Age, sex, economic status, position in the community matter little ; the criterion of entrance is spiritual worthiness, nothing more, nothing less. Who determines the right of entrance? Suppose a Mormon from Norway, say, happens to arrive in Utah, and wants to enter. In all probability he would have to bring with him a certificate of character from his bishop. Three particular ceremonies take place in a temple, vicarious baptism, "endowment," and "marriage unto eternity." A young man or woman, of proved

---

[4] In Utah the church owns recreational facilities alone valued at thirty million dollars. Most meeting houses also serve as libraries, gymnasia, and the like.

faith, may be endowed at the age of eighteen or nineteen; the ceremony lasts six or seven hours, and is secret. Thereafter, insignia is worn for life in the underwear (though nowadays some of the young women don't like to deface their lingerie). As to marriage, the Mormon church recognizes two kinds, the ordinary "till death do us part" ceremony, and one linking man and wife *beyond* death, i.e. unto eternity. Any Mormon bishop may unite believers in "simple" marriage, but a marriage unto eternity can only be performed in a temple, with the president of the church or one of the twelve apostles officiating. Quite often, young couples go through the ceremony of endowment and are then "sealed" unto eternity the same day. The philosophy of marriage unto eternity is of course that of carrying the community on. Mormons believe implicitly that they will continue to bear children in heaven, since they never die. Thus marriage unto eternity is a kind of spiritual substitute for polygamy which, as the world well knows, the church was forced to give up.

Divorce is, strange as it may seem, permitted in the Mormon church, though the divorce rate is very low, especially in regard to marriages performed in the temple.

Vicarious baptism is a story in itself. Put bluntly and crudely, it means that upon "death" a good Mormon's status in heaven depends to a certain degree on the number of relatives he can muster. Thus, most Mormons dig back into the past to unearth ancestors, who, if proved acceptable, may be vicariously baptized in the temple, whereupon they make part of the heavenly company. This has led to the fantastically acute Mormon interest in genealogy. Believers all over the world assemble genealogical data, unearth new ancestors, and are baptized in their stead. An immense research library exists on the subject in Salt Lake City, and I have seen ancestries traced in all seriousness back to 173 B.C. Perhaps fittingly, it is the very old members of the church who dig up their antecedents with greatest fervor.

The organization of the church is concrete and fixed on a pyramidal basis. At the head are three men, the president and two counselors, who are collectively known as the first presidency. Immediately below comes the council of twelve apostles, which also has a president. The first presidency and council meet every Thursday, from 9:30 A.M. to 1:30 P.M., like a cabinet; the meeting opens and closes with prayer, and transacts the running business of the entire church. The apostles serve for life, and are chosen by revelation to the president, in his capacity as living prophet; criteria for choice are a clean life, absolute conviction, and Call from God. The president himself is, on his side, chosen from among the apostles, which makes for a very close-knit organization indeed. The other two members of the first presidency (that is, counselors) are also, as a general rule, former apostles, but the rule is not invariable. For instance, the potent J. Reuben Clark, Jr., became a counselor although he had never been an apostle; of Mr. Clark more anon. When a president dies, the first presidency is automatically dissolved, and the counselors are relieved of their duties; temporary headship passes to the president of the twelve apostles who as a rule is the senior and who is then nominated as new president of the church. The ceremony is brief; the other eleven apostles lay hands on his head. Then, at the first subsequent general conference of the church, the name of the new president is submitted to a vote of the total membership. As soon as a new president is "sustained and set apart" in his office, he chooses two new counselors—or reappoints the old ones—and a new first presidency is formed.

Seniority and venerability are greatly respected by the church; but the real secret of Mormon vitality lies in the children. From the cradle to the age of twelve they are organized into primary associations, which merge into the celebrated MIA's (mutual improvement associations) for adolescents. Beginning at about six, a boy is trained for the priesthood, and any male child may become a deacon of the church at twelve, and an elder at nineteen.

Problem in the Past

In pious times . . . before polygamy was made a sin.
—Dryden, *Absalom and Achitophel*

When I arrived in Utah I was warned by Gentiles never to mention "plural marriage" to members of the church, because they were still so sensitive about it. What I found out was, of course, that almost all Mormons were crazy to talk about the subject, once it was broached.

I met one stalwart believer who told me, "My father died thirty years ago, but I'm still running into half-brothers I never knew I had." I met another whose father had had five wives and thirty-four children, and at one dinner party a businessman astonished me (it was my first evening in Salt Lake City) by stating suddenly, "My father had seven wives."

A vast lot of nonsense has been written about polygamy. A case may well be made that, far from having debauched the community, it contributed greatly to the sternly moral standards and high level of citizenship that prevail in Utah today. It made adultery unnecessary, and juvenile delinquency was practically unknown. Also, quite seriously, the position of women was often bettered by plural marriage rather than the opposite. For one thing, it meant that almost all women had a chance to marry; there was very little old-maidism among Mormons. For another, women had wide latitude in the choice of husbands. Finally, polygamy protected women economically, since only the more courageous and capable men, with considerable earning power, could afford more than one wife. As a matter of fact, less than 3 per cent of all male believers were practicing polygamy when the practice ceased. Another point frequently forgotten is that in theory no man could undertake plural marriage without (a) consent of the first wife, and (b) the church's consent which was strictly contingent on his economic status. Some Mormons loathed the institution from the beginning; for instance Joseph Smith's own son vigorously denied (though we know today that the denial has no basis in fact) that the prophet had ever been polygamous. Brigham Young had forty-seven children by seventeen wives,[5] but most Mormon historians say that Young did not "serve," i.e. have sexual relations with them all; even so, the ratio works out to 2.7 children per wife. Incidentally, plenty of Young's grandchildren are still around; two, in fact, married present apostles of the church, Albert E. Bowen and John A. Widtsoe.

But did not women in the old days resent the intrusion of new wives; were they not subject to the ordinary emotions of jealousy, exclusiveness, and possessiveness? Of course. I talked to one lady who could recall quite vividly when her father took a second wife; her own mother was bitterly hurt, but stoical, and instructed her to call the interloper "Auntie." First wives had, and still have in retrospect, a kind of moral priority, it would seem. For instance, one fourth-generation Mormon told me proudly that his father was the son of his grandfather by the grandfather's *first* wife, and that his mother was a daughter of a *first* marriage also.

Why did the Mormons advocate polygamy? First, for the complex theological motives outlined above. Second, for strictly economic and demographic reasons. A hunted people, they were colonizing a vast new territory and of necessity they wanted to populate it hard and fast.

Deep in their hearts, some few Mormons today still believe in polygamy, and would secretly like to see it reinstated. They are nevertheless punctilious in obeying the law, and any polygamist who comes to light is ruthlessly excommunicated. Groups of fundamentalists, as people still polygamous are called, crop up every once in a while; when the church finds one, it informs the secular authorities immediately and assists in applying the law; polygamists are prosecuted under whatever federal statute may apply, for instance the Mann Act or the Lindbergh Kidnapping Law, or under local statutes against bigamy or unlawful cohabitation.[6] One cluster of twenty-six was unearthed ten or twelve years ago. They might have escaped detection forever, hiding out in the Arizona "strip," but when the depression came along they applied for federal relief, and the curiosity of the government was naturally

---

[5] According to the *Encyclopaedia Britannica*. Other authorities give larger numbers.

[6] The United States Supreme Court has, however, recently thrown out several convictions of Utah fundamentalists arrested under these laws.

aroused when an applicant stated that he had thirty-one sons and daughters. Members of another group, which published its own magazine called *Truth*, and which had a total of 55 wives and 287 children, began serving jail sentences as recently as May, 1945.

Polygamy was abolished by the church in the 1890's, more than fifty years ago. The theological dilemma was distressing in the extreme, since God's will, by revelation to Joseph Smith, had to be reversed. The church had no choice—after a fierce struggle—but to submit to federal pressure. Six times between 1849 and 1887 Utah sought to become a state; each time it was rejected because the Mormons practiced—and refused to give up—plural marriage, which federal statutes of course forbade. Finally it became clear that the church could not exist without Utah, and Utah could not exist without statehood. Polygamy was, in a word, abandoned as the price for admission to the union.

Present Politics of the Church

The president of the Latter Day Saints today, George Albert Smith, is a man without guile, seventy-six years old, clear spoken and practical, with an oval gray beard on a long thin jaw. His power derives not merely from his personality, which is agreeable (one of his most fervent admirers, a member of the faith, told me without any irreverence, "the thing to keep in mind about the president is that he's a grand old boy scout"), but from two other factors. First, by Mormon doctrine, God speaks to him as to every believer, and when this comes in the form of a revelation, he is infallible. Second, a descendant of the first prophet's family, he is the third Smith to hold the presidency, and Smith is a name to reckon with in Mormon circles. It's hard to keep Smiths down.

I had the privilege of a brief meeting with President Smith in Salt Lake City; he read me scripture, and talked with lively clarity about the unique characteristics of his community. He thinks that the United States is a chosen land, and that the coming of the Pilgrims was not an accident; he denied that the church has any direct interest in politics in "any way, shape, or form," adding that it simply carried on because God, at the moment, was not on hand, and that baptism does not change the structure of men's brains as between conservatism and liberalism; he is convinced that God will fight our battles if we behave well, and that all men must pay for their crimes on the Day of Judgment, which may come at any moment.

Smith was a successful businessman in his youth, with little thought of an ecclesiastical career, but in his middle years he became an apostle. He spent considerable time as a missionary in England, where he distinguished himself as a teacher with a great executive ability; he succeeded to the presidency in May, 1945, on the death of eighty-eight-year-old Heber J. Grant. A defect of the Mormon system is that leadership is restricted to the very old; almost all presidents live to a great age indeed; there have been only a total of eight since 1830, and if Smith should die his successor would probably be George Richards, president of the council of the twelve apostles, who is eighty-two.

President Grant was, in his last years, old and tired. To this circumstance is often attributed the rise in power of J. Reuben Clark Jr., the present first counselor of the church. Mormon politics are today a kind of tussle between Clark, on the extreme right wing, and the liberals, and an important contemporary question is whether Clark's dominance will survive the new Smith administration.

Under Herbert Hoover, Clark was under secretary of state and ambassador to Mexico; in fact he was called into the first presidency of the church while ambassador. He stumped Utah against the League of Nations in 1919 and was an implacable isolationist. Once Brigham Young paid tribute to his vigorous grandfather (the Clarks are of old Utah stock), by saying "Toss his body in a river; it will float upstream." The same thing might well be said of Clark himself today.

He owes much of his church career to the fact that when he was a boy, Heber Grant liked him. Then he became an extremely successful man of affairs; Grant admired strong personalities who made a great show in the world, and came to rely on him more and more. But in those days the church had a powerful liberal wing, led by a counselor named Anthony W. Ivins; when the Republican party in Utah nominated Clark for senator, he was told by Ivins that, if he ran, he would have to resign as counselor of the church. Clark was in New York, and argued with Ivins by long distance phone. The position of the church was that, although the celebrated Reed Smoot had once been both an apostle and a senator, such a doubling of jobs was improper and unwise; it would be like a cardinal running for president. Clark, forced to choose between a senatorship and his position in the church, withdrew from the senatorial nomination though it had already been accepted on his behalf.

Clark's great days came in the period of Grant's senescence. Ivins died, and from 1934 to 1945 he practically ran the church singlehanded. Not since the days of Brigham Young have the Latter Day Saints known such vigorous rule, I heard it said, and as a consequence Clark became highly unpopular in some circles. An old dictum attributed to Joseph Smith says, "I teach correct principles; then let the church govern itself." The rank and file wanted more chance to govern than it got. On the other hand, one should note that Clark is an absolutely sincere and able man, who has given a generation of devoted service to the church; also, opposition to him comes, not so much from liberals within the church, but from liberals outside. He is disliked on political grounds, not religious.

A counterweight to Clark to some extent is the benign old second counselor, David O. McKay, a middle-roader. He was born and raised near Ogden, began life as a schoolteacher, and was an apostle for almost thirty years. The balance of power on the council is probably held by Apostle John A. Widtsoe, who, interestingly enough, was not born a Mormon. He immigrated to the United States from Norway, and is a convert.

When we turn to the council of the twelve we find that it is pretty well packed with Clark men; of these the most conspicuous is Mark E. Petersen, whose secular job is general manager of the *Deseret News*. Petersen is the mouthpiece of the hierarchy, and as such has great power. Other Clark spokesmen are commonly thought to be Ezra T. Benson, Harold B. Lee, and A. E. Bowen who was a former law partner. Most of these are men in their forties; Petersen, the youngest, is for instance only forty-four. Thus the Clark machinery hopes to perpetuate itself, since apostles hold their jobs for life, or until promotion to the presidency.

Whether an apostle is a Democrat or Republican is, as a rule, a question never asked; nor is there much prying as to a member's finances or early education. All three members of the first presidency today are Republicans and so are nine out of the twelve apostles, it is thought. Several apostles are university graduates; more are not. Petersen is without private means, living on his modest *Deseret News* salary; one of his colleagues is quite rich, the operator of a big automobile business who also owns a cemetery.

The church denies that it intervenes in politics; but of course it does, as I shall soon point out and as, indeed, the most cursory reading of the *Deseret News* will prove. Let us summarize the inner issue. The Mormon theology is based on acceptance, not on free thought; anyone who fights the hierarchy is apt to be squeezed out (for instance by being sent abroad as a missionary), and the dead weight of reactionary influence is still a great drag on LDS affairs.

Turn now to public trends. In the church, the stranglehold of the hierarchy remains; in the state, it is noticeably lifting. The Mormons are, of course, very shrewd politically, and by tradition they work well with whatever party is in control. Members often run against one another, though this means as a rule that one is a "church" (i.e. Republican) candidate, the other is a Democrat; about 60 per cent of the church membership is supposed to be Republican. In an election between a Mormon and a Gentile, each community tends to support its own candidate; progressives in the church are inclined to deplore this, since it preserves a line of religious demarcation in what should be strictly a lay affair. Utah has, incidentally, had two non-Mormon governors since statehood, George Dern,[7] who was Roosevelt's first secretary of war, and Simon

[7] Dern once ran against a man named Mabey. So his campaign slogan was, "We want a Dern good governor, and we don't mean Mabey."

Bamberger, one of the very few Jews ever to be governor of an American state.

To prove that the hand of the hierarchy is not so strong as it once was, on a political plane, one need only turn to the record. Before 1932, Utah was generally Republican; in 1912 for instance it was one of only two states, the other being Vermont, that went for Taft. But since 1932 it has been strongly Democratic; it returned Roosevelt all the four times he ran. The reason is not far to seek. Utah is a poor state. More than 40 per cent of its farms are mortgaged (the third highest rate of farm mortgages in the union), and in 1932 not less than 21 per cent of the population was on relief. So—no matter what the upper level thought— Mormons as well as Gentiles voted for relief. This brings up the ancillary point that the hierarchy, though paternalistic in the extreme and though Brigham Young was one of the most signal exponents of made-work in American history, violently opposed such New Deal measures as the WPA. There were two main reasons for this, first the fear that the federal bureaucracy would cut into its own vested privileges and power, second a desire to take care of its own poor in its own way, independently and alone. And indeed, every Mormon bishopric has a storehouse, or cache, of sugar, canned goods, winter vegetables, and the like, so that the indigent—in theory—never suffer.

But the rank and file didn't follow theory. They wanted WPA, and they voted Roosevelt, Maw, and Elbert Thomas in.

On one great national issue the Church of Jesus Christ of Latter Day Saints did take a formal and united stand. This was prohibition. Yet, by strange chance, Utah was the thirty-sixth state to ratify the 18th Amendment, much to Mormon shame.

Morals and the Mayor of Price

An example of direct church intervention into local politics, in the interests of public morality and good government, came in the 1944 gubernatorial election, when a man named J. Bracken Lee, the Gentile mayor of a town called Price, ran against Governor Herbert Maw. Price is in the coal country, and like most mining towns it bears sin lightly. Zealots in the church thought it should investigate Lee's record there. The motive was almost purely moral, inasmuch as the hierarchy was at the same time strenuously opposing Maw, Lee's opponent. Much as it disliked Maw, the church feared that if Lee got in, he might become a creature of the liquor and gambling interests, and make Utah a kind of Nevada, a thought never to be borne.

A group of churchmen made two trips to Price, and issued a choice little leaflet called *Morals and the Mayor*. I have a copy before me now. It regrets "involving a Utah city in the publicity of a shameful situation . . ." but states that the looseness and corruption of the community was such that thirteen-year-old boys "had been allowed beer." The churchmen concluded by urging Mr. Lee's defeat, even at the price of electing a candidate they didn't like, and he was beaten though by a scanty margin.

L'Affaire Gaeth

In August, 1944, Arthur Gaeth, one of the best-known radio commentators in the West and for many years a leading Mormon, led a clothing drive for Russian war relief. This was sponsored by the American Legion among other organizations; President Smith was a member of the committee; nothing could have been more respectable, and 416,000 pounds of clothing were collected.

On August 23, the *Deseret News*, the official church newspaper, printed a leading article, "Just How Friendly to the U.S. are the Soviets?" Its implication was that the Russians were pretty selfish folk, and, though it did not mention the clothing drive specifically, it hinted that generosity to Russia might well be wasted. So several perplexed churchmen telephoned to Gaeth, asking him what the editorial was driving at; were the clothing contributions, piled up with much labor and sacrifice, merely going down the drain?

Gaeth waited a few days, and on his next regular broadcast over the Intermountain Network, of which he is vice president, he explored the issue, trying to allay fears of the flock. The broadcast was reasonable enough, though vigorous in tone. Whereupon ten days later, the *News* came out with a front page editorial, something almost unprecedented, and attacked Gaeth by name in two thousand furious words, insinuating that he was a Communist sympathizer and practically denouncing him as an apostate. And Gaeth had been head of a church mission for ten years! In the whole history of the Mormon church, there is no similar record of attack by the hierarchy on an individual. Reason? The hierarchy mortally hated (and hates) Stalinist Russia, and thought Gaeth a pink.

Gaeth had crossed swords with his superiors once before. Some years ago he worked for KSL, the church station. When, after the German attack on the U.S.S.R. in 1941, he welcomed Russia as an ally, he was warned that the brethren might insist on editing his broadcasts. A little later he brought up a controversial domestic issue, the need of transition in Utah from agriculture to industry, something that some Mormons oppose though it would almost certainly raise the standard of living of the community. Gaeth was told, "The brethren are dissatisfied." He offered thereupon to put himself at the disposal of the first presidency. But he was given no appointment. Then, informally, he went to Counselor McKay. But McKay had never heard about the argument, which indicated that although pressure was put on Gaeth in the name of the first presidency, a member of the first presidency had not been consulted. Gaeth's boss at this time, the manager of KSL, was Ivor Sharp, who is J. Reuben Clark's son-in-law.

Footnote on the Deseret News

This is one of the most remarkable newspapers ever printed anywhere; I know nothing like it except, possibly, the old Denver *Post*. It has existed since 1850, and is the official church paper, supposedly reaching Mormons not merely in Utah, but everywhere in the United States. Yet its circulation is only forty thousand daily, in a region where it could reach at least five hundred thousand readers. For many years it had an annual deficit, and it is apparently disliked by many in the community; in fact I was told that a petition demanding a change in its editorial policy would get fifty thousand signers.

The *Deseret News* is, of course, dominated (through Petersen) by Clark. It carries no liquor or tobacco advertisements; it is full of news of genealogy; it prints nothing against morals. It was violently isolationist before Pearl Harbor, and I was told that for three solid years, 1942 to 1945, it scarcely printed a single editorial attacking Hitler or Nazism, though it denounced Roosevelt scores of times. The only columnists it publishes are Pegler, Rukeyser, and Sokolsky, and when I asked President Smith why its columns were closed to Walter Lippmann, Dorothy Thompson, and Samuel Grafton among others (who after all are not Communists), the aged head of the church looked bewildered. Then his explanation of the paper's policy was that "the church owns it, but people on the staff have their voice" (that is, Reuben Clark's voice), and that "it didn't want to get embroiled in the rest of the world."

Any of a hundred *Deseret News* editorials will show quickly the paper's slant, tone, and method. I choose one from the issue of July 23, 1945:

POISONED VOTE BAIT

The plain, unadulterated bunk that is being peddled today by so-called responsible men in government to the effect that Congress must pass legislation that will provide jobs for all, is simply sickening. Congress might pass an emergency measure that would employ everybody for a few months or a year or two, but neither Congress nor the government has a dime to employ anybody until it first takes it away from the people in taxes . . .

Hitler's Germany would be a kindergarten compared with the tyranny that would develop in any country that provided jobs for all . . .

Maw, Utah Power, and Thomas

By three years, Governor Herbert B. Maw is senior to his state; Utah became a state in 1896, and is thus fifty years old; Maw, one of the most interesting of contemporary governors, is fifty-three. He is a former professor of oratory and one of the best public speakers in the United States. In both physical appearance—he has a broad tanned forehead and a vigorous, well-cared-for body—and in deliberation of manner, plus confidence, he resembles Harold Stassen. And, like Stassen, he is a comparatively isolated figure; few people seem to know him well, and he keeps himself pretty inaccessible. When a man does get close, Maw will be apt to win him. A Republican worthy, visiting him recently, said, "It isn't till I get away from Maw that I can make up my mind that I'm *not* going to vote for him."

Maw, a tough and honest people's man, is a typical western-type New Dealer. He was a poor boy, who wanted to be a surgeon; from the ages of ten to fifteen he sold papers on the street, and then worked nights to pay his way through college. Once again the self-made man! He had to give up a medical career because he could not afford the laboratory fees. Then he turned to law and teaching. He is, of course, a Mormon; he was one of three LDS chaplains in the U.S. Army in World War I.

But the top layer of the church fights him bitterly. For many years he belonged to the general boards of both the MIA and the Deseret Sunday School Union (one of the most important of all Mormon groups); but when he came out for the governorship in 1940, the hierarchy demanded that he resign from his ecclesiastical posts. Maw's theory of this is that the church was punishing him for being a New Dealer. Then, on becoming governor Maw, a fighter, retaliated by refusing to reappoint two apostles as regents of the University of Utah, McKay and Richards. The church leadership considered this an unforgivable affront, and in the 1944 campaign the *Deseret News* opposed him with sustained ferocity.

A great many Republicans voted for Maw, a Democrat, in this complex election, because they favored his industrial development program, and without these votes he would have been beaten, inasmuch as many Democrats opposed him, though he was their candidate. But the Democratic party is severely split in Utah, and Maw was widely scratched against by his own people. What, then, is the basis of his support? First, loyal Democrats generally. Second, church and nonchurch liberals, particularly the young element. Third, the old folks. Utah, like California, does a lot for its aged and indigent, from which Maw benefited. The very young and very old comprised the wings of his coalition.

There has been no real political "machine" in Utah since Reed Smoot, and the chief pressure groups today are: (*a*) the Utah Power & Light Company; (*b*) the sheep interests, who control southern Utah; (*c*) the education lobby; and (d) the liquor interests. The importance of these last may be appreciated from the fact that the Utah Liquor Control Commission made a profit of $2,373,423.41 in 1944. Recently, an odd minor point, a bill was introduced but not passed to set up a new liquor tax which was to be exclusively assigned to paying for *temperance* propaganda.

Maw runs the state, insofar as he runs it, mostly by careful use of his power over the Liquor Commission, the pensioners (through the State Welfare Department), and the State Road Commission. Almost all governors work through similar agencies. Suppose the roads get bad in the fall. They may, in your community, be repaired or not, depending on whom your community voted for. Utah does not do things so crudely, but the pattern exists almost everywhere else in the United States.

When Maw first became governor in 1940, he cleaned house, and practically everybody attached to the previous ultraconservative Democratic administration got the sack. The joke was, "Everything was kicked out of the capitol but the statuary." Maw had two motives in this—first to install his own people, second to reorganize the apparatus of administration. But his reorganization was so drastic that at the end jobs were scarce even for his own men, and they too became aggrieved. Also the legislature became saddled with a permanent budget commission, set up *sine die* as a kind of watchdog on Maw's plans. To this day, it is all but impossible to determine accurately whether his reforms have saved the state money or not, or how worth while they have been otherwise.

Maw, as a result of all this, is himself the chief political issue in the state; the only real cleavage is Maw or anti-Maw, and he is both extolled and hated almost as Roosevelt was.

Another struggle was between Maw and the Utah Power & Light Company, until recently a subsidiary of that enormous spidery octopus, Electric Bond & Share.[8] Maw won. He has been fighting Utah Power off and on ever since he entered politics; he was a senator for ten years before becoming governor. In fact, he first ran for governor because of irritation at what was going on in the legislature. He happened for instance on one occasion to overhear a lobbyist for the Taxpayers Association, who was Republican, calmly inform five Democrats how they were to vote. Once he wrote a bill to increase Utah Power's taxes by a minor amount. What followed may, *mutatis mutandis*, be taken as an example of the technique of the power lobby all over the United States. First, though he had not told a soul about his bill, the company knew every detail of it—so he swears—before he had finished drafting it. Second, lobbyists invited him to a lavish dinner, and tried to persuade

---

[8] Utah Power is itself a minor octopus. It owns and operates electric power and light companies in Idaho and Wyoming as well as Utah, and it wholly owns the Western Colorado Power Company.

him to withdraw it. Third, they organized opposition to it in the legislature. Fourth, they asked the president of the university (where Maw
was a professor and dean of men) to call him off. Fifth, when all this
failed, they tried to get his job.

But Maw stuck it out. Moreover, as a direct result, because enough
people liked what he was doing, he became governor. Virtue, even in
American politics, is sometimes its own reward. Meantime he had been
striking back all the time. He was convinced, for instance, that Utah
Power, like Montana Power as we have seen, was grossly overcapitalized
(the big capitalization gave it, of course, an excuse for high rates);
when he said so in the senate, not a paper in the state would print his
speech, though every reporter knew that he was stating facts. In the end
the Federal Power Commission in Washington ordered a reorganization
of the company, squeezing out a lot of water; then Maw helped to force
through a rate reduction that saves the people of Utah about $1,500,000
per year; moreover, the reduction was made retroactive, and every
utility customer in the state got a refund.

Elbert D. Thomas, the senior senator from Utah, is a very different
type of man from Maw, but he too is a Mormon liberal. And the fact that
he has won three successive senatorial races against conservatives (all
Clark men) shows how the Utah winds are blowing. Thomas was a
professor of classics for many years; Utah runs to professors in politics.
One of his distinctions is his expert knowledge of Japanese; he spent a
considerable time in Japan as a missionary, once taught English in the
Tokyo War College, and is the author of a religious book in Japanese,
Sukui No Michi. During World War II he broadcast regularly to Japan
in Japanese, for the OWI.

Thomas, tall, lean, gray, and grave, is of English stock; his father was
a London draper, and he is quite proud of the fact that he is one of two
Utahans in the British *Who's Who*. He has always been a Jeffersonian,
an interventionist, and a strong prolabor man. As chairman of the Military Affairs Committee of the Senate he played a powerful and constructive role during the war; he had more to do with the writing of the
Selective Service Act than any other civilian. In 1942 he sponsored the
Thomas-LaFollette bill which, if passed, would have imposed criminal
penalties on labor spies and would have prohibited yellow-dog contracts
and hiring of strikebreakers.

What Thomas believes in most is Mormonism, which he thinks gives
a man more individual dignity than any other religion; a man of grace
and erudition, he is greatly respected both in Utah and the Senate; he is
a bit inclined to be pleased with himself, and with considerable good
reason.

Utah had another strong liberal senator in Abe Murdock (also a
Mormon) until 1947; he was beaten in the 1946 midterm landslide. In

a chart prepared by the *New Republic* in February, 1946, he was one of only four senators who was credited with a 100 per cent perfect progressive voting record. The other three were Green of Rhode Island, Tunnell of Delaware, and Mitchell of Washington.[9]

What an enormously diversified country is the United States, even in respect to an item so small as this! Green is a traction magnate and millionaire aristocrat; Tunnell a public school teacher who became a vigorously successful bank president; Mitchell is the son of a civil servant; Murdock, a poor boy, was born on a farm.

Life Among the Gentiles

There are, of course, other forces in Utah aside from the Mormon church. Take the Catholics. The bishop of the Diocese of Salt Lake City, Duane G. Hunt, is probably one of the ten most important people in the state; he is a convert (from Methodism) who in 1945 celebrated the twenty-fifth anniversary of his conversion. And, among lay Catholics, consider John F. Fitzpatrick, who was once a railway conductor and who now runs the great Kearns estate. The Kearns interests today, operated by Fitzpatrick, include the Silver King mine, one of the biggest mining properties in the world and the foundation of the wealth of Salt Lake City, and the two Gentile papers there, the *Tribune* and *Telegram*.

I have mentioned that a Jew, Simon Bamberger, was once governor of Utah. And Salt Lake City once had a Jewish mayor. The Bambergers, a rich and influential family, own the electric railway between Salt Lake City and Ogden, and have large mining interests. One of the brothers at the head of the family is married to a grandniece of Heber Grant's.

Also consider agriculture. Only about 13 per cent of Utah is arable (at least 75 per cent of the territory of the state is still public domain, incidentally); only 3.3 per cent of the total area is actually tilled. To double this area, which is what most progressives want, would cost about 400 million dollars in irrigation projects. Most Utah farms are very small, under twenty acres. The chief crop is sugar beets.

There must also be a word about the railways. Salt Lake City is equidistant, within forty or fifty miles, from San Diego, Los Angeles, San Francisco, Portland, and Seattle; and as any boy knows who has ever looked at a railway map, Salt Lake City and Ogden are the headquarters of a gigantic fork of routes spreading out to the Pacific coast. Seventy per cent of all transcontinental traffic in the United States goes through this Utah fork. The dominant railway is, of course, the Union Pacific; it is almost as important to Utah as, say, is the Pennsylvania to

---

[9] Eight senators are given a similarly 100 per cent negative record—Millikin (Colo.), Willis (Ind.), Hickenlooper (Iowa), Reed (Kans.), Hawkes (N.J.), Moore (Okla.), Bushfield (S.D.), Robertson (Wyo.).

New Jersey. Its headquarters are in Omaha, Nebraska, but it was incorporated in Salt Lake City, and Utah is its spiritual home. The Mormons at one time attempted to compete with the Union Pacific by building their own line (the Utah Central) south from Salt Lake City. Long ago they gave this up, and the church and Union Pacific have co-operated closely ever since.

Does the Mormon church oppose industrialization? This is a gravely argued point. On the surface it would seem absurd that anybody with the basic interests of the community at heart should resist any such development. But industrialization means a labor influx since, after all, machines cannot be run without men. In the 1920's, the population of Utah was 75 per cent Mormon; today, as we know, it is 60. And the more the state is opened up, the more will Gentiles filter in, thus further diluting the church majority. Also, an auxiliary point, industrialization usually means a shift in voting power, since labor is inclined to vote Democratic and—very important from the LDS point of view—a big labor immigration might bring about a breakup in the social structure and, Mormons say, a decline in moral standards.

The two greatest industrial complexes in Utah, about which space forbids any but the briefest mention though I visited them both, are the Utah Copper Company and Geneva Steel. Utah Copper, at Bingham, is absentee owned (by Kennecott and allied eastern interests); its great mine is an enormous declivity, one of the most remarkable sights I ever saw, which looks like the Great Pyramid of Egypt in reverse; it is by all odds the largest open pit copper mine in the world, having produced well over five billion pounds of copper since its foundation in 1906. The ore spooned here from the open earth is smelted in part by another great eastern corporation which maintains a plant near Salt Lake City, American Smelting and Refining. Utah Copper distributes millions of dollars per year in dividends; of this, nothing but a fraction stays in Utah. Yet 50 per cent of the state's population depends for livelihood on the mining industry.

Geneva Steel is something else again. The copper mine seems in some indefinable way reminiscent of the past; its atmosphere is obsolescent. But the great new 220 million dollar steel plant is as contemporaneous as tomorrow's newspaper; it is, in fact, incomparably the most modern steel works in the world. It was built from scratch near Provo for purposes of World War II, and was operated during the war by the United States Steel Corporation (through a subsidiary, Columbia Steel), for the Defense Plant Corporation. Visiting it, I saw the 150-foot-long slabs of steel shoot through the rolling mill at the rate of 1,200 feet per minute, in a thunderous and sizzling roar, in appearance like gigantic strips of well-smoked salmon. You can tell the different stages of combustion going on by the multi-colored smoke pouring out of the chimneys—

orange, black, brownish, gray. Geneva Steel was the angry focus of the kind of struggle between eastern and western interests that I have already noted in connection with Henry Kaiser. After the war it lay inert for a long interval, waiting for a purchaser. Westerners hoped that Kaiser or some other western company would—or could—buy it, and so assist the integration of a growing steel industry for the entire West. Following a great deal of obscure and difficult negotiation Geneva was knocked down by the War Assets Administration to United States Steel for $47,500,000, which represents less than 25¢ on the dollar, although a Los Angeles company (New York *Times*, May 2, 1946) bid more than $200,000,000 for it. Kaiser did not bid. The upshot of this is that Big Steel, even more than previously, is master of the western steel industry, such as it is.

. . . .

So now to conclude with Utah. From everything I have said, the essential point rises clear and sharp. The Mormon community, with so much at stake, with its tremendous contribution in pioneering, colonization, devotion to standards, and plain hard work, is hanging tenaciously onto the unique preserve it created. But the astringent winds of a new world, which bewilder the older believers, are beating mercilessly at the pillar they drove into the desert.

Chapter 14

—But Scenery Is Not Enough

wwwwwwwwwwwwwwwwwwwwwwwwwwwwwwwwwwwwwwwwwwwwwwwwwwwwwwwwwwwww

To fling-Ossa upon Olympus, and to pile Pelion with all its
growth of leafy woods on Ossa.

—*Odyssey, XI, 315*

They came to the Delectable Mountains.

—*Pilgrim's Progress*

COLORADO, the most spectacular of the mountain states, lives on
many things—scenery, beet sugar, gold, molybdenum, livestock,
tourists, and tuberculosis. As to this last I heard an ungentle and taste-
less Coloradan complain, "Some fiend in human form discovered that rest,
not altitude, was the best cure for t.b., and so the tuberculosis cases don't
come to Colorado so much any more, and the economy of the state
suffered terribly as a result, so I suppose you could say that t.b. is killing
us, not the patients."

Very little in the world can compare to the scenery of Colorado. The
vistas here stretch the eyes, enlighten the heart, and make the spirit
humble. Colorado has more than 1,500 peaks—literally—more than
10,000 feet high, and of the sixty-five in the United States higher than
14,000 feet, it has not less than fifty-one. This is indeed the top of the
nation. Colorado has the highest automobile road in the country, the
highest automobile races, the highest ski courses, the highest astronomical
laboratory and the highest railway tunnel and the highest lake and the
highest yacht anchorage and the highest suspension bridge. It has two
national parks and six national monuments, fourteen million acres of
national forest and more than seven thousand miles of fishing streams.
And no matter where you turn, up and down or left and right, the overwhelming variety and magnitude of the view makes you blink. But—
the state has had to learn these past years that scenery alone, no matter
how stupefyingly dramatic, does not pay the bills. Scenery alone is not
enough.

Colorado, like Oregon among the western states, is distinctly on the
conservative side. It is conservative politically, economically, financially.
I do not mean reactionary. Just conservative—with the kind of conserv-
ativeness that does not budge an inch for anybody or anything unless
pinched and pushed. For instance, one point among several, Colorado
is the thirty-ninth state in amount of state aid to education. Or con-

sider reconversion. Washington and California, as we know, worked hard and concretely on postwar planning, to ease the gap toward peace. Colorado did almost nothing—and was proud of it. It has ridden for year after year on its prestige, its reputation. Nothing better illustrates this than affairs in Denver, as we shall soon see.

But to return to scenery and tourist traffic for a moment. In a normal year tourists bring into the state something like sixty-five million dollars. This sum is not to be sneezed at, but it could be greater. I heard complaints generally that "Colorado has missed the boat on tourism." Scenery is to Colorado what sunshine is to California, but it makes nothing like California's effort to capitalize on this asset, dramatize and buttress it. There will be many, I grant, who will congratulate Colorado for its lack of organized booster spirit. But progressive Coloradans themselves worry about how the state is becoming a backwater. Until quite recently, for instance, it employed no director of public relations and the governor had no press advisor. This was mostly the result of negative influence by the Denver *Post*, which held that it, exclusively, provided enough publicity for Colorado; it vehemently opposed creation of any other agency. As a consequence the state paid comparatively small attention to roads, country hotels, and the like; it built no enterprises like Sun Valley, and the general mood was to give the visitor a quick glimpse of Pike's Peak, and then let him get out.

Colorado is divided down the middle by the sharp and impenetrable spine of the continental divide; its western and eastern sections differ considerably, though the cleavage is not so sharp as in Washington. The western slope faces Salt Lake City, the eastern Denver. The west, behind the divide, is mostly mining and livestock country; the east is irrigated and merges into the Great Plains. The western slope is dominated by two or three land-owning families; the eastern—including Denver—has one overriding magnate, Claude K. Boettcher. I use this somewhat old-fashioned word, "magnate," because Mr. Boettcher so precisely evokes its spirit. The word "tycoon" connotes a touch of the parvenu, the adventurous. Boettcher is no parvenu. He is solid like a plinth, adhesive, and pachydermous. If I were a casting director in Hollywood and wanted a type to play one of the railroad barons of the last century, I would hire Mr. Boettcher at once. This margrave of the sugar beets, this padishah of cement, potash, mining, what not, one of the richest men in America and one of the least known, is a magnate like the antique Astors and Vanderbilts.

But the chief element of difference between eastern and western Colorado is water. Touch water, and you touch everything; about water the state is as sensitive as a carbuncle. Water—as is true all over the West—is everybody's chief preoccupation. In the briefest kind of summary, the situation is that western Colorado has more water than it can use, eastern less than it needs. Hence the east must have irrigation and the problem—this is reminiscent of California—is to get the water over. This the west resents. It thinks it is being milked of water for the benefit of capitalists in Denver which, in many respects, is almost as "foreign" a city as Wilmington, Delaware or Brookline, Massachusetts. The east replies that the water is "spare" water and that the west wastes it anyway.

Water is blood in Colorado; only California among American states has a greater irrigated area. And I know no state with quite so many water issues:

(1) The Big Thompson Diversion project. This is a thirteen-mile tunnel through the divide, built by the Bureau of Reclamation to tap the Colorado River headwaters. It will, in effect, make the river pump itself backward through the mountains, to provide three hundred thousand acre-feet per year for irrigation on the eastern slopes. The project is built, but the war delayed the finishing touches, and as of the moment it is not yet in operation.

(2) A still larger diversion scheme is planned for the Blue River, a northern tributary of the Colorado, with a twenty-mile tunnel that will produce 500,000 acre-feet per year. This is a joint project of the Bureau of Reclamation, the state of Colorado, and Denver; it will irrigate 320,000 acres now insufficiently supplied with water.

(3) The Gunnison River project. This, according to plans, will do for the Arkansas River valley (in southern Colorado) what Big Thompson and Blue River will do for the north.

(4) MVA. The conservative interests of course oppose MVA, and Denver has been the focus of more propaganda against it than any other city. MVA, it is claimed, would upset Colorado's own irrigation schemes; the issue is not only fear of government authority, but loss of water. That MVA would interfere with Colorado irrigation has, however, by no means been proved. Governor John C. Vivian, whom I would rank as one of the dullest American governors I met, told me, "The courts have held for fifty years that the man who makes beneficial use of water owns not the water itself but the use of it. Now this MVA thing comes along and three men in Washington could take our water away. What do we care about navigation up around Fargo? We want our own water here!" The governor, incidentally, once publicly said that, to beat MVA, he would spend the whole state surplus of nine million dollars if necessary.

(5) Colorado, Wyoming, and Nebraska have been at each other's throats for a quarter of a century, arguing in the courts about disposition of water from the North Platte; each of the three states, by long-established "filings," gets its "take" of North Platte water. Colorado says (in the person of Magnate Boettcher who put it this way to me): "We've

been here for seventy years. We made the prairie bloom. We turned sagebrush into sugar beets. We did all this when Nebraska and Kansas were nothing but territory fit for jack rabbits." Wyoming, too, bitterly resents what it calls Nebraska's "grab." But by a recent Supreme Court judgment Nebraska is to get 75 per cent of North Platte water, with Colorado and Wyoming dividing the remainder.

(6) The Colorado River Compact and the Mexican Water Treaty. This we shall mention later where it more properly belongs, in connection with Arizona.

Historically Colorado is of mixed origin; in whole or in part it has variously belonged to Spain, France, Mexico, and Texas. There is still a strong Spanish underlay in the southern tier of counties; all these bear Spanish names.[1] Its modern annals begin with the discovery of gold in 1858, nine years after the California Gold Rush, and the mines at Leadville and Cripple Creek became a mud-and-canvas Mecca. It is an interesting revelation of the national character—James Truslow Adams makes a point of this—that California and the far West, though farther away, should have been settled *before* the states of the Rockies and Great Plains. It is as if a crazy impetuosity carried the first frontiersmen as far as they could possibly go geographically; they swooped straight across the continent without pause (of course this generalization is too broad); then later a second wave, less volatile, descended on the states between.

Coloradans are proud of being Coloradans, and the state has a large proportion of citizens born within its borders. This is in acute contrast to Oklahoma and Arizona, say. A very real cleavage, especially in Denver, is that between old-timers born locally and those who moved in from outside; I felt this more strongly in Colorado than anywhere else in the country, except possibly New England. This prompts one to a word about the Indians who, after all, were in Colorado even before the first families of Denver got there. Colorado is the only western state where I never once heard the word "Indian" spoken, which is the more interesting in that the Utes were the only Indian tribe in the United States—like the Araucanians in Chile—never conquered. Today they play no role in state life at all.

The total wealth of Colorado was estimated in 1937 at $3,434,000,000 and the foundation of the state's economy is not, as one would be apt to think, mining, but agriculture. Mining began to decline thirty years ago. The easy gold got scooped out; the easy money ended when it

[1] Spanish (or Mexican) influence versus British is another Colorado cleavage. British influence has always been strong in the north and east: for instance the streetcars in Denver are called tramways. An odd point is that the Catholic Mexicans in the south were permitted, by special dispensation, to eat meat on Fridays, since the area was too dry for fish. For this note, as well as for much else in this chapter, I am indebted to my friend Roscoe Fleming.

became necessary to use complex and expensive metallurgical processes to refine ore.[2] People turned instead to sugar beets and livestock. Today, it is not gold or even comparatively rare metals like uranium and vanadium that are the heart of the mining industry that remains, but prosaic coal. Colorado is the first state in the union in coal reserves, with—in theory—enough deposits to last forever.

Colorado has more big game than any other American state, and Denver is the biggest manufactory of fishhooks in the world; Colorado Springs is the glisteningly suave "Newport of the West," and the greatest man the state ever produced was Judge Ben Lindsey, who was of course reviled by the city he worked so hard to improve. Once, when he sentenced a utilities executive to jail, the executive shouted in the courtroom, "This state has more sunshine and more bastards than any place on earth!"

"Top of the Nation"

I drove into Denver along the sharp steel-blue curtain of the divide. We saw antelope; we saw the B-29's drilling invisible holes overhead; we saw the turkeys. These are herded just like sheep, thousands to the herd, and they have commendable utility; they eat grasshoppers out of the wheat, and then are duly eaten themselves. We saw something that I would not have believed could exist—a coal mine protruding through a wheat field; we saw the untidy beet dumps in clusters around the small, ugly, chugging sugar factories. We passed fields of crest grass, for which the government furnishes seed as part of the soil conservation program; we passed haystackers at work and ghost villages that the automobile assassinated. In the horse-and-buggy days a village with a post office and general store could support itself, but not now, inasmuch as people with a car can drive greater distances to a bigger or more advantageous market. We looked at a hamlet called Nunn, with a bold sign WATCH NUNN GROW on the water tower. The population of Nunn is exactly 196.

The wheat looked different from that in Washington or Montana. Here it is harvested by a binder, which leaves the shocks in the field to be threshed later. Colorado does not go in for combines much. First, a combine leaves no straw, and there is a big demand for straw in Denver; second, a binder can cut wheat while still moist, whereas it has to be bone dry before a combine can handle it; the binder thus makes harvesting possible a few days earlier, and lessens the risk of damage by bad weather. Hail can kill a county full of wheat in half an hour. If hail could be abolished, there would be no beets or corn in Colorado. People who

[2] A striking illustration of this is the way the names of mines changed. At first they had such names as Ace of Diamonds, Invincible, Golconda. Then they became Last Chance, Grubstake, Hard Times. *These United States,* II, p. 374.

bought wheat farms at twenty dollars an acre last year have paid for their land already, with one tremendous crop.

Later I drove from Denver out to Boulder and Central City to see the forests. Colorado has hundreds of thousands of acres of virgin timber —much of it in carefully protected national parks—and scarcely a single mill. From the point of view of conservation this is admirable. Consider the depraved looting of Oregon by contrast. But it isn't just conservation that keeps processing mills out of Colorado; freight rates are the major reason. Ship unprocessed timber to the East, and the rate is favorable. Make a plank out of a log, let alone pulp or paper, and it jumps prohibitively.

We watched the cattle in the high pastures. They are born and raised here, fattened in the local feed lots, slaughtered in the Colorado yards, and sold all over the country, including Denver—as Kansas City beef! We watched the sheep. The herders bring them up to government-owned land, near the snow, every winter, where grazing is free except for a nominal charge. Here too, freight rates become a problem. To ship raw or unprocessed wool east is comparatively cheap, but to clean wool takes three-quarters of the weight away, and on this "scoured" wool, the rate goes up. The railways prefer to ship the heavier wool anyway, since it makes a bigger freight load. So Colorado has no wool scouring plants.

At Boulder, one of the most briskly lovely towns I have ever seen, we visited the university, which is the seat and fountainhead of much of what liberalism obtains in the state, and which has become a kind of intellectual capital (like Chapel Hill in the South) for the whole mountain region. There has been a lively issue lately over academic freedom; the episode resembles to an extent the famous brawl at the University of Texas, which we will deal with in due course—but it has a different ending. Regents at the University of Colorado are chosen by what is known as the "Michigan system," i.e. they are elected by vote of the people on a party basis. Nominations were, however, usually reserved for deserving party hacks; to get on the board of regents was something like being promoted to the House of Lords. But in 1944 the character of the board changed. President Robert L. Stearns was on leave of absence with the armed forces—where he made a brilliant record—and the president in his absence was R. G. Gustavson, professor of chemistry and a vivid and hard-hitting progressive. Gustavson later became dean of the faculties at the University of Chicago, and then (September, 1946) chancellor of the University of Nebraska. The regents, with two new reactionary members, began to stir up trouble, and it became known that four professors had been passed over for routine promotion and salary increases. That this was pure discrimination and that the four were being disciplined for "liberalism" could not be doubted. Of the four one was a Jew, Joseph Cohen, professor of philosophy; one, Clay Malick, was called a "radical" because he once told a political science class that the British cabinet system was as good as ours; one, Professor Edwin Walker of the department of religion, had been instrumental in inviting Harry Bridges to address a student assembly; one, Professor Morris E. Garnsey, chairman of the department of economics, was an adherent of MVA. Indeed partisanship over MVA had a good deal to do with the whole issue. In the end—from the point of view of academic freedom—all turned out happily. President Stearns came back and took a strong line in favor of the "radical" professors, public opinion became aroused, the board of regents backed down, and the four duly received their promotions.[3]

Central City is totally something else again. This is a shadow town like Virginia City in Nevada. Sagging boardwalks and yellowish torn curtains over cracked windows; stairways frayed and broken; dog-eared timbers holding back yellow mud in what was once one of the great mines of the world. Central City had been dying for a long time; the War Production Board ban on gold and silver mining killed it. But Central City is celebrated for two reasons other than the mines. The Teller House, an ancient and proud hotel, contains the original Face on the Barroom Floor; it's still there to see. Everybody knows the old ballad this evoked:

'Twas a balmy summer evening, and a goodly crowd was there
Which well-nigh filled Joe's barroom on the corner of the square,
And as songs and witty stories came through the open door,
A vagabond crept slowly in and posed upon the floor.

And at the end—

Another drink and with chalk in hand, the vagabond began
To sketch a face that well might buy the soul of any man,
Then as he placed another lock upon the shapely head
With a fearful shriek he leaped and fell across the picture dead.

Also, until the war, Central City had a theater festival that brought summer visitors from everywhere. The opera house—how revealing it is that these old mining towns should all have had their formidably ornate operas!—was refurbished for the occasion, and performances were put on like *Othello* with Walter Huston, *The Merry Widow* with Gladys Swarthout, and *A Doll's House* with Ruth Gordon. All this in a deserted mining village tucked high and almost invisible in the Rocky Mountains!

Colorado is, as a matter of fact, a state famous for theatrical talent.

---

[3] The University of Colorado at Boulder is not to be confused with the University of Denver, which is an altogether different institution. It too has an able president, Dr. Ben M. Cherrington.

The Elitch open air theater in Denver has a sumptuous history, and Douglas Fairbanks, Ernest Truex, Fredric March, Harold Lloyd, Fred Stone, Edward G. Robinson, are among figures of stage and screen who are, or were, Colorado born.

Some Factors in Colorado Politics

(1) Seventeenth Street. This is the Denver financial and banking center, the equivalent of Wall Street; for years it pretty well dominated the state. But nowadays, though still powerful, it doesn't always have its own way. And although it absolutely controls the state legislature, it doesn't carry so much weight in the city; for instance FDR carried Denver every time he ran. I asked one eminent Seventeenth Street tycoon whether it was really true that his brethren ran Colorado, and he sighed in reply, "Ah, if it were only true!"

(2) The Denver *Post*, which for years occupied itself largely by grinding out hate.

(3) Industry, which is of course tied up with Seventeenth Street. For decades the most important single enterprise was the Colorado Fuel and Iron Company in Pueblo, owned by the Rockefellers. The Rockefeller people sold it in 1945, however, to other eastern interests. Colorado Fuel and Iron made two things indispensable to the growing West— barbed wire and rails—and hence prospered. One should also mention the cement companies in which Boettcher is the main figure, and the utilities. The chief power companies are the Southern Colorado Power Company and the Public Service Company of Colorado, which was recently separated by the SEC from the Cities Service Company (Doherty interests) and is now autonomous.

Colorado has some superb railways, and nothing is more brilliant than the record of the lustrous streamliners which bore their way to Chicago, 1,052 miles away, every day in fifteen hours—the Burlington Zephyrs, the Union Pacific streamliners, and the Rock Island Rockets. But the railways have, in a way, less influence in Colorado than elsewhere in the West, if only because the first transcontinental lines did not cross it. The Union Pacific by-passed Denver for Cheyenne, and the Santa Fe went through New Mexico. Naughty politics played no role in this; the obstacle was simply the barrier of the mountains.

(4) Sugar. By far the biggest Colorado company is the Great Western Sugar Company, a Boettcher concern. In fact it was the Boettcher family and other German settlers at the turn of the century who first brought sugar beets to the state. The industry grew prodigiously during and after the shortages of World War I, and since that time, as everybody knows, sugar has been a headache—nationally and internationally—of migraine size. To tell the story in any detail would take a book, and

I must beg indulgence for attempting to foreshorten into a paragraph a subject of the most dense and abstruse difficulty. The long and short of it is that sugar, more than any other product used in America, is supported by a fantastically artificial price. The story has ramifications all over the place. For instance it was the large domestic sugar producers who assisted greatly in the movement for Filipino independence; the first idea—though it hasn't quite worked out that way—was that commonwealth status would push Filipino sugar outside the American free-trade area, so that it would be able to compete with domestic sugar only after climbing a tariff barrier. At the moment, however, Filipino sugar comes in duty free; a preferential tariff will begin to operate in 1954. Meantime the American consumer—and taxpayer— is helping to pay for sugar subsidies to Hawaii and Puerto Rico, and for a price arrangement with Cuba, to keep Cuba from exploding, which it always does if it cannot sell enough sugar to the United States. Without these arrangements, beet sugar, a highly synthetic industry to say the least, could hardly survive. Finally, there is the domestic subsidy to the American cane and beet producers. This was set at $4.00 per ton for beet sugar in 1945, though the sugar growers wanted it higher. The farmer at present receives $13.50 per ton of sugar beets. Of this roughly $6.90 comes from the processor, $2.60 from the federal government under the Sugar Act, and $4.00 as a subsidy payment (also federal) by the Commodity Corporation. But both growers and processors want further help. Late in 1946 sugar was the only commodity in the United States still on the ration list. Despite every stimulus to the domestic industry, there isn't enough to go around, though plenty of cheap sugar is grown in the world.

The sugar bloc in Congress, comprising western and southern senators both, has a legislative power—and veto power—like none other in the country except possibly the silver bloc. And, even more than the silver bloc, it represents an extreme minority of interest. Only 3 per cent of American farmers grow sugar beet and cane; the entire processing industry employs no more than twenty-five thousand people. But sugar is spread through many states—beets grow in seventeen, cane in two—which gives it thirty-eight senators out of ninety-six,[4] and they can certainly make a noise.

(5) The Colorado Education Association (an organization of schoolteachers founded in 1875), the American Legion, and groups similarly familiar in many states. We might also mention hangovers from the Ku Klux Klan; for Colorado more than any northern state except Oregon and Indiana, had a strong Klan movement after World War I. One former governor, an overt Klansman, was arrested on a stock fraud

[4] See "The Sugar Shortage and Politics," by Hubert A. Kenny, *American Mercury*, May, 1946.

not long ago and sentenced to jail. Also one might include old age pensionnaires—who are protected by quite generous legislation—and the liquor interests. Finally, the wool and cattlemen's associations.

(6) A sizable Spanish-American vote, and a considerable Catholic influence. There are at least twenty-five thousand "Mexicans" in Denver alone.

(7) Labor. The CIO membership in the state is only about eight thousand, that of the AF of L more and of the Railway Brotherhoods somewhat less. But labor is an active and growing force, and the CIO takes credit for cutting some Republican majorities in half in the last election. The legislature passed in 1943 the Colorado Labor Peace Act—so-called although there had not been a single wartime strike—that wiped out every labor gain since the Ludlow Massacre in 1914; it set a record in the nation for antilabor legislation, and was even denounced by West-brook Pegler. The courts nullified some sections of it after a time, and no substitute bill has ever been passed—which Colorado labor counts as a considerable victory, if negative. The CIO itself is badly split. One wing lines up with the United Steel Workers, another with the International Mine, Mill, and Smelter Workers, a union which is itself divided. The wage scale for miners is the lowest in the nation. A man at Anaconda gets only $7.75 per day; but at Pueblo or at the molybdenum works at Climax (which produces 85 per cent of the world's molybdenum), the rate may be as low as $5.00.

(8) The legislature. This is overwhelmingly conservative and Republican. Several members are wealthy lawyers with corporation practices, like Robert G. Bosworth and Arthur H. Laws who helped write the labor bill; others are the state's biggest dry farmers and cattlemen. It is comparatively rare in the United States for men of such beam and caliber to bother with active participation in a legislature. But Seventeenth Street watches its interests hard.

(9) The parties and personalities. In sixteen national elections up to 1944, Colorado went Democratic eight times, Republican eight times, so it is touch-and-go on the presidential level. Roosevelt carried it, as we know, in 1932 and 1936, but Willkie won by about fifteen thousand votes in 1940, and Dewey in 1944 by about thirty thousand. One interesting politician is a Republican liberal, former governor Ralph L. Carr who was beaten for the senate recently, in part because he took a strong pro-Nisei stand when Japanese exclusion was a burning issue. Once, when a flash strike seemed to be getting out of hand, Carr sent state troops to protect labor, instead of intimidating it, something almost unheard of in Colorado.

About Colorado's senators little need be said, except that Edwin C. Johnson (Dem.) is one of the most extroverted men in Washington. He has never been beaten in an election; nobody in Colorado could possibly beat him, if only because he gets the upper echelon of Republican as well as Democratic votes. At the moment Johnson is fighting a clamorous civil war with Eugene Cervi, the liberal state chairman. The Republican senator is Eugene D. Millikan, an extreme conservative. His wife, whose name was Delia Schuyler, must be one of the very few American women ever to have married two senators; her first husband was also a Colorado Senator, who died. Millikan was his law partner.[5]

Denver: Notes for a Portrait

I don't know any other American city quite so fascinatingly strange. Not merely because yellow cabs are painted green or because the fourteenth step on the state capitol bears the proud plaque, ONE MILE ABOVE SEA LEVEL. Or even because it has luxuriant shade trees (every single one of which had to be imported), or because it is full of people who think that Ray Clapper and Ernie Pyle were Communists (and that Eric Johnston and Henry Kaiser are), or because the *Rocky Mountain News* prints the most original Advice to the Lovelorn column in the United States, or even because of Zeitz's Buckhorn Cafe. This estimable establishment is run by the last living survivor among Buffalo Bill's scouts; looking at you as you dine, and dine well, are stuffed animals which are the rustic equivalent of Antoine's medals in New Orleans, and which include some splendid snakes and a fine two-headed calf.

The Brown Palace Hotel in Denver is quite possibly the best hotel in the United States. It was run for years by a legendary character named Moxcy Tabor; this was the son of H.A.W. ("Haw") Tabor, one of the creators of Colorado, a man who had never heard of Shakespeare and who named his daughter Silver Dollar.[6] A carpenter in Colorado Springs took a vacation prospecting, and discovered the first vein in Cripple Creek; his name was Stratton, and he made about five million dollars, very quick. In the Brown Palace one day Mr. Stratton kicked up even more of a rumpus than was usual, and Tabor told him he would have to get out. Insulted, he walked across the street, went to the bank, and bought the hotel from under Tabor's head. This was a good many years ago. The Boettcher interests bought the Brown Palace in 1922, and have been running it ever since.

The remarkable thing about Denver is its ineffable closedness; when it moves, or opens up, it is like a Chippendale molting its veneer. This is not to say that Denver is reactionary. No—because reaction suggests

[5] Perhaps strangely Colorado was one of the few states with Democratic victories in 1946. John A. Carroll, a former Denver district attorney and a pronounced liberal who ran with Cervi's support, even displaced a Republican congressman.

[6] She was almost as renowned a creature as her father. She died a violent death in a Chicago brothel. Cf. *Silver Dollar*, by David Karsner.

motion, whereas Denver is immobile. We will in the course of this book come on other cities, like Tulsa, that really are reactionary; but Denver is Olympian, impassive, and inert. It is probably the most self-sufficient, isolated, self-contained and complacent city in the world.

It was named for General James W. Denver, an old-time governor of Kansas, whom scarcely anybody has ever heard of. (Similarly Dallas, Texas, takes its name from a politician almost unknown in life, but immortalized by a city.) It has a very peculiar unity, being both a city and a county, both a congressional and a judicial district. The story is that Byers made Denver a camp, Tabor made it a town, and Speer a city. W. N. Byers was the founder of the *Rocky Mountain News*, and he persuaded visitors—in those hoary and dynamic days—to stay. Tabor incidentally died broke; he was the city's postmaster and still illiterate. Robert W. Speer was its greatest mayor.

The mayor today is a man who gave me the impression of gliding on his oars, Benjamin Franklin Stapleton; he has been mayor for almost a quarter of a century—since 1923 in fact, except for one four-year interval. Stapleton runs the most unusual municipal machine in America, in that it is both completely impregnable politically and just as completely non-partisan. Laborites know that Stapleton won't send the police after them, and Seventeenth Street knows that he will do what he can on taxes. Only one city post in Denver is elective; Stapleton appoints everybody else; this helps to give him his considerable power.

But the greater power in Denver lies in the tightly knit, family-interlocked financial structure. The city is one of the half-dozen richest in the nation; most of its money—as in Boston—is tied up in trust funds, and a great deal is held by women, daughters and granddaughters of the gold and silver kings. Denver has the largest number of bond houses per capita of any American city; its major banks put most of their money into bonds and are extremely chary of loans—which is one reason the city doesn't grow; the attitude is to hold tight, stand pat, discourage new industry (that might compete), and keep expensive labor out. The ruling class in Denver has, it should also be noted, a distinct sense of *noblesse oblige*, that is to say it spends a considerable amount of conscience money; hence the parks, Civic Center, and well-kept hospitals.

In Denver, almost for the first time since California, we may detect signs of religious crackpotism on a lively scale. One church has a "Department of Psychoanalysis," and I saw advertisements for Back to the Bible broadcasts, tent meetings by wandering evangelists, Rosicrucian and Holiness Camp lectures, and—something that even Los Angeles hasn't got—a church with drive-in services. We may find political crackpotism too, associated with "religion" exactly as in California. One preacher, a henchman of Gerald L. K. Smith, runs both a large church and a newspaper, the *Western Voice*, which is a typical anti-

Negro, anti-Jewish, anti-Catholic, anti-United Nations, and antilabor smear sheet of the reactionary fringe.

The Denver *Post* is difficult to write about just now, because it is in process of rebirth. This was for many years the most lunatic paper in the United States, as well as one of the most conservative. Its front page looked like a confused and bloody railway accident; it had no editorial page at all; its slogan was Denver Post—First in Everything. I was particularly entranced, while in Denver, at its chauvinism about the weather. It printed a box every day with the rubric *'Tis a Privilege to Live in Colorado*, and then the words "There *are* exactly 14 hours and 12 minutes of sunlight in Denver on Monday." [Italics mine.] This would appear *on* Monday afternoon! The *Post* cared not a whit if God should not oblige. In fact, the announcement of the amount of sunlight due was often followed in the next line by an actual forecast predicting rain.

The *Post* was founded by two raucous and pyrotechnic adventurers, a rapscallion bartender named Harry Tammen and the celebrated F. G. Bonfils, a lottery promoter. For a generation, howling and screaming, they splattered Denver with red ink, and made a vast fortune by so doing. The paper, as lascivious politically as any in the nation, maintained most of its idiosyncrasies even after they died. Though it printed every lucrative comic (= continuity) strip it could find, it would (like the Chicago *Tribune*) buy no columns, and its readers lived in an intellectual vacuum of a kind comparatively rare in the United States. Of course the Denver *Post* could not have been expected to print anybody like Lippmann, Mark Sullivan, Edgar A. Mowrer, the Alsops, Tom Stokes, Pearson, Ernest Lindley, Lowell Bellett, Winchell, Grafton, or Eleanor Roosevelt; but it didn't print Pegler or Sokolsky either. Its presentation of news was often murderously vindictive. Its favorite weapon was to ignore. For instance in a hot and news-worthy campaign in 1944, the *Post* never once mentioned Charles A. Graham by name, though he was the perfectly respectable Democratic candidate; it considered him a "radical." Once, during a bizarre circulation war, the *Rocky Mountain News* called Bonfils a rattlesnake and Bonfils sued for libel. A distinguished attorney named Philip Van Cise represented the *News,* and from that day on, the *Post* never printed Van Cise's name. Bonfils died in 1933. The *Saturday Evening Post* wrote that a lot of people came to the funeral to see for themselves if he were really dead—and hoping he was buried deep.[7]

E. Palmer Hoyt, formerly of the Portland *Oregonian*, became publisher of the Denver *Post* in 1946. Already he has changed the paper beyond description. The first thing he did, Roscoe Fleming reports, was to put doors back on the toilets. Bonfils had taken them off to keep his beloved employees from sneaking any time off.

[7] "Papa's Girl," by Mary Ellen and Mark Murphy, December 23, 1944.

Perhaps we should end this section on a different note. Two other things make Denver distinguished. The National Opinion Research Center, the third of the great American poll-taking organizations like Gallup and Roper, has its headquarters at the University of Denver and the city is the home of the National Farmers Union, the most progressive of American farm groups, and of its remarkable leader, James G. Patton.

Playground of the Republic

I have not mentioned in this book so far that all American states, house proud and retentive of tradition, have their own flags, flowers, slogans, and the like. For the record and as an example—all are similar in kind—we might list those of Colorado. Flag, stripes of blue and white with a red C and a golden circle; nickname, Centennial State; great seal, a shield with mountains and miner's tools; flower, the Rocky Mountain columbine; motto, *Nil Sine Numine* (Nothing without God); bird, the lark bunting; song, "Where the Columbines Grow"; and tree, blue spruce.

Chapter 15

"Stop Roaming, Try Wyoming"

〰〰〰

> God give me mountains
> With hills at their knees.
>
> —Leigh B. Hanes

HERE is America high, naked, and exposed; this is a massive upland almost like Bolivia. The state rests about a mile high; it is eighth in size in the country, and covers almost one hundred thousand square miles. But the population is only one-tenth that of Brooklyn, and in all the intermontane emptiness there is a total of only 327 inhabited places; of these not less than 161 have populations under 100 souls. The population of Cheyenne, the capital, is about thirty-five thousand today; that of Casper, the next biggest town and Cheyenne's craggy rival, about twenty-four thousand. In many places in the state, says *Wyoming* in the American Guide Series, it is still possible "to ride 50 miles or more without seeing a dwelling of any kind."

Aptly enough Wyoming, which was the forty-fourth state to enter the union, has been called a child of the transcontinental trails. This garland of trails has magnitude and color. Oregon, Overland, Mormon, Bridger's, Bozeman—all these bisected the area, and so did the route of the Pony Express and the cattle highway up from Texas. Come forward to today. Geography remains immutable, one relatively fixed factor in a world of change, and Wyoming is still a state of the great trails, though they are of a different type. Cheyenne is a kind of iron pivot bound in buckskin. It is a principal stop in the Union Pacific's run across the West, and also that of United Airlines. US 30, the chief American transcontinental highway, intersects at Cheyenne with US 85, the main north-south highway that runs from Canada down to Mexico where it becomes the Pan-American highway and stretches almost to the Panama Canal. Then consider rivers, which are also trails. A spot the size of a card table exists south of the Yellowstone where rivers rise that eventually reach both the Pacific and the Gulf of Mexico. Almost all the great western rivers are born in or near Wyoming: the Snake (which becomes the Columbia), the Green (Colorado), North Platte, and Yellowstone.

In a good many ways Wyoming differs from Colorado, its bulky neighbor to the south. Incidentally, these are the only two states in the nation to form perfect rectangles; there was no nonsense out this way about "natural" or "strategic" frontiers. Wyoming is less sophisticated than Colorado, less cosmopolitan. It is more open, more "western," closer to the frontier, less tight-fisted. Colorado has both mines and irrigation; Wyoming has oil and low-grade coal,[1] but its irrigated area is small, and it has less agricultural diversification. It still lives mostly on cattle and sheep; it is in fact, of all American commonwealths, the livestock state par excellence. Finally, Colorado has a good deal of industry, Wyoming almost none.

Less sophisticated than Colorado? Perhaps. But in Cheyenne, which at first sight—especially during the Frontier Days Celebration when I happened to be there—seems to be a pure and unadulterated cowboy town, I went to as civilized a dinner party as could be imagined, and certainly the Cheyenne folk were more perceptive, more inquisitive, more tolerant, than most of the top-of-the-world, last-ditch aristocracy of Denver.

Wyoming is the friendliest state I have ever been in, even friendlier than Texas or Nevada. Almost everybody, one point among many, has a nickname. The governor is "Doc," and nicknames are often printed on calling cards. I have before me that of William "Scotty" Jack, secretary of state. Visiting the capitol one morning I heard about the substitute janitor, filling in during the regular janitor's vacation. He is a former governor of the state, now come on hard times![2] But maybe this story is apocryphal.

Wyoming has a lively history, with a quite conglomerate parentage. The flags of four countries besides the United States have floated over all or part of it—Spain, Great Britain, Mexico, and France—as well as the territorial flags of Utah and Dakota, and the state flag of Texas. The two great forces making for settlement were the iron thrust westward of the Union Pacific from 1867 to 1868, and the great cattle drives north from Texas in the early 70's.

The first pressure group in Wyoming history was a lady, by name Esther Morris. She lived in South Pass City, and alone and unaided she prevailed upon two men, Colonel William H. Bright and Captain H. C. Nickerson, to promise, if elected to the legislature, to give women the vote and the right to hold office. This energetic lady later became the first woman justice of the peace in the country. Nickerson and Bright were as good as their pledge, and the state's first territorial assembly voted for woman suffrage in 1869, after a venom-sparkling fight. Thus Wyoming was the first state to give equal political rights to women;

---

[1] Also it is the first producer in the nation of a mineral called bentonite.

[2] Once in territorial days two men claimed the governorship. The candidate who thought he was being cheated out of the job crawled through a window in the capitol at night, locked himself in, and refused to budge, while his rival sought to conduct the business of the state in the corridors outside.

many years later, in 1925, it was also the first state with a woman governor, Mrs. Nellie Tayloe Ross.

The present governor, Lester C. Hunt, who has a knowing and sympathetic interest in local history, showed me with amused pride his collection of Wyomingana; he possesses the photograph and signature of every delegate to the 1889 convention that brought statehood. They make a stimulating gallery. Only one delegate, so far as Hunt knows, is still alive. He is William E. Chaplin and he now lives in retirement—he must be nearly eighty—in Van Nuys, California. One delegate, Melville C. Brown, went to Alaska and there, according to the local folklore, became the prototype of the villain in *The Spoilers*, a noisy novel by Rex Beach. Another, George W. Baxter, was governor of the state for sixty-five days and then got kicked out because he dared to fence in the public domain, thus outraging the cattlemen. Two others, Clarence D. Clark and Francis E. Warren, were senators for interminable years, and another, who retired from politics in a huff because he didn't get a committee job, is the father of California's present-day senator Sheridan Downey. Another, named H. E. Teschemacher, was a doughty oldster and rich livestock man who once proclaimed in the Cheyenne Club, "I have enjoyed every sensation that human flesh is heir to, except childbirth and the consolations of religion."

Historically the chief issue in Wyoming has been the "war" between sheep and cattle. Cattle got into the state first; immense ranches—at the beginning financed mostly by British and Scottish capital, because the British were in those days willing to lend money at considerably lower rates than bankers in New York—were established and some still exist, like the vast Warren property near Cheyenne. The cattlemen resisted invasion by sheep because sheep crop the grass clean, leaving nothing for cattle to feed on. They saw, to their horror, the limitless rich grass of the open range disappear down the gullets of countless rams and lambs. Climax came about forty years ago at the "battle" of Ten Sleep, in the Bighorn region; cattlemen sacked the sheep area, murdering herders and exploding dynamite among the flocks; thousands of sheep were stampeded and "rim-rocked," i.e., killed by being driven over precipices. Nowadays, with the open range no more, cattle and sheep co-operate. Most of the great ranchmen maintain both, and the legend is, "There's romance in cattle, money in the sheep." Sheep are both "close-herded" in Wyoming and "migrated" as in Washington. They wander from place to place during the long winters, under escort, both within their own fenced ranges and on public land made accessible by the Taylor Grazing Act.

Wyoming is, naturally, extremely sensitive about anything to do with wool. This is in strict reality a wool-gathering state—no pun intended. Cattlemen in Wyoming once had a civil "war" all their own, the Johnson County War in 1892. People in Cheyenne still talk about it as if it had happened yesterday, and some are still ashamed of it. What happened was that the big ranchmen, resenting competition from small independents, hired Texas gunmen to get rid of them. The Texas bad boys were imported in sealed boxcars, but never quite fulfilled their mission; the fracas was so lively that federal troops had to be summoned to restore order. The cattlemen today are not so touchy. The big owners still monopolize the industry, but they don't shoot competitors. About the only thing that will make a Wyoming cattleman reach for his gun nowadays is to call him a "farmer." A "rancher," he wants it clearly understood, drinks only canned milk, never eats vegetables, and grows nothing but hay and whiskers.

Here is what the *New Yorker* might call some Incidental Intelligence. The Wyoming flag shows a bison with the state seal on his flank, and automobile license plates carry a vigorous stencil of a bucking horse. The highway police, an admirable body, was once known as the Wyoming Cowboy Courtesy Patrol, and a recent president of the senate never had shoes on in his life—only boots. The biggest ranch in the marvelous Teton area is supposed to be that of John D. Rockefeller, and there are towns named Pitchfork, Hell's Half Acre, Jay Em, and Atlantic City (population 50). Wyoming is the birthplace of Thurman Arnold, and one of its towns, Lander, is reputed to be both the coldest and the hottest spot in the United States. There are few citizens not American born, but in the mining town of Rock Springs sixty-four different nationalities are said to be represented. Wyoming has two "inland" counties not touched by any railroad, and dude ranches play a large role in its economy. It is one of the three states in the union (the others are Louisiana and South Dakota) where no driving license for automobilists is required, and it is basketball crazy. Its university won the world's intercollegiate championship in 1942, and the local radio station, subsidized by the merchants, follows basketball games play-by-play all over the Rocky Mountain region, even those between high-school teams.

Gun-toting is still quite legal in Wyoming, incidentally, provided that the weapon is not concealed. Aliens, however, of whom there are not many in the state, may not carry unconcealed weapons except while herding sheep.

Wyoming Growing

Lester C. Hunt, governor of Wyoming since 1943, and one of the few Democratic governors in the country to break through the Republican landslide and win in 1946, is an able, aware, and modest man. He was born in Illinois and educated in Missouri; he supported himself for a time playing semi-pro baseball, and became a dentist. Once more—we will see it many times again!—we have the spectacle of the altogether self-made man. Hunt came out to Lander, Wyoming, and set up dental practice just before World War I; he interested himself in politics, and in 1932 was elected to the legislature. He served two terms as secretary of state—during which time he really put this office at the disposal of the people—and then became governor. Dr. Hunt, pleasantly assisted by his wife, is a friendly and efficient host. His nineteen-year-old son had a recent serious illness with a bone infection; Hunt repeatedly underwent operations at the Mayo Clinic for bone grafts to assist his boy's recovery.

Anybody can walk into Hunt's office, where his secretary, Zan Lewis, welcomes visitors. The governor gets to work at 8 A.M. and puts in a long, conscientious day. Like so many politicians in the West—and unlike so many hearty citizens—he is bone dry, never having had a drink in his life.[3]

A powerful figure in Wyoming politics, and along with Hunt one of the most interesting men in the state, is Tracy S. McCracken, the Democratic national committeeman, a hotel owner and real estate man, and proprietor of KFBC.[4] What makes him count particularly is the newspaper situation. McCracken came out to Wyoming without a nickel; today, he controls journalism in the state. He owns the Laramie *Boomerang*, which was named for its previous proprietor's favorite mule; the Laramie *Bulletin*; the Rock Springs *Rocket* and Sunday *Miner*; the Rawlins *Daily News*; and the northern Wyoming *News* in Worland, which has a circulation of 4,200 in a town of 3,500. Also more important, McCracken has a 50 per cent interest in the two Cheyenne papers, the morning *Eagle*, which is stanchly Democratic, and the evening *State-Tribune and Leader*, which is vehemently Republican, and which between them dominate the state. The other 50 per cent is owned by Merritt C. Speidel, who is also proprietor of papers in cities as widely scattered as Reno (where he owns both dailies), Poughkeepsie, Ohio City, Fort Collins (Colorado), and Salinas (California). McCracken started the *Eagle* as a throwaway sheet to compete with the strongly entrenched *Tribune*. Eventually he beat the *Tribune* and bought it, and today runs both.

That one man should, with apparent impartiality, control the only two newspapers in a capital city, and papers which take diametrically opposite sides politically and compete zealously for circulation and advertising, is of course a striking American phenomenon. It is not, however, uncommon. For instance roughly the same situation obtains in Evansville (Ind.), Lancaster (Pa.), and Phoenix (Ariz.). McCracken's rival

---

[3] Another dry western governor is Ford of Montana.
[4] Among other reasons why broadcasting is so important in Wyoming is the weather. Cattlemen in miles and miles of empty country must rely on radio for warnings of blizzards and flash storms. Wyoming considers itself underprivileged in allocations of wave lengths by the FCC, and there are many districts which radio does not reach at all.

twins are printed in the same shop, with a joint operating procedure
for the sake of economy, but they have completely separate identities,
each with its own editor in chief and staff. I asked McCracken
if his Republican friends didn't object to this system. His reply was that
without it the Republican party would have no organ at all, and that he
himself never interferes politically in any way; the *Tribune*'s editor, a
lifelong Republican, has complete editorial authority. Does this mean,
then, that McCracken himself has no political convictions? Not at all.
He has been deep in Democratic politics since the Year One. What it
does mean is that many American businessmen have a unique capacity
to compartmentalize themselves. The European mind will recoil from
this, and see something fishy in it. Imagine a newspaper proprietor in
prewar Paris owning both the *Matin* and *Humanité*—and letting
Humanité say anything it wished. But American papers, particularly in
smallish towns, are seldom party minded in any exclusive way; they have
about as much domestic political slant as a department store. For
instance a great many print Pegler and Winchell side by side—which
would also give our friend the man from Mars (or Moscow) a headache
—exactly in the way the proprietor of a shop puts two competing brands
of breakfast food or neckties on the same counter.

There is no boss in Wyoming, no rule by machine; the people are too
independent and individualistic for that. Here we are still in the wide-
open spaces where a man tries, at any rate, to think for himself, and
ends up as a rule by voting for his neighbor. No governor in the state's
history has ever served two full terms, and most electoral results are
extremely mixed; for instance Hunt, a Democrat, has to govern with a
legislature overwhelmingly Republican. Of course—no matter how
individualistic Wyoming may happen to be—there are special groupings
of individuals. The Mormons (here as in Idaho they have spilled outside
Utah) are a distinct influence; mostly they take a broad view and vote
for what is best for all. The biggest lobbies are those of Union Pacific,
the oil companies, and of course the sheep and cattlemen, which as
always are a force for extreme conservatism. Incidentally there is a curious provision in the Wyoming statutes forbidding the state treasurer to
succeed himself. In the old days the explanation was that anybody ought
to be allowed to steal for a while, but that four years are enough. Another
curiosity—which was noted by Lord Bryce many years ago—is that
"logrolling" is forbidden by explicit word of the constitution.

The livestock men are so conservative because, as in Texas, only a
generation separates them from gun-and-saddle days, and they are very
proud of being rugged individualists who hate any kind of government
interference or regulation. They do not, however, object to such items
in government "shackling" as the tariff on Australian wool, or the
strictures that exclude Argentine beef from the country. During the

depression the federal authorities gave local relief by building wells, fences, and so on. But this made the ranchmen even more resentful and suspicious than formerly. They had never heard of a man improving any property not his own, and they cagily figured out that the public works program must be a prelude to expropriation. Now, however, many of these same folk, who still complain loudly about government interference, are the first to run for help when they get into trouble. In any case Wyoming, dominated by livestock, was a safe and sound Republican state until 1932. Then Roosevelt carried it three times. He lost to Dewey in 1944, but only by a few thousand votes. And he probably would have won except for what is known as the Jackson Hole dispute.

This is the kind of local *cause célèbre* which, the necessary allowances being made, exists in practically every American community. It is the Wyoming equivalent—on a different level—of sewage disposal in Pittsburgh, the drinking water in Philadelphia, or smoke abatement in St. Louis. And, like all such issues, it arouses the most vigorous kind of partisanship and is of considerable complexity; I must foreshorten the details drastically. In 1926, John D. Rockefeller Jr. bought thirty-four thousand acres near Grand Teton National Park, with the intention of giving it to the nation as a scenic monument, but pressure by Wyoming congressmen held up acceptance of the gift. In 1943, President Roosevelt, largely under the persuasion of Mr. Ickes, created by proclamation the Jackson Hole National Monument, to comprise the Rockefeller holdings together with 170,000 acres of federal land, and some 17,800 acres privately owned. The proprietors of this latter were, of course, promised full and equitable recompense, with no loss of grazing rights; their land, though within the boundaries of the monument, was not to be considered part of it. But the local cattle interests opposed the proposal with biting intensity and began a fierce campaign against it; the state of Wyoming even filed suit against the government to test the validity of the presidential proclamation. Then Congress passed a bill to nullify the whole thing; FDR vetoed this, citing as authority the Antiquities Act of 1906, by which every president since Theodore Roosevelt has created national parks and monuments—eighty-two in all—in the public interest. That Jackson Hole is of unrivaled scenic beauty as well as utility—for instance in preserving game and wild life—is hardly disputable, and it belongs to the nation, safe from spoliation, as much as do Yosemite or the Grand Canyon; it fills, wrote the New York *Herald Tribune*, "every requirement of scientific and historic interest" that the Antiquities Act requires. But Wyoming, which ordinarily believes in conservation devotedly, still hopes to block and if possible eradicate the project under pressure of the grazing interests. This story has a moral, or else it would not be worth telling. It is that even the best-principled and most austere of public servants are at the mercy of their constituents on a *local* issue if it burns deep enough. No Wyoming official could dare whisper a word for Jackson Hole, no matter what he might think privately, because it would mean political suicide. Yet it is not the people of Wyoming as a whole who are against the monument, but only a splinter fraction.

Petroleum is another big issue in Wyoming, and a standard complaint —the same complaint about absentee ownership heard all over the West —is that millions upon millions of barrels of oil are drained off to other parts of the country and processed there; the eastern companies get the great bulk of the profits with only a small remainder left for Wyoming, the originator and producer. The chief companies operating are Standard of Indiana, Standard of New York, Texas Company, Continental Oil Company, and Sinclair Oil Company. The state has, however, a considerable income out of oil—though it is not so big as it might be— because it owns 3,200,000 acres of school land, given it by the federal government on being admitted to the union; oil has been found on this property, pledged in part to the support of the schools, and the state gets a royalty; the total royalty in 1945 was about $1,500,000. Another issue has to do with our old friends, the utilities. Cheyenne gets power partly from a steam plant, partly from a reclamation project on the Platte River. Handling both is the Cheyenne Light Fuel and Power Company, which is owned by the Public Service Company of Colorado; this in turn, as we know, was once part of the Cities Service Company operated by Henry L. Doherty. Wyoming is potentially an enormous producer of natural gas. But Cheyenne has to obtain its gas by pipeline—one of the pipeline companies is also a Public Service Company subsidiary—all the way from Amarillo, Texas! The retail price in Cheyenne is $7.32 for 15,000 cubic feet. At towns like Lander in the north, which taps its own limited fields, the price is $5.98.

Another Wyoming issue is MVA, though it is quiescent at the moment. Still another—it may seem minor but let us mention it in all seriousness; education is a vital matter to the West—is whether or not to expand the university, which is at Laramie. A junior college recently began functioning independently at Casper. But Wyoming is not sure that it can, or ought, to afford further branching out. Idaho, we saw a few chapters back, was perplexed recently by the identical issue—how much a state justly feels it can invest in higher education.

Labor, which till recently played no role at all in Wyoming, has become a considerable factor; Tracy McCracken told me, in fact, that it actually holds the balance of power in the state. Yet to talk of the CIO in Wyoming—heart of the virgin West, where people used to think a union was something to go with the word "jack"—seems as anomalous as to talk about a rodeo in East Chicago. But the coal miners at Rock Springs, the chief coal town west of the Mississippi, are now organized, and the Railway Brotherhoods, as in all western states, carry heavy weight. These latter were largely instrumental in killing a recent $160,000 bond issue to repave Cheyenne's badly worn streets, which are as full of holes as any I have seen in America. It was the first bond issue of its kind ever beaten in Cheyenne. Reason: the brotherhoods didn't want to spend the money.

The Indians have the vote in Wyoming, as in Montana, and candidates for office campaign actively among them. The Shoshones, who have a reservation almost half the size of Delaware, tend to be Republican; the Arapahoes on the same reservation are mostly Democratic. The first Indians I saw in Wyoming were performers at Frontier Days Celebration, the annual Cheyenne festival which is the most dramatic affair of its kind in the entire West. Event No. 18 was a Squaw Race by Ogallala Sioux. The names of the contestants were Zona Afraid of Horses, Zena Wounded, Julie Gray Eagle, and Alice Red Water.

Traditionally Wyoming has one senator for cattle, one for sheep. But Joseph C. O'Mahoney (born in Massachusetts) is big enough to outride the usual categories. O'Mahoney, by any count, is one of the two or three ablest men in Washington, and by all odds the first figure of the state. The second senator is Edward V. Robertson. He was born in Wales of Scotch parentage and naturalized after emigrating to America. A very rich, conservative and charming gentleman, he owns something like 150,000 acres of sheep and cattle land. Once he was manager of a small trading company.

Finally, in the general sphere of politics, Wyoming has one unique attribute. It is the only state where some proceedings of the legislature are broadcast in open session, and in the evening the secretary of state, "Scotty" Jack, gives a commentary on what happened, though not in his official capacity. Once a cowboy legislator was led to the microphone. He had never seen one before, and asked the KFBC official, in a voice that could be heard over three counties, "Do you want me to talk into that son of a bitch of a thing?"

The horrified official whispered hastily, "Take it easy, buddy," but the legislator went on amiably to murmur, "Well, don't think I'm *afraid* of the little son of a bitch! Why, the little thing—"

Nobody cut the switch. And not a line of protest ever reached the station.

Note in Autobiography

I saw Wyoming for the first time more than twenty years ago. I remember the snow slashing against the wet sides of the train and the choking purity and sharpness of the high night air. I was an extremely junior reporter on the Chicago *Daily News*, and this was my first out-of-town assignment. I was going to write the story of Teapot Dome.

Nobody remembers much about Teapot Dome nowadays, but the

scandal boiled out of the teapot over the country as a whole. Corrupt members of the Harding cabinet were milking the Navy of its oil reserves, through leases to such men as Harry F. Sinclair. The first paragraph of the first story I sent from Casper makes me shudder now, from the point of view of style: "Forty-two miles from Casper by flivver or mule pack, midway between the Laramie Rockies and the Montana border, in the heart of the desolate Wyoming wasteland, lies a shallow basin with a hundred million dollars in it." And I could not resist writing that Teapot Dome had no resemblance whatever to a teapot, and none whatever to a dome.

I used in this story a weather anecdote that I have seen half a dozen times since, in various forms. "They have a twenty-foot pole at Salt Creek with a log chain at the top," one of the drillers told me. "When the chain stands out at right angles to the pole, the wind is normal. When the links start to snap off, the wind is considered strong."

But it is not the Dome itself that prompts me to this small reminiscence. Looking back today the thing that seems extraordinary is, in a way, the fact that there *was* a scandal. Because, up to that point in American history, depredations of this type, though perhaps not on quite so regal a scale, were not only fairly common but were generally ignored or accepted. Since Teapot Dome we have progressed considerably. There are petty malefactors on war contracts but nobody does much wholesale tinkering with basic natural resources. If anything at all has been established during these past twenty years, it is that this country belongs as of right to nobody but itself. As the Beards say in their *Basic History*, it is no longer possible "for private persons or corporations to enter into secret connivance with government officials"—as had been almost a matter of routine for fifty years—"and gain titles to huge sections of the public domain without risk of exposure and retribution."

.   .   .   .

So now we take leave of the mountain states, and it is fitting that we do so in Wyoming, which is the most unspoiled and typical of them all. One could write about the West indefinitely, but it is time to climb downward toward the plains.

Chapter 16
The Miraculous Dakotas

NOTHING is more remarkable in the United States than the difference between the Dakotas. These are the two least-known states in the country, and many people think of them casually as a kind of "bloc," which they most certainly are not. North Dakota is probably the most radical state in the union, and South Dakota is one of the most conservative. North Dakota has two transcontinental railroads; South Dakota has none. North Dakota lives on wheat and is, to an extent, a "colony" of Minnesota; South Dakota lives on wheat too, but on livestock, mining, and above all pheasants in addition. Both states produce political characters of remarkable eccentricity, but the North Dakotans are eccentric in a different way. There are more idiosyncrasies per square inch in North Dakota than in any state I know.

What is more, the two Dakotas, though coterminous for 330 miles, have practically no contact with one another. South thinks that North is inhabited exclusively by raging Bolsheviks; North thinks that South is a preserve for all people to the right of Hoover. South looks down across the river to Iowa and southward to Nebraska; it never looks upward to North at all, if it can help it. I met one South Dakota editor who has been an important personality in the whole area for twenty years; never once has he crossed the line and set foot in North Dakota. It was impossible, so far as my own experience went, to find North Dakota newspapers in Sioux Falls or South Dakota papers in Bismarck, though in both you could easily buy the Chicago *Tribune* and the Omaha *World Herald*.

Finally, extraordinary as it is to tell, travel between the two states is difficult in the extreme. When I was there no bus or air lines connected them at all. Try to get from Pierre, say, the capital of South, to Bismarck, the capital of North, by rail. In a manner of speaking railways do exist, but you will not thank me for the suggestion.

Glimpse of North Dakota

Quite possibly this cross-grained, inflammatory state is the most complex in the entire nation. Contrasts are sharp in almost every field: for instance the state capitol is a handsome skyscraper built by Holabird and Root; the governor's mansion near by is a small white frame house that would be modest even for a farmer of very modest means.[1] Its public men are among the most refractory in America, and much of its political history can only be characterized by some such word as wacky.

I spent several bewildered days in Bismarck and elsewhere in North Dakota; my cicerone on several occasions was Gaylord Conrad, the editor of the *Capital*, and I met people of every camp. No state except possibly Oklahoma has a history so bursting with furor. I learned that it once had, in a period of a few months, no fewer than four governors; of these one served only fifteen days before he was expelled by an outraged citizenry. The recall has only been used four times in American history for the removal of an important public official; three of the four occasions were in North Dakota. Senator William Langer, whose ornery career is inextricably enmeshed with the life of the state, stood criminal trial three times on a technical charge relating to the collection of funds, and was once sentenced to eighteen months in a federal prison, before the judgment was reversed and he was finally cleared. The three trials produced every possible kind of flaming charge and countercharge. Langer even lost his citizenship for a time—though he had just been nominated governor!

But out of a background of confused scandal, the most savage kind of internecine feuding, and berserk demagoguery, has come strikingly advanced government. The people fought for good works, and they got them. North Dakota is the reform state par excellence. Along with Minnesota, Nebraska, and Wisconsin, it is traditionally the chief repository of progressivism in the United States.

It maintains the only state-owned bank in the nation, which has resources of 71 million dollars and is the biggest bank between the Twin Cities and the West Coast; it controls all public funds and is the state's fiscal agent. Similarly North Dakota maintains the only state-owned flour mill in America, and the only state-owned grain elevator. This, at Grand Forks, was established to relieve farmers from the pressure of absentee elevator interests in Minnesota. All public officials in North Dakota, down to the pettiest, must be bonded by the state, and all public buildings, including the county courts and schoolhouses, carry compulsory state insurance. North Dakota insures its farmers against the risks of fire, hail, and tornado; it has an admirable workman's compensation law, and a highly developed system of co-operatives. It is in fact, to sum up, almost as thoroughly socialized as Sweden.

Behind all this is of course agriculture and its concomitant in hard times—agrarian radicalism. For mile after mile through the state I passed the prodigious bread factories, i.e., wheat farms.

North Dakota is divided into two distinct spheres, dry (western) and

---

[1] The governor's salary is $333 a month.

wet (eastern), by the 98th meridian. Another demarcation line is made by our old acquaintance the Missouri River. The eastern area is the greatest producer of hard durum wheat in the world; this is the indispensable binding ingredient for products all the way from cake flour to macaroni. Wheat in North Dakota is usually moved to the machine (a fixed thresher) rather than vice versa; combines aren't used much. The state has 57,000 farms, and the total agricultural income has exceeded 500 million dollars every year since 1943. It worked out in 1945 to the dazzling average of $7,600 per farm.

But wait. These past years have been exceptional. North Dakota has not forgotten others in the 1930's. It may be an exaggeration, but one farmer told me, "It didn't rain for seven solid years." The risks of weather make for a bizarrely vulnerable economy; I heard of one man who, in 1939, declared his assets to the state bank as $320; in 1944, four crop years later, he was worth $47,920. In the 1930's farmers sold Liberty Bonds at 60¢ or even 50¢ on the dollar. In one group of counties big insurance companies still hold at least 30 per cent of the entire area, as a result of foreclosures. I have before me a pamphlet, *Buy Now for Security*, published by the University and School Land Department. I know nothing like what this contains except the Florida newspaper advertisements after the real estate boom and collapse in Miami—thousands of holdings are listed for sale at minuscule prices, holdings that were once the property of small landowners closed out.

A statue exists in North Dakota to an anonymous Indian[2] who watched an early pioneer turn up pasture land for wheat, and who grunted in simple comment, "Wrong side up!" Later we shall meet the Dust Bowl in the southwestern states. The Dakotas had their own grisly experience of a dust bowl. Land that should never have been plowed in the first place flew off and became new top soil in Indiana and Ohio. I have described what toll the Missouri River takes of soil. Wind erosion has cost the nation just as much. In the whole Great Plains area, it is calculated, there were once 400 million acres of tillable land. The tremendous droughts of the 30's destroyed forever about 10 per cent of this. Some 200 million acres were badly damaged, and 40 million simply blew away.

Non-Partisan League, Politics, and Langer

The political history of North Dakota is mostly the history of the Non-Partisan League. This peculiar institution was founded in 1915 by A. C. Townley, who lives these days in Minnesota; for a time its influence spread to a dozen states. Townley was a salty and effective organizer. Somebody told him once, "You ought to read history." His reply was, "History? I don't care to read it. I make it." Once a rebellious farmer

[2] *Life*, August 13, 1946.

rose in a league meeting and interrupted him: "A.C., I paid up sixteen dollars to join this thing, and what did it ever give me?" Townley replied, "It gave you the courage to get up and ask that question."

Townley was a farmer at Beach, and an old-line Socialist. Most league planks derive from the platform of the Socialist party of North Dakota, as worked out at a famous convention at Minot in February, 1914. Townley set out to arouse the countryside. To become a member of the Non-Partisan League a man had only to be a farmer and pay sixteen dollars. Basically the movement was one of protest. A North Dakota senator once scoffed at some complaining farmers, "Don't talk about things you don't know about. Go home and slop your hogs." It was this kind of attitude that Townley fought against. At first his men were called the "sixteen-dollar suckers."

But not for long. The movement found roots and life in the soil and spread. By 1918 it controlled both houses of the legislature, and it is the source of most of the North Dakota reforms. In many ways it was a precursor of the New Deal, which came along a quarter of a century later. The ever normal granary is an extension of Townley's idea for a state elevator; the Federal Crop Insurance Law embodies the league's ideas on hail insurance; the Federal Deposit Insurance Corporation and the Federal Housing Administration applied on the national level what had already been worked out locally in North Dakota.

But the Non-Partisan League always operated within the *Republican* party, and as a splinter instrument of that party. The details are confusing. I heard a dozen versions of what happened from 1920, say, to date. The leaguers chose to work with the Republicans because Democrats were as rare in North Dakota as ocelots.[3] Then came fissures and dissension. Townley himself seldom ran for office; the league's political boss and spearhead was usually Bill Langer, though he once spent eight "wilderness" years outside its fold. Formidable sho-guns like Nye and Lemke were also leaguers at the beginning. In time a faction known as the Independent Voters Association (IVA) broke off from Langer, and he and Nye became adamantine enemies. Later this IVA, which embodied the conservative end of the movement, became resurrected as the Republican Organizing Committee (ROC) and elected an anti-Langer governor. The league and the regular Republican organization both hold conventions, and usually the primary is a race between a "regular" conservative and a league radical. To make it more fun, the loser as a rule tries to work out a subsequent deal with the Democrats, so that he can help defeat the primary winner in the general election. Langer, in fact, was once actually elected governor as an independent after being beaten in the primaries. The local Democrats are, by and large, suspicious of the league because it is more liberal than they

[3] But—a Democratic governor did hold office from 1939 to 1945.

are. But though the league supported Roosevelt in 1932, it did not do so thereafter. Hold your head.

Today the Non-Partisan League is at a very low ebb, and it has not elected a governor since 1937. Several things aside from inner splintering damaged it: (1) It was pre-eminently "a hard-times outfit," and worked best in periods of depression; (2) The New Deal outdid it in its own field; (3) Its old-timers seemed incapable of keeping pace with a fast-changing world; (4) Its isolationism, always ferocious, steadily became more sterile.

Bill Langer is an extremely complicated personality. One source of his power is his strong record as a people's man. He was the first American governor to declare a moratorium on foreclosures for debt; he called out the National Guard to prevent forced sales of farm property by local sheriffs; once, during a labor dispute, he used state troopers to protect workers who had been getting wages as low as 28¢ an hour. Like that of so many grass-root radicals, his Washington record is inordinately mixed. He voted for the confirmations of both Henry Wallace and Aubrey Williams; he has always voted for FEPC and against the poll tax; he supported veterans' housing and opposed the Case bill. Of course, an isolationist pure and undefiled, he fought the British loan, and he was one of two senators who voted against the San Francisco Charter.[4] Once he called the UN a "production of pure bunk." But after voting against the Charter, he announced that, since it was the law, he would support it—a position exactly opposite to that taken by Wheeler, incidentally.

Here is what Langer said about himself once. It appears in the neat little handbook that North Dakota publishes at all elections, explaining the issues and allowing each candidate a page to state his own position.

> I am a firm believer in the . . . Townsend Plan. I stand for money reform and a Bank of the United States . . . For years I was the attorney for the Brotherhood of Railway Trainmen. I have rarely been retained by the corporations . . .
>
> When I was elected Attorney General I was endorsed by the Scandinavian Total Abstinence League, the Farmers Educational Union, the Progressive Republican Party, the Woman's Christian Temperance Union, and the Non-Partisan League.
>
> I promise to uphold the dignity of a North Dakota United States Senator, and will not endorse any brand of cigarette, snuff, perfume, or whisky; and I also promise not to become a candidate for President of the United States within two weeks after I assume the duties of office.
>
> If elected, I will devote my time to the duties of office, and will not rob the taxpayers of the time that is due them by giving one

---

[4] The other: Henrik Shipstead of Minnesota.

hundred speeches a year . . . at two hundred and fifty dollars a speech.[5]

Not everybody in North Dakota likes Langer—by any means. One favorite local story (pre-1945) was, "Heard the wonderful news? Roosevelt died, and Bill Langer got killed going to the funeral."

Langer, despite cataclysmic failings, is a much more substantial man than Gerald P. Nye. Nye was an outright America Firster; Langer, perhaps strangely, never was. Nye, who was born in Wisconsin, was defeated for re-election in 1944, after twenty years in the Senate; in 1946 he ran to regain his seat, and was badly beaten—Nye, Shipstead, Wheeler, and LaFollette were, as we know, all casualties at about the same time. Nye's comment on Pearl Harbor, delivered immediately after news of the attack, was that it was "just what Britain had planned for us," and that "Britain has been getting this ready since 1938."[6]

Farmers Union and the Co-ops

North Dakota is the premier Farmers Union state, and its headquarters at Jamestown, under the able Glenn Talbot, are a pivot in the organization almost as important as Denver or St. Paul. Of the 57,000 farmers in North Dakota, more than 30,000 are members, which must be something of a record for saturation in any movement. The Farmers Union is by far the biggest single force in the state, and its North Dakota unit is probably the strongest farmers' organization in the whole country on a state level, though several others, like the Illinois Farmers Association, may be wealthier. It plays no direct role in politics, though it supports some issues like the MVA; it never takes a line as between candidates for office.

To many this seems a pity. Should the Farmers Union come out forthrightly against a man like Lemke, it could beat him, because it could, if politically organized, beat anybody. The confusion exists that, whereas it favors MVA, the governor of the state is against it, though he is a Farmers Union member. The attitude of the union seems to be that the local citizenry is not yet ready to tie political and economic issues together; people take their political allegiances very seriously, and are accustomed to think that the union functions on an altogether different plane. The organization is in a way fearful of risking its own great force by tossing it into the unpredictable political whirlpool that North Dakota is.

The fields it does cultivate are: (a) those that similar farm organiza-

[5] This last was a slap at Nye, his fellow senator, who had been making money on the lecture platform. A whole chapter might be written on the intricate frenzies of the Langer-Nye civil war.

[6] New York *Times*, December 8, 1941.

tions attend to everywhere, like rural education, electrification, technological improvement; (*b*) insurance; (*c*) the co-operatives. It maintains its own flourishing life insurance and other insurance companies, and its co-operatives are a whole big story in themselves. "The co-ops rule North Dakota," I heard it said. The Farmers Union has co-operatives in everything from hospitals and creameries to credit unions and funeral homes.

Here we touch on a subject hitherto unmentioned. But this book cannot be expected to deal with co-operatives in general on any scale. That there are an infinity of different kinds of co-operatives in the United States, ranging from a huge business like the Central Cooperative Wholesale Association in Wisconsin to the small consumer co-operatives in California, is known to everybody. The Farmers Union co-ops in North Dakota arise, by and large, from the immediate wants and needs of the local citizen; they are short on theory, and long on practical results. Take the gasoline co-ops. The union maintains about 120 of these in North Dakota, and they are a thriving institution. A man pays $25.00 to join; of this, $5.00 is checked off as Farmers Union dues, and is applied to an education fund. Or a purchaser may buy his gas and oil, also hardware and farm supplies, from a co-operative although not a member; when his "patronage dividend" reaches $25, this will serve as his membership fee, and he gets one share of stock, one vote, in whatever the local co-op happens to be, for instance the Farmers Union Oil Company of Bismarck. The "patronage dividend" is what the co-operative as a whole turns back to its membership in lieu of profit. Normally each member gets 9 per cent of his total purchases for the year back in dividends; if he spends $100 on gasoline his refund is $9.00.

Naturally this has become big business. The union owns its own oil wells and refineries in Kansas and elsewhere, and its own distributing system, the Farmers Union Central Exchange in South St. Paul, Minnesota. In North Dakota the co-ops have about half of all retail gas business. One result is that prices have been forced down. When I was in North Dakota gas cost 21¢ as against 25¢ in adjacent states, and what the big commercial oil companies thought about it can't be printed.

Bigger and more important, however, are the grain co-ops. Fifteen per cent of all grain marketed in the Twin Cities is handled by the Farmers Union on a nonprofit basis, and North Dakota has a total of 316 local co-ops dealing with grain—more than any state except Illinois, more by a good deal than Kansas or Iowa though their population is considerably greater.[7] The nucleus of the system is the Farmers Union

---

[7] *Cooperative Grain Marketing in the United States*, a pamphlet issued by the Farm Credit Administration of the Department of Agriculture, p. 3.

Grain Terminal Association in St. Paul, headed by M. W. Thatcher. This celebrated institution markets grain for members, stores it for them (in six million bushels of storage space), operates a durum mill for semolina flour, and maintains 150 local elevators all over the Northwest. Members receive dividends exactly as do those who belong to the gasoline co-ops, if the elevators make a profit. The idea behind all this was concentration. It was to exert pressure on the terminal market. "Follow the wheat all the way to the terminal, instead of selling it at the gate," was an early motto. Also the system has served to modify abuses and discriminations. A member is free of middleman and commission charges, and he escapes the "dockage" racket. Dockage is the extraneous matter that gets into wheat like mustard seed, oats, and so on. Standard tests now determine what "dockage" shall be assessed against the farmer by the miller, in contrast to the former system in which it could run to almost any amount.

A Line on Other Factors

About 40 per cent of North Dakotans are Scandinavian in origin (predominantly Norwegian); about 30 per cent are German or "Volga German." Bismarck was actually named Bismarck in order to attract German immigrants; tickets could be bought Bremen-to-Bismarck direct.[8] During World War I, some Germans sought to evade the draft, and many refused to buy war bonds; by the time of World War II this situation was much ameliorated. A good deal of anti-Semitism exists in North Dakota.[9] The Volga Germans (who are basically of Russian descent) "will" trade with Jews, I heard; the non-Volga Germans won't, if they can help it.

Other North Dakota forces and influences might be listed as follows: (1) The railroads. The Great Northern, largely because of the memory of Jim Hill and because it is famously a "railway man's railroad," is highly regarded throughout the state. (2) The chain banks. During the 1920's, as in Montana, hundreds of small banks failed; most were eventually bought up by two large banks centered in the Twin Cities, the Northwest Bancorporation and the First Bank Stock, Inc. These have very considerable local power. (3) The Greater North Dakota Association, which is a kind of over-all chamber of commerce for the state. (4) The absentee millers. (5) The Lutheran Church. (6) Women. As I got on the train in Bismarck, a lady handed me some resolutions just passed by the ninety-seventh anniversary meeting of the

[8] Bryce (II, p. 837) records that in the 80's Bismarck was destined "to be the metropolitan hearth of the world's civilization."
[9] But one of the leading citizens of the state, William Stern, a Fargo banker and the former Republican National Committeeman, is Jewish.

Seneca Falls Convention. One demanded a woman's equal rights amendment to the constitution; another asked for government subsidies for housewives. (7) The various groups working for MVA, which was by all odds the greatest issue in North Dakota when I was there. As always, the stratifications caused by MVA are very sharp, and I heard liberals say, "We're done for, if MVA goes out." So far as conservatives are concerned, to advocate it is to become a leper.

Finally, journalism. North Dakota was, as of the time I visited it, the only state in the union with no Blue Network (American Broadcasting Company) outlet, and so the citizenry never had opportunity to hear Raymond Swing, John W. Vandercook, Winchell, Pearson, Dorothy Thompson, Elmer Davis, or LaGuardia. One local paper of interest is the *Leader,* the organ of the Non-Partisan League, not so much by reason of its opinions, which are what anybody would guess, but because it employs a paragraphist of great talent. Western journalism has always been notable for a dry, pithy, understated type of paragraphing. Here are two examples from the *Leader*:

EAST IS WEST

E. V. Eastman and C. F. Westman, neighbors, got together and built a wall dividing their property. Eastman lives on the west of the wall and Westman lives on the east.

HORSE JUMPS ON AUTO

Frightened by a bus, Dave Sanders' workhorse made a lunge. He landed on top of an automobile in one bound and, had it not been for the fact that he had a clumsy old wagon behind him, he would have set a hurdle record.

South Dakota: Everything But Pheasants

"South Dakota," writes Hayden Carruth,[10] "is the heart of the prairie region of North America. Take a pair of compasses and on your map set the legs to cover six hundred miles. Plant one in the middle of South Dakota, and swing the other around, and in your great circle, twelve hundred miles in diameter, you will have the prairie. . . . South Dakota in the exact middle of this great plain of the world should be its very heart and soul, and is."

In fact the state has set up a monument near Pierre (pronounced Peer), the hamlet that is the capital, to mark its geographic middle and "the approximate center of North America." From this point "more than a thousand miles from any ocean," the prairie "spreads endlessly

[10] In *These United States,* I, p. 269.

in every direction." But actually there is much in South Dakota that is not prairie exclusively. What chiefly differentiates it from North is a certain diversity and variety. It has timber stands, a packing industry, mountains, and mineral deposits, all of which its northern sister lacks.

Also South Dakota contains the Bad Lands. This largely uninhabited district in the west of the state, beyond the Missouri River and on the dry side of the 98th meridian, was once described by General Custer as "a part of hell with the fires burnt out." On the authority of *Life* (which, in a pictorial essay on South Dakota, once printed some of the best photographs of American terrain ever taken), exactly eleven human beings live in this wilderness, who have to haul even their drinking water "from sixty miles away"; the area is populated only by "rabbits, rattlesnakes, birds of prey, and the wailing wind and coyotes."

Behind the Bad Lands lie the Black Hills, so called not because of black rock but by reason of their dense black-green covering of pine and fir. Here are both natural and artificial wonders—rackety towns like Deadwood, which was the home of Wild Bill Hickok, and Lead (pronounced Leed), the site of the Homestake Mining Company. On Mount Rushmore is "the most impressive monument ever executed by man," in the words of a local pamphlet—the four heroic statues hewn on the mountain by Gutzon Borglum, depicting Washington, Lincoln, Jefferson, and Theodore Roosevelt in 480-foot blocks.[11] South Dakota is proud of its Black Hills, and though it is an extremely isolationist state it tried hard to make them the site of the UN world capital.

Also in western South Dakota is gumbo. This is a type of soil very hard when the weather is dry, and at other times the opposite. In gumbo, during drought, "you can see a nickel two miles away," I heard it said, but when it rains, the grass grows so fast that "you have to part it to see a cow." You can't stand on really wet gumbo, because it is too slippery, or get it off your hands, because it's so sticky. Anybody born in the gumbo country will be long legged: he gets so much exercise pulling his legs out. One friend told me, "Drive over a gumbo hill, and you'll take the road right with you."

The Homestake mine is the largest gold producer in the Northern Hemisphere. It was once owned by William Randolph Hearst; control is now largely dispersed. Homestake is probably the dominant enterprise in the state, not merely from the point of view of economics but politically. Until 1937 it paid no tax whatever on the ore it produced (such was its power in the South Dakota legislature); then a small tax, 8¢ a ton, was affixed, but with the first 50,000 tons exempt, in theory

---

[11] The only thing remotely resembling this in America is the unfinished sculpture on Stone Mountain outside Atlanta, Georgia, which is also by Borglum.

to encourage smaller mines. Lately this tax was reduced to 4¢. Homestake has a terrific lobby, but it operates very smoothly. Its labor is not
organized. If any union organizer should appear in Deadwood or Lead,
so I heard it put, "he would simply be thrown in jail." I have mentioned
in Chapter 11 the policy and tactics toward labor of Anaconda in
Montana. Compared to Homestake, Anaconda is the CIO. One auxiliary
point, not without interest, is that the legislative district of Francis
Case, the South Dakota representative who wrote the Case bill, includes
the Homestake properties. The mine has always been a substantial
money maker, except during the war when gold mining was shut down.
Its dividends spread all over the country. Gold is a heavy metal, but
very volatile.

Glance at another field—no play on words intended. I have seldom
seen anything lovelier than the shocks of grain in South Dakota. Flying
into Sioux Falls, I looked down and saw the fields dotted symmetrically,
in patterns that might have been designed by the Museum of Modern
Art in New York, with what seemed to be golden marbles—the oats,
barley, wheat, cut by the binder, stacked, and waiting to be picked
up. On an immensely magnified scale, they looked like the fruit and
beans in a Mexican market such as that at Toluca, with every object
artfully spaced, every color and shape balanced with delicate harmony
and precision.

South Dakota is full of "foreigners"; it has 140,000 folk of German
extraction (out of a total population of roughly 650,000), and 90,000
Scandinavians. Also, like North Dakota, it has a considerable Indian
population, mostly Sioux; Indians hold one-tenth of all land in the
state. A general still alive fought the last campaign against the Sioux
in the Dakotas—the date may seem incredible—as recently as 1890.
His name is John J. Pershing.

South Dakota is today almost as Republican as, say, Alabama is
Democratic. Nevertheless, there were Democratic governors in 1926,
1932, and 1934, and FDR carried it twice. In 1940, when Willkie ran, it
gave him the largest proportionate majority of any state; the percentage
even exceeded that of Vermont and Maine. Also South Dakota is
extremely conservative; when it does elect Democrats, they are very
conservative Democrats, you may be sure. Once it had a brief liberal
interlude, during the hegemony of Peter Norbeck, who died in 1935.
Norbeck, a progressive Republican, took over some of the policies
of the Non-Partisan League. South Dakota, like North, had hail
insurance for a time; it had a rural credit law and a bank deposit
guaranty law. Then came a conservative back swing, and what liberalism
Norbeck gave the community was lost; even the measures covering hail
insurance and rural credit were repealed. Today, the successor to Nor-

beck's Senate seat is Harlan J. Bushfield, who is quite possibly the most reactionary man in Washington.[12]

For all its conservatism, South Dakota is not machine run. Lobbyists are obliged to register, and a favorite political maneuver is to embarrass your opponent by alleging that he does belong to a machine. As strong an influence as anything in the state is its leading newspaper, the Sioux Falls *Argus-Leader*. The cattlemen are of course important, and so are the various agrarian groups.

South Dakota: Pheasants

But easily South Dakota's greatest distinction is in the realm of—pheasants! It is a curious story. There are some 50 million in the state,[13] and Sioux Falls is the "pheasant capital of the world." One friend told me, "We have more pheasants than Republicans—and you can't even count the Republicans!" The open season varies from year to year; an average is two months, beginning from October 15, with a bag limit of five birds a day. South Dakota is a paradise for the maladroit marksman; the pheasants are so thick that nobody can possibly miss. Residents pay $1.00 for a shooting license; outsiders pay $20. The hunters come from all over, and in a normal year some 40,000 out-state licenses are issued—so it may be seen that pheasants bring the community a very handsome revenue.

This revenue is controlled strictly. It goes not to the state as such, but to the Game, Fish, and Parks Commission, which uses it for wild life shelters, lake improvement, and the development of more pheasants. One can easily imagine what opportunities for graft the "pheasant fund" would provide in a really corrupt state, like Illinois in older days or Pennsylvania. Of course the Game, Fish, and Parks Commission, handling its funds with absolute probity, deals with other birds and animals besides merely pheasants. The state has set aside more than 400,000 acres for "the protection and propagation of migratory water-fowl, game birds, song birds, and game animals."[14] There is even a law to protect frogs. South Dakota produces, protects, and then duly shoots

[12] The Great Plains states do still produce radicals, of course, but mostly they move out. I do not know if Maxwell Anderson, the playwright, or Professor Alvin H. Hansen of Harvard would classify themselves as "radicals," but they have their roots in North and South Dakota respectively. Nebraska has a big export of radicals, and Earl Browder, the deposed head of the American Communist party, is a Kansan. But beware of such generalizations. John D. M. Hamilton, former chairman of the Republican National Committee, is a Kansan too.

[13] North Dakota has plenty of pheasants too, but they are neither so concentrated nor so exploited as those in South. Even so, its pheasant "harvest" was over a million birds last year, brought down by some 30,000 hunters. North Dakota considers itself, in fact, just as important a "gallinaceous" state as its neighbor.

[14] According to an attractive pamphlet compiled by the State Writers' Project.

chukar partridge, Hungarian partridge, prairie chicken, grouse of several types, sage hen, quail, wild turkey, and all manner of geese and ducks. One of the handsomest brochures ever put out by an American state is *Wild Ducks,* issued in collaboration with the American Wildlife Institute, and containing fascinating material about the four great "flyways" ducks like to use.

But to return to pheasants. In World War II came a severe shortage of shotgun shells; this crippled the local industry. But in a normal year, about 15,000 birds are killed every hour during the season; guns shoot at the rate of 75,000 shots per hour. Since the first open season in 1919, something over 20 million pheasants have been legally slaughtered; this is the equivalent—I am relying on the pamphlet cited above—of some 3,000 carloads of beef. This whole development has arisen in forty years or so from an investment of about $20,000, and mostly as a result of the acumen of three men, Peter Norbeck, a Doctor Zitlitz, and a man named Rothschild. Previously there had been a prodigious undiscriminating slaughter of wild life. Sensible people wanted to stop this, and, if possible, replenish the stocks of game. The pheasant that helped do the job was, originally, an alien from China; its name is still the Chinese Ring-Necked Pheasant. As early as 1880 an American consul general in Shanghai shipped a few of these birds to Oregon, as a gift to friends, and by 1892 there were enough in the neighborhood to provide an annual kill of 50,000. Pheasants, in a word, are great multipliers. In 1898, Dr. Zitlitz brought into South Dakota two males and four females. They were carefully-bred, and then ten birds in all were released into the wilderness. Similar experiments took place elsewhere. A handful at a time, the pheasants were turned loose. This went on until 1914-15 when the state itself purchased and released 7,000 birds. We know the rest. Today, you can shoot pheasants in South Dakota while driving an automobile.

I hope I have not given the impression that South Dakota, with its extreme political conservatism, is a staid state. Sioux Falls is one of the least staid cities I have ever seen. At the airport gates I looked warily at a sign, ANY PERSON ATTEMPTING TO ENTER OR DEPART AT ANY OTHER POINT SUBJECT TO BEING SHOT, and commercial airline passengers actually were unable to leave the field except under military convoy. F. C. Christopherson, editor of the *Argus-Leader,* invited me to a party the day I arrived. This, it happened, turned out to be V-J Day. I had seen V-E Day in New Orleans, a notably tumultuous town. But nothing that I saw in New Orleans or, for that matter, that I have ever seen anywhere else, rivaled what went on in Sioux Falls that night. For someone to tear out a public drinking fountain by the roots and hurl it playfully down the streets was only a quiet episode.

Addendum on a Great State, Nebraska

Former Governor Dwight Griswold let me ride by highway patrol from Omaha to Lincoln[15] and we spent most of a day together. I admired "O" Street which is part of US 34 and which runs sixty-nine miles without a turn, and so is called the longest and straightest street in the world. I admired the state capitol also. Like that in Bismarck (also Baton Rouge) it is a skyscraper, and, rising out of the wide green-tawny flatness of the plains, it is strikingly dramatic. A story goes with it too. It cost eleven million dollars and took eleven years to build, since it was paid for, year by year, by a special property tax calculated to yield exactly a million dollars annually. The doughty Nebraskans don't believe in debt, and they built, penny by penny, as they got the money. The portals of the building bear the legend, THE SALVATION OF THE STATE IS WATCHFULNESS IN THE CITIZEN, and atop the dome is a large statue of the "Sower."[16] This too shows what Nebraska thinks about.

Griswold left office in January, 1947. He had previously been beaten in a run for the Senate by Hugh Butler, an extreme diehard. What defeated Griswold was the British loan—mostly. Butler, a fierce isolationist who not only voted against the loan but against selective service, Lend Lease, and Bretton Woods, made isolation the chief issue. Griswold, a liberal Republican of the Stassen school, took a strong internationalist line, and lost three to one.

Of course Griswold, who was one of the best governors in the nation, will return to politics some day. Let me write about him briefly as an example of a modern Great Plains-corn-belt chief executive. He was a "sand hill" boy; his parents were homesteaders who settled in western Nebraska before the railroads came. That, in high school, he won a $100 prize for an essay "How to Lay the Foundations of Good Government," shows how character patterns may be forecast in childhood. Except while governor, he has lived in a small town called Gordon since 1901, and is chairman of the board of the local bank and publisher of the Gordon *Journal*, with a tiny but important circulation. Griswold's tough independence reminded me to an extent of Sumner Sewall, who was then governor of Maine, though he isn't so rambunctious or iconoclastic. He was one of the few governors (Kerr of Oklahoma is another) who did some hard spadework on the questionnaire I sent him. Always, before seeing governors, I submitted a small list of questions. I would ask what their state contributed to the union and so on. Griswold sent these questions all over Nebraska, and collected an interesting anthology of answers.

[15] Several other governors did me similar courtesies, notably Blue of Iowa and Dempsey of New Mexico.
[16] The Vermont state capitol has a similar figure on the dome.

He is a stubborn man (like Osborn of Arizona); he had to run for the governorship three times before he made it. Then he was re-elected twice. Once he received 74.8 per cent of the total vote cast, and once 76 per cent, an all-time record for Nebraska. He was one of the few Republican governors to "go along" with FDR on foreign policy, and his secretary was a registered Democrat. The international question was not the exclusive cause of his defeat. He had had three terms as governor and people thought that this was enough public office for the time being. Nebraska is a fickle state.

What runs Nebraska is—the weather! I do not mean this as a wisecrack. The state differs markedly from its neighbors South Dakota and Kansas in that it has no mineral wealth, and there are few foaming, power-producing rivers in the interior.[17] All Nebraska has to live on is its eight- to twelve-foot-thick rug of soil.

On this it lives quite well—provided the weather smiles. It is the thirty-second state in population, and yet the sixth in production of foodstuffs; what supports it is, in other words, export of corn, wild hay, wheat, alfalfa, feeder cattle, feeder hogs, butter, eggs. It is, after Wisconsin and New York, the third dairying state. More than a billion dollars are invested in the 121,000 Nebraska farms, which are tended as carefully as lawns in Connecticut. These farms average 191 acres in size incidentally—more than twice that of farms in the country as a whole—and they are mechanized 61 per cent more than the national average.

Driving back to Omaha I looked at some farms and decided that my synonym for the word "rich" hereafter would be corn growing in southeastern Nebraska. But not all of it is so lush and fertile. The state is half West, half Middle West. The western half is dry ranch and sand hills country, with thousands upon thousands of acres that have never seen a plow.

No wonder weather is such a preoccupation. It can almost literally be a matter of life or death. I saw the clouds burst open one day; out of sunshine came water that was three inches deep in half an hour. The first copy of the Omaha *World Herald* I picked up had three weather stories on its front page, and the local radio broadcasts weather news all the time. Incidentally an Omaha hotel is the only one I have ever known with radios in the elevators. Out in the country, the fact that there are comparatively few trees, no big stands of timber, and no mountains for a windbreak, makes the impact of weather more dramatic; nothing screens you from what may be elemental violence. The summers are as brutally hot as the winters are brutally cold. The drought of the middle 30's hit

[17] It differs from Iowa, another neighbor, chiefly in that aside from producing grain it is predominantly a livestock state. A further differentiation from Kansas is that its chief crop is overwhelmingly corn, as against wheat; for Kansas the situation is exactly the reverse.

here just as it did in the Dakotas; nobody has forgotten the "black blizzard" dust storms. Of course, as in all agrarian states, weather equals politics, and bad weather equals radicalism. James E. Lawrence of the Lincoln *Star* went east in 1936 to do a series of articles on Alf Landon's chances. When he left, the corn was green. When he returned it was black. He knew then that Landon's chances were gone with the corn, "fried out."

The name Nebraska means Flat Water; the Otoe Indians called it this, for the Platte and its famous characteristic of flowing "bottom side up."[18] Originally the state was a "Louisiana orphan," being in that part of the Louisiana Purchase which Congress first set aside as Indian country. The first homestead in the United States (1863) was in Nebraska, at a town named Beatrice, pronounced today Be-*at*-rice.

There were two main streams of settlement. First, Civil War veterans who sought homesteads. Nebraska, unlike Kansas, had no slave problem. There is scarcely a county seat today without the imprint of the Grand Army of the Republic. Second, German, Scandinavian, and to a somewhat smaller degree Czechoslovak settlers. These had an enormous yearning for land, their own land; they cared little for cities, and pushed straight out into the flat wilderness. Some early villages were so small that, for a time, each had only one church; Catholics and Protestants worshiped in the same room, with half the pews facing an altar at one end, half a pulpit at the other.

This was all sturdy stock. It believed in health, hard work and education. Anybody who has read the early novels of Willa Cather knows what the circumstances of life were. Today, Nebraska has more folk of German extraction than any state except Wisconsin, and about 11 per cent of the total population is of Czechoslovak origin. Most of the Scandinavians are Swedes, though both Norwegian and Danish communities exist. Some counties are almost solidly Czech, and Czechoslovak is spoken almost as commonly as English; one county is half Czech, half Swede. The Germans are largely Lutheran, and their political affiliation varies. Woodrow Wilson, I heard it said, made Republicans out of them; then prohibition made them Democrats; during World War II they were divided. There was no discernible disloyalty among the Nebraska Germans, though plenty were strongly isolationist, in 1941-45; the Bund was not a problem. In World War I many Germans had thought well of the Kaiser, but Hitler alienated Lutherans, Catholics, Jews and all. During World War I when the German newspapers were a real power in the state, a law had to be passed proscribing foreign language schools and papers. This wasn't necessary in World

[18] Cf. "Nebraska, the Cornhusker State," by Leo A. Borah, in the *National Geographic*, May, 1945.

War II. In a sense, the old German Turnverein and similar societies, which had played a substantial role in Nebraska for well over a generation, never regained their former influence after 1919. A striking point—the American melting pot does melt—is that even after Lidice, Germans and Czechs in the same Nebraska town got on perfectly well together.

Nebraska is, like most western states, exceptionally hospitable and friendly. The atmosphere is quite different from that in some parts of Iowa where, if a stranger passes, the suspicious citizenry assemble to discuss him. A hotel in one western Nebraska town has a big sign on the door, HUNT AND FISH AS YOU DAMN PLEASE. WHEN THE BELL RINGS COME IN TO DINNER.

Any innocent traveler from the East who thinks that Nebraska is a stick-in-the-mud state politically will get some surprises. Somehow the illusion exists that it is overwhelmingly Republican and conservative, which is absurd. Simply recollect that this is the state not only of George W. Norris but of William Jennings Bryan.[19] It had a series of Populist governors, Roosevelt carried it twice, its leading newspaper is Democratic (though strongly anti-New Deal) and Democratic and Republican governors have tended to alternate. Except for Butler and the loud-mouthed Wherry (the other senator) it has scarcely ever elected an outright reactionary to public office. It dislikes Republicans with a Wall Street flavor, and it is the only state ever to have elected a federal senator (Norris) as a nonpartisan. On the other hand it has recently shown a strong antilabor tinge, and in 1946 it was one of three states to adopt a constitutional amendment outlawing the closed shop.[20]

In the old days what ran Nebraska was the railways. This was inevitable, in the pattern the reader knows well: the railways got the land, then populated it, then exploited it. For many years, the Union Pacific and the Chicago, Burlington & Quincy divided the state between them; the UP was always supposed to elect one senator, the Burlington the other. One thing that broke down railway dominance was the direct primary; the parallel here to California is very close. Another lively factor was the growth of the automobile, which made free railway passes less valuable and desirable. A chief minor weapon of the railways everywhere in the nation was, for many years, the free travel with which they bribed legislators and practically anybody else. South Dakota once went to the length of making all members of its legislature swear by the constitution not to accept railway passes.

The chief uniqueness of Nebraska today is that it is the only state with

[19] The first lines of Bryan's celebrated "cross of gold" speech are known to everybody; not so many may know those that follow: "The great cities rest upon our broad and fertile prairies. Burn down your cities and leave our farms, and your cities will spring up again as if by magic; but destroy our farms, and the grass will grow in the streets of every city in the country."

[20] The others: South Dakota and Arizona.

a unicameral legislature.[21] Largely George Norris was responsible for this. Senate and assembly were abolished in 1934, and a one-house system with forty-three members came into operation. Norris developed the idea when, in Washington, he saw bills dear to him killed in committee or hopelessly weakened by compromises; he thought that the "special interests" would have less room in which to operate in a single chamber. I found people in Nebraska somewhat divided on this subject. Most agree that the unicameral idea, as it has worked out, makes for a higher class of legislator (since fewer are to be elected) and greater efficiency and economy generally; some thought however that the system, by giving the lobbyist a single target to aim at, and by eliminating the possibility that special interest legislation which manages to pass one chamber will get stopped by the other, has not been so effective as Norris would have hoped.

The Cornhusker State has plenty of other political distinctions. The legislature (like that of Minnesota) is elected on a nonpartisan basis; a man does not stand as a Republican or a Democrat, and there is no division in the chamber itself on party lines. Another important reformist item is that debate on all bills must be public; this is I believe something unique in the nation; Nebraska has no "executive sessions" (where so much bad legislation is worked out in other states) or private committee meetings. Once again, we see western ideals of democracy demanding expression in concrete form. The *people* insist on running things. All judges and educational officers in Nebraska (as in California) are also elected, like the legislators, on a strict nonparty basis. Another singular factor is that the constitution limits the bonded debt to $100,000; Nebraska cannot undertake expensive public works without specific authorization from the people. Sometimes the passion for pure democracy and complete popular control of the procedures of government leads to picturesque exaggerations; for instance the Omaha ballot in November, 1946, was thirteen feet long and contained 26,000 words. One proposal on this ballot was that the state should contribute $40 per year to the support of every child in the public schools.

Recent big issues have been (*a*) prohibition, and (*b*) public power. A referendum to make the state dry was beaten three to one in 1944; Nebraska has many do-gooders, but it is not dominated by them as, for instance, Kansas is. As to public power, a subject of cardinal importance, the simplest thing to say is that Nebraska has it. Behind this "simple" sentence are years of struggle, violent affrays with the utility companies, convoluted maneuvers by Electric Bond and Share, an irresistibly expanding sentiment for rural electrification, pressure by the Securities Exchange Commission, establishment of people's power districts like the PUD's in the Northwest, and finally the transfer to public

[21] But both Pennsylvania and Georgia were unicameral before 1789.

ownership of the Nebraska Power Company, one of the great old-time behemoths. The result is that Nebraska (not Washington or Oregon which might claim the distinction or Tennessee which does claim it) is the first public power state in the nation.

Finally a word on Omaha (population 223,844). This is one of the most masculine cities in America. It is a great place for aggressive hijinks on Saturday night; it has more night clubs, so-called, than any city between Chicago and San Francisco except, perhaps, Kansas City, Missouri. Omaha is one of the most active cattle markets and meat-packing centers in the world; it is the jumping-off place of the Union Pacific; nine other major railways serve it (of which seven were insolvent in 1937[22]). It is full of dust, guts, noise, and pith; what it lacks mostly is effective civic leadership. Omaha, like Kansas City, is one of the biggest cities in the country where local journalism is a monopoly; the only newspaper (it exists however in morning and evening editions) is the *World Herald*. Its leading citizens are, aside from the distinguished editors of this paper, a real estate and department store man named George Brandeis, and of course William Martin Jeffers of the Union Pacific, who started work as a janitor and who is reputedly so tough that he breaks half dollars with his teeth.

[22] Cf. *Five Cities*, by George R. Leighton, p. 229, which contains a masterful sketch of Omaha.

Chapter 17

On the Extreme Particularity of Kansas

Kansas is the child of Plymouth Rock.
—William Allen White

Kansas had better stop raising corn and begin raising Hell.
—Mary Elizabeth Lease

I WAS in Denver with Topeka as my next stop. I didn't know a soul there and so, after some hesitation, because I hated to disturb a busy man whom I had never met, I sent a telegram to Alf M. Landon, explaining what I wanted. A reply came back so fast that it seemed to bounce: CALL ME ON ARRIVAL UNNECESSARY FOR YOU TO IDENTIFY YOURSELF. So I telephoned Mr. Landon when I got there and he asked if I would come over that evening and "meet some of the fellas." What followed was one of the best bouts of talk I have ever had in America.

In fact there was good talk everywhere in Kansas. Landon thought that perhaps I was getting too one-sided a picture, and he telephoned the university at Lawrence, so that I could meet several folk with other views. Then I had a productive meeting with the then governor, Andrew Schoeppel (a former Walter Camp All-American by the way), and a group of railroad men, packers, and agriculture officials. I spent most of one afternoon with a political journalist of radical tincture, W. G. Clugston, the author of *Rascals in Democracy*, and with Dr. Karl A. Menninger, the psychiatrist whose Topeka clinic is one of the best known in the country. Then William E. Long, head of the Industrial Development Commission, filled in his side of the picture for me, and two of his assistants had the courtesy to drive me into Kansas City.

A word further on Mr. Landon. I have seldom met anybody more likable. Certainly he is a conservative, and I think his views on foreign policy are mostly wrong. But anybody who calls him a mossback or a Bourbon is grossly misinformed. He was overwhelmingly defeated by Roosevelt in 1936, even losing his own state, but FDR would have beaten anybody overwhelmingly in that year. Landon still has a strong influence on the Republican party in the Middle West, chiefly through his close relationships with members of the state organizations. This influence may not always be attuned to the times. But again, do not underestimate him. Raymond Swing, no less, once called him as attractive a man as he had ever met in American public life,[1] and in 1924, believe it or not, Landon bolted the GOP and voted for Wheeler and LaFollette!

One thing surprised me. William Allen White, the late editor of the Emporia *Gazette* who was one of the soundest as well as most delightful Americans of modern times, seemingly has less of a reputation in Kansas than out. Several times I heard him sneered at as a "pseudo-progressive" and so on; perhaps this was no more than an *ex post facto* sprouting of local jealousies. But I heard intelligent liberals say seriously that the "decline and fall" of Kansas could be dated from the appearance in 1896 of White's most famous editorial, "What's the Matter With Kansas?" which was, it is true, an explosive outburst against the ragamuffin radicals, and which appealed to the conservative class against them. But to argue that this editorial was the *cause* of subsequent reaction in Kansas (and the state isn't always so reactionary) seems jejune and silly. The text of "What's the Matter With Kansas?" may be found in White's posthumous *Autobiography*, which is a wonderfully meaty lot of reading matter for the money. Anyway, no matter what his political reputation may be within Kansas, he wrote "Mary White," and that will keep him alive anywhere in the world where people admire the human heart and effective prose.

Of course I asked everybody I met the single simple question, "Who runs Kansas?" No question could be more innocent, and it never ceased to perplex me that so many people found in it overtones of the sinister. It seemed to embarrass them, and their answers usually showed bad conscience, not merely in Kansas but almost everywhere. Either they would deny being "run," or that they "ran" anything, or would retreat into a cloud of clichés; they appeared to think that it was indecent to pry further. After I left Topeka the *Daily Capital* and other newspapers printed pious editorials denouncing me even for having asked the question, and replying that " the people" ran Kansas. Of course. But what I wanted to find out was, "Who *are* the people?" The conventional answer, as given by one paper, "Old John Q. Public in the ballot box," simply isn't good enough, as any intelligent citizen should realize. Then John Harris, publisher of the Hutchinson *News-Herald*, came to my defense, more or less:

> John Gunther, the writer who has a genius for grinding a plausible chapter out of a 24-hour visit [sometimes it's a shade longer, Mr. Harris] spent a day in Kansas recently. . . . The question he had in particular to ask was "Who runs Kansas?" To which two of the

[1] In two remarkable articles in *The Nation* printed during the 1936 campaign. These got Mr. Swing into trouble, because eastern radicals who had never been west of the Mississippi River couldn't bring themselves to believe that Landon's record was so liberal.

state's better-known papers immediately donned their haloes, picked up their golden harps, and made melodic reply.

One hates to inject a sour note into such heavenly music, but from this bassoon comes a singular word, NUTS!

Kansas, Mr. Gunther, is much like other states. That means it is populated by human beings. Most of them are politically so disinterested that what dominating they require is so gentle they don't know what is being done to them. The dominators are a self-perpetuating group from both parties who through recent years have been of such uniform mediocrity that no one of them has emerged as a boss. The group sways . . . to the pressure exerted periodically by organizations representing, respectively, some 25 percent of the farmers, a few of the senior unions, the professional drys, the large industries and utilities, certain reactionary newspapers and the organized oldsters.[2]

The first thing I saw in Kansas, even before the airplane landed, was a huge establishment belonging to International Harvester. The second was a lonely little Salvation Army parade, grinding its way through the hot streets of Topeka. Both these details are, as we will see, not without significance.

Backdrop to the Sunflower State[3]

> To understand why people say, "Dear old Kansas!" is to understand that Kansas is no mere geographical expression, but a state of mind, a religion, and a philosophy in one.
>
> —Carl Becker

In the strict topographical sense Kansas is the heart of the United States, as well as being a kind of gravity point for American democracy. The geographic center of the nation is in Kansas; so is the geodetic center, from which official latitudes and longitudes are reckoned. The state is a huge "tilted slab," sloping downward from the west. People customarily think of it as totally flat and unvaried; actually the highlands near the Colorado border reach 4,135 feet. In shape it is an almost perfect parallelogram, "with one corner nibbled off by the Missouri River."[4]

Kansas (the name means People of the South Wind) is bounded neatly by Oklahoma, Colorado, Nebraska, and Missouri, and because

[2] This small episode is described in *Facts You Should Know About Kansas*, a brochure by W. G. Clugston.

[3] Kansas has six other accepted nicknames—Central, Cyclone, Squatter, Garden, Grasshopper, and Jayhawker. A good many American states have, like this, more than just one nickname; for instance Mississippi has six in all, Connecticut three besides Nutmeg and Constitution, and Arizona five aside from Valentine and Baby. See Odum, *Southern Regions*, p. 540, a book of which I shall make much mention later. For nicknames Odum draws on *State Names, Flags, Seals, Songs, Birds, Flowers, and Other Symbols*, by George E. Shankle.

[4] William Allen White's introduction to *Kansas*, in the American Guide Series, p. 1.

most of the chief roads and railroads go east and west, the pull of Colorado on western Kansas, and of Missouri on the east, is very strong. The pressure from north and south is much less. The Kansas puritans "get along fine with Oklahoma," I heard it said—though of course they are apt to think that Oklahoma is noisy and on the brazen side. When I asked Kansans about Nebraska they looked puzzled and were almost inclined to say "Where's that?" There are few first-class roads leading up to Omaha, and Nebraska as a whole seems almost as distant as Montana.

Kansas is, in a way, unique in the United States, because it has no real metropolis, though Wichita has 115,000 people and Topeka 68,000; this serves to increase the enormous influence—on eastern Kansas in particular—of Kansas City, Missouri. This great and extraordinary city, while not the capital of its own state, is in effect the capital of another, a situation without parallel in the country. A minor illustrative point: part of the University of Kansas is not located in Kansas itself at all, but in Kansas City, Missouri. For a word on Kansas City, Kansas, the singular community across the river from Kansas City, Missouri, see Chapter 22 below.

Where did Kansas come from? From New England and the South, in a proportion of three or four to one. The abolitionists pumped in, armed with "Beecher's Bibles" (rifles) and the printing press, an equally important weapon, to keep the state free; they waged their own pre-Civil War with the Southerners already there. Everybody knows the story of John Brown of Osawatomie. After the war, emigration from the North continued; any federal veteran was entitled, after 1865, to settle on 160 good acres of Kansas land, and there came—as in Nebraska—a great influx of Grand Army of the Republic officers and men. The first New England stock became diluted with that of Iowa, Indiana, and Illinois.

Nevertheless southern influence has always remained fairly strong, though not so strong as in Missouri, say. As of today, there are Jim Crow theaters in Topeka. The remarkable thing is that Kansas did become so homogeneous. It is an extraordinarily well-integrated state, overwhelmingly "Nordic," middle class, and Protestant. One factor making for homogeneity was of course the ineffable richness of the land. The soil of Kansas absorbed, colored, and made virtually identical the Methodist preachers from Iowa small towns, the younger sons of the Salem clipper captains, workmen from the Susquehanna, and even Ozark crackers from Arkansas. The Kansan is, as has been well said, the most average of all Americans, a kind of common denominator for the entire continent.

Only two "foreign" groups of any consequence exist today, the Mennonites and the Volga Germans, though there are a few Mexican workers

in the railway yards. There is no great Scandinavian element as in the
states to the north. The Santa Fe Railroad (which dominated the state
for more than a generation) brought in the Mennonites, and the
Union Pacific the Volga folk. Both groups were brought over as a result
of direct negotiation in Europe by the railways, which badly needed population to fill out their vast land grants; out of population would come
crops, and out of this, freight. The passenger fare was made as tempt-
ingly low as $11.00 from New York to Kansas, to suck the emigrants in.
The Mennonites, a tightly knit and curious community, came originally
from both North Germany and the Crimea. They disbelieve in most
forms of political participation, and until about twenty years ago many
refused to vote. Most Mennonites are farmers; they are in particular
great producers of Turkey wheat.

The various processes of assimilation, of wresting a commodious life
out of soil, of chaining new communities to the plains, weren't always
easy. On one occasion[5] a Russian grand duke came to Kansas to hunt
buffalo. The lieutenant governor, honoring him at an official banquet,
pointed to a banner on which was emblazoned the state motto, *Ad Astra
per Aspera*, and explained, "Duke, them there words is Latin, and they
mean to the stars after a hell of a lot of trouble."

Kansas Puritanism, probably the most intense in America, derives
from the abolitionist tradition, the New England background, and a touch
of fundamentalism from the South. Not only did Kansas help to produce
John Brown; it produced that hatchet-carrying granny and holy crone on
broomstick, Carry Nation. The state is, of course, "dry." I will describe
later why I print "dry" in quotation marks. Gambling is forbidden, and
so for a time were cigarettes and even the sale of cigarette paper. In some
directions the Puritan impulse was less cranky; for instance one famous
Kansas crusade was against the old-fashioned roller towel, and the state
was the first in the union to pass an effective Blue Sky law.

When we reach New England we will find that plenty of Puritans are
radical. Kansas is a strongly conservative state, yes, and it is ordinarily
overwhelmingly Republican; nevertheless a considerable base of progressive legislation does exist. It is certainly nowhere near so radical as
North Dakota or even Minnesota, but also it is nowhere near so reactionary as Indiana. There is very little complacency in Kansas. Of course
reformist legislation and "radicalism" are, as we know, strictly and
specifically dependent on the price of crops. Very few farmers are
radical when wheat hits $1.80. But let agricultural prices drop sharply,
and the Kansas (and Iowa) man of the soil can become, almost overnight, a flaming and embittered opponent of the existing order.

Kansas was the original home of Populism, and it was one of the first
states to demand direct election of senators. It does not have the initia-

[5] Paraphrased from Clugston, *op. cit.* p. 5.

tive and referendum, but a good many other Populist planks are in the statute books today—put in by Republican legislatures for the most part! A real estate mortgage law protects farmers from being dispossessed for a full eighteen months after notice of sale; municipal ownership of utilities is widespread; schoolbooks are free.

Does "Bleeding Kansas" still bleed? Will it still rise to fight injustice? I asked this question generally, and one answer I got was, "Oh, we still have a hemorrhage once in a while."

John Steuart Curry, whose death in 1946 at the age of forty-eight removed from fruitful activity a first-class American painter, and a Kansan born and bred, was once commissioned to do a set of murals for the Topeka capitol. The work covered a span from Coronado (the first white men to see Kansas were the Spaniards) through John Brown to twentieth century farmhands destitute and miserable. The panels were never finished, and Curry refused to sign them. Official criticism had been that they were "far too blunt."[6]

Why—a remarkable fact about the United States and one which is worth underscoring from time to time—are even the American underpossessed (except in times of acute economic crisis) inclined to be so stubbornly conservative? One answer is of course that they don't really consider themselves "underpossessed." Another, applicable all over the Middle West, is the extreme social fluidity of America and a consequent progressive dimming out of categories; the hired hand marries the farmer's daughter. Another, which has particular reference to Kansas, is Puritanism. The poor man goes to heaven easier than the rich.

Folklore and the Kansas Jayhawk

Almost for the first time in this book we mention now the tall tale; most of these are based on an exaggerated prowess by frontiersmen struggling against nature, and no country is so rich in them as the United States. Kansas of course provided an apt background for tall tales; the early cattlemen ended their long hell-for-leather treks at towns like Dodge City and Abilene. In Chapter 15, I mentioned that Wyoming has been called a child of the transcontinental trails. But look at Kansas! Not only did the Santa Fe and Oregon trails make their historic junction in Kansas; the state was crossed by the Pony Express, the Osage Trail, Pike's Route to Pawnee Village, Holladay's Overland Line, the Santa Fe Cutoff, and Butterfield's Overland Dispatch Line, to say nothing of the Texas cattle trails. "Home on the Range" was originally a Kansas song.

[6] The Diego Rivera murals in Rockefeller Center, New York, once similarly provoked a public storm.

The Kansas equivalent of Paul Bunyan is Lem Blanchard.[7] Once in mid-July when the corn was growing at its fastest Lem climbed a stalk, the better to survey his field; after looking into the next county, "he was horrified to find that the stalk was growing upward faster than he could scramble down." In one version, the denouement is that Lem is rescued by a balloonist; in another, his neighbors, having at last located him on high, shoot him to save him from slow death by starvation.

There were grasshoppers in Kansas as big as mules, who after devouring the corn crop "insolently pick their teeth on the barbs of the wire fence." There were farms so large that, "by the time the mortgage was recorded on the west side, the mortgage on the east had come due."

But most Kansas legend centers on the Jayhawk—the wondrous native bird that flies backward, and so doesn't care where he's going, "but sure wants to know where he's been!" The Jayhawk has, of course, no wings; he wears bright yellow slippers, and his yellow beak is very large. A Kansas primer begins with this:

> I am a Jayhawker.
> I do not have wings.
> I can sing.
> I can run.
> I can laugh.
> I was born in Kansas.
> All boys and girls who were born in
>   Kansas are Jayhawkers.
> Are you a Jayhawker?

Then there are many Jayhawker songs, like:

> I'm a Jayhawker boy from the Jayhawker state;
> I wear Jayhawker hats on a Jayhawker pate;
> I ride a Jayhawker horse in a Jayhawker way;
> In the Jayhawker state I have settled to stay.

The Kansas historians have much grave fun with this famous animal. In *The Mythical Jayhawk*, by Kirke Mechem, secretary of the State Historical Society, one may find passages like, "There was an epoch when the Jayhawk flew in our troubled atmosphere. It was a bird with a mission. It was an early bird and it caught many a Missouri worm. . . . Geologists are familiar with the representative of the class Aves called *Jayhawkornis kansasensis*. . . . The brow of those of the commonest size is two palms across from eye to eye, the eyes sticking out at the sides, so that when they are flying they can see in all directions at once. . . . The theory that the Jayhawk is a Phoenix has divided scientists into two schools of thought, both fiercely incognito." Mr. Mechem's monograph

---

[7] My source for these stories is *Kansas* in the American Guide Series, pp. 100-101.

also includes a blank space under the notation, "Invisible Jayhawks on Their Way to Plant Volunteer Wheat."

The Jayhawk folklore has, as is quite proper, moved up to date with the times, and many are the B-29 pilots near Wichita who have miraculous adventures with these monsters. Of course they can easily outfly any B-29, and some have jet-propelled motors and retractable yellow-claw landing gear.

Kansas Has Statistics Too

Here we really get into the booster area. No state is prouder of itself than Kansas, and I have seen no propaganda in any other quite so handsomely prepared as, for instance, the folio-size booklet *Let's Look Into Kansas* issued by the Industrial Development Commission. One of its mottoes is "Kansas—Where East Meets West, and Farm Meets Factory"; another is the dubious pun, "Resourceful Kansas." From documents issued by this commission, and from other sources, the reader who does not object to handouts (I love them myself) may glean much curious material. For instance Kansas possesses the only pipe organ factory in the western United States, and a law has been on the books for a quarter of a century (of course it is never enforced) "making it a felony to fly the Russian flag within the state." Kansas has a State Beautification Project, and it contains, near Atchison, a huge limestone cave, air cooled and capable of storing 50,000 *tons* of food or anything else—come an atomic war—that the government might want to keep there.

What is the average American proud of in his state? I picked up an official set of postcards, bound with a slip INVESTIGATE KANSAS. They show "The Beautiful Musical Tower in the Center of the Topeka, Kansas, Two Million-Dollar Senior High School Building (Educational Advantages Offered in Kansas Rank Among the Best in the Nation), Topeka's Nationally-Known Rose Garden in Gage Park (Is Typical of Similar Scenes in City Parks Throughout Kansas), A Portion of the 206 Million-Bushel Wheat Crop (Kansas, Greatest Wheat-Producing State, Raises About One-Fifth of the Entire Nation's Crop), Assembly Lines of a Kansas Airplane Factory, and Well-Improved Farms Dot the Kansas Landscape (Attesting to the Fertility of the Soil and the Importance of Agriculture."

Agriculture is important—yes. But more striking because far more unexpected are the state's industrialization and mineral resources. The Boeing plant at Wichita (employment 52,000 at peak) built more B-29's than any other three similar plants, and the Sunflower Ordnance Works at De Soto make the ticklish explosives that go into rockets. Actually Kansas produced, from Pearl Harbor through August, 1945, more than four billion dollars worth of industrial goods—without a single strike. One sizable booklet (*Kansas Buyers Guide*, 131 pages) itemizes some

Kansas-made things; I looked at the listings under J, an unlikely letter I thought, and found glass jars, concrete jetties, janitor supplies, pumping jacks, jewelry, "jail and cell-work—steel," and expansion joists. Another pamphlet lists more than a hundred "industries applicable to Kansas," among them air-conditioning units, dehydrated alfalfa, dog food, grave markers, and bows and arrows.[8]

The notion that Kansas is nothing but a vast prairie boiling with wheat and corn is, to Kansans, laughable. What lies underneath the land is almost as important as what grows on it. For instance Kansas is the fifth petroleum-producing state; every "major" operates in it except Humble—Magnolia, Texas, Continental, Gulf, Shell, Sinclair. It actually outranks thirty-nine other states in mineral output, with an annual production worth 175 million dollars which is five times that of Alaska. Take salt. Kansas has 5,000 *billion* tons of salt reserves, enough to cover the entire state with a layer 17 feet thick, or to build a wall around it 1,000 feet wide and 200 feet tall. "There is enough salt in Kansas to supply the entire United States for 500,000 years" is a statement in one publication. Then too it has the largest natural gas field in the world (though Texas may dispute this); it is the third state in zinc and lead production and among the first three in cattle; it is first in flour milling and among the first in number of tractors on farms, carbon black, "tame hay," and railroad mileage; it produces coal, various clays, volcanic ash, chalk, and such rarefied items as tripoli, chat, and diatomaceous marl.

Kansas flaunts statistics in other realms too. It has the most college students per capita of any state, and it claims "the nation's best public health record." It has forty daily newspapers, which makes it the first in America in newspapers per capita, and it is fourth in percentage of high school graduates. It maintains five different schools on the university level, and it has unique publishing houses like that of Haldeman-Julius at Girard. It has produced (or strongly influenced) a considerable number of writers—for instance Dorothy Canfield Fisher, Ed Howe the rustic philosopher,[9] Professor Carl Becker, Langston Hughes and Claude McKay among Negroes, and in a different literary category Charles M. Sheldon, whose *In His Steps* is by far the greatest best seller in American history.

Also—to move into another field—Kansas is the home state of two men well known for being good citizens. Milton S. Eisenhower, president of Kansas State College, and his brother Dwight.

---

[8] A complication is of course discriminatory freight rates. Kansas City is the second largest livestock city in the world. But its hinterland has no leather industry whatever, because freight rates are so high. A Californian, I heard, could come into Kansas, buy live hogs, ship them back, slaughter them in California, and ship the processed meat back to Kansas and still sell cheaper in Topeka than Kansas City can.

[9] For the doings of Howe's son Gene see Chapter 47.

Very Well: What Does Run It?

Kansas used to believe in Populism and free silver. It now
believes in hot summers and a hot hereafter.

—Julian Street

(1) The congeries of forces generally alluded to by Mr. Harris above,
agriculture in particular.

(2) The Capper interests. Senator Arthur Capper is eighty-one; his
views on some subjects are roughly those of Beowulf or General Grant;
after the November 1946 election he became chairman of the powerful
Agriculture Committee of the Senate. But Capper's position in Kansas
does not rest on his Washington reputation—and a quite lively reputation it is in some respects. It rests on his formidable power in local
journalism.

A well-informed man in Kansas is, I heard, one who reads a Capper
daily, a Capper weekly, and a Capper monthly. The range and influence
of this press is astonishing; yet few folk outside Kansas or professional
farm groups have ever heard of it. First, Capper is publisher of the
leading Topeka daily, which is both the "official" state and county paper,
the Topeka *Capital*, and he owns the local radio station. Second, he
publishes *Capper's Weekly*, with a circulation (as of the date I was in
Kansas) of 353,000. Third, he publishes two monthlies, *Household* and
Capper's Farmer, with circulations respectively of 1,850,000 and 1,250,-
000; the advertising rate for a full page in *Household* is $7,500,
which should make several national (= eastern) magazines take notice; a
coupon on one of its advertisements recently brought 52,000 replies.
Fourth, Capper publishes a group of farm weeklies in various sections of
the Middle West and East Central states, like the *Michigan Farmer* (circulation 142,000), the *Ohio Farmer* (152,000), the *Missouri Ruralist*
(116,000), the *Pennsylvania Farmer* (141,000), and of course the *Kansas
Farmer* (106,000). Altogether, the venerable senator's publications are
believed to have a minimum of 400,000 readers in his home state
alone. I asked a man who knows him well what Capper himself felt about
all this. Answer: "He sits on the fence, with ears to the ground on both
sides."

As interesting an afternoon as any I had in forty-eight states was
one spent in Topeka with a group of Capper editors. We didn't talk
politics much, but what these folk didn't know about agriculture could
be locked up in the inside of a penny.

(3) Alf M. Landon among Republicans and Harry H. Woodring,
who for an unhappy period was Mr. Roosevelt's secretary of war and
who is a former governor, among Democrats.[10]

---

[10] I inquired naïvely who were other Democrats in Kansas, and had the reply,
"Go to the federal building." In other words most federal appointees during the

(4) As far as big business is concerned, oil and the utilities. Once, according to a story possibly apocryphal, a division of the university made a survey recommending that a severance tax be placed on petroleum. The next year appropriations for this department of the university mysteriously disappeared from the budget.

(5) The great insurance companies, who are of course intimately involved with agricultural finance.

(6) The Methodist church.

(7) Closely allied with this, the do-gooders in general who, a Kansan worthy told me, "were a fine collection of wonderful old ladies, who will chew your eyes out."

(8) To an indeterminate degree, the Masonic orders.

(9) The noon-day luncheon clubs. It has taken this book far too long to get around to more than general mention of such universal American institutions as the Kiwanis, Lions, and Rotary. Generally, they fit in with the local chamber of commerce, which means that they tie up with the banks, department stores, utilities, and so on, throughout the state.

(10) Obscure and complex social pressures. Suppose a young politician's wife wants to become a member of the local country club. The young politician is not likely to affront wantonly the insurance executive who, it happens, is chairman of the membership committee. Suppose a farmer takes a strong public stand for municipal power. He may not find himself such a jolly good fellow at the next meeting of the local Grange. Or suppose the pastor of some small church, mildly liberal, says that maybe the Russians had something worth fighting for, since they fought so well. The local bank may not actually buy advertisements in a county newspaper to denounce such an obvious miscreant, though such things have happened; what is more probable is that the pastor's wife will be snubbed, and his children pointed out as "different."

(11) The Legislative and Research Council. This, a bipartisan group of about thirty members, led by the president of the local senate and the speaker of the house, works *after* the adjournment of the legislature; it devotes itself to research on impending problems, and is a kind of permanent connecting link between the widely spaced legislative sessions; no major laws are likely to pass the new legislature without its approval. Kansas is the innovator of this sensible device, and eleven other states have so far copied it.

(12) Finally, and above all, the Kansas City (Missouri) *Star*. This potent newspaper, one of the most distinguished in the United States, has

more influence in Kansas than in its own state, and its Kansas circulation, around 170,000, is as big as that of any three Kansas dailies put together. Not only is Kansas a "colony" of Kansas City, Missouri; it is the "colony" of a newspaper, something that exists nowhere else in the entire country. The head of the Kansas Department of the *Star*, Lacy Haynes—incidentally, Will White's brother-in-law—was for years a king-maker, and it is hard to name any Topeka politician, Democratic or Republican, whom he didn't help to put in office, or keep from getting it.

Politics and Prohibition

> Oh, they chaw tobacco thin
> in Kansas.
> Oh, they say that drink's a sin
> in Kansas.
> —Kansas folksong

By all odds the leading Kansas issue is prohibition. Here too the influence of Missouri is paramount, inasmuch as it is almost universally accepted in eastern Kansas that "Missouri keeps us dry, so that we have to go there to buy our liquor."

In fact, during the whisky shortage in 1945 and 1946, it was almost as easy to buy good Scotch and bourbon in dry Topeka (though at higher prices) than in wet Kansas City. Cars and trucks shuttled day and night across the border; Topeka and other Kansas towns bloomed with bootleggers, speakeasies, bars, and it was said that to keep liquor from being run into the state "at least 1200 federal agents would be necessary." Hundreds of Kansas liquor dealers (in a dry state!) actually posted retail licenses on their walls; the sixty-six-year-old state prohibition law became, in short, a joke. This was too much for the Alcohol Tax Unit of the United States Treasury, and late in 1946 an attempt began to clean it all up—through the familiar device of prosecuting bootleggers for tax evasion. On one occasion, federal agents made an exhibit of a thousand cases of hard liquor they had seized—and invited the state authorities to come and look. Meantime, Kansas county attorneys and so on were promised actual "bonuses" for bringing prohibition violators into court, viz., they were bribed by the state itself to enforce the law.[11]

All this became the pivot of the 1946 gubernatorial campaign. Harry Woodring ran for governor on a platform urging repeal of the prohibition act. The Anti-Saloon League, the WCTU, the State Temperance Society,

---

[11] See columns by Doris Fleeson in the New York *Post*, January, 1946. A detail is that, on one occasion, "some righteous members of the liquor syndicate forced hijackers to return their booty because the victim, a night club operator, had paid his protection," i.e., paid the police. Negotiations for this deal actually took place in the county jail, with "the county paying the expense of a long-distance call to Kansas City to close the transaction."

and similar organizations went into ferocious action, and he was soundly beaten.

The most revealing sidelight on law enforcement I heard was that "If you get caught with a quart, you get six months; two quarts, three months; a five-gallon jug, a week; a case, a day; a truckload, nothing." There have been crazy politics in Kansas on other levels. Does anybody these days remember John R. ("Doc") Brinkley? A notable character, Doc Brinkley was the great goat-gland specialist; his treatments, which cost up to 750 dollars, restored waning virility to the credulous. For a time the goat population of Kansas abruptly declined—so anyway people told me in Topeka—as Brinkley's expanding and lucrative practice demanded the sacrifice of more animals. The Doc entered politics in 1930, and, in a three-cornered race, only narrowly missed being elected governor.[12] Also he was, I believe, the first American demagogue to use radio for political purposes in a big way. Kansas eventually ran him out of the state for malpractice. He moved to Del Rio, Texas, and then across the border to Mexico, where for a time he maintained what he called the most powerful radio station in the world. Brinkley died some years ago. Whether or not he used goat glands on himself is unknown.

Life of the Kansas Land

Really Kansas is two states, or maybe even three. One line of division is of course that which cuts through the Dakotas and Nebraska too, the 98th meridian. Western Kansas is short-grass country, sparsely settled, with scanty rainfall and big mechanized farms, based on wheat. The east is moist, with thick alluvial soil; here we touch the corn belt. In between is an area more difficult to define, "central" Kansas, which is mostly (of course I am oversimplifying) alfalfa and grazing country.

South of Kansas is cotton, and north is spring wheat; Kansas grows neither, and its two great crops are of course winter wheat and corn. The gist of the Kansas "story" is, in a way, a struggle between wheat and corn, although plenty of farmers grow both. Corn is cultivated in every county now. It doesn't, however, come anywhere near the importance of wheat in the state's economy, and Kansas is the greatest wheat state in the union by far.

Wheat, as we know, is a crop not without risks; also, in Kansas at least, it used to be called a "lazy man's crop." In the old days you planted it in September, whereupon there was nothing to do until you harvested it the next summer, whereupon you paid off the bank. Not now. Wheat

[12] The background of this bizarre episode, including details of tawdry political interlockings and the role played in exposing Brinkley by the Kansas City *Star*, may be found in Clugston's *Rascals in Democracy*, pp. 148 *et seq.*

farmers are busy all the year. They have hogs, soy beans, sheep, lespedeza, and sorghums like feterita, to lessen their dependence on wheat, and to provide an income the year around. Above all, land planted in wheat (until it starts to "joint") may be used for grazing; the wheat is green before the snow comes, and then again in spring; a most remarkable thing in this part of the world is that the more you pasture wheat, the better will be the wheat produced; it does wheat good to be eaten as it grows!—almost as cropping a beard in an adolescent makes the beard stronger. This technique of growing livestock on growing wheat means, in effect, that the wheat farmer gets two wheat crops a year, one in the form of meat.

I asked the Capper editors what distinguished Kansas farmers as against those of any other state. They replied: (1) aggressiveness; (2) willingness to experiment; (3) the gambling instinct, imposed of necessity by the risks of wind and rain; (4) modernity. It may seem a poor figure, but at least one-third of Kansas farms are electrified.

But now we are very close to the Middle West—that broad thick mattress of corn and hogs, great cities, the Mississippi basin, and reputed isolation. Let us proceed.

Chapter 18

Mind of the Middle West

〜〜

> The Americans are a queer people; they can't rest.
> —Stephen Leacock

> The essential factor in the destiny of a nation . . . lies in the quality and quantity of its will.
> —H. G. Wells

> This country with its institutions belongs to the people who inhabit it. Whenever they shall grow weary of the existing government, they can exercise their constitutional right of amending it, or their revolutionary right to dismember or overthrow it.
> —Abraham Lincoln

TO DEFINE the Middle West is comparatively easy; it is the upper basin of the Mississippi and its tributaries. The region cannot, however, be precisely bounded by state lines, though commonly it is assumed to consist of Minnesota, Wisconsin, Iowa, Missouri, Illinois, Indiana, Michigan, and Ohio. But the eastern fringes of the Great Plains states—the Dakotas, Nebraska, and Kansas—also belong to the Middle West by most standards. Conversely part of Minnesota (which calls itself the "Northwest" or "Upper Midwest" incidentally) hardly seems middle western at all, and Missouri has, as we shall see, pronounced characteristics of the South. Ohio is in a category mostly its own. Most Ohioans, at least in the rural areas, think of themselves as Middle Westerners, but towns like Akron and Cleveland belong much more to the orbit of the industrial East, and Cincinnati is southerly as well as eastern. One remark I heard is that Toledo is "where the Middle West ends." All this being true, we shall abide by those authorities who consider the Middle West to be the eight great states named above.

There are other criteria, of course, aside from the Mississippi basin. It might be said that the Middle West is that part of the nation where moist black soil of great depth and richness is to be found, in contrast to the red soil of the South, the mongrel stone and sand of New England, and the red, yellow, or dry sparse soil of the West. But there is plenty of middle western soil, like some in Minnesota and the marginal southern areas of Indiana and Missouri, not black at all. Another definition might be that it is that part of the country mostly laid out in townships six miles square;

it is where the farmer owns his own quarter-section (160 acres) and works it himself. But there are plenty of middle western farmers with more or less than 160 acres, to say nothing of the fact that the whole region is pre-eminently one of great cities too. Another simple definition might be that the Midwest is the broad flat area blocked off by the Rockies and the Alleghenies at each end, where people tend to look inward rather than outward, where few ever see the sea. Similarly a narrow delimitation might be that it is an area coterminous with the circulation belt of the Chicago *Tribune*.[1]

At any rate one thing is corelike and indisputable. This great block of states is the central pivot and umbilicus of the nation.

Great Lakes and Great River

> Rolling, rolling from Arkansas, Kansas, Iowa
> Rolling from Ohio, Wisconsin, Illinois,
> Rolling and shouting:
> Till, at last, it is Mississippi,
> The Father of Waters; the matchless; the great flood
> Dyed with the earth of states; with the dust and the sun and
>   the seed of half the states.
>
> —Stephen Vincent Benét

Many years ago in London I happened to be telling an English lady about Chicago, and how its most challenging feature was the great imperturbable expanse of lake. "Lake?" she asked. "What lake? Can you see across it?" (It was this same lady who was similarly astonished to hear that in Chicago we could see some of the best Renoirs in the world, hear Chaliapin and Galli Curci regularly although New York did not, watch Katchaloff and Moskvin of the Moscow Art Theater in the flesh, and go to a university with three Nobel prize winners on its staff.)

Lake Michigan (22,400 square miles in area) is bigger by a comfortable margin than Spanish Morocco or Switzerland, and as every American knows it is one of five, with a total area of 95,160 square miles —almost twice the size of England. These lakes, called "Great" with reason, are the fresh-water Mediterranean of the western hemisphere, as has nicely been said. They are the Middle West's equivalent of a coastline.[2] Of course they are more than merely a midwest phenomenon, since Pennsylvania abuts on one, and New York on two. They carry the Middle West right out into the Atlantic, and they are as important to Canada as to the United States. Originally, a couple of hundred thousand years ago, they were hollowed out by the glaciers which at the same time

---

[1] Baseball provides another definition. Nothing could possibly be more middle western than seven of the eight cities whose teams play in the American Association—Indianapolis, Milwaukee, St. Paul, Columbus, Toledo, Minneapolis, and Kansas City (Mo.). The eighth, Louisville, is a border city.

[2] Cf. *Who Are the Americans*, by W. D. Whitney, p. 66.

ground the rocks into what is now fine soil. They are the source not merely of a prodigious commerce but of mythology; Paul Bunyan is a Great Lakes character. One extraordinary thing about them, as de Tocqueville noted a century ago, is that unlike almost all European lakes they are not walled in—they merge flatly into the plains and prairie. But do not think that they cannot be angry! I have seen weather on Lake Erie that made the China Sea seem calm. Normally one does not associate such turbulent outbursts of nature with a mechanical civilization, but Lake Erie is also the greatest industrial waterway in the world, a lake almost as big as Palestine with a cordon of railways drawn tight around it like a noose.[3]

Define the Middle West again. It is where industry and agriculture both reach their highest American development and coalesce. This theme, even if I do not mention it explicitly, will recur time and again in the chapters following. The Great Lakes are so important because, aside from much else, they feed half the nation with (*a*) grain and (*b*) steel. From the western tip of Lake Superior, at Duluth (Minnesota) and Superior (Wisconsin) flows an inordinate, colossal tonnage of iron ore and wheat destined for the furnaces and breadbaskets of the East. In return, coal flows up. The life of the freighters carrying this cargo has an authentic romance hard to match in contemporary affairs. Also it is a fact perhaps hard to believe, and realistic in the extreme, that Duluth-Superior is the second biggest port in the United States. Lake Superior is artificially connected with its sisters by the Soo Canal at Sault Ste. Marie. This canal, which charges no tolls, carries more traffic than the Panama and Suez Canals combined.[4] Professor Hatcher makes the point that, if the locks here had been destroyed during the war, the United States might have lost it. More than 90 million tons of iron ore, destined to become steel, passed through the Soo Canal in 1942 alone.

Finally think of the great cities on the lakesides. "Blot out of the North American continent the cities that rim . . . the Great Lakes and it is astonishing to consider how much would be lost," writes Hatcher. "The heart of Canada would cease to beat." On the American side forget the medium towns—dozens like Racine, Ashtabula, Sandusky, Marquette, Gary, Menominee, Ashland, Erie, Ludington, Escanaba, Niagara—and reflect merely on the goliaths: Milwaukee, Chicago, Detroit, Toledo, Cleveland, Buffalo.

The Mississippi River, which we must also mention briefly now, has never been described better than by Mark Twain seventy-odd years ago:

[3] For this subject see *The Great Lakes* and *Lake Erie*, by Harlan Hatcher, books so solid, conscientious, and alive, that few things in American regional writing can compare with them except, say, the best work of Carey McWilliams.
[4] *Life*, April 22, 1940.

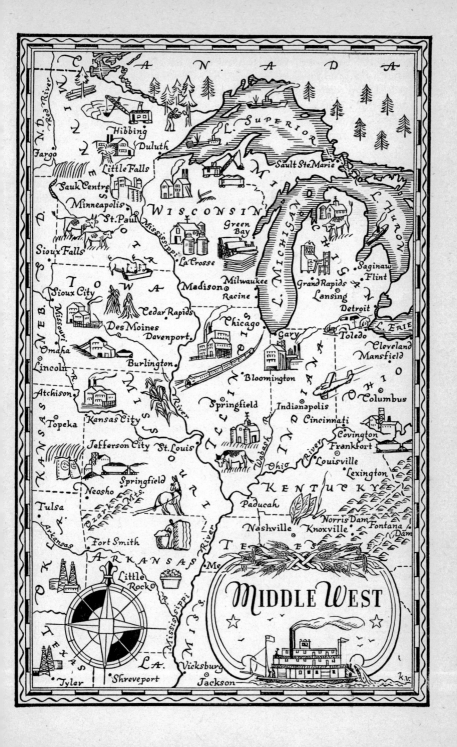

MIDDLE WEST

The Mississippi is not a commonplace river. . . . Considering the Missouri its main branch, it is the longest river in the world—4,300 miles. It seems safe to say that it is also the crookedest river in the world, since in one part of its journey it uses up 1,300 miles to cover the same ground that the crow would fly over in 675. It discharges three times as much water as the St. Lawrence, 25 times as much as the Rhine, and 338 times as much as the Thames. No other river has so vast a drainage basin; it draws its water supply from 28 states and territories, from Delaware, on the Atlantic seaboard . . . to Idaho on the Pacific slope.

The Mississippi receives and carries to the Gulf water from 54 subordinate rivers that are navigable by steamboats, and from some hundreds that are navigable by flats and keels. The area of its drainage basin is as great as the combined areas of England, Wales, Scotland, Ireland, France, Spain, Portugal, Germany, Austria, Italy, and Turkey.

It is a remarkable river in this: that instead of widening toward its mouth, it grows narrower . . . and deeper.

Mark Twain, who was a prescient reporter, also mentions that as of his day the Mississippi empties every year 406 million tons of mud into the Gulf of Mexico. Change the word "mud" to "soil," and we are up to date. It is a striking commentary on the way that rivers don't change that the best contemporary figure on soil loss is almost precisely that which Mark Twain uses, 400 million tons. Harnessing of this mastodon of rivers and its tributaries remains, as Professor Brogan has said,[5] incomparably the greatest engineering problem in the western world.

Another description of the Mississippi is that of Charles Dickens in the 1840's. He sees it first at Cairo, Illinois, "a slimy monster hideous to behold." Mr. Dickens pays his respects to Cairo ("a hotbed of disease, an ugly sepulchre, a grave uncheered by any gleam of promise") and proceeds:

But what words shall describe the Mississippi, great father of rivers, who (praise be to Heaven) has no young children like him! An enormous ditch, sometimes two or three miles wide, running liquid mud, six miles an hour; its strong and frothy current choked and obstructed everywhere by huge logs and whole forest trees . . . now rolling past like monstrous bodies, their tangled roots showing like matted hair . . . or wounded snakes. The banks low, the trees dwarfish, the marshes swarming with frogs, the wretched cabins few and far apart, their inmates hollow-cheeked and pale, mosquitoes penetrating into every crack and crevice of the boat, mud and slime on everything . . .

For two days we toiled up this foul stream.[6]

[5] In *The American Character*, p. 37.
[6] *American Notes*, p. 183.

Dickens would find a change or two today, though the river is certainly a "Big Muddy" still, and it remains what it always was—a kind of huge rope, no matter with what knots and frayings, tying the United States together. It is the Nile of the Western Hemisphere. Its banks and levees are not all that they might be, and it still shows an uncontrollable tendency to spit and wander, but Dickens would be interested in two developments at least—the way it has become a tremendous industrial waterway, fit for two-way navigation the year around, and the proposal made last year to build a "Mississippi River Parkway," an automobile road that would be a "scenic highway" along its total length, through ten states. But when one stops to reflect, it is rather odd that such a parkway has never been proposed before.

Three Brief Observations about the Middle West

(1) More than any other American region, except possibly New England, it represents the full flowering of the "gadget mind." Most American boys, and in particular those from midwest farms, are born mechanics; they can do anything with their hands. Out of this and much else has come what Detroit, let us say, symbolizes better than any other American city—the assembly line and mass production.

Perhaps the "mechanical approach" is the curse of modern America. It has put a sharp metallic edge on events and phenomena in many fields, and it serves to make utility, practicalness, the dominant American measuring stick in almost everything. What really runs this country, one might say, is the spirit that wants to know what makes an automobile go. What really distinguishes the Middle West is the combination it affords of black soil *and* the tractor; it is where corn *and* the jeep work together.

Details in this field are innumerable. The skyscraper was invented in Chicago. Henry Ford once made the nation laugh, witlessly, by talking about the synthetic cow. The scientific work that most interested Charles A. Lindbergh was on an artificial heart.

(2) The most interesting single thing about the Middle West is probably its actual middleness, not only in geography or in the sense of moderation, but in its averageness, its typicalness. This is America uncontaminated. Here sounds the most spontaneous natural note in the nation. Any good politician knows that, if he can't carry the Middle West, he can't carry anything. The region has, as a result, a profound veto power over the rest of the country. Another aspect of this "middleness" is that, since the Midwest is like a governor controlling the oscillations of a wheel, it is the part of the nation that most strongly resists change. One might also say that, for the Japanese to have assumed that an attack on Pearl Harbor could win a war or for the Germans ever

to have had any idea of beating the United States at all, proves that they knew nothing of the Middle West whatsoever.

This middleness can be expressed in another dimension. The Mississippi Basin was filled by the pushing out of the first thirteen states, and therefore it became a kind of bridge between New England, Virginia, and the migrations later. The influence of the South is often ignored, but it is considerable, particularly in Ohio, Missouri, and southern Illinois and Indiana. The father of the Middle West was, as Graham Hutton points out, none other than Thomas Jefferson, and Patrick Henry (believe it or not!) was the first governor of Illinois.[7]

New England, however, outranks the South as a progenitor. In a way the Midwest is exactly what one would expect from a marriage between New England puritanism and *rich* soil.

Middleness in still another direction is expressed by the suggestive fact that the area is, all at once, a producer, processor, distributor, and consumer. Two-thirds of the entire retail market of the nation, Hutton calculates, is in the middle states. The West is as we know primarily a producer; the East is primarily a consumer; the Middle West is both, and also the link between them.

(3) It would be absurd to call the Melting Pot specifically a Midwest phenomenon; it exists conspicuously in New England and all the industrial cities of the East; from this point on until we reach the South many chapters hence, the foreign-born and the sons of foreign-born will never be far absent from these pages. But the challenge of opening up and settling a continent was first met in the Middle West. Some of the earlier strains, like those of the French and Dutch, are recessive nowadays. But think of the Scots, Germans, Irish, Italians, Canadians, Russians, Scandinavians, Bohemians, Poles, that came later!

Except for a few Indian full-bloods, *all* Americans are, of course, the product of foreign immigration—Puritan, Cavalier, Chinese, Greek, Negro, Montenegrin, or what you will. This point, though astonishing to some outsiders, need not be labored. "The United States," a British historian wrote once, "is the greatest single achievement of European civilization."

A phrase every middle western boy hears a thousand times is "the old country," uttered by his elders usually in a tone of nostalgic affection plus relief that it is far away plus a desire to return for a visit someday but not to stay. The United States is a country unique in the world because it was populated not merely by people who live in it by the accident of birth, but by those who willed to come here.

How well the melting pot has melted is a question not the province of this chapter. "The temperature at which fusion takes place," as André

[7] See Mr. Hutton's balanced and lucid *Midwest at Noon*, pp. 24 *et seq.*

Siegfried wrote once,[8] varies according to locality and the nature of the stock. But surely, of all American achievements in the past century and the early years of this, the successful absorption of millions upon millions of immigrants is the most notable. Free primary education was, of course, a major factor in this. What is the more remarkable is that this ponderous influx was assimilated without a declension in the national standard of living; indeed, the standard actually went up. As recently as 1927, Siegfried thought that the problem of assimilation was still the most onerous that America had to face. In 1945, all that he would have had to do was glance at the crew of almost any B-29.

There are, however, some striking examples in the Middle West today of foreign-born and foreign-descended groups still tightly cohesive. If the reader happens to be a Chicagoan, he will know what an American city is like when it contains a Greek city, a Lithuanian city, a Sicilian city, a Slovak city, a Hungarian city, and a Negro city. Chicago is the biggest Italian community in the world after Milan, and the biggest Polish community after Warsaw. According to Hutton, two-fifths of *all* Chicagoans, even today, do not customarily speak English at home.[9] Or take the massive and extremely American state of Michigan, where more than *half* the entire population is foreign born or had parents foreign born. Michigan has one community that, in a literal sense, is unique: Hamtramck. This has a population of roughly 50,000, almost exclusively Polish. Hamtramck is entirely surrounded by Detroit geographically—it is impossible to get in or out of it without going through Detroit—but it is a quite separate and independent community, no part of Detroit politically. It has its own city council, laws, and mayor.

Cities, Nomadism, and Labor

> But for my children, I would have them keep their distance
>   from the thickening center; corruption
> Never has been compulsory, when the cities lie at the monster's
>   feet there are left the mountains.
>
> —Robinson Jeffers

The important midwest cities are not merely those on the lakes; they are deep in the interior, too, like Indianapolis, which is one of the few big American towns not on any navigable waterway at all. Of fourteen cities in the country with more than 500,000 people, five are in the Middle West; of the ninety-two with more than 100,000, twenty-seven; of the 197 with more than 50,000, fifty-eight.

One of the most exasperating of familiar criticisms of the United States is that the cities are so much "alike." Some in the Midwest are indeed alike physically—and for this there is a good reason, that they were built

[8] In *America Comes of Age*, p. 22.
[9] *Op. cit.*, p. 143.

at roughly the same time, and as products of the same westerly march. But most will be found to be highly contradistinctive and dissimilar—even those close together in the same state—if one knows them well.[10] I cannot imagine any two communities more unlike than Kenosha, Wisconsin, and Green Bay, Wisconsin, though both have almost the same population and both are on the water within a hundred-odd miles of one another, or Muskegon, Michigan, and Jackson, Michigan.

The medium middle western cities, with what H. G. Wells once called their "long defiles of industrialism," are the ugliest, least attractive phenomena in the United States. They represent more bluntly than anything else in the country the worst American characteristics—covetousness, ignorance, absence of esthetic values, get-rich-quickism, bluster, lack of vision, lack of foresight, excessive standardization, and immature and undisciplined social behavior.

Because so many American cities are painfully crowded, noisy, and packed with dirt and squalor, thousands of Midwesterners are constantly on the move, not so much fleeing the cities for the country, however, as seeking other cities. The United States is, as is notorious, a nation on wheels. Often we have mentioned nomadism. This is not so important for its own sake, perhaps, as for the concomitants it brings. One of its results, paradoxical as this may seem, is the deep-seated American instinct to join—clannishness. People are forever fleeing from one residence to the next, and so more than normally they seek some kind of identification. This country, as a New York friend of mine put it recently, is the most "overclubbed" in the world. Think merely of the great fraternal orders like the Elks and Moose. The national foot-looseness has another consequence in that rootless people have little interest in local civic problems; corruption in municipal affairs, the generally low level of the local judiciary, defective public services, juvenile delinquency, slum conditions —all these may be explained in part by this phenomenon. But also, it is only fair to mention on the other side, nomadism and the flight from city to city are one of the chief centripetal forces, like chain stores and comic strips, that binds the United States together.

The Midwest discharges itself outward without halt. If I were asked to mention the most typical "middle western" phenomena I know, I should answer first a country club in Westchester, New York, and second, on a different level, a pier dance in Los Angeles.

Finally, a word on labor. Here in the choked midwest urban areas, we come across labor as a really major political and social force for the first time. Of course this is mostly for the good. But one should at least mention in passing two factors that, more than anything else, have damaged the labor movement in the United States: (1) Exploitation by criminal racketeers; (2) Communist infiltration.

[10] Cf. Hatcher, *The Great Lakes*, p. 260-1.

Mail Order and Machines

Nobody can possibly understand the Middle West who has not, for fun or profit, once looked through the catalogue of a great mail order company. Houses like Sears Roebuck and Montgomery Ward are beyond doubt one of the chief unifying and co-ordinating of all American forces. Sears normally puts out about seven million catalogues (they are as bulky as a telephone book) twice a year, and Ward about six million.[11] They are free, of course, and the printing bill is one of the biggest in the United States.

The cover of a recent Sears catalogue is a mellow autumnal scene by Inness; inside is a pretty girl in blue, wearing an Ann Barton Sears Famous Dress, price $4.98. It looks very fetching too. A heavy paper insert describes how to measure linoleum, and the inner back cover explains the Sears Easy Payment Plan. Perhaps I have not looked minutely enough, but in the more than nine hundred closely printed pages the most expensive item I found was a 3½ carat diamond ring for $3,800. There is also a 1/100 carat ring for $12.25. The cheapest thing I saw was a nail hole patch at 8¢. But on one page (Get More Eggs and Meat with 4A Grade Trapnest Pedigree Sired Chicks) are day-old baby chicks at 14¢ in lots of a hundred. In between is a luxuriant variety of material. Americans take this for granted. Non-Americans, not so lucky, may not. The span runs from duck and crow calls (Authentically Toned Bean Lake Duck Call, $1.95) to vaginal suppositories, from window sashes to shrubs for fall planting, from automobile insurance to the Peoples Book Club to Slumbersound Mattresses, layer-felted for resilience, inner straps for durability, 54-inch mattress, only $18.95.

About the differences between Sears and Ward, pages might be written. Sears had behind it for years the tradition of a truly great and sound man, Julius Rosenwald. Its chairman of the board nowadays, General Robert E. Wood, was as everybody knows once president of America First. Ward's president too gets his name in the papers quite often. He is none other than that antique fogram Sewell L. Avery.

My friend Lloyd Lewis, historian of Sherman and the Lincoln legends, told me once that the wholesale dry goods business, which along with the meat packers traditionally dominated the Chicago commercial world, has been all but squeezed out in recent years, having been caught between the mail order houses and the small merchant in the minor cities. Mr. Lewis explains this by saying that obviously the old wholesalers can no longer survive in the contemporary "Expense Account Era." Macy's and the other big New York stores take the small out-of-town buyers to

[11] Total merchandise sales in the calendar year 1946 were $1,666,458,120 for Sears, $1,021,584,833 for Ward. *Moody's Industrial Manual.*

the Stork Club, no less, and the old-time wholesalers can't compete with that.

Another force not to be neglected in any survey of midwest affairs is agricultural machinery. International Harvester, McCormick-Deering, Oliver, Ferguson, Allis-Chalmers, John Deere, and the other great manufacturers are important factors in several ways. For one thing they assist the industrialization of agriculture, which should mean greater earning power for the farmer. For another they promote a healthy diversification of crops because, the more varied a man's crop is, the more will he need different types of farm machinery. For another their advertisements bring a considerable revenue to the agricultural newspapers and magazines. One healthy trend is the development of new types of *small* machinery for small farms, together with prefabrication of farm buildings.

Note on Religious Influences

All the principal Protestant denominations are active in the Middle West; ditto the Catholics; ditto the Jews. Cultist extremism is fairly widespread. Most folk who grew up in or around Chicago will remember the Holy Rollers in Benton Harbor, Michigan, and the Voliva community near Waukegan, Illinois, which believed that the world was flat, and where automobiles were forbidden. Today, in Minneapolis (a quite effervescent town religiously, and one with strong tinges of anti-Semitism), you may hear "Catechism Comes to Life" on the radio, and attend services at the River-Lake Tabernacle of Cowboy Bill Durbin, "Famous Western Cowboy Evangelist and Former Radio Singer." In Des Moines you may go to the "First Church of the Open Bible" and listen to tabernacle ceremonies of "Christ Centered"; in Detroit (the most touchy and violent of midwest cities) you may applaud a southern evangelist who has a "rapier-like wit and inimitable style" (adv.) and listen in to an institution known as "the GospelLiteHouse of the Air."

The situation of Jews in the Middle West, especially rich Jews, is peculiar. The plain fact of the matter is that they are, in effect, segregated. Near the University of Chicago when I went there, a handsome, dignified, stately residential district existed that was almost as Jewish as Tel Aviv; here lived—and pursued very useful lives—a cluster of Rosenwalds, Adlers and so on almost as dynastically interlocked as Hapsburgs. In Chicago certainly, and in other big middle western cities to an extent, the Jews who could afford it were driven by *goy* prejudices and discriminations not only to establish their own clubs of various sorts (downtown and country), schools, kindergartens, and college fraternities, but even neighborhoods.[12]

[12] There is, however, so far as I know, no exclusively Jewish university, as Notre Dame in Indiana is a Catholic university.

There are some notably liberal Roman Catholics in Chicago and the other midwest cities; there are some notably illiberal. A sharp line of demarcation is that provided by Franco Spain; some of the most militant Catholic propaganda about Spain comes out of the Middle West. The Missouri State Council of the Knights of Columbus (St. Louis) recently published advertisements in eastern newspapers pleading the Franco "case" and urging action *now* "before another Christian nation is enfolded in the foul embrace of the Red Fascists." In Cincinnati the *Catholic Telegraph-Register*, official organ of the archdiocese, similarly bought space to accuse the republican government that preceded Franco of "killing 300,000 citizens." One advertisement begins with a grammatical error that has greater impact, perhaps, than the rest of the text: "Looting, pillaging, violation of women, the burning and burial of people alive (people like you and I)—these are the horrible historical facts!" And so on for half a page.

Finally, let it not be forgotten, the Detroit area is the home base of two men whose names—and reputations—are flavorsomely known, Father Charles E. Coughlin and the mucid Gerald L. K. Smith.

Midwest Miscellany

Years ago in *Inside Europe*, writing about that baffling country England, I listed some forces and things heard and seen in British public and private life. One might do likewise for the Middle West:

Church suppers.

County and state fairs—particularly on Governor's Day as in Iowa.

The ole swimmin' hole, the red brick schoolhouse, and the ritual of "working one's way" through college.

Juke boxes.

Cartoons like that by John McCutcheon of the Chicago *Tribune* about Indian Summer, football teams like the Green Bay Packers, and social phenomena like wrong-side-of-the-trackism in regard to where a person is born.

Canals and the memory of portages.

The tradition of great independent newspaper editors, living and dead, like Charles H. Dennis and Henry Justin Smith of the Chicago *Daily News*, H. E. Newbranch of the Omaha *World Herald*, William T. Evjue of the Madison (Wisconsin) *Capital Times*, W. W. Waymack of the Des Moines *Register* and *Tribune*, and Oliver K. Bovard of the St. Louis *Post-Dispatch*.

Small lakes in northern Indiana like saucepans full of limp bathing suits; the lawns, six inches deep with autumn leaves, before frame houses with big porches in middle-sized Wisconsin towns; the rows of pumpkins outside the filling stations in Ohio villages.

Country (as distinct from city) clubs.

The recreation and travel industry, which produces an income of 300 million dollars a year in Michigan alone.

The great state universities, their athletics and their alumni.

Bulletin boards in the local post offices, with their wide variety of reading matter—reports on migratory birds, advices on criminals by the FBI, and civil service jobs open at $1,140.25 per year.

Automobiles with wooden bumpers in the winter of 1946-47—as strange a sight as an eagle wearing gloves.

Splendid teachers (to name only a few from a single university) like Robert Morss Lovett, Frederick Starr, the late James Weber Linn, Charles E. Merriam, Ferdinand Schevill, Edith Foster Flint, and Anton J. Carlson.

Nuggets of political conversation like "Don't know if he can vote his own wife, but he carries a lot of punch," "When we're in a war I'm for the president as long as it lasts," "There's a pretty high brand of government in this here state," (how many times did I hear that!) "He's the best rough-and-tumble swivel-chair lawyer in the country," and "The guy is so honest that there's nothing he'd steal but an election."

Utterly nauseous conditions in the state insane asylums.

The use of the word "visit" as a synonym for the verb "see."

Public worship of vitamins, golf, and Frank Sinatra.

The signs in hotel lobbies, made of small white letters set into black felt, like MAX BERKOVITC BRKL KNIT SWEATERS CHIC TOGS BLOUSES 590, and those in hotel restaurants, like LUNCHEON GUESTS WITH A 75¢ MINIMUM ARE INVITED TO PLAY CARDS FROM 2 TO 4:30 P.M.

The fact that the most conservative vote is not, contrary to general opinion, that of the farmers but of businessmen in small towns.

Middle western (and American) awe of a really good department store, like Marshall Field's in Chicago.

The elevator boy in Indianapolis who said of his car, "This jitney o' mine is a piece o' junk."

Painters like Grant Wood, John Steuart Curry, and Thomas Hart Benton.

The stupendous effect of women on *adult* education, in that it is generally women who promote lecture tours by visiting celebrities and the like.

The look on the GI's face when the MP poured his bottle of bourbon down the toilet in a Pullman washroom between Elkhart and Toledo.

The crushing social pressure exerted on youngsters by the corner drugstore.

Place names like What Cheer, Iowa, and Peculiar, Missouri.

Night schools—especially their courses in law.

Motels and tourist camps, which, what with hypocrisy, puritanism, and the housing shortage, have become the chief haunts of the amorous.

The hired man who comes to work at 7:50 A.M. or 8:02 instead of 8 sharp, to "avoid regimentation" and demonstrate his independence and equality.

Slovenly cemeteries in remote Indiana villages; Iowa streets absolutely silent after 7:30 P.M.; bank nights in an Ohio hamlet (population 2,172) with a pot of $635.55; weddings performed in Missouri on an open truck.

Fishing.

The fact that the United States is the country where most luxuries are cheap.

A great instinct for horseplay and a terrific gambling impulse in most Americans.

The gap between a basic good will in citizens and a lack of concrete know-how; the gap between sound and generous social ideals and inadequate performance; the gap between what most people believe in as regards political and civic affairs, and what they actually do.

Note on Politics

Considering the Middle West to be twelve states instead of merely eight, with the Great Plains thus included, it will control about a third of the delegates to the next party conventions. It is not without interest that, in January, 1947, the Republican chairmen in these states met and adopted in Chicago a resolution to the effect that their nominee should be "one who is symbolic of the ideals and heritage of the Middle West." In fact as of the moment of writing all serious contenders for the Republican nomination, except Warren of California, are Midwesterners by birth if not residence: Vandenberg, Taft, Stassen, Bricker, and Dewey who was born in Michigan.[13]

Also, the political leverage exerted by the Midwest was shown sharply by the chairmanships assigned to congressional committees after the 1946 elections. The position of Taft and Vandenberg in the Senate is well known. In the House, Charles A. Halleck of Indiana (a Dewey man) won the majority leadership after a contest with another Middle Westerner, Clarence J. Brown, the Ohio favorite. Leo E. Allen (Illinois) became chairman of the powerful Rules Committee, and Leslie C. Arends (Illinois) the party whip. All told New York got two chairmanships out of nineteen, New Jersey four, Massachusetts one, the Pacific coast one, and the Midwest all the rest—eleven. Five went to Michigan alone. Of course seniority was the prime reason for all this. Of the eleven Midwest chairmen, two at least are vehemently narrow and intractable

[13] See Luke B. Carroll in the New York *Herald Tribune*, January 19, 1947.

isolationists, Clare E. Hoffman of Michigan and Harold Knutson of Minnesota.

Negroes in the North

> Eenie, meenie, minie, moe,
> Catch a nigger by the toe,
> If he hollers make him pay
> Fifty dollars every day.

Between three and four million American Negroes live north of the Mason and Dixon's line, and we must make brief mention of those in the Middle West. The great northerly migration of southern Negroes began after World War I, and has continued intermittently ever since, though no mass movement occurred after World War II to compare with that of the early 1920's. Most educated Negroes, looking at the Negro problem from the broadest point of view, think that this hegira is healthy. It makes things better for those Negroes remaining in the South, by thinning them out. It proves that the Negro can learn skills and earn a living in new fields. Above all, it distributes the Negro problem better over the whole country, by "nationalizing" it.

Some old-time Negro residents of Chicago or Milwaukee or Cleveland fear and resent the newcomers, however. For one thing most of them are undereducated and they serve to lower the common denominator of the community. For another they add painfully to the difficulties of a housing situation already grievous. I heard Northerners say, almost with desperation, that they "simply couldn't take any more Southerners in." Yet a steady continuing influx is inescapable. More and more Negroes are being forced out of the South by the mechanization of agriculture, and experts say that, of the seven and a half million now on southern farms, only four million will, within a predictable future, be needed there. How, the North asks, can it possibly feed and house and send to school three and a half million Negroes on top of those it already has?

By and large the northern Negro is much better off and more secure than his brother in the South. First, the living standard is higher, and there are more opportunities for jobs. Second, whereas in the South segregation is a matter of law, in the North (though it can be highly unpleasant as we shall see) it is one mostly of habit and procedures. A Negro can be a juror in the North; he can be a policeman; he escapes a considerable number of the indignities we shall inspect when we reach the South; his children may, with luck, even be able to go to a tolerable school. Another difference is that very few Negroes in the North go into agriculture. Southern whites say, of course, that Northerners mistreat Negroes "worse than we do." But such ill-treatment is not, as a rule, based on *law*. Also the fact that Negroes may often suffer injustices in the North, to say nothing of murder and mutilation in race riots, does not excuse the South for the way *it* handles the selfsame problem.[14]

Northern Negro communities are, because of greater advantages, considerably more variegated than southern; there are at least half a dozen lines of stratification:

(*a*) Color. Here the pattern is roughly the same as in the South. Most Negroes have a lively sense of shadings within color, as we shall see later. Like members of all depressed classes, they are acutely conscious of anything that contributes to their caste status.

(*b*) Social "class." What makes a northern Negro an aristocrat? Of several hallmarks, which are complexly blended, one is certainly nonslave origin. The Negro whose forebears were freed *before* the Civil War is, as a rule, likely to think of himself as superior. Many slaves became freedmen in pre-Civil War days, and some were sent north by their masters to get an education; their descendants are apt to say "*My* people were never slaves!" Then again, under slavery in the South, house servants among Negroes were the superior class; the farm workers were the proletariat. The cook's children mingled freely with the white master's children; sometimes they learned to read and write together. One may, in the North today, meet two Negro physicians or Ph.D.'s; one will be self-conscious in a mixed gathering, one will not; like as not the one *not* self-conscious derives from this special servants' class.

(*c*) Education. Obviously the Harvard graduate has a better position in the community than an illiterate sharecropper out of Arkansas. Similarly a Negro whose father and mother *both* went to school is above his fellows.

(*d*) Rich and poor. Overwhelmingly the Negro community in the North is poor, though not so poor as in the South. Wealthy Negroes are extremely rare anywhere in the United States, though a few do exist. The richest American Negro is probably the president of an insurance company in Durham, North Carolina; running him close—but again I must write "probably"—is a publisher and real estate owner in New York. Insurance is, by and large, the business in which most northern Negroes make the most money; an important item in this field is funeral insurance.

(*e*) Religion. Most northern Negroes, like their southern brethren, are Protestant and predominantly Baptists.

(*f*) Attitude to segregation. Here, perhaps, we find the chief difference between North and South. Northern Negroes are of course more outspoken and radical. They can afford to say publicly what most Southerners could not possibly risk saying, and they sometimes criticize them for "weakness" on the segregation issue. But like as not the miserably crushed southern Negro has no choice. But in the North, too, a few of

[14] See *An American Dilemma* by the Swedish sociologist Gunnar Myrdal. Word about this book is in Chapter 41 below.

what modern Negroes call the "take-it-easy boys" still exist, those who want "to stay in good" at all costs, who will accept white strictures without protest, who for instance consent to ride in the freight elevator of a hotel. Some compromisers on segregation are called "handkerchief heads." This relates to the bandannas traditionally worn by old mammies, and among the political minded it is the worst of epithets.

(g) *Politics.* In the 1944 elections the country-wide Negro vote was Democratic by the staggering figure of 80 per cent. This onesidedness may not last. Negroes of course range from conservatives to radicals, within both parties, exactly as do whites. There are Bourbons among Negro political leaders, middle-roaders, Communists. Also, a point not generally appreciated, there are some 250,000 Negroes (mostly northern) in the federal civil service.

The most pressing Negro issue in the North is housing. Negroes in Chicago, in Detroit, in Pittsburgh live in what are in effect ghettos. These are not as a rule directly established by the municipality; they rise through restrictive covenants set up by white landlords, many of them absentee. A real estate group or local association of landowners will, for instance, get every owner in a district to sign a contract limiting, say, tenancy to "people not of African descent" for a period of years. Negroes have protested the legality of this, but unsuccessfully on the whole. The result of such closing off of Negroes from opportunities in housing is, first of all, the *equivalent* of segregation in the South; the Negro community is forcibly cooped up in whatever districts it now inhabits, and cannot spread no matter how much it multiplies. This, in turn, means that schools in the closed area become solidly Negro, exactly like the segregated schools in the South; it means congestion, violently high rents, the perpetuation of slums, breakdown in municipal facilities like street repair and garbage disposal, hoodlumism especially among the young, and serious problems in police and fire protection.[15]

One interesting minor problem has to do with sports. Negroes are admitted to college football, and are often very good at it. A northern team with a Negro member will not, however, be able as a rule to play a southern team, at least in the South. On the other hand, by an unwritten Big Ten rule, Negroes are excluded from basketball. This is an indoor sport, and taboos are strong (though not so strong as in the South) against any contact between half-clad, perspiring bodies, even on the floor of a gym. Probably Ohio State, among the great midwest universities, has the best record in these matters. A Negro was president of one of its chief student organizations last year, and a Negro girl led its YWCA. Negroes at Ohio State may go into the swimming pool (the sudden explosive vibration you hear is caused by a southern white read-

---

[15] See pamphlet, *Hemmed In*, the ABC's of Race Restrictive Housing Covenants, published by the American Council on Race Relations.

ing this), live in dormitories, and even go to proms—with Negro partners.

The worst racial outbreak in the United States for many years occurred in Detroit in 1943. Six hundred people were injured, mostly Negro, and thirty-one were killed, twenty-five of whom were Negro. A race riot is, to paraphrase Myrdal, "urban lynching." A superb account of the Detroit riots, well worth the most serious attention still, may be found in *A Primer for White Folks*, by Earl Brown. The most shocking thing about the whole ugly episode was, as Mr. Brown reports, the fact that "such an outbreak had been foreseen for more than a year before it occurred." Detroit is the most explosive town in the Western Hemisphere, Buenos Aires not excepted; it is here, more than anywhere else in America, that the Negro problem is exacerbated by what is called "three-dimensional incompatibility." There were many contributing factors to the disorders. The behavior of the police, for the most part, was the most disgraceful ever known in an American city. That, overwhelmingly, most aggressors were white is proved by the briefest glimpse of photographs in *Life* of the massacre, among the most remarkable photographs ever printed in a magazine. Detroit is packed with southern white hillbillies, who had never in their lives seen Negroes on a quasi-equal level; many of its policemen were southern; it has an angry tradition of labor violence; it is full of company thugs, ex-Bundists, and Ku-Kluxers; and it houses the automobile business, which means that life is tremendously competitive with rewards high and accustomed to being fought for.

Middle West and Isolation

With foreign policy as such this book does not deal; there must, however, be a word about isolationism. That the Middle West is the most isolationist area in the country is usually taken for granted; whether this is really so is not certain. Actually, whether you like it or not, isolationism to some degree exists wherever America exists. Polls carefully made by the Gallup and Roper organizations do not indicate that the Mississippi Basin states are much more decisively isolationist than other areas, except perhaps the South and Texas which are of course interventionist in the extreme. Questionnaires in Iowa do not have results much different from those in, say, upper New York state or Oregon. Consider too the personal item that three of the most outspoken and ardent internationalists of our time—Willkie, Wallace, Stassen—were or are all Middle Westerners.

Let us say a word first about the tenacious grip that isolationism can indubitably exert. It is old stuff to most of us; it may not be such old stuff to the man in Zanzibar. For instance during the whole of World War I the United States was never an "ally" of Great Britain and France, but only an "associated power." Until just before Pearl Harbor.

32 per cent of the American people thought it was more important to stay out of war than to beat Hitler.[16] Some small personal items seem, nowadays, almost too singular for belief. No American distinguished himself more for friendship to Britain during World War II, or more endeared himself to the British public, than Herbert Agar, once editor of the Louisville *Courier-Journal*. But before the war Mr. Agar—I mean no reproach—had been a convinced and quite vocal isolationist. No paper has a more broadly generous record of public service than the St. Louis *Post-Dispatch*, but even this newspaper attacked with ferocity, as late as 1941, the arrangement whereby we "gave" Britain fifty overage destroyers. Thousands of Americans of every stamp and category, in the prehistoric days before 1939, failed to realize that the Atlantic Ocean, in the false sense of security it gave, was one of the worst enemies the United States ever had.

To an extraordinary extent classifications became mixed. It is a tribute to the depth and width of the issue that before Pearl Harbor, Colonel McCormick, Norman Thomas, the Communist party, distinguished folk like Charles A. Beard and Stuart Chase, the La Follettes, Oswald Garrison Villard, and William Randolph Hearst, were all in the same camp. In the interventionist camp, be it noted, was an equally odd assortment—J. P. Morgan & Co., the liberal weeklies, almost all non-Communist radicals, Yankees to whom the word "radical" connoted a touch of hell, the cotton millionaires, most Jews, William Allen White, and southern senators full of frounce.

Shrill isolationist notes may still be heard. Consider the following bleat from a Missouri congressman named Dewey Short:

> I am against it [the UNRRA appropriation] with all my heart and soul. I talk as I vote and vote as I talk. So long as I know they have crown jewels of the King and the Czar—and I have seen them —they are brilliant and would bring a neat sum on any market today, enough to run any government for quite a while—as long as they wear ermine and emeralds in London and Moscow, as long as foreign assets are hidden in nearly every country of the world, I am not going to vote for $1 to take butter and bacon, cornpone and sowbelly out of the mouths of my poor people.[17]

The leading forces behind isolationism, with particular reference to the immediate pre-Pearl Harbor period in the Middle West, might be listed as follows:

First, and above all, the simple factor of geography. The Midwest is, as Hutton puts it, "surrounded, shielded, insulated," by the rest of the country. Probably not 1 per cent of the people of the eight central

[16] *What America Thinks*, by W. A. Lydgate, p. 64.
[17] This was plucked from the *Congressional Record* of December 6, 1945, by the vigilant *New Republic*.

states have ever seen New York or San Francisco. There were no submarine nets in Lake Michigan, or bombs in Calumet, and the idea that the United States could be in any physical danger seemed (and still seems to some) preposterous.

Second—so I heard it put once—the Middle West was so rich that "it could afford not to care."

Third, powerful religious influences, both Protestant and Catholic. Innumerable preachers told their flocks that it was morally wrong to fight and taught the evilness of war. Probably this had as much to do with the growth of American pacifism, which in many instances became identical with isolationism, as any single factor between 1919 and 1941. In addition many Catholics had strong appeasement tendencies, and appeasement in Europe was what most isolationists wanted or tended to defend.

Fourth, racial background. This country is largely populated by people (and their descendants) who left Europe to find a new life; hence, they resisted vividly anything that brought them back to Europe. Also formidable numbers of Middle Westerners are of German background, and many of these had German sympathies. Again, the region is full of Scandinavians, who were traditionally isolationist even in Europe itself. One should not, however, draw too sweeping conclusions about this. Nebraska is a strongly German state, and Kansas has scarcely any Germans at all; yet Kansas was much more isolationist than Nebraska. Usually, in a community where isolationism was abnormally acute, several factors were at work in combination. Milwaukee for instance is a town even more markedly Polish than German; also the Catholics are powerful there and so is the Chicago *Tribune*.

Fifth, a curious lack of self-confidence among Americans generally as far as things international are concerned, an innate provincialism. I have heard people say, "We don't really know what we are ourselves, and so how can we throw our weight around in the rest of the world?"

Sixth, the paradox alluded to early in this book to the effect that so many American Westerners, particularly liberals who might have been expected to be strongly internationalist, were on the contrary powerful conservative influences in the field of foreign affairs, because they hated the eastern banking interests and the big cities of the East. Also, absorbed to the hilt in the field of domestic reform, they had no energy left for other matters. Mr. Willkie's "one world" idea simply did not exist; rather, there *was* only one world, and it was the United States.

Seventh, ignorance, fed by ill-educated leadership. Think back to some of the moonshine prophecies made before the war, and what a burlesque atmosphere they led to. Father Coughlin said (January 15, 1942), "We lack the guns, tanks, ammunition, without which an army can be slaughtered like sheep. We have not the ships to transport a mass army." Herbert Hoover said (June 29, 1941): "Does any sane person believe that by military means we can defeat two-thirds of the military power of the whole world in even years and years?" Charles A. Lindbergh said (April 19, 1941): "This war is lost. . . . It is not within our power today to win the war for England, even though we throw the entire resources of our nation into the conflict." Former Governor La Follette of Wisconsin said (June 6, 1941): "Nothing that Britain can do now can pull the chestnuts out of the fire. It matters nothing to America which group controls Europe, be it England or Germany."[18]

Eighth, in contrast to the feeling that England was bound to be defeated, a widespread hands-off sentiment existed on the ground that Britain was bound to win in the end anyway and so why worry.

Ninth, the United States, in so far as it faces anywhere, has during all its history faced the Pacific. Europe is what is behind it. This may have contributed to the phenomenon whereby almost all isolationists turned into fervent admirers of General MacArthur, and urged more and more support to him even if this meant weakening American forces in Europe. Once the war was under way, most isolationists thought that it was much more important to beat Japan than Germany. (On the other hand, the late General Patton was also a hero to most isolationists, maybe because they felt that he too hated Europe, or perhaps because they are so often apt to be hypnotized by flamboyant military figures, no matter whom.)

Tenth, domestic political considerations. People hated Roosevelt; therefore they hated "his" war.

Eleventh, international considerations. A few isolationists, at least, foresaw that Stalin was going to reap the chief rewards from the war, and hence the great number of folk who hate and fear Russia on a wide variety of grounds opposed American intervention, on the ground that this would ultimately serve to further a "Russian" victory.

A fascinating turnabout has come in this realm. The professional Russia-haters, who were once ardent isolationists for the most part, and many of whom were pro-German, are now equally ardent interventionists, since they want to beat the Soviet Union down, and think that the United States should do so.

Equally, former interventionists who favored Russia generally are now, after World War II, under considerable compulsion to face around and become isolationists, because anything that serves to diminish American influence in Europe will serve to strengthen the Russian position there.

Twelfth, the McCormick dialectic and the influence of papers like the Chicago *Tribune*.

[18] These gems are from *PM*, August 19, 1945, and the Milwaukee *Journal*, August 26, 1945.

Tweaking the Lion's Tail

Beyond all this is still something else, the zealous anti-Britishness of so many midwest Americans. Many people who are classified as isolationists are not so at all. They are merely anti-British.

Not one American in ten thousand ever looks at the *Congressional Record*, and so most citizens are dulcetly unaware of some of the concrete shapes Anglophobia may take.

Fred Bradley, Congressman from Michigan, said during the debate on the British Loan (July 13, 1946): "Britain still owes us from the first World War $6,500,000,000 in principal and interest that she has not made one single move to repay . . . but she has unmined gold reserves worth at least $15,000,000,000 and $8,000,000,000 in diamond reserves." Gerard W. Landis (Indiana, July 12, 1946), said: "Why should we make this loan to Britain? The British are by no means strapped . . . They own 1,500,000 shares in United States industries: General Motors, 434,000 shares; Radio Corporation, 177,000 shares; Amerada Petroleum, 133,000 shares; Chrysler Corporation, 36,000 shares; Standard Oil of New Jersey, 198,000 shares; Socony Vacuum Oil Co., 130,000 shares; Standard Oil of Indiana, 315,000 shares; American Telephone & Telegraph Co., 70,000 shares; U.S. Steel Preferred, 21,000 shares."

Time and time again, during this debate, midwest senators and congressmen submitted lists showing what the loan would "cost" each county in their constituency. The figures were ingeniously worked out, down to the last alleged cent. Representative Karl Stefan of Nebraska (July 2, 1946) put it this way:

> Mr. Speaker, calculated upon the basis of 1940 census figures, and utilizing the accepted figures of $2,000 for the share of each individual in the Nation in the Nation's debt and $28 for each individual in the Nation as his share in what will be taken from the Nation by the proposed British loan, Nebraskans must assume $2,631,668,000 as their share of the national debt and $36,843,352 as their share of the loss to this country through the British loan.

Broken down into counties, this means:

COUNTY	SHARE OF NATIONAL DEBT	SHARE OF BRITISH LOAN
Adams	$49,152,000	$687,128
Antelope	26,578,000	371,092
Arthur	2,090,000	29,260

Mr. Stefan's list of counties then fills a solid column. Marion T. Bennett of Missouri proceeds further and presents a similar list subdivided by cities:

The share of each community in my district can be computed in the same way. The present estimated population of Springfield, Mo., my home town, is 76,450. Springfield's share of the British loan would therefore be $2,140,000.

I do not mention these details to give circulation to the financial views of these congressmen, or to rebut their premises which would be easy enough. Foreign policy—good foreign policy anyway—cannot be measured in dollars and cents. I do mention them to demonstrate on what a specific and particularized intimate local level midwest politicians are apt to consider any matter having to do with (a) international co-operation (b) world peace.

We return to slightly broader vistas. Nobody, it would seem, can easily be an isolationist in an era when you can cross the Atlantic between lunch and dinner and when the atomic bomb can make mincemeat of any ideology. Chicago is as near Moscow by air as New York. Foreign policy is, or should be, as much a matter of survival to the Middle West as the price of corn. Many points may, in fact, be adduced to show an internationalist trend everywhere in the nation, the Midwest included. Not only were Wheeler, La Follette, Shipstead, and Nye beaten recently, as we know; so, among other isolationists, were Danaher, Gillette, Holman, Davis of Pennsylvania, Clark of Idaho, Clark of Missouri, Walsh of Massachusetts, and Ham Fish. Of the thirty-one senators who voted against Lend Lease in 1941, only thirteen are still in the Senate, and of these several are much less intransigently isolationist than they once were.

As a counterbalance to the congressional views quoted above I am tempted to mention, though it does not have any official status, a remarkable pamphlet called *Crossroads Middletown*.[19] It begins with the sentence, "This booklet is the story of the awakening of the people of Middletown, Ohio, to the realization that they are today at the crossroads between peace and war." It describes then, with vivid impact, the various steps Middletown took to inform itself of the nature of the crisis, its education of local opinion toward effective international collaboration, the town meetings it held and the "quota force plan" it suggests for establishing an "effective world authority" with the United States participating. And hundreds of middle western communities feel exactly as does Middletown, though not all have expressed themselves so effectively.[20]

[19] Not to be confused with the "Middletown" of the Lynds, which I believe was Muncie, Indiana. This Middletown is an actual community in Ohio.

[20] Not the least interesting aspect of this is the variety of bodies that co-operated. I print a list of them not merely for its connotation in this particular issue, but as an example of the number of clubs and associations a typical midwest town may have. American Citizens Club, American Hellenic Educational and Progressive Association, American Legion Post 218, Ancient Order of Hibernians, Armco Employees Independent Union, Armco Girls Association, Blythe-Williams American Legion Post (colored), Business and Professional Women's Club,

Two polls taken recently by the Roper organization should be noted:

1945

Which one of these comes closest to expressing what you would like to have the United States do after the war?

	PER CENT
a. Enter into no alliances and have as little as possible to do with other countries	9.7
b. Depend only on separate alliances with certain countries	4.8
c. Take an active part in an international organization	71.8
Don't know	13.7

1946

If every other country in the world would elect representatives to a World Congress and let all problems between countries be decided by this Congress with a strict provision that all countries have to abide by the decisions whether they like them or not, would you be willing to have the United States go along on this?

	PER CENT
Yes	62.4
No	19.8
Don't know	17.8

But to conclude. Is isolationism finally, actually, and completely dead in the Middle West? Of course not. It is, however, much tempered and diluted. Perhaps the fundamental emotional bias has not changed. But there has been a distinct change in practical attitudes. A man who has had a succession of bad colds will carry an umbrella the next time he goes out into the rain. This is a rough approximation of the way the Middle West is feeling. The UN may not be a very good umbrella. But at the moment it is the only thing it has.

Chamber of Commerce, City Commission, Civic Association, Civitan Club, Congress of Industrial Organizations Middletown Chapter, Co-Operative Club, Fabricating Foremen's Club Armco, Federation of Women's Clubs, Independent Unions, Industrial Council, Insurance Underwriters Association, Junior Chamber of Commerce, Kiwanis Club, Lions Club, Ministerial Association, N. A. L. C. Branch No. 188 (postal employees), Poasttown Grange, Real Estate Board, Red Cross, Retail Merchants Association, Rotary Club, Spanish American War Veterans, Sulphite Paper Workers Unions (AF of L), Trades and Labor Council AF of L, Veterans of Foreign Wars Miami Valley Post, Veterans of Foreign Wars Hunter Clark Post.

Chapter 19

Stassen: Young Man Going Somewhere

〜〜

A SLOW-MOVING, hard-thinking moose of a man named Stassen (which in Minnesota is pronounced Stossen), is one of the most interesting and valuable personalities in the United States. Late in 1945 Captain Harold Edward Stassen, three times governor of Minnesota and a liberal Republican white hope for 1948, left the Navy after more than two years' hard service. So, like millions of other young Americans, he returned to the national scene unemployed in a manner of speaking, with the tremendous experience of the war behind him, and the uncharted world of a turbulent peace ahead. What next for Stassen? There are many people who would like to know the answer.

Stassen is six feet three and weighs 220 pounds without a cubic inch of fat. He has a big skull with sparse, sandy hair. His step is quiet; he pauses a long time between questions, so that you can fairly listen to the muscles in his big head working; his large clear eyes stare straight at you, with the look of a man very sure of himself, but not quite so sure of others. If you think of him as a kind of King of the Woods, but as stalking instead of being stalked, the analogy is not so far-fetched, because he is one of the best rifle shots alive. At the University of Minnesota he made a target record that has never been excelled.[1]

He believes in three things: (1) himself; (2) world peace; and (3) the people—if you give them an even break. What is more, he probably believes in these things in this order.

The Minnesota moose, like most men who appear simple, is far from being so; "simple" men are seldom simple. He can be ruthless in political dealings—if ruthlessness is necessary in a fight on principle—and yet he is one of the kindest men alive. He operates a good deal on hunch; yet he is the least impulsive human being anybody ever met. He is somber, with a lot of Scandinavian mysticism; but he can laugh with the best, and he was easily the most popular American at the San Francisco Conference, where his record was outstanding. The word

[1] Once he and a friend, also a superlative shot, hung some tinsel ornaments on another friend's head, and then shot them off in an exhibition shoot. "The act was a sensational success from the point of view of the spectators but the school authorities stopped it after one performance." Charles Van Devander in the New York *Post*, February 13, 1943.

went around that while a delegate Stassen was "running for president in 1948"; but this didn't detract from the quality of his performance.

The extreme right, even in his native Minnesota, distrusts and dislikes him; so does the extreme left. He is above all a reasonable man of the middle. But don't think this means he is not capable of vigorous leadership. He came out for an international organization with real teeth before Roosevelt did; he is one of the very few politicians to date who has had the guts, and real faith in America, to suggest that we might give up some of our own precious national sovereignty. And this from a Minnesota Republican—the representative of a state where not to be an isolationist had long been considered the kiss of death.

Stassen is not, oddly enough, a phenomenal vote getter in the sense that, say, Saltonstall in Massachusetts is a great personal vote getter— for instance a shift of 4 per cent in the last two Minnesota elections would have beaten him—but he certainly knows how to exert power, once he has it. This faculty is closely associated with three of his prime qualities, candor, courage, and a great gift for taking the public at large into his confidence.

Consider for instance the Ball episode in 1940. Senator Ernest Lundeen[2] was killed in an airplane accident, and Stassen, as governor, appointed his friend Joseph H. Ball, a St. Paul newspaperman who had never held public office and had no party standing or support, to be his successor. People thought that Ball had been appointed purely as a stopgap, and that the governor himself would run to succeed him in 1942 when the senate term expired; in other words that the two had made a deal. Besides, they said, Ball couldn't win; the Old Guard didn't like him and he was virtually unknown to the state at large. But Stassen *wanted* him to be a senator; he liked his views and his record and he thought that it was time that Ball, as a useful citizen, should not only write but "get in and pitch." So what did Stassen do? To forestall opposition to Ball, he calmly announced—two years in advance!—that not only was he appointing him, but that he would support him for re-election. He said in effect, "Not only are you going to accept this man; I'm sticking with him and so will you." And two years later Ball won.

To tell another story I must dive briefly into the confused inner byways of Minnesota politics. But it is perhaps worth telling because it illustrates in one episode Stassen's forthrightness, his political ruthlessness, and his conscientious sense of public duty.

In early 1942, almost a year ahead of time, Stassen told the people that he would definitely run for governor again; simultaneously he added that if elected he would only serve four months of the two-year

[2] Incidentally Lundeen's widow later married another isolationist senator, Holman of Oregon.

term! As soon as the legislature had completed its session, he declared, he would resign and seek active service in the Navy. "This is a young man's war, and I want to help fight it," he said. That Stassen should win an election in which he publicly warned the electorate in advance that he would serve only four months out of twenty-four is a startling enough example of his popularity. And not only did he win himself, but it was a triple victory, because he pulled Joe Ball in as senator and also, as lieutenant governor, his friend Edward J. Thye.

Now in regard to Thye more should be told. Of course since Stassen was going to serve only a few months, the real election issue was the choice of lieutenant governor, who would automatically succeed him. And the lieutenant governor at that time was a man named C. Elmer Anderson, whom Stassen did *not* want as his successor. Anderson was a worthy enough small businessman in Brainerd, an upstate town, but little else. The story was that he had been elected in the first place for one reason only, that the Scandinavian vote is large and his name was Anderson. Also he was a sympathizer of the Old Guard, according to the Stassenites. In any case Stassen decided to get rid of him, and he picked Thye, a sturdy farmer but an unknown quantity politically, to run against him. This meant in turn that the Stassen crowd had to campaign *against* Anderson, their own lieutenant governor. Anguished howls from the betrayed Anderson camp reverberated through the state. But Stassen's motive was of the best, to leave Minnesota in good hands. Also, of course, he was serving to perpetuate his own machine.[3]

Thye, to bring this story ahead, came into national prominence in 1946 when, as Stassen's candidate, he beat Henrik Shipstead, one of the most famous of the old isolationists, in the primary race for the Senate, and proceeded to election in November. He will be a moderate liberal in the Senate's new Republican majority.

One key to Stassen's character is certainly his seriousness. This young giant—he is only forty today—is no wisecracker. I have met him only twice, but each time these qualities—earnestness, seriousness—were the first things I felt. The basis of much of his success is a belief that people, the great mass and bulk of people, *can* be convinced on a serious issue. What a real leader should do, he thinks, is above all to give the people a chance to inform themselves; his first duty is to interpret issues to the people, and give them the opportunity to take sides, even if he himself is beaten; the leader, he feels, should be one who concentrates in himself the deep inner yearnings of the people, their own unexpressed impulses and desires. Out of this comes what is probably

[3] An item in minutiae is that some Old Guardists, hating Stassen, were delighted to vote for him on the chance that Anderson *might* squeeze in too, since on Stassen's resignation Anderson, their own man, would then be governor. But it all came out Stassen's way.

his greatest asset: that his actions follow resolutely his own reigning body of conviction.

Now I shall attempt briefly to tell the story of Harold Stassen, but first there must be a line or two on his native Minnesota.

Background on the North Star State

Minnesota is a state spectacularly varied, proud, handsome, and progressive. The French explorers came in first, and then both French and English fur traders; the British flag flew over some trading posts until 1815, as if two wars had not been fought. It had a lumber era and a railroad era, and its economy today is based on grain, milling, dairy farms, and the largest deposits of iron ore on earth—it is Minnesota which is the basic source of wealth for such relatively distant phenomena as Big Steel. There are at least six different Minnesotas geographically, and its racial stock is a mixture of Yankee, Irish, Germans in great number, Poles and Czechs, Italians, and above all Scandinavians— Swedes and Norwegians in particular. Minnesota is also the Lutheran state par excellence. It is a state pulled toward East and West both, and one always eager to turn the world upside down; a state with a highly virile liberal tradition, where 37 per cent of the voters are classed as "independent," and where both the steelmakers and farmers' co-operatives wield great power; and a state where the two chief cities, Minneapolis (milling, Scandinavian, Republican by and large) and St. Paul (railroads, Catholic Irish, Democratic by and large) are famous rivals.

The natural result of all this is to make Minnesota extremely volatile politically. For instance Elmer A. Benson was elected Farmer-Labor governor in 1936 by roughly 250,000 votes; two years later, Stassen beat him by an almost identical majority. Another point of importance is the state's unique electoral system. Anybody can enter a Minnestoa primary by paying a small fee, and it is the only state in the union, except Nebraska, where the *legislature* is elected on a non-party basis. Running for the legislature in Minnesota (and also for municipal and judicial offices) you do not file as a Democrat or Republican or Farmer-Laborite; the primaries are open and these distinctions do not exist. (But candidates for governor and federal offices do wear a party label and do run on party tickets.)

The state was overwhelmingly Republican till the early 1930's; then came Roosevelt who carried it all the four times he ran. On a state level the Farmer-Labor party, an offshoot of the Non-Partisan League in North Dakota, had begun to climb rapidly, following the agrarian miseries of the depression; its leader was a remarkable man, Floyd Olson, who was elected governor three times, serving from 1930 to 1936.

Olson, an able radical, died of cancer during his third term; his successor was his first disciple, Elmer Benson. It is a shame to have to foreshorten so drastically one of the most fascinating episodes in recent American history. Benson was a kind of Henry Wallace to Olson's FDR. Olson had got himself surrounded by a riffraff of Communists, Trotskyists, labor crooks and other undesirables. But, a man with charm, fists, and force, he could boss them. Benson, one of the most high-minded men alive, was not quite strong enough to do so.[4] His record was good enough, but the Farmer Labor party itself began to disintegrate. Also Benson lost control of labor in the towns. There came an angry, vicious upsurge of strikes, vandalism, and gang assassination. An AF of L local, the celebrated Teamsters 544, ran wild, and farmers couldn't get their produce in. The fabric of government seemed almost at the point of being ripped apart.

It was at this juncture that Stassen—only thirty—entered the big pit for the first time, as a clean-up candidate for governor.

Early Life and Works

Harold E. Stassen was born in West St. Paul on April 13, 1907. His father was a German of Czech descent (the grandfather came to the United States from Austria in 1871); his mother, by name Mueller, was born in Germany but had some Norwegian blood. For Stassen's future career, this was a perfect political and biological combination, since it meant both German and Norwegian votes.

The father, William Stassen, is still alive. He is a truck farmer living near West St. Paul, who still wears overalls when he comes into town. He had three other sons besides Harold, all of whom live today in the St. Paul area. One, William, is a metal worker; another, Arthur, drives a milk wagon; the third, Elmer, is a grocer. Nothing aristocratic about the Stassens! These are good men close to the earth, who work with their hands. In Stassen's first campaign literature a particular point was made that two of the brothers were members of local AF of L unions, William in the Sheet Metal Workers Local 76, Arthur in the Milk Drivers 546.

Harold went to the public schools, then worked his way through the University of Minnesota, emerging after six years with a law degree. He was an exceptionally brilliant and pertinacious student, and his industry was colossal. He never joined a fraternity, and was never a "big man" on the campus in the undergraduate sense of the term. He had to earn a living, and the tough Czech-Norwegian-German strain began to show. He worked as a Pullman conductor, as a laborer in a

[4] Today this worthy character is president of the National Citizens Political Action Committee.

bakery, as a pigeon salesman. Also, his ambition was considerable from the beginning. Friends say that while still an undergraduate he told them that he intended to be governor of Minnesota before he was thirty-five. He made it at thirty-one. (But while still in college he didn't know whether he would be Republican or Farmer-Labor.)

He set up law practice in 1929, entered politics at once, and in 1930 was elected county attorney for Dakota County. His partner, Elmer J. Ryan, an Irish Catholic, is still, incidentally, his closest friend—people who dislike him say that Ryan is his only friend. Because, as we shall see, this Stassen is a lone wolf, who chooses among men warily. Ryan got so close to him by campaigning for him when he had a short siege of tuberculosis; Stassen still has one damaged lung.

Dakota County is a tough and rowdy spot; it includes South St. Paul and the stockyards and was a wide-open haven of gangsters, but this didn't faze Harold Stassen, as a half-forgotten episode reveals; when I asked him to name some of the turning points of his career, he mentioned this first of all. The milk farmers in the county were up in arms, since milk prices had collapsed; highways were blockaded and farm trucks were waylaid and the milk spilled out. A meeting was held, and an outside agitator urged further violence. Someone said, "But what about the county attorney?" The answer came, "Lynch him!" But it happened that the county attorney, young Mr. Stassen, was sitting quietly in a back row; he had entered the meeting place unnoticed, wanting to see what went on. It was the most difficult decision of his life to get up, announce himself, walk to the platform, and say that if anybody wanted to lynch the county attorney, he was right there in the room. Stassen then placated the gathering. Moreover he promised that if they would be temperate a bit longer, he would represent them in litigation without fee. Eventually he got an agreement in eleven counties and raised the price of milk by 25 per cent.

But already he was looking outward. For instance he began early in the 30's to cultivate a group of country editors and the county weeklies are very influential in Minnesota. They reach grass-roots via the most personal kind of old-style journalism. By ones, twos, or threes, Stassen would invite such editors to "visit" with him. He was looking outward in other directions too. It is surely an indication of his character that at twenty-six he fought—and won—a hard case before the Supreme Court in Washington.

Following the Republican debacle of 1932 came the Republican debacle of 1936. All seemed lost to the party in Minnesota, as Elmer Benson swept the state for a fourth consecutive Farmer-Labor victory. A Republican acquaintance of Stassen's exclaimed sourly, "Let's quit, and give Minnesota back to the Indians." Stassen said, "We can't quit." Someone plaintively put in,

"But we haven't got a candidate—who can possibly beat Benson in 1938?" Stassen replied, "I'll take the rap, if necessary."

Almost at once he got to work, but very quietly. In August, 1937, he called on Roy E. Dunn, Republican national committeeman, a veteran political strategist, and one of the ablest men in Minnesota. He asked Dunn a million questions about politics on the gubernatorial level, but not by any gesture did he disclose that he had any serious aim for the job himself. He was too young. He was unknown outside Dakota County. No one would take him seriously. On Thanksgiving day he asked Dunn to dinner, announced calmly that he intended to run for governor, and asked him to help manage his campaign. It was as if an understudy at the opera should invite Melchior to coach him for the role of Tristan, while Melchior was still singing it.

This put Dunn in a quandary. He couldn't take on Stassen's campaign without giving up the national committee; also, he didn't want to do anything against either of the two other Republican candidates, each of whom had strong party claims for support. One was Martin A. Nelson, who had been beaten by Olson in both 1934 and 1936 and who, having held the party together during the lean years, wanted his reward. Indeed, before Stassen had popped up, the organization had begged Nelson to run once more.

I asked Minnesota friends who finally did manage Stassen's campaign. Reply: "Stassen."

That 1938 campaign was one of the most blistering in local annals. As I write I have the literature from both sides before me. And it is worth describing briefly because this was Stassen's first important run and it tells a good deal about him. That he wanted Dunn's assistance is not uninteresting. He wanted advice from a professional. Yet he himself ran in the most nonprofessional manner possible. He was willing enough to accept assistance from the Old Guard—on his own terms, with no strings attached—but he knew that people were sick and tired of the Old Guard. They wanted new faces. And he made them want his own.

First came the primaries. The regular Republican organization did not support Stassen at first. The fat boys thought he was muddying the waters, splitting the vote. He paid no attention to them, campaigning all over the state in an ancient Ford until people began to wake up. Then came a crucial need for money. Stassen and his crowd were penniless. The big money of the millers and the steel men was wary. Nobody wanted to waste a campaign contribution on an untried outsider, a youngster of thirty. Yet everybody wanted unity and above all a winner. So the money waited. After a while Stassen was told bluntly that if he could hold out for three more weeks, funds might be forthcoming. In three weeks, the Old Guard thought, they would know how much of a chance he had. He replied, "I'll eat hamburgers on a side road to economize." The three weeks passed, with Stassen clearly out in front, and substantial help was then forthcoming.

One eminent Old Guardist first became convinced that Stassen would win following an organization dinner at Sauk Centre for all the candidates. Stassen's speech was superb; he ran away with the performance. Then photographers came with the coffee. Young Stassen couldn't be found to be photographed. He was at the front door, shaking hands with the crowd outside. The next day, practically every citizen of Main Street boasted of having met him "personally." This, one might add, is a technique that he still follows. Instantly after a speech he darts to the nearest door and greets the folks who weren't able to get inside.

Stassen got a Buick, with dictaphone, to help in the remainder of the campaign. The story is that when it was over a spot on the front seat was worn off where, dictating in back, he would stretch a long leg forward, rubbing the upholstery.

Now for another item. The Farmer-Labor party was at this time seriously split. On his side of the primary, Benson had opposition too, in the person of a remarkable creature named Hjalmar Petersen of Askov, the rutabaga center of the world. An old-style isolationist, Petersen led one wing of the Farmer-Laborites. Thousands of Republicans switched party and went into the Benson-Petersen primary instead of their own—thinking that the really important thing was to beat Benson, whereupon any Republican could win the subsequent election.

Stassen gained as a result, since most of the deserters were anti-Stassenites. Even Republican money went into the Farmer-Labor primaries to beat Benson, who was thought of as anti-Christ at least. In a way Stassen won the primaries, and later the governorship, because a lot of Republicans voted Farmer-Labor![5]

Stassen and Benson ran it off in a fierce, gouging campaign. Benson was beaten for several reasons that had little to do with Benson, mostly the gang warfare in Minneapolis. Also this was the year when progressives had a hard time everywhere; La Follette was beaten in Wisconsin and Frank Murphy lost in Michigan; there was a temporary national swing away from Roosevelt. Also Stassen's campaign pledges were substantial, intelligent, and attractive. He promised (a) real jobs instead of the WPA, (b) reform of the civil service, (c) economy in administra-

[5] A specialist in complexities might be interested in further details. Many Republicans thought at the last moment that Hjalmar *would* beat Benson (as a result of their support), and they hastily sought to close the money bags and switch ranks again, on the ground that (as the campaign was turning out) Petersen might after all be harder for them to beat. The mind bends under the weight of this. Minnesota, as I have said, is an extremely volatile state politically. The main point to seize is that Stassen profited enormously from (a) fedupness of Republicans at the Old Guard; (b) Farmer-Labor loss of prestige and self-division.

tion, (d) labor peace. Besides, people liked him. This sandy hulk was something new.

The campaign was unpleasant in that some of his supporters—but never Stassen himself—went in for some Jew-baiting. Benson is about as Jewish as Greta Garbo, but he had several Jewish secretaries and friends, and these were unmercifully slashed at. One campaign song went as follows:

> Hi ho, hi ho
> We join the CIO
> We pay our dues
> To the goddam Jews
> Ho hi, hi ho.

Then a big worthy in the Republican party, Ray P. Chase, who is still a conspicuous Minnesota officeholder, published a pamphlet under his own name—I am looking at a copy now—called *Are They Communists or Catspaws?* It was frankly and defiantly labeled "A Red-Baiting Article," and it sought to tie Benson in with the Communists and other stuff and oddments. Stassen had no responsibility for this pamphlet—indeed he disavowed it late in the campaign—but to an extent he was its beneficiary.

Anyway he won, and won thumpingly. One of his first acts as governor was to appoint a Democrat as a private secretary, presumably to help keep Republican office seekers out! This man's political courage and extreme independence are never to be ignored.

Progress toward the National Scene

So Harold Stassen became governor of the splendid state of Minnesota at the age of thirty-one. Then came the "ninety days." The state never saw anything quite like them. He booted out the crooks, sent several Benson holdovers to jail for corruption, and saw a Labor Conciliation Act through the legislature. He reorganized the state government and created the job of state "business manager"—the first such job in America. Economy, a rational approach, moderation, security plus opportunity were his watchwords.

But it is time now to consider Stassen from a broader angle. He became a national figure almost overnight; a political child-in-arms, he somehow got himself into the federal scene. Partly this was because his local record was so good. But what else? How account for his amazingly quick and sweeping rise?

In 1939, during his first term, he was elected chairman of the Governors' Conference, a considerable honor; the next year he brought the conference to Duluth, in his own state. He went east once or twice, and political writers sought him out as a kind of curio. They came to stare, and went away to admire. At a Gridiron Club dinner, the redoubtable Paul McNutt was the chief speaker on one side, Stassen on the other. And in a speech packed with humor (which is not usually pronounced in him) the Minnesotan all but obliterated McNutt.

In the summer of 1939, Roy Dunn, the national committeeman, got a long distance call from Henry P. Fletcher, counsel of the Republican National Committee. Fletcher spoke from the offices of his friend Sam Pryor, the Connecticut leader. "Can you come to New York?" Fletcher asked Dunn. "When?" Dunn replied. "As soon as you can," said Fletcher. In New York Fletcher and Pryor told Dunn, "It's time to talk about this man Stassen. What would you think of him as keynoter for the next [1940] convention? We want a young man and someone from the West. But is he a free lance, or is he bound to anybody?"

Dunn traveled back to St. Paul and sounded out Stassen, who was naturally pleased, and then wired New York, "Governor answered all questions satisfactorily." So it came about that a man who was too young to run for president himself became keynoter at the Philadelphia convention that nominated Willkie. (He was at the time thirty-three and by constitutional limitation a president must be thirty-five.)

Then an astonishing thing happened. By inflexible tradition, the keynoter at a national convention is a kind of neutral, and in particular is supposed never to support anybody himself until balloting has begun. Meanwhile, however, Stassen and Willkie had become friends. The intermediary who first interested the governor in Willkie was the late columnist Raymond Clapper. Clapper drifted through Minnesota about six weeks before the convention and had a long talk with him. One of his friends asked him later what he had asked Stassen about. "I didn't ask him a darned thing," Ray replied. "I'm up to my neck for Willkie, and all I did was tell Stassen that Willkie ought to be the nominee." Also John Cowles of the Minneapolis *Star-Journal* had a good deal to do with promoting Willkie sentiment.

On that vivid day in June, 1940, when Stassen made his keynote speech, the Minnesota delegation was split three ways: seventeen out of twenty-two for Vandenberg, the rest divided between Bob Taft and Dewey. Someone said, "Where does Stassen stand?" The answer came, "He has one foot in Taft's camp, one in Dewey's, and a third with Willkie." The night before the balloting, the governor sat in informal conference with the four Minnesota newspapermen who had covered him from the beginning. The newspaper men split 2-2 for Willkie, but there was no hint from Stassen himself as to his preference, no indication of any kind. Then he spent some hours with Dunn. Though he said nothing specific, Dunn thought that he was going to come out for Dewey.

But at 10:55 the next morning he told Dunn that he would support Willkie. Dunn was thunderstruck. If he had let Dunn know a little in advance, things might have gone more smoothly. But a meeting of the Minnesota delegation had been set for 11 A.M. which gave Dunn only five minutes to break the news and smooth things over. Stassen forthwith announced to the delegation that he would work for Willkie, and this caused literal pandemonium; one woman screamed, "You can't do that!" and people practically pulled each other's hair. Dunn asked, "Are you speaking only for yourself, or for the delegation?" "For myself," Stassen replied. Then at noon—just one hour later—it was announced that he had become Willkie's floor manager! This must have been known to Stassen; but he never told his own crowd about it. Finally at 4 P.M. he asked Dunn to swing the entire delegation to the Willkie candidacy.

A lone wolf? Yes. Ruthless? Yes. But—no one influenced Stassen in this course of action except Harold Stassen. Some Dewey people—and also some Minnesota politicians—have never forgiven him for what they call this doublecross.

There is a poignant footnote to this tale, in that Stassen and Willkie fell out later. Willkie stopped in Minneapolis on his round-the-world flight in 1942, and John Cowles arranged a dinner where they met, but both were somewhat cool; Cowles worked hard to get Willkie to write Stassen a nice letter, but he wouldn't. Later Stassen reviewed Willkie's book *One World*, criticizing it, and Wendell felt affronted. In 1944, though Stassen was out in the Pacific, his enthusiasts pushed him into the Wisconsin primaries as a presidential candidate, and the new lieutenant commander said that he would accept the nomination if he got it, which hurt Willkie badly. Willkie's theory about this was that the Old Guard feared *he* might win in Wisconsin, and hence produced Stassen to draw off the liberal-internationalist vote, such as it was. Actually, Stassen outran Willkie in this race, and Willkie never quite forgave him.

Stassen went into the Navy, as we know, early in 1943; previously he had been a reserve officer. He waited till the Minnesota legislature adjourned its session; then he signed bills till midnight, resigned the next day at noon, and left the state house in uniform at 4 P.M. A remarkable item is that the Navy was able to accept him, since he had been tubercular. But Secretary Knox had wanted him acutely for a long time; the Navy badly needed first-class administrators. Stassen became flag secretary and assistant chief of staff to Admiral Halsey, and his record was distinguished, though he did not see much actual fighting. Halsey is reputed to have said at first that he didn't want "any damn politicians" in his fleet; later, they became warm friends.

Personal Qualities of Stassen

His wife, whose maiden name was Esther Glewwe, was a childhood sweetheart. She is an unassuming woman of great sweetness of character, who has developed step by step with her husband; they have two children, Glen (aged nine) and Kathleen (three and a half), and live in a small house in South St. Paul financed in part by a modest FHA mortgage. Before that, the Stassens had lived in a five-room cottage. The plain people of Minnesota are a frugal lot, and the governor was criticized for "ostentation" when he moved; the new house was called "Stassen's palace." The charge is ridiculous. Nothing could be further from his character than ostentation, and the house is the kind that anybody might buy whose salary was $8,500 a year, which is what he got as governor.

Stassen has no private means, and so far as one can tell he has utterly no interest in money for money's sake. If he wanted to be rich he could quit politics tomorrow and easily earn a hundred thousand dollars a year at law.

He is a Baptist. He drinks little, and smokes not at all; he eats carefully, and likes a lot of milk. He can relax in a second, and sleep anywhere. He seldom goes to the theater or to the movies or to the great Minneapolis symphony. He reads a good deal, but mostly on strict vocational lines. One book—on some such topic as German war guilt, say—will send him to another. He writes every word of his speeches, which indeed have a highly individual style.

I asked several times in Minnesota who his best friend was, and the nonserious answer I got was "Stassen!" Probably those closest to him are Elmer Ryan, a long-time companion named Radebaugh, a dentist who was chairman of the Republican state committee during his administration, and—until recently at least—Joe Ball. But nobody gets too close. He has the greatest admiration for men like J. Russell Wiggins[6] in St. Paul and Gideon Seymour in Minneapolis, two of the ablest newspapermen in the country, but he holds everybody off to some extent. "Just when you think you're really close to Harold," one friend told me, "he trips you up." The retreat into sudden enigmatic coldness is never explained. Then two weeks later he will be warm again.

His chief defect, most of his associates think, is his intense ambition, which serves to make him seem too calculating. Next to this is the seeming coldness. He is not in the least shy, but he is reserved, and some old acquaintances say that he lacks "human" spark.

Like practically all good politicians he is a superlative brain picker. What he likes to listen to—above all—are facts. He seldom talks much

[6] Mr. Wiggins recently became assistant to the publisher of the New York *Times*.

in a group; but he is a formidably acute and spacious synthesizer. He drove some of his own experts mildly crazy at San Francisco; they would pass him notes suggesting courses of action; he would read them carefully but never make any sign of reply at all.

One of his positive qualities is of course courage. Another is his stubborn determination, his fixity. He has a divine capacity never to be bored by what he is doing. Other people, fatigued at grappling with an issue, may drop by the wayside; he holds on to the finish. He is full of Teutonic thoroughness. And he is very seldom diverted by side issues. Call him a Fascist, call him a Communist—he will pay absolutely no attention, but continue to plug steadily down the middle. Nor will he go down the line for anybody, except out of deep conviction. It is impossible for him to pretend.

He thinks more slowly than any other man I have ever met in public life. I asked him a question in San Francisco; he swung one big leg over the other, cupped his chin in a fist, and stared levelly out of the window for what must have been sixty seconds before uttering a word. But when he finally does answer, it's usually something worth waiting for.

Then there are other qualities, for instance his spectacularly good memory. In the summer of 1945, he reported to the Governors' Conference at Mackinac on the San Francisco charter. He spoke for an hour and a half, without notes. Two governors told me later quite independently, that this was the finest intellectual performance they had ever heard.

Stassen is an excellent executive and administrator; once he assigns duties, he seldom interferes. He is methodical in the extreme; for instance, in the old days, his campaign speeches lasted twenty minutes each, almost to the second. He knows politics inside out, and he is that rarest of things, a spontaneous and natural leader; this is one reason why the die-hards are always fearful of what apple carts he may upset. And, above all, he has the ability to visualize the moods and needs of the average citizen. He has faith in the people and their good will, plus frankness in telling them—even if he doesn't tell his intimate advisers —what he's going to do.

Another of Stassen's traits is self-confidence; another is his consistency (few people have ever seen him out of character); another is his directness, his rapidity of pace. Consider the following, which is from the *first* paragraph of the first big speech he ever made on international affairs, in Washington in 1943:

In response to your invitation, I bring you tonight a message from the Middle West. It is this . . . The overwhelming majority of the people of the Midwest know that the walls of isolation are gone forever.

Stassen has made enemies on both sides in Minneapolis, if only because he *is* a liberal. Old Guard Republicans think of him as a kind of half-adopted pinko who has forced his way into the house, who has made the party in Minnesota a springboard for his presidential aspirations. Left wingers on their side are apt to dig up the past and say that he once campaigned in Nebraska against George Norris, and never once had a word to say for Loyalist Spain, whereas Benson stuck his neck out on Spain and took a severe beating for so doing. They assert that his tax program has favored the steel company, that Minnesota is one of the few states with no enabling act to take advantage of federal housing, and that his famous labor law is antilabor. Finally, they point to the way he entered the Minnesota scene, taking advantage of a labor crisis to "ride roughshod over opposition"; they hint ominously that this is a "Fascist" pattern, that he could seek to become a dictator.

The main provision of the labor law is to provide a mandatory ten-day cooling-off period before any strike may be declared—a thirty-day period if the governor decides that the industry involved is "vital to the public interest." Labor, naturally, claims that this bill nullifies its most precious prerogative, the right to strike, but in practice it has worked out fairly well, and few moderates want it changed. In all fairness to Stassen it should be pointed out that he put this bill through to forestall passage of another much worse. And—something not to be ignored—the CIO itself supported him in both 1940 and 1942, though it would probably not support him now (and though one reason for its support was that his opponent, Petersen, was an isolationist).

Criteria of "liberalism" may differ, but if you take a broad view I heard expressed in Minneapolis and categorize people into four classifications—radical, liberal, conservative, reactionary—it is impossible to think of Stassen except in category number two.

What Next?

I met Stassen for the first time at a party in New York given by Sinclair Lewis in 1943. The room was filled with people who had spent all their lives studying foreign affairs. Who was this amiable, slow-spoken youngster listening with such intent interest? Then people began to ask him questions. It was not surprising that he should be so interested in technical European matters; what struck everybody was that he *knew* so much, and knew it with such precision. Someone asked him why the old League had failed. "For three reasons," he answered succinctly, and then named them without hesitation: point one, point two, point three. What was impressive was his unrehearsed command of a subject that seemed very remote from Minnesota.

A few weeks later came the speech in Washington which I quoted above. A Republican governor from the Middle West forthrightly stated that isolationism in the Middle West was dead. Maybe he was wrong; time alone can tell; the point is (*a*) he believed it, and (*b*) dared to say so. This was the speech in which he sketched a program not merely for a world "organization" but for a "permanent United Nations government," which out-Roosevelted FDR. At about this time a group of Republican old-timers, meeting him in Washington, pleaded with him not to go so far. He "was driving himself out of public life." Stassen replied, "Okay. If you fellows win, Hitler will be boss of the United States, and I'll be delighted to be out."

As an officer in the Navy, Stassen could not of course continue speechmaking. But on March 8, 1945, just before the San Francisco Conference, he made an astonishing talk in Minnesota that, so far as I know, outreaches anything in the field ever said by an American politician. He hit at the shibboleth of national sovereignty, saying that all of us are "citizens of the world," and suggesting

> that we do not subscribe to the extreme view of nationalist sovereignty, that we realize that neither this nation, nor any other nation, can be a law unto itself in the modern world, and that [italics mine] *we are willing to delegate a limited portion of our national sovereignty to our United Nations organization.*

He went on to qualify himself and deny that he favored setting up any super-state; he was not advocating any abrogation of the American right to be independent. But, he proceeded, "true sovereignty rests in the people, and the people know that for their own future welfare they must exercise a portion of that sovereignty on a world level in place of a nationalist level." And, "the extreme principle of absolute nationalistic sovereignty is of the Middle Ages and it is dead."

Stassen's appointment by Roosevelt as a delegate to San Francisco flabbergasted him. He is said to have felt that to accept it would be a political liability; yet he announced, "It is as much my duty to take an assignment to work for a successful peace as to work for a successful war." At once he set out to build a kind of bridge between himself and the rest of the party, and he saw that the conference might be a vehicle toward his dearest aim—liberation of the Republican machine from its stick-in-the-mud backwardness in social policy and foreign affairs.

Stassen got out of the Navy, and ever since has been putting in titanic labors all over the country—writing articles, making countless speeches, meeting friends—to further (*a*) what he believes in; (*b*) his run for the presidency in 1948. The difficulties are immense, for, by ordinary rules, it would seem that he has to take two sides at once—be "conservative" enough to win the nomination in an Old Guard convention, and then "liberal" enough to beat the Democratic candidate, if nominated. But Stassen does not work by ordinary rules. What he has done—with prodigious, never-ceasing energy—is to keep pounding away at the Republican party from within, to vitalize it, bring it up to date, pump fresh air into its tight corners, make it an authentic contemporary force.

His friends think that, in 1948, he can make a first-class race. They say that he got Minnesota out of just the kind of mess that the United States as a whole may find itself in; they claim that he is just the man to hang on to the real gains of the Roosevelt revolution, and yet scour out the barnacles and sediment; they adduce his courageous vision on international policy; and they think that, with luck, he can get more labor votes than any other American, more farm votes, more Republican votes, more internationalist votes, and the service vote to boot.

But Stassen cannot win with Stassen alone. Without an organization the case is hopeless. So he has set up "Republican Open Forums" all over the country, which are "Stassen clubs"; William H. Vanderbilt, a former governor of Rhode Island, is helping to raise money; hundreds of associates are hard at work. The Stassen forces suffered a severe defeat in Nebraska in June, 1946, when Senator Hugh Butler won re-election; they won a weighty victory when Thye beat Shipstead in Minnesota. The Old Guard observes most of this with contempt. They don't concede Stassen one chance in a million; they will stop at nothing to beat him down; and they know that the better are prospects of Republican victory in 1948, the less are Stassen's own chances for the nomination—since, if victory is certain, there is no temptation to choose any but the "safest" candidate.

Chapter 20
More About Minnesota, Plus Wisconsin

THERE is more to Minnesota than just politics, Stassen and the Twin Cities. Consider merely what Sinclair Lewis calls the "radiant, sea-fronting, hillside city of Duluth." I drove up to Duluth from Minneapolis, and in fact it was Mr. Lewis who was my host there. We looked at what is called Minnesota Point from a tall bluff, and watched the freighters come in with coal, and go out again with their mammoth burdens of ore, against the swelling blue backdrop of Lake Superior. Duluth is the end of the line. Here is the extreme westernmost tip of the Atlantic Ocean. Duluth, together with Superior (Wisconsin), *is* a seaport, though its shining water is fresh, not salt. But it is difficult, up in this piney stillness, to appreciate the well-known fact that this is the second biggest port in the nation; there is something incongruous about its commercial activity. "Port" connotes smoke and slums and men hurrying down greasy cobbled streets, whereas Duluth tingles with openness, the atmosphere of campfires, placid sunshine, and the free spirit of the viking north.

Second busiest American port! But, if the local folklore is to be believed, Duluth is also a city where bears wander in from the woods every spring, push their way into back yards, and imperturbably invade the lobby of the chief hotel. Greatest iron ore city in the world! But the booster pamphlets call it "America's air-conditioned city, in the Hay Fever Haven of America."[1]

Speaking of folklore, one might mention a renowned speech in the House of Representatives by Proctor Knott of Kentucky on January 27, 1871, and several times reprinted in the *Congressional Record*. A proposal was being debated for railway development in the Duluth area. Mr. Knott opposed the bill on the ground that nobody knew where Duluth was, and embroidered his theme with the kind of exaggeration common to American rhetoric at the time:

Duluth! The word fell upon my ear with peculiar and indescribable charm, like the gentle murmur of a low fountain stealing forth in

[1] This whole region is hay-fever conscious. Papers in Minneapolis print a daily "pollen count."

309

the midst of roses, or the soft sweet accents of an angel's whisper in the bright, joyous dream of sleeping innocence. Duluth! 'Twas the name for which my soul had panted for years, as a hart panteth for the waterbrooks. [Renewed laughter.] But where was Duluth? Never, in my limited reading, had my vision been gladdened by seeing the celestial word in print. [Laughter.] And I felt a profound humiliation in my ignorance that its dulcet syllables had never before ravished my delighted ear. [Roars of laughter.] . . . I rushed to my library and examined all the maps . . . but I could nowhere find Duluth! Nevertheless, I was confident that it existed somewhere, and that its discovery would constitute the crowning glory of the present century, if not of all modern times. [Laughter.]

I knew that if the immortal spirit of Homer could look down from another heaven than that created by his own celestial genius, upon the long lines of pilgrims from every nation of the earth to the gushing fountain of poesy opened by the touch of his magic wand; if he could be permitted to behold the vast assemblage of grand and glorious productions of the lyric art called into being by his own inspired strain, he would weep tears of bitter anguish that, instead of lavishing all the stores of his mighty genius upon the fall of Ilion, it had not been his more blessed lot to crystallize in deathless song the rising glories of Duluth. Yet, sir, had it not been for this map kindly furnished me by the Legislature of Minnesota, I might have gone down to my obscure and humble grave in an agony of despair, because I could not nowhere find Duluth. [Renewed laughter.] Had such been my melancholy fate I have no doubt but that, with the last feeble pulsation of my breaking heart, with the last faint exhalation of my fleeting breath, I should have whispered, "Where is Duluth?" [Laughter.]

Originally the Duluth area was Sioux and Chippewa country. The French explorers came in early, and in 1679 Daniel de Greysolon Sieur du Lhut raised the French flag near where the city named for him now stands. But not for 138 years did a white settlement become permanent in the region, when the well-known German immigrant John Jacob Astor set up a fur trading post on the St. Louis River.

Mesabi: Iron on the Range

From Duluth, through the courtesy of officials of the Oliver Iron Mining Company, I drove to Hibbing to look briefly at the Mesabi Range (sometimes this puzzling word is spelled Mesaba, and sometimes Missabe, as in the name of the railway serving it).[2] Again, let me allude to the tranquillity, the remote sylvan calm of this area. Then reflect that this is the essential heart of the steel industry of the United States. From these gentle meadows and serene hills comes, basically, the wealth of General

[2] Cf. *Iron Brew*, by Stewart H. Holbrook, p. 91.

Motors, J. P. Morgan & Co., and the United States Steel Corporation, to say nothing of the American industrial effort generally in war and peace.

The Lake Superior region, comprising the Mesabi, Vermilion, and Cuyuna ranges in Minnesota (range means district, not hill), the Gogebic range in Wisconsin, the Marquette and Menominee ranges in the upper peninsula of Michigan, produce normally 87 per cent of the iron ore in the United States. Minnesota alone produces 65 per cent. In the peak year 1942, when the region as a whole produced 92 million tons of ore, an all-time record, Minnesota produced almost 70 million tons. This is about triple the average annual production of all Soviet Russia. By far the biggest company operating is Oliver, which is responsible for about 48 per cent of all production. Along with the Duluth, Missabe, & Iron Range Railway and the Pittsburgh Steamship Company, which transfer the ore from the mines to Duluth and then to the Lake Michigan and Lake Erie ports, Oliver is a subsidiary of the U. S. Steel Corporation, and is by far the greatest iron-ore-producing organization in the world.

Route 53 leaps out of Duluth northward. A great fire destroyed the forests here in 1918, eating its way into the outskirts of Duluth itself, and burning up whole towns like Cloquet. So the timber is all second growth today—poplar, birch, tamarack. To the north is the watershed of the great divide; on the far side, the rivers flow to Hudson Bay; on the near, to the Mississippi. We saw a gray bulge on the horizon—this is the range. In the near-by farmers' gardens, gladioli make bursting sprays of salmon pink. We drove briefly over a section of road actually paved with iron; this was an experiment of the 1930's. The surface is of corrugated steel bricks, laid on a concrete base. It will last for all time.

We visited first the town of Eveleth. Here, my guides told me, we stood right on "the ore body." All this land was covered by an ice sheet during the era of the glaciers. The first mine we saw, known as the Spruce, gave us a nice geological cross section. At the top of the open pit is the "overburden" or glacial drift. This is stripped off, and the brownish-red ore lies exposed. At one mine we saw how naked ore comes right up to the roots of the grass, and in the bottom of another grass was actually growing. From this point we could see the "twist" in the range itself, as it swings around. Once the towns here, like Virginia, were timber cities, with the greatest sawmills in America. The mines—lucky country!— started to be big business just as the timber gave out as a result of merciless spoliation. What will succeed the mines, if they too give out some day?

Then at Hibbing we saw "the biggest hole ever made by man," one of the most extraordinary sights on earth. "This," my guide said with a kind of flip reverence, "is the real reason why the United States is great, and maybe it's the baby that won the war."

The Hull-Rust-Mahoning Open Pit Iron Ore Mine, as it is officially
called, is about three miles long, half a mile to a mile wide, and 435 feet
deep; it covers 1,250 acres, and has 55 miles of railway track in its
exposed bowels; out of it have come, to date, more than 650 million
tons of material, more than the total excavations of the whole Panama
Canal. We stood on the rim. The huge trough looks as if it has been
stamped into the earth by a terraced skyscraper upside down. Clawing
at its sides and hollows—to change the metaphor—are what seem to be
ice cream scoops. We drove down into the actual pit, along bumpy zig-
zags, and saw that the scoops are 350-ton slowly rotating electric shovels
that eat 16 tons of ore at a snap.

Several companies—in fact a good many—wallow competitively in this
pit. Bethlehem has 51 per cent of the Mahoning area. Two tracts are
owned by the Northern Pacific Railroad. Oliver is however the biggest
holder. Most of the properties are held on lease, not owned outright.
There are no discernible frontiers between the rival properties, and so
engineers from each keep a lookout. Originally, long before people knew
they were standing on the greatest deposits of iron ever known, this was
forest land. Owners who held the stumpage, even after the trees were
felled, became heir to the ore underneath. Directly on the edge of the pit
today are several houses, the owners of which still refuse to move or sell.

The ore is shoveled into railway cars, which switch back and forth to
reach the top; the "shovel runners" who operate the scoops are the
highest-paid men in the pits, getting about $1.50 an hour. Near the end
of the Oliver tract, we saw a rock hill, of pinkish purple, in the middle
of the ore, which the shovels nibble up to, and then let severely alone.
Finally—the sight must be seen to be believed—a corps of women sweep
the last bits and specks of ore out from tiny crevices, so that no ounce
will be lost, the way a child licks a chicken bone. "We have a very clean
type of mining here," my guide said.

Up top, the ore is sampled, tested, "beneficiated" in some cases, and
then shipped. Part of these processes were explained to me in the laboratories; I hope I understood them. Actually while the cars are en route
to the loading docks at Duluth, it seems, samples are analyzed, so that
the shipment may be properly classified and graded on arrival. Then each
special type of ore awaits its passage down the lakes; usually a ship
carries only one type of ore. The mines fill a freighter to meet the exact
specifications of the purchaser, set out in advance, so that there will be
no delay at Gary or South Chicago.[3]

Hibbing, the town, has had curious adventures. For one thing most

[3] Underground mining goes on all the year, but the open pits only keep up a
limited activity during winter. Of course shipping is impossible for the five or six
months when the lakes are frozen. Sometimes the cars full of ore freeze. These
must be thawed out by steam, because frozen ore won't go through the hoppers.

of it was once moved—bodily picked up and physically moved, house by house. The Hull-Rust open pit was getting bigger, so big that it was on the point of swallowing Hibbing itself. So Oliver bought a forty-acre tract covering about three-quarters of the town as it then was, and moved building after building to a new area a mile and a half away.

The Mesabi range presents a nice demonstration of how capricious history may be. But for a famous accident most of this region would belong to Canada. A British scientist named John Mitchell, mapping the region in 1755, thought that the Lake of the Woods led directly into Lake Superior by way of the Pigeon River. He was, it happened, wrong. When, in 1783, Benjamin Franklin negotiated the Treaty of Paris, which first delimited the American-Canadian frontier, he and the other commissioners accepted this map as accurate, although it would have been more logical to follow the line of the St. Louis River further south. One story is that Franklin, somewhat of a sharp dealer, knew well that the original map was wrong, but saw to it that it was accepted anyway. So the Minnesota "arrowhead" went to the United States.

The Minnesota ranges have in the sixty-odd years since their discovery produced just under a billion and a half tons of "merchantable" iron ore.[4] The existing reserves are calculated at 1,150,000,000 tons. So considerably more has gone out than remains. If the average rate of production continues on a prewar level, Minnesota ore will last only another thirty-five or forty years; if production should ever again be that reached during the war, it will last only another fifteen years. Naturally this somewhat alarming rate of drain, at best, gives pause not only to conservationists but to anybody who realizes how cardinally the basic strength of the United States is hinged to steel. On the other hand steel is durable. It will not, like wood, catch fire or rot. As scrap, it can be used again and again. Also immense deposits of inferior iron ore, including a variety with a low iron content known as taconite, exist widely. Iron, next to aluminum, is the most common of all minerals; 5 per cent of the entire earth's surface is iron. But at present the process of extracting steel from low-grade ores is too expensive to be practicable, i.e. profitable. On some future date, new technologies may be discovered that will change this picture. Even as of the moment, Minnesota officials advocate "a gradual shift" to production from taconite by companies whose reserves of "merchantable" ore are getting low.

Oliver is, of course, an overriding factor in the economy of the state. Its attorney, Elmer Blu, watches its interests carefully; he is one of

[4] These figures and several that follow are from a pamphlet called *Economic Analysis of the State of Minnesota*, published by the Minnesota Resources Commission. For a contrary view on most of these matters, see a brochure *Minnesota, a Duped State*, published by the Civic Association of Northeastern Minnesota in Hibbing.

the most influential men in Minnesota. The chief issue is of course taxes. Oliver, by far the biggest local taxpayer, thinks it is paying quite enough; its critics think it might well pay more. The Oliver people point out they pay four different kinds of state tax, and that the total may reach as much as 25 million dollars a year. Their opponents argue that the company itself, since U. S. Steel is both producer and consumer, both seller and purchaser, is in a position to set the price on which taxes are based. Half the internal politics of Minnesota, for years, devolved on whether what is known as the "Lake Erie price" was, or was not, fairly calculated.

I heard commonly that Oliver "ran" Minnesota. The best proof that this is not really true is that taxes *are* as high as they are. If the company could run the state as it chose, they would of course be lower. Almost everywhere in America, the power of the great industrial companies is tempered to an extent by the power of the public interest. This is not to argue that Oliver should not make a greater contribution than it does. And although Minnesota is not remotely a "colony" of Oliver or anything else, it is indisputable that the company has a wide influence in the legislature, in particular the senate. It would be difficult to pass a bill in Minnesota that it actively opposed.

Old Eagle's Nest

I drove from Hibbing to Sauk Centre, where I wanted to see the prototype of *Main Street*; on the way Sinclair Lewis suggested that I drop in at Little Falls, where Charles A. Lindbergh grew up. The Lindbergh house rests in a grove—now a state memorial park—on the Mississippi. It was built and lived in for many years by Lindbergh's father, a Minnesota congressman who was a kind of Minnesota La Follette. It has a very pleasant, screened-porch rocking-chair canoe-in-the-boathouse atmosphere.

Lewis, who as everybody knows is a Minnesotan himself, published in 1915 *The Trail of the Hawk*; it was the first serious novel about aviation ever written. H. G. Wells and Jules Verne had written fantasies, but this was not a fantasy. Yet, in a way, it was. Because its hero, by remarkable coincidence, happened to be a lonely boy named Carl (=Charles) who after a spectacular career in aviation marries an eastern heiress. The resemblances between this imaginary character and Lindbergh are quite striking. But when Lewis, with the strange prescience of the artist, wrote *The Trail of the Hawk*, Lindbergh himself was only thirteen years old; the two could not possibly have ever heard of one another, though they lived only thirty-nine miles apart, and at that time Lindbergh had probably never so much as seen an airplane. Incidentally Lewis had great admiration for Lindbergh's father. "Only man in Little Falls with a decent library; only man in town with sense enough to build a house on the river, not away from it."

Main Street Up to Date

How has Main Street—the street, not the book—changed in a quarter of a century? What would Dr. Will Kennicott and Carol find if they walked today in Gopher Prairie? *Main Street* was published in 1920, and a whole generation of Americans has grown up since the phrase imbedded itself into the language. The model for Gopher Prairie was of course Lewis's own birthplace, Sauk Centre. The house where Lewis was born is still in good shape and is lived in today by a mail carrier; the one to which he moved later is now the residence of the local manager of Swift & Co. I talked with a dozen of his oldest friends, and tried to find out how, if at all, the community has changed. Does the tawdry provincialism and vulgarity that shocked Carol still exist? Do the good qualities symbolized by the stout Kennicott—devotion to hard work, neighborliness, frugality, deep roots in sound native soil—still play their role?

First, the population has scarcely risen; it is still about 3,000—3,016 to be exact. ("3,000 swell folks—and 16 skunks!" is the way I heard this subdivided.) The railway station is as it was, but the bus service is new, and, wonder of wonders, Sauk Centre is soon to have its own airfield, with a half-mile landing strip! The lines of elms have grown twenty-five years older, and Kennicott would marvel at the overhead lights on the road leading into town. The post office is new; the library is a vast improvement on what it was. How proud Carol—who saw that indecent author, Balzac, driven from the shelves—would be to learn that it now has the largest per capita circulation of books of any community in Minnesota!

Nothing is livelier in *Main Street* than the ironic passages purporting to come from the local newspaper. But today's paper is a quite substantial sheet, and not at all uncivilized. There was no Rotary Club in Gopher Prairie; today, Sauk Centre has one. The old town had neither a golf course nor a hospital; today, its citizens can play golf (for nine holes), and a hospital is being organized.

Remember the barbed and glittering description of the shops on Main Street, as Carol took her first walk downtown? Today she would see few buildings that existed twenty-five years ago; the old frame structures have given way to brick. She might look for Hedine's, where Kennicott had his shoes resoled; now it's a Ben Franklin store. Of all the buildings on the west side of Main Street between Third and Fourth, she would remember only three: a bank, Hanson's Home Brand Foods, and the corner drugstore, drugstores being imperishable. On the east side every shop but one would be new to Carol, including a Chevrolet agency, a neat mortuary, and a movie.

Take a trip from Sauk Centre to the lush dairy farms surrounding it. The standard of living has jumped to a level that would leave Kennicott incredulous. Remember how he charged one of his country patients $11.00 for an operation, and told him he could wait till next year to pay up—if his crop was good enough? Today the mortgages and "barnyard loans" are largely paid off.

There are several reasons for this prosperity; one is the phenomenal growth of co-operatives, in everything from telephones to coal, and another is rural electrification, which began on a substantial scale in the late thirties. Not all farms are electrified, by any means; but the good ones are. A family with rural electrification is at one jump removed from peasanthood, because not only does electric power bring "luxuries" like telephones and running water; it means cream separators, milking machines, and twice as many pigs per litter.

Three other main elements have contributed to the development of Sauk Centre—and a thousand other middle western Main Streets—since Lewis wrote his book.

(1) Enormous advance in the use of the automobile. No one who has read *Main Street* will easily forget its arduous winter journeys on horse-drawn sleighs. Today, these have virtually vanished. Automobiles did, of course, exist in Carol's time, but they couldn't be used in winter. As motoring became universal, more and better highways cut across the land, and the whole picture of rural society was altered irremediably. The automobile—plus good roads—changed Sauk Centre from a village into a metropolis; instead of being an outpost, it became a pivot. On the other hand, the automobile came near to killing the near-by hamlets, with populations of two hundred to five hundred, because their people could drive into bigger towns to market. This phenomenon we have already observed in Colorado and the West.

(2) Chain stores. These were of course unknown in Kennicott's day. I heard two contrary points of view about them. The chain store obviously makes it easier, more economical, for Main Street to shop. In 1920, a shopping tour for outright necessities could be a day's work; now, it takes half an hour. The other attitude is that the chain store undermines civic spirit; it has made small business migratory, and thus destroyed the town's homogeneity. The manager of a chain store will stay in Sauk Centre, say, for six months to a year; then he moves on, never having become a real ingredient in the life of the community.

(3) Movies and radio. It is almost unthinkable, but neither Will nor Carol ever saw a newsreel. Nor could they have ever heard a radio show. Main Street itself may not have moved very much; but the world

itself has moved to Main Street's door, and people have become broadened, willy-nilly.

These factors have helped to modify another aspect of the former life of Main Street—it does not have to hibernate in winter. Winters in Minnesota are still bitterly long and trying, but no longer does the citizen have to dig in and insulate himself from the outside world for five or six solid months. The roads are open, and he can even keep warm at home. (An incidental point is that the relative comfort of modern living has given rise to the illusion that "Minnesota's climate is getting milder!")

The automobile has contributed, so Sauk Centre admits, to juvenile delinquency. Sixteen-year-old girls wander down Main Street nowadays in red slacks, or even shorts! Other social patterns have changed too. In 1920, the town's bar was a refuge for the healthy male seeking to get away from home for an hour or so; today, it is no longer a masculine inner sanctum—the youngsters, boys and girls both, swarm all over it. Again, in Kennicott's time, an important and distinctive role was played by the lodges and fraternal organizations, not only at business meetings but on picnics and excursions. Now the social functions of the lodge have been largely usurped by the movies, luncheon clubs, automobile drives, and golf.

One Sauk Centre veteran lamented what he called a decline in the "pioneer spirit." In the old days, he told me, two men who quarreled would go into the back yard and slug it out. Then, like as not, they would be arrested—briefly—for disturbance of the peace. But in the last few years, only one fist fight and consequent arrest has taken place in the whole town!

The gist of *Main Street*, the book, was Carol's revolt against the ironclad taboos of her environment. Has Main Street, the town, grown up at all in this respect? Yes. Carol would certainly be talked about, today as in 1920, but the criticism would probably be more diffuse, more tolerant. A suggestive confirmation of this is that Lewis himself was, of course, reviled and calumniated when his book appeared. Today he is something of a hero, and is considered by all to be the most distinguished citizen the community has ever produced. There was even a movement to change the actual name of Sauk Centre to Gopher Prairie! Some years ago Lewis returned for a visit. He wrote a brief inscription for the new movie theater, which the town proudly cast in bronze, and which adorns the wall today:

THESE ARE THE PORTALS OF IMAGINATION.
RECOVER HOPE, ALL YE WHO ENTER HERE.

Minnesota Medley

Minnesota has millers like Pillsbury and General Mills, families like the Heffelfingers, and quite possibly the best public schools in the nation. In Minnesota are both the Mayo Clinic at Rochester and the Hormel packing plant (Spam) at Austin. Minnesota gave birth to the modern bus industry, and was the original home of Greyhound; it is the home today of one of the most aggressive air companies in America, Northwest Airlines. It has the Cowles papers in Minneapolis, and also the Ridder chain. Minnesota has co-operatives ranging from the immense Land o' Lakes Creameries, Inc., one of the largest and most conservative in the nation, to the six hundred small burial associations. It pays 575 million dollars per year in federal taxes, and has both the biggest calendar printing business in the world and the biggest law book printing business. Its fiercest local political issue is over liquor licensing, and it has 10,000 lakes, including Itasca, the headwater of the Mississippi. In Minneapolis is the only skyscraper I ever saw built to taper like an obelisk, and one of the best mayors in the nation, H. J. Humphrey Jr., the leader of the Democratic-Farmer-Labor coalition.

In the St. Paul telephone book I saw a melting pot item not without interest: CURTIS (see also CURTICE—CURTISS—CURTS—KERTESZ—KURTZ).

Brief Mention of Wisconsin
Where there was nothing there is something.
—Charles McCarthy

Wisconsin is a splendid, virile, and sometimes a cross-grained state. I could write about it at considerable length, if only because I vacationed in it for many years, and a dozen Wisconsin towns—Sheboygan, Manitowoc, Green Bay, Ephraim—are indissolubly part of the America I once knew best.

Wisconsin is the state of a remarkable eighty-four-year-old governor, Walter S. Goodland, of the La Follette dynasty now out of power, and of a long-standing guerilla war between butter and oleomargarine.[5] It is a state full of cream and cheese and containing bland cities like Milwaukee and superlative beer like Van Merritt. It is also a state so strongly industrialized, though people usually think of it as overwhelmingly agricultural (it is of course the first dairying state and produces 12.5 per cent of all milk in the union), that not less than one-half of all its wealth comes from manufacturing. It has an erosion problem—where Lake Michigan chews steadily into the shoreline—and a road problem; a long-standing political issue is the "highway lobby," and a newer one has to do with slot machines. It is a state packed with vitality, hard-

---

[5] The ravages of this famous conflict extend into Iowa and other states.

headed, with dreamily beautiful country landscapes and two of the longest and most stubbornly fought strikes in the history of the American labor movement.

Among widely known Wisconsin industrial enterprises are Fairbanks Morse at Beloit, Parker Pen at Janesville, Kohler bathtubs at Kohler, Oshkosh trunks at Oshkosh, Nash Motors at Kenosha, Johnson Wax at Racine, and the great paper companies at Neenah, near Appleton, the home of Kotex and Kleenex and the Sensenbrenner family with its unique local influence. One should also mention H. L. Nunn in Milwaukee, a shoe manufacturer with an enviable record for good relations with labor; the A. O. Smith Co., which is a famous maker of automatic machinery and the like; the great Milwaukee brewers like the Uihleins (Schlitz) and the makers of Blatz and Pabst; and of course the cheese processors, like Kraft and Borden. There were once some 2,700 cheese factories in Wisconsin. Amalgamations and so on have reduced the number to about 1,800.

On December 26, 1945, workers at the J. I. Case Company, manufacturers of agricultural machinery at Racine, went out on strike. As of the moment of writing, fourteen months later, this strike is still rancorously going on. The Case company is a kind of feudal principality, run strictly as a one-man show by Leon R. Clauson.[6] He was born on a farm in 1877; he has been dictator of Case for a quarter of a century. A compromise might possibly be effected on wages (the workers want a 25¢ an hour raise, and Case offers 13¢), but the management has refused to consider other demands by the union. The present strike is the fifth since 1934. The only contract the company ever gave labor was one imposed by order of the National Labor Relations Board. A year after the present strike began this board ruled against Case, ordering it to bargain with the union.

Workers of the Allis-Chalmers Manufacturing Company near Milwaukee, one of the most important industrial units in the country, similarly began a long and obstinate strike early in 1946. These two strikes cut down by one-quarter the production of all farm machinery in the United States, at a time when such machinery was more urgently needed than at any time in decades. Demands for the federal government to seize and operate the struck plants came naturally from all over the country, and particularly from the Middle West; in fact, a seizure order was prepared in regard to Case in midsummer, but the cabinet split on the issue and Mr. Truman never signed it. The unions involved in these disputes are both locals of the United Automobile Workers, CIO, but they are very different. At Case is Local 180, a strong right-wing and anti-Communist union; at Allis-Chalmers is Local 248, just as distinctly on the left. There was, however, little of the political in either

[6] Cf. Luke Carroll in the New York *Herald Tribune*, August 24, 1946.

strike. The principle at stake was of the simplest—basic and primitive labor rights.

Wisconsin is probably the most isolationist of American states. It breeds senators like Wiley and congressmen like O'Konski, with his superb melting pot name and his record not so superb. It makes conspicuous in the person of several representatives one of the ugliest paradoxes in America : that those same men who voted against every defense measure, who opposed Lend Lease and Selective Service, who would not budge one inch or spend one cent to assist Roosevelt and the administration to prepare for American defense were exactly those who in the Pearl Harbor inquiry and on other occasions whined the worst about the lamentable condition our defenses happened to be in.

Wisconsin is also one of the two or three best-run and best-governed states and, on almost all domestic issues, one of the most liberal. For this the La Follette tradition is to a great extent responsible. Wisconsin had the first workman's compensation law in the United States, the first direct primary law, the first state traveling library, and the first state unemployment insurance. Its legislation was very hard boiled. When companies found that it was costing them money if workmen got killed in industrial accidents on their premises, they saw to it soon enough that fewer workmen got killed. Wisconsin has more credit unions than any other state, the lowest syphilis record, the second highest literacy rate, and the best record in state aid to education. It was the first state to revoke the old charter of the Ku-Klux Klan, when this uncomely organization began to re-emerge in the 1940's. It was one of the first states, after World War II, to organize direct relief, hospitalization services, and educational aid for its veterans, and it is the only state, so far as I know, where public school students are insured against accidents in athletics.[7]

Like Minnesota, Nebraska, and the Dakotas, the Badger State has a formidable basic German-*cum*-Scandinavian coloration. But it differs from these neighbors in that it was settled earlier and came into the union earlier ; it was populated in the first instance by Yankees, as one may see by observing old tombstones ; for instance Bob La Follette's great-great-grandfather fought in the Revolutionary War. Mostly the Germans came after 1848. They not only brought sound agricultural techniques but they are the foundation (as in southern Ohio) of the state's highly diversified craft industries. The Scandinavians were more purely agricultural. There are today solid German counties completely ringed by Norwegians. But Germans, Norwegians, Poles (the south side of Milwaukee is 97 per cent Polish) were not the only folk who came to Wisconsin. There are Finns in Superior, Danes in Racine, Canadians

[7] This insurance covers fourteen sports, and the fee is $1.00 a year, or only 50¢ if you don't play football. Benefits range from $15 for a broken nose to $200 for injury to an eye. Cf. *News-Week*, August 27, 1945.

almost everywhere, and an astonishing community of Swiss in Green County. Here, not anywhere in Switzerland, is the Swiss cheese capital of the world. Its atmosphere is, indeed, much more Swiss than anything I ever saw in Zurich or Geneva. Swiss from the old country sent emissaries here many years ago, who tested one Wisconsin area after another until they found a place where conditions of soil and water most closely resembled those in Switzerland itself. Then they moved over and have lived happily ever since. The smallest whisper in Green County is still a yodel.

Perhaps Wisconsin gives an aroma of the staid, the bourgeois; actually it has produced or strongly influenced a remarkable lot of individualists. One factor in this is the university at Madison, which for a generation anyway ranked as the most progressive of all American state universities. Among well-known public servants associated with Wisconsin are Lloyd K. Garrison, David E. Lilienthal, and Julius A. Krug, whose father was the local sheriff and who is still assistant state fire marshal. Among artists and literary people and professional men are, or were, Thorstein Veblen, Frank Lloyd Wright, Edna Ferber, Zona Gale, the Lunts, Professor Frederick J. Turner, Emily Hahn, Thornton Wilder, and, among military folk highly picturesque, General MacArthur, whose father lived in Milwaukee, and the late Admiral Marc A. Mitscher.

Word About the La Follettes, Past and Present

Roughly from the Civil War to 1900, Wisconsin was dominated by the railroads and, until the forests were denuded, by the timber interests; these controlled the Republican party, and ran the state government.[8] Came a new era in 1900, with the election of Robert Marion La Follette as governor. La Follette was a young lawyer who rose steadily in public jobs. Probably because it was richer, Wisconsin has never been as belligerently radical as North Dakota or even Minnesota; La Follette was a liberal. Milwaukee had a strong Socialist nucleus—in fact it had a Socialist mayor, Daniel W. Hoan, for twenty-four years—but only incidentally did this contribute to the Progressive movement.[9] La Follette was more than a great man. He became a myth. His technique was, by and large, to take up specific concrete issues one at a time. For instance, his first considerable campaign was for regulation of the railroads; then he fought for the direct primary and direct election of senators; then he forced the railways to pay their fair share of taxes, and to modify the rebate system whereby the big companies were favored as against the small. Theory meant little to him, and his approach was seldom ideo-

[8] In the entire history of the state there have been only two Democratic governors.
[9] Also Victor L. Berger of Milwaukee was the first Socialist ever to sit in Congress.

logical. He did not, like the Socialists or Communists, present a program
as the corollary of a theory. But he was a profound believer in both
expert knowledge and education; he was one of the first American men
of politics to build up a brain trust, and he believed heavily in the
scientific method. One of his tenets was that the government should
be able to step in and help the people solve a given problem, by having
at hand an expertly worked-out applicable program. Also he sought to
educate the people as a whole so that they might truly understand what
the issues were. Hence, when he himself went on to Washington and
the national scene, his domestic reforms stayed put. Conservative governors that followed him could not write his reforms off the books, because
the citizenry had become sufficiently educated to see that they remained.

From 1901 until 1946, for almost half a century, a La Follette was
either senator from Wisconsin or governor of the state. No record quite
like this exists in American history.

La Follette's two sons, Robert M. Jr., the elder, and Philip F., have
always complemented one another nicely. Bob equals Washington in
La Follette language; Phil equals Wisconsin. Bob was his father's secretary for some years, and then senator; Phil has been governor three
times. Bob, I heard from friends of both, resembles his mother in character and temperament; Phil is more like his father. Bob is studious, more
reserved, gentler; Phil is volatile, quick minded, capable of some extremely errant judgments, more ambitious probably, and less sound.
In a curious way, though the elder, Bob has usually tended to defer to
Phil. Possibly this is because, midway through college, Bob had a long,
almost mortal illness; he never got a university degree (whereas Phil's
scholastic record was exceptionally brilliant) and did not think he had the
stamina for public life, which Phil had amply. The whole family is very
devoted. Phil married before Bob, and had a son first. Bob insisted that
he be named Robert Marion La Follette III although Phil wanted to
leave the name free for the time Bob should marry and have a son.
Indeed Bob has two sons today; their names are Bronson Cutting La
Follette and Jo Davidson La Follette. One of the boys, while working
his way through school, became ill. Father Bob got up at three in the
morning and delivered his son's paper route.

The story of the creation, rise, collapse, and eventual disappearance of
the Progressive party may be told briefly. The movement started back
in the 1890's. Its spearhead was, of course, Bob Senior. But he was first
elected governor as a Republican, and during most of his political life he
worked *within* the Republican party.[10] Hence most electoral issues were
decided in the primaries; a Progressive would oppose a conservative
("stalwart") Republican; the general election was mostly a formality,
since both Republican wings would generally unite to beat whoever was

[10] Of course he ran for president as a Progressive in 1924.

the Democratic candidate. But in 1932 the Progressives, after Phil was beaten in the primaries by a conservative, bolted the Republican ticket, and two years later the Progressive party was formally organized at a convention at Fond du Lac. Phil ran for governor and Bob for the senate as Progressives, and both won handsomely. They supported the New Deal on various measures; FDR smiled upon them, and presently, instead of being a splinter Republican party, the Progressives became close allies of the New Deal. Bob didn't agree with Roosevelt on foreign policy, certainly. But even in 1940 he ran with New Deal blessing, and folk like Harry Hopkins assisted his campaign.

But I am getting ahead of the story. Phil wanted to build up a real countrywide party. He called it the National Progressives of America, and it was launched in 1938. He invented a device, a cross within a circle, as an insigne, which was supposed to signify, among other things, the ballot box, "the multiplication of wealth" and "the unity of the nation." But promptly it was dubbed a "circumcised swastika" by folk who didn't take Phil as seriously as he took himself. At about the same time, as a Wisconsin friend of mine put it, he "began to talk a lot of damn strange stuff." He had visited Europe and old-line Progressives were horrified to hear him speak in accents that seemed unduly to reflect European influences of the time. He told friends that democracy had become too cumbersome, that it needed more direction, that people liked to feel in a positive way that they *belonged* to a movement, and that maybe new techniques in uniforms, pageantry and the like might be useful. At this period it was never quite clear whether the National Progressives were to remain an independent movement, rescue the Democratic party from the town bosses, or go back to the Republicans. Some of Phil's old comrades said that, since FDR had put into the law of the land most of what his father had fought for, any attempt to fight him would be lunatic. It was during this time, I was told in Madison, that Phil thought that the procedure of government in Wisconsin might be made simpler if the governor, not the legislature, should initiate legislation; the function of the legislature would merely be to approve. Shades of the Reichstag! At the mass meeting where the movement was launched, a big banner, with Cross in Circle, was spread out behind the stage; uniformed ushers, spotlights, and a band were part of the regalia. It was all somewhat ridiculous and somewhat Caesarian.

After the 1940 campaign and then Pearl Harbor the Progressives began to decline seriously. Phil went into the Army and became an officer on the staff of General MacArthur. Bob, however, stuck to his knitting as a senator and an extremely able one. In 1944, instead of being a force that could tip the balance either way (after all, the Progressives had been the chief influence whereby Roosevelt carried the state three times) they were ground out between the two big parties, and got only 6 per cent of the vote. Once again, it was proved that no third party in America can succeed for long, unless it ties onto a national ticket. The political picture became highly fluid. Progressives on the conservative side slipped out and joined the Republicans; the liberals joined the Democrats. This disintegration went on for some time, and in March, 1946, the Progressive party met in convention at Portage and voted by a large majority to kill itself. So ended, after twelve years, the life of the only third party organized on a state basis in the United States. Phil, back from the wars, was lying low and saying little. Bob ran for re-election to the senate—as a Republican—and was beaten.

Phil's political plans are, as of the moment, not precisely known. What he talks about mostly is MacArthur. For this general he has, like almost all isolationists and Europe-haters, an admiration frenzied and idolatrous.

Bob will be grievously missed in the new Senate. He is a man of pith and substance. Few public servants have ever done a sounder domestic job. For one thing it was he, along with Monroney of Oklahoma, who was mostly responsible for the recent congressional reform bill. Bob was never quite the overt isolationist that most people believe him to be; he was never so violent as Phil. He likes to recall that his father introduced a bill back in 1916 favoring a League of Nations, that both he and his father wanted recognition of the Soviet Union as long ago as in 1922, and that it was his father who was largely instrumental in getting American troops out of Siberia after World War I. Bob voted for, not against, Bretton Woods, the reciprocal trade treaties, and the Charter. On the other hand he opposed the British loan.

What beat Bob? There were several factors, among which isolation was merely one. His opponent in the primaries, who later won the election easily, was Joseph R. McCarthy,[11] a farmer's son who at twenty-nine had become the youngest circuit court judge in the history of the state. He entered the Marines as a private, and came out as a captain with a brilliant record. Naturally he was able to make use of this with advantage. But isolationism was not nearly so decisive an element in La Follette's defeat as in the cases of Shipstead, Wheeler, et al. The best proof of this is that several extremely isolationist Wisconsin congressmen, like O'Konski and Keefe, were re-elected easily. One factor obviously contributing to the result was that Bob, completing a long job of work on the Congressional Reorganization bill, selflessly thought that it was his duty to stay in Washington and see it through; he made no real campaign, and did not even visit Wisconsin except briefly. Another was that plenty of Progressives disapproved of the coalescence with the Republicans so strongly that they went into the Democratic primaries. Hannegan, incidentally, had wanted Bob to run as a Democrat, with

---

[11] Not to be confused with the Charles McCarthy who was one of the founders of liberalism in Wisconsin.

administration support; this he would not do. Finally, by an irony cruel enough, what beat him was labor, though he has as liberal a labor record as any senator. He came into Milwaukee with a light lead; Milwaukee turned against him by some nine thousand votes, and that finished him. Some urban Catholics opposed him (McCarthy is a Catholic incidentally) because he had taken a stand against Franco Spain; more importantly, the strong Communist-inspired fringe of the Milwaukee CIO went all out to beat him, because he had often attacked Stalinist Russia.[12] At any rate he was defeated. For the first time in more than a generation, there is no La Follette in the U. S. Senate.

Wisconsin is not an easy state to take apart and diagnose. The Republican state chairman, Thomas E. Coleman, is a wealthy industrialist, the president of the Madison-Kipp Company. He has been anti-La Follette practically since childhood; almost all reactionary interests in the state are marshaled behind him. Coleman worked hard, in fact, to prevent the La Follettes from re-entering the Republican party; he even got a bill through the legislature (the governor vetoed it, however) that would have served to keep them out. What beat Bob was, in short, strange as it may seem, a kind of Catholic big business Communist coalition.

Coleman, I heard it said, runs the legislature, but he does not run the governor. No one runs this tough old man. In fact Goodland, the Republican governor, whom La Follette opposed, was also opposed by the Republican machine. But he won easily—although he endorsed his own Progressive opponent! Figure it out for yourself. Goodland is a craggy character indeed. He made no campaign speeches in 1946, and returned all campaign contributions.

The Case of Mr. Crowley

The most powerful figure for years in Democratic politics in Wisconsin, though this influence was expressed mostly on the national level, was Leo T. Crowley, at one time or another Alien Property Custodian, chairman of the Export-Import Bank, head of the Federal Deposit Insurance Corporation, head of the Board of Economic Warfare during part of World War II, and then Foreign Economic Administrator. Many first-class American business and professional men went to Washington during the war, giving up their jobs, sacrificing their homes in some cases and their savings, to work for the United States of America and freely give every inch and ounce of themselves for victory. The honor

[12] Foreign affairs and Communism are noisily acute issues in Milwaukee. One Polish-descended Democrat, alleged to be a Communist, beat another of Polish origin in the last Congressional primaries, in part because the community is divided almost as much on Polish as on Wisconsin issues. At the 1946 state convention of the CIO, however, the Communists were sharply spanked down.

roll is impressive. Think—to pick a few among dozens—of John J. McCloy, Dean Acheson, Byron Price, Patterson and Lovett in the War Department, Thomas K. Finletter, Elmer Davis, Adlai Stevenson. There were also folk like Leo Crowley.

Crowley was a poor boy born in Milton Junction, of Irish Catholic parentage.[13] He had a talent for politics and business both. He became head of a paper jobbing firm and then expanded into real estate and banking; he was president for a time of an important bank in Madison. When, in the 1930's, the big bank chains, in Wisconsin as well as Minnesota, started buying up small banks, Crowley's institution was taken over by the Wisconsin Bank Shares Company. How successful Crowley was as a businessman is difficult to assess from one point of view, since he accumulated substantial debts. He turned to politics, and became secretary to a Democratic governor, Albert G. Schmedeman, in 1933. He went to Washington a good deal, became close to Roosevelt during the banking crisis and in 1934 was appointed head of the Federal Deposit Insurance Corporation. His appointment to a second important federal job, Alien Property Custodian, followed some years later.

Also Crowley had other interests. He became chairman of the board of the Standard Gas & Electric Company, a big middle western utility, in 1939. His salary was $50,000 for a time and $75,000 later. This job he held along with his federal jobs. He would not, he announced, accept his salary as Alien Property Custodian while working for Standard Gas & Electric; he did, however, for a time at least continue to keep the $10,000 a year he got from FDIC. Behind Standard Gas is a complex personal and financial panorama. This company, once controlled by H. M. Byllesby and Co., was later taken over by the well-known promoter Victor Emanuel. Standard Gas, when Emanuel and his friends took it over by formation of a holding company called U.S. Electric Power Corporation, became "part of a utility empire stretching over 20 states and worth $1,119,000,000."[14] The depression came along, however. So did the Securities Exchange Commission. Standard Gas "went into reorganization," and Victor Emanuel stepped out of the chairmanship, which then went to Leo Crowley.

That any man should accept a very large salary from a private utilities company, while at the same time accepting another smaller one from the federal government, which through the SEC often had brushes with utility companies, naturally provoked some criticism. Also that Crowley, whose own banking record was not too brilliant, should be head of just such a federal agency as the FDIC, seemed peculiar to some. Moreover as Alien Property Custodian he had to deal with several foreign companies,

[13] He is today a Knight of St. Gregory, K.C., and Knight Commander with Star of the Order of Pius IX.
[14] *Time*, October 7, 1946.

like I. G. Farben, that had been interlocked in one way or another with some of the people who formerly ran Standard Gas.[15]

In 1943, after the quarrel between Henry Wallace and Jesse Jones, Crowley became head of the short-lived Board of Economic Warfare. This was merged, along with Lend Lease, into the Foreign Economic Administration, which he ran until the end of the war in a style best described as lumbering. Recently he gave up all his public jobs, and returned to private life.

Wisconsin state income tax returns are open to the public, by law. Anybody can look at anybody's in the state house or the regional tax districts. It is, therefore, possible to survey details of Crowley's financial life. In one year, 1942, his listings of "interest paid" amount to $19,-436.40, which would indicate that his debts at the time totaled a considerable sum. Three among the payees are large insurance companies. From 1940 to 1942 inclusive Crowley's return under "wages and salaries" includes $10,000 each year from the Federal Deposit Insurance Corporation, and from Standard Gas and Electric $50,000 in 1940, $65,625 in 1941, and $75,000 in 1942.[16]

When FDR turned the Board of Economic Warfare over to Crowley, the *Capital Times* of Madison printed several of the details given above, and concluded, "Can anything be more incongruous than a situation in which a high personage in the Roosevelt administration is receiving $75,000 a year from a vast holding company empire when the Roosevelt administration itself has taken the position that holding company set-ups . . . are against the public interest and should be broken up?"

Why did Roosevelt give Crowley so many jobs? The late Harry Hopkins once gave me a quadruple answer to this. First, he never got into trouble; none of his agencies ever had any public fracases. Second, he did what FDR wanted him to do, without fuss or argument. Third, he was a powerful middle western Catholic. Fourth, he got along well with Congress.

[15] Details of most of these interrelations were first revealed by I. F. Stone in *The Nation* and *PM*.
[16] In July, 1946, Crowley was barred by the Federal Power Commission from continuing as a director of three other utility companies, because he had not attended the minimum number of meetings that FPC regulations require, as a result of his duties in Washington. *PM*, July 9, 1946.

Chapter 21

Iowa, Corn and Pigs

∿∿∿

> There's talk says Illinois
> Is there says Iowa.
>
> —Archibald MacLeish

> The Corn Belt is a gift of the gods—the rain god, the sun god,
> the ice god, and the gods of geology.
>
> —J. Russell Smith

IOWA spells agriculture, and agriculture in this part of the world spells corn. This is the heart of agrarian America. We have touched the edges of the corn belt in Nebraska; here in Iowa it actually is.

It was very hot that August afternoon in Des Moines, blisteringly hot. The waitress saw me sweltering. "Never mind," she said, "this is the kind of weather that's good for the corn." Later I drove out in the country, and the chauffeur said, "Our corn is going to have to hurry to get in on time." Never have I felt with such primitive and searching force the inexhaustibleness of America. "The corn gathers speed like a long freight train going downhill," I heard it said. You can practically hear and feel it growing. And it is everybody's chief preoccupation.

Corn is the greatest of all American crops; it grows in every state and in both value and production it outranks wheat, oats, rice, and rye combined. Glance at a Department of Agriculture map, showing the total American acreage of corn, with a black dot for every ten thousand acres. Parts of the map look like the ink blot tests used in psychiatry. The central puddle is Iowa—Iowa is so solid with black that you cannot see where the state begins or ends. Then smears and blobs drip over into adjacent areas, particularly in Nebraska and Illinois.

Corn is everything in Iowa; it is eggs, milk, breakfast cereals, cattle, meal, chemicals, syrup, starch, liquor, and pork. But the chief thing to know about it is that it is not corn. It is hogs. The "corn-hog ratio," which can be worked out by a child on a blackboard, dominates corn as the formula $E = mc^2$ dominates the production of atomic energy. Corn grows on 11 million acres in Iowa, but only an infinitesimal fraction of these produce corn to be eaten as corn—in the shape of corn on the cob, popcorn or sweet corn. The enormous preponderance of production goes to "field corn," viz., corn fed to animals—chiefly hogs. Corn is not a corn problem at all. It is a pork problem and to some extent a beef and poultry problem.

The chief characteristic of Iowa agriculture is that the great cash crop is hogs, not corn. What really lifts the mortgage on an Iowa farm is hogs. The "ratio" varies year by year. In theory, the farmer may withhold corn from his hogs, if the price of meat does not hold a favorable ration to that of corn per se. Normally this ratio is highly favorable. For instance if corn is worth $1.00 a bushel as corn, it may be worth $1.40 in the form of hogs. The Iowa farmer is much more than a farmer; he is a processor of meat.

Proceed now to the story of hybrid. This is the key to everything today. The evolution of hybrid corn is one of the great contemporary American adventures.[1]

Corn, a very peculiar plant, is a kind of hermaphrodite; each stalk has both a male and female element and fertilizes both itself and neighbors. The male is the tassel at the top; the female is the soft silk attached to the ear; normally corn is fertilized when pollen from the tassel falls naturally on silk in the same stalk. But, since millions upon millions of particles of pollen are released when wind ripples through a cornfield, many ears may be fertilized by tassels not their own. So, even in the same field, different stalks of corn may have different characteristics; some are tall, some scrawny; they grow ears at different levels, making mechanical husking difficult if not impossible. Inevitably agronomists began to experiment toward production of a corn more uniform, sturdier, easier to cultivate—and so came hybrid. The details are too technical for inclusion here; I can describe only what I saw. The corn is planted in rows arbitrarily called "male" and "female" by the seed farmers, and these are "segregated" carefully. Then the "female" stalks are detasselized. Workers go through the fields, capping all the tassels. This is hard and expensive work—but worth it. As a result, only chosen male pollen (from the stalks *not* detasselized) is free to settle on chosen female silk. Thus a carefully controlled crossbreeding is effected. Farmers resisted all this for a time. For generations, they had grown their own seed; it cost them nothing, whereas hybrid seed is fairly expensive. I asked my guides what brought them over. They laughed shortly. "The man not using hybrid grew thirty or forty bushels to the acre and looked across the fence and saw his neighbor, who used hybrid, getting sixty–eighty."

Seldom has any innovation met with such quick and sweeping success.

[1] See "Revolution in the Corn Belt," by Kurt Steel, *Harper's Magazine*, August, 1945, for a brilliant brief description of hybrid. Mr. Steel also points out that corn, hybrid or not, "is an orphan among grains, belonging to no known family." Like wheat and cotton its origin is unknown. But unlike them it "has never been found growing wild." It has existed everywhere in the world from the earliest times— "corn is the one global plant"—but it cannot grow "without man's help." The implications of this are mysterious in the extreme.

Hybrid matures in whatever period is best suited to the area; thus it greatly decreases risks from weather. Its rate of growth is almost mathematically precise; the height of the stalks and the size of the ears is more uniform; the roots are vastly stronger; it resists wind better; the mechanical picker can handle it much more easily; above all, different hybrid varieties can be developed to fit the special soil characteristics of any region. In 1933, when hybrid first came in, 143,000 acres or about one-tenth of 1 per cent of the total corn acreage of the nation were planted with it. In 1946, the hybrid acreage was 62,680,000, or 67.5 per cent. Different states responded to hybrid with varying alacrity. Corn in Nebraska is now 85 per cent hybrid, in Minnesota 91 per cent, in Ohio 96 per cent, in Illinois and Indiana 98 per cent. The figure 100 per cent is difficult to attain in any category; complete saturation points are rare. But Iowa's hybrid figure is so near an actual 100 per cent today that statisticians accept it as the figure.

One result: the nation's corn crop as estimated for 1946 is 3,496,820,000 bushels. This overrides a previous all time high by some·300 million bushels. Iowa itself has had the greatest harvests in its history recently. The crops of 1942, 1943, and 1944 each broke preceding records, and 1946 beat all three.

Henry Wallace, the well-known Iowa boy who has entered many fields with distinction, who was editor of a farm publication years ago and who is now editor of the *New Republic*, Mr. Wallace who has been secretary of agriculture, secretary of commerce, and vice president of the United States, has been called a "theorist" and a "visionary" by his enemies. So put it down that he is one of the two or three men in the United States most concretely responsible for hybrid. He helped develop it from the beginning, not only as a public servant but as a practical farmer in the field, and his pioneer seed corn company is one of the biggest in the business.

Visit to a Farm

Forrest Seymour, who succeeded Mr. Waymack as editor of the Des Moines *Register* and *Tribune*, J. S. Russell, its longtime farm editor, and Harry D. Linn, secretary of the state department of agriculture, drove me out to a farm owned by Scott Ellis. I think they chose it because it was so "typical." I can only hope it is. Mr. Ellis's establishment is so superior, so well run, that Iowa is indeed a lucky state if it is typical. Mr. Ellis works with his head as well as his hands; one might think him a prosperous banker if it were not for his cap and overalls; incidentally his mother helped herd cattle in this same region when it was still an open range.

Mr. Ellis showed us his property—inevitably it looked like something painted by Grant Wood—and explained his techniques. He plants eighty acres to corn, forty to oats, and forty to clover, and rotates on a four-year schedule. If you plant corn, you cannot plant anything else on the same land in the same year. The oats are used mostly as feed for young pigs. "We wean 'em on oats, instead of sow's milk," Mr. Ellis said. "Corn makes 'em fat, but it's the oats that make 'em grow." One-third of the clover is left for hay; the hogs use the rest for pasture. As to the corn about two-thirds are fed to the hogs and poultry; the rest goes to "deficit areas" in Missouri and the East or to the cereal mills.

A farm like this is vastly different from those we have glanced at in the West. It is thickly green and luxuriant. There is less need to irrigate or fertilize or keep half the land fallow. "Our ground is all sweet," our host pointed out. It grows legumes easily and the droppings of the animals at pasture provide most of the fertilizer. It has, of course, every conceivable type of mechanized equipment—ensilage cutter, hay mower, hay buck, manure loader and spreader, and binder, as well as milking machines. A long, electrically wired fence keeps the livestock from roaming out of bounds. An animal touches it, and is jolted back by a slight electric shock.

We drove over an alfalfa field, and then into Sudan grass. We saw the green mats of clover, solid underneath brown oats; the clover isn't damaged when the oats are harvested. Finally came the corn itself, a waving sea eight feet tall—as high as a man on horseback. We watched girl workers in white hats pulling the tassels off the female rows, in the fields where commercial hybrid was growing. The detasseled rows give them a certain striped, illogical appearance, as if someone were dressing Nature up in fancy tweeds.

Mr. Ellis has one hundred Holsteins. All are calving—but none has ever seen a bull! They are inseminated artificially. All over Iowa farmers club together to maintain a "bull ring" with six or eight bulls, for artificial insemination. The semen is drawn off in a catch-valve contrivance, which the bulls wear; it is then mixed with an egg-saline solution, kept at a constant temperature, and sold to farmers with dairy cows, at need. The price is $6.00 per cow, for three injections. "The system saves a lot of transport," one of our party sagely observed.

In winter the Ellises keep beef cattle too, some 150 head, in feeder lots. The steers (when I was there) cost about 10¢ a pound; they weigh about 750 pounds when they come in, and go out at 1,100. "We buy 'em from Wyoming, and put 350 pounds of corn fat on 'em in three months."

I wanted to know where Mr. Ellis gets his electricity from—he uses and needs a lot. For many years, in the pattern so familiar all over the United States, the utilities would not put power into rural communities until they had a certain minimum number of customers; three "units" to the mile was the rule in Iowa. Now however the Iowa Light & Power Company will sell electricity almost everywhere. The Rural Electrification

Administration came in and helped to force rates down. But, my guides told me, the utilities make more money even with rates lower, because so many more customers can now afford to buy. I asked Mr. Ellis what his politics were. He voted for Roosevelt in 1932, Landon in 1936, Willkie in 1940, and Roosevelt again in 1944.

Later I had another Iowa outing, driving with the state highway patrol westward from Des Moines. I watched the bright yellow straw which the combines had left, after chewing off the oats; I heard of farmers who still resisted growing soybeans, because they feared that these gave an oily taste to meat. I saw glimpses of another side of Iowa too; one coal mine, two brick factories, and in eighty miles no fewer than eleven towns. Along this road, the officer driving me said, some of the strangest traffic ever known used to come. Convoys of B-29 fuselages and bomb bay sections, too big for the railways, had to go by truck all the way from Akron to the assembly plant at Omaha. When they passed, the whole road was closed. Also I heard (this was in the summer of 1945) that radio commentators in New York determined to an extent how much work the Iowa highway patrol had to do. If the war news sounded good on the air, the farmers drove carelessly, with spirits high, and there were plenty of accidents. When it was bad, driving was slow, sullen, plodding—and free of crashes! Iowa gave 275,000 men to the armed forces. We hear much of the militancy of Texas and the southern states, but this figure, on a basis of proportionate population, is one of the highest in the country.

Agriculture in the United States is of course a subsidized industry. Why should it not be?—Iowa farmers ask. After all manufactured goods are protected by the tariff or by other measures. Agriculture has, indeed, always been assisted by some kind of subsidy. What was the Homestead Act but an enormous over-all subsidy to agriculture?

Yet I found many troubled consciences. Basically most farmers do not like subsidies; they would much prefer getting a good price in the open market without government support. To a man, for instance, they express theoretical dislike of the Department of Agriculture's Crop Adjustment Program. But here we encounter one of the most typical of all manifestations of what might be called American "psychology." Unanimously, farmers talk about the evils of government "control." But I never found one who didn't accept the checks the government sends out.

The root problem of American agriculture as seen in Iowa is that the national stomach cannot possibly, in normal times, contain everything that the farms produce. The most pressing issue is that of surplus. In other words, the greatest of all agricultural problems lies outside agriculture, since, strictly speaking, "surplus" simply means lack of consumption. What agriculture needs above all, to become self-supporting, is full employment and a greater earning power by the non-agricultural communities of the United States, so that more people will buy more food.

Corn Belt Dialogue

During the agitated summer of 1946 the New York *Times* gave James Reston, its well-known expert on international affairs, a brief change of scene. It sent him to the wilds of the Middle West, which is of course fully as exotic as Tibet. Mr. Reston's lively and sensible reporting deserves a place in the anthologies. One story, written about Kansas, applies equally to Iowa with a change or two:

Farmer—Well, young man, what's new Down East?

Reporter—OPA's dead.

Farmer—That's fine. Now we can get more for our wheat and meat.

Reporter—Yes, but the President says you'll probably have to pay more for what you buy. Maybe $225 more for cars and 13 per cent more for farm machinery.

Farmer—They can't do that to us. Prices are too high already. What we want is price control on what we buy and no price control on what we sell.

Reporter—That's what labor wants. Price control on your wheat and no price control on their wages. Same with industrial management, price control on labor's wages and your wheat but no price control on its products.

Farmer—That makes it tough, don't it? Who killed OPA?

Reporter—The President vetoed it.

Farmer—I thought he was for it.

Reporter—He was and he says he's just begun to fight for it, but he wanted more price control so he killed what there was. He blames Senator Taft for the trouble.

Farmer—How's that? I thought Taft was against price control.

Reporter—No, he says now he's for price control.

Farmer—I've missed a lot during the harvest. Whatever happened to that fellow Bowles?

Reporter—He quit.

Farmer—But I thought you said the Administration was just beginning to fight for price control. Isn't Bowles for price control?

Reporter—Sure, but he recommended that the President veto the price control bill and then he quit. . . .

Farmer—We've had a whopper of a wheat crop.

Reporter—That ought to make you happy.

Farmer—Happy hell! We're sore. We're restricted by the Government in everything we do. A guy has to be an accountant to run a farm these days.

Reporter—You're getting a good price for your wheat, aren't you?

Farmer—Almost $2 a bushel at the elevator, but if they'd keep off these restrictions and stick to the good old democratic law of supply and demand we'd be getting $2.50 like we did during the last war.

Reporter—What did you get in 1931?

Farmer—Don't even mention that year. That was when we had "two-bit wheat." Yes, sir, we got 25 cents a bushel.

Reporter—Wasn't the law of supply and demand working then?

Farmer—Sure, but these restrictions from Washington drive a man crazy. It ain't right. It's an infringement on a man's personal liberty.[2]

Iowa: More Facts and Figures

Three millions yearly for manure
But not one cent for literature.
                               —Ellis Parker Butler

Iowa, a really fecund state, throws its corn over into Nebraska and Illinois, and its old folks all the way to California. We know what Iowa has done to California; the question might well be asked: what has California done to Iowa; what effect have the great outgoings had? The answer appears to be: very little. When I asked Governor Robert D. Blue, a friendly and able man, why so many Iowans left Iowa, he replied with local spirit, "Because they've never seen it!"

He meant that Iowa, lying uniquely between the two great middle western rivers, is somewhat more diversified than most people think. In the north, the "cash grain area," there is a fairly strong Scandinavian underlay, and in the south a Missouri hillbilly influence; people speak with a more pronounced drawl, and go barefoot in the mud. The state is predominantly Protestant, but many Catholics live in the cities. Prohibition makes another dividing line; the river counties are mostly wet, the southern dry. Also there are two unusual foreign-derived groups. One is the cluster of Dutch centering on Pella southeast of Des Moines. These have been there since 1847; they hold an annual tulip festival; they wear wooden shoes on ceremonial occasions, and their children may not speak a word of English till they are old enough to go to school.[3] The other is the German community living near Amana. Here is one of the comparatively few places in the United States where, it seems, the melting pot did not quite melt. The Germans who formed the Amana Society came out of Pennsylvania some eighty years ago; they were an offshoot of the Amish and the Mennonites, and for many years they maintained a completely communal organization, isolated and self-sufficient. A joint kitchen served each group of members, religious faith

---

[2] New York *Times*, July 1, 1946. Reprinted by permission.

[3] Similar pure Dutch colonies exist elsewhere in the Middle West, notably in Michigan towns like Holland.

was strong, and the products of work belonged to the community as a whole.

One-tenth of all the food in the entire United States is produced in Iowa; the state's list of agricultural firsts is remarkable. It is Number One in:

> Agricultural products per capita
> Cash farm income
> Eggs (7 per cent of the United States total)
> Grade A land (a full quarter of the total in the nation)
> Prime beef
> Hogs
> Horses
> Marketing of grain-fed cattle
> Oats
> Popcorn
> Red clover and timothy seed
> Soybean hay
> Poultry (8 per cent of all in the United States)

As well as being second in butter production and soybeans, and third in milk.

But do not think that agriculture is the whole Iowa story. The state is not so strongly industrialized as, say, Kansas, but it has flourishing and diverse industries. Most are, of course, closely associated with agriculture—cereal processing (as in the Quaker Oats plant at Cedar Rapids), meat packing (Ottumwa, Mason City, Sioux City, Cedar Rapids, Des Moines) and agricultural machinery (John Deere at Waterloo). But also Davenport[4] has railroad yards and pearl buttons; the Maytag Company calls its headquarters at Newton the "Washing Machine Capital of the World"; Red Oak has a calendar-printing industry known all over the nation; there are famous publishing houses in Des Moines; some of the biggest gypsum deposits in America are at Fort Dodge; Fort Madison has Sheaffer Pen. Two items little known: Iowa has a lively grape-and-wine industry near Council Bluffs, and it is a big fur-producing state, since its shallow creeks are alive with muskrat, mink, and skunk.

Issues and Ideas in Iowa

The major concern of Iowa is, and must be, the welfare of its corn, hogs, and farmers, and the dominant political factor is agriculture of course. This ramifies in almost every direction; for instance the state

[4] Which with Rock Island and Moline in Illinois across the river makes a single community.

department of agriculture is even charged with supervision of the hotels, and farmers make up at least half the legislature.

Iowa is an extremely conservative state, but it is not quite so overwhelmingly Republican as most outsiders believe. It went for FDR in both 1932 and 1936, and Democratic governors held office from 1932 to 1938. The farm vote, which is usually decisive, hangs in close balance; it was 70 per cent for Roosevelt in 1932, 62 per cent in 1936, 49 per cent in 1940, and 47 per cent in 1944. A great deal depends on the weather, in particular on the state of the harvest and roads. Corn is a late crop. A farmer may not be able to get into the polls if he is busy in a rainy November.

Then, too, the immediate economic situation—as in all agrarian states—plays an incisive role. When the farmer is rich, he placidly votes Republican by and large. When poor, his vote will be a protest vote.[5] "The Iowa farmer is a quiet man," I heard it said, "but if he starts going broke, *can* he yell!" The state saw, in fact, the nearest thing to a Jacquerie the United States has known since, let us say, Shays's Rebellion in 1786. The banks and insurance companies started closing out farms in the early 1930's; this happened elsewhere too, but nowhere did it meet such fierce and concrete resistance as in Iowa. These farmers have a covered wagon tradition. They are a stubborn and determined folk. They were ready to use violence to save their homes. Mobs assembled on the courthouse steps, armed with shotguns and carrying coils of heavy rope; the sheriffs as a rule took one look, and decided not to go on with whatever forced sale was scheduled.

A cogent force in Iowa, though it does not often express itself on a direct political level, is the state branch of the American Farm Bureau Federation under the leadership of one of the ablest men in his field in the country, Allan B. Kline. The Farm Bureau, probably the most powerful of the three great national farmers' organizations, has a position in Iowa (and in most middle western states) parallel to that of the Farmers Union in North Dakota and the Grange in New England. Iowa has ninety-nine counties, and the Iowa Farm Bureau has ninety-nine local offices.[6] Mostly it exerts influence through the "county agent" (in Iowa called the county extension director), who all over America is a kind of father and mother to the farmer; he is an official of both the "Extension Service" of the Department of Agriculture and the Farm Bureau. Thus the latter is an indispensable link between the farmer and the multifarious services that can be rendered him by Washington and the local land grant college. Again, the Farm Bureau is, like the Farmers Union, extremely active in such matters as insurance and co-operatives. It inaugurated its own life insurance company in 1945, to sell insurance

[5] For instance a few counties traditionally Democratic went *Republican* in 1932.
[6] It misses one county, however. In another big county there are two offices.

to members at cost; within a few months, it had 26 million dollars worth in force. The commercial insurance companies did not like this development, but they could not easily attack it without seeming to make all insurance vulnerable. The Farm Bureau co-operatives have a very substantial business in Iowa. One handles gasoline as in North Dakota; another has an elevator in Des Moines roughly like that in Minneapolis though not so big; another distributes veterinary serum and biologicals.

Some businessmen resent hotly the entrance of the Farm Bureau into business. Its answer is that anything that increases the wealth and earning power of the farmer will increase the wealth and earning power of the merchant too. The small businessman (who is jealous of the farmer anyway, in that his taxes help pay the farmer's subsidies, and of the Farm Bureau anyway, in that this is supported in part by public funds) replies in turn that he is being progressively squeezed out by the big chain stores on one hand, and the co-ops on the other. Also it wounds him grievously that the co-ops are exempt from most taxation.

Another strong Iowa force is journalism. John M. Henry of the Des Moines *Register* and *Tribune* did me a useful service, when he let me sit in, during most of a day and then at dinner, with a group of country editors from all over the state. In Chapter 17, I mentioned the Capper press in Kansas; there is no concentration of power quite like this in Iowa, but several publications, like the Meredith family's *Successful Farming* and *Wallace's Farmer*, which is the Henry Wallace paper, have great influence; the latter has a circulation coverage of not less than 93 per cent in Iowa, and almost as much in adjacent states.[7]

As to the Des Moines *Register* and *Tribune*, owned by the Cowles brothers who also own *Look* and all the dailies in Minneapolis, they comprise one of the most celebrated newspaper properties in the United States. John Cowles takes care of the Minneapolis end, and Gardner Cowles ("Mike") runs the *Register* and *Tribune*. The Cowles duumvirate is the fountainhead of liberal Republicanism in Iowa; the Des Moines papers, together with their radio stations KRNT and WNAX, have a strong enlivening influence on almost everything in the state. When the Cowles paper *and* the rural press agree on an issue, they are virtually unbeatable. As far as journalism itself is concerned, the Des Moines papers have established an imposing variety of records. Taken

[7] Then too I discovered some remarkable oddities. Several times, for instance in Cheyenne, we have come across men who own "competing" papers in the same city. In Indianola, Iowa, this development reaches a unique peak. On Wednesdays and Fridays, from the same publishing house under the identical ownership, appear the *Record Herald* and the *Indianola Tribune*. On Fridays, the name *Record Herald* is printed in 72-point type, and the name *Indianola Tribune* in 10-point; on the Wednesdays, the order of type is reversed. It is the same paper, but since the name in the smaller type is all but invisible, it appears to carry a different identity in alternating issues. Moreover the two editions oppose one another editorially; one is as Democratic as the other is Republican.

together, the *Register* and *Tribune* have (*a*) the largest daily mail circulation of any. metropolitan newspaper in the United States, (*b*) the largest daily farm circulation of any newspaper in the United States, (*c*) the largest Sunday home-delivered farm circulation in the United States. The *Sunday Register* maintains more than a thousand rural routes, and is delivered by automobile to more than 90,000 individual farm homes. Every "town" in Iowa (850 in all) that contains more than seventy-five families gets "home delivery." There are fifty-five cities in the nation larger than Des Moines; only nine have papers with a larger Sunday circulation.

Another powerful element in Iowa is Masonry. Of 108 members of the lower house of the legislature, about seventy belong to the Masonic lodge, though nobody ever runs "as" a Mason, and only seldom is a man asked directly if he is one or not. Governor Blue is a Mason; so is the attorney general; so is every supreme court justice. Two things explain this: (1) Masonry is a kind of badge of respectability, not only in Iowa but in almost all the Mississippi basin states; (2) a man comes up through the local Masonic lodge and, if he shows leadership, is pushed outward to the legislature almost as a matter of course.

Other Iowa forces are like those we have encountered so many times: the American Legion (both Senator Hickenlooper—a first-class senator by the way—and Blue had strong legion support), the Methodist Church, the education lobby, and the Iowa Manufacturers Association, which is the local equivalent of the NAM. The most conspicuous lobbyist in the state is Edward A. Kimball, who is secretary of this last, and who holds, or held, several other jobs. Kimball, I heard it said, "camps on the capitol steps," and "is in and out of the governor's office two or three times a day."

The boss of the Republican party in Iowa is Harrison E. Spangler, a former chairman of the Republican National Committee. A friend, not an Iowan, once described him to me as follows: "He is a fine old man. He hasn't had a new idea since 1902." The strength of the Republican machine rises from the county courthouse rings; this is a phenomenon we shall encounter later in the South, though a different party of course holds sway there. Politics in Iowa is based on patronage as controlled by these rings. Anybody in state employment, no matter how minor, must have the approval of the precinct chairman, the county chairman, and the district chairman—all three! Even to be a janitor you have to have political support. Actually patronage is based on a point system, according to the vote rolled up. For example, a job paying $2,000 a year counts for five "points"; each county and so on gets jobs to distribute strictly on the basis of the "points" it accumulated in the last election.

The Republican party in Iowa, I heard it said by everybody including most Republicans, lacks vision, ideals, courage, progressiveness, faith, leadership, and *élan*. It has been too tightly stratified for far too long. Also the traditional pattern wherein a man works himself up—legislator, house leader, speaker, lieutenant governor, governor—kills off bright spirits.

One important issue is schools, and another is, of all things, roads. Iowa has the highest literacy rate in the union, 99.3 per cent, and it has some splendid colleges; yet almost everyone I met said that the state starves education. The Iowa schools are in the main supported by the local communities; the state itself contributes very little. In Kansas, the biggest, smartest, and best building in almost every rural town is the school. Not so in Iowa. The Farm Bureau and other organizations set out recently to put through a reform educational program, with increased state aid, better pay for teachers, and so on. The business interests (especially those representing real estate which might be taxed) moved against this, and in the end, as against $12,000,000 asked for, the schools got only $3,500,000.

Roads make a curious story; they are a chief political preoccupation of the state. It may seem hard to believe, but a powerful wing of opinion is *against* good roads, because roads cost money, i.e., taxes. In the north where they can be surfaced with material locally available, the secondary roads are generally quite good. But in the south, which has no gravel, thousands of miles of dirt roads exist which, when it rains, become muddy lanes almost impassable. This in Iowa—the first agricultural state of the union! Naturally the southern counties have for years agitated for road improvement. Iowa is forbidden by its constitution to go into debt except for a minor amount; so to get money means raising it out of the local pocketbook. The Northerners, who came to be called the "Mud Roads" group though they live in the "Good Roads" belt, resisted for a long time even a modest "farm-to-market" road program for the south. "The crisis over this had me plumb scared to death," Governor Blue told me. Finally a compromise was worked out, a penny tax was added to the price of gasoline, and road improvement got slowly under way.[8]

The United States is a country where good roads seem to be as much part of the essential landscape as bread or baseball. But actually, except for the great interstate highways and the parkways leading into the larger cities, American roads are apt to be quite bad. Of course road building is a comparatively new development from any long-range point of view. They became vital only after the automobile became vital;

[8] 3,500 Iowa farmers now have their own airplanes. One reason is that the roads are so bad. They are, in a manner of speaking, attempting to skip right over the roads era.

it is astonishing to think back and realize that, as recently as during the early 20's, most American roads off the beaten track were as atrocious as those in, say, Jugoslavia or Venezuela now. It was more than merely the automobile that brought the present superlative network of major highways to America. It was grants in aid to the states by the federal government.

Chapter 22
Notes for a Portrait of Missouri

^^

MISSOURI has the reflexes of its own celebrated mules; this is a
state with a kick to it. Here, moreover, you will find almost every
American problem in peppery miniature. Rural development versus
urban; two great cities with contrasting points of view; politics at their
most ferocious; erstwhile machine bosses of Neronian magnificence; a
close equilibrium between Catholic and Protestant communities; sectional
rivalries between north and south—all this is in Missouri.

In Washington, D. C., I met a trim, small, graying man with shiny
spectacles and an alert inquisitiveness. He stood by a big wall map, and,
as affectionately as a father poring over the photograph of a beloved
child, pointed out various lights and shadows, bumps and hollows, in the
Missouri landscape political and otherwise. One thing I know about Mr.
Truman is that he loves Missouri.

"Let me give you a cross-section," this modest, friendly man who was
going to be president of the United States three weeks later said, working over the map and reeling off names faster than I could take them
down, "Let me tell you about the why and wherefore." Mr. Truman has
visited every Missouri county—114 in all. He talked about friends I
should call on, who were the apple of his eye. "They're ornery, mean
folk!" he chuckled. "They're against everybody but themselves!" I asked
Mr. Truman what they were for. "Missouri!"

In Missouri for the first time in these pages we touch the South. This
is emphatically a border as well as a middle western state. "Missouri
would lose something if the Civil War were ever entirely settled," wrote
the Kansas City *Star* not long ago. The Missouri boot heel digs directly
into what is veritably the "old" South, and one region is called "Little
Dixie." Missouri came into the union as an offset to Maine. The War
Between the States split it savagely asunder; it gave 118,000 troops to
the Confederate army, 116,000 to the federal.[1] In blunt fact the Bushwhackers and others in Missouri fought their own Civil War, within
the state's own frontiers, and traces of this still show.

In St. Louis I first heard about the mechanical cotton picker and its
terrifying wonders.[2] Cotton is the gravest domestic problem in the

---

[1] Mr. Truman's figures. He mentioned also that Kentucky went 96,000 to 94,000
the other way.
[2] See Chapter 46 below.

economic sphere in America, and Missouri knows this well. One-third of the entire cotton crop of the nation is, believe it or not, produced in the area of the St. Louis Federal Reserve District.

One Missouri peculiarity becomes manifest at once when you look at a map, that each of its two great cities (like Omaha in Nebraska) is on an extreme edge of the state. Europeans will, I daresay, find this more striking than Americans. Try to name any European capital located directly on a land frontier. Americans take for granted what most Europeans envy—the impregnable security of United States frontiers.

The northern tier of Missouri counties is wonderfully rich agricultural land for the most part. Mr. Truman described to me where the glaciers stopped, along the line of the Missouri River, and how they left soil that practically has no bottom. The southern tier, settled in large part by Virginia and Tennessee mountaineers, is less productive. But the state is a literal checkerboard, the crossroads of almost everything; there is scarcely a county without some special interest or distinction. One largely German area is called the "Rhineland." In one region are the largest lead and zinc mines in the world. Another has (I am quoting an eminent local patriot) "more blue grass than Kentucky and Tennessee put together." There are Mennonites in most of Missouri; many farmhouses have two front doors side by side, one for use on Sundays only. I once visited a remarkable community in the extreme southwest of the state, called Neosho.[3] It was the Confederate capital of Missouri, and lies in what my military mentors called "traditional guerilla country." Also it produced some famous desperadoes and bank robbers in the civilian sphere, like the James boys. Nevertheless the local citizenry is of a strong religious bent and puritanical in the extreme.

In the southeastern corner of the state, near Sikeston, is a village of 104 families, 62 white, 42 Negro. In this cluster are represented thirty-seven different religious denominations.

The Ozarks are a world in themselves. These are, as everybody knows, the only block of moderately high land between the Alleghenies and the West; they are older mountains than the Rockies, and they are the backbone of the state. Perhaps oddly, there is little mineral wealth in the Ozarks except zinc and lead; the oil, I heard it put, "drained out to Kansas a couple of million years ago." There is not so much human wealth either. The Ozarks are the Poor White Trash citadel of America. The people are undeveloped, suspicious, and inert. There are children aged fifteen who have never seen a toothbrush.

In *These United States*, the compendium edited by Ernest Gruening a good many years ago but a book still very contemporary and stimulating, I find this somewhat mordant passage about the Ozark mountaineers:

[3] St. Clair McKelway once described this community brilliantly in *Life*, May 26, 1941.

They . . . (Hoosiers, Crackers, Pikers, and so on) were descendants of the bond-servants of colonial days, and being of low degree sought their own kind. . . . They settled in the malaria swamps of Indiana and Illinois but that was on the highway to empire, and civilization drove them out. They colonized again in Pike County, Missouri, and made the name "Piker" notorious throughout the West as denoting a fellow of feeble wit and feebler initiative. "Crackers," descendants of the Georgia convict colony, also found refuge. . . . The mountain people, too, came gradually onward, proliferating in their beloved highland till they crossed the Mississippi and peopled the Ozarks. They are simply a highland race that loves solitude and scorns comfort, literature, and luxury.[4]

One should have a word for the singular town of Independence, which as everybody knows is Mr. Truman's own home base. The president's attitude to it may be guessed from his remark to me that Kansas City is "one of its suburbs." Independence is the place which, as we know from Chapter 13, many Mormons think will be the scene of the Resurrection; also a Latter-Day Saint community lives in it to this day, comprising those who split off from the original church mostly on the issue of plural marriage; its tabernacle is the biggest building in the town. Also Independence was the jumping-off place for three of the greatest American trails, the California, the Santa Fe and the Oregon. Lewis and Clark started out from Missouri, and so did the first covered wagons to California. The great city of St. Louis grew from a population of 300 to its present 816,048 in the first instance because it was the *entrepôt* which outfitted the early westward trekkers. Independence has, among other things, a spirited Confederate tradition; Truman's father was a veteran, and his mother lives near there still. It has incidentally its own method of dealing with the Negro problem. Recently a very old Negro died; white men, including the president's brother, were his pallbearers.[5]

Rural journalism in Missouri is something quite special. Everywhere I heard stories about Arthur Aull, editor of the Lamar *Democrat*, who writes personal notes that have considerable tang. He likes nothing better than to report the marriage of a couple that has just had a baby, or to describe, with names, various misadventures of the inebriated. One item, as reprinted in *Life* tells of a local worthy who got a divorce because his wife ran off with her brother-in-law while he and the children were at the Baptist church.

Leonard Hall, who does a weekly column about the Ozarks for the St. Louis *Post-Dispatch*, recently described one mountaineer who "had six marriages go bad on him but . . . wouldn't mind to have another

[4] Vol. II, p. 357. By C. L. Edson.
[5] Roy Roberts told me this anecdote and added that the *Star* hardly gave it a line because nobody thought it was a "story."

woman if she's a good one, for they air the best piece of property a man can have around the place."[6]

On Pendergast and Certain Corruptions, Past and Present, in American City Politics

Boss Pendergast, the old man, is dead, but it is impossible to write about Missouri or indeed the United States without mentioning him. Why have so many American cities been so fabulously corrupt?

My own memory goes back many years: I remember with curious sharpness the first time I ever ran into crooked politics. Our high school in Chicago had a magazine and I, for some reason never explained before or since, was its business manager. We made up the magazine each month, and took it to a small neighborhood printer, who was an old-school honorable craftsman; we worked long hours with him; he liked us, and we loved him. Then one month the principal of the high school called me in; I still remember how his face was averted, as if he were ashamed of what he was going to have to say. No more could our magazine patronize that small, conscientious, patient printer. There were no complaints. Our printer's price was reasonable, and his work first rate. But a new city administration had just taken office and its members had various interlockings and interlacings and political debts to pay. So an order came from on high obliging all the small amateur school papers to transfer their business forthwith to a large commercial printing house downtown. What was our total business worth? Not more than a few hundred dollars a year. Enough. The big commercial printer wanted that few hundred dollars from each of the schools, and was in a position to demand it. And that was that.

All over America I ran into little stories about urban politics. I didn't have to collect them; they stick to the ears.

Item: In one New England city, the new mayor told his crowd on accepting office, "Now, boys, no ——— ———, everything's got to be clean from now on, for two months."

Item: Nugget of conversation about the mayor of a great middle western city: "Oh, the old boy ain't so bad, he got rich *before* he was elected."

Item: In 1936, the St. Louis *Post-Dispatch* won a Pulitzer prize for exposing "padded registrations," of which there were found to be 45,000 in St. Louis alone. It printed picture after picture of deserted empty houses—each the address of a hundred "voters."

Item: In one city until very recently, if some institution should be so unwise as to resist a shakedown, the number of things gravely wrong with its elevators and plumbing, which would instantly be pounced upon

[6] This is also from *Life*, May 27, 1946.

by the building inspectors and which might well lead to condemnation of the property, was remarkable.

Item: In one city, when a drugstore proprietor did not contribute to the local machine, policemen stood outside his premises and searched outgoing customers for narcotics, which did not make business flourish.

The chief reason for the growth of corrupt political machines was inertia in the citizen. Bryce wrote about "the fatalism of the multitude," and years later men like Pendergast proved his point. A factor contributing to civic apathy and consequent graft was the large percentage of urban foreign born. These were too ignorant, too lazy, or too busy trying to earn a living, to care who ran the place, and their immense voting power, bought by favors if not by outright purchase, could swing most elections.

Four things—of course the generalization is too rough—have led to the serious weakening today of most of the old-style crooked machines. (1) The steady Americanization of the foreign born. (2) Civil service. (3) The decline in influence of the party system as such. (4) That well-known experiment in socialism, the public schools.

Return to Missouri in general and Kansas City in particular. Actually Kansas City is a clean and well-run town these days; it jumped from being one of the worst cities in America to one of the best. Its mayor, though a Democrat privately, runs as a nonpartisan—it was he who led the revolt against Pendergast—and its administration is in charge of an entirely apolitical city manager, L. P. Cookingham. One former source of corruption was a dishonest state judiciary, since it is usually a combination of city boss plus state patronage that makes a machine work. Missouri put in a new judicial system some years ago, by which district, appellate, and supreme court judges are appointed by the governor on recommendation of an impartial committee, whereupon they must go before the people. Later, as their terms run out, they are obliged to run again on the simple and direct issue of whether or not they shall be retained. This arrangement has, it seems, done a great deal to take the state judiciary out of spoils politics.

Pendergast was a symbol. He had little importance in himself—though it is indubitable that, had he not shoved Harry Truman ahead some years ago, Truman would never have become president. One of the reasons that he liked Truman was, of course, that Truman is one of the most honest men alive; all political machines with shadowy edges like to have men of impeccable character "in front." Thomas J. Pendergast was born in St. Joseph in 1870. He went to St. Mary's College, a small Catholic school, and became a bouncer in a Kansas City saloon run by his elder brother, Jim. This Jim was a satrap of considerable eminence. Tom was bright and ambitious and he soon saw where the big money lay. He ran a liquor business with one hand, and went into politics with the other. By 1900 he was a street commissioner and a councilman. His patron in these days was James A. Reed, then the mayor and later a famous Missouri senator. Pendergast was both burlier and sharper than most of his confreres. He was an operator on a really big scale and he soon squeezed out all the small fry. Mostly he made his "legitimate" money out of a cement business.[7]

Almost all Americans will understand at once what this means; the man from the moon may not. Counties like Jackson and cities like Kansas City do an immense amount of public as well as private building. Pendergast was the boss. Therefore, it well behooved any contractor to see that he bought his cement and concrete exclusively from the boss's companies. The pattern is almost pitiably simple; I will not go into the minutiae. But also "T.J." had other interests—liquor, gambling, prostitution; Kansas City was a brilliantly wide-open town. Mr. Westbrook Pegler once wrote an outraged column describing a "public restaurant in which the waitresses stripped to their high-heeled shoes." Suppose you were a neighborhood saloon keeper. You had to buy your liquor from one of Pendergast's firms, use his cement if you wanted to repair a wall or extend your premises, and pay his lieutenants "protection" if your establishment included vice and gambling. The Pendergast crowd even "put the lug" on the corner policemen. These made $60 dollars a month salary perhaps, 10 per cent of which went to the local ward or precinct "club."

One of the most remarkable sights in America is Brush Creek, the shallow, winding waterway that leads into Kansas City from the west for fifteen miles. Some years ago it was *paved* by Pendergast!

My friend Jay Allen delivered a lecture in Kansas City in the early 1940's, and talked about the collapse of France. Someone in the audience, seeking a pious explanation of this, asked, "But wasn't France frightfully corrupt?" Mr. Allen's reply was, "Am I speaking in Kansas City or am I not!"

On the political side Pendergast throve and proliferated. He was, even more than Hague and Crump, the most powerful American boss of his generation; he controlled politics on the city, county, state, and national level. He had, at one time, no fewer than 60,000 "ghost" votes; the names were taken out of the cemeteries. He never took important public office himself (unlike Hague and Crump) but he was a major behind-the-scenes figure in every Democratic National Convention for a generation. Missouri is a pivotal state presidentially, and "T.J." had Missouri in the calloused hollow of his hand.

I asked people in Kansas City what beat Pendergast. "He got swell." Also he got careless. A wildly extravagant love of racing gripped him,

[7] That Big Tom was originally a bouncer is from the New York *Times*, January 26, 1942.

and for years he was accustomed to bet some $50,000 *per day*[8] on the horses; sometimes he lost, and this cost money. The breakup came in 1939, when the federal income tax authorities went after him; he pleaded guilty to tax evasion, and was sentenced to fifteen months in Leavenworth. He died shortly after being released on parole. The pivot of the affair was a $430,000 bribe he reputedly received from some fire insurance companies for "settlement" of a rate issue. The case has a certain relevance in the kinds of tie-up it adduces. The New York *Herald Tribune*, not a muck-raking organ but one that guards zealously the public interest, wrote as follows:

> This settlement had its genesis in 1929, when the State of Missouri opposed an increase in fire insurance rates by 137 companies, and, pending settlement of the litigation, a United States District Court impounded the rate-increase money. By 1935 this impounded money had amounted to $9,500,000.
> Half of the impounded money went to the companies involved; 30 percent more went into a trust fund for the companies to pay lawyers' fees and expenses—and among the expenses, government agents charged after their investigation, was an item of $430,000 that went to Boss Pendergast for arranging the settlement.
> Under the original settlement of the insurance rate case approved by the Federal court, only 20 percent of the impounded money went back to the policy holders, but shortly after Pendergast's release from prison, a three-judge Federal court in Kansas City ordered $8,000,000 refunded to the policy holders on the ground that the insurance companies could not "enjoy any fruits from the decree procured by fraud." The companies also were ordered to pay interest and costs, estimated at $1,000,000.

We turn now to today. What remains of the Pendergast machine, cleaned up, is run not by T.J.'s son but by his nephew, James M. Pendergast, a lawyer. It sought to "come back" in both 1942 and 1944, but not with great success, and it has comparatively little influence in the city nowadays. However, in 1946, it marshaled all its remaining strength to help Mr. Truman "purge" Representative Roger C. Slaughter, and he was duly beaten by Enos A. Axtell, the Truman candidate. But then in November Axtell himself was beaten by a Republican.

When the city machine began to deliquesce, the Pendergasters put their hope in Jackson County, where they controlled the courthouse. But the 1946 Republican upsurge also knocked them out of this, at least for the time being. Six out of eleven Jackson County seats in the legislature went to the Republicans, and the Pendergast people lost, with one minor exception, all the local jobs that count.

This was part of a national trend of course. The great Democratic

[8] New York *Herald Tribune*, January 26, 1942.

machines in New York, Chicago, and Jersey City took tremendous beatings too; almost everywhere the urban bosses were repudiated. Partly this was a natural swinging of the pendulum; in part it was, as we know, caused by the death of Roosevelt, to whose star Pendergast, Kelly-Nash, and Hague always clung hotly; partly it was because so many women, with their great voting power, were sick and tired of food shortages, standing in line, and OPA. An interesting conjecture is what the Republican party will do with its new city victories. "The proletariat went Republican," I heard it put. Will it stay Republican? Many folk in the Middle West do not, it seems, think that the GOP strength in the congested urban areas is very deeply fixed or based, especially if hard times should come again.

More About Missouri Politics and Similar Confused Topics

To describe what Missouri lives on is easy enough. In the Show Me State we are out of "colonial" territory at last. The banks, both in Kansas City and St. Louis, are powerful, big, and home owned. Missouri is, incidentally, unique in having two federal reserve bank district headquarters; two out of the twelve in the union are in this state. Missouri lives on coal (also home owned) and other minerals, on shoes, flour, brewing, and chemicals (for instance Monsanto in St. Louis), on strongly developed and diversified small industry, on agriculture and cattle and meat packing, on jobbing and distribution in general, and on the railways—both Kansas City (served by twelve major lines) and St. Louis are great railway towns.

Missouri is one of the least predictable of states politically; most electoral races are extremely close, and—like Idaho for instance— Missouri is so representative of stresses and fermentations in the country at large that it has gone the way the country went, on the presidential level, in every election for some forty years. Roosevelt carried it all four times. But it is very touch and go otherwise. Until the elections of November, 1946, one senator was Republican, one Democratic, and of the House delegation seven were Democrats, six Republicans.[9] Though the result is almost always uncertain to the very last minute, the pattern is usually the same. Kansas City runs up a large vote one way, and St. Louis the other; the rural counties swing the balance. These are themselves acutely mixed. "Little Dixie" is as solidly Democratic as South Carolina; the Ozark area is predominantly Republican.

The legislature is dominated by agriculture, the rural districts, and the "county rings." Another lobby is that of the brewers; this is the first time, I believe, that we have come across brewing as an influence.

[9] As of today both senators are Republican, and also nine of the thirteen congressmen.

As I heard it said, "The guy for the St. Louis breweries is always the biggest single guy in the legislature." Also—another first—a powerful lobby is that of the loan companies, which in the good old days blossomed with interest rates as high as 300 per cent a year. The Baptists in the Bible belt play a role, as do the Catholics in St. Louis, and so do the school teachers and the League of Women Voters. The American Legion is not so strong as in adjacent states. Labor has been a comparatively minor force until recently; the war, however, gave a heady boost to industrialization and hence to unionization; in the 1944 campaign, the CIO was the biggest single factor in carrying the state for Roosevelt.[10] Finally, two great newspapers, the Kansas City *Star* and the St. Louis *Post-Dispatch*, are as influential in their special areas as any in the land. Superfinally, one should remember the sometimes neglected factor of the common man himself, the small citizen, the independent voter. A real issue in Missouri has always been politicians versus people. As much as in any state, the unorganized and uninstructed and unpledged individual voter, for all his failings and futilities, is a potent and pervasive force.

Missouri gave itself a new constitution in 1945. Many state constitutions are, as we know, hopelessly outmoded; that Missouri should have gone to the trouble to make a new one is an indication of its gumption. The new document, over which eighty-three delegates spent a year of work, replaces that of 1875. It provides for a considerable number of reforms; for instance seventy former state agencies are now grouped in fifteen executive departments; justices of the peace who lived on their own fees (this immoral characteristic exists almost everywhere in the Middle West) are replaced by salaried magistrates; the state commissioner of education is appointed on a nonpartisan basis; patronage is presumably checked and a merit system in public appointments encouraged. The provision that caused most struggle was one which aimed to cut down the exorbitant fees charged by the loan companies.

Let us, on the state level, mention only one episode in Missouri's opulent record of political scandal. This was the celebrated and somewhat comic attempt to "steal the governorship" after the 1940 election. The *Post-Dispatch* lifted its voice to full thunder, calling it "the most gigantic attempted political steal in the history of the state." A Republican, Forrest C. Donnell, now a senator, won the governorship[11] by a very slim margin, some 3,000 votes. The legislature was Democratic. The St. Louis Democratic bosses met in the conventional "smoke-filled" room (at the De Soto Hotel to be precise) and worked out a scheme

[10] Of the forty-nine international unions in the country eighteen have units in Missouri now. Biggest is the UAW, because of the Ford and Chevrolet assembly factories and the great sprouting of aircraft plants. At one time Pratt & Whitney at South Kansas City employed 22,000 workers.

[11] Not to be confused with Phil Donnelly, the present governor, a Democrat.

whereby they hoped to keep Donnell from being installed. The case, which had highly convoluted aspects, boomeranged and after much delay Donnell was able to take his seat. One explanation of this is that the St. Louis machine got worried halfway through, because the local repercussions were too inflammatory; their attitude became, "To hell with the governorship, if this thing is going to beat us in *town*!" Indeed the affair ended with the expulsion from power in St. Louis of the incumbent bosses. They tried to steal one election, and lost another! This may lead the innocent observer to reflect that, after all, the episode has a proper moral ending. Actually it is not so simple. National eminence and copious rewards have, as it has worked out, come to several of the participants.

No political reporter can visit Kansas City and St. Louis without hearing lively talk about the men whom Mr. Truman has fetched out of the wilds of Missouri into, or near, the White House. The list is impressively long—Hannegan, Symington (the son-in-law of Jimmy Wadsworth incidentally), Vardeman, Snyder (who is very well liked and respected locally), Judge Collet, Vaughan, and Clark Clifford. But here we enter the national field; this book must, unless it is to be a million words long, draw the line somewhere, and Truman and the personalities around him are not our province now. Of course jokes about the Missourians in Washington are without end. The one I like best I heard in St. Louis. Two high Washington officials were having a policy dispute. One said metaphorically, refusing to yield to the other, "Okay, you've made your case, but I don't agree with you—I'm from Missouri." His colleague replied with brisk aplomb, "Tell me anybody who isn't!"

The Two Missouri Queens

What makes cities differ? What makes one somnolent and another gay; what makes one as raw and effervescent as another is sober and sophisticated? Age; geography and history; contrasting types of settlement; relation to the hinterland; demographic variations; also factors mysterious and unanswerable. Kansas City and St. Louis, though in the same state and separated by only a few hundred miles, differ as drastically as any two great cities in the nation.

KANSAS CITY (population metropolitan area 634,093; city limits 399,178) is, or was, a wild buckaroo town, a great railhead for the cattle trade, and "the meanest, most lawless" city in the United States. Among adjectives I have heard for it are compact, dynamic, and obscene. It is also one of the friendliest cities I have ever been in. Above all it is full of restlessness and bounce. ST. LOUIS (population 1,367,977 metropolitan area; 816,048 city limits) is much bigger, calmer, more seasoned, with a wealth more deeply entrenched; it gives a sense of civilization like that of Cincinnati, grave and mature. St. Louis was founded by the French, but coloring it strongly is a very large German-descended population. Also it has intimate Deep South colorations, whereas Kansas City is almost purely western. The emphasis in Kansas City is on raw materials; that of St. Louis on manufacturing and finance. Kansas City faces west; St. Louis faces east and south. One reason why the latter didn't have the cattle market is that the Ozarks cut off the range. Kansas City is essentially Protestant; St. Louis essentially Catholic. Kansas City is the heart of Democratic power in Missouri, St. Louis the heart of Republican. Kansas City is full of boosters and go-getters; St. Louis, with a certain stagnancy, isn't so self-conscious or aggressive—except about its baseball teams when they are winning.[12]

One curious anomaly lies in a point of difference between the Kansas City *Star* and the St. Louis *Post-Dispatch*. The *Star*, once a great crusading paper, was left to its employees by its founder, William Rockhill Nelson; nobody may own a voting share of its stock without being a working member of the staff. The result of this was to make the *Star* progressively more conservative, because, as I heard it put, the editorial employees naturally come to take a front-office view. The *Post-Dispatch*, on the other hand, a Pulitzer property and baronial in management, is probably the most effective liberal newspaper in the United States. This is no country in which to make loose generalizations about the influence of property on politics, or vice versa.

The admirable *Star* reminds me a good deal of my own newspaper, the Chicago *Daily News*, in older days. It resisted comics for a long time; for years it printed line drawings instead of photographs; even today, its headlines are so conservative as to be almost invisible. Nobody, not even the president of the company or Roy A. Roberts, the fabulous managing editor, has an office. Everybody's desk is open and exposed on a vast armorylike floor.

The *Post-Dispatch*, its editors told me, does not play quite such a direct political role as the *Star*. The *Star* really tries to run Kansas City —and run it well—and its influence on eastern Kansas is, as we know, profound. In Kansas City itself it is a monopoly. One item is that the *Star* will accept no liquor advertising because this might damage its prestige and circulation in the Kansan wastes. Mr. Roberts is a potent influence not only in local politics, but in national. The *Post-Dispatch* has considerable national influence too, but in a different way. The East St. Louis hinterland is not Mr. Pulitzer's private colony. The paper leans over backwards, in fact, to avoid direct commitments in local affairs. For instance the owner of the leading St. Louis department store told me that he has never once so much as laid eyes on either of the two senior editors of the *Post-Dispatch*, and he has met Mr. Pulitzer only

[12] St. Louis is one of the five American cities with teams in both major leagues.

once. This is in acute contrast to the habit in most middle western cities where the top publishers and businessmen are usually members of the same clubs, guests at the same parties, and in general close associates. This aloofness on the part of the *P-D* has even led to the legend that "it isn't interested in St. Louis!" Actually, though its temper *is* national rather than purely local, it has largely set the tone of St. Louis for two solid generations.

What appears on the masthead of the *P-D* every day is worth quoting:

> I know that my retirement will make no difference in its cardinal principles; that it will always fight for progress and reform, never tolerate injustice or corruption, always fight demagogues of all parties, never belong to any party, always oppose privileged classes and public plunderers, never lack sympathy with the poor, always remain devoted to the public welfare; never be satisfied with merely printing news; always be drastically independent; never be afraid to attack wrong, whether by predatory plutocracy or predatory poverty.
>
> —Joseph Pulitzer

The record of the paper's citations and crusades is almost endless. It won so many prizes that for a time it withdrew from the Pulitzer competitions. Its cartoonist, Daniel R. Fitzpatrick, is one of the two or three best in the world, and it has one of the most highly developed senses of smell in journalism; at the slightest sniff of graft or scandal, the nostrils of the *P-D* quiver. When it goes after someone, it all but throws the printing presses. Some of its better-known crusades were those over Teapot Dome, smoke abatement, municipal vote frauds, a utilities scandal (it sent the president and vice president of a power company to jail), Pendergast, and, more lately, the tidewater oil affair. It supported Roosevelt three times, and opposed him once.[13] From the beginning, though it has had a large Catholic circulation, it has reported and interpreted the Russian Revolution as intelligently as possible, and for years it has been incisively and copiously anti-Franco, no matter what its Catholic readers may think, and will remain so until Franco is where he belongs, out of office or out of Spain.

Naturally the *Post-Dispatch* makes enemies. One story describes the Negro who, informed by his doctor that he has syphilis, is jubilant at the news. The doctor is much puzzled by this until the Negro explains, "Well, suh, the *Post-Dispatch* has always been against syphilis, so I'm for it."

St. Louis, a real metropolis—once it was the third city in the nation, and even today it is eighth—has a quality rare in America: tolerance. It is a great town for civil liberties, and the intellectual climate is practically all that a civilized person can ask. The city is 13 per cent Negro; yet there are no race riots, and the Negro problem is nowhere near the

---

[13] In 1936. It did not, however, support Landon either.

preoccupation that it is in Kansas City. It is 50 per cent Catholic, but several local Catholics collaborated closely with the PAC during the last presidential campaign. St. Louis is the town where Communists speak on Twelfth Street with police protection, and where the liberal press insists that Gerald L. K. Smith has a perfect right to hold a mass meeting.

The Germans are about half the total population. The telephone book is full of Eberts, Muellers, Vogts, Fritsches, Kolbes; I counted sixty-seven solid columns of names beginning with Sch. The Germans came (as they came to the other river cities) after 1848, a sound folk with an advanced culture; they were largely responsible for keeping Missouri federal in the War Between the States; their impact remains very strong, not so much in politics but in giving the city its interest in education, fine craft work, beer, and the arts. The dominant German was for many years the late Adolphus Busch, who arrived in St. Louis in 1857, married a brewer's daughter named Lilly Anheuser, and organized what became the largest brewery on earth.

St. Louis has two universities, Washington (nonsectarian) and St. Louis (Jesuit); they are friendly rivals rather like Tulane and Loyola in New Orleans. In 1944, by odd and striking chance, a professor in the medical school of each won a Nobel prize. For a long interval we seem to have been in an area where the big cities have only one newspaper. But there are three independent competing papers in St. Louis. The *Globe-Democrat* is a lusty sheet, and the *Star-Times*, an excellent paper, is as liberal as the *Post-Dispatch*, though not so prominent on the national scene.[14]

I like Kansas City too—the red lights atop its skyscrapers at night (St. Louis doesn't have many skyscrapers), its war memorial that looks like a silo, its sense of being a gateway, its progressive social-minded bankers, its flavor of Dallas and Fort Worth in one. Its leading hotel, the Muehlebach, is one of the most satisfying in the nation. Also, despite reforms, it is still a kind of middle western Babylon, the nearest place where Texas and Oklahoma can go on the loose. Experts in these matters tell me, too, that it is the best boogie-woogie town in the United States. I went to one Corybantic bar where, under Pendergast, horsebooks and dice tables flourished, and the croupiers, without even bothering to take off their green aprons and eye visors, went out to lunch and nobody paid attention.

Quite a different atmosphere is that in one of the most peculiar com-

---

[14] One inexplicable point about St. Louis is that the British government considers it one of the four cities in the United States "unhealthy for purposes of leaves of absence." The others are New Orleans, Jacksonville and Savannah. This is completely mystifying. An explanation may be that the reference to St. Louis got in the Foreign Office Handbook forty or fifty years ago, and through oversight has never been removed.

munities in the United States, Kansas City, Kansas. Its main street is called Minnesota Avenue; like almost all Kansas main streets it is straight and enormously broad; also, more than any other American street I ever saw, it connotes the derelict. This whole neighborhood seems ship-wrecked. A good many shops are walled up and most are dreary; within a block are a line of credit shops ($1.00 down on furniture), automobile loan agencies, and three "Unclaimed Freight" stores.

It is almost impossible to tell in some areas where Missouri ends and Kansas begins, or vice versa. Kansas City (Kansas) is so exploited by its ambitious sister that even the streetcars are routed to go through the Missouri retail district. The frontier actually goes down the middle of the livestock exchange, one of the biggest cattle markets in the world; I know nothing like this in America except the remarkable hotel on Lake Tahoe which is partly in California, partly in Nevada, with the line going through the dining room—you can qualify for a divorce on one side, but not on the other.

The right to vote is determined in the two Kansas Cities by residence, and taxation by where you earn your money. So a Missouri executive who lives in the fashionable part of the Kansas sector lives, at best, a double life. He will pay a Missouri income tax on his salary, and a Kansas income tax on whatever other income he may have. The post office disregards state lines. Mail addressed to Kansas City (Missouri) will be delivered without interruption to residents of, say, Johnson County, Kansas.

Nowadays the night clubs and bars in Kansas City (Missouri) do actually stop serving liquor at midnight, on Saturday. So folk in the midst of diversion simply pick up bottles and proceed across the state line into "dry" Kansas, where they may drink unfettered. I visited a fine old pub called the Last Chance on Southwestern Boulevard, very close to the frontier. I am not sure of my notes at this point, but my impression is that, come midnight on Saturday, all you do is move a few inches down the bar, and although there will be no more Missouri liquor, 3.2 per cent Kansas beer begins to flow.

Negro Problem and Education in the Show Me State

Negroes call Missouri a "southern state with northern exposure." It was a slave state in 1860, and laws prohibiting intermarriage between black and white are on the books. Segregation is the rule in schools, theaters, restaurants, and hotels; on the other hand there is no Jim Crow in transportation. Conductors on southbound trains try, however, to persuade Negroes to sit in the same car, to save the trouble of moving them into a Jim Crow coach when the South proper is reached.

In Kansas City I asked friends what the chief local issue was, and it took some time before they were willing to admit that it was the Negro problem. The whites were, by and large, defensive; they didn't like to talk about the subject. Yet there was an obvious fear that Kansas City might, like Detroit, explode into tragic riots. People said that Negroes because of postwar prosperity, with increased earning and spending power, were becoming markedly aggressive; there were rumors (as in New York) of "Thursday night bumping." This is the usual maid's night out, and department stores are open till 9 P.M.; Negroes, on Thursday in particular, were supposed to have developed the habit of bumping into whites on the streets. As it turned out the "bumping nights" were almost as much of a myth as the similar legendary "Eleanor Clubs" in the South.

In Swope Park, one of the biggest municipal parks in the country, the swimming pool and tennis courts are not open to Negroes; one of the two golf courses is. Reports spread thickly last summer that the Negro community, organized into "push clubs," intended to invade the park, jump into the pool forthwith, and play tennis. So seriously were these rumors regarded that the police went out to the area in force, prepared to quell disturbances. Nothing happened—because the Negro community itself had never heard of the "plot."

Negroes are of considerable particularized political importance in Kansas City; for instance the Negro vote was decisive in beating Roger C. Slaughter for renomination in the Fifth Congressional district in 1946.[15] It was not merely Truman and Pendergast leftovers that knocked Slaughter out. What really beat him was the Negroes, as a ward-by-ward analysis of the vote will prove. Why did the unanimous Negro vote turn against Mr. Slaughter? That he was an anti-New Dealer who had done everything possible for a long period to impede and defeat Roosevelt-Truman measures was not all. The thing that counted was that he had vehemently opposed legislation to keep alive the Fair Employment Practices Commission. He is quoted as saying, "I sure as hell opposed the bill for an FEPC, and I'm proud of the fact that my vote killed it."

Kansas City (Missouri) provides, all in all, a glimpse of almost every aspect of the Negro problem—from growing awareness by Negroes of their constitutional rights to growing awareness by whites of what the problem means in terms of conscience as well as legality. One CIO organizer told me, "By God, during the 1944 campaign we had to work with 'em and I even learned to call 'em Negroes instead of niggers myself!" Kansas City (Kansas) across the river presents a sharp contrast to most of this. It is more heavily Negro by a good deal (about 17.4 per cent as against 11.9 per cent for Kansas City, Missouri), but the

[15] See the New York *Herald Tribune*, September 8, 1946, for an analysis of this by Bert Andrews.

Kansans are on the whole more tolerant and the sense of incipient tension is much less.

The most interesting over-all aspect of the Negro issue in Missouri is in education. The situation is moderately complex. The University of Missouri at Columbia refuses (like all southern state universities) to admit Negroes. The University of Kansas at Lawrence, Kansas, does admit them. The University of Kansas City (Missouri) does not admit Negroes, nor does Washington in St. Louis. St. Louis University (Catholic) does. At Jefferson City, some thirty miles from Columbia, is Lincoln, a state university exclusively for Negroes. In 1936 a Negro named Lloyd Gaines, on being graduated from Lincoln, applied for admittance to the University of Missouri law school. He was refused. He thereupon sued the university. The case reached the Supreme Court, which in 1939 made a historic ruling, to the effect that the state of Missouri was obliged to give its citizens, white or Negro, equal educational facilities. But a loophole continued to exist, whereby the state could pay the tuition of a Negro at some institution *outside* the state, instead of admitting him to one of its own white schools; this is the reason why so many Missouri Negroes go to the University of Kansas. But the Gaines case made further action necessary. Missouri was forced to set up a branch of its law school, *for Gaines alone,* in St. Louis!—in order that the campus at Columbia should continue to remain lily white. This must be the only case in history of a school designed for a student body consisting of one person. Gaines, however, did not appear in St. Louis to take up his unique position.

Then a lively young girl named Lucile Bluford, at present on the staff of the Kansas City *Call,* applied for admittance to the University of Missouri school of journalism, which is incidentally one of the best in the nation. The registrar did not recognize her application as being from a Negro, and she was accepted. Then, when the school term opened and she arrived on the campus, she was promptly informed that she could not, of course, be admitted. Miss Bluford renewed her application, was refused, and then sued the university. To evade implications of the suit, the state then set up a separate school of journalism at Lincoln—which still exists—again with the intent of keeping, at all costs, any Negroes from infecting the home campus. This segregated school of journalism had only five or six students to begin with; yet it had to be specially maintained with a staff of teachers and the like. Miss Bluford, however, would not attend the ersatz school. It was set up for undergraduates and she was qualified to be a graduate student. So she applied for admittance to the university's graduate school. Again she was refused. So she filed another suit. Fearing to lose the suit, in which case it would have had to accept her, the university proceeded to abolish (temporarily) its own graduate school of journalism.

Lest this whole episode appear purely incredible, as well as asinine, we should point out again that Missouri is a border state. When we reach the South it will become clearer why such monstrous procedures continue to exist.

Smoke and Railways

Most of the great cities of the Middle West and its periphery have the same problems, in whole new fields that this book has scarcely touched as yet—traction, law and order, slums, water pollution, motor traffic, garbage (believe it or not, the chief issue in the 1945 mayoralty election in Pittsburgh was garbage, no less), honesty in administration, airports, and smoke. Of all American cities, St. Louis has the best record in ameliorating the smoke nuisance; it has, indeed, practically abolished it. Think of Cincinnati or Pittsburgh by contrast!

St. Louis lies close to the great bituminous field in southern Illinois, and coal from this fed its industry for decades. It was, as a result, a city where you had to change your shirt three times a day, and where, literally, it was often impossible to see across the street. There are only two practicable ways to reduce smoke. One is to use more expensive (but more efficient) smokeless coal. The other is to use smoky coal only in conjunction with a stoker or other mechanical contrivance that reduces the amount of smoke produced.

The story of what happened to smoke in St. Louis, in all its detail and interplay, is one of the most interesting in America; if I were a professor of political science I would turn my students loose on it as a classic example of how the public interest, long frustrated, *can* rise on an issue like this, force political action to be taken, and win hands down.

The situation had become intolerable. The *Post-Dispatch*, using its familiar one-two punch technique, opened up with an angry editorial and an even angrier Fitzpatrick cartoon. There had been campaigns to abate the smoke evil before, but they were ineffective. The mayor of the time then set up a new apparatus, in which two men distinguished themselves, James L. Ford Jr., a banker with a strong sense of civic interest, and Raymond R. Tucker, professor of chemical engineering at Washington University. Eventually new ordinances came into effect, which forced the citizenry either to use smokeless coal or, in furnaces not hand-fired, to install devices that take the smoke out of "high volatile" bituminous from Illinois. When St. Louis does see smoke these days, it is largely that which blows over from East St. Louis (Illinois), which curious municipality—one of the most backward in the United States—has persistently refused to co-operate.

The chief interests fighting smoke abatement were of course the bituminous operators in Illinois. They were bitter enough for a time to threaten a boycott. St. Louis responded by threatening a boycott in turn, i.e. to buy nothing but anthracite. The fight was in effect won when a clause was incorporated into the projected ordinance empowering the municipality of St. Louis, if necessary, to go into the coal business on its own. Actually the bituminous operators have not suffered. It was the householders and industrial consumers who had to pay for the installation of smoke-removing stokers. Moreover when a person buys a stoker (average cost, $125) it means as a rule that he will not be tempted to change to oil or gas for some little time.

For the romance of railroads, St. Louis is the first city in the nation. At the Union Station the sleek trains are lined up like race horses in adjoining stalls—the Pennsylvania's Spirit of St. Louis and the New York Central's Knickerbocker to New York, the Baltimore & Ohio's Diplomat to Washington, and all the streamliners: The Rebel (Mobile & Ohio) to New Orleans, the Ann Rutledge (Alton) to Chicago, the Burlington Zephyrs to the Twin Cities, the Colorado Eagle (Missouri Pacific) to Denver, the Green Diamond (Illinois Central) to Chicago, and several to Texas and points south and west.

"No train ever passes through St. Louis." This was a boast once. The Union Station had the largest traffic in the world, because in Chicago, crossing the continent, a traveler had not only to change trains but stations; in St. Louis, only the change of train was necessary.

Many times in Europe I have taken the Orient or the Simplon-Orient Express. With a minimum of fuss, one may traverse the entire continent, from Calais or Paris to Athens or Istanbul, across eight or nine different countries, without once stepping out of the *wagon-lit*. But, until 1946, it was physically impossible for a person to cross the United States, the most acutely transportation-minded of countries, without changing trains. Fruit and cattle could make the trip without transfer, but not a man or woman. This has been modified now, largely as a result of initiative by Robert R. Young of the Chesapeake & Ohio, and a few transcontinental trains have been set up to go through both St. Louis and Chicago without the former long delays profitable only to the hotel and transfer business.

Last Words on MVA

Near St. Louis, as everybody knows, the Mississippi and Missouri meet. It is, oddly enough, somewhat difficult to visit the actual site of the junction. Also St. Louis, more than any other place in the nation, is the home of MVA. This was another *Post-Dispatch* crusade, and its campaign was so effective that the St. Louis Chamber of Commerce, by a majority of 76 out of roughly 1,500 votes, actually came out for MVA. But the issue as a whole moved out of St. Louis and Missouri into national politics, as we know, with results still uncertain. So far as this book is concerned, we take leave now of rivers and river valleys and river authorities for a considerable time to come.

Chapter 23

Chicago *Tribune*, Illinois, and Indiana

〰〰〰〰〰〰〰〰〰〰〰〰〰〰〰〰〰〰〰〰〰〰〰〰〰〰〰〰〰〰〰〰〰〰

Chicago is stupefying . . . an Olympian freak, a fable, an alle-
gory, an incomprehensible phenomenon . . . monstrous, multifarious, unnatural, indomitable, puissant, preposterous, transcendent . . . throw the dictionary at it!

—Julian Street

There is no peace in Chicago. It is a city of terror and light,
untamed.

—W. L. George

WHAT the Chicago *Tribune* reminds me of most is the state of
Texas. We must talk of this newspaper in considerable detail,
because it is impossible to understand America without knowing something about it. The *Tribune* is more than a mere newspaper, more even
than the "World's Greatest Newspaper," as it fondly calls itself; it is a
property in several dimensions, a domain, a kind of principality. Like
Texas, it is aggressive, sensitive in the extreme, loaded with guts and
braggadocio, expansionist, and medieval. Also, like Texas, it has its own
foreign policy—though one very different.

Another thing Colonel McCormick's *Tribune* reminds me of is Soviet
Russia, which it has such a brilliantly good time attacking. It is, like
Russia, big, totalitarian, successful, dominated by one man as of the
moment, suspicious of outsiders, cranky, and with great natural resources
not fully developed; it has a strong nationalist streak, a disciplined body
of workers, a fixed addiction to dogma, hatred of such assorted
phenomena as the idle rich, the British, and crooked bourgeois politics,
and a compelling zest to fight for its own. Colonel McCormick even goes
in for paternalistic reforms. Every *Tribune* employee has his teeth cleaned
free twice a year.

One word on the *Tribune's* sensitiveness. A British author, Hilary St.
George Saunders, visited America during World War II and wrote an
appraisal of what he saw, called *Pioneers! O Pioneers!*[1] The reader is
astonished on page 78 to find that the text breaks off, and does not
resume again till page 85. On each otherwise empty page is a brief note
to the effect that the author's description of his conversations with Mr.
Stoltz, chief editorial writer of the *Tribune*, has been omitted in "defer-
ence to his request . . . backed by the threat of legal proceedings." This

[1] New York, the Macmillan Company, 1944.

359

made me curious enough to get a copy of the English edition of *Pioneers!*
O Pioneers! also published by Macmillan, which is not cut, so that I
might find out what Mr. Leon Stoltz and/or the *Tribune* had objected to.
The affair is still a mystery as far as I am concerned. There is nothing in
the offending passages except mild ironic chitchat about gangsters, German restaurants, and the difference in status between Negroes in Chicago
and those under British imperialism in Africa. The *Tribune* itself is
scarcely mentioned, and Mr. Stoltz himself is not even named.

On November 14, 1945, the *Tribune* printed an editorial about Robert
St. John, war correspondent and radio commentator, under the title
"In Which We Skin a Skunk." It calls Mr. St. John a "deliberate and
contemptible liar," a "pipsqueak" who "persuaded a physic vendor to
buy time for him on the National Broadcasting chain," and who also
"picks up a few stray dollars" lecturing. Actually, St. John is one of the
best paid lecturers in the country, as well as a distinguished and perfectly reputable author. What was his offense? He had asserted in a
lecture that the *Tribune* was trying to foment a war between the United
States and Russia.

Perhaps Mr. St. John's remark was ill-advised. He may have been
misquoted. I do not know. This does not nullify the point—the ferocity
of the *Tribune's* counterattack under criticism. The editorial concluded,
"The National Broadcasting Company, either willfully or because it is
being blackmailed by fellow travellers . . . caters to Communists and has
almost as disreputable a list of speakers as the discredited Blue Network." What did NBC do in the face of this preposterous assertion? So
far as the public or Mr. St. John knows—nothing.

I have heard stories about Colonel McCormick since, it seems, I was
four. I worked in amiable conjunction with Chicago *Tribune* reporters
for years, all over Europe. Among foreign correspondents who, at one
time or other, were *Tribune* men (the character of the list will surprise
many) were Jay Allen, Edmond Taylor, William L. Shirer, George
Seldes, Vincent Sheean. Many of these have gaudy tales to tell of what
"service messages" from the Colonel could be like, as well as personal
reminiscences of vibrant quality. Several too were truncated from the
Tribune in circumstances highly sudden and dramatic.

Colonel Robert Rutherford McCormick, now sixty-seven, is a seigneur
of seigneurs, with a very grand manner indeed. His eccentricities are
famous. Once, welcoming some guests at a picnic on his estate near
Wheaton, he emerged from a moving van—on horseback. The van let
down a ramp, so that the mounted Colonel could prance out and greet
his astounded company.

Once one of his favorite foreign correspondents was peremptorily
summoned to escort him across the Atlantic. The colonel was found
sleeping one evening in the bathtub, because the woodwork in his

bedroom creaked. He had carefully lined the bathtub with a mattress snatched from one of the beds.

McCormick was born in Chicago in 1880. (He believes incidentally that the second *c* in Chicago should be pronounced as an *s*.) The family interrelations are profound and complex; McCormicks of various breeds have been part of Chicago history from the beginning. The colonel's father, Robert Sanderson McCormick, was an American diplomat—a point not widely known—and served as ambassador to France and czarist Russia. Young Robert, who from an early age became afflicted with the nickname Bertie, spent some boyhood years in Europe; perhaps it is not too fanciful to assume that this may have contributed to his perfervid hatred of most things European today. He went to a British public school for a time, and then to Groton and Yale. Another point little known is that he was one class removed at Groton from another American with a partly European background, who made a different use of it, Franklin Delano Roosevelt. Whether McCormick and Roosevelt saw much of one another at Groton is uncertain.

McCormick's brother was Medill McCormick, who was an isolationist senator from Illinois for some years. Their grandfather on the mother's side was Joseph Medill, the first great editor of the *Tribune*. He had two daughters; one married the colonel's father, the other married Robert W. Patterson, Medill's successor as *Tribune* editor. Joseph Medill's will created a trust, the income of which, as it worked out for some years, went equally to Colonel McCormick, his two cousins—Captain Joseph Medill Patterson and Eleanor (Cissy) Patterson (the children of the Patterson named above)—and Mrs. Ruth Hanna McCormick Simms, Medill McCormick's widow. Captain Patterson, as everybody knows, became in time publisher of the New York *Daily News*, and his sister Cissy of the Washington *Times-Herald*. Thus three grandchildren of Joseph Medill became publishers of three of the most powerful, rich, and aggressive newspapers in the United States. This cousinly McCormick-Patterson-Patterson axis is not, however, quite so solid as one commonly thinks; the *Daily News* and the *Times-Herald* print identical editorials and cartoons daily, but the *Tribune* sticks to its own. Patterson, who died in 1946, differed strongly and often from Cousin Bertie. For one thing he had a Socialist past. For another he supported the New Deal ardently until the fight over Lend Lease.[2]

Colonel McCormick is a very tall man, about six feet four, shy, with considerable charm if he wants to exert it, aloof, handsome in a riding-

---

[2] The most complete and fair-minded account of the Colonel I know is contained in two *Saturday Evening Post* articles, July 19 and 26, 1941, by Jack Alexander. They do not discuss one curious and seldom-mentioned fact, that an interest in the *Tribune* was held for many years by William Bross Lloyd, a famous old-line Chicago Socialist.

to-hounds sort of way, and with something of a British accent. The radio critic of the New York *Herald Tribune*, John Crosby, had much innocent fun with him recently, when he listened in to one of his broadcasts, and could not understand until he gathered it from the context who "Colonel George Washton" was.

McCormick, on graduation from Yale in 1903, went into law in Chicago, and then politics; he was an alderman for a time, and from 1905 to 1910 president of the Sanitary District, at which he did a good enough job. During the war, commissioned in the Illinois National Guard, he saw service in France; he is still intensely proud of this military experience. Meantime Robert W. Patterson had died, and the colonel and Joseph M. Patterson inherited the *Tribune*. They ran it together, editing it on alternate months for some time; then in 1925 Patterson went to New York to found the tabloid *News*, and the *Tribune* has been McCormick's exclusive one-man show ever since.

Vast wealth, vast prestige, vast influence have come to him. In 1944 the Colonel, a widower,[3] married a lady recently divorced; various McCormicks—Chauncey, Fowler, and so on—came to the ceremony, and Patterson was best man. In July, 1945, a public dinner was tendered the colonel by the upper Chicago citizenry on the occasion of his sixty-fifth birthday. Among the guests were three representatives of Quebec (the *Tribune* has heavy paper interests in Canada) including the apostolic vicar of the Gulf of St. Lawrence, Mayor Edward J. Kelly, Senator C. Wayland Brooks, its special favorite among senators, and such eminent and retrorsed figures out of the Chicago past as Silas H. Strawn. A congratulatory message came from General MacArthur, and Governor Dwight H. Green of Illinois, another *Tribune* pet, made a speech. The *Tribune* itself covered the event with sober words. "Speakers dwelt upon phases of Colonel McCormick's career as soldier, editor and publisher, and citizen. They weighed the achievements of the colonel and the *Tribune*, the latter now approaching the century mark, wrapped into the history of America as the voice of the midwest."[4]

The colonel's furious Americanism and patriotism, the fact that no matter how much one may disagree with the *Tribune*, "it is for America first last and all the time," which was the theme song of the dinner, make a fascinating and at times perplexing study. Once he disapproved so strongly of an event in Rhode Island that he ordered one of the stars in the *Tribune's* big American flag torn out. Later frightened lawyers told him that mutilation of the flag was an offense, and the colonel, baffled, ordered the Rhode Island star to be sewn in again.

Let us explore further. It is not without interest that Gerald L. K. Smith, who stands against almost everything that most Americans are

---

[3] He gave his first wife a funeral with full military honors.
[4] Chicago *Tribune*, August 1, 1945.

for, once drew up a "Hall of Fame," with the colonel first on the list.[5] Repeatedly during the war—many quotations could be supplied at this point—the German and more particularly the Japanese press and radio praised the *Tribune* warmly. Once the Tokyo radio said, "There is no doubt that Robert McCormick is an extremely charming character. I think America today needs many more characters like this Chicago veteran."

Not long ago I met in Washington a diplomat newly assigned to the United States. He had never seen a copy of the *Tribune* until I showed him one. He glanced at the front page cartoon. His comment after a pause was, "But does the *Tribune* hate the United States?" Indeed the impact of its political cartoons can be startling. Time after time, Uncle Sam is presented as a dupe, a ninny, a sucker, a stooge, a gull, an easy mark. In a hundred cartoons America is portrayed as being swindled by the "international slickers," as the credulous moron-minded victim of vastly clever European cutthroats.

As to *Tribune* cartoons specifically about Europe, they are quite a study too. The one on November 14, 1945, is captioned, THE BRUTISH EMPIRE'S BOMBING OF JAVA.[6] In another Mr. Attlee is presented, flag in hand, addressing a wilted and witless Uncle Sam with the words, "Let's bribe Stalin with your two billion dollar atomic bomb so Russia will let England rule Europe with the five billions you're going to lend us without interest." One on October 2, 1946, entitled "Monument to Stupidity," shows a pedestal marked *German Martyr* and inscribed with the words "Nazi Criminal Convicted by a Biased Court Composed of Germany's Enemies in an Illegally Conducted Trial, Upon Unlawful Evidence Illicitly Procured." This was the *Tribune's* comment on—the Nuremberg trials and verdict!

The headlines are sometimes startling too. On March 3, 1945, the banner head, in enormous type, was KILLS WOMAN, BURNS BODY. The second head, much smaller, was "Report Yanks Cross Rhine; Nazis Flee Before 9th Army."

Tribune editorials, the heart of the paper, are hard hitting and they name names: a recent one pungently took to task one of the greatest of American corporations, the wealth of which derives from the Middle

[5] Others: Father Coughlin, Gerald Winrod, Joseph M. Patterson and Eleanor Patterson, Martin Dies, Charles A. Lindbergh, Hearst, the editors of the Brooklyn *Tablet*, and Father Edward L. Curran of Brooklyn. Whether or not the colonel was pleased by being associated with everybody on this list is not known. *Time,* May 25, 1942. One honorable thing about the *Tribune* should be mentioned: it has never been anti-Semitic. One or two of the folk named above are, as is notorious, ferocious anti-Semites. The *Tribune* has never been touched with this taint. Indeed for many years several of its most powerful executives were of Jewish origin.

[6] But the *Tribune's* Anglophobia does not keep it from occasionally printing dispatches from Reuter's, the official British news agency.

West but which maintains its executive offices in New York. Also they can distort issues with a cunning that can only be described as masterful, and with nonsequiturs of astounding range. One *Tribune* judgment is that "the line from Roosevelt to Bilbo . . . is plain," in that FDR, "while posing as the great friend of the Negroes to win their votes, was seeing to it that their most virulent enemy was getting a bribe." Often the *Tribune* bows in the direction of New York:

> Under the pretense of air raid precaution, a dictatorship has been established in New York City such as never has been dreamed of on this continent. Fiorello La Guardia has recruited a political force of 235,000 air raid wardens. There is no legal curb on the conduct of the wardens in pushing the citizenry around or insulting and molesting women . . . New York is now almost . . . completely under the tyrant's heel.

Once an editorial praised the British dominions for knowing more of liberty than England itself, except New Zealand "where liberty has been overthrown by Fascism (!) and enormous graft." The comment on Russia's entrance into the war against Japan ended with the paragraph, "Surely no one can find the slightest parallel between Stalin's announcement and Mussolini's attack on France after the fall of Paris." A few months later the paper was writing, "Conditions are so bad in Germany that our troops probably will soon be shooting hostages and then every ideal of the American Republic will go overboard."

About imperialism in any form, the *Tribune* can turn cogent phrases:

> The Japanese are being used in Indo-China to help the British Indian troops kill the revolutionary natives until the French, now enjoying the privilege of stretching their legs out of German clutches and shooting their own people, can get back in force to say whose land Indo-China is.

On one occasion the *Tribune* admitted grudgingly that the only positive accomplishment of the UN so far is the replacement of the old mandate system by trusteeships. But, it goes on, "the change is in name only, not in actuality," and colonial exploitation still goes on. Then comes the remarkable conclusion:

> It was for this that the fleet at Pearl Harbor was betrayed; that the garrison on Bataan was left to its fate; that a quarter of a million American boys were killed; that this nation was brought to the edge of bankruptcy. And it is for this that more than half a million of our young men have been snatched from school and productive work to learn immorality in garrisons overseas.

Tribune news columns can make fancy reading too. A recent dispatch from Paris, after the French Communists received a temporary setback, quotes an anonymous Quai d'Orsay diplomat with the words, "If the communists had won a clear-cut majority, you Anglo-Saxons would have had no bridgehead on the continent in about 1964 in which to come to grips with the Red Army."

Often the *Tribune* slants its news stories. The best extant handbook on Washington journalism, that by Leo C. Rosten, records that it is second only to Hearst as "the least fair and reliable" newspaper in the country, in the view of Washington correspondents themselves. The Chicago *Times* once offered the *Tribune* a $5,000 reward for proof of "facts" in a story about American Communists and Roosevelt. It was never collected.[7]

Milton Mayer of the University of Chicago, writing in *Common Sense*, tells how the *Tribune* consistently put phrases like "so-called" before the names of government agencies, to discredit them, even when this meant tampering with AP copy. For instance the NLRB was referred to as the "so-called National Labor Relations Board." Let Mr. Mayer proceed:

> Now the *Tribune* did this not only with its own . . . dispatches but also with AP stories . . . I collected a bunch of AP stories so distorted in the *Tribune* and sent them on to Kent Cooper, the AP general manager. Mr. Cooper wrote me that the complaint had been referred to the member paper and that I would hear from him, Mr. Cooper, as soon as the member had replied. Of course I never heard from Mr. Cooper, but I did get a letter, obviously written so that a carbon copy could be sent to Mr. Cooper, from Bob Lee, the managing editor of the *Tribune*. Mr. Lee's letter said that this "mistake" had been traced to a new copy-reader on the paper, who had inserted the expression as his own idea.

The colonel's own writings and radio addresses, under his own signature, make lively reading. By sending a dollar to the *Tribune*, anybody can get a compilation of seven McCormick lectures on "The American Revolution and Its Influence on World Civilization." This brochure and another like it state the most extreme faddist type of isolationist-imperialist chauvinism. They have passages of good sense, given the premises, together with an almost deformed bravado and capriciousness. One of the colonel's points is that a "British monarchical faction" exists in the United States which was given great impetus by the marriage of wealthy American heiresses to impoverished British peers. "Heiresses brought from America . . . would bring money into the country [England] without introducing any unpleasant social and political repercussions," such as would happen if the British "impecunii" [of the ruling class] broke their own caste barriers by marrying *British*

[7] *Time*, December 1, 1941.

women. The colonel calculates the British gain from these emotional precursors of Lend Lease as 15 billion dollars. In the middle of the argument comes a paragraph that I have read a dozen times, and which I am not yet sure I understand:

> About the middle of this corruption, the infamous Cecil Rhodes conceived the plan to give free education to Americans in Oxford and make them into English cells, boring from within. He builded better than he knew. Thinking that there were still only 13 states, he provided a scholarship for each state. In consequence he has trained four times as many agents as he planned for.[8]

But to return to the unwavering magnificence of the colonel's Americanism. He said recently, "All of the important land and naval victories [in the Pacific war] were American victories. All the distinguished admirals and generals in this war are Americans." It appears further that the good colonel considers that he himself has something to do with these victories. The *Atlantic Monthly* printed in June, 1942, a letter he wrote to a Chicago citizen:[9]

> You do not know it, but the fact is that I introduced the R.O.T.C. into the schools; that I introduced machine guns into the army; that I introduced mechanization; I introduced automatic rifles; I was the first ground officer to go up in the air and observe artillery fire. Now I have succeeded in making that the regular practice in the army. I was the first to advocate an alliance with Canada. I forced the acquiring of the bases in the Atlantic Ocean.
>
> On the other hand I was unsuccessful in obtaining the fortification of Guam; in preventing the division of the navy into two oceans. I was unable to persuade the navy and the administration that airplanes could destroy battleships.
>
> I did get the marines out of Shanghai, but was unsuccessful in trying to get the army out of the Philippines.
>
> Campaigns such as I have carried on inevitably meet resistance, and great persistence is necessary to achieve results. The opposition resorts to such tactics as charging me with hatred and so forth, but in view of the accomplishment I can bear up under it.

On December 4, 1941, the *Tribune* printed a dispatch from Washington which revealed in explicit detail the war plans of the American general staff in the event that we were attacked. The *Tribune* prides itself greatly on being a *news*paper. It likes scoops—of course. But

---

[8] From an address broadcast over WGN and the Mutual Broadcasting System, May 5, 1945.

[9] From "Chicago Patriot," by Robert Lasch. Mr. Lasch makes well the points that the *Tribune*, though advocating victory of course, always portrayed the war as senseless and idiotic, and that the Colonel "supported the war, but fought anything which might give it meaning."

that it should have printed a scoop such as this seemed to imply that its journalistic fervor—and implacable hatred of Roosevelt—outran its patriotism. Something of the same sort occurred on June 7, 1942, when the *Tribune* (also the New York *Daily News* and the Washington *Times-Herald*) printed what appeared to be complete details of the disposition and strength of the Japanese fleet in the Battle of Midway. This, it then seemed, might well imperil the whole course of the Pacific war, since it would indicate to the Japanese that the American Navy had broken their code. The Japanese, however, never caught the full implications of the story. A vast commotion was caused in Washington, however. The Bureau of Censorship cited the *Tribune* for breaking the censorship code (but later withdrew its charge), and the Navy, furious, insisted on a grand jury investigation to determine if the Espionage Act had been violated. The Department of Justice put the FBI to work and appointed William D. Mitchell (who had been Hoover's attorney general) to take charge of the case; this was presumably to forestall any charges of animus that might have come if a New Dealer had been named prosecutor. A federal grand jury did in fact meet in Chicago.[10] The colonel was triumphantly cleared! Meantime the Navy decided that the best thing to do was let the matter rest. It should also be stated that, according to general belief, the *Tribune* regretted having printed this story, and McCormick himself has said that it would never have got into the paper if he had seen it first.

The December 4, 1941 leak was alluded to by Mr. Stimson in his statement on Pearl Harbor of March 22, 1946. The language of the former secretary of war is so remarkable that it should be quoted:

> Our General Staff officers were working under a terrific pressure in the face of a global war which they felt was probably imminent. Yet they were surrounded, outside of their offices and almost throughout the country, by a spirit of isolationism and disbelief in danger which now seems incredible. A single incident gives striking evidence of this.
>
> During the very last week before the Pearl Harbor attack there was made a most disloyal and almost unbelievable attack on the chief work of the Staff. For months the General Staff had been laboring over the construction of a strategic and tactical plan for the fighting of a global war in case it should eventuate.
>
> The making of such a plan is the highest and most important duty of a General Staff—the chief purpose for which it exists. It is also naturally the most highly secret paper in the possession of the government. On December 4, 1941, the Chicago *Tribune* published practically in full a copy of that plan.
>
> The impact of such a blow was very severe. It involved implica-

---

[10] See Charles A. Michie in *PM*, September 9, 1945, and an article in *Harper's Magazine*, October, 1944, by John Bartlow Martin.

tions which stretched far and suspicions (happily not fulfilled) of disloyalty in the Army itself.

Next to the New York *Daily News*, which leads the whole field, the *Tribune* has the largest daily circulation of any newspaper in America, and it is the biggest non-tabloid by far. Its circulation is over a million daily, half inside Chicago itself and half out, and on Sunday about a million and a half.[11] Pick up a copy of the *Tribune*. Cartoons and editorials aside, what will you find? It is well put together on good paper, expertly written, and legibly made up. It has, and has had for decades, features that are indissolubly tied up with the life of Chicago, from the Line o'Type or Two founded by the greatest of all personal columnists, B.L.T., to the Voice of the People, the How to Keep Well column, the advice to the lovelorn of Doris Blake, the beauty department of Antoinette Donnelly. Its financial and sporting pages are edited with great elan—its sports department is one of the best in the country—and, above all, thanks in part to the prescience of Captain Patterson, its comics are extremely strong. Some are, in fact, such formidably valuable properties that the colonel will not allow their syndication anywhere in the Chicago area. This means five states, what he calls "Chicagoland." For these comics you must buy the *Tribune* itself, or do without.

Finally, a word on the *Tribune's* direct and immediate local political influence. There is a simple way to state this, namely that it is profound. A great many Chicagoans despise the *Tribune*. But they buy it every day. Many loathe almost everything it says editorially, and it is one of the few American papers ever to have been burned in the streets. But its circulation steadily goes up, not down. Graham Hutton, in his *Midwest at Noon*, makes play with a conceit and in his whole book never once mentions the *Tribune*; I understand very well the reason for this, but I think it gives a false impression. To write about the Middle West and leave the *Tribune* out is like playing *Hamlet* not only without the prince of Denmark but without Polonius. The governor of Illinois and one Illinois senator are *Tribune* friends. It is commonly said that it "cannot elect a mayor," and Kelly is of course a Democrat, the product of a Democratic machine in a Democratic city in a Democratic era; nevertheless, Kelly and the *Tribune* get along. In fact he and McCormick have been warm friends for years; the colonel once saved his job when he was a young engineer in the Sanitary (= sewage) District. Moreover when the *Tribune* sets out to beat anybody, its enmity can be crushing, although it does not always win.

[11] A British reader, accustomed to the huge London circulations—*Daily Express* 3,000,000, *Daily Mail* 1,700,000, *News Chronicle* 1,425,000, to say nothing of *News of the World* 4,000,000—may find these figures small. But by American standards they are very large indeed. For instance the circulation of the New York *Times* (daily) is only 551,699, the New York *Herald Tribune* 338,667. That of the New York *Daily News* is 2,176,903.

I am not sure where, but I think in an article by Joseph Wood Krutch in the *Nation* some years ago, I read a revealing passage to the effect that a great many writers, even though they have never actually read Marcel Proust, have been strongly influenced by him. The same thing is true of the Chicago citizenry and the *Tribune*. Even if you don't actually read it, you feel its permeating influence. Its potency is subcutaneous. Another point is that it would be a grave error to assume that the *Tribune* "creates" the various moods it describes. It certainly can build up a case for or against anything or anybody, and it most deliberately seeks, by every possible means, to mold opinion. Nevertheless it also *reflects* a prevailing Chicago and Middle West sentiment and mythology, which greatly augments its power.

The colonel, as a person in his own right and not merely as publisher of the *Tribune*, has been more active politically in the past few years than ever before. His interests go far beyond Chicagoland. For instance, a minor point, he recently gave a $5,000 contribution to the campaign fund of Senator Bushfield of South Dakota.[12] McCormick hopes to play a great and intimate role in the 1948 Republican race. Repeatedly he describes why Stassen and Vandenberg and even Dewey are impossible as candidates. Taft he appears to like. His word on all these matters should be watched. Illinois has a big vote in the Republican national convention and Colonel McCormick is official leader of the party in Illinois.

Chicago and Illinois: Things in General

Chicago . . . a mushroom and a suburb of Warsaw.

—Arnold Bennett

Great injustice is done to Chicago by those who represent it as wholly given over to the worship of Mammon, as it compares favorably with many American cities in the efforts it has made to beautify itself.

—Baedeker in 1893

Hog-Butcher for the world
Tool-maker, Stacker of Wheat,
Player with Railroads . . .
City of the Big Shoulders.

—Carl Sandburg

Having seen it (Chicago) I urgently desire never to see it again. It is inhabited by savages. Its air is dirt.

—Rudyard Kipling

About Chicago itself there is so much to be said that the task of compression becomes hopeless. This is the greatest and most typically

[12] Other contributions to the campaign of this notable citizen were $8,000 from the Pennsylvania Pews, $9,000 from the Mellon family, $4,000 from Lammot Du Pont, and $2,500 from Alfred Sloan. *New Republic*, April 2, 1945.

American of all cities. New York is bigger and more spectacular and can outmatch it in other superlatives, but it is a "world" city, more European in some respects than American. Chicago has, as a matter of fact, just as many foreign-born as New York, but its impact is overwhelmingly that of the United States, and it gives above all the sense that America and the Middle West are beating upon it from all sides.

Being a Chicagoan born and bred I can recall much. The city has the most intense vitality and energy of any I have ever lived in. The icy wind screaming down snow-clogged boulevards; the sunny haunch of Lincoln Park near the yacht moorings in torrid summers; the automobilelike horns on the Illinois Central suburban trains; the steady lift of bridges, bridges, bridges; holes and bumps and mountains and earthquakes and yawning pits in the streets; the piercing whistles of angry traffic cops; the marvelous smooth lift of the Palmolive Building and how the automobiles seem to butt each other forward like long streams of beetles; the tremendous heavy trains of the North Shore whipping like iron snakes through the quivering wooden suburban stations; the acrid animal smell from the stockyards when the wind blew that way, and the red flush of the steel mills in black skies—all this is easy to remember.

It is above all the span of Chicago—in space, in time, in people, in variety of experience—that is so striking. This city has produced or made famous folk in a gamut from Jane Addams, the founder of Hull House, to Big Bill Thompson, who was going to paste King George V on the snoot; from Louis Sullivan, one of the fathers of modern architecture, to the Everleigh sisters, who operated the most distinguished bordello in the world; from great liberal prelates like the late Cardinal Mundelein to profiteers like the late Samuel Insull; from philanthropists like Charles R. Crane to good public servants like Carter Harrison to merchants like Levi Z. Leiter who became the father-in-law of the Marquess of Curzon to singers like Mary Garden to criminals like Dean O'Banion and Al Capone. (Nor are we through with Chicago names.)

Chicago, with a population of 3,396,808 in 1940 (metropolitan limits 4,449,126), is the second largest city in the United States and the fourth largest in the world; its area will, according to careful estimates, hold 6,200,000 people by 1960. It contains a number of veritable small towns within its own interior, and its expanding suburbs, like Evanston and Winnetka, which will dislike being called suburbs, are models of their kind. Chicago is not compressed into a designated mold, like New York, by rivers. In fact it has spread out to become a kind of state, including parts of Wisconsin, Indiana, and even Michigan. Everything from Racine to La Porte is really Chicago.

This goliath of the corn-fed plains has various magnitudes and curiosities. Bigness itself is not a notable characteristic. Hercules was big, but a fool. Chicago is not a fool. It is of course the greatest railway center in the world, the greatest meat-packing center—and meat packing is the third biggest American industry—and the greatest convention city. No fewer than nineteen times have either the Republicans or Democratic parties chosen Chicago for their conventions. It is the home of the greatest printing press in the world; among other things this prints the *Encyclopaedia Britannica* and most of the telephone books of the nation. Its budget for the current year is $237,458,637, which is more than those of Mexico, Chile, and Colombia combined, with 30 million people. Its harbor handles almost as much traffic as the Panama Canal, and it must be the only city in the world that has made its river run backward, by means of the celebrated Drainage Canal, so that the flow of sewage will not run into Lake Michigan.

The motto of Chicago is "I Will." A brief bibliography of the city takes sixty-nine closely printed pages, and it is the headquarters of the Council of State Governments, the Governors' Conference, the American Medical Association, Rotary, and the American Library Association. Its principal internal problem has always been traction. The elevated lines and streetcar system have been bankrupt for years. It is staggeringly tax-delinquent, and its standard of public morality, amid all the grandiose development, is such that for a notorious long interval it did not even have the money to pay its schoolteachers. Predominantly it is a foreman's town and strongly AFL; everybody in the CIO is likely to be called a Communist. It has vistas of the most sublime magnificence and also the worst slums I have ever seen, not excluding those of Glasgow, Istanbul, and Lodz.

The age of the dinosaurs has mostly passed. The new dinosaurs are well brought up and watch their manners carefully. What a gallery the Chicago titans make! The line stretches from the first Marshall Field, in a descending arc, to Wrigleys (chewing gum) and Hertzes (taxicabs). Most of the early builders were invaders from the East, as indeed they had to be. George M. Pullman was born in Chautauqua County, New York, and Gustavus Swift in Cape Cod, Massachusetts; the first great Armour came from rural New York, Potter Palmer from New York, Nelson Morris from Germany, and the incomparable Field himself from Conway, Massachusetts.[13] The Chicago gentry never knew who—or what—was coming next. No place but Chicago could have produced a character quite like Mrs. Rockefeller McCormick. Society was an extremely explosive thing. Also the Chicago hierarchy was laced and whipped together by an extraordinary series of marriages. Not only did McCormicks marry Rockefellers but Pattersons married Higinbothams and Fields married Spragues, while Stillmans, Deerings,

---

[13] Which is the present home of Archibald MacLeish, who was born in a Chicago suburb. The patterns of migration change.

Guggenheims, Phippses, Fairbankses, Carpenters, MacVeighs became intermixed in the social pool.[14]

Despite all this, Chicago has never lost a certain roseate naïveté. When General Charles G. Dawes reached the age of eighty some time ago, the newspapers roared their delight once again in recalling that he had refused to wear knee pants at the Court of St. James's, and had hired a comedian pretending to be a trick waiter to entertain guests in the London Embassy.

Recently I asked an eminent Chicagoan what ran the city, and he answered "State Street and the Irish." The great merchants in the Loop (the downtown area still bound by anachronistic elevated tracks) have great influence, together with their allies such as the packers. It is extremely typical of Chicago, incidentally, that Marshall Field's is called "The Cathedral of the Stores." What the State Street oligarchy tries to stand for is civic and social leadership. The tycoons live in subdued beautiful estates along the Lake Shore or on the "Gold Coast" in town; it is they who sponsor such manifestations of civic energy as the Chicago Planning Commission and the like; their impregnable inner citadel is the Commercial Club. The Irish meantime, the most articulate of the great immigrant bodies that grew up under the layer of oligarchs, allied with other racial groups, run the city politically. There is a kind of unspoken, unwritten deal. "We let the Irish have the government, if they let us do what we please," is one way I heard it put.

Politics per se need not detain us long. Merit in this country is chosen by popular vote, which means, in most of the great machine-run cities, that the voters seldom get it. Politics in the United States is a profession out of which most politicians expect to make money. The historic days of the Chicago party bosses are, however, over—though there are still some precincts where the total vote may exceed the total registration. Hinky Dink Kenna is dead, Bathhouse John Coughlin is dead, Pat Nash, the sewer contractor, is dead, and Ed Kelly himself is in the background. The 1947 mayoralty race was between new candidates virtually unknown.

The basic pattern in Chicago follows roughly that which we have just explored in Kansas City; there were hoodlums, filchers, footpads, hatchet men, caitiffs, and gorillas. Hinky Dink, a saloon keeper, left a fortune of $1,003,535, of which $426,770 was in cash. Not long ago a man who had been Cook County clerk for twenty-four years, a leading Catholic layman and seemingly a sound citizen of German descent, was found $414,129 short in his official accounts. Tried by a criminal court jury, he was acquitted. When Special Prosecutor Frank J. Loesch started his investigation of City Hall payrolls, he found that 16 out of

[14] For family backgrounds, see Wayne Andrews, *Battle for Chicago*.

every 100 names were fictitious; in one office, 75 per cent were "fraudulent or irregular."[15]

The Kelly-Nash machine goes deep into Chicago roots. It came out of the Roger Sullivan–George Brennan–Tony Cermak organizations. Its basis of operation was the fifty Chicago wards. Over each, the party committeeman, depending on what party was in power, was absolute dictator. Kelly himself, mayor for almost fourteen years, was considerably superior to his fellows. One thing that might well be mentioned was his superb record of hospitality to servicemen during the war. Every GI who went through Chicago, eleven million in all, had to change trains, and Kelly and Chicago took good care of them. Another thing worth mention is that Mr. Kelly once had to pay the United States Treasury $105,000, as settlement for having forgotten to pay taxes on $450,000 "earned" between 1926 and 1928, when his job was that of a Sanitary District engineer at $15,000 a year.

Perhaps I should, at this point, include briefly something about the other Chicago newspapers; lusty journalism exists in the Windy City outside the *Tribune* tower. There are five in all, and competition among them can be agitated. The *Daily News*, after its Lawson era, its Strong era, its Knox era, is owned by John S. Knight, publisher too of powerful papers in Miami, Akron, and Detroit. Knight doesn't believe in inheriting feuds, and one of his first acts as publisher of the *News* was to drop the "Colonel McCosmic" cartoons with which Colonel Knox was wont to heckle McCormick.[16] The *Times*, edited by Richard J. Finnegan, is a vivid and effective tabloid, that deserves more of a national reputation than it has. The *Herald-American*, the Hearst paper, is a cut above other Hearst papers. The *Sun* of Marshall Field III, which entered the picture in 1941, is a whole long story in itself. The *Tribune* had had no morning competition for many years; thirteen different rivals had died or been killed off, and for the *Sun* to beard it in its chosen morning field was a gallant enterprise. The *Tribune* sneered at the *Sun*, grunted at it, snarled at it, but could not keep it down. I have often wondered what would have happened if Field's, the store, had refused to give advertising to the *Tribune*, or if the *Tribune* had boycotted Field's. But the rivalry, bitterly intense as it was, expressed itself only in journalistic and political terms, not in commerce. Field's as such has no financial interest in the *Sun*.

For a brief giddy period Chicago was the "literary capital" of the

[15] "The Plunder of Chicago," by Walter W. Liggett, *American Mercury*, March, 1932.
[16] Knox and McCormick, the two rival colonels, were not on speaking terms. McCormick resented it fiercely when Knox, a Republican and a former candidate for vice president, became Roosevelt's secretary of the navy. McCormick and his present rival, Marshall Field, meet occasionally in mixed groups. I am told that they bow but do not shake hands.

United States. There were several factors in this. Harriet Monroe edited *Poetry* in Chicago, and Margaret Anderson edited the *Little Review*; the University of Chicago turned out writers as various and distinguished as Glenway Wescott, Elizabeth Madox Roberts, and James T. Farrell; in addition an older Chicago "school" existed, going back to William Vaughan Moody and Robert Herrick. Also Chicago was rich in writers not particularly associated with any single institution, like Sherwood Anderson, Vachel Lindsay, Edgar Lee Masters, and Vincent Starrett. Burton Rascoe was for some years the coruscating literary editor of the *Tribune*, and the old *Evening Post* had an imposing succession of literary editors, including Henry B. Fuller, Francis Hackett, and Floyd Dell. Ring Lardner was a sports writer on the *Tribune*. But incomparably the chief incubator of Chicago talent for many years was the Chicago *Daily News*.[17]

The list of writers who, at more or less the same time, worked on this great newspaper, under the beneficent guidance of Henry Justin Smith, is indeed extraordinary; it includes Ben Hecht, Carl Sandburg (who was the movie editor), Keith Preston, Howard Vincent O'Brien, Meyer Levin, Sterling North, Lloyd Lewis, and Harry Hansen. Consider too its foreign correspondents, some of whom served it faithfully for many years—Robert J. Casey, the Mowrer brothers, Junius B. Wood, Leland Stowe, the late John T. Whitaker, Raymond Swing, Negley Farson, William H. Stoneman, M. W. Fodor, A. T. Steele, the late Hiram Motherwell, Carroll Binder, Wallace R. Deuel, Helen Kirkpatrick, and Hal O'Flaherty. No newspaper in the United States, or in the world for that matter, can come anywhere near this record. I remember with pleasant nostalgia a day when Mr. Smith was happy. Fourteen Chicago *Daily News* authors and foreign correspondents were having books published in one season!

Finally, a word on affairs downstate, in other words on agriculture. Illinois is the second corn state in the union, and a very large producer of other agrarian products. Also it is the third industrial state, third in coal, second in railway mileage, and surprisingly enough, sixth in oil. The intensely flat greenness of Illinois—it is so level that a railroad once built a hundred miles of track without having to move an inch of dirt—also has some interesting cities, like Peoria, one of the toughest towns on earth. Readers who fail to grasp some of the bignesses of the Middle West may be reminded that the Illinois River at Peoria is wider than the Danube at Budapest.[18] The volume of this river is as nothing, however, to what Peoria turns out in liquor. It is one of the great

---

[17] Ernest Hemingway was born in Oak Park, a Chicago suburb, and John Dos Passos in Chicago itself, but neither is customarily thought of as a "Chicago" writer.
[18] Cf. Hutton, *op. cit.*

whisky-producing cities of the world. Consider also Rockford, where the late Mrs. Ruth Hanna McCormick Simms, who combined two great Republican dynasties in her person, was a leading citizen; Bloomington with a famous newspaper, the *Pantagraph*; Elgin (watches), Springfield (Abraham Lincoln), East St. Louis (already alluded to) and Urbana (University of Illinois).

The chief political issue on a statewide basis is redistricting. Cook County and the Chicago area is overwhelmingly Democratic and rural Illinois is just as overwhelmingly Republican. So the average politician tries to straddle; a campaign becomes an exercise in catch-as-catch can. The state has not been redistricted since 1901, though the constitution says that this shall be done every ten years, with the result that the rural counties have grossly disproportionate political power. Cook County has a shade over 50 per cent of the population of the state, and pays 53 per cent of its taxes, but it is allowed only ten congressmen out of twenty-six. So, in voting power, a Chicagoan is only about 75 per cent a citizen. This has led in turn to prodigious corruption, since the system is unworkable as it stands, and the only way Chicago can operate in the legislature at all is to try to buy it.

University of Chicago

A university is a community of scholars. It is not a kindergarten; it is not a club; it is not a reform school; it is not a political party; it is not an agency of propaganda. A university is a community of scholars.

The greatest university is that in which the largest proportion of these scholars are most competent in their chosen fields.

A college teaches; a university both teaches and learns.

—Robert M. Hutchins

Some day I would like to take a year off, return to Chicago, and write a book about the University of Chicago, which by any reckoning is one of the three or four most outstanding in the world. In doing so I would have considerable fun in trying to analyze the character of its chancellor, Robert Maynard Hutchins, a man sensitive, often wrongheaded, stubborn, with as bright a mind as ever you met, and one who will talk back to God, Mammon, or the devil. Hutchins is so much an egotist that it is sometimes difficult for him to be a participant. He boils with vision, likes idiosyncrasy, and is absolutely fearless, honest, and independent. Once I heard him described as a "cosmic mountaineer." He has a curious juvenile streak which makes him like to affront dull people and say things he doesn't really mean. He can charm moneybags out of any millionaire, and argue with any professor until the cows come home.

The University of Chicago was founded in 1890, and grew as a result of the impingement of three forces—a Baptist organization which contributed the idea; John D. Rockefeller who contributed the money; and the first president, William Rainey Harper, a Greek scholar out of Yale and one of the foremost educationalists of his or any time, who contributed almost everything else. Many years ago, when I was an undergraduate, I wrote for the old *Smart Set* an article describing the University of Chicago, in which I tried to make clear Harper's original ideas:

> Harper implied at the outset that his university would be like no other ever witnessed by the eyes of man. He announced, first of all, that it would be primarily a graduate school. At this time, it is important to note, there were only two genuine graduate schools in the country. . . . Further than this, the University of Chicago would abolish the old system of four classes, and establish instead two colleges, Junior and Senior, and the Junior would, if possible, be later eliminated. Harper did not stop here. He demanded the most complete possible co-education; a system of exchange professorships; a system of extension work by which lectures under the auspices of the University would be given all over the Middle West; the foundation of a complete university press, not only to take care of official publications, but to nurse a troupe of scholastic journals and books; an extensive correspondence school system; and the establishment of a downtown college to take care of part-time students.

Hutchins, it will clearly be seen from this, built on the Harper foundation. Various explosive innovations and developments have taken place since 1929, when he became the university's fifth president at the age of thirty. Not all of his reforms have stayed put. In essence, his belief was that every "student should obtain a liberal education before being permitted to specialize." He encouraged by such devices as the courses in "Great Books" a broad basis in the humanities; at the same time he did much to speed up the curricula, so that education for the professions could get promptly under way when the time was right. As was said of him once, what Hutchins wanted was "more educated A.B.'s and fewer uneducated Ph.D.'s."[19] He even looked forward, as someone else put it, to the time when Ph.D.'s would really be doctors of philosophy. He hated "uneducated specialists." What interested him was not vocational education, but an irreplaceable substratum of ideas. This is not to say that he was old-fashioned. The University of Chicago, with its interlockings into broadcasting and the *Encyclopaedia Britannica,* is as modern as a dynamo. Hutchins worked out a scheme whereby a high school graduate could enter college when fit to do so, not after a stipulated period; he gave bachelor's degrees after two years of study

[19] *Life,* July 16, 1945.

if the student was good enough; he waived old-style regulations in regard to class attendance and examinations.

Hutchins, whose father was also a university president, was dean of the Yale Law School at twenty-eight. Here his regime was iconoclastic too. It was largely the perspicacity of Harold H. Swift, a contemporary luminary of the packing family, that brought him to Chicago. Mr. Swift once told me the story of how he found him; the major problem was to persuade the other trustees that a boy of thirty should be given such a job. What eventually won the trustees was not young Mr. Hutchins' brashness, but his poise and dignity. Later his more intellectual qualities became manifest; the fact that he believed above all in the rational approach, that he was a firm moralist, that he didn't believe that man was purely an economic animal. Some of his proposals aroused fierce enmity. He abolished football—brave man!—and once suggested the abolition of rank among professors, so that each would be equally "a member of the faculty of the University of Chicago," no more, no less.[20] Above all he sought to keep the university young. He himself stepped out as president in 1945, to become chancellor, and he noted with satisfaction that in the administration then set up, of the six top men, only two had passed the age of 45.

Various brushes in and out of public life have brought Hutchins to national attention. Roosevelt offered him the headship of the NRA; he turned it down. Once, during a local "red" hunt when Professor Robert Morss Lovett was under attack by the Hearst press and by some minor plutocrats, Professor James W. Linn told him, "Bob, if the trustees fire Robert Lovett, you'll get twenty resignations from the faculty in twenty-four hours." Hutchins replied, "No, I won't. My successor will."[21] A man of principle, he believes deeply in academic freedom and civil liberties, and he resigned recently from the university's own faculty club, because a candidate for membership was rejected for being a pacifist. He was for some time a governor of the New York Stock Exchange, as a nonmember representing the public at large; he resigned when he felt that the Exchange did not act strongly enough in the case of Richard Whitney, who had been sentenced to Sing Sing for grand larceny. His point was that other members of the Exchange must have known of Whitney's "criminal conduct" months before it became known to the public, and should have done something about it.

Hutchins has a long record as an isolationist. This did not, as one observer has pointed out, keep him from giving a job to President Beneš of Czechoslovakia during his exile. He has been called a Communist often, and a Fascist several times. What his party politics are

[20] Benjamin Fine in the New York *Times*, May 27, 1944.
[21] Milton S. Mayer, "Hutchins of Chicago," *Harper's Magazine*, March and April, 1939.

I do not know. Once he said that he would vote for Norman Thomas, if the major parties did not offer better platforms.

Hutchins has been accused of being "antiscience"; this has an odd ring now. Actually the atomic age may be said to have begun at 3:25 P.M. on December 2, 1942, in one of the converted squash courts under the stadium at Stagg Field. For a considerable time the university, under Hutchins, had been working hard on "trans-uranic" chemistry and physics; Professors Arthur Compton, Fermi, and Urey were all Chicago men, and it was on this date, one of the most pregnant in history, that the uranium-graphite pile constructed and operated in total secrecy first created a chain reaction.[22] No single person can claim credit for having made practicable the fission of the atom and the bomb this produced. But Hutchins and the university certainly had a great deal to do with it. The Manhattan Project had reached the point where it was necessary to construct a large pilot plant. Several universities and industrial organizations, which the War Department approached, felt that they could not accept the responsibility. Hutchins did. This was one of the most onerous decisions any man ever made. He made it purely on his own and it had to be secret. An agency known as the Metallurgical Laboratory was set up, for which the university, in Hutchins' own subsequent words, acted as "host and contracting agency." The great Clinton Laboratories at Oak Ridge, Tennessee, where the pilot plant was duly built, was administered by the University of Chicago, little known as this fact is, until June 30, 1945.

Hutchins himself, when I talked to him, had much to say about the bomb, and some of his reflections were what one might call, for want of a better word, philosophical. If atomic power, in a world of peace, becomes overwhelmingly cheap and plentiful, what will happen to the doctrine that life is a process of salvation by work? On the concrete side, I believe, he felt strongly that the bomb should have been "demonstrated" before being used against the Japanese. Incidentally Mr. Hutchins is an isolationist no longer. "Isolationism as a national way of life," he wrote recently, "is an anachronism in the atomic age, and if we are finally to survive, we must now, as never before in history, act our age."

Here is the conclusion of a discussion at the University of Chicago Round Table, August 12, 1945, a few days after the first bomb was dropped:

Mr. Hutchins: Up to last Monday I must confess that I did not have much hope for a world state. I have believed that no moral basis for it existed and that we had no world conscience and no sense

---

[22] Compton informed President Conant of Harvard of the great event by using the following "code" on the telephone. He said, "The Italian navigator (Fermi) has just landed in the New World." Conant replied, "Did he find the natives friendly?" "Everyone landed safe and happy," Compton concluded. Chicago *Sun*, November 6, 1945.

of world community sufficient to keep a world state together. But the alternatives now seem clear. One is world suicide; another is agreement among sovereign states to abstain from using the bomb. This will not be effective. The only hope, therefore, of abolishing war is through the monopoly of atomic force by a world organization.

Mr. Ogburn (professor of sociology on the faculty) : But that is a thousand years off.

Mr. Hutchins: Remember that Leon Bloy, the French philosopher, referred to the good news of damnation, doubtless on the theory that none of us would be Christian if we were not afraid of perpetual hellfire. It may be that the atomic bomb is the good news of damnation, that it may frighten us into that Christian character and those righteous actions and those positive political steps necessary to the creation of a world society, not a thousand or five hundred years hence, but now.

Crime in Chicago

And then suddenly Chicago is a dark smear under the sky . . .
—H. G. Wells

Next to the *Tribune*, what Chicago is best known for is, of course, crime. I wrote an article for *Harper's* a good many years ago, of which the opening line was, "I have lived in Chicago off and on for twenty years, and I have never seen a murder." (Once I did see a hanging, though.) No innocent bystander in the Chicago hoodlum wars was ever shot. But, I went on, "Murder in Chicago costs from $50 up. The more important the victim, the steeper the price. To kill me, a newspaperman, would probably cost $1,000. To kill a prominent businessman might cost $5,000, a prominent city official $10,000. To kill the president of a large corporation, or a great power magnate, would cost a great deal more, probably $50,000."

This article[23] scarcely mentioned Capone, Nitti the Enforcer, or the other more notable brigands of the era. In Chicago we took these folklore creatures for granted, more or less. What I was trying to explore was something newer, more concrete, more intimate, more expensive to the average citizen—the growth of rackets. These were not a Chicago invention, but it was in Chicago that they first proliferated. "Racket" has degenerated nowadays into a' noun meaning almost anything; originally it had a very explicit definition—simple extortion based on simple threat. A system of criminal exploitation, based on murder, arose in Chicago to seize the ordinary citizen—who paid no attention at all to the biggest gangsters—by the pocketbook if not the throat.

[23] It was written in collaboration with James W. Mulroy, who won a Pulitzer prize for his work helping to solve the Leopold-Loeb case, and who is now assistant managing editor of the *Sun*.

Suppose you had a small business selling tires and batteries. Suppose I am a member of a "mob" in a position to hire thugs and gunmen. I decide suddenly to charge you $100 a month for the privilege of selling your tires and batteries. I do the same to all other dealers. Soon I control your business, and you are utterly helpless in the matter. Or even suppose you have a small shop selling jewelry. I walk in one day and announce that hereafter half the proceeds are mine. What are you going to do about it? If you resist, I will of course shoot or bomb you. Go to the state's attorney or the police? Don't make me laugh! I pay them out of the loot I extract from you!

Soon the rackets became an immense business, and tributes extracted from the citizenry (because, of course, prices had to go up in any racket-controlled industry) ran to millions upon millions of dollars per year. Rackets muscled in on everything from candy jobbing to several great labor unions, from the clothes-pressing business to kosher butchers. They could not have survived, of course, without political protection. The racketeers simply extended into the criminal field some political practices that were already fairly common. When a famous Illinois politician (now dead) got the city council to give him a franchise for a new gas company (which never existed) so that the old gas company was forced to absorb this "rival," was it "business" or "racketeering"—which?

In 1934 I came back to Chicago after a long time abroad. I visited the city hall and police headquarters, I went out on gambling raids and attended sessions in various courts. This whole experience seems like a weird dream today. Events were too fantastically improbable. (In Chicago at the same time, during the Century of Progress World's Fair, you could go to half a dozen admirably done plays by Shakespeare every day, since they were presented in versions cut to a half an hour!) Recently I reread the stories I wrote at this time. Some of them make no sense. Largely the reason was that it was impossible to tell who among officials was honest, and who not. Let it be recalled that in one year there were 367 murders in Chicago, and not a single execution of a murderer. Let it be recalled that the Gennas, a gang of six Sicilian brothers who crashed in on O'Banion, and of whom four were killed in various skirmishes,[24] once gave a Lucullan banquet to the state's attorney of the time, at which a judge of the superior court was present and at which the state's attorney (flanked by four of his own detectives, in case anything went wrong) made a grateful speech. At another notable "mob" banquet the guest of honor was a detective who later became a chief of police. What brought organized gangsterism to Chicago was, in the main, prohibition. It is quite true that, in the Colosimo-Torrio days, prostitution was also a lively source of income, and that, under

[24] The funeral of one Genna cost $100,000, excluding the thirty carloads of flowers.

Capone and carrying through to the present, the gangs branched out into gambling, road houses, and the labor movement. But the great flood of cash came with prohibition. It was the insane lucrativeness that drove men crazy and made the risks worth while. Capone did a business of about 100 million dollars a year, of which 30 million was paid out in graft. No wonder the big mobs were able to control the police, the courts, and above all the political machines—though, be it said to their honor, some officials, and plenty of cops, stayed honest to the end.

What killed gangsterism was, first, repeal, and second, the depression; between them the wonderful easy flow of money was cut down. Also the respectable business community played a role. It became clear that what the hoodlums, in particular the racketeers, were striking at was the very essence of business enterprise in the United States. The special prosecutor who really frightened the gangs for the first time was a lawyer for the Pennsylvania Railroad. Something close to vigilantism also entered. For instance out of the Chicago Association of Commerce came the organization known as the "Secret Six," which assisted the regular law-"enforcement" bodies.

Today Chicago is much quieter, and the back of big organized crime has been broken. Most of the erstwhile great have met the chopper, i.e. machine gun. Anthony (Mops) Volpe, one of the old nobility, still pops up in the news occasionally, and so does "Bugs" Moran. But "Machine Gun" Jack McGurn, "Schemer" Drucci, John Scalise, Jack Zuta, Joe Aiello, Hymie Weiss, James (King of the Bombers) Belcastro (once Public Enemy No. 4) are all, happily, dead.

Nonetheless the "Syndicate" certainly still exists, composed of remnants of the old gangs, plus their young who have come to maturity, plus interlopers. The city's crime bill is estimated at 500 million dollars a year,[25] and at least a thousand gambling joints are still supposed to exist in the city, some, it is proudly asserted, "with full wire services." The last copy of the Chicago *Daily News* I picked up had three crime stories on its front page. But by comparison to the gaudy days, this is small-time stuff. Chicago is as full of crooks as a saw with teeth, but the era when they ruled the city is gone forever.

Reaction in Chicago

New York is, as everybody knows, the chief spawning ground in the United States for Communists and fellow travelers of varying shades; the American Communist Party operates out of the 12th Street neighborhood in Manhattan—it is a riven sect, operating under a dogma imposed from above, composed largely of people unwilling or unable to think for

[25] This figure may seem unbelievable, but it is in the New York *Times*, January 2, 1947.

themselves, and subservient to a policy constantly and vexingly liable to shift. Chicago, but not in quite so well defined a way, is similarly the chief breeding area and headquarters of Fascism in the United States, though Detroit and Indianapolis run it close. The Communists would be of small significance if they did not have the party in Russia and elsewhere to lean on. The forces and institutions that American Fascists, sub-Fascists and semi-Fascists lean on are more diffuse, and perhaps more dangerous because they are internal, not external. No actual Fascist "party" as such exists in the United States. Instead there are organizations like the former Bund and the Klan, isolationist survivals, some extremist elements in the Catholic Church, groups passionately enamored of Franco Spain, some big-business organizations, and a fringe of demagogues.

Nobody could fairly call American Action, Inc., which rose in Chicago in 1946, "Fascist" in the normal meaning of the term. It is merely a would-be political organization of extreme reactionary views, set up originally as a kind of counterweight to the PAC. Its activities were hush-hush for a time; then the Chicago *Sun* lifted the veil, with a story headlined SECRET AMERICA FIRST BORN, and the subhead, "Big Financiers Aid Movement—Million Raised for Purge of 187 Congressmen." The repercussions were sharp, since the 1946 elections were impending; Senate and House committees threatened to open investigations to see if the Corrupt Practices Act had been violated; then both the movement and the attacks on it seemed to peter out. American Action planned "to work through the veterans' organizations as much as possible" and only to put its weight, such as it was, into electoral contests if one of the candidates were "subversive." It specifically disclaimed any desire to influence foreign policy. Many of its members are, however, fervent long-time isolationists.

A tempest in an inkpot? The usual snort-worse-than-bite frivolous rightism? The temptation is to dismiss American Action with such words. Then one notes some of the people who compose it. They have a considerable substance. American Action is a kind of Liberty League brought up to date, with admixtures of America First, and it ties into the so-called National Economic Council of New York. The folk who think that it was Roosevelt personally who sank the American fleet at Pearl Harbor, the least sophisticated tycoons and really rabid anti-New Dealers, the would-be totalitarians and secret or not-so-secret sympathizers with Coughlin, Gerald L. K. Smith, et al., applaud its aims.

The president of American Action is, or was, Edward A. Hayes, former national commander of the American Legion; its treasurer is, or was, W. Homer Hartz, former president of the Illinois Manufacturers Association. The New York *Times*[26] says that among its contributors,

[26] In an article by the Pulitzer prize winner James Reston, October 10, 1946.

aside from General Robert E. Wood of Sears Roebuck, "are said to be Ernest T. Weir, chairman of the board of the Weirton Steel Company, and Colonel McCormick," and *Time* names Lammot Du Pont, chairman of the board of E. I. Du Pont de Nemours, as a "supporter." One member of its Executive Committee is Robert Harriss, a New York businessman with a Coughlinite past, and another is Robert Christenberry, president of the Hotel Astor in New York and of the Broadway Association, who once told an interviewer that he had collected "a lot of money" for the organization.

Here is part of a letter written by Robert E. Wood, who of course was the pre-Pearl Harbor chairman of America First, to an addressee whose name is withheld, as published by the New York *Post*, October 7, 1946:

Confidential

Dear ———

It looks as though finally a national political movement has been started that you and I will want to support. It is called AMERICAN ACTION . . .

The thing I like about it is that it is not "just another organization" of propaganda, but one of direct political action within Congressional districts. It appears to be sound in that it is concentrating in the marginal districts where there are good chances for success and as fast as funds are sufficient to do a thorough job it is expanding to other districts where real American Congressmen are being threatened with the PAC purge.

The movement has been discussed with and *has the blessing of the topmost Republican* and Constitutional Democratic leaders in both houses of Congress and the support of many people you know. [Italics mine.]

I am contributing a substantial amount to the movement and hope you will join me in contributing whatever you wish. Checks should be payable or stocks transferred to W. Homer Hartz, Treasurer, and sent to him at 1215 Board of Trade Building, Chicago 4, Illinois.

Sincerely yours,
R. E. Wood

Further comment is, it would seem, unnecessary.

Negroes in Chicago

The economic situation of the Negroes in America is pathological.

—Gunnar Myrdal

Dr. Metz Lochard, publisher of the Chicago *Defender*, invited me to meet with half a dozen leading Negroes, and we talked most of a morning. The Chicago patterns of segregation are in general those we have already discussed. Segregation does not apply in theaters or movies (some big theaters actually advertise in the *Defender*); it is the rule in most hotels, bowling alleys, taxis, taverns, and soda fountains except in the chain stores. There exist Negro police, but they are confined mostly to Negro districts; this is also true of Negro schoolteachers. In the entire city, one high-school principal is a Negro, but no grade-school principals.

It is housing that is the exacerbating issue. In Chicago there are 350,000 to 400,000 Negroes; be it noted that only about twenty cities in the country have a *whole* population bigger. Of the Chicago Negroes, some 250,000 are squeezed and jammed into a small area on the south side, roughly between 22nd and 67th streets, and between Cottage Grove and Wentworth avenues. This same district held only about 125,000 people in 1925; the population has doubled, but the living space hasn't increased by an inch. So the entire area bulges at the seams. This is the most concentrated "Black Belt" in the world; Harlem is bigger, but it is more diffuse.

The landowners are 85 per cent absentee whites, and their basic tenet is that of most landlords everywhere, to charge what rent the traffic will bear, and blame society at large for outrages that may occur. There is one house, at 3323 Calumet Avenue, built originally with eight apartments to contain eight families, that contains today fifty-four families; in near-by houses, with rooms divided by beaverboard partitions, there may be one toilet for thirty families. The schools must of course operate in double shifts. Hooliganism, overcharging by merchants, "jitney" cabs, overcrowded streetcars and parks and churches, inferior police protection, the numbers racket—all such excrescences of an urban civilization rise inevitably.

Two Chicago wards are almost solidly Negro, and this has had political effects somewhat paradoxical; first, the machines sought for years to vote the Negroes *en bloc*, which tended to prevent their self-assertion; second, the Negroes were so important that they had to be rewarded, and so became assertive anyway. Two aldermen out of fifty are Negro, one county commissioner out of twelve, one municipal judge out of thirty-six, one civil service commissioner out of three, one state senator out of fifty-one, four representatives out of 153, and one congressman out of twenty-six. One result of machine rule is that the quality of the vote deteriorates. I asked Dr. Lochard and his friends why, at least in so far as Negroes are concerned, an attempt could not be made to counteract this. One answer is that Chicago became a dumping-off spot for illiterate Negroes from the South. Another: "We don't turn enough spotlight on our own leadership." Another: "Increase in white prejudice."

The Chicago newspapers are friendly to Negroes, more or less, except the *Tribune*, which used them as a stick with which to beat the New Deal whenever convenient. Recently an appeal went to all local papers for the screening of routine news unfavorable to Negroes—in crime stories and the like—so that racial tensions that seemed to be growing dangerously might be minimized. Every paper agreed to co-operate except the *Tribune*. The colonel's refusal was based on his zealous regard for "freedom of the press."[27]

Indiana Briefly

> There is about it a charm I shall not be able to express . . . This is a region not unlike those which produce gold or fleet horses or oranges or adventurers.
>
> —Theodore Dreiser

The yellow sea of corn out of Iowa still pours high, and sweeps across Illinois into Indiana. But not only is this one of the foremost agricultural states; it is ninth in industrial production. Lake County, southeast of Chicago, smoke-blinded, taut, a metallic jungle, is a manufacturing area comparable to Pittsburgh. Gary is like Magnitogorsk. Then consider South Bend (with Studebaker and Bendix), Whiting (refineries), Fort Wayne and Muncie and Evansville and Indianapolis itself. The state's most distinguished citizen is an industrialist, Paul Hoffmann, president of Studebaker—the kind of modern executive who is testimony to the fact that, despite everything, the free enterprise system *will* work, if you think of it in terms of enterprise for the many, not just the few.

Also in South Bend is, of course, the most famous Catholic university in the world, Notre Dame. Why, I have wondered, are Notre Dame football teams called the "Irish"? Here is a recent lineup—Skoglund, Mieszkowski, Mastrangelo, Walsh, Rovai, Berezney, Cronin, Dancewicz, Colella, Augsman, Ruggerio. Well, out of eleven, two *are* Irish. Perhaps one should add for the benefit of the visitor from outside that one of the most illustrious of recent Notre Dame players was named William Shakespeare.

The concept "Hoosier" is by no means easy to define. I have quoted Dreiser above. With his home state, he is very gentle; he saw it in more romantic terms than most of us. He writes, in an essay on Indiana's "soil and light,"[28] putting the words into the mouth of a friend, "I insist that the Hoosier is different mentally and spiritually to the average American. He is softer, less sophisticated, more poetic. . . . He dreams a lot. He likes to play in simple ways. He is not as grasping as other Americans. . . . That may be due to the fact that he is not as practical, being as poetic and good natured as he is. . . . In a crude way, perhaps, he has the temperament of the artist."

[27] It is an impertinence to try to deal with the Negro problem in Chicago in such brief space. Luckily a superlative book, *Black Metropolis*, is available everywhere with 782 pages on the subject.

[28] *These United States*, II, p. 264.

Many Hoosiers themselves would differ with Mr. Dreiser; the average Indianian by no means thinks of himself as a soft fellow. I asked several friends in Indianapolis what they thought were particular Hoosier characteristics, and almost all replied "shrewd" and "independent" first, and then added "conservative," "God-fearing," and "unostentatious." Also most Hoosiers have a marked local "nationalism," like residents of Texas and Missouri. Ernie Pyle, an Indianian born, interpreted the Hoosier character very well, but authorities on the spot say that he was not a real type himself. Indiana has a powerful substratum of Germans, particularly in the south; these can have lived in a community for a hundred years, but they will not be Hoosier. I asked one expert to name the most typical Hoosier he knew. Answer: a waterworks' executive born in Boston, who spent most of his life in Akron, Ohio.

Booth Tarkington, George Ade, James Whitcomb Riley, Meredith Nicholson—the Indiana literary school had great mellowness; its members may seem old-fashioned now. Tarkington and Riley often had a companion, in the forgotten days, for amiable conversation; his name was John L. Lewis. Indiana is also, like Kansas, a state famous for newspapermen, radio commentators, and editors. One need only mention Elmer Davis, Byron Price, Kent Cooper, "Stuffy" Walters, and Roy Howard. The Indianapolis *Times*, ably edited by Walter Leckrone these days, is still Howard's own favorite among the whole Scripps-Howard chain, and the only one, aside from the New York *World Telegram*, in which his name appears on the masthead. Howard was a poor boy born in Indianapolis, very proud now that he came from the wrong side of the tracks.[29]

Indiana has one social characteristic which, though not unique by any means, reaches a pitch of development unrivaled elsewhere in the Middle West—clannishness. The Hoosiers are tremendous joiners. The state is one of the few where almost all eligible people, adults, set great store twenty years later by what fraternities they belonged to in college, and where flourish literally thousands of clubs; Indianapolis is one of the most "organized" cities in the world. You do not meet with three neighbors to play bridge; you organize the Upper Tenth Avenue Bridge Club, with a membership of four, and choose your president and secretary-treasurer. Then there are the "Sub-Deb" clubs, organizations of girls of high school age; of these actually seven hundred

[29] Indianapolis, like St. Louis, has three independent rival newspapers. In Evansville the process of consolidation in journalism reaches a new development; there are, I am told, two competing papers which operate a printing plant jointly and publish a combined Sunday paper with *two* editorial pages. In some of the smaller, grimmer Indiana cities, where the McCormick-Lindbergh atmosphere equals anything in Illinois or Wisconsin, the standards of journalism are not what you would term elevated; in one is a paper that might easily be called a really isolationist edition of the Chicago *Tribune*.

exist in Indianapolis alone, and they bear names like GCP (Gotta Coppa Poppa) and ZANY (Zealous, Adorable, Nice and Yummy).

Indianapolis, the largest capital city in the United States except Boston, is several things. It is the home of two of the most trenchantly conservative labor leaders in the United States, Daniel J. Tobin, general president of the International Brotherhood of Teamsters, and "Big Bill" Hutcheson, president of the United Brotherhood of Carpenters and Joiners and first vice president of the AF of L. Indianapolis is an unkempt city, unswept, raw, a terrific place for basketball and auto racing, a former pivot of the Ku-Kluxers, and in it you may see the second ugliest monument in the world. It is the former bailiwick of Paul McNutt. It contains the national headquarters of the American Legion —the Legion and its sizable pay roll are big business to the city—and one friend, who has lectured on political affairs all over the country, told me that it is the "worst" audience in the United States.

On the other hand, Indianapolis has several admirable book shops, and it is the seat of one of the few publishing houses in the country with a general book business not on the eastern seaboard, Bobbs-Merrill. In fact, university presses aside, I cannot think of another. Recently the University of Chicago set up one of its "Great Books" courses in Indianapolis; two professors travel down every fortnight, to minister to a group of forty citizens, and the idea has spread throughout the state. Indiana is one of the few northern states which has laws like those in the South forbidding intermarriage between whites and Negroes, and segregated schools; yet its record in race relations is quite good. Anderson and Maynor sing in Indianapolis auditoriums; Negro boys often win in the Golden Gloves tournament held every year, and in 1945 a crack Indiana University football team, the best in its history, had three Negro stars. A local hotel refused once to put up Paul Robeson. The governor of the state and a dozen other whites promptly volunteered to do so. The hotel then withdrew its ban. A wealthy lady on one occasion asked her Negro maid to be sure not to miss a current movie. But Jim Crowism exists in some local theaters, and the maid was not admitted. The wealthy lady, previously unaware of this, became so indignant that she threatened not to renew the theater's lease; it happened that she owned the property. Small personal incidents like this can do more to ameliorate local race conditions than a bushelful of committees, and a good many have occurred in Indianapolis and other Indiana towns.

Antilabor sentiment can be savage in Indiana. The following advertisement, of which I quote only a small section, actually appeared in the New York *Times*. It was signed by H. N. Light, president of The Light Co., South Bend:

If I ran for the Presidency of the World, following would be my platform, Nationally and Internationally:

STRIKES MUST BE OUTLAWED

No. 1. Why should a man pay his hard-earned money to give a big, fat man a big, fat salary of $75,000 a year plus an unlimited expense account, which could easily double his annual salary. Think!!! Don't just listen to some flowery orator. THINK!!! That is why God gave man his brain—to work out his own Salvation.

The religious advertisements fill whole pages of the Indianapolis dailies. One boasts of a "Great Singspirational Rally Featuring Bishop Marston and the Girls' Trio."[30]

Indiana is one of the most "professional" states in the union politically; this is a community—with occasional respectable interludes—ruled by grab and spoils. It has, however, some good men in Washington. One is, or was, Charles M. La Follette, a distant cousin of the Wisconsin La Follettes, a dissident Republican and one of the most outspoken liberals in the 79th Congress; the Old Guard beat him down when he ran for the Senate in 1946. Also Indiana has had some choice reactionaries. Probably nobody on its delegation is so unutterably sordid as, for instance, McKellar of Tennessee, but several run him close.

The chief local lobbies are liquor and insurance. There is no civil service in Indiana, which means a virtually clean sweep of office holders with every new administration. The most lucrative profits are in the liquor business. A wholesaler must have a state license; this will not come easily unless the county chairman nods approval, and passes the word along. In fact, licenses simply are not issued "unless the guy is right." Hence the big wholesalers who know their way around make contributions to both political parties as a rule. Once they are "in," they are set for four years at least. But to keep on being "in" they must "co-operate," and a wholesaler who does not do so may simply have to go out of business when the administration changes. It was this sort of thing which, a quarter of a century ago, helped to bring prohibition. Indiana was at that time one of the most implacable and frenzied dry states in the union, which meant that it was also hard drinking in the extreme.

A good many medium and small insurance companies have home offices in Indianapolis. During a World War II bond drive, the prize was part of an original manuscript by Ernie Pyle. It went to an insurance company for $10,525,000!—and another insurance firm was runner-up. The insurance lobby has promoted one reform that has provoked much

[30] The town New Harmony is in Indiana incidentally. This is where the Rappist cult once existed, and where Robert Owen, the great Scottish reformer, set up his short-lived Utopia.

controversy. The Indiana motor liability insurance law is probably the most rigorous in the country; there are severe penalties for accidents, and every driver must carry insurance worth $11,000. In another field the insurance companies have not been so socially minded. They fought and killed a measure which, if passed, would have greatly furthered cheap hospitalization, which the companies oppose if it competes with their own activity.

The present governor, Ralph F. Gates, a Republican, came into office after twelve years of Democratic administrations. He is competent enough, conservative, an honest man, and ambitious. Many Indianians think that he has a close eye on the vice presidential nomination in 1948, and may well get it.

Indiana was, as everybody knows, the northern state most infected after World War I with the virus of the Ku-Klux Klan. In fact the Klan actually captured the state government for a time.[31] The spoils were, as the word is, colossal. Think what economic power an organization like the Klan, if successful, can exert, and what loot comes to its leaders. Suppose you have 200,000 members. Each pays $10 for admittance, $10 per year for dues; moreover, the rake-off on the regalia is to be considered. Then consider the "take" if, in addition, you control the entire state apparatus and its patronage. The business was almost as lucrative as alcohol. No wonder what chiefly broke up the Klan were racketeers and hi-jackers who muscled in. The Indiana Klan, with its infantile mess of Klavalcades and Klaverns, fought the Catholics and Jews (the Negroes were not so conspicuous an "enemy" then), just as today it chiefly attacks "reds" and Communists under the guise of "patriotic" witch hunting. In practice what it really stood against was anybody who opposed it. One Indiana Klan official had a sophistication so acute that he once remarked, "We're not against you Irish Catholics, but just them *Roman* Catholics!" The Klan also went to pieces in Indiana because its grand dragon, David C. Stephenson, got into certain troubles. He ran off with a girl and raped her; she took poison and died. Stephenson was exposed by the *Times*, arrested, tried for murder, and convicted, although he boasted that "he" was the law in Indiana.[32] He was sentenced to life imprisonment, and is still serving his term. His adherents have made numerous (actually twenty) efforts to get him out,

[31] For a brief word about the Klan in general see Chapter 45 below.
[32] After his conviction the national Klan organization tried to drop him. A remarkably illuminating account of Stephenson is "Beauty and the Beast," by John Bartlow Martin, *Harper's Magazine*, September, 1944. "On April 17, 1924, that is to say on the Deadly Day of the Weeping Week of the Appalling Month of the Year of the Klan LVII, His Lordship H. W. Evans, Imperial Wizard . . . signed an edict ordering the Evansville Klavern Number One to try Stephenson, and addressed it to All Genii, Grand Dragons and Hydras, Great Titans and Furies, Giants, King Kleagles and Kleagles, Exalted Cyclops and Terrors, and to All Citizens of the Invisible Empire, in the name of the valiant and venerated dead."

but no Indiana governor will risk the explosion that would presumably attend his release. When motions for parole are made, papers like the Indianapolis *Times* write drily, "Isn't the girl still dead?"

Indiana, even more than Michigan and Illinois, boils with Fascist and sub-Fascist movements. One was led by the late Carl H. Mote, who died in 1946. Mote was a minor telephone executive, and he had money, which made him valuable. He published a magazine called *America Preferred*, which was saprogenically anti-Semitic and contained passages like "I am ashamed to be an American. . . . The war has demonstrated one thing, that the Germans are superior to the Americans physically, intellectually, aesthetically, and morally."[33] Mote tried for a time to maintain a national farmers' organization "to lead a strike against strikes. One goes into the background of a man like this, and tries earnestly to explore the reasons for such an evolution. In most cases, it seems that the whole performance rose in the first instance out of simple antipathy to Roosevelt and the New Deal. These would-be demagogues really thought that the "Jews and Communists" were going to take the country over.

Court Asher of Muncie, Indiana, still publishes a sheet called *X-Ray*. He was neatly taken apart recently in a *Harper* article. Asher is an eccentric. His ancestry is hillbilly. During the war he was one of those indicted in Washington for sedition, and went on trial in the celebrated case terminated abruptly by the death of the judge. The indictments were all dismissed. Asher once served time briefly on a charge rising out of bootlegging, and was closely involved years ago with Klan activities. One can measure his mind easily enough by glancing at *X-Ray*, which uses such original phrases as "Jew York" and "Jew Deal."

Considering some of these things, it seems remarkable that a man like Wendell Willkie could have risen out of the Indiana wastes. Willkie, as a matter of fact, only carried his home state by the narrowest of margins in 1940. I went to Rushville, to look at the house he lived in. It is comfortable, of red brick, ivy-bound, shaded by sturdy elms, and with a white-pillared stoop and an iron rail along the steps. A point that would astonish Europeans who know little of the normal topography of middle western towns is that, though in a good residential district, it is only twenty yards from the railroad tracks. I reflected on the astonishing mutability of America, and wondered whether or not Willkie would have become president in 1948, had he only lived.

[33] New York *Post*, April 30, 1946.

Chapter 24

A Talk With Vandenberg

~~~~~~

WHAT manner of person is Vandenberg? What does he stand for, and what does he believe in most? What are the determining characteristics of this man who is senior senator from Michigan and the Republican party's chief spokesman on foreign affairs—the man who, ticketed for years as an isolationist, has lately been a leading American delegate to the UN Conference at San Francisco, the Foreign Ministers' Conference at London, and the "Peace" Conference in Paris?

I called on the senator in Washington recently, hoping to find out. We sat in black leather chairs in the president's room in the Senate, and talked an hour. It goes without saying that, since November 1946 and with the Republican party in control of Congress, Vandenberg's importance has steeply risen. He and Taft run the Senate.

Vandenberg has written two books about his greatest hero, Alexander Hamilton; the title page of one carries the motto, *Nationalism—not "Internationalism"—is the indispensable bulwark of American independence.* But this was written in 1921, since which date both Senator Vandenberg and the world have traveled a considerable way. In 1939, addressing an American Legion convention, he proclaimed, "This so-called war is nothing but about twenty-five people and propaganda. They [presumably the Europeans] want our money and our men." This from the senator who has spent almost every moment of the last two years working with Europeans!

Actually Vandenberg, a temperate and discriminating man, has never been an isolationist of the blindly implacable type of Hiram Johnson or Henry Cabot Lodge. There is little of the intransigent or irreconcilable in the big Michigander's character, and his voting record on international issues has been mixed. He vigorously opposed revision of the Neutrality Act in 1939, during the *Sitzkrieg*, but, though this is not always recollected, he voted *for* Lend Lease, and he was one of six Republican senators who favored United States participation in the World Court. Also Vandenberg, by far the most influential Republican in the Senate on foreign issues, worked staunchly for UNRRA and was to an extent responsible for putting UNRRA through.

The most severe criticism of Vandenberg I have come across is by Milton S. Mayer in *The Nation* of May 11, 1940. "Vandenberg is liberal (for a Republican), enlightened (for a politician), and industrious (for a senator). But you can't find out what makes him go. Dewey and Taft have cores; you may not like them, but they're there. Vandenberg doesn't add up to anything. He cancels out. . . . On domestic problems you can't locate him at all. He has stood squarely on both sides of every issue for the past ten years. He has been against subsidies to the farmer and for the payment of equalization fees; for the RFC and against pump priming; for economy and against reorganization; for devaluation and against "repudiation"; for housing and against the spend-lend theory (and for and against housing); for the SEC and against marginal trading and holding company regulation; for tariff and loan benefits to the suffering poor (and for and against relief); for and against federal control of relief; for budget balancing and at the same time for a general pension; for and against income tax publicity; for higher surtaxes and against taxation of tax-exempt securities."

But this was written almost seven years ago. What Vandenberg himself is proudest of in his senate record, in the domestic field, is his fatherhood of the Federal Deposit Insurance Corporation law, which is usually thought of as a New Deal measure. The Michigan senator considers that this act has contributed more to the economic stability of the United States than any other single measure in fifty years. Yet, in the early days of the Roosevelt administration, the proposal that the federal government should insure bank deposits was considered little short of insurrectionary by many of his Republican colleagues. Today, hardly a finger in the land would be lifted against it. Vandenberg expands and grows; so does the country grow, through the fierce education imposed by threat of disaster.

Arthur Hendrick Vandenberg is a large, solidly built man, now sixty-two, who wears his age well. If I had to describe him in a sentence I would be tempted to say that he looks exactly like what he is—a senator. White hair combed laterally across a bulging brow; a heavy gold watch chain worn laterally across a massive waistcoat—these are as familiar as black pants. But he has nothing of the blowsy look of some "professional" senators. He has dignity; he never uses words vapidly; and though he is a large hunk of man he is also tidy. No one would ever mistake him for a McCarran. And his intensely dark eyes look at you with a shiny glare at once searching and beneficent. Vandenberg gives at one and the same time an impression of power—an easy and affluent kind of power—plus an irreverent wit and comfortable good humor, a note of laziness (despite his unrivaled reputation for industry), and a very definite and alert sophistication.

"My whole life," the senator told me, "was underlined by my having to go to work at the age of nine, while supporting my mother and father. As a result of this, I solemnly promised God Almighty, first, that if it lay within my power, I would never permit what happened to my father to happen to me. This resolution has made a permanent notch in my character. Second, I gained a lot of early equipment in self-confidence, and ever since I've held to the conviction that if you really want to go somewhere in life, you can."

For a man to have perfect self-confidence means, as a rule, that he also has acute knowledge of his own limitations, which indeed Vandenberg has. But he went on:

"My experiences as a child bent me two ways, if I assign myself to any political category. I know from bitter experience what it feels like to have nothing in your pocket, but also I know the value of enterprise, and how enterprise can protect old age. I'm half a conservative, half a liberal. The liberalism derives from my having been poor, the conservatism from having got moderately rich."

He went on to describe his early days; he was born in Grand Rapids, Michigan, in 1884; his father was an old-style harness maker. The family came originally from the Mohawk Valley. The harness business developed into a good thing, and young Vandenberg grew up in a comfortable home with all normal conveniences until he was nine, when the crash of 1893 wiped his father out. The family home became a boarding house, his mother had to find work as a laundress, and Arthur saw his tormented father become quickly a broken old man. So he became the main support of his family, at the age of nine.

"What kind of a job did you get?" I asked.

"A damned good job! I ran a pushcart, in the hours after school, delivering shoes from a wholesale house to the freight yards. By the time I was twelve, three others boys worked for me. By the time I was a senior in high school, I was getting fifteen to twenty dollars a week, which was a lot of money for those days."

The Horatio Alger pattern is as clear in this story as it is in a thousand others. But Vandenberg's career turned out to be Alger with reverse English. Because his next step forward came as a result of getting fired for disobedience. It is astonishing how many Americans owe much of their good fortune to having lost rather than gained a job.

"In 1900, Theodore Roosevelt was running for president, and I was a tremendous TR fan. I was out of high school by this time, working as a billing clerk in a cracker factory. There was a TR parade in town, and I asked the boss for time out to see it. He refused. I went anyway. I came back, and he fired me. I had to have another job right away, and I got one as an office boy on the Grand Rapids *Herald*."

Young Arthur's subsequent career as a newspaperman was rapid, to say the least. At twenty-one he was city hall reporter and political writer, and as such covered the senatorial campaign of a Republican dignitary named William Alden Smith. Smith took a considerable

fancy to Vandenberg, bought the paper in 1906, and made the young
man publisher, manager, and editor—when he was twenty-two.

"What a chance for a youngster!" Vandenberg exclaimed. "The
paper dominated the morning field in western Michigan, and here was
I, twenty-two years old, running it! A break like that can't happen to
more than one person in a million. I've been a creature of great good
fortune. Just the same, I could have lost the whole thing the next year—
or any other year—if I had been a flop. When I say to my wife nowadays that I've been lucky, she replies that I was so indefatigable that
something would have had to give way to me, no matter with luck
or not."

I asked him when he first became interested in politics, and he
answered with a kind of good-humored, retrospective assurance that his
ambition was to be a United States senator from the first moment he
had a conscious thought. "Public life in the broad sense has always
appealed to me." He made speeches and won oratorical contests when
still in high school, and by odd coincidence took part in 1899 in a
debate on the Peace Conference at The Hague. "Forty-six years later,
I signed the San Francisco charter for my own country."

Though Vandenberg had a good job on the Grand Rapids *Herald*
for twenty-five years he did not make any enormous amount of money,
and though he was resolute in his determination to go into public life
some day, he was just as resolutely determined never to run for office
until he could easily afford it. As he put it, grinning at his own epigram,
"I decided not to go into public life until I was independent of public
life." As early as 1907, however, though not running for office himself,
he campaigned throughout Michigan for the Republican party, and
became a member of the state central committee. Nine years later, in
1916, he was so well known that all factions urged him to run for governor, on the assumption that only he could mend a local bull moose
split, but he refused. Not till 1928 did he come out for senator, when he
was perfectly certain (a) that he would win, and (b) that he had
means enough to support the job. His opponent in the 1928 elections
would have been Woodbridge N. Ferris, a hard Democrat to beat. But
Ferris died just as the campaign began, and Vandenberg was appointed
by the then Republican governor to be his successor—another example
of his good luck. Then, running for the new term, he won handily, as
he did again in 1934, 1940, and 1946. In 1934 he was the only Republican
senator in the whole country to win re-election.

Vandenberg says today—with his fingers crossed—that he is not a
presidential candidate. He declined the Republican nomination for vice
president in 1936 (it went to his good friend Frank Knox instead),[1]
and, as he jokingly puts it, "he was declined" for the presidential

[1] He and Knox were cub reporters together on the Grand Rapids *Herald*.

nomination in 1940, when Willkie took it on the run. But the Michigander got seventy-six votes for president in the 1940 convention. And though—today—he claims that he has no burning desire to be president himself, he wants to have a lot to say as to who the Republican candidate shall be, especially since, at the moment of writing, a 1948 GOP victory seems inevitable. In 1944, as is well known, he came out for MacArthur, but the MacArthur movement sputtered out after brief fireworks. Could Vandenberg be "persuaded" to run himself in 1948? Of course—if all the circumstances are propitious.

I asked Vandenberg what his basic political conviction was and he replied that what he believed in most was the essential dignity of the individual citizen, and his right to have the kind of free opportunity "to go places" he himself has had. "You can't regiment 'em into a slot." He thinks that the American constitution is still the most progressive document in the history of the world, and that the American republic is still the most progressive country in the world. He wants to resist all efforts to "standardize us into bureaucratic tyranny." On the other hand, he concedes that any presidential candidate must hereafter take heed of the times by being "socially minded," and he thinks that "the whole world has moved into a new relationship between state and citizen, which cannot be ignored." This relationship should, however, be adjusted within the old framework, he insists. "We don't have to be Communists to be broadminded." Finally, he seems to be aware that any total reversion to the ideas and ideals of 1929 would—for the time being anyway—be altogether impossible and ruinous.

I wanted to know how Vandenberg relaxed, since a man's play will often tell as much about him as his work, but he said that nowadays he had no time for hobbies. For seventeen years what he liked to do was travel, not merely for fun but for self-improvement. He traveled in a very special way; every year he went to a different country and stayed there for two months, sticking to the one place. He did this for seventeen consecutive years, and so it may be presumed he has today a fair enough acquaintance of seventeen different foreign countries.

Next to travel, what he likes most is writing. His first book on Hamilton, called *Alexander Hamilton, the Greatest American*, was prompted in part by Gertrude Atherton's *The Conqueror*. The late but not lamented President Harding, of all people, contributed the preface to this largely forgotten volume. Vandenberg loved both the research and the writing attending his literary work. His other books are *If Hamilton Were Here Today*, published in 1923, and *The Trail of a Tradition* (1925), a highly nationalist tract on foreign policy, which I imagine the senator would not like to have quoted against him today.

A good many people were surprised when Vandenberg was selected by Mr. Roosevelt as an American delegate to San Francisco—and more surprised still when the Michigan senator accepted.

But after the presidential elections of 1944, Vandenberg found himself in a quandary. Roosevelt had been overwhelmingly re-elected, with all that that showed as to the temper of the country. All senators, if not in their dotage or unless cranks, want to be re-elected—this is their first law of life—and Vandenberg was coming up in 1946. He had been influenced gradually to believe in international conciliation and a modified American participation in the world structure; yet, as leader of the Republican opposition in the Senate, he could not possibly jump with both feet on the Roosevelt bandwagon. He studied hard, thought things over, and scouted around for a compromise. Then on January 10, 1945, he came out with one of the most important speeches on foreign policy ever made by an American, putting himself on record for an immediate alliance between the United States and the other great powers (including Russia) for the future control of Germany by permanent armed force. He even went so far as to suggest that the president might, if necessary, enforce the future peace treaties by use of American military strength without consent of Congress.

A brief time later, Roosevelt appointed him to the San Francisco delegation. The invitation appealed at once to Vandenberg's vanity, his genuine sense of public duty, and his politics. Nor has he ever regretted accepting it. He is as proud as punch, still, of being a signatory to the charter. He tells friends, "They can't take *that* out of history!" Another point is that San Francisco taught him a lot, and men who are capable of intellectual growth in their sixties, capable of acquiring new knowledge and new points of view, are rare indeed.

In January, 1946, Vandenberg went to London, this time as a delegate to the UN. Previously he sought assurance from President Truman that we were properly safeguarding our knowledge of the atomic bomb. He was still, in other words, a kind of Republican watchdog, a brake on the delegation as a whole; later this was his role in Paris too, though he co-operated well and cordially with Byrnes. Looking at him in large perspective, it can hardly be denied that his contribution over the years is substantial, if only by contrast to what happened in 1919. Today, the United States is not only part of the contemporary equivalent of the old League of Nations; the United States Senate passed the San Francisco charter by eighty-nine votes to two. No development in American history more cardinally represents a greater change of point of view in the short span of twenty-six years. Suppose Vandenberg had been a Lodge. He *could* have wrecked the treaty. Negatively at least, the Michigander is as much responsible for American participation in the present cycle of peacemaking, however shaky this may turn out to be, as any American now living.

To summarize, Vandenberg's brain is better than the puddings some senators have inside their skulls, and he has never lost the advantage of the half-a-generation head start he got in life, as a result of having had to go to work at the age of nine. Most lucky men tend to become complacent, but Vandenberg worked hard to make his own luck hold. What caused the great "sea change," the transposition in adult years from a narrow kind of nationalist approach to his present position? Surely the answer is not hard to find. The keynote of his whole life and career has been security—the loss of security, the search for it, the gaining of it, and the canny weighing of every decision to the inch, so that security shall not be lost again. Vandenberg would hate to think of the world, and his own country, going to ruin just at the juncture when he is in a position to enjoy it most and serve it best. Security in the personal sphere has simply been transposed into security nationally and internationally. The only way any man can be secure himself—in this robot and atomic age—is to help make the world secure, if he can.

Chapter 25

World on Wheels: Ford Dynasty and UAW

wwwwwwwwwwwwwwwwwwwwwwwwwwwwwwwwwwwwwwwwwwwwwwwwwwwwwwwwwwwwwwwwwwwwwwwwwwwwwwwwwwwwwww

> When a man dies, it means that a part has worn out.
>
> —Henry Ford

> Nothing has spread socialist feeling in this country more than the automobile . . . they are a picture of the arrogance of wealth with all its independence and carelessness.
>
> —Woodrow Wilson in 1906

FORD isn't always easy to see. Some years ago I went out to Dearborn from Detroit in a company car. The officials had been evasive as to whether I had an actual appointment or not. Probably they didn't know either. The chauffeur kept talking about Ford, and, though we were some miles from the plant, refused a cigarette because he said there were spotters everywhere and if he were caught smoking he'd be fired.

The Ford story is the greatest in America. Any newspaper man will understand what I mean by this. It is not the most important story. That is probably TVA or foreign policy. The Ford story is the "greatest" for the simple reason that it has never been written. A Ford bibliography could fill a library, but, even so, much about the old man is not known; much else that is known cannot, for various reasons, be freely told. It is still extremely difficult to get facts on Ford; the mythology is boundless, and three different people, all supposedly well informed, will give you three different versions of the same circumstance or episode.

Henry Ford is a very old man now, almost eighty-four, and still the richest in the world, the Nizam of Hyderabad possibly excepted. The president of the company today is Henry Ford II, his thirty-year-old grandson. In the span between the two Fords an era was born, the automobile age, the era of both mass and precision production, of the world on wheels. What would the United States be like today if Ford had never lived? Someone might have arisen in the same field with roughly the same accomplishment. Maybe. It is possible. Just the same Ford's peculiar idiosyncratic personality as well as his work, his peculiar *Zeitgeist*, have left a mark on this continent that will never be effaced.

In 1914 occurred two seminal historic events. One was the outbreak of World War I. The other was the announcement that Ford would pay a $5.00 per day minimum wage—for which he was, of course, denounced as a crackpot or a monster by the entire manufacturing, commercial, financial, and propertied class. I am not sure which of these two events, in the long run, will be remembered as the more significant.

I reached Dearborn, and had conversation with Ford men. I was told that Mr. Ford, who at that time bore no company title of any kind, only seldom used his office; instead he just "circulated." Most of the offices had glass partitions, and you could see anybody approaching a half mile off. Ford likes visibility. Yet I did not see the old man come near the room where I was waiting. He is swift as a shadow. I do not remember now much that he talked about, but the physical impression remains very vivid. He is taller than one thinks from his pictures. He is lean, with a stomach long and flat like an ironing board; his hair is carefully kept and lustrous; the years have written long, deep parentheses at each end of his quick, sensitive mouth. He is able neither to sit or stand still for long. When he stands, his hands flutter across his chest or by his sides. When he sits, he crosses and recrosses his legs, making gestures practically with his toes.

Mr. Ford disappeared after half an hour or so and one of the executives, with a kind of frightened reverence, took me tiptoeing to his private office. On the floor were neat copies of old bound magazines, *Harper's* and *Leslie's Weekly*, and the window seats were full of toys, rubber dolls and animals. Ford gives them to children in the village when he is out walking. The desk contained two telephones, a Detroit phone book, and a few folios of papers. What impressed me most was the table adjacent, which was covered from rim to rim with—old watches! Ford still loves to tinker with watches and slowly, carefully, take them apart.

I visited Dearborn again in 1945. This time I noticed in the whole establishment a considerable relaxation, a slackening of the tension. I was allowed to smoke. Unless my memory misleads me some Ford officials actually smoked too, right there in the building. The relaxation, the humanization, expressed itself in other and more important fields. The executives seemed to be of a new and much more reasonable stamp. This was at a time when a great inner revolution, or convulsion, had just occurred, as Henry II was taking over and when Harry Bennett, of whom more presently, resigned. Ford used to be a shop where "anybody could fire anybody," where no schematic organization existed at all, where one executive could countermand the orders of all the others. "You got your head lopped off if you talked to the wrong guy," as I heard it said. Nowadays this has all changed drastically. The intimidation days are gone, too, so far as labor is concerned; the plug-uglies have disappeared. "Ford won't be a roundheel in labor relations," one of his top men told me, "but he'll play fair. If labor works, we work, and vice versa."

Finally, though as we shall see Ford does not "have" to make money in the manner of other more mundane companies, the organization is determined to get out in front again, and regain the position of undisputed leadership it held for so long.

But about the entire titanic Ford plant there is still an aura of uniqueness, of differentiation. Ford is like no other industrial undertaking in the world. He was, or rather is, a kind of government—and much more powerful than many governments. The annual budget of the republic of Brazil before the war was about 160 million dollars. Ford's was at the time at least three times greater. The total value of the imports of the kingdom of Jugoslavia, prewar, amounted to about 580 million dollars. So did Mr. Ford's. Switzerland normally spent about $270,000 per day to run itself. Ford spent, and still spends, about one million dollars a day on payroll alone.[1] Since its foundation, the company has grossed more than 11 billion dollars.

The overriding phenomenon that, in abrupt analysis, makes Ford unique is that no stock is held outside the family. This is why the company can take losses, as it did for many years. This is why almost all his competitors eventually have nervous breakdowns, because nobody can ever predict what Ford will do. If he suddenly lowers the price of his cars, as happened without warning in early 1947, the rest of the industry lurches with dismay because, whereas Ford can do this, they may not be able to do so—or rather, even if they can, they may not want to. Ford has no outside stockholders to satisfy, no banking interests to appease, no interlocking directorates to keep in order, no meetings in New York of bondholders or directors, and, above all, no dividends to pay outside the family. Ford could start giving automobiles away tomorrow for nothing, or pay people a premium to buy them; all that would happen would be that the family fortune, which probably amounts to 800 million dollars or more, would be cut into. But General Motors and Chrysler and the other great companies have stockholders for whom dividends must be earned. Ford doesn't even publish a balance sheet for general attention. He doesn't have to, except in certain states like Massachusetts which demand a limited declaration, since nobody trades in Ford securities. Nobody even knows what the family dividends may be.

Ford—to put it somewhat mildly—is a very strange person indeed, an "off-ox" as I heard it put. This is the last of the spectacular, ornery American individualists. For a generation he carried a billion-dollar business under his hat. A lone wolf of lone wolves, he never even joined the Automobile Manufacturers Association. But every Ford patent, of

---

[1] One odd distinctive minor point is Ford's attitude toward public relations in this public-relations-choked era. In Ford's public relations department are employed exactly five men. Any comparable corporation has a staff of hundreds.

which there are thousands, is available absolutely free to anybody in the world who wants it.[2]

Greenfield Village

> History is bunk.
> —Henry Ford

> If only Ford himself were properly assembled! If only he would do in himself what he has done in his factory!
> —Samuel S. Marquis

Greenfield Village, a few miles from Dearborn, is one of the most singular sights in the United States. It is a far cry from the black furnaces and grunting machines of Willow Run and River Rouge; it is something in a different and blander sphere—Ford's attempt to resurrect the American past, the America he knew as a boy and which, as much as any man, he helped to obliterate.

"Well now, let me see," Mr. Ford said jerkily when I asked him about the origins of this project which is at once stupendous and in a curious way absurd. "I haven't thought much about that. I suppose it began in my head twenty-five years ago. It occurred to me to try to get together some early American furniture and industrial equipment. We went seriously to work on it six or seven years ago. Oh, it will take years to complete—years and years!"

Ford, more than any other man, typifies the era of machines; now, next door to his birthplace, he goes back to horse and buggy, venerating what he destroyed. Ford created the automobile assembly line and, just as important, the standardization and interchangeability of parts, which made the early automobile practicable, and which today is one of the giant bases of the industry. Now, in his old age, out of some kind of psychological displacement or nostalgia, he tinkers with his fingers in a blacksmith shop and looks for old-style locomotives that go puff-puff. The man who made the Model T allows no automobiles in Greenfield Village, except in the museum. You go from exhibit to exhibit behind a horse.

Of course the whole thing is almost insufferably grandiose. Here the criteria of the millimetre gauge is applied to antiques. The first thing I saw was a sixteenth century Cotswold cottage, brought over from England bodily, and set up stone by stone. Every timber and bit of plaster is of course original. It is not a replica of the Cotswold cottage. It *is* the Cotswold cottage. Such devotion to the minutiae of genuineness is, one need not point out, a familiar enough American characteristic; Hearst has it too. But Ford goes further. Was it necessary to

[2] According to *Fortune*, June, 1944.

bring over from the Cotswolds an authentic herd of Cotswold sheep, which now graze on the sunny Greenfield slopes? Anyway they are sheep alive and of undeniable authenticity.

Ford's idea was to show the development of American institutions. I saw an original Mississippi River boat, complete, and the original log cabin where W. H. McGuffey of the McGuffey Readers was born. Here is a building in which Lincoln practiced law, Luther Burbank's office, and the cottage where Steinmetz performed his experiments. Carried to its logical conclusion Greenfield Village should, of course, include the Alamo, Mount Vernon, and Independence Hall. Well, Independence Hall *is* here, down to the very crack in the Liberty Bell—but in replica, alas. Maybe Mr. Ford couldn't persuade Philadelphia to surrender the original.

The prize of the whole village, which covers 220 acres and contains several hundred thousand objects, is the group of structures associated with Thomas Edison, Ford's hero. Here is the entire Menlo Park laboratory, complete with the very test tubes and mortars that the great inventor used, and including the whole train (!) which Edison set on fire as a boy, the original hawker's basket in which he sold newspapers and bananas (bananas absent), and a few square rods of his own red earth, imported reverently from New Jersey.

Of course there are acres of automobiles, quiescent, including some wonderful-looking old juggernauts (do not forget that, in the United States alone, more than two thousand different makes of automobiles have been built and sold in the past fifty years—today only about a dozen survive); there is No. 999, the Ford in which Henry himself set the world's record for the mile in 1902; there are the ten millionth Ford and the twenty millionth Ford and hundreds of other Fords for some reason notable. Also I saw near by the first car Ford ever built. Occasionally, to amuse visitors, Ford (sometimes Mrs. Ford watches), carefully priming it with fluid out of an eyedropper, starts its engine. It still runs very well.

Aladdin of the Tin Lizzie

If you will study the history of almost any criminal, you will find he is an inveterate cigarette smoker.

An army or navy is a tool for the protection of misguided, inefficient, destructive Wall Street.

—Henry Ford

Ford's father was an Irish immigrant; his mother was of Pennsylvania Dutch extraction. He has a younger brother, William, whom scarcely anybody has ever heard of; his wife, with whom he has lived more than half a century of undiluted happiness, was named Clara

Bryant. The outline of his early life and struggles, his first puttering with the horseless buggy, are too well known to bear repetition here. Ford, like so many American boys, got ahead by quitting jobs rather than by revering them. Almost overnight, from being an obscure mechanic, he became the most famous man in the world. Does anybody remember the inundating cycles of Ford jokes when the Model T first swept the roads?

Ford sued the Chicago *Tribune* for a million dollars for having called him an "anarchist," and got 6¢ damages after an elaborate trial; an incident in this was that, trapped in cross examination by smart *Tribune* lawyers, he didn't know who Benedict Arnold was. He organized the Ford Peace Ship expedition, with which he hoped to stop World War I.[3] Indirectly, through the medium of the Dearborn *Independent*, he waged a long campaign against the Jews; not until 1927, when a reputation for anti-Semitism was cutting into his business gravely, did he publicly recant. He ran for the Senate as a Democrat in 1918, and was only just beaten by Truman Newberry; a generation later, one of his grandsons and a Newberry scion were classmates at Hotchkiss, in Connecticut. Wall Street and the bankers sought to buy into old Henry or break him or get him, and for decade after decade he hated Wall Street, in the conventional western way, hated it more than anything on earth except, maybe, organized labor. When the UAW first sought to organize Ford, he put notices in the pay envelopes warning every worker that unionization was just like Wall Street, "two ends of the same rope," only worse; he has long since come to terms with labor, but his hatred of absentee capital and the financial world of the East is still implacable.

The Ford Motor Company was incorporated on June 16, 1903, with a thousand shares of stock at $150 per share, of which Ford held 255 shares. The Dodge brothers had a hundred shares, and James Couzens, whose career was to be interlocked with Ford for many years, had twenty-five. Couzens started life as a $10-a-week car checker for Michigan Central. I would like very much to know what has happened to a man named Alex Y. Malcomson.[4] He too had 255 shares in the original company, an amount equal to Ford's, and he was its first treasurer. It seems that he was a coal dealer, and Couzens was a clerk in his office. Ford must, of course, have bought him out many years ago, as he bought out Couzens. I was unable to find anybody in Detroit who knew anything further about Mr. Malcomson. But it has been calculated

[3] Not many will recall that William C. Bullitt, who many years later became ambassador to Soviet Russia and France, was a member of this party.

[4] A 1,075 page handbook, *Report on the Motor Vehicle Industry*, prepared by the Federal Trade Commission, is the indispensable source for almost all details of this kind about the automobile industry.

4

that any original Ford investor who held his stock even for sixteen years, till 1919, made a return of 355,000 per cent on the investment.[5]

It is natural enough that Ford, like General Motors later, should have been the proving ground for many who became famous in the industry. The Dodge brothers I have just mentioned. William S. Knudsen, later to become a lieutenant general and among other things an early partner to Sidney Hillman in war production, was of course a Ford man for many years. So was Charles E. Sorensen, whom many think to be the actual inventor of the assembly line. Knudsen left Ford for General Motors, and presently sales of Chevrolet (named for a French racer of the day) passed Ford's. Ford, which had once sold 40 per cent of *all* passenger cars in the United States, has never recovered its lead; in 1941 its share of the total business was only 18 per cent. Malcolm W. Bingay, editorial director of the Detroit *Free Press*, told me that someone asked Ford once if he had not regretted letting Knudsen go. "That's a good question, a very legitimate question," Ford replied. "I'm not surprised that Chevrolet has passed us. Mr. Knudsen is the best production man in the United States. But he was getting too big for me. I spent more energy trying to handle him than my competitors."[6]

In 1920 the Ford accumulated surplus was more than 200 million dollars. In 1937 its surplus balance was more than 600 million dollars. But, over a period of eleven years ending in 1937, according to the Federal Trade Commission, Ford operated at a net average *loss* of 0.80 per cent. But since the reserves were so enormous and there were no hungry shareholders to pay off, this did not matter much. The Ford empire continued to grow, and its wealth in real terms remained literally incalculable. As everybody knows Ford has, or had, companies in Great Britain, Canada, Germany, and Japan, a large coal business so that he would always have his own access to coal, steamship lines, and rubber plantations in Brazil. The total assets of the company, as calculated by the New York *Times*, were still conservatively estimated at $1,021,325,159 in 1945.

Unorthodox hints to young men studying to be executives, who may like to know of Ford's business habits: He hates paper work, almost never writes a letter, very seldom issues an order and never keeps appointments unless he really feels like it.[7]

Perplexities increase when we leave the domain of pure business. Ford has an anti-Semitic past; yet at least one of the associates whom he most admires is Jewish, the architect who built most of his plants—

[5] Cf. *Combustion on Wheels*, by David L. Cohn, p. 83. Every dollar became $3,550.
[6] See Mr. Bingay's lively *Detroit Is My Own Home Town*.
[7] One of his secretaries was once put to work going through three waste baskets full of Ford's personal mail, some of which had been unanswered for two years. Cf. *Henry Ford*, by Samuel S. Marquis, D.D., p. 123.

Albert Kahn, one of the foremost industrial architects in the world.[8] He has been accused of being anti-Russian; yet Ford was the first big American industrialist to do business with Soviet Russia. He brought Russian engineers to Detroit by the sackful, taught them mass production, and sent them back to establish the Ford plant at Nizhni Novgorod, now called Gorki. Ford's theory was that anything that would assist Russia to become stable was a good thing; he liked to say, "It never hurts to put someone to work again." One result was that he got about 350 million dollars worth of Russian business—before the rest of the United States and the NAM woke up.

He is accused of being anti-Negro, but he has insisted on a substantial number of Negro workmen in all his plants since about 1914. One charge, a shade fanciful, might be argued against him—that he is antifeminist. Until World War II at least, extremely few women were employed at Ford's.

But now to other and more serious matters. Shortly after the outbreak of the war Ford said, "There is no righteousness in either cause. Both [sides] are motivated by the same evil impulse, which is greed." He began to show a most extraordinary catholicity in hiring people. Fritz Kuhn got a job at Ford's shortly after he arrived from Germany, and was a Bund leader in Detroit. There is no record, however, that Ford knew of his subversive actions. Colonel Lindbergh was a close friend and trusted employee at Willow Run for years. Ford had a great impulse to take in anybody who was in trouble no matter how disreputable the trouble might have been. For instance he promptly gave a job to an army officer who, following gunplay at Selfridge Field, was forced to give up his commission. Admiral Kimmell and General Short—who are in a totally different category of course—found jobs with Ford after Pearl Harbor.

Then there is the extraordinary tropism toward athletes. That such an imposing number of athletes are, or were, on the payroll, may however be more the result of the influence of Harry Bennett than of Ford himself. Athletes may be converted into healthy assistants. Ed Cicotte, the "Black Sox" pitcher, worked for Ford. A famous ex-hockey player named Stewart Evans was a director of labor relations for a time. A member of the Ford private police, Charlie Bernard, was once a Michigan All-American, and Bennett's secretary was also a football star. A celebrated ex-prize fighter, Kid McCoy, was a Bennett employe, and one of his friends, Harry Kipke, who had been coach at the University of Michigan, became a member of the university board of regents.[9]

[8] Also he likes to give athletes like Hank Greenberg winter jobs. Harry Newman, a former Michigan All-American, is labor relations director in one of the big units at River Rouge.
[9] According to John McCarten, *American Mercury*, "The Little Man in Henry Ford's Basement," May and June, 1940.

We know well Ford's fierce autochthonous puritanism. Once he threatened (but did not put the threat into effect) never to build a car again if prohibition were repealed. Is it too fanciful to associate this puritan impulse, the worship of a strong body, with his fondness for athletes? But if this is so, one is entitled to ask why so many people, no matter how superb physically, were hired whose moral qualities were not exactly puritan.

In any case the consequences of all this spread, even into politics. Detroit elections are city-wide and nonpartisan, and almost anybody with a big name in the world of sports is a good candidate. Two city councilmen today are Billy Rogell, a former shortstop of the Detroit Tigers, and Gus Dorais, formerly of Notre Dame, the University of Detroit, and the Detroit Lions.

Of course Ford is, in his own field, a man of authentic genius, and like many genuises he is apt to stray when he enters other fields. Basically he is a wily but simple-seeming peasant with an excessively developed mechanical skill. "Mr. Ford reads a machine the way a bibliophile reads a first edition," one of his men told me. Knudsen thinks that his greatest single characteristic is a tremendous ability to concentrate; others talk of a superlative intuition. I heard it seriously stated that if half a dozen carburetors were put on a table, identical in appearance but five good and one bad, Ford could tell by *looking* at them which one was defective. I also heard that, walking down the street and seeing a brick wall, he can compute instantly, within a margin of 1 or 2 per cent of error, how many bricks it contains.

Bennett, Internal Politics, and the Succession

I do nothing because it gives me pleasure.

—Henry Ford

Few characters in American industrial history have had more mysterious careers than Harry H. Bennett. He helped erect Ford's "iron curtain," and for years he operated behind it. Bennett has been a sailor, waterfront hanger-on, deep-sea diver, lightweight boxer, clarinet player, draftsman, and artist. He still paints. He keeps both lions and tigers on his estate. He was once shot in the stomach and seriously wounded, and was almost brained on another occasion when his guards sought to break up a labor demonstration.[10]

Bennett joined Ford in 1917 or thereabouts, and became in time head of what was known as the service department. This was the Ford police, which has been described as "the most powerful private police force in the world." Bennett, a tough boy, assembled around him a group of

[10] The only extended account of Bennett I have ever seen is the McCarten article cited above. *Fortune*, however, handled him with gingery caution in an article on the Ford heritage in June, 1944.

tough boys. Some were uniformed; some were not; that all members should wear insignia was one of the main points that the UAW insisted on in its first contract with Ford. Bennett and his men were, at first, primarily a security organization. The Ford family, with grandchildren growing up, feared kidnappers, and the Bennett group was in a position to know what, if any, gangs might be moving in on Detroit. But Bennett, who always called himself "Mr. Ford's personal man," nothing more, nothing less, was much more than a detective with underworld connections. First, his organization inevitably became the Ford spearhead against labor; second, it developed into a kind of palace guard. Bennett controlled appointments, labor relations, and personnel. He was the grand vizier who had the decision on the most important of all things in a structure like Ford's—access. For years, very few people ever saw the old man until they had been screened by Bennett's group, with its giant illuminated switchboard and system of telephones. A minor proof of this is that any newspaperman who had even a semblance of approach to Ford—or Bennett—was always sure of a good job in Detroit. Anybody near the throne was a kinglet.

Many people have sought to explain the hold Bennett had on Ford. The most reasonable and probably the best is simply that Ford liked him. Then, as he grew older, and was perhaps not quite so alert as in earlier years, Bennett's influence grew, and so did Ford's dependence on him as the one man he could trust. I asked several people in Detroit what "ran" much in the Ford organization—until two years ago. The answers were all but unanimous: "Harry Bennett."

The upper hierarchy of Ford executives did not accept this situation lightly, and at least one very important production man hated Bennett. So on the top level there came to be two camps, Bennett and anti-Bennett, with the Ford family itself involved.

Ford's only son was Edsel. He took over the presidency of the corporation in 1919, and was at least its titular head until his early and unexpected death in 1943. This was a crushing blow. The old man himself had to step out of "retirement" and take over. Edsel and Bennett were not close friends. One story is, in fact, that the real struggle at Ford was sometimes between the old man, supporting Bennett, against his own son. Another, highly suggestive, is that Ford *wanted* Edsel to demand that he, Ford, choose between Edsel and Bennett, as a test of Edsel's character, but Edsel, a notably decent and gentle character, could not bring himself to do so. Edsel's widow, a lady with great good sense, dignity, and courage, and the mother of Henry II, found herself in a key position. One widespread Detroit rumor, of course impossible to substantiate, is that she once threatened to sell her Ford stock on the open market, which would have compromised forever the closed character of the corporation, if Bennett's wings were not clipped.

On September 21, 1945, Henry Ford II, having reached the age of twenty-eight, took over the presidency of the company from his grandfather. A few days later, Bennett was "relieved of his position" as director in charge of administration, and in October he resigned. The board of directors was reshuffled, and several of the "Bennett" men among top executives were shelved. In other words young Henry moved in with a broom. The old guard began to scatter. Two years before, John S. Bugas, a young Wyoming lawyer who had become head of the FBI in Detroit, was hired by Ford as Bennett's chief assistant. When Bennett went out, Bugas succeeded him as director of personnel and labor relations, and has admirably handled the job ever since. John Edgar Hoover once publicly called Bugas "the best man in the FBI."

Finally, a word about young Henry. He is a careful, well-brought-up, plump young man, who takes with extreme seriousness his responsibilities. The old Ford hands, delighted to see the Bennett regime ended, call him "the world's greatest young fellow." Henry II went to Yale. He did not like to study much, and never was graduated. He enlisted in the Navy in 1941, and served two years; then he had a brief novitiate studying the Ford ropes, before acceding to the presidency. I have read several of his speeches. They are somewhat guarded, very much on the proper side, and conventionally well written. Some of them are so earnest that, even in the printed versions, the italics young Mr. Ford made for emphasis are preserved. When he gives an interview, he is quoted in the third person only. Little by little, his poise and confidence have been built up. A well-meaning and friendly person, he reveres the memory of his father, and it goes without saying that his mother is a signal and healthy influence. Mrs. Edsel, it might be said, is the spiritual mainspring of the Ford company today.

Young Henry, when he was still at Yale, fell in love with a girl named Anne McDonnell, one of fourteen children of James Francis McDonnell, a wealthy New York broker, and one of sixty-three grandchildren of an inventor, Thomas E. Murray. Miss McDonnell was, and is, a vigorous Catholic, whereas the Fords are Methodist. Monsignor Fulton J. Sheen, the prelate who assisted at the conversion to Catholicism of Heywood Broun and Clare Boothe Luce, gave young Henry instruction, and he was admitted to the Catholic church. *Time* printed a remarkable photograph of the wedding party, with Sheen among the guests. Henry's Catholicism, which is devout, is very little talked about in Detroit. At first people wondered what his grandfather would say. The old man, a masterfully oblique character, waited until several weeks after the wedding, and then, after many years of unsuccessful attempts to persuade him to do so, consented to enter the thirty-third degree of Masonry at an imposing ceremony at which all the thirty-third degree Masons in Michigan were present.

What will happen to old Henry's fortune? About this there is as much mystery as anything in Detroit. Something exists known as the Ford Foundation. This owns Greenfield Village and the Edison Institute (the village, one sees, may turn out to have a utilitarian aspect after all), and as such is a nonprofit organization and is tax exempt. When Ford dies, it is generally believed that most of his wealth will be left to this foundation; if so, the huge estate may escape most inheritance taxes. This procedure will also presumably insure that no Ford stock will have to be dumped on the market to meet enormous tax charges. The old man is believed to own 58 per cent of Ford stock today, and the foundation, on his death, will almost certainly be the richest in the world.

Biggest Union in the World

We come now to the International Union, United Automobile, Aircraft and Agricultural Implement Workers of America, CIO, the biggest labor organization in America. From 15,000 dues-paying members ten years ago, it jumped to 1,250,000 during the war. The figure is considerably less today, mostly because of contraction in the aviation industry. But it is not size that makes the UAW so important. What counts is its power, leadership, heterogeneity, and explosiveness. This is the most volcanic union in the country.

Into Detroit, from the time that Ford announced the $5.00 day, have streamed for years the most miscellaneous types of labor; hence the UAW contains everything from Ku-Kluxers to Trotskyists, from political theorists of the most advanced type to hillbillies who can scarcely read. The UAW is a "rank-and-file union," in which power rises from the bottom; its leaders, unlike those in the United Steelworkers for instance, have to deal with a constantly shifting body of men who demand the most complete democratic freedom of expression; this has imposed at times an extreme strain on the leadership, in that its first duty has had to be to educate, to teach responsibility.

Also the newness and the speed of rise of the UAW, its enormousness (after all its "population" is twice that of the city of New Orleans or Minneapolis) and its association with an extremely volatile industry, have made fissures inevitable, and a right wing and a left wing have developed. For a time the criterion was whether a member was anti-Communist or not. Now this is not nearly so true. None of the top UAW men are Communists. The Communist philosophy was smartly beaten down at the last Atlantic City convention. Actually differences of view among leaders, though expressed with vociferousness on occasion, are based mostly on personalities, as we shall see.

What is remarkable, in fact, is not so much the degree to which the UAW is split, but its cohesiveness in spite of all the centrifugal rivalries. One factor making for unity is the character of Detroit itself, a city packed with hate, and representative of the "tycoon mind" at its most backward. Here, men who could scarcely understand a newspaper headline became millionaires wielding vast economic power overnight. The great automobile companies for years were not only vehemently antiunion; they thought of labor simply as an inanimate commodity. A Detroit skyscraper, one of the tallest buildings in the world, was built largely by scab labor brought in from Canada, and paid about 20 per cent under the American scale. A mild indication of the kind of thing that went on was that, according to testimony heard by the La Follette Civil Liberties Committee of the Senate, General Motors alone paid $839,764 for detective service in a two-year period. A workman never knew whether or not the man next to him on the assembly line was a spy.

Resentment against all this and much else in Detroit helped hold the UAW together. Richard T. Frankensteen told me during his race for the mayoralty that, among other things, the city was "the rat capital of the world." He did not mean human rats. He meant those that feed in alleys on the city's garbage. Detroit has one acre of playground per thousand population (the figures are approximate) compared to New York's twelve, Chicago's eleven, and Cleveland's nine. It has two outdoor swimming pools—for 1,623,452 people. Its transportation systems are even more dilapidated than those of Chicago and, in 1945, on the opening day of school, 30,000 children could not get in, because there wasn't any room.

It isn't easy to work out the fissures in UAW leadership on a straight "left" or "right" basis. A more satisfactory division would be between Reutherites, Thomasites, and anti-Reutherites. Walter P. Reuther, the president today, is both a socialist and a marked conservative. Like social democrats in Europe, whom he strongly resembles, he is a Marxist in theory, but what he hates most in the world are Communists. He calls the American species "prostitutes" and "saboteurs" and points out that *they* did not defend Stalingrad. In return Reuther is the Communists' Public Enemy No. 1, and, he says, they spent $50,000 (unsuccessfully) to beat him at the last convention. Yet, by most newspaper readers and by opinion generally throughout the country, Reuther is thought of as on the extreme *left* wing.

Actually the leftist leader is the former president and present vice president, R. J. Thomas. He too is very far from being a Communist, however. His role was mostly that of moderator, at least till the 1946 convention. Associated with Thomas are Richard T. Leonard, an able man who for years was head of the union's Ford department and who is now another vice-president, and George F. Addes, who has been secretary-treasurer and the second-ranking officer almost from the beginning. Addes is supposed to be the most leftist of all, and usually he is backed by the Communists. It is an interesting point that he should also be an ardent Catholic.

In 1946, Reuther won the UAW presidency by 124.4 out of 8,765.2 votes. The voting was hairline close right down the line. Leonard, a Thomas supporter, squeezed in by fewer than fifty votes. So today UAW is run by Reuther and an anti-Reuther cabinet. The supreme ruling body is a board of twenty-two men, elected on the basis of the per capita contribution of every affiliated local union. Of the present twenty-two, Reuther's men are a small minority. This does not mean, however, that he does not have great power.

A further word on Thomas. When I saw him he said that factionalism was less acute than at any time in the history of the union. I do not know if he would say the same thing today. Early in 1947, amid hurly-burly over the Allis-Chalmers strike, Reuther called him "false, malicious, and irresponsible," and Thomas replied in kind.[11] Originally Thomas was a Murray-Hillman man. He was a worker for years in a Chrysler body plant. He would rather be president of the CIO some day than of the Ford Motor Company, or, doubtless, the United States. Some people think that, like labor leaders in England, his duties and responsibilities have made him too standpat and stodgy.

A further word, too, on Frankensteen, another UAW vice president until recently. The name is pronounced to rhyme with "bean," incidentally. A point somewhat extraordinary, considering the name, is that his assistant when he was a big union figure was named Dragon. During the 1945 mayoralty campaign, his enemies called him a Jew in the German districts of Detroit, and a German in the Jewish districts. Actually Richard Truman Frankensteen is an Episcopalian, though most of his family is Catholic; his mother is of Irish stock. Frankensteen is one of the most extroverted men in the American labor movement. He is a very large, handsome youngster, bursting with cheerfulness and vitality; he was a football star at both the University of Detroit and the University of Dayton; he likes night clubs and conviviality in moderation and has written several plays, including a musical comedy called *Gypsy Moon*.

Frankensteen, along with Reuther, was beaten up in a famous fracas by company police, at the "Battle of the Overpass," sometimes called the "Battle of Bull's Run," outside Gate No. 4 at River Rouge in 1937. What happened is all a matter of public, though confused, record. Frankensteen, Reuther, and their comrades were passing out circulars and handbills as part of an organizing drive. This procedure was against

[11] New York *Times*, February 17, 1947.

the Dearborn ordinances. Later, however, such ordinances forbidding circularization were declared unconstitutional by the Supreme Court. Ford men broke up the demonstration, and the UAW boys were mauled and set upon.[12] Frankensteen, who is handy with his fists, is indignant to this day that he couldn't fight, because someone got him from behind and pulled his coat over his head, imprisoning his arms.

Frankensteen ran for mayor in 1945. Whether this was with official UAW blessing is disputable. He ran, so I heard it put, "without much previous consultation." Some CIO right-wingers voted for him on the theory that, if he won, he would have to leave the union. But Frankensteen is not much interested in ideology one way or the other. He won the primaries neatly, but was beaten in the runoff.

History of the UAW, as such, begins in about 1936. I have heard its steep climb described as the "greatest surge forward of the under-possessed" in the history of industry. Here Ford enters the story again, because he was inevitably the crux and the test. In 1928 there were 435,000 automobile workers, mostly unorganized; their average pay was $33 for a forty-four-hour week. Came the depression. In 1933 only 244,000 had employment; they worked only thirty-three hours a week, and their take-home pay was $20.10.[13] After prodigious struggles in the 1930's the UAW managed to organize a few plants, and some successful small strikes followed—against Bendix at South Bend, and Midland Steel and Kelsey-Hayes in Detroit. The first great General Motors strike was centered at Flint and was won on February 11, 1937. Reuther played a conspicuous role in this as we shall see. A sit-down at Chrysler followed, equally successful. By the end of 1937, the UAW was in full swing, and had won contracts with four hundred companies.

But Ford held out. This was the tough nut to crack. He was the lonely patriarch of the business. To organize Ford became a consuming ambition from the psychological as well as practical point of view. Ford broke up a UAW organizing drive in 1937. Then came periods of acute dissension in the UAW, which all but wrecked it. In 1939, however, "strategy strikes" were successful against both GM and Chrysler, and the union knit itself together. Ford still fiercely resisted unionization. Finally the UAW became strong enough to force the issue, and, in 1941, after a short strike, the National Labor Relations Board ordered an election, and Ford workers voted for UAW-CIO by three to one. The Ford folk had to accept this or be in contempt of federal law. Then—to everybody's immense surprise—Ford, as if giving up the fight for good and all and accepting in good spirit the fact that he *was* beaten, gave the

[12] Pictures of both Reuther and Frankensteen, with bloody shirts but looking victorious, were printed in *Life*, September 10, 1945.
[13] Figures from a pamphlet by Edward Levinson, *The Rise of the Auto Workers*, quoting statistics from the Automobile Manufacturers Association.

union practically everything it asked for, including the first union shop and the first dues checkoff in the automobile manufacturing industry. Ford's relations with the UAW have been fairly good ever since—with occasional spasms and though there have been plenty of wildcat strikes. Leonard and Bugas get on together well, and Ford still pays the highest wages in the business and is still the only company operating a union shop.

The UAW grew hard and fast after this. With Ford organized, very few other manufacturers dared to stand out.

Man Named Reuther

Walter P. Reuther, a modest but ambitious redheaded young man with an earnest smile and a beguiling sort of self-confidence, is one of the most stimulating men in American labor. For several reasons his story is worth telling briefly. In a way, despite the most obvious differences, he is almost as typical an American as Ford, if only for the qualities of savvy, industriousness, and enterprise.

Reuther (pronounced Roother, not Royter), was born in Wheeling, West Virginia, forty years ago, the son of a German brewery worker and devout old-school Socialist. Young Reuther had the polemics of the working class drilled into him from the cradle, and when he was still a schoolboy he organized a local shop. Then, finding the Wheeling horizon too limited, he set out to make his way in the world. He went to Detroit, and became an expert tool and die maker at Ford. He knew, however, that work was not enough. There was something known as school. So, while working an eight-hour day, he also worked his way through high school and three years of Wayne University. He got up at dawn, caught his first class at eight, did his school work till one, and then put in his stint at Ford from 3 till 11:30. After this—homework! His brother Victor, who is now director of the education department of the UAW, kept house and did the cooking. Before long, Walter stood first in his class, and was earning $12.00 a day. Then Ford fired him for "union activity."

Reuther passed his final examinations, drew every cent he had out of the bank on the day before the Detroit banks crashed in 1933, and then, with Victor, set out on a trip around the world. The Reuther boys were away for thirty-three months. As Walter says today, "We wanted to find out how the world was living." A trip like this is a fairly conventional thing for young Americans to do, but few have ever done it quite so thoroughly as the Reuther boys. They arranged their itinerary as a "tour in social engineering." It was a serious vocational attempt, very German and Socialist, to get underpinning for a future career. The boys worked their way across the Atlantic, bought pushbikes, and cycled 12,000 miles in western Europe. Only twice in nine months did they sleep in hotels. If they ever bothered to look at the "sights," like the leaning tower at Pisa, this was mere frosting on the cake. What they really liked to do was visit mills in Lancashire and mines in Gelsen-kirchen. Whenever they were broke they paused to get a job. They slept at student hostels in Germany, joined workers' groups, helped organize them, and, as Hitler was rising to power, made contacts in the Socialist underground. Victor spoke excellent German but, as Walter laughs about it today, "with such a wonderful West Virginia accent that the Germans thought we came from some remote part of Swabia."

Next, Russia. The boys traveled 18,000 miles in the Soviet Union. They are among the very few Americans who, in those days, reached Central Asia and saw Samarkand. Being skilled mechanics, they had no trouble getting jobs. Walter became, in fact, an instructor in the Ford plant at Gorki, and showed Russian boys how to build gasket dies with tolerances to one-seven-thousandth of an inch. "It was darned delicate work," he says today.

One day the Reuthers got a letter from another brother, Roy, telling them that the automobile situation was popping and to come home. They took the Trans-Siberian to Manchuria, bicycled briefly through Japan, and eventually arrived back in Detroit.

By 1936, Reuther had become an important cog in the stirring UAW. He organized a small local on the west side of Detroit. This he merged with six other locals, and so created the first Reuther "machine," membership seventy-eight. He borrowed three hundred dollars, opened an office, and bought a typewriter. In nine months he had 32,000 paid-up members, with organizations in forty shops. "To be a union leader in those days," he reminisces, "you had to run like blazes to keep up with the membership."

Reuther's first signal coup was the Kelsey-Hayes strike in December, 1936. He tied up Kelsey-Hayes, which makes wheels and brake drums for Ford, and which had some 5,000 workers, though he himself had not more than thirty-five men in the plant. This was one of the first three considerable strikes the UAW won, and it presaged the organization of the whole industry.

This is how Reuther did it. He was busy passing out leaflets and making speeches at street corners. Such activity did not satisfy him. He wanted something more decisive and dramatic. But he had only a handful of people in the plant, and he could not get in himself, having been blacklisted as a notorious organizer. What the workers were protesting about most was not wages but the speed-up. Reuther had an idea. He was helpless unless he could contrive to get inside. He suggested that a girl on the day shift, in department 49, a brake-shoe line, should faint at the exact moment when the pace was fiercest. If the superintendent was duly deceived by this artifice he would pull a switch and stop the assembly line. Then there would be a scramble and the workers would quit and demand that Reuther, their leader, be called in.

The scheme worked to perfection. The girl "fainted" on schedule. Reuther was waiting at the end of a telephone. After much commotion the dialogue with the personnel director of the company went something like this:

Director: "Workers in 49 won't work. They say to call you up."

Reuther: "What do you want me to do?"

Director: "Put 'em back to work."

Reuther: "How can I? Will they listen?"

Director: "They listen to you on street corners."

Reuther: "I can't talk to 'em from here. Will you let me in?"

The company obligingly sent a car for him and by the time he arrived the strike had wild-fired, with several thousand workers milling around; Reuther climbed on a pile of boxes, and started to make a speech. The personnel director grabbed him by the coat, yelling, "What's going on here? You said you'd put 'em back to work!" Reuther's single-line reply has become a classic in Detroit folklore: "I can't put 'em back to work," he shouted, "until I get 'em organized!"

The rest of the story I have no space for, though it is full of punch and color. Reuther made a deal for a meeting between company and workers the next morning, and, as the night shift arrived, managed to harangue its members too. By morning, 2,000 men and women were organized. Then the negotiations failed. Reuther ordered his members (a) to stick by their machines, and (b) not to work at them. This, the most notable of the early sit-downs, lasted ten days, whereupon the company gave in.

Reuther strategy had a good deal to do with the great GM strike that followed in January, 1937. One incident is still recalled as "Reuther's feint." The key plant at Chevrolet was no. 4, which makes the actual motors. This became Reuther's object of attack. But he carefully contrived that everybody should think that he was going after no. 9, a bearing plant, not no. 4. Such stratagems were forced on him because he was not at all sure of his own men. Of key men in the Chevrolet local, he trusted only a few; some others might be stool pigeons. The upshot was that, by feinting at plant no. 9, he not only managed to win no. 4, but to find out who his traitors were. They tipped the guards off to protect no. 9, whereupon Reuther and his loyal cohorts promptly made for no. 4, half a mile away, which was denuded of protection. By the time the police got back, Reuther and his group were safe inside. They held out till the end of the forty-four day strike. This strike, which was national in scope and which was not predominantly fought on the issue of wages but on the right to unionize, turned the balance for the whole industry. The UAW was really "in" from this time on.

Another well-known Reuther accomplishment was the "strategy" strike in 1939, during the interval when GM was tooling for the next year's production. Reuther persuaded his colleagues that it was at this exact time that the industry was most vulnerable, and that by drawing out a few key men, tool and die makers, he could tie up the whole GM structure. He did so, and General Motors capitulated after an interval.

In these days violence was plentiful. Things have moved so fast that it is almost impossible to realize that, until the Flint strike, the great companies did not even answer letters from unions. Labor "negotiations" were matters for plug-uglies. Think by contrast of the great 1945-46 strike which Reuther also led against General Motors. Not a single person was hurt in a tie-up that lasted 113 days. There was not one bloody nose.

An attempt to beat up and possibly kill Reuther was made in 1938. Walter, Victor, and a group of friends were quietly celebrating a birthday in the family. Somebody ordered chop suey over the telephone. Half an hour later came a knock on the apartment door. Victor opened it, thinking the food had arrived. But two sluggers pushed their way in. One snapped, "We want Walter Reuther," and the other pointed out, "There's the ——— ——— in the corner. We're taking you for your last ride tonight." The sluggers, armed with a blackjack and gun, herded family and friends against the wall, and then appeared to lose their nerve. Remarks came like "We can't get him out of the room with all these people here," "Shoot him here," "Not before all these witnesses," and "Well, kill him with the blackjack." Reuther grabbed the blackjack from one of the thugs, and a struggle started. He was being beaten when a UAW man jumped out of the second-story window, and called the police. The sluggers ran. It took an hour and a half before the police came.

This episode was thoroughly aired in court subsequently. The two thugs were arrested and identified, and Reuther, who had not been badly hurt, got a telephone call from an anonymous informant, describing who had hired them, for what price, and why. After fierce commotions, the pair agreed to plead guilty, provided that the charge was made something less than assault with intent to kill, which carries a twenty-year sentence in Michigan. Reuther refused to reduce the charge. When the case came to trial the two men were acquitted. Some months after this, one of the sluggers called Victor on the telephone. He said that he hoped the Reuther brothers had no hard feelings, that he was simply carrying out a routine assignment, and he wanted to make amends by asking them out to dinner.

For the last half dozen years the outline of Reuther's career is well known. In 1940 the "Reuther plan," a project for the conversion of empty automobile plants to aircraft production, aroused national attention. It is an interesting fact that, when Charles E. Wilson, president of General Electric,[14] was running the War Production Board, he wanted Walter Reuther as vice chairman. Meantime his philosophy has solidified. Expressed in a sentence, it is to the effect that industrial and economic democracy must operate unhampered in the United States, if political democracy is to survive.

General Motors: First Glimpse

The business of the United States, Mr. Coolidge said once, is business; above all, this is the country of the giant corporation. General Motors is, in the words of the Federal Trade Commission, "the world's most complicated and most profitable manufacturing enterprise." Its monumental office building is the central citadel of Detroit,[15] and it carries the ball for the entire industry, as it were. No matter how idiosyncratically important Ford may be, GM is much more important in setting the tone for the business as a whole. Ford is big, but General Motors is twice as big.

It would be inaccurate, however, to think of Motors as a peculiarly Detroit phenomenon, or of Detroit as predominantly a GM town. The capital of General Motors is New York. Of its stock, between a fifth and a quarter—representing something like 600 million dollars at today's prices—is held by the Du Ponts of Delaware. It has 102 plants all over the nation, and its biggest money-maker, Chevrolet, lives in Flint, not Detroit. Flint is also the principal site of Fisher Bodies. General Motors has always believed in autonomy within autonomy; Buick and Cadillac and their kin, up to a certain level, make their own decisions. Outside the office building, probably not more than 25,000 out of General Motors' 250,000 employees and workers live in Detroit at all.

I heard a labor man say admiringly once that "GM is the most brilliantly operated company in the world." Automobile men laugh with scorn when you compare it to U. S. Steel. Steel, they say, started out as a virtual monopoly, and today holds only about a third of American steel production; General Motors started from nothing, and today approximately 45.6 per cent of *all* automobile business in the country is in its hands. Thirty-five per cent of *all* reconversion in America was a GM job, and its 1945 balance sheet shows assets of more than two billion dollars. Motors has an invested capital of $1,440,000,000, "a sum greater

[14] Not to be confused with the Charles E. Wilson who is president of General Motors.

[15] An odd point is that the UAW headquarters are a small low building just across the street, lying as it were in GM's shadow. It is so modest that it doesn't even have an elevator.

than the combined bonded debt of New York, California, and Illinois."[16]
In 1941, the last "normal" year, its net sales were $2,437,000,000 which
amounted to about 7 per cent of all American manufacturing sales. From
1936 to 1944 inclusive, it earned an average of 16.3 per cent on its
invested capital, to the benefit of some 426,000 stockholders; for the
years 1942-44, its average net profit was $161,000,000. Some earlier
comparative figures are:

Name of Corporation	Average Profits, 11 Years
General Motors Corporation	$173,236,252
American Telephone & Telegraph Co.	150,524,232
Standard Oil Co. (New Jersey)	86,811,276
United States Steel Corporation	48,586,563
American Tobacco Co.	29,395,625
International Harvester Co.	26,668,811
Chrysler Corporation	24,213,767
Goodyear Tire & Rubber Co.	8,144,037

The automobile business is, as is well known, not only the most
competitive but the most lucrative in the country. Calculations by the
Securities Exchange Commission covering the total profit per $100 of
invested capital in a group of industries, are as follows: Automobiles,
25.54; Office Machinery, 19.54; Agricultural Machinery, 16.93; Cigarettes, 16.63; Chemicals and Fertilizer, 15.95; Mail Order Houses, 15.17;
Containers and Closures, 13.06; Oil Refiners, 10.67; Motion Pictures,
10.63; Sugar Beet Refiners, 10.60; Steel Products, 7.53; Tires and
Rubber Products, 7.18; Department Stores, 6.37; Cement, 5.96; Meat
Packers, 4.90.

In 1944 the Treasury's list of top money-makers in the country
put Charles E. Wilson of GM fifth, with a salary plus bonuses of
$362,954. Two other Motors executives were in the first ten, Ormond
E. Hunt ($287,745), and Albert Bradley ($276,018); five more, including Charles F. Kettering, were among the first twenty-five, all
having received more than $200,000 in the year.[17] One might mention
that Walter Reuther's salary, as president of UAW, is $9,000. Also the
GM men suffered sharp reductions in 1944 as against 1943. Wilson's
income in 1943, when he was the second highest paid man in the country,
was $459,041; only Louis B. Mayer exceeded him. An auxiliary point
is that the salaries at their regular jobs of the three distinguished men
who comprised Mr. Truman's fact-finding commission in the General

[16] Keith Hutchison in *The Nation*, December 8, 1945. Figures on average net
profit are from a round table discussion by Charles E. Wilson.
[17] Over-all leader in the 1944 returns was Leo McCarey, motion picture producer
and director of *Going My Way*, whose total income was $1,038,035. Second was
Charles H. Strub, founder and executive vice president of the Los Angeles Turf
Club.

Motors strike, and who in effect determined the course of automobile wages for the immediate future, probably do not run to more than $10,000 each. The three were Milton Eisenhower, president of the Kansas State College, Lloyd K. Garrison, former dean of the University of Wisconsin law school, and Judge Stacy of the North Carolina Supreme Court.

Even more than Ford, General Motors has been an opulent pool for various fantastic careers and fortunes. De Tocqueville, in one of his prophetic passages, mentions "how an aristocracy may be created by manufactures." Kettering, perhaps the greatest of all GM men, the man who invented the self-starter and much else, started life as a cash register mechanic. William C. Durant, whose history runs in and out of Motors like that of an erratic and often victorious racehorse, was a grocer's clerk. The father of the seven Fisher brothers operated a village livery. K. T. Keller, the present boss of Chrysler, was a GM man for years. Walter Chrysler himself, who was once head of production for Motors, a Kansas boy, was an engine wiper who got five cents an hour. When he left the organization he sold his interest for 18 million dollars.[18]

General Motors has almost four and a half million stockholders; these own the business, but they do not control it. It is a familiar American phenomenon that, in any very large corporation with diffused ownership, a minority group of stockholders may exert control. The average GM stockholder has 1,094 shares; a great many have much less. But Du Pont has a solid block of 10,000,000 out of the 44,986,373 shares outstanding. Seven GM officers or directors are also Du Pont directors, and 37 Motors men hold 192 interlocking directorates in other corporations. As an indication of the immensity of this network here are a few of them—J. P. Morgan, Drexel & Co., the Bankers Trust Co. of New York, the Guaranty Trust, the National Bank of Detroit, the Bank of Montreal, the Pullman Co., Imperial Chemicals Ltd., General Electric, the New York Stock Exchange, the Lawyers Trust Co., the Emigrant Industrial Savings Bank, Ethyl Gas, the Yellow Truck and Coach Co., Kennecott Copper, the Pennsylvania Railroad, Consolidated Edison of New York, Bell Telephone of Canada, United States Steel, International Nickel, and the New York Central Railroad.

Note on Sensitiveness

One singular point is the extreme sensitiveness of most of the great American corporations. I do not mean General Motors in particular. Almost all have their tenor notes. At the least whisper that, even in the most legitimate way, they may be "running" things, they jump

[18] Most of these details are from Bingay, *op. cit.*

and quiver. One intimation about their internal life, no matter how legitimate or correct, and these monoliths shudder like aspens in the breeze. They may be fat as Japanese wrestlers, but they shy at criticism like featherweights.

Faces Without Names

There are too many names in this book. Let us have a word for people nameless. My mind rolls back through the lights and shadows of long middle western years, and I remember—

The biology teacher who was going to win a Nobel prize some day, and who drank, just a little, and who was the only happy cynic I have ever met, and who watched with icy glee the miserable shortcomings of his students, when he knew that he was not going to win a Nobel prize some day.

The young woman almost thirty, who had three children in a Wisconsin town, whose husband had been killed Christmas Eve, who was cool and crisp and who conceded absolutely nothing, but whose eyes were frightened, because she earned a living running a small airport, and the only pilot she trusted was a Negro.

The old men on piers, very old, fishing in Lake Michigan when the steamer from Mackinac came in, and talking about the war, with grave grumbling nods of the head, in thick German accents, and the restless, taut, dissatisfied schoolgirl on the upper deck, who restlessly thumbed through a book by Proust, with her chic hair tossing, and who would be off to Vassar next year, and whose father had had a much thicker German accent.

The Minnesota official, frugal and prominent in state affairs, who hitch-hiked with his four growing sons through five states in order to see TVA.

The stewardess on the airline who had waited for three years to get a job on the airline, and she was twenty-two, and she had lived in eleven cities, and this was her twenty-seventh job, and she was going to hold onto it forever, that is until she got married.

The young student at the university, who had headaches every afternoon at a certain hour because of the excitement of reading new books, who talked long dreams to himself and wanted to do good for the world.

Generalizations in Drypoint

Perhaps we are far enough along now to risk brief generalizations about the United States as a whole, with particular reference to the Middle West. Three dominant problems are:

Item: How, if a period of sharp depression should come again, with widespread and damaging unemployment, to reconcile economic and political democracy—how, in other words, to maintain a democratic system if the economic machine breaks down.

Item: How to maintain military power and at the same time give it up, viz., how to use the tremendous military predominance of the United States *for* the furtherance of world organization and peace.

Item: How to reconcile the pleadings and pressures of special interests with the legitimate needs of the people as a whole, under a democratic political system—in other words, how to make democracy work and maintain the essential unity of the United States.

Chapter 26
Men and Politics in Ohio

Ohio's deeper boom was there . . .
—Maurice Thompson

FRANK J. LAUSCHE,[1] governor from 1945 to 1947 of one of the great master states, Ohio, is a character like no other in American public life—something of an athlete, something of a poet, something of a gypsy. What he seems to possess above all is a quality both mysterious in origin and of inestimable value to a politician—a very considerable personal vote-getting capacity. Lausche won the Ohio governorship in 1944 against the most varying of obstacles; for instance he was the first Roman Catholic ever elected governor, and also the first son of an immigrant.

Lausche, pronounced like Low-she, is not nearly so well known outside Ohio as in, though gradually he is being talked of on the national plane. But within Ohio, particularly in and around Cleveland where he was mayor for some years, he is a legendary figure. A small joke makes the point. A teacher told her first graders that the next day was Columbus Day, and that they wouldn't have to come to school.

"Who was Columbus?" a child asked.

"He discovered America."

"Nuts!" replied the child. "America was discovered by Frank J. Lausche."

Background, Heritage, Career

The Lausche saga begins in Slovenia. His father came from a small band of Germans who lived in the Gottschee, an Alpine valley behind the Adriatic near Fiume, in what is now Jugoslavia; the clan moved into Ljubljana, the capital of Slovenia, about a hundred years ago. A small Teutonic island in a Slavic ocean, it maintained an exclusive German culture and strict use of the German language for a time, and then intermarriage began to take place. Lausche's father was half-German, half-Slovene; his mother was pure Slovene.

[1] Lausche lost his campaign for re-election in November, 1946—tribute indeed to the overwhelming nature of the Republican midterm sweep. Lausche got more than a million votes, however, and lost by only about 35,000, in the closest gubernatorial race Ohio has seen in a quarter of a century. No one should think that he is permanently retired from public life. As a matter of convenience I am letting this chapter, which was written before the elections, stand largely as I wrote it.

422

Anybody who knows that part of Europe will understand what this heritage means. The mountain folk of Jugoslavia, particularly those whose valleys climb down to the sea, have a complex personal distinction. People like the Lausches have a fine appetite for meaty, sauce-laden food; they like to drink, to saunter across meadows blanketed with flowers, to climb mountains in the spring; they are passionately fond of music and hand-embroidered costumes; they have vitality, a love for healthy indolence, and a great gift for happiness.

Lausche's father came to America in 1885, and Frank was born in Cleveland ten years later. The father worked in the steel mills, and died when his son was twelve. Also he edited a Slovene-language newspaper, with a neighborhood circulation in Cleveland, for a time; the fact that his father was an editor—and a radical editor who always took his own side, that is, the side of the underpossessed—had a profound bearing on Frank's life. Young Lausche had to earn a living, in the Cleveland slums, practically from the time he can remember. There was a brood of younger sisters and brothers. His mother, whose memory he adores, ran a small wine shop to help support the family.

Look at the Lausches today. One of Frank's sisters, Mrs. Josephine Welf, is a musician who has made a specialty of recording Croatian and Slovene folk songs; her husband is a referee with the State Industrial Commission. (This was a civil service appointment; Lausche had nothing to do with it. There is not the faintest trace of nepotism about him; no relative has ever been given any kind of job.) The family has a close spirit of kinship, and one thing binding it together is music. One brother, Dr. William J. Lausche, a dentist, is also a composer; another, Charles, is an attorney who plays the piano and is also one of the community's leading bowlers. One sister is the wife of a doctor (of Jugoslav origin); another brother, Harold, works in the Fisher Body plant.

Lausche himself married a girl of Scotch-Irish descent—once again we witness the extraordinary miracle of the American melting pot—named Jane Sheal. She is not a Catholic. She plays the piano, and often accompanies her husband at the violin. For many years the Lausches did not have a house of their own; they lived in Cleveland with Mrs. Lausche's father, an engineer, on 100th Street. It did not embarrass them in the least when the neighborhood began to break down, so that a Chinese laundry is next door today. Lausche's wife, a highly competent young woman, has been of the most signal service to his career, and a strong liberal influence; she goes to all his political meetings and some people in Columbus like to say that she should be the governor, not he. The Lausches have no children. The fact that she is not a Catholic has made a minor political issue. Lausche himself has never paid much attention to religion in the formal sense.

Reminiscing a bit in Columbus, the governor told me that there had been two great turning points in his life, following two great decisions he had to take.

As a boy he was fascinated by athletics; he played marbles, horseshoes and corner lot games of every kind (and today he shoots golf in the middle 70's). Growing up, he found that he was pretty good at baseball, and he became a semi-pro. Then he got a job as third baseman with Lawrence, Massachusetts, and later with Duluth. Came the First World War. Lausche was learning to be a soldier at Camp Gordon, Georgia. A scout named Charlie Frank, who is now owner of the Atlanta Club in the Southern League, was the camp's recreational director and manager of its team. Lausche, one of sixty thousand men, made the team; Frank promptly signed him for Atlanta when the war should be over. Lausche was discharged from the Army in January, 1919, and had to decide whether or not to accept the Atlanta offer, and formally adopt professional baseball as a livelihood. Finally, after much turmoil in mind and heart, he chose not to do so. He went back to Cleveland, attended law school at night, and started what became a political career.

Lausche was admitted to the bar in 1920, placing second highest in the state examinations, and practiced until 1932. He was then appointed to a judgeship in the municipal court to fill an unexpired term; the next year, running for office for the first time, he was elected to the Cleveland bench (he led the ticket) and served till 1937, when he moved up— also by election—to the court of common pleas, which is the Ohio equivalent of the supreme court in other states. He held this post till 1941, when he became mayor. Lausche was an admirable judge. For one thing, he loved the law; for a time he taught judicial equity at the John Marshall School of Law. He discovered by so doing that the first thing a teacher must learn is to keep ahead of his own students, a lesson he has sought never to forget. In time, other lawyers came to send their difficult cases to him. As a judge what he liked particularly were laborious cases in equity. Most of his colleagues preferred simple personal injury cases and the like; Lausche took on the difficult ones where, without a jury, he had to decide both facts and law. His most famous decision was probably that in the so-called Crosby case, when he laid down the principle that picketing was illegal if undertaken by members of unions not employed at the place picketed, or if it could be conclusively shown that the employer involved had amicable relations with his own employees. After years of tussle, this decision was reversed by the Supreme Court.

The second great turning point in Lausche's career came in 1935. He could have gone on being a judge all his life. But a group of civic-minded citizens, and Cleveland is probably the most civic-minded city in the country, urged him to run for mayor. He was very hesitant. He had never held administrative office; he had no idea whether he had the talent necessary. (And indeed, his worst fault today is lack of interest in administration.) Finally he decided not to run. Harold Burton, now a Supreme Court justice, ran instead, and won handsomely, with Lausche cordially supporting him. In 1937 and 1939 friends again urged Lausche to try for the job himself. He refused. Then Burton went on to the Senate, whereupon Lausche was sounded out once more. He happened to be en route to San Jose, California, for a holiday with his wife's aunt, and he told his supporters that he would give them his decision when he returned. One day he dropped into an old church near Monterey; he heard the chant of the liturgy, and saw the warm rays of the sun pouring through windows bound with ancient iron. He began to meditate, finally made up his mind, and decided that he would not run for mayor. Then he returned to Cleveland. Something "clicked," as he puts it, when he saw his home town again; what it was, he does not know till this day. But he reversed himself, and announced his candidacy.

Lausche, a profoundly honest man, resigned from his judgeship, a twelve thousand dollar job—more than he got as governor—before he was nominated. He felt that it would be morally wrong to run for one office while holding another, though the opposite example has been set by, let us say, a hundred thousand other politicians who hold onto whatever job they have as long as possible. Nowadays Lausche sometimes regrets his decision. He substituted for the serenity of the judicial chamber—its "absorption and dignity," as he says—the turbulence and clamor of a hot municipal campaign. He didn't like a lot of things. But anyway, he was elected mayor, and by a thumping 61 per cent majority; he got the biggest vote in the history of the Cleveland mayoralty. In 1943 he ran again, and was even more thumpingly reelected; he received 71 per cent of all votes cast, which is probably a record for any big city election in our time.

Then, the next year, came the first race for governor. I shall go into this for one reason only, to illustrate Lausche's attitude toward (a) professional politicians, (b) money.

While mayor of Cleveland he had paid no attention whatever to the regular Democratic machine; he kept all ward heelers and party hacks as far away as possible. This led to strain and resentment both; on one occasion he flatly refused an offer of three thousand dollars for campaign expenditures by the Democratic National Committee; thereafter the party leadership in Washington let him severely alone. But to fight an election in Ohio costs a staggering amount of money. Lausche nevertheless set up a kind of rule, that no contribution should exceed one hundred dollars. Once Marshall Field (whom he has never met) gave him $1,000, and there have been a few donors of $250 or $500, but by and large the $100 limit remained in force. Hence the great bulk of Lausche money had to come from little people who gave small sums; most contributions were under ten dollars, and there were plenty of half-dollars and even quarters. Lausche set up another rule, that under no circumstances would he accept money from gambling or racketeer interests, or from any person doing business with the state. All told, in the 1944 race, he spent only $27,162.75, a minuscule sum for Ohio. His Republican opponent, Mayor James G. Stewart of Cincinnati, together with the statewide Republican party, spent not less than $988,000—and lost!

Once during the campaign Lausche was offered a thousand dollars by the Political Action Committee of the CIO—the CIO was supporting him at the time (albeit coolly), but he turned the money down. On the day after election, his headquarters literally didn't have a nickel left; it could not buy an airmail stamp, and it was in debt $3,700. Then the Democratic National Headquarters, impressed by the decisiveness of his victory, telephoned him from the Biltmore in New York, offered to let bygones be bygones, and volunteered to help pay the bills, *ex post facto*, insisting, however, that any check they sent should be payable to the local executive committee of the party. With this group Lausche had had absolutely nothing to do, and he refused the money.[2]

No wonder New York and Washington were impressed. Roosevelt lost Ohio to Dewey by 11,500 votes, but Lausche won the governorship by 112,000. This is the only instance in the 1944 election of victory by a local Democrat when the president was beaten; almost everywhere else, in fact, it was Roosevelt who carried the local candidate through. But Lausche outran FDR by 33,000 votes.

Some Qualities of Lausche

How account for a success like this? There are several reasons; at the moment let me confine myself to one. I heard the same story twice, in two different cities, and no doubt the same thing happened several times.

Everybody in Cincinnati thought that Jim Stewart would win the governorship hands down. He was widely popular, Ohio is normally a strong Republican state, and he had been working for the post for years. Lausche did not even announce his own candidacy till six weeks before the primaries. Then he arrived in Hamilton County. He completely ignored the regulars and old-line politicos and, instead, made just two talks. One was at the Women's City Club, with an audience of scarcely a hundred. But these were key women. And Lausche "burned them up." The other was at the Commercial Club, which is the Cincinnati equivalent of the Union League in Philadelphia or the Somerset Club in Boston. Hardly any Democrat had ever been seen within its portals. It ate Democrats for breakfast. Lausche spoke for an hour. A member who was present told me, "Before he came, it was a dead sure shot that 90 per cent

---

[2] While campaigning for governor, incidentally, he returned to the Cleveland city treasurer his pay for each day that he was absent from the city hall.

of the people there would vote against him; when he left, 90 per cent were on his side." Among the guests, incidentally, was Mr. Stewart himself, his opponent.

Lausche then called on the publishers of the chief Cincinnati papers, which are arch-Republican. To each he said simply, "I know you're against me, of course. All I want is a fair deal."

Everywhere he went, he followed the same technique. He would stay a day or two; by the time he left, the town would be buzzing with his name. He won friends everywhere by a quality of the heart.

But he had very serious barriers to overcome. People said that he was too ambitious, too clever, too impetuous, and a "narrow-horizon man." They were aghast that he practically refused to speak to Al Horstman, the powerful Democratic state chairman; they asserted that he was "woolly minded," a "terrible administrator" and "all things to all men." Some people disliked him for being Catholic, and a lot of Catholics disliked him for having a non-Catholic wife. Some labor people said he should have done more for labor, antilabor people said he did too much, and the AF of L refused to take any stand at all. He was accused both of being a parvenu (the snobs could not forget his foreign and plebeian origin) and a slave to the Chamber of Commerce. In industrial cities he praised Roosevelt highly; in the rural communities he never even mentioned Roosevelt's name—particularly in the America First belt of Ohio, in the western tier of counties—and so he was accused of opportunism and equivocation.

In fact, when you analyze it, everybody in the state was altogether dubious about Lausche—except 1,603,809 voters.

Personal Life of the Former Governor

Frank Lausche is a big man physically, with heavy shoulders, a nice waistline, and the easy grace of an athlete. He plays golf twice a week, and has had only one serious illness in the past twelve years; the doctor had a hard time keeping him in bed. His smile is grave, yet very warming; charm and vitality are the first things a visitor is apt to feel. He speaks slowly, feeling for words with care, most of the time, and then is likely to spurt into an erupting cloud of rhetoric. Mostly he is direct and simple, but, with his big hands waving and his dark, Indianlike face aglow, he can shoot right off the earth.

He works like an ox and his day is long. Up at seven, he is usually at his desk by 8:15. He seldom goes out to lunch, and he sees people hour after hour. They queue up outside his office, and a great percentage of them are neighborhood folk; they arrive in overalls or workers' clothes, saying that they must see "Frank" himself; many are foreign born, and few are ever turned away.

Lausche's only hobby, music and golf aside, is poetry. He enjoys reading, and burrows into the classics every chance he gets. A curious point is that he likes to read Shakespeare in winter but not summer. Poetry supplies something, he told me, that makes it possible for him to be sympathetic to any kind of problem or point of view; he reads it because it makes him mellower. Current magazines and books do not occupy him much, and he goes through newspapers like a buzz saw.

He has no nicknames; people who know him well simply call him Frank. He has no pets, except an English setter. He drinks well, and loves a heavy dinner. Until recently, he smoked about twenty five-cent cigars a day; he practically ate them, and never smoked anything that cost more than a nickel. For the time being he has given up smoking. He plays poker occasionally, but never craves it; sometimes—but rarely —he sneaks off to see a baseball game. He never goes to movies or the theater.

His closest political friend is probably John E. Lokar, his executive secretary. Lokar, also of Slovene origin, was the son of a crony of Lausche's father; they played in the streets together when both were children, though Lokar is younger. Lausche's technique with political associates is to listen carefully, but only seldom does he ask advice. When he meets with his cabinet he says, "Boys, tell me what you think," but no one influences him much; as a rule he sits on a problem for twenty-four hours, then announces what he will do. He likes a considerable number of people; and an enormous number of folk, dating from the time when he was a judge, dote on him, but he relies on nobody.

He has no interest at all in money, though the time may come when he will have to worry about security in his old age. His governor's salary was $10,000, of which—on payday every two weeks—he got exactly $302.96. The rest went to taxes, and saving was all but impossible. He owns no property, and in Cleveland he drove a 1939 Chevrolet, so tattered that it scarcely looked respectable, even when he was mayor. When he moved into the gubernatorial mansion in Columbus, he had exactly one extra suit of clothes and two pairs of shoes. (Bricker, moving out, had ninety-two suits, I heard it said.)

I asked one friend about his finances. Answer: "Why, the guy don't have nothin'!" Another said, "Whatever money you may have in your pocket at this moment, I will make you a wager for any amount that Frank Lausche is carrying less."

What distinguishes him most is probably his compelling sympathy for the underdog; he told me that he had absorbed this mostly from his father. Once, when he was about fifteen, he fought what he calls "the fist-fight of my life." An immigrant boy, in peasant clothes, had just arrived from Europe; an older boy in the neighborhood bullied him, and

Frank took on the older boy. "And I beat him, though he was a foot taller!" When Lausche tells this story today his eyes literally gleam with pride.

One could go on to list other good qualities that Lausche has, for instance his whimsy, boyishness, and considerable (political) sex appeal for women. Another is his instinct for making use of political enemies. His two chief opponents in the last Democratic primary were Frazer Reams and James W. Huffman. He appointed Reams to be state director of welfare, one of the most important jobs in Ohio, and named Huffman to the Senate! To forgive and forget is a basic item in his philosophy.

Also he has very definite defects; mostly these derive from a lack of academic education and a disinclination to think abstractly; he is a man of emotion, not of mind. He is little more than a child as regards foreign policy: his views on world affairs are parochial in the extreme. On some domestic issues he seems to take every possible attitude at once, and on others he is confused, undecisive and indeterminate. I asked him what was the rock-bottom basis of his political thought; he replied that "he had steeled himself to refuse to be alarmed or stampeded by the threats of any single group." He has, in fact, a terror of seeming to be the candidate of any particular force or interest, no matter how worthy, which makes him far more guarded than necessary. He told me, with a curious touch of self-pity, "I may be battered all to pieces one of these days." Then he added, pondering, "Defeat can be a victory if you are rebuffed by the wrong kind of people."

I heard someone say, "Everybody is crazy about him—and wonders why." I heard someone else say, "Was he a really good mayor? No one knows. But he'd be elected again any time he ran." I heard a third friend say, "You can get so mad at him you'll call him every name in the world, and five minutes later be the best of friends. The guy who knocks him most says, 'He's mine!'"

Of course other than personal qualities have brought Lausche power. He owes a great deal to the simple fact that he comes from Cleveland; he inherits its great tradition of good government as exemplified by Newton Baker and Tom Johnson, and derives strength too from its huge industrialization and reservoir of foreign born. Most of the Germans vote for him because he has a German name, and most of the Slavs because they know he's Slav.

What does he believe in most? First, honesty. Second, the spirit of American institutions. What does he stand for most? The principle that public office is a trust.

Man of the Future?

Governors in Ohio serve for two years only, and hence most of them start their campaign for re-election the very minute they are inaugurated.

Lausche, who is after all a politician, was no exception. Yet, relying on heart, prestige and friendship, he did not seek to build up any actual "machine." Of course his ambition runs beyond the governorship, and many people think he may be a good vice-presidential possibility in 1948. But he himself is apt to disclaim such futurities. He told me that he had "a sort of abiding conviction that when you aspire too covetously, it is a rule of nature that you'll be deprived of the enjoyment of your ambition." He smiled, "There are lots of things we'd like to do that we can't do."

Lausche's record as governor was moderate and unsensational, with good appointments on the whole. He was—it should be pointed out —a Democratic governor with a Republican majority in the legis- lature, which never makes for happiness. Strangely enough, consid- ering his instinct for the underpossessed,[3] his chief struggle was with labor; the issue was revision of the Unemployment Compen- sation Law which, as it stood on the books, provided sixteen dollars in weekly payments for eighteen weeks. The CIO wanted this raised to twenty-five dollars for twenty-six weeks; Lausche fought for and got an exact mathematical compromise, twenty-one dollars for twenty-two weeks. He said that he thought the CIO plan, which would have increased the cost of unemployment insurance by 140 per cent, was too expensive; he told me, "I believe in giving, but not to the point of exhausting the body that gives." Then he changed the metaphor, saying, "There can be such a thing as too much reform, if it takes the wheels off the wagon."

So much for Frank Lausche in midstream. Now only forty-nine, he is obviously a man to watch. The United States doesn't have so many capable and honest men in public life that it can afford to neglect any favorite son particularly if he comes from Ohio. Lausche, like Stassen on the other side of the fence, seems to be a political natural, despite his defeat in 1946.

Taft and Bricker

Put on your old gray bonnet
With the Hoover button on it
And we'll hitch old Dobbin to the shay.
When the New Deal's over
We'll be back in clover—
On inauguration day.

—Gridiron Club ditty

Either of these good gentlemen may well be the next President of the United States, which to many is a somewhat horrifying thought. As these pages go to press, Taft overshadows his colleague as a Republican contender, but in a convention deadlocked between Taft and Dewey, say,

---

[3] When the housing shortage reached its most acute and exasperating state in Columbus, Lausche opened an unused wing of the state executive mansion to put up veterans' families rent free.

Bricker might quite possibly emerge as a compromise. Neither Ohioan has, as of January, 1947, had the candor to announce his candidacy openly, as Harold Stassen so forthrightly did, but each is as much in the fight as a baseball team in the first division racing for the pennant.

Naturally, to preclude the possibility of the two Ohio senators fighting one another at the finish and thus canceling each other out, negotiations began immediately after the November 1946 elections for one to withdraw in favor of the other. This has happened before. In 1940, Bricker stepped aside for Taft. But Dewey blocked Taft off, and Willkie became the nominee. In 1944, Taft withdrew in favor of Bricker, and a similar arrangement was confidently predicted early in 1947, with Bricker giving way to Taft. But nobody made any public move. Neither wanted to split the powerful Ohio delegation, but neither, on the other hand, was willing to surrender his own precious chance. With the White House and its glories seemingly almost within reach, the intramural Ohio tensions inevitably became more acute.

A truly remarkable example of the vagaries of American politics and journalism came on Christmas Eve, 1946. Two stories filed from Columbus at the same time were published in two different New York papers the same morning. One distributed by the International News Service was headlined, BRICKER YIELDS TO TAFT IN PRESIDENTIAL RACE. The other, a United Press dispatch, was headlined BRICKER WON'T BOW TO TAFT. Pay your money and take your choice.

It is impossible to understand Robert Alphonso Taft without reference to Cincinnati, which splendid city I will mention in the next chapter, and to his extraordinary family background.

For the first time in this book on an important level—later we shall see the same thing with Saltonstall in Massachusetts—we confront the phenomenon of the Great Political Family. In Poland, Hungary, Great Britain, Japan, Argentina, this phenomenon is, or was, as common as soap; in the United States it is comparatively rare. Bob Taft is to politics and public eminence born. Everybody knows that his father, William Howard Taft, was governor general of the Philippines (Bob grew up in Manila), secretary of war under the first Roosevelt, and the only American in history to be both president of the United States and chief justice of the Supreme Court. Incidentally it is remarkable, considering the number of exalted positions he held, that the elder Taft won only two elections in his life, as clerk in an Ohio court and for president.

The contrast to Lausche is of course extreme. Lausche, Taft, and Bricker represent three utterly different and contrasting poles in American life and origins—the urban melting pot, the political aristocracy, and the barefoot-boy old-red-schoolhouse tradition.

Other ramifications of the Taft family are not so well known. They spread out like Hapsburgs or white mice. Suppose we start two generations back. Taft's paternal grandfather, Alphonso, a Vermonter, was secretary of war and attorney general under Grant, and minister to both Austria and the Russia of the Czars.[4] One uncle, by name Louis More (brother of the arch-Tory essayist Paul Elmer More), was dean of the Graduate School of the University of Cincinnati. Another, Horace, founded the Taft school for boys in Watertown, Connecticut, and was its headmaster for many years. Another, Charles Phelps Taft, is the source of most of the contemporary wealth of the family; he married an heiress named Annie Sinton, bought up large amounts of Cincinnati real estate, became a traction magnate, and built the Cincinnati *Times-Star* into a markedly lucrative and influential property. Bob Taft married Martha Bowers. One of her distant forebears is Jonathan Edwards, the theologian; a great-great-grandfather was Timothy Dwight, president of Yale; her grandfather (born in Ireland) was chief justice of Minnesota and her father, Lloyd Bowers, was solicitor general of the United States under William Howard Taft. Bob's brother, Charles, is a well-known public figure in his own right, his sister (Dr. Helen Taft Manning) is a professor of history at Bryn Mawr, and his cousin, Hulbert Taft, is publisher of the *Times-Star*.

The brightest star in the family is a lady, Bob's wife Martha. His debt to her is beyond compass. She is not only one of the most delightful women alive: politically she is indefatigable and indispensable. She is a much more accomplished speaker than her husband, and has assisted in all his campaigns. Once, going to a political rally, her car skidded as she swerved sharply to avoid a dog; the car turned over three times, but she miraculously escaped injury. She proceeded to the meeting, and said imperturbably, "Well, anyway, this ought to get us the Society for the Prevention of Cruelty to Animals vote." Once, before an audience of coal miners, her opponent boasted that he was just an ordinary, humble man. Mrs. Taft's response was instantaneous: "My husband is not a simple man. He did not start from humble beginnings. He is a very brilliant man. . . . Isn't that what you prefer?" After Taft's first run for the Senate, one Ohio newspaper headlined the event simply, BOB AND MARTHA WIN.

The Taft family lived originally in a heavy, lawn-surrounded stone house built by Alphonso in Cincinnati. Here Bob played as a child with his father (who weighed 312 pounds) and his delicate, beautiful mother who was a school teacher named Nellie Herron and who was called "Fascinating Nellie." Today, when not in Washington, the Tafts live

---

[4] Sources for this genealogical material are mainly an article in *Time* (January 29, 1940), an article in *PM* by Alexander H. Uhl, October 4, 1942, and "Taft and Taft," by Joseph Alsop and Robert Kintner, *Life*, March 18, 1940.

at Sky Farm, a modest suburban estate in the Little Miami Valley near Cincinnati, where they grow strawberries for fun and profit. Taft was not rich when he and Martha bought Sky Farm in 1916; it cost every cent they had, and didn't even have electricity. The neighborhood was an outpost then; today, as Cincinnati has expanded, it has become fashionable, and Martha likes to say that buying the house is the only fashionable thing she and her husband have ever done.[5] The Tafts spend their summers, when they can find the time, at Murray Bay, Canada. Here, for years, their children and other children of the family, in almost Rooseveltian profusion, had their holidays. Bob and Martha Taft have four children; Charlie (who often disagrees with Bob politically) has six.

Sons of politically famous fathers often, it seems, find their parentage an encumbrance. They are marked for the limelight too early if they adopt political careers themselves, and also their fathers overshadow them, no matter how deep the mutual affection and admiration. Both Bob and Phil La Follette will attest to this, and so will several Roosevelts. Bob Taft is an extremely reticent man (politics aside), shy, and not given to advertising privacies. Once he asked Alice Longworth, "What *do* you say when someone says they knew your father and how much he meant to them?"

Robert was something of a child prodigy. He was a sober, orderly and precise youngster with a great gift for mathematics. He went to the Taft School (inevitably), Yale, and the Harvard Law School. In all three, he was first in his class; he has been called, next to Brandeis, the most brilliant student the Harvard Law School ever produced. He practiced law for a time, was rejected for military service because of faulty eyesight, went briefly to Europe for Herbert Hoover's Relief Administration, and set up a law firm in Cincinnati with his brother Charles. Almost at once, he interested himself in politics. He became a legislator, speaker of the house, and state senator. This was at a time when the Ku-Klux was almost as strong in Ohio as in Indiana, and his first notable service was a vigorous offensive against the Klan, which took courage. This Klan episode, largely forgotten now, would be well worth recounting in detail if space were available. In 1938, Taft ran for the United States Senate. He won handily. In 1944, running for re-election, he won again—but his majority slipped from 178,000 to 18,000, and a better opponent would probably have beaten him.

Taft is a hard and tireless worker. Not only has he brain power; he knows how to organize it. His sincerity is absolute.[6] He has the strength

---

[5] See *Life*, cited above, and an article by Alice Roosevelt Longworth in the *Saturday Evening Post*, May 4, 1940.

[6] But Arthur Krock has reported in the New York *Times* (October 8, 1946), "Up to a point Mr. Taft plays obvious or even opportunist politics."

of a man who believes in things even when they are the wrong things; he knows the virtues of discipline and order. In formal debate, especially on any financial topic, he is pertinacious and formidably acute; he needs preparation, however, and as an extemporary speaker—or in any field that needs lightness of touch—his record is not happy. One lawyer told me, "The way to win a case against Bob is to get him mad; then he blows up." He is much more "professional" a politician than most people think; he spends a considerable amount of time and energy keeping his Ohio fences in good repair. Sometimes he takes the line that his job is to vote as his constituents want him to vote, that it is his major duty to reflect their opinions; this is not, however, any excuse for some of his more errant judgments. One famous remark about him is that "he has reached more wrong decisions more ably" than any other man in public life.[7] He is intricate and clever; for instance he attacked the British loan from the flanks as well as frontally, by putting forward a "substitute" gift idea that would have cut it to $1,250,000,000. Alice Longworth once said that, if he became president, Taft would follow Roosevelt like a glass of milk after a slug of benzedrine. But milk connotes richness, warmth, the upspringing of life, and mellowness; and Taft is not what you would call a warm or mellow man. One of his chief defects was, in fact, pithily expressed once by the *New Republic*—that "he is about as magnetic as a lead nail."

From this point forward we deal in the inexplicable and the disconcerting. That Taft should be a conservative is quite understandable— though other leaders with just as authentic an aristocracy-intelligentsia background have not been conservatives. That he should have been an isolationist is also understandable, though it does not jibe well with much of the family tradition. What cannot be explained in Taft are his majestic wrongheadednesses, his Brobdingnagian bad judgments. I confine myself strictly to the record:

On April 14, 1940, he said, "I am opposed to the Selective Service bill because in my opinion no necessity exists requiring such tragic action."

On February 16, 1941, he said, "It is simply fantastic to suppose there is any danger of an attack on the United States by Japan."

On February 22, 1941, he said, "An invasion of the United States by the German army is as fantastic as would be the invasion of Germany . . . by an American army and as unlikely to be undertaken."

On August 1, 1941, he said, "My opinion is that the situation today . . . looks infinitely safer. . . . I cannot understand the statement that the situation is more perilous today than it was a year ago."

[7] Cf. "Taft: 20 Degrees Colder Inside," by Carroll Kilpatrick, *The Nation*, December 23, 1946.

On September 22, 1941, he said, "There is much less danger to this country . . . today than there was two years ago; certainly much less than there was one year ago."

Taft is a rationalist; one cannot dismiss him, as one may dismiss Wheeler, as the mere slave to an isolationist obsession. Taft keeps his eyes (on other matters) well above ground; one cannot call him an ostrich or a fool. Taft is honest; one cannot blame these fantastically bad judgments on politics. The clue is probably ambition and a false identification with the temper of the times, plus a certain Philistinism and an almost pathological setness of vision and stubbornness.

Taft was also, it should be pointed out, conspicuous among those isolationists who, "by declaring war on December 8, conceived that they were thus absolved of all their past stupidities and error and were enfranchised to go right on committing just the same kind of error and stupidity thereafter."[8] He has clung right onto his old line, with a persistence that one responsible, conservative, and highly Republican commentator calls "sheer and cantankerous." Consider some other items in the record:

He voted against Lend Lease, against the ship seizure bill, against extension of the draft, against revision of the Neutrality Act, and even against the confirmation as secretary of war of that eminent fellow Republican, Henry L. Stimson.

He voted for limiting the use of armed forces to the Western Hemisphere, and for limiting the training of drafted men to six months; he voted against the destroyer transfer, and against the arming of our merchant ships.

He spoke at America First meetings (though he was never a member); he led the opposition to Bretton Woods, and sought to block American participation in the world bank and the international stabilization fund. He voted for the San Francisco charter, but soon thereafter introduced an amendment (rejected by the Senate 41 to 18) that would have removed its teeth so far as effective action by the United States is concerned.

In October, 1946, Taft called the Nazi trial at Nuremberg a "miscarriage of justice which the American people would long regret," and overtly deplored the death sentences. Even Joe Martin, speaker of the house since January, 1947, whose record matches Taft's in most respects, never went so far as this.

On domestic affairs his record is somewhat contradictory. His first Senate speech was against TVA, which is the most generous work of man in the United States. He favored permanent FEPC legislation, and then turned against it. He led the attack on the confirmation of Henry Wallace as secretary of commerce; this produced a spirited controversy with Walter Lippmann, who wrote, "What Senator Taft does not know

[8] From an editorial in the New York *Herald Tribune*.

on this subject, as on a good many others, is most of what there is to be known about it."

Taft was the author of the well-known Section V of the Soldier Vote law, which gave the army power to censor books, movies, and the like. Taft's motive was "to quarantine the GI's from any federally financed political propaganda." The result was such absurdities as a veto by the army on films like *Wilson* and even a comedy, *Heavenly Days*, starring Fibber McGee and Molly. The law became an ass.

On housing, OPA, labor, and similar domestic issues Taft has slipped and slithered. His record is certainly more liberal than that of senators like Bushfield. This does not, let me add at once, make it very liberal. He helped write the Case bill, voted to amend the Full Employment bill, and fought price control. On the other hand he has several times taken a mild prolabor line; once or twice he has even supported Administration measures favoring labor. He joined Senators Wagner and Ellender to write a housing bill, which though it does not promise much does promise something, and he made a remarkable coalition with two progressive Democrats (Thomas of Utah and Hill of Alabama) to introduce a bill for a modicum of federal aid to education.

John W. Bricker is a totally different article. He and Taft are both conservative senators from Ohio; this aside, there is scarcely any resemblance between them. One can scarcely mention them in the same breath from the point of view of intellectual capacity. Little record exists that Bricker has ever said anything worth more than thirty seconds of consideration by anybody. Intellectually he is like interstellar space—a vast vacuum occasionally crossed by homeless, wandering clichés.

"Honest John" is his nickname; any American (except Lincoln) with such a nickname will, one may be sure, be on the dull side. One remark about him, credited to a famous Washington lady of society, the same distinguished lady who called Dewey "an ornament on a wedding cake," is that Bricker is "just an honest Harding." A better description might be a "Harding who has no embarrassing friends." Bricker is the man who—to repeat another well-known phrase—puts his foot in his mouth every time he opens it.

Just before Christmas, 1946, when the Taft-Bricker rivalry became a big story, the senator-elect spoke before the Gridiron Club. Nobody unfamiliar with America can easily understand what a singular function Gridiron dinners perform, and with what effortless but merciless precision the invited guests survey presidential timber. Dewey, it is recorded, once spent a hundred solid hours preparing and rehearsing his first Gridiron speech. Bricker's Gridiron performance was, observers say, something almost too horrible to talk about. The comment of Harold L. Ickes was, "Before his speech . . . Bricker thought he was running for the

Republican nomination for President. Now he is not only walking, he is limping. . . . The Republican Party's Bricker-without-straw could not have done better for his rivals. . . . In future lexicons 'Bricker' will doubtless appear as a refinement of 'boner.' As a presidential candidate, Bricker is a mere flicker."[9]

John William Bricker, six feet two inches tall, white haired, handsome, the only Republican ever to serve three consecutive terms as governor of Ohio, was born a poor boy on a farm near Mount Sterling, in central Ohio, on September 6, 1893. He worked on his father's farm, taught school briefly, and went to Ohio State University—which institution he recently said "has become indoctrinated with un-American philosophy." During World War I, Bricker was a chaplain. This was because, although a lively athlete and baseball player,[10] he was rejected for ordinary military service because he has an abnormally slow pulse, about fifty-five beats to the minute. This, perhaps, contributes to his placidity, his present-day habit of mostly unspotted calm. A friend ordained him into the ministry of the Congregational Christian church, whereupon the Army took him as a chaplain. He served as an athletic instructor too, and was discharged as a lieutenant. After the armistice he took a degree in law, practiced briefly, and almost at once began a steady, plodding, quite honorable but quite undistinguished political career.

A great deal can be understood about Bricker's personality and the milieu from which he comes by the fact that he was president of the YMCA when a young man, and that the girl he married was president of the YWCA. She was a schoolteacher named Harriet Day. A charming and able woman (like Mrs. Lausche and Mrs. Taft) she has been of the most substantial help to his career. Once a politician said of her, "Harriet is the only woman I know who hasn't a single enemy in the world and whom I like anyway."[11]

Most American politicians—or shall we say most Americans?—are much dominated by women. The "Mom" chapter in Philip Wylie's *Generation of Vipers* comes to mind. Bricker's mother managed the family farm for twenty-seven years, after her husband's death; she died in 1941. Until then, out of respect for her principles, Bricker never took a drink, and never went to a Sunday baseball game. Since her death he has relaxed somewhat; he will go fishing on Sundays now, and even drink a glass of beer.

[9] New York *Post*, December 27, 1946. But one should point out that recoveries have been made from Gridiron catastrophes. In fact, in 1940, Taft made a similar failure; it was talked about then as Bricker's was six years later.

[10] Like Lausche, Bricker was catcher on an Ohio State team that won the state championship.

[11] See a brilliant study of Bricker, which tells more about him than anything I know, by Eliot Janeway in *Life*, June 11, 1944, and an article by Malcolm Logan in the New York *Post*, March 20, 1943.

"Honest John" first became governor in 1939, after having served as a town solicitor, assistant attorney general and then attorney general for four years. He got the governorship partly because Ohio, which has known scandals in its time, could no longer stomach the violent corruption of the preceding Democratic administration.

When we inspect his gubernatorial record there is little to write about except "economy." Bricker came in facing a 40 million dollar deficit; when he left this was a 65 million dollar surplus, which sounds impressive. But several qualifying points arise. First, his administration put in a 3 per cent sales tax, and during the war the money rolled in unendingly. Second, in spite of economies, the budget somehow grew greater every year. Third, the huge Bricker surplus was made possible by starvation of some essential services.

So far, except in passing, we have not mentioned the penitentiaries, insane asylums, homes for the blind and the like, that all states maintain. Mostly their status—particularly insane asylums and homes for the deficient—is a scandal and a disgrace. I will not say that those in Ohio are the worst in the nation. They are certainly among the worst. Not only are the institutions themselves evilly kept up, filthily overcrowded, and operated almost without reference to the human spirit; there are not enough of them. I heard a devoted public servant say in Cincinnati, "Mental disease is so far ahead of us that we can't possibly keep up with it." Some states manage much better than Ohio. "Our penitentiary, compared to the one in Michigan, is an oubliette out of the dark ages," a Columbus editor told me.

What does Bricker believe in? One may guess. It is not, however, easy to pin him down on any concrete issue. He would not even take a stand for or against daylight saving, when this was a controversial point tying up the legislature week after week.[12] At first the observer assumes that, like most favorite sons, Bricker hesitates to commit himself on most things for fear of prejudicing his chances for the presidency. But many Ohioans have come to believe the real reason is something else and simpler—that he takes no stand because he literally has none, that in actual fact he is devoid of convictions on most problems. Everybody knows where Taft stands on everything. But no one knows much about what Bricker believes even on such a matter as foreign policy.

Outside Ohio, in Washington, I heard a potent Republican publicist defend Bricker on the ground that he was an "idealist." For what? Again, the answer did not come forth. There are moments, indeed, when it is almost impossible not to dismiss Bricker as Simple Simon. He was asked once what he intended to do about the bureaucracy. His answer, in all

[12] Cf. an article by Potomacus in the *New Republic*, June 28, 1943. In many states, for instance Arizona, there were similar attempts to turn back to standard time.

seriousness, was "One of the best solutions of the problem of a bureaucracy is less bureaucracy."

As a result of situations and fermentations not within the province of this chapter, John William Bricker, all that he is and isn't, was nominated for vice president by the Republican party in 1944. He was the hero of the convention, and was vastly more popular with most delegates than Dewey. His "simplicity," if that is the proper word, seemed irresistible. His subsequent campaign was unbelievably packed with malapropisms. He seemed an actual Throttlebottom come to life. He embarrassed Dewey continually—for instance by welcoming support from Gerald L. K. Smith —and the two scarcely spoke during the campaign.

In 1946 came his election to the Senate. He won overwhelmingly. But as a freshman senator, with the White House beckoning, Bricker will have his troubles. For one thing Taft will be more in the public eye; for another, his intellectual weaknesses are apt to become more and more conspicuous vis-à-vis Taft in the Senate chamber. But, so strange a country is the United States, the very circumstance that Bricker is less intelligent than Taft, together with the fact that he is far more "human," may make him a better presidential candidate.

Politics, Politics, Politics

I'll say we've done well.
—Sherwood Anderson

Ohio, as everybody knows, has produced more presidents from the point of view of birthplace than any state except Virginia—seven. Moreover if one thinks in terms of where presidents actually lived when they were elected, Ohio leads the nation, with six as against Virginia's five. As to the seven "native" Ohio presidents, all were Republicans. It is indeed a remarkable tribute to the state's impact on the Republican party, or vice versa, that since the Civil War *every* Republican president except Hoover elected for a first term (excluding those who acceded to the White House from the vice presidency, like Theodore Roosevelt and Coolidge) was either born in Ohio or elected from Ohio. Ohioans are very prone to tell the visitor things like this. They are not nearly so prone to admit that none of the Ohio presidents had much distinction, and that the administrations of two at least were embarrassed by the most heinous scandals.[13]

Ohio is such a tremendous state presidentially for three reasons: (1) It is fourth in the union in population, and hence its twenty-five electoral votes carry pivotal weight. (2) Despite its production of Republican

---

[13] The seven: Grant, Benjamin Harrison, Hayes, Garfield, McKinley, Taft, Harding. Another point is that of the last fourteen presidents, Republican or Democrat, excluding FDR and Truman, actually seven—50 per cent!—were from Ohio.

presidents it is a state very volatile and touch-and-go. Anybody who can so much as read a comic strip can usually predict how New York and Pennsylvania will go nationally. But nobody is ever sure of Ohio. Once the manager of a presidential candidate, arriving in Columbus, asked the local boss if he could "deliver" Ohio. The legend is that the local boss took a deep protesting breath, curled up his toes, and on the spot died of heart failure. (3) It was formerly famous for its bosses, like Marcus A. Hanna of Cleveland, who wore a president like McKinley practically as a watchfob. But Ohio has no all-state bosses now, and so it is doubly unpredictable.

A curious and suggestive point, which I heard first expressed by former Senator Burton, is that Ohio senators are very short lived politically. As of January 3, 1941, when Mr. Burton himself entered the Senate, Ohio had had forty senators since statehood in 1803. Of these twenty-four or 60 per cent served one full term or less; only eight or 20 per cent ever got two full terms or more. This has had a serious political effect in that the state seldom develops the seniority it deserves, and that the southern states have in such full measure for example. Its turnover is too quick. This means too that its senators usually lack seniority not merely in the literal sense but in experience.

Ohio politics cover a very broad span. For instance before Lausche gave Burton's senate seat to Huffman, he offered it to two other men, both of whom declined. One was the brilliant young air corps officer who more than any other man was responsible for the strategic bombing that demolished Japan, Major General Curtis LeMay. The other was none other than James M. Cox, the newspaper publisher who (not one American in a thousand will remember) was the Democratic candidate for president to succeed Wilson in 1920, and whose running mate was Franklin Roosevelt.

To ask the question "Who runs Ohio?" is to get into the same kind of problem in differential calculus that applies to most middle western states. The education lobby is a powerful force; it must needs be, since Ohio spends the staggering sum of 55 million dollars per year on schools, the universities not included. The labor movement and in particular the CIO are gravely split. For years a dominant factor was the Anti-Saloon League, and the coal operators are a substantial force. Big business is a potent lobby, and so is agriculture. At least two-thirds of all Ohioans live in cities; nevertheless the farmers, called the "Cornstalk Brigade," are the biggest single force in the legislature.

I met a good many political worthies in Cincinnati, Cleveland, and Columbus. When I left Ohio a telegram from one followed me: IF YOU HAVE REALLY FOUND OUT WHO RUNS THIS PLACE FOR GOD'S SAKE DON'T KEEP IT CONFIDENTIAL. KINDLY WIRE TEN THOUSAND WORDS COLLECT.

Chapter 27

—and More From the Ohio Mill

wwwwwwwwwwwwwwwwwwwwwwwwwwwwwwwwwwwwwwwwwwwwwwwwwwwwwwwwwwwwwwwwwwwwwwwwwww

> Ohio is the farthest west of the east and the farthest north of the south.
>
> —Louis Bromfield

BASICALLY, Ohio is nothing more nor less than a giant carpet of agriculture studded by great cities, and few states are so impressive statistically. Let us gulp down a few figures. It has 93,041 retail stores doing about 20 billion dollars' worth of business a year, 53 museums, 11 state-owned lakes, 684 parent banks, 13 major railroads, 272 tax-supported libraries, 90 power companies (of which about 50 are municipally owned), 300 square miles of public parks, 14,000 restaurants, more than 1,000 newspapers, 1,700 hotels, 85,500 miles of road, 33 radio stations, and 1,600,000 telephones, which latter figure is greater than the number in the entire continent of South America.

Three things made Ohio historically: (1) emigration from New England, (2) settlement by the veterans of the Revolutionary War, and (3) incursions from the South. Similarly the state falls into three geographic spheres: (a) the north, centering on Cleveland, where the New England heritage is strongest; (b) the "military lands" in the middle, with Columbus as a focus; and (c) the south which pivots on Cincinnati and its river culture with a strong German overlay. The New Englandish north may in turn be subdivided into the "Western Reserve," which in the beginning was an actual geographic extension of New England, and "the Firelands," where property was taken up by Connecticuters whose homes had been destroyed during the Revolution. Consider names like Ridgefield, Bridgeport, Danbury, Greenwich. These are Connecticut names of course. They are also names of towns in Ohio.[1]

The whole United States flows through Ohio; the Buckeye State gives you an almost perfect sense of what the country is as a whole. The state motto was once "an empire within an empire," and Ohio prides itself greatly on its self-sufficiency. But by and large Ohioans do not, if I may generalize roughly, think of themselves much in state terms. They are not so self-conscious regionally as, say, Hoosiers in Indiana. Ohio is rich in writers. But one thinks of Sherwood Anderson as a

[1] Cf. Hatcher, *Lake Erie*, p. 66. Among other Ohio place names straight out of New England are Salem, Montpelier, Springfield, Cambridge, Middletown.

"Middle Western" rather than an "Ohio" author, of Louis Bromfield as an "American" rather than as an "Ohio" novelist.

I went out to Mr. Bromfield's farm near Mansfield, and admired his boxers, cook, and agricultural techniques. I will not describe Pleasant Valley since Mr. Bromfield himself has done this so amply. What impressed me most was the feeling this part of Ohio gave of being a crossroads. Take Mansfield. This town of 37,154 people is on the main line of both the Pennsylvania and Erie railroads, with direct service to New York and Chicago both; it is on a branch line of the Baltimore & Ohio, and the New York Central is only twelve miles distant. A stone's throw away northward is Norwalk, a pure New England town; a stone's throw away southward is Mount Vernon, a pure southern town. Consider, too, crossroads in another dimension. Mansfield has sixty industrial plants, but it is the center of one of the richest agricultural areas on earth.

Agriculture in Ohio is, of course, a tremendous business; the total investment is about two billion dollars. But in industry the record is even more formidable. This state is a nucleus for 70 per cent of all industrial activity in the nation. It is first in an extraordinary variety of products and enterprises—machine tools, rubber, publishing of periodicals, ceramics, nuts and bolts, steel barrels, washers and rivets, oilcloth, sporting goods, cranes and derricks, playing cards, china, and, among oddities, sewer pipe and false teeth. The craftsmen in this last industry, in Columbus, are largely porcelain workers originally from Belgium. Ohio is the second state in motor vehicles, steel, and blast furnace products; third in paints and varnishes and job printing; fourth in chemicals, aviation, men's clothing, and bakery goods; fifth in footwear; sixth in paper.[2]

Industry means cities and in these, too, Ohio is extraordinarily rich. There are no fewer than fifty-one with populations between 10,000 and 100,000, and ten between 100,000 and a million; only Pennsylvania has as many in this latter category. The Ohio cities, scattered over the whole state, range from Toledo (population 282,349) to Van Wert, "the peony capital of the world";[3] from Dayton (210,718) to historic river towns like Marietta; from Youngstown, the second greatest steel city in the world (167,720), to remarkable communities like Steubenville, which is famous equally for pottery and vice; from Akron (244,791) to places with names like Napoleon and Greasy Ridge.

[2] Think back to Iowa's agricultural firsts as an indication of the way American states complement each other.
[3] How many similar "capitals" exist in the United States! I have already mentioned several, and a good many more are to come, for instance the rose, barbecue, and natural gas "capitals." In California is the "artichoke capital" of the world, and in Texas the "honey" capital. Carrying this further, a shop in Manhattan calls itself the "stationery" capital of the world.

About any of these and others, pages might be written. Canton (108,401) is the home of Timken roller bearings and also of one of the notable *causes célèbres* in modern American journalism, the murder in 1926 of Don Mellett, editor of the Canton *Daily News*. Toledo has the most mature and provocative city planning program in the United States, as worked out by Norman Bel Geddes and others; what is more no city needs one more badly. Akron is of course the rubber center of the universe, and is like nothing else on the face of the earth; until the war at least, 90 per cent or more of all American tires and tubes came from Akron. This illustrates an odd tendency among great American corporations, particularly those which are intense competitors—that of huddling together in the same community, like automobiles in Detroit, or sheep.

The Two Great C's

I said in the foreword to this book that, if possible, I always tried to see people in every camp, and that it was an ideal day professionally when, for instance, I was able to talk to the CIO in the morning and the chamber of commerce in the afternoon. Three times in Ohio, once in Cleveland, once in Cincinnati, once in Columbus, I had the good fortune to go this experience one better. Through the courtesy of friends a small round table was arranged, and I found myself talking to people of both camps at one and the same time. All I had to do was ask a question or two, and then sit back and listen to my hosts flail away at each other. When, four or five hours later, the plaster began to fall off the wall, it was time to go home, and I knew more than I had known before.

Cleveland (population 1,214,943 metropolitan area; 878,336 city limits), which has roughly 1 per cent of the total population of the country, is the sixth largest American city and from any point of view one of the most important. I have already made mention of its civic spirit; I know of no other metropolis with quite so impressive a record in the practical application of good citizenship to government. Next to New York, it is probably the best-run big city in the country.

Cleveland has one of the finest civic centers in the nation, and it was the founder (back in 1913) of the community chest idea. It takes culture very seriously indeed, and its symphony has the highest endowment of any orchestra in the world; it spends $2.27 per capita per year on its public library, as against 51½¢ in New York. It is an excellent town for book buying, and its Citizens League watches public affairs sharply. It has a good City Club (on the model of Town Hall in New York), the first Health Museum in the United States, an admirable art museum, the Western Reserve Historical Society, and the Cleveland Council on World Affairs. This last organization, aiming to bring an intimate knowledge of international problems directly into the community, has 3,383 active members; by contrast the Chicago Council on Foreign Relations has 2,334 and the Foreign Policy Association of New York 4,496, though both these cities are of course much larger.

The Cultural Gardens of Cleveland are another uniqueness. The city is one of the most heterogeneous in the nation; roughly 50 per cent of its population is foreign born, and another 30 per cent is of the second generation. But no single nationality group has more than 15 per cent of the total in either category. The British and the Czechs each have 15 per cent, closely followed by the Germans. The Poles make up 13.2 per cent of the combined total, Italians 8.9 per cent, Jugoslavs 6.2 per cent, Hungarians 6.4 per cent, Russians 5.6 per cent. The idea behind the Cultural Gardens is to harmonize the different foreign groups into a kind of orchestra, rather than to melt them down. Some years ago a grove in one of the public parks was dedicated to the memory of Shakespeare, and subsequently a Jewish memorial was laid out in the same area. Then came a German garden, planned as a shrine to Mendelssohn. An association was then formed to tie together other projects of the same type, with the city giving space, on the understanding that each memorial must celebrate a figure in the world of culture, not a military man. There are fifteen so far. That of the Italians is to Virgil, that of the Hungarians to Liszt. The Czechs and Slovaks have their separate groves. That of the Irish is in the form of a Celtic cross, since they couldn't agree on any one person as a dedicatee.

Cleveland, I heard it said, responds to movements for the millennium better than any other city in the world. One joke is that a group of civic-minded citizens will presently set out "to organize the weather," which is apt to be notably capricious and unpleasant. Another is that Cleveland is the city where every rich burgher, returning home at night, catechizes himself with a dutiful prayer, "Have I co-operated well today?"

Reasons for all this are several. One is the tradition of good government laid down by such men as Newton D. Baker, and another the spirit of *noblesse oblige* fostered by the earlier Cleveland tycoons, like Samuel W. Mather, one of the few men ever to have been a director of both United States Steel and Bethlehem Steel at the same time. John D. Rockefeller was of course a Clevelander. And many "medium" millionaires, I heard, have given the city much more than Detroit ever got from its much richer automobile barons. Frederick C. Goff, a former Rockefeller attorney and president of the Cleveland Trust Company, one of the half dozen leading banks of the nation, set a precedent when he said on one occasion, "I am more concerned that the Cleveland Trust Company shall fulfill its obligations to the community than make money for stockholders." Another point is that Cleveland was never dominated by a *single* financial group, like the Mellons in Pittsburgh; industry is diversified, wealth is widely dispersed, and there was lively competition in good works.

Cleveland has always produced and helped make famous financial folk (including some not so generous) of the most varied and dramatic types—like the super-bucket-shop promoters Oris P. and Mantis J. Van Sweringen, who made astonishing forays into both railroad and financial morals, and, in a totally different category, William S. Jack and Ralph M. Heintz who have been called "the Katzenjammer Kids of U. S. Industry"[4] and whose "Jack and Heintz" did remarkable work in war production. There are also a number of heads of smaller corporations who conduct management on a highly personalized level and who have a strong sense of social responsibility—men like James F. Lincoln of the Lincoln Electric Company, where employees have averaged wages of $5,800 per year; Franklin G. Smith of the Osborn Manufacturing Company, about which Julian Street once wrote a provocative pamphlet; and Robert Black, the son of a miner, whose White Motor Company has an enviable record in labor matters.

Take a ruler. Lay it across a map from the Mesabi Range to the Pennsylvania coal fields. It will hit Lake Erie precisely at Cleveland, and this of course is the principal reason for its phenomenal development. One odd point is that Cleveland might very well have had the automobile industry, instead of Detroit, had it not been for the kind of trifling personal accident on which industrial as well as political history often turns. This, at least, is the Ohio version of the story. In 1908, Jim Packard arrived in Cleveland, looking for property on which to build an automobile factory. He called on Colonel J. J. Sullivan, then the head of the chamber of commerce, asking for assistance. Sullivan's reply was, "Nothing doing!" Cleveland, he said, wasn't interested in any such newfangled contraption, and besides it had just induced the largest clothespin manufacturer in the country to build a local plant!

Cleveland, like all industrial cities, can go in for remarkably technical language on occasion. Here are some details of surplus war goods advertised in a local paper:

Hot Rolled Strip

184,553#—.118×5⅝″ HR Coiled Dead Soft Strip. SAE 1010 Mill Edge Oiled. 275#/Coil $2.31/CWT
160,879#—.065″×1¹¹⁄₃₂″ HR Mill Edge WD 1010, Pickled and Oiled. Approx. 235#/Coil $2.10/CWT

Cold Rolled Strip

476,500#—.120# ±.003″×3¾″±.010″ Strip, Cup, Steel Case, 4SCCS, Cal. 45, Hardness Not Over Rockwell B60. Material FXS-486

[4] *Time*, April 8, 1946.

The city is quite well served in newspapers: the *Plain Dealer* (conservative Democrat) and *News* (Republican) are vigorous competitors, though owned by the same company, in the pattern familiar all over the United States. Scripps-Howard is very important in Ohio, with three papers, the Cincinnati *Post*, Columbus *Citizen*, and Cleveland *Press*. This last, a good liberal sheet, is supposed to be the biggest money maker of all Scripps-Howard properties; it was founded by the original Scripps himself, and was famous for years as a penny newspaper. One curiosity about journalism in Ohio is that so many papers use dispatches from Reuters, the British news service.

The city is a great one for homes (as against apartments), and it attracts able men from all over the nation. For instance at a lunch with fourteen civic leaders, I found that only one had been born in Cleveland. Probably its most distinguished citizen today is a rabbi, Abba Hillel Silver.

Cleveland lives in the competitive orbit of Detroit, Buffalo and Pittsburgh more than with the rest of Ohio. I asked Cleveland friends what they thought of Cincinnati. Answer: "We're quite friendly to Cincinnati, when we happen to think about it."

Cleveland has about as much charm as an automobile cemetery or the inside of a dynamo; CINCINNATI (population metropolitan area 789,309, city limits 455,610) is packed with charm. Like all the river cities partly German in origin (Louisville, St. Louis, Milwaukee), it has a certain stately and also sleepy quality, a flavor of detachment, soundness, and *je m'en fiche*-ism. Many years ago Longfellow called it the Queen City of the West, and for all its Germanness, it is one of the most truly American cities in the nation; for instance—in acute contrast to Cleveland—it has a higher proportion of native-born citizens than any city of similar rank.

Cincinnati was a handsome young matron before Chicago even existed and when Cleveland was a helter-skelter village. By 1820, it was the biggest town in the country north of New Orleans; for some years it was headquarters of the government of Northwest Territory; in 1860, it was one of three cities in America with a population greater than 100,000. This was partly because, in the early years, the Ohio River was the Main Street of the nation, and at Cincinnati three distinct and highly civilized groups converged—Virginia younger sons, Welsh Quakers from Pennsylvania, and New Englanders. The great German wave of migration came later, between the 50's and the 70's. These Germans were mostly cultivated and luxury-loving folk. Many chose Cincinnati because of the vineyards nearby, and some went into the brewery business; many because it was a flourishing center of crafts that needed skilled labor, like carriage-making. Cincinnati began to give way to Chicago and the north at about the time of the Chicago fire; Chicago, like a Phoenix out of the ashes, built a modern industrial equipment from scratch, and ran away with much of its trade. Also the main line of westward movement shifted to the north. The Buffalo-Cleveland-Toledo-Chicago lake and railway channel replaced the Ohio River as Route No. 1 to the West.

In 1945—just after World War II was won!—the following letter appeared in the Cincinnati *Enquirer*:

Your editorial entitled "Relentless Propaganda," surely gets many a reader's "goat" because it seems to be the style of many editors, including yourself to "kick" the Germans around, and at the same time, we should have love for all races. I am American born, German descent and have loved ones both relatives and friends in Germany, and feel that the German people could not help what their leaders did any more than what we could help for what Roosevelt did . . . and why should correspondence not be opened between the German people and Americans. The Germans are just as fine a race as any other race, and when it comes to science, engineering, mechanical work, they take their place in the world the same as any other nationality, but jealousy and hate has been stirred and continued by you. Be a U.S.A. citizen and practice what you preach.

Cleveland is proud of its culture with much justification as we know; Cincinnati has plenty of culture too, though it does not advertise it with such self-consciousness. Its literary club (which has more distinction than such clubs usually have) will be one hundred years old in 1948; it was the first town west of the Alleghenies to have a symphony, and its municipal university, founded in 1819, is the oldest (and one of the best) in the United States; it had the first law school and the first medical school in Northwest Territory. Cincinnati history is rich with names like Stephen Foster, Harriet Beecher Stowe, and John James Audubon.

Nor is Cincinnati today an industrial backwater by any means. It has a stupendous soap business (Procter & Gamble), one of the biggest shoe factories in the nation (United States Shoe), and the largest machine-tool plant in the world. This latter is the Cincinnati Milling Machine Company; it has been operated for three generations by the Geier family in a tradition patriarchal in the extreme, with a staff of German mechanics almost as patriarchal as their bosses. Also Cincinnati is the biggest coal distributor[5] in the country, and it is the seat of the Crosley Corporation, which makes automobiles, airplanes, and various electrical devices.

[5] Another unique feature is that the city owns a railway, which goes by the imposing name of Cincinnati, New Orleans, and Texas Pacific; colloquially the line is known as Cincinnati-Southern, and the municipality owns the tracks as far as Chattanooga. This railway development came about when the community fathers saw the necessity of changing over from a river to a railroad era. Today, the railway income pays the service on the city debt.

WLW, the Crosley radio station, is the biggest in the nation in dollar volume of business; it even exceeds the great stations in New York, though Cincinnati ranks only seventeenth among American cities in population, and New York is first.[6]

One leading problem today is slum clearance, and another is sewage. Some new industries that might have been attracted to Cincinnati (for instance Fisher Body recently chose Columbus as a new site instead) went elsewhere because of an exasperating situation over zoning. The zoning ordinances, originally designed to save people's homes, now serve to perpetuate the slums, and these are among the most insufferable in the nation; 40 per cent of buildings on the river front and in the "Basin" are substandard. The labor groups—a conspicuous Cincinnati labor leader is Jack Kroll, state president of the CIO, who succeeded Sidney Hillman as national director of the PAC—and liberals generally want to clean out the slums under a long-range housing program, and make available new sites for industry. What holds this up is largely the propertied class, which is in a cleft stick; it too wants new industry, but on the other hand it won't give up its rents. Americans, it seems, can solve anything except a problem so simple and elemental as where citizens shall live.

Sewage is a lively issue. The city gets its water from the Ohio River. Also it dumps its refuse into this river. "Cincinnati's own untreated sewage," writes George Sessions Perry in the Saturday Evening Post,[7] "goes into the river only a few hundred yards below the intakes for the city's water plant."

Should a big city get bigger? Isn't a city of half a million people big enough? What would it profit Cincinnati to become a Detroit? Is Cleveland really happy—with one-third of its population forced to live outside its own city limits, with its upper bracket of rental values suburban? Cincinnati, which is not a booster town, ponders these questions gravely, and is inclined to answer in the negative.

Cincinnati politics are crazily fascinating. The story is too long to tell with any aroma here. The municipality is run by nine council members who are elected on a nonpartisan basis and, uniquely in America except in New York, by proportionate representation, as a result of the Charter reforms. "PR" is of course a thicket of pitfalls for politicians amateur or professional. Under "PR," as I heard it said, if you make one friend and seven enemies, you win. What it does is ensure effective minority representation.

The nine councilors choose one among themselves as mayor, whose function is ceremonial, and hire a city manager who really runs the town. The mayor gets $6,000 per year, the city manager $25,000. Cincinnati has been very lucky in its managers; it has had only three since

[6] Consider also what Cincinnati contributes to radio in terms of soap operas!
[7] In the Cities of America series, April 20, 1946.

the system started twenty-odd years ago, and all were, and are, first-class men: Colonel C. O. Sherrill, an army engineer; Clarence Dykstra who was president of the University of Wisconsin and is now provost of the University of California (L.A.); and the present incumbent, a railway man and administrator who had previously managed the Union Station, Wilbur M. Kellogg.[8]

What really makes the fur fly in Cincinnati is something else—Charter. This was born out of adversity in the early 1920's, when the city lay prostrate under bad government. Liberal citizens organized a reform movement, against the Republican bosses then in power and, aided greatly by woman suffrage which had just come in, won an election to amend the city charter as it then existed—hence the name "Charter." In 1925, Charter transformed itself into an overt political party, which it still is, in the shape of a Democratic, independent, and liberal Republican coalition. It held a majority in the council for twelve years, from 1926 to 1938; as of the moment it is the minority party, with four seats to five held by the regular Republicans.

I happened to be in Cincinnati at the time of the last municipal election, and I was forthwith inducted into these mysteries. Republicans and Charterites each put up a slate, and the voter, under "PR," must indicate by *number* his nine preferences; there is no such thing as an "X" on the ballot for councilmen. Each party seeks naturally to choose candidates who will reach special categories of voters; each presents as a rule one labor man, one Negro, one Republican Catholic, one Democratic Catholic, and so on; the real contest is then between the rivals in each of these special "pools." Charter did not, however, put up a Negro candidate in the last election, on the theory that the Negro community preferred *not* to vote on racial lines; instead it supported a strong labor man, Rollin H. Everett, who had both AF of L and CIO support. One leading Republican told me, "If Everett noses out *our* Negro, we're done for." Everett did indeed do so, but the Republicans maintained a council majority anyway. Incidentally Cincinnati is 13 per cent a Negro town, and the Negro vote usually carries the balance of power.

Cincinnati's most distinguished citizen today is probably Charles Phelps Taft II, Bob's brother. The two Tafts differ strikingly. For instance Charlie is, and has been for years, a leading Charterite; he sits on the council as a Charter member now, and is thus cheek by jowl with the CIO. This is not to say that he is a flaming radical. He is, however, enormously more liberal than Bob. Bob has always been fiercely anti-Charter. Charlie Taft served during most of the war in the State Depart-

[8] Cincinnati is the biggest American city to have a city manager. Others are Kansas City (Mo.), Norfolk, San Diego, Rochester, and Oakland. The city manager system began to all intents and purposes in Ohio; Dayton was the first considerable town in the country to have one, largely as a result of initiative by the Patterson family that runs the National Cash Register Company.

ment (as director both of the office of transport and communications and as chief of Wartime Economic Affairs) and has often worked at New Deal jobs. He takes a broad liberal view both nationally and internationally; he supported Roosevelt in part, and has been an attorney for the Amalgamated Clothing Workers. It is, indeed, extraordinary that two brothers—and partners in the same law firm—can have views so widely divergent, philosophies so contradistinctive, and still remain close friends. Basically Charles, though full of warmth and charm, is a do-gooder. He has always been a big YMCA and local church-and-charity man, and in December, 1946, he was elected president of the Federal Council of the Churches of Christ in America, the first layman ever to hold this exalted post.

Another Taft out-of-the-ordinary is Hulbert, half-cousin to the brothers and publisher of the *Times-Star*. This wealthy newspaper blankets southern Ohio almost as the Cleveland *Plain Dealer* blankets northern. What the *Times-Star* believes in, its publisher says, is only one thing—"the American middle class." Hulbert Taft is the most conservative man I met in forty-eight states. He told me that, driving through Cincinnati, you could tell which neighborhoods were "Republican and *Times-Star*" by the fact that they would be "clean and self-respecting." He once wrote a letter to Alf Landon saying that he would gladly "remain" a Republican if the party didn't elect a "radical" like Dewey; he thinks that the nomination of Willkie in 1940 was "treasonable" and that Lindbergh would make a president almost as good as Calvin Coolidge.

I asked some Cincinnati friends what they thought of Cleveland. Reply: "Cleveland is contentious, introspective, and not really part of the United States!"

Columbus and the Wolfes

The capital of Ohio, COLUMBUS (population metropolitan area 365,796; city limits 306,087), does not think of itself as a metropolis; it is in transition from what Cincinnati was to what Cleveland is. Originally it was called Franklinton, and it became the capital only after a vivid struggle with two rival towns, Worthington and Dublin. One story is that Dublin was chosen first, but lost its claim when its representatives were beaten by Franklinton in a poker game, while deluded with drink.[9]

Columbus today is a spacious and friendly town; a big issue is apt to be whether or not to cut down the trees and so make a street broader.

[9] This type of story is told of several state capitals, for instance Sacramento. A bill to make a town named St. Peter, rather than St. Paul, the capital of Minnesota, was once passed by the Minnesota legislature. But the St. Paul adherents kidnapped the engrossing clerk, kept him drunk for a week, and so prevented the bill from being properly drawn up.

It is a fanatic and frenzied football town; if you don't go to football games on Saturday, people think you're an odd fish and a pariah. It is a strong religious town; there are more Methodists, I heard, within a one-hundred-mile radius of Columbus than any other city in the world. Roman Catholic influence, though not nearly so weighty as in Cincinnati, is also considerable; for instance the film *Mission to Moscow* was withdrawn from exhibition after one day's showing. Later, however, it was resuscitated in small neighborhood theaters. As to politics, the "Catholics can nominate, but not elect," I heard it put. Finally, Columbus is 11 per cent a Negro town.

No fewer than 3,500 different Columbus organizations are represented in an over-all correlating agency, the Community Services Board, the aim of which is to "broaden the basis of the city's culture." It includes 88 parent-teacher associations, 700 separate church organizations, 135 Negro groupings of various kinds, and great numbers of patriotic, Masonic, fraternal, neighborhood, and other units, like the Columbus Council for Democracy, the Columbus Town Meeting, and the Council of Social Agencies. This is archetypically American and archetypically middle western. It healthily represents a familiar preoccupation with "co-operative" thinking, a desire to create leadership which is the chief community problem almost everywhere in the United States, and an attempt to overcome apathy and develop in citizens a sense of responsibility to the city as a whole.

One of the strangest and least-known stories in America is that of the Columbus Wolfes. Talk about the self-made man, or men! The Wolfe dynasty (contrary to some opinion, the family is not Jewish) was for many years the greatest single force in Columbus politics, journalism and business, and its political influence seeped widely into the state at large. Several times when I asked people who ran Ohio, the answer was, "the Wolfe interests." But this was an exaggeration. One qualifying remark I heard was, "After all the Wolfes have to clear with the Taft machine in Cincinnati and Cleveland doesn't pay much attention to them," and one eminent man of politics told me, "Sure the Wolfes boss the town, but if you want to get licked, just get the *Dispatch* (one of the Wolfe papers) on your side." Again one may note the way Americans in general tend to oppose anybody who is *known* to be bossed.

Two Wolfe brothers initiated the dynasty. Both are dead, and a group of sons and nephews now carry on the family. Robert F. Wolfe fell or jumped off the top of the *Dispatch* building some years ago. Harry Preston Wolfe died in his bed, aged seventy-three, in January, 1946, after a New Year's Eve party. They began as poor boys; Harry got his start in life as a lamplighter in a remote Ohio village. Robert got his, in a manner of speaking, in the penitentiary; he served a term for manslaughter, having shot someone who had insulted his sister in a barroom brawl; while a prisoner, so the story goes, he learned how to make shoes. Robert's wife, incidentally, was a sister of Thurston the magician.

Robert, emerging from jail, joined forces with Harry, and they founded the Wolfe Wear-U-Well Shoe Corporation. This was almost fifty years ago. As of today the same company is one of the biggest and most successful in the country, serving thirty-eight states with 3,600 retail outlets. The Wolfes became interested in publishing as far back as 1903; eventually they came to control the *Dispatch*, the *Ohio State Journal*, and several radio stations including WBNS. They turned to politics too, and their summer place, known as the Wigwam, was a kind of Republican headquarters; here Landon, Hoover and innumerable other party dignitaries have been entertained. Also at the Wigwam the Wolfes kept —pet wolves!

Banking was another interest; in 1929 the Wolfes organized *BancOhio* which today controls some twenty Ohio banks, including the biggest in Columbus; it has branches in seventeen Ohio cities, with capital resources of 275 million dollars.[10] Finally the Wolfes were prominent in civic affairs (donating stretches of parkway to the city and so on), in university circles (but they were never able to control the university though one Wolfe man was a prominent trustee for some years), and agriculture. The Wolfe Farms, also known as Agricultural Lands, Ltd., is supposed to be the biggest single farming operation east of the Mississippi.

As I heard it put in Columbus, there was nothing sinister in any of this. But that a single family should have set the tone and pace of an entire capital city, almost without opposition or qualification, for more than a generation, wasn't quite what you would call pure democracy either.

Note on Buckeye Character

Never underestimate the homeliness of Americans. In contrast to the Wolfe story consider the life and works of the late Alvin Victor ("Honest Vic") Donahey, three times Democratic governor of Ohio and Senator once. Mr. Donahey, according to legends that have grown about him, is the only man the state ever sent to Washington who never made a speech there. When governor, he would divide bills into two piles, those "for the people" and those against; his "policy" was simply to support one pile, and throw the other out. His favorite political motto was, "You can't win a campaign with creased pants." Once, when he was state auditor, an official submitted an expense account that included a notation, "Baked Potato—35¢." The unhappy creature had been charged this amount on a railway diner. Donahey disallowed the scandalous item, saying that nobody should or could spend such a sum for a

[10] New York *Times*, January 10, 1945.

mere potato, became known as "Honest Vic," and was launched instanter on a long and noteworthy political career.

Ohio: Miscellaneous

One important Ohio issue is something vicious known as strip mining, and another, indirectly related, is a proposal for an Ohio Valley Authority on the model of TVA.

Enormous quantities of coal lie very close to the surface in the United States: "strip mining" is simply open-air mining whereby such coal is shoveled or scraped off by bulldozer, steam shovel, or even a man with a pick and a wheelbarrow. One-fifth (roughly 110 million tons) of all coal produced in America today is strip mined, which fact came to close national attention during John L. Lewis's seventeen-day coal strike late in 1946. Mr. Ickes among others suggested that the best way to circumvent Lewis, if the strike continued, would be to assign army and navy to strip mining in Ohio and the other great strip-mine states. But strip mining has manifest evils and disadvantages. It makes a violently controversial issue.[11]

For one thing, unless local legislation forces the strip miners to do something about it, the process defaces the countryside by leaving unsightly mounds and ridges where the bulldozers pass—like the detritus of the gold mining dredges in Montana on a vastly larger and uglier scale. For another, strip mining obviously ruins agriculture: a power shovel, according to the article just cited, will chew up "an entire 300-acre farm to a depth of 75 or 80 feet" in a year. Again, the natural growth of trees is destroyed, which in turn means loss of topsoil and stimulus to erosion. Still again, the strip mines "lower the water table" and this can lead eventually to floods and dislocation of the entire balance of nature in an area.

Strip mining is certainly a problem in Ohio—the coal operators only just managed to beat two different bills last year which would have abolished it—but it is not quite so frightening a problem as in Indiana, Illinois, and particularly Missouri, where *good* land is being totally destroyed. In Ohio the phenomenon is still mostly limited to marginal, nonproductive land in the hillbilly counties near the West Virginia border. Of course the strip miners themselves assert vigorously that they are helping, not hindering, the farmer. They pay him well for his land, and in twenty years or so, they say, the "spoil banks" will be green again.

OVA is not a burning local issue. It may very well become one, however, if strip mining causes future floods. The Ohio River is, at

[11] A fair-minded account of the whole topic is "The Battle of the Spoil Banks," by Alfred H. Sinks, *Harper's Magazine*, as condensed by *Reader's Digest*, July, 1946.

best, notorious for periodic devastating floods; one of these all but drowned out Cincinnati and Louisville ten years ago. But it won't be easy to establish an OVA, whether for flood control or other reasons: the valley of the Ohio is intensively industrialized, and you cannot easily make lakes out of towns (though the floods may do so temporarily!); also the Ohio's fall of water is much less than that of the Tennessee, which makes for difficult engineering problems. The chief non-Ohio force arguing intermittently for an OVA is the New York *Daily News*.

On Education in Ohio

The state has no material resources at all comparable with its citizens, and no hope of perpetuity except in the intelligence and integrity of its people.

—Ohio State University Motto

Ohio boils with colleges and universities; it has forty-three, more than any state except Pennsylvania, and five are actually state universities. First came Miami University at Oxford and Ohio University at Athens, in the southern area where the state was settled first. Next Ohio State University, the biggest and best known of the five and one of the great universities of the country, was established at Columbus; originally it was a land-grant college, and its emphasis on agriculture is still very marked. Fourth, in 1912, the northeastern part of Ohio demanded a university of its own, and the normal school at Kent was given this status. Fifth, Bowling Green University was similarly set up for the northwest. All five today are quite separate and distinct institutions; they compete with vigor for students and for funds from the state treasury, though a single board superintends their finances.

Then consider the city universities in Cincinnati, Akron, and Toledo as well as Western Reserve at Cleveland, and a number of smaller schools, some of them denominational like Capital University (Lutheran) at Columbus. Many of these have a signal individuality. Antioch at Yellow Springs is one of the most distinctive colleges in the nation, and Oberlin was the first educational institution in the United States to admit women on equal terms with men, and Negroes on equal terms with whites. Wilberforce, near Xenia, is one of the best-known Negro institutions in the country, and it is supported in part by state funds. Also there are Ohio Wesleyan at Delaware, Wooster (where the Compton family of university presidents sprang from), Heidelberg at Tiffin, and Denison at Granville.

Ohio State is a colossus. It has more than seventy buildings, upwards of 14,000 students, a stadium that seats 74,000, its own radio station, a "twilight school" for evening classes, and a vice president—"in charge of education"! It teaches liberal arts and agriculture first, and then anything that makes for a good living or extension of the wealth of

Ohio. The variety of curriculum, though a commonplace to Americans and perfectly typical of all middle western state universities with a strong vocational slant, will astonish any European. Among courses offered are:

> Ice Cream Manufacturing
> Elementary Russian
> Introduction to Clothing and Textiles
> Factors in Successful Marriage
> Motor Carrier Organization
> The Social Work Approach to Life Adjustments
> Pliny and Catullus
> Driers, Kilns, and Theory of Firing
> Education of Exceptional Children
> Epidemic Diseases in Warfare
> Principles of Taxonomy: Monocots and Dicots
> Intermediate Japanese
> Anatomy of the Horse
> Old Provençal
> Woodlot Management

Tuition at Ohio State, as in most state universities in the nation, is of course (nominal charges excepted) absolutely free to residents of the state. Americans take this phenomenon for granted, but it is another point of unceasing wonder to almost all Europeans.

So to conclude with the Middle West, though we shall touch middle western characteristics elsewhere, notably in Pittsburgh, before this book is done. We take a long jump now to the baffling, astringent, and tightly productive world of New England.

Chapter 28

Inside New England I

God hath sifted a whole nation, that he might
send choice grain into this wilderness.
—William Stoughton, Governor of Massachusetts
1694-1701

New England is a . . . house divided against itself.
—Howard Mumford Jones

OF COURSE what the man from Mars will find out first about New
England is that it is neither new nor very much like England. Nor
does it much resemble nowadays the conventional concept of "New
England," that very special embodiment of tradition and culture established so firmly in most American minds by generations of observation
and acceptance. New England is many things—an area, a congeries of
precedent, a symbol, and, as has so often been said of Boston, a state
of mind. Also, like every American region, it is full of the unexpected,
infinitely complex and variegated. I never ran into anything in Costa
Rica or Albania quite so exotic as Boston; I found that the Saltonstall-
Tobin Axis, if one could have called it such, was almost as curious and
intricate a political phenomenon as the old Popular Front in France.

What else is New England? It is both a region of entrenched Puritan
conscience and of Sacco and Vanzetti. It is a region both of a fibrous
aristocratic tradition and of a tremendous influx of the foreign-born.
It is the region where for many years every Connecticut voter had to be
certified as of good moral character, and where until 1820 Massachusetts
had property and religious tests for officeholders. It is a region of the
craggiest kind of civic virtue, made manifest by such institutions as the
town meeting, and of characters like James Michael Curley, who represents a great many things of which civic virtue is not one. It is the
region of enormously conservative financial power—and also of such
majestic speculators as Joseph P. Kennedy. It is a region of wonderful rivers like the Housatonic, long winters so severe that they
warp the character, octogenarian hotel clerks and bell hops, and more
mildly crazy people than anywhere else in the nation. It is a region
profoundly devoted to specialized skills in small craft industries; but
it contains the biggest magazine press in the world, the biggest shoe
factory in the world, and the biggest watch factory in the world. It is,

as everybody knows, a region with a splendid self-reliance on the one side, and of a good deal of smugness, bleakness, and provincialism on the other, but it has a greater tolerance for eccentricity than any area in the country. It is a region where 190 savings banks in one state, Massachusetts, have deposits of more than three billion dollars, and where the same state announced in 1946 that it was preparing to take legal action to clear the names of those wrongly accused of witchcraft in Salem in 1692. It is the region of antique furniture shops, glowing bowls of fruit on tightly curving narrow roads, and that well-known silversmith, Paul Revere. It is the region of red cherry jam from the Boston firm of S. S. Pierce, the first antivivisection society in the country, and of Plymouth Rock, the brothers James, William Dean Howells (born in Ohio), Emily Dickinson, Brook Farm, Edna St. Vincent Millay, and extraordinarily bright and industrious young men like Arthur Schlesinger Jr.

Also New England is still other things, if only because it is changing, and changing fast, and finally it is an extremely difficult section of the country to write about, because there is so much to say and so little space. Half the paragraphs that follow could easily be expanded into whole sections, and half the sections into chapters.

Some Basic Characteristics

New England is a finished place. Its destiny is that of Florence or Venice, not Milan, while the American empire careens onward toward its unpredicted end. . . . It is the first American section to be finished, to achieve stability in its conditions of life. It is the first old civilization, the first permanent civilization in America.

—Bernard DeVoto

New England is the most closely knit group of states in the union; it has the dimensions of an entity, with sharp, concise frontiers. As we well know it is almost impossible to define the "West" conclusively; even such a comparatively homogeneous area as the "Southwest" leaks over state borders, and we shall see when we reach the "South" that no two authorities quite agree as to what it is. But every school child knows what the six New England states are, and what is the knifelike boundary of the region as a whole. Or compare New England with that loose and conglomerate geographical expression "the Middle West." Among other things the Middle West has no single "capital." But New England most certainly has—though the influence of Boston is, on the whole, declining, especially in Rhode Island and Connecticut.

This is not to say that the six New England states do not differ vividly among themselves. They do, as we shall see.

Three qualifying points arise. One is that, despite their geographical and historical affinities, the New England states only seldom express themselves in Washington with political unanimity. The "silver" senators from the West make a single dogmatic bloc; the New Englanders do not, which may be a result of Puritan individualism among other things.

Second, though the region may seem very closely tied and interlocked together, there are some staggering disunities in such a simple matter as, for example, transportation. One thinks of New England as a kind of Switzerland; one assumes that travel is easy from almost any point to any other point in a few hours, by road or rail. Which is a great illusion. To get from Augusta (Maine) to Concord (New Hampshire), say 130 miles as the crow flies, you have to ride two long sides of a triangle through Boston. To get from the capital of Vermont to the capital of Connecticut means a bus ride and three changes of train, on three different railway systems.

Finally, from the point of view of geography and industrialization, there are two New Englands. The north (Maine, Vermont, and to some extent New Hampshire) is predominantly rural—an area of solid forests and small diversified farms. The south (Massachusetts, Connecticut, Rhode Island) is, on the contrary, very thoroughly and heavily industrialized (though, again, almost every sentence in a survey like this needs to be qualified); there is plenty of *small* industry in southern Maine and in New Hampshire. I heard an argument once made that Vermont should by geographical criteria belong to New York—any Vermonter will rise to arms at the suggestion—and that New Hampshire is in reality "part" of Maine. But debate on such points could be endless.

Many chapters ago I quoted from an address by Professor Kenneth Murdock of Harvard. Perhaps I may insert here another passage from the same speech, because it describes aptly another New England characteristic. Most people think that the area is altogether drab and colorless physically. But listen to Mr. Murdock:

Outsiders . . . accept as an article of faith that it is always winter, always raining or snowing or at least cloudy, east of the Hudson River. Black, white and grey sum up for them the colors to which New England attains; they explain the colorlessness they discern in her poets by pointing to the Puritanism in their blood, and the drabness of their environment. Apparently the flaming New England salt marshes in October, the brilliant mosaic of inland hills at the same season, the riot of color when crimson maple buds and the yellow and green of a New England spring do their best to cheer the unfortunates who live among these scenes, the infinite variety of fruit and shade in a summer landscape in New Hampshire or Maine—all have nothing to do with color; to find it one must, apparently, go to Manhattan Island or the Pennsylvania mine fields.

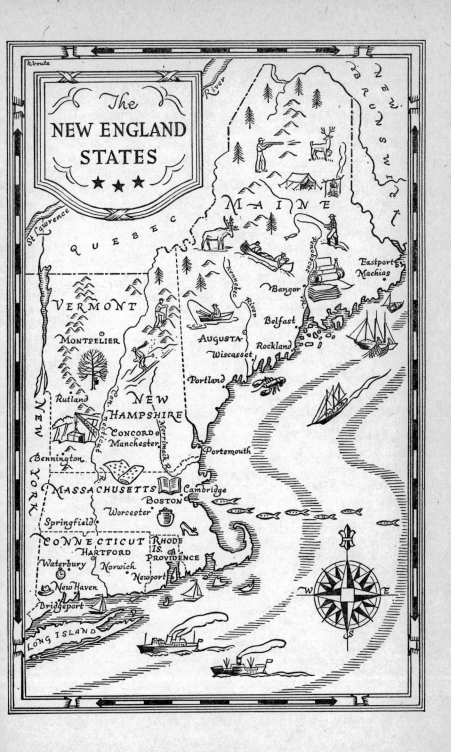

That shrewd and courageous Yankee, Wilbur Cross, former governor of Connecticut, suggested quite seriously some years ago that all the New England states should combine to make one; he pointed out the saving this would entail in legislative expenses, the efficiency and directness in administration that would result. He was violently shouted down. But out of his idea came the practice whereby the six New England governors now meet regularly, two or three times a year. Once they all called on Mr. Roosevelt for a conference. Several of the governors had never met the president before, and some were shy. FDR broke the ice by counting them and saying, "What! All six! You're not going to secede, are you?"

Perhaps oddly, close-packed and samesome as the region is, it has no outstanding newspaper that serves all six states, though the Boston *Herald* reaches fairly far. But there is no New York *Times,* no dominant paper with a pan-New England point of view. The Boston *Transcript* might well have seized this place, but when the *Transcript* died in April, 1941, of journalistic cirrhosis of the liver, its total circulation was exactly eighteen thousand.[1]

Puritan Tradition and Nonconformist Conscience

What have Puritanism and democracy in common? Both respect the individual . . . both recognize the ultimate authority of reason . . . both respect the dignity of man. Both are equalitarian and leveling, for to the Puritan salvation was dependent on merit or grace, not on wealth or class or talents, and to the democrat equality was part of common humanity. . . . Both, finally, gave their allegiance to ideas or principles rather than to men or institutions.

—Henry Steele Commager

We proceed to a kind of tentative analysis of that quality known as "Yankee" or "New England" character. The dominating items are almost too obvious to need mention—frugality, individualism, hardiness, eccentricity. But perhaps our mythical reader in Johannesburg, South Africa or Asunción, Paraguay (or Chattanooga, Tennessee) is not so well informed.

"The courage of New England is the courage of conscience," wrote Daniel Webster. And James Truslow Adams has a fine sentence in his *Epic of America*: "As time went on (in New England) the gristle of conscience, work, thrift, shrewdness, duty, became bone." One joke is ancient but nevertheless apposite. "The Pilgrim Fathers fell first on

---

[1] A famous limerick is to the point:

> There was a young maid from Back Bay
> Whose manners were very blasé;
>   While still in her teens
>   She refused pork and beans
> And once threw her *Transcript* away.

their knees and then on the aborigines." Other things being equal, this duality of attitude still applies today.

No one should forget three factors. First, the early New England settlers were men of the highest intellectual quality; the Calvinist tradition insisted upon and promoted not only such homely virtues as honesty and diligence, but also intelligence; the basic pattern was set early—brains count: no sloppiness; out with the mental riffraff. Second, the New England states (among the other original thirteen) had long experience of self-government *before* the federal union. The first thirteen had a really concrete adolescence; they learned how to make good government in practice. More than any other American region, New England owes its present to its past. Third, as has been many times pointed out, New Englanders love to be "agin things"; they still stand by Thoreau who said that the individual's first duty is to "live his life as his principles demand," and by Emerson who believed above all that there should always be "a minority unconvinced."

Two details to illustrate nonconformity: (*a*) A good many New Englanders who believed violently in the innocence of Sacco and Vanzetti were blue-bloods; President Lowell was as vehemently attacked by some members of his own faculty as by members of any other group. (*b*) It was the *Atlantic Monthly* which first gave Ernest Hemingway commercial publication after his story "Fifty Grand" had been rejected by every other magazine in America—just as it was the *Atlantic Monthly* that published Bret Harte's "Luck of Roaring Camp," after Harte's own west coast had refused it.

We should have a word too about that celebrated New England phenomenon the town meeting, as an example of the Puritan tradition. In 93 per cent of the corporate communities of New England, the town citizens elect their selectmen and other administrative officers in the most direct and literal way; there are no primaries, no conventions, no balloting as a rule except by show of hands; this is immediate personal democracy, the immediate choice of a few individuals by another few. Of course the Town Meeting system can apply only where communities are small.[2] And of course the purity of the process varies with localities. Massachusetts for years fined qualified citizens who neglected to attend town meetings. Elsewhere they have become intermixed with elements of the bogus. For instance in at least one community the time and place of the meeting are only announced to the public in microscopic type in the most inconspicuous corner of the local newspaper; doors are closed instantly the meeting comes to order, and a local machine puts through its slate almost as in Kansas City or Chicago.

---

[2] Towns of greater population than 5,000 have what is called the "representative town meeting," in which the procedure is not quite so direct. Cf. *Fortune*, February 1940.

Brahmins and Middle Yankees

We are *thin* . . . we are pale, we are sharp. There is something
meagre about us; our line is wanting in roundness . . .
—Henry James

What is a Boston Brahmin? It isn't easy to define the term, since
copiousness of ancestry is not, as might be expected, the chief criterion.
Mr. Conant, the president of Harvard, had three forebears on the *Mayflower*; but Mr. Conant is not a Brahmin. But his predecessor, A.
Lawrence Lowell, who couldn't trace many ancestors beyond the Revolution, most certainly was. The joke in Boston is that the Brahmin ranks
closed in about 1820; nobody has been taken in since. People often
assume that to be a lineal descendent of a *Mayflower* passenger means,
ipso facto, that you are an aristocrat. But this isn't true by any means;
the *Mayflower* Pilgrims were mostly very simple folk. And the hallmark
of aristocracy became subtly overlaid and underlaid with politics (for
instance with such a consideration as what side a family took during
the Revolution), with social pretensions, and of course with wealth.

The Brahmins today make a wonderfully close-knit archaic group,
which nothing in the United States quite rivals. Harvard and trusteeships; the world placidly revolving around Back Bay; the Apley-Pulham
spirit; aridity and charm and a Bloomsbury cultivation; above all, profound family interweavings. I met one eminent Brahmin who told me
that his grandfather had 226 nieces and nephews, and one gentlewoman,
whose husband is absolutely beyond dispute the quintessence of Brah-
minism, informed me quite seriously that, though she had lived in her
exquisite house in Brookline for thirty years, and borne six children
into the family, she was not yet finally "accepted"—because she had
been born in Rhode Island!

One story pleased me! I hope it's not apocryphal. A gallant old lady
whose family tree is as thick with eminent ancestors as a hedgehog with
bristles, was knocked down by a thug one winter night. She did not
deign to rise; lying there in the snow she exclaimed simply, "My man!
Do you not realize who I *am*!"

As typical a Brahmin as any is Charles Francis Adams, the most
distinguished living Bostonian, the great-great-great-grandson of President John Adams, a former secretary of the Navy, and a director of
some forty corporations. Men like Mr. Adams and women like Mrs.
Homans, his sister, have every distinction, grace and elegance. Nor
should anyone be so naïve as to assume that the Adamses are old-fashioned
or illiberal; let no one think that because a man is a Brahmin he may
not be a rebel too. With absolute simplicity one member of the family
told me, "We *are* rather a splendid people, don't-you-know." But the
Brahmins as a whole realize that most of the finite world has passed

them by; they concede that few of their fellow citizens appreciate their fastidiousness, their sophistication. They live in a shrinking backwater, and they know it. There are thirty-seven Cabots in the Boston Social Register; but there are forty-one Browns and Brownes.

Has the ancient blood itself run dry? Not quite. A Saltonstall is, after all, senator from Massachusetts; and an Endicott Peabody was an all-American football player not long ago. I heard it said that "the Lowells and Adamses have run out biologically, but the Cabots are still prolific."[3] It seems that the life strain is still capable of bursting out after long periods of lethargy; consider for instance the contemporary entrance into politics and public affairs of some first-class Brahmin youngsters. A Choate is editor of the Boston *Herald*. Henry Parkman Jr. (descendent of Francis Parkman) was head of OPA in Massachusetts, and then a state senator. One of the best men in New England, Robert F. Bradford, a lineal descendent of the Governor Bradford who wrote the *History of Plimouth* [*sic*] *Plantation*, became governor in 1947. In Springfield you will find Roger Lowell Putnam, a Bostonian who went west (that is, he went west one hundred miles), married a Catholic, and became—of all things!—the town's Democratic mayor. I do not know what relation William Phillips is to Wendell Phillips. But when the contemporary Phillips went to India as Roosevelt's ambassador, something in him, impeccable and intricate blue-blood that he is, made him break out in indignation at the injustices he saw.[4] Many Brahmins are still abolitionists at heart.

The Melting Pot and How It Melts

Late one November afternoon I strolled across Boston Common; no site in the United States can have associations quite so stirring. A young ensign stopped me with "What place is this, sir?"

I said, "Boston Common."

He said, "What's that?"

I said, "Where we all come from, in a way."

[3] I take the following from the Raleigh (N.C.) *News and Observer*, April 15, 1945. "It seems that some Russian with the unpronounceable name of Furnoffsky or something that sounded like that applied . . . to be allowed when he took out his papers as an American citizen to bear the honored name of Cabot. As he had become a hundred percent American he wanted to be known by a Yankee name with the American name blown on the bottle, so to speak. So he selected the name Cabot. . . . But a fellow named Cabot interpleaded and said it would be an insult to let the noble name of Cabot be borne by a Russian immigrant who had never heard of Plymouth Rock. . . . Finally the court held that the Cabot who objected had no legal monopoly on the name."

[4] Exactly the same kind of spirit brought men like Francis Biddle out of the swamps of Philadelphia.

He looked blank a moment and then said, "Oh." In twenty minutes I overheard a dozen foreign accents.

A few weeks later I visited Hartford, Connecticut. In three blocks on a single street I saw these shop signs:

> Kutz Music Store
> John Campo. Custom Tailor
> P. O. Postma. Jeweler
> P. J. Dooley. Rathskeller
> Paul A. Zazzaro. Permittee
> Calfas. Hatter
> McCoy's. The House of Music
> Witkower's Old Book Store
> Gung-Ho. Chinese Restaurant
> Donchian. Rugs
> R. G. Sceli & Co. Radio & Electronic Parts
> Gustave Fischer Co. Office Equipment
> Dr. George E. Woerz. Optometrist
> Leo Celio. Groceries

Here are German, Jewish, Greek, Irish, Italian, Chinese, Armenian, and Polish names.

In his indispensable and massive *North America*,[5] Professor J. Russell Smith makes a list of some births recorded in one month in a New England factory town:

A daughter, Ida, to Quintu and Amelia Perline.
A daughter, Vittoria Luigia, to Antonio and Luigian Musante.
A son, Albert Joseph, to John and Amelia Kottman.
A daughter, Hilda M., to John and Elsie Balster.
A daughter, Stanislawa, to Wlodslow and Mary Dictk.
A daughter, Annie, to Joseph and Mary Groszek.
A daughter, Helen, to Nikolay and Sophia Smey.
A daughter, Sophie Justine, to John W. and Louise F. Kempt.
A son, Joseph, to Redolf and Mary Govin.
A daughter, Katie Mary, to Nicholas and Joseph Moriscato.
A daughter, Victoria, to Mathew and Joanna Styfcka.
A daughter, Eugeniusz Jo, to Volente and Mary Borcz.
A daughter, Cecilia, to Peter and Anne Nasiadka.

My friend Edward A. Weeks Jr., editor of the *Atlantic Monthly*, took me to lunch in Boston; he said he'd show me "the real New England." I thought I would meet Cabots and Lowells, and, since I had seldom met any Cabots or Lowells, my curiosity was pleasantly aroused. Mr. Weeks introduced me to his friends. One was a Greek importer, one the brother of a Jewish judge, one an Irish businessman. Not a Brahmin in the lot.

[5] New York, Harcourt, Brace and Company, Inc., 1925.

All over New England the foreign-born have laid themselves on the land; this fact is paramount and basic. No visitor can avoid the generalization that the "Yankee-land" is no more "Yankee-land"; the old stock has been inundated with waves of Irish, French Canadians, Italians, Polish, Portuguese. In Manchester (New Hampshire) there is a solid block of Greeks; in Waltham (Massachusetts) a solid block of Armenians. Providence (Rhode Island) has practically the texture of an Italian town, and so have parts of New Haven (Connecticut). The Polish-language newspaper with the biggest circulation in America is published in Boston, and so is the biggest Armenian paper, which incidentally was the first in the country to print William Saroyan; the biggest Finnish paper appears in Fitchburg, Massachusetts; and the biggest French at Fall River, Massachusetts. There are towns in New England named Berlin (but pronounced *Ber*-lin), Calais (pronounced Callus), Paris (pronounced Pay-rus), and Peru (pronounced Peeru).

Figures for Massachusetts are particularly relevant; one out of every five persons is foreign born. Some details as to country of birth:

Eire	103,000
Northern Ireland	10,500
Sweden	28,000
Poland	53,000
Russia	64,000
Lithuania	20,000
Italy	114,000
Portugal	24,000
Syria, Palestine & Turkey	18,700
Canada (French)	81,000
Canada (other)	142,000
Azores	12,000
Greece	15,000
Hungary	1,100
Germany	16,000
France	4,600
Finland	10,000

One thing that surprised me was that, by and large, the foreign communities do not mix much—at least in the towns. The new archbishop of Boston, Dr. Cushing, told me with great pride that his chauffeur, Lithuanian born, had married an Italian girl; but such marriages are quite rare even when Catholicism is a common denominator. Intermarriage across both a religious and a racial frontier—say between Irish and old Yankee, or between Portuguese and Swede—almost never happens. There have been no marriages between Saltonstalls and Vanzettis. The melting pot does melt in that the foreign-born most certainly do become American citizens, their children learn the American language in American public schools, they are unchallengeably American in mores, style and spirit. And Poles, Czechs, French Canadians (the most parochial and unassimilable of all racial groups), and Jugoslavs do of course meet professionally and, to a certain extent socially, at least in the upper brackets. But in the great towns they don't intermarry much. In rural districts the case is somewhat different; in villages, a lone Spaniard or Turk has a better chance to be absorbed.

Most people think of the foreign-born as predominantly urban and industrial, but plenty of immigrants and sons of immigrants are New England farmers; the countryside is fairly choked with them. There are splendid farms near Concord, Massachusetts, owned by the Irish, and the French Canadians have pitched camp in rural Vermont, Maine, and New Hampshire. Most of the farming on Cape Cod is done by Portuguese and Spaniards; in Rhode Island by the Portuguese; and in the Connecticut Valley by Italians and Poles.

The tremendous influx of foreign-born has certainly changed the face of New England. But also New England has changed the face of the foreign-born. The equation works both ways. There are Polish shopkeepers in Westport, Connecticut, and Irish gardeners near Pittsfield, Massachusetts, who, in a generation or so, have become more Yankee than the Yankees.

Paragraph About the French Canadians

Probably this unique minority group, almost unknown to the nation at large, is the most tenacious in the entire country. There are 908,386 French Canadians in the United States, of whom the great majority are Roman Catholic; and almost all are clustered in New England. Most of them came to the United States for the same reason that the Irish did—they were hungry, they needed jobs. And (I mean no offense) they represented communities in Quebec which for two hundred years had had extremely little opportunity for social or intellectual development. Look at parts of Quebec itself today. The French Canadians now in this country almost never intermix; they hold with the utmost stubbornness and obstinacy to their own folklore, customs, language. A good many are farmers, but some are urban dwellers; almost all vote Democratic, and they are a considerable source of power to the political machines in Maine and New Hampshire towns. I heard many stories of French Canadian adhesiveness. Let us choose only one. About ten years ago, the head of the Catholic church in the Rhode Island diocese was compelled to excommunicate some sixty laymen in the Woonsocket area— where the French Canadians constitute what is practically a state within a state—because of a bitter struggle over teaching of French in the parochial (not the public) schools; the community had insisted on holding onto French and keeping English excluded. The bishop (of Irish extraction) took the line that American citizens of no-matter-what origin must learn English! But the French Canadian leaders had refused to agree; hence the excommunication. Thereafter, English was duly taught.

"Reverse Lend Lease"

Now to another field. Plenty of conspicuous New Englanders, particularly the Middle Yankees, are of basic American stock but they were not born in New England. For instance Dr. Karl T. Compton, president of the Massachusetts Institute of Technology, was born in Ohio, and Van Wyck Brooks, the distinguished historian of New England literature, comes from New Jersey. Edward A. Weeks of the *Atlantic Monthly* was also New Jersey born; so was Charles E. Spencer Jr., the president of the First National Bank of Boston, the behemoth that is the sixth largest bank in the country. Or take Donald K. David, the dean of the Harvard Business School, one of the ablest men in Massachusetts. He came to Harvard from Moscow, Idaho! And John P. Marquand, no less, was born in Delaware.

This brings up an astonishing contributory point. One thinks of Harvard as the essence and incarnation of New England. Yet, Mr. Conant told me, eleven out of twelve Harvard deans never went to Harvard College! (On the other hand, all twelve are graduates of a Harvard graduate school in the specialties they teach.) To name a few— Dean Paul Herman Buck (Arts and Sciences) comes from Columbus, Ohio; Dean Alfred Chester Hanford (Harvard College) from Makanda, Illinois; Dean Edmund Morris Morgan (Law) from Mineral Ridge, Ohio; Dean Charles Sidney Burwell (Medicine) from Denver, Colorado. A point on the other side—no *president* of Harvard has ever come from outside Massachusetts.

During the last century New England went, as it were, west; it sent people out, everywhere in the United States, as we well know from many passages in this book. It became a kind of concentrated breeding ground of human resources, fertilizing great cities like, for instance, Cleveland and Portland, Oregon. As a result Kansas is today, in some respects, more "New England" than New England itself; just as parts of California are more Kansaslike than Kansas. As the New Englanders energetically pushed out, their own area became necessarily drained of much vitality and talent. When people talk of the alleged "decay" of New England this is what they usually mean. Like a blood donor who gives too much, it got weak.

To fill the vacuum, other people of course came in; the process was a kind of reverse lend lease in the human sphere. Hence men like the Comptons, the Spencers, the Davids. "We have a way of life here a hell of a lot of people crave," one sage New Hampshire editor told me. But he proceeded to point out that most of the blood that comes nowadays to New England is old rather than new blood. People settle in Boston or Cambridge *after* having made their fortunes, *after* having reached the highest distinction in science or the professions. Hence, they are not so vitalizing a force to the community as younger men might be.

Another able editor suggested that the test of modern New England will be whether or not the "new" American from South Boston or Aroostook County will measure up to the old. Will the sons of the Irish be frontier builders like the Yankees? Will the Portuguese and Greeks and French Canadians send their children out to create new business empires in the West—or even blast or chip their way through granite to make small tidy farms in Vermont? The answer I got in the main was—no.

Hypodermic Needles, War, and Cranberries

Quintessentially New England is, as everybody knows, a region of small varied industry and small varied agriculture; this naturally arises from the physical characteristics of the area—from the inflexible juxtapositions of land, geography, climate. What are the natural resources of New England? Answer: very few, except woods and water power. There is no coal, iron,[6] or oil in any of the six states (though quarrying is an important industry in Vermont).

The soil is sparse and frugal, the climate rigorous. So New Englanders had to count on what they did have with special emphasis: (*a*) access to the ocean; (*b*) lusty rivers. As a result came the tremendous nineteenth century growth of textiles, as well as shipping and commerce generally. The area must import food, fuel, raw materials, to live. So the people perforce learned to be good traders, lively businessmen, and manufacturers of almost everything.

Even agriculture in New England is of a very specialized and subdivided kind. Consider potatoes in Maine, wrapper tobacco in Connecticut, apples in Massachusetts and New Hampshire, cranberries near Cape Cod, fluid milk and maple sugar in Vermont. But a disconcerting recent phenomenon is that much New England agriculture is declining. Whole villages—for instance in New Hampshire—once dependent on a single crop have collapsed into decay, as the soil wore out. Thousands of small holdings have had to be abandoned, with resultant social transformations at once profound and, so far, comparatively little observed. As a consequence some slight pressure has arisen for a Valley Authority

[6] But a small iron mine near Salisbury, Connecticut, operated from pre-Revolutionary times till about 1900.

in New England like TVA. Shades of the Puritan nonconformists! Congressman Thomas T. Lane of Lawrence, Massachusetts, introduced a bill for a Merrimac Valley Authority in July, 1946. It didn't get very far.

As to industry, most New England plants are very small; the great majority employ five hundred men or less. The emphasis is, and always has been (except in textiles) on quality, precision, craftsmanship, durability. Many concerns have remained in the same family for generations; they rigidly resist mergers and combinations, and their emphasis is still on individuality of enterprise. Later we shall mention superlative New England accomplishments in producing everything from hypodermic needles to woolen socks.

The war naturally gave New England's economy a monumental boost—something that was very welcome and useful considering what had been a serious progressive decline in such things as boots (many of the great shoe manufacturing companies had moved west) and textiles (which as a rule were not successfully passed on from generation to generation). In the winter of 1944-45 New England held 9.2 per cent of the total war supply and facilities contracts of the entire United States; the amount involved was roughly sixteen billion dollars. Of this, aircraft accounted for four billion, shipping three billion, ordnance three billion.

Harvard and Yale: Presumptive Influence

These great universities do not belong merely to New England; their influence is national. Locally, their most important contribution—aside from an overriding dedication to national service during the war—is that New England is intellectually the most reasonable area in the country. Of course, dozens of smaller universities and colleges have assisted in this process. You can have temperate and rational and detached discussion about anything under the sun with most educated New Englanders; they will take up with calmness the pros and cons of almost any subject, no matter how startling or controversial. They will not get red in the face if you mention Bolshevism or the Ku-Klux Klan; they like to look at both sides of every question; in fact, they are quite capable of taking either side in any argument, and supporting it with clarity and vigor. For this beneficent climate of mind, Harvard and Yale are probably the factors most responsible.

Harvard is a national university, yes; but as I heard it said, it is a "provincial college." That is, roughly 75 per cent of students in the graduate school are *not* New Englanders; roughly 75 per cent of undergraduates in Harvard College are. Harvard is run by its president and the six members of the corporation, who are a kind of self-perpetuating oligarchy unique in the world. One interesting and little-known point[7] is that only about 12,000 out of roughly 62,000 Harvard alumni regularly vote for the board of overseers, or subscribe to the alumni bulletin. The president of Harvard, James Bryant Conant, is one of the ablest, most intelligent, and most useful men in American public life, though many younger scientists thought that he took too conservative and conventional a line on postwar developments attending the atomic bomb. With the bomb itself Conant, like Vannevar Bush, had much to do.

In mid-1945 came publication of *General Education in a Free Society*, a book sponsored by Harvard and written by a group of faculty members who gave two years of research and study to the job. It made a considerable impact in the world of education all over the country; its contents are both too tightly knit and too ramifying for discussion here. What it appealed for most, in its earnest endeavor to broaden the basis of American education as a preparation for true citizenship, was, first, less strictly vocational education in high schools; second, broad compulsory courses emphasizing root subjects—the humanities, science, and the social sciences—in the universities. Harvard itself prepared to modify its elective system, under which a bright student had previously been able to study almost anything he chose, and so did Yale.

How do Harvard and Yale differ? For one thing, Harvard is a good deal bigger, with 8,500 students[8] as against Yale's 3,331. But Yale has 1,052 teachers to Harvard's 1,871. Again, Harvard is more closely interlocked with Boston and Cambridge than is Yale with New Haven. Without Harvard, Boston wouldn't be much more than a provincial town; Harvard permeates every line of Boston's better being. But Yale seems less tied up with New Haven and the neighborhood. Finally, I heard it said, "they teach better at Yale, but Harvard is more cosmopolitan and it spreads a richer feast."

The president of Yale, Charles Seymour, is a distinguished historian and editor of the Colonel House journals. On his faculty, as at Harvard's, are seasoned and bright rebellious spirits both, and the Yale University Press is one of the most discerning in the country.

The New England Senators

These are a formidable miscellany of extremely distinctive individualists, and most are very able. Of one, Saltonstall, I shall talk in

[7] Another point not generally recognized is that Cambridge, the city, is not quite what one would imagine from photographs of Harvard Yard. Mostly it's a slum. A curious item, according to *Fortune* (February, 1940) is that a resolution was once adopted by the Cambridge city council "banishing from the sacred precincts of the city all printed matter in which appear the words Lenin or Leningrad."

[8] Up to 11,700 late in 1946. Of the total 75 per cent are war veterans.

detail in the chapter following, not because he is the most typical but because he illustrates best the tensions within his own great state. Almost all deserve much fuller treatment, and I hope to return to several in another place. This summary attempts nothing more than the briefest kind of composite sketch.

Wallace A. White of Maine is titular leader of the Republican party in the Senate; a pleasant, mild, and pious man of seventy, he is popular on all sides; his chief function is to hold the balance between two much more dominant and vivid men, Taft and Vandenberg, especially since the 1946 elections. Everybody likes White; few people pay much attention to him. *Owen Brewster*, the junior Maine senator, is a totally different matter. Colorful, ambitious, hard-set, he has a complex voting record, and a career that may go almost anywhere. Brewster was a valuable member of the old Truman Committee; on the other hand he was a moving spirit of the Pearl Harbor investigation. Brewster had an isolationist past; but he voted to lift the arms embargo and for both Lend Lease and selective service. He has taken a strong pro-Zionist line on Palestine, and on most domestic affairs he is liberal. For instance he voted to confirm Henry Wallace for secretary of commerce in 1945 (so did five out of the eight Republican New England senators), and he thinks that for his party to tie itself to the extreme reactionary Democrats of the South is a painful form of slow suicide.

No two men could be in greater contrast than the two Rhode Island senators, *Peter G. Gerry* and *Theodore F. Green*, though both are very rich men and both are Democrats. Gerry is a Bourbon of Bourbons, one of the most reactionary men in Congress, a man of enormous inherited wealth and withal a very civilized old gentleman. He announced his retirement in 1946. *Theodore F. Green,* though seventy-eight years old, is junior to Gerry in point of service; just as Gerry is one of the extreme reactionaries in the Senate, Green is one of the extreme liberals. I have mentioned that his voting record on progressive legislation was recently judged 100 per cent perfect by the *New Republic*. Green is an out-and-out New Dealer; some Yankees practically think of him as a traitor to their class. His family is one of the most distinguished in Rhode Island; he is that rarest of things, a Brahmin Democrat. Both Theodore Roosevelt and Woodrow Wilson asked him to handle the Rhode Island campaign in 1912; he chose Wilson. Once he was president of the American Bar Association; and he is a celebrated connoisseur of Chinese painting and ceramics.

Brien McMahon (Democrat) of Connecticut is still another quite different type of man, a young politician (he is only forty-three) who did a good job as a gang-busting attorney, and who saw the Atomic Energy Bill through the Senate. McMahon went to Fordham and Yale, and became a protégé of Attorney General Homer Cummings; he helped prosecute remnants of the Dillinger gang in Chicago and in Kentucky investigated the Harlan County coal operators who were accused of violations of the Wagner Act. McMahon reached the Senate in 1944 by beating John A. Danaher, a Republican wheel horse and well-known isolationist. In 1946, McMahon, an ambitious man, was supposed to have been a chief force in breaking up the movement to run Chester Bowles for governor of Connecticut.

Both the New Hampshire senators are vigorous men too, with such highly variegated records that they are hard to classify. *Styles Bridges* (Republican) was born in Maine, and went to New Hampshire to devote himself to scientific agriculture. He had political interests from the beginning, and in 1934 became governor of New Hampshire at the age of thirty-six; at that time he was the youngest governor in the country. Bridges is an aggressive reactionary on most issues. In 1946 he introduced a bill for a constitutional amendment the upshot of which, if ever carried through, would be to throw off the Supreme Court bench the four justices most recently named. He hates pressure groups: he was one of the very few senators who voted against "neutrality" legislation before the war; and he is pertinaciously engaged in a continual running fight with the CIO, the Roosevelt family, and the Union of Soviet Socialist Republics. *Charles W. Tobey* (Republican) is a much more reasonable man, whose voting record has been consistently progressive; he is an old-style craggy individualist. Though a Republican senator from New Hampshire, he speaks widely under the auspices of the National Citizens Political Action Committee; and although he has an isolationist past he believes firmly now in good relations with Russia and full co-operation. It was Tobey, more than any other man, who blocked Ed Pauley's nomination as under secretary of the Navy; for this Mr. Truman among others has not forgiven him.

Vermont has two splendid senators. *Warren R. Austin,* one of the most useful men in Washington, was appointed in 1946 to succeed Edward R. Stettinius as American representative on the United Nations Security Council. In the Senate Austin was a kind of George Norris in reverse; very liberal on foreign policy, much more conservative on things domestic. He is a lawyer by profession, born in 1877. In Mexico in 1945, he saved the Chapultepec Conference from disaster singlehanded—mostly by being sane. *George D. Aiken* is almost the precise inverse of Austin. He was an intractable isolationist (before Pearl Harbor) and in domestic policy is a very strong liberal. But Aiken, like so many Vermonters, is full of idiosyncrasy. In December, 1944, he was one of three senators to oppose *all* the nominations made by Stettinius, who had just become secretary of state, for assistant secretaries; he voted "Nay" not only to MacLeish and Clayton, but also to Dunn, Holmes, Grew, and Rockefeller. What kind of State

Department Senator Aiken wanted is unknown. Austin's record, incidentally, was exactly the opposite. Who says that Vermont isn't an individualistic state? For Austin was one of the very few senators who voted *for* all six Stettinius nominees. Senator Aiken is a farmer, specializing in fruits and wild flowers; he is the author of two books, *Pioneering with Fruits and Berries,* and *Pioneering with Wild Flowers.* During one Vermont election campaign he reported his expenses as exactly thirty cents; in another, he spent exactly nothing. Early in 1945 he came out for an overhaul of the whole structure of federal government and suggested the creation of four new cabinet posts (Transportation, Banking and Insurance, Social Welfare, and Public Works); early in 1946, searching out a way for peace, he said that our foreign policy was too pro-British. This man is a character.

Vermont, a lucky state, has as successor to Austin a new senator, *Ralph E. Flanders,* self-educated and self-made, a machine tools manufacturer who is supported by the CIO, and who is one of the most remarkably sound and able men in America. Flanders worked on the precursor of the War Production Board for a while, handling machine tool priorities (he probably knows more about machine tools than any other man in the country) and quit because he couldn't get along with the bureaucracy. Later Roosevelt made him a member of the Economic Stabilization Board (though he is an emphatic Republican) and in time he became president of the Federal Reserve Bank in Boston, chairman of the New England Council, and a major actor in the Committee of Economic Development. Flanders was a strong Willkie man, and is a stout liberal with closely trained and productive brains who knows his way around.

David I. Walsh, Democratic senator from Massachusetts from 1918 to the end of 1946, is a wholly different type of person. He was born in 1872; he is old, burdened with an awkward past, disappointed, and rejected. But for years his Massachusetts popularity was so great, among Brahmins and Irish both, that he was unbeatable; in 1940 he even ran ahead of Roosevelt. But young *Henry Cabot Lodge Jr.,* who had previously resigned a Senate seat to go into the Army, ran against him in 1946 and beat him soundly.[9] I heard a friend say of Lodge once, but with admiration and affection, "Cabot thinks that only two people exist in the world, Cabot Lodge and his grandfather, Cabot Lodge; and of these two, one is dead." His voting record in the Senate was very mixed. I quote *Time* (July 7, 1942): "He voted to limit the use of U.S. forces to the western hemisphere, to restrict transfer of naval craft, to make a two-billion loan instead of Lend Lease. Then he voted for Lend

[9] His brother, John Davis Lodge, won a Connecticut seat in Congress in the same election.

Lease, then to retain the neutrality act, then to declare war, thus taking all sides."

New England has or had some remarkable folk in the House of Representatives too. Consider Congressman Joseph W. (Joe) Martin Jr., of Massachusetts, for long the minority leader and scheduled to be the new Speaker in 1947, who has as purely negative a record as any important man in Washington; consider a group of men and women like Chester E. Merrow of New Hampshire, Margaret Chase Smith of Maine, Charles A. Plumley of Vermont, Edith Nourse Rogers of Massachusetts, and Robert Hale of Maine; consider John W. McCormack, the ex-majority leader and the first Roman Catholic in history to have held that post, whose brother is a South Boston publican with the nickname Knocko; and consider that lovely, spectacular, and very useful lady Clare Boothe Luce.

During the 1946 debate on the British loan McCormack had a slight brush with Representative Gordon L. McDonough of California:

Mr. McDonough: Mr. Chairman, will the gentleman yield?

Mr. McCormack: I yield.

Mr. McDonough: What I have in mind is this: There is more of a desirability to have an association between the British and the Americans, politically and financially, than with any other nation on the face of the earth: is that the gentleman's contention?

Mr. McCormack: What does the gentleman think?

Mr. McDonough: I am asking the gentleman.

Mr. McCormack: What does the gentleman think?

Mr. McDonough: The gentleman from Massachusetts is speaking.

Mr. McCormack: What does the gentleman think?

Mr. McDonough: I am asking you.

Mr. McCormack: What does the gentleman think?

Mr. McDonough: I think there is.

Mr. McCormack: Then all right. I will not challenge the gentleman's answer to his own question.

Mr. McDonough: The gentleman ought to be fair and give us his opinion.

Mr. McCormack: I said I did not challenge the gentleman's own answer to his question.

Mr. McDonough: Then there is a political significance?

Mr. McCormack: There is no political significance about this as intended. The gentleman, I am sure, is capable of drawing a distinction between intent and results.

Mr. McDonough: Is this a gift?

Mr. McCormack: Why, the gentleman now shifts. Of course, it is not.

Mr. McDonough: Is it a loan?

Mr. McCormack: Why, the gentleman knows it is.

Mr. McDonough: In the hearings Mr. Will Clayton, of the State
Department, referred to it not as a gift, not as a loan.

Mr. McCormack: Is my friend going to vote for the agreement or
not?

Mr. McDonough: I will decide that when the roll is called.

Mr. McCormack: Then I have hopes that I may convert my friend
because if ever in the last several hundred years we needed a spirit
of constructive conversion it is today, not only in America, but elsewhere, based upon those truths in which we believe.

The Chairman: The time of the gentleman from Massachusetts has
expired.

What New England Was and Is

First, the New England states—a kind of long-time working laboratory in the procedures and techniques of practical government—helped to
father most American political institutions. Second, its contributions to
literature and science have been literally without parallel. Third, it gave
financial brains and managerial capacity to the nation. The Burlington
and Union Pacific railroads were largely financed by Boston; for years
both AT & T and General Electric had their head offices in Boston; so,
still, have such corporations as United Fruit, now run by that fabulous
outlander, Sam Zemurray. The First National Bank of Boston still helps
to finance Hollywood, and New England money still dominates traction
in Houston, textile mills in Memphis, and shoe factories in St. Louis.

But there are two more serious contributions that, perhaps above these
others, New England may be said to make today. Both, it is interesting
to note, embody concepts which particularly distinguish the New
England character; both have a strong symbolic significance. One is
insurance. Hartford, Connecticut, is still the insurance capital of the
world. The other is education. I have mentioned Harvard and Yale.
But think also of Radcliffe, Mount Holyoke, Smith, and Wellesley, of
Amherst, Williams, and MIT (Mass.), of Dartmouth (New Hampshire), Bowdoin (Maine), and Brown (Rhode Island). Think also of
the great boys' schools—Deerfield, Andover, and Groton in Massachusetts, Putney in Vermont, Phillips Exeter in New Hampshire, and
a round dozen in Connecticut. Boys from all over the country get their
basic character patterns out of the New England way of life.

So to conclude this general summary. If anyone should ask "Where
is New England?" the answer might well be "in the bodies and minds
of men everywhere in the nation."

Chapter 29
Saltonstall

~~~~~~

L EVERETT SALTONSTALL, three times governor of Massachusetts, senator from Massachusetts since January, 1945, and a
mild Republican white hope for 1948, is a tall, swift, skinny man of
fifty-four with hard red cheeks, absolute honesty, and the gift of being
popular. He is practically the nicest person anybody ever met. I never
heard of anybody who disliked him—after years of hurly-burly in one
of the toughest political states in the union. You talk about Saltonstall
in Washington or Boston and sometimes wonder where the nigger in the
woodpile is. It seems almost too much to believe that any politician can
have so many good traits, and so few bad ones. He has, it seems, everything: wealth, industriousness, Yankee shrewdness, and, above all,
character. Then you discover that in 1944 he won the greatest vote in
Massachusetts history up to that time; the cliché has it that when Saltonstall is running, you don't count the votes, you simply weigh them. And
finally you discover that he, a blue-blood of blue-bloods, achieves these
astonishing results in part through the support of those who it might be
supposed would most vigorously oppose him—the Boston of Irish
descent.

I heard some pleasant stories about John H. Corcoran, the Democratic
mayor of Cambridge who was rash enough to oppose Saltonstall for
senator. They met shortly before the campaign began; Mr. Corcoran
spoke up anxiously: "You don't mind if I run against you, do you, Lev?"
In another campaign—this must certainly be apocryphal—his opponent
told a friend, "I don't know whom *you're* going to vote for, but *I'm*
for Saltonstall!"

How shall one explain stories of this kind? Saltonstall is the most
complete possible contrast to the popular conception of the successful
American politician. How did he get that way? Let us explore.

The Gift of Modesty

For one thing, Saltonstall has the great and precious gift of modesty;
for another, he gets on well with almost all kinds of people. When still
governor he took me out to Needham where he made a noonday speech.
Afterward I overheard two bits of dialogue. One man said, "Governor,
thanks for your check." Saltonstall looked puzzled. "I'm your elec-

trician," came the response. At the same moment another guest called out, "Any chance of playing tennis sometime this week, Lev?"

A few days later I ran into him in the lobby of the Somerset Club. Nobody who has ever seen him could possibly forget him; his face is extraordinarily distinctive. But before I could say a word he strode up, and introduced himself! "Maybe you've forgotten me," he said with complete genuineness, "I'm Leverett Saltonstall."

His wife is as modest as he is. I met someone who has known them well for years, who said, "I have seen Lev and Alice come into a room together about a hundred times, and I never saw either look anything but shy." In one election campaign Saltonstall's opponent kept graciously making Mrs. Saltonstall gifts of nylon stockings.

Family Tree of Family Trees

One hears much of Cabots, Lowells, Adamses, but actually from the point of view of seniority the two greatest families in New England are not these; only the Winthrops and Saltonstalls are, as the phrase is, "arms-bearing"; they brought their coats of arms from England. "My God, they *are* a family!" one friend told me, explaining that they were so impeccably sure of their perpetuity that they named their children for their grandparents, not the parents.

The Saltonstalls trace descent back to 1343. Sir Richard Saltonstall founded the Boston suburb of Watertown in 1630, and on his death left his fortune to Harvard College; for ten successive generations the Saltonstalls, father and son, have gone to Harvard. During the Revolutionary days the family—very intelligent and prescient—supported the American side. Leverett's great-grandfather was once president of the Massachusetts senate and mayor of Salem; his grandfather was collector of the Port of Boston by appointment of Grover Cleveland. Both grandfather and father were Democrats, odd as this may seem.

The Saltonstall wealth came from his mother's side of the family; she was a Brooks, and so Leverett's tidy background is interlaced not only with Saltonstalls but Brookses and Adamses. The considerable family fortune was founded not in Massachusetts, but in the Middle West: the Saltonstalls were early and highly successful speculators in Chicago real estate and western railroads. Leverett and his mother are supposed to be worth anywhere between five and ten million dollars today.

Seldom have I seen in America a more compactly packed parcel of family ground than the Saltonstall colony in Chestnut Hill, Newton, just outside Boston. Gray stone gates lead into a small park; an artificial ditch lies across the road, so that automobiles must slow down to protect children playing. Saltonstall's grandfather laid out in this neighborhood five simple plots for his five children; on one is Leverett's house today—a gray frame structure with three red chimneys, cream window frames, and a comfortable railed porch—and his mother, Mrs. Richard Saltonstall, resides next door. More Saltonstall properties and houses lie close by: a cousin, George West has one, and three more relatives, Mrs. Henry Fessenden ("Cousin Kitty"), Mrs. Reginald Grey ("Cousin Rosie"), and Mrs. George S. Mumford ("Cousin Bella") occupy the others.[1]

For all this extreme tincture of family exclusiveness Leverett had a very normal upbringing. A Boston newspaper asked some eminent New Englanders if they had ever been punished when they were children. These were the governor's answers:

"Ever spanked or whipped?"	Yes.
"With what?"	Father's slipper.
"By whom?"	Father.
"What age?"	Old enough to remember and while Father was still young enough to do the job.
"Where?"	Father's bedroom.
"What for?"	Stubborn disobedience.

In 1903, Saltonstall met a young girl named Alice Wesselhoeft at a dancing school, and he fell in love with her on the spot. He was then eleven years old. He has been in love with her ever since. They were married in 1916, and had six children; one, Peter, was killed in Guam in the summer of 1944. Several others, like Leverett Jr. and Emily who was a radio operator in the Waves, had active service records; the youngest were still in school during the war.

I talked to Saltonstall several times and each time I tried to explore the pattern of his convictions. The central core is always, it seems, associated with his family: the family that produced him and the family he produced. And he has reached a simple philosophy more or less to the effect that a good family spirit is what produces good communities which in turn is what should produce good government. Naïve? Perhaps. When I asked him "What do you believe in most?" he scratched his head and looked puzzled. "Well, it might sound more impressive if I

[1] In the immediate vicinity are both a large reservoir and also the former German Consulate, where Dr. Herbert Scholz, one of the most active Nazis in the United States before the war, had his headquarters. Saltonstall told me that this proximity disturbed him greatly and helped to awaken him to the German menace in pre-Pearl Harbor days; he feared the Nazis might blow up Boston's water supply.

said something like 'democracy' or 'the country,' but let's not be pretentious—what I believe in most is Harvard and my family."

A Steep Rise in Career

Saltonstall was conventionally graduated from Harvard in 1914, and was secretary of his class. His scholastic record was not distinguished, nor did. he do anything notable in athletics, though he played hockey and captained the first and only crew ever to win the Henley cup. He read for the bar, and worked for a few years as an attorney and—of course, Boston being Boston—as a "trustee."

But politics bit and scorched him early. It is in the blood. He happened once to find an old newspaper—of date 1875—in the family archives; it described how his grandfather, on being sworn in as collector of the port, made a stirring appeal for integrity in public office. This made a considerable impression on Leverett; from that time on, so he says, he wanted to follow his forebear's footsteps. I asked him how his political life began, but I do not vouch for all the details that follow—he is both so swift in speech and so shy that it is somewhat difficult to nail him down. It seems that one of his uncles, Endicott Peabody Saltonstall (the whole story is pivoted on family relationships), once set out to run for district attorney. When James Michael Curley, the celebrated Irish boss of Boston, heard that Endicott Peabody Saltonstall might get this job, he snorted, "What! All three of him?" But Uncle Endicott got in. Then Leverett became an alderman. Endicott gave him a post in the district attorney's office, and in 1923 he ran for the Massachusetts legislature and won.

In 1936, having risen to be speaker, Saltonstall entered for the lieutenant governorship; he was defeated in a close race by an Irishman who, ever since, has lived on the reputation of being the one man who ever beat him. For Saltonstall has never lost another election. His rise has been astonishingly swift and steep. He ran for governor in 1938 against Curley, and won by a tremendous vote—in part because so many Bostonians had become sick of that grotesque old man. Running for re-election in 1940, Saltonstall got in again, but only by a narrow margin; his opponent, Attorney General Paul A. Dever, was an excellent man—which goes to show that when Massachusetts has to vote between two good candidates, the result will be close. In 1942, running for governor a third time, Saltonstall beat Roger Lowell Putnam, the mayor of Springfield. Then came the senatorial race in 1944.

This election filled the seat originally held by Henry Cabot Lodge Jr. who, a capable and highly complex and ambitious young man, resigned in February to enter the Army. Saltonstall might easily have quit as governor, whereupon the lieutenant governor could have appointed him to the Lodge vacancy—which would have meant a senate seat without a fight. But, says Saltonstall, "I didn't quite like to do it." So he decided to stay on as governor until his term was finished, and take his chances running as a regular candidate. To fill the vacancy he appointed his friend Sinclair Weeks, with the understanding that Weeks would not subsequently run against him. His victory in the race that followed was prodigious. He carried Massachusetts by a 2-to-1 majority—something all but unprecedented. And it was the more impressive in that Roosevelt carried the state by 113,946 votes against Dewey, and Mayor Maurice J. Tobin of Boston (a Democrat of course) won the governorship overwhelmingly; taking the Roosevelt-Tobin figures as a criterion, Saltonstall ran ahead of his ticket by three hundred thousand votes. No such personal triumph had been known in Massachusetts history, and Saltonstall became the greatest personal vote getter the Bay State has ever known.

Saltonstall seconded Dewey at the Chicago convention (1944), but he was something of a Willkieite at heart. During the campaign he inadvertently caused Willkie great pain, however. In an interview in New York he predicted that Dewey would carry Massachusetts by getting so-and-so many votes more than Willkie got in 1940. Saltonstall did this because if he had said anything else everybody would have known at once that Dewey was as good as beaten. But Willkie was hurt at what he thought was a slight from a friend, and because he thought Lev was showing himself a shockingly poor prophet. (Willkie was right, of course.)

We come now to a question that demands answer. *Why* did Saltonstall run so far ahead of the ticket? What accounts for his hold on Massachusetts voters? It appears that there are several reasons:

(1) His obvious merit. He gave the state six years of excellent administration. People liked him because he was wholesome and upright. His popularity overran party lines.

(2) He was careful not to say anything much against Roosevelt. He always worked closely with Washington on national defense.

(3) A moderate liberal, he caught most of the middle-roaders. Some of his speeches sound as if they had been written for, not against, the New Deal.

(4) His labor record was good, and although the Political Action Committee, which was very strong in the state at the time, did not overtly support him, it did little to oppose him. (The CIO, incidentally, did support him in 1942.)

(5) Above all, the Irish-descended community did not fight him with much punch. Motives for this date back a long way. Many honest Irish were mortified by the records of previous Democratic governors; they wanted a decent upstanding man. And some Irish, looking up to

the Yankees, voted for Saltonstall out of a curious inverted snobbery—they enjoyed being on the Brahmin side for a change; they were eager to line up with Beacon Hill.

(6) A last complex point. *Some* of the Irish voted for him, even if this meant a diminished vote for the Democratic ticket, because they hated FDR.

Incidentally Saltonstall is a member in good standing of the most venerable and celebrated of Irish institutions in Boston, the Charitable Irish Society. He dug up an Irish ancestor some years ago and thereupon became eligible for membership. The small joke is that it was quite a strain to find his Irish strain.

Things Mostly Personal

I have mentioned Saltonstall's house in Chestnut Hill, but when in the Boston area he much prefers to spend what time he can on his ninety-acre farm near Dover. When he was governor he always spent week ends there, even if it meant leaving the state house at three o'clock Saturday morning, when his work was finally done. On the farm, he ʼked to relax by pitching hay and cutting wood; more lately he has dropped exercise so strenuous. For years he and Mrs. Saltonstall rode to hounds. But they gave it up in 1939 when, Lev told me, "I fell and broke my neck and the Missus fell and broke her leg."

His weekday routine (as governor) was more or less as follows. He took a Boston & Albany suburban train from the Chestnut Hill station, and got off at Huntington Avenue, one stop before the terminus. From here it is a mile to the state house; he usually walked it, since this provided the only fresh air he was apt to get. He arrived at his desk at 9:20. Then he worked till six, eight, ten, as the day demanded.

He drinks moderately, smokes very little, and eats anything. He has a drawl and pronounces the word law "lawr." He is fond of the theater but never gets time to go. He told me, "But the Missus gets to the symphony every once in a while."

What he likes best are familiar things. When he was governor, if he happened to be in New York or Springfield, he would always try to catch the last night train, so that he could sleep at home in Boston.

He has little time to read anything except official papers. But he goes through *Time* cover-to-cover, and glances at *Life*. It takes him a very long time to read a book. Sometimes he picks up a heavy volume, usually on a political subject; it will last him months. "My wife jollies me about it," he likes to say.

He seeks to persuade good people to help him write his speeches; then sometimes this embarrasses him. Boston's new archbishop, Dr. Cushing, drafted his last Thanksgiving Day proclamation; but when this was widely praised he felt that Cushing should have had the credit.

Saltonstall is not much of a churchgoer. Technically he is a Unitarian. But his faith, in the Puritan tradition, springs out of himself rather than from any obedience to a dogmatic creed.

His sense of humor is fairly acute. Once he got letters from President Roosevelt and Mrs. Roosevelt on successive days, expressing totally different views on the same matter. Saltonstall exploded, "Can't those two *ever* get together?"[2]

I asked him what he wanted most out of life that he didn't have. He replied with a disarming simplicity, "To be of service, and to leave a good name."

His friends are legion, partly because his own friendliness is effortless. He told me that he probably knew about ten thousand people in Massachusetts by name and face, but that now, as he gets older, his memory sometimes fails him. He has a nice homely touch, comparatively rare in blue-bloods; he is neither stuffy nor a backslapper. Probably his closest political friend and adviser is Henry J. Minot; I asked what Minot "did" and got the reply, "Oh, he's just a gentleman." Minot's brother is a Nobel prize winner in medicine. He held no official job when Saltonstall was governor; he carried no title or salary, but simply kept a desk in the state house.

Another person very close to him—and this is a good example of Saltonstall's wide gamut—is Allan Larrivee, his aide and chauffeur. You can tell a good deal about a man from the amount of proprietary interest taken in him by people of his entourage; and Larrivee worships him. No detail in Saltonstall's life, from high politics to what he has for breakfast, escapes Larrivee's attention, and he wants any visitor to like and above all understand his boss just as he does. Larrivee is "new" in Saltonstall's service; that is, he has been with him a mere six years. The other chauffeur has been with the family thirty-four years. Saltonstall, Larrivee told me, "is the most considerate man who ever lived." He will take the most extraordinary pains to see to the chauffeur's comfort, and so on. Larrivee, of French descent, is Catholic. Ted Stavredes, a sergeant in the state police who was his bodyguard, is Greek in origin.

Saltonstall has a good puritanical sense of the value of industry; also of time. He has one habit that sometimes annoys the entourage. "He drives us crazy catching trains." If a train is to leave at 2:37, he will not dream of getting to the station until 2:36½.

He works "like a jumping jack," his friends told me; he is doing something day and night, and one of the few criticisms I heard is that

---

[2] As to his sense of humor he wrote in the *American Mercury* (August, 1946), that like all senators who work in the Senate Office Building, he sometimes gets mail addressed "Senator Saltonstall, S.O.B., Washington, D.C."

he tries to do too much himself. He is so conscientious that he finds it difficult to delegate authority; he likes to fuss around. He can't keep his fingers out of things—another New England trait.

He has considerable capacity to turn unfriendly comment to his advantage. On one occasion his inveterate opponent Curley called him a "blue-blood with a South Boston face." (In college, Saltonstall's nickname was "Horseface.") He replied to the effect that he certainly wasn't afraid to show South Boston just what his face was like.

Saltonstall has come a long way quickly and he still has much to learn, his friends say. At the beginning, because of his shyness, he didn't like rough give-and-take; he was the world's worst public greeter. The legend is that two friends hired a suite in the Parker House, installed a soap box in a locked room, ripped off Lev's coat and shirt, hoisted him up on the box, and kept him there shouting and gesticulating till he got used to it. Another story is that one adviser sought to curb him from ever saying anything extemporaneous; Saltonstall had made some wisecrack that didn't quite catch fire. The adviser cautioned him, "Lev, any time you ever think of another quickie, call me up, and next day I'll let you know whether or not to use it."

There is a cliché about Saltonstall: that he has everything—except brains and top-flight intellect. I have read everything I could find about him, and almost all critics assert that he is neither brilliant nor profound. But good senators are seldom "brilliant" or "profound." His chief defect, if you can put it that way, is what I would describe as a lack of essential bulk. He does not lack stamina; but his shoulders are not very broad. He could never be like Theodore Roosevelt, say—a prodigiously full man capable of taking violent risks, of making tremendous mistakes, of creating explosive cataclysms. Saltonstall is not a genius. (Few men are.) He is not an Olympian; he will never mimic Prometheus. The blasting fires of creation do not rage in his lean belly.

Nevertheless, in recapitulation, we may summarize the chief sources of his considerable power. First, integrity. He never pretends to be what he isn't. Second, modesty and friendliness. Third, a canny man, he never promises anything. He told me that in three campaigns for governor, he had made only one specific promise, to repair a stretch of local road near Holyoke. Fourth, he draws support from both sides, because of his essential moderation. Fifth, though wealthy, he is very frugal, and he gave Massachusetts the strictest financial administration since Coolidge. He has never in his life wasted a cent—something which appeals to Yankees. Sixth, he has a kind of naïveté more precious than the most refined sophistication. I heard him say once that he had sent two chickens from his farm to Washington by air express, so that a relative might have them for Thanksgiving. The express bill was $3.88. He added quite seriously, "The chickens weren't worth $3.88 themselves, but I sent them anyway."

Saltonstall would be pleased to be president in 1948. Probably he has very little chance. Anyway the prospect frightens him almost as much as it attracts.

A Word or Two on the Record

Saltonstall's record as governor for three terms was commendable, and he is particularly proud of his state's contribution to the war. I asked him what had been his biggest crisis; he replied that the first six or seven weeks of his first term were the hardest, when he had to clean house and establish the level of government on a new, sanitary basis. This aside, his worst crisis came over birth control. Massachusetts and Connecticut are the only two states in the nation where the practice of contraception is still technically illegal; after years of effort a birth control act finally passed the legislature. The governor believed personally in the bill, but after a stiff struggle w th himself he vetoed it. His reason: its enactment would have hopele   divided the state just when political unity was most necessary at the   ginning of the war.

He is very proud of some of the men   e got to work for him like Thomas F. Sullivan, a distinguished engineer and former chairman of the Boston Transit Commission, whom he made Boston's chief of police. Oddly enough, it is the governor who fills this municipal post in Massachusetts; Saltonstall, by appointing an Irishman of irreproachable character, pleased almost everybody, rural Republicans and urban Democrats alike.[3] Another interesting appointment was that of Matthew W. Bullock as chairman of the State Parole Board. Bullock, a graduate of Dartmouth and the Harvard Law School, and a man with an outstanding civic record, is a Negro.

On January 9, 1945, Leverett Saltonstall was sworn in as junior senator from Massachusetts. When he and his wife arrived in Washington they were met at the train by their daughter Emily, who had temporary leave from her post in the Waves. Saltonstall's first remark to reporters was characteristic: "I'm not here to make news; I'm down here to try to learn. All I know is that I'm on the honeymoon. No commitments; no promises of any kind."

He took a strong liberal line on foreign policy at once; one of his first acts was to join a round robin of freshman senators pledging support to the administration on international affairs. I asked him in Boston how

[3] Boston is the only great city in the country where the governor of the state, not the mayor, appoints the chief of police. The rural Republicans, who thought that their governors might not be safe in dangerous Boston in the old days, put this measure through in the first place, and rural jealousy of urban political power has kept it on the books ever since.

he happened to become an interventionist long before Pearl Harbor, in 1939. His answer was disarmingly simple. He kept hearing airplanes fly over his house. And he knew they were en route to Europe. Well then, Europe couldn't be so far away! He represents a seaboard, a mercantile community. Therefore he couldn't afford to blind himself to what went on abroad.

Early in his Senate career Saltonstall showed (*a*) that he was willing to be heterodox with the courage of his convictions, and (*b*) that he was a liberal on some domestic issues too, by being one of the few Republicans to vote for confirmation of Henry Wallace as secretary of commerce after the fight with Jesse Jones. Finally, it is extremely typical of him that he waited for more than a year, until April 25, 1946, before making a major speech in the Senate. He was feeling his way cautiously, exploring the unfamiliar ground. When he did speak at last it was in support of the British loan.

Chapter 30
Inside New England II

〰〰〰

> To my mind Maine is the most beautiful state we have in this country, but even more appealing is its homeliness.
>
> —Booth Tarkington

MAINE, a sturdy state, has special characteristics all its own. For one thing it is much bigger than most people think; it is, in fact, almost as large as the other New England states combined (33,215 square miles for Maine, 33,393 for the other five); it is bigger than South Carolina, and almost as big as New York or Ohio. A single one of its counties, Aroostook, celebrated for its potatoes—its potato yield makes it the third wealthiest agricultural county in the whole country—is bigger than Connecticut and Rhode Island put together.

Maine's chief distinction is, however, not size but character. One element in this is intrepidity. The state is largely marked by fingers of land poking out into the sea; in the most literal sense its lobstermen and other fishermen make their living by combat with the elements. Another factor is the complete simplicity and financial integrity of almost all old Maine citizens; money doesn't count for everything in their scale of values; people will spend their last cent on a coat of pale yellow paint for their houses; drop a pocketbook in the streets of Augusta, and a dozen passers-by will return it. Another element is humor. This is not as wry and bitter as is humor in Vermont, say; it has a glow; it has been softened by the Atlantic fogs. Still, it can be sharp. For instance Bert Sinnett, an old retired lobsterman and a member of one of the ancient families of Maine, was once called as a witness in a lawsuit.

Q. Your name is Bert Sinnett?
A. Yes.
Q. You live in Bayley Island?
A. Yes.
Q. Lived there all your life?
A. Not yet.

Finally, Maine has great pride. Almost all its people are proud, from the marmoreally entrenched aristocracy of Bar Harbor to the lonely professor living in a shack on a deserted beach. Brunswick spells its main street "Maine" Street, and every school child is obliged to study for a specified time the state's history and accomplishments. (Also, something unique in America, an old statute has it that every teacher must give ten minutes a week to instruction in kindness to birds and animals.) As to Maine's history, it contains some little-known points and curiosities. A pamphlet called *Facts About Maine* asks us if we know:

That Sebastian Cabot visited Maine in 1497.
That in 1607, thirteen years prior to the landing of the Pilgrims, the Popham colonists settled at the mouth of the Kennebec.
That the first chartered city in America was York, Maine, in 1642.
That a gaol built in 1653 is the oldest public building in New England.
That the first pile bridge built in America was built at York in 1761 and is still standing.

Maine is the habitat of novelists like the late Booth Tarkington and Kenneth Roberts; it has fabulously cold winters and is also, by some strange paradox, the home of Palm Beach cloth; along its swift rivers the windows of its mills are painted blue, to keep sunlight out; 21,611 deer were killed in Maine last year, and there are estimated to be 150,000 deer still roaming at large, more than when the white man came; it produces more sardines than any other state, and more blueberries; Maine was part of Massachusetts till 1820, and the pull of Boston is still very strong; it was the first state to appropriate sums for tourist and vacation advertising, and the only eastern state with an official trade-mark, to distinguish "State of Maine" apples and potatoes; it is the state from whose ports, like Bangor, old-time sea captains went to the West Indies with cargoes of top hats and, believe it or not, ice; it has 17 million acres of forest, 2,500 lakes, 5,147 rivers, few leading families, and fewer millionaires.

To get from Portland, Maine, to the northern edge of Aroostook County, on the border of Canada, takes a full day by train. The farmers there are like few elsewhere in the union—individualists, fatalists, and gamblers, all at once. Too much rain or lack of it may seriously injure the potato crop, and Governor Horace A. Hildreth told me that it gave him quite a thrill, when he was campaigning in 1944, to hear a farmer say, "Well, if we don't have rain this week, we lose thirty million dollars." Of course, ideally, Maine agriculture should be more diversified. The state has what is known as a potato tax, installed in 1937 to promote potato sales and propaganda; the potato grower pays it himself, one cent per barrel. In 1943 the tax brought in $170,000, and it is a sidelight on New England character that the total cost of administering it was $102.

Politically, a unique item about Maine is that it holds its gubernatorial election in September, two months before any other state; thus arose the apothegm, "As Maine goes, so goes the nation." Of course Maine votes in November too for national offices. One reason for this anomaly is that the Republicans are pretty sure as a rule to carry state posts (though there was a Democratic governor as recently as 1933), and the Republican organization likes to flaunt a Maine victory to the country, before the national polls.

It would probably be a mistake, however, to assume that Maine will always remain impregnably Republican. Dewey only carried it by a narrow margin; Willkie likewise. The trend—in Maine as elsewhere in New England—is all toward urbanization, industrialization, which, as we know, usually means more Democrats. Maine has changed fast; consider for instance the great influx of war workers into Portland. The state used to be predominantly agricultural; now, what with boots, textiles, shipbuilding, it is not less than 60 per cent industrial. Potatoes are important—yes—but Maine's most valuable industry by far is paper; the great paper mills in their massive half-hidden forest empires are the pivots of the state economy.

There are, it would seem, four chief elements in the political life of Maine:

(1) The propertied class, which, in general, has the power to give jobs and which almost always votes Republican.

(2) The French Canadians, called in Maine "Francos." They are, as always, practically unassimilable, and they constitute a considerable political force. The French Canadian vote is split—some upstate Francos vote Republican, but in Portland and the big mill towns they are violently Democratic; they completely dominate Biddeford and Lewiston, and have roughly half the vote in Waterville. Biddeford is run by a French Canadian boss, Mayor Lausier, practically in the way Frank Hague runs Jersey City.

(3) The rural districts, which dominate the legislature and prevent any fair distribution of voting power because of their suspicion of "big-city ways." Portland, with 73,643 people and 8 per cent of the population of Maine, has only 7 votes in an assembly of 133. This is not only a typical New England phenomenon, but one characteristic of the country at large as we know.

(4) The Central Maine Power Company, a surviving fragment of the old Insull empire, which supplies power to most of the state, controls various enterprises, and maintains "legislative agents" who are a big influence in the legislature. Probably this company is the strongest single political factor in the state.

One Man of Maine

One of the most attractive and original men in American public life is Sumner Sewall, governor of Maine for two terms from 1941 to 1945.

In 1942, campaigning for re-election, he won the greatest majority in the history of the state. He did not enter the 1944 race, largely because he needed to recoup his modest private fortune—once again we may note how this country loses the services of good men by not paying them enough—and, in part, because he thought "the job was done."

Sewall, who is nearing fifty, is an explosively energetic man. He comes from an old and distinguished shipping family; his grandfather, a Democrat, once ran for vice president under Bryan. His remarkably interesting wife is Russian; though the wife of a Republican governor, she proudly kept on display in Blaine House—the gubernatorial mansion in Augusta—an autographed portrait of Eleanor Roosevelt, which considerably titillated the local society. Sewall volunteered as an ambulance driver in France in World War I; then he joined the first American air squadron, and became an early ace. After the war he dug for oil in Mexico, grew sugar in Cuba, and worked in South America and Spain. Returning to the United States he reverted to his first love, aviation; he helped organize Colonial Airlines, and has been mixed up in commercial aviation ever since. He went into Maine politics "for the hell of it," serving first in the local legislature, then the senate. He became president of the senate in 1938, and then governor.

Sewall first came into national prominence during the 1944 presidential campaign when he made a strong prolabor speech in Detroit. Previously he had been very active, like most of the young Republican governors, for a positive foreign affairs plank at the Chicago convention. His theory about the CIO—which dumbfounded his conservative supporters in Maine—was, and is, that nothing in the world was more sensible than that American labor, seeking more jobs and better wages, should directly attempt to express itself in politics. Sewall's range of ideas and interests is wide, vivid, and provocative. He told me that during the war German prisoners in Aroostook got better "wages" in the potato fields than native farmhands, which he thought was a pretty crazy demonstration of how things can go wrong in American economy; that no one is ever going "to slip things over" on this country again as in the 20's and 30's; that there is just as keen a need for government-trained men to go into business as for business-trained men to go into government; that as a kind of dynamic substitute for war, Americans with hope and ideals still cryingly need opportunity for "adventure"; that the people by and large are a hundred miles ahead of the politicians; and that most citizens have "more than a dollar sign in their blood" and that if they really want good public services, they will be willing to pay for them.

Sewall's administration was, despite his rambunctious irreverence, a model of solid government. He put the state on a clean financial basis (having inherited a mess of scandal), and most of his appointments were commendable. His chief trouble was finding good men. Maine pays no salary higher than six thousand dollars, and it isn't easy to persuade successful young lawyers or engineers to give up their practices for that. One thing he is proud of is a minimum wage law for teachers; and it is something of a commentary on New England that he succeeded, after a gigantic fight, in raising this to—$720 per year! To get the money he proposed an increase in the inheritance tax (though his own family is wealthy), a cigarette tax, and a tax on electric energy. Perhaps Sewall included this latter item with tongue in cheek; he loved brawling with the power company. The company beat down his proposal, but at one point during the fight Sewall, obviously a wicked man, threatened to install his own electric generator in the State House, rather than use electricity from Central Maine.

On retiring from the governorship Sewall became president of American Overseas Airlines; then at considerable sacrifice he went to Germany as first civilian director of military government. That some day he will return to elective office on the domestic scene is almost certain. It is all but impossible to keep a man like this away from public service, and there is a flashing glint of tomorrow in his eye.

A Word About New Hampshire

Who runs New Hampshire? Answer: the voters. Who runs the voters? Answer: all sorts of things. This prickly and hardheaded little state is famous for elections with the closest kind of finish. In 1916, it went for Woodrow Wilson by exactly 56 votes; in 1944, a lady named Mrs. Mary C. Dondero became mayor of Portsmouth, the state's only port, by a majority of exactly seven.

New Hampshire is ordinarily coupled with Vermont, but the illusion that it is invariably Republican is—an illusion. Manchester, the chief city, has been electing the same mayor for years—a French Canadian Catholic Democrat—and some New Hampshire towns are almost as solidly Democratic as towns in Alabama or Mississippi. In 1932 the state elected Hoover, but Roosevelt won by close margins in 1936, 1940, and 1944. In 1944 the whole local Republican slate came in, but Dewey himself was defeated by about 9,000 votes.

What distinguishes New Hampshire among all American states is its legislature, which is the largest deliberative body in the world. It numbers 443 men and women—in a state the total population of which is only 491,524![1] The reason for this is, of course, that every local community insists on its own representation. Because the legislature is so

---

[1] Jonathan Daniels has calculated that if Congress were chosen on the same basis there would be over one hundred thousand Congressmen in Washington. Cf. *A Southerner Discovers New England*, p. 69.

enormous it is hard to control; the pressure groups can operate in the senate—membership twenty-four—to some extent, but the lower house is too unwieldy. In the early days the rural areas were solidly Republican. But this is changing now. Most of the French Canadian farmers are Democratic, and they control about one-third of the total vote. The Irish are split almost evenly between Republicans and Democrats; there is a strong Polish enclave in Manchester, which votes predominantly Democratic; also in Manchester is a large Greek community, solidly Republican.

New Hampshire, which like most of New England has its cranks, has produced some strange attempts at crank legislation. For instance a bill was introduced in the 1923 session of the General Court (as in Massachusetts this is the name the legislature goes by) to regulate hours of sleep. Section 1 reads that "eight out of each 24 hours shall be the minimum of time for sleep"; Section 2 that "failure to observe this injunction shall be sufficient ground for the charge of negligence in case of sickness." (The bill did not pass.)

Labor plays no great role in New Hampshire; nor, on the other side of the fence, is there much conservative pressure from corporations or entrenched family groups. I asked what "the interests" were. First, the Boston & Maine Railway. For years this organization had a completely dominant influence on the legislature, but now this is diminishing. Second, a utilities lobby. But the New Hampshire Public Service Company has nothing like the power of Central Maine, say, in Maine. Third and most importantly, Rockingham Park, the race track. Taxes on racing contribute about 15 per cent of the state's total revenue.

When I visited New Hampshire—work on this book started a good long time ago—the governor was Dr. Robert O. Blood, who will probably return to politics some day. He has three careers—politician, surgeon, farmer. While governor he kept up his medical practice, sometimes taking time off from the state house to do an emergency operation; also he worked hard on his farm, three miles from Concord, where he breeds "the best darned cows in the United States." One of his prize Ayrshires gave more milk and butter than any other animal in the United States in 1943; another sold in 1944 for a record price. Dr. Blood is one of the few American governors who won both the Distinguished Service Cross and the Croix de Guerre in World War I; he was once national vice commander of the American Legion, and, like almost everyone of prominence in New Hampshire, he went to Dartmouth. He is the best type of extreme conservative, and he gave the state a good administration, though some people thought that his economies were too stringent.

New Hampshire—Massachusetts and New York aside—has probably

contributed more men to American public life than any other eastern state. Consider the late Chief Justice Harlan Stone, former under secretary of state Joseph C. Grew, and Ambassador John G. Winant. Probably the most conspicuous living New Hampshire resident is Dr. Ernest M. Hopkins, former president of Dartmouth. But the old Yankees say that men of this caliber are dying out, that progressive Republicans like the picturesque Winant are getting more and more rare; people told me that the incoming of foreign-born is changing the character of the state irremediably. Good Yankees describe urban labor as "all that slum stuff" and I heard more anti-Semitic talk in New Hampshire than anywhere else in New England; Dartmouth, in the summer of 1945, got into a noisy peck of trouble because it was applying the quota system to limit attendance by Jewish students.

New Hampshire was the first of the original thirteen states to declare independence from Great Britain, and the ninth and deciding one to ratify the federal Constitution. About 40 per cent of its people are engaged in industry, and though the fact is seldom realized, it is the third most highly industrialized state in the union in proportion to population. The biggest textile mill in the world, Amoskeag, functioned in Manchester until Christmas Eve, 1935, when the company collapsed —of hardening of the arteries—and the state has not yet fully recovered from this disaster.

New Hampshire is the state where the people vote every seven years to decide whether there shall be a new constitution, and where you may find some of the finest skiing country in the world as well as wonderful vacation opportunities in general—the novelist Robert Herrick once acidulously called the whole state a "summer boarding house." It contains the house in which both Ralph Waldo Emerson and Samuel F. B. Morse got married, and more old people in ratio to population than any other state except California and Florida; it produces fifty million dollars worth of shoes a year, and more magazines than any other state; it has two Shaker communities, and no saloons.

New Hampshire humor is a good deal like that of Maine and Vermont. A character witness at a trial refused once to answer a question. He was told that he would be in contempt of court if he refused to say exactly what he thought of the person involved. Reply: "He's this kind of feller. He raises a lot of hogs. But he don't fatten 'em up inside the way some do; he lets 'em run loose in the fields. Sometimes he wants to look 'em over in the barn. When he does, he has to have the hired man call 'em over, because them hogs don't put any reliance at all in anything he says."

The New Hampshire Yankee is, in fact, a special breed. I met one estimable official who kept talking about "Theodore"; I was puzzled until I realized that he was referring to Roosevelt I. Then he explained that he had hated Franklin too much ever to use the actual name "Roosevelt" aloud.

Note in Aesthetics

I have seen some lovely towns in New England; I have seen some appallingly ugly towns. Usually, it seems, when they are very ugly it is not because individual buildings are graceless or unsightly, but because the town as a whole was built with total disregard to uniformity or plan.

Concord, New Hampshire, has the ugliest state capitol I ever saw. Around the central square one may note the following types of architecture:

> An old-style granite post office
> Public library—a low building of whitish stone
> State library—in brown stone, Italian style, with an
>   amazingly hideous bell tower
> A Pennsylvania Dutch town hall built of red brick
>   with white windows
> A & P supermarket
> A dingy red Unitarian church, with tall steeple
> An atrocity of a barn
> A Christian Science church
> A highly modern, functional office building, sleek
>   and shining
> A red brick schoolhouse down at the heel

The whole effect is that of a junk shop filled with jarring varieties of junk.

Vermont and New Hampshire: How They Differ

Half a dozen times I sat down in New England with wise men, like Ralph E. Flanders, the new Vermont senator, and James M. Langley, editor of the Concord (New Hampshire) *Monitor.* I asked them to pretend that we were in Buenos Aires, say, and to explain to me the differences between the New England states, their essential qualities and particularizing characteristics, with exactly the same perspective with which one might discuss how Chile differed from Argentina, or Peru from Ecuador.

So far as the "twins," New Hampshire and Vermont, are concerned the main point of difference is that New Hampshire is much more heavily industrialized; Vermont is still an essentially rural state—the only state in the union that, in a way, the industrial revolution never hit. For another point we must go all the way back to the age of glaciers; the ice cap didn't scrape off the top soil of Vermont as it did that of Maine and New Hampshire, with the result that Vermont is richer. In New Hampshire the mountains are, by and large, heavily wooded; 87 per cent of the total area is forest. But in Vermont, with better soil, the pastures run right up the sides of the hills, and the hills themselves are softer, friendlier. From the windows of the capitol in Montpelier one may see cattle placidly grazing; Vermont is the only state in the country with more cattle than human beings.

Generalizations are risky, but the Vermont Yankee is, one may say safely, the most impregnably Yankee of all Yankees. In New Hampshire many farms look run down and dilapidated; but in Vermont (as in Maine) almost everything is neat, spick and span. In New Hampshire the Puritan strain has been severely diluted, but in Vermont overwhelming evidence of nonconformist origin is still to be seen on every hand. And Vermont has fewer French Canadians, fewer foreign-born, fewer big towns; there are only three cities with more than ten thousand population: Barre (10,907), Rutland (17,082), and Burlington (27,686).

Charm and Virtues of Vermont

Vermont has smooth and gentle dulcet hills—yes. But underneath is slate, marble, granite. This granite is solid in the state character. Hit a man with an ax; he will practically chip off like a block of stone.

Most Vermonters live close to the soil and therefore they understand cause and effect; they know what two extra weeks of snow will do to crops; they have an instinctive cognizance of weather, seasons, and the cruelties of flood and frost; so, by and large, they are folk who anticipate, who know how to plan and prepare. The state is one of the poorest in the country; less money changes hands during an average year than in any other. But the triumph of Vermont is a kind of richness in character—richness that is nevertheless stern. The typical Vermonter is rugged, reticent, suspicious of outsiders, frugal, intensely individualistic, and with great will to survive.

A contrary characteristic is neighborliness. If a farmer gets sick, his neighbors will milk his cows. "Vermont is the cosiest state," I heard it said. People (including servants) don't work for you; "they help you out."

Vermont, as almost everybody knows, was an independent nation for fourteen years from 1777 to 1791, coining its own money, running its own postal service, carrying on diplomatic relations with "foreign" governments. New York, New Hampshire, and its other neighbors coveted Vermont territory, but Ethan Allen, its greatest hero, kept it intact and free. It was the first American state to forbid slavery, and it sent more troops per capita to the Civil War than any other in the north. This attitude and spirit carry on to date. On September 11, 1941, for instance, two months before Pearl Harbor, the Vermont legislature officially declared "a state of belligerency with Germany" (!), in view of America's "armed assistance" to Great Britain.[2] Before selective service, Vermont contributed more volunteers to the Army than any other state, in ratio to population.

Vermonters are really something quite special and unique.[3] Ethan Allen once proclaimed, "I am as determined to preserve the independence of Vermont as Congress is that of the Union; and rather than fail I will retire with my hardy Green Mountain boys into the caverns of the mountains and make war on all mankind." This state bows to nothing: the first legislative measure it ever passed was "to adopt the laws of God . . . until there is time to frame better." Nor do its people bow to anybody; there is the story of the couple in Barnet who on their sixtieth wedding anniversary boasted that they had never in their married life bought one pound of meat, flour, or sugar. A list of eminent men born in Vermont is almost endless; this tiny state has produced 31 chief justices of *other* states, 33 senators, 144 congressmen, 60 governors, and 80 college presidents. Vermont was the first state to advocate civil service, one of the first to establish a normal school, and the first—we jump to modern times—to found a central plasma bank.

The instinct for continuity in Vermont life is considerable—to put it mildly. The first white child in Vermont, by name Timothy Dwight, was the son of Timothy Dwight, the first permanent white settler in the state. He was graduated from Yale in 1744, and he married the daughter of Jonathan Edwards, the theologian. Their eldest son—named Timothy Dwight also—became a president of Yale, and one of their daughters became the mother of Timothy Woolsey, who also became a Yale president; and so did one of their lineal descendants! But do not think that this state does not also produce types of people extremely divergent from the "typical" Vermonter. For instance both Joseph Smith and Brigham Young, the Mormon leaders, were Vermont born, strange as this may seem.

Vermont still has a fine spirited tradition of doing what it pleases. A sorority at the University of Vermont produced something of a national storm early in 1946 by admitting to membership a Negro student; it was penalized and put on probation by the national sorority organization, but refused to budge or compromise. Also Vermont can

[2] It is extraordinarily striking that Texas, also an extremely militant state, should have been the only other to have had an extended period of independence.
[3] For the material in this and the next paragraph I am indebted to ex-Governor M. R. Proctor.

be superbly, enormously provincial. A college professor on holiday, with a Norman Thomas banner on his automobile, went to the movies one evening in the little town of Hardwick, near Greensboro. Inadvertently he parked next to a fire plug. A policeman went into the movie and called out what he thought was his name, "Norman Thomas!"

I have mentioned frugality. Let me quote from a recent news story, describing how new curtains, drapes, and furniture are being installed at the state house in Montpelier. "The drapes . . . will replace those hung *85 years ago* [italics mine] when the State House was rebuilt following the fire of 1857. Cost of the new drapes . . . will be $760, slightly less than the $768.75 paid *to curtain the same windows in 1859.* Expense for the other windows will approximate that of the 1859 purchases. However, the 85-year-old drapery now being replaced is material . . . of a quality unobtainable at the present time."

Vermonters are frugal in speech—or at least so it is always said. Actually they can be as loquacious as Texans if the conversation is on a point that interests them. But they have little "small talk," nor are they particularly interested in people who have nothing to contribute; they pay absolutely no attention to rank, title, or position. President Coolidge once crossed a toll bridge near Springfield; this bridge, incidentally, is still operated under a charter granted by King George III, as are many land titles in the region. "Fifteen cents, please," the toll keeper asked the president. No one paid the slightest regard to the fact that he was (*a*) a Vermonter by birth, and (*b*) president of the United States.

Vermont is reticent, yes. But when it has a justifiable pride in something, it doesn't necessarily whisper. In Montpelier I saw a bakery, on the side wall of which was neatly painted:

ESTABLISHED 1828 MONTPELIER CRACKERS

CROSS BAKING CO.

BEST IN THE WORLD

Vermont possesses—so it is usually said—the purest racial stock in America; in this stock, however, are various strains. There are three different quarrying industries, and each brought in a different foreign colony. With slate came the Welsh; Barre, in the granite area, was settled by Scots from Aberdeen; marble brought in Swedes and some Italians. Of course the war intensified industrialization—even in Vermont. The town of Springfield had a prewar population of 5,182; it has three machine-tool plants, and during the war the population trebled. And this town with exactly three small factories exported seventy million dollars worth of machinery in one year, 1943! So in the public library of Springfield, in its drugstores and on its busses, Vermonters heard accents they never heard before.

But the basis of life in Vermont remains agriculture; this in turn is based on fluid milk. Most Vermont dairy farms are small, worked by their own owners, and often held in the same family for generations. The farmers are well organized; most belong to the Grange. During the war many worked in war industry throughout the long winters; in summer, people who earn wages in village factories still go home in the evening to their own land, their own cow. In a way, like Maine in regard to potatoes, Vermont is too dependent on one commodity; its milk brings in thirty million dollars a year, and most of it goes to the great city markets, New York and Boston; but sensible Vermonters want to diversify their economy. The soil is getting thin on the hillsides; year by year, more farms become worn out and have to be sold, if any buyers are to be found. And deforestation is a problem; it is becoming more and more necessary to think in terms of the forests as a crop, not as a mine. But even though the typical Vermont farmer may be poor he will go through almost any hardship to educate his children. His interest in electrification, co-operatives, public health, is mature and serious; here the procedures of government really do begin right in the shallow dales and sparkling meadows.

The dome of Vermont's state capitol is surmounted by a bulky statue of the goddess Ceres. The original, the work of a local sculptor, was blown off in a storm some years ago. It was replaced in 1938 by a copy hewn out of granite by the state sergeant-at-arms; it is somehow typical of Vermont that when he did this job he had reached the age of eighty-seven.

Green Mountain Politics and Men

In the 1946 primaries Governor Mortimer R. Proctor was roundly beaten for renomination, and for the first time in the modern history of Vermont a chief executive was refused a second term. Reason: a remarkable upsurge of modern-mindedness; the same positivist swing brought Flanders in as senator. Proctor was and is a civilized and able man. But the voters wanted something fresher. So they elected as governor a forty-five-year-old war veteran of solid performance and promise both, Colonel Ernest W. Gibson, who had once been senator for a brief time, who was severely wounded during long service in the South Pacific, and who, a political outsider, was practically unknown to the regular Republican organization.

Proctor himself belongs to the dominant family of Vermont, and was to the capitol born. His father, his grandfather, and an uncle were all three governors of Vermont, and one forebear was a senator and secretary of war. The Proctors, who have been in Vermont for six generations, founded Proctorsville; and thirty-three miles away, on the other side of "the mountain," they developed the marble collieries near the town of Proctor. The ex-governor himself went to Yale and then into the marble business; his wife was a newspaperwoman who worked in the press bureau of the legislature. Some people, I found, though everybody respected him, were somewhat shocked at the amount of money that he, a rich man, spent on the 1944 campaign—$14,000. This to get a job that pays only $5,000 a year! Vermont is frugal.

It is typical of America that Proctor's predecessor, the late William H. Wills, had a completely different background—yet one which is just as strikingly "American." Wills spent fifteen years as a drygoods clerk; then fifteen more as an insurance salesman. His family lived in Vermont for three generations, but he himself was born in Illinois; his grandfather, it seems, invented a horseshoe nail-pointing machine, and sold the patent to a Chicago company which—I quote from the family records —"employed him as master mechanic in their works." Young Wills came back to Vermont at the age of seven, after his father's death; his mother had four young children to support. She scrubbed floors and washed windows in the town of Vergennes; the family lived in a house (rent, three dollars a month) with a roof so leaky that the children had to sleep under an umbrella. Wills left school at fourteen, and worked for a living from that date until his death in 1945. "My education is the world," he told me. He was a liberal, and when he retired as governor, FDR gave him a job on the Federal Communications Commission. He thought the Republican party was doomed if it did not recognize its own liberating forces; he kept on saying, "the yeast is in the dough; let it work."

The basis of political power in Vermont is, of course, the overwhelmingly Republican and rural legislature. This legislature is not so monstrously swollen as that of New Hampshire; yet it has 246 members, one for each "town" in the state. Burlington (population 27,686) has precisely the same representation as Stratton (population 8). As a result the senate has turned out to be a more representative and democratic body than the lower house, because it is elected on a more rational basis. The determination of each community in the state to retain its place in the legislature is fixed, fierce, and permanent; there are eight Vermont "towns" with a population of less than one hundred each—but each has its own stubborn legislator in Montpelier.[4]

The Green Mountains run straight down through Vermont, splitting

---

[4] Two "towns" were, however, legally voted out of existence recently, because their populations had diminished to the point of consisting of a single family. The two had, and have, the fine old English names of Glastonbury and Somerset.

it. The focus of the west side is Burlington; the east is more diffuse. By convention, to keep everybody happy, Vermonters choose senators and governors alternately from different sides of "the mountain" as it is always called. Of course the real struggle is always in the primaries, since the Republican candidate is bound to win. Usually the Democrats, in a race for governor say, choose a distinguished citizen simply as a gesture of honor; their recent candidate, a doctor in Barre, only accepted the nomination on condition that he would not have to make a campaign. Yet one should not ask idly who Democrats in Vermont can possibly be. There are plenty. Franklin County (with a considerable population of French Catholics) has voted Democratic since the days of Al Smith, and Burlington went Democratic in 1944 largely because of the Bell Aircraft plant which brought in war workers by the thousand. Dewey carried Vermont by 71,000 votes to 53,000, but if industrialization proceeds further, if more foreign-born and more labor filter in, it is not beyond the realm of possibility that Vermont, the most impregnable stronghold of Republicanism in the United States, *might* eventually go Democratic.

Vermont is one of the few states in the country that has no comptroller. Various governors have wanted to install this post; the people wouldn't hear of it, insisting that the governor should be his own comptroller. In the entire history of Vermont, no official has ever filched a cent of graft.

Minuscule World of Rhode Island

Nothing could be in greater contrast to Vermont than Rhode Island, the smallest state in the union and—what is not so commonly known— the most highly industrialized. Rhode Island, it seems, has almost everything that Vermont has not: glacially aristocratic families, huge conglomerations of industry, government almost completely in the hands of the Irish, a Democratic administration, and a great substratum of foreign stock. There are fifty thousand first or second generation Italians in Providence alone, and of the population of the state as a whole, not less than 75 per cent is of foreign origin. In some respects Rhode Island seems to be an offshoot of Massachusetts; yet the pull toward New York is probably stronger today than that to Boston. Many people—at least those prosperous enough—go to New York rather than Boston to shop, though it is three times farther away; they read the New York *Times* more than the Boston *Globe*; and the Democratic hierarchy pays more attention to Mr. O'Dwyer than to Mr. Curley.

The official name of Rhode Island is "The State of Rhode Island and Providence Plantations," and it takes its somewhat cantankerous history very seriously. It refused to attend the Constitutional Convention of 1787; it held on to its colonial charter until 1842, refusing to create a state constitution instead; in the same year it had to suppress a lively insurrection, the Dorr Rebellion, by mild force of arms; it maintained a property tax as a qualification for voting till 1888. Rhode Island is the birthplace of the textile industry in the United States, and the biggest jewelry-manufacturing community in the world.[5] It contains Brown University and the Narragansett race track; it is the most densely populated of American states and, perhaps because it is so small, the state capitol in Providence, built by Stanford White, is not only one of the most handsome but the biggest capitol building in the nation, with the possible exception of that of Texas.

The uniqueness of Rhode Island lies in its size; Bryce wrote that it might become the first American "city-state." Everybody is packed close together; almost everybody knows everybody else. An administrator— the governor, say—is at the beck and call of anybody; he must go and see for himself in an emergency, because everything is within fifty miles of his office. Yet, though their state covers only 1,214 square miles, the Rhode Islanders—who are as particularistic as any people in New England—have had no fewer than four different capitals. For a time (like Connecticut) they insisted on having two at once, Providence and Newport, with the legislature holding alternate sessions in each. Newport (which was once a bigger city than Providence or New York!) was the center of colonial culture; Providence represented the expanding energy of a new and more restless age.

When I visited Rhode Island the governor was J. Howard McGrath, who subsequently became solicitor general of the United States; in 1946 he won the Senate seat being vacated by Peter Gerry. McGrath was born in Woonsocket, Rhode Island, in 1903; he began his public career as an attorney, and was governor three times; once he beat William H. Vanderbilt (now an able member of the Stassen brain trust) for the job. He is a Democratic machine politician of a conventional but superior type: urban, of Irish descent, Catholic; he is a serious man, with big gray eyes, balanced and concise. The dominant note in all three of his administrations was close attention to politics and progressive social legislation. After I talked with him he said that I must call at once on the Republican state committee, to "get their side of the picture"—a pleasant example of the fairmindedness of much in American public life.

Originally the struggle for power in Rhode Island was that of Yankee versus Yankee. The state was dominated by Brown & Sharpe, one of

[5] Some of these details are from *Rhode Island*, in the American Guide Series. Another uniqueness is that Rhode Island officially celebrates Independence Day on May 4 instead of the Fourth of July.

the greatest machine tool factories in the country, and by far the biggest enterprise in the state; by tremendously entrenched families like the Metcalfs and that of John Nicholas Brown (who when a boy was known as the wealthiest child in the world); by old-time millionaires of almost mythical conservatism like Nelson W. Aldrich who for thirty years "ran" the United States Senate; and by the Hope Club which like the Somerset Club in Boston is the irreproachably sacrosanct and impenetrable inner citadel of the aristocracy. (Once ex-Governor McGrath made a somewhat pointed allusion to this Hope Club saying that there were clubs in Rhode Island to which he, the governor, was not admitted. Someone told me, "The Hope die-hards will keep McGrath dangling. But if they *have* to take him in, they will.")

After the Yankees came the Irish. And for a time Yankees and Irish struggled. The only direction in which the Irish could express themselves was politics—the story is roughly the same as that of Boston—since "society" life and big business were barred. Then came Portuguese, Italians, French Canadians—all, like the Irish, predominantly Catholic. Rhode Island is about 50 per cent Catholic today. At first the powerful Irish resented the newer and more Mediterranean breeds; they still tend to call the Italians "black fellows." Inevitably, however, the Italians and south Europeans will in turn reach their share of power; indeed, the governor who succeeded McGrath is named John Pastore. One can almost predict how long the time lag will be. For instance the first "Irish" mayor of New York City (which is like a Providence enormously intensified and magnified) was Gaynor. This was in 1910. Twenty-four years later came LaGuardia. Now in Rhode Island the pace seems to be accelerated.

The Yankees are a diminishing political force today; they co-operate freely with the Irish because otherwise they would get no share in politics at all. Consider the situation. The chief justice of the state is Irish. The presiding justice of the superior court is Irish. The judge of the federal district court is Irish. So is the attorney general, and so are the mayors of both Providence and Newport. Also the Irish are closely knit, with fewer schisms than in Massachusetts, say. As a result the Yankees have no recourse but to get along. They like someone who is efficient and whom they can deal with: so they vote for people like McGrath. The Providence *Journal*, one of the worthiest—and most conservative—newspapers in the United States, supported him in both 1942 and 1944; it advocated a split ticket in 1944, coming out for McGrath *and* Dewey. Incidentally Rhode Island furnishes an illuminating instance of the so-called power of the press in contemporary America. Rhode Island is overwhelmingly Democratic; yet there is no Democratic daily in the entire state.

The Nutmeg State

Connecticut . . . the little spot . . . that makes the clock peddler,
the schoolmaster, and the senator. The first, gives you time;
the second, tells you what to do with it; the third makes your
law and your civilization.

—Alexis de Tocqueville

Probably Connecticut is the least "typical" of the New England states.
Its southern border is only twelve miles from New York City, and the
shoreline from Greenwich up to Westport belongs in almost every respect
to the New York area. Part of Connecticut is in the New York Federal
Reserve district, and the frontier region near Rye is a kind of peaceable
American Alsace-Lorraine.

Connecticut is coterminous with Massachusetts for roughly ninety
miles, and it has, as is natural, many resemblances to its northerly sister.
But there are differences too:

(1) Connecticut has no mass industries as big or as profoundly interlocked with the community as the textile mills of Lowell, say, or
Lawrence.

(2) There is much less church influence in politics, and less dominance
by a single city.

(3) By and large it is much better run—at least according to Connecticutters.

Connecticut is a very worthy little state, compact, efficient, and with a
splendid history. Proudly it claims that its "Fundamental Orders" of
1639, embodied in a charter issued by Charles II in 1682, was the first
democratic document of the kind in American history; by terms of this
charter Connecticut's western "boundary" was, as all its citizens know
well, the Pacific Ocean! Here are some other things Connecticut is
first in :[6]

1640.   First American public election in defiance of royal courts
held at Wethersfield.

1670.   First survey made for first turnpike to be completed in
America.

1680.   First American carding mill established and (1727) first
American copper coins minted.

1738.   First American theological seminary established.

1775.   First American warship, the *Oliver Cromwell*, with 16
guns, built at Essex.

1789.   First American juvenile publication, the *Children's Magazine*, published; ditto (1796) the first American cookbook. (This
latter was republished in 1937.)

1794.   First cotton gin patented by Eli Whitney.

[6] As listed in *Connecticut: A Guide to Its Roads, Lore, and People,* in the
American Guide Series, p. 111.

1817.   First American school for the deaf founded.
1830.   First American hoop skirts made.
1844.   First use of nitrous oxide gas as an anaesthetic.
1848.   First cylinder lock invented and (1856) first commer-
cially successful condensed milk produced.
1861.   First American degree of Ph.D. conferred by Yale, and
first American boys' camp established.
1863.   First American accident insurance issued.
1878.   First commercial telephone switchboard installed.
1899.   First tackling dummy for football practice invented by
A. A. Stagg at Yale.
1901.   First American speed limit for automobiles put in force:
twelve miles per hour (but eight in cities).

Above all today Connecticut is the home of specialized industry; it is
the gadget state par excellence. It produces revolvers, typewriters, sub-
marines, and a multifarious variety of objects that demand immense
precision in manufacture, immense skill in labor. It is a tremendous state
for work in brass, as witness the city of Waterbury, and various Connecticut communities are famous for auger bits, clocks, hooks and eyes,
gold leaf, bedsprings, toothbrushes, coffins, ball-bearings, hats, and saddlery. Though it is forty-sixth in the union in area and thirty-first in
population, it is not less than eighth in industrial production.

Also Connecticut is an exceptionally well-governed state; like the
rest of the original thirteen, it learned the art of government by actual
trial and error. Nowadays, like much of the rest of New England, it
suffers from disproportionate representation. For instance the city of
New Haven has only two representatives in a legislature of 278, though
it is Connecticut's second biggest city (population 160,605); but the
rural county of Tolland (population 31,866), the smallest county in the
state, has 22. The rural folk justify this by saying that they must watch
that "none of that crazy stuff" from the towns "gets by."

Who runs Connecticut? Historically it was once divided between two
rival "city-states"; then came the era of railroad dominance, emergence
of a handful of big families, and the utilities. But today there are no
financial octopuses of markedly aggressive nature and no big pressure
groups. The people have a strong community sense, and the basic
struggle is the same as elsewhere in New England—rural Republicans
versus urban Democrats. Connecticut did have a boss until quite recently.
He was a spectacular example of the old wheel-horse titan. His name
was Roraback; he controlled the legislature and the lobbies; he killed
himself in 1937. From 1931 to 1939, for four terms, Professor Wilbur
Cross of Yale University was governor. This salty old Democrat—he
was sixty-nine at his first inaugural—had unique quality. Read Con-

necticut Yankee, his autobiography, which he published at eighty-one. People thought that Cross was a joke, a crank, a "dear old gentleman" down from Yale. The crusted worthies laughed at this venerable upstart, but he was elected again and again because he believed in a practical conception of people's government, practically applied; he was supported by Republicans who were sick and tired of the "machine" as well as Democrats. Once in office, as I heard it put, "the politicians couldn't get at him," and this became a basic source of his strength and popularity. One of the strangest American paradoxes is that though the power of politicians depends on people, the people don't like politicians.

Connecticut is a nip and tuck state politically. It voted for Hoover in 1928 and 1932, and for Roosevelt in 1936, 1940, and 1944. Raymond E. Baldwin (Republican) was governor for three successive terms; he was re-elected in 1944 even though Dewey lost the state. This was the more remarkable in that the voting machine used in Connecticut makes it comparatively difficult for a citizen to split his vote. Yet enough people wanted a Democratic president and a Republican governor to say so. Similarly Hartford elected a Republican mayor (a liberal) although it went for Roosevelt. In other words—as we have found elsewhere in New England—Connecticut voters are discriminating. The fact that Baldwin should have won whereas all other state offices went to the opposition (except the attorney generalship which was held by a Republican holdover), also reflects another familiar contradiction, that very often an American governor is not the head of a real cabinet, but has to work with associates belonging to the rival party.

Clare Boothe Luce and Baldwin are the two Republicans of consequence in the state. Baldwin ran for the Senate in 1946 and won; the nomination could have been Mrs. Luce's, but after long consideration she decided not to take it. She would almost certainly have won the senatorship easily, and would thus have become the first woman in American history ever originally elected to the Senate (a lady from Arkansas, Hattie Caraway, was once appointed, and then re-elected); but for a variety of good reasons she did not become a candidate. Few people, unless they read the *Congressional Record* carefully, realize what a good congresswoman Mrs. Luce was; she was at a disadvantage most of the time in that she became a victim of her own reputation, versatility, and beauty; her long hours of conscientious work never got in the papers; the wisecracks did. She certainly has blind spots, but even so she was a much better legislator than many people give her credit for.

Baldwin is a big man in his early fifties, hearty, straightforward, and agreeable. He was a leader among the young Republican governors, and his record was progressive in most respects. To have remained in public life has been a considerable sacrifice for him; he has no private fortune, and several times he has wanted to go into the insurance business, out

of the direct necessity to support his family. I asked him once what he
thought of Willkie; he replied that Willkie was not only the greatest
American of this century, but "the greatest man since Lincoln." One
thing he is proud of is the Connecticut labor record during his governorships. Next to that of Michigan the state's manpower problem was
the most difficult in the country, but its record of man hours lost by
strikes since 1941 is the lowest in the nation.

On the Democratic side the most interesting event lately was the
squeezing out of Chester Bowles as candidate for governor. As a sidelight on the way American politics are operated behind the scenes, I
quote the following from a letter to the *New Republic* (September 30,
1946):

Chester Bowles lost at Harvard. He lost—and this is the real reason—because the delegates sized him up and decided that although
they thought he was probably a first-rate fellow, they would rather
have Snow as their candidate. Oh, the bosses ganged up on Bowles,
but not in any cutthroatedly efficient fashion. There was a business
of putting up favorite sons to keep Bowles from getting a majority
on the first ballot; but if he had got the majority they would have
backed him.

He lost the nomination on Monday afternoon, the day before the
voting. The candidates had set up headquarters along Asylum
Street in Hartford: Snow and Dodd at the Bond, which is the
biggest hotel, and Bowles a few doors away at the Hotel Garde.
He came into the real campaign too late to rent headquarters at the
Bond; that was his first mistake. The second mistake was that his
campaign was being run by amateurs. The crowd went to his headquarters first, sampled his excellent liquor, nibbled at or wolfed his
sandwiches, then found that there was nobody to talk to, yes,
nobody. Bowles himself appeared, with a nice shy smile and a firm
handshake, but after having smiled and shaken hands, he had
nothing to say. The crowd drifted over to the Bond, went into the
Snow headquarters, sampled his liquor, ate his sandwiches and
were buttonholed and pledged by Snow himself. . . .

The delegates figured this way: Snow is our sort; he's campaigned
at one time or another in every one of the I think it is 167 Connecticut towns, including Bozrah; while Bowles is a nice guy, but
an outsider, and some people will vote against him on account of
the OPA. In the background there were dickers for delegates—
probably if Bowles had been nice to the Hartford bosses or promised the lieutenant-governorship to the mayor of Waterbury, he
still could have been nominated.

On the floor of the convention, Bowles had another piece of bad
luck. All his strength was concentrated in the big towns of the 3rd
and 4th Congressional Districts. But the roll was called beginning
with the little towns of the 1st and 2nd Districts, where Bowles had

practically no strength at all. . . . The lucky thing for us Connecticut Democrats is that we got a candidate as good as Wilbert Snow, as intelligent and as liberal. It's one of the few times on record when the party bosses and small politicians went down the line for a liberal college professor.[7]

Is Connecticut changing? Yes—profoundly. Before the war it had 370,000 people in industry, Baldwin told me; today the number is 600,000 or more, of whom from 30 to 40 per cent are women. Year by year more foreign-born pump in; and as far back as 1930, only 34.1 per cent of Connecticutters were of native American stock. Another item —a cardinal point almost everywhere in southern New England—is the growing decentralization of cities. The well-to-do go out into the suburbs; big parking lots disfigure empty blocks in the towns, where buildings have been torn down because the owners cannot pay taxes; and the towns spread out voraciously into the mellow, undulant countryside.

Every once in a while a territorial dispute between states comes up in American politics, and the metropolitan dailies have great fun writing about "plots for territorial revision" and the like. A recent example was a petition by residents of Fisher's Island, New York, for annexation to Connecticut. The island is a small one near the end of Long Island, three miles off the Connecticut shore; its natural links are across the Sound. Baldwin took the matter up with Dewey. He explained that no defection in loyalty to New York state was intended by the inhabitants of Fisher's Island, and that New York itself must of course agree to this "loss of sovereignty," before he would consent to take the island in.

Finally Connecticut has other things. It is the state of place names just as dramatic as any in the West (for instance Dark Entry, Jangling Plains, Cow Shanty, Dodgingtown); it is the state of twenty-six daily newspapers including the Hartford *Courant*, founded in 1765, the oldest American paper of continuous publication; of ten billion dollars worth of insurance in forty-five insurance companies; of the graves of J. P. Morgan, Tom Thumb, and Noah Webster; of a host of New York writers, artists and millionaires who escape New York in the vicinity of Westport; of strong Jewish influence (Hartford has more Jews per capita than any American city except New York); and of the only important city in the nation, Bridgeport, with a Socialist mayor, the picturesquely named Jasper McLevy.

Some other Connecticut developments recently have been (*a*) a successful strike in Norwalk by the schoolteachers, who had been shockingly underpaid; (*b*) vivid emergence in local elections of war veterans, like Captain Emilio Quincy Daddario (who bears a nice melting pot

[7] This letter, signed only by initials, was written by Malcolm Cowley incidentally. Professor Snow, a teacher for many years at Wesleyan University, was defeated for the governorship by its former president, Dr. James L. McConaughty.

name), a hero of the Italian campaign who became Democratic mayor of Middlesex in 1946; (*c*) suppression in both New Haven and Bridge-port of performances of *Uncle Tom's Cabin*, as a result of Negro protests, and (*d*) bitter opposition by lush landowners in the Greenwich-Stam-ford area to the possibility of the United Nations moving in.

Chapter 31

Natural History in Massachusetts

〜〜〜

> Only Bostonians can understand Bostonians and thoroughly
> sympathize with the inconsequences of the Boston mind.
> —Henry Adams

> Boston State-house is the hub of the solar system . . . That's
> all I claim.
> —Oliver Wendell Holmes

NOTHING could more sharply reveal the antipodal poles in Massachusetts public life than the 1946 gubernatorial race between Maurice J. Tobin, the incumbent, and Lieutenant Governor Robert F. Bradford. From the point of view of background, and though the two men are good friends, this was among much else a straight-out struggle between the Catholic Irish and the Brahmins of Beacon Hill. Bradford won.

I saw Tobin, a former mayor of Boston, when he was still functioning in the City Hall. Functioning? Yes indeed. I sent him a telegram asking for an appointment; a day later the telephone rang and one of the pleasantest voices I've ever heard said, "This is Mayor Tobin. My private number is such and such. Call me up, and I'll see you in a day or two." I called several times; the phone may have been there but not the mayor. Then one day talking to Saltonstall I said that I hadn't yet met his successor. Saltonstall volunteered to arrange a meeting, and called him at once, but at a different number. A voice said that Tobin would call right back. Saltonstall grinned saying, "They know where he is, of course. It's just a little ritual to protect him." Tobin called back in 45 seconds; Saltonstall asked him to see me and he said to come right over.

He was in a suite at the Parker House, not at the City Hall. Instantly I remembered days when I was a cub reporter in Chicago twenty years before. This was politics. These were politicians. A knot of big men, wearing big hats and smoking big cigars, perched buzzardlike in the living room of the suite. Every four or five minutes, the door popped open, and Tobin (with no secretary or other intermediary) said to whomever was next in line, "Come in, Joe," or "Okay, Bob, five minutes." At 3:12 my turn came. Tobin said, "I haven't had lunch yet." We went down to a lunchroom in the basement. We were interrupted half a dozen times.

I was impressed and fascinated. In what other country of the world could anything quite like this go on? This was politics, yes—the hardest-boiled kind of politics—but also it was democracy in action. The Negro waiter brought the check. He said, "You know my wife." "Oh, sure," Tobin replied. (She was a political worker somewhere.) The waiter asked the mayor a small favor, and Tobin at once agreed. Then an elderly man approached; he said that one of his sons, in the Merchant Marine, wasn't getting his proper pay, because he had "lost" his own first name (!) and couldn't be identified. I understood no head nor tail of what followed, but Tobin scribbled on a chit of paper, "Take this to so-and-so." The man looked dubious. "It's okay; they know my hand-writing; you'll get in," the mayor said. "The old guy has two other kids in the service," Tobin mentioned when the man left. Then he paused and said with great earnestness and emphasis: "After all we're their servants. The government works *for* the people! That old man hired *me!*"

Tobin is a handsome, hard-working and elusive youngster of forty-five. He is intensely proud that in 1944 he carried such traditionally Republican strongholds as Gloucester and the fishing counties, Berkshire County, and even Provincetown. People enumerate several reasons for his success (*a*) He had the solid Irish vote, of course. (*b*) He did a good job as mayor for two terms. (*c*) He campaigns with great zest and vigor; for instance he visited 300 out of the 349 incorporated communities in the state. This campaign cost a considerable sum, something over $174,000, incidentally. Thirty-nine different people gave him one thousand dollars each.

Tobin is the son of a carpenter—once again we see the self-made man! He had to get a job at the age of nine, as a newsboy; he had one of the longest routes in Boston, and took the "owl car" at 4:30 A.M. to get to work; he went to school at night. Politics fascinated him from the start, and he was a member of the state legislature at twenty-six while he earned a living working for the telephone company.

Americans close to politics are traditionally irreverent; to the visitor from abroad, this is one of our most striking traits. I asked a Brahmin about Tobin. Reply: "If he makes as good a governor as he was mayor, he'll be a national figure, but the gang around him will pull him down." I asked a big newspaper publisher about him, and he replied calmly: "Has he character enough to keep really honest men around him?" Another comment back in 1944 was, "But Curley will wrap himself around Tobin's neck, and that'll be too bad." Actually Tobin kept just as far away from Curley as he could, and denounced him often—and his record as governor was commendable.

Robert F. Bradford, the governor since January, 1947, is now forty-three, a Harvard man, a scion of one of the most potent and distinguished of all New England families, a lively straightforward person whose blood is not merely blue but purple, and a splendid type of unselfish public servant. Though he is of necessity a politician too, he carries nothing of the extremely professional aura that enwraps Tobin. Bradford, a lawyer by trade, was for some years partner to a former governor of Massachusetts, Joseph B. Ely; out of this same law firm came Horace A. Hildreth, the governor of Maine—an example of the close inter-locking of New England politics. Bradford has a pleasant and com-fortable manner; he takes an adult and reasonable line. Politics in Massachusetts is expensive: his 1944 race for lieutenant governor cost $47,601.43. Bradford became well known locally in the 1930's; he is still, however, so inconspicuous on the national scale that he does not even appear in the 1946-47 *Who's Who*. In 1938 he was prevailed upon to run for district attorney of Middlesex County, the most heavily populated county in the entire United States. The courts there (New York *Herald Tribune*, August 25, 1946) were only averaging a 26 per cent conviction record. After being in office a year, Bradford had raised this to 93 per cent, and in 1942 he returned to the county $166,000 in un-spent appropriations. Running for re-election, he won like a tidal wave. American citizens, no matter what one may say to the contrary, do in the long run appreciate good and clean local government. As lieutenant gov-ernor too, though in this post a person has little to do, Bradford served admirably. This is a man to watch. Any good governor of a key state like Massachusetts is worth watching. *Who's Who*, put him in.

Another Word on Bay State Politics

The first thing to reiterate about politics in Massachusetts, an ex-tremely distinctive and important commonwealth, is the crucial posi-tion of Boston and its urban vote, which is so big that Massachusetts as a whole is one of the few states with a Catholic majority. Statistics aren't always reliable, but Boston is probably 75 per cent Roman Catholic at least. Thus the struggle for power in Massachusetts is, and for many years will be, that of the predominantly Republican hinter-land versus Catholic, Democratic Boston. One of the most emancipated critics of local politics I met, W. E. Mullins of the Boston *Herald*, says that the basic and irreducible Republican vote is 800,000, the Democratic 700,000. This makes for bitterly close races. Also it makes for divers-colored results in an oddly checkered pattern, with Republican and Democratic victories alternating through the ticket. Massachusetts has gone Democratic in every presidential election since 1928, and Senator Walsh has been a terrific vote getter; yet Saltonstall's victories were also tremendous, as we know, and seven out of the last nine lieutenant governors[1] have been Republican. Moreover, the Republicans *always* win a majority in the General Court (legislature) and in the House of Representatives.

[1] Boston *Herald*, November 29, 1944.

Massachusetts, alone among American states except for New Hampshire and Maine, preserves an institution known as the executive council, a relic of colonial days. It grew up before the Revolution because the citizenry demanded the right to vote for and choose a council among its own kind, as a check on the royal governor sent out from England. Nowadays this executive council has little power except in approving gubernatorial appointments, yet it is an interesting survival. Saltonstall had a 7-1 majority on the council; Tobin had it 5-3 against him. Any time a Republican governor takes office with a Democratic council or vice versa fireworks are likely to occur.

Because the contending forces are so evenly balanced the way to play politics in Massachusetts is to nail down your own party first, then make raids into your opponents. Saltonstall was absolutely sure of Yankee Republican support; so he could afford to do favors to Democrats, hoping to entice them over the wall. Conversely, Tobin contended hard for Republican support, since most Democrats voted for him anyway. In other words the secret of Massachusetts politics is the cultivation of your enemies. Carried to its logical conclusion this results in the paradox that no Massachusetts politician can gain office unless supported by his opposition.

Last of the Buccaneers

The fantastic and incredible James Michael Curley, at present mayor of Boston, sues for libel at the drop of a hat; so I will proceed cautiously. But *Time* (November 20, 1944) dared to write, "As onetime mayor he helped himself to $30,000 of political graft," and so far as I know *Time* was never sued. Curley is a kind of rank perennial that cannot be weeded out; a typical American *condottiere* of the old school; a wonderfully charming old man when he wants to be; and a jailbird among much else. One of the abundant legends about him is that he was actually in prison when, many years ago, he was first elected to public office; the offense was minor—a technical charge. Curley conducted his campaign—he was running for the city council—from his cell in jail.

Curley, who is seventy-one now, has been governor of Massachusetts once, mayor of Boston on four different occasions and a Congressman several times. He has had plenty of defeats as well as victories:[2] he was beaten once for Congress, twice for governor, once for senator (by Henry Cabot Lodge Jr., whom he liked to call "Little Boy Blue"), and three times for mayor. Saltonstall beat him for governor; Tobin beat him for mayor twice. Yet the legend persists that "only Curley can beat Curley"; if things go right he is almost irresistible; he bursts out like an unquenchable and explosive stream.

In November, 1945, Curley was once more elected mayor of Boston.

[2] Boston *Herald*, December 8, 1944.

He was also Democratic representative in Congress from the 11th Massachusetts district; thus he held one job that paid twenty thousand dollars a year, and another that paid ten thousand dollars. On February 18, 1946, very shortly after he took office as mayor (he won this fourth term by an unprecedented majority) he was sentenced by a Washington, D. C., federal court to six to eighteen months in prison, on conviction of a sixty thousand dollar mail fraud in connection with war contracts. Curley at once appealed; then, free on bail, he took the train for Boston. On February 21, ten thousand of his wildly cheering supporters met him at South Station, tied up traffic for half an hour, and took him home with a brass band playing "Hail the Conquering Hero Comes."

Before this Curley had been in trouble too, if he would call it trouble. The local courts ordered him to pay back to the city of Boston $42,629, part of which he "improperly received" during a previous term as mayor. It took him a long time to pay; he was in court no fewer than nine times in regard to arrears and other details. Was Boston ashamed of all this? Not much.[3] Curley cannot be removed from office as mayor, since the city charter contains no provision for a mayor's recall. Mostly the newspapers kept their mouths shut after the 1946 federal conviction, though the *Herald*, which was once sued by Curley, did dare to say that "it would perhaps be a little regretful that a city of 770,816 should be run from a jail." (*Time*, September 2, 1946) Howard Brubaker commented in the *New Yorker*, "Bostonians have again disproved the charge that they are narrow-minded people. They . . . can see merits in James M. Curley not visible to anyone else." Governor Tobin, however, did attack Curley. His plaintive reply was, "I don't think any man could be more vicious and cruel than he has been to me."

Curley came into prominence when the great Irish-descended population of Boston first began to assert itself; for many years he was the undisputed champion of the local Irish, and his basic source of power was his identification with all the resentments closely cherished by the Irish underpossessed. And, be it remembered, the Irish and people of Irish stock were indeed severely discriminated against; there were signs in Boston ONLY PROTESTANTS NEED APPLY FOR JOBS and so on; no Irishman could get anywhere in economic or political life because the Brahmins and middle Yankees held the doors tight shut; the Boston Irish fifty years ago were in almost the position of the Mexicans in San Antonio today. What Curley did was to crash through all this. His rise was an absolutely proper and inevitable phenomenon, and he has always been perfectly frank about his methods.

Curley was totally self-educated. In his thirties he spent two evenings a week in the home of a Boston utilities magnate; he roamed through the library, and reported like a schoolboy on the books he absorbed.

[3] Our friend the man from Mars—or Moscow—may well be given pause by this.

During his great dictatorial years his influence was, on the whole, to the good. But his power began to fade when, a few years ago, the late great Cardinal O'Connell appeared to be disapproving of his general line. Nevertheless, Curley retained the faculty of pulling not only himself but everybody else up by the bootstraps.[4] A fantastically effective speaker, either to great crowds or alone with friends, he had—and has —a gift of gab almost unrivaled in America. I heard one man say of him with a kind of wistful affection, a man who certainly had no reason to be fond of him, "I suppose that fellow is the damnedest single human being I ever met."

The Boston Irish

Nowhere else in the United States does a single community dominate a metropolis in quite the manner that the Irish Catholics dominate Boston. No Anglo-Saxon Protestant could ever conceivably be its mayor, and Boston is probably the only city in America where, in order to have a frank political talk with anybody, you have to begin with the question, "Are you a Catholic?"

There is a little joke.

"What is Boston?" someone asks.

Answer: "Part of South Boston." South Boston is, of course, the major stronghold of those of Irish origin.

Some years ago *Kitty Foyle*, Christopher Morley's well-known novel, was offered for serialization to the Boston *Globe*; its canny editor instantly turned it down. But another Boston newspaper bought the novel sight unseen, because of its reputation as a best seller. A big promotion campaign began. Then abruptly it was stopped; the book never appeared. No outside pressure caused this, nor was there any public explanation. What happened was simply that, on actually reading it, the editor of the second paper knew that he couldn't possibly risk printing a serial in which a Catholic girl has an illicit love affair.

Yet, for all their immense power, the Irish-born and the second-generation Irish do not play much of a role in nonpolitical affairs. They "permeate without controlling," I heard it said; they are a kind of minority—except in political offices—although a majority. They have entered all fields; but they don't quite "take them over." For instance, only one small Boston bank is Irish owned, and only four out of thirty directors of the Chamber of Commerce are of Irish descent. There are few dominating Irish figures in law, medicine, or finance, and none of the big department stores are Irish controlled; not a single Irishman is an officer, a committee chairman, or a member of the executive committee of the New England Council.

[4] And nevertheless Franklin D. Roosevelt once offered to make him ambassador to Poland.

The Irish in Boston derive from a very special background; they go far back, and the Charitable Irish Society is older than the Daughters of the American Revolution. But the great bulk of immigration did not come until the middle of the last century; in one year alone, 1849, 28,917 Irish arrived.[5] They came packed like animals in ships that charged eighteen dollars as fare from Queenstown; most were ignorant, destitute—a starving rabble. They got jobs as ditchdiggers on the canals and railways, or at the lowest kind of menial labor. And they stayed *in* Boston instead of moving on, because: (*a*) they were too poor to move on; (*b*) they had had their fill of farming under famine conditions in the home country, and they liked urban living. For a time they found Boston an extremely hostile habitat. I have heard it seriously proffered by a non-Irishman that the Boston Irish of the last century were the worst-treated white minority that has ever existed. Not only could they not find jobs but they were forbidden actual entrance into whole districts; people said, "So long as we live, no Catholic shall enter here." The Irish died in state hospitals without benefit of last rites, until in the 1860's a law insisted that priests be allowed to enter such institutions; previously it had been forbidden. But the Irish proliferated nevertheless. Many remained poor—the great majority in fact—but some got rich. The "lace curtain" Irish replaced the "cattle Irish"; they moved slowly through Boston like a glacier. Then came the "suburban Irish"; and finally the Irish on Beacon Hill. There are men today whose fathers sold buttons on the streets who have splendid mansions in the most fashionable part of town.

What do the Irish want? Their fair share of power. That and to be let alone. They resent slurs like a famous one made by Rudyard Kipling, "Anything dirty will buy the Irish vote." Why do the Irish sometimes make trouble? Because, as I heard it said, "they are a people who love to contrive things so that there will be no solution." But actually they don't make "trouble" often. If they ever should choose to be a serious nuisance they could hamstring the city in a day; consider merely what would happen if they should boycott non-Irish shops.

Politically the Irish may be closely influenced by what happens "at home" in Eire; Mr. De Valera's moods can strongly affect South Boston. On the whole they are much less anti-British today than in 1914-18 when hatred of Britain was dense, intense, and bitter. During World War II the Boston Irish were notably loyal; a personal reason for this may have been the previous appointment of a home boy, Joe Kennedy, to the Court of St. James's, and the splendid war record of his sons, though Kennedy himself was for years an isolationist.[6]

[5] Cf. *Boston's Immigrants 1790-1865, a Study in Acculturation,* by Oscar Handlin.
[6] One son, John F. Kennedy, an attractive youngster of twenty-nine, ran for Congress in 1946 and won Curley's former seat.

Inextricably bound up with the Irish question is the Catholic question. It is a subject almost never brought out into the open, particularly by Boston newspapers. But that the city is 75 per cent Catholic is an overwhelming fact, and the *Pilot*, the official organ of the archdiocese, is one of the most influential periodicals of its kind in the United States. Most Boston Catholics are vehemently and irreversibly anti-Russian—which can produce a considerable effect in Washington. Ex-Governor Tobin's views on foreign policy are as parochial as his environment was bound to make them. Another point is the dislike of most Irish and many Catholics for Harvard; a reason for this is, of course, that Harvard is the great rival of the archbishopric for intellectual control of the community. "I don't know why Harvard *should* dominate the city, but it does," one famous prelate sighed not so long ago. In the whole history of Harvard, only one Catholic, a New Yorker, has been a member of the corporation. And the Irish say that Harvard "discriminates" against them.

Certainly the church watches its interests with extreme solicitude and care, no matter on what level. Consider the following from the *Congressional Record* of June 12, 1946:

LAWRENCE, MASS., JUNE 10, 1946

Federal Communications Commission,
Washington, D. C.

MY DEAR SIR: I am herewith enclosing editorial from the *Pilot*, official organ of the Catholic Archdiocese, of Boston, relative to the program Duffy's Tavern, over the NBC network, and sponsored by the Bristol Myers Co., of New York.

I have written this concern regarding their sponsoring of this offensive program, which, in our opinion, is a direct insult to people of Catholic faith and Irish ancestry, but a reply from them states that they are unable to control this person who broadcasts under the name of Ed Gardner, and are, therefore, unable to remedy the situation.

The Bristol Myers Co. admits that the program is offensive but that they are unable to do anything about it, as this person, Gardner, persists in his weekly insults, with the full knowledge that the program is offensive.

A letter to NBC brought no satisfaction.

I am bringing this matter to your attention in order that some action might be taken to prevent our people of Catholic-Irish faith and ancestry from being lampooned and insulted over the air waves. Will you kindly advise.

Respectfully,

PATRICK J. SCANLON

In January, 1946, Superior Court Judge John E. Swift, supreme knight of the Knights of Columbus, in a public speech accused Russia of "international robbery and unblushing enslavement of whole nations." Several times previously this somewhat extroverted judge had been in the news, notably when in 1941 he committed three children, whose parents were members of Jehovah's Witnesses, to a reformatory because they did not salute the American flag in a public school. Judge Swift's outbreak brought forward a sharp Russian protest, and lost Boston whatever chance it might have had to be the UN capital.

The Irish were certainly persecuted in their own country, they were certainly persecuted in Massachusetts (where incidentally the Congregationalist church was not disestablished until the 1830's), and it is an unfortunate fact that almost every racial or other group that has been oppressed takes on a subsequent tendency to be an oppressor. So among other things Boston was, and is, probably the strongest Coughlinite city in America, which was one reason for much hoodlumism in the city and its environs and of an ugly outbreak of anti-Semitism in the spring of 1944. These "riots" were minor and nobody got killed; but the atmosphere was sinister enough. Mostly the police dismissed the incidents as "kid stuff"; and indeed, ordinary juvenile hooliganism was conjoined with them. A gang of a dozen alley rats would run into a pair of Jewish boys, and beat them up, or windows would be stoned at the Jewish Home in Dorchester, or offensive words would be scrawled on synagogues, including of all things loud chalkings of "Hitler" and "Gestapo." A seventy-year-old Jew was assaulted on a streetcar by three young roughs, and two Harvard boys were beaten up by eight Cambridge toughs. Now episodes of this kind, though they went on for a considerable time, were concealed behind a thorough news blackout. Not a single Boston paper printed a line about any "incident" until the New York newspaper *PM* blew the story open, and most Bostonians, when they heard the news, were sincerely shocked. The whole story has been so well told that there is little need to recapitulate it here; a full and objective account may be found in the *Atlantic Monthly* (July, 1944) by Wallace Stegner. Though this article was fair-minded in the extreme, it was bitterly attacked in Boston; so was a mild enough essay in *Life* (January 15, 1945) which did little more than mention that some of the Boston Irish were underpossessed.[7] The supersensitiveness of Boston and its great Catholic community is at a flash-point level on such matters, which is a healthy sign perhaps. When I asked Tobin about the

---

[7] The riots provided, incidentally, the only known occasion when Leverett Saltonstall publicly lost his temper. A *PM* reporter called on him presenting various affidavits and asking for a statement; the governor had him thrown out of the office. But—note well—Saltonstall immediately opened an investigation, called for action, and apologized to the reporter a day later. "I had a rude awakening," the governor said.

disturbances he first seemed shocked that I should even mention them; then he asked me "not to be taken in by all that talk."

The Christian Front headquarters in Boston had a considerable responsibility in this whole matter, let me repeat; the passions aroused were more political than religious. For years the Coughlinites had pumped out vicious streams of slander against the Jews, and Boston is reputed to have been Father Coughlin's chief single source of income. A man named Francis P. Moran, formerly Boston leader of the Coughlinites, once publicly charged Roosevelt with treason and denounced him as a Jew. Of course no local Catholics of any responsible position had anything whatever to do with the "incidents." The only charge brought is that the hierarchy might have taken a stronger line to discourage miscellaneous hoodlums. For instance a Jewish butcher in Dorchester had his windows regularly broken once a week for a period. Neither the police on the beat, the local relief organization, nor the insurance company were able to halt this vandalism. Then someone had the bright idea of appealing to the parish priest, and it stopped at once.

A further word on anti-Semitism. Popularly Boston is supposed to be the most anti-Semitic town in the United States—though this situation is probably changing for the better, and I am not sure but what Minneapolis, Portland (Oregon), and several places in the South are worse. In most American cities it would excite no comment if a rabbi and a priest were to be seen publicly together; in Boston, this event occurred at a recent book fair and it was considered not only a new development but a sensation. Mr. Stegner points out that the Jewish "problem" in Boston is almost as difficult as the Irish "problem"; there are, for instance, sixty thousand Jews packed in a single "sociological enclave" in one Boston district, who form the most solidly Jewish community in the whole country. And not only are some Boston Catholics anti-Semite; so are many Brahmins. I asked one blue-blood if Felix Frankfurter could become a member of the Somerset Club, the inner citadel of Beacon Hill. Answer: "Certainly not, but I would be perfectly willing to take him to lunch there and, as a matter of fact, he lunches there quite often." Mr. Justice Brandeis, be it noted, never got an honorary degree from Harvard. But this may have been because Brandeis was what Dr. Lowell called a "radical," not because he was a Jew.

William Henry, Cardinal O'Connell, one of the most powerful and pervasive dignitaries in American church history, a remarkable old potentate about whom a whole picturesque section might well be written, died at a great age in 1944.[8] His successor—as archbishop but not yet

---

[8] One big insurance company in Boston neglected to pull down its American flag to half-mast on the news of his death. It was so inundated with telephone calls of protest that it closed down entirely for the whole day of the funeral as a mark of belated respect.

as cardinal—is the Most Reverend Richard James Cushing, D.D., a stalwart man of great dignity, common sense and good humor. His manner can be quite informal. In the autumn of 1944 he called at the state house to be sworn in as corporation sole of the archdiocese; this is an ecclesiastical position but the incumbent must be installed in a civil ceremony. A group of stenographers left their desks, crowding around the new archbishop and kneeling so that they might properly kiss his ring. He greeted them with the words, "My name is Cushing." To another gathering, when he was asked if he belonged to the great Cushing medical family, he once replied, "No, I am from the South Boston Cushings."

Dr. Cushing was one of eleven children. (So, incidentally, was O'Connell.) His father was a blacksmith on the horse cars, who worked from 6 A.M. to 7 P.M. seven days a week for a seventeen dollar wage; the fact that Dr. Cushing should have risen to his present exalted position from this humble background is, one scarcely needs to point out, a characteristic American phenomenon. Archbishop Cushing is unusual in that he has never been to Rome; normally it is considered essential that an archbishop should have studied in the Eternal City. When I saw him he recalled days when convents had been burned in Massachusetts; he insisted that Catholics in Boston today have very little *economic* power, and talked mostly about the indubitable good qualities of the local Irish, for instance their love of home life and simplicity.

Dr. Cushing's formidable predecessor, Cardinal O'Connell, had an officially registered "lobbyist," Frederick W. Mansfield (a former mayor), who performed his liaison work with the legislature and the like. It is thought that Dr. Cushing's relations to politics are not quite so concretely close.

A final odd point is that many of the Irish, especially those prosperous and those who have moved into solidly Republican suburbs like Beverly, become Republican. This is of course because they are passionate politicians and they would be permanently excluded from political life and patronage if they remained Democrats. Exactly the inverse of this happens in communities in Florida, say, where Republican in-migrants turn Democratic.

Why Books Are Banned

There are several censorships in Boston; the most notorious is that of the New England Watch and Ward Society. But censorship of books is more stringent in Boston than anywhere else in America for another and broader and very obvious reason, namely that censorship is one field in which both Catholics and Puritans agree and have an identical objective.

Only rarely—if ever—is original action taken against a book by the authorities; instead, a private person or organization brings a blue-stocking suit. Watch and Ward has taken steps against four books recently, *Forever Amber, The History of Rome Hanks, Strange Fruit,* and Erskine Caldwell's *Tragic Ground.* In December, 1944, a municipal judge refused to support the attempt to suppress this last; this was the first time a Massachusetts court failed to back up Watch and Ward since Walt Whitman's *Leaves of Grass* was banned in 1881. But in 1945 the Supreme Judicial court upheld the suppression of *Strange Fruit,* and at the moment of writing the *Forever Amber* case is still *sub judice.*

I asked why, if Boston is so puritanical about books, it permits burlesque shows, which are forbidden even in that latitudinous modern Babylon, New York. Reason: an innocent mind may be corrupted by a book unwittingly picked up, but anybody going to a burlesque show knows what he is in for, and the danger of damage to both public and private morals isn't quite so great.

Late in 1946 the municipal censor ordered the exclamation "Oh, God!" cut from the celebrated play *Life With Father,* after it had played in Boston for many months. A substitute interjection, "Oh, fudge!" was proposed instead.

Hub of the Universe

We say the cows laid out Boston. Well, there are worse surveyors.

—Ralph Waldo Emerson

It is not age which has killed Boston, for no cities die of age; it is the youth of other cities.

—W. L. George

Perhaps I have neglected to note a quality in which Boston seems to me to outrank any other city in America—charm. Stroll around Louisburg Square on a tranquil autumn afternoon. This is the central haunt of Brahmins; there is nothing in the country to rival it for a kind of lazy dignity, intellectual affluence and spaciousness, velvetiness, and above all a wonderful lacquered sense of responsibility to its own past. Of course it suggests rather than overstates. Indeed the quality of understatement characterizes much in Boston life, including its humor in particular.

After two hours of sturdy talk with Erwin D. Canham and R. H. Markham in the *Christian Science Monitor* offices I wanted a cigarette badly.

"Can I smoke?" I asked.

Mr. Canham, executive editor of the *Monitor,* replied gently: "Of course. But no one ever has."

Also I have neglected so far to give any description of that unique Boston phenomenon—the trustee. Trustees exist in other cities, notably

Philadelphia, but not to the same extent; nowhere else in the United States is the trusteeship such a "cherished tradition" (as the phrase goes), such an inextricable part of the life of the privileged community.

The great Boston fortunes were made in textiles, in boots and shoes, and by the China trade. A young clipper captain might well retire with a sizable fortune after not more than two or three trips to the Orient; the turnover was enormous and immediate. Then the millionaires of the day tended to put their capital into long-term trusts, which were nurtured by trustees with scrupulous conservatism and efficiency; succeeding generations of beneficiaries spent the interest, but as a rule could not touch the principal. Now this process is breaking down, and such well-known modern crudities as taxes are beginning to cut in. I heard it put this way (by an irreverent Brahmin lady): "We were confronted by the dire alternative of living on our interest—say twenty-five thousand dollars a year, which of course is penury—or by something equally unpleasant, digging into the reserves. So we curse contemporary civilization and dig into the reserves."

It was presented to me on all sides, notably by trustees themselves, that the institution of trusteeship has a curiously subtle and intricate psychological basis. Many fathers of the last century and the early days of this distrusted their own children fearing that they would turn out to be either (a) namby-pambies, or (b) radicals, which would be worse. Yet they had a strong fixed family sense. Thus they contrived through the medium of the trusteeship to ensure that their sons could not maraud through the family fortune, and at the same time to arrange that the grandchildren would be provided for.

Most of the great trustees would not, I heard it said, invest in anything that they couldn't see outside the window. So billions of dollars of Boston money became sterilized. There was very little impulse, by and large, to invest capital creatively, and partly for this reason, New England industry began to dry up. The trustees' idea was above all to keep capital safe, not to risk it. Suppose a trust had a million dollars to invest in 1914. It will be proud today if that million is still a million. But think what it might well be today, if it had been invested in automobiles or some other such expanding industry!

If it is true that trusteeship is founded on the unwillingness of parents to believe in their own children, one should also point out a corollary phenomenon—that trusteeship made a generation of youngsters doubtful in turn of their own parents. Not only did it serve to make many young people distrustful of their own families, since they themselves were being distrusted; it made them skeptical and distrustful of something more important—of institutions in general, of institutions as *such*. This generalization, if correct, leads to a fancy paradox: that something intended above all to give enduring faith to institutions—what could be more of an "institution" than a long-term trust fund?—should have tended on the contrary to destroy this faith and to damage the institution itself.

Financial note: At the corner of Federal and Franklin streets in the core of central Boston is an empty lot. Here once stood the building of Lee, Higginson, & Company. Nothing could demonstrate with more startling pictorial impact how times—and Boston—have irremediably changed.

Two more items deserve brief mention. First, much of Boston seems physically ragged, dilapidated, and, in a way, deserted; on Commonwealth Avenue, I counted twenty buildings that seemed empty. This is partly the result of crushingly high urban taxes.[9] Rows of houses that were once handsome are frowsy and down-at-the-sill, because people can no longer afford to keep them up; one can easily trace the collapse of whole neighborhoods as successively poorer waves of tenants drifted in—first the Irish, then Italians, then Greeks and Poles, finally the Negroes. The middle class tended to move out into near-by towns or suburbs; only the very rich and the very poor, as I heard it put, could afford to stay within the city limits. This of course has produced profound sociological results: it is not healthy that a great municipality should lose its middle class.

Which leads to point two. Technically the population of "Boston" by the 1940 census is 770,816. But it is a complete delusion to consider this the actual figure. If its statistics were calculated as they are in Los Angeles, for instance, the population would be about 2,300,000, and instead of being the ninth city in the United States, Boston would be third or fourth.

The fact that so many thousands of "Bostonians" live in suburbs and adjacent communities—like Cambridge, Dedham, Melrose, Newton, Brookline, Belmont—has produced political problems of staggering complexity. Within fifteen miles of Boston City Hall there are no fewer than forty incorporated municipalities—which means *forty* different police and fire departments, boards of health, and school systems! The resulting confusions, like those in Los Angeles, are anarchic. It also means that countless men and women who earn their living inside Boston proper, and who contribute cardinally to its wealth, social energy, and civic prestige, cannot vote there. The people with the biggest stake in the municipality have no opportunity to express themselves politically on municipal affairs.

In an effort to clear up this and other irrational anomalies an eight thousand dollar prize contest was held in 1944, under the auspices of Boston University, for plans to reorganize the city. About ninety projects were submitted by various groups; the chairman of the board of judges, Charles Francis Adams, read every line of every one. The winning prize

[9] The real estate tax is $42.50 per $1,000 of valuation.

went to a Harvard group headed by Professor Carl Friedrich; its major proposal was that sixty-six cities and towns of the Boston area should be united into a single metropolitan authority.

One stout Bostonian told me, "Thirty years from now, if we don't do something, Boston will be so red that Muncie, Indiana, will think we're Bolsheviks."

Boston Labor Leader

The most important labor leader in New England is probably the Massachusetts boss of the CIO, an eloquent man of forty-seven, by name Joseph Salerno.

It happened that I saw him on the same day that I saw Charles Francis Adams. The contrast was a stimulating exercise. Adams—so sere, meditative, delicate, cultivated, and unchallengeably devoted to public service. Salerno—so blunt, confident, and unchallengeably fixed in doctrinaire convictions. Adams—great-great-great-grandson of one president of the United States and great-great-grandson of another. Salerno—born in Sicily and on arrival in Boston at the age of ten not knowing a word of English. Yet—I do not need to labor the point—each is a perfectly good American.

Salerno worked first as a waterboy in a factory; he had to quit school at twelve. Then he got a job in a pants shop, working from 6 A.M. every day "till the clock broke down." He has participated in a dozen strikes; he has been an organizer from the earliest days; he is a good Catholic. Like many self-educated men he has a feeling for aphorisms, a love of the apothegm. Samples of his talk:

"Words become action; then action becomes history."

"The purpose of life is more life."

"No one has stopped believing in God because the postman brings you a letter for three cents. Is that collectivism?"

"What we of the CIO have done here is induce a new mental climate. Labor can't be prosperous unless the rest of society is prosperous too. Life means jobs."

"If you have a message that hits people both in pocketbook and ideals, they'll act."

Salerno also talked a good deal about the church. No longer, he says, does an Irish priest automatically come to the defense of an Irish cop when the cop bashes someone in the head on a picket line. "The church can't afford it any more." The great majority of Irish Catholics voted for FDR in 1944. Why? "Because most of them are working people; they want security." And Salerno seemed to think that, rationally, there was no reason why church and CIO should not work together since—in Boston anyway—both have their strongest roots in the urban proletariat.

Composite Portrait of a New England Legislator

He is tall, gaunt, wrinkled, and there are great reserves of character in the face and raspy voice. He earns a living in a garage, and also owns a bit of real estate. His salary as legislator (which in New Hampshire would be two hundred dollars a year plus traveling expenses; in Vermont four hundred) is an important addition to his income. His wife is a farmer's daughter from the next county; they have been married twenty-four years and have three children. The eldest son was a carpenter's mate first class, another son is in his third year at the public high school, and is crazy about gliders; the daughter wants to go to Vassar. Our legislator has two brothers: one is a lobster fisherman in Stony Creek, Connecticut, and the other left Massachusetts many years ago, and is believed now to own a small farm in Iowa. Several generations back there were some complex marriages in the family; one distant relative is Greek born, and another married a Finn; but also our legislator is related to no less a personage than a former governor of the state. He believes in paying his bills on the dot, in the inherent right of his children to a good education, and in common sense. He gives ten dollars a year to the Red Cross, believes that "Washington ought to let us alone," knows that very few Americans are peasants, and feels that the country has enough inner strength to ride out any kind of crisis. In several respects he is somewhat arid; but no one has ever fooled him twice. He is a person of great power. Because, out of the community itself, power rises into him. What he represents is the tremendous vitality of ordinary American life, and the basic good instincts of the common people.

So much for New England. We proceed now to the most important and difficult subject in this whole wide and interwoven panorama. New York.

Chapter 32

New York: Dewey and the State

vvvvvvvvvvvvvvvvvvvvvvvvvvvvvvvvvvvvvvvvvvvvvvvvvvvvvvvvvvvvvvvvvvvvvvvvvvvvvvvvvvvvvvvv

> Crazed with avarice, lust and rum,
> New York, thy name's Delirium.
> —Byron R. Newton

> If you wish to make democracy conservative, you must give it
> something to conserve.
> —Lord Randolph Churchill

I DROPPED in to see Mr. Dewey at the Hotel Roosevelt in New York City on a bright morning not long ago. I had useful talk with two of his exceptionally able and friendly associates, Paul E. Lockwood and James C. Hagerty, and then an hour with the governor himself. Dewey is an alert and aggressive conversationalist. He covered a gamut from the effect of weather on politics to Hindus in India to what makes a best seller to whether or not Anaconda runs Montana. He has sharp, positive opinions, and he sometimes says, "I don't agree with you!" He mentioned Roosevelt once, with a curious abstract and impersonal half-bitterness, saying that FDR had stolen the faith of people, seduced from them their self-confidence. Once he paced to the window and looked down at the street, with its hurrying crowds in the thin, electric sunshine. "Mecca!" he exclaimed. But he did not go into what particular holy stone, what especial tablet of the devout, drew the thronging millions to New York. He looked steadily at the people crowding and weaving their way four abreast down the sidewalks. "Anybody who thinks this country isn't fundamentally okay is crazy. Sure there are a few crazy reactionaries and a few crazy left-wingers, but you could put the whole bunch in Grand Central Station."

Mostly he talked about New York state, its historical piquancies, its heft and beam, its truly imperial variety. "Why, this state is as big as countries in Europe that fight wars!" He mentioned his own farm, near Pawling, and described (the phraseology is his), "the soft loveliness, the incomparable rolling dairy country" of Dutchess County. "My farm is my roots." About agriculture Governor Dewey had much to say. "The heart of this nation is the rural small town." New York is one of the leading agricultural states in the union, but 60 per cent of its agriculture is marginal dairying; half the farmhouses need a paint job badly, and one-third have no electricity—in the Empire State, the most favored in the land! This, Mr. Dewey thinks, is outrageous. "Electricity and a vacuum cleaner mean whether or not the farmer's wife dies at fifty with a broken back." He talked about the work of H. E. Babcock, chairman of the board of directors of one of the best universities in America, Cornell, whom he called "the Kettering of American agriculture." He mentioned the extraordinarily high level of the state's agricultural schools, the research that was going on in grasses and hay, and the need, rich as New York is, to import grain. He reverted to his own farm, and how proud he was that his farmers "milk standing up," that his cows don't sleep on wet concrete but on soft, dry, warm straw. He pleaded the necessity of improving the quality of stock, and talked of research and developments in this direction. "You can get any cow artificially inseminated in every county in this state, at cost. The best sixty bulls in the state serve every farm."

About New York City, the governor did not say a great deal; I have an idea he doesn't like it much. "New York City isn't a melting pot, it's a boiling pot." Nor did he talk about contemporary politics at all. He mentioned the old corrupt machines with contempt; he pointed out of the window again, saying "No crook can get away with buying *that* any more!" and meaning by "that" the broad mass of moving people. Dewey is acutely conscious of the great historic tradition he inherits. From De Witt Clinton to Al Smith, New York has had notable chief executives. He talked about Smith warmly. New York has, he mentioned among other things, a much better budget and financial system than the federal government. "And we don't use New Deal methods either!"

Mr. Dewey has, I was told by those close to him, some positive reformist ideas about the structure of state governments. That a state may have a governor belonging to one party, and a lieutenant governor to another, seems to him little short of idiotic from the point of view of rational administration. If I gathered correctly the line of his thought, he believes (1) that primaries should be abolished in favor of the convention system, (2) that all governors should have four-year terms, not two, because two hardly give a man time to move around in, (3) that the organization of state government should follow the federal pattern more closely, with only governor and lieutenant governor elected among administrative officials, and the others, including judges, appointed, subject to confirmation by the state senate and to some such system as that in Missouri, which gives the electorate a chance to review a judge's record. Mr. Dewey is a strong believer in executive authority—very strong. But, just as strongly, he wants decentralization and community authority, for instance in such matters as juvenile delinquency and what it derives from—poor housing. For some elected representatives of the people on a local level, Mr. Dewey has considerable contempt. "There are bums that make you cringe."

What runs New York? Public opinion, Mr. Dewey thinks. What runs

Dewey? Dewey. What does Dewey believe in most? I didn't ask him directly, but I imagine the answer would include two items at least, himself and efficiency.

Dewey: Four Sources of His Power

Mr. Dewey, as of the moment of writing, is probably the most important Republican in the United States and a strong contender for the presidency in 1948, though he is not an avowed candidate. Several factors contribute to this:

(1) In both foreign and domestic policy he falls roughly in the middle between extreme conservatives like Taft and Bricker, and the liberal wing of the party represented by Stassen.

(2) Dewey or no Dewey, any New York candidate goes into the convention with a great head start.

(3) His strategic position vis-à-vis putative opponents in Congress is excellent. He does not have to expose himself to public inspection on a variety of issues; he does not have to vote. Moreover, on the side-lines so to speak, he can buttress his own record. His administration as governor will continue to be good; he can easily go out of his way to be attractive to all manner of special groups; he can avoid committing himself on controversial issues.[1]

(4) His personal qualities, including in particular the mainspring of a powerful ambition.

Brief Outline of Career, Record, Attributes

Thomas Edmund Dewey was born in Owosso, Michigan, a town of some eight thousand people, on March 24, 1902. His father, George Martin Dewey, was the local postmaster and also the editor of a weekly newspaper; his paternal grandfather helped found the Republican party when it was organized at Jackson, Michigan, in 1854, and a remote cousin was the Admiral Dewey made famous by the war with Spain. On his mother's side Dewey's descent is mostly Irish; his maternal grandmother was born in County Cork. The family traces its origin to a forebear named Thomas Dewey who landed near Boston in 1634, and hacked out a clearing near what is now Dorchester. The name was spelled "Duee" then. The governor was not named for this Thomas Dewey, however. He takes his name from his mother's side of the family.

The Deweys thus have roots. The family was not, however, nor did it

---

[1] Of course there are contrary factors. For one thing the Republican party is loath to give a second chance to any candidate who has ever been defeated. For another Taft controls much of the national machine. Carroll Reese, the chairman of the national committee, is a Taft man, and so, almost without exception, are Republicans in the South.

ever pretend to be, of any considerable wealth or distinction. Tom grew up in a pleasant enough house on a pleasant enough street, where his mother still lives; his upbringing was as conventional as that of any normal middle western boy. He set type in his father's shop, sold magazines, did farm chores, and went to the public schools. He did, however, show leadership and ambition above the average; by the time he was thirteen, he had a crew of nine other youngsters working for him. Also the bent of his mind, from earliest days, was toward argumentation and debate. His high school yearbook, published in 1919, gives him the motto, "First in the council hall to steer the state, and ever foremost in a tongue debate." Dewey himself was editor of this yearbook.

Childhood bites deep into a man. Few people have capacity for basic change. The hardest thing to conquer is a man's own genes. These bromidic remarks are called forth by a minor circumstance: I have just looked at two pictures of Mr. Dewey in *Life*. They were taken some thirty years apart. But Mr. Dewey as an infant of three, and Mr. Dewey as a nationally known prosecutor, have the identical facial expression, and even point an index finger to the cheek with the selfsame gesture, as *Life* points out.

Dewey went on to the University of Michigan, and did well both scholastically and otherwise. What interested him most was singing. He had a good resonant baritone voice, and placed first in a Michigan singing contest; this encouraged him to pursue voice as a career. He followed his singing teacher, Percy Rector Stephens, to New York, and at the same time began to study law at Columbia. Briefly he sang as a cantor in a New York synagogue; he didn't know Hebrew, but spelled out the syllables in phonetic English. The time came when he knew that he must choose between the two professions, music and law. He was conscientious enough to know that he could not do well at both. One legend is that he had a bad sore throat when about to sing a concert; this frightened him because it showed on what minor accidents a musical career could depend. At any rate he chose law, took a degree at Columbia, and started practice in 1925. He still likes to sing for fun. There are strong traces in him of the artist who never quite became an artist.

A man who gives up art puts a load on his subconscious. I do not mean to be too fanciful, but that Dewey is one of the neatest men who ever lived would suggest to any psychologist that he is still overcompensating for old artistic impulses, driving down and suppressing former tendencies to abandon. One of his biographers even records that he kills flies neatly, so that they will not make a spot on the wallpaper. That he drinks sparingly, and carefully limits himself to a package of cigarettes a day, is another indication of the rigorous will with which he controls himself, and avoids disarray. Consider too his extreme self-centeredness and self-consciousness. Mr. Dewey (it is an admirable trait) will never be "one of the boys." This too connotes a tendency to be on guard, or rather a fear of being caught off guard. To the point is the fact that he is violently camera shy. For years he had trouble with photographers. The New York camera men—a grim crew they are—once boycotted him for a time, or only snapped him in the most fearsome and unbecoming poses, with his mouth wide open or blowing his nose.

Dewey's speaking voice, as every American knows who ever listened to the radio in the last two presidential campaigns, has a full, rich quality; yet it sounds schooled. It is full of vitality, yet the delivery seems contrived, like that of an elocutionist. In depth of tone it strikingly resembles that of his friend and neighbor, Lowell Thomas. One early joke about Dewey was to call him "Lowell Thomas E. Dewey."[2]

The interlude with voice also led to Dewey's marriage. His wife, Frances Eileen Hutt, a grandniece of Jefferson Davis, who was born in Texas and raised in Oklahoma, was a promising young mezzo-soprano, also studying with Stephens. She sang in New York churches and, under the name Eileen Hoyt, had small roles in several of the John Murray Anderson revues and, of all things, in a road company of George White's Scandals. She married Dewey in 1928, and gave up her musical and stage career.[3] The Deweys have two children, and their home life has been very happy. For a time they lived in the Tuxedo neighborhood; they gave it up because it was too stuffy and fashionable, and later bought the farm at Pawling. It cost $3,000 cash, with a $27,000 mortgage.

Here perhaps is place for another personal item. Two things gravely hurt Dewey in his first presidential run in 1940, jokes about his youth and about his size. To attack him on either score was, of course, hardly fair. There is nothing reprehensible about a man younger than forty running for the presidency. But when Mr. Ickes announced to the nation that he had tossed his diaper into the ring, all was lost. As to his size Dewey is five feet eight, which is not so very short. It was preposterous to attack him as Dollfuss or a dwarf. Yet the jibes were merciless. He posed for *Life* in a very deep chair in the Executive Chamber at Albany; when the magazine announced that the governor was sitting on two telephone books, the country tittered. Dewey keeps a very large dog, Canute, and so the story rose that "he rode it to work." He was called "the chocolate soldier of Albany." One joke was that he had a "tinker toy approach" to foreign affairs, and another was, "I don't mind changing horses in midstream, but what about a Shetland pony?" Dewey once told Leonard Lyons of the New York *Post* that, of all the things

---

[2] *Time*, October 23, 1944.
[3] Noel F. Busch wrote in *Life*, April 22, 1940, "If Dewey is inaugurated next January 20, Mrs. Dewey will be the first ex-show girl who has ever entered the White House as its mistress and easily its most decorative occupant since Dolly Madison."

Lyons had ever written about him, he resented only one—a statement that he wore built-in high heels.

Dewey, while still a struggling young lawyer, became interested in Republican politics, and worked doggedly at small party jobs, starting at the bottom as a watcher at the polls. Presently he was chosen chairman of the New York Young Republican Club. He comes by his Republicanism honestly enough. During the 1946 gubernatorial campaign, the well-known New York *Times* illustrator S. J. Woolf asked him "Why are you a Republican?" Dewey answered: "That's a question I have never been asked. I believe that the Republican party is the best instrument for bringing sound government into the hands of competent men and by this means preserving our liberties. . . . But there is another reason why I am a Republican. I was born one."

The great racket-busting days, the Dewey-splashed-over-the-national-landscape days, began in 1931. The late George Z. Medalie, a famous New York public figure, liked him and, when Medalie was appointed United States district attorney for the Southern District of New York, took him on as his chief assistant, at the period when federal authorities were vigorously going after gangsters and racketeers for income tax evasion. Dewey leapt into this work with fervor. He chose some able young assistants, built up a staff fanatically loyal to him, established good techniques in teamwork, and began to become known as an aggressive, fearless, incorruptible prosecutor. Medalie resigned in 1933, and for a brief interval Dewey succeeded him as United States attorney.

Historical accidents are always provocative to explore. I do not mean that Dewey is an accident. I mean merely that in July, 1935, the time, place, and circumstance were all propitious. New York was bursting with corruptions; as in Chicago, thuggery was destroying the reputation of the city. What is more, the rackets struck at the very heart of the business interests of the community; the gangsters were getting rich not merely at the expense of other gangsters, but at that of the free enterprise system itself. All this was made possible, of course, by the co-operation, active or passive, of politicians. A grand jury investigation broke down, and the jury asked the governor of the time, Herbert H. Lehman, impeccably able and distinguished, to appoint a special prosecutor to handle the rackets issue. Lehman set about to find a man. A Democrat, he asked four Republicans in a row to take the job, Charles Evans Hughes Jr., Judge Thomas Thacher, Charles H. Tuttle, and finally Medalie; all four turned it down. Then the offer went to Dewey, who accepted. Where would Dewey be today if Lehman had not chosen him? Where would he be today if Hughes, Thacher, Tuttle, or Medalie had taken the post? It is a rare circumstance indeed that national power and eminence should come to a man as a result of a personal decision not by *one* other man, but by four.

Dewey went into action and put on a very impressive show, with Star Chamber and Blue Ribbon overtones. All the paraphernalia, the hideouts and tapped telephones and so on, became famous. More than any other American of his generation except Lindbergh, Dewey became a creature of folklore and a national hero. What he appealed to most was the great American love of *results*. People were much more interested in his ends than his means. They liked the impression he gave of being a man always in strict training, a zealot. Another key to all this may be expressed in a single word: honesty. Dewey was honest. That he was also relentless, able, dramatic, and full of guts and tricks, hardly mattered. Plenty of people might have been relentless, dramatic, and full of guts and tricks. What I am saying is of course a considerable reflection on the state of civilization in New York City as of that time. What staggered everybody—including the defendants—was that a prosecutor actually *was* an honest man, who could not be fixed or bought, and with no strings attached except his own. He had no ax to grind except that which ceaselessly hewed out his own career.

On the other hand, fighting fire with fire, Dewey used methods which today seem slightly sensational to say the least. Witnesses were held under exorbitant bail; some highly dubious things went on; there is no doubt that some civil rights were violated. The most famous case was that of Lucky Luciano, the vice king. This gaudy episode could be described at vast lubricious length. After Luciano was convicted and safely salted away, it became known that some, at least, of the confessions that helped put him in Sing Sing were wildly, almost comically fraudulent. Also celebrated was the later prosecution of Jimmy Hines. Dewey had to do this job twice. The judge at the first trial threw the case out. To get a conviction against Hines, who was not only deeply involved in the policy racket[4] but a Tammany chieftain of exalted rank, was certainly an achievement. But Hines might not have gone to jail except for evidence from associates who got some very fancy favors from the Dewey staff. Dewey's record was spectacular in some respects. As special prosecutor he is supposed to have gained seventy-two convictions out of seventy-three cases tried. But these figures are not quite so impressive if the details are analyzed closely. Another point is that, after the second Hines trial, Dewey himself seldom appeared in court. He left the actual mechanics of prosecution to his extremely able young assistants.

Dewey ran for public office for the first time in 1937, when he was thirty-five, and was elected district attorney by an overwhelming vote, running on the Republican, Fusion, City Fusion, Progressive, and American Labor Party tickets. That he was supported by the ALP at this time, only ten years ago, will be a surprise to many. Also it may be

---

[4] It is not generally known that this word comes from the Italian, *polizza*. Cf. *Fortune*, New York City issue, July, 1939.

a source of astonishment that the man who led the ticket, running for mayor, was none other than the celebrated Little Flower, Fiorello La Guardia, later to become one of Mr. Dewey's mortal enemies, and vice versa. The whirlpool of New York politics tosses up strange combinations. Dewey was not so active as district attorney as he had been as special prosecutor. For one thing he spent a good deal of time campaigning and running for other offices. He ran for governor in 1938, and was beaten—after a tense, close fight—by Lehman. In 1940 he campaigned all over the country for the Republican nomination for the presidency, but Willkie squeezed him out.

Nevertheless, as one looks back, Dewey's achievement as a prosecutor is substantial. In one category he prosecuted Wall Street's Richard Whitney; in another Federal Judge Martin Manton, who was forced to resign from the bench and who got a stiff prison sentence; in still another Charles E. Mitchell, former president of the National City Bank, over income tax. Mitchell won an acquittal in a criminal suit, but in a civil case was forced to make large restitution to the government. As to gangsters the list is as long as an ape's arm, all the way from "Waxey" Gordon to "Legs" Diamond in the early days to the late Arthur Flegenheimer, alias "Dutch" Schultz, once the boss of those racketeers whose particular prey was restaurants.

Dewey: the National Scene

That Dewey should have proceeded into major politics was of course inevitable. This is a country where, even if you have never had ten minutes of administrative experience, you are a good political candidate if you are celebrated enough. The district attorney's office is almost as conventional a springboard to higher office in New York state as is the governorship to the presidency. The wheels were in full motion by 1940. Some of the professionals did not, however, take Dewey as seriously as did members of his own entourage, when convention time approached. "The original plan," it has been written, "was to use him as a stalking horse and trade him off later." But Dewey was not to be handled in any such cavalier way. One of the Republican hierarchy said, "We drafted this monkey, and, by Jesus, he took us serious."[5]

Dewey ran for the governorship of New York state (after Willkie could not be persuaded to run) in 1942, and won handily. So at last—and he was still only forty—he had reached great office. He was the first Republican governor since 1922, and proudly he took up residence in Albany in what was once called the Stadt Huis. In 1944, as everybody knows, he finally won the presidential nomination, ran against Roosevelt,

[5] This anecdote appears in both a *Harper's* article by Richard H. Rovere and in a merciless *New Yorker* profile by Wolcott Gibbs and John Bainbridge.

and was defeated.[6] In 1946 he ran for re-election to the governorship of New York, and won by the greatest majority known to the history of the state.

We have mentioned Dewey's ambition several times. It is only fair to point out that he has never made the slightest attempt to capitalize his enormous fame, except politically. Even when temporarily out of office, in the middle 1930's, he rigorously resisted any temptation to be vulgarized or exploited. He is by no means a rich man, and he has a healthy regard for the power money brings. He could easily have become a millionaire several times over by succumbing to various movie and radio offers; he would have had to do nothing except give permission for movies or radio serials to be built around his career and name. Be it said to his honor, he never did so. Nor has he ever accepted any of the innumerable invitations to lecture that might have brought him a small fortune.

What beat Dewey in 1944 was not so much Roosevelt as the war. As Irving Brant once wrote, "The choice was not simply between Roosevelt and Dewey, but between Roosevelt and Dewey at Teheran."[7] On the conduct of the war and foreign policy Mr. Dewey was, naturally, in a cleft stick. He could not possibly afford to take nor would he have wanted to take a defeatist line; yet he had to continually attack Roosevelt for the way the war was being conducted. He could not easily condemn the whole structure of the international coalition; thus he was restricted to sniping along the edges, and some of this sniping was pretty silly, as for instance when—mispronouncing the name—he went out of his way to mention a Russian general who had taken part in the Rumanian armistice negotiations. It was revealed later, by John Chamberlain in *Life*, that Dewey had become privy to the secret that the United States had broken the Japanese codes, and had patriotically made no disclosure of this fact during the campaign, though it might have gravely embarrassed the administration. General Marshall, in highly secret and dramatic circumstances, did in fact communicate with Dewey urging him not to speak out. But had Dewey divulged the story, this would almost certainly have cost him more than it would have won, in that people could have said indignantly that he was sacrificing the national interest for private political gain.

Also Dewey had his own awkward past in the field of foreign relations to live down. He was never so overtly isolationist as Taft or Lindbergh. Yet there were some compromising statements on the record. For

[6] But, on becoming governor, he had categorically stated that he intended to fill out his full four-year term, and *not* be a candidate for the presidency. This pledge, as made on December 11, 1942, is absolutely explicit as regards the nomination. Arthur Krock quotes it verbatim in the New York *Times*, June 24, 1944.

[7] *PM*, July 30, 1944.

instance on January 10, 1941, he said that Lend Lease "would bring an end to free government in the United States and would abolish the Congress for all practical purposes." Later of course he changed his mind. Dewey has slipped and slithered a good deal in matters of this kind. Dorothy Thompson, in a famous speech delivered during the campaign, made pointed allusion to certain of these shilly-shallyings:

> What do you think of a campaign in which the candidate accuses the president of not being tough enough with Japan while his supporters suggest that he provoked Japan into war against us?
>
> What do you think of a campaign that suggests that the Republicans in Congress might support a world organization on the Dumbarton Oaks model if Mr. Dewey is president, and might not if Mr. Roosevelt were re-elected?
>
> After the European war was well under way, and the situation of Britain and France was terribly dangerous, I had more than an hour's talk with Mr. Dewey about foreign policy. . . . Mr. Dewey was at that time against any aid to either Britain or France beyond cash and carry . . . He did not believe that the fall of Britain or France would directly menace the United States . . .
>
> All men live and learn. I do not intend now to cast any aspersions upon Mr. Dewey's honesty at that time, however unintelligent I thought his attitude was.
>
> But when Mr. Dewey now attacks the president for not going far enough—at the very time when Mr. Dewey thought he was going much too far—I can only consider it a brazen impertinence.

Dewey, it should be mentioned on the other hand, took a strong line in slapping down men like Gerald L. K. Smith and Hamilton Fish. He forthrightly repudiated Fish, who was running for re-election to Congress, which took courage. There were some notable isolationist Democrats whom Mr. Roosevelt did not quite dare repudiate at the same time, like Walsh of Massachusetts.[8] After Dewey's running mate, the ineffable Bricker, had said that he would welcome Gerald L. K. Smith's vote, Smith's America First party nominated him as its own vice presidential "candidate," without his permission of course. Not one American in a thousand will recall that Bricker was thus a candidate for vice president on two "tickets." Dewey denounced Smith for this in resounding terms—as well he might.

On domestic policy too Dewey had to do some fancy side-stepping. Halfway through the campaign it became clear that it would be suicidal to attack the whole New Deal as such. The people were, at that time at least, in no mood to sacrifice the reforms that had come in twelve long years of effort. In an extraordinary speech on the west coast, Dewey practically came out for Roosevelt's own domestic program. Howard

[8] Cf. *Public Men, op. cit.*, p. 387.

Brubaker commented in the *New Yorker*, "Governor Dewey's visit to the Pacific Coast was fraught with peril. He was in a train wreck in Washington and in California he accidentally swallowed the New Deal." This caused some gnashing of teeth among the more reversionary Republicans, naturally. One columnist wrote, "The new Republican leader accepts definitely the principle of governmental intervention in the economic life of the nation," and another, using his own very special definition of "liberalism," said, "Already, even such a measure as the Wagner Act, which is vicious from the standpoint of American liberalism, is indorsed by Mr. Dewey."

Dewey: Personal

A blunt fact about Mr. Dewey should be faced: it is that many people do not like him. He is, unfortunately, one of the least seductive personalities in public life. That he has made an excellent record as governor is indisputable. Even so, people resent what they call his vindictiveness, the "metallic" and "two-dimensional" nature of his efficiency, his cockiness (which actually conceals a nature basically shy) and his suspiciousness. That Mr. Dewey is crammed with ego is well known. His voice is baritone, but he can sound tenor notes. People say that his sense of humor is vestigial, and that he is as devoid of charm as a rivet or a lump of stone.

I talked to a good many public men during my trip, Republicans and Democrats both, who had worked with Dewey at various conferences. All, to a man, respected his abilities; almost all—perhaps jealousy enters into this—seemed to dislike his personality. During one governors' conference, when each chief executive's car was supposed to take its place in line according to the seniority of the state, he insisted nevertheless on being first. I heard one public official say, "Tom Dewey is the only man I ever met who can strut sitting down."

There are plenty of vain and ambitious and uncharming politicians. This would not be enough to cause Dewey's lack of popularity. What counts more is that so many people think of him as opportunistic. Most Americans like courage in politics; they admire occasional magnificent recklessnesses. Dewey seldom goes out on a limb by taking a personal position which may be unpopular on an issue not yet joined; every step is carefully calculated and prepared; he risks almost nothing; he will never try to steal second unless the pitcher breaks a leg.

But in conclusion there is something else to be said: people may not "like" Dewey, but (*a*) an inner core of advisers and friends, including some extremely distinguished people, have a loyalty to him little short of idolatrous, and (*b*) he is one of the greatest vote-getters in the history of the nation.

Tentative Glimpses of the Empire State

New York, the city, overshadows New York, the state. This is natural, but a pity. The Empire State has, as the phrase is, everything—from a history varied and colorful in the extreme to contemporary statistics that rock and tease the imagination—and some of its wonders ought to be better known. It has spacious frontage on two great lakes; it has Niagara, which in the original Indian means "bisected bottom lands," and that most majestic of all American rivers, the Hudson; it has Long Island nibbling into Manhattan from the Atlantic like a trout with a double tail; it has two husky mountain footstools, and open country astonishingly beautiful, tender, and diverse. It is only the twenty-ninth state in size, but it holds 10 per cent of the population of the United States; every tenth American is a New Yorker, and every twentieth is a resident of New York City.

Think of California with its glowing diversity of agriculture, and Ohio or Pennsylvania with their immense industrial accomplishments; throw the two together, and you have New York. But the Empire State is richer. Its citizens and corporations pay approximately almost a fifth of all federal income taxes, and its industrial development may be gauged from the fact that during World War II it held 9.9 per cent of all war contracts in the nation. As to agriculture, New York has various superlatives. A fantastic proportion of all the ducks eaten in America are raised in a Long Island enclave covering hardly more than a hundred acres, and its dairy business is worth about two billion dollars a year. This is roughly equal to the income from the garment trade. Diversity! In New York City, the sewing machines clatter and the needles fly, producing almost 75 per cent of all the clothes American women wear. A few score miles away, the milk trains thunder all night across the countryside.

New York history goes far back, as everybody knows, to the Dutch and British. To appreciate quickly the nature of the Dutch contribution in one field, we have only to think of names like Roosevelt or Santa Claus—no connection between the two intended. As for the British bedrock consider merely that the present court of general sessions has never missed a meeting since 1776, when it took over without interruption from the royal court of general sessions. Of the 308 battles of the Revolutionary War, ninety-two were fought on the soil of what is now New York state.[9] We have talked in this book about historical markers like those so picturesque in Utah and Montana. New York has six thousand similar markers. Before the Dutch there were, of course, the Indians. Normally we associate Indian lore with the Dakotas, the West, or even the upper middle western states. But New York had the

[9] *New York,* in the American Guide Series, p. 64.

Iroquois, the Algonquins, and the Five Nations Confederacy; there are at least five hundred Indian place names in the state today. New York still maintains an Indian Affairs commissioner, and there is an Indian reservation (Shinnecock) within eighty-five miles of New York City.

The American West is, we like to think, the region par excellence of expanses of property almost limitless. But New York (in great contrast to New England incidentally) was also the home of enormous land grants. We instinctively turn to California when we think of the old railway builders, their exploits and depredations. But New York has a railway story so choked with purple scandal that California's seems like a Sunday school recital by comparison. Recall Gould, Fisk, Drew, and Vanderbilt, to say nothing of some early journalism by a bright young muckraker named Theodore Roosevelt. We think of various religious manifestations and these too we are likely to associate with the West. But the Shakers, the Mormons, the Lily Dale spiritualists, the Oneida Community, and the Millerites who waited for the end of the world on a hilltop, all came out of New York. (So did Chautauqua and the woman's suffrage and temperance movements.) We think of political corruption and Chicago comes to mind. But recollect Boss Tweed. We think of New York—it is almost impossible to think otherwise—as pre-eminently industrial. But its first wealth was built on furs.

The story of California is, we have seen, the story of migrations. That of New York is one of communications and transportation. It is not so much the migrations of people that have made New York, not of people on foot anyway, but the intercommunication of peoples made possible by machines. One need only recall the *Clermont* and the *De Witt Clinton*. Consider too such a phenomenon as the Erie Canal. We have scarcely mentioned canals in this book so far. They played a consummately important role in American development. The Erie Canal, which became in a manner of speaking the Barge Canal of today, was opened in 1825; its function was to lay a water-level route across the state, link the Great Lakes to the Hudson, open up the Mohawk Valley, and tap the dormant hinterland. History repeats itself on ascending planes. Today one of the biggest projects in the state is the tremendous "thruway" which, if it works out as planned, will perform precisely this same set of functions, but by a multi-laned road instead of water, and at seventy miles an hour instead of three.

The assessed value of property in New York state is 24 billion dollars, and it produces 23 per cent more manufactured goods than any other state. It holds 19 per cent of all the factories in the country, and handles more than a third of all American foreign trade—33 per cent of imports, 41 per cent of exports. It has the highest per capita savings in the country, and by far the biggest pool of skilled labor. It has more millionaires than any other state, the greatest volume of retail sales

(13.3 per cent of the American total), and the greatest volume of wholesale trade (26.3 per cent). Its allotment to education is the highest absolutely and proportionately of any state ($169 per pupil-year), and it was the first to establish its own rent controls. It has roads, like the parkways in Westchester, that cost $300,000 a mile to build. Also it has Jones Beach; Sing Sing and Ticonderoga; seventy state parks; the memory of Yankee Doodle and Rip Van Winkle; thirty fish hatcheries; West Point (which is the Fort Knox of silver); the highest waterfall east of the Rockies; celebrated colleges for girls like Vassar; Fire Island and the contemporary mythology of Wolcott Gibbs; and among historical monuments everything from the Battlefield of Saratoga to the home of the author of "Home Sweet Home."

New York is, as everybody knows, a great state for cities, but it has more dude ranches than Wyoming. "The country around New York is surpassingly and exquisitely picturesque," Mr. Dickens wrote more than a hundred years ago. It still is. Fly from La Guardia Field; glance down for a moment at the bridges and the skyscrapers and the roads built by that beneficent Caesar of the parks, Robert Moses; then in an instant you are flying over forest. New York City is the supreme apotheosis of a civilization based on ferroconcrete. Yet there are deer crossings twenty minutes out of Manhattan, and on the tip of Long Island I have seen vegetation literally subtropical.

Finally, the cities. New York state is broken down into eight great economic "areas" by the state Department of Commerce, and seven "districts." Most of these hinge on a city. These hinge in turn on a single industry or complex of industries for the most part, which makes their economy extraordinarily vulnerable. Let the industry shut down, and overnight the city is dead as Baalbek.

BUFFALO (population metropolitan area 857,719, city limits 575,901) is, however, strikingly diversified. It is a great town for milling (it mills more grain than Minneapolis), steel, airplanes, waterpower. Buffalo is, in fact, the eighth industrial city in the nation; in any other state it would have a much greater reputation as a metropolis than it has, but being in New York it is overshadowed by Manhattan, though the latter is 398 miles away. In another direction too Buffalo is diversified; it is one of the most polyglot cities on earth; I had a letter recently asking me to speak at one of its public schools (No. 51), at which children of *twenty-six* different racial stocks are pupils. The chief groups are the Germans (originally from Alsace, the Rhineland, and the Palatinate) and the Poles; whether in East Prussia, Pomerania, or Milwaukee, Poles and Germans seem always to be mixed up together. Buffalo grew slowly; its foundation was the furniture trade and other handicrafts; it is not a toadstool like Detroit. It has several distinguished citizens, like members of the Schoellkopf family (Niagara Falls Power Company),

General William J. ("Wild Bill") Donovan, the wartime head of the Office of Strategic Services, and John Lord O'Brian, a public servant who has worked and worked well for every president since Wilson. Buffalo, according to one of its own councilmen, has the worst rat problem of any American city; its rats "take the tops off the peanut butter jars and dive into the Buffalo River and catch fish." It is a city with a very strong presidential tradition. Fillmore and Cleveland, though not born in Buffalo, lived in it, and Cleveland was once Mayor; McKinley was assassinated in Buffalo, and Theodore Roosevelt was sworn in there. Recently it had a schoolteachers' strike that gained—and deserved—national attention. Its leading politician for years, and a man who came closer than anybody since Thomas C. Platt to being a boss on a statewide level, is Edwin F. Jaeckle, the former Republican state chairman. An old-timer and a hardboiled citizen, he was once close to Dewey, but is not close now.

In ROCHESTER (population 411,970 metropolitan area, 324,975 city limits) we have, as everybody knows, Eastman Kodak. Close to Lake Ontario, and the chief town of the Genesee Valley area, it is an attractive city, a rock-ribbed Republican stronghold for many years, and, in a social sense, something of a center of New York feudalism. People still ride to hounds near Rochester. It is, of course, what with Eastman, one of the great centers of scientific research in the world, and it has a splendid university. Also it is the headquarters of Frank Gannett, father of the so-called Committee for Constitutional Government, who is probably the most reactionary newspaper publisher in the United States.

In central New York is SYRACUSE (population 258,352 metropolitan area, city limits 205,967). Anybody who ever went by rail to Chicago, until about ten years ago, knows how the New York Central trains ground through Syracuse directly on the street level; one was reminded of Rudyard Kipling's furious denunciation of Omaha for permitting the same kind of thing. This has been remedied now. Syracuse, like Rochester, is strongly Republican; it too has a flourishing university; its personality is not quite so distinct as that of Rochester; it has L. C. Smith typewriters and Solvay chemicals, and dozens of other industrial enterprises making everything from traffic signals to building blocks.

The charming town of AUBURN, the headquarters of the Finger Lakes area, is not far away; south of this is ITHACA, with Cornell, which has what is probably the most beautiful university campus in America. Ithaca, nobody will remember, was an early seat of the movie industry: it was here that early serials like the *Exploits of Elaine* were filmed. In the Mohawk valley are ROME and UTICA. Next we reach SCHENECTADY (population 431,575 metropolitan area, 87,549 city limits) which means to most people just one thing, the General Electric Company, as near to being a model corporation as any in the land. Also Schenectady

has a second very large industrial undertaking in the American Locomotive Company. It is a town still redolent with the memory of Dutch
patroons. Nearer Albany is TROY, a famous textile town, and the place
where the detachable shirt collar was invented; it has been severely hit
by various depressions.

The capital, ALBANY (population metropolitan area 431,575, city
limits 130,577), has a varied industrial development; it makes dominoes,
toilet paper, chemicals, billiard balls, and felt. Its history has been rich
since the days of Peter Stuyvesant, and it has a heavy shipping traffic;
boats from all over the world come up the Hudson to its great port.
Otherwise it lives on politics mostly. Not only does it have the
legislature; it was for years a kind of political cloaca maxima, besides
which Kansas City seemed almost pure. Spirited struggles are, as of
this moment, still progressing between the Republican administration
of the state, and the Democratic machine entrenched deeply in the city.

All this is but a top skimming of the New York urban cream. There
should at least be mention of towns like Gloversville (leather), Amsterdam (rugs), Saratoga (society and spas), Hudson Falls (wallpaper),
Pleasantville (*Reader's Digest*), Saranac (tuberculosis), Rheims (wine),
Corning (glass), Poughkeepsie (Roosevelts and regattas), Endicott
(shoes), and Binghamton and Elmira in the "southern tier," i.e. the
counties off the beaten track near the Pennsylvania border, which are
as different from, say, northerly New York towns like Lake Placid as
is Dallas from San Antonio.

Superfinally, a word on Long Island. Here is one of the richest counties in the country (Nassau), and the bailiwick of one of the most prominent state political leaders, J. Russell Sprague. Without Sprague, Dewey
would be much less than he is. Parts of Long Island are slums; parts are
small poultry and rabbit farms almost like those in California; parts are
as delightfully drowsy with fog as Martha's Vineyard; one part at least
is Shangri-La. The North Shore of Long Island, like Newport, is a
suburb of Wall Street, or rather of what is left of Wall Street after the
SEC got through with it; here, in circumstances of entrenched privilege
and luxury of a type growing increasingly rare in the Western world,
lives a unique moneyed society. An essay might some day be written
on the difference between the great Long Island country houses and
estates, from the Roosevelt (Theodore) area near Oyster Bay to the
former Morgan preserves at Glen Cove, and similar houses and properties near London; one difference is that so many of the Long Island
houses, even when lived in, seem like mausoleums. A striking item in
the unexpected came recently when the Soviet Purchasing Commission
rented the 316 acre Morgan estate as a week-end spot for Russian
missions in the New York area. To most of Long Island, this was as if
Caligula or Jack the Ripper had moved in. Lately the Russians an-

nounced that they are giving up the Morgan properties, and moving into the $354,000 Pratt estate near by, which is equally sanctified and opulent. It seems that the Russians have decided to stay. Whereas the Morgan property was rented, the Pratt estate was bought.

St. Lawrence Waterway in 606 Words

Thousands of controversial lines have been written about the St. Lawrence project; the problem is one of the most interesting in the United States. Its gist may be expressed very briefly, though this is not to minimize its importance. What the project would do is open up the Great Lakes to deep-draft ocean traffic, and provide abundant cheap power to the New York and New England areas.

At present a handful of small, shallow-draft ocean vessels do manage to sail up the St. Lawrence and eventually reach Chicago and Duluth; this traffic is, however, as nothing compared to what it might be if sizable ships could get through the fierce 113-mile stretch of rapids between Ogdensburg, New York, and Montreal. Build locks and a great dam here, by-pass the International Rapids (as the Welland Canal, built by Canada, by-passes Niagara), and a 2,300-mile deep-water seaway, striking deep into the heart of the continent, linking the lake ports directly to Montreal and Liverpool, to say nothing of other ports all over the world, would be the result. Think merely what an advantage this would be to the Middle West in freight rates.

On the face of it, nothing more sensible than opening up the St. Lawrence can be easily imagined. The cost (probably some $400,000,000) is not prohibitive, and the engineering problems not insuperable; the advantages to various communities, to Canada, and the American nation as a whole, could be considerable. Quite possibly the project would in time, by giving it direct access to the deep sea, make Chicago the greatest port in the world. Every chamber of commerce from, say, Detroit westward wants the St. Lawrence waterway; in Duluth and the further cities, the cry for it is intense. Presidents Coolidge, Hoover, and Roosevelt favored the project, and so does Truman; so do many eminent citizens of New York, including Mr. Dewey and Mr. Lehman. Those who oppose it have, however, so far managed to keep action from being taken. The opposing forces include the railways, the railway brotherhoods, the power companies, and practically everybody who has a stake in the Port of New York, which means a lot of powerful people, not only in New York City itself but in New Jersey. Antagonists of the scheme assert that it would cost the Port of New York about a sixth of its present volume of traffic. Some opponents of the waterway live far afield, for instance southern senators who think that, just as Chicago and Montreal would be benefited, southern ports like New Orleans would suffer.

But the real issue behind the issue is the familiar one of power. As at present planned, the St. Lawrence project, utilizing the immense weight of water descending from the Great Lakes and concentrated into a short, narrow gorge, would produce more power than Grand Coulee or Boulder. Almost certainly, what with the way the contemporary winds are blowing, this would be put in the hands of some public agency like the TVA. Hence, the private power and utility lobbies have vigorously opposed the idea. Incidentally local power rates in Ontario, which has public power, are only about half those in New York state across the river. That the St. Lawrence project would bring power rates down is indisputable: one authority, Congressman Rankin, says that it would save consumers in New York state alone 153 million dollars per year; the state Power Authority puts the figure at 25 million dollars. Rates in New England, which are the highest in the country today, would also presumably decline. So liberal senators like Aiken of Vermont vigorously support the St. Lawrence project; the conservatives similarly oppose it.

New York Politics in General

Five presidents have been given to the nation by the Empire State; four of these (Van Buren, Cleveland, both Roosevelts) were also governors.[10] Another governor, Samuel J. Tilden, was elected president by popular vote, but he never reached the White House. Also New York is a great state for presidential candidates who don't quite win (Hughes, Al Smith, Dewey), and for vice presidents. Run through the lists of presidential and vice presidential candidates of both parties in each election this century. There are few indeed in which a New Yorker is not one of the four contestants. Also New York's terrific impact lies in the fact that it has more electoral votes than any other state, forty-seven. Nobody has much chance of being elected president (or vice president) of the United States without New York support.[11]

The leader of the New York delegation in Washington today is the senior senator, Robert F. Wagner. A German immigrant boy who rose slowly through power of character and warmth of intelligence, Wagner is one of the best public servants in America, and one of the very few men not American born ever elected to the Senate. No senator has ever done more for labor. He told me once, reminiscing about the Wagner Act, "I've always tried to do what I can for the working fellow." I mentioned to him that one of his colleagues had said that what he believed in most was people—if you give them an even break. "Yes," Senator Wagner

[10] The fifth: Millard Fillmore.
[11] One odd point is, however, that nobody has ever been elected president who had a voting residence in New York *City*. Cf. Noel F. Busch in *Life*, April 22, 1940.

replied, "but try to get 'em an even break." In 1946, in his seventieth year, Wagner was converted to Catholicism.

The junior senator, Irving M. Ives, is still an unknown quantity as far as federal politics are concerned; he holds considerable promise. He was the first Republican elected to the Senate from New York in twenty-six years. It was Ives, now fifty, who set up the School of Industrial and Labor Relations at Cornell, and who was the author of New York's anti-discrimination bill and father of the State Commission against Discrimination. For a time Ives was majority leader in the state legislature, and then speaker, whereupon he became majority leader again. His record has been liberal for the most part. Ives is New York born; his father was a coal merchant in a small town near Syracuse. That Dewey should have picked Ives and insisted that he run for the Senate in 1946 is an important credit item in the Dewey ledger.

Of New York's forty-five congressmen twenty-eight are Republicans, sixteen are Democrats; the odd man is of course Vito Marcantonio of the American Labor party. All the Democrats but one come from Manhattan, Brooklyn, and the Bronx. The delegation as a whole covers a dizzyingly wide arc. Consider such divergent types as the extremely party-linish Mr. Marcantonio, a neighborhood boss powerful enough to have won both Republican and Democratic as well as his own American Labor party nomination; the conservative James W. Wadsworth, a former senator, who would be ranked by almost everybody as among the ten ablest men in the House; the veteran Sol Bloom, a wise and generous man who started work at the age of seven, who wrote the original "Hootchie Kootchie" ballad and who was an entrepreneur at the Chicago World's Fair half a century ago; and another lively veteran who is beginning his thirteenth consecutive term, Emanuel Celler of Brooklyn. Among others are fuddy-duddies who pinch nickels till the metal squeaks, grimly backward upcountry Tories, a handful of careerists who sweat politics from every pore, and isolationist survivors who see a Red—and also the British lion—under every bed. Some of these last hate the Russians much more than they ever hated Hitler. Some perform the delicate intellectual adjustment of putting fear of Russia above all other considerations, while at the same time opposing such things as the British loan; apparently it does not occur to them a weak Britain will tend to increase relative Russian strength.

On the state level the main thing to say about New York politics is that the struggle is mostly one between upstate and New York City. Indirectly at least it is the legislature in Albany that decides what salary a Manhattan traffic cop shall get—to take one of dozens of similar anomalies available. Yet the city is markedly underrepresented in the overwhelming Republican legislature; it has 67 out of 150 members of the assembly, and 25 out of 56 in the senate. This underrepresentation is moreover permanent and statutory; it constitutes a serious discrimination against democracy. The struggle is, I heard it put, one of people against acreage. More than this, the hinterland is not merely geographical. It is often a peripheral area barren in ideas. And even from the purely geographical point of view, suspicion of New York City, the wicked Babylon, can be as acute thirty miles away in Westchester as in the most remote villages of the Adirondacks.

All this finds its hottest, most pointed expression in the standard issue of taxation. What it amounts to in fact is taxation without representation. New York City has something over 55 per cent of the population of the state, and it contributes 74 per cent of all state taxes. Yet, from the state, it gets only 57 per cent of state aid. An area of 365.4 square miles contributes to the state, in other words, nearly three-quarters of the revenue of an area of 49,576 square miles. Or, to put it another way, of every dollar the state receives, and spends, New York City has contributed 74¢, but it gets only 57¢ back. Moreover it costs proportionally much more to run a big city than a rural community. A dollar goes further in Chipmunk Falls than in the Bronx. It costs much less to govern two people in a community of 2,000 than two people in a community of two million. Problems of street repair, police protection, and the like increase almost in geometric proportion to the number of people governed.

"As a sovereign power," writes Leo Egan in the New York *Times*,[12] "the state prescribes what taxes the city can levy and, in many instances, specifies how they shall be used. On the other hand, the city has no control over taxes the state can impose nor can it say how they shall be spent."

What New York City wants is help. The state is rich. The city is not so rich. The current state budget is $671,439,557, and its accumulated surplus is expected to reach 485 million dollars in 1947. New York City's budget is—another paradox—much larger than that of the state, or of any other state; it was $856,960,298 for the present year, and is estimated at $970,000,000 for the next. It has to spend much more money than the state. Mayor O'Dwyer, hat in hand, went to Albany early in 1947 to plead his case. Presently came revealing headlines, like one in the New York *Daily Mirror*, NOT A CENT FOR N.Y.C.—ALBANY. The situation is made the more glaring by the fact that the city may not raise its own revenues, for instance by a boost in the sales tax, without the legislature's permission. Into all this is locked the question of subway fare, as we shall see.[13]

[12] February 9, 1947.
[13] Further technical or financial details are hardly the province of this chapter. They could be written about for pages. O'Dwyer's last request was for an increase in state aid of 102 million dollars. Dewey's reply was that the legislature "should" grant the city permission to install "nuisance taxes" calculated to yield

Turn now to Albany. Not one New Yorker in ten thousand knows the name of his assemblyman; perhaps this is why the legislature, even if New York is the Empire State, is of such indifferent quality; apathy in the public, as we know, induces apathy in government. I talked recently to a highly respected citizen, an expert, who has been in and out of state politics for years; he ticked off, one by one, some of the members of senate and assembly. One, a Christian Fronter. Another, a nonentity from the Bronx with a gambling past. Another, an upstate ward heeler and paid agent of lobbying groups. Another, a survivor from Hines-Davis days, still on the make. "It scares you," my friend said. "No one would believe it if you would tell them what really happens in Albany. Are the people asleep?"

Another experienced observer and critic put it a shade differently: "The New York legislature represents everybody *but* the people."

But New York state as of today has no single effective boss. Like California, it is too big, too various. Even Jaeckle could not establish real authority on a statewide plane. Nor, since about 1906, has any single special interest been able to dominate New York. That was the year (Jimmy Wadsworth was speaker) when the railways were forbidden to issue passes, with which they had bribed multitudinous people. Before this New York had probably been the most corrupt of all states, if only because it was the richest. Things were fought out naked, and plunder really reached baroque proportions.

Also—let us turn to another side of the picture—New York has had some superbly public-minded and courageous servants. The list ranges from Cleveland and the first Roosevelt through Charles Evans Hughes to FDR and the present. Probably the greatest from a local point of view was Al Smith. One remarkable aspect of Smith's career might well be studied by Mr. Truman in the White House today. Smith was a liberal who had a hostile reactionary legislature to face. He got, however, almost everything he wanted, and he put through some markedly liberal measures directly in the teeth of his own lawmakers, by being willing and able to demonstrate, from time to time, that he was a chief executive elected by the people who represented the people, that what he stood for was the people, and what he drew power from was the people.[14]

A final point might be that religious and racial considerations probably play a greater role in New York state—and city—than anywhere else in the nation. Traditionally each party presents a ticket to include as wide

---

24 million dollars. The basis of New York City public finance is the real estate tax. But, another complication, this is held to a certain level, by statutory limitation.

[14] A curious point is that Al Smith almost always warily kept out of New York *City* politics.

a net as possible. For instance the Democrats in 1946 ran a Catholic for governor (Mead), a Jew for senator (Lehman), an Anglo-Saxon Protestant for lieutenant governor (Corning, the mayor of Albany, and one of the best mayors in the nation), and an Italian—by origin at least— (DiGiovanna) for attorney general. Dewey, on his side, was criticized by some Republicans for having no Catholic, no Italian, among leaders on his list; he won anyway, so it didn't matter. But it was unusual that the party should have headed its ticket with two men (Dewey and Ives) both Protestant and Anglo-Saxon.[15] One Jew was, however, conspicuous on the Dewey list—Nathaniel L. Goldstein, the attorney general, and one of the ablest attorneys general the state has ever had.

Nothing could better illustrate all this than the present administration in New York City. The three top men are O'Dwyer (Irish Catholic), Lazarus Joseph (Jewish), and Vincent R. Impelliteri (Italian).

New York Daily News and Vox Pop

I have made frequent passing references to the New York *Daily News*, which by all odds has the biggest circulation of any newspaper in America. On Sunday it is around 4,750,000. I wonder how many people read carefully the department which I like to turn to first, the Voice of the People, one of the saltiest things in American journalism. Here are shrieks, moans, and whistles that cover every conceivable variety of topic. I do not print these letters critically. The *News* is extremely fair in presenting all sides in its correspondence columns. Its letters prove something well known to most Americans, but occasionally ignored, and also something which many foreign observers don't realize at all, the enormous capacity of American citizens to take sides on public issues with ferocious vigor.

Following are some recent judgments by *News* readers on international affairs:

PRESENT FOR RUSSIA

Manhattan: Russia shows by its spy activities in Canada that it badly wants the atom bomb, so I say give the bomb to Russia the same way we gave it to the Japs.

AGREES WITH CHURCHILL

Manhattan: Churchill was right. F.D.R. was the best President England ever had.

---

[15] Widespread pressure was exerted, in fact, to run General William J. Donovan or General Hugh A. Drum, both of whom are Catholic, instead of Ives, though not by any means purely on religious grounds. But Dewey, it seemed, did not want any folk quite so conspicuous. He wanted it to be a clean sweep for Dewey and no one else.

CHECKING OUT

Newark, N. J.: Strikes, discrimination, prejudice, superiority complexes—that describes the United States . . . I'm going to England next month to become a British subject. God save the King, and long live Great Britain!

WANTS SOLDIERS BACK

Orange, N. J.: If we taxpayers were consulted, there wouldn't be one U.S. soldier on foreign soil. . . . We should announce in plain words that if ever again a nation attacks us every man, woman and child in that nation will be condemned to death the same as Goering & Co. have been. Incidentally, it was Japan, not Germany, that attacked us. How come we condemn Goering, but not Hirohito?

RUNNING AWAY FROM WAR

Queens: War with Russia for U.S. and British oil in Iran? Listen; any jackass in Washington, D.C., who thinks I'm sweating out another war is batty. Stand for hours for horse meat, swilly pork, frozen, slimy, stinking chickens? . . . Hell, no! As soon as I see a war looming, I am going to take a plane to Cuba post-haste, and then to South America, and I'm never coming back.

On things domestic, *News* readers are not less vocal:

RADIO HATE LIST

Hartford, Conn.: The public is taking an awful lot of abuse from the radio. Crooners, preachers, politicians, commentators, swing music, and Reds should simply be swept off the ether waves.

REDS VS. UNCLE SAM

Manhattan: Inasmuch as everyone knows the Communists are out to destroy our Government, what is the Government waiting for? Why doesn't it just execute all Communists guilty of direct or indirect attempts to overthrow it?

But:

WANTS VITO FOR PRESIDENT

Manhattan: Why can't we have Vito Marcantonio running for President in 1948? We should have Vito in the White House, and other men like him in Washington, for better conditions.

The *News* supported FDR in 1932, 1936, and 1940, and then turned violently against him. Its readers still find him a favorite object of attack:

WANTS SOULS TO ROT

Bronx: No matter how many crimes the Nazis committed, they never stooped so low as to execute captured generals. That fiendish action remained for the maronic [*sic*] Roosevelt clique to do. May their souls rot in hell forever.

ROOSEVELT AND DISASTER

Manhattan: What do you mean, News, by that crack in your editorial "Pearl Harbor Snafu" that Roosevelt was only partly to blame for the disaster? Why, FDR was the greatest warmonger of all time, was itching to get us into the slaughter from 1933 on. Didn't he keep blasting away at Hitler? Didn't he give the order as early as September, 1941, for the Navy to shoot Axis ships on sight? . . . Why, you dumb oxen, have you forgotten so soon? Pearl Harbor was only a smoke-screen for his devilish World War II plans! Wake up, you dopes, to the truth.

PRESIDENT JOE

Trenton, N. J.: Why not elect Joe Stalin President of the United States in 1948? Then we'll be sure to have a President with courage, prestige and dignity who will work for America first—something neither Roosevelt nor Truman ever did. He is the most courageous man of our time, as witness the fact that he scared Roosevelt to death at the Yalta conference.

Many *News* readers had violent feelings about the UN when it moved into the New York area:

HYDE PARK: DEATH VALLEY

Queens: If the United States MUST be saddled with this white elephant, the UN, then by all means let the world capital be at Hyde Park, N. Y., the graveyard of America's independence. . . . On second thought, how about Death Valley as a world capital site?

Not all *News* letters are on political topics by any means:

EXIT THE LITTLE WOMAN

Bronx: After almost two years overseas, I recently returned home expecting to rush into the arms of my loving wife, only to find that she had cleaned out our bank account and run off with a man who is married and the father of two children. What fools these mortals Le! I still love her.

WANTS HIS MUSIC

Milltown, N. J.: There should be more soft, sweet music on the radio after 11 P.M. How can a fellow cuddle up to his girl with some news commentator yapping in the background?

TURN OFF THE BABIES

Manhattan: Isn't there some way to keep married couples from producing children? All they want is to have little images of themselves running around. What egos!

Finally, the *News* takes great delight in printing attacks on itself:

SAYS THEY WERE NO GOOD

Iselin, N. J.: What a lousy sheet The News has turned out to be! . . . And your so-called Voice of the People is a big fraud and frameup, too. Many people I know have sent you letters praising the Democrats but you did not print any of them. I dare you to print this, you stinkers.

SAYS WE'RE COMMIES

Brooklyn: I think your paper is a dirty, filthy, crummy rag, and it stinks like hell. . . . You are a bunch of Communist rats. I hate everything connected with you, from the editor all the way to the newsboy who sells this stinking paper. I can make my language stronger, but some children might read this.

BOOST FOR BILBO

Brooklyn: Mr. Bilbo was legally elected Senator, so where does Mr. Irving Ives get the right to kick about him? . . . I think The News is owned by Republican millionaires who force The News to keep out all letters to the Voice which are against the Republican Party.

SAYS WE'RE DECADENT PUNKS

Manhattan: Are the editors of The News a bunch of decadent intellectual punks, or are they fitted to direct the people into a better life? I think they are decadent punks, and if we lived in a virile country where dueling was legal I would enjoy meeting these decadent punks in a duel . . .

GOT PLASTERED

Bronx: News, when I realized that your fondest wish would not come true, that you could not soak the people with the 10¢ [subway] fare, I felt so sorry for you that I went out and got stinking drunk.

SAYS WE'RE OPIUM-COATED

Bronx: The News reminds me of an opium-coated poison pill, with sex and crime stories and comic strips covering up malicious columns that work against the people's interests. Your paper exists as a monument to the stupidity of the human race.

As Others See Us

Recently I have been asking visitors from abroad what impressed them most about the United States, with particular reference to the New York area:

An Austrian diplomat: The copiousness and variety of foreign accents heard in the streets.

A German novelist: Space. *Lebensraum.* The impression that no crisis can be really severe or permanent in this country because people are free to move around so much.

A young English girl: The steam rising from manholes in the streets, and the fact that so many policemen are so fat.

A foreign correspondent returning after seven years away: Rise in number and conspicuousness of Negroes, and a breakdown in standards of etiquette.

A wealthy central European refugee: "In the law courts, they have to prove *me* wrong!"

A Norwegian: The lack of capacity of Americans for stable personal relationships.

An English labor leader: "Suburban gardens have no hedges, and children are not taught to be responsible."

A Russian official: The alleged influence of public opinion, and does it actually serve to control events?

A radio commentator returning after long absence: That the United States is the only country that raised its living standard during the war.

A Brazilian: Road signs like those warning motorists, DEATH IS SO PERMANENT.

A British aristocrat of great distinction and long lineage: That so many Americans do not seem to realize that any new war, for instance against Russia, will almost certainly destroy what this country would presumably be fighting for, democracy.

Chapter 33

New York: Sketch of Megalopolis, with a Word on Wall Street

wwwwwwwwwwwwwwwwwwwwwwwwwwwwwwwwwwwwwwwwwwwwwwwwwwwwwwwwwwwwwwwwwwwwwwwwwwwwwwwwwwww

> Submit to no models but your own O city!
> —Walt Whitman

> New York is all the cities.
> —W. L. George

SO NOW we come to New York City, the incomparable, the brilliant star city of cities, the forty-ninth state, a law unto itself, the Cyclopean paradox, the inferno with no out-of-bounds, the supreme expression of both the miseries and the splendors of contemporary civilization, the Macedonia of the United States. It meets the most severe test that may be applied to definition of a metropolis—it stays up all night. But also it becomes a small town when it rains.

Paradox? New York is at once the climactic synthesis of America, and yet the negation of America in that it has so many characteristics called un-American. One friend of mine, indignant that it seems impossible for any American city to develop on the pattern of Paris or Vienna, always says that Manhattan is like Constantinople—not the Istanbul of old Stamboul but of the Pera or Levantine side. He meant not merely the trite fact that New York is polyglot, but that it is full of people, like the Levantines, who are interested basically in only two things, living well and making money. I would prefer a different analogy—that only Istanbul, of all cities in the world, has as enchanting and stimulating a profile.

Also I have heard New York characterized as nothing but "a cluster of small islets in the North Atlantic." These at any rate fling their luster far. The most important single thing to say about Manhattan in relation to the rest of the United States is that it dominates what, for want of a better phrase, may be called American culture. New York is the publishing center of the nation; it is the art, theater, musical, ballet, operatic center; it is the opinion center; it is the radio center; it is the style center. Hollywood? But Hollywood is nothing more than a suburb of the Bronx, both financially and from the point of view of talent. Politically, socially, in the world of ideas and in the whole world of entertainment, which is a great American industry needless to say, New York sets the tone and pace of the entire nation. What books 140 million Americans will read is largely determined by New York reviewers. Most of the serious newspaper columns originate in or near New York; so do most of the gossip columns, which condition Americans from Mobile to Puget Sound to the same patterns of social behavior. In a broad variety of fields, from serious drama to what you will hear on a jukebox, it is what New York says that counts; New York opinion is the hallmark of both intellectual and material success; to be accepted in this nation, New York acceptance must come first. I do not assert that this is necessarily a good thing. I say merely that it is true. One reason for all this is that New York, with its richly cosmopolitan population, provides such an appreciative audience. It admires artistic quality. It has a fine inward gleam for talent. Also New York is a wonderfully opulent center for bogus culture. One of its chief industries might be said to be the manufacture of reputations, many of them fraudulent.

The field of culture or quasi culture aside, New York City's tremendous importance has traditionally been based on four factors:

(1) It was by far the greatest point of entry for European immigrants. Karl Marx, writing in the New York *Tribune* a good many years ago, predicted not only that these would come, but that the great bulk of them, having arrived, would tend to remain in the New York area.

(2) It was by far the greatest American port for exports, primarily of wheat. New York was the city where people came in, and goods went out.

(3) It was the financial and credit capital of the United States.

(4) It was a great place for residents of other American cities to visit, shop in, and throw money at.

New York has to some extent lost ground in all these categories. First, immigration was largely cut off. Second, wheat and other exports turned to other ports (though New York is still the biggest ocean port in the country). Third, Washington replaced it as the financial capital, as we shall see. Fourth (though still the Number One American tourist attraction),[1] New York has lost something of its inevitableness as the place that all Americans want to see before they die.

This situation makes it clear incidentally why New York made such a fight to get the UN. The city is not exactly what you would call moribund, and actually the UN will serve to further its transformation from merely a national into a world metropolis. Nevertheless, most of New York was glad to have the UN safely tucked in between the East River and shabby old Turtle Bay.

[1] "New York is a bigger summer resort than Atlantic City and a bigger winter resort than Miami." Simeon Strunsky, *No Mean City*, p. 52.

"Little Old New York"

More than anywhere else in this book, the author must now steer tightly between Scylla and Charybdis, between saying too much and too little. How can we talk about the Statue of Liberty without seeming ridiculously supererogatory? But how can we omit Brooklyn Bridge and still give a fair, comprehensive picture? One must either take the space to mention something that everybody knows everything about, or else risk omission of things that everybody will think ought certainly to be included.

Park Avenue in summer near Grand Central, a thin quivering asphalt shelf, and the asphalt soft, a thin quivering layer of street separating the automobiles above from the trains below; avenues as homespun with small exquisite shops as Madison, and streets as magnificent as 57th; the fat black automobiles doubleparked on Fifth Avenue on sleety afternoons; kibitzers watching strenuously to see if the man running will really catch the bus; bridges soaring and slim as needles like the George Washington; the incomparable moment at dusk when the edges of tall buildings melt invisibly into the sky, so that nothing of them can be seen except the lighted windows; the way the pace of everything accelerates near Christmas; how the avenues will be cleared of snow and actually dry a day after a six-inch fall, while the side streets are still banked solid with sticky drifts; how the noon sun makes luminous spots on the rounded tops of automobiles, crowded together on the slope of Park Avenue so that they look like seashells; the shop that delivers chocolates by horse—all this is too familiar to bear mention.

That Manhattan was discovered by Henry Hudson in 1609, and bought from the Indians for $24 in 1626 I refuse to enlarge upon. Not so well known are such details as that the city's flag still bears the Dutch royal colors (orange, white, and blue), and that, in 1811, it was decided that only three sides of the City Hall need be finished, since surely there would be no more movement of the city northward. Of course New York has been pushing outward like a swarm of bees ever since, and not merely to the north. It covers 365.4 square miles today; it has upwards of five thousand miles of streets.

As of 1940 the population of New York City within city limits was 7,454,995; as of early 1947, it is estimated at 7,768,000. Only two states, Pennsylvania, and California (aside from New York state itself) contain more people; of the seventy-five nations in the world, it has a greater population than forty-one. By 1970, according to census estimates, the population will have risen to 8,500,000; after 1980, along with that of the rest of the country, it is expected to decline. These figures refer to city limits only. As of 1940 the New York "metropolitan district" actually held 11,690,520 people and an estimate today is that 12,500,000 people live within a radius of thirty-five miles, making the area by all odds the greatest urban concentration the world has ever known. Newark and Jersey City are, to all intents and purposes except politically, subdivisions of Manhattan; I have heard a Pennsylvanian say that even Scranton was "part of New York"; speaking in the broadest way, "New York" includes the whole region from Bridgeport to Trenton and beyond.

Turn now to racial fusions. The best remark I know in this field is from Bryce, that New York "is a European city, but of no particular country." He might of course have said, "but of many countries." Details are well known. For instance *two hundred* newspapers not in English are published in New York. We have talked about enclaves like Hamtramck in Detroit. New York is full of Hamtramcks. More than two million New Yorkers are foreign born; more than two and a half million others are of foreign or mixed parentage. Of the foreign-born the largest group is Italian (more than 400,000), followed closely by Russian (395,-000), and with Germany (225,000), Eire (160,000) and Poland (195,000) next. Those of mixed parentage follow the same order. There are 26,884 foreign-born Czechs, 28,593 Greeks, and 12,000 Chinese. All told there are representatives of at least seventy nationalities in New York, from Bulgarians to Yemenites. Cutting across national categories are the Jews, of whom the city has about two million; New York is, as everybody knows, overwhelmingly the first Jewish city in the world.

A grave and estimable Bourbon of my acquaintance put it to me a few days ago, with internal frothings but probably with tongue in cheek as well, that the most powerful single influence in the United States today is that of Minsk, the provincial capital of Byelo-Russia. His train of thought went like this. Minsk is the birthplace of Max Lerner, the well-known editorial writer and political scientist. Lerner runs *PM*. *PM* runs the American Labor party. The American Labor party runs New York City. New York City runs New York state. And New York state of course runs the nation.[2]

Hamilton Fish Armstrong, writing in *Foreign Affairs*, once had some illuminating things to say about the New York potpourri. One is that, in spite of all that has been added, the basic Anglo-Dutch stock still gives marked coloration to the city. Another is that New York's conglomerateness dates from the very beginning, and has given it a tolerance unmatched by any other American city except one much smaller, San Francisco. From the early Du Ponts to Otto Habsburg, from Leon Trotsky to Haya de la Torre, Manhattan has been traditionally generous to refugees. It has a cosmopolitanism of the mind as well as pocket. It may be built on islands, but it is not insular.

New York of course has religions in profusion too. It is a very strong

[2] David Sarnoff, one of the most enlightened capitalists in the United States and president of the Radio Corporation of America, was also born in Minsk.

Roman Catholic and Episcopalian as well as Jewish city. It is the headquarters of the Collegiate Reformed Protestant Dutch church, and it
has a powerful upper sprinkling of Christian Scientists. The best indication of the importance of religion in New York is real estate. Stroll
down Fifth Avenue. In block after patrician block are churches of
various denominations occupying sites of the most prodigious value.
Or—as an instance of the influence of religion in another secular field—
consider Christmas shopping.

It is a proud boast of New York that, what with its enormous pools
of foreign-born, any article or object known in the world may be found
there. You can buy anything from Malabar spices to stamps from
Mauritius to Shakespeare folios. A stall on Seventh Avenue sells about a
hundred different varieties of razor blades. Also it is incomparably the
greatest manufacturing town on earth; in an average year it produces
goods valued at more than four billion dollars. It houses no fewer than
36,000 different industrial concerns, representing more than 312 different
manufactures—even if, as noted in the chapter preceding, you can see
deer in Westchester a few miles away. Also it is by far the first city in
the nation in the service industries. Manhattan alone employs more wage
earners than Detroit and Cleveland put together; Brooklyn more than
Boston and Baltimore put together; Queens more than Washington and
Pittsburgh put together.[3] The two most important New York industries
are printing and the garment trade. To attempt to describe Manhattan,
without at least one mention of the Garment Center, is impossible.
Everybody knows how, on the one hand, mammoth trucks choke the
streets between 34th and 38th, and how, on the other, men on foot push
through the crowds with their movable racks hung with clothes. The
Garment Center means also that New York has two of the most powerful unions in the country, the Amalgamated Clothing Workers which
was Sidney Hillman's union, and the International Ladies Garment
Workers Union run by as able a man as American labor knows, David
Dubinsky. This union has elaborate extracurricular activities, like its
famous summer camps. Once it produced a musical comedy, *Pins and
Needles*, that became a great Broadway hit.[4]

In *Inside Asia* I had a small passage describing the variety of strange
occupations in India, like grasshopper selling. I have just thumbed
through the classified New York telephone directory, a volume 1,600
solid pages long. Among occupations in New York are cinders, chenille
dotting, bullet-proof protective equipment, breast pumps, bungs, boiler
baffles, glue room equipment, abattoirs, flow meters, eschatology, mildew-
proofing, pompons, potato chip machinery, rennet, spangles, solenoids,

[3] New York *Herald Tribune*, June 21, 1945, quoting *A Survey of the New York
Market* published by the Consolidated Edison Company.
[4] A *New Yorker* cartoon of the time presented two girls sweating at their sewing
machines. One says to the other, "Now what's my cue line after your song in
Act II?"

and spats. Also this book contains literally twenty-two columns of associations of one kind or another.

Items in Physiognomy

No king, no clown, to rule this town!
—William O. Bartlett

Well, little old Noisyville-on-the-Subway is good enough for me.
—O. Henry

As almost everybody knows, New York is divided into five counties called boroughs. The extraordinary tongue of MANHATTAN is only 12½ miles long and 2½ miles wide, but by 1947 estimates it contains 1,906,-000 people. It has twenty bridges, roughly 100,000 out-of-town visitors a day, 915 night-clubs, Columbia University, and Central Park, which many people think is the most satisfactory park in the world, with its 840 acres spread out like a carpet for the skyscrapers to tiptoe up to. It has subdivisions as divergent as Kips Bay, the Gas House District, Hell's Kitchen and Greenwich Village. BROOKLYN (estimated population 2,798,000) is of course a world in itself, with local bosses like Peter J. McGuinness, a fierce local nationalism, the Dodgers, the Bush Terminal, Coney Island, and the *Tablet*, one of the most reactionary Catholic papers in the country. Geographically Brooklyn, which was once spelled Bruekelen, is the huge, bumpy, watery "head and shoulders" of Long Island. It covers 88.8 square miles; merely to list its street names takes 192 pages in a pocket guide. It delivers the biggest Democratic vote in the nation, and is a famous haunt of Christian Fronters; the viceroy of this formidable province, who died in 1946, was Frank V. Kelly. The BRONX, which borders on Westchester County and is the only borough on the mainland, covers 54.4 square miles and has 1,489,000 people. It is heavily Jewish like Brooklyn, and likewise a great community for baseball, having the Yankee Stadium; it contains sub-Bronxes like Throg's Neck, Morrisania, Clason's Point, and Mott Haven. It has its own flag, a well-known zoo, the Hall of Fame of New York University, and seven hundred miles of streets; for a proud interval it called itself the capital of the world, when the UN sat at Hunter College.

In the Bronx, one might say in parenthesis, live two notable New York politicians, Edward J. Flynn and Michael J. Quill. Mr. Flynn, its boss for many years, has craggy importance on the national level too; he is a former chairman of the Democratic National Committee, and FDR once named him ambassador to Australia. He was rejected by the Senate, however, because some Belgian paving blocks got found in the wrong place. Of all the great American municipal bosses, Flynn is the most superior, the most civilized and cultivated man. Mr. Quill is on the left-wing side of the political fence. He was born in County Kerry in 1905, and was a soldier in the Irish Republican Army; he came to New York, and got a job as a subway worker. Quill is two things today: head of the powerful Transport Workers Union, which threatened a serious strike in 1946, and a city councilman.

QUEENS, the biggest borough in area (126.6 square miles), has 1,456,000 people; it is the most diffuse of the boroughs, the least distinctive.[5] It has La Guardia Field and Forest Hills, the tennis capital of America; it has 196 miles of waterfront, and relentlessly unending rows of ugly small houses; in Queens, as well as anywhere in the country, you may see how a great city frays at the periphery; no community has more untidy edges. Finally, RICHMOND (population 186,000) which is another world in itself, Staten Island. A curious community, half an hour away by boat, Richmond has only one vote out of sixteen in the Board of Estimate (the governing body of New York City); this it resents, and occasionally it threatens to secede.

One should, at this point, at least mention the other New York islands; they are untidily picturesque—Governor's Island, North Brother Island, Randall's Island, Riker's Island—to say nothing of Ellis, Welfare, and South Brother. Then too there are the great and vital rivers, the Hudson, "like a state highway" as a writer in the *Times*[6] said aptly, and the East, "synonymous with poverty and ugliness," "churlish and oil-pocked," "treated with no more reverence than . . . a subway excavation, and traditionally New York's watery main street."

Finally, the Port. Here, once more, we reach what Hollywood (or New York) would call the supercolossal. "This is at once the front door of the nation and its service entrance."[7] The Port of New York, run and run well by its unique authority, is the biggest natural harbor in the world; it comprises "seven bays, four river mouths, four estuaries"; it covers 431 square miles of water, has 307 miles of shore line, and 1,800 docks. Out of it, in a normal year, travel some 60 million tons of goods on 13,000 ships, to carry 41.7 per cent of the entire foreign trade of the United States.

New York, Neighborhoods & Spectacle

> The city like a ragged purple dream, the wonderful, cruel, enchanting, bewildering, fatal, great city.
> —O. Henry

> Vulgar of manner, overfed,
> Overdressed and underbred.
> —Byron R. Newton

A point to make now is New York's extreme brittleness, its vulnerability. As fascinating as any story in America is how it gets its water;

---

[5] Four subdivisions of New York City are, it will be seen, greater in population than any American cities except Chicago, Philadelphia, Detroit, and Los Angeles.
[6] Article by Murray Schumach, January 19, 1947.
[7] *New York City*, in the American Guide Series, Random House, p. 410.

the supply system represents an investment of two billion dollars, and some water comes from points at least a hundred miles away. What might a small bomb or two, at any of several strategic points, do to this enterprise? Also the city's life depends on water in another direction, that is, on the bridges and tunnels by which water is traversed. New York learned grimly about its vulnerability in this respect during a tug-boat strike early in 1946. A handful of 3,500 workers, manning three hundred tugboats, paralyzed the city from stem to stern; the entire Atlantean metropolis was forced to shut down for 16 hours. Most neutral observers thought that the operators had as grave, if not a graver, responsibility for this strike than the AF or L workers who struck; but this is beside the point. What counted (and could count again) is that the city, without these tugboats, cannot live. New York uses about 34,500,000 pounds of food a day, 98,000 tons of coal, and 4,000,000 gallons of oil, which help provide its gas, steam, and electricity. Seventy per cent of all this is moved by tugs and barges. Consider too elevator strikes; a brief one occurred in September, 1945. New York City has more than 43,000 elevators (about 20 per cent of all in the country), which carry about 17,500,000 passengers daily. Their shafts, put end to end, would stretch 1,600 miles; they go halfway to the moon, 125,000 miles, every day. When the elevators stop, New York stops too.[8]

At the Manhattan skyscrapers, every name in the book has been thrown. They have been called "the inconceivable spires of Manhattan, composed, repeating the upthrust torch of Liberty," "gypsum crystals," "a mass of stalagmites," "a ship of living stone," "an irregular tableland intersected by shadowy canyons," "dividends in the sky," "a giant cromlech," and, best of all, "a pincushion."[9] A more utilitarian-minded description is one by H. G. Wells; the skyscrapers reminded him irresistibly of the commercial nature of our civilization, being like "piled-up packing cases outside a warehouse."

Last Christmas I sent a lady a book. She lives in the Waldorf-Astoria Towers but the bookstore didn't understand me on the telephone, and, remarkable as it may seem, the book was dispatched not across the street but a distance of some 2,500 miles, to Mrs. So-and-So, Waldorf-Astoria, Taos (New Mexico). When it was retrieved I could not but reflect that, after all, American history is little more than the record of progress from Taos to Towers. Progress? New Yorkers, cliff dwellers still, have simply moved into a new type of pueblo.

[8] These figures and details are all from the New York *Times*, September 30, 1945, and February 10, 1946. A remarkable point is the safety record of the New York elevators. The ratio is one person killed to 196,000,000 carried.
[9] These phrases are from a brilliant essay on New York by Vincent McHugh. It was originally published in the New York City volume of the WPA series, and was later reprinted by Clifton Fadiman in his anthology, *Reading I've Liked*.

No city changes so quickly as New York; none has so short a memory or is so heartless to itself; it has an inhuman quality. Very few New Yorkers pay the slightest attention to the historical monuments that fill the city. Most know very little about its wonders. How many realize that, by a simple mathematical trick, anybody can calculate where house numbers on the avenues are? How many ever recall that Theodore Roosevelt was born at 26 East 20th Street,[10] or that the oldest building in the city is on Peck Slip, or even that a three-million-dollar treasure ship is supposed to be lying in the East River near 53rd Street? My publisher lives in the east 30's. I had been in his delightful house fifty times before I learned that James Monroe had once lived in it.

Glance at Baedeker's *United States* of 1893. To what sights does this worthy guide give its severely rationed stars? What was the 1893 equivalent of Rockefeller Center? Let the reader go to the public library and find out. But as to other details the midtown hotels starred are the Everett House, the Westminster, and the Windsor. ("Fees to waiters and bellboys are unfortunately becoming more and more customary in New York hotels.") The first uptown restaurant starred is the Café Brunswick; the chief "oyster saloon" is Dorlon's; the first theater mentioned is Daly's ("Shakespearean and modern comedy—Miss Ada Rehan"). As to shops, Baedeker says, "Many of the New York shops are very large and handsome, easily bearing comparison with those of Europe." As to baths it mentions that "hot and cold baths may be obtained at all the hotels (25¢-75¢) and large barber shops."[11]

One extraordinary phenomenon all over New York is its unequal rate of growth. On one side of a courtyard in the east 60's is a glittering modern apartment house where, I doubt not, you could find a tolerable small place to live for a rental of $5,000 a year, if apartments were available at all. On the other side, not fifty feet away, is a dirty balcony hung with laundry, part of a frowsy tenement built over squalid shops.

I live in midtown Manhattan; I have just walked around the block to see concretely what illimitable variety this neighborhood affords. Within a hundred yards I can go to church, have my hair cut, admire flowers, visit two banks (both low Georgian buildings in red brick), and dine in one of the supreme restaurants of the world or at Hamburg Heaven. Within a slightly greater radius I can buy a Cézanne ($55,000), a chukar partridge ($7.50), a pound of Persian caviar ($38), or a copy of the Civil Service *Leader* (10¢). Within two hundred yards are three competing pharmacies comfortably busy, a shop for religious goods and

---

[10] Strunsky, *op. cit.*
[11] Another item is that the average Englishman will find offensive the American habit of spitting on the floor, but that the Americans are now keenly alive to this "weak point" and are "doing their best" to remove it.

missals, a delicatessen squeezed into a four-foot frontage, windows full of the most ornately superior English saddlery, a podiatrist, a good French bookstore, a Speed Hosiery repair shop, and, of course, the inevitable small stationery shop with its broad red band across the window advertising a variety of cigar.

New York is so volatile, so diffuse, that it has no more recognizable social frontiers; it is too big a community to be a community. As *Fortune* once observed, even the greater millionaires no longer live in houses for the most part, but in apartments; the *Social Register* contains upward of 30,000 names. Fifty years ago the "400" constituted a genuine enough inner nucleus. Today practically anybody who can buy a drink at "Twenty-One" or be seen in the Cub Room of the Stork Club is a member of society, because the criterion is no longer merely wealth or lineage. It is not Mrs. Vanderbilt who draws attention at the opera; it is a visiting movie star. Nor does it matter much nowadays where people live; anybody who has the money can buy a house in the east 70's (if he can find the house). People shoot up; people shoot down. Ask any New Yorker to list the dozen leading citizens of the town. The variety of names you will get is astonishing.

Finally, what are the chief New York issues today, political, semi-political, and otherwise? First, traffic. The violent snarled congestion in bursting streets costs the city at least a million dollars a day. Second, housing. Mayor O'Dwyer estimates that the city has an "absolute shortage" of 150,000 apartments, which means that about 500,000 people are living "under the crudest and most difficult conditions." Another estmate is that 450,000 families, or roughly one-fifth of the total population, live in "subhuman" tenements or houses. Third, a complex internecine struggle over airport development and the future of the great airport now being built, Idlewild. Fourth, the subway fare. It costs the city about 70 million dollars a year to maintain this ("Biggest Ride in the World," about twenty-five miles) at a nickel.

"Go East, Young Man"

New York City sucks in humanity from all over the world, as it sucks in New Orleans prawns and Idaho potatoes. This city, a parasite, would die without new blood. New Yorkers born in New York City are, as is notorious, rare. Consider some distinguished citizens in various fields and where they came from. John J. McCloy, presumptive president of the world bank, was born in Philadelphia, James A. Farley in Grassy Point (New York), Judge Sam Rosenman in San Antonio, Herbert Bayard Swope in St. Louis, and Gustav Metzman, president of the New York Central, in Baltimore. Henry R. Luce was born in China,

Elsa Maxwell in Iowa, and Judge Learned Hand in Albany. Harold Ross, editor of the *New Yorker*, comes from Aspen, Colorado, and Lewis W. Douglas from Bisbee, Arizona. H. V. Kaltenborn was born in Wisconsin, George Jean Nathan in Indiana, Bruce Bliven of the *New Republic* in Iowa, and Winthrop W. Aldrich, probably the most important banker in the city, in Rhode Island. Among great churchmen John Haynes Holmes was born in Philadelphia and Harry Emerson Fosdick in Buffalo. The Van Doren literary family derives from Illinois, Mary Simkhovitch from Massachusetts, and Mrs. Ogden Reid of the *Herald Tribune* from Wisconsin. Walter S. Gifford, president of AT&T, was born in Massachusetts, former governor Charles Poletti in Vermont, Sherman Billingsley in Oklahoma, John W. Davis in West Virginia, and Arturo Toscanini in Parma, Italy. There are, of course, a few exceptions. Robert I. Gannon, president of Fordham University, was born on Staten Island, and former comptroller Joseph D. McGoldrick in Brooklyn. Born actually in Manhattan are Gilbert Miller, the theatrical producer, Arthur H. Sulzberger, publisher of the New York *Times*, Hamilton Fish Armstrong, and Charles G. Bolté, the brilliant young chairman of the American Veterans' Committee.

Mayor Bill O'Dwyer and City Politics

Countless times in this book we have mentioned people with a great variety of experience, but I know none who quite matches O'Dwyer for abundance in this respect. He was born in 1890 in Bohola, County Mayo, Ireland, one of eleven children; both his parents were schoolteachers.[12] He ran off to Spain when a boy, and studied for two years with the Jesuits at the University of Salamanca; he planned to be a priest. But he changed his mind, took ship for New York, and arrived here in 1910, twenty years old, with $23.35 in his pocket. In the next few years he held every possible sort of job. First he became a handyman in a Bronx grocery at $9 a week; then he worked as a deckhand on a freighter in the South American trade, as a stoker, and later as a fireman on the river boats between New York and Albany. Meantime, he studied stenography at night school. He had a turn as a hod carrier and plasterer's apprentice, working on a building near Maiden Lane; he can look out from the City Hall today and see where the scaffolding was, and he still holds his membership in the Plasterers Helpers Union, AF of L. Also—it pleases him to recall this now—he was a bartender for a brief elegant period in the Hotel Plaza.

Then came a great decision. O'Dwyer decided to become a cop. He

[12] Two of his brothers, who also emigrated to America, met violent deaths; one, John, was killed by gunmen in a Brooklyn holdup some years ago; another, James, a New York City fireman, lost his life while answering a false alarm.

had been granted United States citizenship in 1916, and he joined the New York police department a year later. Also he kept on studying at night, now at Fordham Law School; it was a long grind, but he was graduated in 1923. Finally, in 1925, after great ardors and sacrifices, he was admitted to the New York bar.

The fact that Mayor O'Dwyer, who has the nice numerical luck to be the one-hundredth elected mayor in New York City history, was a policeman has considerable importance. It means, first of all, that he knows cops. One can talk about issues and involvements like housing, subways, or what you will, but basically the mayor of any great American city stands or falls by his police department. Any time a police department, through horrible circumstance, chooses to embarrass a mayor by lying down on the job, the mayor is beaten. There are 19,000 policemen in New York City, and it is no easy thing to keep that many men, who may be continuously exposed to temptation, honest all the time. The average New York cop gets $3,420 a year. Twice a week, in the old days anyway, he may have had to turn down a hundred-dollar bill. The police have nice distinctions in graft. Gambling money, so the legend goes, is "clean"; vice money is, however, dirty. The terrific difficulty of dealing with gambling may be illustrated by one small point, that at Mr. La Guardia's request the Stock and Curb exchanges for a brief time published no daily sales totals except in round numbers, so that the tens of thousands of people in the "policy" racket couldn't use the last digits as the basis for their calculations.

But to resume. Mr. O'Dwyer knows cops and understands them and likes to deal with them. He was an honest cop himself and he has an honest police force now. He took over the commissioner appointed by Mr. La Guardia, Arthur W. Wallender, gave him a free hand to do a good job, and backed him up.

O'Dwyer's political career may be outlined briefly. In 1932 he was appointed a city magistrate, which meant that he was politically "right." Governor Lehman promoted him to the county court in 1938; later he won an election to a fourteen-year term on this bench. This was a well-paid job, and he could have looked forward to security and a pleasant routine existence for years and years. He dropped it the next year, however, to run for the district attorneyship of Kings County (Brooklyn), and won. His record in this post—though a subsequent investigation accused him of mild inefficiencies—made him famous. The job he did as a prosecutor is fully as remarkable as Dewey's, though he never sensationalized it as Dewey did. Brooklyn had, in those years, a gang nicknamed Murder Incorporated, led by a notable killer named Louis Lepke and including some fancy folk like Abe "Kid Twist" Reles; that O'Dwyer got first-degree murder indictments against Lepke who was later duly electrocuted, and several of his lieutenants, is as unprecedented in its field as Dewey's conviction of Jimmy Hines. Altogether, O'Dwyer's friends say that he solved eighty-seven murders. His opponent in the 1945 mayoralty race, however, charged widely that his record was spurious in several important respects, that most of the real work was done by an assistant prosecutor, and that wily folk behind the scenes, who were the masters of the actual front-line killers, were never touched. However, the fact remains that Murder Incorporated was broken up.

In 1941, O'Dwyer ran for mayor; La Guardia beat him. Came the war. O'Dwyer volunteered for service the day after Pearl Harbor, and was presently commissioned as a major; the Army put him to work investigating contract frauds, and by 1944 he was a brigadier general. Then Roosevelt sent him as his personal representative to the Allied Control Commission in Italy, and later he was appointed executive director of the War Refugee Board. He ran for re-election as Kings County district attorney in absentia while still in the Army; Democratic, Republican and American Labor parties all endorsed him. Then came the mayoralty race of 1945. (New York, like most American cities, has its mayoralty election in off-years.) O'Dwyer won—there were some highly special circumstances connected with this election as we shall see—with an absolute majority of 285,000, and the biggest plurality in the history of the city.

His first year in office, at what is generally considered the third biggest and most difficult job in the United States, was certainly trying enough. He had the tugboat strike to deal with, and then the threat of a subway strike. His wife, who had been a telephone operator at the Hotel Vanderbilt when he met her in 1916, died after a long and exhausting illness. His appointments were excellent on the whole; he kept some of the best La Guardia men, like Bob Moses; he got William H. Davis, former head of the War Labor Board, to work with him on transportation. He fired two of his cabinet members, one following a scandal in professional football, the other after a tenement collapsed with the loss of thirty-seven lives. He worked hard to bring the UN to New York; it might not have come, however, had not John D. Rockefeller Jr. made possible the purchase of the site through an $8,500,000 gift. He did what he could on taxes, sought to bring a showdown on subway fare, and raised the pay of city employees to meet the advancing cost of living. In a city like New York, however, very little of this really matters. What does matter is the relation of a mayor to what is behind him. O'Dwyer is, after all, a Democrat. What everybody wanted to know was what he was going to do with Tammany. "A vast, corrupt organization, starved through twelve long years, is panting for its revenge," wrote the New York *Herald Tribune* when he assumed office. During the La Guardia years, Tammany was of course frozen out. Was Mr. O'Dwyer going to let it in again, and if so in what form? The answer to this came in early 1947, after prolonged sub-surface struggles. The mayor pushed out the old Tammany leaders, shook the organization up from top to bottom, removed some of its more adhesive members, and became, in effect, Tammany chieftain himself with the slate washed clean.

I went down to the City Hall the other day and had an hour with O'Dwyer after not having seen him for several years. He is a shade grayer, a shade stockier, and still a grand man to talk to—easy-going, bluff, friendly, and informal. He wore a light brown sports jacket; he was as relaxed—working a fourteen-hour day—as a character in the *Crock of Gold*. O'Dwyer has heavy, very short, blunt fingers, a decisive nose, and expressive, eloquent blue eyes. He is full of Irish wit and bounce. Also he is very modest. Mostly we talked about things personal. But occasionally there were remarks like, "How the hell *does* democracy work, anyhow?" This was not, I hasten to add, said with any lack of faith. The mayor is a very gregarious man, and he loves people; especially he loves those who have fought their way out of a bad environment. What he hates most are stuffy people. ("I am sorry for the selfish ones; they only see one side.") I asked him how he took the load off. "A thousand ways!" One is music and another books. Then suddenly Mr. O'Dwyer was reminiscing about his childhood. "It was all a series of breaks . . . you know how rebellious Irish kids are . . . and every-body yearning for a piece of poetry." He wanted to be a doctor. Medi-cine, the mysterious agencies of disease, the world of pain, fascinated him, and he was bursting with humanity for the sick, though "healthy as a trout" himself. To contribute to that field, he thought, would be some-thing. "What is it that makes people happy? To contribute!" He couldn't afford the long years of schooling that medicine entailed; he chose the law as the next best thing. "When a guy gets along in his twenties he begins to get uneasy; people stare at themselves, and know that they'll be sore as hell at life at sixty if they don't do something to improve themselves." He asked himself, while a cop on a beat, "Is life just a process of eating and destroying food?" The urge to get ahead stirred him, as he put it, "like a bug on an elephant's tail." And to do some-thing for the little fellow. As a magistrate he had the power to be a tough guy, "to swing a hatchet." When youngsters and old men came into his court he tried to "soothe 'em down." Then suddenly O'Dwyer was talk-ing about what is, as he knows and everybody knows, the dominant problem of our time, the relationship of government to the people. I asked him what he was proudest of in his record as mayor so far. He hesitated. "The guy who follows me will find a million things wrong, of course." Again he paused. "One thing I kinda like—it might be a con-tribution." This is a system he has worked out for dealing with potential labor troubles before they reach a climax; a body called the division of labor relations goes to work a month before the expiration date of any collective agreement so that, if there is the possibility of a strike, early discussions may avert it.

A word now on the 1945 mayoralty election that brought O'Dwyer in. Of all crazy elections in the history of New York City, this was certainly the craziest. He was the candidate of both the Democratic and American Labor parties, which was interpreted by anti-O'Dwyer folk as meaning that he was the candidate of (*a*) Tammany and (*b*) the Communists, unnatural as this coalition may seem. Of course O'Dwyer is about as Communistic as Saint Peter or Monsignor Sheen. In the old Brooklyn days the Christian Front boys vociferously sided with him for the most part. Nevertheless, he was bracketed with Vito Marcantonio, the industrious leader of the ALP. O'Dwyer, a good vote-getter with a good record, was obviously going to be a hard man to beat. After ponderous deliberations (in which Governor Dewey of course shared) the Republicans chose a judge of the general sessions court, Jonah J. Goldstein, to run against him.[13] This was in part a device to catch the Jewish vote which is roughly 30 per cent of the total city vote as a rule. The only trouble with Judge Goldstein was that he was a Democrat! This fact may not be believed by the man from Mars, but it is true. Judge Goldstein, the Republican candidate to beat O'Dwyer, was a member of the Democratic party until the night before the nomination.[14]

Meantime, of course, much finagling had been going on in higher reaches of the Democratic party too—Roosevelt, Hannegan, Flynn, Kelly, all played a role. O'Dwyer would not consent to run until after a stiff fight with both Kelly and Flynn, who wanted to put people on the slate he wouldn't have. Finally O'Dwyer (Democrat-ALP) and Goldstein (Republican but a Democrat) squared off against one another. Also behind Goldstein were the Fusion and the Liberal parties—which, however, were not at the time parties! All seemed simple. Then entered a new and disruptive factor—the Little Flower. Previously Mr. La Guardia had announced the names of a dozen people who he thought would make good mayors and whom he would support, among them Adolf A. Berle Jr., Lewis W. Douglas, Robert Moses, Gordon S. Rentschler, chairman of the board of the National City Bank, General Brehon Somervell, and Newbold Morris, then president of the City Council. Now Mr. Morris (an able and amiable man, about whom the crude witticism was spread that he had been born with a silver foot in his mouth) decided to enter the race himself. This made the struggle triangular. La Guardia vigorously supported Morris, who ran as a "No Deal" candidate. He knew of course that this would split the opposition,

---

[13] Not to be confused with Attorney General Goldstein mentioned in the last chapter.
[14] *Time*, September 24, 1945.

and help elect O'Dwyer; the only explanation is that (though in theory
a Republican himself and a mortal foe of Tammany) La Guardia disliked
the Dewey-Goldstein brand of Republicanism so much that he was
willing to see a Tammany Democrat elected. O'Dwyer would have won
anyway. Nevertheless, Morris' candidacy did what Mr. La Guardia
hoped it would do, and the New York *Herald Tribune* was soon writing,
"The fundamental reason why William O'Dwyer is mayor today is that
Mr. La Guardia willed it."[15]

Tiger Tamed; Wigwam Sublet

> They have such refined and delicate palates
> That they can discover no one worthy of their ballots,
> And then when someone terrible gets elected
> They say, There, that's just what I expected.
> —Ogden Nash*

> A reformer is a guy who rides through a sewer in a glass-
> bottomed boat.
> —The late James J. Walker

> Voters of the laboring class in the cities are very emotional . . .
> In the lower wards [of New York City] where there is a
> large vicious population, the condition of politics is often fairly
> appalling, and the local boss is generally a man of grossly
> immoral public and private character.
> —Theodore Roosevelt in 1886

Of various puppets and ephemeral riffraff in New York City politics
this book tells nothing. Nor have we the space to mention here how
proportional representation makes a goulash of elections to the city
council, how New York (just like a village) has big red signs near the
polls telling people not to loiter, how Fusion is not something that you
can call up on the telephone, how the Greater New York City Charter was
first set up and how the city has a triple central government the interrelations of which can only be calculated by a slide rule, how the well-
known entrepreneur of slot machines, Mr. Costello, lost $27,200 in a taxi
and finally got about $150 back, and how the Liberal party broke off from
the American Labor party (the father of which was Mr. La Guardia)
after a vicious left-right split.

But about the institution known as Tammany and its camorra we must,
if only for the record, have a brief line. Actually Tammany goes back into
American history as far as the federal government itself. One of its
founders was Aaron Burr, and it was a quite worthy organization in
older days. Bob Wagner and Al Smith both came out of Tammany.

---

* Copyright, 1933, by Ogden Nash.
[15] A minor but illuminating item is the way the New York newspapers lined
up during this campaign. The *Times* backed Morris; so did the *Post*. *PM* supported
O'Dwyer until a day or two before the election, and then switched to Morris. The
Brooklyn *Eagle* supported O'Dwyer and so did the *Daily Worker*. Supporting
Goldstein were the *Herald Tribune* and the *Sun*. What line the *News, Mirror,
World-Telegram*, and *Journal-American* took was difficult to figure out.

It was first the classic example of the American political machine, and its role was the orthodox one of being a bridge between the newly arrived immigrant and citizenship. It taught him how to vote and for whom. Also it really rendered service. If Sally Snooks of West 98th Street got measles, the district leader saw to it that she was taken care of. Tammany purveyed help, if not justice. Whether or not the corner cop would let your youngster play under the water hydrant on a hot day depended on Tammany. It could do anything for a man from granting a bus franchise to a suspension of sentence for a serious crime; whether or not you could build a skyscraper—and how cheaply or expensively— or a chicken coop, depended on the Tiger. The Seabury investigation told much about the sale of judgeships. Then, after a long period of satiety and deliquescence, came the crushing blows of fifteen years ago. Judge Seabury demonstrated that it was extremely unwise for politicians to maintain safety deposit boxes with big amounts of cash in New York City. Jimmy Walker resigned rather than be forced out of office by Mr. Roosevelt, and the great days of Tammany were over.

Aside from scandals and witless leadership three major factors have contributed to the collapse of Tammany:

(1) The movement of people out of Manhattan itself into Brooklyn and the Bronx. Tammany is, of course, the Democratic machine in Manhattan only.

(2) Mr. La Guardia, who was beaten by Tammany in 1929, beat it in 1933, 1937, and 1941—which drove it into the wilderness.

(3) Above all, the New Deal. Tammany favors were small stuff compared to public works through the WPA. These latter, moreover, were administered honestly.

Wall Street, the Solar Plexus

I must atone for my wealth.

—Otto Kahn

There was a time, I am told on good authority, when John D. Rockefeller was getting one million dollars a day; and still, I have reason to believe, they buried him in a pair of pants.

—Milton Mayer

A bank is the thing that will always lend you money if you can prove you don't need it.

—Joe E. Lewis

The main thing to say about Wall Street today is that it is not what it once was. Much of the brutal golden power, the sheen, is gone. Consider as typical of a whole great evolution what has happened to the "Corner," i.e., the House of Morgan. J. P. Morgan himself, the Younger, died in 1943, and his will was made public in 1947. After deduction of tax, debts, and expenses, his net estate amounted to the bagatelle of

$4,642,791. Nothing could more dramatically illustrate how times have irremediably changed.[16]

About American finance and business in general, monopoly, profits and the like, I hope to write in another place. Here is room only for the briefest highlights on Wall Street itself. The United States is the last stronghold of the capitalist system left in the world. We cannot but inspect its liver and solar plexus.

Wall Street is, strange as it may seem, so called because Peter Stuyvesant, in 1653, built a wall roughly where it lies today. It is a narrow, noisy, trenchlike little chasm, scarcely six hundred yards long. Here, or in the immediate neighborhood, are banks like Chase ("the most influential bank in the United States"),[17] the National City, and the Guaranty. (Mr. Bell's essay tells much about who owns these banks, for instance of the Giannini holdings in National City, and which are "Morgan banks" and which are not.) Here are potent underwriting houses like Halsey Stuart and Morgan Stanley; here is the Stock Exchange, on which are listed 200 billion dollars' worth of securities and which transacted business worth 15 billion dollars in 1945. But another index of the way things have been going is that in 1929 the price of an Exchange seat was $625,000, and today is about $68,000. At the depth of the depression a seat cost $17,000. Details like these are as familiar to most Americans as the trademark of a brand of cigarettes, but let us point out once more that outlanders may not be so well informed.

In the vivid, fragrant days before 1929 Wall Street was, though disliked and distrusted by many people, an object of profound veneration to the business world. To become a Morgan partner, or even a Kuhn Loeb partner was for most rising young men of the East practically like becoming a cardinal, only more so. The path was well beaten for any really bright and ambitious youngster, and it was often a golden path— St. Paul's or Lawrenceville, Yale or Princeton, and then the Street. Bankers were really looked up to in those days. Now of course they have to spend most of their time explaining themselves. Morgan and Kuhn Loeb had the juiciest parts of the investment business almost without competition, with Morgan concentrating on British and domestic industrial issues mostly, Kuhn Loeb on German and Scandinavian issues and some railroads. Another pregnant point is that in this era bankers played a very definite role in international political affairs. The House of Morgan was like the Board of Trade in England; to all intents and purposes it was a silently functioning agency of the American government itself. A Morgan partner could have much more influence than,

---

[16] The best single thing on Wall Street in short space I have ever read is an essay by Elliot V. Bell in an anthology called *We Saw It Happen*. Mr. Bell was a financial reporter for the New York *Times* when he wrote it. He is now a leading member of Governor Dewey's brain trust and the head of the New York State Banking Department.

[17] See *Life* in a useful pictorial essay, January 7, 1946.

say, an assistant secretary of state. Mr. Bell, if I may allude to his essay once more, makes mention of the way Wall Street kept in close touch with Washington, and told it, bluntly if necessary, what it was to do. Now as to the domestic side we must mention railroads in particular. The railway empires of the country were also more or less divided between Kuhn Loeb and Morgan, though other firms in time pushed their way in. The railroads could not promote their massive issues without money, and it was Wall Street which gave them money. Finally— and this is of course still true today—the bankers, through interlocking directorates and otherwise, had germinal influence on the affairs of almost all the great American manufacturing corporations.

Where do the bright youngsters turn today? A good many, if they hope to become millionaires some day by a conservative route, go into law. (Many, not exclusively interested in making money, more interested in making *things* or public policy, go into small businesses or government service, after a period at law.) The great law firms of Wall Street still pick the best brains in the nation. They have consummate power, ability, and intelligence. Their profits may still be enormous; since the SEC, a great deal more legal work attends financial issues than heretofore.[18] One point to reflect on, though, is their inhospitality to Jews. Many big law firms—and to a certain extent banks—rigidly exclude Jews; even Jewish underlings and clerks are uncommon. In no American milieu is this more conspicuous. For a Jew to get into a good legal firm below Chambers Street is almost as difficult as to get into the Ku-Klux Klan. The upper reaches of the law in Wall Street are the last frigid citadel of Anglo-Saxon Protestantism.

To proceed. In 1930 James W. Gerard, formerly ambassador to Germany, made a national sensation—it will seem very tame now—by listing the sixty-four men who "ruled the United States." He included only one politician (Mellon); he did not include the president, Mr. Hoover. These shoguns, he said, were the real powers behind the throne, too busy to run for office themselves but decisive in determining who did run, and in utter control of the nation's purse strings. Perhaps the list has relevance today:

John D. Rockefeller Jr.
Andrew W. Mellon
J. P. Morgan
George F. Baker, banker
John D. Ryan, copper magnate
Walter C. Teagle, president of Standard Oil of New Jersey
Henry Ford
Frederick E. Weyerhaeuser, lumber
Myron C. Taylor
James A. Farrell, U.S. Steel

Charles M. Schwab, Bethlehem Steel
Eugene G. Grace, Bethlehem Steel
Harry M. Warner, movies
Adolph Zukor, movies
William H. Crocker, San Francisco banker
O. P. and M. J. Van Sweringen, railway magnates
W. W. Atterbury, president of the Pennsylvania R.R.

[18] *Life, op. cit.,* says that the charge for preparing a prospectus may be $100,000.

Arthur Curtiss James, large holder of
railway securities
Charles Hayden, financier
Daniel O. Jackling, president of the
Utah Copper Co.
Arthur V. Davis, president of Alcoa
P. M. Gossler, president of the Colum-
bia Gas & Electric Corp.
R. C. Holmes, president of the Texas
Corp.
John J. Raskob
Seven members of the Du Pont family
Edward J. Berwind, financier
Daniel Willard, Baltimore & Ohio
Sosthenes Behn, IT&T
Walter S. Gifford, AT&T
Owen D. Young, General Electric
Gerard Swope, General Electric
Thomas W. Lamont
Albert H. Wiggin, banker
Charles E. Mitchell, banker

Samuel Insull
The seven Fisher brothers
Daniel Guggenheim and William Loeb,
mining magnates
George Washington Hill, American
Tobacco Co.
Adolph S. Ochs
William Randolph Hearst
Robert R. McCormick
Joseph M. Patterson
Julius S. Rosenwald, merchant
Cyrus H. Curtis
Roy W. Howard
Sidney Z. Mitchell, chairman of the
board, Electric Bond & Share
Walter Edwin Frew, Corn Exchange
Bank
A. P. Giannini
William Green and Matthew Woll,
labor[19]

What are the main reasons why Wall Street has declined so notably in prestige, authority, and influence? Following are a few. They are not listed chronologically or in order of importance:

(a) First, of course, the crash and the depression, which not only obliterated a great proportion of the national wealth, but drastically lowered confidence in bankers.

(b) Scandals. It was a severe blow to Wall Street that men like Richard Whitney, a former president of the Stock Exchange, and in a different category Charles E. Mitchell, the president of the National City Bank, no less, went on public trial. Something was wrong. When Whitney first got into trouble people said, "Oh, the Morgans will never let him go to jail." But he went.

(c) Income tax. It is, after all, almost insuperably difficult nowadays to accumulate a fortune. It may not be impossible to make big money; to hold on to it is a different matter. What does it profit a man to spend thirty years trying to make money in large amounts, and have his major earnings go to taxes?

(d) More pertinent than any of these items so far, the transfer of much of the control of credit from Wall Street to the government. "Freedom to speculate" became severely limited. Moreover the government extended its direct financial power through such agencies as the RFC (created by Mr. Hoover). Many corporations didn't have to go to Wall Street any more. They went to Washington.

[19] It is not uninteresting that while making out this list, Mr. Gerard was the guest of General Cornelius Vanderbilt at Newport, Rhode Island. One singular point is that none of the great insurance companies are represented.

(*e*) The growth of corporations themselves. Plenty of companies, especially new companies (like Kaiser) do of course still come to Wall Street for underwriting. But the colossi like AT&T are big enough to be their own bankers for the most part. In the old days a middle western railway could be as dependent on Morgan as a cripple on a crutch. Nowadays even small corporations do their banking locally. Financial power has become much more diffused. Also Ford (a special case of course) financed himself in an emergency through his own dealers.

(*f*) Various regulatory devices, initiated by the New Deal for the public interest. We accept these today, it has been said, almost as automatically as we accept—and welcome—the strictures of the Pure Food and Drug Act. But think back to 1929! A private bank did not even have to make public its condition. There was no federal regulation whatever of the issue of securities except of certain minor types.

(*g*) Among specific acts, the Banking Act of 1933, which enforced a separation of banks of deposit from investment banking ("and so took all the gravy out of Wall Street") and the Securities Act of 1934 which set up the SEC. Today—something so obviously correct that it seems barbarous that it did not exist fifteen years ago—every underwriter is under strict legal compulsion to declare in the most minute detail every relevant fact about an impending issue. "It is the underwriters themselves," notes *Life*, "not the corporation, that are legally liable for false or misleading statements in such a prospectus." Every material fact bearing on an issue must be made known.

(*h*) One might also mention the Investment Trust Act and similar acts, regulating the operation of investment trusts and councilors, and forbidding the latter to act as brokers, and also, in another and wider field, the Johnson Act, which cut off loans to foreign nations in default on obligations to the United States.

(*i*) Competitive bidding. Except in isolated cases the railroads and utilities are no longer able to negotiate their financing with banking houses of their own choice. Instead they must offer their securities publicly to the highest bidder. This, as much as anything, has served to upset old banking ties, lower the morale of the Street, and cut profits to the bone.

(*j*) During the hearings of a subcommittee of the United States Senate investigating the banking business and the stock market, a lively press agent managed to put a midget on J. P. Morgan's knee.

Perhaps this last item marked the turning point. With that midget, an impregnability was shattered, a myth was broken, an era ended. The Pecora hearings were the Great Divide, Wall Street has never been quite the same since.

Some testimony by Mr. Morgan and his associates during this astonishing investigation shows nicely what a Divine-Right-of-Kings world we lived in then:

Q. Should not private banks be examined and forced to publish statements of their condition?
A. Possibly.
Q. What assurance has a depositor of the solvency of Morgan & Company?
A. Faith.
Q. Are not depositors entitled to statements of Morgan & Company's condition?
A. They can have them if they want them; no one has ever asked.
Q. Has any public statement ever been made . . . since the Elder Morgan testified before the Pujo committee twenty years ago?
A. No. That was the only public statement we have ever made about anything.

It was at this hearing, incidentally, that the country learned with a burning incredulous shock that neither Morgan nor any of his great partners, men like George Whitney and Thomas W. Lamont, had paid any income tax during the depression years 1931 and 1932, and that in 1930 their payments had totaled only $48,000. This was, of course, because the partnership had taken advantage of the capital gains and losses provision in income tax regulations. The late Senator Glass of Virginia snapped in icy disgust, "The fault is with the law." (It should also be noted that few among those outraged by this nonpayment of taxes for two years paid much attention to the fact that from 1917 to 1927 members of the firm had paid taxes of more than 50 million dollars.)

Also in this investigation it became known that the Morgan partners followed the practice of offering certain stocks to a group of selected friends at prices considerably below market, before issuing them. The question was asked, "Was not the offer of such shares at wholesale prices a kind of bribe?" The answer was, "No. The shares were only offered to clients and friends who could afford to take a risk . . . regarded as too speculative for the general public."[20] Among Morgan acquaintances— who got Standard Brands at bargain rates—were Calvin Coolidge (3,000 shares), John J. Raskob (2,000), General Pershing (500), Colonel Lindbergh (500), Bernard M. Baruch (4,000), Norman H. Davis (500), Cornelius S. Kelley of Anaconda (2,000), Charles E. Mitchell (10,000), Alfred P. Sloan (7,500), Clarence H. Mackay (2,000). Similar bargains in Allegheny Corporation stock went to Charles Francis

[20] One of Morgan's own statements about this was the following: "Our lists of private subscribers naturally were composed of men of affairs and position; but they were selected because of established business and personal relations and not because of any actual or potential political relations. We never had any occasion to ask favors from legislators or persons in public office, nor have we ever done so." From the obituary of Mr. Morgan in the New York Times, March 4, 1943.

Adams (1,000), Newton D. Baker (2,000), and Owen D. Young (5,000).[21]

Morgan partners in 1933 held 167 directorships in 89 corporations, it was revealed, with aggregate assets of about 20 billion dollars. Among the 89 were 15 banks and trust companies, 7 miscellaneous holding companies, 10 railroads, 5 public utility holding corporations, 8 public utility operating companies, 38 industrial companies and 6 insurance companies. Asked about this, Mr. Morgan himself said that he disliked having his partners serve as directors; they did so "only by the earnest request of companies which wanted them as financial advisers." But, according to *Time*, "The Morgan-First National influence in 1935 was estimated by a National Resources Committee report as still reaching into $30,210,000 worth of U. S. railroads, utilities, industries, banks. Yet some of the proudest Morgan nurslings, like General Electric, had long since outgrown their Morgan link."[22]

Meantime the 1933 Banking Act was passed. "J. P. Morgan & Co.," wrote the New York *Times* in its obituary of Mr. Morgan, "had to choose between its security underwriting business, the leading business of its kind in the world, and its private deposit banking." It decided to remain a private commercial bank, and therefore had to drop its investment business. Morgan's son Henry and two other partners resigned from the parent house to form a new investment firm, totally independent, Morgan Stanley & Company, Inc. Morgan's other son, Junius, stayed on with the parent bank, which was still "the largest private bank in the world."

In 1940 came another bruising and revolutionary step. The financial writers cried, "*Götterdämmerung!*" What happened was that the Morgan bank decided to incorporate itself. This was as if Carry Nation had done a midnight strip tease at Leon & Eddie's. Morgan no longer a private bank! It applied to the authorities for a charter of incorporation and then moved into the sphere of "government supervision and growing accountability to the public." The *ancien régime* was no more. This was Louis XVI's head bouncing into the cart. "It was understood," wrote the New York *Times*, that "the firm was incorporated because death and inheritance taxes raised difficulties of keeping the bank's capital intact as partners died or withdrew. The firm had deposits of more than $600 million at the time of this change from a purely private bank to a state-chartered institution." Some time after this—another shock to the old-fashioned—J. P. Morgan & Company, Inc., offered stock to the public for the first time, and in 1942 it was admitted to membership in the Federal Reserve system.

[21] This list has been printed often. Here I am following *Time*, June 5, 1933.
[22] February 26, 1940.

Now to conclude. No one should think from the above that Wall Street is powerless these days. By no means! It is still incontestably the most powerful financial center in the world. It still has an influence on America pervasive, tenacious, and articulate. All that has happened is that it can no longer play its game exclusively its own way. It must obey house rules.

As to the place in the national economy of some great corporations not so directly in the Wall Street arc, though most are based in or near New York, the most interesting presentation I have seen is that in a pamphlet prepared by Senator O'Mahoney's Temporary National Economic Committee. Some of this material also appeared in the *Congressional Record*.[23] There were, as of that date, forty-one American corporations with total assets of a billion dollars or more. In the year preceding there had been thirty-eight; in 1941, thirty-two. There are, of course, other and perhaps better ways of measuring the size of a corporation than by its assets. But considered strictly from the point of view of assets, the biggest—and the largest enterprise in the United States— is the Metropolitan Life Insurance Company, with almost six and a half billion dollars in assets; next comes Bell Telephone, with more than six billion; next comes the Prudential Insurance Company with more than five. A fingerful of banks are runners-up, with more than three and a half billion each; then come two more insurance companies, with more than three billion. The first railway on the list is the Pennsylvania, with assets of $2,800,000,000 plus. The first industrial corporation is Standard Oil of New Jersey, with $2,300,000,000 plus. General Motors is thirteenth on the list; U. S. Steel fourteenth; the New York Central fifteenth; the Santa Fe twenty-third; the Union Pacific twenty-fifth; Consolidated Edison twenty-seventh; Du Pont thirty-eighth; and Ford forty-first. Senate statisticians made much play with this list. They showed, for instance, that only six American states (New York, Pennsylvania, Ohio, California, Michigan, Massachusetts) have a total assessed valuation of property greater than the assets of Metropolitan Life. Both AT&T and the Prudential Insurance Company have greater assets than all but thirteen states. Assets of Chase National run nip and tuck with those of Kentucky, and Standard Oil (New Jersey) is richer than Virginia. The Northwestern Mutual Life Insurance Company of Milwaukee has assets almost equivalent to those of the state of Georgia; similarly the Chemical Bank & Trust Company of New York runs neck and neck with Florida; the Baltimore & Ohio Railway with Washington; and Commonwealth & Southern with Colorado. As of 1942 there were thirty-two American corporations with considerably greater wealth than eighteen states. Mr. Berle, the former American ambassador to Brazil and assistant secretary of state, said once that two hundred companies

[23] February 12, 1945.

owned half the wealth of the United States. Probably he was not far wrong.[24]

What happened to Wall Street and the nation during 1946 is hardly part of our story here. The long bull market finally collapsed. Pages might be written about the reasons for this. One striking fact is that the market did not climb, but actually sagged, after the Republican victory in 1946. What will happen next? This country has at hand at least some of the techniques that might prevent a new crash or a new depression. It remains to be seen, however, if it will use them. Plenty of people still hate the idea of government controls so much that they would rather ruin themselves—and everybody else to boot—than make use of them.

The Harlems

Harlem has a black belt where darkies dwell in a heaven and where white men seek a little hell.
—Alfred Kreymborg

There are several. One is Puerto Rican, one Haitian, and another, verging into what might be called the Marcantonio territory on the east side, Italian. I drove through this area before the 1946 election; loud speakers brought campaign speeches—in warm whole-toned Italian —out into the dreary, chilly streets. (It was in this neighborhood that a Republican election official, Joseph Scottoriggio, was killed in mysterious circumstances.) Also there are Russians in Harlem, Spaniards, Mexicans, a considerable salting of Chinese, some Japanese Nisei who do not want to return to California, and, of all things, the largest Finnish community in the United States. Take the Benjamin Franklin High School on the East River Drive. It may be doubted if any school in the country has such a bizarrely commingled student body.

Next to the Negroes, the biggest group in Harlem is that from Puerto Rico, which numbers about 100,000. Negroes and Puerto Ricans get on well together by and large. One Puerto Rican told me that this was natural because his people want to get Americanized as quickly as possible, and the Negroes represent Anglo-Saxon culture! Another item in this general field is probably apocryphal. Harlem had a small angry upsurge in 1943 which, but for instant sharp work by Mr. La Guardia and the police, might have become a serious riot. The Negro community seemed to feel so secure and confident of adequate protection,

[24] As to concentration of ownership the *New Republic* states (September 2, 1946) that of the two hundred largest nonfinancial corporations in the country, 6 per cent of the common stock is owned by the upper 1 per cent of registered stockholders. Three family groups—Du Ponts, Mellons and Rockefellers—still control fifteen of these two hundred biggest corporations, with assets of eight billion dollars. In 1935 nearly a third of the directorships of the two hundred largest nonfinancial corporations and the fifty largest financial corporations were held by only four hundred men.

however, that a Chinese laundryman is supposed to have hung a sign on his shop, *Me Colored Too!* Still another point in Harlem mixedupness is the fact that a well-known small community exists of Negro Jews.

Though not necessarily the biggest, Harlem is by all odds the most important concentration of Negroes in America. Roughly from 110th Street to 155th on the east side, and from Madison Avenue to St. Nicholas, live some 310,000 Negroes. This is more than the population of whole cities like Atlanta, Dallas, or Portland, Oregon. Yet Harlem holds only about half the total number of Negroes (600,000) in New York City as a whole; there are approximately 150,000 in Brooklyn, about 30,000 in the Bronx, and about 30,000 in Queens. Years ago, New York Negroes lived in a few scattered and isolated enclaves: Minetta Lane in Greenwich Village, "San Juan Hill" on West 63rd Street near the river, and some areas in German Yorkville (especially on East 88th near Third). Now, as everybody knows, they have spread all over the city. Harlem itself is expanding all the time. It has no fixed frontiers.

Since "Harlem" has become a kind of abstraction (like "Hollywood"), it is extremely difficult to describe. The easiest thing to say is that it is a profoundly complex cross section of the whole of New York in black miniature. People are tempted to think of Harlem as exclusively a slum; it is also talked about as if it were a cave full of night clubs. Many Harlemites have of course never seen a night club. Some parts of it are indeed slums, and one block, near Lenox and 143rd Street, is commonly said to be the most crowded in the world. A recent commissioner of housing and building visited a sixty-four-year-old tenement in the neighborhood of Fifth and 117th not long ago, and found it "infested, scaly, shabby," a menace to health, a disgrace otherwise, and a fire trap. Rats were so much in evidence that the remark was reported, "They not only come here to eat, but I think they cook their own food, too."

But Harlem as a whole is by no means a slum. This is not the Bowery. A good many apartment blocks, built long before the district became Negro, are still in good shape; the trouble is that they are viciously overcrowded and badly maintained. For instance there will be only one superintendent for six buildings, jammed with sublet flats, and containing literally hundreds of families. Also Harlem has several handsome, modern, and well-maintained apartment buildings. One, at 409 Edgecombe, is in the area known locally as "Sugar Hill"; here lives, as I heard it put, "the glamor set of Black America."[25] But this description makes Sugar Hill sound frivolous, which it is not. A great number of eminent Negroes live there—Walter White, the competent discerning

[25] For much detail on this and similar matters see Roi Ottley's *New World A-Coming.*

secretary of the National Association for the Advancement of Colored People, Municipal Judge Charles E. Toney, Roy Wilkins the editor of *Crisis*, one of the best-known Negro lawyers in the country Thurgood Marshall, William T. Andrews who is one of the senior members of the state assembly, and W. E. B. Du Bois. The rents on Sugar Hill are perhaps $85.00 a month, for something very much like apartments on Park Avenue, and which on Park Avenue would cost $300.

I went up to Harlem with two Negro friends a few evenings ago, and tried to learn a little. It is a community constantly in motion. Like New Rochelle, it is a kind of bedroom for the rest of New York; people live here, and work downtown. It has several Negro newspapers, including the conservative *Amsterdam News* and the radical *People's Voice*. There is no Negro department store; most of the shopkeepers on the main street (125th) are Jews. Almost all real estate is white absentee owned, though one Negro businessman, A. A. Austin, is a substantial owner; there is no Negro bank (but local branches of the great white banks employ Negro personnel); about seventy-five saloons and one movie house are Negro owned, but no more; the chief hotel is a remarkable establishment called the Theresa, almost exclusively Negro, but it is white owned, and several whites live in it. The chief Negro business in Harlem on a broad level is insurance (unless you want to count religion as a business), and on a narrower level hairdressing.

The whole community is, of course, strongly labor conscious. At least 50,000 Negroes in New York City are members of unions, including laundry workers, garment workers, hod carriers, longshoremen, painters, maritime workers, and members of the United Office and Professional Workers, CIO. Probably some single streets in Harlem have more Negro trade unionists than the entire state of Georgia. In New York as a whole there is probably less discrimination against Negroes, in employment and otherwise, than in any other city in America. In fact many familiar forms of anti-Negro discrimination are illegal in New York. Of course some discriminations, illegal or not, do continue to exist.

Harlem has no single political boss, any more than New York City itself has a single boss. You can find every shade of opinion on any question. Some Harlemites are "handkerchief-heads"; some frankly call themselves "antiwhite." Once the community had a picturesque creature, Abdul Hamid Sufi, who was called the Black Hitler, and who, despite this name, operated a "Temple of Peace and Tranquillity." There are extremely conservative Negroes, like Dr. Clilan B. Powell, editor of the *Amsterdam News,* a member of the State Boxing Commission, and assistant publicity director of the Republican National Committee, and there are equally some extreme radicals, as well as many who defy classification. The president of the New York City Civil Service Commission, Ferdinand Q. Morton, is a Negro, and so is a member of the state Committee

Against Discrimination set up by the Ives Bill, Elmer Carter (who also lives on Sugar Hill incidentally). The only Communist on the New York City council is a competent and accomplished Negro, Benjamin J. Davis Jr. Also Davis, who played football at Williams and is a graduate of the Harvard Law School, is publisher of the *Daily Worker*. His father interestingly enough, an Atlanta publisher, is an important Republican politician. In a recent councilmanic election, under proportional representation, Davis's vote was only topped by that of Stanley M. Isaacs, an able Republican who has been entrenched in New York politics for many years.

On a street corner near the Theresa we listened to a campaign speech by Congressman Adam Clayton Powell Jr.[26] Many Negroes dislike Powell, and call him a spellbinder. He has a blistering hot voice; he never pauses a second between sentences; he gestures like a piston. This evening, with his words reverberating up and down the street, he denied with ringing animosity that his wife, Hazel Scott, a well-known Negro pianist, was white (as some silly people had alleged); he excused some absences from Congress by saying that, after all, his constituents ought not mind that he had taken a brief honeymoon—how the crowd roared! —and, anyway, his mother was very ill. "Any Negro born of a Negro," Powell cried out, "must be a Negro, must be a radical, must be a fighter, all the time!" Powell has fire and courage. By profession he is a preacher, as was his father before him. His Abyssinian Baptist church has, in fact, what is believed to be the largest Protestant congregation in the world, numbering at least ten thousand. Like almost all Negroes running for office in 1946, Powell was vulnerable on the score that the Democratic party was also the party of Mr. Bilbo, an embarrassing paradox indeed. But he squeezed through, and is now serving his second term in the House of Representatives. He was the first Negro councilman in New York City, and is one of two Negroes in the Congress.

To sum up: the chief characteristic of Harlem is that, by and large, its Negroes (and others in New York) have greater opportunities in more fields than in any comparable city; they have better chances in education, jobs, social evolution, and civil service; they are the nearest to full citizenship of any in the nation.

New York Olla Podrida

New York City has more trees (2,400,000) than houses, and it makes 18,200,000 telephone calls a day, of which about 125,000 are wrong numbers. Its rate of divorces is the lowest of any big American city, less than a tenth of that of Baltimore for instance, and even less than that in the surrounding countryside. One of its hotels, built largely over railway

[26] No relation to the Powell named above, I believe.

tracks, has an assessed valuation of $22,500,000 (there are 124 buildings valued at more than a million dollars in Manhattan alone), and it is probably the only city in the world that still maintains sheriff's juries and has five district attorneys.

New York City has such admirable institutions as the New School for Social Research, the Council on Foreign Relations, Cooper Union, the Museum of Modern Art, and the Century Association. It has 17 billion dollars' worth of real estate, and a black market in illegitimate babies. It has 492 playgrounds, more than 11,000 restaurants, 2,800 churches, and the largest store in the world, Macy's, which wrote 40,328,836 sales checks in 1944, and serves more than 150,000 customers a day. It has the Great White Way, bad manners, 33,000 schoolteachers (average pay $3,803), and 500 boy gangs.

New York makes three-quarters of all the fur coats in the country, and its slang and mode of speech can change hour by hour. It has New York University, a wholly private institution which is the second largest university in the country, 13,800 Jews in its student body, 12,000 Protestants, and 7,200 Catholics, and a great municipal institution, the City College of the College of the City of New York, one of four famous city colleges. In New York people drink 14 million gallons of hard liquor a year, and smoke about 20 billion cigarettes. It has 301,850 dogs, and one of its unsolved murders is the political assassination of Carlo Tresca.

New York has 9,371 taxis and more than 700 parks. Its budget runs to $175,000,000 for education alone, and it drinks 3,500,000 quarts of milk a day. The average New York family (in normal times) moves once every eighteen months, and more than 2,200,000 New Yorkers belong to the Associated Hospital Service. New York has a birth every five minutes, and a marriage every seven. It has "more Norwegian-born citizens than Tromsoe and Narvik put together," and only one railroad, the New York Central, has the perpetual right to enter it by land. It has 22,000 soda fountains, and 112 tons of soot fall per square mile every month, which is why your face is dirty.

Chapter 34
The Not-So-Little Flower

〰〰

THE MAYOR asked me if I'd like to come down to City Hall and spend a day with him. I sat at a corner of his desk for eight consecutive hours and twenty minutes, and took as full notes as I could on everything that happened.[1]

Fiorello Henrico LaGuardia, the most spectacular mayor the greatest city in the world ever had, has characteristics and qualities so obvious that they are known to everyone—the volatile realism, the rubber-supple grin, the flamboyant energy, the zest for honesty in public life, the occasional vulgarisms, the common sense. But the mayor I spent these uninterrupted hours with showed more conspicuously some qualities for which he is not so widely known. He picked what he called a "desk day" for me to sit in on. He did not inspect a single fish market or visit a single fire. What he did was work at his major job, administration of the city of New York. What he did was to govern, to put in a routine day as an executive. Routine? Yes—but wait.

"Everybody talks about the mayor's 'temperament'—which doesn't exist!" Reuben A. Lazarus, one of his closest associates and his legislative aide, told me. Mr. LaGuardia really runs the entire machinery of New York City, in all its dazzling complexity, singlehanded or, let us say, with his own two good hands. Temperament? There's no time for it—unless it happens to serve a useful purpose.

Just once during my ten hours the mayor lost his temper (ten because I had two more hours with him after his official day was done). Then in a second he was grinning. "When I get excited and blow off like that," he winked, "it was all planned two days ago."

The mayor said he'd pick me up at my apartment, and his car came by at 9:12 A.M. With him was Robert Moses, commissioner of parks, one of the ablest and most devoted public servants in the United States. It was seventeen above zero outside; the mayor wore no overcoat but he kept a warm rug on his knees. We swept downtown while Moses went through a pile of papers and the mayor rapidly gave his decision on point after point.

---

[1] This sketch was written in February, 1945, when *Inside U. S. A.* was first getting underway. Of course Mr. LaGuardia is no longer mayor. But I am letting what I wrote stand as written. Most of the people in the chapter have changed, but the problems and issues remain the same.

Sample of the talk:

Moses: "You can't do that. There's a constitutional inhibition." The mayor: "Can't I? Well, work it out yourself." Moses congratulated him about something mildly. The mayor: "I know I'm good. Go on." Then a difficult decision. The mayor: "Okay! But God Almighty!"

Then—in six or seven minutes as we rolled along—rapid questions and answers on subjects ranging from Brooklyn tenements to how to build a playground.

Mr. LaGuardia's car is something. A steel desk swings out over the back seat, and a reading lamp that looks like a small searchlight can focus on it. A special radio of course—which intermittently barks out news of police alarms and fires. A fan, a locked compartment full of guns, and a telephone. I asked the mayor if it worked. He told me about an occasion when he had called the lord mayor of London, from the moving automobile in the streets of New York, to invite him over for a visit. "My dear fellow," replied the lord mayor (and Mr. LaGuardia reproduced his accent with ripe and luscious flavor), "I'm only in office for a year, don't-you-know, and I have 2,500 social engagements already!"

We arrived at City Hall at 9:29. A man was waiting for LaGuardia on the outside steps. The mayor bounced right past him; one might say he bounced right through him. Bits of conversation floated behind "Hizzonor" like darting minnows. "I want to talk to Patterson about that. Bob will follow up. Write him a sympathetic letter." We were in the mayor's office by 9:31.

It's one of the pleasantest offices I've ever seen—a large room painted white, with a coal fire at one end; it's on the ground floor, but is nevertheless extraordinarily quiet. Also it was hot—very hot. The mayor doesn't like too much fresh air. The fire boiled and bubbled. On one wall hangs a portrait of President James Monroe, and on an easel is a charcoal sketch of Puccini. Next to the mayor's desk is an immense wooden contraption built like a trough; it contains the active files for which there is no room downstairs. Then on a mantel I noticed a violin, a gift from Jascha Heifetz. It is made of aluminum and is the substitute violin Heifetz used when traveling in the tropics. He told LaGuardia that he wanted to contribute it to New York City's scrap metal drive, but the aluminum is hardly worth more than a nickel or so, and the mayor decided to save it for auctioning to some charity after the war.

On the mayor's desk are the following objects:

A large Bible, full of slips of paper to mark passages
A small clock
Calendar pad, conspicuously tilted on top of a couple of books
2 corncob pipes and a can of Rexey mixture
2 small snapshots of his children

A baby microphone
A couple of batons
Extra glasses
A model airplane
Bottle of white pills
Yellow ash tray, shaped like a rubber life raft
Marked copies of the New York *Times*
A miniature totem pole
A small silk American Flag
A big dark book, the New York City Charter and Administrative Code
A roll of maps

The mayor's technique of work is this. First, he has no telephone—at least none is on his desk. During eight hours and twenty minutes, he only used the phone once. When he does use it, the call comes outside in the anteroom where Miss Betty Cohen, a secretary, who reads his mind with electric swiftness, stands faithful guard; the door between the office and this anteroom is always open, and the mayor marches briskly in to take the call. Miss Cohen leaves her cubbyhole and walks to Mr. LaGuardia's desk fifty or sixty times a day. The distance between them is about seventy feet, so she must walk about three-quarters of a mile between nine and five. The mayor seldom leaves his chair. But while seated, he goes through a considerable amount of movement. He sits back, pounces forward, swings around. He leans back so far that his feet leave the ground. Without actually leaving the chair, he goes through practically every physical motion known to man. Meantime his face and hands are perpetually active. His glasses fly up over his forehead; he shoots his fists out; he grimaces, chortles, frowns, nods, shrugs, beckons, leers. There is never a lost second between one appointment and the next. I was fascinated to see how this was arranged, because there are no audible buzzers or bells. But a light flashes on Miss Cohen's desk when the mayor wants something. A new visitor is announced by the expedient of Miss Cohen walking into the room and slipping a piece of paper with a name on it on top of the appointment pad. The name is never mentioned aloud. So there is no interruption of talk with whatever visitor is with him at the time.

I sat most of the day at the corner of the big desk. No one paid any attention to me except to smile. Sometimes the mayor introduced me; sometimes he did not. Only seldom did I get a chance to ask him some of the questions I badly wanted to ask. There was never enough time.

From this point on I shall try to give a picture of the LaGuardia day by listing each appointment and activity exactly as it came.

9:43. "Get me Judge Wallace on the phone." This to Miss Cohen.

9:43. He started going through his mail. He gets five hundred to six hundred letters a day, which his secretaries winnow to forty or fifty. They attach to each of these a pink slip, summarizing the contents. The mayor goes through the forty or fifty with intent and conscientious care, but swiftly. I never saw anything more efficient. Three secretaries stand by the desk. Miss Cohen superintends operations generally, and Miss Beatrice Resnick and Miss Gertrude Keane take the dictation. Usually Goodhue Livingston Jr., the mayor's executive secretary, hovers near by, and so do Charles F. Murphy, his legal secretary, and Inspector James Harten, his police aide. The group works like a casual yet beautifully co-ordinated machine.

This is the way the mayor's talk went, more or less, as he went through the mail. "Tell him to work up something, quick." "I'll want to write to Stimson on this." "Memo. Ed. See me." "Tell Jones to come in today." "All fixed for tomorrow at two?" (The mayor was going to Washington.) "When are you returning me?" Then picking up a letter he scowled and paused. It was from someone in San Francisco, asking advice on crime prevention. He dictated a succinct reply. Of twenty-odd letters this was the first he answered.

9:47. Judge Wallace was on the phone and the mayor left the room to talk to him.

9:49. More letters. He sorted them like playing cards. "I'll want to talk to Anna Rosenberg about this." "No." "This is for Brundage." "You can reach him in Washington if you want to." "Just put this in his file with the voucher." "Write a pleasant answer." Then a long pause; he read a four-page letter, and put it aside carefully without comment. More short letters. "If it's on the sidewalk, it's the duty of the abutting owners to clear the sidewalk." "Look into this; I don't think it's very serious." "It's my impression I asked you to comment on this tax memo, *in re* schools. Please return, with constructive suggestions." A gesture of scornful dismissal: "Never heard of this guy." Then: "Please investigate. Police to move for revocation." "Give this to Newbold Morris." "I want comment on this today." "I don't know if this is a police job or FBI job. Deserves careful study, skillful investigation." Then (rattling a paper): "Please remember this name. Underline it. I want you to be able to identify him." On something else: "Let it sleep." Then: "Confidential." "Children's Museum, Brooklyn." "Breaks in water main. Let's get a special file on this. I want a comparison for the last ten years." "Oh, for goodness' sake, we never answered this. 'My dear Mrs. X . . .'"

10:27. Letters seemingly finished. Then came one more, to his good friend Montemezzi, composer of the opera *Love of the Three Kings*. "Okay, girls, that cleans us up." As the secretaries left the room, he called to Miss Cohen, "I want to see Chester Bowles tomorrow. If he says lunch, say 'No'; it's hard on him." Then a second instruction: "Can I see Ickes? Tell him it wouldn't be a bad idea to have X. X. there." Then to somebody new who popped into the room and whom I was not able to identify. "This is manpower. This is testimony. This is very good on police."

10:28. The mayor leaned back. I asked him about the big trough of files. "I'll tell you a little story. Files are the curse of modern civilization. I had a young secretary once. Just out of school. I told her, 'If you can keep these files straight, I'll marry you.' She did, and so I married her."

10:35. Instructions to Miss Truda T. Weil, his education aide. "We've been planning a vocational high school for the maritime trades, to train stewards for the Merchant Marine and so on. . . . But will this be necessary after the war, considering the number of men to whom the Navy will have given training?" He and Miss Weil talked it over. He ordered her to dig up background.

10:39. Press conference. Eight or ten reporters, the men regularly assigned to City Hall, came in and asked questions about gambling in connection with basketball. The mayor demonstrated a fierce and aggressive puritanism. "We *must* protect amateur sports; we can't have people corrupting kids who are playing *games*!" Then a violent onslaught against the "tin-horn chiselers, the big mouths, the procurers." "What's wrong with the newspapers and the courts?" "Sneers and jeers of editorial writers." "People abuse the police for doing their duty and enforcing the law; they abuse me when what I am doing is to protect the home." Then an onslaught again, "Dirty little pimps who say their constitutional rights are being violated when as a matter of fact all they've got is good connections!"

10:55. The mayor said, "This is a lull. I had planned to open a tunnel." So I had a chance to ask some questions. But not many. Lull lasted until 10:58.

JG: "What's the hardest decision you ever had to make?"

LaG: "Damn it all, I've never been able to keep a diary. The days are too crowded. There are tough decisions every day. I could write a book, about twenty of 'em. . . . When I came into office this city was bankrupt. Its revenue was hypothecated. I had to put it on a pay-as-you-go basis. Taxes. Everybody thought, 'That damn fool of a new mayor is committing suicide' . . . I didn't give it a thought. Usually when you ask a public official what he plans to do, he'll think in terms of the next election. I've never worried about the next election. I've never belonged to any political party for more than fifteen minutes. . . . Why do good public servants break with political parties? It's so simple. The political people never ask you to do anything that's *right*—and that you're going to do anyway! No. What they want you to do is all the things that are wrong."

10:58. Dr. Ernest L. Stebbins, commissioner of health, and Judge Robert McCurdy Marsh. Discussion of meatless days, enforcement, etc.

The mayor was silent for six or seven minutes, listening to Stebbins hard; this was his longest period of silence during the entire day. The judge was about to be sworn in as a member of the Board of Health. Someone asked, "Are you going to ask the press?" and the mayor replied, "Let's not make a secret of it." The newspaper men entered, and he swore Judge Marsh into office. The mayor said: "You know why I picked Marsh for this job? Because he's a fine upstanding fellow."

11:35. I asked the mayor how he accounted for his own hold on the electorate. "There's a fundamental political fact about the City of New York. The stratification isn't by parties. Ultraradicals, ultraconservatives: they both vote *for* me! Otherwise I could never break through. A well-informed electorate understands that the essence of municipal government is housekeeping, to make a city clean and keep it that way. What am I proudest of? Oh, well!" He grinned, and then became serious. "That I raised the standard of municipal government everywhere in this country, by raising it in New York and so proving it could be raised!"

11:37. Man announced. "Oh, I don't want to see him now." Pause. "Well, if he's here, let him in." Man entered. "Hello, Fiorello." Five minutes' chat on textbooks, leading to the point that "education must *not* be rationed," and on the curious fact that there seemed to be plenty of paper for racing sheets and stock market reports, but none for reprints of modern classics for the schools. "What I'm thinking of is the class of 1957. Teach 'em English from Grade 1A up. Proper English. I don't care what kind of accents they have. But English so that a kid can learn what language is for, that is, to convey thoughts."

11:47. Miss Weil again. Maritime school again. Miss Weil said, "I drafted the report. Thought you wouldn't have time to look. But . . ." The mayor read through the draft. Miss Cohen came in. Signing checks, fixing up petty cash. Then a minor crisis. The mayor (an angry mutter): "If they don't know my stand on that by *this* time!—"

11:50. Mary Dillon, president of the Board of Education. To me in parenthesis: "Remember, you're to write about the city, not the mayor." Then fifteen minutes of vivid argument with Miss Dillon. Expostulating, "Mary—after what we've gone through together!—" Points at issue: lunchroom situation; centralized purchase of food; transfer of personnel. "Let me handle him. You'd have trouble with that hombre." Then a quarrel full of violent comedy over whether somebody should, or should not, be hired for a job which would entail raising his salary from $6,500 to $7,500 a year. The mayor fought like a tiger to keep the figure down. But Miss Dillon explained patiently that the man was, at the moment, indispensable and his appointment an absolute necessity. The mayor kept refusing. Miss Dillon suggested a compromise at $7,000. The mayor scornfully kept on saying "No!" Then she left the room after discussion of other matters and at the very last moment, at the door, she called over her shoulder, "$7,000?" The mayor grunted, "Well—okay!"

12:05. Dictated a memo on books. "Pick your books as you would your friends. Have Emerson in your home. Ever see a movie that was a bit over your head? Well—it was because you haven't read enough."

12:12. Henry M. Brundage, commissioner of markets. Quickly followed by—

12:15. Delegation of eleven retail butchers and chain store representatives. But interrupted by—

12:16. An official whom I did not identify. He popped in for exactly thirty seconds, breathless, saying only "How about ODT?" and then adding a quick interjection, "Yes, but the road to Rockaway!"

12:16½. Butchers' delegation resumes. Long, tangled, tortuous discussion on the meat shortage. Problems: How about Kosher stores? Can chain stores just close their meat counters on meatless days? What about the unions? What about fish? ("Anybody here know anything on fish?") How about the men who boned the meat the night before? What about local autonomy in the AF of L union? "We've screamed our heads off at OPA!" Why weren't cod and haddock available at the retail prices the mayor gave during his last broadcast? Why can't you use the neck bones that the Army discards? Long argument with butchers on just how a neck is boned. The mayor showed them how.

12:50. Miss Cohen and Miss Resnick. Dictation. "How do you spell calisthenics?"

12:53. Resumption of talk with me on municipal politics and what really makes power in New York. Everybody said in 1934 it was hopeless. Corruption and contagion. But was it hopeless? Look how municipal government has improved everywhere. Los Angeles; Boston under Tobin; Cleveland under Burton; Detroit, Seattle: all first class. A sudden bursting but modest smile. Politicians don't like it. Of course not. "*Why* are the machine politicians against me?" (A bray of laughter.) "They've been on a very strict diet, and you know what it is to starve!" Basis of New York politics used to be patronage. Favoritism in contracts; fortunes out of nepotism. "But I harass the bums!" New York City today has $1,126,000,000 in war contracts. Think of the loot—if old-time crooks and gangsters could get their hands on it! "We need constant vigilance, constant supervision."

12:54. Lunch. That is, the mayor had a cup of black coffee, nothing else, and I had a sandwich (of cheese, since it was a meatless day).

12:56. Last year, in 127 days of racing, 400 million dollars were spent on gambling in New York. Most of it in little bets—two dollar bets and so on. "So—I keep after it." Why? "Because those two dollar bets should have been spent on food, clothes, shelter, and a smile at the family table in the evening. A guy loses his money; he's ashamed to face his wife; so he drinks; he gets arrogant and they quarrel in front of their kids."

12:58. I asked why New York City did not permit sharing of taxis. The mayor snapped, "Police problem."

1:09. A representative of the Carey Coach Company. Talk on local transportation, how to ease the rush near Pennsylvania and Grand Central stations.

1:15. Four physicians, led by Dr. Edward C. Costelloe of the Fire Department. Discussion about men discharged from the army returning to work. After Dr. Costelloe left I asked, "Don't you ever get tired, Mr. LaGuardia?"

"Toward sundown."

1:58. Patrick Walsh, fire commissioner. A man with a lovely brogue: "So your specific orders, mayor, are—?" "My suggestion is to get a court decision." But—"If we go into court on this with one of those political judges, we'll get it in the neck!"

2:05. Miss Weil again. More statistics about maritime trades, and a projected curriculum for the school. I walked with Miss Weil to the door. She whispered in admiration, "All day long—just to get the proper background for whatever decision he will take. What a field he covers! What a grasp he has!"

2:06. Edwin A. Salmon, chairman of the City Planning Commission and city fuel administrator. Report on fuel supply. "What's the temperature outside?" "Higher." Eleven hundred carloads of coal in today, which is wartime normal. "But what is it going to be on Friday?" The theaters have a five-day supply at the moment: how to keep them open? Orders: "Get in touch with K. before he has kittens. Then see me once more." Other complicated details. "Damned good, Salmon!"

2:09. An aide in shirt sleeves came in with a bag of tobacco to fill the humidor. "I didn't want to disturb you before." The mayor tossed him half a dollar and said, "Get me some matches."

2:15. William Wilson, commissioner of housing and buildings. He stood while talking. "Well, major." (Lots of people call the mayor "major.") Up to this point, incidentally, except for one phone call and when he swore in Judge Marsh, LaGuardia himself had not once stirred from his chair. Mr. Wilson leaned over the desk, shuffled, paced, roamed around, prowled, edged forward on tiptoe, and presented about thirty different matters for attention, judgment, and decision. Most were in the personal sphere, like cases of dispossession and wrangles over property; the mayor took the most prodigious pains to be fair. "Interesting case here, major. Thought you'd like to hear about it." LaGuardia looked at a chart describing a certain property, showing the sun area at 9 A.M., 6 P.M., and so on, for different days of the year. The mayor (awake to every tiny detail but impatient over one dossier): "Do you want to go

on with the long-haired boys or the skinflint boys?" Then he took time
out to dictate a memorandum to Reuben Lazarus, his aide in Albany:
"Keep your eye on all bills affecting multiple tenancy." Then to Wilson:
"Call your file Special War File, Pending Availability, Impending Material." Zoning orders. "God damn it, I don't want to hear about it."
But he listened. He began to be restless, tapping his knuckles on the desk.
Wilson: "Here's a little headache." LaGuardia: "Okay, you stick your
neck out." Glasses up on hair. Wilson: "I have my budget. I hope you
won't trim it." LaGuardia: "I won't trim it much." Wilson: "I'm still
coming back for more money on demolition, but the budget is smaller
than last year." LaGuardia: "I'll give you every break I can." Wilson:
"You bawled me out over this last time, but listen, the man is over
seventy; forty-two years in the service, an absolutely clean record. Here's
his card." The mayor looked at the photograph attached. "When this
picture taken?" Wilson shrugged. "Okay," the mayor sighed. "If you
want him another year, keep him on."

2:38. A lull, arranged for my benefit.

JG: "Whom do you hate most?"

LaG (grunting): "Hitler."

"What do you like most?"

LaG: "Music."

"What do you believe in most?"

LaG (smiling): "Children."

2:44. John McKenzie, commissioner of marine and aviation. Everything from the latest plans for Idlewild, which will be the biggest airport
in the world, to an alleged injustice to a blacksmith. "Let's smoke 'em
out." "Put a burr under that guy's tail." "Iron it between them if they're
competitors."

3:03. Miss Cohen brought in a letter. "Well, for God's sake! It's from
Eleanor!" He spoke warmly and admiringly of Mrs. Roosevelt. Then
fished in his desk, pulled out the small green Official Directory of New
York City, and carefully checked a detail.

3:03½. Inquiry from WPB, Washington, on statement about restricted lighting.

3:04. (By this time all appointments were about half an hour late).
William W. Mills, president of tax commission. Made his report.
LaGuardia (swiftly): "Congratulations!"

3:06. He rose abruptly, and retired for about a minute to wash his
hands.

3:07. Brundage again. What's to be given to the newspapers on meat
crisis? Quick dictation of a memo.

3:10. Arthur Popper and Adrian Burke, representing Youth House.
What to do with tough kids, thirteen or so. Very volatile; you can't
reason with them as you can with delinquents a few years older. Report

on Public School Number X, which seems to have more incorrigible boys than any other. Report on an unsatisfactory teacher. The mayor broods: "I'm thinking big along those lines." Suggestion. "Yes, that sure would help some." Then a quick change of mood and a funny story.

3:36. Meeting of the Mayor's Committee on Race and Religion; chairman, Charles Evans Hughes Jr. Points discussed: Pushcart peddlers and a new Harlem market; problems involving pickles in fancy glasses; Coney Island; what's the best municipal library in this country; housing problems for families who live on less than $2,500 a year; savings bank mortgages and their relation to housing projects; discrimination against Negroes in employment; the numbers racket; origin of Irish and Italian gangs; how to build a proper community spirit. During this appointment (the longest of the day) the mayor ran every gamut of emotion and expression. He was arch—as when he said to Mr. Hughes, "Can I talk to the committee about the things you thought I was so emotional about last time?" He was gloomy—as when he wrapped his hands about his head and groaned about the need for social workers. He was anecdotal—as when he told a spirited and irreverent story about General Charles De Gaulle. He was ironic—as when he said, "Now, let's be good Anglo-Saxons; don't lose our heads like all those Latins (!) up in Albany." He was contemptuous—and with highly appropriate gestures—talking about "the fakers in the housing racket, experts who couldn't build a doghouse!" He was gay—again with fitting gestures—when he tantalized the committee by saying, "Now go ahead and make your own mistakes!" He was enigmatic—as when he said blandly, "The publishers say, 'We have to print the news.' But there are two ways to print it!" He was sacerdotal—as when he murmured, "I believe in what you will find in St. Luke, but don't ask me what it is." He was impish with paradox when he grinned wickedly, "The Republicans didn't know me very well then, so they thought I was a member of their party, when I was!" And finally, he was intensely sober. His fist smashed down on the desk, and he called out angrily, "So long as I'm the mayor, regardless of race or religion, everybody in this city gets treated on merit and alike!"

4:42. A secretary entered the room and paused pointedly at the door, as if to indicate that time was slipping by. This was the only time this happened all day.

4:43. John Delaney, chairman of the Board of Transportation, and (4:44) Newbold Morris, president of the Council. Talk on budget. The mayor rapped an envelope. "There's 72 million dollars in this stack of paper!" Then his feet went up on the desk and he yawned. He smiled at me questioningly: "Tired?"

5:01. Grover Whalen and a delegation. Whalen was the only man all day for whom the mayor rose. Civilian defense. Ice show at Rockefeller Center. Building projects. Gossip.

5:32. Signing the day's letters; Miss Cohen and Miss Resnick stood next to him as he went through the pile. An official popped in. "Talk fast," the mayor said. Then, not seriously, "What do you mean by coming in at this unseemly hour?" The official grunted, "I've been waiting since four-fifteen, major." Then last-minute details. Miss Cohen to remind him about something regarding the St. Lawrence Waterway. Somebody dismissed as a *Dummkopf*. Wild rage—a literal frenzy—on discovering that liverwurst sandwiches had been available in the municipal cafeteria today, though it was meatless. Then good humor again: "Betty . . . change this. I said I wanted to write a sharp letter . . . well, never mind."

5:39. C. R. Beardsley, Commerce Department. Last appointment. Then a final call to Miss Cohen. "What do I have to take home with me? Oh, say, don't forget, prepare that second thing for Bowles."

5:46. The mayor stretched and said to me, "Come on, let's go." Then to various aides and secretaries: "Have car ready. No curb interviews."

5:58. Silly item from a news agency that demanded last-minute attention. Then: "I guess I'm tired too."

5:59. Out of the building and into the car. The mayor took me home with him, to have a drink, eat some antipasto, and meet his wife and children. We rolled up the East River Drive and suddenly he grabbed the telephone, calling Miss Cohen on something he'd forgotten. We could hear her, but she couldn't hear us; LaGuardia was as disappointed as a child that the phone didn't work. We reached Gracie House. Then we talked till 7:55 about Tom Dewey, the war, Bill Bullitt, good food, what are the sources of Mr. Roosevelt's power, summer camps for kids, Henry Wallace and Jesse Jones, Russian foreign policy and the Atlantic Charter.

I left at about eight. The mayor was going to have a bite of supper. Then he had paper work facing him till midnight and beyond. I felt that I had had one of the most remarkable—and remarkably full—days I've ever gone through. And that Fiorello H. LaGuardia is one of the most original, most useful, and most stimulating men American public life has ever known.

Chapter 35

Hague Machine and New Jersey

wwwwwwwwwwwwwwwwwwwwwwwwwwwwwwwwwwwwwwwwwwwwwwwwwwwwwwwwwwwwwwwwwwwwwwwwwwwwwwwwww

FRANK ("I am the Law") J. HAGUE, boss of Jersey City since 1917 and its mayor for eight successive terms, is no longer quite the law in New Jersey, now that the twilight of the great city bosses has seemingly set in. But, even if he is an anachronism today, this satrap of the urban spoils still runs a machine that for many years was the most successful in America, and that still has weighty pull, push, and power not only in city and county but in state affairs.

Hague is such a formidable institution that he has, as it were, become disembodied. He is often referred to, not by name, but merely as the "Hall," i.e. City Hall. One of his more notorious remarks is, "I decide—I do—*me!*"[1]

Let us summarize his personal characteristics briefly, if only because he is not at all a boss "type" in several respects. The Hall is a tall lean man with a ruddy face, so excessively well dressed that you notice it. To conceal baldness, he almost always wears a hat. His collars are stiff and high, even on the hottest of days, because he has a hypochondriacal fear of throat infections. Twice a year, if possible, he goes to a sanitarium in Michigan, and he likes Florida for long holidays in winter. Mr. Hague is a teetotaler, and has not smoked for a quarter of a century. He likes good food, and often comes into New York for lunch at the Plaza, where, as a rule, he sits in the Oak Room just inside the door. He loves racing and ball games. For years he took a brisk walk, actually for six or seven miles every evening after supper, whereupon he went promptly to bed. He likes to rise early, and the whole Hague machine is often alerted by telephone at seven in the morning. He can abuse the English language marvelously on occasion. Like all great city bosses he rules by having jobs to give—and take. Like most of them (except Crump) he is an ardent Catholic, and the fact that Jersey City is 70 per cent a Catholic town has something to do with his hold on power.

Hague's father and mother both came from County Cavan, and he was born in 1876 in a Jersey City slum called the "Horseshoe." The Hall was expelled from public school as an incorrigible at the age of thirteen,[2] and his biography in *Who's Who* says that his education was

---

[1] Cf. article by Prof. Dayton David McKean in *Public Men*, p. 440.

[2] According to John McCarten in the *New Yorker*. This two-part profile, which appeared early in 1938, is an indispensable source for material on Hague. Also

continued by "private tutor." He went into politics practically by the time he was shaving, and was collecting votes before he could vote himself. For some years he was City Hall Custodian (=chief janitor) and in 1911, the first great step, he was elected street and water commissioner. A mayor in Jersey City does not run as such. Five commissioners are elected, who then choose a mayor from among themselves. Hague became mayor for the first time in 1917, though another commissioner, A. Harry Moore, got a bigger popular vote. He and Moore became close friends and remained so for years, and Moore is the only man who has ever been a governor of New Jersey three different times.

Guess who delivered himself of the following:

> There are no alibis in politics. The delivery of the votes is what counts. And it is efficient organization in every little ward and precinct that determines national as well as local elections. National elections, national politics are just . . . a city on a big scale. It boils down to the wards and precincts. The whole thing is to have an organization that functions in every ward and precinct. That's where the votes come from. The fundamental secret is to get the vote registered—and then get it out after it's registered. That's all there is to it. All the ballyhoo and showmanship such as they have at the national conventions is all right. It's a great show. It gives folks a run for their money. It makes everybody feel good. But the man who makes the organization possible is the man who delivers the votes, and he doesn't deliver them by oratory. Politics is a business, just like anything else.

Actually it was not Hague who said this. It was Boss Pendergast of Kansas City. But every word might easily have come from Hague's mouth.[3]

Politics is not only a business in most American cities; it is also a business often corrupt. Lincoln Steffens in his *Autobiography* has a relevant passage about another town, much smaller and of a totally different kind, Greenwich, Connecticut. The stout burghers of Greenwich indignantly denied Mr. Steffens' allegations (of course this was a good many years ago and now Greenwich is an honestly run city), whereupon he summoned a mass meeting and explained exactly what he meant. A young journalist who, as a volunteer leg man, had helped him collect his material and had assisted his lecture, then drew a diagram on the blackboard. I wish I could reproduce it here, for it demonstrates

---

see the essay in *Public Men* just cited, and a chapter in *The Big Bosses*, by Charles Van Devander.

[3] From an interview with Pendergast by Ralph Coghlan of the St. Louis *Post-Dispatch*, the best interview with an American boss I have ever read, except possibly one with Boss Murphy of New York in the New York *Times* many years ago (April 7, 1924) by Richard Barry. Mr. Coghlan's interview has been reprinted in *Running the Country*, p. 287.

as well as anything I have ever seen the various intercoggings that can exist among business, taxes, politics, police, and the community at large. Incidentally the young journalist was Walter Lippmann.

Boss Hague, it will be said, copiously renders "service" to his flock. Indeed, ward heelers deal adequately with local complaints, and pass out cookies to the children of the poor. Nobody need be cold on Christmas Eve, and the fire department is zealous. There is no vice, no prostitution, in Jersey City, and dance halls and night clubs are severely frowned upon. Mr. Hague wants a nice clean town. Saloons, of course, proliferate, because they are good places in which to promote friendliness among Democratic voters, but women are discouraged from attending them. On the other hand Jersey City has slums as filthy and debasing as any in the East. Thirteen per cent of all its buildings are, according to a federal survey, "unfit for human habitation."[4] Gangsters find short shrift in Hague's citadel; sometimes they are met at the ferry, and expelled back to New York in a downright ungentlemanly fashion. But Jersey City is one of the biggest "handbook" towns in the nation. "It is," writes Mr. Van Devander, "the home and sanctuary of the nation's biggest handbook horse race betting syndicate." "The Horse Bourse," writes Westbrook Pegler, "is a protected racket handling millions of dollars, and it would not exist for an hour if the local administration were not interested in its preservation."

What counts above all this is the cost. Jersey City pays through the nose to be, depending on the point of view, "Hague's paradise" or "the worst city in the country." The local tax rate is the steepest in America, having risen from $21 per $1,000 in 1917 to the glittering and almost unbelievable sum of $76.80 in 1947. The city spends more on itself on a per capita basis than any other in the United States, by far. Listen to *Newsweek*, not a muckraking or insurrectionary organ:[5]

The reasons for Jersey City's plight are so numerous that they almost defy cataloguing. To build his machine, Hague in 1917 began loading up the city and county payrolls with political workers. . . . To finance the bulging payroll (there have been 'cuspidor cleaners' at $1,950 a year, a judge drawing two salaries at once, a multitude of henchmen receiving fat pay for questionable municipal tasks while operating private businesses on a full-time basis) the tax rate has risen . . . to the highest in the nation. Property assessments have risen correspondingly until they now approximate 100 per cent of true value, and, in some proven cases, more. Jersey City's bonded debt is the highest per capita in the nation, and its financial rating is so poor that it pays premium interest rates to holders of its bonds. In return, the city receives the benefits

---

[4] *New Republic*, January 31, 1944.
[5] May 21, 1945. The comparable tax rate in New York City is $27.00.

of a gigantic municipal hospital, operated at costs far in excess of comparable units, enjoys the worst-littered streets in the nation and the most antiquated school buildings, but is "protected" by the largest and most expensive (for the city's size) police force in America, which devotes itself to searching innocent motorists and pedestrians without provocation.

How does Hague rule? How does any boss rule? By pulling in the votes. The Hall has a solid block of 100,000 Hudson County voters. Hague does not go in for really rough stuff—there are no "pineapple primaries" as in Chicago—nor does he, as Pendergast did, have to call on "the cemetery vote."[6] He doesn't need to. Except when he is in a jam, the vote is his anyway. It is, as the phrase goes, "beautifully regimented." But the question is not yet fully answered. Jersey City is a broken-down city of ramshackle tenements with magnificently excessive taxes. Why does the citizenry continue to vote for Mr. Hague? The simplest answer is that he is an utter master at all the political devices that can be used in a city (and county) which has never known superior or even decent government. Most Americans love what I once heard described as "an extra portion of prestige." The Hague faithful receive little "niceties" in police protection, their children get the best school-teachers, and they are assigned low number license plates.[7] Conversely, anybody who is known to oppose Hague openly—or worse, surreptitiously—may encounter discomforts. You may get a parking ticket no matter where you park. Or, if your offense is more serious, you may be subjected to a variety of discriminatory sanctions. Or, if you become an overt political antagonist, you may go to jail. The renowned Longo case is to the point. Mr. Hague is one who knows all, sees all. He is nobody to fool with, unless you really mean it.

Again to proceed. Hague has the votes, but what else? I quote now an extremely responsible journalist, James Kerney Jr. of the Trenton *Times*. The Kerneys, father and son, have been distinguished in New Jersey public life since the days of Woodrow Wilson.

Hague has for years manipulated the juries, prosecutors, judges, election boards, and tax assessors of Hudson County. They were outright agents of the machine, and powerful ones. Any critic of His Honor was likely to find his tax assessment raised, his right to vote impugned, and he was lucky, indeed, if he wasn't arrested for fraudulent voting or gambling, or any of a dozen other offenses.[8]

[6] Mr. Coghlan (*op. cit.*) mentions two specific wards in Kansas City where 41,805 votes were cast by the 38,401 babies, children, adults, and dead men living there. The registration was greater than official census figures for the population.

[7] A whole essay might be written on the strange snobbery implicit in this phenomenon.

[8] The *Nation*, August 26, 1944.

Of course taxes are a prodigious weapon. Until recently, the Hall controlled both the Hudson County Tax Appeals Board and that of the state. During Governor Walter Edge's administration Hague lost this latter. In the picturesque idiom of a member of the governor's staff, "What we did was cut into Hague's tax territory." One does not need labor the point why taxes are so important. Any business, any family can be sent to the poorhouse if the tax assessor puts the tax high enough, and if there is no recourse to honest courts. A quarrel over 34 million dollars in delinquent railway taxes has been a thorn in the New Jersey body politic for almost twenty years. The railways—five main trunk lines—*must* go through Jersey City to reach New York. They can't move. So what they can or should pay in taxes becomes a major battleground between Hague and the city on one hand and the state on the other. Prudential Insurance, one of the great insurance companies of the world, threatened to pick up bag and baggage and quit the near-by city of Newark forever, in February, 1945, unless taxes were reduced. It was complaining about state taxes, however, not Hague's. Standard Oil of New Jersey has moved four times in recent years, because of what it thought were exorbitant local taxes. I do not say that these great corporations should not pay their proper share of the tax burden: I am saying merely that they considered conditions to be intolerable. For instance Jersey City could, by arbitrary procedure, suddenly lift an assessment on a company, as it did in one case, from $1,500,000 to $14,000,000 overnight, while at the same time reducing to a bagatelle that of another which it favored.[9]

One reason why Hague is no longer so powerful as before is that, as he grows older, and his absences in Florida become more pronounced, he finds it more difficult to impose discipline on his own men. Also many of his cronies and henchmen, who got their jobs a generation ago, are getting older too. Hague is loyal, however, and will not sacrifice them. As a result the younger men in the machine, the district leaders who actually get the vote out, find promotion very slow. All they can look forward to, as I heard it put, is funerals.

Turn now to the state. The simplest way to illustrate Hague's power on a pan-New Jersey plane is to point out that six out of the last ten administrations were supported by him, including those of the aforementioned Mr. Moore.[10] But since 1941 Hague has not had such easy sledding with governors. A notably decent man, Charles Edison, the son of the inventor and a former secretary of the navy, took office then, and refused to be bossed by the Hall, although a Democrat. The noise of

[9] According to the *New Yorker*, which names the names.
[10] A wonderful glimpse of Moore's political philosophy may be gathered from his opposition to social security on the ground that "it takes the romance out of old age." *Public Men*, p. 442.

the ensuing three-year quarrel could have been heard in Saturn. Then came Edge, a stalwart old Republican and a former ambassador to France, who fought Hague stubbornly for three years more. This was the first time that Hague had been faced by two hostile governors in turn; before this, even if unfriendly administrations did exist, he had managed to get one of his own men in between. Finally, in November, 1946, Hague got the beating of his life, when Alfred E. Driscoll, another able and hard-hitting Republican, succeeded Edge.

Few states have more volatile and energetic politics than New Jersey. Even United States senators pop in and out of office like balls in a pin game. The number that have held office in the past twenty years is beyond belief; there have literally been thirteen since 1929. Then consider judges. I could make this chapter fifty pages long. I will not do so. To trace out the interrelations among various members of the judiciary, pro- and anti-Hague, since the Hall has controlled most of the courts, is an adventure like going through the maze of Hampton Court blindfold and full of marijuana.

New Jersey governors, uniquely in the union, serve three-year terms. They may not be re-elected until after an interval. The legislature, especially the senate, is elected by a rotten borough system which favors the rural districts, and is invariably controlled by the Republicans. Now the power of the governor rests almost solely on appointments. But all appointments to the judiciary and in fact to all really good jobs in the state must be confirmed by the senate. Customarily the governor and senate, even if of the same party, are as suspicious of each other as blackbirds, and therefore, to prevent a governor from slipping through appointments it may not like, the legislature remains almost continuously in session. In fact it usually stays alive until five minutes before its successor convenes, to obviate the possibility of *ad interim* appointments by the governor. There are more than seventy-five different state bodies in New Jersey, many of them overlapping, to which appointments may be made. So jobs are plentiful and keenly fought for. Some governors, instantly on being elected, set out to build a machine of their own, so that (*a*) they will be sure of a satisfactory job on leaving office, and (*b*) will be in a good position to run for re-election after the three-year interval. As a rule a governor wields effective power only in his first two years of office. After that, nobody pays much attention to him, since everybody is concentrated on maneuvering for the succession.[11]

Now this whole situation plays perfectly into the hands of a boss like Hague. He can balance almost anybody against anybody else by promising favors in return for support, to say nothing of the fact

[11] The fact that New Jersey gubernatorial elections are held every three years has another odd effect; they only jibe with Presidential elections once every twelve years, instead of every four.

that appointees all over the state are still his men, appointed by "his" governors. Moreover there are many consequential Hague *Republicans* in New Jersey, not only in the rural areas but in cities like Atlantic City. Hague has, or had, cordial relations with Enoch L. ("Nucky") Johnson, the Republican chieftain there who went to the federal penitentiary on an income tax conviction in 1941, and with lesser princelings in other towns.

Finally, we reach the national level. Why should a man great and serene like Roosevelt, who compares to Hague as the Parthenon to a chicken coop, have stooped to the level of dealing with the Hall? Do not be innocent. Mr. Hague has a steely grip on the Democratic state machine; he has been the leader of the New Jersey delegation to every national convention since 1920. Mr. Roosevelt had to deal with him because the structure of American politics imposes on every president the necessity of being a politician, and all folk running for office not only like votes but *surplus* votes, even when they're not necessary. As a matter of fact FDR would not have carried New Jersey without Hague's support in several campaigns. In 1932 for instance he won the state by only 30,000; Hague's plurality in Hudson County was a walloping 117,000. About the various shenanigans that accompanied the candidacy of Mr. Edison (after FDR "toured the state by telephone"), and some excessively opaque and unsavory matters in federal patronage, we cannot speak here for lack of space. One extraordinary fact is that Hague himself was once an Al Smith man, violently anti-FDR. He arrived at the 1932 convention stating that, if nominated, Roosevelt "would not carry a single state east of the Mississippi, and very few in the West."[12]

The way Hague plays with politics is accepted by many Americans with a certain moral lethargy; when he started playing with civil liberties sharper resentment was aroused. Some years ago, in consequence of a vindictive campaign to drive the CIO out of New Jersey, the Hall among other things passed an ordinance forbidding public meetings without a police permit. Later this was declared unconstitutional by the Supreme Court. But not until fierce local alarums had been sounded. It is one of the strangest of strange developments that, years later, the CIO should have re-entered the state in a quite different role, as a vehement supporter of Hague and the Hague machine. Of course this was to assist Roosevelt's re-election. Politics makes—but you finish it.

The Hall has a son, by name Frank Joseph Hague Jr. This young man, who subsequently did a perfectly good and correct job as an official in Leo Crowley's Foreign Economic Administration, was in 1939 appointed by Governor Moore to a seat on New Jersey's highest court, that of errors and appeals. He was at this time only thirty-four;

[12] *Public Men, op. cit.*, p. 447.

he had only begun to be well known as a lawyer; he had been unable
to finish Princeton, and to make a place for him on the bench a vast
and complex reshuffling was necessary, with repercussions that reached
Washington and permeated judicial affairs all over the state for years.
That this young man, whose legal experience can best be described as
meager, should have been given this appointment to a court as proud of
its historic tradition and impeccability as any in the land naturally provoked comment. Judge Hague resigned his post in January, 1945, just
before his term was to expire. His chances of being reappointed by
Governor Edge were not considered good.

Most New Jersey observers do not think that the junior Mr. Hague
will be the successor to his father; the succession rests, it is thought,
with the Hall's nephew, Frank Hague Eggers, the old man's secretary
and a member of the city commission. One description I heard of him is
that "he is personable in a Jersey City sort of way."

Hague's salary as mayor of Jersey City, the only public post he holds,
is $8,000 per year. Yet his fortune is estimated by such an authority as
Professor McKean of Dartmouth, author of *The Boss,* at four million
dollars. Hague lives in an expensive Jersey City apartment building,
which he owns; his summer house at Deal cost, according to public
record, $125,120.50 cash. Several times he has had brushes with the in-
come tax authorities; in 1929 he was fined $60,000 for tax delinquency.[13]
He has been questioned on occasion as to sources of his income and once,
when accused of having accepted financial help from the bookmakers, he
replied, "It's all a goddam lie. I'd be crazy to take that kind of money.
Hell, if I wanted to be dishonest, I could have dealt with the big companies whose assessments I raised." Hague's own explanation of his
wealth is that well-informed friends gave him tips on the Stock Market.

To recapitulate: Hague himself is important not for his own qualities,
or lack of them, but as a type. He is the end product of a system of
society rather than a protagonist. But the system he represents is an
affront to the Democratic party, to the American political system, to the
memory of Mr. Roosevelt, to President Truman and the Democratic
National Committee, and to civilization in the United States.

Note in Futurity

If, like Enoch Soames in Max Beerbohm's famous story, I could be
projected a hundred years into the future, to find myself browsing in a
library, one of my first curiosities would be about a man like Hague.
What will Hague—and Jersey City and so many other American cities
large and small—look like in the perspective of a new century? What

[13] According to the *New Yorker,* February 12, 1938. This is also the source for
the quotation that follows.

we of 1947 can hope for, at least, is that in 2047 our present modes of political behavior, our manner of life in great cities, will seem as museum-like, as silly and archaic and also profanely cruel and wasteful, as conditions of child labor in England during the industrial revolution, or the peasantry in Russia under the czars, seems to us today. A clean brightness and briskness of civic spirit; enlightened and orderly democratic processes; tenements and slum encrustations abolished; scientific criteria for city management; a more generous community interest; schools well built and teachers well paid; the rubble of old neighborhoods torn out and rebuilt according to broad plan—all this can be in 2047, if people in 1947 will only will it so.

Garden State Foreshortened

New Jersey, a raucous little state, is marked off on its whole western edge by the sharp bending ribbon of the Delaware River, and is, in a manner of speaking, almost an island. The Gulf Stream warms the Atlantic along most of the Jersey shore; there is a 20 per cent difference in temperature between the water at Sandy Hook and Cape May; ice-breakers are at work near Bayonne when the strawberries are blooming below Atlantic City. The ocean frontage not only means a great fishing and tourist industry, but also a considerable income to the state from riparian rights.

As Edmund Wilson once wrote in the days when he was Edmund Wilson Jr., New Jersey is the slave of two cities. It is the commuter state par excellence. Hundreds of thousands of its citizens lead a "hybrid" life between New York, Philadelphia, and their homes in Jersey itself; at least a third of the population is suburban. Newark is as much a part of New York City, as we have already noted, as the Empire State Building. The Port of New York Authority embraces, with full New Jersey co-operation of course, the whole Hudson River estuary, and Newark was for years New York's chief airport. To get to Times Square, say, from Jersey City, takes much less time than from the outer fringes of the Bronx or Staten Island. One odd point is that Jersey City, with its 300,000 people, has no department store. It must be the only American city of such size without one. Macy's, Gimbel's, Wanamaker's, Saks, all the others on Manhattan, are only a half hour away.

Anybody who has ever doubted that American civilization is industrial has only to take a train from New York to Philadelphia or, better, get lost driving in the Newark-Jersey City area, underneath the Pulaski Skyway. The roads here are, I think, incidentally, the most confusingly marked of any in the United States. Here the fangs of industry really bite. There is not a blade of grass, if one may exaggerate slightly, in a dozen square miles. In a small car, at dusk, as the giant trucks and trailers grind their way through loops in smeary roads, one feels like a grasshopper caught in a stampede of iron elephants. The whole area is a kind of demonic metal shambles. Then it is almost impossible, emerging, not to reflect on one of the sharpest of all American paradoxes: the illimitable profusion of wealth in this country, created by men as well as machines, and the degrading poverty that accompanies it or, put in slightly different terms, the titanic amount of energy that goes into industrial production, compared with the meager residue allotted to the amenities of life. Look at any of the sleek factories on the road to Trenton. Then glance at the creaking black hovels along the tracks where people live.

New Jersey, though only the forty-fifth state in area, is sixth in value of manufactured products. The historic reason for this, aside from proximity to the sea, is that its axis is the shaft of a kind of dumbbell, of which New York and Philadelphia are heads; New Jersey feeds them both. It produces a greater variety of industrial products than any other American state, from steel rope to television sets (New Jersey will be "the first television state," I heard it said), from battleships to silk to calculating machines, from gasoline to industrial tape to jinrickshas. Passaic and Paterson are great textile towns, famous for early struggles in the labor movement, and it has no fewer than seven cities greater in population than 100,000.

Then—two minutes off this seething industrial highway—New Jersey bursts open like a rose. It produces a multifarious agriculture, mostly in vegetables, poultry, and dairy products. Not only agriculture. When the small-game season opens every autumn, at least 100,000 people hunt. New Jersey is a great state not merely for electronic tubes but for pheasants, rabbits, quail.

Much else about New Jersey should be said. It has one town, Flemington (the site of the Lindbergh kidnapping trial), which was once the home seat of some ninety corporations, including Standard Oil of New Jersey, because its property taxes are so light. It has the biggest court of last resort in the United States, with sixteen judges ("slightly bigger than a squad, slightly smaller than a mob"), of whom six lay members need not be lawyers. It has part of the Hudson Palisades, than which nothing in the eastern United States is more dramatically beautiful, the headquarters of the Gallup Poll, and the home of Walt Whitman. It has an important Ukrainian newspaper, and it is one of the few states where the Communist party, as such, advertises in the local press; it has one city, Hoboken, where there is a bar for every 207 citizens, the "Yarb Folk" of the southern shore, and a law obliging all high school students to take two years, not merely one, in American history and government. It has a strong Quaker underlay, also a strong Dutch underlay, and it believes so strongly in states' rights that it once appropriated $25,000 to test the constitutionality of the Social Security law, while its citizens were benefiting from its provisions.

Finally, consider education. New Jersey has Rutgers, founded in 1766 and later a land grant college, which is one of the largest universities in the country with 16,000 students, and also the Institute for Advanced Study where Einstein works with a handful of exalted spirits. Princeton, the most sophisticated of all American universities as well as one of the best, is of course a New Jersey institution. Sometimes this pleasant school is referred to as a kind of ivory tower plus a country club. Nothing could be further from the truth. About a third of Princeton's boys are on scholarship, and many wait on table eleven meals a week. Princeton differs from Harvard and Yale first because it is so much smaller, with attendance normally limited to 2,400, second because it is rural, not urban. Princeton, about which pages might be written, is crammed with strange distinctions; for instance every president has either been a Presbyterian minister or the son of one. It takes its splendid history for granted, and the campus has no statue, monument, or tablet to Woodrow Wilson.

Chapter 36
The Great State of Pennsylvania

vvvvvvvvvvvvvvvvvvvvvvvvvvvvvvvvvvvvvvvvvvvvvvvvvvvvvvvvvvvvvvvvvvvvvvvvvvvvvvvvvvvvvvvvvvvvvvvvvvvvvvvvvvvvvvvvvvvvvv

> The public must and will be served.
> —William Penn

WHENEVER I go to Philadelphia, which is as often as I can, be-cause I like it, I stroll down Chestnut Street and look at Inde-pendence Hall. Here, on June 10, 1775, George Washington became commander-in-chief of the American Revolutionary forces; here, on July 4, 1776, the Declaration of Independence was adopted; here, on November 3, 1781, the twenty-four British standards captured at York-town were presented to Congress, and here, on September 17, 1787, the Constitution of the United States, which still rules us all, more or less, was signed. One plaque in the central lobby goes farther back, the "Frame of Government" of William Penn:

GOVERNMENT IS FREE TO THE PEOPLE . . . AND MORE THAN THIS
IS TYRANNY OLIGARCHY AND CONFUSION

Look across Chestnut Street, and travel several hundred years in twenty yards. In the block facing the red brick Hall, I noticed these 'buildings and signs:

Scottie's Restaurant—Pure Food—Coca-Cola
Krug's Parking
Sandwiches Toasted Grilled Large Variety of Desserts
Land Title Bank and Trust Co. Chartered March 10, 1812. Charter
    Perpetual
Ben Gurk's. Sandwiches, Platters, Souvenirs.
For Rooms, Read *Bulletin* Want Ads

Perhaps, for the vigor of its industrialization, its patchwork mixedup-ness, America pays a large price in the sacrifice of esthetic values. But this line of small shops and offices, nondescript and heterogeneous, is proof just as much as Independence Hall—the birthplace of the United States in all its classic tranquillity and grace—that this is a country still based on personal energies and ambitions and explorations, on freedom and the rights of man.

Some Characteristics of Pennsylvania

Pennsylvania, literally a keystone, one of the two or three most important of all states, one of the four commonwealths, lies like a rectangular wedge, a matrix, linking the Great Lakes and the Atlantic, embracing rivers as lovely as the Susquehanna and mountains like the Appalachians, and above all tying together steel and coal. Pennsylvania is bigger by a third than Hungary, more populous than the Netherlands, and as self-sufficient as any but a handful of nations. It runs a stout and exhilarating gamut from the quiet enchantment of the scenery in Bucks County to the flat ugly black roofs of Pittsburgh, from the aluminum and glass works along the Allegheny to the greatest collection of modern French painting in the world, that of the renowned Dr. Albert Barnes near Philadelphia.

To a degree the story of Pennsylvania is the story of iron, coal, and steel. Yet, of its 26 million acres, almost half is forest! This is a Commonwealth almost always thought of as overwhelmingly industrial, but it contains some of the richest agricultural land on earth. Pennsylvania beats and throbs with its Herculean production of locomotives, steel blooms and ingots, printing presses, great boats, electrical machinery, and every variety of textile from rugs to cotton lace. Also you can go out in its woods and shoot, not merely grouse and pheasant, but deer and bear. From two to three hundred bear are killed in Pennsylvania every year on the average, and some 30,000 deer; in one season in 1931, 200,000 deer were shot, just to thin them out.[1] Talk about the gargantuan span of America, its variety!

Pennsylvania belonged successively to the Indians, the Netherlands, Sweden, and England, and France claimed part of it for a time. A great man named William Penn arrived in 1682. The story is well known. He obtained a grant for most of what Pennsylvania and Delaware cover today, to settle a debt of £16,000 owed his father by Charles II. He wanted to call his vast tract New Wales (indeed Welsh influence was strong in the area for generations; witness such names as Bryn Mawr), but he was overruled, and Pennsylvania became the name. For his immense preserve, Penn agreed to pay the king "Two beaver skins to bee delivered att our said Castle of Windsor, on the first day of January, in every yeare, and also the fifth parte of all Gold and Silver Oare, which shall from time to time happen to be found."[2]

---

[1] As interesting as any specialized publication I know is the monthly *Pennsylvania Game News*. It contains sentences like "Raccoons may be hunted at night, with a noon-to-noon daily limit," and "Traps must not be placed closer than 15 feet from the waterline of any established beaver house." The State Game Commission has an elaborate "predator control" system to protect important fur-bearing animals like minks. Bounties were paid in a recent season for 8,032 gray foxes and 16,509 weasels.

[2] *Pennsylvania* in the American Guide Series, pp. 22-24.

Pennsylvania, bulging down the middle with its mountains, is a sharply divided state; Philadelphia in the seaboard orbit, is at one extreme end as everybody knows, and Pittsburgh, close to the Middle West, is at the other, with Harrisburg in between. I asked Senator Edward Martin, when he was governor, how Harrisburg happened to become the capital; he answered amiably, "Darned if I know," and then suggested that, in prerailway days, canals usually determined the sites of cities. Soft coal is at one end of the state, anthracite at the other; steel is in the Pittsburgh area, and textiles in Philadelphia, though Philadelphia has plenty of heavy industry too, for instance the Baldwin locomotive works and the Budd Company that makes stainless steel trains. One geographical curiosity is the abutment to Lake Erie. Pennsylvania is not a Switzerland; it has its own outlet to an inland sea.

However markedly divided the Keystone State may be geographically, the ideological divisions are not less acute. The gap between conversation at a Main Line dinner party and what you will hear in a bar at Altoona, to say nothing of talk in a miner's yard near Shenandoah, is as broad as the Rubicon. Also political stratifications are various. You cannot say simply, as you can with New York, that the rural areas are Republican and the cities Democratic, and that politics are a struggle between these balanced forces. The commonwealth is much more complex than that.

Pennsylvania is packed with great cities; it has ten metropolitan districts holding more than 100,000 people, like the Scranton–Wilkes-Barre complex and Allentown–Bethlehem–Easton. It is the home not merely of Independence Hall but of two other of the greatest historical sites in the country, Gettysburg and Pittsburgh Point. In Pennsylvania, Lord Halifax went fox hunting, and one great town, Hershey, lives on chocolate. Beethoven once intended to write a symphony, "The Founding of Pennsylvania." It is not merely the state of Benjamin Franklin, but of the Whiskey Rebellion, the Molly Maguire riots, and the Homestead Massacre. The first daily newspaper in America was published in Philadelphia, and the first radio station, KDKA, ever to make regular commercial broadcasts is in Pittsburgh, though others have disputed this claim. Pennsylvania has the *Saturday Evening Post,* and also one of the outstanding educational institutions of the nation, the International Correspondence Schools at Scranton. In Pennsylvania, you will find fascinating things to eat like scrapple; a strong Finnish underlay in some areas; the home of the Conestoga wagon; the Pennsylvania, one of the best run and operated railways in the world; towns with names like Seven Stars; the site of Washington's first battle (Fort Necessity); and politics at their most dissolute. It is the original oil state, and both Army and Navy threatened during World War II to put its capital out of bounds, because the venereal rate was so high there. It is the state of

Kitty Foyle and of both the pretzel and pickle "capitals" of the world, and another of its cities aside from Philadelphia—York—was once the seat of the national government. It has a supremely good symphony orchestra, the Liberty Bell, mines where children of six worked a twelve-hour day as recently as forty years ago, the greatest linoleum factory in the world, and the birthplace of Daniel Boone.

City of Brotherly Love and Much Else

Philadelphia, the first capital of the United States and its first metropolis, the third biggest city in the country today[3] and the twelfth largest in the world, is really something special. Often it is compared to Boston, and it is, like Boston, a kind of casement to American history, with a copious intellectual tradition and social aristocracy. But in many ways it differs substantially from Boston. For one thing it is much bigger; for another it is much more heavily industrialized. Like Boston it has an aroma, a patine, a lacquer of charm and mellowness, but it is more relaxed, and also dowdier. Boston is, as we know, a compound of Yankees and the Irish; Philadelphia is more complex, with intermin-glings of Pennsylvania Dutch, other Germans, Scots-Irish, and plain British. Most of Boston stood for the Revolution while it was going on; Philadelphia, like New York, was full of Quislings. Boston has an ag-gressive civic pride; Philadelphia has almost none. Both cities, but for different reasons, have a marked puritanical front; not until the crusades of the late lamented *Record* was Philadelphia's "Black Sunday" light-ened; there is still no alcohol on Sunday, and movies don't open till 2 P.M., so that the devout may not be seduced into entertainment until they have gone to church. Both cities have a great nucleus of consolidated wealth, which is slipping away—in Philadelphia faster. Boston is Catholic, Congregationalist, and Unitarian; the leadership in Philadelphia is Quaker or Episcopalian. Boston, as we know, is a Democratic stronghold par excellence; Philadelphia is the only great American city where the political machine is Republican. Finally, Philadelphia, a distinctly smug and self-satisfied city, is jealous of nothing, whereas Boston is jealous of one thing anyway, Cambridge.

Philadelphia, like Boston, despises New York, and is indifferent to it, though Manhattan draws off a good deal of its wealth and talent. "New York is simply an island full of clip joints," I heard one Phila-delphian aver. J. David Stern, former publisher of the *Record*, who for years was as strong a liberalizing influence as the city had, told me once never to forget that Philadelphia was "the most Chinese city in the United States," surrounded by its own impenetrable wall, and that "Seattle was much nearer to New York."

[3] But the next census may well put Los Angeles and Detroit ahead.

Innocently enough, I asked a group of eminent Philadelphians on one occasion what they thought of Pittsburgh. Answer: "Pittsburgh? Where's that?" Then came howls of laughter.[4] Indeed, Philadelphia is apt to think that anybody beyond the Schuylkill is a red Indian.

In the Philadelphia suburbs, set in an autumnal landscape so ripe and misty that it might have been painted by Constable, in Germantown and Chestnut Hill and along the Main Line, lives an oligarchy more compact, more tightly and more complacently entrenched than any in the United States, with the possible exception of that along the north shore of Long Island. But Long Island, whether in fact or not, gives a seasonal impression, an impression of being a summer refuge, and its more affluent millionaires maintain establishments in town too. The Main Line lives on the Main Line all the year around. It stretches on either side of the right of way of the Pennsylvania Railroad to Paoli, for about forty miles. It is one of the few places in the country where it doesn't matter on what side of the tracks you are. These are very superior tracks. The aristocracy of Chestnut Hill and Germantown (not strictly on the Main Line) is perhaps more civilized and dignified; I heard one member murmur ironically, "We went slumming for the first time in years last night . . . dined with people on the Main Line." The plain fact of the matter is that the Main Line has a deplorable icing of nouveau riche. One of its most conspicuous recent Timons started life as a trolley-car motorman in Indiana. Shades of Drexels, Biddles, Cassatts! What does the whole Main Line believe in most? Privilege.

Main Line or non-Main Line, Philadelphia maintains some remarkable atavisms. There is the City Troop, the pre-Revolutionary regiment which is the escort of every president of the United States who visits the city. It gritted its teeth when Roosevelt came along. There is the Assembly, the rules of which are stricter than those of Buckingham Palace, and which can be compared to nothing in America except, possibly, the St. Cecilia Society in Charleston. Boat racing still survives, and so does cricket. I asked a gentleman who might have stepped out of the ruins of Persepolis why cricket had declined. "Because," he answered dryly, "America consists today of people who want to be at bat all the time." Then there are the clubs, like the Sunday Breakfast Club, which of course meets on Wednesday evenings, the Racquet Club (of some 1,100 members perhaps a dozen voted for Roosevelt in 1944), and the Union League (not Union League "club"), where every member must attest that he has never voted for anybody not a Republican, and above all the Philadelphia Club, which admirable institution is the holy of holies, the inner hall of halls. There are stories, doubtless apocryphal, of grim millionaires who died in anguish, after years of bruising their knuckles

[4] Later I repeated this to a stanch citizen of Pittsburgh, who replied, "Philadelphians? Oh, them!"

trying to break through these delicate portals, and never succeeding, and who in revenge punished the entire town by leaving their fortunes elsewhere. Fun to watch in the Philadelphia Club are old gentlemen playing sniff, which appears to be a form of dominoes. An authoritative book on the game is Chew on Sniff.

Once I asked some Philadelphians who was the indisputable grand old man of the community, like Charles Francis Adams in Boston. An embarrassed silence came and then a wrangle. Philadelphia has no single captain of this rank. Several names were mentioned, and all were distinguished enough—Dr. Thomas S. Gates, president of the University of Pennsylvania, Mr. Justice Owen J. Roberts, who has not, however, been directly associated with the city for a good many years, and of course former senator George Wharton Pepper. Still feeling for names, I asked what, if anything, descendants of Benjamin Franklin might be doing in Philadelphia these days. One answer was (I report it literally): "We consider Mr. Franklin to have been of a somewhat shady family."

All over Philadelphia one may hear gems of this kind. A Main Liner in, I believe, one of Philip Barry's plays says, "We don't pay any attention to our daughters, but we train good horses, by Gad!" I asked about Gifford Pinchot, Pennsylvania's late great governor and conservationist, and got the reply, "He offended me as a trout fisherman; the fellow actually fished downstream." At one dinner party I heard the remark, "The trouble with Stokowski is that he *is* a damned good musician!" At another I listened to William Penn being referred to affectionately as "Billy," and learned that Hitler and Mussolini were representatives of the common people and that consequently the common people are to be damned, that of course Roosevelt was "a traitor to his class" (this cliché popped up actually in this form), and that American elections are a farce, since the majority, even if it is only 51 per cent, can overrule the minority. Dave Stern once printed, strictly as satire, a letter purporting to come from a local Croesus urging that the unemployed be sterilized. To his horror, dozens of people took it seriously. At one gathering, with my own ears I heard a frigid snob call the president of the United States "that haberdasher." In forty-eight states, over thirteen months, in talk with a thousand people, I heard this remark only here.[5]

Does the aristocracy of Philadelphia live up to its civic obligations? Parts of the city, so frowsy and derelict these days, look like an old man losing his teeth. But municipal decay is a complex phenomenon; no single group has responsibility. The fact that for many years Philadelphia was ruled by a political machine monstrously knavish certainly played a

[5] Philadelphia has an admirable Jewish community, it might be added, philanthropic, civic minded, able. Consider Rosenwalds, Gimbels, Masbaums, Wolfs, Fleishers, Felses. One historic colony of seven Jewish families lived for years on what was called "Jews Hill." Some of these turned Christian however.

role. The Main Line and the aristocracy are factors largely through their absence, one might say. "The people who own the city," writes George Sessions Perry, "have abandoned it."[6] This phenomenon is not, of course, peculiar to Philadelphia; we have noted it in Boston and Chicago. In city after city, the ruling class moves out to escape the pressure of urban taxes. The Main Line settled itself in its beautiful homes and formal gardens, continued to make its money in the city, and left it to decay. One theory I heard was that "the automobile has killed Philadelphia," by making it easier to flee from. "Everybody with $3,000 a year lives in the suburbs." Of course this is an exaggeration, but it expresses the prevailing mood. Meantime the oligarchy has not had everything its own way financially, by any means. The trustees of Philadelphia, like those of Boston, invested the old family fortunes with extreme conservatism. They did not go in for anything so daredevil as automobiles or banks. The basis of the ancient wealth was real estate; a sound mortgage was venerated in Philadelphia practically on the same level as the Episcopal church. But now, with the city deliquescing, the value of urban mortgages has been drastically reduced, and the Main Line suffers along with everybody else.

In any case Philadelphia is full of troubles. The valuation of real and personal property dropped from almost five billion dollars in 1930 to roughly three billion in 1944, and the city is tax-delinquent by millions. This has, of course, played havoc with revenue, and public works, even in the simplest matters of street repair, consequently suffer. Yet, a proud city that hated the New Deal, Philadelphia flatly refused a 60 million dollar offer from the Public Works Administration during the depression. This spirit carries right on to date. Philadelphia has fifteen times the population of Camden, New Jersey, across the Delaware River; 22 years ago Camden set out to reorganize its approaches to the bridge connecting the two cities, and employed as good engineers as were available. But Philadelphia has still to do the same thing at its end. A subway spur along Locust Street, built at a cost of eight million dollars, was never finished; the tunnel is still there, empty, derelict, without tracks or stations. In 1930, twelve years after World War I, Philadelphia started a campaign to build a veterans' hospital. Today, two years after World War II, it still hasn't got one. Some 400,000 veterans of both wars live in the city; for them, 550 hospital beds are available.[7] Conditions in Byberry, the hospital for mental diseases, make it a kind of Bedlam, as the reports of Albert Deutsch in *PM* recently disclosed. On the other hand, Philadelphia is very self-conscious about its pigeons. In

[6] In his lively Cities of America series, *Saturday Evening Post*, September 14, 1946.

[7] Philadelphia *Record*, October 14, 1945.

order to weed them out, an ordinance was passed recently forbidding the citizenry to feed them.

Finally, water. Philadelphia drinks its own sewage, chlorinated. The City of Brotherly Love is, in fact, the only one of similar rank in the nation where the quality of the drinking water is a compelling problem. Both the Delaware and the Schuylkill are filthy rivers, slimy with industrial and human waste. One expert recently termed the Port of Philadelphia "the largest, vilest, and foulest fresh water port in the world"; its water is so tainted that, literally, it damages the steel walls of ships. Every day, some 350 million *gallons* of raw sewage pour into the rivers that are the city's only source of water supply. To create a proper supply, and to avoid the necessity of chlorination which affects the taste of the local water even though making it safe enough, would cost 150 million dollars. The industrial plants upriver would have to change their techniques in getting rid of waste, which is at present simply dumped into the rivers, and so many of them oppose projects for amelioration and reform.

A heavy blow came to Philadelphia in 1946. Wholeheartedly, almost with desperation, the city hoped to be the United Nations capital. The entire community bestirred itself, from top to bottom, to gain this prize which might have served to revivify it and renew its ancient distinction. But though Philadelphia wanted the UN, the UN didn't want Philadelphia.

Society of Friends

No community of people in America has a more substantial record in good citizenship than the Quakers. This goes all the way back to William Penn himself; Penn's laws were a hundred years in advance of his time, and the Quaker precepts of diligence, modesty, and firm belief in the fundamental goodness of man worked their way deep into the life of the commonwealth. Came the Revolution, and the Quakers resigned in a body from the legislature rather than support any military action. Then opened what historians call the "Period of Quietism," and gradually Quaker participation in public affairs diminished. Meantime, however, the faith spread widely. For a time the Friends dominated New Jersey and Delaware as well as Pennsylvania; they held the balance of power in Maryland, and had considerable importance as far afield as Rhode Island and North Carolina.[8]

Today Pennsylvania is still the citadel of Quakerism, though some other states have more members, for instance Indiana. Mostly the influence of the Friends, in and around Philadelphia, is intangible, an invisible

---

[8] This is the more remarkable in that the Friends, unlike the Mormons whom they resemble in some respects, were never direct colonizers; they never went into politics or worldly affairs as an organization.

permeation of the atmosphere; Quakers are respected, and a great many old Philadelphia families have Quaker blood. A big source of their power is, too, the fact that many non-Quakers, often without realizing it, have absorbed Quaker characteristics. The frontiers of the sect are not closely defined. Trying to assemble a list of leading Quakers, I asked some important members if, for example, M. W. Clement, the president of the Pennsylvania Railroad, was a Friend. Nobody knew.

More directly, Quaker influence is spread by its splendid schools. Swarthmore and Haverford are both Quaker institutions, though you don't have to be a Quaker to attend either; Bryn Mawr was founded by Quakers, though it is not a Quaker college today. Then, among secondary schools, the role is profound in the community of the George School, the William Penn Charter School, and the Germantown Friends School. To several of these the upper level of Philadelphia citizenry, whether Friends or not, send their children, and have done so for generations.

Strawbridge & Clothier (one of the big local department stores) is Quaker owned, and the Provident Trust Company is a Quaker bank. In most other long-established Philadelphia banks, for instance the Girard Trust or the Corn Exchange, there will be a Quaker or two on the board of directors; this is also true of the big insurance companies, like that which still maintains the honored name "Pennsylvania Company for Insurances on Lives and Granting Annuities." Despite all this, the main weight of Quaker influence is cultural. The president of the Philadelphia board of education is a Friend; so is the president of the art museum, and so are several leading professors at the university. The leader of the Quaker community itself is the venerable Rufus M. Jones, honorary chairman of the American Friends Service Committee.

The Quakers were long divided amongst themselves; the "orthodox" or Arch Street Friends made one wing, and the Hicksites or Race Street Friends the other. The theology of this is not our concern; more than a hundred years ago a man named Elias Hicks led a revolt against what he thought was the increasingly formal theology of rich Quakers in the towns. But now this fissure, after much hard-headed pondering, has at last been healed.

Quakers still maintain unchanged a good many of their original characteristics, though of course they no longer wear broad-brimmed hats or otherwise dress differently from their neighbors. Alcohol and tobacco are in theory proscribed, and good Quakers say "thee" and "thou." There is no tithe as in the Mormon church, and no collections; the ministry is unpaid, and all financial support comes from voluntary contributions. The meeting houses have no altar or formal service, and the organization is democratic to an extreme degree. For instance the faith has no official head, and issues are settled by discussion and compromise, never by formal vote or even by raising of hands. A subject will be aired, pro and con; nothing is accepted save by unanimous consent. This makes progress sure, if slow.

Politics of the Pennsylvanians

I don't like Joe Pew's brand of politics.
　　　　　　　　　　　　—Wendell Willkie

As of the time I did my research in Pennsylvania, the dominant political personalities were three men named Joe—Joe Pew, Joe Grundy, and Joe Guffey. In 1946, however, Senator Guffey, a strong New Dealer, was beaten for re-election by the Republican governor, General Martin, and the three Joes became two, with Pew and Grundy at the top of the heap again.

Pennsylvania probably has the most confused and internecine politics of any state, and it is one of the most difficult in the union to administer. When I asked who or what ran it, one answer was, "Nobody—it just runs"; another was "Everybody—pulling it by the nose," and a third was the simple word, "Corruption!" Pennsylvania has public men as ambitious as Brewster, as reactionary as Bridges, as stubbornly prejudiced as Taft, and who leave spoors almost like that of McKellar. Above all it is a big-money state, and its politics ring with cash. For a generation or more, almost as Republican as Vermont, it was the most "dependable" big Republican state in the union; hence most of the more volcanic struggles took place within the GOP itself, which led to intricate and stormy splits and fusions, often with the Republican command biting itself in half.

The names flicker in and out of history: Matthew S. Quay, the first statewide boss, who like William S. Vare was refused a seat in the Senate "even when it was controlled by his own party," so dubious was his reputation;[9] the late Senator Boies Penrose, who ate himself to death, and whose statue faces the capitol at Harrisburg today, in significant symbolism; the coal masters like Frick and the iron masters, oil masters, railway masters; in a different category eruptive romantic youngsters like William C. Bullitt, who was beaten recently for the Philadelphia mayoralty by an unholy coalition between tycoons and Communists; ancient and glacial magnates like Andrew W. Mellon, "the meanest man in the world," and odd characters who sat next to him in the Cabinet like "Puddler Jim" Davis, former secretary of labor and ruler of the Loyal Order of Moose.

The main background element in all this is that Pennsylvania was built substantially by manufacturers; the manufacturing class in turn based its existence on a high tariff, and was ferociously Republican. For years, the bosses were able to dominate affairs by the simple expedient of going

[9] Cf. *The Big Bosses*, by Charles Van Devander, p. 135.

to the great manufacturers, and threatening to raise taxes if campaign contributions were not forthcoming. Or, as it developed, the manufacturers themselves entered politics freely, and gave without the necessity of being asked or threatened, in order to implement their own control. Political and industrial bossism merged.

Then came Roosevelt. He was beaten by Hoover in 1932, but he carried Pennsylvania the other three times he ran. In 1934, Guffey became the state's first Democratic senator in more than fifty years, and the next year George H. Earle, a close friend of Bullitt's and Dave Stern's, became the first Democratic governor since the turn of the century. This was revolution. Earle, a notably picturesque character to put it very mildly, forced through laws—amid the most violent hurly-burly—restricting child labor, establishing the forty-four-hour week for women, and enlarging the scope of workmen's compensation, unemployment relief, and the like. Pittsburgh went Democratic too, for the first time in its history. Later Earle's regime collapsed, to the tune of wholesale scandal among underlings, but the mayor of Pittsburgh today is David L. Lawrence, who was secretary of the commonwealth under Earle and who is still state chairman of the Democratic party.

The magnates had, of course, gone too far. Until Earle, the big "interests" had had everything their own way; above all they were able to write their own tax bills. The immense, beneficent force of Roosevelt carried into Pennsylvania, but it did not last, if only for the reason that the statewide Democratic organization can never be as strong as the Republican, because it does not control Philadelphia. In 1946 came the inevitable reaction, and the resurgent Republicans swept the state almost clean. Yet, since 1932, much ancient ice has been broken. Nobody can predict what will happen next. Chester County, along the Main Line, used to go Republican by twenty to one. Now it goes Republican by two to one, or less. One of the grand old men of Philadelphia told me, "But it wasn't just the war. It wasn't just Roosevelt. This country is changing. People change."

Money is still, however, the biggest factor in Pennsylvania politics. The following is from a speech by Senator Guffey, made on the Senate floor on March 8, 1945:

> The Republican leaders in Pennsylvania are preparing to buy or steal the election of 1946. For that purpose they have accumulated a corruption fund of $875,000 for which they do not expect to account. This corruption fund was distributed by the Pews and the other oily fat cats . . . as part of the 1944 campaign fund but has been held over for future use . . .
>
> In that election [of 1944] the various Republican state organizations have reported expenditures to a total of $2,367,539.12. These figures are admittedly incomplete . . . I mention these facts pri-

marily to remind the Senate and the country . . . of the multimillionaires, the fat cats, who seek to buy political power by spending
money on politics. Just to make the point clear, it would seem that
the 1,835,048 votes they garnered for Governor Dewey . . . cost
them almost $2 a vote.

The various Democratic committees in Pennsylvania spent a
total of $520,000 in 1944, to which I will add the $92,000 spent by
the Political Action Committee, making a total of $612,000 . . . This
was used to produce a total vote for Roosevelt of 1,940,479 or little
more than 30 cents per vote. If we had had more money I do not
know what we could have done with it unless we had used it to
corrupt the voters.

What I want to know is why the Republicans needed $2 a voter
to lose the election while the Democratic party needed only 30 cents
a voter to win.

The dean of Pennsylvania bosses, Joseph Ridgway Grundy, a Quaker,
a bachelor (like Guffey), an amateur historian, and a wealthy Bristol
textile manufacturer, is over eighty. He is in the grand line, coming
down from Penrose. For many years he was president of the Pennsylvania Manufacturers Association; he led the fight against reform of the
child labor laws; his contribution to American history may be judged
from the fact that, more than any other man, he was responsible for the
Smoot-Hawley tariff bill, which was a major provoking cause of the
world economic crisis of the 1930's and the subsequent depression.
Mr. Grundy is still interested in the tariff. He wrote the tariff plank at
the 1944 Republican convention.[10] Like most bosses, Grundy does not
run for office often. In 1930, he was appointed to fill a Senate vacancy;
but in those days there was a mile-deep and disorderly schism between
the state organization and his machine, and he was badly beaten by the
one-time iron worker, James J. Davis.[11]

Joseph Newton Pew Jr. is a comparative newcomer to the Pennsylvania scene; he did not enter as a major actor until the middle 1930's.
What Pew is is Mr. Money Bags. He and Grundy work together, and
more or less divide their functions; Grundy is a chieftain on the state
level, Pew in Philadelphia. Pew is also a very wealthy man, the vice
president of and a large stockholder in the Sun Oil Company, one of the
richest corporations in the country. Also he has big shipping interests
and is a publisher of considerable power, through his agricultural
journals the *Pathfinder* and *Farm Journal,* which have a very substantial

[10] According to *PM*, May 13, 1946.
[11] Mr. Davis must be one of the greatest joiners in American annals. Not only
does he run the Moose, but he is a member of the Masons, Mystic Shrine, Grotto,
Odd Fellows, Knights of Pythias, Elks, Eagles, Foresters, Protected Home Circle,
Knights of the Golden Eagle, Woodmen of the World, and Maccabees. See Van
Devander, *op. cit.,* p. 142.

national circulation. Pew is about sixty. He voted for Roosevelt,[12] *horresco referens*, in 1932; then he went to Washington to help draft the petroleum code under NRA; this experience disillusioned him, and he became a perfervid Roosevelt hater. For a decade in fact Mr. Pew was one of the fiercest anti-Roosevelt crusaders in the country. He thinks of himself as saving the nation from FDR even now.

Many Pennsylvania men of affairs are inclined to minimize Pew, I found. They dismiss him as a mere plutocrat. He really thinks, as he said once, that only 1 per cent of the country is fit to rule, and that they should. Some people say that he is not a "real" boss, because his influence is so totally negative. But after all he has been the chief mechanism for keeping the Republican party in the state alive financially. People say that "he has even less imagination than Bob Taft," that, despite his services, he is a dead weight on leadership, and that he treats Philadelphia like a corporation in bankruptcy.

A federal law forbids any individual from giving more than $5,000 in campaign contributions to any group. Mr. Pew has, I am perfectly sure, never broken any law, and would not do so. Nevertheless his campaign contributions to the party in the past ten years are estimated at more than a million dollars. He is the chief Republican angel of modern times. How is such largesse legally distributed? First, contributions may be given in the name of relatives or friends; second, they may not be gifts at all, but loans. If a loan should happen not to be repaid that is, of course, a matter for private settlement. No law is broken. The Republican City Committee in Philadelphia is supposed to be in debt to Pew for a very considerable sum, which serves, naturally, to keep it in perpetual fief to the creditor. But nobody has broken any law.

The Philadelphia *Record* printed a report in 1944 that Clinton Anderson, at present secretary of agriculture and at that time a member of a Congressional Committee investigating contributions, had proof, in the form of four canceled checks, that scurrilous post cards attacking the late Sidney Hillman had been paid for by persons close to Pew, in the office of the *Pathfinder*. Pew bitterly "resented and repudiated" the charge, and denied categorically that he had anything whatever to do with the affair. John W. Owens in the Baltimore *Sun,* one of the most irreproachable political reporters in the country, had previously charged that Pew, or members of the Pew family, had given varying sums to such a strange (but maybe not so strange) miscellany of organizations as the Liberty League, the National Committee to Uphold Constitutional Government, the Sentinels of the Republic, and the Farmers Independence Council, which last had fought the social security laws, child labor reform, and agricultural relief. Mr. Owens also stated that the Pew family had contributed more than $300,000 to the Landon cam-

[12] According to Potomacus in the *New Republic*, May 8, 1944.

paign, and that its contributions to the Willkie funds (though Pew had frantically opposed Willkie at the Philadelphia convention), amounted to $113,000, spread through ten states. New Jersey got $16,000 and Missouri $14,000. Vermont and South Dakota (safe!) had to be content with $1,000 each.

Turn now to Harrisburg and the legislature. I heard one former governor say calmly that "it was 80 per cent honest." What the biggest lobby is depends on which is threatened most. But trades between various special interests and the lawmakers cannot be performed so crudely now as heretofore. One famous device was "the pinch bill." This was a threat to write legislation militating against some group of manufacturers, or any other group, which was then called upon to buy off the projected legislation. Another device was a promise by legislators, favorable to the interests of some special group, to initiate legislation *against* this group, in order to gain the support of do-gooders who were opposing it. Then, a few days before the session closed, when it was too late to begin anew, the bill would be mysteriously withdrawn and killed.

Finally, Philadelphia. Here we must go back to the immortal Penrose and even before: Bryce was writing about Philadelphia corruption fifty years ago. Penrose, an extremely clever and able man (but not clever enough to avoid being photographed once emerging from a fancy house, which was a minor embarrassment during one election), had machines both in city and county, so that if he lost in one, he could recoup through the other. Then he cultivated what contemporary Philadelphians call the "weak liberals"; in fact he set up a so-called "independent" liberal committee all his own, in order to control this wing of the vote too. Old citizens of the town and political connoisseurs despise the degeneration that followed Penrose; they consider it beneath Philadelphia's dignity that a subsequent ring of bosses, the Vares, based their operations on the city's garbage collections, and worked in similar unbecoming media.

Another Penrose device was the staggering of elections. They are still carefully arranged so that, most of the time anyway, the local polls do not coincide with the national vote. For instance a slate of county officers like coroner, controller, and some magistrates, comes up in, say, 1945. Governor, members of the legislature, and half the senate, however, do not come up till 1946. Then in 1947 it is the turn of the mayor of Philadelphia, district attorney, recorder of deeds, and the like. By the time the presidential election rolls along, when the vote is sure to be much bigger and when the Democrats would have more chance, most Republicans are safely in. The Democrats, of course, if they get the opportunity, make use of this arrangement exactly as do the Republicans.

The vote of municipal officeholders themselves, though small, is another important item. There are some 21,000 citizens in the employ of Philadelphia, from firemen to the janitors who, it seems, crowd every inch of the City Hall without keeping it clean, and one of their duties is not only to vote themselves, but to get out the vote of others. Promotions in several categories depend on a nod from the precinct committeemen, and most of the division leaders, ward heelers and so on, are of course deeply imbedded in the public payroll. In the old days, as in most great cities, terrific sanctions could be taken against anybody who strayed from the machine, or defied it. In a flash the sanitation department could find your plumbing unsatisfactory, and rip your bathroom out before your very eyes.

Chapter 37

Pennsylvania: Steel and Pittsburgh

〰〰〰〰〰〰〰〰〰〰〰〰〰〰〰〰〰〰〰〰〰〰〰〰〰〰〰〰〰〰〰〰〰〰〰

Our forefathers were pioneers.
So are we.
—Haniel Long, *Pittsburgh Memoranda*

WHAT is steel?" I asked Harold J. Ruttenberg, research director of the United Steelworkers of America and now vice president of the Portsmouth Steel Corporation. He answered promptly, "America!" Eighty-five per cent of all manufactured goods in the United States contain steel in one form or another, and 40 per cent of all wage earners in the country owe their livelihood to steel, directly or indirectly. But this is not what Mr. Ruttenberg was driving at. The basic power determinant of any country is its steel production, and what makes this a great nation above all is the fact that it can roll over 90 million tons of steel ingots a year, more than Great Britain, prewar Germany, Japan, France, and the Soviet Union *combined*. The United States Steel Corporation alone makes twice as much steel as the entire U.S.S.R.

This is a steel age; the whole of modern industrial history, which often means political history, is based on steel. The Civil War was an iron war. Every war since has been a steel war. The day that iron ore was discovered in Brazil, the only important source in the Western Hemisphere outside the United States, we became an imperial nation. We do not control Brazilian production (though one American ore firm has big Brazilian holdings), but we could not afford to let any other country control it. Almost the same thing might be said of the deposits of bauxite in Dutch Guiana. The State Department would not admit this in so many words, and pious adherents of the Good Neighbor policy would of course deny it, but not conceivably could we ever permit any but a friendly power to remain in these areas.

Pittsburgh is Gibraltar. Where the Allegheny and the Monongahela join to form the Ohio a vast ragged umbrella of soot tells you that this is indeed steel's own citadel; civilization based on industrial aggrandizement reaches here its blackest and most brilliant flower. Why? The chief reason is the structure of the rivers, and the great coal deposits near-by. Even so, Pittsburgh is not nearly so "ideally situated" for steel as is, say, Birmingham, Alabama, and it lacks several of the advantages of Cleveland. In Minnesota I heard people say that the "great tragedy of the last century" was the creation of the steel industry so far away from its major supply of iron ore, the Mesabi Range. But there was a good reason for this, in that in the beginning it was cheaper to ship ore to coal than coal to ore. Still, many people in the Northwest yearn for the industrialization that might have been theirs. Perhaps oddly, Pittsburgh did not become the steel capital of the world out of any characteristics inherent in the city itself. Why did automobiles come to Detroit? One reason is that it was already the home both of a considerable foundry and a considerable carriage industry, with skilled craftsmen in both trades available; and an automobile is, after all, as I heard it put in Detroit, nothing but a stove (a foundry product) in a wagon. But Pittsburgh became what it is largely through forces released by nature rather than expressed by man.

Small iron manufactories were built in the Pennsylvania hills near the coal mines a hundred years ago; one can travel a short distance from Pittsburgh today and see furnaces that have not been operated since 1853, but which are still in good repair. In those days a furnace did well if it made eight hundred tons of iron a year. Today, a furnace that doesn't do 50 per cent more per day is obsolete. If an owner didn't have cash with which to pay his workmen in the old days, he gave them actual chunks of pig iron, which was traded in for groceries at the near-by store —"iron money" in the most literal sense. Today, iron is made for a penny a pound. A few years later the Pennsylvania Steel Works at Steelton made its first Bessemer blow, and in 1871 the Pittsburgh Steel Casting Company organized the first steel foundry in the United States. By 1889, American production of pig iron for the first time passed that of Great Britain, and in 1900 we passed the British in open hearth steel. New century, new industrial era, new equilibria in world politics came all at once.

But go back a bit. Steel, in its natural form of iron, is, like wheat, primordial. Iron, in connection with Tubal Cain, is mentioned in Genesis, and crude saws and sickles found in the Pyramids date back at least five thousand years. One authority says, in fact, that iron was known in Egypt from about 7,000 B.C. onward; it was certainly known in both China and India from about 2,000 B.C. Homer is full of iron. Jump forward several thousand years. Iron works are known to have existed in Schasslau, in what is now Czechoslovakia, in A.D. 677, and by the middle of the fourteenth century cannons were used in France and needles in Norway. The first discovery of iron ore in North America appears to have taken place in North Carolina in 1585; members of Sir Walter Raleigh's expedition found it. By 1608 the Virginia Company at Jamestown was actually exporting iron to the East India Company at £4 per ton. The first blast furnace in America was probably built in Pennsylvania near Pottstown in 1720. Four signers of the Declaration of Independence were ironmasters, and in 1795 the first nail mill west of the Alleghenies was built at Brownsville, Pennsylvania. By 1830 there were fourteen steel furnaces in the United States, with a capacity of 1,600 tons of steel; by 1855 the American Iron Association, which was to grow into the present immensely powerful American Iron & Steel Institute, was organized; by the 70's Frick and Carnegie were in action and in 1875 the first sixty-foot steel rails ever rolled in America were produced at Braddock, Pennsylvania. Only seventy-odd years ago![1]

United States Steel

The simplest thing to do is look in the Pittsburgh telephone book. Here is what I saw:

US Steel Corp Subsidiaries
   Amer Bridge Co
   American Steel & Wire Co
   Atlas Lumnite Cement Co
   Carnegie-Illinois Steel Corp
   Carnegie Natural Gas Co
   Cyclone Fence Division—
      Am Steel & Wire Co
   Frick H C Coke Co
   Hostetter Connellsville Coke Co
   Natl Mining Co
   Nat Tube Co
   Oil Well Supply Co
   Pgh Limestone Corp
   Tennessee Coal Iron & Railroad Co
   Union Supply Co
   US Coal & Coke Co
   US Steel Supply Co
   United Supply Co
   Universal Atlas Cement Co
   Wilson-Snyder Mfg Corp

But this does not tell all the story. It does not, naturally, mention that Carnegie-Illinois is the largest unit of its kind in the nation; it gives no conception of the enormousness of American Steel & Wire nor American Bridge. Figures, names become meaningless and dull. It matters little that United States Steel manufactured nine million tons of coke in 1901, had operating expenses of half a billion dollars in 1910, owned 61,999 railway cars in 1918, and in 1945, with assets of more than two billion dollars and 279,000 employees, had gross sales of $1,700,000,000.

[1] Most of these details come from an invaluable privately printed booklet, *Chronology of Iron and Steel*, by Stephen L. Goodale and J. Ramsey Speer, Pittsburgh, 1920.

What does matter, even if General Motors and some bigger companies should disagree, is that U.S. Steel is the world's premier corporation. In the words of *Life*[2] it is "the most fabulous giant yet produced by the industrial revolution. It runs the world's biggest steel plant (at Gary, Indiana), the world's biggest soft coal company, the world's biggest cement company . . . and makes nearly a third of the nation's steel."

U.S. Steel was put together mostly by the heavy, intuitive fingers of the senior J. P. Morgan. Steel was a prodigious advancing business, and various consolidations and abstruse competitions were going on in the 1890's. The ore in a furnace was hardly in a greater state of flux—and heat—than were the jealous interweaving steel men of the day. Andrew Carnegie, I heard it said in Pittsburgh, was "the Sewell Avery of his time," but he was an Avery with a keenly developed sense of public relations—he even projected his reputation into posterity. Henry C. Frick was mainly a coal and coke man. He and Carnegie worked together, but once he told the sharp little Scot that he would see him in hell some day since he knew surely that both would be there. The Carnegie interests coalesced in 1892, and five years later came the "great wire consolidation," with the formation of the American Steel & Wire Company. Still, frictions and abrasions disturbed these mammoths. A contemporary chronicle says, for instance, "The Lackawanna Works broke up the rail pool. The price of rails dropped from $27 to $17 a ton." Another weighty factor was the Rockefeller family, which had bought heavily into the iron ore properties in Minnesota. In the end, J. P. Morgan bought out Carnegie at a considerably inflated price, almost 500 million dollars—the grandiose Morgan despised Carnegie's small shrewdnesses—and in 1901 the United States Steel Company was formed, the first billion-dollar corporation in all history.[3]

Labor people often have, it seems, a nice paradoxical loyalty to the corporations they are pitted against. In Detroit I heard UAW leaders call General Motors "the most brilliantly run of companies." Similarly, in Pittsburgh, United Steelworkers called U.S. Steel the most "intelligent" and "advanced" corporation in the industry. U.S. Steel was a merger of other mergers, but the men who made it were not all economic libertines. Certainly they sought to freeze wages in the holy name of "stabilization," but gradually they developed institutional ideas. They had to. For a time United States Steel actually had more employees than the United States government. In a way, Morgan wanted Big Steel to be so big in order that it should influence all other industries in the nation. At the same time—the paradox is not too difficult—it tried consistently not to be too big in its *own* major field, steel. As we know,

---

[2] November 11, 1946.
[3] The Morgan fee for its services was $62,500,000. See Beard, *op. cit.* p. 308.

it had twice as large a share of the industry's business in 1901 as it has today.

U.S. Steel ramifies of course through the whole fabric of American finance and enterprise, just like General Motors. A list of its twenty largest stockholders, as printed in that suggestive and useful book *The Modern Corporation and Private Property*,[4] is extraordinarily revealing. The largest individual shareholder was the late George F. Baker. Myron C. Taylor had 40,100 shares, or about 0.37 per cent of all stock outstanding. The twenty largest holders of preferred held only 1.7 per cent of the total preferred shares, and only 8.8 per cent of the common. But, though the ownership steadily became more and more diffuse, the management remained fixed and concentrated.

Judge Elbert H. Gary, Morgan's man, was chairman of the board of U.S. Steel, its chief executive officer, and chairman of the finance committee. He was never president. Perhaps as a result of this, perhaps by reason of almost fortuitous development, the company has always been run by triumvirs. Its presidents, like kings—it has only had five since 1901—have been somewhat undistinguished men since the electric and restless Charles M. Schwab, who resigned in 1903. Hardly anybody remembers the other names—William E. Corey (1903-1911), James A. Farrell (1911-1932), William A. Irvin (1932-1938). The president today, whose name is of course in the contemporary news a good deal, is Benjamin S. Fairless. He was a miner's son who taught school in order to be able to go to college, and who became an engineer. He did not join Big Steel till as recently as 1935.[5] But whereas the actual presidents were relatively obscure, other steel executives became very well known indeed, like Edward R. Stettinius Jr., the son of a Morgan partner, who later became secretary of state among other things, and Myron C. Taylor, who has distinguished himself at many types of public service, and who is now the president's ambassador to the Vatican.

When Gary died in 1927 at eighty-one, the high command was split three ways; J. P. Morgan Jr. became the chairman of the board, Farrell the chief executive officer, and Taylor the chairman of the finance committee. A decade later, when Taylor himself resigned, the company maintained this self-division, and three much younger men took over: Stettinius as chairman of the board, though he was only thirty-eight at the time, Fairless as president, and Enders M. Voorhees, a former accountant, as chairman of the finance committee. Of course what this system does is to insure checks and balances. No president is ever the number one man. The notion that any pirate or lone wolf could "invade" Big Steel and seize it, even though steel is a famously anarchic industry, is of course absurd. But a three-way leadership is a sensible precaution.

[4] By Adolf A. Berle Jr. and Gardiner C. Means.
[5] *Life, op. cit.*

The triumvirs today are Fairless, Voorhees, and Irving S. Olds, a Morgan lawyer who has only been with Steel since 1936, and who became chairman of the board in 1940. Behind these men are other directors too, like James B. Black, president of the Pacific Gas & Electric Co., Cason J. Callaway, a Georgia textile manufacturer, one big Chicago banker, one big New York banker, Sewell Avery, and a former governor of New York state, Nathan L. Miller.[6] Finally, there is Thomas W. Lamont, chairman of J. P. Morgan & Co. Of all names mentioned so far, right back to Gary, Lamont is probably the most important. If there is any supreme decision for Big Steel to take, Mr. Lamont's word will probably be decisive. And certainly his counsel will be sage.

From the Pittsburgh point of view Big Steel is, obviously, absentee controlled. Its liver and lights are in Pennsylvania, but the heart and brains are in New York.

Steel, Big and Little

Little Steel is not so little; all the Littles combined are, for instance, as big as Big. By customary definition, Little Steel comprises Bethlehem, Republic, Youngstown Sheet & Tube, and Inland. Weirton is not, as a rule, considered to be in Little Steel, although it certainly is an independent. The word "Little" is not only a misnomer; it becomes absurd when applied to a corporation like Bethlehem, which has assets today of over two billion dollars. Late in 1946, during the portal-to-portal crisis, one of the largest single suits in the country was that filed against Bethlehem, for 200 million dollars.

Schwab moved into U.S. Steel; then he moved out. When he took over Bethlehem it had only one important customer; soon he built it into the second biggest steel company in the world. The president of Bethlehem today, Eugene G. Grace, runs his mastodon strictly as a one-man show, almost as Gary ran his before the era of triumvirates began. Grace is probably as relentless a labor-hater as any in the industry. Big Steel has, it need not be pointed out, no particular sentimentality toward labor, but it appears to have accepted for good the principle of collective bargaining; none of its executives talk quite in terms of going back to the turn of the century and abolishing unions. But seemingly Grace would like to drive the Steelworkers out of existence. What he stands for is complete reaction and resurrection of the open shop.

The Little Steel companies compete vigorously in some respects, and work together in others. Many of their executives, through the great eastern banks, are interlaced with Big Steel men. Perhaps oddly, Little

[6] Others: George A. Sloan of Bankers Trust and Goodyear Rubber; ex-president Irwin; Mr. Taylor; Robert C. Stanley, president of International Nickel; and several Morgan partners.

pays on the whole better salaries than Big. The top U.S. Steel salaries are, if you look at them with appropriate perspective, quite "moderate," being in the $100,000 to $200,000 class. Look at some figures for 1932, the worst year of the depression. Myron Taylor got $197,203. But Schwab's salary was $250,000 in that year, and G. G. Crawford, an executive of Jones & Laughlin, another formidable independent, got $247,225. In 1940 Grace got $478,144 and in 1941, $537,724; in both these years he was the second highest-paid man in the nation.[7]

Best of the Unions

About the United Steelworkers of America, which a Pittsburgh management man told me was the "most adult labor organization in the United States," we could write much. Nothing more dramatically illustrates the sharp, heady rise of American labor than its organization of the steel industry. In 1900 men worked twelve hours a day seven days a week. Think merely of the stupendous development that has taken place within the last decade; it is necessary to take hold of oneself sternly, and look backward with vigilance, to appreciate all that has occurred. In 1936, after two disastrous strikes (one in 1892 at Homestead, one in 1919 led from Chicago), the steelworkers were still unorganized. Then came the evolution of the Committee for Industrial Organization, later to become the CIO, and its powerful, well-thought-out, well-executed drive into steel. The steelworkers' organizing committee, led by Philip Murray, represented an insurgent wing of an old AF of L craft union, the Amalgamated Association of Iron and Steel Workers. Assisting Murray, who was at the time vice president of the United Mine Workers, were men who became famous in the CIO later, like Lee Pressman and Van A. Bittner. Big Steel fought the drive hard for a year. But it didn't want a catastrophic strike, after years of the great depression. On one of the supreme dates of labor history, March 1, 1937, Myron Taylor, chairman of the board of Big Steel, signed a contract agreeing to collective bargaining. The workers got a forty-hour week and a substantial wage rise. The repercussions of this have sounded ever since. The man who signed for labor was John L. Lewis.

Little Steel could scarcely contain itself with rage; it thought of Taylor practically as a wrecker, a saboteur. It refused to treat with labor during most of 1937, and severe strikes took place in several independents. Tom Girdler of Republic was Little Steel's spearhead in those days. The companies contended that they could not "afford" labor boosts. On Memorial Day occurred the tragic massacre at South Chicago, at the gates of the

[7] These figures are from *PM*, January 1, 1946, and the *New Republic*, February 18, 1946.

Republic mills, when police fired into crowds of men, women and children, killing ten and wounding forty. Finally the National Labor Relations Board ordered Republic to bargain collectively and by the end of 1942 all of Little Steel had followed Big into labor contracts. The fight was won, and no serious setback to unionization in the industry has occurred since, though two sizeable independents are still non-CIO.

Meantime the United Steelworkers of America, CIO, was born out of this struggle and grew. From the beginning this great union had characteristics very distinctive. Its mood and organization were, and are, quite different from those of the United Auto Workers, which was winning its first victories in Detroit at roughly the same time. Workers by the thousand poured into the UAW, which grew practically by a process of mass rebellion, as we know. But the Steelworkers were organized little by little by skillful and devoted leaders who went into the mills and stayed there. Nothing remotely like the confusions and rivalries of the UAW exists in the Steelworkers. Their union is run, and run well, from the top; it believes in what I heard called "centralized decentralization"; it has the kind of unity you can't get by hammering people down, and its sub-leaders can move, stick their necks out, and take subordinate decisions without risk—all of which embodies lessons Walter Reuther might well learn. The rank and file is educated and soberminded, and almost everybody has some share of responsibility. Mostly this is the result of complete confidence by the membership in the courage, integrity, and good judgment of Philip Murray.

Murray is probably the most seasoned and civilized of contemporary American labor leaders. This is not a man for whom unionization could ever be a promotion racket. One source of his power is that he has almost complete authority—and practically never uses it. Murray is, of course, president of the CIO itself as well as of the Steelworkers. He was born in Scotland in 1886, and came to the United States with his father in 1902; he worked in the mines as a boy and educated himself by correspondence courses. His father was, incidentally, president of a miners' union in Lanarkshire, and he himself went to his first labor meeting at the age of six.[8] Murray is a strong Catholic, and in 1946 he received an award as "outstanding Catholic layman of the year." He has always kept Communists severely down in the Steelworkers, and is a marked, steady influence against Communist troublemakers and malingerers in the CIO at large. In the long run Murray has, it would seem, only one thing to fear—John L. Lewis, his former leader.

During the war, the no-strike pledge was of course in effect. The Steelworkers were notably loyal. But they did not forget that, from 1924 to 1929, in one of the richest periods of industrial expansion the

[8] *Time,* January 21, 1946.

country has ever known, steel did not grant a single wage increase. As to later years a pamphlet published by the union says that the national income rose 132 per cent between 1939 and 1943, from something over 72 billion to 168 billion dollars; the income of corporations, before taxes, rose 302 per cent, from 6 billion to more than 23 billion dollars; that of the farmers, 179 per cent, from over 4 billion to 12 billion dollars; that of labor only 72 per cent—and much of this as a result of overtime —which meant a lift in average annual earnings only from $1,372 to $2,360. Labor, Mr. Murray likes to point out, did not profiteer during the war.

On the other side profits, before taxes, of Republic Steel rose 779.6 per cent between 1940 and 1942, as against the 1936-39 level. The analogous figure for Bethlehem is 320.4 per cent; for United States Steel, 151.5 per cent. Mr. Girdler of Republic got $275,000 salary in 1942, an increase of 60.7 per cent over 1936-39; Mr. E. T. Weir similarly got $275,000 or an increase of 52 per cent. Other figures published by the Steelworkers compare the five war years, 1940 to 1944, to the five years 1935 to 1939 from the point of view of profits. Profits before taxes for the steel industry as a whole rose not less than 276 per cent, from 933 million dollars to more than three and a half billion, in these years; profits after taxes rose 113 per cent. Dividend payments rose 82 per cent; total assets rose 22 per cent; undistributed profits rose 81 per cent. Look at wages by contrast. Careful investigation showed that the average steelworker's earnings in January 1945 were $50.85 a week, of which federal taxes took $4.93. Compared to 1941, and taking into account the decrease in purchasing power of the dollar, his income actually was substantially lower, not higher, than it had been in 1941.

All this, together with much else, led to the twenty-six-day steel strike of 1946, which, when it began, was called freely the "greatest strike in history." Yet, so vivacious is the pace of events these days, that, looking back only a year later, one can scarcely remember what the details were. Several days before the strike, during the most arduous and acrid negotiations, Mr. Truman suggested that a compromise be reached on the basis of an 18½¢ an hour pay raise. Murray had asked 25¢; Big Steel offered to pay 15¢. Later the union cut its proposal to 19½¢, but Steel refused to move forward from 15¢ and the strike began, on January 23. It tied up 1,292 companies in thirty states. The Truman offer made interesting headlines—and in some unexpected places. *Life* captioned one editorial "Mr. Fairless should pay 18½¢; right or wrong, the President picked it, and we've got to get on with the job." The New York *Daily News* said simply, FAIRLESS MADE A BIG MISTAKE. The only three steel companies that maintained operation during the strike were Henry Kaiser's plant in Fontana, California, Weirton in West Virginia, and the American Rolling Mill

Company in Ohio. The negotiations that went on between government, industry and labor, to say nothing of those between the Iron & Steel Institute (Mr. Grace), Big Steel, and Little, while the strike was on, cannot be dealt with in this space. Formula after formula was worked out and rejected, and the president overruled his own fact-finding board. The whole question became mixed up with OPA, since the industry insisted that it could only pay more if it were allowed to charge more for its product. It held out for a $6.25 per ton rise in the price of steel; OPA held out for $4.00; finally Steel got $5.00. The strike came to an end on February 15. That it was a labor victory though by no means clearcut, could scarcely be denied; workers' pay was lifted by $32 a month, the largest single raise in the history of the industry.

Pittsburgh Plus

But Pittsburgh is much more than just steel. In fact its root strength is not in steel at all, per se, but coal. It is the home of Westinghouse and its intricate nucleus of industries, of great glass works, and above all of Alcoa, which is a whole tremendous story in itself. Look at the telephone book again. We have scarcely mentioned in these pages one of the supreme concentrations of wealth in this country, and one of the least known and most curious. Not only will you find the name Mellon in the book; you will find the Mellon National Bank, the Mellbank Corporation, and the Mellbank Surety Corporation. Then note the listings of the Koppers Company and the Koppers Gas & Coke Company, which are Mellon firms, with their divisions ranging from butadiene to couplings from tar and chemicals to wood.

Thinking of Alcoa, I asked innocently enough what other interests the Mellons had. Answer: "All they are interested in is everything." They have profound ramifying investments in petroleum (Gulf Oil is a Mellon concern), railways, banks, coal, utilities, and steel. Recently the Rockefellers joined the Mellons to form a new insurance company specifically designed to compete with Lloyd's and handle risks too great for smaller firms; recently, too, the First Boston Corporation, one of the notable investment houses of the nation, joined up with the Mellon Securities Corporation, owned by Richard K. Mellon, the nephew of old Andy. Also in 1946, two Mellon banks, the Union Trust and the Mellon National, announced plans to merge and thus give Pittsburgh its "first billion dollar bank."[9] Mellons, through the Mellbank Corporation, a holding company, control eighteen other Pennsylvania banks also. Finally, Mellon announced recently the formation of a private organization to be known as T. Mellon & Sons, the name of the original

[9] *Time*, July 8 and 22, 1946.

banking house founded by old Andy's father, as a voluntary kind of family team for co-ordination of all the Mellon enterprises.[10]

Perhaps oddly, the Mellon clan keeps itself carefully under wraps. Customarily it has not, like the Du Ponts, participated much in the life of the community. Nor are the Mellons active politically in any direct manner, though, as is more than obvious, their power, should they choose to exert it financially, could be overwhelming. W. L. Mellon, another nephew, was for some years the Republican state chairman. But the Mellons like to keep out of the news, perhaps because they are sensitive about Andy's reputation, and they have withdrawn from most relationships in public affairs.

Pittsburgh is a vulnerable city. Lay off steel, and everything lays off. Its industrial life is not, like that of St. Louis or Cincinnati, diversified. The rash of strikes in 1946, culminating in that of an independent union in the Duquesne Light Company, which cut off power, left the community irritable and sullen. December 8 was the first day in a solid year that Pittsburgh did not have some strike or other.

There are all manner of curious Pittsburgh distinctions. From the point of view of tonnage handled, it is by far the greatest port in the world, though hundreds of miles from any ocean and 150 miles from the nearest lake. The Pittsburgh locks, like those at Sault Ste. Marie, handle more traffic than the Panama Canal. The city is, as everybody knows, one of the most shockingly ugly and filthy in the world; most of the time, like London, it lies under a grim tart canopy of smoke and fog. Its approaches are the most forbidding of any city I saw in America, and its traffic arrangements the worst. In the environs, near steel mills like Irvin, are cemeteries of motorcars, thick with rusting carcasses. Pittsburgh has the biggest neon sign in the world, and no locally owned newspaper. Its Catholic community has liberal elements; recently the official organ of the archdiocese went so far as to attack General Franco as an "undisguised dictator." Its university is in the form of a forty-two-story skyscraper, and is called "the Cathedral of Learning"; it has an admirable symphony orchestra, and its Carnegie Exhibition is one of the chief annual events in the American world of art.

Never, until I came to Pittsburgh, had I heard the phrase "industrial folklore." Its heroes are such Paul Bunyans of steel as Joe Magarac, who could toss a locomotive off the tracks with his little finger. Magarac is a Hungarian, and his formidable rival is a Jugoslav, Steve Mestrovic, who can twist a five-hundred pound iron bar into a pretzel. Both comb their hair with traveling cranes, and boil their eggs in a Bessemer converter.

[10] New York *Times*, July 14, 1946.

Negroes in Pittsburgh

I went to see William G. Nunn, managing editor of the Pittsburgh *Courier*, to ask about Negro problems in the community. The main thing to say is that, in his view, the situation of Negroes in Pittsburgh is probably better than in any comparable American city, certainly better than in Chicago or Detroit. There are about 65,000 Negroes in Pittsburgh proper (roughly 10 per cent of the population), and some 35,000 more in a fifty-mile radius. Negroes live almost everywhere in this whole area; there is no ghetto like Harlem or the Chicago "Black Metropolis," though plenty are indeed clustered in the "Hill" district. No discrimination exists in streetcars or elevators; the good hotels accept Negroes without much question; admittance to concerts, the theater, and football games is normal. Other items in segregation are determined by individual neighborhoods. Negroes go to the public schools in circumstances of theoretical equality, and to the university. Three Negro boys were on a recent University of Pittsburgh football team, and one, miraculous to relate, made a touchdown against Notre Dame.

Detroit is the home par excellence of the skilled worker; Pittsburgh of the unskilled. The Pittsburgh working class, with its immense foreign-born and foreign-descended population, seems to tolerate Negroes better than that of any major industrial city. The most hostile foreign communities are the Poles and Italians; the Irish and the Germans are the friendliest. Catholic influence is active; any Negro can go to any Catholic mass in Pittsburgh, and many Negro children go to the parochial schools. As to labor, the pattern is familiar. The CIO welcomes membership by Negroes, and no CIO union in the region would refuse one; many Negroes are, in fact, officers in CIO locals. But the big AF of L unions, particularly the plumbers and bricklayers, continue to resist Negro participation. As to politics, Negroes in Pittsburgh (and in Pennsylvania in general) are not quite so conspicuous as, say, those in Illinois. There are no Negro congressmen, and only one legislator at Harrisburg is a Negro. Partly this is because the community is so widely dispersed; it does not have the geographical impact that it has in Chicago in several wards. But Pittsburgh has plenty of Negro policemen, including a few officers and even motorcycle cops; these serve all over the city, not merely in the Negro districts.

The *Courier* is one of the best known of American Negro newspapers, and this is, perhaps, a good place for brief mention of the Negro press in general. There is only one Negro daily in America, the Atlanta *World*. Most of the others are weeklies, which means two things: (*a*) they cannot deal much in spot news, so that their readers are obliged to take in a white paper too; (*b*) they compete hotly with one another in overlapping areas. Most Negro journalists whom I met, all over the country, think that the *Journal and Guide* of Norfolk is the best Negro paper in the nation, with the Chicago *Defender* as runner-up. The *Courier,* with a circulation of about 280,000, is the biggest, followed by the *Afro-American* group in Baltimore. Often the Negro press is attacked for its sensationalism and stereotyped way of handling "color" news. On the other hand it seldom prints flagrant cheesecake, and does not go in for the more salacious gossip columns.

Of course the *Courier* is a national institution; it prints thirteen different editions which go all over the country. Next to Pennsylvania itself, its biggest circulation is in Florida. It was Republican until Roosevelt, and liberal Negroes sometimes attack it as the organ of the black *petite bourgeoisie*; it supported Dewey in 1944, largely because its editors resented the dragooning of Negroes by southern white Democrats. Not everybody knows the work of George S. Schuyler, the manager of the *Courier*'s office in New York, and one of the best—and most provocative—political writers, white, black, or of any color, in the nation. The following is a fair example of his style. It was written some years ago in protest at the way most white newspapers identify Negroes in the news as Negroes.[11]

This is a subtle form of discrimination designed to segregate these individuals in the mind of the public, and thus bolster the national policy of biracialism. Thus, Paul Robeson is not a great baritone; he is a great "Negro" baritone. Dr. Carver is not just a great scientist; he is a great "Negro" scientist . . . Langston Hughes is not a poet merely; he is a "Negro" poet. . . . No other group in this country is so singled out for racial identification, and no one can tell me that there is not a very definite reason for it. No daily newspaper refers to Mr. Morgenthau as the "Jewish" Secretary of the Treasury or New York's Herbert H. Lehman as the "Jewish" governor, or Isador Lubin as a "Jewish" New Dealer. . . . There would be considerable uproar if Senator Robert F. Wagner were termed "New York's able German-American solon," or Representative Tenerowicz dubbed "Detroit's prominent Pole."

We shall hear more from Mr. Schuyler soon, when we reach the Negro problem itself in Chapter 41.

The Plain Sects

And be not conformed to this world.
—Amish precept

I drove to Lancaster, city and county, and there sought to learn something of the Plain Sects, or Plain People, as they are sometimes called. The placid, swelling fields here—Lancaster is the second richest agricultural county in the entire United States—are, needless to say, an

[11] From Myrdal, *op. cit.*, II, p. 1184.

acute contrast to the pistonlike atmosphere of Pittsburgh. Here are
farmers among the best on earth, irremovably fixed to the soil from
life to death, who for the most part have never even seen the belching
mills not far off—still another American study in differentiation and
amalgam.

It would be a rash person who would attempt to define the term
"Pennsylvania Dutch." The criteria are racial, religious, and linguistic
intermixed, with language—the famous "schoenste lengevitch"—probably the most important factor. But use of this tongue is declining.
Courses in it are still given, however, in the Franklin and Marshall
College at Lancaster. The Pennsylvania Dutch (or Pennsylvania Germans more properly) derive mostly from the Palatinate and Wurttem-
berg, and their migrations date from 1720 or earlier. Simple people like
the Quakers, frugal, pious, they constitute one of the most striking
communities in America. Some of their place names are Paradise,
Bird-in-Hand, Perkiomenville, Gap, Intercourse, and Fertility. Mostly
they are aloof, polite, and interested in nothing so much as accumulat-
ing a property for their children. They take beautiful care of their
farms, come into Lancaster to markets like those in Balkan provincial
capitals, build magnificent modern barns—and decorate them with
various abstruse symbols to ward off the hex-women and the evil eye.
They are among the most progressive farmers in the world, but to list
even the more conspicuous of their superstitions would take a page.

All manner of sects live in this neighborhood. There are Mennonites
of sixteen different types (and they want you to be very clear about
which they belong to), Dunkards, members of the Church of the
Brethren, Schwenkfelders, Moravians, Seventh-Day Adventists, Brinsers, and Weinbrennarians.[12] Most are extreme pacifists, and believe
devoutly in nonresistance. During World War II, if they refused to wear
uniform, they were as a rule assigned to the civilian public service corps
set up under Selective Service. The Quakers started work on this system a year before Pearl Harbor, and it cost them almost five million
dollars to administer it before the war was over. Ninety per cent of
Mennonites were conscientious objectors. The figure for Dunkards and
Church of Brethren was somewhat less, that for the Quakers themselves
about 25 per cent.

The most interesting group is the Amish, of whom there are about
3,500 in the Lancaster environs; these are in turn divided into the "Old
Order" or "House Amish," and the "Church Amish" or "Amish-Men-
nonites." They practiced contour farming and soil conservation long
before the Department of Agriculture did, but tractors and other agricultural machines are still forbidden; that is, tractors "may be owned

[12] Cf. *Pennsylvania* in the American Guide Series, p. 63.

and operated for belt power, but they may not be used to operate implements in the field."[13] This—near the inmost heart of industrial America!

The Amish smoke, but do not drink, and they are liable to excommunication if they marry outside the sect. No Amish may, except in cases of *force majeure*, sleep outside his home, and domestic servants are called "livers." It is an odd experience to hear one Amish say to another, "Is your liver in or out?" Mennonites may have telephones—but I talked to one leader of the faith who told me how for years his father had resisted installing one—and freely drive in automobiles, but in theory at least, no Amish may own or use any mechanical contrivance, not even radios or vacuum cleaners. The Amish can use buggies to move about in, but these must be open, and dashboards and whipsockets are forbidden. They are not supposed to read anything whatever except the Bible and Bible stories. They do not vote or participate in any way in civic affairs. The House Amish (who worship in their own homes) do not use electricity, and their children may not even play with manufactured dolls. They do, however, use water pumped from wells, and in some other respects the purity of their nonmechanical isolation is breaking down.

Above all, the Amish manner of dress and appearance is unusual. Members are not allowed to wear buttons, which might be considered a sign of display; instead, hooks and eyes are used. The girls wear black bonnets, with a white cap underneath; the men wear broad black hats. In some circumstances, however, the Amish may make use of bright colors, for instance purple and green; but there must be no design, no pattern, in the material. The men wear their hair long, parted in the middle; unmarried men shave, and then, upon marriage, never cut their beards again. They do, however, always continue to shave their mustaches.

Lancaster itself, a flourishing industrial town and the center of a great tobacco region, has much of interest. Its four-square-mile boundary has not been changed since 1718, and every street, so the saying goes, leads to a cemetery. Its population, in extreme contrast to Pittsburgh, is 93.2 per cent of native white stock, and it bounces with vitality. Cattle would be sent here all the way from Texas, because the grass is so rich, except for the cost of fencing; even so, Lancaster has the biggest stockyards in the nation east of Chicago. Also it is a great nucleus for cork manufacture. The newspaper situation is curious in the extreme. All three papers are owned by the Steinman family; the *Intelligence Journal*, founded in 1794, the morning paper, is Democratic; the evening paper, the *New Era*, is Republican; the Sunday paper, the *News*, is independent.

[13] See a fascinating Department of Agriculture Pamphlet, *Culture of a Contemporary Rural Community*, by Walter M. Kollmorgen, 1942.

Chapter 38
Atlantic Seaboard

THE saga of the Du Ponts, a family retentive, continuous, and intricately prolific, is like no other in America. Its members have played a conspicuous role in public and private life for almost 150 years, and far from having reached any ebb, they are as interesting today as they ever were. Du Pont and Delaware seem virtually synonymous; actually there are thirty-six different Du Ponts in the Wilmington telephone book alone. The state is usually considered a kind of caliphate of the family, and an old joke is that only two political parties exist, the Du Ponts and anti-Du Ponts, with the proviso that many Du Ponts themselves belong to the anti-Du Pont faction.

Delaware, the second smallest state in area and the third smallest in population, is a curious little community; an unkind critic once called it a "flea-bitten sandspit." It has three counties[1]—and only two at high tide, as the saying goes—and about half its 265,000 people live in Wilmington. The population of the capital, Dover, is only 5,517. Along with the Eastern Shore of Maryland and the tip of Virginia, it is more or less cut off from the rest of the United States by Chesapeake Bay; the whole Delmarva peninsula dangles out in the Atlantic like an elk's tooth on a watch fob. The major streams of traffic push from New York and Philadelphia through Wilmington to Baltimore and Washington; scarcely anybody visits the backwash area below Wilmington, where its self-sufficient people grow fruit, vegetables, broilers and other species of poultry, and mind their own business. A gentleman of considerable distinction, who has been a citizen of Delaware for thirty years, stood for office not long ago. He was beaten on the ground that he was not Delaware-born and therefore could not really represent the state. Finally, in Delaware (Maryland also) we touch the fringes of the South. The Mason and Dixon's line runs just south of Wilmington.

Also Delaware has a highly particularized history. It was one of the three proprietary colonies and its settlement goes back, as everybody knows, to the Dutch and Swedes; it was New Sweden once, part of the overseas empire of Gustavus Adolphus. Delaware is very proud of the fact that, at least according to its own version of the story, it cast the deciding vote to accept the Declaration of Independence, and it was the first state to ratify the Constitution. It maintains a good deal of indi-

[1] With the names Newcastle, Kent, and Sussex.

vidualistic legislation; for instance it still has the whipping post, though it is only rarely used.

Above all, with a population less than the total number of employees in some really big companies, Delaware is famous as a home for great corporations, and the notation "incorporated in Delaware" may be seen on any number of distinguished letterheads. This is mostly because the state has very generous tax laws in regard to capitalization. Ford is a Delaware corporation; so is Coca-Cola; so are Commonwealth & Southern, the American Snuff Company, American Radiator, Bethlehem Steel, Pullman, Allis-Chalmers, Wrigley, Associated Gas & Electric, and a multitude of others. Competitors, as we know, tend to cluster together. Consider automobiles in Detroit or rubber in Akron. Similarly, both Hercules Powder and Atlas Powder exist side by side with Du Pont in Delaware, and so does American Viscose, its great competitor in rayon.[2]

Something special among corporations is International Latex of Dover, Delaware, under the presidency of Abraham N. Spanel, which as a public service regularly publishes long two-column advertisements in the newspapers. These do not mention Latex; they do mention the necessity to conquer cancer, the Maternal and Child Welfare Act, contemporary chronicles of scientific progress, and the need for world organization in the atomic age. In effect these advertisements are editorials; many, in fact, are actual reprints of editorials from other newspapers, or articles by specialists. Their impact is all toward social progress. Advertisements of this type on such a scale are a characteristic American phenomenon; I do not think they exist anywhere else in the world.

But to return to the Du Ponts. An astonishingly versatile and enterprising Frenchman named Pierre Samuel Du Pont de Nemours, fled France a step ahead of the guillotine in 1789, and came to America hoping to establish a tract for emigrants in the Shenandoah. This Du Pont, who was the son of a watchmaker, is today considered the father of the family. He was a close friend of Thomas Jefferson's, and many letters that he exchanged with Jefferson survive. They had one point in agreement among many, that agriculture should be the basis of national life, and it is a striking irony that, out of Du Pont's loins, should have arisen one of the most conspicuous industrial organizations in history. Pierre Du Pont had a son likewise remarkable for individuality

---

[2] "It is absurd," writes Professor Brogan in *The American Character*, p. 93, "that the three counties that make up Delaware should be empowered to charter corporations to do business all over the Union on terms more profitable to the corporations' comptrollers than to the body politic." William Dwight Whitney, in *Who Are the Americans?* writes, "The tamer state legislatures, such as that of Delaware, have . . . not merely imposed very low duties for incorporation under their laws, but have provided that the shareholders and directors of a Delaware corporation may meet wherever they choose, and have made innumerable other most carefully drafted provisions to meet the convenience of company management. Indeed, Delaware has been as preeminent in this field as Nevada in divorce."

and enterprise, Éleuthère Irénée Du Pont de Nemours. It is his name that the company bears today. E.I., as he is usually referred to, had studied chemistry in France under Lavoisier. In America he set out to find a job when his father's ventures failed. It happened that the gunpowder then being made in America was very inferior; the only good powder was a British monopoly. The United States wanted independence from Great Britain not only in politics, which was being steadily achieved, but in explosives. So in a mill on the Brandywine, in 1802, E. I. Du Pont set up a factory for the manufacture of gunpowder; this particular site was chosen largely because of a willow grove in the neighborhood, since willow makes good charcoal.[3]

What happened then was that the business—and the family—grew exactly as American industrialization grew. As roadbuilding increased, as the mining industry developed, finally as the railroad era opened, explosives became essential. At first the Du Ponts sold only black powder for firearms and blasting in land clearance. They progressed to all manner of refinements. The expansion of America in the nineteenth century was assisted not only by steel and coal, but by explosives, especially after Nobel invented dynamite. Nobody could quarry rock or build a railroad without blasting; nobody could mine coal or iron ore without something with which to tear open the earth.

Both E.I. and his father were striking characters; even more striking was E.I.'s wife, Sophie Dalmas, the daughter of an innkeeper. I have heard a present Du Pont say fervently that Sophie was just what God intended the family to have; without her, it would be as nothing. She and E.I. had three sons, Alfred Victor, Henry, and Alexis Irénée. I am glancing at a simplified genealogical table of the last four generations of male Du Ponts. It is as full of names and lines as a factory blueprint. The three sons of Sophie had nine sons among them, and each founded new proliferating branches of the family. To take just one example, one grandson, Lammot I, had in turn five sons. One of these, Lammot II, similarly had five sons.

There were two distinguished Du Ponts in the nineteenth century— Henry, a West Pointer and a severe disciplinarian, who laid down the rules that, like the house rules in the Rothschild or Mitsui families, still help to keep it together, and who was largely responsible for giving the company the dominant position in the explosives business it still holds, and Lammot I, a chemist and inventor, much more progressive than Henry, who turned the Du Ponts toward modern developments like dynamite, and who was killed in an explosion. Another member of the family of this period, Samuel Francis, was an admiral, for whom Du Pont Circle in Washington, D.C., is named.

Later came a famous family feud; the details are too remote for inclu-

[3] See a sketch by Gerald W. Johnson in his *American Heroes and Hero Worship* for an account of these early Du Ponts.

sion here. An angry dispute occurred between Pierre S. and Alfred I., two cousins, when T. Coleman Du Pont, a nephew of Lammot I, tried to dispose of his stock. Before the case was finally straightened out, it had been carried all the way to the Supreme Court. Personal and marital difficulties were also involved. The feud left Alfred, who had been a rebel all along, on one side of the fence, and Coleman and Pierre on the other. I do not mean "fence" figuratively. Actually two branches of the family set up citadels on different sides of the Brandywine and for years never spoke.

Coleman had always been interested in politics and public life, and was for some time a senator. When he ran, Cousin Alfred actively campaigned against him, and even bought a newspaper to assist this endeavor. Also Coleman had strong social instincts. The wedge of Delaware below Wilmington was virtually untapped, like a lost county in the South. In those days *noblesse oblige* counted for something; paternalists could really be paternalistic. Coleman, with his vast wealth, simply built a road bisecting Delaware from tip to toe, and presented it to the state. Similarly Pierre was interested in education. He set about reforming the state school system, and contributed more than one-third of the 18 million dollars that Delaware spent on new schools between 1921 and 1935. When tax collections for support of the schools became difficult, Pierre assumed the post of tax collector, set up and staffed an office at his own expense, and lifted collections from about $1,500,000 a year to more than $7,000,000 in eight years.

Alfred, meantime, went off to Florida. On one occasion he built a waterpower plant on his estate there to save $15 a year in electric current. The plant cost $100,000.[4] The wealth of the Alfred Du Pont interests in Florida alone was estimated at 50 million dollars in 1945, during a suit for control of the Florida East Coast Railway.

Three brothers are at the head of the family today, sons of Lammot I. They are the Pierre S. named above, Irénée, and Lammot II. Pierre, the eldest, was born in 1870. He married in 1915 Alice Belin, a first cousin. They had no children. Brother Irénée has, however, eight daughters and one son. Brother Lammot II has five sons and five daughters. Pierre became president of the company in 1915, when Coleman retired, and it is a revealing indication of the durability and inner cohesiveness of the family, despite feuds, that Pierre himself, on retiring as president four years later, was succeeded first by Irénée, one brother, and then a few years later by the other, Lammot II. The three brothers were all presidents in turn. All three have formidable establishments near one another in the Wilmington area. Pierre's home, Longwood (in Pennsylvania though only twelve miles from Wilmington), is one of the florif-

[4] New York *Times*, November 30, 1941, review of *Alfred I. Du Pont*, by Marquis James.

erous show places of the eastern seaboard. Irénée, however, lives these days mostly at Xanadu, a promontory he bought in Cuba. He too married a first cousin.[5] When Pierre, on the death of his father in 1884, became head of the family, his two younger brothers fell into the habit of calling him Papa. They still do, though Irénée is seventy-one and Lammot sixty-seven.

Consider politics now. Despite its obviously interlocked texture, the family is somewhat too big nowadays, too diffuse, to operate as a unit; its members take both sides. The company itself rigorously avoids any political entanglements or commitments, and a member of the family may follow any political line he pleases; if he makes campaign contributions, it's his own business. Pierre Du Pont gave $92,500 to the Republican party back in 1916.[6] and Lammot, as we know, has contributed to the funds of senators like Bushfield. But Pierre became an Al Smith man, and he supported Roosevelt in 1932. Franklin D. Roosevelt Jr., as everybody knows, married a Du Pont girl. For forty-five years John J. Raskob, one of the outstanding Democrats of the nation, was a great power in Du Pont affairs. Sometimes the family produces sharp critics. For instance Ethel B. Du Pont of the Kentucky branch bought full-page advertisements in various journals in late 1945, including the *New Republic,* denouncing General Motors in trenchant terms, and appealing to customers, stockholders and citizens to support the strike of the United Auto Workers. Miss Du Pont in fact wrote particularly from the point of view of a stockholder, saying that "many stockholders find it embarrassing to have to admit that, in spite of being considered one of the richest corporations of the world, General Motors has refused to accept the responsibility it owes to its country, the consumer, and its employees."

Does the Du Pont family and/or company "run" Delaware? The company is by far the biggest corporation and biggest taxpayer in the state, and without it Wilmington would be a whistlestop. It owns the chief hotel, which is indeed part of its own building, and the local playhouse, and its position in the community is so conspicuous that any movement, no matter of what kind, must needs turn to Du Pont for support. But it is not so directly aggressive in public and political affairs as many people think. The family, through an agency known as the Christiana Securities Company, a syndicate formed by Pierre when he took over Coleman's stock, and which is the holding company for the personal properties of Pierre's branch, owns two of Wilmington's three newspapers, the *News* and *Journal.*[7] C. Douglass Buck, a former gov-

[5] There were so many of these cousinly marriages that, after a time, they were stopped by family ukase.
[6] Lundberg, *America's Sixty Families,* p. 131.
[7] These two papers stand near the top nationally in travel advertising, which is an illustration of the cosmopolitan and substantial nature of the Wilmington community.

ernor and now a senator, married into the family; he did not, however, get elected on that basis. Another Delaware senator, James M. Tunnell (defeated in 1946) was as progressive a New Dealer as the country had.

E. I. Du Pont de Nemours & Company

What really makes Du Pont, the company, live and breathe is—women! Its history is a development from dynamite to nylon, at least in times of peace. Of course explosives are still an important part of the business, but its biggest department is rayon, which includes nylon and cellophane.[8] Organic chemicals, including dyes and synthetic rubber, are second, fabrics third, heavy chemicals fourth, plastics fifth, and explosives sixth. So, by strange paradox, the women, not the men of the world, are the ultimate determinant of Du Pont policy. Much more than on dynamite, the company rests on housewives. Plastics, house paint, nail polish, perfume, fabrics, dyes—these are the things making up the bulk of its activity today.

Nylon, a Du Pont invention and monopoly, is a plastic as well as a material for stockings. There is plenty of competition between nylon and other fibers, but none within the nylon field itself. Out of it, as everybody knows, anything can be made from paintbrush bristles to unbreakable cups and glasses; its potential development is almost illimitable. The man primarily responsible for its creation is a company chemist, Dr. Charles M. A. Stine.[9] Duco is also an original Du Pont development and so in large part is cellophane. This last was invented in France; Du Pont bought the American rights to the process, and developed techniques whereby it could be moisture-proofed and sold at a fraction of its original cost. The history of cellophane, and all that it dovetails into, is one of the most fascinating of modern industrial stories. Another Du Pont product is lucite. Also the company is the largest American manufacturer of DDT and of a long list of materials for pharmaceutical products, like Vitamin D. Tanks full of wood pulp, limestone, sulphuric acid and other evil-smelling chemicals come into Du Pont by the carload, and go out as synthetic musk, soapless soaps, lacquers for automobiles and plastics for the boudoir.

The great strength of Du Pont is, in fact, its multiplicity, its diversity. American Viscose is bigger in rayon; Sherwin-Williams is bigger in paint; Eastman makes more film and Allied Chemical and Dye more ammonia; but none of the three thousand chemical companies in the United States can touch it on an over-all basis. Chemicals are, incidentally, the eleventh industry in the United States according to value of

[8] Between 1920 and 1941, the peace years, sales of military explosives were only 2 per cent of total Du Pont sales.

[9] The name "Nylon" was chosen by Du Pont executives quite arbitrarily, out of about a hundred suggested.

product. Du Pont has eighty-four factories in twenty-five states; of the eighty-four only three are actually in Delaware itself. These are a pigment plant at Newport near Wilmington, a titanium plant at Edgemoor, and a great nylon plant at Seaford. The largest single Du Pont works is the Chambers plant at Deepwater, New Jersey, just across the river from Wilmington, originally built to make dyes.

In the early days of the Manhattan Project, General Leslie R. Groves came to Wilmington and told the company something of his problem. The Du Pont reply was that they were chemists, not nuclear physicists; the company went into the atom business with considerable reluctance. Finally, under the general supervision of the University of Chicago, Du Pont agreed to build the pilot plant at Clinton, Tennessee, near Oak Ridge, and then the 350 million dollar installation at Hanford, Washington; this has been called "the biggest and most difficult industrial enterprise ever undertaken." Why did the War Department come to Du Pont first? Answers: (1) It had always been accustomed to creating its own machinery; (2) the War Department knew it well and favorably over many years; (3) it was best fitted for the job, with no rival in over-all facilities except, perhaps, Standard Oil of New Jersey; (4) it had, of course, massive experience with explosives. Du Pont did not, however, agree to participate in the Manhattan Project except on two conditions. First, that it should derive no patent rights out of what developed, second, that its fee for each undertaking should be $1.00.

Du Pont has 80,000 stockholders, but the control rests in the family; some 40 to 50 per cent of the stock is still held by descendants of E. I. Du Pont, the founder. Nor do the Du Ponts branch out much into other corporations except General Motors. Pierre, for instance, is a director of only six other companies in all. One of these is the Wilmington Trust Company, and two are near-by railroads; he resigned his directorship in Motors in 1944. As to Motors, the Du Ponts bought ten million GM shares in 1921, which they have held continuously to date. This is regarded in Delaware purely as an "investment," but that it gives the Du Pont family effective control of GM cannot be gainsaid. Du Pont has often been linked with I.G. Farben in Germany. It vehemently denies that any such link still exists.

The president of Du Pont today is Walter S. Carpenter Jr., who has been with the company for almost forty years; only once before has Du Pont had a non-Du Pont president. His salary is $150,000 a year. Carpenter has no family connection except that his brother, R. R. M. Carpenter, now retired, married a Du Pont. The theory seems to be that, for top jobs, as between two people equal in merit, one of whom is a Du Pont, a member of the family will be chosen. If, however, no member happens to be available for a particular job, the choice will fall outside. The company is run by an executive committee of nine members including the president; a curious point is that none of these has any formal administrative duties. "This is a corporation," as I heard it said in Wilmington, "that believes in the theory that the top management has to have time to think."[10]

The family is hard on itself as a rule; it judges its own by severe standards. The youngsters start usually in small jobs. As a rule they go to MIT—at least twenty present members are MIT graduates—and then in the French tradition which still survives, work up. Du Pont girls are encouraged to marry young executives not of the family.

Maryland Free State

I testify . . . first for Baltimore.
—Henry James

Maryland looks like a squat leftward-pointing pistol with a jaggedly divided butt. The division is, of course, Chesapeake Bay, which comes near to splitting the state in two; the Atlantic side is the singular region known as the Eastern Shore, or Sho'. Maryland is a small state, but it has, on account of the convolutions of the Bay, a very long coastline, and through it flow a remarkable number of idiosyncratic little rivers. Some have highly pungent names, like Transquaking, Annemessex, Tred Avon, Plaindealing, Rockawalkin, Tedious, and Goose.

The Eastern Sho' held, until recently at least, a stable and gracious kind of life. Now it has been a good deal spoiled by the invasion of vulgar rich Pittsburghers and New Yorkers. South of the Choptank, it is almost indistinguishable from Alabama; one jumps from the industrial age to the life of the deep South in the space of a county or two.

This region is notable for two things among others, waterways and food. Somehow, because the weight of material has become so pressing, we have not mentioned the Inland Waterway in this book so far. Not many Americans know that, by means of this reticulated series of bays, canals, inlets and small rivers, a medium-sized boat can sail all the way from New England to Florida without once touching the open sea. As to food, nothing in America can rival the area except New Orleans. Maryland is the home of Chincoteague oysters, terrapin (never put cream in the sauce), stuffed ham, and beaten biscuits, the dough of which must be spanked with a paddle for a solid half hour.[11]

Maryland has, as everybody knows, a rich and sophisticated history.

---

[10] Also note a remark in *Fortune*, February, 1940, "The remarkable collaboration between research, engineering, and selling for which the company is famous has been forwarded chiefly by spreading responsibility, but also by such coördinating devices as a special development department."

[11] *Maryland* in the American Guide Series is authority for the statement that the cook should know when to remove terrapin from the pot "by the ease with which the toenails can be pulled out."

Its statehouse is the oldest in the nation after that of Massachusetts, and its state flag, which antedates the Stars and Stripes, contains the coat of arms of the Calvert family, and is, I believe, the only heraldic state flag in the United States. Always in Maryland it is supposed to fly side by side with the national flag. British influence has been strong; most of the counties, like those in Delaware and New Jersey, bear British names; two are named for British princes and queens, and portraits of members of the British royal family decorate the capitol at Annapolis. Also French influence is considerable; twice groups of French, fleeing insurrections in the West Indies, found refuge in Baltimore. The strong Catholic tradition goes back, of course, all the way to the Calverts. The Marylanders have a lively and self-conscious local patriotism. One phrase is that they are "citizens of Maryland and subjects of the United States," and it is a proud boast that state laws, by tradition going back 308 years, must be "consonant with reason." The locution "Maryland Free State" is, however, of comparatively recent origin; it was invented by Hamilton Owens, the present editor-in-chief of the Baltimore Sun-Papers, which, as every civilized person knows, are among the best newspapers in the land.

Maryland lives on poultry (like Delaware again), beer, tobacco, fishing (like New Jersey), and above all on vegetables; it is the first vegetable-canning state. It was the first state to disestablish the church, and the first to institute universal male white suffrage. It has the Naval Academy at Annapolis, one of the great seats of learning in the world in Johns Hopkins, and St. John's College, run by Stringfellow Barr, with its "Great Books" courses like those at the University of Chicago, only more so. Also (as in Delaware) horseracing plays a conspicuous economic role as well as socially and in the realm of the picturesque. Maryland has a good deal of riding to hounds, and the Maryland Hunt Club is famous for its steeplechasing. The Pimlico track, where the Preakness is run, is of course in Baltimore, and Havre de Grace is not far off. Finally, politics. Maryland is a state in nobody's pocket. Baltimore (like Wilmington in Delaware) holds half the total population, and so the balance of forces is equally divided. If either side gets rambunctious, the other can knock it off.

H. L. Mencken, by all odds its most distinguished citizen, once wrote an essay classifying Maryland—which of course he is violently fond of—as the most "average" of the states. In percentage of native-born whites, percentage of illiteracy, number of the blind, salaries of high school teachers, average temperature, and number of automobile licenses, Maryland is median. "It is," writes Mr. Mencken, "in the middle of the road in an annual average of murders, suicides and divorces, in the average date of its first killing frost, in the number of its moving picture parlors per 100,000 of population, in the circulation of its newspapers, in the ratio between its street railway mileage and its population, in the number of its people converted annually at religious revivals, and in the percentage of its lawyers sent to prison yearly for felony."[12]

In Baltimore, one of the pleasantest cities in America and the seventh biggest, Mr. Mencken was my cicerone, together with several amiable doctors from Johns Hopkins. The first thing everybody notices, at least in the residential districts, are the solid rows of houses with white stone steps; of these there are literally thousands, row on row. A marble quarry exists a few miles out of town, which makes marble the cheapest stone. Most of these houses are owned, if own is the proper term, through the extraordinary mechanism known as "ground rent"; the leases are unto perpetuity. Some of the street names have nice distinction, like Johnny-cake Road, Featherbed Lane, Rolling Road, and Cider Alley, and one street, Mr. Mencken assures me on his word of honor, has successively been known as Charles Street, Charles Street Avenue, Charles Street Avenue Extended, and was once called Charles Street Avenue Road. Also Baltimore, with its eighteenth century atmosphere, is the only city in America I know where one may see names in the phone book like Hurst, John of W., or Fisher, Frank of J. This is a survival from older and gentler days, when members of the squirearchy couldn't tell themselves apart except by identifying the father by initial.

To treat of Maryland and Baltimore in these few words is of course absurd. Not since Minnesota have I so disliked having to say good-by to a community. But we have only dealt with thirty-two states so far, which means, after all these multitudinous pages, that there are still sixteen to go. We turn now to a great border state, Kentucky, and then to the broad bosom of the South.

[12] *These United States*, Vol. I, p. 14.

Chapter 39

Romance and Reality in Kentucky

^^

Heaven is a Kentucky of a place.
— from *Kentucky* in the American Guide Series

I ASKED a mild-mannered, perspicacious friend in Louisville, "Who runs Kentucky?" His answer was, "It doesn't run—it limps." I asked him what was its chief distinction, and he replied, "Braggadocio." I mentioned that a recent Gallup poll showed that more Americans would prefer to live in Kentucky than anywhere else in the union, and he responded, "Of course—they don't know that the reason we're so backward is that Kentucky is infected with Kentucky."

The authentic romance of America!—You have more of it packed into a tighter space in Kentucky than in any other state. Toll off a few words, names, images—Daniel Boone, Kentucky "colonels," the gold in Fort Knox, and moonshine; Cumberland Gap, the Mammoth Cave, and Henry Clay; mint juleps, blood feuds, Churchill Downs, the Derby; the birthplace of both Lincoln and Jefferson Davis (and both married Kentucky girls); Big Sandy, "My Old Kentucky Home," and mountaineers who allegedly pronounce bear "bar" and can spit Burley juice ten yards in a crooked line.

But there are realities as well. Kentucky is par excellence a border state—and not merely the border between North and South, East and Middle West, but between fruity myth and brutal fact.

A Garland of Statistics

Recently a group known as the Committee for Kentucky was set up under the leadership of Harry W. Schacter, president of the Kentucky Merchant's Association; one of its vice presidents is H. Fred Willkie, a distillery executive and Wendell's brother. The committee includes some fifty member units, crossing the political gamut all the way from extreme Republican to extreme Democratic, and including Negro, university, labor and agricultural groups, with a total membership of 350,000. Some of its findings are the following:

42 per cent of Kentucky farms are not reached by improved roads of any kind.
Kentucky is the forty-seventh state in literacy; only one other state (Mississippi) has more illiterates.

42,009 Kentucky farms had no toilets or privies of any kind in
1940, and 97 per cent of all farms have no toilets inside the house.
[Italics mine.]

Its population decreased 10 per cent between 1940 and 1943, and
more than 25 per cent of its state-born citizens have left it.

Kentucky is the 46th state in death rate from tuberculosis, and in one
area a single doctor serves 11,500 people. One hundred thousand
Kentuckians have syphilis and there are fifty thousand gonorrhea
cases per year.

34 per cent of all Kentucky farms are worth less than $300, only
25 per cent have electricity, and only 16 per cent have telephones.

The average farm income per agricultural family was *$12 a week*
in 1940.

And more particularly in regard to education—

In 1932, 114,000 children started first grade; by 1944, when they
should have reached twelfth grade, only 14,000 were still in school.
Not less than 100,000 had to drop out, largely on account of bad
roads, lack of transportation, and poverty.

37 per cent of Kentucky school children fail to finish elementary
school.

The average number of days a pupil goes to school in Kentucky
is 129 (as against 150 for the U.S. as a whole and as against 170
in Michigan, for instance).

In Kentucky, 78 per cent of children of school age are enrolled in
school. (National rate is 84 per cent; that of Idaho 96.)

For each 1,000 children between 14 and 17, the number who go to
school is 412 in Kentucky, 679 for the nation, 952 in the state of
Washington.

Ideally, about 8 per cent of children enrolled in a twelve-grade
school should graduate each year. The proportion for Kentucky is
2.5 per cent.

Average number of pupils enrolled per teacher is 32 in Kentucky,
29 in the nation, 17 in South Dakota.

Average teacher's salary is $1,014 in Kentucky (as against $1,599
in the country as a whole, and $2,697 in New York).

Did the Bluegrass State rise in self-indignant shame on hearing these
statistics, and attempt then to bestir itself? It did not. Instead the general comment was only too likely to be, "Why worry about being 'progressive'?" The only two important organizations in the state that did
not, by the way, join the Committee for Kentucky are the Kentucky
Bankers Association and the Associated Industries of Kentucky, the
local equivalent of the NAM. The committee held a big meeting recently to explain its work and findings. One hold-out corporation took
an advertisement in the papers the next day, telling the committee
"We're all right, thank you," and to shut its mouth.

Blueprint of Bluegrass

Look at Kentucky on a map; it is shaped, as that celebrated Kentuckian Irvin S. Cobb once said, like a camel lying down. It isn't very big geographically, but seven other states adjoin it (and look at a map again to see of how many other American states this may be said), and an immense amount of variety is squeezed into its area; to take just one instance, no fewer than twenty different railways cross it, and it has more miles of navigable river than any state.

Where did Kentucky come from? Mostly from Virginia; in fact in its early days it was a kind of Virginian satrapy; later of course came crossfires of immigration, up from the south, and across the Ohio river from the north. Its proud history began early, and Kentucky calls itself, not a state, but a "Commonwealth"; for a time it wanted to be an independent republic, and it was the second state to enter the union after the original thirteen, as well as the first to be created beyond the mountains. It has always had a vivid sectarianism; for instance it did not vote for Lincoln even though he was a native son. The legend is that it was neutral in the Civil War; this is not quite true, since what really happened was that the Bluegrass State fought on both sides, and fought well.

Today there are, by customary definition, three different Kentuckys, and none of the three is apt to agree on anything, except the glory of Kentucky. First, reading right to left, is the eastern or mountain section; second, the Bluegrass region centering on Lexington; finally, the river country to the west. The state is, so far as I know, the only one in the union where one small segment, cut off by a loop of the Mississippi, is not territorially adjacent to the rest. You have to go from Kentucky to Kentucky through Missouri or Tennessee, as in former days you had to cross Polish territory between Germany proper and East Prussia. But in the United States, there are, luckily, no Polish corridors.

Actually Kentucky could be subdivided into more than merely three distinct provinces. For instance the Louisville *Courier-Journal*, one of the best newspapers in the country, issues six different Kentucky editions (as well as one for Indiana across the river). And its Louisville edition in turn subdivides state news into six or seven grand divisions, and prints a "Kentucky All Over" section too. This in a state with a population of less than three million!

South of Louisville, and stretching out westward, is what is known as the Pennyrile, named for a species of wild mint. It is a "pastoral land cut through by deep winding streams,"[1] merging to the north with the Western Coal Field, and to the west with the Jackson Purchase, called

---

[1] From *Kentucky* in the American Guide Series, p. 315.

usually just the Purchase, a flat region bought originally from the Indians, and closed in by three giant rivers, Mississippi, Ohio, and Tennessee.

The most "typical" Kentucky region is, of course, that generally described as Bluegrass. No two local zealots agree on its precise frontiers, though it is partially enclosed by hills known as the Knobs; it is called "blue" because the rich grass has a bluish cast in spring. "Underneath this Bluegrass turf" (I quote the *Kentucky* Guide) "is a layer of rare Ordovician limestone, a shell deposit laid down millions of years ago when the region was an ocean floor"; this gives the soil its very high content of calcium and phosphorus. The Bluegrass grows good tobacco, the commonwealth's most important crop next to corn, and superb race horses, which are its most spectacular pride. Some thirty million dollars are invested in horse farms of the Bluegrass country. Most Kentuckians who are not residents of the Bluegrass are jealous of it, because of its wealth; on the contrary all patriotic Kentuckians spurn the idea of being jealous of the similar Bluegrass region in Tennessee, which is even richer.

The curse of Kentucky is backwoodsism, and its gritty mountaineers in the east form a narrow provincial world all their own. They are of the most poor and primitive type of Anglo-Saxon stock; they adhere closely to their isolated mines, stills, and mountains; they have, by and large, both the meanness of the typical peasant and the suspiciousness of the mountaineer; above all, they are fantastically inbred. One famous mountain center is "Bloody" Harlan, where a coal strike was viciously crushed in the 1930's after years of intermittent strong-armism by company guards, violence, and terrorism.

In *The Kentucky* by Thomas D. Clark,[2] is the following nuggety passage. A man named Haggin of Breathitt County, to support his candidacy for county jailer, adduced that "among those to whom I am related by blood and marriage are the . . . Bachs, Lovelys, Allens, McQuinns, Pattons, Landrums, Stampers, Watts, Watkins, Manus, Crafts, Calhouns, and Nichols," while his wife, a Crawford, has relatives in such clans as "the Jetts, Johnsons, Combs, Griffiths, Terrys, Amburgys, Bowmans, Heralds, Spences, Lawsons, Capes, Hargises, Days, Haddixes, Evans, and many more." Indeed the politics of Kentucky are apt to be a family affair.

About one-quarter of the state's present legislature is mountaineer. Some members still carry arms, and guns were pulled in the chamber seven times during one robust debate, over the sales tax, during the governorship of "Happy" Chandler. An ambitious governor like the immortal Laffoon can go a long way toward control of the legislature by giving jobs to the mountain members (also of course to nonmountain

[2] Farrar and Rinehart, New York, 1942.

members). The mountaineers particularly love getting extra pay as "penitentiary guards," which also means that they can carry arms unconcealed.

Politics in the Bluegrass Commonwealth

The song birds are the sweetest
in Kentucky;
The thoroughbreds are the fleetest
in Kentucky;
Mountains tower proudest,
Thunder peals the loudest,
The landscape is the grandest,
And politics the damnedest,
in Kentucky.

—Song by Judge James H. Mulligan

Fred Vinson, the eminent Kentuckian who seemed for a time to be holding practically all big federal jobs and who is now chief justice of the Supreme Court, told me a little story the other day. He once asked a prominent Kentucky politician whom he was going to support in a primary election a few weeks off. Answer: "I don't know yet. I'm waiting to see what the opposition does, so I can take the other side."

Paul Porter, formerly chairman of the Federal Communications Commission and then head of the truncated OPA, strove to find out from the late Desha Breckinridge, editor of the Lexington *Herald*, what line he would take on an impending local issue. The answer came, "Haven't made up my mind. But when I do, you can count on it we'll be damned bitter about it!"

Another Kentucky worthy, who will prefer to be nameless, told me in Louisville, "If Jesus Christ were running for sheriff here, he'd get opposition."

In 1900 occurred an episode obstreperous even for Kentucky. Two men claimed to have been elected governor. One, William Goebel, had waged a tremendous campaign against the so-called moneyed interests and especially the Louisville & Nashville Railroad; he was shot while the last votes were being counted. He managed to keep alive until the legislature declared him elected; the oath of office was then administered and he died. Previously Goebel himself had shot and killed a political opponent. The disaffection and estrangement following these two murders led to what such a sober authority as the *Dictionary of American Biography* calls "the verge of civil war." For a time there were two acrimonious rival governors and two "governments." And this, let it be remembered in our prosaic era, took place only forty-six short years ago.[3]

---

[3] According to one authority the Goebel people so hated the Louisville & Nashville that they refused to have his body moved to its last resting place over its tracks; the funeral train took a roundabout way from Louisville to Covington instead. See *The Kentucky*, p. 357.

Kentucky is basically and normally Democratic (assisted by a bit of gerrymandering) but many mountaineers are Republican, and most election results are mixed. The present governor, Simeon Willis, is a Republican; but his legislature is powerfully Democratic. The present mayor of Louisville, successor to the admirable Wilson Wyatt, is Democratic (he got in by exactly 205 votes out of 93,000); but his board of aldermen is Republican. Moreover politics never stop. The gubernatorial and mayoralty elections take place in odd-numbered years, and hence do not correspond with national elections; Kentucky is one of the few places (New Jersey also) where this is true. There's never a dull moment—in Kentucky. Incidentally it was the first state to make FDR's birthday, January 30, a legal holiday.

The commonwealth boasts that Louisville was the first city in the country to introduce the Australian ballot, and an Honest Election Committee composed of 217 nonpartisan volunteers watches every vote, but politics in Kentucky at large have been fabulously corrupt. Thomas L. Stokes of Scripps-Howard won a well-deserved Pulitzer prize for his report on the Barkley-Chandler primary in 1938. The most outrageous thing about the report of the special committee that made a subsequent investigation—and which showed outrageous corruption—was that nobody in Kentucky was outraged. In the fat old days the bosses did not bother with anything so crass or rudimentary as mere stuffing of ballot boxes, precinct captains did not rummage around in the cemeteries or fabricate single names. They simply certified as cast, *en bloc*, the grand total of votes they needed! Today, as a result, a new electoral law is in force. Votes are not counted in precincts at all, but instead are sent to a central courthouse under triple lock, where they are opened publicly, one at a time, and then publicly tabulated. Kentucky is, in consequence, usually the last state nowadays to report electoral results; if a race has been close, it may be four or five days before anybody knows who won.

A crippling item in Bluegrass political life is the old constitution, which has been in force since 1891. It is, like constitutions in so many states, almost completely out of date today; one proviso, as an example, is that anyone running for state or even municipal office must swear that he has never fought a duel. This constitution imposed a top limit of five thousand dollars on salaries for public officials in the state, except the governor; five thousand dollars was a lot of money in the 1890's, but it isn't so much now, and as a result it has been difficult to get anybody good to run for office. Despite great pressure, there are two groups today that resist any attempt to modernize the constitution: (*a*) the lawyers, who thrive on its extreme complexity; (*b*) the rural areas generally, which fear that rewriting it will give more strength to the towns.

A vivid rivalry between town and countryside is, in fact, a permanent factor in Kentucky politics. Louisville contains about 12 per cent of the total vote, but the hinterland makes it fairly difficult for a Louisville man to win state or federal office.

Who and What Run Kentucky?

Against this background, what, then, are the dominant forces in the political and economic life of the state? In rough summary, one may mention at least seven:

(1) The great swashbuckling days of the Louisville & Nashville are gone forever, but this railroad interlaces the commonwealth so tightly that it still remains a considerable factor. For instance (like the railroads in Tennessee) it fights the truck companies, and the resultant trucking issue is a chief preoccupation of Kentucky politics. The railroads (including others beside the L & N) forced a bill through the legislature severely limiting the amount of freight the competing truck lines may carry; the limit is eighteen thousand pounds, much less than that in states adjoining, and hence the truckers must either unload and redistribute their cargoes at the Kentucky line, or drive scores of miles out of the way.[4] The trucking lobby plays politics on its side too. For instance it made big contributions to the campaign fund of a Democratic candidate for governor some years ago; the *Courier-Journal* published photostats of checks he had received, although he had denied getting any. The affair was, of course, irregular, since the truckers are regulated by a public agency, and for any party to receive a contribution from a corporation doing business with the state is against the law. There was, however, no prosecution because of the statute of limitations. But the resultant scandal split the Democratic party, and so a Republican got the governorship by a tidy margin.

The L & N is, by the way, no longer owned by Kentucky capital but by the Atlantic Coast Line, which is in turn a Wall Street railroad. So once more we come across economic absenteeism and its sundry phenomena.

(2) The race track and all the racing interests—in other words the Jockey Club. Matt Winn, the youngest man of eighty-four anybody ever met, is the great spirit behind the Kentucky Derby and Churchill Downs, and the magnitude of his success is such that the racing people don't have to play much politics any more. In older days, during a long fight over pari-mutuel, and when anti-race track agitation was pronounced, the Jockey Club maintained a potent lobby; for years every candidate for governor, Republican and Democratic alike, was its man. The lobby does go into action nowadays if any tax bill threatens it, like a recent

---

[4] But in 1946 a new bill raised the limit to 42,000 pounds; this was one of the worst beatings the L & N has taken in the history of the state.

proposal to put a 5 per cent tax on pari-mutuels. The race tracks contribute to state revenue of course, but the contribution is pretty small. The Jockey Club has exclusive gambling privileges at every track in Kentucky; handbooks are forbidden, and there is no other legal gambling.

(3) The liquor interests. Liquor, though absentee owned for the most part, is big business in Kentucky; indeed the commonwealth manufactures 40 per cent of all the whisky produced in the United States. But the distillers are less powerful a direct political force than is generally believed, and they are split. One wing, the "Bottle and Bond" people, produces only straight whisky; the other, including firms like Seagram's,[5] makes blends. In the old days even to suggest that a stanch Kentuckian should so much as sniff a drop of blended whisky at a distance would, of course, have been an insult more mortal than impugning the honor of his grandmother; but times, as they say, change. The blenders have to buy straight whisky in considerable quantities, and so the two wings, though rivals, get along. Blended whisky is not so strong as straight; hence some temperance interests, if forced to a choice, favor the blended side. Strangely enough there is a very marked prohibitionist element in Kentucky, mostly in the rural areas; the figures may seem incredible, but 88 counties out of the state's 120 are dry by local option. The Bible-belters are bone dry on moral grounds, and mountaineers in a few localities make a profit on illegal moonshine and would make a killing if prohibition were ever to return. Many citizens of course drink wet but vote dry, for complex theological-political reasons; this phenomenon, far from being peculiar to Kentucky, is something we shall find almost everywhere in the South.

(4) The Louisville *Courier-Journal*, the dominant newspaper in the state and a splendid liberal force. This is "Marse Henry" Watterson's old paper, and under Barry Bingham, the present owner, and Mark Ethridge, the publisher, its valiant tradition is vigorously carried on.

(5) The coal operators and, outside of Louisville, the Kentucky Utilities Company. But the coal people are less powerful than in former years, first because coal itself is not so important in the economy of the commonwealth, and because the operators, within the industry, are not so strong vis-à-vis their own miners. Labor (predominantly AF of L) is fairly strong.

(6) There are some miscellaneous forces. For instance the country doctors and lawyers, who are in the main dependent for livelihood on the railways, are an important conservative factor; correspondingly, a liberal factor is the Kentucky Education Association, with seventeen thousand members. It stands, like all genuine education lobbies, for more public expenditure and hence more taxes; thus it is usually opposed

---

[5] It was this house which printed widespread advertisements when the movie *The Lost Weekend* was released, urging some people not to drink.

by business interests which want to keep taxes down, in a pattern adumbrated in this book many times.

(7) Religious influences. Here too, as in the matter of prohibition, we are getting close to the South, and religious factors in general may better be discussed later. In Kentucky the Baptists and Methodists, though perhaps declining in strength, still dominate the rural areas together with those offshoots known as Disciples of Christ and Campbellites. Sectarianism is tremendous; there are, for instance, no fewer than five different subdivisions among the Presbyterians. In Louisville, Roman Catholicism is strong; next to New Orleans, it is the chief Catholic city south of the Mason and Dixon's line.

Finally, a word on people. Next to Vinson, the most conspicuous Kentuckian in national life is Senator Alben W. Barkley, former majority leader and an able and useful citizen. One man to watch is a provocative youngster, Edward F. Prichard Jr., who, of all the brilliant secretaries that Felix Frankfurter ever had, is probably the most brilliant; Prichard, shot through with politics in every ounce of his 250 pounds, was successively the astute and unquenchable assistant to Attorney General Biddle, Jimmy Byrnes, and Vinson; he is at present counsel to the Democratic National Committee.

One Kentucky congressman is John Robsion, from the mountaineer country; he is slightly more isolationist than the Chicago *Tribune*. Another, Virgil Chapman, elected from the Bluegrass year after year, watches tobacco with vigilance, and is apparently interested in little else. And of course Kentucky is the home state of Congressman Andrew J. May, the wretched homunculus who, early in 1946, found himself involved in the Garsson scandals. But long before this May and his characteristics were well known to political connoisseurs. He was probably the most prolific cliché maker in the entire House, no mean honor; his career is a standing reminder of the extreme necessity of reforming Congress so that seniority alone shall not decide the chairmanship of a committee.[6]

From Laffoon to Buffoon

I have mentioned the remarkable "Happy" Chandler, the ex-governor and ex-senator who succeeded Judge Kenesaw M. Landis as "czar" of baseball. His history is illuminating. When he finally quit the Senate for active duty at the baseball commissionership (he held both jobs, salaries ten thousand and fifty thousand dollars respectively, for an intervening six months), the *Courier-Journal*, in tolerant mood, spoke as follows:

The imprint of Albert Benjamin Chandler upon Kentucky politics had a pattern so personal, familiar and sharp that it is hard to

[6] May was defeated for re-election in November, 1946.

believe it first was stamped only fifteen years ago, and that Happy
Chandler, departing from the scene, himself is only 46 . . . Neither
the local scene nor perhaps the United States Senate will be quite
the same, now that Happy Chandler has chosen to leave one game
for another.

"Happy"—and one of his secrets is that, without any self-examination
whatever, he is a happy person—first reached prominence in about 1935,
when he was lieutenant governor, through a complex machination that
eventually brought him the governorship. He waited until the fabulous
Ruby Laffoon who created a thousand colonels, and who was governor
at the time, was out of the state, became acting governor himself, and
jammed through a change in the electoral law to favor himself. In 1939,
when he was just finishing his own term as governor, Senator M. M.
Logan conveniently died, and Chandler, resigning the governorship,
was promptly appointed to the vacant seat. (The year before, running
against Barkley, he had taken a terrific beating.) In 1942 he ran
for the full Senate term, and won. And there are several people
in the penitentiary today, convicted of frauds attending this election.
Did this embarrass Happy? He has never been embarrassed in his
life. The word for such a contretemps (even in reference to those
still in jail) is, "Oh, it was just politics." Then came another episode.
Chandler was a member of the Senate Military Affairs Committee,
and it became revealed that a Louisville contractor named Ben Collings
had presented him with a swimming pool. This was at a time when steel,
brass, and other materials used in swimming pools were supposed to be
rationed for the use of the armed forces and the nation as a whole. At
first, horror struck, Happy is reported to have exclaimed that he had
never even heard of the swimming pool, though it was built on his own
grounds at Versailles. In the immortal words of a *Saturday Evening
Post* writer, "You could have knocked Happy over with the springboard." Next, he protested plaintively that "the people of Kentucky aren't
going to get mad at me over a little old swimming pool." Investigations
began, counterinvestigations followed. At first the War Labor Board
reported that construction of the pool did not violate priorities; then it
reversed itself by saying that the use of "8,000 pounds of steel and considerable brass" had hampered and impaired the war effort. Finally,
the Truman Committee itself, nothing less, whitewashed everybody
concerned.

In the Senate he took as strong an antiadministration line as he dared,
and he was an avowed and outspoken isolationist. In May, 1943, he made
a speech urging that the war in Europe be called off, in effect, so that
more aid could go to MacArthur, one of his great heroes. The New
York *Herald Tribune*, which is not an administration organ, seldom
flays a man without good reason, and only rarely does it advocate that

a senator be shot. What it said on the occasion of this speech, under the heading "The Wrecker," is worth repeating:

> Senator A. B. (Happy) Chandler of Kentucky consumed three hours of the Senate's supposedly valuable time . . . in what, by any rational standards, could only be regarded as an attempt to wreck the war plans, alienate the Allies, and give aid and comfort to the enemies of the United States. What his motives were we do not know. . . . His performance, however, was of the kind for which in less enlightened states a person would be taken out and shot at the following sunrise.

Why did baseball choose the ineffable Happy to follow Landis? Because he is "colorful," "popular," and "in the know." Baseball wanted somebody as unlike the rigid Landis as possible, someone who, by example, could bring recruits to the big leagues by encouraging the sport in every sand lot in the land.

Wilson Wyatt of Louisville

Now out of this hotchpotch of provincialism, fake glamor, and poverty of purse and spirit that has so often afflicted Kentucky has arisen a man. His name is Wilson Watkins Wyatt Jr.; he was born in 1906, and he served from 1941 to 1945 as mayor of Louisville. Early in 1946, Truman called him to the Washington scene as national housing expediter, one of the most difficult and important jobs in the country, and then as chairman of the National Housing Agency, from which he resigned in December, 1946.

Wyatt, one of the most attractive men I have met in American public life, gave Louisville a stunningly good administration. Like Harley Knox in San Diego, he is a phenomenon profoundly healthy, if comparatively rare—the citizen of merit who volunteers for public service, at great personal sacrifice, and attaches himself to whatever is most vital in his community.

Louisville has great charm—like all the river cities with considerable German populations—and a history of distinction. It was the first American city to have its own university, and in the old days its own packet ships sailed down the Ohio and Mississippi to New Orleans and beyond; there was even a direct service Louisville-Liverpool.[7] It became a stable city, not given to getting excited easily, half-southern, and in recent times fraying at the edges. The old society crumbled; and today, every once in a while, some last survivor of a family dies, leaving a fortune made in alcohol, horses, or tobacco, of whom the present generation has scarcely even heard.

[7] Cf. *Five Cities*, by George R. Leighton, p. 50.

Wyatt picked Louisville up by the scruff of its drowsy neck and shook it. He and the war came in together; together they revivified, resuscitated the town. From being an isolated and moribund city living largely on its reputation, it became the center of troop concentrations, wartime industry, middle western bustle. One of the first things Wyatt did was to help redress the balance between city and state. Louisville pays roughly 33 per cent of all Kentucky's taxes (but gets back only 11 per cent); it supported the state, in effect, but it was seriously under-represented in the capitol. Wyatt sought to close ranks between city and hinterland, and to increase its representation in commonwealth affairs.

Wyatt is a lean, talkative, effervescent man of forty with a sharp nose, sharp ears, and one of the brightest smiles ever seen anywhere. He is a Presbyterian. He went to the public schools, fell in love, refused to marry until he was earning five thousand dollars a year, and promptly earned it as a lawyer, after studying at night and working as a railway clerk. He became a member or director of practically every organization in Louisville worth belonging to, and was on the way to becoming rich. He never ran for office until the mayoralty race in 1941, when he was elected by the largest majority in the history of Louisville.

At once he was called a traitor to his class. This was because he proceeded immediately to get entangled with what he likes to call "the vulture wing." He had been an attorney for Louisville Gas and Electric (a subsidiary of Standard Gas and Electric and an intermediate Delaware holding company); promptly on becoming mayor, he set out to buy the company for the community. So, in Louisville as in a dozen cities we have mentioned, private power vs. public power became the dominant issue. Wyatt figured out that, if Louisville Gas and Electric were municipally owned, the advantage to the rate payer and taxpayer would be roughly twenty thousand dollars per day or almost one thousand dollars per hour. The original proposal for municipal ownership was first made by the board of aldermen on a nonpartisan basis, but it was bitterly fought later by the Republicans; during the last two years of his term, Wyatt was constantly at loggerheads with a new board with a strong Republican majority.

Wyatt came into office with a twelve-point program; all have been carried out. To go into them in detail is beyond the province of this chapter. Suffice it to say that they included a bond issue for a flood wall (to prevent recurrence of such a catastrophe as the Louisville flood of 1937), reduction in the streetcar fare, consolidation of city and county health and public service agencies (thus avoiding wasteful duplication), and equalization of salaries of Negro and white schoolteachers. Wyatt cheerfully worked fourteen to sixteen hours a day, intermittently making direct reports to the people via radio, reports which are a model of their kind, and—an unorthodox touch—during all four years was never on time to an appointment.

I asked Wyatt once what had led him into public life. He could easily earn ten times his salary in private practice, and most of his savings have been spent. He answered that, living in Louisville, he became conscience stricken every time a new mayor was elected; he would say to himself, "They aren't doing the job *well* enough! I'd like to have a shot at it myself." And he was profoundly irritated by the prevalent American assumption that politics, particularly municipal politics, were not "respectable" as a profession. He felt that any American who sneered at politics per se was also sneering at democracy; and this he knew to be wrong. He wanted to get down to the level of the people themselves, and encourage their active participation in their own government; the failure to do this is the greatest misfortune in American public life.

Kentucky Miscellany

Kentucky is the state where a brother of John Keats was a bank director, and where ladies may enter the Pendennis Club, the chief meeting place of tycoons, only by a side entrance; where the WCTU demanded that bathrobes be draped on show window models in low-cut bathing suits, and where Man o'War is worth five thousand dollars per time at stud; it is the state where the first enameled bathtub in history was manufactured, where river towns like Covington give you a wonderful glimpse of sky's-the-limit river life, and where roast opossum and raccoon are still great delicacies.

Chapter 40

The South: Problem Child of the Nation

〰〰〰

O for a beaker full of the warm South!
—John Keats
Bright and fierce and fickle is the South.
—Alfred Lord Tennyson

WE FACE now the South. The simplest over-all definition of this complicated and engaging area is that it consists of ten states below the Mason and Dixon's line—Virginia, North Carolina, South Carolina, Georgia, Florida, Alabama, Tennessee, Mississippi, Arkansas, and Louisiana. Underlying most of it is the harassing pressure of the Negro problem.

As we know well by now, and as is the case with every American region except New England, the regional "frontier" does not follow state lines with exactitude. The South, like the West, is a fluctuating entity; it spills over. St. Louis, Washington, D.C., and Louisville are almost as southern in some respects as Atlanta; and Miami, the most southerly of important American cities from a geographical point of view, is about as "southern" as the Bronx. Indeed purists will object to almost any definition of the South, and refinements can be listed ad infinitum. Maryland, Kentucky, and Missouri often consider themselves "southern," and indeed they are marked by some conspicuous southern characteristics; however, for purposes of this book, it is easier to call them border states. One conventional definition is that the South consists of the eleven confederate states that seceded from the union; these are the ten I have listed above plus Texas. But Texas is, as we shall see, too much of a world of its own to be included here, though east Texas is certainly more "southern" than eastern Tennessee. Another definition is that, politically, the South consists of the seven poll tax states; similarly the "white primary" states make a unit. André Siegfried says in his *America Comes of Age* (p. 91) that the South "comprises Maryland (southern section), Virginia (eastern), North Carolina (eastern), Texas (eastern), Oklahoma (eastern), Missouri (southern), Kentucky (western) and Tennessee (western)," aside from the more obvious states; he excludes from the "South" the whole Allegheny area, cutting across four states, because there are so few Negroes in the Alleghenies. By this listing only seven states remain purely of the South—South Carolina, Georgia, Alabama, Florida, Mississippi, Louisiana, Arkansas.

Gunnar Myrdal, in *An American Dilemma* (of this prodigious tome more anon) makes his definition by applying the following criteria: secession in the Civil War; slave states in 1860; states that maintain laws prohibiting intermarriage between white and Negro; segregation in the schools; and Jim Crowism in both railways and local transportation. He might easily have added another—cotton culture. Texas, Oklahoma, and even West Virginia are southern by several of these criteria, though West Virginia is by most accepted classifications a northeastern state. Maryland, Delaware, and Kentucky were slave states, but they did not secede; they still prohibit intermarriage and have Jim Crow laws, but they grow no cotton. Missouri has segregation in education, but no Jim Crow.

The greatest authority of all from a regional point of view, Professor Howard W. Odum of the University of North Carolina, divides the entire United States into six big regions, and he supplies a fantastic amount of data to prove that there are only six—Northeast, Middle States, Northwest, Far West, Southeast, Southwest. He puts Texas, Oklahoma, New Mexico and Arizona into "Southwest," and in "Southeast" includes the ten states I have named, plus Kentucky. Interestingly enough the Mississippi River is not the boundary between Southeast and Southwest, since Arkansas and most of Louisiana, both of which are indisputably southern states, lie west of it.

To proceed and considering the South to be only ten states, we may of course subdivide them further. By normal definition, the "upper" South consists of Virginia, Tennessee, and North Carolina; the "deep" South is Florida, Georgia, Alabama, Mississippi, Louisiana, Arkansas, and South Carolina. Let us keep the region as a whole in mind. It has, in any number of respects, a most remarkable homogeneity. The total area of the ten is 485,214 square miles, and the total population about 26,500,000 by 1944 estimates. Thus the South comprises roughly 16 per cent of the nation in area, and contains something over 19 per cent of its people. Of the total population about one-third is Negro.

The region is extraordinarily homogeneous, yes; but there are also extraordinary sectional differences and distinctions. Once again we observe the incomparable variety of America. Of the ten states VIRGINIA has the richest history, and it likes to think of itself as the most "superior" southern state, with somewhat dubious justification. Virginia has a more diversified economy than most of its neighbors, and it is pulled almost as much toward Washington, D.C., as toward Richmond.

NORTH CAROLINA is in most respects the most progressive southern state. It has tobacco as a great staple crop, a considerable amount of industry, and a splendid university at Chapel Hill which is a kind of intellectual capital for the whole South. In contrast, SOUTH CAROLINA, a stubborn and rebellious entity with pronounced sectionalisms, is very

The
SOUTHEASTERN
STATES

backward by most criteria. It is a curious kind of graveyard of various economies, having successively lived on indigo, turpentine, and rice, as well as cotton. GEORGIA is the crossroads of the South, "the State of the Angle," where the north-south railways turn off toward the West. Its capital, Atlanta, has a great distribution trade; its former governor Ellis Arnall is the most considerable man of politics the South has produced in many years. In FLORIDA we find a totally different background; Florida is a special case: a playground, a citrus grove, a cattle ranch all in one. It has a strong underlay of Spanish culture, and it is the only southern state with an Indian problem.

ALABAMA, a highly important state, with a sizable iron and steel industry at Birmingham, is in the process of political upheaval and economic fermentation. In MISSISSIPPI, "the worst American state," we will find Rankin, Bilbo, and the most discreditable statistics. TENNESSEE, a virile, lively, and strongly bifurcated state, is one of the most complex and fascinating in the entire union; it contains TVA, the river culture of Memphis, Vanderbilt University, and Boss Crump. As to LOUISIANA it is like Florida something quite special and distinct, largely because of its French and Creole background. ARKANSAS, a kind of inland Mississippi, is probably the most untouched and unawakened of all American states; the South is inclined to be ashamed of it and says that it belongs more properly to the West, which it doesn't.

It will be almost literally impossible for an outsider, whether a man from Mars, the moon, Moscow, or Jersey City to understand the South, if he does not accept as a concrete and contemporaneous living fact the cataclysm of the Civil War or, as it is usually called by die-hard Southerners, the War Between the States, together with what followed. Perhaps the four years of actual warfare were not quite so important as the aftermath. For instance—a minor but suggestive item—I happened to be in Richmond on an important anniversary of Appomattox; the event got no more than an inconspicuous few inches tucked far inside the newspapers. But nobody in the South ever forgets Reconstruction. To this day the South has not recovered from Reconstruction. This was one of the most cruelly outrageous episodes in all the wantonness of history. Lincoln, had he lived, might have been able to make a generous peace. The peace that came was far from generous; and the roots of white supremacy, the Negro problem, and a dozen other inflamed and derivative issues, are all to be found in what occurred in Reconstruction days. The South lost a quarter of its adult male population during the war; the property loss is calculated at six billion dollars. Bad enough! But what came after was much worse. The carpetbaggers began to arrive in about 1867, and in 1870 the 15th amendment, which enfranchised the Negroes, went into force. The South was divided into five districts, under rule of the United States (i.e. Northern) Army, and white Southerners themselves, classified as rebels, were not allowed to vote.

If you read the history of those days you must inevitably be reminded of contemporary analogies: Atlanta in the 1870's must have startlingly resembled Budapest or Warsaw under the Nazis in the 1940's. I do not mean to be invidious. But chopping up the South and ruling it by an absolute dictatorship of the military, while every kind of economic and social depredation was not only allowed but encouraged, is so strikingly like what is going on in Germany at present that the imagination staggers. "The war," writes James Truslow Adams, "left the South prostrate; Reconstruction left it maddened."[1] The period of Reconstruction lasted for varying periods in different southern states. Georgia was not finally readmitted to the union until 1870, and federal troops were not withdrawn from Florida, Louisiana, and South Carolina till 1877.

One brief word about secession as an instrument of policy. Comparatively few people in the United States, whether of the North or South, associate the idea of secession with that of outright treason, strange as this may seem to a non-American. On the whole secession was accepted as a fairly respectable phenomenon, though of course the North lamented it and fought it bitterly. But the New England states had several times talked of leaving the union, on different issues. The southern point of view about this may take extreme forms. Plenty of Southerners like to argue that it was the North that seceded, not themselves. The idea of an enveloping and overembracing American unity was seldom forgotten, even in the fiercest days of warfare;[2] this is one reason why Southerners today seek to avoid such terminology as the "Civil War," hate to be called rebels, and insist on such euphemisms as "War Between the States." The official American name for the war is, incidentally, "War of the Rebellion."

Red clay roads curving around unkempt hills and time passing slowly; lazy drawling accents and Jim Crow water taps; brides marrying in the evening and the drooping of moss; moldy lawns and crinolines and broken-down greasy shacks near the railway tracks; names like Shiloh and Chickamauga; afternoons hot as cotton—these are familiar stigmata of the South. They are part of what might be called the Magnolia Myth. But the South is more than just hot biscuits. I must add, however, that I did actually meet one antediluvian colonel who, rocking on the soft rotting boards of a sagging back porch, gave me a mint julep mixed by someone who was obviously Uncle Remus himself, while we stared straight at a grove of magnolias blatantly in bloom. But if we are to apply sandpaper and emery to much of the so-called "romance" of the South,

---

[1] *Epic of America*, p. 286.
[2] One little-known fact is that three of Lincoln's brothers-in-law were killed fighting with the South; two half-sisters-in-law were married to southern officers. See *The United States of America*, by R. B. Mowat, London, 1938.

we must operate similarly with the realities; the debunking should go both ways. The South is no longer full of elegantly fainting ladies—if it ever was. On the other hand the South is not Omaha or Pittsburgh. The South contains some wonderfully courageous and emancipated liberals, as we shall see. On the other hand it does indubitably contain Mister Bilbo.

Great commotion came to the region recently when the Richmond *Times Dispatch* printed a brief editorial about that distinguished contemporary southerner Senator Claghorn:

CLAGHORN, THE DIXIE FOGHORN

For years, yes, decades, we've been battling to bring some measure of rationality into the fried-chicken-watermelon-mammy-magnolia-moonlight-mocking-bird-moon-June-croon school of thinking on Southern problems, and now we've run up against the toughest proposition yet. We refer, of course, to that bombastic bumbling, brou-ha-ha of the air waves, Senator Beauregard Claghorn, "from the deep South, that is." . . .

This amazing character on the Sunday evening Fred Allen program must have given millions in the North and West the notion that southern Senators spend their time in making frightful puns, and bellowing "That's a joke, son!" and in such professionally southern deliverances as: "When in New York ah only dance at the Cotton Club. The only dance ah do is the Virginia reel. The only train ah ride is the Chattanooga Choo-Choo. When ah pass Grant's tomb ah shut both eyes. Ah never go to the Yankee Stadium! Ah won't even go to the Polo Grounds unless a southpaw's pitchin'."

We "southrons" have been kept sufficiently busy asserting to our northern friends that we aren't all morons and degenerates *à la* Tobacco Road, or banjo-picking mammy-singers, *à la* Al Jolson, but now we have to go around protesting that we aren't all raucous nitwits and foghorns like Senator Claghorn, "from the South, that is." Gad!

I suspect that my friend Virginius Dabney wrote this skit, but I'm not sure. At any rate Mr. Dabney was obliged to report later in the New York *Times* that his paper had been swamped with protests, especially when a chauvinistic southern congressman caused the offending editorial to be inserted in the *Congressional Record*. Mr. Dabney stuck to his point, but he did handsomely admit that Claghorn brought in plenty of laughs, for instance when he said, "In college ah was voted the member of the senior class most likely to secede and ah was graduated magnolia cum laude." (New York *Times*, May 4, 1946.)

The South, I once heard it put, is full of people whose only profession is to be southerners. Once or twice, traveling from town to town, I felt that I wasn't in the United States at all, but in some utterly foreign land. Yet, more than any other region, the South highlights almost every American problem—education, nutrition, the valley authority idea, the growth of industry, religious impulses, agricultural techniques, the Negro of course, and also the culture of the white. It is a kind of laboratory, an exotic testing ground. Also the South lives dangerously—I don't know any other American area about which this may be said in quite the sense I mean it. That it is *the* problem child of the nation is of course indisputable. But how it resents being told so!

How "solid" is the solid South? From the point of view of sociology and basic economic patterns it is, as I have said, by far the most homogeneous of American regions. Nowhere else, not even in New England, is it so comparatively easy to generalize over a broad body of states on the basis of such similar characteristics; the South is a genuine region in the strict sociological meaning of that term. From the point of view of politics, however, the solidarity is not quite so great as is commonly supposed. In fact, if we want to be pedantic, the really "solid" South should be defined as comprising only seven states. Virginia, North Carolina, Florida, Texas, all voted for Hoover and against Al Smith. Of course some very special circumstances attended this election. The fact remains that as recently as 1928 four extremely important southern states went Republican, and I have heard several responsible Southerners say, "The South is breaking up hard and fast."

Some Generalizations About the South

We Southerners are of course a mythological people.
—Jonathan Daniels

Nevertheless, if it can be said that there are many Souths, the fact remains that there is also one South.
—W. J. Cash

(1) The foreign-born and sons of foreign-born, who have been traveling along with us for most of the course of this book, now leave our story to all practical intent. The South is overwhelmingly of native-born Anglo-Saxon origin; this, along with cotton, poverty, and the Negro question, is a major common denominator for the entire region. I say "Anglo-Saxon"; I might add, "predominantly of Scots-Irish, Ulster, or Celtic stock." There are towns in North Carolina almost as Scottish as Aberdeen; there are backwoods in Tennessee and Arkansas as implacably Celtic as anything in Wales. Most southern states are, moreover, extremely proud of their background. I think it was in Mississippi that I first heard someone say, "The state of Mississippi has a smaller proportion of foreign-born than any other American state." I then heard the precisely identical remark in three other states. The detailed figures do

not matter; in every state except Florida and Louisiana 90 per cent or more of the white citizens come of parents who were both American born. The figure reaches 98.7 per cent in Arkansas, if Arkansas statistics are to be believed. That Arkansas should also be one of the most unquestionably backward of American states naturally gives the observer slight pause, and makes one wonder what peculiar characteristics the Celts and Gaels, when transported, contribute to a civilization.

Of course minor qualifications are necessary to all of the above. The seaports, like Mobile and New Orleans and even including Charleston, have a definite foreign sprinkling, and industry during the war brought in some alien workers. The Bell aircraft plant at Marietta, Georgia, just outside Atlanta, once employed 28,000 men and women; it was bigger than Willow Run, incredible as that may seem; even so, a large proportion of the workers were backwoods Anglo-Saxons, and the number of foreign-born was not so great as might have been assumed. That this overwhelming preponderance of English-Celtic-Gaelic background should have produced corollary phenomena in several fields goes without saying. For instance it means that there is no buffer foreign group between the ruling whites and the Negro. Nor, politically speaking, are there any "foreign blocs" to be delivered, like the Poles in Buffalo or the Czechs along the Monongahela. Another relevant point is that the under-educated semimountaineer Scots-Irish are, almost beyond question, those who believe most firmly in "white supremacy," and are therefore a continual exacerbation to the Negro problem.

(2) Some early landowners among the original American immigrants —a Cavalier from a British dukedom was, let us point out, just as much an immigrant as is a Greek shoeshine boy from the slums of Athens—were distinctly of aristocratic blood and they definitely maintained and nurtured an aristocratic tradition, but the idea that all old-line southern planters were, or are, of a superior social class is of course nonsensical. An oligarchy of wealthy planters did indeed grow up, who worked their land mostly through factors, but they were a minority, and only an infinitesimal proportion were substantial slave owners. More often the pattern was that of a lonely Virginia or North Carolina pioneer working his land to the limit, and then pushing west when it was exhausted. Successively a family might own, and ruin, a tract in tidewater Virginia, then in the Virginia mountain country, then in Tennessee or Kentucky bluegrass, then in Ohio or Missouri; its present descendants may, in fact, have very well carried on this process in the Okie and Arkie migrations of the 1930's. The origin of Tennessee was in this movement, and Tennessee itself is responsible for other westward marches. To revert: the notion that the majority of the southern ruling class came from "columned mansions" is very far from the truth. Take such a representative and distinguished family as that of splendid old Josephus

Daniels, who has been inextricably conjoined with the life of North Carolina for fifty years. Mr. Daniels' father was a ship's carpenter in Rhode
Island. He helped build the *Merrimac*. He died of blood poisoning when,
after a wound, he refused to have his arm amputated, since this would
have meant that he could no longer work at his trade. So his widow went
to Wilson, North Carolina, where she became the postmistress, and so
supported—and sent to the university—her three sons.

(3) Intervention and the martial spirit. The South was, as everybody
knows, the part of the nation that from the beginning and most vividly
took the allied side in both World War I and World War II. This
phenomenon, which we shall elaborate upon when we come to Texas,
has deep and legitimate natural origins. Several southern states have
military records which even rival that of Texas. For instance in 1940-41,
according to the well known Birmingham journalist John Temple
Graves,[3] the proportion of volunteer enlistments to induction under
selective service was 49.8 per cent for the nation as a whole; the corresponding figure was 85.3 for South Carolina, 92.6 per cent for Georgia,
98.6 per cent for Texas, and not less than 123.4 per cent for Kentucky.
In October 1941, by terms of the Gallup poll, 88 per cent of Southerners
thought that it was more important to beat Germany than to keep out of
the war, as against a national average of 70 per cent. Mr. Graves has
an interesting chapter wherein he asks various southern specialists
of great renown how they account for such striking figures. One factor
is obviously the Anglo-Saxon origin of most Southerners. Another (this
we shall also see in Texas), is that southern economy is based on the
export of raw materials, chiefly cotton and tobacco, of which Europe in
general and England in particular have been immemorially important
customers. Still another is the peculiar and ineffaceable persistence of the
martial tradition, the fighting impulse. The South has always been fond
of military heroes, and it has produced generals by the carload, from
Andrew to Stonewall Jackson. General George C. Marshall is by residence a Virginian—and incidentally the Virginia Military Institute at
Lexington has an importance in the training of American officers second
only to that of West Point—and General Douglas MacArthur was born
in Arkansas. But read the first chapter of Mr. Graves' book. It is an
illuminating anthology. For instance Mark Ethridge, publisher of the
Louisville *Courier-Journal*, gave as his reason for southern militancy
that "we know better than anybody else that war settles questions," and
Professor Odum replied that "the South has been invaded so often . . .
by thousands of reformers and accusers that it is automatically prepared
to defend itself."

Dr. Douglas Southall Freeman, the eminent biographer of General
Robert E. Lee and his lieutenants, told me a nuggety little anecdote per-

[3] See *The Fighting South*, published by Putnam, New York, Chapter I.

taining to the Army maneuvers held in Louisiana in 1941. A farmer asked a visiting northern newspaperman what all the excitement was about. "We're training," the newspaperman replied. "For what?" "We think we may be getting into this European war." "I thought so! Been thinkin' so for a good long time. But one thing bothers us down here. Do you reckon that when we do get in, you Yankees are goin' to help us any?"[4]

Another point worth making is that just as the South is vehemently pro-British, in peace as well as in war, so it is at the moment vehemently anti-Russian. Nowhere else in the country except in Catholic Irish groups such as those in Boston, did I find such belligerent and effervescent anti-Russian sentiment.

(4) *Poverty.* This is a most salient and pervasive item. The South is by all odds the poorest region in the nation; for instance the average income per capita in ten southern states was $716 in 1944, as against $1,284 in New England, $1,459 on the West coast, and $1,117 for the country at large. In almost every species of conceivable statistic having to do with wealth, the South is at the bottom. Professor Odum, in his massive *Southern Regions,*[5] prints a munificent galaxy of charts and maps; in map after map after map, drawn to illustrate various economic indices, the South appears as a solid bloc ranking lowest in the nation. This bloc, in some maps colored white, in some black, but always demonstrating the South's deficiencies, is precisely coterminous with similar maps showing the extent of cotton culture, the percentage of white native stock, and the heaviest concentration of Negroes. Professor Odum uses hundreds of criteria; among literally dozens of categories in which the South is lowest in the country are per capita bank resources, per capita savings deposits, wages per wage earner, value of product per wage earner, number of automobiles (Florida excepted), gross agricultural income, average value of land, amount of life insurance in force (Oklahoma, Arizona, New Mexico join the South here), number of families per radio (not, as it might be in the North, number of radios per family), percentage of farms with telephones, taxable property per capita, estimated true wealth per inhabitant (Texas is also included here), average value per farm of domestic animals, horsepower available per worker, retail sales (Florida again excepted), and milk production. In

---

[4] This story also appears in Graves. Incidentally it was these Louisiana maneuvers that first brought General Eisenhower to the foreground. He was a lieutenant colonel then, and his work on the staff of one of the competing generals was so brilliant that he was pulled forward to Marshall's personal attention.

[5] *Southern Regions of the United States,* by Howard W. Odum, published for the Southern Regional Committee of the Social Science Research Council, University of North Carolina Press, Chapel Hill, 1936. This book is of the most stunning value. But I should perhaps point out that most of its vast plethora of statistics, of date 1930 and thereabouts, may be somewhat outmoded today. On the other hand nothing else has been assembled that even approaches Odum's work.

value of farm property per farm, Mississippi is the forty-eighth state, Arkansas forty-seventh, and Alabama forty-sixth. (Nevada first, California second, Iowa third.) In percentage of farms having tractors, Mississippi is forty-eighth, Alabama forty-seventh, Arkansas forty-sixth. (North Dakota first, South Dakota second, Montana third.) In average annual wage per wage earner in all manufactures, the three lowest states are North Carolina, South Carolina, Georgia. Conversely, in percentage of families receiving unemployment relief from public funds (as of 1933), the three highest states were South Carolina, Florida, and West Virginia. A final almost unbelievable figure, not from Odum but from Dabney[6] and more up to date, is that eleven *million* Southerners have annual cash incomes of $250 or below.

From statistics like these we may derive much ancillary matter. One item is that, as in the West, most of the bright young men get out, if only because the simple circumstances of earning a living are so onerous. Erosion of the southern soil is an important problem, as we shall see; so is the erosion in human beings. A second item would have to do with a complex mass of intellectual dilemmas. Why is the South so flame headed, obdurate, and irrational so often? Because, if I may paraphrase David L. Cohn in a recent article in the *Atlantic Monthly*, it hasn't the means to afford the golden mean.

(5) At this juncture a word about agriculture is essential, though we shall mention cotton in a separate section later. Overwhelmingly the South is rural. We are far away now from the thickets of great cities in the Middle West. In fact, the whole South has only three cities over 300,000 in population by the 1940 census, and one of the Odum charts shows that only 29.8 per cent of Southerners live in urban areas, as against a figure of 67.2 for the far West and 74.4 for the northeastern states. Southern agriculture is a good deal more diversified than most people think—consider for instance peaches, melons, citrus, peanuts—but cotton and tobacco are still the two great staple crops. Now both these crops, it happens, cause extremely heavy loss to soil. We have talked almost endlessly of soil erosion in this book, it would seem, and we know well how dangerous a problem it is in the West. But erosion in the South is incomparably more dangerous. Fully half of all the eroded land in the nation is in the southern states, and loss to the soil is calculated at something like 300 million dollars per year;[7] significantly enough the poverty-smitten South, which is such a laggard in so many statistics, leads the country in the amount of fertilizer it has to buy. Former Governor Arnall of Georgia has cogently pointed out that the average south-

[6] *Below the Potomac*, by Virginius Dabney, p. 291.
[7] The figure 300 million dollars is from *Fortune*, "The Industrial South," November, 1938, p. 49. The Arnall calculations are from the *Atlantic Monthly*, "The Southern Frontier," September, 1946.

ern farmer pays $2.71 per year for fertilizer (making the total fertilizer bill a staggering 160 million dollars), and loses $9.00 worth per year of exactly the same substances he is putting in—potash, phosphate, nitrogen derivatives, and the like.

One encouraging new sign has been a swing to cattle. Under cotton culture, the number of work days per year is comparatively small; about 180 days out of 365 grows a cotton crop. So the average cotton worker is idle half the year; no wonder living standards are so pitiably low. The problem has been one of diversification not only from the point of view of soil, but of soul: to give more men more kinds of work. Live-stock provides a possible solution, inasmuch as cattle require plenty of at-tention, and except in those areas where erosion has made the earth look as barren as the blank face of the moon, they can live on marginal land. At any rate cattle have become an energizing and lucrative southern in-dustry. Florida lives on cattle today almost as much as on citrus or even the tourist trade and gambling; the figure may seem hard to believe, but 40 per cent of Georgia's present farm income derives from livestock, as against 32 per cent from cotton; Montgomery, Alabama, has become the cattle capital of the Southeast, and is a miniature Fort Worth; the eyes of men in Memphis glisten when they talk of Herefords, and some Tennessee cattle, of all things, won prizes last year in a Texas cattle show.

There is poor land in the South; there is land that is not even land, like the notorious area around Ducktown, near the Tennessee-Georgia border, where nothing whatever remains but savagely gutted and defiled dirty gullies; there is also the land of the Delta, as rich as Croesus. The Delta which, oddly enough, is not a delta, is the area adjacent to the Mississippi River between Memphis and Vicksburg; it is a region of large farming rather than small, and it is where the mechanical cotton picker is working one of the cardinal revolutions of our time. Nothing quite like the Delta exists in the nation except, perhaps, Central Valley in California, but Central Valley depends for life on artificial rainfall, as we know. In the Delta the rain still comes from God and heaven.

Almost all southern problems interlock; and the future of agriculture in the South is very closely wrapped up with the future of the Negro. Let more Negroes become small landowners, owning their own small farms, and the lot of both agriculture and the Negro will be improved.

(6) This brings us to two phenomena famous in the South: the luck-less, miserable group of millions known as poor whites, and share-croppers and tenant farmers. Poor whites live in the towns too of course, but it is in the rural districts that their gross poverty is most conspic-uous; the rural slums of the South are almost beyond doubt the most revolting in the nation. No one can define the term "poor white" with much precision; originally poor whites were the small landowners who did not own slaves or the frontiersmen who reached the mountain areas

and did not progress further; they do not live like most Negroes in segregated enclaves, but spread their poison through the whole community; they exist almost everywhere in the South, perhaps more conspicuously in the Piedmont than in any other specific region; they are the whites who hate and fear the Negro most; many of them bear the most gallant and distinguished of old Scottish names; they are a living exemplar of a famous remark by Booker T. Washington, "The white man cannot keep the Negro in the ditch without sitting down there with him." The kind of piquant sociological detail known to readers of William Faulkner still crops up in the news from day to day. While I was in Atlanta the papers printed a handsome little story about nine sisters, all of whom were prostitutes in the same room. Lillian Smith, the author of *Strange Fruit*, told me in Clayton, Georgia, of a recent case in which a baby died. The parents left it on the bed to rot. They were not rendered helpless by grief. They made no effort to bury the body because they simply didn't know any better.

The line between the sharecropper and the tenant farmer isn't always easy to draw. Both derive, in first analysis, from slavery and the plantation system that was for generations the chief hallmark of southern agriculture. Always the area has had a substantial big landowner class, and also a very large completely landless element, both white and black. The process arose whereby the owner of a sizable plantation, having more property than he himself could till, let out part to a tenant, who then worked it; the owner as a rule contracted to supply a house to the tenant, and the tenant on his side supplied tools, perhaps a team, and his own labor. But, the key to the system as it operates today, the tenant does not pay rent for the use of this land; what he pays is a share of the crop he grows. The usual bargain is that the tenant pays as rent one half of the cotton he himself grows, and about one third of the corn, if corn is part of the crop. This ratio may, however, vary according to locality and the price of the commodity. Of course this procedure is, from the point of view of the tenant, completely heathen, in that he provides both tools and labor and yet is permitted to retain only one half (or some other variable proportion) of the rewards of his own endeavor.

There are other evils. The average tenant, holding the use of the land for a limited interval only, attempts to suck out of it all he can; operating under short-range tenure, he can eviscerate a property, ruin it utterly, with three or four successive cotton or tobacco crops. There is no incentive to scientific agriculture, no stimulus to soil conservation or rotation. Another factor is migrancy. Most tenant farmers are continually on the move. They proceed from property to property because nothing fixes them to the soil; hope (since most are miserably poor) sometimes spurs them on; sometimes they quarrel with the landlord.

Usually contracts are made in the near-by rural town on a Saturday night at the end of the year. A tenant hears of a new landowner in the next county. He goes to him, saying, "I'm tired of working for Mr. Tom. Any farm land open on your property next year?" The new landlord, if he wants a tenant, straightens things out with Mr. Tom, and makes the bargain. Then early in February the new tenant moves over. Each move is calculated to cost about fifty dollars. Some tenants move every year. It is an expensive way to farm.

In Chapter 30 above, quoting the opinions of a typical New England legislator, I said that he knew that no peasants existed in the United States. Perhaps my New England legislator is wrong. He has not met some black belt[8] sharecroppers. These, he might find, are not merely peasants; they are peons. And at one time there were eight million sharecroppers in the South, most of them clustered in a wide series of pools lying outside the Piedmont, and stretching—with interruptions—all the way from North Carolina to east Texas. This is the shrunken core of what was once the slave area. A sharecropper differs from a tenant farmer in that he has no tools, no teams, no stock. He has, in fact, nothing whatever except his own labor. Thus his bargaining power is less than that of the tenant farmer, and he gets as a rule less favored treatment. His house, hardly even a dilapidated shack, may be part of a deserted bus, or almost literally a heap of packing crates; he has no cash, and has to live exclusively on credit; often he cannot educate his numerous children for the simple reason that he cannot afford to buy them clothes decent enough to permit school attendance. The tenant farmer is in a bad enough situation; the plight of the sharecropper is a good deal worse. For one thing, he gets a smaller share of the crop as a rule. For another, no matter how intolerable his circumstances, he can't afford to move; sharecroppers in the strict sense are seldom migratory. The only hope for a sharecropper, and it is a slim one, is that he may pull himself up the ladder one rung by becoming a tenant. But to do this he must be able to buy tools and a team. Which is difficult considering that interest rates in his locality may run as high as 40 per cent.

(7) Out of poverty in the material domain arises inevitably poverty in education. I gave above some few of Professor Odum's electrifying indices on economic factors, and similar chartings are available in regard to schools. Using no fewer than 152 different indices, Odum finds that the South (including Texas in most charts) is at the very bottom of the nation, not only in the general amount of expenditure on public education, but in such items as total enrollment in high schools, per capita expenditure on public day schools, length of the school term, and teachers' pay. In percentage of white literacy, South Carolina is the

[8] Black in the sense of black soil, not Negro.

forty-eighth state, Louisiana the forty-seventh, New Mexico the forty-sixth, Mississippi the forty-fifth, Alabama the forty-fourth. An auxiliary item, not covered by Odum so far as I know, is textbooks; all over the South textbooks are a lively issue. Huey Long early in his career set out to provide textbooks for the children of Louisiana *free*; this was a substantial contribution to his rise in power. In several southern states scandals over textbooks, free or otherwise, have made angry political crises, as we shall see.

(8) Similarly in such matters as public health, the South is at the bottom of the heap. It is lowest in the nation in number of hospital beds, and in physicians per unit of population; it is highest in maternal deaths in childbirth, infant mortality, and venereal disease.[9] As of selective service records, Louisiana, Mississippi, Georgia, South Carolina, and Florida had up to 171.5 cases of syphilis per 1,000 of men examined. The corresponding rate in thirteen northern and western states was under fifteen.

(9) We come now to the general rubric of culture, which overlaps some of the foregoing material. H. L. Mencken once wrote a famous essay, "Sahara of the Bozart," in which he slaphappily throws at the South everything about the *Boobus americanus* he can think of; he began with the little jingle:

> Alas, for the South! Her books have grown fewer—
> She ne'er was much given to literature.

Among Mr. Mencken's choicest remarks are that the South is "an intellectual Gobi or Lapland," that its culture is like that of "Asia Minor, resigned to Armenians, Greeks, and wild swine," and that "one could no more imagine a Lee or a Washington in the Virginia of today than one could imagine a Huxley in Nicaragua." But as to the lack of southern writers, Mr. Mencken might have to change his tune today. Consider Thomas Wolfe, Ellen Glasgow, Margaret Mitchell, Erskine Caldwell, William Faulkner, Eudora Welty, Roark Bradford, Allen Tate, Harnett T. Kane, Hamilton Basso, Julia Peterkin, Marjorie Kinnan Rawlings, Lillian Smith, Josephine Pinckney, to say nothing of Negroes like Richard Wright. I am not saying that all these writers are of the very first flight; I will say that contemporary American literature would be considerably the poorer without them.

In some other fields, however, many of the Mencken strictures still apply. There are sixteen major symphony orchestras in the United States; not one is in the South. There is no southern philosopher of consequence. There is no southern theater worthy of the name, and there are comparatively few painters, sculptors, or other artists of talent,

[9] *The Southern Patriot*, May, 1945.

though some southern architects have considerable distinction. The South has become highly self-conscious about these lacunae in cultural fields, it might be added; for instance the Atlanta *Journal,* a lively and progressive paper, includes "a symphony orchestra, expanded art museums, and libraries" in the "Platform for Georgia" that appears under its masthead every day. North Carolina has the only orchestra in the United States supported by the state (it does not count among the majors), and Virginia has decided to set up a state theater.

We must, finally, turn once more to Professor Odum's terrifying charts. In one passage he takes twenty-six widely differing cultural criteria, and finds that the South (Texas, West Virginia, and Kentucky included) is lowest in every one; in another, with no fewer than 130 indices "selected to represent all aspects of culture from land use . . . to educational institutions," he finds Mississippi to be the lowest state culturally, with South Carolina next and Georgia and Arkansas closely following.[10] Take the single item of libraries. The south is lowest in the union in per capita expenditure for public libraries, in per cent of population registered as library borrowers, and in number of libraries of all kinds.

(10) Religious factors. Just as the South is the region of Anglo-Saxon white stock *in excelsis* it is also the region par excellence of militant protestantism. More than three-quarters of the population of Arkansas, Mississippi, Alabama, Georgia, and the Carolinas are either Baptists or Methodists; in the other states the rate is over half. Six southern states, it is interesting to learn from Bryce, once excluded from public office any person who did not believe in the supreme being; the whole area today, especially the Piedmont, is still the "Bible belt," the "infant damnation belt," and the "total immersion belt," replete with Bible marathons, revivalists, Gaelic fundamentalism, and a fierce retentive hostility to other creeds. This is the region where Al Smith was thought of as an agent of the Pope, and where a young schoolmaster named Scopes, was, not so many years ago, tried and found guilty of the crime of teaching evolution in the hamlet of Dayton, Tennessee. Tennessee's present junior senator, Tom Stewart, was incidentally the prosecuting attorney at this celebrated but now largely forgotten trial. And be it noted: the law forbidding evolution to be taught still stands on the books of the sovereign state of Tennessee.

A passage from the cross-examination of William Jennings Bryan is illuminating:

Q. Do you claim that everything in the Bible should be literally interpreted?

[10] *Southern Regions*, p. 565. Again let us point out that the utterly blank spaces on the Odum maps are precisely coterminous with the areas of cotton culture and lowest per capita income.

A. I believe that everything in the Bible should be accepted as it is
   given there.
Q. But when you read that Jonah swallowed the whale—or that the
   whale swallowed Jonah—excuse me, please, how do you literally
   interpret it? . . . You believe that God made such a fish, and
   that it was big enough to swallow Jonah?
A. Yes, sir. Let me add, one miracle is as easy to believe as another.
Q. Perfectly easy to believe that Jonah swallowed the whale?
A. If the Bible said so.

Perhaps the reader who chances to pick up this book in Mukden or
Tirana and who has never heard of Mr. Bryan may be reminded that
he was the Democratic party's most important leader for a generation,
and ran for the presidency of the United States three times. Also in
his earlier days he was unquestionably a great man.

An unusual number of southern papers carry a daily quotation from
the Bible at the head of their editorial columns. Among them are the
Raleigh *News and Observer* (the Daniels paper), the Florida *Times-
Union*, the Tampa *Morning Tribune*, and the Nashville *Banner*. I make
this observation as a matter of interest to the reader, not in a critical
sense.

The Methodists and Baptists in the deep South not only have, by and
large, a yeasty suspicion of other religions; they can attack their own
kind savagely. Politics gets mixed up in this. Dr. Louie D. Newton,
president of the Southern Baptist Convention and thus a man of no
mean substance, returned from a visit to Russia recently and said that
he had detected evidences there of a growing religious freedom (New
York *Times*, August 25, 1946). As a result, even though he attacked
Communism as such, Dr. Newton was picketed when he spoke at the
Atlanta municipal auditorium, and placards were borne, Is LOUIE
D. NEWTON SELLING COMMUNISM TO THE U.S.A.? At about the same
time clubs were organized in Knoxville, Tennessee, to prevent a public
appearance there of no less a personage than Dr. G. Bromley Oxnam,
bishop of the Methodist church and former president of the Federal
Council of Churches of Christ in America.[11] It was alleged that Bishop
Oxnam, a great many years ago, had belonged to some mildly leftist
political organization.

Roman Catholics are a minority in most of the South (of course
Louisville and New Orleans are heavily Catholic towns); the Celtic
backwoodsmen resent them fiercely. There would appear to be three
reasons for this aside from religion per se. First, most Catholics are
wet. Second, Catholic children in the South have a fair chance of getting
a better education than Protestant, since the quality of the public schools

[11] Lowell Mellett in the New York *Post*, August 27, 1946.

is generally so low. Third, Catholics by and large are more liberal than Protestants in regard to Negroes, and they proselytize the black communities with vigor. Let us explore. Baptist and Methodist churches in the South operate, of course, under segregation; most Negroes are Baptist or Methodist but they have their own separate church organizations and churches. But any Negro may go into *any* Catholic church, and, though he may not be enthusiastically welcomed, he will not as a rule be rebuffed. Catholics do, however, accept the segregation principle in their schools and hospitals, and they maintain many exclusively Negro churches.

Jews play less of a role in southern life, on the whole, than in any other American region except the West. Some big department stores, particularly in Atlanta and Richmond, are Jewish owned; a few rich plantation owners are Jewish (Bernard Mannes Baruch of South Carolina for instance); some able journalists are Jews. But by and large—let us repeat it once and for all—the South is Protestant, of English stock, and above all rural. This does not mean that biting anti-Semitism does not exist. It does exist. It is the hallmark of the backward in the South as everywhere else in the nation. The Ku-Klux Klan has, as everybody knows, three enemies—Negroes, Catholics, Jews.

(11) Prohibition. This is of course closely associated with religious factors, and the South is technically the driest area in the country, the stronghold of the Anti-Saloon League and the Woman's Christian Temperance Union. Partly, this is a result of a general Puritan inheritance; the South is, or has been, fundamentalist not only about God and whisky but about card playing, dancing, and cigarettes; at one time Coca-Cola was forbidden Sunday sale in Richmond. Another aspect of the close association between drinking and religion is, as a wise lady once pointed out, that Catholics (and also some Protestants in the upper echelons) use wine in celebration of the Mass; the backwoodsmen hate Catholicism, and hence hate wine too, with which they associate the Catholic ritual.

Everywhere I went in the South I asked why it was so dry, legally speaking, and I got a considerable variety of answers. One was that Southerners fear outbursts of drunkenness by Negroes. Surely what this means is that they also fear outbursts of drunkenness by themselves. Lillian Smith, when I visited her school and camp in Georgia, had some pertinent remarks to make in this field. The Freudian hypothesis, she points out, provides a useful tool. The South contains a great number of pronouncedly schizoid people; the whole region is a land of paranoia, full of the mentally sick; most Southerners feel a deep necessity to hate something, if necessary even themselves. Their hatred (=fear) of alcohol is partly a reflection of bad conscience; the South fears that liquor will release its own most dangerous inhibitions. The Negro problem is inextricably involved; so is the sexual problem. A Southerner will, perhaps without expressing it consciously or concretely, work out an equation something like the following: "We are not going to give up the Negro; therefore we must give up something else. We will not give up fundamentalism, sex, white supremacy, or slavery; so we give up rationality instead."

All this being mentioned, let me at once add something else, namely that "dry" as the South may be in some spots, it is also the hardest-drinking region I have ever seen in the world, and the area with the worst drinking habits by far. There are no bars permitted in most cities; hence, people drink by the private bottle, and as always hypocrisy begets disorderly behavior. Never in Port Said, Shanghai, or Marseilles have I seen the kind of drinking that goes on in Atlanta, Houston, or Memphis every Saturday night—with officers in uniform vomiting in hotel lobbies, seventeen-year-old girls screaming with hysteria in public elevators, men and women of the country club category being carried bodily off the dance floor by disinterested waiters.

Similarly in sexual affairs the South combines a heavy puritanical façade with almost epochal lubricity. In one hotel, one of the best in the nation, I found a printed manifesto, "Persons Entertaining Visitors of Opposite Sex Must Notify Office to Prevent Possible Embarrassment." In another city, the most renowned of the local restaurants has a big sign on the door, UNESCORTED LADIES NOT ADMITTED.

(12) Coca-Cola. All through the South, socially and economically and even politically, Coca-Cola has an importance hard for Northerners to appreciate; this drink is one of the few things that the South developed of itself, and that the North hasn't taken over. Almost everywhere below the Mason and Dixon's line the Coca-Cola dealer (or maybe the local cotton ginner) is the richest person in town; quite often one man fills both these posts, and he has something of the position that the Ford agency proprietor once held in the North. O. Max Gardner, till recently under secretary of the treasury and one of the most distinguished of contemporary Southerners, has filled usefully many jobs; he was once governor of North Carolina, and the nearest thing to a boss that state ever had; he was for a time president of the Cotton Textile Institute of the United States; also the fact that he was one of Coca-Cola's lawyers certainly didn't diminish his power and fame. Late in 1946 Mr. Gardner was named ambassador to the Court of St. James's.

(13) Crime and civil liberties. In both these categories the South is probably the darkest place in the nation. According to Dabney,[12] six of the eleven major "centers of repression" in the United States as listed by the American Civil Liberties Union are in the South—Harlan County in Kentucky, the area in Arkansas where the sharecroppers sought to organize, New Orleans, Birmingham, Tampa, and Atlanta—and as

[12] *Below the Potomac*, pp. 128, 192, 247.

to crime it leads every other area; even excluding lynchings, the murder rate from Kentucky through Texas (but not in the Virginias or North Carolina) is the highest in the land. Charlotte, North Carolina, was once known as the "murder capital" of America; a savory touch is that it also calls itself "the greatest churchgoing town in the world, except Edinburgh." This noteworthy and curious community contains about 100,000 people and has 114 churches; it has been legally dry for forty years, and in 1940, sixteen of its forty-seven murders took place on a single street corner. As to more general figures W. T. Cash has some remarkable comparisons in his *Mind of the South*. For instance in 1935, according to the FBI, the murder rate in certain sizable towns in the eleven confederate states was 23.23 per 100,000. The analogous rate for New England was 1.3.

(14) We should add a brief note on weather. I thought I had seen some cataclysmic storms in Montana; but the noisiest weather I ever did encounter was in Alabama. I thought once that the roughest trip I had ever taken in an airplane, in several hundred thousand miles of flying, was across the Andes in Bolivia; but a recent trip near Miami made Bolivia seem dulcet. For a time, traveling in preparation for this book, I thought I had emerged with a splendid new generalization about the United States as a whole: that this is the country where the South is cold, the North hot. This was after I had come near to freezing to death in South Carolina and when I was broiling at 104 degrees in Bismarck, North Dakota. Seriously of course the general temperateness and mildness of southern climate is an extremely important factor in economy and behavior. Most homes in the South don't, at least in theory, need central heating during the winter; if they did, the circumstances of life in a hundred areas would be very different. Why don't more poor Southerners move north, and thus allay their privation and discontent with the better wages of northern industry? A highway policeman near Montgomery, Alabama, gave me one answer: "I'm scareda coal weatha."

(15) Sport. The South, like the West, is excluded from major league baseball, though teams in St. Louis, Cincinnati, and Washington, D.C., certainly impinge on the southern frontier. But as to football the South has tremendous teams. These, and this is true elsewhere in the nation, help to subsidize education, in that wealthy alumni give more money when the football scores are best. Among teams consider the formidable records of Duke, Alabama, Georgia Tech, Georgia. In 1945 the historic Army team, with Blanchard and Davis, won four places on Grantland Rice's All-American. But of the other seven four were from Texas or the South, and Blanchard is from South Carolina.

(16) Economic factors aside from agriculture. The South has considerably more industry than most people give it credit for having. The list is virile—cotton shirts and sheets and towels in the Carolinas,

cigars in Tampa, chemicals and aluminum in the Tennessee valley, bathtubs and agricultural machinery in Chattanooga, cigarettes in Durham
and Richmond, lumber in Alabama and Mississippi, bauxite in Arkansas,
shipbuilding in Virginia, petroleum in Louisiana, iron and steel in Birmingham, and Coca-Cola bottling almost everywhere, to say nothing of
potential atomic by-products from Oak Ridge, Tennessee. Most responsible Southerners both hope for and fear further industrial extension; they
don't want any more slums like those in the Carolina milling towns.
What they would prefer as an ideal is development of small decentralized
industries making use of southern resources at present only partly
tapped—such as mica, specialized types of timber like black walnut,
pottery clays and so on. The South does not want to industrialize à la
New England; what it seeks is a balance between the present overwhelmingly rural economy and the growth of new industry in modest
semiurban units.

Of course the war changed things vastly. As in the West, the federal
government planted fabulous amounts of new industry in localities never
industrialized before; eleven billion dollars went into southern installations. But some Southerners are apt to make acrid complaints in this
general field. One is that the Defense Plant Corporation, for reasons best
known to itself and Jesse Jones, but which were perfectly legitimate,
strongly favored Texas as against other states in distributing new industry. Mark Ethridge[13] has calculated that Texas got 31 per cent of the
total war investment, though both North Carolina and Georgia out-
ranked it in prewar industrial employment. On a per capita basis Texas
got $103.37 in new industry, Kentucky $66.33, Alabama $27.12, Georgia
$1.44, and Mississippi 81¢. Many of the new southern war plants were,
after the war, forced to shut down. There was no possibility of reconversion, and this too is something that the South laments, though there is
very little that anybody can do about it.

Another standard and general grievance is freight rates; for the background of this the reader is referred back to Chapter 10, since the situation in the South exactly parallels that of the West, except that, if possible, discrimination is more severe. Merchandisers in Arkansas, I heard,
operate under what is in effect a penalty of 75 per cent; I even
heard that to ship a gasoline engine from Little Rock, say, to
Chicago, costs fifty dollars more than to ship the same engine
from Chicago to Little Rock. Other figures, like those I gave in Chapter 10, are equally remarkable. For instance if a textile mill in Macon,
Georgia, and one in Philadelphia both ship goods to a point in the Middle
West an identical number of miles away, the freight charges from Macon
will be 39 per cent greater. The South resents the manifest injustice of

[13] In a speech to the Georgia Academy of Political and Social Science, February
16, 1945.

this; also it resents (like the West) the aspect of "double squeeze"; for instance it has to pay a stiff differential in shipping out its own raw materials, and then must pay a further stiff charge when these raw materials are shipped back in the form of manufactured goods. It was, as we know, former Governor Arnall of Georgia who first catapulted this vexing matter to national attention. But perhaps the chief interest in Arnall's celebrated suit was not so much that he brought up the freight rates question as such, but that he set a precedent whereby an American state was permitted to plead as an aggrieved party against a private monopoly.

Finally, like the West, the South has complaints in the realm of absentee ownership and "colonial economy." The great Tennessee Coal, Iron & Railroad Company in Birmingham, Alabama, is a subsidiary of United States Steel, and several of the chief utility and private power companies link up with holding companies in New York. About one-third the total number of cotton spindles in the South (18,100,000) are owned in the North, and more are being transferred to northern control month by month. One of the largest cotton plantations in the world, in the Mississippi delta near Greenville, is British controlled. Mark Ethridge in the speech cited above asserts that "85 per cent of Georgia" is owned by people outside and that 50 per cent of money on deposit in Georgia banks is northern. During the depression, I heard in Atlanta, when thousands upon thousands of small farms were foreclosed, at least half the land in the state came under ownership by northern insurance companies. Why didn't southern insurance companies enter into this? Because they were not large enough to lend money on such a scale.

(17) Labor. Inescapably conjoined with this is the Negro question. Labor in the South consisted first of white indentured servants; it took them seven years to pay for their passage to America, whereupon their owners turned them loose; as a rule they were given an ax and a pair of jeans, and they pushed behind the coastal plantations and hacked farms out of the Allegheny wilderness. Second came the slaves. Third came developments that followed invention of the cotton gin. As cotton production thus became "mechanized," and as big plantation owners, employing slaves, reached out for more and more land, the original whites became displaced. Some, as we know, went west. A good many, however, stayed; many of these went into the towns and constitute, by and large, the origin of the white mill-working class today. The first big industry was textiles, and labor in the textile mills is still overwhelmingly white and violently Negrophobe. It became established that work in a mill was a white man's business; a mill such as that at Inca, North Carolina, making rayon, is still 97 per cent white. Negro labor went into different types of industry; for instance the fertilizer plant at Henderson, North Carolina, is 95 per cent black.

Another point is the extreme dearth in the South of trained and skilled craft workmen. Before emancipation, if a slave owner wanted an iron balustrade wrought, say, he trained a slave to the job, which was less expensive than hiring a white craftsman. But when slavery ended, this procedure necessarily died out; emancipation put a premium on the exercise of skills by whites for a time, and the great majority of Negroes turned to agriculture. But then the whites got lazy, and many forgot their specialized aptitudes. Meantime, in another swing of the pendulum, many Negroes returned to industry in the towns when their land wore out. As a general result of all of this, the great body of southern labor today is the least skilled in the civilized world, and its wages are the lowest.[14]

No one can understand the present labor situation in the South without some appreciation of this background. In the Alabama coal mines the United Mine Workers accepted white and Negro members both, and this precedent was followed when iron and steel were organized at Birmingham. This provoked bitter resistance and animosity on the part of the companies, and especially of their white foremen; presently the companies, to break the back of the unions, began to encourage racial rifts. Nevertheless the CIO endorsed mixed unions, despite obvious dangers and embarrassments, from the beginning, and many CIO unions—for instance in cotton-seed oil, peanut processing, some furniture plants, and shipbuilding—are mixed to this day. The majority of AF of L unions are on the contrary white. Textiles are the biggest southern industry; textile labor is overwhelmingly white; this is why the AF of L has led the CIO in the unionization of textiles by five to one, and it is the chief handicap against the CIO in its present drive to organize the South.

The organization and procedure of a mixed union are curious. A white is usually president, a Negro vice president; a white is secretary-treasurer, and a Negro is the chaplain; the posts alternate right down the line, to "inner" and "outer" guards. As a rule most participation by Negroes in union activity is in the local, and meetings of locals, even in the CIO, are semisegregated; that is, Negroes sit on one side of the aisle, whites on the other. There is very little, if any, mixed social participation, and no fraternization after the meeting is over. The white chairman will seldom call a Negro member "Mister"; he uses the euphemism "Brother" instead. At a recent Atlanta meeting, a speaker addressed a Negro as "Mister" by mistake, and simply added, "I mean Brother." There were no protests one way or the other. Despite this type of equivocation, the CIO system has done a good deal for racial harmony. People in analogous jobs come to trust one another; simple acquaintance on the business level

[14] For much of this material and for some preceding passages I am indebted to George S. Mitchell, for many years an official of the Farm Security Administration and later regional director of the Political Action Committee in Atlanta.

of union activity makes for friendlier relations. At any rate the CIO intends firmly to abide by its policy of no discrimination, and to maintain and encourage mixed unions in every direction possible.

At least three southern states have recently passed drastic antiunion legislation; one reason for this is resentment by the ruling whites against the CIO, because it *has* tended to break down segregation to an extent. The CIO is nice to "niggers"; hence down with it! Also of course white supremacy addicts know well that the CIO is a powerful influence furthering the right of Negroes to vote; it persistently propagandizes on such questions as the poll tax and white primaries. At best, the white rulers of the South hate labor unions. When labor unions start mixing up in political and racial affairs, they are twice accursed.

For all these reasons and several others, the CIO effort to increase its power in the South, which began as a major campaign in the spring of 1946, proceeded slowly. Van A. Bittner, leader of the drive, with four hundred organizers in twelve states, set about to acquire one million new members; the cost of the project was estimated at a million dollars. The movement was at any rate successful enough to prompt an immediate counter drive by the AF of L.

(18) Suppose we conclude now on a different note. Somehow we must take the curse off those earlier statistics, their aroma of clamor and despair. Consider the quality of charm. Despite everything, the South probably leads the nation in this respect. Life doesn't move too fast, and people take more time to live. I know few things in the nation more delightful than the plantations outside Charleston, or restaurants in New Orleans underneath their ancient iron balconies, or the way the placid roads in North Carolina look painted by Cézanne.

Politics Southern Style

The South, the poor South!
—Last words of John C. Calhoun

Famously the South is the land of demagogues, of cumulus-cloudy politicians who emit wads of opaque cotton wool every time they open their mouths. Think back a little, to the time when men now mostly forgotten were household names—"Cotton Ed" Smith of South Carolina, who was probably the worst senator who ever lived, no mean honor; Tom Watson of Georgia and Tom Heflin of Alabama, one of the most fanatic reactionaries in American history, especially about things religious; John Sharp Williams of Mississippi, Cole L. Blease of South Carolina, one of the typical "spittoon senators," and of course Huey Long of Louisiana.

Also the South contains men of politics not demagogues, but of dwarf-like character and an intelligence positively wizened. There are do-nothing governors in the South today who are little more than nimble ferrets; some have about as much spine as an Eskimo pie. Sprinkled through the South are soapy miscreants who want a war with Russia for the fun of it, and irresponsible wretched politicians who talk about "Communists" exactly in the accents of the late Dr. Goebbels fifteen years ago, who invent a myth in order to have excuse for demolishing not merely the myth but such realities as civil liberties.

But—the point is important—the South has a good many first-class liberals too. The notion that the area is a debauched hinterland occupied exclusively by reactionaries is as far from the truth as the notion that everything above the Mason and Dixon's line is progressive. Jonathan Daniels once asserted in conversation that the South is in fact the most radical area in the United States. There is hyperbole in this statement of course; also there is truth, and much of the South is foaming today with a progressive crisis. Consider some southern liberals. The region has senators like Spessard Holland of Florida, John J. Sparkman of Alabama, young Bill Fulbright of Arkansas, Lister Hill of Alabama, who might well be considered to be as good a liberal as any man ever sent to Washington by any state, Alben Barkley of Kentucky, and particularly Claude Pepper of Florida. The South contains congressmen like Priest, Kefauver, Folger, administrators like David Lilienthal, university presidents like Frank Graham, Supreme Court justices like Hugo Black, mayors like de Lesseps S. Morrison of New Orleans, and a circle of useful editors—Dabney and Ethridge whom I have named several times, Ralph McGill of the Atlanta *Constitution* and the whole group that edits the Atlanta *Journal,* Jennings Perry, formerly of Nashville, and Hodding Carter, editor of the Greenville (Mississippi) *Delta Democrat Times* and the Greenwood *Star,* and author of *The Winds of Fear,* one of the ablest progressives not merely in the South but in the nation. Consider too such an organization as the Southern Conference for Human Welfare in Nashville and the Southern Regional Council in Atlanta. The president of this latter is Professor Odum; one of its vice presidents is Carter Wesley of Houston, Texas (Negro); its executive director is Guy B. Johnson (white); his assistant is Professor Harold Trigg (Negro). The work of mixed organizations of this kind is of particular importance because a good many Southerners are what Westbrook Pegler once called "Jim Crow liberals"; that is they are "liberal" up to the frontier of the Negro problem, but not beyond. Bodies like the Southern Regional Council do what they can to destroy this line of demarcation.

All this being said it should also be said that, so far as the national scene is concerned, the over-all impact of southern influence is conservative in the extreme. Take Congress. That the representation of the South is largely reactionary is something we all know, but it is not so commonly known that quite aside from its reactionary quality this representation is also very powerful—so much so that it may be fairly said that the southern bloc of Tory Democrats is the chief single factor in the United States militating against the progress of the nation as a whole. When this cohesive and impenetrable southern bloc votes against FEPC, for instance, it is not merely exercising a racial bias; it is exercising a direct dominance in basic national affairs. This it does mainly by coalition with the Republicans. The *New Republic* printed a chart on September 23, 1946, demonstrating the combined southern Democrat plus Republican vote on recent Senate issues. It was a Republican-southern Democrat coalition that passed the Case antistrike bill, that defeated unemployment compensation and that killed minimum wage legislation. A similar coalition in the House approved the bill to establish the permanent Wood-Rankin (ex-Dies) committee, and a bill to legalize speculation on housing prices. Only 21 southern Democrats of 117 in Congress "consistently supported the administration in social legislation."

Why did the South become Democratic in the first place? How can it be both Democratic and reactionary at the same time? How can it vote for Roosevelt with one hand and Bilbo with the other? These questions comprise one of the great paradoxes of American life, and their roots go variously into history; everything from the Jeffersonian tradition to Andrew Jackson to the tariff to the Negro issue is involved. In the early days the southern Democrats were an agrarian party representing that part of the nation which lived by exports abroad and hence wanted free trade. Came the Civil War and the Democrats became the white man's party, in contradistinction to the northern Republicans who freed the slaves. This, in a convoluted way, produced a development in which the whole South became a kind of split personality; on one set of issues it was liberal, and on the other conservative to the last bitter ditch.

An exceptionally important factor in all this is that the South operates under the so-called one-party system; practically all electoral decisions come, as everybody knows, in the primaries. Why, since the southern Democrats comprise such disparate groups, do they not divide and make two parties? One answer is of course that this would mean loss of patronage and seniority. There is no real contest in many constituencies, no real opposition; hence the incumbent stays on in office for year after year. Why is the South so powerful in Congress? Why is the South so conservative? Because the one-party system naturally serves to produce oldsters who hang on and above all because it leads to seniority in committees. There are forty-eight standing and seven select and special committees in the House of Representatives. In the standing committees twenty-eight out of forty-eight chairmen are southern Democrats; in the select committees seven out of seven.

One brief word about Republicans in the South. They cannot control any southern state; nevertheless they are by no means without specialized local power. No fewer than thirty-eight Tennessee counties are Republican; so are seventeen North Carolina counties. The Republicans are by and large of three varieties: a peppering of bankers, manufacturers, merchants; the mountaineers, "Valley farmers," and backwoodsmen; and office holders. We shall have more to say about Republicans in this third category when we come to Texas. After all, the federal administration in Washington controls a great number of appointments all over the nation, from judges to postmasters; until Roosevelt, this had been Republican for twelve long years. Hence—though most are getting old now and the group has thinned out considerably—the South was filled with Republican office holders (federal). An auxiliary point is that, by terms of the American electoral system, the Republican voter in Mississippi, say, is in effect disfranchised in national elections. His vote can never count for the presidency, because (under normal conditions) his state's total electoral vote will always be Democratic.

Another curious paradox is that the South, so solidly Democratic, carries very little weight in a Democratic national convention. This is because the national party leadership knows that the South will vote Democratic anyway, no matter what happens (unless Al Smith is running), and hence does not need to buy it off with big favors. Only one man born in the South has been president of the United States since the Civil War, Woodrow Wilson. It is very rare for a southerner even to get the vice presidential nomination. The last one I can think of is Joe Robinson of Arkansas, though Cactus Jack Garner is of course a Texan.

That a great many southern conservatives feared and detested Roosevelt and the New Deal is well known; there was a definite but abortive movement in 1944 to bolt the ticket, for instance in South Carolina; the idea was that a split vote might throw the election into the House of Representatives. But when election day came Roosevelt carried South Carolina by fifteen to one. People may have loathed him; but to vote against him meant cutting their own throats. (In Texas, however, the revolt, though unsuccessful, did become concrete and actual.) Roosevelt on his side attempted famously to purge some southern senators, like George of Georgia; he too was unsuccessful. A final extraordinary point is that Roosevelt would have won in 1944, and also in his earlier campaigns, even if the solid South had voted solidly against him. The South, despite its hatred of the New Deal, gave tremendous majorities to Roosevelt; but on the basis of electoral college figures it had no responsibility whatever for electing him.

Chapter 41

Negro in the Woodpile

~~~~~~

The Negro problem is a white man's problem.
—Franz Schoenberner

It is a peculiar sensation, this double-consciousness, this sense
of always looking at one's self through the eyes of others. . . .
One feels his two-ness—an American, a Negro; two souls, two
thoughts, two unreconciled strivings; two warring ideals in one
dark body, whose dogged strength alone keeps it from being
torn asunder.
—W. E. B. Du Bois

It is not good to be a Negro in the land of the free and the
home of the brave.
—Rudyard Kipling

THAT the United States is very nearly 10 per cent a black nation is
known to everybody and ignored by almost everybody—except maybe
the 10 per cent. There are more than 13 million Negroes in this country;
roughly every tenth American man, woman, and child is a Negro.

I had heard this often enough but until I reached the South I had no
real perception of what it means.[1] I had heard words like "discrimination" and "prejudice" all my life, but I had no concrete knowledge, no
fingertip realization, of what lies behind them. I knew that "segregation" was a problem; I had no conception at all of the grim enormousness of the problem. The phrase is trite, but I know no other: the
Negro in the South has to be seen to be believed.

Dr. Ira de Augustine Reid picked me up in Atlanta one morning,
and we spent some hours together. Dr. Reid, chairman of the department of sociology at the University of Atlanta, is a scholar of considerable distinction; he is a Columbia Ph.D., and the successor to Dr. W. E.
Burghardt Du Bois as editor of *Phylon*, the Negro quarterly. But Dr.
Reid (I know that this sounds innocent, but spend a few days around
Atlanta yourself) was of course unable to accept my invitation to have

[1] The reader who chances to pick up this book at this point is asked to glance
first at the chapter preceding. Also there are passages about the Negro in Chapters
18 and 33 above, as well as briefer mention in 3, 22, and 37, and some additional
material in 45, 46, and 49. As to the present chapter, almost every sentence could
be expanded into a page. To compress into a chapter any attempt to describe the
Negro in the South is like trying to squeeze a sponge into a matchbox.

a cup of coffee. He could not even meet me in my hotel room. He parked his car outside, contrived in some manner to send a message up, and waited on the street.

Atlanta University consists of seven different Negro institutions; Dr. Du Bois writes that "between 1900 and 1925, no work on the Negro and no study of the South was published which was not indebted in some respect to . . . Atlanta University." I had good talks with its president, Dr. Rufus E. Clement, and with the president of one of its units, Dr. Benjamin E. Mays of Morehouse College. Both have great capacity—I thought that Dr. Mays was as intelligent as anybody I met in the whole South—and both, it goes without saying, are men of courtesy as well as erudition. I would have liked extremely to repay their hospitality. But it was not possible for me to do so in Atlanta, because I could not take them into any public place.

Atlanta is supposed to rank fairly high among southern cities in its attitude toward Negroes, but it out-ghettoes anything I ever saw in a European ghetto, even in Warsaw. What I looked at was caste and untouchability—half the time I blinked remembering that this was not India.

Consider the case of Professor X, who is *any* Negro professor at Atlanta University. He works in close conjunction with several whites; but meeting him on the street after hours, they will not be likely to recognize or greet him. In a hotel, he must take the freight elevator, and under no circumstances can he eat in any but a quarantined restaurant or lunchroom. He is too proud to go to a Jim Crow theater; therefore he can scarcely ever see a first-run movie, or go to a concert. If he travels in a day coach he is herded like an animal into a villainously decrepit wooden car. If he visits a friend in a suburb, he will find that the water, electricity, and gas may literally stop where the segregated quarter begins. He cannot as a rule try on a hat or a pair of gloves in a white store. Not conceivably will a true southern white shake hands with him, and at a bus terminal or similar point he will, of course, have to use the "colored" toilet, and drink from a separate water fountain. He is expected to give the right of way to whites on the sidewalk, and he will almost never see the picture of a fellow Negro in a newspaper, unless of a criminal. His children must attend a segregated school; they could not possibly go to a white swimming pool, bowling alley, dance hall or other place of recreation. When they grow up, no state university in the entire South will receive them.

I mentioned Dr. Mays above. Recently ex-Governor Arnall (one of the best progressives in the South!) had occasion to write him an official letter. Arnall was in a quandary. He could not, of course, address Dr. Mays as "Mister" or "Doctor," even in correspondence. The taboo on this has been ironclad for years. Finally he hit on the device of simply calling him "Benjamin."[2]

Dr. Du Bois, who has a position almost like that of Shaw or Einstein, being the most venerable and distinguished of leaders in his field, tells in one of his autobiographical passages how he was not allowed to enter the Atlanta public library. Dr. Du Bois is, of course, a Harvard Ph.D. who also went to the University of Berlin and who holds three other doctorates.

Turn to the white side briefly. I asked a young, intelligent, and quite "liberal" politician to explain some aspects of all this on a strictly personal basis; I tried to get from him exactly what he would and would not do. Eat with a Negro? Good God, no! Go to a Negro's house? Not under any circumstances. ("Ah couldn't afford it; might get known.") Go to a reception for, say, Paul Robeson? ("Couldn't happen here; if it was in New Yohk Ah might go if it was a big crowd and Ah wasn't known.") Shake hands with a Negro? ("Ah shook hands with one in Pohtland, Oregon, last year; fust time in mah whole life!") Sleep with a pretty Negro girl? Answer confused.

The basic pattern of segregation in the South is unwavering and absolute, though minor modifications come from time to time. Technically segregation is simply a term to denote the various strictures separating Negroes from whites, and it has manifestations all the way from the laws prohibiting intermarriage to such taboos as that which commonly forbids a Negro to argue with a white man. It has existed since the first Negroes arrived at Jamestown in 1619; slavery was simply the first form of segregation. It not only includes Jim Crowism in schools and places of amusement, but such items in "etiquette" as the principle that a southern Negro must go into a white man's house by the back door. Return to such a matter as transportation. In Atlanta, taxicabs driven by whites serve whites only.[3] As to busses Negroes are of course obliged to squeeze into the back seats everywhere in the South; in Mississippi they may actually be separated from whites by a curtain. The analogy to India—purdah!—comes to mind again.

But in some respects segregation is breaking down. I watched Negroes shopping in the best Atlanta department store (they could not, however, work as clerks there), and whereas before World War II it was almost unthinkable that a Negro girl should serve whites at a drugstore fountain or similar establishment, this is now fairly common. I saw Negroes and whites standing together in lines at post-office windows and at

[2] Some southern business firms are, however, coming to use "Mister" in letters to Negroes. This is partly because the big mail order houses in the North pay no attention to the ban on honorifics and so are getting much Negro business. Cf. Brogan, *U.S.A.* p. 22.

[3] But some Negro drivers also refuse Negro passengers.

Western Union counters, and while I was in Atlanta the *Journal*, for the
first time in its history, gave a Negro woman the title "Miss." In
another field Negroes may now join some of the great fraternal orders.
Mostly the loosening up of strictures favors rich Negroes. For instance
those who can afford Pullman space do not have to ride in segregated
cars though they will usually be given a compartment and thus sterilized
off from the rest of the train, and, as is obvious, those who have automobiles are relieved of much Jim Crow nuisance, though some filling
stations may refuse to serve them. An illuminating minor point is that
such an organization as the Southern Regional Council, with white and
black membership, evades segregation by having its mixed meetings in
Negro houses or places of assembly.

The economic cost of segregation is of course preposterous and
staggering. It is a cardinal reason why the South is so poor. In effect, it
means that *two* sets of everything from schools to insane asylums to
penitentiaries to playgrounds have to be maintained.

Of course, too, whites make use of segregation as a pretext for
economic discrimination and exclusion; the caste system is applied to
jobs. A white employer will say, "Why, yes, I'd like to employ good
niggers, but how could I have them in the lunchroom?" Similarly consider cultural matters. The white will affirm, "Sure, I believe in education for Negro kids, but!—" The "but" in the unfinished sentence
expresses the social (which becomes an educational) taboo.

Segregation—we are by no means finished with this subject; of
necessity it will carry through this whole long chapter—has one aspect
sometimes neglected, that thousands upon thousands of good white
citizens never have any contact at all with Negroes except with servants
and employees in the service trades; they become as isolated from the
Negro community as from a tribe of Bantus; whites and blacks of
similar professional interests almost never meet. There are 55,000 Negro
college graduates in the United States.[4] Most southern whites have
never seen one.

One effect of this has, naturally, been to drive Negroes into what
Myrdal calls "self-segregation," as a means of preserving what is left of
their self-respect. Listen to Du Bois: "In a world where it means so
much to take a man by the hand and sit beside him, to look frankly into
his eyes . . . in a world where a social cigar or a cup of tea together
means more than legislative halls and magazine articles and speeches—
one can imagine the consequences of the almost utter absence of such
social amenities between estranged races, whose separation extends
even to parks and street cars."[5]

Not long ago, but before World War II was over, a young Negro

[4] Lillian Smith, *These Are the Things to Do*, p. 5.
[5] In *The Souls of Black Folk*, p. 185.

girl was asked how she would punish Hitler. Answer: "Paint him black and bring him over here."[6]

Word about a Book

In Washington, D.C., when I was starting my trip and long before I reached Atlanta, I asked a group of friends what I should look out for most. One was a justice of the Supreme Court, one an assistant secretary of state; they all know this country much better than I do, and in giving me advice they mentioned the Mississippi Delta, wheat in Montana, mill towns in New England, the TVA, rehabilitation in the dust bowl; similarly they recommended various people and institutions; finally they said that one thing indispensable to understanding of the United States was a book—*An American Dilemma*, by Gunnar Myrdal.[7]

This study of "The Negro Problem and Modern Democracy," by a Swedish sociologist who worked for several years in the field with a competent staff, runs to 1,483 large, full, tight-packed pages; there are 258 pages just of footnotes. I know no book quite like it. As the last word in analytical insight on a subject it resembles to a degree Sir George Sansom's superb *Cultural History of Japan*, and though it may lack the latter's grace it outranks it in exhaustiveness. Nobody has much right to discuss the Negro in America until he has looked into Myrdal's book. (I say "looked into" rather than "has read" because to read it takes at least a month.)

Myrdal makes a major hypothesis at the outset—that the Negro problem is above all one of morals, heart and conscience. He describes with great acuteness the "American Creed," the body of belief in liberty and equality embodied in law that chiefly distinguishes the United States from all other nations, and proceeds, "Though our study includes economic, social and political race relations, at bottom our problem is the moral dilemma of the American." He says too, "The reading of this book must be . . . an ordeal to the good citizen." The enormous discrepancy it reveals between what Americans preach in regard to the Negro and other issues, and what they practice, is painful to survey. "The American Negro problem is a problem in the heart of the American."

An American Dilemma is so extraordinarily copious that it may be unfair to pick out only one other major point—Myrdal's belief that the Negro is not, per se, inferior to the white man, but that his seeming inferiority is the result of poverty, lack of education, and discrimination. Like all modern anthropologists, Myrdal attacks the myth of race—

---

[6] Walter Winchell, New York *Daily Mirror*, March 26, 1945.

[7] Written with the assistance of Richard Sterner and Arnold Rose, and published by Harper & Brothers, New York, 1944. The work was made possible by a grant of the Carnegie Corporation of New York.

incidentally the word "race" itself is less than two hundred years old—
and together with an elaborate amount of other material he adduces
various United States Army tests to indicate that some *northern* Negroes
are more intelligent than some *southern* whites.[8] Be this as it may. A
contrary view exists. Negroes may resent my saying so, but many
observers will hold it to be undeniable, in some parts of the country at
least, that many Negroes *are* of less capacity than whites. Of course this
may indeed be the result of generations of grinding white pressure, of
segregation and all the perjuries of the human spirit this entails, of the
appalling uglinesses that occur when a whole community is forced into
perpetual Coventry. The real point is something else. Whether the
Negro is at present "inferior" or not is not the issue. The issue is that,
no matter how "inferior" he may or may not be, he is still entitled to
civil liberties, equality of treatment, and the ordinary privileges of
American democracy. The status of imputed inferiority is no excuse for
the prejudices that make him a third-class citizen.

Violence: the Record

All I ask for the Negro is that if you do not like him, let
him alone.
                                        —Abraham Lincoln

Here are some advertisements that Charles Dickens found in American newspapers in 1842:

Ran away, a negro woman. A few days before she went off I
burnt her with a hot iron on the left side of her face. Tried to make
the letter M.
One hundred dollars reward for a negro fellow, Pompey. . . .
Branded on left jaw.
Fifty dollars reward for the negro Jim Blake. Has a piece cut out
of each ear.
Twenty-five dollars reward for my man John. The tip of his
nose is bit off.[9]

Today, 105 years later, here are some things that still happen:
Item: A twenty-eight-year-old Negro named John C. Jones was
arrested in Minden, Louisiana, because of "suspicion" that he had tried
to break into the house of a white woman. No formal charges were
brought, and Jones and Albert S. M. Harris Jr., a seventeen-year-old
friend, were released. Both were then "picked up by unidentified persons."
Jones's body was found in the woods a few days later. Both his hands had
been chopped off, and he had been killed by application of a *blow*

[8] A point in an allied realm is that Mound Bayou, Mississippi, one of the few
all-Negro towns in the United States, is also one of the few with no jail. Dabney,
op. cit. p. 196.
[9] From *American Notes*, p. 245 *et seq.*

torch to his head, throat, and body. Harris, though badly beaten, was still alive, and the National Association for the Advancement of Colored People immediately brought the case to country-wide attention. The local authorities made no arrests, however, and discovered "no clues in connection with the reputed mob action."[10]

Item: Near Lexington, Mississippi, a thirty-five-year-old Negro tenant farmer named Leon McAttee was flogged to death by five whites; his body was left to rot in a bayou. The five assailants were indicted for manslaughter, inasmuch as they admitted that they had hit their victim "a few licks," and were brought to trial. A jury acquitted them after being out ten minutes. McAttee had been accused of the theft of a saddle. After the trial two other people confessed to the theft.[11]

Item: Because of libel laws, I cannot describe what is probably the most outrageous lynching in the United States in recent years. Two citizens of local prominence were interestingly involved. It occurred in Tennessee.

Item: In Athens, Alabama, in August, 1946, two white boys and a Negro had a scuffle. An honest white policeman refused to arrest the Negro, on the ground that he was not the aggressor; he did arrest the whites. A mob numbering between 1,800 and 2,000 thereupon stormed the city hall, forced the release of the white boys, and began to riot; Negroes were chased off the streets and between fifty and one hundred were injured. When order was restored nine whites were taken into custody on charges of "unlawful assembly." They were released later. Eight were teen-agers; the youngest, thirteen years old, "carried a club and knocked Negroes down."[12]

Item: In Columbia, Tennessee, the home town of President James K. Polk, a Negro woman complained of incivility in a white shop, and a fracas occurred. That night, in February, 1946, mobs penetrated into Mink Slide, the Negro quarter; frightened Negroes feared a pogrom because the town has a bad race relations history, and, after they had been fired on, they opened ill-organized fire with shotguns on the white intruders. Nobody was seriously hurt. But state troopers and police "cleaned up" the district the next day, smashing houses and wantonly destroying shops and stores, in a savage little reign of terror. Twenty-five Negroes were arrested for "attempted murder"—while two others were actually murdered in the town jail![13] The trial of the twenty-five took place at Lawrenceville, Tennessee, and became a nation-wide *cause célèbre*, because almost every aspect of the Negro problem was distilled and concentrated in its proceedings. For instance the defendants had to travel fifty-three miles each way every day, since Lawrenceville, a small

[10] Quotations from the New York *Times*, August 15, 1946.
[11] New York *Times*, October 24, 1946.
[12] New York *Times*, August 11, 1946.
[13] *Time*, March 11, 1946.

hamlet, had no facilities for handling them; the Negroes and their lawyers had no access to toilets, a lunchroom, or even drinking water. Twenty-three of the twenty-five defendants were acquitted after a two-week trial. Vincent Sheean, describing this episode in the New York *Herald Tribune*, contributed to the nation some of the finest journalism of our time.

Item: On February 12, 1946, a Negro veteran named Isaac Woodard, who had received his honorable discharge papers only a few hours before and who was still in uniform, took a bus at Atlanta for his home in South Carolina. When the bus stopped at a hamlet Woodard asked the driver if he could go to a rest room. The driver refused and a violent quarrel ensued. At the next stop, Batesburg, South Carolina, the driver called a policeman, saying that Woodard had made a disturbance; the policeman took him off the bus, started beating him, carted him off to the local jail, and *ground out his eyes* with the end of his club. Woodard as a result lost his eyesight. This case too became a country-wide scandal. A mass rally held in the Lewisohn Stadium in New York raised a purse of $22,000 for the blinded veteran. It did not restore his vision.

Attorney General Clark and the FBI instituted an investigation, after much public clamor, and the Batesburg police officer was identified, arrested, and brought to trial. His name was, and is, Lynwood E. Shull. The charge, brought "in a criminal information filed by the Department of Justice," was that Shull violated Woodard's "civil rights" by beating him. Shull's reply was that he had acted in self-defense. A United States district court jury acquitted Shull in half an hour.

This whole saga took place in the home state of former Secretary of State James F. Byrnes, during a year in which Mr. Byrnes was active in the extreme pleading for justice, democratic procedures, and fair play in regard to Bulgarian elections and the frontiers of Trieste.

Another type of mob outrage sometimes occurs in the South: clandestine or "underground" lynching in which a Negro who has broken taboos simply disappears. There is no *corpus delicti*, and no scandal. The body is never found, and people say that the victim has "moved" somewhere. For a time members of the Ku-Klux Klan were most distinguished for this kind of affair.

* * * * *

Why cannot the federal authorities act more effectively in lynching cases? Why, if the FBI can ferret out the secrets of the most intricate spy rings with remarkable dispatch, cannot it identify successfully a handful of thugs in Monroe, Georgia? This is a question that the stranger to America may legitimately ask. The answer is complex. For one thing the average southern community will seal itself into a protective web against any outsider with truly impenetrable effect. More important is that old bugaboo, state rights. Crime in this country is a matter for each individual state except in such categories as income tax evasion, counterfeiting, kidnapping across state lines, and the like. The federal government cannot bring anybody to trial on a murder charge except in special circumstances. "There has never been a successful federal prosecution of lynching, *per se*," according to the New York *Times*.[14] The Department of Justice can intervene in a lynching, under federal civil rights statutes, only if an official or agent of the state is involved, and southern states, notoriously touchy, do not easily admit such involvement. Even if they do, convictions are extremely difficult to obtain before a white jury—especially when the case may be handled by local officials of the federal government whose sympathies are those of the white community.

The effect of World War II is one point worth noting. Almost every victim of lynching since the war has been a veteran. The Negro community is probably more unified today, more politically vehement, more aggressive in its demand for full citizenship—even in the South—than at any other time in history. Roughly one million Negroes entered the armed services. They moved around and saw things; they were exposed to danger and learned what their rights were; overseas, many were treated decently and democratically by whites for the first time in their lives; the consequent fermentations have been explosive. Also since Negroes were presumably fighting for democratic principles on the international plane, it was difficult to keep them from wondering why the same principles were not applied at home. It wasn't easy for an intelligent Negro to accept that he was fighting for democracy—in a largely Jim Crow army. The glaring crudity of this paradox became the more striking as the war went on. One famous remark is that of the Negro soldier returning across the Pacific from Okinawa. "*Our* fight for freedom," he said, "begins when we get to San Francisco."

The war shook up southern whites too. Consider merely the vast plantings of new industry with many thousands of Negro workers, and the fact that, because of the climate, a substantial percentage of Army training camps were located in the South. Negroes—who on occasion threw their weight around—became disconcertingly numerous and conspicuous. The very fact that they *were* soldiers (though 90 per cent were confined to labor battalions, construction work and so on) was bitterly resented. All this served to stimulate postwar mobbism. In a sense the recent lynchings were a retaliation by whites for an increased aggressiveness in the Negro community as a whole.

In this picture any amelioration is good news, and it is only proper to report changes for the better. Recently in North Carolina (where even burglary may be punished by the death sentence) a Negro boy raped a woman who was eight months pregnant. He confessed and was sentenced

[14] Article by Cabell Phillips, August 3, 1946.

to die. The governor, R. Gregg Cherry, promptly commuted the sentence to life imprisonment, on the ground that though the crime was revolting, "part of the blame arises from the neglect of the state and society to provide a better environment." What is more, Mr. Cherry's action was generally commended by the white citizenry, not condemned.

In the South there were six lynchings last year. This is certainly an ugly figure, especially as it came after a succession of years in which mob violence was rare. Gradually, until 1946, a steady statistical improvement has taken place. When Dr. Du Bois was a student at Atlanta, the fingers of lynched Negroes might be seen in white butcher shops, and the country as a whole averaged five lynchings *a week*; in 1892, there were 235, without a single case being punished. Compare 1941, with four lynchings, or 1945, with only one. Decent Southerners themselves have of course worked hard and well to reduce violence; one of the most interesting organizations in the United States is the Association of Southern Women for the Prevention of Lynching. Other groups public and private—notably the NAACP—are busy all the time, especially among the helot whites.

However, let us not be too complacent. The significance of lynching is often not the crime itself, horrible as that may be, but the terrorizing and demoralizing effect of the *threat* of lynching on a community. Also the double standard still exists strikingly, and whites generally go scot free for crimes that Negroes are butchered for. As an example, the Negro wife of a Negro serviceman overseas was raped by four whites in a small town in Alabama in early 1945; the case made a minor furor, but nobody was ever punished.

Shades of Spartacus

> Some doubt the courage of the Negro. Go to Haiti, and stand on those fifty thousand graves of the best soldiers France ever had, and ask them what they think of the Negro sword.
>
> —Toussaint l'Ouverture

Outlanders may be shocked and surprised at some of the indignities Negroes suffer in the South; likewise they may be affronted and shocked at the outspokenness of some modern Negroes. To anybody who does not watch the Negro press carefully, the line taken by such a man as George S. Schuyler, one of the nation's outstanding journalists, must indeed be astonishing. Listen to Mr. Schuyler:[15]

By a peculiar logical inversion the Anglo-Saxon ruling class, its imitators, accomplices, and victims, have come to believe in a Negro

---

[15] "The Caucasian Problem," in *What the Negro Wants*, a symposium edited by Rayford W. Logan, University of North Carolina Press, 1944. Reprinted by permission.

problem. . . . While there is actually no Negro problem, there is definitely a Caucasian problem.

Continual reference to a Negro problem assumes that some profound difficulty has been or is being created for the human race by the so-called Negroes. This is typical ruling class arrogance, and . . . has no basis in fact. It has been centuries since any Negro nation has menaced the rest of humanity. The last of the Moors withdrew from Europe in 1492.

The so-called Negroes . . . have passed few if any Jim Crow laws . . . set up few white ghettoes, carried on no discriminatory practices against whites, and have not devoted centuries of propaganda to prove the superiority of blacks over whites. . . .

While we may dismiss the concept of a Negro problem as a valuable dividend-paying fiction, it is clear that the Caucasian problem is painfully real and practically universal. Stated briefly, the problem confronting the colored peoples of the world is how to live in freedom, peace, and security without being invaded, subjugated, expropriated, exploited, persecuted, and humiliated by Caucasians justifying their actions by the myth of white racial superiority.

The term Negro itself is as fictitious as the theory of white racial superiority on which Anglo-Saxon civilization is based, but it is nevertheless one of the most effective smear devices developed since the Crusades. . . . Of course "white" and "Caucasian" are equally barren of scientific meaning. . . . There are actually no white people except albinos who are a very pale pink in color . . .

Do not, friends in Macon or Mobile, jump out of the window at this and say that Mr. Schuyler must be a "Communist," which would be another smear device. Actually he is a prosperous and perfectly respectable citizen who, I believe, often votes Republican.

Mr. Schuyler of course states an extreme view. But consider other straws in the wind: (a) in Washington, D. C., recently a Negro dance hall refused admittance to a white, on the ground that "discrimination (!) in the nation's capital must go"; (b) the NAACP opposed vigorously a plan to train Negro pilots in their own squadrons at Tuskegee, on the ground that this served to perpetuate segregation (normally one would have thought that Negroes would have been delighted to have their own aviation cadets); (c) wounded Negroes at Anzio and on Iwo Jima on several occasions refused to accept white plasma.

In Atlanta it was interesting to learn that Lillian Smith's *Strange Fruit*, which whites considered extremely Negrophile, was deeply resented by many Negroes. They didn't like it that the heroine, a well-brought-up, college-educated Negro girl, should do anything so disgraceful as have an affair with a *white* boy! Actually a well-known Negro actress refused to play the part when a drama based on the book reached Broadway.

Negro "nationalism" takes extravagant form sometimes. I once asked a northern Negro for a list of eminent but little-known members of his race, and he proudly included two or three Negro criminals! Seriously one should never neglect the fact that Negro prejudice against the ignorant poor white in the South is probably as deep rooted and active as that of the poor white against the Negro.

Statistics, Sex, and Segregation

The rape which your gentlemen have done against helpless black women in defiance of your own laws is written on the foreheads of . . . millions of mulattoes, and written in ineffaceable blood.
—W. E. B. Du Bois

Of the total of roughly 13 million Negroes in the United States, somewhere between nine and ten million live in the South; in ten specific states the approximate proportion is as follows:

Mississippi	49%	Florida	29%
South Carolina	46%	North Carolina	29%
Louisiana	37%	Virginia	27%
Georgia	37%	Arkansas	26%
Alabama	36%	Tennessee	18%

Tension between white and Negro is most acute, of course, in the states with the higher percentages. Yet this does not tell the whole story, since there are plenty of *counties* in several states where the population is 50 per cent Negro or more; some Mississippi counties have a Negro proportion of 80 per cent or greater.[16] It is in these (*pace* Mr. Schuyler) that the Negro "problem" is to be found in its most extreme and exacerbated form.

There were approximately four million slaves in the South when emancipation came; free Negroes numbered about half a million all over the country. Less than three generations ago, in other words, nine out of ten Negroes were a lump of property; Negroes today, eighty years later, are still overwhelmingly of slave origin. This is an emotional factor not to be ignored, and it plays a considerable role not merely in the demarcation between black and white, but in the stratifications of the Negro community itself.[17]

How deeply do American Negroes today feel their roots in Africa, and

[16] See Chapter 46.
[17] During Reconstruction the Negroes were a majority in three states. Some communities had black "control." Out of the excesses then practiced by carpetbaggers and others, as mentioned in the preceding chapter, came the chief rationalizations whereby the South excuses itself today for lack of progress. It is only fair to state that a "revisionist" school of historians differs sharply from its predecessors in this matter. They assert that professional Southerners have violently exaggerated the outrages of Reconstruction.

do many want to return there? Very few. The Bilbo "solution," that of forcible mass transplantation of the entire Negro population to Liberia and the Gold Coast, has utterly no support among responsible people. A "return to Africa" has, however, been a recurrent theme in arguments over the Negro ever since Thomas Jefferson founded the Africa Colonization Society; even Lincoln flirted with the idea of an African hegira. During World War I a remarkable pure black man named Marcus Garvey, who was born in Jamaica, started a "Back to Africa" movement; his cohorts wore uniforms, marched in Harlem, organized an African "government," and even bought a steamship line. But very few actually set sail, and eventually Garvey was sentenced to prison for using the mails to defraud. (Later he went to Great Britain, where he stood for Parliament on one occasion.) Today, practically all remnants of his or any similar movement have disappeared.

* * * * *

We reach now a field of extreme and forbidding difficulty. It is virtually impossible to get accurate figures, but the best estimate is that roughly 6 million out of the 13 million Negroes in America are mulattoes. Intermarriage is forbidden in every southern state (and some northern), and so what this enormous figure means is that a very considerable amount of extramarital lovemaking and extralegal childbearing has been going on. A corollary point at once arises—how is a Negro to be defined? Almost half the Negroes in the United States today have what Myrdal calls Caucasoid (=white) blood. Lots of folk have been intimate with lots of folk! What is a Negro? For almost *50 per cent* of the community, the answer is—someone partly white!

Mixed marriages occur in the North; there are, in fact, about 15,000 in the country today.[18] Frederick Douglass, one of the first great Negro educators, had a white wife, and so did another Negro scholar, William Scarborough, a professor of Greek who married Sarah Bierce, principal of the Wilberforce Normal School—this last did not, Du Bois writes tartly, provoke any "social catastrophe."[19] Jack Johnson, former heavyweight champion of the world, had *two* white wives. Of course taboos on this subject are still violent. If you want really to infuriate a southern white, all you have to do is mention casually that several well-known contemporary Negroes have white wives—for instance Mr. Schuyler, the novelist Richard Wright, and William Grant Still, the musician. Mention that such a wife may be a *southern* white woman, like Mrs. Schuyler, and almost literally there will be blood vessels, or something else, broken in the room.

[18] According to George S. Schuyler in "The Caucasian Problem," cited above, p. 290.
[19] *What the Negro Wants*, p. 66.

Many Negroes, however, it should be added at once, dislike miscegenation as much as do whites.

As to extramarital relationships they too make a complex story, and the roots go far back. One of the first legal actions in the history of Virginia was the punishment of a white planter found with a Negro girl; he was ordered to be thrashed, "for the discipline of his body, and for sinning against the glory of the Lord." There are Negro families in the United States today that have had white blood since before the *Mayflower*. The whole subject is cloaked by hypocrisy; yet that there should have been sexual connection between white and black was altogether inevitable. Even today, many southern white boys grow up with "Mammies," and this can make for much emotional confusion, in that, as Lillian Smith once put it, their first "intimacies and restraints come from two people, one from each race." A boy grows up, and pressures of the most varied sort—from the "daredevil" attitude that it is "the thing to do" to the virginal restraints of white girls of his own class—drive him to the arms of Negro women. Still later, after marriage, there may be continuing influences prompting him "to break the color line." But usually a liaison with a black girl gives a white man a strong (though perhaps subconscious) sense of guilt, which may express itself later in the form of the most violent Negrophobia. The errant puritan punishes someone else for his own profligacy.

Lillian Smith and Paula Snelling write:[20]

> No white Southerner with a trace of decency in his soul can feel guiltless before the knowledge that there are six million brown Americans in this country today whose white ancestors, with few exceptions, abrogated every human obligation of parenthood, not only leaving the physical, financial, psychic and moral burden of their individual rearing to the Negro mother and her race, but passing segregation laws and entrenching customs whereby their blood-children are excluded from opportunity to develop their full potentialities as human beings.

Many Negroes—once again I am having to foreshorten crudely a subject of the most delicate complexity—have hatred and contempt for white women. They and their ancestors have had to sit by for two hundred and fifty years, and watch white boys take mistresses among Negro girls, while they themselves could not possibly touch a white woman. They lost their own women, and a transition to resenting white women too, and holding them partially to blame, was inevitable. Several times southern women, those emancipated enough to have mixed committee dealings and so on, told me that only rarely will even an educated Negro approach them without self-consciousness. Their eyes "don't

[20] In *South Today*, Winter 1942-43.

touch." The women may feel self-conscious too. One lady informed me that the first time a Negro ever "looked" at her, she felt "naked." Finally, in mixed gatherings a Negro will sometimes be markedly aggressive, as a compensation for his instinctive fear and feeling of inferiority, and of course his vanity may be inflamed vastly if a white woman likes him.

What is the attitude of a "pure" Negro toward the mulattoes? Opinion can be very divergent here. On the one side, it is all but indubitable that many black Negroes hate their own blackness, and as a general rule those already mixed tend to "marry as light as they can." That the woman is lighter than the man in at least two-thirds of all Negro marriages is sufficient proof of this, and it is a familiar locution that "the blacker you are, the harder things are for you." Many Negroes speak of "good" and "bad" hair, and are proud of a child born with hair straight and not kinky. On the whole, too, the very dark are apt to be jealous of the lighter. A Negro can be a militant fighter for equality vis-à-vis whites, but he may try to get his hair straightened just the same. Then he will apologize to his black fellows with some such glancing remark as "Straight hair is easier to comb!"

On the other hand there are plenty of Negroes—chiefly intellectuals —who profess great pride in pitch blackness, and who despise octoroons who "pass" or try to "pass." Most of those to whom I talked about mulattoes found the subject painful; it seemed to be a symbol of shame and defeat, meaning essentially that their women had betrayed them. "Passing" is a whole subject in itself. No Negro would despise Walter White for passing; of course Walter White, who could pass easily, never does. Before the war, a good many light Negroes thought that it was "smart" to pass; this tendency is believed to be diminishing. Some Negroes pass in the South, because they will not submit to the indignities of Jim Crow, but not in the North; some pass only when traveling; some very pale Negroes pass by accident, as it were. A conductor will say, "White coach this way," and the octoroon obeys because to do differently will provoke too much fuss.

A proud but healthy attitude to variation in color is that of Du Bois. He wrote once of the joy given him by "the whole gorgeous color gamut of the American Negro world; the swaggering men, the beautiful girls, the laughter and gaiety, the unhampered self-expression . . . to be among people of my own color or rather of such various and extraordinary colors . . ."

Negroes can almost invariably tell who is a Negro, no matter how light. One Negro friend of mine, who lives in the North and who can pass without effort, made a business trip recently to Memphis. He had a quick lunch at the hotel drugstore. Several whites sat beside him, without dreaming that he was a Negro. The Negro counterman, however, detected him instantly, and showed his appreciation of the situation by saying casually, "Good mawnin', *suh!*"

* * * * *

Segregation equals sex. Or perhaps one should say merely that sex is the basic reason for segregation. The strictures that forbid whites and Negroes to eat together, drink together, play together, talk together are at bottom the result of white fear that such intimacies will lead to a breakdown in sexual barriers, and the involvement of blacks with white women. A dozen times I heard whites say, "Of course I want full equality for Negroes—but under segregation!" Many years ago, visiting the United States, H. G. Wells reported the remark, "If you eat with them, you've got to marry 'em!" Indeed the issue is so distorted that, in the South, almost anybody who takes a strong line against segregation is apt to be accused of "advocating mixed sexual relations."[21] But, as pointed out above, to most Negroes themselves intermarriage is not a vital preoccupation; it is an issue as remote as the Himalayas. What the overwhelming mass want is not a chance to marry a white woman, but equal treatment and justice in the realms of economics, politics, and law, and opportunity to educate brown children decently.

Last word on sex. The illusion is widespread that rape and attacks on white women are the chief cause of lynching. As it happens this is not true. Of 2,522 Negroes lynched during the past twenty-six years, only 477—a shade under 20 per cent—were even charged with any sex offense.[22]

Black on White

The Negro is a problem to himself.
—Gunnar Myrdal

What does the Negro himself think of segregation? Agreement is all but universal among leaders: they say simply "Segregation must go," and have this as the alpha and omega of their position. But there are some oldsters, the "Uncle Toms" and "handkerchief heads" who "want to stay in good" with the ruling whites and who equivocate on the issue; also a smattering of "Quislings," Negroes who take the white side. I have heard the phrase, by one Negro about another, "He sold out on segregation."

Actually it is sometimes quite difficult, and understandably so, to get a frank statement about the subject. Most Negroes, through bitter experience, have become suspicious of white curiosities; they will

---

[21] Of course, as Langston Hughes once pointed out, millions of northern Negroes manage to go to the polls without cohabiting with white women.
[22] Sketch of Walter White, in *Thirteen Against the Odds*, p. 87.

answer questions in controversial fields by saying what they think the white man wants them to say; in order to survive at all, the Negro has always had to lie. A good many try to avoid being pinned down by saying that all they want is genuine "equality of opportunity." But the catch here, which they don't always appreciate, is that real equality of opportunity isn't possible unless segregation goes. The white man continues to impose segregation partly because it automatically serves to maintain discrimination in economic as well as social fields.

Almost all Negroes agree on a general strategic aim, the eventual abolition of segregation; they may vary in techniques and procedures. The radicals want direct action; the moderates put faith in gradualness. Most Negroes realize that Jim Crow cannot be done away with overnight; I heard the president of a famous Negro university say, "There are easier ways to take a fortress than by direct assault." Also the attitude of a given leader, like that of Du Bois, may change from time to time as circumstances change. The policy of most responsible Negroes today is to do what they can to ameliorate the evils of segregation, while living within its structures, or, in more technical words, "to work for full equality within the bi-racial pattern, in every field where discrimination takes place."

I have used the phrase "direct action." But what direct action could Negroes take? One possibility might be a nation-wide withdrawal of their children from the public schools, which would almost certainly provoke a first-class crisis. But that the community would gain by such a drastic measure, even granting that the boycott could be made permanent, is very doubtful. A generation of Negro children would grow up without education, and education is their strongest need and greatest weapon for the future.

What are the chief Negro grievances aside from segregation? One could make a list pages long, as to wit:

To a considerable extent, Negroes are relegated to the worst kinds of work, for instance in turpentine camps and fertilizer factories. If a factory lays men off, the Negroes will most likely lose their jobs first, and a tradition has it that they shall not be paid more than 75 per cent of what whites get for the same work. Some types of employment are altogether closed, especially to women, who can scarcely ever get white-collar jobs—for instance as stenographers. This means that most of them have to go into domestic service.

Average life expectancy for the Negro is 50.52 years, as against 60.6 for whites. Deaths in childbirth average 33 per 1,000 for Negro women, as against a white rate of 11.3.

Negroes cannot possibly get the truth told in any but a handful of southern or other newspapers, on any controversial point involving race.

They are the permanent target of white demagogues like Bilbo and such a creature as the late Mr. Talmadge, without having any way to answer back.

In the United States as a whole $80.26 is spent per year per pupil on education. The amount for Negroes in ten southern states is $17.04.

What the South needs above all is doctors, teachers, dentists, veterinarians, engineers. But only after surmounting the most savage handicaps can Negroes get degrees in these fields.

Suppose a Negro is traveling by car, and, outside his own community, has a traffic accident and is arrested by a white policeman. The consequences may not be pleasant. As much as anything, the Negro dislikes his "unprotected status." Take Atlanta. There are 100,000 Negroes there, and not a single Negro policeman.

He resents it that his wife is called a "Negress" and his child a "pickaninny," and he doesn't like the terms "high yaller," "darkie," or "quadroon."[23]

What does the Negro want? Several different phrases express the same idea, and I heard them universally—"equal rights without reservations"; "real participation in American life"; "integration into the United States"; "first class citizenship"; "full citizenship." As to details:

(1—Political). Abolition of the poll tax and the white primary for which see hereunder.

(2—Educational). Assistance to the school system, if necessary by the federal government.

(3—Judicial). Fair play in the courts, and a federal antilynching law.

(4—Jobs). FEPC and a decent chance at occupational opportunity.

(5—Enlightenment). Acceptance by whites of the theory that, if Negroes get proper education and jobs, an immense economic improvement for the whole South, white and black alike, will result.

(6—Social). Better housing, better public services, better transportation.

(7—Propaganda). In the words of Mary McLeod Bethune, "government leadership in building favorable public opinion."

Things are hard for the Negro in the South—yes. They could scarcely be much harder. On the other hand the point might be made that, for the most part, Negroes are better off in America than in any other country in the world, if only because the chance to rise is greater. There is less discrimination in France, true, and no segregation or race prejudice at all in Brazil, but in no other country—despite everything—have

[23] To say nothing of coon, jig, dinge, Sambo, shine, crow, smoke, boogie, ape, jazzbo, jigaboo, moke, kinky head, spade, eight ball, Zulu, skunk, and seal. Cf. Myrdal, II, 958, and an essay by H. L. Mencken, "Designations for Colored Folk," *American Speech*, October, 1944. One term I heard often is "nigra." This is a compromise used by whites who don't like either "Negro" or "nigger."

most Negroes quite so much potential opportunity as in the United States. Very few American Negroes ever want to leave America. Of course it goes without saying that this should not serve to excuse further ill-treatment of Negroes by the white community.

White on Black

> Southern conservatism is a unique phenomenon in western civilization in being married to an established pattern of illegality.
>
>   —Gunnar Myrdal

Whites in the South have several attitudes on the Negro problem. At one extreme is the fanatic who shouts, "We're going to maintain our white supremacy at all costs!" Next comes he who says, "We must maintain white supremacy, but we're going to be just!" Next, perhaps, is the compromiser who wants to do something for the Negro but who fears to do so, because he may be saddled with the worst epithet the South knows—"nigger lover!" Finally, there are numerous decent Southerners to whom the issue is a permanent excruciating dilemma, who take it wrenchingly to heart, and in whom a fierce struggle of conscience rages. In almost every southern town there is at least one white group earnestly trying to improve things. Then too there are plenty of whites who, on more sentimental grounds, have a genuine deep affection for the Negro. Some envy him. "They can be happy on nothin'! Listen to 'em laugh!"

To most southern whites, segregation is simply considered a matter of decency. It is bred in the bones. A southern child learns about segregation practically as he learns about God and sex. I heard one governor of a state burst out passionately. "The Lord created it—their damned color!" But also I heard one man, by no means a governor, remark, "The blacker they are, the better I like 'em!"—meaning, of course, that such blackness gives additional pretext for discrimination.

A revealing item is the "Eleanor Club" legend. An invisible monsoon swept the South a few years ago; the black kitchen and household help, so the stories flew, were "organizing" in the name of Mrs. Roosevelt, and planned to desert their pots and pans and romp off to work in war industry or, at the minimum, form labor unions of their own. The rumor mongering about these "clubs" was, no doubt, caused partly by fear that Negro servants *might* strike for better wages. In actual fact, after investigation by various competent authorities, no single "Eleanor Club" has ever been found. The entire business was myth out of the whole cloth.

Lillian Smith[24] once asked a number of white citizens a group of questions. The results were various in the extreme:

[24] *South Today*, Winter 1942-43.

Question: Do you call Negroes "niggers"?
Answer:
1. "Of course I do—what else is there to call one?"
2. "I have never used the word. No well-bred Southerner would."
3. "No, I don't say 'nigger.' I say 'darkie,' though."
4. "I call them 'niggers' behind their back; never to their face."
5. "Yeah, by God—and I'll call them 'niggers' till I die."

Question: Do you mind sitting by a Negro in a street car?
Answers:
1. "No. I prefer to sit by people who don't have colds; that's about all I'd ask of a street car."
2. "I personally don't mind. But you know you can't start that kind of thing down in the South."
3. "If you let a nigger sit where he wants on street cars and buses, next thing you know he'll be wanting to marry your sister—see?"

Question: Would you call a Negro "Mister"?
Answers:
1. "Certainly. What else could a well-bred person call one?"
2. "Call a nigger 'Mister'! I'd be —— —— first."
3. "I wouldn't mind doing it. Never have, however."

Question: What do you think of co-education of the races?
Answers:
1. "My God! 'Scuse me, lady, but you honestly oughtn't to ask that question round here. Personally, but don't quote me, I really wouldn't care."
2. "Co-education! I don't think a decent person would discuss it!"

One familiar southern attitude is, "The Negro is *our* problem. We have to live with it, and let *us* solve it." Also Southerners say, "You Northerners didn't grow up with this thing in your hearts; therefore you can never understand it." Indeed, interference or advice from the North is tenaciously resented. Yet, no matter what the South may have done of itself, the record would certainly seem to indicate that it is not enough. Another familiar phenomenon is the "vicious circle" attitude. People refuse to give opportunities to a Negro, on the a priori assumption that he cannot make use of them, blaming him the while. The pattern becomes, "We cannot train Negroes for this type of work, since they won't be able to do it if we train them!"

The most interesting program for amelioration of the whole problem that I heard in the South came from a white professor. It consisted of four clauses: (*a*) Enforce the law, i.e., prevent illegal discriminations; (*b*) As to segregation, try to do first things first; (*c*) Encourage migration to the North, until approximately one-third of the Negroes now in the South have moved; (*d*) Don't mistreat Negroes, but don't baby them either.

Politics, Poll Tax, and White Primaries

On the level of national legislation three dominant issues involving Negroes confront the country, an antilynching bill, FEPC, and a bill to abolish the poll tax.

A federal bill aimed against lynching has passed the House of Representatives several times, but each time it has reached the Senate it has been killed by filibuster. One may well ask how any senator, even Bilbo, can assume a position which seems to favor lynching, but this is not the way it works out. Projected antilynching bills concentrate mostly on the setting up of federal machinery for prosecution, taking this out of the hands of the local state authorities. So of course the southern senators are able to protest that their precious state rights are being infringed, and it is mainly on this ground that they filibuster, and keep any bill from coming to an actual vote.

As to legislation to make the FEPC permanent, it is moribund on the national plane, though in several states (notably New York and Massachusetts) local organizations are working well. In Washington the proposal remains hopelessly bottled up in committee, and it can be resuscitated in the 80th Congress only by reintroduction of the measure and beginning all over. The Fair Employment Practice Committee has a curious history. Early in 1941, when anti-Negro discrimination in national defense industries was becoming more and more severe, A. Philip Randolph, president of the Brotherhood of Sleeping Car Porters and one of the most controversial of modern Negro leaders, threatened to organize a "March on Washington" in protest. Mr. Roosevelt as a result called a white-black conference of industrial and labor leaders and government officials, and issued an executive order which formally "abolished" discriminatory practices in industry and government departments. This was, incidentally, the first executive order by a president having to do with Negroes since the Emancipation Proclamation. Subsequently the FEPC was set up to enforce the order and superintend its application. But it never got anything like the appropriations it needed, and the southern senators sniped at it and chivvied it unmercifully. Finally, after the war, a bill to extend the act was beaten by filibuster. Anybody who wants to undergo the distressing experience of learning what southern conservatives really think can do no better than read the *Congressional Record* containing the accounts of this gruesome debate, which held up all other Senate business for eighteen entire days early in 1946.

The poll tax is a whole long story in itself. A bill to abolish the poll tax by federal authority has passed the House three times, but each time the Senate killed it, again by filibustering. It is extremely striking that none of these three major proposals for ameliorative legislation—antilynching, FEPC, and poll tax—has ever actually reached a full *vote* in the Senate; the Bilbos and their like have always managed to squash them *before* they reach the voting stage.

A "poll tax" is an annual tax imposed as a prerequisite for voting. Seven states still retain it—Arkansas, Alabama, South Carolina, Mississippi, Virginia, Texas, and Tennessee, though in Tennessee it only remains in force by virtue of some of the choicest legal skulduggery ever known. The amount of the tax differs state by state, and in some it is retroactive; for instance in Alabama, though the annual tax is only $1.50, it may cost as much as $36.00 to vote if a man has failed to pay over a long period. The highest annual tax ($2.00) is in the poorest state, Mississippi. Now, to a comfortably well-off Northerner, these sums may seem small. But they can mean a good deal to a sharecropper who earns $20.00 a month and whose children have no shoes. Moreover other factors make the payment a nuisance. In some states no notice is sent out; the initiative rests with the voter, and often he is too ignorant to pay. In some the tax is lumped with other taxes, and the citizen may not even know that he has paid it. Also, as a rule, it must be paid well in advance, and very few of the Negro underpossessed or poor whites pay *anything* ahead of time. Finally, many Negroes hesitate to pay because this puts them on the general tax rolls, and may make them subject to other levies.

What this system serves to produce is, of course, disproportionate representation and a limited electorate. At least ten million potential voters are disfranchised in the South as a whole;[25] to take a specific example, Mississippi has about 1,250,000 people of voting age, but in the last elections only 180,000 went to the polls. In other words Bilbo was elected by less than one-sixth of the electorate. As another example, Walter F. George was elected senator in 1944 by 14 per cent of the total potential Georgia vote, or less than 8 per cent of the people of the state; similar figures for Ellender of Louisiana are 6 and 3 per cent.

Most politicians love the poll tax. For one thing it leads to a small, easily influenced electorate. A machine may take its choice: (*a*) assume that the tax will keep enough people *from* the polls, or (*b*) simply "buy the vote," that is, pay the tax for a bloc of voters big enough to decide an election. For years, this latter practice was a favorite method in Tennessee. Negroes by the thousand (with poll tax duly paid by somebody else) were herded into busses and hauled wholesale to the voting booths. In South Carolina recently 25,000 poll taxes "were put up," as

[25] Cf. *The Southern Frontier*, January, 1945. Figures on George and Ellender are from *PM*, January 23, 1946.

the phrase is, at the last moment to decide an election that seemed uncertain. This was the election where a Negro candidate, Osceola McKaine, ran for the Senate under the aegis of the "Progressive Democratic Party" and actually won about 12,000 votes.

Also the poll tax increases the power of the South in Congress. Take South Carolina. It has 989,841 citizens over twenty-one, of whom only 99,830 voted in 1944. But South Carolina has precise equality of representation in the House—six seats—with the state of Washington, with 793,833 voters out of a total voting population of 1,123,725! Similarly Georgia gets ten seats for 312,539 votes; Wisconsin gets ten for 1,941,603.[26]

Finally consider the political morality of all this. Plenty of good Southerners hate the poll tax hotly, if only because they sincerely think that it is sinful, under democracy, to make people pay for the privilege of voting. What the poll tax really means, in the words of Jennings Perry, is that "the *majority* of people in seven states have no voice in government."

Of course the white supremacy addicts, on their side, defend the poll tax with great vigor. If, conceivably, Congress should ever abolish it, they will retaliate promptly by imposing a literacy tax as a substitute. They must, at all costs, continue to prevent the Negro from voting, because once he is in a position to exert full voting power, he will in time vote white supremacy out. There is, however, one interesting qualification to this. If any local movement to get rid of the poll tax seems on the point of winning, as in North Carolina in the 20's, Florida in the 30's and Georgia in the 40's, the professional politicians join the movement with alacrity, because they cannot risk facing a free electorate with a record of having just voted against a free electorate.

The poll tax disfranchises whites too; in fact, it actually prevents more whites—about six million in all—from voting than it does Negroes, which is a striking commentary on the poverty of whites in the South too.

Another device severely limiting the vote in several southern states is the residence requirement. Numerous tenant farmers move every year, which means that many, even if they have paid their poll tax, never get a chance to vote. In Alabama, for instance, a voter must be a resident of the state for two years, of the county for one year, and of the actual district for three months.

Finally consider the white primary. This is an instrument even more decisive than the poll tax in depriving Negroes of the vote, and it still exists in South Carolina, Arkansas, Georgia, Mississippi, and Louisiana; in Florida (and parts of Texas and Alabama) it is breaking down; it no longer exists in North Carolina or Tennessee. The white primary is not so much a matter of statute as of party regulation. To exclude

[26] *What the Negro Wants, op. cit.,* p. 158.

Negroes from general elections, on the ground of race, would of course be unconstitutional. But it is the primaries that decide all elections in the South, and so, if Negroes can be excluded from these, they are duly cut off from effective suffrage. This is easily done if the local Democratic party passes bylaws, say, eliminating Negroes from party membership or privileges. Lately, however, in the celebrated Texas case the Supreme Court of the United States has decided that such strictures by the local party are illegal. Consequently various southern states are, at the moment, trying to work out new legal artifices to keep the primaries white and "pure." They have not been too successful. More Negroes voted in 1944 and 1946 than at any other time in history.[27]

Except vestigially in South Carolina, no movement toward a Negro political party exists in the United States. That this should be so is a perpetual puzzle to non-Americans. They wonder why, since the Negro is so manifestly discriminated against, he does not rise in the classic American manner and express his dissatisfaction in perfectly legal but overt political terms. This has never happened. There is no "Negro party" for the simplest of reasons. Such a party would have no real cohesion except in the South, and it would almost certainly defeat its own putative end by formally putting the race issue into politics and so arousing the united white South to intensified opposition. I have yet to meet a responsible Negro, southern or northern, who wants a black party, any more than I have ever met anyone who wanted a "California" party or a "South Dakota" party. The future of Negro politics lies within the existing parties, and shrewd Negroes know well how these may be played against one another.

This is not to say that Negroes do not have substantial political power. They do, though in the South, under a one-party system, they cannot easily influence results. But in the North, according to such a sober authority as Walter White, Negroes hold the balance of power in no fewer than seventeen states, with a total of 281 electoral votes (and to elect a president only 266 are necessary). What Mr. White means is that in a hotly contested state where a few heavily industrialized precincts may tip the scales one way or the other, the Negroes may be able to do this, exactly as can the Poles in Buffalo or the Czechs in Pittsburgh.[28]

[27] Such artifices as the white primary are by no means new. For years, until the Supreme Court declared it unconstitutional in 1915, most southern states restricted Negro voting by use of the "grandfather clause." This kept from the polls all Negroes whose grandfathers were not American citizens—which meant automatic exclusion of the vast majority who were descendants of slaves at the time of emancipation.

[28] Myrdal, with his customary thorough sagacity, takes issue with Mr. White on this point (II, 1330), saying that the seventeen-state estimate "is based on the dubious assumption that all Negroes of voting age do vote, that the Negro vote is perfectly organized and flexible, that white voters are always divided closely . . .

One point that good white politicians keep in mind is Negro sensitiveness. With what avidity Negroes leap to support a leader who tells them nice things! Any white who really does something for Negroes (Roosevelt) or promises them something (Willkie) can overnight build up a landslide vote.

What the Future Holds

> The haughty American nation . . . makes the Negro clean its boots and then proves the . . . inferiority of the Negro by the fact that he is a bootblack.
>
> —Bernard Shaw

Now in conclusion let us say with emphasis that, in spite of everything, a slow but progressive steady amelioration of the Negro problem is a fact. The social upheavals and new distributions of peoples caused by the war (for instance during the war a million Negroes worked side by side with whites all over the nation); the greater awareness by Negroes of their own rights; the pace of urbanization in the South; bad conscience among many whites; the findings of modern science which dissipate the racial myth; the Negroes' own achievement in various fields —all this makes a leaven, a yeast, which contributes to progress and reform.

Forty years ago when President Theodore Roosevelt invited Booker T. Washington to the White House the event was a national scandal. No such scandal would arise today from a similar incident. As a matter of fact Booker T. Washington became in 1940 the first Negro ever elected to the Hall of Fame. Atrocious things still happen, but that there has been some measure of advance can hardly be denied. Recently two Negro judges became members of the American Bar Association, and the American College of Surgeons in 1946 broke a famous barrier by electing eight Negroes to its membership. For the first time in history Baptist ministers, Negro and white, met in Georgia recently for a joint session. Jackie Robinson, a Negro shortstop, became in 1945 the first Negro in organized baseball, and the Supreme Court ruled in June, 1946, in what is known as the Irene Morgan case, that passenger busses engaged in interstate travel have no right to enforce Jim Crow restrictions. A Negro girl presided not long ago over a mixed meeting at the University of North Carolina, the first time this has ever happened, and in Tennessee the American Veterans Committee voted in favor of mixed chapters.

---

and that white voters would be uninfluenced if an organized Negro movement were afoot." On the other hand one should never underestimate the extreme vulnerability of the American political system to minorities of all kinds. In November, 1946, for instance, it seemed for a time that control of the Senate would rest on the electoral outcome in the single state of Nevada, with a population of 110,000 out of 138,-000,000.

Amelioration does not mean solution. The Negro problem is nowhere near being "solved." To solve it will take generations, if only because, as Myrdal says, it is indissolubly part of all other American problems, part of a universal evolution in "social self-healing."

One thing, it would seem, is certain. The days of treating Negroes like sheep are done with. They cannot be maintained indefinitely in a submerged position, because they themselves are now strong enough to contest this position, because the overwhelming bulk of white Americans are, in the last analysis, decent minded, and because of education. It is impossible at this stage to halt education among Negroes. But the more you educate, the more you make inevitable a closer participation by Negroes in American life as a whole. In slightly different terms, this is the problem that the British Empire has faced in various colonial areas; once mass education gets under way the route to freedom becomes open, and the more you educate, the more impossible it becomes to block this road. The United States must either terminate education among Negroes, an impossibility, or prepare to accept the eventual consequences, that is, Negro equality under democracy.

There will never be a "solution" of the Negro problem satisfactory to everybody. But improvements, no matter how fitful, must continue if American democracy itself is to survive. Discrimination not only contaminates the Negro community; it contaminates the white as well. There were people in the Middle Ages who thought that the bubonic plague would not spread to their own precious selves. But there is no immunity to certain types of disease. A cancer will destroy a body, unless cured.

Chapter 42

The Southeastern Marches

In Dixie land, I'll take my stand,
And lib and die in Dixie,
Away, away
Away down south in Dixie.

—Daniel D. Emmet

INCONTESTABLY what runs Virginia is the Byrd machine, the most urbane and genteel dictatorship in America. A real machine it is, though Senator Harry Flood Byrd himself faced more opposition in 1946 than at any time in his long, suave, and distinguished public career.

Virginia is, of course, the "mother of states"; it is one of four in the union to call itself a commonwealth, and it has produced eight presidents, more than any other state. Its history goes back to Jamestown, the first Anglo-Saxon settlement in America, in 1607; the colony was named for Elizabeth, the virgin queen, and its citizens established an effective representative government several years before the Puritans in New England. Ever since it has prided itself on an aristocratic tradition, a seasoned attitude toward public life, administrative decency, and firm attachment to the regime of law. Virginia breeds no Huey Longs or Talmadges; its respect for the forms of order is deeply engrained. One subsidiary point is that the Virginians, it seems, were not so philoprogenitive as their New England counterparts. Boston is, as we know, choked with Cabots, Adamses, and Lowells. But there are no Washingtons in Richmond; George Washington, as a matter of fact, left no children. Jefferson had direct descendants, but none with the name Jefferson play any consequential role in Virginia life today. There are no Madisons, Monroes, descendants of John Marshall or Patrick Henry, or even Lees, in the contemporary political arena.

Outside the Executive Mansion in Richmond, one of the most impeccably handsome buildings in the country, a tablet tells the story:

On this spot have lived four Presidents of the United States Jefferson Monroe and Tyler Each of Whom Served as Governor and William Henry Harrison while his Father Benjamin Harrison signer of the Declaration of Independence was governor.
Here Also Lived Governors Patrick Henry and Henry Lee Father of Robert Edward Lee.
The Present House First Occupied by Governor James Barbour

in 1813 has been the Home of Chief Executives of Virginia since that Date.

Here have been Entertained Lafayette King Edward VII when Prince of Wales Presidents Hayes Cleveland McKinley Roosevelt and Taft Lord Balfour Marshals Foch and Petain General Pershing and the Daring Airmen Lindbergh and Byrd.

Several times I heard well-informed people say, "There is no excuse for Virginia"; by this they meant that the commonwealth, with its immensely opulent political tradition, and by reason of the fact that it is comparatively rich from a financial point of view as well, has small legitimate reason to be as backward as it is in many respects. It possesses Monticello and Mount Vernon and Duke of Gloucester Street in Williamsburg; it also possesses rural slums and antiquated one-room schools as hopeless as any in America. It is one of the few states that till very recently at least flogged convicts, and prisoners, white or black, may still be shackled; Georgia has abolished chain gangs, but not Virginia. Early in 1946 a youngster who was serving a four-year term for embezzling two hundred dollars escaped and found refuge in another state. When recaptured he tried to avoid extradition back to Virginia by testifying that, while a prisoner there, he had several times been hung from a post for 72 hours at a time, "barely standing on his toes." Virginia produced not only the Declaration of Independence (through Thomas Jefferson) but, in a manner of speaking, the Bill of Rights. The state has been aware of intellectual fermentations for a good long time; for instance a lecturer at the University of Virginia taught "Socialism and Communism" way back in 1892; this must have been one of the first courses of such nature anywhere in the South. But in 1946 two Virginia schoolteachers were ousted from their jobs (because of pressure from local posts of the American Legion and the Veterans of Foreign Wars) for having been conscientious objectors during World War II. I do not, of course, mean to generalize too widely from such particulars; several states have worse records in civil liberties. Early in 1945 the College of William and Mary at Williamsburg, the second oldest university in the United States, temporarily suspended publication of the campus paper because its editor, a twenty-two-year-old Michigan girl, wrote an article saying that the time should come when Negroes would attend William and Mary, "join the same clubs, be our roommates, be in the same classrooms, and marry among us." (New York *Herald Tribune*, 2/12/45.) The storm this caused was black and ferocious, but the young editress was not expelled from school.

Senator Harry F. Byrd incarnates the cavalier-First-Family-of-Virginia tradition, except in one important particular. The Byrd family has a heredity like that of a Middle Europe princeling; indeed, for some generations, the ancestral estate at Westover resembled nothing so much as, say, an estate like that of the Potockis' outside Warsaw. Byrd's initial ancestor, William Byrd I, arrived in Virginia in 1674, and he and his son, William Byrd II, were powerful pre-Revolutionary characters. But early in the nineteenth century the family began to disintegrate. The present Byrd, lacking nothing in aristocratic heritage, did lack something that usually attends an aristocratic heritage—money. The family, grown poor, had scattered; Byrd's father was Texas born, and he himself was born in West Virginia. Yet always the Byrds were tightly enmeshed in the old tradition. At the age of fifteen, young Byrd took over a newspaper in Winchester, Virginia, that for a long time had been unable to make ends meet and put it on its feet. He never had opportunity to go to high school or college. Byrd made the newspaper a successful property, and branched out in other fields; he is a very wealthy man today, and his Shenandoah Valley home, Rosemont, near Berryville, is a Virginia showplace. His fortune derives mostly out of apples. Virginia as a whole is the fourth apple-growing state in the union, and Byrd himself, with 200,000 trees and a million bushel a year crop, is believed to control about 1 per cent of all American production.[1] The outline of Byrd's career, especially in its motivations, is strikingly like that of his friend in the Senate, Arthur Vandenberg. Vandenberg also struggled for a living as a young man, as we know, and a consequent impulse toward security has dominated his behavior ever since. In Byrd's life story we may similarly find a characteristic that distinguishes him above anything else—his extreme obsessive hatred of debt, his dogged fixation on economy. He had to struggle for bitter years to get a family property out of debt. Both the United States Senate and the commonwealth of Virginia have seen the results of this transmuted into other spheres.

Byrd interested himself in politics early, and he became a state senator and then in 1926 governor of Virginia. He is an able man (in industriousness and abstract competence he strongly resembles Taft of Ohio) and his record as governor was in several respects notable. He fought the gasoline and telephone companies, to drive rates down and thus save the public money; he put through an admirable antilynching bill, the first such bill in the South, making any member of a lynch mob subject to state authority and indictment on a charge of murder. As a result Virginia has not had a lynching for twenty years. Roosevelt liked Byrd at this time and wanted him in the federal Senate; as a result, when Claude A. Swanson was elevated to FDR's cabinet in 1933, Byrd got his Senate seat. He has been a senator ever since. He began to break with Roosevelt when the New Deal got under way, and within a few

---

[1] Cf. "Senator Byrd of Virginia," by Gerald W. Johnson, in *Life*, August 7, 1944, an admirably informed article. Harry Byrd has two brothers, incidentally, named nicely Tom and Dick. Tom is a successful businessman; Dick is the celebrated admiral and explorer.

years had become the most important and powerful of all his enemies among Senate Democrats. For session after session he intransigently bored away at Roosevelt budgets, Roosevelt appropriations, Roosevelt administrative agencies. Yet, a gentleman, he never attacked FDR blatantly. His good manners made him the more dangerous an antagonist. He could not be dismissed as a demagogue or spiteful partisan. At the 1944 Democratic convention, he got eighty-nine votes for the presidential nomination; he was—and still is—the obvious candidate and hero of the Bourbon South that is Democrat in name only. He voted against the party leadership on 61 per cent of all roll calls in sixteen months in 1945-6.[2]

When Byrd first entered Virginia public life the roads were in a shocking state, and pressure was great for a bond issue to improve and augment them. He opposed it. The pinchpenny motif dominates his entire public career, in state as well as federal affairs. He wanted good roads; but he insisted that they should be paid for out of taxes, inch by inch as they were built. At about the same time North Carolina promoted a very substantial road-building campaign which, in contrast to that in Virginia, was financed by bonds. As of today the state of North Carolina is certainly no worse off than Virginia financially; it has a considerably better road system; easy transportation encouraged the building up of rural industry; on the whole its standard of living is better than Virginia's. Take schools. Byrd and his machine have not been what you could call generous to education, and since economy has always been a major criterion, most efforts to reform the grotesquely inadequate school system have failed. Virginia was the forty-second state in "draft rejections because of educational deficiencies"; this is one of many similar indices available. One reason why Virginia—like all southern states—is so poverty stricken and backward in education is of course Negro segregation, which makes it necessary for the state to supply two different sets of schools and teachers. End segregation, and educational statistics will sharply improve.

The Byrd machine is a highly efficient organization; it runs the commonwealth as effectively as Pendergast ever ran Kansas City or Kelly-Nash Chicago, though with much less noise. In fact, from the point of view of its adhesive power in every Democratic county, its control over practically every office, no matter how minor, it is quite possibly the single most powerful machine surviving in the whole United States. Virginia, I heard it said, is the only "aviary" in the country; it is a cage the netting of which, though almost invisible to outsiders, is extremely close spun; the commonwealth is, so a friend in North Carolina told me— the remark is somewhat bitter—not only the cradle of American democracy, but its "grave." Byrd has never forgotten his Virginia interests. He pays as intimate and inflexible attention to state affairs as to

[2] This figure is from *PM*, June 23, 1946.

federal. The machine works something like this. Its major instruments are, as always, jobs and patronage, plus the Virginia poll tax. First, through the Democratic National Committee, Byrd controls federal patronage. Next, he pretty well decides the choice not merely of governor but of most members of the general assembly (legislature). The governor, who in Virginia today cannot be other than a Byrd man, in turn controls the appointment of some thousands of state employees, and circuit court judges are chosen—for substantial eight-year terms—by the legislature; these in turn appoint the school trustees, county electoral boards, county welfare boards, and trial justices. In each county there is a fixed ring of six or seven machine men. Some county officers like sheriff and tax assessor are elected but their salaries and expense allotments are, within limits, established by the State Compensation Board, also appointed by the governor under Byrd's control. The pattern makes a full interlocking circle. Nothing could be neater or more complete.[3]

Yet the whole structure would crash to ruin if it were not for (a) the one-party system and (b) the poll tax. The one-party system means that, in the majority of counties (some few areas are Republican, but there are only five Republicans in a legislature numbering 140), the machine need worry only about one side of the fence. The poll tax means in turn a small, easily handled vote. The tax amounts to $1.50 per year, and it has to be paid well in advance of the voting; hence many people, even if they could afford to pay it or were willing to pay, forget to do so. In addition the mere task of registration is sometimes made formidably difficult. Lowell Mellett once described (New York Post, February 20, 1945) some of the obstacles, medieval in the extreme, that a would-be voter has to overcome. As a result of all this and the general indifference induced by the one-party system, the proportion of Virginians who actually vote, as compared to those who would be eligible to vote if poll taxes were paid and other requirements met, is only about one in five. In the 1946 senatorial primary only about 230,000 Virginians voted. But the total population is 2,677,773.

Another important factor contributing to Byrd's dominance was, for long, the senescence of Carter Glass. This crotchety but enormously able old American, stricken by illness, did not sit in the Senate from June, 1942, until his death in 1946 at the age of eighty-eight. Innumerable times in the *Congressional Record*, the first word recorded after prayer was the statement that the senior senator from Virginia was absent on account of illness. But Glass, an obstinate man, would not resign, and his prestige was such that for a long time no one would dare ask him to. As a result Virginia had in effect only one senator, Harry Byrd, for four crucial years.

[3] Some of the material for this paragraph is derived from a chart in *PM*, June 23, 1946, part of a series of articles about Byrd by Gordon H. Cole.

Consider the Byrd obsession with economy once more—but in a different light. Political machines can be expensive. The commonwealth ranks very low in almost all statistics on education, public health, and the like; but it stands very high in number of office holders. It is the nineteenth state in population; it is the ninth in state employees. According to Marquis W. Childs (New York *Post*, August 3, 1946), Virginia is first in the nation in number of state employees per capita; it has one for every 164 citizens. The corresponding figure for New York is 241, for Massachusetts 255, for Illinois 376. Virginia has no fewer than seventeen *thousand* state office holders; this is more than the total number in New Jersey, which is certainly a politics-ridden state, and one with a considerably greater population.

The Virginia machine is impregnable, yes; but it had a bad scare in 1946. Byrd introduced a stringent antilabor bill; for this and other reasons (for instance he was one of the few southern senators who voted against the British loan—another instance of the fetish for economy) the CIO made him number one on its list of men to be purged. One might think that this would have redounded to his benefit. But for the first time in his Senate career, and indeed for the first time in the commonwealth for a quarter of a century, a contest in the senatorial primaries took place. A Richmond lawyer named Martin A. Hutchinson ran against Byrd as Democratic candidate. Byrd got roughly 150,000 votes. But Hutchinson got more than 80,000. Byrd lost the city of Alexandria, across the Potomac from Washington, D.C., and only narrowly won Richmond.

One result of this situation is to make the poll tax the chief political issue in Virginia. Traditionally the Byrd machine has stood vehemently against lifting it. But winds of disaffection, winds of change, still reach the state that once was Jefferson's. Early in 1946 a legislative suffrage commission urged repeal of the poll tax by an overwhelming majority. But actually to repeal it will mean amendment of the constitution, and the procedure for this is weighty; a long time ago Virginia (like the United States) took precautions to make constitutional amendments difficult in the extreme to pass. Both houses of the legislature must approve a new amendment; then it must also pass a legislature subsequently elected. So nothing can be done for two years at least.

Another recent issue is that of flood control on the Potomac. Congress asked the Army engineers to work out a project in this direction after serious floods took place; the engineers produced a plan that, while it did not embody the valley authority idea, did envisage power development for the region and multiple-purpose dams and reservoirs. The total cost would have been about 250 million dollars. The project would, among other things, have served to ameliorate serious pollution in the Potomac, and to improve the Washington, D.C., water supply. The proposal was enthusiastically voted down. First, small farmers in the

Shenandoah Valley didn't want to lose their land. Second, the Byrd machine led the opposition.

When I visited Richmond the governor was Colgate W. Darden Jr., a civilized and decent man, well equipped for the job and honestly devoted to public service. He was a Byrd lieutenant, and in fact he managed the 1946 primary campaign; but Darden is not quite so obsessive about economy. On one occasion the Byrd-dominated assembly reduced state payments to surviving widows of Confederate veterans from fifteen to eight dollars a month. Mrs. Darden offered to make up the sum. That she is a rich woman, a member of the Du Pont family, does not detract from the graciousness of her gesture. Darden, by Virginia law, could not succeed himself; he could have had Carter Glass's old senate seat, but did not want it. The governor who succeeded him was William M. Tuck, an organization wheel horse. He had the support of the machine, and nobody of real stature could be found to run against him; the nomination (and election) went largely by default. Personalities were not involved; what grieved Virginia liberals was that there could be no effective raising and airing of public issues. Tuck came into wide notoriety in the spring of 1946, when a strike was threatened in the Virginia Electric and Power Company. The governor proclaimed a state of emergency, and issued orders for mobilization of the "unorganized militia," which would have meant forcible impounding of would-be strikers into a semi-military force of strike breakers. This outrageous situation did not come to a head, inasmuch as last-minute negotiations called off the strike.

Howard W. Smith, Virginia Congressman from the Eighth District, is an extreme die-hard, who was co-author of the Smith-Connally law, the author of an original draft of the Case antistrike bill, and a powerful member of the House Rules Committee; as such he was a leading spirit in preventing the FEPC bill from reaching a House vote. Smith stands for almost everything old-fashioned in Virginia and the South, and it is perhaps an indication of a fresher spirit that he was badly beaten in an effort to succeed Carter Glass. The man who did succeed to the Glass seat was A. Willis Robertson, a respectable enough conservative. Oddly enough both he and Byrd were born in the same town (outside the state), Martinsburg, West Virginia, within a few days of one another.

Look at Richmond

Broad-streeted Richmond . . .
The trees in the streets are old trees used to living with people,
Family trees that remember your grandfather's name.
—Stephen Vincent Benét, *John Brown's Body**

Very few cities in America can compare with Richmond, a stately rectilinear town, for concentration of historical allusion. It has celebrated

* Copyright, 1927, 1928, by Stephen Vincent Benét.

monuments to Lee, Jefferson Davis (for Richmond was the second capital of the Confederacy), and Stonewall Jackson; General Lee's home, now the headquarters of the Virginia Historical Society, is here, and so is that of Edgar Allan Poe. It contains the John Marshall house, designed by the great chief justice himself, and the University of Richmond.[4] But what I liked best, next to the incomparable executive mansion, is the heroic (and heroically ugly) equestrian statue of George Washington, which was cast in Munich of all places, and which now stands in Capitol Square. The general's eyes look sternly at the state house and his finger, like a flail, points to the penitentiary!

Richmond is not a very large city, but it has great wealth; most of the modern fortunes come from tobacco. It is heavily industrialized, and is the biggest cigarette manufacturing center in the world; there is, however, little sign of any urban proletariat. One curious point is that, though it numbers only 200,000 people, there are 285 streets with duplicated names. Richmond has, or had, another twin distinction, one in the realm of beautiful letters. I thumbed through the telephone book, and found these entries:

> Cabell James Branch 3201 Monument Av 4-5421
> Glasgow Miss Ellen 1 W Main 3-3118

"Tobacco, Divine, Rare, Superexcellent Tobacco!"

Tobacco is, in a quite literal sense, a kind of weed. It produces a small pretty flower; part of its science of cultivation is to keep the flower from developing, to keep the plant, in other words, from going to seed, to force its vitality into the lower leaves. Tobacco must be planted every year, and, as is well-known, its effect on the soil is exhausting. It is predominantly a warm weather plant, but in actual fact it grows almost everywhere on earth—even Sweden! One of the most remarkable things about tobacco is the size of the seed; a single plant may produce a million seeds, and one teaspoonful will plant ten acres.

Tobacco is a small man's crop; the average holding in the American South is about three acres. In Virginia and western North Carolina most growers are owners; in Georgia they are mostly tenants. There are no great tobacco "plantations" like cotton plantations. The harvest comes in late summer; the farmer hangs his crop up in his shed or kitchen, practically sleeps with it while he cures it, ties it in bundles called "hands," and then—as radio listeners are well aware—auctions it at a central market. The wholesale buyers give it further treatment by steam and otherwise, and hold it for anything from a few months to a few years.

---

[4] Not to be confused with the University of Virginia, which was founded by Thomas Jefferson, at Charlottesville; its rector at present is Edward R. Stettinius Jr. Another famous Virginia university is Washington and Lee at Lexington.

Ninety-five per cent of American cigarette tobacco is blended with Turkish or other oriental breeds. Virginia tobacco, of the variety called Bright, is more sugary than that from Kentucky say; it is supposed to hit the taste buds in the front of the tongue whereas less sweet tobaccos strike further back. The chief demerit of tobacco as an agricultural product is, aside from its cost to the soil, the fact that it is a cash crop; if the price goes to pieces, the small farmer faces ruin.

Lucky Strikes are made at Richmond, Durham (N.C.) and Reidsville (N.C.); Chesterfields and Old Golds at Richmond and elsewhere; Camels exclusively at Winston-Salem (N.C.); Philip Morrises entirely at Richmond. The total annual United States production is something over 250 billion cigarettes. There is, I heard in Richmond, more mumbo-jumbo and hocus-pocus associated with the cigarette business than any other in the world, and estimates of rival sales vary widely; generally it is thought that Lucky Strikes and Camels are paired at the top, with Luckies in the lead by a slight margin (as of the time I was in Richmond); probably 80 billion Luckies are sold per year. Chesterfield and Philip Morris are similarly neck and neck in a lower echelon. Both Luckies and Camels have a higher proportion than the others of Kentucky tobacco. The percentage of labor costs to dollar of sales is, I was told, lower in cigarettes than in any comparable American industry, being something like five to seven cents as compared to about forty cents in automobiles. One plant in Richmond probably produces 12 per cent of all American production; yet it employs only about five hundred workers. The average profit to the manufacturer is believed to be something like a half a cent per pack.

The great tobacco magnates do not, like the automobile behemoths of Detroit, play much of a community role in a town like Richmond. Liggett and Myers are not like the Fisher Brothers. There is no Liggett, and no Myers. The major tobacco and cigarette companies are run from the North. Forty or fifty years ago there were a number of local independents. Then the fabulous J. B. Duke came along, and consolidated the tobacco business almost as Rockefeller consolidated oil. The Duke interests, concentrated in the American Tobacco Company, not only controlled most of United States production but British as well. In 1908, by terms of a Supreme Court ruling, they were split into various segments, like Liggett and Myers (Chesterfields today), Lorillard (Old Golds), and the Reynolds Company (Camels). But remaining to the American Tobacco Company as of today are Lucky Strikes, Pall Malls, and Melachrinos; among pipe tobaccos Bull Durham, Tuxedo, Blue Boar, and half a dozen others; among plugs and twists Piper Heidsieck and Penny's Natural Leaf; and among cigars La Corona, Chancellor, and Henry Clay.

According to the *New Republic* (February 18, 1946), in a letter by George L. Knapp called "Salaries, Wages and Depressions," which cites figures from the Federal Trade Commission and the Bureau of Labor Statistics, four leading officials of the American Tobacco Company received in 1932, the worst year of the depression, salaries respectively of $825,607, $473,472, $473,422, and $100,000. The average annual pay of the full-time tobacco worker at the same time was $614.12. The man who got the $825,607 was the renowned and supereccentric George Washington Hill, who invented most of the Lucky Strike slogans, and who died in 1946.

In June, 1946, the Supreme Court rendered a decision to the effect that the American Tobacco Company, Liggett and Myers, and the R. J. Reynolds Company had formed a monopoly in violation of the Sherman Antitrust Act. This followed six years of involved "trust-busting" litigation by the Department of Justice (New York *Herald Tribune*, June 11, 1946), and came as a result of an appeal by the three companies (who had already been fined upwards of $250,000) against previous convictions by other federal courts, which the Supreme Court upheld by a six to zero vote. The three companies, according to this verdict, had "set up a price monopoly on leaf tobacco . . . and conspired to restrain their competitors."

1946 saw tobacco at an all-time high; the crop, worth more than 600 million dollars, reached an estimated total of 1,300,000,000 pounds. The consumption of tobacco in the United States has never been greater. Yet one should always remember that roughly one-third of all American production goes abroad.

A Word About West Virginia

Coal is portable climate.
—Ralph Waldo Emerson

By most criteria, West Virginia is a northern state but it has a few southern characteristics too; I include it at this juncture mostly as a matter of convenience. West Virginia is shaped like a squid or some other odd marine animal. It has not merely one but two panhandles. One is a northerly sliver ending in a pinpoint above Wheeling; the other is to the east. Historically the reason that the three "overhanging" counties of this eastern panhandle are part of West Virginia, instead of Virginia itself, was that they controlled the westward approaches to Washington during the Civil War. The main line of the Baltimore and Ohio Railway went through this strip and still does; General Lee once broke it at Harpers Ferry.

West Virginia's peculiar geographic characteristics have given rise to a well-known toast:

Here's to West Virginia.
Its northernmost city, Chester, is farther north than
     Pittsburgh, Pennsylvania, therefore she's a northern state,
Its easternmost city, Harpers Ferry, is farther east than
     Rochester, New York, therefore she's an eastern state,
Its westernmost city, Kenova, is farther west than
     Cleveland, Ohio, therefore she's a western state,
Its southernmost city, Bluefield, is farther south than
     Richmond, Virginia, therefore she's a southern state,
But be she east, west, north, or south, she's a damn good
     state for the shape she's in!

The West Virginia motto is *Montani semper liberi*, and the state is one of the most mountainous in the country; sometimes it is called the "little Switzerland" of America, and I once heard an irreverent local citizen call it the "Afghanistan of the United States." The precipitous upland nature of the terrain makes naturally for three things: (1) poor communications; (2), fierce sectionalism; (3), comparatively little agriculture. West Virginia lies mostly in the Ohio orbit; all but eight of its counties drain into the Ohio River, and a pressing problem is strip mining, as in Ohio. On the other hand, the state has, it is hardly necessary to point out, little of the prodigious urban development of Ohio, and at the same time no great rural blocs such as those that dominate the Ohio legislature. The pull of Pennsylvania is also very strong, particularly near Wheeling which, like Pittsburgh hard by, is based on steel. Finally, in this geographical realm, one should not think of West Virginia as being "western" Virginia. It is a totally distinct and separate entity. Virginians themselves, as a matter of fact, pay almost no attention nowadays to their craggy neighbor.

West Virginia became a state in a very special way, and not, as is customarily believed, exclusively by reason of the War Between the States; the western mountaineers had talked about splitting off from Virginia for fifty years. They did not feel closely akin to the tidewater aristocrats. They did not relish control by absentee planters. Virginia had 350,000 slaves east of the mountains; the west had only about 15,000. The actual split was of course furthered by the war; when Virginia proper seceded from the union, the Allegheny counties organized a rump regime which they called the "restored government of Virginia." This nullified the Virginia secession ordinance, elected an administration, and was recognized by Washington. Technically, by terms of federal law, no new state may be created out of the territory of an existing state without the consent of the parent. But no one paid much attention to this during the war and West Virginia was formally admitted to the union in 1863. Its governor functioned first at Alexandria, Virginia, and then at Richmond during the northern occupation. After Appomattox Virginia tried to get West Virginia back. But the West Virginians declined to abandon their new separate status.

The most astonishing thing about West Virginia today is the extent of its industrialization. The Kanawha Valley centering on Charleston, the state capital, is like nothing I have ever seen, except perhaps the southern lip of Lake Michigan; its development has been phenomenal. Chemical industries always tend to cluster because one is apt to use by-products of the other. So one factory on the Kanawha sits immediately adjacent to the next in a close thicket exactly as in the tumultuous region around Harrisburg. Of all state capitals in the nation, Charleston, according to Charleston statistics, was the greatest single seat of war production; it is the world's biggest center for synthetic chemicals. Together with its environs it produced all the lucite made in the nation, all the "vinylite" resins, all the polyethylene resins, and every drop of nylon ever known to the world; the raw material for every stocking made since nylon began comes from the Kanawha Valley. Likewise this extraordinary industrial complex produced during the war one-sixth of America's total production of synthetic rubber, more than half the Navy's armor plate, most of the strontium peroxide used in tracer bullets, more than a million gun-barrels, millions of gallons of Prestone, Zerone, and other antifreezes, and millions of tons of ammonia, chlorine, and various alcohols. All these products leave West Virginia in raw form; the nylon and resins are liquid and go out in tanks.

One by one I passed units in this imposing constellation. Twelve miles up-river from Charleston is the Du Pont Belle Ammonia plant, which makes "nylon intermediate." Union Carbide and Carbon has three factories in the area operated by different subsidiaries; one, the largest synthetic rubber installation in the country, is at the town of Institute; another at the appropriately named town of Alloy manufactures ferroalloys; a third in South Charleston makes oxygen for industrial uses. Also near by are the United States Naval Ordnance plant at South Charleston; the American Viscose Company, making staple rayon out of acetate; and the largest flat glass plant in the world, owned by the Libby-Owens Glass Company.

Oddly enough considering all this, Charleston is one of the few major cities in the United States without an airport. About thirty flights a day pass over it and several companies want to come in, but during the whole period of the war there was no place for planes to land. One reason was the mountains; another was that former airport facilities had been taken over by the government for a synthetic rubber plant. An airport is now being built; the job, half complete when I saw it, is described by loyal West Virginians as the "biggest airport development in the history of America." Four separate mountains had to be removed;

the site looks somewhat like the Mesabi pits in Minnesota upside down.

West Virginia's economy rests fundamentally on coal; the state is first in the nation in bituminous coal production. For this reason among others, John L. Lewis, though he doesn't live there, is a powerful local personality. West Virginia has no fewer than 117,000 miners, who belong to the United Mine Workers to a man; coal is a billion-dollar industry, and 117,000 miners make a lot of voters for so comparatively small a state. Coal is one of the most competitive industries on earth. Most of the great coal properties were bought originally by men who had no idea that coal was there. They bought for timber on the face of the land. Ownership today is divided among a good many rivals; the largest company doesn't control more than one-eighth of the total state production. One important factor is Koppers (Mellon interests) and all the railroads that cross the state, like Chesapeake & Ohio and Norfolk & Western, are closely involved in coal; several have their own "captive" mines. Two or three of the biggest coal companies are eastern owned, but West Virginia doesn't complain about "colonial economy" as much as do western and southern states. The profits may leak out but most of the wages stay, and are spent inside West Virginia. Coal is overwhelmingly the biggest distributor of wages in the state; the labor bill last year amounted to more than 300 million dollars.

From this we may turn to a contrasting sylvan note. West Virginia must be the only place in the union where bears are still hunted with dogs. Also in Watoga State Park near the Virginia line, deer may in theory be shot by bow and arrow; archers, that is, are allowed a week's season before the regular open season. But no archer has ever actually brought down a deer.[5]

Politically, for obvious reasons, West Virginia is a sharply riven state. It was mostly Democratic from the Civil War to 1896, and then Republican most of the time until Roosevelt; FDR carried it all four times he ran. The chief pressure groups, aside from the coal interests and the miners, are the power companies, the railroads, and the West Virginia Manufacturers Association. Politics are very personal, and complex family and other loyalties play a considerable role. The most distinguished West Virginian in politics today is Senator Harley M. Kilgore, whom we shall view in another place. The governor, Clarence W. Meadows, was born in the coal fields and, after a career as a lawyer, became attorney general and circuit judge. Kilgore was his scoutmaster when he

[5] West Virginia has a peculiar gun-toting law, by the way. Homicides among the backwoodsmen used to be disconcertingly numerous, so a law was passed whereby no citizen may carry arms except by permission of the local court, and after a sizable bond is posted.

was a Boy Scout, his commanding officer when he was in the National Guard, and a judge in the Raleigh County criminal court when he was a state prosecutor. Also Meadows is indirectly related to Chapman Revercomb, the Republican senator. Meadows and Lausche of Ohio are friends; one reason is that Meadows plays almost as good a game of golf.

West Virginia has assorted distinctions in other fields. It contains the fabulous community of Weirton, run by the equally fabulous E. T. Weir, which is probably the most conspicuous company town in America. Also the state has a capitol building of remarkable dignity and beauty, designed by Cass Gilbert. The chandelier in the dome weighs four thousand pounds, and the 60 by 26-foot rug in the governor's reception room—incidentally the pleasantest room of this kind I saw in the whole United States—is said to be the largest and heaviest one-piece rug in the world.

Politics and Affairs in the Tar Heel State

I found quickly that North Carolina was a state various in the extreme. Also it is beyond doubt one of the most important, alive, and progressive states in the union. First let me mention some incidental matter. The first thing I saw in North Carolina was a sign outside a group of bungalows, MOTOR COURT—MORALLY PURE. "Motels" and similar institutions all through the South and Texas are traditionally haunts for the amorous. The next thing I saw was an admirable bookshop in Raleigh that had been in the same family for seventy-eight years, passed down from father to son for three generations. The third thing I saw was Chapel Hill. The fourth was a newspaper clipping. An eight-year-old boy in Randolph County dropped a dead cat down a well, where it remained for a matter of two fruitful weeks. The boy, frightened, failed to mention this occurrence to his uncle, under whose custody he lived. But the youngster avoided drinking water from the well; the uncle became suspicious. The boy then confessed, whereupon the uncle made him dredge the animal out, and eat one of its hind legs. "Then he made him wash his mouth with peroxide." The case reached the courts, and the uncle, convicted of "assault," was sentenced to thirty days on the roads.

In several dimensions North Carolina is bigger than is generally thought. With 3,571,623 people (1940), it is the eleventh state in population; moreover this figure has increased by 12.7 per cent in the past ten years—a rate of increase which, incidentally, leaves Virginia far behind. Not less than 99.6 per cent of its people (by North Carolina figures anyway) are native born; it has been called the "most American of all the states." Geographically it has three distinct divisions: first, as it slopes gradually from the Appalachians to the sea, come the mountains (there are 43 peaks higher than 6,000 feet, and 125 higher than 5,000), with parks, forests, and a handsome resort industry exploiting the Great Smokies; second, the great Piedmont plateau, packed with lumber, water power, and industry of several types; third, the coastal plains with the Inland Waterway, cotton, and tobacco. The state's tobacco crop was worth 350 million dollars in 1945. The public finances are in commendable order; industry is decentralized and diversified, and the community as a whole has a better protection against depression than any other southern state.[6]

North Carolina maintains an aggressive and well-handled publicity and advertising system; on the whole it runs its public relations better than any other state I know. Above all it is a state of small cities: Winston-Salem (cigarettes); the Raleigh-Durham area; Charlotte, the biggest town in the state, which I have mentioned in Chapter 40; Fayetteville (a pure Scots-Irish enclave); Greensboro (chemicals, textiles, and the third largest women's college in the world); Asheville (the western mountain center); Newbern (almost solidly Swiss); Gastonia (textiles). There was once a movement to shift the capital from Raleigh to Greensboro. A Republican state senator threatened, "We're not going to leave a thing in Raleigh except the insane asylum, the penitentiary, and the *News and Observer*."

North Carolina was once famously described as "a vale of humility between two mountains of conceit"; the "mountains" referred to are, of course, Virginia and South Carolina. I'm not sure that North Carolina is humble, but it certainly does differ from its neighbors. The Tar Heel State and Virginia like to snipe at one another. Mostly the differences arise from the circumstances of early settlement (exactly as with the differences between Utah and Nevada, say). North Carolina never had the kind of big-plantation economy that Virginia had; it has much less of the tidewater tradition; its society was broadly speaking more plebeian. As to North and South Carolina, they are (perhaps I exaggerate slightly) almost as different as North and South Dakota. A single illustration: in North Carolina divorce may be granted simply on the ground of absence of cohabitation; South Carolina is the one American state in which divorce is not possible.

That North Carolina is by a good deal the most liberal southern state will, I imagine, be agreed to by almost everybody. The reasons for this are several:

(1) Geography and origins. Consider, for instance, the point—which

---

[6] One example of specialized industry is cigarette paper. Until World War II, practically all the cigarette paper used in America, a prodigious amount, came from France. Now most of it is manufactured in North Carolina in new plants on the banks of the Davidson River, near the Pisgah National Forest. One company makes paper for Camels, Chesterfields, Philip Morris, Old Gold, and Lucky Strikes.

is rather odd when you come to think of it—that North Carolina has never had any considerable seaport, though it fronts the Atlantic for a good long way. But Virginia to the north had Norfolk; South Carolina on the other side had Charleston; the Tar Heel State was left comparatively isolated in between, and as a result it developed a kind of adventurous frontier sense. This meant more freedom, and dissenters of several types began to filter in.

(2) Settlement. The northeastern part of the state was settled mostly by insurgents from Virginia; North Carolina became the "quintessence of Virginia's discontent." To the southeast came English stock, some by way of New England, some from Bermuda. To the upper Piedmont came Quakers, Moravians, Palatinate Germans, and pre-eminently the Scots, mostly by way of Pennsylvania. These were all sturdy folk, who had fought kings in their time, and who took their civil liberties with seriousness.

(3) Few original settlers were rich. They had pride instead, religion, and firm democratic instincts.

(4) In modern times, however, North Carolina has become a wealthy state. The total taxable property was about three-quarters of a billion dollars in 1900; by 1940 it was almost four billion dollars. Certainly wealth does not of necessity produce liberalism, but the fact that the state was never so grindingly poor as its neighbors has, naturally, tended to produce better standards of education.

(5) Most North Carolina farms are small, and, except in a few areas, they are predominantly worked by owners, not by sharecroppers or tenants. This also tends to produce a healthy economy which in turn may, with luck, promote liberal rather than antiliberal instincts.

(6) Climate. North Carolina covers a very wide gamut geographically, which also makes for reasonableness. A subordinate point is that the roads are good, which gives the population more mobility than in most southern states, and mobility can be an additional factor leading to moderation.

(7) The influence of independent newspapers like the Raleigh *News and Observer*. This is the Daniels paper. Surely it is one of the pleasantest of personal sidelights that, after Josephus Daniels resigned the active editorship to his son Jonathan, he took it over again at the age of eighty-three so that Jonathan might be free to become Roosevelt's press secretary in the White House. Old Josephus had, of course, been secretary of the navy and FDR's chief many years before.

(8) There were comparatively few slaves in North Carolina. It has plenty of Negroes now, but on the whole it has had better luck with the Negro problem than any other area in the South. Its facilities for Negro schools are the same as for white, at least in theory (sometimes the Negro

buildings aren't what they ought to be); Negro teachers get the same pay as white teachers, something unique, and the state supports a Negro college.

(9) Several strongly liberal governors, like Charles B. Aycock, set a pattern for progressive government a good many years ago.

(10) Finally, the influence of the University of North Carolina, at Chapel Hill, the oldest state university in America.

Who runs North Carolina? This is an extremely independent state. It refused at first to accept the federal Constitution (like Rhode Island) and was in theory a sovereign commonwealth for a brief period; its legislature voted *against* secession when the War Between the States began, and it did not join the rest of the South until the Northern armies invaded Virginia. All over America we have seen tenacious and deep-rooted suspicion by the people toward executive power; North Carolina probably carries this further than any other state. For one thing its governor has no veto. For another he may not succeed himself even after an interval. Most southern states forbid a governor to have two *consecutive* terms; North Carolina won't let him have two no matter when.

The South, by and large, is sensitive about being bossed; most states, even those worst bossed, are ashamed of being so. "If it's known that you belong to a machine, you're licked" is a familiar motto, except in Tennessee and Virginia. North Carolina accepts this hostility to bosses to an extreme degree. If you say of any man that he "runs" the state, he'll turn black in the face trying to deny it.

Most of the main political factors are familiar. The textile industry on the extreme conservative side, together with the tobacco companies and the utilities—these are the main economic groups behind the legislature, and those putting up the most money for political campaigns. A counter-weight to an extent is agriculture. If you can get the farmers aroused, they can be a lively influence. The veterans are beginning to be a force, though they have not been so conspicuous as in Tennessee. The Baptist church is another element, and so are the liquor interests.[7] Finally, the nearest thing to a machine that North Carolina has is the so-called "Shelby crowd." Shelby is the seat of Cleveland County, a textile nucleus; in the past few years the speaker of the local house, several judges both state and federal, former Governor Max Gardner and his brother-in-law Senator Clyde R. Hoey, have all come from the Shelby group. North

[7] A great local issue is of course prohibition. Recently the finance committee of the senate, after a vivid fight, voted down a proposal for a state-wide prohibition referendum. The situation has elements of the picturesque, in that the counties most eager to make the whole state dry were those most replete with illicit stills. Seventy-five of North Carolina's one hundred counties are dry at present. In the others the ABC (Alcoholic Board of Control) stores have the monopoly of the liquor traffic. Old Mr. Daniels calls these the "Alcohol Brutalizes Consumers" stores.

Carolina has not been distinguished for its federal senators lately; one almost begins to wonder if the state is so liberal after all. One senator is Josiah W. Bailey, and till recently the other was Robert R. Reynolds, founder of the American Nationalist party and a reactionary full of fustian.

I have mentioned the University of North Carolina (Chapel Hill) so often that any further word seems supererogation. Yet this institution is not only the single most noteworthy thing in the state; it is one of the best of all American universities. Here, under Frank P. Graham (who took time out during most of the war to help run the War Labor Board), the "North Carolina renaissance" has its focus; Chapel Hill really fulfills the function of a true university, in giving a spirited and pointed leadership to the whole community. "Members of my faculty can say anything they please," Mr. Graham told me, "and what I hope is that boys and girls who come here will always have an inner commitment to the freedom of the mind." His attitude is that the university belongs to *all* the people; when I was there delegates from white and Negro colleges in thirteen states met to form a "Conference of Southern Students," and elected a Negro chairman. There was no explosion, though by state law no Negro student may actually be admitted to Chapel Hill. Graham himself probably laments this. He says, "I don't have great racial consciousness myself. I obey the law." Above all he believes in his university as an "agency of the commonwealth"; what he wants is "to take it *to* the people."

Duke University at Durham near by is more conservative, but the influence of Chapel Hill is a steady leaven. Duke was, as everybody knows, once called Trinity; the stream of tobacco millions poured into it, and it changed its name; Duke has a bigger endowment now than Princeton. In physical plant, the two Carolina institutions provide the sharpest contrast. Chapel Hill looks informal, comfortable, and a bit down at the heel. Duke looks like a 1947-model chromium-plated castle; it has glittering carved paths instead of Chapel Hill's dusty shaded lanes; it maintains two separate campuses, with men and women students segregated; Chapel Hill on the other hand looks like a somewhat careless happy family. Duke is run from New York, where the trustees meet, more than from North Carolina. The two institutions collaborate quite closely, in the exchange of teachers and library facilities, and remain fierce football rivals.

Finally a footnote in another world, that of the mountaineers. Pick up a book called *The Great Smokies and the Blue Ridge*, discerningly edited by Professor Roderick Peattie and including some beautiful passages by his brother, Donald Culross Peattie.[8] The chapter that struck me most is by Alberta Pierson Hannum; it contains sections of a diary—"more

[8] Published by the Vanguard Press, New York, 1943.

tanagra than diary"—kept by an old mountaineer named Jacob Carpenter. Whenever a mountaineer in the district died, Mr. Carpenter, may he rest in peace, wrote down a brief obituary. I beg leave to quote a few:

Wm Davis age 100.8 died oc 5 1841 war old soldier in rev war and got his thie brok in last fite at kings monton he war farmer and made brandy and never had drunker in famly

Franky Davis his wife age 87 dide Sep 10 1842 she had nerve fite wolves all nite at shogar camp to save her caff throde fire chunks to save caff the camp war haf mile from home now she must have nerve to fite wolf all nite

Steven buckanen age 70 June 5 1898 he war precher babtis

Margit Ollis age 60 died July 10 1899 work on farm all of her days

South Carolina and Its Charleston

This is a case apart; South Carolina is one of the poorest of American states, and probably the balkiest. Like its big sister to the north, it has pronounced sectionalisms; the chief division is between the "low country," that is the coastal area, and the "uplands"; one might also mention a third region, the sand hills above tidewater, where poor folk called "sandlappers" live. These segmentations arise out of history as well as geography. The state was first settled in 1670, by the English, and for half a century the new arrivals hugged the coast; the sea has always meant a great deal to South Carolina, and for years little penetration of the interior took place. The first colonists thought of themselves, interestingly enough, not so much as inhabiting the southern tip of America, but the northernmost tip of the West Indies—and West Indian influence is still very distinct in Charleston to this day. "We have the finest climate in this part of the Indies," wrote one old chronicler. The back country, on its side, was settled (as in North Carolina) mostly from the north; the Scots began to filter down from Pennsylvania and Virginia. Then a Connecticut artisan named Eli Whitney invented the cotton gin. This carried the plantations, and the slave system, into the interior. A corollary item is that many early South Carolina planters hated slavery. They were free men, packed with idealism, and they strongly disapproved of slavery on moral grounds, though they lived with it.

The low country people and upland people are still at loggerheads. One reason is poor communications; nobody can quite understand this point until he tries, by rail, to cross the inland area. Charleston, on the coast, dominated everything until half a century ago; Columbia was made the capital to satisfy the hinterland. The uplands today make a kind of "cross roads society" and are spotted with industry to an extent, for instance in textile towns like Greenville and Spartanburg, across from Gastonia; Spartanburg is the home of James F. Byrnes, among other things. The "lintheads," as the mill workers are called, are among the most poverty blanched and backward folk in America. There are 38,931 homes in South Carolina without a toilet or privy.

I have mentioned that South Carolina lucklessly had one economic factor after another shot from under her. Turpentine and the trade in ship's stores declined when sail gave way to steam. Indigo, once an extremely important item, was killed by the advent of aniline dyes. Then rice, after a time, could not compete against the "highland" rice of Arkansas or Texas, where harvesting was possible by machinery; cultivation in South Carolina had to be done under water, by hand, as in Japan. Finally, Sea Island (=long staple) cotton was mostly destroyed by the boll weevil thirty years ago, and subsequent techniques in spinning made this variety of cotton less valuable than it had been before.

Perhaps I am sounding too dour a note. South Carolina, for all its poverty and ill luck, has a certain somber and shadowy magnificence. Josephine Pinckney, author of *Three O'Clock Dinner* and a descendant of one of the most irrefragably distinguished of Charleston families, wrote an article during the war to introduce the state to British readers, which is well worth quoting:

> Physically the Low Country retains its glamorous air under the scourings and sweepings of industrial change. 'Down on the salt,' as they say, the sea-islands still offer their long, palmetto-fringed beaches and their wide green marshes to the enormous sky. A little way inland the dense woods hung with grey Spanish moss, the nostalgic ruins of plantation houses destroyed by war or fire, the cypress pools of clear black water in which the herons stand like fabulous white blooms on their stalks—these trappings of the Gothic romances have their old power to stir the imagination.

Miss Pinckney proceeds to talk of Charleston, its Georgian houses so startlingly like those of London, meandering piazzas, soft walled gardens, and the memory never far away that this was a town built by the Lords Proprietor.

Charleston is in fact a gem; it is also a kind of mummy, like Savannah. I heard one unkind friend nickname it "Death on the Atlantic," and call it "a perfect example of what the South must never be again." Be this as it may, it belongs in that strange eclectic category of American "sights" not to be missed, practically like the Taos Pueblo and Niagara Falls. Once it was the fourth biggest city in America, and probably the most brilliantly sophisticated; today much of its polish has worn off, though it still retains a cardinal quality of grace. Also, a city on a narrow island between two small rivers, it has great local pride. "Charleston, sir," one of the local worthies once told a Yankee interloper, "is that untarnished jewel shining regally at that sacred spot where the Ashley and the Cooper join their majestic waters to form the Atlantic Ocean."[9] Once Charleston was known as "Capital of the Plantation"; but it is a seaport, and so has been vulnerable to the incursions of the foreign-born. The leading commercial family today derives from a group of six Sicilian brothers, who own theaters, hotels, automobile agencies, and the like; there are also Chinese, Greek, Portuguese, and Sephardic Jewish communities. Many of the great old houses are, one by one, being sold or boarded up. Some were used during the war by the Army and Navy (Charleston played an active and honorable role in war activities); some, leased by northern owners, are empty most of the year; in some the last entrenched survivors of the old society—in the main wealthy widows who inherited fortunes made on rice—still hold out.

The town keeps up, however, a considerable intellectual and social life. It has never heard of Minneapolis or Akron, of course, and is just coming to recognize Atlanta; but it has a good art gallery and a theater. It contains one of the best clubs in the country, the oldest St. Andrew Society outside Scotland, and the oldest surviving home of Scottish Rites Masonry. One Charleston editor told me that if he joined every club in town, not including secret societies and organizations like the Kiwanis, his annual dues would amount to eight hundred dollars or more. The most famous of Charlestonian social institutions, and a survival like nothing else in America except the Philadelphia Assembly, is the St. Cecilia Society which was organized in 1763. It holds (in normal times) three massive and ornate balls a year; its membership is the cream of the cream, and its etiquette super-rigidly formal; no Charleston newspaper ever prints any report of its events or invitations, and when I asked what *Life* would do if it "went" to a St. Cecilia party, the reply was, "*Life* would be thrown out on its neck." Invitations to these fabulous affairs must still be conveyed by hand, smoking is not permitted, and needless to say every young lady has a chaperone.

"Society" in Charleston lives below what the irreverent call "the Drain," that is, south of Broad Street, where the great houses are. Once an admiral in charge of Charleston Navy Yard, a native of a town about a hundred miles away, met a lady. She was impressed by his Carolina accent and proffered, "Admiral, I live in Connecticut, but I'm not a Yankee; I was born in Maryland south of the Mason and Dixon's line." The admiral calmly replied, "I, Madame, was born north of the Mason and Dixon's line—in Florence, South Carolina." The lady, puzzled, asked how that could be. "Madame," the admiral proceeded with gravity, "in my part of the world we have always been given to understand that the Mason and Dixon's line runs through Broad Street, Charleston."

[9] *Reader's Digest*, May, 1940, quoting *Collier's* magazine.

Politics in South Carolina need not concern us greatly. This is a "white supremacy" state par excellence (though it did manage to retire an atrocity like Cotton Ed Smith) ;[10] it is one of the few states (Alabama is another) where a person must have a certain amount of property to vote. Nevertheless South Carolina has a curious eruptive quality. For instance one senator, Olin D. Johnson, was once a mill hand, and the new governor, J. Strom Thurmond, a youthful war veteran, is a distinct liberal. I asked a Charleston friend why Cotton Ed Smith had not left a machine. Answer: "Because he never had one." The chief political issue today is the white primary. When the Supreme Court decided in the Texas case that Negroes could not legally be excluded from primaries, South Carolina evaded this by repealing its own electoral laws; by so doing, the pretense was put forward that the primary is purely an affair of the Democratic party, with which the state has nothing to do; hence, it is not bound to intervene if a "private organization" like the Democratic party chooses to restrict its "membership."[11]

The Negro community is, on its side, self-conscious and adult, and South Carolina is the only state in which Negroes have, in effect, sought to establish their own political party. This striking development came in 1944. Membership in this Progressive Democratic Party, as it is now called, includes whites also; that it had a considerable success was a painful shock to traditionalists. South Carolina had, incidentally, no fewer than three different "Democratic" parties in 1944: the regular organization, the Progressives, and the "southern" Democrats who wanted to bolt the Roosevelt ticket and vote for Byrd. The background of this cannot be appreciated easily without cognizance of the fact that South Carolina for many years had a Negro majority. This dwindled, however, from roughly 150,000 in 1910 to about 46,000 in 1920; numerical preponderance then passed to the whites, and the white majority today is about 227,000. But this is too narrow a margin for white comfort. I heard one doughty citizen of Charleston say, "If we could only have primaries that would eliminate 90 per cent of the Negroes, and also 50 per cent of the whites, all would be well!"

A saltily picturesque character is W. W. Ball, editor of the Charleston *News and Courier*. This veteran is accused of "not knowing yet that the War Between the States is over," and of being a "damned up-country-man"; his office is in the building where South Carolina voted for secession, and his views are idiosyncratic in the extreme; he likes

[10] Mr. Smith once walked out of a Democratic National Convention because the invocation was delivered by a Negro preacher, muttering, "Hell, he's as black as melted midnight!" Then he told his constituents, "The Negro minister was not put there to invoke divine blessing . . . He was asking for *primary* blessing." From *Public Men In and Out of Office*, p. 347-48.

[11] Cf. Stewart Alsop in the New York *Herald Tribune*, September 16, 1946. The constitutionality of this artifice is yet to be tested.

to say that he is the last surviving Jeffersonian Democrat and has "to go to my sister-in-law, a Vermonter, to find anybody who talks my language"; he recalls wistfully a half-forgotten demagogue, remarking, "He trampled on me, but I'd thank God to have him back"; he delivers himself of statements like "We white Southerners just carry the blacks on our shoulders, exactly as if they were still slaves," and "It's a pity that Mr. Lincoln didn't set the white-men free"; he likes to quote a remark, "Well, when the last cargo of niggers leaves the South, damned if you won't find me hanging onto the platform!"

Ball writes half a dozen brief editorial paragraphs daily, which are full of prejudice and pith. For instance:

> As an opponent of class legislation, the News and Courier insists that no state hospital for alcoholics shall be established and maintained at taxpayers' expense unless it shall also accept the custody of and be responsible for hoboes of all varieties. No good argument for the social security of drunks . . . can be offered.

And in April, 1945:

> The News and Courier hopes that President Truman will appoint our Mr. Byrnes secretary of state in his cabinet. We wish him to prove that he is not one of those "sectional" partisans opposed to Southern white men having a chance to be president and it would delight in seeing a deserved and sharp rebuke administered to the Harlemites . . . and boycotters of Southern white men.

The Special Entity of Florida

The singular characteristics of the great state of Florida are so well known that we can risk being brief. Visitors from the North are apt to take one look at that Heliogabaluslike organism Miami Beach, and say, "Florida isn't part of the South at all." Actually, the Peninsula State is very much part of the South; it contains not merely most of the familiar southern stigmata, but much else particularly and distinctively its own.

Florida has by far the longest seaboard of any American state which fact alone, giving it a kind of ocean culture, distinguishes it markedly. It has a history stretching far back indeed: there were 306 years between Ponce de Leon and proprietorship by the United States; St. Augustine is the oldest town in North America, having been founded in 1565. More than any other southern state except possibly Louisiana, Florida has variety; it combines an old Spanish underlay, the atmosphere of the deep South, and most important of all, a tremendous incursion from the North. For these and other reasons, it has more vitality than any southern area, with the possible exception of Tennessee in the valley region.

Consider some of the things Florida has, in various but accordant fields. Baby alligators for sale; the Seminoles who, deep in "the cypress," maintain their own so-called law, and have no treaty with the United States to this day; the great naval air base at Pensacola; sugar cane and 30,000 lakes; wonderful tarpon, sailfish, and white marlin fishing; winter headquarters for the circus and most major-league baseball teams; freakishness in everything from architecture to social behavior unmatched in any American state; aloof and benign haunts of an etiolated aristocracy at Palm Beach; two million cattle valued at 60 million dollars; the highest syphilis rate in the nation; violent quarrels between rival railroads; the bizarre excesses of the annual run of tourists from the North; political conflict between the Crackers (technically anybody born in Florida is a "Cracker," but the term has come to signify the poor whites of the interior); the Hemingway country near Key West; 328 different kinds of trees; the solidly Jewish resort towns and, until recently at least, the grisly back streets of Miami with their signs in rooming house after rooming house, GENTILES ONLY; a considerable jealousy of California in the realms of citrus fruit and of the weather; petroleum in the Everglades; Lake Okeechobee west of Palm Beach, called by local chauvinists the most fertile spot on earth; tennis players at Rollins College at Winter Park; Jacksonville and its growing importance as a port; a large proportion of the people living high for three months during the tourist season and then living very low on fish and grits the rest of the year; flamingos, hibiscus, labor goons, and the late Al Capone; an annual farm income of 300 million dollars produced on 7 per cent of the land; a substantial business in turtles, shrimp and sponges; no sales tax, no income tax, no tax on small homesteads, no state land tax, no poll tax; and above all sunshine.

Politically there are several struggles for power in Florida. One is that of the "turnstile boys," the hotel proprietors, and the "Fountain of Youth folk" against the rest of the community. Florida spends nowhere nearly as much as does California, say, or Pennsylvania on tourist propaganda; nevertheless the sum is considerable and many "Floridians" (not Floridans) resent that this should come out of taxes, as a state expense, instead of being paid for by those particularly dependent on the tourist trade. Another is, as in so many states, that between the rural and urban communities; Dade County, which contains Miami, pays 25 per cent of the entire tax bill of the state but has only one senator. The big towns— Jacksonville and Tampa as well as Miami—dislike being in an inferior position vis-à-vis the "cow counties" just as New York City hates to be at the comparative mercy of Oswego.

Florida politics can be fancy in the extreme. One point is the considerable power of the governor. Uniquely in America, sheriffs and some other county officers are subject to gubernatorial confirmation; a man may, for instance, spend a Cyclopean amount of money to get elected sheriff but he cannot assume office until the governor agrees to his appointment. A system leading more beautifully and inevitably to the possibility of graft can scarcely be imagined. Florida has fanciness, too, in other fields. Early in 1945 the Florida Power Corporation, the dominant utility in the state, was ordered by the SEC to divest itself of nine million dollars worth of stock. The power corporation officials moved into New York with "souvenir boxes of Florida fruit preserves" and in a cavalcade led by "Miss Florida of 1945" trimly caparisoned in a bathing suit.[12]

A curious item is that Florida, like California a mecca for the aged and underpossessed, has nowhere near the Golden State's share of political crackpotism. Townsend clubs do, it is true, exist, and they have at times exerted considerable local power, but they have nothing of the impact and prestige of similar groups on the west coast. One reason for this, oddly enough, is gambling. In some Florida counties, particularly in the south, gambling is by all odds the chief political force and factor. Technically gambling is illegal, but to say this is like saying that alcohol is "illegal" in Kansas or Mississippi. Miami and its environs have for years been the most explosively and pictorially gambling-dominated communities in the United States. A tremendous industry is horse racing. I happened to be in Miami when the season opened last year. The first day at Gulfstream Park brought in $805,866. The Hialeah track is of course one of the most famous in the nation. Now, by Florida law, 85 per cent of the horserace "take" goes back to the bettor; 15 per cent is distributed otherwise, of which the track gets 7, the state the other 8; of this 8 per cent, 5 per cent is earmarked for old age pensions. Similarly, the old folks get a share—but a very small share—of proceeds from the dog tracks, which are another part of the Miami saturnalia.

The total Florida income from horse racing was something like 100 million dollars in 1945, so, from this source alone, the state got eight million dollars, and the old folks five million dollars. For many years, the state's share in racing was only 10 per cent. This was raised to 15 per cent four years ago, against the stormy protests of the track interests, with the extra 5 assigned to the old and indigent. Hence, gambling in Florida supports the aged.

Miami has, of course, another and a more sober side, one aspect of which is aviation. Not only has it become one of the great international airports of the world; it is the home base of Eastern Airlines, and during the war Pan American's local pay roll was close to 25 million dollars a year. Most of the companies flying north from Miami have a service stop at Jacksonville. There is a reason for this—that Florida charges no state tax on aviation gasoline. So the big liners take on in Jacksonville all the fuel they can hold.

[12] *Life,* November 5, 1945.

The convoluted history of Miami and Miami Beach—in particular their intramural rivalries and the way the latter was created by a unique adventure in speculation—is too familiar to deal with here. What the whole community, so blessed by a lucent climate, so wonderfully picturesque and choked with such blatant incongruities, fears most today is another crash. The Florida winter of 1945-46 saw the most spectacular and savage spending in American history. Most of this came from black market money being unloaded in the so-called amusement industries. But the boom spread over into real estate too; northerners, released from the burden of war at last, free to travel, heavy with cash, fought to buy an inch of land. The story has ominous overtones of the familiar, in that exactly this kind of development took place in the 20's; then, too, vacant lots in scrubby neighborhoods sold for $25,000. In 1926 came the Florida crash; it took the state more than ten years to recover fully. I have before me a Miami *Daily News* of date May 15, 1939. In it are thirty-two solid columns of fine type listing properties sold for taxes. Most of the lots—literally thousands—went for prices like $5.43, $4.16, $7.46, and most owners were given as "unknown." The point need not be labored that responsible Floridians don't want any such catastrophe to occur again.

Finally, let us mention weather. Florida is a heaven of sunshine even more heavenly, in part, than California. Perhaps a small and old story is to the point. An eminent Chicago gangster, having succumbed to vices inherent in his trade, was to be buried not in Chicago but in Miami. A very large and imposing funeral was arranged by his Florida companions. But he rose like a jack-in-the-box from the coffin just as the burial began. Florida's sunshine had penetrated right through the heavy casket and revived him.

Chapter 43
Model TVA

vvvvvvvvvvvvvvvvvvvvvvvvvvvvvvvvvvvvvvvvvvvvvvvvvvvvvvvvvvvvvvvvvvvvvvvvvvvvvvvv

> Too little is understood about social momentum as a force in
> human affairs; I really think we have it down here.
> —David E. Lilienthal

> The South is tired of the dark.
> —Jonathan Daniels

THE most remarkable single thing about the Tennessee Valley Authority is, in a way, the quality of its acceptance. This immense and
beneficent project, the largest agency of its kind in American history,
has in its time aroused some formidable opposition. It cut across zones
as sensitive as states' rights, political patronage, and the utilities industry.
TVA still has powerful antagonists, like the aged and suffering Senator
McKellar and, since November, 1946, it faces for the first time a non-
Democratic Congress. But the fact remains that the TVA is, as it were,
there. It is an accomplished fact, and it works. As Mr. Willkie once said
a few years ago, "It doesn't matter what I think any more. You can't
tear those dams down!"

Quality of acceptance? Quantity of acceptance? For the record a few
items should be put down firmly. The TVA operates in seven southern
and border states, and the governors of several of these are, it need
not be pointed out, conservative in the extreme. All seven were asked
recently what they thought of TVA; all seven responded with vivid
pro-TVA views. The governor of Tennessee agreed that "the rights of
this state and its citizens, far from having been restricted or violated
. . . have been enlarged." Ellis Arnall of Georgia said, "The only complaint I have regarding TVA is that its influence has not permeated this
state further." Chauncey M. Sparks of Alabama said, "Conducted . . .
with vision and regard for local agencies, it has made a tremendous
contribution to public welfare." In another recent test of opinion all
newspaper editors in the region were asked to report their feelings;
every reply was favorable, out of several hundred, except three. If a
general plebiscite on TVA were taken in the valley, the pros would win
by 95 per cent, one famous—and conservative—politician told me. Early
in 1945, when the authority was under minor particularist fire in the
Senate, the St. Louis *Post-Dispatch* asked for opinions from local businessmen. The response in favor of TVA was overwhelming and unan-

imous; among those replying were one bank president, one Coca-Cola bottler, several contractors and lawyers, the president of the Tennessee Manufacturers Association, and no fewer than eleven presidents of chambers of commerce in the region.

Recently, while the Northwest was discussing the pros and cons of an authority like TVA for the Columbia, the Yakima (Washington) Chamber of Commerce wrote its fellow organization in Chattanooga. Reply of the Chattanooga Chamber of Commerce:

> There is no question but that this agency has contributed more to the economic development of the Tennessee Valley than any other single influence. . . . It is generally conceded that the establishment of TVA has accelerated the growth and progress of the region by as much as twenty-five years and possibly more. . . . This . . . has been accomplished with a minimum of political domination, control, or interference.

This from a chamber of commerce! Shades of socialism! But the reason is not far to seek:

> The power generated by TVA is sold principally to such municipal distribution systems as the Chattanooga Electric Power Board. . . . In the five and one-third years of Power Board operation, Chattanooga customers have saved $14,876,000 in their power costs, or more than the $14,000,000 invested in the system.

David E. Lilienthal came up for reappointment as chairman of TVA in the spring of 1945, at the time of Roosevelt's death; whether or not to reappoint him was Truman's first great decision, and strong pressure against Lilienthal—including threats—was put on the new president by irreconcilables like McKellar. Reaction to this in the valley area was illuminating; practically every newspaper in the region, even in the innermost precincts, anxiously urged Lilienthal's nomination. From beyond the valley too people came to his defense. I know few Americans in public life with such a copious variety of support. In New York for instance his work was commended heartily by the New York *Times* and *PM* alike, and by the *Daily News* together with the liberal weeklies and a Catholic professor in the *Sun*.

Eleven million visitors have seen TVA since its foundation, and a vast literature surrounds it; yet, in a peculiar way, it isn't quite so well known as it ought to be. At the beginning, it attracted more attention abroad than at home; the *Times* of London was greeting it as a "great American experiment" as far back as 1935. Chinese, Russian, Indian, and European experts have inspected it by the hundred; most outsiders, no matter what their nationality, grasp at once its implications to their own local scene. At bottom, there is little difference between a farmer in Alabama and one in Bihar, a hydraulic engineer in New Zealand and one in Knoxville; a professor in Chungking will like decentralization as much as one in Muscle Shoals. The point remains that Americans, it would seem, know less about TVA than non-Americans. Courses on it are given in European universities; but the American Association of University Professors has never sent a delegation to see "the greatest development in large-scale social planning" ever undertaken. During my trip for this book I met several distinguished Americans—one a musician, for instance, one an actress—who had never so much as heard of the authority. Some of my colleagues and friends in New York, like Dorothy Thompson, William L. Shirer, and Vincent Sheean, know every corner and cranny of Sweden, Poland, and Siam, but I don't think any of them have ever visited TVA.

Shorelines of the Future

A river has no politics.
—David E. Lilienthal

TVA has a meaning in several spheres. A simple limited definition would be that it is a decentralized federal project, cutting across seven states in an area as big as England and Scotland and containing about 4,500,000 people, for the harnessing of a river and development of its valley for the service of the people as a whole. The New Deal passed into history with the last congressional elections; the Tennessee Valley Authority will probably turn out to be its most permanent and enduring monument.

The Tennessee is, or was, an obstreperous angry river with an angry history; it was long called America's "worst river." It is formed by the junction of the Holston and the French Broad just above Knoxville, and the 42,000 square miles it drains include portions of Virginia, Kentucky, Alabama, Georgia, North Carolina, and Mississippi, as well as Tennessee itself; in the north, it almost touches Illinois; in the south, it dives deep into cotton country. The Powell, the Clinch, the Holston, the French Broad, the Hiwassee, the Little Tennessee pour into it, down the mountain slopes; eventually it reaches the Ohio at Paducah, and then the Ohio carries its waters on into the Mississippi. Its valley is fed by a soaking rainfall, 84 inches a year in some areas, and its tributaries charge downhill at a torrential pace. The drop is from roughly 6,000 feet to 933 (at Knoxville) in a hundred miles.

Congress set up the Tennessee Valley Authority in 1933, with intent to master this foaming Goliath. As much as any man, FDR aside, the father of the project was George Norris of Nebraska, who for almost thirty years had devoted himself to ideas for flood control on the lower Mississippi, and who sensibly thought that this should begin where the floods had their origin, i.e., in upper rivers like the Ohio and the Tennessee. Also there was a recurrent desire to make' use of the nitrogen and fertilizer plant at Muscle Shoals, Alabama, built in World War I, which had become obsolete and was lying idle. Two bills to reconvert and utilize Muscle Shoals passed Congress; Coolidge vetoed one, Hoover vetoed the other. Finally Roosevelt gave an enveloping and energizing spark to the whole idea; the concept gradually arose that flood control, Muscle Shoals, and various other factors might be combined in a single over-all development.

So TVA came into being on May 18, 1933, when Roosevelt had been in office only a few months, and while the country was still prostrate with depression. The wasteful, dangerous giant of the Tennessee was going to be put to work. Running waters were to be "made to walk," as a TVA pioneer expressed it. But from the beginning the conception went far beyond mere control of a river, though that was job enough. The great germinal and creative idea was regional development; TVA was the first real planning agency in the United States. The act not only gave TVA jurisdiction across state lines, under unified control, but "across existing lines of federal bureaus and departments."[1] A totally new principle was envisaged, that of a "seamless web," in which "one strand cannot be touched without affecting every other strand for good or ill." The act called for (a) the maximum amount of flood control; (b) the maximum development of the river for navigation purposes; (c) "the maximum generation of electric power consistent with flood control and navigation"; (d) the proper use of marginal lands, i.e., development of new agricultural techniques; (e) reforestation; and (f) "the economic and social well-being of the people living in the river basin."

A large order!

But this is not quite all. Mr. Roosevelt, in his first directive, asked that the new authority be a corporation "clothed with the power of government but possessed of the flexibility and initiative of a private enterprise." TVA was authorized to acquire real estate, to construct dams and reservoirs, to operate transmission lines, and to sell its surplus power with states, counties, and municipalities as favored buyers. Also it was to put Muscle Shoals into operation, for purposes of national defense. Perhaps we take all this for granted now; the revolutionary character of the agency, as well as its beam and bulk, is difficult to appreciate

[1] Most of these quotations are from *TVA—Democracy on the March* by David E. Lilienthal, Harper & Brothers, 1944. This is one of the best books of its kind ever written. Time and time again the commentator on TVA, trying his utmost to describe some phase of its philosophy or operation, returns to Lilienthal to find that he has already said it better. See also an admirable survey by R. L. Duffus and Charles Krutch, *The Valley and Its People*, Knopf, 1944. A first-class picture paying special attention to financial points is "A Hard Look at TVA" by C. Hartley Grattan, *Harper's Magazine*, September, 1945.

without hindsight. A British observer, writing in the *New Statesman* years ago, listed—as if catching his breath—the eleven basic aims the new development seemed to embody. I will quote four of them:

(1) An attempt to create a demand for electrical power in back-woods rural areas and the like, among poor farmers, to an extent . . . hardly dreamt of.

(2) To ensure that prices charged for electrical power by dis-tributing agencies, public and private, are reasonable instead of excessive, by providing a yardstick, in the form of economic federal prices, with which private agencies must compete, and by which their charges may be judged.

(3) To reafforest lands not really suitable for other forms of agri-culture, and to convert to pasture lands not suitable for arable farming . . . with the further purpose of preventing soil ero-sion, which is another vital problem of twentieth century America.

(4) In connection with the foregoing to re-settle poor families, white and coloured, now cultivating so called sub-marginal lands (i.e. lands which cannot now yield a reasonable return, and which ought to be returned to pasture or forest), on fresh and better tracts (such as those made available by irrigation).

The history of TVA has included brisk and lively interludes ever since passage of the act in May, 1933. A tense internal struggle led to the withdrawal of the first chairman, Dr. Arthur E. Morgan, in 1938; he was succeeded by Lilienthal, who had been a board member from the beginning. Externally, as was inevitable, the chief struggle was with the power companies; these were spearheaded by Willkie, who was then president of Commonwealth & Southern, the leading utility in the area. Lilienthal and Willkie became, as a matter of fact, good friends; they spent day after day in argument and exploration. In the end Willkie found himself in something of a cleft stick: He told Congress that he was, in effect, being expropriated, while at the same time he got an excellent bargain for his stockholders. For a time he could not "under-stand" Lilienthal; he thought that there must be "a nigger in the wood-pile" somewhere; it was almost impossible for him to conceive (this was back in the middle 30's) that a man like Lilienthal, who could easily have made twenty times his salary in a private job, cared for absolutely nothing but public service. Of course the issue outran personalities. It was basic—whether or not TVA was constitutional, whether or not it had the right to operate and sell power as it did. The federal courts finally supported TVA, which then took over the Tennessee properties of Commonwealth & Southern. Lilienthal handed Willkie a check for $78,600,000. Willkie's comment, as he put the check in his pocket, became famous: "Quite a lot of money for two middle western farm boys to be handing around."

Consider now, in purely physical terms, what TVA has done in the fourteen years since its foundation, at a total cost of about 750 million dollars. The job is incontestably the biggest in American history, from the viewpoint of sheer size. In Chapter 8 I quoted some impressive statistics about Grand Coulee. But the TVA dams as a whole used ten times the amount of material in Grand Coulee, and thirty-five times that in Boulder Dam. There are, at present, twenty-six immense dams in the TVA system, sixteen of them built by TVA.[2] The amount of concrete, earth, and rock they contain would, Director James P. Pope told me, fill a hole 10 feet in diameter straight through the earth from the United States to China; the concrete alone is two and one-half times more than was used in the entire Panama Canal; another remarkable statistic is that the amount of TVA construction since 1935 equals that of the entire railway development of the United States for a hundred years.

The best way to describe TVA in detail is to quote Lilienthal. His written work is not merely that of an engineer and administrator and a passionate but cool-headed believer in twentieth century social aims, but also that of a philosopher and poet:

> In heat and cold, in driving rain and under the blaze of the August sun, tens of thousands of men have hewed and blasted and hauled with their teams and tractors, clearing more than 175,000 acres of land, land that the surface of the lakes now covers . . .
>
> The work of the builders has made of the river a highway that is carrying huge amounts of freight over its deep watercourses. . . . Huge modern towboats, powered by great Diesel engines, move up and down the channel, pushing double columns of barges, and the cargo is no longer limited to raw materials. Billets of steel and cotton goods come from Birmingham, grain from Minneapolis, millions of gallons of gasoline, oil, machinery, merchandise . . .
>
> Quiet cotton towns of yesterday are now busy river ports. . . . Millions of dollars have been invested and thousands of jobs created as new grain elevators, flour mills, and oil terminals have been erected along the river's banks. At Decatur in Alabama, on land where a few years ago farmers were raising corn and cotton, now newly built ocean-going vessels go down the ways into "Wheeler Lake" and thence to their North Atlantic job.
>
> And on these same lakes are thousands of new pleasure craft of every kind—costly yachts, sailboats, homemade skiffs. Nine thousand miles of shoreline—more than the total of the seacoast line of the United States on the Atlantic, the Pacific, and the Gulf of Mexico— are available for the recreation of the people. . . .

[2] Five belong to Alcoa, and are operated by a co-operative arrangement. TVA has complete jurisdiction over matters of flood control and the like. The other five were acquired by TVA.

Lilienthal was born in a small town in Illinois in 1899; he went to Harvard Law School, and then practiced law in Chicago until 1931, when he became a member of the Wisconsin Public Service Commission. He was only thirty-four when, in 1933, Roosevelt put him on the original TVA triumvirate. To say that he has been heart, brain, and soul of the institution ever since would be an exaggeration, since in a curious way TVA has a special heart, soul, and brain all its own; but certainly without Lilienthal it would be less today than what it is.

That TVA helped make the atom bomb is known to everybody; the great city plant at Oak Ridge, Tennessee, utterly without existence in 1941 and now one of the most interesting communities in the United States, was of course dependent on TVA power, just as Hanford, Washington, was dependent on Grand Coulee.[3] So it was natural for Lilienthal's name to be considered when the future and peacetime use of atomic energy became a pressing national issue. First he became chairman of the State Department's atomic energy committee and, as such, was largely responsible for drawing up the Acheson-Lilienthal Report, early in 1946. This document became the bedrock of American atomic policy; out of it came the Baruch recommendations to the United Nations. A few months later President Truman created the Atomic Energy Commission of the United States and made Lilienthal its chairman. There is certainly no more important position in the nation, and Mr. Truman could not have made a more appropriate choice.[4] Among other things the commission is exclusively empowered to supervise and conduct atomic research, to license operations on all fissionable materials, to make atom bombs for the armed forces, to regulate use of all plutonium and uranium in the country, to distribute atomic material for medical or other use, and to control the "dissemination of secret information."

So many Americans become spoiled or destroyed by money, by abuse of the acquisitive instinct. Lilienthal is a poor man, who had two children to educate, but he seems to have absolutely no interest in money as such. He is tall, spare, muscular, industrious, and has a manner at once direct and shy. Long before he took the atom job, he wrote that mankind had a fundamental choice: to use science either for good or evil. A person of deep liberal conviction, he believes that "men *can* make themselves free," and that "democracy is a literal impossibility without faith that on balance the good in men far outweighs the evil."

[3] TVA personnel kept the Oak Ridge secret marvelously well. Almost everywhere else in the country where activity on the bomb was intense, a visitor would hear vague (and quite harmless) whispering; but not in the Tennessee area. The first hint to outsiders that something very big was going on came when newspaper editors in other regions noticed that the Knoxville papers seemed to be getting an abnormally large amount of newsprint.

[4] Lilienthal's appointment must of course be confirmed by the new Senate.

Another clue to his thought is his belief that "the real revolution of our time, the dominant political fact of the generation that lies ahead," is that people all over the world will demand for themselves the fruits of technology applied to natural resources. "No longer do men look upon poverty as inevitable, nor think that drudgery, disease, filth, famine, floods, and physical exhaustion are visitations of the devil or punishment by a deity. Here is the central fact with which statesmanship tomorrow must contend."

Lilienthal was succeeded as chairman of TVA by Gordon R. Clapp, for some years its general manager. This was a good career appointment. For a time it was thought that Bob La Follette (who gave Lilienthal his first public job) might get the post; this would have been a good appointment too. The other board members today are former Senator Pope of Idaho, and the venerable Dr. Harcourt A. ("H.A.") Morgan, who has been a TVA director since its inception. Morgan, Canadian born, was formerly president of the University of Tennessee; he is a specialist in the philosophy of agriculture, and he and Lilienthal formed an inseparable partnership. "I'm two years older than his father," Dr. H.A. likes to say. "Why, from the moment we started this thing together, I tucked his shirttails in."

The Range of Accomplishment

This is very wide, and a great many factors come into play. The first and simplest thing to say is that TVA raised the income level of the 3,225,000 people in the valley proper by something like 75 per cent in ten years, as against a national increase of 56 per cent. Compare some present figures with those of 1933. Wages went up 57 per cent as compared with 47 per cent for the rest of the nation, retail sales 63 per cent as against 47, value of manufactured products 68 as against 54, and wholesale trade 80 as against 46 per cent.

One specific element is rural electrification, and a proportionate advance in the urban use of electricity. Some 125,000 valley farms are now electrified, and Chattanooga and Knoxville are like Portland and Seattle; cheap rates have made electric current available in unprecedented quantities. Other very big items are the new 650-mile navigation channel and the network of "soil clinics" and 29,000 demonstration farms. Still others are introduction of a cheap new hay drier, a tremendous boom in fishing, the development of a tannin industry, following laboratory research on waste products from timber mills, and the planting of about 150 million trees. Or consider such a factor as malaria control. Malaria in the region, once a menace, has been virtually wiped out. This was done partly by conventional airplane spraying, partly through a wonderfully ingenious system whereby the water level is temporarily but sharply reduced along the lake rims, which leaves the mosquito eggs high and dry, and kills the larvae.

Consider too another factor—education. TVA is a kind of university; its whole staff is a research faculty. The curse of most universities is departmentalism and segmentation. But TVA, which has a central philosophy, based on the broad unifying force of a single idea, is something different; also it co-operates fully with most laboratories and institutions of learning in the region and in particular the land-grant colleges. Georgia Tech is doing research in clays (for aluminum production); the University of Tennessee on kitchen appliances (including a small portable flour mill) and on new electrical devices for farms; Tuskegee on cheap vegetable paint; others on articles as varied as laminated flooring and briquets out of sawdust.

TVA has also promoted an interesting library development. It wanted to get books out to its workers on the dams, and worked with the near-by county authorities to do so; out of this, as construction moved up and down the rivers, came mobile library units—the bookmobiles. The influence of these on isolated rural communities can scarcely be over-estimated; in 1940 one area of twelve counties had no books at all; now it has 52,000. One Tennessee county, Meigs, with a population of six thousand, has no railroad, no telephone, and no newspaper. This in twentieth century America! But it does have the TVA-inspired libraries and bookmobiles. "The bookmobile and the grapevine are our only means of communication," one Meigs citizen wrote Lilienthal. "If we lose the bookmobile, how will we know what is going on in the world? Talk about country people not reading! In Meigs county we read 4,000 books a month"—thanks to TVA.

Then look at flood control, perhaps the most dramatic of all manifestations of authority activity. Recall the 1937 floods, which made a million people homeless in the Ohio and Mississippi valleys; or think back to those of 1943, which inundated four million acres of land in Illinois, Missouri, Arkansas, and Indiana, and ruined 160,000 homes. Such catastrophes would be almost impossible on the Tennessee, now that TVA's great dam-network is complete; they are a danger almost as remote as an epidemic of bubonic plague. In January, 1946, occurred one of the great floods of the river's history, but the new dams held the flow; there was no disaster; the river had become the pliable servant of man, not its master.

Again, let Lilienthal tell the story:

In the winter of 1942 torrents came raging down this valley's two chief tributaries, in Tennessee and Virginia. Before the river was controlled this would have meant a severe flood; the machinery of vital war industries down the river at Chattanooga would have stopped, under several feet of water, with over a million dollars of direct damage resulting.

But in 1942 it was different. Orders went out from the TVA office of central control to every tributary dam. The message came flashing to the operator in the control room at Hiwassee Dam, deep in the mountains of North Carolina: "Hold back all the water of the Hiwassee River. Keep it out of the Tennessee." The operator pressed a button. Steel gates closed. The water of that tributary was held. To Cherokee Dam on the Holston went the message: "Keep back the flow of the Holston." To Chickamauga Dam just above the industrial danger spot at Chattanooga: "Release water to make room for the waters from above."

. . . Reports came in from hundreds of remote rain-gauge stations, telephoned in by a farmer's wife, a crossroads store merchant, a woodsman. From well-nigh inaccessible mountain streams ingenious TVA-made devices send in their reports by short-wave radio without human intervention. . . .

Day by day till the crisis was over the men at their control instruments at each dam in the system received their orders. The rate of water release from every tributary river was precisely controlled. The Tennessee was kept in hand.

All of this is important—very. All of it should be stimulating and heartening. But we have not touched the heart of the story yet. The heart of TVA is not a river at all, but soil; not techniques in electric power or navigation but in agriculture.

TVA, Soil, and Life

First I went to Norris, to see the beautiful dam there, one of the earlier colossi, and then to Fontana, where the newest dam was just being completed; I flew to Muscle Shoals, and saw the chemical establishments. Everywhere I went, my guides talked mostly about agriculture and the soil and, above all, Dr. Harcourt Morgan did his best to explain these mysteries.

In this atomic age the Einstein formula, $E = mc^2$, is well known; it means that energy equals mass multiplied by the square of the speed of light. Not so well known is another formula equally important to the valley: $nCO_2 + nH_2O = (CH_2O)n + nO_2$. Which means that carbon dioxide and water plus oxygen combine to produce the life of plants.

The case might easily be made that the most important single thing in the world is chlorophyll. This is the green coloring matter in plants, as every school child knows; it has never been synthesized, and it is in conjunction with chlorophyll that the foregoing formula works. A plant lives on carbon dioxide in the air together with moisture in the earth, but this process is dependent on chlorophyll, which is a kind of mysterious catalyst imprisoning the energy of the sun. It transforms solar light into agriculture, i.e., life; sunshine is captured by the green of leaves. Thus a plant grows—like grass—and becomes beef, eggs, milk, and man.

No living thing, animal or vegetable, can live without air, water, soil. Air and water are inexhaustible; but soil is not. We may think of soil as simple dirt; actually, it is one of the most highly complex of substances. In effect soil is life; certainly its character may determine the quality of life. That it behooves us to conserve soil is well known; equally well known is our reckless and prodigal waste of soil, this most basic and irreplaceable of all commodities. Soil has several enemies, of which man is one, and another water. Mother Earth is like "eternal" snow; apply water, and "she" will melt. In a thousand areas in the United States today water is slowly, silently, eating away the life blood of the people. In the Tennessee Valley the average rainfall is 52 inches; this means that six thousand tons of water per year fall on each acre of land, and the cultivatable top soil of this land only weighs about one thousand tons itself; nothing can stand up against such extreme odds, without help. The water, falling on the land, ruins the land, and the land in turn, flowing out into the rivers, ruins the rivers. What TVA stands for, in a word, is reversal of this process. What it seeks above all is to capture and utilize all the lost and wasted energy, to put the forces of nature back in harmony. Capture and make use of all that errant water! Capture and make use of chlorophyll, plants, and soil!

This is the chief essence of TVA. Its real meaning is man and nature working together to restore life to land.

Now another item: consider phosphates. Every plant lives not only on sun and water, but on rock; 2 to 5 per cent of every living thing is mineral. Thus to produce a healthy agriculture (= life), soil must have a healthy mineral content. For reasons which we need not go into here, most types of soil lack phosphate among necessary minerals. Phosphate rock deposits are found, however, only in a few areas of the country; 80 per cent of all American soil is deficient in it. One aim of TVA (and other agencies) is to remedy these and other insufficiencies by the scientific development of a substitute in the form of a phosphate fertilizer.[5]

Let erosion continue at its present rate, and the United States will not be able to feed itself in fifty years. For food (= fuel) the 140,000,000 people of this country, plus its livestock population, need the equivalent of 800,000 tons of coal per day, or something over five trillion calories.

When TVA came in there were counties in the valley more than half destroyed by erosion; some few spots were totally destroyed. The authority has so far saved something like three million acres; millions

[5] But so far as TVA is concerned the idea is not merely to get a bigger crop or put more money into the farmer's pocket; it is to correct and remedy a *fundamental* soil weakness throughout a region.

more will be saved in time. "The gullies are being healed, the scars of erosion are on the mend." The small terraces on small hillside farms are a work of engineering exactly comparable to the monumental dams; both seek to avoid peril from water, and each puts live water to fruitful work.

Lilienthal's own words about the general philosophy behind this are the following:

There is a grand cycle in nature. The lines of those majestic swinging arcs are nowhere more clearly seen than by following the course of electric power in the Tennessee Valley's way of life. Water falls upon a mountain slope six thousand feet above the level of the river's mouth. It percolates through the roots and the sub-surface channels, flows in a thousand tiny veins, until it comes together in one stream, then in another, and at last reaches a TVA lake where it is stored behind a dam. Down a huge steel tube it falls, turning a water wheel. Here the water's energy is transformed into electricity, and then, moving onward toward the sea, it continues on its course, through ten such lakes, over ten such water wheels. Each time, electric energy is created. That electricity, carried perhaps two hundred miles in a flash of time, heats to incredible temperatures a furnace that transforms inert phosphate ore into a chemical of great possibilities. That phosphatic chemical, put upon his land by a farmer, stirs new life in the land, induces the growth of pastures that capture the inexhaustible power of the sun. Those pastures, born of the energy of phosphate and electricity, feed the energies of animals and men, hold the soil, free the streams of silt, store up water in the soil. Slowly the water returns into the great man-made reservoirs, from which more electricity is generated as more water from the restored land flows on its endless course.

Such a cycle is restorative, not exhausting. It gives life as it sustains life. The principle of unity has been obeyed, the circle has been closed. The yield is not the old sad tale of spoliation and poverty, but that of nature and science and man in the bounty of harmony.

I visited several demonstration farms, and marveled. One had been "uncovered" five years ago; its land was steadily washing away, right down to the barren clay. My guide, W. M. Landess, an eloquent man who had seen it all from the beginning, kept murmuring, "What a transformation!" The neat terraced fields, once deserted, were growing corn; the nontilled land was resting; part was "under cover" with soil-protecting and water-holding crops, like crimson clover. Before TVA came in, the farmer had simply retreated, year by year, before the marching forces of erosion; now he is attacking. The back part of his 125 acres had been abandoned; it grew only "poverty-land" crops like sassafras. Now it's producing hogs and beef. "If only I could convey it to you!" he exclaimed.

No farmer in the area is obliged thus to improve himself. The TVA has no authority—or desire—to coerce. A demonstration farm is strictly a volunteer proposition. What happens is that a group of farmers get together (if they so wish) and meet with the county agent; the TVA field man is at their disposal, to give technical advice and to furnish superphosphate free. The idea is, "You organize your community, pick an area for demonstration, and let us help." Farmers were reluctant to co-operate at first. Then they saw what happened—just as Iowa farmers, suspicious of hybrid corn at first, became quickly converted when they realized what hybrid was doing for their neighbors.

Here are some comparative figures, furnished me by Director Pope, covering various items in Limestone County, Alabama:

	1933	1943
Acres terraced with power equipment	0	47,500
Acres terraced, all sources	11,500	91,357
Acres of pasture improved	351	5,986
Acres small grains planted	2,297	113,677
Tons of lime used	450	49,723
Tons of 16% superphosphate used	160	13,580
Value of legume seed saved	$330	$306,570

At Fontana, F. C. Schlemmer, the project manager who built the fourth biggest dam in the world and the biggest in America east of the Rockies practically with his own two hands, took us around; he loves Fontana as Major Hutton loves Grand Coulee. Schlemmer was one of the first six men hired by TVA; this is the kind of public servant the country should be proud of. Once he left the authority briefly to take a $25,000 job with a private company; he came back because life without TVA, where his salary is a great deal less, seemed literally meaningless.

I will not describe the Fontana dam itself, because we have looked at dams in this book several times before. It weighs more than eight million tons; but it is so sensitive to various pressures that it will tilt one-quarter of an inch upstream when the sun strikes the downstream side. What interested me most was the housing situation. Here, deep in the uninhabited Smokies, in an inaccessible mountain fastness, 3,700 workers had to be housed. I remembered the slovenly huts like a line of scum around the California war industries, the unspeakable wretched hovels near Detroit, Chicago, and Atlanta. TVA does things differently. I had a foretaste when, coming up the road, two trucks each containing half a prefabricated house complete down to doors and bathrooms, drove past. Instead of a car passing a house, a house passed a car!

TVA builds several types of prefabricated house; one costs $2,200 to build, and rents at $27 per month, and I have seldom seen anything more serviceable or comfortable. The houses come in two sections (of TVA's own design), and are demountable; they contain a living room-dining room, a bedroom, kitchen, and bath. Most of the furniture, like the bed, is built in; on delivery the house has lights in the closets, screened doors, and insulated cupboards, as well as electric hot water. The villages made by a cluster of these houses are strikingly compact and functional; the houses fit together as if the whole community were prefabricated; for instance drugstore, bank, and beauty shop are all of a piece.

The area around Muscle Shoals is as different from Fontana as can be imagined. Here is flat and torpid cotton country. When it was thought that Henry Ford would take over the old nitrogen plant after World War I, a real estate development began; property was sold at crazy prices until the crash came, and paved sidewalks and lampposts still stretch into a deserted wilderness. So Muscle Shoals is probably the only point in the world where you can shoot quail and other game from concrete pavements.

Muscle Shoals exists not merely for the valley, but for the nation; its fertilizer is distributed everywhere. It makes phosphates, ammonium nitrate and (during the war at least) calcium carbide for synthetic rubber; it is one of the biggest industrial operations owned by the American government.

A final common denominator about TVA is the simple tablet that each of its units wears: BUILT FOR THE PEOPLE OF THE UNITED STATES.

Power Companies, Taxes, and the Opposition

Power, we should realize by now, is not the main gist of TVA, but power is the issue its enemies usually seize on, on the assumption that it is most vulnerable in this direction, hoping thus to draw a curtain over its achievements in other fields. In the public mind it is ordinarily thought of as predominantly, or even exclusively, a power project, which it is not. Nevertheless power is a very important element in the organization, since its sale pays the bills. TVA is, in fact, the biggest power-producing system in America; the only private company that runs it close is at Niagara. It sold 35 million dollars worth of power in the 1946 fiscal year, to eighty-five cities and forty-six co-operatives, with a net income around 16 million dollars. It does not, of course, sell electricity retail; like Bonneville, which was patterned on TVA and which we have already inspected, it simply transfers power to a local community, which then distributes to the public. TVA electricity covers about a quarter of Alabama, a third of Mississippi, one-tenth of Georgia, a quarter of Kentucky, virtually all of Tennessee, and small areas in North Carolina and Virginia.

The competing private systems are controlled by Commonwealth & Southern (which still operates in Georgia, Alabama and Mississippi, as well as Indiana and Ohio). In a sense the situation has been stabilized, and the frontiers defined. TVA has, of course, served to drive rates down, just as public power in the Northwest drove rates down; in areas where TVA and private power exist side by side, there is virtually no difference in rates; in places more remote, private rates, though much lower than they were, are still 10 per cent or more higher. It is when you compare TVA rates with those of a community totally outside the valley that you see the difference; I gave an illustration of this in Chapter 12. Another, closer home, shows what people in Memphis pay for power (under TVA) as compared to those in an Arkansas town just across the river, Marianna, which the authority doesn't touch, and which is served by Arkansas Power & Light:

Kwh per month	25	40	100	250	500
Memphis	$0.75	$1.20	$2.50	$5.00	$ 6.90
Marianna	1.58	2.10	3.95	7.58	10.08

Also, exactly like Bonneville in the Northwest, TVA has greatly stimulated the use of power. At .0178¢ per kwh (as against a national average of .0331¢) more people can afford to buy; the private companies of course benefit from this, and make more money. For instance the two biggest utilities adjoining TVA were ordered in 1944 by their state public service commissions to make rate reductions of roughly $1,400,000, and to refund not less than $1,500,000 chiefly to domestic consumers, because of "prospective high federal income and excess profits taxes." The Ford principle, that the cheaper you make a good commodity the greater will be your returns to a point, applies as always to most *new* industrial undertakings.

But opposition to TVA by the private utilities remains fierce and ineradicable; again, the story closely parallels that in the Northwest. One utility executive told me that what he objected to most was TVA's "glamor"; he thought that a prosaic businessman shouldn't have to compete with anything so "romantic." This is puzzling; the serious ground for opposition is of course that TVA is akin to socialism, and extremely effective socialism at that. The power companies no longer play politics in the region quite as they used to. To go back a bit, Southwestern Gas & Electric helped finance Huey Long, and Bilbo once made the press agent of Mississippi Power & Light president of the University of Mississippi.[6]

But elsewhere in the United States the power lobby is as active as it ever was; consider evidence from the "Electric Hour" on the radio to propaganda agencies like that of the Hofer Company in Oregon which

[6] Raymond Swing, *Forerunners of American Fascism*, pp. 104, 115.

reaches thousands of American publications with anti-TVA handouts. Nobody can write an article in any national magazine, even one of such stature as the *Atlantic* or *Harper's*, that even remotely touches TVA or the power issue, without getting some kind of reply, from the Edison Electric Institute up or down. For example, when I began writing this book, an amiable spokesman of an advertising agency representing a power company immediately got in touch with me. This is a very minor point. I mention it because the power lobby was the *only* pressure group in the country to pay any attention to what I was doing or what I hoped to do.

The most effective opposition TVA has had recently came in Kentucky. Here, after several attempts, a "ripper bill" reached the legislature which, if passed, would have prevented cities and municipalities from buying TVA power. The president of the Kentucky Utilities Company "admitted frankly that the bill had been prepared by the company" (New York *Times,* February 16, 1946); this is an example of a kind of *direct* political activity becoming rare. A great many respectable Kentucky institutions—none of which particularly wants high rates for electricity —came vigorously to TVA's defense, and the bill was beaten.

TVA officials themselves deny that they oppose the interests of private industry in any way. The authority has worked closely with Alcoa from the beginning; it worked with dozens of business enterprises at Oak Ridge. Once again, Lilienthal phrases the issue best: "The TVA . . . has sought . . . to harmonize the private interest in earning a return from resources with the public interest in their unified and efficient development . . . and to make affirmative action in the public interest both feasible and appealing to private industry." At any rate Tennessee itself, the heart of the institution, sees little dangerous or subversive in it. It was Boss Crump himself who triumphantly brought TVA into Memphis, and Tennessee advertisements in national magazines, designed to invite business into the state, use the slogan THE FIRST PUBLIC POWER STATE.

Finally, taxes. As in the case of Bonneville, the cry is raised that TVA doesn't pay any taxes, and so has an enormous and unfair advantage over the private companies. This is not true, though it is true that TVA pays no federal taxes as such since it is owned by the federal taxpayers and its entire income is the property of the federal government. In 1945, its net income represented 45 per cent of its gross power revenues. This income went of course to the government, exactly as if it were a tax, and an additional point to make is that this percentage of return to the government is considerably greater than the average return of the private companies; for instance in 1944 the utility companies of the country paid in taxes only about 23.8 per cent of their total operating revenue. Then consider state and local taxes. TVA *does* pay these—most distinctly; this is almost always ignored by private utility propaganda, but it is a simple matter of recorded fact. Technically (because no federal agency is obliged to pay local taxes) these payments are described as being "in lieu of taxes"; they are taxes nevertheless and the amounts are quite substantial. For instance in 1944, TVA paid state and county governments $2,168,824, which was $790,311 *more* than the former ad valorem taxes on these properties; in 1945 the corresponding figures were $2,137,484 and $762,127.

Another allegation in this realm is that TVA "doesn't pay for itself," that its accounts are juggled to conceal "operation at a loss." This is far from being true, and the charge can be made only by someone who willfully neglects to mention how its costs are allocated. Final note: the utility companies, before mentioning such matters, might well look into their own books. In 1943-45 inclusive they earned enough money (by charging rates high enough) to pay an average of 180 million dollars per year in *excess profits* taxes.

Esprit de Corps

The greatest thing about TVA is something I haven't specifically mentioned yet but which is implicit all along—the factor of morale. Never in the United States or abroad have I encountered anything more striking than the faith its men have in their work. To explain this we may list several factors:

(1) The quality of personnel is very high. TVA picks its employees with as scrupulous care as any corporation; its standards are at least as high as those, say, of the United States Steel Corporation or, in a different field, the University of Chicago or Harvard University.[7] At the beginning, its men were hired during the deepest pitch of the depression; hence, it was able to pick the cream of the national crop among engineers and the like.

(2) Autonomy. TVA makes its own decisions, and makes them promptly. It is in first and last analysis subject, of course, to control by Congress, but in the field and in day-to-day administration it is wholly its own boss. Nobody has to ask permissions from a distant bureaucracy in Washington. Nobody breathes down anybody else's neck.

(3) Decentralization, a point that needs important emphasis. TVA is very big; also it is very small, in that every unit has its roots in the immediate local problem. Americans, in general, dislike remote control; they appreciate having things close to home; TVA is run by men actually in the field and on the spot.

(4) No interference with private business interests. TVA spreads the socializing concept, but it doesn't threaten anybody. There is no attempt

---

[7] In point of fact the first TVA personnel director was a University of Chicago professor.

to dominate. Nobody in the valley thinks it has a foot behind the door. Man and nature work together; so do government and private property.

(5) No politics. This factor is absolute and paramount. All TVA appointments are on the exclusive basis of merit and experience; there are no political jobs of any kind; patronage does not exist, and no employee may undertake any political activity at any time.

(6) Above all, the nature of the job. People are happy because they are doing something creative, something bigger than themselves. You cannot legislate morale; you cannot impose from above the kind of loyalty TVA gets from almost every worker.

Coda: What Next for TVA?

The phase of major construction is coming to an end, but in the larger sphere TVA's work, after fourteen years, is just beginning. The plant is there; now should come the period of full use. Consider one detail only. When the authority came in, 3 per cent of valley farms were electrified; the figure today is 24 per cent; but this means that there is still 76 per cent to go. Similar expansion is possible, and is in fact impending, in such fields as dispersal of small industry, forest conservation, and research on almost every branch of agriculture.

The future of TVA is of course more TVA's, in the pattern sketched in this book several times. We have talked about the Columbia and the Missouri; an even more pressing case might be made for the Arkansas. TVA is not, Lilienthal says, a "cookie cutter," and different rivers may need different methods; but the idea is there for anybody to pick up and use. The range of the concept is indeed almost boundless; it knows no barriers except the selfishness of man, and its horizon could be illimitable. It proves that the idea of unified development works, that national resources can be developed with politics excluded and without prejudice to private enterprise.

It *can* be done. What more should one legitimately ask? Quite possibly the TVA idea is the greatest single American invention of this century, the biggest contribution the United States has yet made to society in the modern world.

Chapter 44

More About Tennessee, Plus Arkansas

~~~~~~

> . . . And evening folded on Tennessee.
> —John Galsworthy

THE case of Mr. Crump is something tart and special. This is a boss in the grand manner—the last of the great city bosses to function unimpaired in the United States.

Actually, Crump is more than just a city boss; he not only runs Memphis, he runs the state of Tennessee. His closely notched machine has always had more than the merely metropolitan importance of Pendergast in Kansas City or Kelly-Nash in Chicago. Boss Hague once dominated most of New Jersey as well as Jersey City, but as we know the November 1946 elections seriously bit into his statewide influence. Crump alone, among the old-style bosses, is still a constringent power on a city, county, state, and indeed a national level.

Two fine old Negroes heard some time ago that the Pope had died.

"Who was he?" one asked the other.

"Oh, a big fellow very important—in a county east o' heah."

"He died, you say? Who do you reckon Mr. Crump is goin' to put in his place?"

How does E. H. ("Ed") Crump run Tennessee? The answer could not be simpler. First, the state is usually Democratic by two to one; the total vote runs about 400,000 of which some 260,000 is normally Democratic; in other words, to win any Tennessee election, all you need is something over 130,000 votes. Of these, Crump has 100,000. So, in effect, he "spots" any candidate he favors with this solid overwhelming mass of voting power. Sixty thousand of Crump's 100,000 votes are concentrated in Shelby County,[1] of which Memphis is the county seat. Time and time again opposition candidates are well ahead until the Shelby vote is counted; they "come in up to Shelby" as the phrase is; then the great Memphis vote drowns them under. Technically, Crump controls this through the kind of organization and behavior familiar in several American cities, but Memphis, 41 per cent Negro, is a special case; it has the largest proportionate Negro population of any southern city. Tennessee is not a white primary state, and the Negro vote is consequently of very considerable value; Crump has controlled it for years,

---

[1] Of course not to be confused with the Shelby in North Carolina.

absolutely. Tennessee is, on the other hand, most distinctly a poll-tax state, and the poll tax is, as we shall see, the chief single element serving to perpetuate the Crump regime.

Beyond all this is much else: Mr. Crump has famous exoteric and esoteric methods. He doesn't, I heard it said, "go in for any rough stuff except in a very nice way," but whether this is true or not depends on your definition of the good word "rough." Suppose, like Edward W. Carmack,[2] in 1946, you are running against a Crump candidate, who in this instance happened to be McKellar. You will find several obstacles in your path, to put it mildly. For one thing, Mr. Crump will buy advertisements in most of the state's newspapers at considerable cost, in which he will call you anything from a "donkey" to a "vulture," with assorted adjectives like "cruel," "treacherous," and "venomous," and will say that you have "no more right to public office than a skunk has to be foreman in a perfume factory." You will find, as Mr. Carmack did, that you can find no arena or other site in downtown Memphis available for speech-making, and that no printer will dare make your campaign posters.[3]

Beyond this, Crump has other powers. He controls federal and state patronage completely, and all state employees are expected to contribute 10 per cent of their salaries to the campaign, while it is going on. Also, citizens like insurance agents, road contractors, liquor dealers, automobile agents, and the like, if they have any business with Memphis or the state, may be called upon for contributions. Then, of course, Crump controls all municipal employees, though he holds no public office at the moment. Memphis distributes its own electricity, water, and gas; therefore the number of city employees at the service of the machine is considerable. The organization works hard and well. Among other things it maintains a card catalogue of every voter in the county.

Let no one doubt the concrete blistering efficacy of all this. In 1936, Gordon Browning, running for governor with Crump's backing, won Shelby County by 60,000 votes. They fell out, and two years later Crump opposed him when he ran for re-election. Browning then *lost* Shelby County by 60,000 votes!

In a more personal field Mr. Crump does things with real zest. He donates boat rides to cripples and shut-ins, organizes opossum hunts for the faithful, and gives a prodigious annual picnic at the fair grounds; at a recent one he distributed—free—30,000 frankfurters and 1,600 gallons of lemonade. He loves to roam around with firecrackers in his pocket, which he tosses to the children, under pennants and banners streaming with the words THANK YOU, MR. CRUMP!

[2] Mr. Carmack's father was a famous Tennessee editor, who was murdered in Nashville in 1908 by a political opponent. The tradition of political violence in Tennessee is, as in Kentucky, never far away.

[3] See a series of columns by Thomas L. Stokes in the Scripps-Howard papers, July, 1946.

MISSISSIPPI
VALLEY
SOUTH

Not long ago a well-known young attorney who was running for the legislature went to an outing given by one of Crump's cronies; he happened to be playing gin rummy when it was announced that all guests would join up in soft-ball teams. The young man, not dreaming that he was committing political suicide, said lightly, "When the boss says you gotta do something, you gotta do it." This remark was reported back, and incredible as it may seem, the would-be legislator was compelled to resign his candidacy and in fact soon found Memphis so uncomfortable that he moved to Nashville. Crump is very sensitive about being a boss; the legislator's remark was not only considered to be *lèse-majesté*, but also an intrusion into the forbidden. The fact that the wretched creature apologized, saying "I didn't realize what I had said," made no difference. One of the Crump lieutenants dismissed the whole episode by announcing, "Our friend made a mistake; he can now go on his way." Such magnanimity!

Of course the Crump machine could not exist unless it did "deliver the goods." The boss is very responsive to public opinion; he watches carefully what people want. A minor instance of this is that, the day I met him, he had spent the entire morning in the Memphis streetcars, riding up and down as an ordinary passenger, because he wanted to check on complaints about inefficiency. There is no doubt that Crump has given Memphis good government at low cost; the city has admirable public services cheap. This is no Kansas City. There is no graft, no corruption; Crump has never taken a cent from the public treasury, nor will he permit anybody else to do so. Gambling is abolished, and crime has been cut down; Memphis is one of the few big cities with no policy or numbers racket, and prostitutes have been driven out. But on this general topic of "good government," more anon.

One must not distort the picture. Crump is relentless, yes, if anybody really gets under his skin; once an entire county was redistricted to get rid of a magistrate he didn't like; once the legislature went to the length of writing specific legislation purely to embarrass one of his enemies. Yet the great majority of citizens feel no threat to their liberties civil or otherwise; there is no atmosphere of tension or reprisal; people, by and large, get along. One of Crump's most consistent critics, on good and legitimate grounds, has been Edward J. Meeman, who has ably edited the *Press-Scimitar* for many years. Crump writes fantastically vituperative letters to him, signed with a giant floriferous scrawl, but Meeman has never been threatened or otherwise interfered with.[4]

[4] One of these letters began, "Your stupidity at times defeats the cold cruelty and cunning evil with which you seek to inject [*sic*] in your news articles and editorials." Meeman replied by printing it. The other Memphis paper, the *Commercial Appeal*, is more cautious in its attitude to Crump. Incidentally Memphis is the only American city in which Scripps-Howard, owning both papers, is a monopoly. The *Commercial Appeal* is, however, the only Scripps-Howard paper that does not use the organization's lighthouse insignia on its masthead.

Crump, aged 72, looks like three apples. He is a very tall lean man, and under a streaming mop of pure white, cotton-wool hair, his hard, round, red cheeks stand out like apples and so does the hard, round, red chin. He is a vegetarian (shades of Hitler and Mussolini!), and doesn't swear, drink or smoke. He is president of E. H. Crump & Company, investment bankers, one of the most prosperous real estate and insurance firms in the South. There has never been any whisper or intimation that the company mixes in politics improperly; its reputation is, and always has been, impeccable. Members of the business community in the Memphis area may be asked for campaign contributions, but there is no evidence that Crump himself ever applies pressure to sell insurance. But it is only natural that people in and around Memphis with real estate to sell or insurance to buy should think that the Crump firm is an excellent one with which to do business.

The Red Snapper

Edward Hall Crump was born in a Mississippi village in 1875; the family came from Virginia originally, and has traces of Scottish and Norwegian ancestry. His mother died at the age of 97. Crump, after working as a farmhand, moved to Memphis when he was seventeen to make his way in the world; soon he organized the E. H. Crump Buggy & Harness Company, and then branched out into real estate. He was about twenty-six when he first went into politics; he was redheaded in those days, and gained the nickname "the red snapper." He was elected to several minor municipal posts, and in 1909 became mayor of Memphis. His hold on the city has never slackened since; for almost forty years it has been his to do with almost as he chose. Does everybody know the song "Memphis Blues"? Actually, this ditty, written by W. C. Handy, the well-known Negro musician, was originally called "The E. H. Crump Blues"; it was written for Crump and dedicated to him, as a marching song. Since 1909, Crump told me, he has run for office twenty-three different times, without a single defeat, and in addition has "taken part" in seventy-nine more elections, all successful. Once he sent out petitions for a mayoralty election with the candidate's name left blank; even so, everybody signed them. In 1940 he ran for mayor; four seconds after his inauguration on January 1, 1941, he resigned the post[5] and took off for New Orleans to see a football game, in the company of McKellar.

Once he superintended an election on a nine million dollar bond issue for a municipal electric system to distribute TVA power. It won seventeen to one. Promptly he renamed a street to honor the day, and in the

---

[5] He wanted to give the mayoralty to a congressman friend who had not been able to run because Crump had asked him to stay in Congress long enough to vote on neutrality legislation then impending.

European manner called it Sixth of November Street. One odd point is
that he has never made a public speech in his life.

Mr. Crump writes famous letters to the newspapers. Those he sends
Meeman are soft as silk compared to the philippics received by Silliman
Evans, publisher of the Nashville *Tennessean*. For Mr. Evans, who
organized and led the poll-tax fight against him, he reserves the really
sulphurous thunder. Mr. Evans has shown me some of these letters. They
are really quite remarkable. Crump delivered one in January, 1945, by
messenger, in order to avoid possible violation of the postal laws, and
after causing it to be read in the legislature as "privileged" matter. He
called Evans a man "with a foul mind and wicked heart," with "ventosity"
[*sic*] as his chief stock in trade. He called Jennings Perry, then the editor
of the *Tennessean* and one of the ablest and most disinterestedly sincere
liberals in the South, "unworthy, despicable, a venal and licentious
scribbler . . . with the brains of a quagga," who writes unintelligently
on any subject "just as one would expect of a wanderoo." Of a third
Tennessean victim, the political columnist Joe Hatcher, Crump said
simply that he had "a low, filthy, diseased mind" full of "ululation" [*sic*].
The three together—I am choosing only the mildest language—were
called "mangy, bubonic rats, yellow to the core." Evans is a doughty
character with no mean sense of humor. What he did was simply print
on his front page Crump's full and unexpurgated text, under pictures set
side by side of Crump, one of Crump's cronies, a "wanderoo" (purple-
faced ape), and a "quagga" (a kind of African wild donkey).

No one should think that Mr. Crump is crazy or even some type of
monster. Actually—the kind of paradox that so often happens—he is a
man of considerable erudition and, when he wants to turn it on, of the
most persuasive and engaging charm. I didn't particularly want to meet
him. I said to a newspaper interviewer that I didn't care much about how
Boss Crump bossed Memphis since the pattern is the same in most cities,
but that I would be interested in what forces, if any, bossed the boss.

The phone rang the next day, and it was Mr. Crump speaking gently,
"So you want to know who bosses *me*!" He said flattering things about
my books, and asked me to come right over. I hesitated and he went on,
"Really, I don't think you can write about Tennessee without seeing me."
Then we had a wonderfully fascinating couple of hours. Mostly he gos-
siped and reminisced. He described his own career; he talked with
admiration of TVA, and said that it was silly for Arkansas, in contrast
to Tennessee, to be at the mercy of a power company; when I asked
about his organization he laughed in deprecating reply, "Oh, we have
friends all over the state," and murmured that he merely likes to "assist
things"; he averred that his only real interest was in building a good
community, and talked of the work he had done for Negroes. He added
that his position was totally unlike that of the usual boss; he has never

made a nickel out of it, he and his family are liked and respected, and he only gives the newspapers "the deuce" occasionally because they don't have "the real interests of the people at heart." He talked of Tennessee history from Andrew Johnson to Cordell Hull, of politics and such in cities as far afield as Duluth and Des Moines, and of Roosevelt, his great friend for many years. "I tried to help him down here," Mr. Crump concluded, "in a minor kind of way."

Of course the boss has given Memphis first-class government—in some respects. But almost all the creditable items are the equivalent of Mussolini making the trains in Italy "run on time." Perhaps they did run on time, and a good thing too. But at what sacrifice?—at what cost to things much more important? Mr. Crump has made Memphis a "clean" enough city. But it is a community that has not really functioned as a democracy for more than a quarter of a century; a whole generation has grown up without fulfilling the first and simplest duty of citizenship, that of exercising political choice. Participation in the American democratic process has passed Memphis by; city and county both have surrendered their most essential prerogatives out of laziness and fear. And for most of this civic infantilism E. H. Crump is alone responsible.

What will happen when Crump dies? There is no discernible successor. Everything depends on the old man himself. Stanley Baldwin once wrote that dictatorship is like a giant beech tree—very fine to look at, but nothing grows underneath.

Poll Tax and Veterans' Revolt

Indissolubly associated with all this is the poll tax. Obviously anything that keeps the vote down and makes it the more easily controlled serves the Crump machine. Tennessee is 82 per cent white, and so, more than in any other southern state, its poll tax is not predominantly a Negro question; what the poll tax does is to drastically curtail the *white* man's vote. Crump is, however, careful always to state publicly that he is in favor of "repeal" (at the same time that he makes repeal impossible); since, if by some miracle repeal *should* come, he doesn't want to face several hundred thousand new voters with a record of having opposed it. In 1943, mostly as a result of a brave and intensive crusade by the *Tennessean*, poll-tax repeal did go through the legislature.[6] Then, following a suit filed by a Crump associate, the bill was held up on a charge of being unconstitutional—though the legislature had, in the most regular manner, passed it. The case went to the state supreme court, which voted three to two to support the allegation of unconstitutionality, i.e., to keep the tax on the books. But the chief justice vigorously dissented from this opinion, and it would not have been made at all had not another justice

[6] This story is told in full detail in *Democracy Begins at Home: the Tennessee Fight on the Poll Tax* by Jennings Perry.

conveniently died; he was happily succeeded by a local Memphis judge who was proudly wont to call Mr. Crump "our leader." One of the dissenting justices, shocked by a decision which implied that a legislature could not repeal one of its own acts, stated that it was of a kind unknown "in the history of English and American jurisprudence." But—the Crump crowd won, and the poll tax still rules Tennessee.

A fine lively fracas, related to this and other issues, came in the summer of 1946, when—the affair made front-page news all over the country—a group of outraged GI's rose in Athens, McMinn County, in the eastern part of the state, and by threats of force and after some hours of violence as nearly justifiable as any political violence can ever be, threw out the members of the incumbent political machine. McMinn County was, for many years, one of the most downright unpleasant communities in the United States, and Athens had a vicious reputation. Three counties in this area are, or were, the impenetrable citadel of Sheriff Burch C. Biggs; customarily he delivered 98 per cent of the local vote to the Crump machine. It was Biggs, a character out of rowdy folklore, who once stopped the clock in the Tennessee senate—actually by poking at it with a long stick—to prevent some early anti-poll-tax legislation from passing. His subviceroy in McMinn County was a man named Cantrell who, with members of his family, had maintained an iron-bound grip on it for years.

Out in these mountain districts, things are really rough. The McMinn sheriffs and other officials lived on fat fees, estimated at $25,000 a year, gouged out of the community and unwary passers-through who did not know that they could be fined $16.05 for going over twelve miles an hour. John Jennings Jr., a Tennessee congressman who fought the Biggs-Cantrell gang, has stated[7] that "during the war, while more than 3,500 boys from McMinn County were serving . . . the machine, bloated with official graft running into the hundreds of thousands of dollars, drunk with power and emboldened by the absence of the young men, kicked, cuffed, slugged, shot, and robbed the fathers and mothers of these boys in every election held from 1940 to and including . . . 1944."

What happened in 1946 was that a group of veterans, led by a young schoolteacher named Knox Henry, and a twenty-three-year-old grocer's son, Jim Buttram, made a coup d'état when it was clear that, once more, the McMinn crowd was preparing forcibly to steal an election. The GI's had been certain that this would occur; they had served ample warning on the authorities, but no one paid attention. Mr. Biggs didn't want to be disturbed, and he is a man with a hasty temper. As outlined in the *Congressional Record* (July 13, 1946) the gang customarily performed its electoral thievery by (*a*) voting absentee ballots for persons fictitious or dead; (*b*) substituting their own whole ballot boxes for others; (*c*) stuffing them; (*d*) keeping opposition judges away from the

[7] *Congressional Record*, August 12, 1946.

polls with guns and blackjacks; (e) allowing boys and girls under twenty-one to vote; (f) destroying election records.

The young GI's—and again let it be said that only these most exigent circumstances can excuse their lawlessness—rose in arms. The machine, protected by imported thugs, grabbed the ballots and started to "count" them in the safest place, the local jail, whereupon the veterans simply stormed it. They used gunfire and dynamite, and twenty-odd people were hurt; nobody was killed. The gang and its deputies surrendered after a six-hour siege, and the GI's took over; Cantrell and a man named Mansfield, the sheriff, fled town precipitously—for days their whereabouts was unknown. Order was promptly restored by the veterans themselves, and young Mr. Henry duly became sheriff; his men have set up a reform administration, and they promise to agitate—legally— for poll-tax repeal.

Pressure was put on the state authorities while the fight was going on to send in the militia. Wisely an order to do so was rescinded. Crump and McKellar dismissed the episode as purely a local matter, but it should have shaken them in their boots for a time.

The Mythical McKellar

The easiest way to describe Senator Kenneth Douglas McKellar, who is seventy-seven now, is to call him an old fusspot, though this word may not carry enough connotation of irascibility; Mr. McKellar is one of the angriest men alive. I have had a good many experiences of one kind or other talking to political dignitaries in thirty or forty countries for the last fifteen or twenty years, but only once in my life has anybody ever "shown me the door." This happened, much to my astonishment, during a brief talk with Senator McKellar, when I called on him in Washington last year. It seems that I made the mistake of asking what I should see in his state "aside from TVA." The aged senator rose from his desk, turned a color between a prune and a plum, and forthwith ordered me to begone.

Short, squat, rubicund, and now serving his sixth Senate term, McKellar is like a wonderland creature out of another age. He was a poor boy born in Alabama. He is a bachelor, a prohibitionist, a Presbyterian, a 32nd Degree Mason, a Shriner, and an Oddfellow.

Drew Pearson once wrote a paragraph describing one of McKellar's adventures in patronage, and on one occasion mentioned that several members of the family were on the old senator's pay roll. McKellar rose in the Senate in July, 1946, and denounced Pearson in language remarkably lurid, even for Tennessee. Among other things he called him "this miserable, lying, corrupt, dishonest scoundrel, claiming to be a newspaper man, but with a dishonest and disordered mentality and with a putrid and corrupt morality." But all that Pearson had done was put down figures. McKellar went on, "No person with the character sufficient to sleep with a hog or to associate with dogs or polecats would write such an article. . . . This paid, low-lived skunk Pearson . . . this unmitigated liar and mercenary, money-making crook . . . the biggest liar in Washington."[8] McKellar said all this under senatorial immunity, and hence could not be sued. But Pearson's brief rejoinder could not have been better: "A hit dog always howls."

It was not, incidentally, just Pearson's allusion to McKellar's family and so on that prompted this rodomontade. What really annoyed the bullfroggish old man was something that the columnist, doing his duty to his public, had written about TVA. The interconnection between McKellar and TVA is somewhat complicated. McKellar claims, now that TVA is a giant success, that he helped to father it; he points out that his Senate committee pushed through the appropriations which made its building possible. This is quite true, and for some years McKellar and TVA got along fairly well together. Then came a straight-out, no-holds-barred fight with Lilienthal over patronage. Lilienthal insisted on putting it down forever as a matter both of philosophy and practice that there should be no political spoils in TVA.[9] Then—the details hardly matter since it is the principle that counts—came a quarrel over the location of a dam. Power, after Pearl Harbor, was desperately needed for war production of aluminum. The best site for water to be put to work quickly was at a place where several prominent Tennesseans, if the dam project went through, would be dispossessed. McKellar, seeking to protect the interests of his constituents, fought to keep the dam from being built; he threatened to hold up its appropriations even after the chief of staff of the Army pled the urgency of the case; finally, it took direct personal intervention by Roosevelt himself to call him off.

McKellar would hardly be worth writing about in detail except for his position; his career personifies the evils and inconveniences of committee seniority. He is Democratic *doyen* of the Senate. For years he was acting chairman of the Appropriations Committee (during Carter Glass's illness) as well as chairman of the Committee on Post Offices and Post Roads, and second in command of the Committee on Civil Service. As a result of all this he had a comprehensive lookout on senatorial business; not only could he pigeonhole appropriation bills, but he could exert influence on almost every other senator by being able to delay their suggestions for appointment to postmasterships. McKellar is of course an ally of Crump's. This does not mean that Crump necessarily admires him although he usually lets him have his way on national legislation. What the Memphis boss does respect is the "prestige" and power that accrues to McKellar by reason of his seniority.

[8] *Congressional Record*, July 16, 1946.
[9] A celebrated member of the early New Deal brain trust, when still in close favor with Roosevelt, once tried to get a job for a relative in TVA. Lilienthal turned him down, and of course has never been forgiven.

The old senator has a shrewd and adhesive eye. Late in 1944 he campaigned quietly to become president of the Senate pro tempore, though no one seemed to appreciate why he was so anxious for this generally thankless job. A few months later Roosevelt died. McKellar, as president of the Senate, then became in effect vice president of the United States under Truman, though of course he had no right of succession to the presidency. But the position gave him 50 per cent more salary, a government automobile and chauffeur, and various privileges. Moreover, while president of the Senate, he still held his committee chairmanships and could make speeches and even vote.

Return briefly to the quarrel over TVA; there is a lesson here. An American politician of the old school needs two things above all vis-à-vis his constituents, first, political credit; second, ability to bestow patronage. Not possibly could McKellar claim full "credit" for TVA. This went where it belonged, to Roosevelt and George Norris. Nor could he get his friends jobs anywhere in the authority. Thus TVA became a kind of permanent symbol and reminder of his own political frustration. He fought back early in 1945 (while still claiming to be an ardent TVA adherent) with proposals for measures that, if passed, would have ruined it. First he demanded that the authority turn in its accounts monthly; second he submitted a bill whereby all TVA salaries over $4,500 a year would be subject to senatorial approval, which—subtle!—would have brought the whole structure under the surveillance of his own Appropriations Committee. Neither bill went through.

After the 1946 primary campaign, Edward W. Carmack, whom McKellar defeated, filed with the Senate an allegation that McKellar's organization had spent wholly unreasonable sums, mostly obtained from the liquor interests. Also Carmack alleged a secret deal whereby McKellar would "throw" Tennessee's twelve electoral votes to the Republican party in 1948 in return for Republican support in the primary. The Senate dropped the charges.

When Truman acceded to the presidency he invited McKellar, as president of the Senate, to sit in at Cabinet meetings. The motives for this were several and, in a sense, understandable. But the Richmond *Times-Dispatch* was not afraid to say, "A hack sits in the Cabinet. . . . Senator McKellar is a vindictive . . . grudge-bearing politician with an incurable itch for spoils . . . a shoddy impresario of the patronage grab."

Tennessee, Its Cities and Geographical Divisions

To cross Tennessee is almost like crossing Texas; the extreme eastern tip of the state is nearer Washington, D. C., than Memphis. The flagships of American Airlines have four Tennessee stops, Tri-City Airport,[10] Knoxville, Nashville, Memphis, and in the old days it seemed

[10] Serving Johnson City and Kingsport in Tennessee and Bristol, Virginia.

inconceivable, flying between these points hour after hour, that one could still be in the same state. Tennessee is in fact a most extraordinarily varied and three-fold commonwealth. Very few Tennesseans call themselves "Tennesseans." They say that they are from "west" or "east" Tennessee. The state is, in actuality, cut into three "grand divisions," not merely two; each is recognized by the constitution as a kind of entity.

West Tennessee is mostly a flat alluvial plain, dominated by Memphis and based on cotton. East Tennessee is the area behind the Cumberland ridge, mountain country almost indistinguishable from that of North Carolina, Virginia and Kentucky, full of Scotch-Irish, small landowners, and Republicans; Tennessee has had two Republican governors within living memory, and Harding carried it in 1920, incredible as this may seem.[11] In east Tennessee some unique survivals are to be found, like the Melungeons, a "tribe" of dark people unlike any other in America. I mentioned Meigs County in the preceding chapter. There is at least one other county without a single telephone, and one that, until very recently at least, had no paved roads.

Look at the Rand-McNally pocket map of Tennessee. "Towns" are solemnly listed—scores of them—with "populations" of four, seven, five, and nine people. Mostly these are mountain outposts.

Middle Tennessee is the heart of the state; this is the blue-grass, mint-julep, big-plantation, old-southern-aristocracy area pivoted on Nashville. Tennessee has some four million acres of blue grass; Kentucky, with about a million, is nevertheless called "the" Blue Grass State. Thirty miles from Nashville, in the southeastern corner of Davidson County, you can see the difference between blue grass and the rest as sharply as you can see the line between irrigated and nonirrigated land in Arizona. The blue grass is so rich that it stays green all winter; hence it is good for grazing, and the animals raised on it have sturdy bones full of lime and phosphorus. Why can't all grass be made "blue"? Cannot enough phosphate be put in artificially? The answer appears to be no. This part of Tennessee is a great fox-hunting region; the Nashville area is also the home par excellence of the Tennessee walking horse. I asked innocently enough if Tennesseans were much prejudiced against other types. Answer: "Kill a non-Tennessee horse and one drop of its blood will poison the Atlantic Ocean."

Clarksville, Tennessee, is the world's largest market for "dark-fired" tobacco; Columbia, Tennessee, notorious as we know for something less pleasant, is the world's largest mule market; "mule day," the first Monday in April, is called "Big Monday." Tobacco, horses, and livestock in general as well as mules, are still sold by auction; a thousand people from all over the country will come to the walking horse auctions in a town like Lewisburg. Auctioneers' jobs, by tradition at least, pass from father to son—it takes heredity to understand the gibberish—and auction-

[11] One county, Sevier, is as solidly Republican as anything in Vermont.

eering is probably the most honorable profession in the state; the legend is that really successful auctioneers end up in the governorship. As a matter of fact, the present governor, Jim N. McCord, is an auctioneer by trade. An auction is of course simply a public market, a kind of stock exchange without a ticker, meeting at fixed intervals. A good auctioneer will get as much as $250 a day.

A word, finally, on Tennessee's fascinatingly varied cities. MEMPHIS (population 293,000), "the Chicago of the South," lives on cotton and timber as well as Mr. Crump. It contains Beale Street, which Negroes almost everywhere consider their "Fifth Avenue," and characters like Alonzo Locke, an eminent head waiter in the Hotel Peabody; Mr. Locke, a Negro, is also a newspaper and real estate man and the vice president of a local bank. Like many southern towns, Memphis is much given to censorship in the realm of the arts; the local movie board refused a permit recently to "Brewster's Millions," because it contains Jack Benny's Rochester and the film as a whole "presents too much familiarity between the races." Finally, Memphis life rests on the Mississippi. I took one look, and realized that the muddy Mississippi is really the Missouri here.

NASHVILLE (population 167,000), "the Dimple of the Universe," has all manner of distinctions. For one thing the Hermitage, the home of General Jackson and one of the most perfect of all American shrines, is near by; for another Nashville ("Wall Street of the South") is one of the largest primary bond centers in America, and like Louisville and Denver is stuffed with ancient money; for another, the "Athens of Dixie," it has no fewer than ten universities and colleges. One is Vanderbilt, another is Fisk, one of the two or three best Negro universities in the country, and a third is Meharry, a well-known medical school for Negroes. Still another (white) is the Gupton-Jones College of Mortuary Science, one of the nation's foremost embalming schools. Recently its undergraduates (many of whom are medical students who flunk elsewhere) went on strike; the slogan was GUPTON-JONES IS UNFAIR TO THE LIVING AND THE DEAD. Finally, Nashville—has any other American city so many nicknames?—is known as "the Protestant Vatican of the South." No man can hold office in Tennessee unless he believes in God, by state law; the Baptists, Methodists, Campbellites, "Cumberland" Presbyterians and other sects are, it goes without saying, of great power politically. Nashville is one of the biggest publishing centers in the United States, because of the great number of religious tracts it prints.

Between CHATTANOOGA (population 128,000) and Knoxville (population 112,000), both in east Tennessee, there is considerable rivalry. Chattanooga ("the Dynamo of Dixie") is a well-run town, full of history (Lookout Mountain), with a genuine social and intellectual distinction, and industry both long established and heavily expanding; it makes everything from ferrosilicon to stockings. And here, in a manner of speaking, the New York *Times* was born.

KNOXVILLE is the ugliest city I ever saw in America, with the possible exception of some mill towns in New England. Its main street is called Gay Street; this seemed to me to be a misnomer. A recent movie, "Ziegfeld Follies of 1946," could only be shown in a cut version in Knoxville, because one sequence shows Lena Horne. Knoxville, an extremely puritanical town, serves no alcohol stronger than 3.6 per cent beer, and its more dignified taprooms close at 9:30 P.M.; Sunday movies are forbidden, and there is no Sunday baseball. Perhaps as a result, it is one of the least orderly cities in the South—Knoxville leads every other town in Tennessee in homicides, automobile thefts, and larceny.

Tennessee: a Word About Its Folklore

The Volunteer State, we have seen, produces some fragrant political invective; it comes by this honestly enough. In the 1860's a famous Kentucky editor, George D. Prentice, disapproved to a degree of William G. Brownlow, a local preacher and reconstruction governor of Tennessee. This is part of what Prentice said of him:

> He never had mind enough to keep his body from rotting—consequently, he was always a mass of putrefaction. . . . All the little atom of sense he ever had—if he ever had an atom—has gone to the grave before him, but not much before him, it is to be hoped, for mankind's sake. He is a loathsome fistula of the body politic . . . a foul bubble floating on the surface of a cesspool. . . . There has never been any more religion or decency in his sermons, or his exhortations, or his talk at death beds, than in the yelling of hyenas, the cursing of pirates, or the objurgations of harlots. . . . Heaven, earth, and even Hell, abhor him—though the latter will somehow manage to gulp him down.

A well-known statue in Nashville is that of John A. Murrell. He was a horse thief and slave thief, so tough that, on being branded once on the palm, he bit the brand out. Caught again, he was branded on the forehead, where his teeth would not reach. But why should the Tennessean community have erected a statue to a criminal who, it would seem, had none of the glamor of a man like Billy the Kid, none of the effective popular appeal of desperadoes like Jesse James? Murrell was little more than a savage; once, in the early days on the Cumberland Trail, he cut a woman's child to pieces before her eyes. Nashville, like Louisville, was at one time the pit of a flaming political conflict over the railroads; Major E. C. Lewis, editor of the old Nashville *American*, led the antirailroad faction. When, years later, one of the railway promoters died, his friends built him a statue. Thereupon Lewis proclaimed, "If that blatherskite is to have a monument in Nashville, then, Heaven being my witness, John A. Murrell shall have one too!" Lewis was chair-

man of the city park board at the time, and so was able to put his threat
into effect.

The biggest man ever known to medical science was a Tennessean,
and also the biggest hog. The man, by name Miles Darden (1798-1857),
was seven feet six inches high, and weighed 871 pounds in 1845; later
his weight grew considerably greater. Up to 1853 (I am quoting a letter
from Albert Williams, a noted Nashville authority on local lore) "he
was quite active and lively, after which, his fat increasing, he was
compelled to stay at home." Previously, when traveling, it took a two-
horse wagon to carry him; when he died, of strangulation caused by fat
around the vocal cords, the side of the house had to be removed, in
order to get the body out. The biggest hog ever known, by name Big
Bill, lived in Lexington, Tennessee, and weighed 2,400 pounds. After
some happy years spent reclining, it tried to rise one day, whereupon all
its legs broke, and it died.

Tennessee, Its Colonizing Force

This is in a way the most remarkable single thing about Tennessee.
The state has, practically since its admission to the union in 1796, produced pioneers who moved out, and in other domains gained stalwart
renown—men like Admiral Farragut and Davy Crockett. When we
reach Texas we shall find how, in a manner of speaking, that gigantic
state is a kind of Tennessee colony; no fewer than seven members of a
recent Texan congressional delegation were Tennessee born. Elsewhere,
too, the Tennesseans have sent out fecund settlers; they have virtually
taken over whole professions—for instance banking—throughout the
Southwest.[12]

Tennessee claims three American presidents, as many as any state
except Virginia, Ohio, and New York. They were Jackson, Polk, and
Johnson; the legend is that Tennessee "ruled the nation from 1830 to
1850." Oddly enough, however, these three all happened to have been
born in the Carolinas, though they became indisputable Tennesseans
later. Indeed Tennessee receives just as it transmits. Both Crump and
McKellar, we have seen, were born outside.

Arkansas, the Wonder State

Arkansas is a highly curious and interesting community. It is one of
the most impoverished of all American states, with an intermontane

---

[12] Boss Crump, mentioning this phenomenon to me, also pointed out the astonishing fact that, at one time, eight United States senators were born in Mississippi—
including men representing Arkansas, Nevada (Pittman), Oregon, and Washington
(Poindexter).

backwoods inaccessible and primitive in the extreme; yet it possesses the greatest reserves in the country of bauxite, the indispensable raw material from which aluminum is made; it contains such a notably fashionable resort as Hot Springs, cotton land as rich as the Mississippi Delta, gambling dens of almost Pompeian splendor, and a senator as good as young James William Fulbright.[13]

Arkansas yields to no other state in its local pride and friendly swagger. Some time ago, an article I wrote on Texas appeared in *Harper's Magazine* and, in severely condensed form, in *Reader's Digest*; I happened to mention erroneously, listing some Texas "firsts," that the Lone Star State produced the biggest watermelons in the world. What a deluge of obloquy and odium descended on my head!—not from Texas, but from Arkansas. I got letters by the dozen; loyal Arkansans wrote me from all over the country, with the rebuke that I must be a miserable creature indeed not to be aware that, incontestably, by mammoth proof over and over demonstrated, a town called Hope, in Arkansas, is the watermelon center of the world, and habitually produces in illimitable profusion the best and biggest watermelons ever known. A recent specimen tipped the scales at 197 pounds.

A few chapters further on I shall mention a provocative pamphlet put out in Houston called *Texas Brags*, a copy of which Senator Tom Connally once gave me. The only similar pamphlet I know on an American state is on Arkansas, edited by Avantus Green of Little Rock, and called *With This We Challenge, an Epitome of Arkansas*. It is full of rare and fascinating gems, under the motto "Let restraint be damned!" Arkansas has the oldest national park in America, it is the first strawberry-producing state, and it has chinchilla farms. It contains the "duck-shooting capital of the world," and within its borders may be found five hundred different varieties of wild flower, including 27 kinds of orchid; 109 different minerals, including diamonds; 61 varieties of "blossoming trees," and though it is two hundred miles from the Gulf, one of the largest oyster-shell beds in the world, with deposits of seven million cubic yards.

An Arkansas farmer and writer named C. L. Edson wrote a pungent essay about his state in the *Nation* some years ago, of which the following is a sample:

> Arkansas has its own popular motto and it is this: "I've never seen nothin', I don't know nothin', I hain't got nothin', and I don't want nothin'." . . . It (Arkansas) just grew out of seepage. . . . A belt of mud prevented Arkansas from having a port and denied to

---

[13] Of course I should balance this chapter with a section on Fulbright, one of the ablest and most levelheaded progressives in Washington, of equal length to that on McKellar above. A whole long essay might be written on the contrasts between them. But space does not permit.

her a metropolis, a civilization, and a history. A people who were willing to foot it a hundred miles through the muck to get nowhere founded Arkansas and achieved their aim. . . . No stream can rise higher than its source, and Arkansas has proved it. . . . Few can read in Arkansas, and those who can, do not.

In *Americana* I find these nuggets. A Little Rock paper reported once:

Warden Evans announced that all electrocutions conducted under his regime would be held strictly according to the law. "People get the idea," he said, "that electrocutions are social gatherings, but none of this kind will be held while I am warden. An execution is a serious matter."

In a back-country town a new ordinance includes these two provisions:

1. Hereafter, it shall be unlawful for any man and woman, male or female, to be guilty of committing the act of sexual intercourse between themselves at any place within the corporate limits . . .
2. This shall not apply to married persons, as between themselves, and their husband and wife [*sic!*] unless of a grossly improper and lascivious nature.

Arkansas is, like Tennessee, packed with folklore, and everybody knows the ancient saga, "On a Slow Train Through Arkansas." Once some miscreants rhymed Arkansas with Kansas instead of saying Arkansaw. An Arkansas representative rose promptly in the halls of Congress:

Mr. Speaker, you blue-bellied rascal! I have for the last thirty minutes been trying to get your attention, and each time I have caught your eye, you have wormed, twisted and squirmed like a dog with a flea in his hide, damn you!

Gentlemen, you may desecrate the grave of Washington, haul down the Stars and Stripes, curse the Goddess of Liberty . . . but your crime would in no wise compare in enormity with what you propose to do when you would change the name of Arkansas! Hell fire, no!

Compare the lily of the valley to the gorgeous sunrise; the discordant croak of the bullfrog to the melodious tones of the nightingale; the classic strains of Mozart to the death bray of an apoplectic mule; the puny arm of a Peruvian prince to the muscles of a Roman gladiator—but NEVER change the name of Arkansas!

Mr. Green's pamphlet contains some other specimens of pictorial braggadocio:

Arkansas chiggers are red-speckled. They are small, about the size of a common Fifth Avenue flea. Anatomically speaking they are composed of nine sets of sharp teeth, a drilling tool, and a brain trained to identify men from north of the Ohio River. Though strictly carnivorous, their habitat is tree foliage, short vegetation, and reclining Yankees.

The Missouri Pacific Railway put a temporary halt to the growing of the really big Hope melons when they refused, at the outset of the war, to consign a flat car for transporting the county prize melon from farm to market. Left on the vine, it soured and last year burst, killing vegetation and animal life over a seven square mile area.

Little Rock, the capital, is a modern-looking town today, with an admirably comfortable hotel (the Friederica), a newspaper (the Arkansas *Gazette*) that has been continuously published under the same masthead for 126 years, and about 90,000 people. Originally it was a French trading post. The most impressive building today gives a hint about the community; it is the Albert Pike Memorial Temple, Ancient and Accepted Scottish Rite of Free Masonry.

Arkansas falls geographically and culturally into two distinct areas; the line of the Missouri Pacific more or less divides them. The state is, I heard it put, both the "West of the Pony" and the "South of the Piazza." The west, a region of open plains, is cow country, and resembles Texas; the Ozark area in the north seems to be a carry-over from Missouri, with small truck and chicken farms and a 100 per cent Anglo-Saxon population, very poor and thrifty. The other great division is the Delta region along the Mississippi, which is pure "old South"—a district of huge plantations (you scarcely count as a cotton farmer unless you have 10,000 acres), and a social system still mostly feudal. Near towns like Wilson, entrepreneurs bought swamp land for fifty cents an acre, drained it, and became millionaires almost overnight. Look at the Negro work hands here, under road bosses, and you will see *Uncle Tom's Cabin* come to life.

The white peasantry—not merely in the Delta but almost everywhere in Arkansas—is not much better off. It was here, some years ago, that American sharecroppers sought to organize for the first time; today, an organization called the National Farm Labor Union is hard at work trying to build an effective labor movement among the poorest of poor whites. But antilabor sentiment in Arkansas is vehement and extreme. As far back as 1944, the state voted on a constitutional amendment to forbid the closed shop; recently a Veterans Industrial Association was set up, with scarcely concealed vigilante aims,[14] and the area was an early stronghold of the Christian American Association, founded by Vance Muse of Texas (whom we shall encounter later on) which forced a bill through the Arkansas legislature providing that even a *threat* of violence by a member of a labor union was a felony, i.e., a penitentiary offense.

The war shook things up. From being a backwater, Arkansas found itself with 400 million dollars worth of war production orders. Labor

[14] Cf. Harold B. Hinton in the New York *Times*, August 26, 1946.

became somewhat stronger as a result since, as we well know, and as even Arkansas came to learn, industrialization isn't possible without a labor movement. The companies working the tremendous bauxite deposits (97 per cent of all the aluminum in America is found in Arkansas) are of course Alcoa and its lively competitor, Reynolds Metals. Both these companies are absentee owned; most of the wealth from bauxite goes outside the state, except local wages. An interesting potential development is the discovery recently of titanium deposits near Eureka Springs. This ore contains considerable portions of both thorium and uranium—which may mean that Arkansas will in time be a great contributor to the use of atomic power.

Next to the Delta farmers and such familiar agencies as the Baptist church, the biggest political force is the Arkansas Power & Light Company, a subsidiary of Electric Bond & Share; nowhere in the union has a utility such influence on a state as in Arkansas. Its boss for years was the late Senator Joe Robinson, a notable vassal of the power company; one recent governor attained office mostly because of resentment at the influence of Arkansas Power & Light on his predecessor. (Americans, when aroused, do move.) The general technique of the company is to watch closely for the rise of any bright young man, a lawyer say and then, quite legitimately, to hire him. Arkansas Power was run for years by a fabulous nabob named Harvey Couch; his regent on the local scene was C. Hamilton Moses, a Baptist who became secretary to various governors and then Couch's attorney. One story is that Arkansas, not Tennessee, might have had a valley development like TVA (in the form of an AVA); but Senator Robinson, who was majority leader at the time, and a very close friend of Couch's, told Roosevelt that the state didn't want it. Arkansas Power & Light is of course absentee owned; I have given in Chapter 43 a typical sample of its rates. Not long ago, it was ordered by the Federal Power Commission to show within a stipulated brief interval why it should not mark off 17 million dollars in its "book value," which is one reason why its rates are high.

Arkansas had a vivid and successful veterans' revolt in 1946 almost exactly corresponding to the one in Tennessee. Combining factors were resentment at big gambling in the neighborhood, the savage poverty of the poor farmers, and contamination of the community by a debauched political machine.

In Arkansas, unlike Tennessee, the white primary is a bigger issue than the poll tax. The situation passes the borderline of the fantastic; in 1946 the state had four separate and distinct primaries, following passage of a law that segregates federal from state elections, in order to evade implications of the Supreme Court's white primary decision, and to continue exclusion of Negroes from state polls.

Chapter 45

Arnall, Talmadge, and the
State of Georgia

wwwwwwwwwwwwwwwwwwwwwwwwwwwwwwwwwwwwwwwwwwwwwwwwwwwwwwwwwwwwwwwwwwwwwwwwwwwwwwwwwwww

Let's get off Tobacco Road.
            —Ellis G. Arnall

Oh, Georgia booze is mighty fine booze,
The best yuh ever poured yuh,
But it eats the soles right offen yore shoes,
For Hell's broke loose in Georgia.
            —Stephen Vincent Benét, *The Mountain Whippoorwill**

OF COURSE the first person I wanted to meet in Georgia was
     Arnall. He was still governor then. We had dinner together in
Atlanta, and several substantial talks. Ellis Gibbs Arnall, only forty,
is one of the best and brightest of contemporary Americans, and that
he will return to public life some day—indeed, in a manner of speaking,
he has never left it—is as certain as that Georgia sunshine makes
peaches grow.

The staggering imbroglio of January, 1947, when for a time Georgia
had two, or possibly three, governors all at once, is still fresh in the
national memory. No more obnoxious mishmash has ever attended
politics in an American state. To tell the story briefly, a word of background is essential. Arnall served as governor from 1943 to 1947, having
succeeded the insufferable Eugene Talmadge, now dead, from whom he
differed as day from night. Arnall, by terms of the Georgia constitution,
could not run for a second term, and Talmadge, except for the accident
of death, would in turn have succeeded *him*. But the extraordinary fact
is that the late lamented Gene, though "elected" governor of the state,
did not win the election that was to put him in, so far as actual number
of votes was concerned. The candidate who did get the largest popular
vote was defeated![1]

Georgia has 159 counties, more than any state except Texas (though
it is only a quarter the size of Texas), and its vote is counted by county
"units"; each county is assigned from two to six units, and the winning
candidate in each county gets its total vote. This is the rotten-borough

---

* Copyright, 1925, by Stephen Vincent Benét.
[1] Man from the moon or Mars, take note.

system in excelsis. Fulton County, containing Atlanta, with a population of 392,866, has six "units"; one cracker county (a single example out of several available) has exactly 241 registered voters, and yet is entitled to two units. A candidate may, in other words, by carrying three counties of this backwoods type, with a total electorate of a thousand votes or so, offset the entire city of Atlanta, with 123,000 registered voters. This preposterous system came into being as a weapon to counteract the old city machines, for instance that of Senator Tom Watson; but as manipulated today it gives an overwhelming preponderance to the hard shells and "wool hats" in the hookworm belt, forces of the most violent parochial conservatism, as against what liberal elements may arise in the towns. Talmadge had what was generally conceded to be an irreducible minimum of about 125,000 wool-hat votes. The Georgia peasants and cotton-choppers are called wool hats because, strangely enough, they like to wear wool hats. The sunshine is broilingly hot. But Negroes have sensibly taken to straw hats, and so the white proletariat sticks to wool.

Two people ran against Talmadge in 1946, a former governor named E. D. Rivers, and James V. Carmichael, the Arnall candidate. Carmichael, a thirty-six-year-old liberal, got 313,389 votes to Talmadge's 297,245 and Rivers' 67,196. Thus Carmichael had a clear and indisputable popular lead over Talmadge, and "Ole Gene" himself received less than half the total vote. But by the unit system Talmadge was credited with 242 county votes as against Carmichael's 148, and so was declared the victor. Similarly an able congresswoman, Helen Douglas Mankin, beat her opponent by a popular vote of 33,675 to 26,175. But she was counted out, because she lost by eight to six county unit votes. This is not mere freakishness. It is democracy stultifying itself and committing an absurd form of Dixie suicide.

The wool hats are not, of course, the only folk in Georgia who voted for Talmadge; many otherwise respectable businessmen certainly supported him, though they would hate to have to admit it. One formidable factor in state affairs is the heavy concentration of wealth (much of it absentee) represented by the Trust Company of Georgia, headed until his death last year by a tycoon named Robert Strickland, and by Coca-Cola. Another force of great consequence is the Georgia Power Company, a subsidiary of Commonwealth & Southern. A wool hat-Georgia Power coalition put Talmadge in. Clark Foreman, one of the most distinguished of southern liberals, the president of the Southern Conference for Human Welfare and a member of the family that owns the Atlanta *Constitution*, said recently as quoted by the New York *Times*, "Talmadge was supported by the Georgia Power Company and every mill owner in the state of Georgia."

This situation has even produced poetry. Here is one jingle I heard:

> The big bugs courted the hookworms,
> And their clandestine embrace
> Produced a governor of Georgia
> Who raised Hell all over the place.

Talmadge, then, was governor-elect. This was in the late autumn of 1946. But he had been in poor health for some time, his condition grew worse, and on December 20, he died. The Ku-Klux sent wreaths to the funeral. Then the brawl started. Georgia has a new constitution, which was supposed to be foolproof, but it made no provision for such a contingency as the death of a governor-elect before his inauguration. Talmadge had a thirty-three-year-old son, by name Herman, who saw service in the Navy during the war, and who managed Ole Gene's campaign. He had always been politically ambitious, and long before his father's death people talked about him as being "trained" for the succession. Now, by extraordinary chance, some few Georgians had written Herman's name in on the ballot—675 to be exact. This was exactly six more "write-ins" than Carmichael got, incidentally; had Carmichael received a few more, there might have been four "governors" instead of only three.

On the basis of his write-in vote, Herman Talmadge claimed the governorship. He took the position that his father's death invalidated the election, and that the choice of governor should be thrown into the legislature. The legislature duly "elected" him, and so Georgia found itself with a "governor" whose total popular vote was—675! The state of Georgia contains 3,123,723 people.

Meantime Arnall had conducted himself with the utmost dignity and correctness. He took the line that, according to the constitution, a governor had a right to continue in office until his successor was "qualified." At this point enters a new character—Melvin E. Thompson. For years he was Arnall's executive secretary; I met him several times and heard him described as "the best progressive in the state." He was elected lieutenant governor in the 1946 race, but whether he ran with Arnall's blessing is not certain. At any rate Arnall announced that, as lieutenant governor, Thompson was the proper person to be certified as governor, and that when this was done he, Arnall, would resign. The legislature elected Herman, however, not Thompson, on inauguration day. So on January 15, Herman strode into the governor's office and demanded that Arnall get out. Arnall refused to go, stating, "I will not turn this office over to a pretender." He yielded the next day, however, under pressure of Herman's state troopers. Previously "his" attorney general had petitioned the courts, which set a hearing for February 7. Herman then announced that he would pay no attention to the courts. He modified this threat later.

On January 17, Arnall, asserting that he was still legally governor, tried to maintain an office in the rotunda of the capitol, and was forcibly kept from using it. One of Talmadge's men roared at him, "Ellis, you remind me of a hawg. Did you ever slop a hawg? The more you give a hawg, the more he wants."

Thompson was finally sworn in as lieutenant governor, on January 18, and Arnall then duly resigned. Thompson insisted that he, not Herman Talmadge, was the true governor, but it was Herman who sat in the executive offices, and Herman who moved into the gubernatorial mansion. Obviously the end of this story is not yet. At the moment of writing Georgia has two "governors." But the real issue and struggle goes far beyond personalities. The contest is one between the old South and the new, between *coup d'état* and constitutional government, between rule by thuggery and rule by law.

Ellis Arnall: Politics and Personal

Bring Georgia back into the United States!
—Ellis G. Arnall

Arnall was born in 1907 in Newnan, a mill town of about 10,000 population forty miles from Atlanta; it calls itself the "barbecue capital of the world."[2] The family had been prominent in the neighborhood for generations, as attorneys and mill executives; one branch makes a well-known brand of towel, called ARNCO. Arnall's father is described in an official biography as "merchant, farmer, banker, and manufacturer"; also he is proprietor of the Krazy Kat Supermarket. When Arnall was inaugurated governor, some seventy relatives attended the ceremonies; blood relationships, let it be said in parentheses, probably play a greater role in the South than anywhere else in the United States.

Young Ellis went to the local schools, and hung up a lively record. In high school he was president of his class four times. He went on to the University of the South, at Sewanee, Tennessee; he majored in Greek, and won a master's degree for a thesis on the English novel. Then he won a law degree at the University of Georgia in 1931. He was the most industrious and enterprising youngster there; he ran everything. He was president of his class, president of most of the students' organizations, and first chief justice of the school's "supreme court." He told me that when he entered the university, he asked classmates what the biggest thing on the campus was. Answer: the Panhellenic Council. Arnall forthwith set out to be president of this; he campaigned for it actively and with subtlety, and won, partly by neglecting his own

[2] The best sketch of Arnall I know is by John Chamberlain, in *Life*, August 6, 1945. "Barbecue capital of the world" is from this. Also see articles by Kenneth Stewart in *PM*, from which I derive the Krazy Kat detail. But my main source for this section and those that follow is conversation with Arnall himself, plus an official gubernatorial biography.

milieu and cultivating poor students, those in Jewish fraternities, and others in categories usually ignored.

Until college, Arnall spent his life with books. He was timid, so he told me (one would not think so now), and "didn't operate much with people." But he wanted a political career. "So I reversed myself, and made books the background." Also he reversed himself in other ways. Newnan is a well-off town, and Arnall grew up in a wealthily conventional planter-manufacturer-Rotary Club atmosphere. But, when he left college and set up law practice, it was the workers whom he sought as clients. He ran for office almost at once, and became a member of the state legislature; in this first campaign, in a field of five candidates, he won 3,164 votes out of 3,510. Until elected to this post, he had never so much as seen the state capitol. He quickly became speaker of the house, assistant attorney general, attorney general, and governor. He was Talmadge's floor leader for a brief novitiate, and it was Rivers (then governor) who appointed him to the attorney generalship; thus do personalities in Georgia interlock.

Arnall is a lawyer. The whole South is jam packed with lawyers. It is the lawyers who make politics, and since most lawyers get a fat share of their business from corporations, it is they who are chiefly responsible when a state becomes corporation ridden. In Georgia an overwhelming proportion of state legislators are lawyers.[3] But although Arnall was a lawyer he never paid much attention to the corporations, or to the other traditional factors of control in Georgia politics, like the liquor and fertilizer interests, the schoolbook lobby, and the 159 county courthouse rings. He played his own lone game.

Arnall has push, charm, alertness, confidence, and brains; also he has luck as a rule. A gubernatorial campaign traditionally gets under way in Georgia with a barbecue in the candidate's hometown. Arnall's at Newnan was a brilliant success. His opponent's a few miles away was drowned out by a sudden cloudburst.

Arnall told me once, "Politics is simple." One good rule, he believes, is never to ask for anything directly, which is what everybody else does; instead, simply send your friends around, saying what a splendid and useful person you are, immediately after you have visited a community. The tragedy of most politicians (and of American politics) is, he thinks, that office holders, once they get in, become too fixed in dependence on their jobs financially and otherwise; hence, their overriding mood is caution, and they run with both hare and hounds. Finally, he says, be careful about money; don't take big contributions from the plutocrats,

---

[3] Other professions represented are funeral director, turpentine operator, naval stores agent, granite business, cross-tie operator, owner freezer locker plant, roofing agent, disabled World War veteran, tire retreading, and feed and chicken business. From a pamphlet *Your Part in Georgia's Politics*, published by the Committee for Georgia.

but try instead for support from a multitude of little people. To become a senator in Georgia, he declares, may cost $150,000. Then the people who put up the big money, i.e., those who wish to exert the real power, make their candidate a prisoner, and he becomes the victim of a machine. Avoid this kind of game, says Arnall. "I've been right free," he told me. Above all, cultivate the youngsters. "You doan' have to lead kids by the nose to the ballot box."

Arnall was one of the best governors Georgia, or any other state, has ever had, but he was almost unknown to the nation at large until 1945. What brought him his first broad million-plus audience was the radio show "Information Please," which program incidentally performed the same service for Wendell Willkie. Arnall's broad southern drawl—the way he pronounced "haidgehog" for instance—was heard throughout the country, and he stole the show. The governor of Georgia, it seemed, knew more poetry by heart than John Kieran or F.P.A. When I asked him to account for this, with the question "Do you still have time to read and memorize a lot?" he answered, "Read poetry? Hell, I *write* it!"

In fact, at dinner after the "Information Please" performance, he quoted a series of stanzas to Clifton Fadiman and the troupe, and demanded to know who the author was. The lines sounded familiar, and guesses took place up and down the centuries, but no one could quite identify them, whereupon Mr. Arnall confessed that he himself was the unknown author.

Arnall is a short, friendly man, very shrewd, earnest, and ambitious. He has a nice sense of phrase; once he called the North "the cold-bread country." His two greatest qualities are probably cleverness and confidence; he has, indeed, been too clever on occasion, and too confident. He was a strong Henry Wallace man—in fact he "delivered" the Georgia delegation to Wallace at the 1944 convention—but lately the closeness of this affiliation has diminished. He dislikes being tagged as an orthodox "liberal," and calls himself a "democrat," with both a big and a little D. What he laments most on the public scene is the dearth of first-class leadership; what he believes in most is the right of the people as a whole "to dignity and contentment"; what he pleads for most is recognition of the essential *unity* of America.

Arnall is a Baptist, and he says grace at meals, but he likes to have a good time socially ("I'm sort of human") and he drinks mildly. He thinks that a man of good will can get anything out of life, if he is willing to make sacrifices, but he is always careful himself not to want too much. He has plenty of courage; he told his first legislative session, "There'll be no pay-offs or shakedowns in *this* legislature!" He likes to improvise rather than plan, and he works in spurts; he is very mobile, and when I asked him what his political plans were, he said, "I'll tell you tomorrow mornin',

but come back in the evenin' and maybe I'll give you a different answer."
He thinks that politics "is like billiards," in that you have to know how
things lie by instinct mostly, and usually his prescience is remarkable. For
instance he guessed, to a man, exactly how the Supreme Court would
vote on his railroads case. On his desk rests a motto, ONE MAN WITH
COURAGE MAKES A MAJORITY, and when he relaxes, he is capable of
reading thirty-two detective stories in seven days. He often disliked the
routine of governorship, the necessity of placating people twelve hours a
day; he says, "I want to *work*, but I cain't work, because too much
detail gets in mah way."

I asked him what was the most important decision he ever had to
make; he said first that a good politician should never get himself into
a position where any decision was difficult. Then he grinned, adding
that the "best" decision he ever made was to go to Orlando, Florida,
some years ago, to attend a friend's wedding. He couldn't make up his
mind, flipped a coin to decide, went, and met there Miss Mildred DeLaney
Slemons, who became his wife; he proposed to her the second time
they met. She is an exceptionally pretty girl, and for a time attended
Lillian Smith's camp at Clayton, Georgia. The Arnalls have two small
children.

What Arnall, jobless at the moment, would seem to need above all
today—like Stassen—is a platform, a forum, to give his views official
emphasis. Mr. Truman offered him the solicitor generalship of the
United States, but he declined it. Perhaps he thinks that it is just as
well to keep out of Democratic politics in Washington for a year or so.

Arnall: On the Record

What a man's sympathies and orientations are does not ultimately
matter, until translated into fact; what does matter, for someone prominent in public life, is what he actually *did* : his record, his accomplishment. Look at Arnall's—long before the lunatic January fracas.

He came in as governor in 1943 with a ten-point plan; twenty-four
days after his inauguration, the legislature had passed each point—
unanimously! Some of them were:

(1) Removal of the University of Georgia from political control.
Talmadge had ousted several teachers because he thought they were
liberal on the Negro issue, and had played politics with the board
of regents; we shall find an analogous situation when we come to
Texas. As a result, the university was discredited, together with most
other educational institutions in the state, and its degrees became value-
less outside Georgia. More than anything else, public indignation over
this led to Talmadge's temporary downfall. At once, on becoming governor, Arnall backed and pushed through a measure setting up a new

regime for the university; he took it out of politics completely, and made it independent of both governor and legislature by giving it special constitutional status under an autonomous board.

(2) Cleaning up of the "pardons" racket. Previous governors had been famous—like governors in other southern states—for the wholesale pardons they were wont to give; this is a classic procedure for gaining political favor. Arnall set up a nonpolitical parole and pardon board, under a former official of the FBI, which altogether takes pardons out of the governor's hands.

(3) Further separation of the governorship from functions previously held. For instance new laws abolished the governor's former right to oust such officers as state treasurer, removed the governor from all boards and commissions operating state departments, and created a new independent system of budgetary control. One result of all this was that, before Arnall's term was over, the state debt of $35,000,000 was paid off.

Note well that the foregoing points, far from increasing Arnall's own grip on power, actually served to restrict it. He was doing something unheard of—appealing to the legislature to curtail, not augment, his own authority as chief executive! One should add, however, that he himself was not responsible for all his reformist legislation. Some years before an organization known as the Citizens Fact-Finding Movement was set up; this did a good deal of valuable spade work, and Arnall not only inherited its findings—he introduced no fewer than twenty-two bills that it recommended—but he rode into popularity on the ground swell the committee helped put in motion. He doesn't particularly like do-gooders, but they have conspicuously helped him.

After the first detail-crowded days, Arnall moved briskly on, as to wit:

(4) He pushed abolition of the Georgia poll tax (with a good deal of help from outside) through the legislature, a really signal accomplishment.

(5) He ameliorated to an extent the celebratedly vicious chain gang system, by a series of penal reforms. When he first took office he appointed a commission to investigate prison conditions, and its report made gruesome reading. "In Tattnell (the state penitentiary) we found an 'Eight Ball Gang,' consisting of approximately twenty-five, wearing the most brutal leg irons to be imagined, and complaining of being beaten and whipped almost daily." Here too sixteen young men had cut their own Achilles tendons, in order to escape the torments of the chain gang, and were found helpless in their bunks. "The punishment at Tattnell . . . was welding of leg irons with long picks on them on the ankles of the prisoners." All this has been modified—though it would be foolish to assert that Georgia prisons today are pleasant rest homes, or that they have been taken out of politics completely.

(6) Arnall cut the voting age to eighteen. His theory was that if boys

of eighteen were old enough to fight, they were old enough to vote. Georgia was the first state to lower its voting age, and the first to have a soldier-vote law.

(7) He increased the teachers' year from ten months to eleven (which meant in effect a 10 per cent raise in pay), established a teachers' retirement system, and set up a state board of education under the constitution, so that in theory at least it could not be tampered with by either governor or legislature.

(8) He introduced and put through the new constitution. Georgia thus became the first southern state to throw off its old constitution; this, written in 1877 and amended three hundred times, had become a hopeless anachronism, unwieldy and contradictory. Arnall won approval for the new one by a typical enough artifice. Good citizens had been yearning for a long time for constitutional reform, but they assumed that this would necessitate calling a convention, which would have meant nuisanceful politics, wrangling, and expense. First, Arnall appointed a committee of twenty-three distinguished citizens who worked for two years to write the new "streamlined" document.[4] Second, he submitted this in entirety, except the preamble, as an *amendment* to the old constitution!—which did away with the need for calling a convention. The new one was then voted upon by the people, at a special election held in August, 1945, and passed overwhelmingly. No one could know—irony!—the role it was to play in the Talmadge eruption later.

(9) Arnall went to the Supreme Court, suing a group of railroads in the name of the state of Georgia, in an attempt to force a reduction in discriminatory freight rates. Explaining the background of this he told me, if I may paraphrase: "We were a conquered and subjugated country after the War Between the States, and so we had to submit to tariff walls. We were relegated to be drawers of water, hewers of timber. Formerly, we could just manage to get along somehow because our labor costs were so cheap. But not now. The South cain't live so long as it costs us 39 per cent more to ship goods than it costs the Nawth."

(10) He brought suit in Georgia to dissolve the Ku-Klux Klan.

With Arnall on Decatur Street

When he was governor, Arnall took me for a drive one evening; he wanted to show me how Atlanta stratifies itself. He drove his own modest car—he thought that we would be too conspicuous if a state trooper came along—and we set forth down Peachtree Street, the

[4] The new constitution contains what are called fifty "major" reforms. But Atlanta liberals point out that it equivocates on the white primary issue; i.e., it makes no mention at all of primaries, which could open the way to evasion (as in South Carolina and Texas) of the implications of the Supreme Court's white primary decision.

renowned main thoroughfare of the town, which incidentally has no
peach trees. Then, where Peachtree meets four other streets, we turned
into Decatur Street and the boiling, teeming Negro quarter.

I have just discovered that Arnall himself, in his admirable and vividly
written *The Shore Dimly Seen*,[5] describes this episode. His object was
to prove to me that the two communities, white and Negro, amicably
live apart in Atlanta of their own volition and free will as well as by
force of circumstance, and that no external pressures produce this
segregation.

> The streets were crowded. I asked Mr. Gunther to notice any
> Negroes he saw. The only Negro he was able to point out to me
> (on Peachtree Street) was the Negro doorman at the Henry Grady
> Hotel. At Five Points we turned into Decatur Street. There were
> literally thousands of Negroes on the street, visiting, shopping,
> and fraternizing. I explained to Mr. Gunther that there was no law,
> no city ordinance, and no prohibition which kept white citizens from
> going on to Decatur Street. Likewise, there was no prohibition
> preventing the Negroes from strolling down Peachtree Street. He
> asked me why it was that they didn't. The only answer that occurred
> to me was that whites preferred to windowshop on Peachtree,
> while the Negroes preferred to visit together on Decatur Street.

Come, come, Mr. Arnall! There is more to it than just this. As anybody who has read Myrdal knows (and I am sure that Arnall knows his
Myrdal well), one of the gravest and most disheartening of all aspects
of the Negro problem is *self*-segregation—the fact that so many Negroes,
hounded and made desperate if they dare to intrude so much as one inch
on white territory, retreat helplessly into the isolation of their own
communities. Perhaps there is no formal "prohibition." But Negroes are
walled off by a body of unwritten strictures even more effective. Legally
they "could" make forays into Peachtree Street. But they know full well
what the cost would be, if only to their own sensitiveness. They might
not be stoned. But they wouldn't feel comfortable.

But I don't want to labor the point. Arnall has ably explained, in considerable detail, his own attitude toward the Negro in his book. His
general line, though more clearly defined than that of most southern
liberals, is still a straddle. He has never been a "nigger-baiter," but
nobody—except white fanatics—would be likely to call him a "nigger-
lover" either. He stands for full legal rights for Negroes, but he is against
FEPC. He still thinks that the Negro problem is primarily "economic,"
which, if I may say so in all diffidence, means simply that he does not
know why it is a problem.

Arnall told me a little story which I hope he won't mind my quoting.

[5] *The Shore Dimly Seen*, by Ellis G. Arnall, pp. 99-100. Published by J. B.
Lippincott Co., Philadelphia and New York, 1946.

Talking to Mr. Roosevelt one day he remarked, "We don't really have any Negro issue in the South; it's white agitators from the Nawth that make the trouble." Mr. Roosevelt (who liked him) turned to him with that well-known twinkle: "You mean Eleanor?"

Atlanta is the nearest thing to a capital that the South as a whole has, and that the Negroes in the whole South have. Of the thirty-two accredited Negro colleges in the United States, seven are in Atlanta, and I have already mentioned some of the personalities and achievements of Atlanta University. Also the city has, as we know, the only Negro daily newspaper in the country, the Atlanta *Daily World*, edited by C. E. Scott.

Another Scott came into the Georgia news recently. He was Aurelius S. Scott, who went variously to Morehouse College in Atlanta and to Ohio State University and the University of Kansas, a former football star and a teacher and educator of prominence, who was so temerarious as to run for coroner in Fulton County in 1946. He could not legally be taken off the ticket. But he was printed on the ballot as "A. S. Scott, *Negro.*" After a vicious little wrangle (twenty-three different white candidates for the job sought to choose one amongst themselves as the sole candidate, in order to forestall the possibility that Mr. Scott might win as a result of a split in the white vote), he withdrew from the contest, so that it would not be fought on a black-white basis and as a racial issue.

In Atlanta I heard two new details about the Negro problem. One is that the only profession having to do with Negroes that whites don't touch is undertaking. They are willing to make money off Negroes, alive, in any conceivable manner; but not Negroes dead.[6] The other is that the segregation spirit is so strong in some parts of Georgia that white children won't cross Negro cemeteries, for fear of being "defiled."

Rapscallion in Red Galluses

This man is darkness. All you have to do is look at him. Lank hair flapping sideways on the forehead; cold malicious eyes full of hate; the strained pouting lips of a Torquemada; a bitter closed tightness of expression and narrowness—above all narrowness: this distinguishes the appearance of Eugene Talmadge, elected governor of Georgia in 1946. Talmadge is the kind of inciter of prejudice that is the curse of the South, that the South must get rid of to be free (but the North need not be unpleasantly smug about this; there are plenty of politically dissolute people in the North too). I wrote the following before Talmadge's death, and before the hocus-pocus of his son's accession. I see no reason to change it now.

In July, 1946, after Talmadge had "won" the primaries, a mob of

[6] Cf. Myrdal, *op. cit.*, I, p. 638.

twenty to thirty whites in Monroe, Georgia, waylaid two Negroes and shot them before their wives' eyes. Apparently one of the women recognized the leader of these knaves; he exclaimed, "Go back and get those bitches," and the women were then hauled from an automobile and murdered too. This was not merely a lynching; it was bald massacre. The Department of Justice went into action, the FBI began a long investigation, and Attorney General Clark promised that indictments would be returned, if possible. The FBI interrogated more than 2,500 people, and 100 witnesses were called before a federal grand jury. But nobody connected with the crime was ever identified, no further action could be taken, and there as of the moment the matter remains.

Talmadge happened to be outside Georgia at the time. Interviewed over radio station WOR, his comment was, "We have officers in Georgia looking out for people. Sometimes it requires several years. I remember when I was a student at the University of Georgia, they caught a murderer after forty years . . . The Bible says we will . . . have crime." Also he delivered himself of an insouciant comment to the effect that, during his three previous terms, there had been no lynchings in Georgia, and that he "sympathized" with Governor Arnall for what must be his "chagrin and embarrassment." Mr. Talmadge was wrong about the lynching record. During his years of office fourteen lynchings did take place in Georgia.

In June, 1942, it became known that 30,000 Georgians had been rejected by Selective Service for illiteracy. Talmadge, to take the curse off these figures, and apparently choosing a target at random, announced that "New York" was the most illiterate state in the union, because a lot of waiters there didn't speak English well. It was Mr. La Guardia who happened to be mayor of New York at this time, and he replied with nice venom, "When it comes to illiteracy, the distinguished governor of Georgia talks as an expert and speaks for his own class."

Once Talmadge, who had a wool-hat background and hated cities anyway, boasted that he had "never carried a county with a streetcar in it." He was a relentless New Deal hater, and he once called Roosevelt "that cripple in the White House." He wrote on one occasion that the movement to give Negroes the vote was promoted by "Asiatic-minded scoundrels and alien-minded perverts," and after his election in 1946 he boasted openly, "No Negro will vote in Georgia for the next four years." His entourage was thick with Klansmen, and once during the depression, when he was asked what he would do about the millions of unemployed, he replied simply, "Let 'em starve!"

Georgia is a state with a splendid history; it is quite proud of the fact that, unlike its neighbors Tennessee and Alabama, it was one of the original thirteen. The telephone number at the capitol is 1776. How did Mr. Talmadge fit into this tradition? The question is almost too painful to explore. How much did he learn from Huey Long? He and Long were never close, reports to the contrary notwithstanding. And he had nothing of Long's undoubted intellectual power, resource, and picturesquely attractive deviltry. There was very little to distinguish Talmadge, the Sage of Sugar Creek, except that he gave his constituents fish fries and took off his coat when making speeches, thus exposing his famous red suspenders.

Georgia is also a state with some statistics to unnerve almost anybody —except possibly the late Mr. Talmadge. Did he know that there are 488,-711 homes in Georgia without running water? Or care? Did he know that Georgia has the highest rate for syphilis among whites in the union, with an average of 145.9 cases per 1,000 as against 4.8 for New Hampshire? Did he know—or care?—that only 170 out of 593 incorporated towns have a public sewer system, and that in a recent three-year period there were 3,000 cases of typhus, a disease almost unknown to civilized communities, and spread by fleas from rats?[7] Or, to turn into quite a different direction, did he know and appreciate anything of the able and constructive work done by some Georgians in other fields, for instance the "Better Farm Units" organized by Cason Callaway, a former textile magnate?

I have been reading—a grim exercise—the miserable four-page parody of a newspaper, the *Statesman* of Hapeville, Georgia, that Talmadge ran. Its masthead read, "Editor . . . The People; Associate Editor . . . Eugene Talmadge," and it carried its heaviest thunder in communications subtly signed, "A. Talmadge Mann." Each issue contained a meandering and half-literate article by Talmadge himself, plus a few letters, a mass of boiler plate (even the editorials were clipped from other newspapers for the most part), and nuggets of miscellaneous wisdom. Three hot "stories" in the issues I have before me are headlined Extra Fat Needed in Roasting Nuts, Short Preparation Needed in Serving Broccoli, and Trojan Horse Ancient Device, History Shows.

Most southern politicians are, as we know, reasonably adult on foreign affairs, but Talmadge took his own special line. As a sample consider the following from his signed editorial on April 5, 1945:

> The Dumbarton Oaks conference provided Great Britain to have twice as many delegates or votes in the peace conference as the United States. why is this? The United States 3 delegates and Great Britain 6. Every country that goes into a peace conference should have an equal number of votes. I notice that the Senate had something to say about this numerical arrangement of votes. I recall in the League of Nations the fatal point about that [sic] was for Great Britain to have more votes than America.

[7] Cf. a recent report, *Building Together*, published by the Committee for Georgia, affiliated with the Southern Conference for Human Welfare, and an article in the *Atlantic Monthly* by David L. Cohn, "Georgia: These Are the Facts."

The leading communication in another issue is a fervid plea from a subscriber asking for information about the number of Georgians serving time for rape.

Marching Through Georgia

The ramshackle house didn't look very good to me, but my guide said, nodding soberly, "He ain't done bad for himself. Got him a hoss."

This was just outside Atlanta, and I was looking at a tenant farm. We had not gone ten miles before I saw expressed, visibly and concretely, all the evils I had ever heard about sharecropping and the tenant system. This is agriculture at its most forlorn and slapstick; actually tenantry is little more than an indifferent substitute for slavery, since it kills hope; almost every year, the small farmer just misses coming out even. For fifty-five years the South has sulked, marked time and staggered while the rest of the nation went forward, at least in agriculture. Farmers in the North got silos, hybrid corn, and mechanization; those in the South got pellagra, hookworm, and malaria.

The first thing I noticed was the outdoor privy. It has a metal ventilator pipe; these were built all over Georgia by the WPA. There is no running water or electricity; an old bedspring leans against a rotting tree; an iron pot—the laundry—sits shakily on burnt stones. We moved on to the house, which is propped up on lumps of rock; if you step firmly on the "veranda," the gray moldering boards give way. A small, cracked mirror is nailed to one of the outdoor posts, since there isn't enough light inside to shave by.

But this tenant farmer did have a horse. So he was a step above his neighbors. He works about eighteen acres, and pays a rent of $100 a year (= one bale of cotton), which is half his total average annual income.

This was a white man's farm; the next one we saw belonged to a Negro. "Hyah, Uncle," my guide greeted him. He had five or six acres in cotton, and in addition grows a hundred bushels of corn a year. In the downfallen villages of Paraguay, a thousand years behind the rest of Western civilization, and in some remote and utterly destitute areas in India, I have seen things like this. No bathroom, no radio, no running water, no electric light, no gas—of course. A crude table, a dipper in a cracked white pail, flies buzzing around, hog meat hanging from the ceiling in white sacks, a small hand-turned phonograph, old trunks and tools are features of the two-room house. There are seven old hens in the yard, and two roosters. This Negro tenant has ten children, and he has ambitions for his establishment; he cleared off part of the woods and put a tin roof on one end of the barn. But he had some bad luck lately. His feet got blistered last year and he put turpentine on them as a kind of ointment; he sat too near the stove one evening, and his slippers caught fire. "I'se never heard of a fool man burnin' up his own feet before!" he exclaimed. Ever since there have been doctor bills and drugstore bills in the village near by. "Costs me a dolluh every time dat doctor write his name!"

Seventeen American states and the District of Columbia have two complete sets of school systems. I don't suppose one Northerner out of a thousand knows this, or realizes the enormity of its implications. That the Negro schools are infinitely less well-equipped than those for the whites goes without saying.

My guide was Sid Williams, director of the Young People's Division of the Democratic National Committee in Atlanta. First we visited a white school, one built by the WPA during the depression and called a "consolidated school"; it has five grades and serves several districts in the county. Busses bring the children in; in theory, at least, this obviates the necessity of having a one-room school in every village. Some bigger "consolidated" schools run right through from first to twelfth grades. This one has 285 children, aged six to twelve. The teachers get just under one hundred dollars a month for ten months, and were looking forward eagerly to the impending Arnall reform whereby they would be paid for eleven months instead of ten.

I walked through the library first. A motto stood against the wall: CLEAN HANDS, A GENTLE TOUCH, SURELY WE OWE A BOOK THIS MUCH. There is a Britannica, and also posters urging safety lessons, bowls of roses on the window sills, and a cheerful, well-kept atmosphere. The playground has good modern equipment, slides and swings and so on, and the children (who incidentally pay 12¢ a day for lunch) looked fairly alert and clean.

Then a few miles away we visited a comparable Negro school. Here four teachers minister to 116 students; the difference is almost literally beyond belief. A shaky warped frame building at the end of a red-yellow unpaved road full of mud and rocks; ancient wooden desks (as against the pleasant movable desks in the white school); a dilapidated iron stove (as against steam heat in the white school); no auditorium, and a piano which is only just barely capable of giving out a tune; no library at all and no playground; and, instead of indoor toilets, two miserable privies thirty yards away.

We talked to the Negro girl who was principal. She was a graduate of Spelman, which is practically the local equivalent of being a graduate of Vassar; she was pleasant, efficient, and a little frightened by our visit. Her salary is 71 dollars a month for ten months, and so she has a little over 700 dollars a year to live on. I asked, "Can't the equipment be improved?" Her answer was, "Well—no!" I walked around and saw a pitiful attempt to build up a science exhibit, looked at signs urging

improvement in social behavior like DAILY DUTIES—PASS THE WASTE-
BASKET and then saw on one blackboard the legend, "The Pilgrims
landed at Plymouth in 1620." So in 325 years, I thought, we have come
this far.

It happened that when I went to see one of the great cotton mills in
the Atlanta vicinity, it was tied up by a sudden strike. The mill had been
organized by the CIO the year before.[8] Most of its workers come originally from mountain farms in Arkansas or elsewhere in the cracker
country; most, when they ask for jobs, are already in their early thirties
—having apparently exhausted any possibility of earning a decent living
in their own communities. They are then apt to remain mill workers
all their lives. They live in a kind of compound, surrounded by barbed
wire; they pay the company 50¢ a week per room, with light and water
free. Wages are 51¢ an hour for a forty-eight-hour week. "Tain't enough
to eat on!" one worker snapped.

This mill carries cotton right through from the bale to cloth, though it
does not cut or finish. I talked to the president and general manager; he
was angry about the sudden strike, defensive and embarrassed; he said
that the mill had already raised wages 50 per cent as over 1941, and that
he couldn't go higher without going out of business. I asked him if mill
work of this type gave any worker a reasonable chance for advancement.
Perhaps I had forgotten I was in America, the country of free enterprise
and equality of opportunity. He answered dryly that he himself had
started work as a mill sweeper at sixteen.

Out in the yard, as sweating policemen watched the lines of workers,
one striker slipped me a copy of their manifesto. Here is part of it:

Dear Friends:
    We, the members of your General Shop Committee elected by
you to represent you before the management of our Company . . .
have reached the end of our rope. We seemed to have reached the
end of our rope several months ago when the management refused
to sign a contract with our Union. In the interest of the war effort,
we refused to agree with you to strike this plant. . . .
    We helped our Union representatives carry your case before the
War Labor Board panel. . . . We went before the Fourth Regional
War Labor Board and again we were upheld. The Company then
appealed to the National War Labor Board in Washington. That
Board denied every one of the Company's appeals, ordering them
to get with the Union [sic] and put into a written agreement, every
section of the contract . . . This, the Company has refused to do.
    WE ARE ASKING THAT YOU REFUSE TO RUN YOUR JOB IN THIS

8 Incidentally one leading official of the Georgia CIO bears the splendid radical
name of Lucy Randolph Mason.

PLANT UNTIL THE MILLS CARRY OUT THE DIRECTIVE ORDERS HANDED DOWN BY OUR GOVERNMENT "THE UNITED STATES OF AMERICA."

Finally, I visited several Negro churches. They don't seem to differ much from white churches on the same plane, except perhaps that the atmosphere is more joyous, with attention directed to heaven more than Hell. One point is that most Negroes, so far as I could tell, think that God is white.

Home of "Gone With the Wind"

Atlanta, the "Workshop of the Confederacy" and a pleasant city with 302,288 people, may be the "capital" of the South but in some respects it is almost as middle western as Chicago. True, it rests 1,050 feet above sea level (quite unlike Chicago), and it is of course the home of much mellow southern sentiment and tradition. But also it is a very lively entrepôt and distributing and mercantile center. Its airport is one of the busiest in the nation; it is the third largest telegraph center in the world and the fourth largest insurance center of the United States; its telephone exchange is the busiest in the South, and it contains more than 2,500 factories which turn out something like 150 million dollars worth of goods a year.

Atlanta, like most cities below the Mason and Dixon's Line, is packed with contrasts. Two or three hundred yards away from Peachtree Street, in all its immaculate distinction, lies a jungle of empty lots with the underbrush boiling in green fury almost like that of Brazil. Along Ponce de Leon Avenue and in the Druid Hills section are the rich, sheltered homes of the Coca-Cola millionaires. Not far away are some of the worst Negro (and white) slums in the nation.[9]

As far as Atlanta is concerned, one of the town's leading businessmen told me, "Sherman is still a cutthroat who was careless with fire." It isn't easy to realize that the city was almost completely destroyed, made into a rubble like Coventry, only eighty-odd years ago. But after the war it refused to stay dead, and became the hub of the resuscitated South. Northerners poured in; I heard one Atlantan say frankly, "You Yankees made us." Like Dallas, it became a chief focus for representatives of northern firms, and its pace today is almost as quick as, say, that of Rochester, New York. One remarkable thing is its continuing capacity to absorb. A Northerner will come in, for instance as local manager for a company like General Electric; he will occupy the house of his predecessor, like as not; in a fortnight he will belong to the right clubs (Atlanta is full of good ones), and in a year will be recognized as a "permanent" citizen of the town; in five he may be president of the Chamber of Com-

[9] An incidental point is that Atlanta is the only city I know in which the leading hotel is named for a newspaperman, Henry W. Grady.

merce, and in ten the mayor. Several times I heard of northern businessmen who, after some years in Atlanta, are offered promotion to better jobs
with the parent organization back home. Some choose to stay in Atlanta,
even if the salary is smaller, because they like its way of life. Anyway
the slogan developed: Atlanta is the city with a southern heart and
northern arms and legs.

Atlanta has two first-class newspapers, the *Journal* and the *Constitution*, which vie with each other not only in circulation but for the honor
of being the more liberal. Both, for instance, claim to have been major
actors behind Georgia's abolition of the poll tax; the *Journal* has the
better case in this regard. The *Constitution* is more widely known outside Georgia, but the *Journal* has the bigger circulation; it is, in fact,
the most widely circulated newspaper in the nation south of St. Louis
and/or Baltimore; it outranks any paper in Washington, D. C., Kentucky, or the whole state of Texas. The *Journal* is owned by former
Governor James M. Cox of Ohio, who is also proprietor of the Miami
Daily News; sometimes 100 per cent Atlantans express resentment that
their largest paper is "absentee controlled."

Finally, a word on a unique educational institution, Emory University.
This was built on Coca-Cola money. It has (like Duke) an expensive
and impressive plant, and is one of the best schools in the South. But
it was forbidden by terms of its foundation to engage in intercollegiate
sports; hence it has no football team and few people have ever heard
of it.

Rococola

I heard it said that the "architecture" of Atlanta is rococola. The pun
is bad, but what the city would be like without Coca-Cola is hard to
conceive.

This is one of the great "success stories" in American history. In the
1880's, when there were only four soda fountains in all Atlanta, a man
named J. S. Pemberton conceived the idea of a nickel drink. He worked
out the formula, which is secret to this day, and his bookkeeper, S. M.
Robinson, named it. He scribbled down "Coca-Cola," and the company's
trade-mark still uses the same script. In 1886 the partners spent $46
advertising Coca-Cola and sold twenty-five gallons of the syrup. Then,
a few years later, Asa G. Candler, an Atlanta druggist, bought out Pemberton and Robinson for a song, and organized the present corporation;
he ran it into a property which, in the early 1920's, he sold to Ernest
Woodruff, then president of the Trust Company of Georgia, for 25
million dollars. The legend is that Candler thought Woodruff was a fool
for paying so much. But when Woodruff, a famously "tight" man, died a
few years ago he was worth, according to reliable report, 200 million
dollars; he was certainly the richest man in the South. His son, Robert

W. Woodruff, is now the chairman of the executive committee. The people who run Coca-Cola are very close-knit. Most have known one another all their lives. In Atlanta alone Coca-Cola has made at least a thousand millionaires.

The present chairman of the board, Harrison Jones, had me to lunch in the central fastness of Coca-Cola. I had half expected to see something like Willow Run. Actually the Coca-Cola building in Atlanta, the heart of the whole vast enterprise over the entire world, is a quite modest structure in a residential district.[10]

Coca-Cola is as international as wheat or taxes. Before World War II, Mr. Jones told me, it existed in seventy-six different nations; the figure today is probably about the same. Its plant in Paris reopened four days after the Germans moved out, and American troops brought it to places as remote as Attu and New Caledonia. Coca-Cola sells when it's 78 degrees below zero in Iceland, and when it's 120 degrees above in Madras; company officials aver that no community has ever been found with a saturation point for it, and only twice in history—both times during a period of sugar shortage—have American sales been less than those of the year before. There is apparently no region of the earth's surface, no race of people or class of citizens from Boston intellectuals to fuzzy-wuzzies in the middle of Africa, immune to its arcane charm.

Coca-Cola consists mostly of sugar and water; a small percentage covers all the flavoring, and of course the formula is closely guarded. What counts, I heard, was the order of mixing of the compound, and it is freely believed that only one man in Atlanta is in possession of the entire technical secret. One gallon of the mysterious inner "essence" will flavor five thousand gallons of syrup, which is manufactured in a number of different factories throughout the United States. Of course Coca-Cola would be a prodigious success nowadays no matter what it contained; you could put almost anything in a Coca-Cola bottle and it would sell, since its vast public acceptance is based on something beyond mere formula.

At first Coca-Cola was sold only in syrup form, and the drugstores and other dispensers mixed it by the individual drink. As a result, since the flavor depended to an extent on the variety of water used, the quality wasn't always uniform. It happened that two lawyers in Chattanooga missed the taste of genuine Atlanta Coca-Cola many years ago, and they went to Candler and suggested the creation of a bottling company. The huge ramifying complexities of what followed are far beyond the province of this chapter. First there were two small bottling plants, one in Chattanooga, one in Atlanta. Today there are 1,056 American bottling plants in 1,056 American cities, and bottled Coca-Cola

[10] Coca-Cola is, like so many American corporations, incorporated in Delaware, but Atlanta is its operating headquarters.

represents about 80 per cent of the total business. Reason: a bottle has mobility.

Coca-Cola bottlers buy or are granted a franchise which, under normal conditions, is perpetual. The system is not quite analogous to that of a Ford or General Motors agency, contrary to general opinion. The great automobile companies can close out their agencies. But Coca-Cola encourages its bottlers to stay with the company indefinitely and put everything they have into it. There are six "parent" bottling companies (which, incidentally, never bottle); it is these, intermediaries between Atlanta and the small bottlers, that give out the franchises. The stock of five out of these six is completely owned by the Atlanta parent.[11]

Coca-Cola, like the New York subway fare at the moment of writing, still costs a nickel; the company has resisted every pressure for a raise in price. Hence among other things it must watch tax legislation carefully since, as I heard it put, "even a tax of a penny plays hell with a kid's nickel." South Carolina imposed such a tax for a time, and so, very briefly, did Kentucky. Several people have been loosely called the "Coca-Cola senator from ————," and so on, but the company keeps clear of politics except in tax matters, and in Georgia at least does not even maintain a registered lobbyist. But its indirect power is, of course, very substantial indeed, since it represents as a rule the chief entrenched wealth of a community.

Why the South likes Coca-Cola so particularly and drinks more of it than any other part of the nation is something of a mystery. Every man, woman and child in Atlanta drinks a hundred bottles of Coca-Cola a year (the figure for New Orleans is 120) as against a total of six for New York City.[12]

Note in Malignancy

> The Ku-Klux Klan has been the vulture of America for almost a century. . . . It is one enemy that has engaged in continual warfare against America since the Civil War. Its ally is hatred. Its weapon is terror. And its aim is the destruction of our democracy. . . . The Klan runs like a bloody thread through the noose every subversive outfit was eager to wrap around America's neck.
>
> —Walter Winchell

I have said that the enmity of the Klan is triple—toward Catholics, Jews, and Negroes. It lives this three-pronged life almost everywhere in the union, though its stronghold is of course the deep South. Georgia has always been its central pivot. But—if I may be forgiven a

---

[11] During the depression Coca-Cola stock was the "salvation" of Atlanta and several other southern towns, I heard it said. It is held very widely and people used it for collateral. Coca-Cola common paid 5.68 per share in 1945, and 2.52 per share in the first six months of 1946.

[12] See Jonathan Daniels' *A Southerner Discovers the South*, p. 91.

minor lapse into autobiography—I remember an episode in Chicago after World War I. A photographer on the paper I worked for, with whom I had done several assignments, carefully sounded me out. He knew that I was not Jewish and not a Negro. With great circumspection he asked me if I were a "Cat-licker," which was Chicago slang for Catholic in those days. When I said no he invited me forthwith to become a member of the Ku-Klux Klan.

The Klan, which represents almost everything repulsive in American characteristics from bigotry to the instinct in otherwise sane people to dress up in costumes that presumably conceal identity and go in for the demonifuge of a secret ritual, has three periods historically. André Siegfried, giving it greater dignity than it deserves, once called it an extreme expression of "Protestant nationalism." The first Klan was organized in the 1860's by Confederate veterans in Tennessee; the first leader was a celebrated southern general, Nathan B. Forrest. The idea was of course to agitate against the carpetbaggers and scalawags, put the newly emancipated Negro back in his place, and re-establish "White (i.e., southern white) Supremacy." Most of the stigmata that distinguish the Klan today date from this period—the burning of crosses on lonely hillsides, the mumbo-jumbo of Klaverns, Kleagles and the like, night riders, intimidation, usurpation of police power, and the whole paraphernalia of a secret terrorist society ostensibly based on a "patriotic" impulse, like the Black Dragon society in Japan.

The first Klan did its work, and by the 1880's had disappeared. In 1915 an itinerant Methodist preacher named William Joseph Simmons (who died in 1946) set out to revive it. His cohorts, masked and in white sheets, burned fiery crosses on Stone Mountain (the movement's Kaaba) outside Atlanta; the new Klan was incorporated in the state of Georgia a few years later, and then had a violent gushing growth. The Klan took in 77 million dollars in this period;[13] it reached a nationwide membership estimated at six million; 85 per cent of all Southerners in public life were members at one time or another; it controlled the politics of whole states. But by the middle 1930's it had broken down again. Three things, in general, wrecked it: (1) a series of internal schisms; (2) a gradual but steady growth of decency in public opinion; (3) racketeers and gangsters got control of it, and the federal government moved in with tax delinquency charges and the like.

The third and contemporaneous Ku-Klux blossoming, if an ulcer may be said to blossom, began surreptitiously in the early 1940's (each Klan period is closely connected with a war, since war, the prime source and fountainhead of all evil, always gives headway to special kinds of subevil), and became overt in 1946. Once more the organization began to solicit members at ten dollars a head—half price to ministers of the

[13] According to Ralph McGill of the Atlanta *Constitution*.

Protestant church!—and summoned the faithful to get out their night-gowns and appear on Stone Mountain to see the crosses burn. Once more, in city after city, in some communities even penetrating to the police force, the Dragons, Kludds, Klokards, Titans, Kavaliers, and Cyclopses got to work.

An illusion exists in the North that the Klan is a "secret" organization. Some aspects of the ritual may indeed be secret; but the fact of its existence, as well as its general functioning and behavior, is not a secret and never was. The words "Ku-Klux Klan," with notes of Klan activity, are printed in the newspapers; in 1939, Klan detachments marched publicly and in full regalia in cities like Miami, Florida, and Greenville, South Carolina. There is nothing "secret" about the whereabouts or lay activities of "Doc" Samuel Green, the state grand dragon of Georgia, who is an Atlanta obstetrician, or in the fact that Senator Bilbo is a member. It is no secret that, on March 21, 1946, an attorney filed with the secretary of state of Georgia a corporate registration for the "Knights of the Ku-Klux Klan, Inc.," and paid the requisite fees covering the years 1943-1946 inclusive,[14] or that in May, 1946, the federal government filed a lien against the Klan for $685,305.08 in back taxes, due since 1921.

Many Klan activities aren't covered up at all. For instance the Ku-Kluxers once presented a flagpole, with tablet, to one of the most illustrious of Virginia colleges. The college accepted the gift and the flagpole is still there, though the tablet acknowledging its Ku-Klux origin has been removed.

The Klan has two new objects of attack these days—Communism (of course) and labor. It has furiously sought to oppose the recent CIO and AF of L membership drives in the South; it has threatened northern organizers, beaten them, and attempted to drive them out of various towns. Who would be a really "ideal" Ku-Klux enemy? Anybody who is at once a Negro, a Catholic, and a member of the CIO.

These are not easy times for the Klan, however. For one thing reputable Protestant clergymen all over the South have risen in opposition; the last conference of the Southern Baptist Convention vehemently attacked it. For another, various state governments have moved against the Ku-Kluxers, and the FBI is watching them with a zealous eye. This goes for the North as well as the South. The state of New York, worried by Klan activity, took a decisive step in August, 1946; four Ku-Klux units had been found operating there, and were forthwith ordered to be dissolved; the names of 1,100 members were turned over to the federal authorities. As of late 1946 the Klan was believed to be operating in a minor fashion in fourteen states, including California (where it used

[14] New York *Times,* May 10, 1946, Associated Press dispatch quoting the State Legislative Council.

the Nisei as the "enemy"); the FBI, to date, has started investigation
of Klan activity in seven, including Michigan, Pennsylvania, Kansas,
and Indiana.

The most significant anti-Klan action yet taken by any southern state
was that of Georgia in the last days of Ellis Arnall's administration, in
the form of a suit to revoke the Klan's charter. Immediately the Klan
said that it was not the Klan. "Doc" Green's organization, the Association of Georgia Klans, claimed that it had no connection with the Ku-
Klux Klan, Inc., led by a worthy who calls himself "His Majesty, Imperial Wizard, Emperor of the Invisible Empire, Knights of the Ku-
Klux Klan." But nobody is fooled by this kind of camouflage inside
camouflage.

One factor that prompted Georgia to move, and that is stimulating
action elsewhere, is the close association alleged between the Klan and
such subversive organizations as the German-American Bund. The
Georgia petition to the courts, aiming to clean out the Klan, specifically
states that, in 1940, certain local units made "a definite, planned effort"
to combine with the Bund in a single "all-Aryan" organization, and in
October, 1946, the Department of Justice announced definite proof
of collaboration between the two organizations between 1937 and 1941
"to promote racial and religious dissension prior to the war."

A proposal was made recently that the Un-American Activities (ex-
Dies) Committee of the House of Representatives should investigate the
Klan. But nothing happened. Congressman Rankin is of course a leading
member of this committee, and he buried the idea by saying that the
Klan is, after all, not "un-American" but "American,"[15] which remark
would seem to be an all-time high in confusion of an issue.

Late in 1946 a "benevolent and patriotic" order known as The
Columbians, Inc., sprang up in Atlanta, with a platform to "create voting
solidarity among all white American citizens." The organization, a kind
of sub-Klan but with more dangerous and violent tinctures, was avowedly
anti-Jewish and anti-Negro; that it should have arisen at all is sympto-
matic—Talmadge's election gave new impetus to all kinds of wrecker
groups. The Columbians, however, promptly got into trouble with the
law, when sworn statements and documentary evidence became available
that this "benevolent and patriotic" association not only had plans to drive
the Negro population out of Georgia and lynch prominent Atlanta
citizens, but actually to set up a Nazi-like "government" by terroristic
means.

[15] According to Drew Pearson, June 11, 1946.

Chapter 46

Cotton, No Longer King, and the Former Realm of Huey Long

~~~~~~

> Cotton farming, we used to say in the South, required three items
> of capital equipment: a strong back, a weak mind, and immunity
> to sunstroke. It involved . . . three operations: cotton was planted
> in the spring, mortgaged in the summer, and left to rot in the fall.
> —J. Mitchell Morse

> The frost that chills cotton and the dew that descends from the
> stars is noted, and the trespass of a little worm on its green leaf
> is more to England than the advance of the Russian army on her
> Asian outposts.
> —Henry W. Grady

COTTON is a tree—a small tree to be sure, but nevertheless a tree, not a grass or a grain. It is also (*a*) by far the chief American cash crop, and (*b*) the worst agricultural headache in the nation.

Something like 1,600,000 of the 6,000,000 farms in the United States, or roughly one out of every four, grow cotton, and some 13 million Americans depend on it for their livelihood, if you include processors and distributors; if you count in every aspect of the cotton industry, at least 21 million people, or more than one-seventh of the total population of the country, live on it. The leverage of figures as big as these is the more weighty because, of course, they apply mostly to the South. Forty-three per cent of all American farmers live in ten southern states where cotton is the standard crop. Seventy-three per cent of *all* farms in Texas are cotton farms, 86 per cent of all Mississippi farms, 85 per cent of all Alabama farms, 80 per cent of all Georgia farms.

The origin of cotton, next to wheat and corn the most important of all things that grow, is, like that of wheat and corn, obscure. Even the derivation of the word is uncertain; it may have come from the Arabic, *qutun*. The use of cotton cloth was known as far back as 1500 B.C. in India and elsewhere in the east, and it has been a prime commodity all over the world for centuries—and not just for cloth and clothes. It is the only crop that produces "food, feed, and fiber." We eat cotton, drink it, write on it, shelter ourselves with it, drive on it, feed it to livestock, tie parcels with it, sit on it, sleep on it, use it in multifarious drugs and medicines and plastics, and shoot it off in guns.

Several times, in Georgia and Alabama both, I went out to see the cotton and talk to the folk who grow it. It is a risky and exasperating crop.

To plant a tree from seed every year, cultivate and harvest it and then let the tree die, is a strange and uneconomical way to farm. Cotton, as a matter of fact, will grow year after year in the tropics, but our winter weather, even in the South, kills it.[1] It is planted in "clean-cultivated" rows, which is one reason why it devastates the soil; weeding between the rows, you turn up the raw soil, and the next rain may carry this away—also cotton is often planted in hilly country, which increases the tendency to erosion. Millions of acres of cotton land have been totally destroyed, so far as their ability to produce cotton again is concerned; one estimate is that an area as big as the whole state of Georgia, once solid with cotton, is lost to the crop forever; another estimate is that one half of *all* surviving cotton land in the United States should, for imperative reasons of public policy, be removed from cotton at once, or it too will be destroyed. The hilly terrain should be turned over to live-stock, fruit trees, and timber, which will keep cover on the land; cotton should be limited to flat, deep, heavy land where row-cropping won't kill the soil.

The small cotton farmer picks his crop by hand, and brings it each autumn to the broker at the county seat. Of each dollar of cotton income, the man who actually produced it gets about $7\frac{1}{2}\textcent$, and if he is a tenant or sharecropper, half his crop is gone before he markets it. The price is of course protected by the "parity" principle. The usual practice is for a cultivator of any size to borrow money from the government on his crop; the system closely parallels that which we described for wheat in Chapter 9. If the price goes up, the grower wins; if not, the government wins. In any case most American cotton ends up in a government warehouse, and the whole national crop is (since the New Deal) controlled by Washington, D.C.

The gist of the cotton problem has been well stated by Claude R. Wickard, former secretary of agriculture and later head of the Rural Electrification Administration:[2]

> Even if farmers received parity for every pound of cotton that could be grown in the South, the incomes of a great many . . . would still be too low to afford an acceptable level of living. And the prospect of marketing at a satisfactory price all the cotton this

[1] For some of this material I am again indebted to George S. Mitchell, whom I mentioned in Chapter 40 above.

[2] From *Cotton*, Hearings before the Subcommittee of the Committee on Agriculture, House of Representatives, Washington, 1945. This report gives some indication of the massive complexity of the cotton situation. Several hundred persons and organizations from all over the country submitted rival cotton "programs," and the text runs to something like 600,000 words in all.

country is capable of producing is, to say the least, doubtful. . . .
Here, then, is a tremendous economic and social problem. . . . For
the immediate future of course, we have the price supporting amendment and the export subsidy. . . . But they are temporary measures.
They do not solve the basic problem.

Normally the United States produces about 12 million bales of cotton
per year, which is about 40 per cent of world production. At the moment
the government has a carry-over of something like 11 million bales in
storage, isolated from both foreign and domestic markets, sterilized and
useless. The long and short of it all is that this country produces
much more cotton than it can sell or consume—this, too, although
the acreage under cultivation decreased from roughly 45 million acres in
1929 to 20,098,000 acres in 1944—a sensational reduction of more than
half. Hence, the price of cotton must be artificially supported. The
government lends money against cotton at 92½ per cent of "parity"; withdraw or modify this parity legislation, no matter how much you may
dislike it, and the bottom could fall out of the cotton market like a hot
coal going through a bag of tissue paper; the basic economy of the South
might well be smashed, with a resultant crisis ruinous to the nation as a
whole.

Meantime, with cotton at a very high price indeed, and with those 11
million bales lying idle, kindly recollect the hapless American citizen
who spent most of 1946 trying to buy a shirt.

Cotton, alone among American commodities of consequence, had no
ceiling price during the war, because the southern senators were powerful enough to keep it exempt. In 1932, during the worst blight of the
depression, cotton sold at around 5¢ a pound. By 1940 it had risen to 9¢,
by 1941 to 14¢, by 1942 to 20¢, and by 1945 to 25¢. Then during the
first nine months of 1946 it roared ahead to reach an almost unprecedented
price—39¢. Such a runaway rise had no relation to economic realities; it
was caused by the wildest kind of speculation. Then came a neat and
nasty little crash. The spiral reversed itself. In October, 1946, the price
fell to 29¢ in two weeks, which meant a drop of about $50 per bale; in
three days southern farmers were estimated to have lost 225 million
dollars; the cotton exchanges in New York, New Orleans, and Chicago
were forced to close. Why? Because economic freebooters, supported
by the cotton bloc, pushed the price up too fast and got caught. Nothing
could better illustrate the extreme vulnerability of the American price
system, if enough greedy people get their teeth into it.

But to return to more permanent realities. Cotton is always full of the
most grinding troubles. The export market, on which so much depends,
has been drastically reduced: the American share in world cotton trade
has gone down 30 per cent in thirty years. By every kind of device we
keep the price artificially stimulated; but still cotton doesn't pay its own

way. Then too consider domestic competition. Shirts are being made of cellulose instead of cotton; multiwall paper bags for flour and cement are cutting into cotton bags; draperies are being made of paper; nylon is being used for everything from rope to diapers; plastics and glass fiber are replacing cotton in armature windings and cable installations; above all, look at rayon. This was once a comparatively expensive product, and the cotton people sniffed at it. But not today. Rayon has become an aggressively dangerous competitor; it is capable of replacing cotton not merely in bed sheets, tablecloths, aprons, raincoats, and the like, but in the cord winding that goes into automobile tires and multifarious other industrial operations.

Finally consider the mechanical cotton picker, the effects of which may be literally prodigious. Slavery eventually became obsolete after the invention of the cotton gin; Eli Whitney was almost as much responsible for emancipation as Abe Lincoln. Similarly the mechanical cotton picker, together with other new devices like the "flame cultivator" that weeds cotton by burning out the trash, may end sharecropping. The cotton picker can pick something like 30,000 pounds of cotton in a twenty-four-hour day; a man, working eight hours, can pick about 120. It costs roughly thirty dollars to pick a bale of cotton by hand; the mechanical picker does it for about five dollars.

The cotton picker was invented by John D. Rust, who worked almost a quarter of a century to perfect it. The machine looks somewhat like a plexiglass turret upside down, with a long elephant's trunk attached. It straddles the cotton rows, travels three miles an hour, and can negotiate hills as well as flat country; it works as easily by night as by day, and costs about $1.60 an acre to operate; it has a wonderfully ingenious selective eye, and while getting 95 per cent of the mature bolls, it doesn't touch those still unripe. Mr. Rust is a longtime Socialist by the way; certainly no other invention of our time is more likely to have a socializing influence.[3] Very few of these cotton pickers are in existence today, because production stopped during the war; now, however, three of the great agricultural implement companies (Allis Chalmers, International Harvester, Deere & Company) are about to start big-scale manufacture of various models, and Mr. Rust is demonstrating his own machines in the Delta near Clarksdale, Mississippi.

The cotton picker will "displace 1,000,000 families in ten years," Mr. Rust estimates; there is no other word for this except revolution. Mechanize cotton fully, and you will cause the greatest social and economic displacement the South has known since the Civil War. Also—with luck—you will greatly increase the standard of living of the entire area, by spreading out the population more evenly. Consider, too, the incidental problems that will be attached, say, to the migration of a million

[3] Cf. Victor Riesel in the New York *Post*, October 15, 1946.

workers of the poorest level, most of them Negroes, from South to North. It is quite conceivable that what we conventionally call the "Cotton Belt" will disappear; cotton will move slowly westward, attracting a better class of labor, and the old cotton lands, far too densely populated and half destroyed anyway, will be taken over by other products.

The scientists work almost as hard on cotton as they do on wheat. One recent development has been the creation of a new fiber, naturally grown, called "Ramie," which has a tensile strength greater than that of cotton and makes clothes that wear much longer. Another is the use of dyes injected into the root of the cotton plant; cotton so dyed keeps color better than that dyed in the mills, and the process is much cheaper. The bewildered visitor may soon see cotton fields blooming in orange, purple, green, magenta, and baby pink! This development was originally worked out by Russian agronomists in the Soviet Union.

The Alabama Scene

The most interesting Alabamians (not Alabamans) in politics today, aside from Lister Hill, are the new governor, James Elisha ("Big Jim") Folsom, and the new senator, John J. Sparkman. Both are, by any fair southern definition, liberals. Alabama is much more diversified than Georgia; it has a very substantial iron and steel industry at Birmingham, a flourishing port at Mobile, well-run textile mills like those of a magnate named Donald Comer, and big advertisements in the Montgomery newspapers—CATTLE AUCTION.

The population is diversified too, within the usual southern limitations. Mobile is strongly Catholic; one southern county is largely German; another has Swedes, Greeks, and Chinese. Not less than 98.6 per cent of the population (despite the steel industry and the foreign enclaves) is, by Alabama figures anyway, native born, and more than 87 per cent of its people were actually born within the state. Alabama is 68.8 per cent rural; of its 230,000 farmers, more than 50 per cent are tenants, i.e., they do not own their own land, and of these tenants, almost half are Negroes. The average length of occupancy is fifteen months; then the tenant moves along, leaving little behind, and taking nothing with him. Two-thirds of the entire population is officially registered as churchgoing; few other states can claim a similar proportion. The chief problem is poverty. For instance it is lowest in the union both in retail sales and in value of school property per pupil. Workers in the Birmingham steel plants get on the average $17\frac{1}{2}\cent$ per hour less than men doing the same work in the North.[4]

Alabama has a quite good state university at Tuscaloosa; one of its best-known teachers is Hudson Strode, who has a nice faculty for

[4] Cf. A. G. Mezerik, New Republic, "Journey in America."

turning out writers of creative English. Also it has its share of violent reactionary crackpots; one paper I saw, called the *Southern Watchman* and published at Greensboro, asked recently for the impeachment of Mr. Justice Frankfurter, whom, of all people, it called a "Rasputin." Another sheet of this defamatory type, *The Crusader*, edited by a priest named Arthur W. Terminiello ("the Father Coughlin of Dixie"), is angrily anti-Semitic; Reverend Terminiello was ordered by the bishop of Mobile, the Rt. Rev. T. J. Toolen, to get out of his parish and resign his pastorate.[5]

One thing Alabama is proud of is a spectacular campaign against venereal disease. A new law obliges all persons between eighteen and fifty to take, at state expense, a Wassermann or similar test, under penalty of a heavy fine; Alabama is the only state with such legislation. The employing class opposed this at first, but now they are glad they have it, since they found that it greatly reduced labor costs and the like. About 30 per cent of the Negro population was discovered to be syphilitic. The campaign to put the law into effect was almost hair-raisingly picturesque; big banners appeared on the streets with slogans like PENICILLIN CURES GONORRHEA IN FOUR HOURS. The father of this movement was a state senator and plantation owner, Bruce Henderson.

An uneasy incipient problem is the fate of the tenant farmers and sharecroppers whom the mechanical cotton picker and the flame cultivator seem certain to dispossess. Five million southern workers will be on relief within the next five years, unless they move, according to the estimates of the Alabama secretary for agriculture.[6] This figure may seem high. But keep in mind that a single flame cultivator may displace five hundred men.

How many American governors, senators, and the like, have been musicians or semimusicians? It is easy to think of three or four. Of these, few are more striking than Big Jim Folsom, governor of Alabama since January, 1947. But whether we should call him an actual musician is open to question, since he himself plays no instrument so far as I know. The five-piece band he used in his campaign is, however, famous, and it helped him greatly to win the governorship. Folsom had two other weapons too, a big corn-shuck mop and a bucket; he would brandish the former as a symbol of his pledge to clean up the state house when he got there and he would pass the bucket for collections. "You furnish the suds," he told his audiences, "and I'll do the scrubbing." After election he explained his victory by saying that everybody voted for him "who had less than five hundred dollars in the bank."

[5] New York *World-Telegram*, December 12, 1945.
[6] Edgar T. Rouzeau in the New York *Herald Tribune*, November 18, 1946.

Governor Folsom is called "big" with reason. He stands six feet eight in his stocking feet—he likes nothing better than to walk around with his shoes off—and in his 1946 campaign he kissed (for political purposes) 50,000 women, according to his own estimate.[7] This may seem to be an impossible figure. But after every campaign meeting, he would kiss all the women who were there. Folsom is thirty-eight and a widower. By trade he is an insurance salesman. He was a poor boy who "chopped cotton and shook peanuts in his youth." But what counts about Folsom is not the free-and-easy vaudeville tincture but his concrete political program—especially if he fulfills it. Seldom has a Southerner reached a gubernatorial chair with such a sweepingly progressive platform. He came out for outright abolition of the Alabama poll tax, utility rates on a TVA basis for the whole state, minimum wages for teachers and bigger old age pensions, and a revision of the constitution long overdue.[8]

Senator John Jackson Sparkman, who took over the seat long inhabited by the late John H. Bankhead, is likewise an honest—and perhaps more serious—progressive, with a mostly admirable record in the House where he was Democratic whip for some years. By an odd constitutional quirk, he was able to run for both House *and* Senate in 1946; winning both races, he naturally chose the Senate. He voted for the Case bill; nevertheless (this takes some figuring out) the CIO backed him. Sparkman was a poor boy in the pattern we have mentioned in this book a hundred times, one of the eleven children of a tenant farmer; he managed however to work his way through college, and has a Phi Beta Kappa key and no fewer than three university degrees. He helped in the fight to keep the military from exclusive control of atomic energy, and is a stanch supporter of TVA.

We must take note of a paradox here. Alabama, a state in ferment, has just elected men like Folsom and Sparkman to big jobs, while one of its neighbors, Georgia, returned Talmadge to office and another, Mississippi, put in for a new term the worst miscreant in American public life, Theodore G. Bilbo. But while doing this Alabama also took a strong backward step on the Negro question, by voting to adopt the so-called Boswell amendment which severely limits Negro voting rights. This amendment is in effect a maneuver to sidestep the Supreme Court white primary decision, by confirming the exclusive right of the registrar in each voting district to determine whether or not a citizen may register. That this will continue in most districts to mean virtual disfranchisement of Negroes, even if Folsom succeeds in killing the poll tax, is of course

[7] *Time*, October 14, 1946.
[8] Like all southern states Alabama, fearful of too much concentration of power in a single man, punishes its governors. Not only can no governor be re-elected until another term has intervened, but for a year after he leaves office he is forbidden to take any state or federal, elective or appointive post.

obvious. For instance the present law governing registration, designed from the beginning to keep Negroes out, provides that an applicant must be able to "read" the Constitution of the United States, and have three hundred dollars in property. By terms of the Boswell amendment the three hundred dollar qualification is dropped—since many Negroes are now in a position to accumulate this sum—but the prospective registrant must not only be able to "read" the Constitution: he must be able to "understand and explain" it. Of course any registrar can hereafter throw out any would-be registrant, by ruling against his "understanding" or "explanation" of any disputed phrase. But to proceed. The point to make is that most Alabama (and other southern) liberals are liberal only up to a certain point, and that point is usually the color line.

Two political curiosities might be mentioned here. One is that Alabama has never ratified the woman's suffrage amendment to the federal Constitution. The other is that, in a legislature of 141, exactly one member is Republican. He comes from a solidly Republican (and ferociously anti-Negro) county called Winston, in the northern part of the state; this county "seceded" from Alabama after the Civil War, and for a time called itself the "Free State of Winston."

Alabama, to conclude, has probably the ablest Washington delegation of any southern state. Naturally its members watched the 1946 Congressional elections with extreme interest, and they point out that a challenging and acid situation has arisen on the Democratic side in that, since so many northern Democrats were beaten, the Southerners have their share of Congress even more bottled up than before. Out of the 188 Democrats in the new House, 115 are Southerners, and 25 out of 45 Democratic senators.

The Negro Oxford

Former Governor Chauncey Sparks, an able and interesting man deeply troubled in mind and conscience by the Negro problem, sent me by highway patrol from Montgomery, capital of Alabama (and the first capital of the Confederacy as everybody knows) to Tuskegee Institute forty miles away. En route, I watched the filling stations and country stores, with their tar-paper roofs, sagging benches on warped verandas, and miserable dogs yelping thinly. The stores are owned by men with fine old Anglo-Saxon or Celtic names. Mostly—though I would not presume to generalize from this—the Negroes clustering at bus stops and in the village streets seemed more animated, better dressed, and had a higher level of courtesy than the whites.

Tuskegee is a pleasantly laid-out community, under big comfortable shady trees. This famous school is not the oldest Negro university in the country (Hampton in Virginia predates it), nor the most influential (a toss-up between Atlanta, Fisk, and Howard in Washington, D.C.), but it has a tradition and distinction all its own, mostly on account of the prestige of its founder, Booker T. Washington, and the scientific work done in its botanical laboratories by Dr. George Washington Carver. Some progressive Negroes think these days that Tuskegee is old-fashioned, for instance in its attitude toward segregation; they resent what used to be called the "Tuskegee machine" and the "Tuskegee Compromise." The main bent of the institute is to emphasize vocational education and to work with the basic economic resources of the region it serves; it trains young Negroes for almost every kind of job, from architectural draftsmanship to child care, from techniques in the leather industry to "fuselage repair and overhaul." Most of its students are from the lower South; still, thirty-two states are represented in its enrollment, together with five foreign countries or colonies.[9] The student body is 99 per cent Negro (there are a few Amerindians); the faculty is Negro exclusively. In both these respects Tuskegee is unusual. For instance white students (mostly Jews) go to Howard in considerable number, and most Negro universities, like Atlanta, have mixed faculties. The president of Hampton is white, and so until recently was the president of Fisk. But Booker Washington wanted Tuskegee to be a truly all-Negro institution, under a benevolent cloak of white "protection," and so it has remained.[10]

President Frederick D. Patterson, a Cornell Ph.D. and a conservative Negro leader, took me around and explained his institution's work. Courses are offered in twenty-three different trades, some for women in particular. The institute has an endowment of about seven million dollars; many prominent whites have contributed to this, such as Julius Rosenwald, Theodore Roosevelt, and railway magnates like the Baldwins. Also Tuskegee gets some financial assistance from Alabama, and it is self-supporting to a degree, both by reason of its tuition fees and because it maintains its own tailor and printing shops and the like.

When I was there Mr. Sparks was still governor of the state, and he was negotiating with his legislature on the one hand, and with Dr. Patterson on the other, toward increase of the institute's appropriation; Sparks realized its valuable contribution particularly in veterinary services and agriculture. Sparks was, and doubtless still is, a last-ditcher on segregation, but he knows full well that the only way out of an impossible economic situation in the whole South is to raise the living standard of the Negro, and so he wants to help Tuskegee. He has helped in other directions too; for instance, until the Sparks administration,

[9] Haiti, China, Liberia, Nicaragua, the Bahamas.
[10] Of course some members of its board of trustees are white. Among eminent folk on the board are Winthrop W. Aldrich, Jesse H. Jones, Basil O'Connor, and Frances Bolton.

Negroes had no toilet facilities in the state capitol. Sparks is quite proud of the fact that he is willing to shake hands with Patterson (who needless to say is an extremely distinguished man) and to call him "Doctor."

The Magnolia State[11]

About Rankin, Eastland, and the unspeakable Bilbo I shall write elsewhere. What else should one say about Mississippi? Plenty! It is, as is notorious, the state with the most damaging statistics; its per capita income is incontestably the lowest in the union. One Southerner, Mississippi born, told me ruefully that it would be a splendid thing for the nation at large if his state should be expelled from the country, because then all American statistics in culture, literacy, wealth and so on would jump precipitously. The proud and loyal Mississippians will not thank me for mentioning this. But let them repair some of their home fences first.

Also I have heard Mississippi described, by Dr. Douglas Southall Freeman, as an exceptionally "gallant" state. This it may indeed be, if you neglect that it elects a jailbird like Bilbo to office time and time again. What Dr. Freeman means, of course, is that Mississippi, so needy, is making a desperate effort, at great sacrifice, to advance itself in such fields as education, industrialization, and agricultural reform.

The one-party system, we do not need to point out, rules Mississippi; this means that the Democratic party itself may tend to split. The conservative faction was led for long by men like Pat Harrison and John Sharp Williams; the "radicals," who represent the poor whites, the wool hats, the hillbillies from the cracker belt, by the Bilbos and their coterie. The governorship usually alternates between the two groups: hence Mississippi has as a rule good and bad governors, term by term.

I heard it said in Jackson, the capital, that "if you shoot a Republican out of season, the fine will be ten dollars and costs." Nevertheless Republicans do exist in Mississippi. They too are divided: one wing is that of the "Lily Whites," who refuse the Negro any voice at all; the other is the "Black and Tans," a largely Negro group led by a Washington, D.C., lawyer, Perry H. Howard, which is recognized by the Republican National Committee. Mississippi has had only one Republican legislator since Reconstruction days; he was, of all things, a former governor of Nebraska who bought a Delta plantation, settled down to enjoy the sunshine, and was drafted into local politics.

What else runs Mississippi, aside from such familiar southern factors as the Baptist church, Ku-Klux sympathizers, and the county rings? There is no state-wide boss or closely entrenched political machine. The

[11] Mississippi has at least five other nicknames: Bayou, Border-Eagle, Ground-Hog, Eagle, and Mud-Waddler. See Odum, *op. cit.*, p. 538.

biggest corporation is of course the Illinois Central Railroad, which owns two-thirds of the state's railway mileage, but it has never played much of a local political role; this is one of the American railroads that has traditionally avoided politics. The dominant utility is Mississippi Power & Light, which was once part of Harvey Couch's empire. As to newspapers we should mention those edited by Hodding Carter, cited in Chapter 40, and the two Jackson newspapers, owned by the same company but printed in different plants and with no editorial connection. The editor of one, the *News*, is Frederick Sullens, an explosive personal journalist (and white supremacy addict) of the old school and of great ability, who resembles in some respects W. W. Ball of Charleston, South Carolina.

Jackson is a curious town. Its population was only 62,107 in 1940, but it has steeply grown since; it possesses a handful of impeccably shining skyscrapers, rising straight out of a muck of Negro hovels and poor-white slums. The pictorial impact is very striking. I shall mention later other cities with a similar skyscraper-slum development, like San Antonio.

Mississippi is, of course, overwhelmingly rural; 90 per cent of the people live on the soil, which means cotton. But the state is doing what it can to press industrial expansion; it has a slogan "BAWI" (Balance Agriculture with Industry) and prints advertisements in the eastern papers, trying to lure capital in; it boasts that Mississippians themselves have invested four million dollars in new industrial plants in the past two years, and that it is "the only state with a plan." Above all, Mississippi looks to petroleum: it is at present the "hottest oil spot" in the entire United States. Oil was discovered in important quantities only about five years ago, and a frenzy of drilling and development began. Some citizens look at the petroleum boom with alarm, pointing to the example of Tulsa and saying, "Oklahoma got oil, yes, but also oil got Oklahoma!"[12]

Mississippi is of course violently addicted to "white supremacy." One reason for this is, we know, that it has the highest proportion of Negroes of any state; Negroes outnumber whites in many counties, and in some they are more numerous by six or eight to one. Also, during Reconstruction days, its Negroes participated more directly in politics than anywhere else in the South; twice, incredible as the fact may seem, Mississippi sent Negro senators to Washington! In its attitude toward the Negro problem, according to one expert, it differs more from North Carolina (using North Carolina as an example of a liberal southern community) than North Carolina differs from Ohio. I heard

---

[12] Timber is another important industry, but vast amounts of forest have disappeared. Fifty years ago the state had the biggest stand of long-leaf yellow pine in the world. This has been completely ravaged, like the similar belt in northern Michigan.

a vehement pro-Negro white say, "Mississippi is the one state that really frightens me!" and I heard a vehement anti-Negro white exclaim, "Can't you understand?—we're being *inundated* here!"

As a matter of fact a great many Negroes have left Mississippi and migrated north; even so, they still number 49 per cent of the population —which serves to intensify "white supremacy" alarm. Many of the old-line whites, however, like those in South Carolina, want to "keep" their Negroes, provided that they stay in their "place" and do not become more "insolent." One friend told me, "If you want to get shot, just try to take a Delta planter's nigger away from him!" Another exploded, "Pass FEPC in Washington, and you just watch, we'll have lynchings galore down here!" Still another asseverated, "You bet your sweet life we will continue to oppose federal aid for schools. That might mean 'nigra' kids getting into *our* own schools!"

Mississippi is a state where, on one occasion, a Bible-reading society passed a resolution to the effect that "Andy Gump, Being 100% American, Should Be Elected President of the United States," and where an eighteen-year-old colored girl was once shot because her brother aroused a gang of whites by refusing to pay 10¢ interest on a loan of half a dollar.

The following small item is not from something printed twenty years ago. It was picked up by the alert *New Republic* from the Natchez *Democrat*[13] late in 1945:

> Tom Jones, 24-year-old Negro . . . was aboard a Greyhound bus from New Orleans, Louisiana. Upon arrival at Woodville the Negro started an argument with the bus driver over the whereabouts of his baggage. The argument became heated and the bus driver went and secured the Town Marshal who . . . upon arriving at the scene found the condition such as made it necessary to shoot the Negro.

But the fact is impressive that, despite the great driving pressures to retain the status quo, Mississippi is loosening up to an extent. A twenty-seven-year-old veteran who lost an arm won a congressional seat in August, 1946, on a liberal platform, and Negroes voted in the primaries in some number for the first time. In December, 1946, the unprecedented and almost unbelievable spectacle was offered of Negroes daring to testify openly in Jackson as to the way they were forcibly prevented from voting in the last Bilbo campaign.

Finally a word on prohibition. Mississippi is, as we know, technically a "dry" state. Nowhere in America does hypocrisy in this regard reach such a dizzily schizophrenic level; though "dry," it actually maintains what is openly called "a black market tax on illegal liquor" (!) and last

[13] This newspaper refused recently to accept an advertisement by Harper and Brothers for *Black Boy*, by Richard Wright, though most other southern newspapers printed such advertisements freely. Incidentally Wright is a Natchez boy.

year, by official report of the state treasurer, this brought in the not inconsiderable sum of $498,966. Mississippi has never repealed the 18th amendment—but more than a thousand local dealers hold federal liquor licenses! Concomitant with this is the fact that it is notably famous for vigorous hard drinking. The situation is crystallized in a remark by Will Rogers, "Mississippi will drink wet and vote dry—so long as any citizen can stagger to the polls."[14]

Blackness in Natchez

Never have I seen a community like this. Natchez, Mississippi, is a museum in several senses of the word. Like Charleston, it is a famous southern shrine, and it imprisons more old Mississippi River culture than any city in the country; the flags of six nations have flown over it, and it is the only considerable American town with no railroad service of any kind.

I liked the crusty old signs in Connelly's Tavern, built in 1795 and restored by the Natchez Garden Club recently, and I learned that in 1819 a barrel of whisky cost $28.12½. Also:

> Fourpence a Night for Bed
> Sixpence a Night With Supper
> No More Than Four to Sleep in One Bed
> No Boots to be Worn in Bed
> Organ Grinders to Sleep in the Washhouse

The tavern was a prominent post on the old Natchez Trace (=trail); here came traders from the Monongahela Valley down to New Orleans, and from New Orleans up to Nashville and beyond. As a defense against both river and "land" pirates, drawbridges were built, and the imprint of the moat is still visible.

Natchez is renowned today mostly for its homes and pilgrimages. The old fortunes were built on cotton and indigo, and most are derelict. So the magnolia-surrounded, anciently rich and placid mansions, which once represented as sweeping a concentration of wealth as anything in the United States, began to go to pieces. Both as a matter of historical pride, and to give aid and comfort to some of the survivors still living in them, the pilgrimages were organized, and tourists came from all over the country to troop through them and admire their dim glory. A visitor may have luncheon in one house, tea in the next, and dinner in a third, for some days, at a reasonable enough fee. A fissure, however, developed in the local citizenry promoting the idea, and for a time there were two rival pilgrimage organizations. Then the war stopped the pilgrimages;

[14] After writing this passage I found almost the identical thing in Myrdal, who says he saw "more hard drinking in Mississippi than he has ever before witnessed." Also Myrdal quotes the Will Rogers line though in different form.

Hitler and Hirohito brought peace, as it were, to the Natchez front.

Most of the houses have an aromatic history, and all are picturesquely named. Rosalie (built in 1820) was General Grant's headquarters in 1863, and is now the shrine of the Mississippi Daughters of the American Revolution; at The Briars (1812) Jefferson Davis married Varina Howell, the "Rose of Mississippi"; Cottage Garden (1793) was the headquarters of the last Spanish governor; Oakland (1838) is still occupied by descendants of Don Estevan Minor; in Hawthorne (1814) General Lafayette once gave a famous party; Propinquity (1790's) was the home of a lady known subsequently as the "Mother of Texas"; Mount Repose (1824) is still lived in by the family of the original owner. Several houses today have passed into somewhat alien hands; one was bought by a retired Chicago schoolteacher. The "King of Natchez," the local Coca-Cola bottler, lives in one (Monteigne), and I visited another (Elmscourt), where the present owner, eighty years old, who got it as a wedding present in 1902, continues to maintain its shadowy, ghost-haunted atmosphere. The most extraordinary, I thought, was Melrose, surrounded by azaleas, loblollies white as wax, and ancient stocky water oaks hung with Spanish moss, and containing furniture and oddments of a sort almost unknown to the modern world— a bateau *tête-à-tête*, a gaming set in which a table fits on a "navel" between two chairs, vases affixed to candelabra, a girandole, and a penholder made of gar scales.

But the antiquity and closed-mindedness of Natchez struck me more particularly in another sphere. I went to a party, and more than anywhere else in the South, or the nation, I heard expressed in their most extreme form the basic issues of the white-black conflict. I happened to mention mildly that there were two sides to the Negro question; I was literally howled and shouted down, and—I hope I am not giving offense to my hosts—several leading citizens of the town almost broke blood vessels to exclaim that I must be a "Communist" or be "influenced by Jews" to hold such a view. At the same time a familiar, curious dichotomy became expressed. Guests cried, "You can't take my nigger away!" at the same time that they cried, "Good-by to white supremacy—we're all doomed!" Again and again I heard that the Natchez area was 60-40 Negro, and that "We can't have our white civilization *overwhelmed*!" An incidental point which seemed to enrage several people present, and to puzzle others to the point of consternation, was that one of the Negro servants had read my books; it was literally unthinkable to them that this evidence of mild literacy by a black underling could be possible.

That evening, for pure hysteria of mood, was the most remarkable I had anywhere in the United States in thirteen months. I left Natchez feeling that maybe the greatest problem in the South was not so much Negro education, but that of whites.

Louisiana: Good-by to the South

Once again the spectacular particularity and singularness of America! I don't know how many times I have mentioned that a state or a community is a "special case," and surely no case is more special than that of Louisiana. Once again I am aghast at the necessity of trying to compress into a page or two material that, if more room were available, could easily fill a brace of chapters. This unique boot-shaped state, Louisiana, has distinctions in many and flamboyant fields—Creole background, the Cajun communities, Mardi Gras, the career of Huey Long, butyl rubber, the shipbuilding and politics of Mr. Higgins, urban politics mythically corrupt, and the fine appetizing restaurants of New Orleans.

There are two varieties of French in Louisiana. The Creoles live largely in New Orleans and the big towns. Technically, by dictionary definition, a Creole is simply a white American of Latin origin; in Louisiana the term narrows down to folk of a superior social class, generally Catholic, whose forebears came from France or Spain.[15] The Creoles came into the area early, at the time of Bienville in the 1690's, and have more or less maintained their own community, very circumscribed and special, ever since. They are the cohesive inner core of New Orleans. Their inherited wealth has, however, tended to fray away, and many, with their estates and plantations gone, have come on hard times. But they remain inflexibly proud of their social prestige, their Faubourg St. Germain manners, and their conservative tradition.

The "Cajuns" (= Acadians) are quite a different matter. They are Catholic like the Creoles, but by and large they are poor folk who have always been poor, and they live mainly in the countryside, not the cities. There is, of course, many a Cajun great-grandfather or mother in the Creole community; but the Creoles don't easily admit this. Most Cajuns came to Louisiana from Canada after 1755; they hoped to find and attach themselves, after a long and difficult migration, to a group of their own kind. But the story is that the Creoles only gave them "the snakes, alligators, and mosquitoes." I have mentioned in Chapter 28 the extreme tenacity of the French Canadians in New England; this tenacity is as nothing compared to that of the French Canadians in Louisiana. Some parishes (the term "county" is not used) hardly seem to be part of the United States. In one congressional district, the Third, the French language is almost as common as English, and along the Bayou Lafourche and near the Gulf of Mexico, there are communities where English is scarcely ever heard. These Cajuns are for the most part a kind of Latin hillbilly. They are like the primitive mountain hardshells in Arkansas and Tennessee—except that they live in swamps and are Catholic. Some of their cultural survivals are picturesque, for

[15] But some "German" Creoles exist today in New Orleans.

instance in the naming of children. One family recently called its four children Carm, Carmel, Carmelite, and Carmedal; another used Antour, Detour, Contour, and Passantour.

Louisiana, an exceptionally complex state, has non-French and Protestant backwoodsmen too.[16] The principal cleavage in local politics is, in fact, that between the Protestant north (largely cotton-growing), and the Catholic south (largely rice and sugar). The headquarters of the south is of course the great romantic city of New Orleans. A complex balance of power exists between the two religious communities; for instance it is a maxim that no Protestant can ever be mayor of New Orleans, and no Catholic governor of the state. The only man who ever ran both state and city was the Kingfish, Huey Long.

The main factors in running Louisiana now might be listed as the following: (1) The Boston Club. This is a New Orleans club, like some I have mentioned all the way from Portland, Oregon, to Providence, Rhode Island, the membership of which is a select distillation of the financial and social power of the area. Interestingly enough, Higgins and some of the aggressive new oil millionaires, who have moved into Louisiana from Texas, are not members, and neither Huey Long nor Robert S. Maestri, a Long cohort and a celebrated New Orleans mayor, ever set foot in it.[17] (2) Until recently, the Choctaw Club, which is a "club" of a totally different category—the New Orleans equivalent of Tammany Hall, and for years the GHQ of Maestri's city machine. But Maestri was not powerful enough in the *state* to elect a governor in either 1940 or 1944. (3) The upcountry, though there are few county rings as in other southern states, and Ku-Klux leftovers. (4) The reformers.

Maestri was, and is, a character. Next to that of Crump in Memphis, his was the most effective municipal machine in the South. But between Maestri and Crump there are considerable differences. Crump, as we know, cleaned up Memphis. Maestri on the other hand lived and flourished in a city which was, to put it with discretion, famous for its liveliness.[18] Crump has always separated politics from business, and was, and is, financially correct. But Maestri has been openly accused of "getting" $1,157,161 from the oil interests.[19] Crump speaks the King's English, and is a well-educated man, even if his epistolary style is

[16] Also there are such splinter communities as the "Redbones" (Indian-Negro crossbreeds), and "Griffes," who are one degree whiter than octoroons.

[17] This establishment produces a club punch which is, if I may say so, the most explosively delightful thing I ever tasted.

[18] In older days a guide to the *bordello* districts, with highly flavored illustrations and advertisements, was freely published and sold, and until quite recently the opening of a new house was a gala occasion with high officials of the police and city administration in attendance. One mayor said of prostitution once, "You can make it illegal, but you can't make it unpopular!"

[19] New Orleans *Times-Picayune*, February 15, 1940. A suit against Maestri brought by the attorney general of the state was dismissed on a technicality.

somewhat floriferous. Maestri once gave Franklin D. Roosevelt luncheon at a great New Orleans restaurant, when the president stopped off on a cruise. He pointed to the luscious plate before FDR and barked, "How you like dem oysters?"

No mayor in the United States was more saltily picturesque than Maestri, and none more thoroughly commingled his own pungent personality with that of the city he ruled, except La Guardia.

A reform wave swept Maestri out of office in early 1946; the same kind of movement made Perrine Palmer Jr. mayor of another southern city, Miami. So, with Maestri, the last important survivor of the Huey Long dictatorship snapped backward out of sight. The man who succeeded Maestri is of an altogether distinct and different type of character, a thirty-four-year-old war veteran, deLesseps Story ("Chep") Morrison, who entered the Army as a second lieutenant and was a full colonel, with Legion of Merit, at thirty-three. No one gave Morrison much chance to win; the reform-and-independent vote elected him, and he was the most surprised man in Louisiana at his victory; the next most surprised was Maestri. One issue was—as in so many American cities—garbage. The housewives (once again let us note the importance of the women's vote) were sick and tired of the city's inefficiency in garbage collection. Also the streets were in bad repair, and every time a citizen felt the springs of his car break, he let out a curse at Maestri— and voted for Morrison later.

Morrison has plans aplenty. He wants to force a reduction in local utility rates, cut out police and municipal graft, and in particular develop New Orleans as a port of entry for Latin America. Between his nomination and election he made a quick trip to Mexico and the Central American states, adducing the geographical and other advantages New Orleans has (over Miami for instance, its great rival) as a market and transportation center. As to gambling, Morrison found himself in a dilemma. First he took the realistic "Catholic" line that the best way to control gambling would be to legalize it, which would serve to reduce graft. But the legislature (largely upcountry and Protestant) refused to approve his proposal to license and tax bookmakers, handbooks, and slot machines. He went ahead independently and, since his authority was complete in New Orleans at least, he shut down all local gambling as the alternative. What the gamblers then did was simply move outside the municipality, where, if a visitor is willing to spend a few minutes in a taxi, he will still find everything yawningly wide open.

I have mentioned musicians among governors. Jimmie (not James) H. Davis, governor of Louisiana since 1945, is not a semimusician, but a professional. A famous crooner, he ran as a reform candidate against a Maestri nominee, and won. I asked a friend what his campaign platform was. Answer: "Mother Love." He carefully avoided any political commitments at all, and fairly sang his way into the governorship. With a small band he toured the state from top to toe, making only the most innocuous of speeches, but singing his well-known "You Are My Sunshine" and other songs in a mellifluous tenor. During the tour he drank, like Gandhi (whom he does not otherwise resemble), goat's milk. Some people feared that Jimmie might desert Louisiana to make a movie, if any offer lucrative enough came from Hollywood; before his governorship, he had roles in several pictures. But since election Davis has stayed close to Baton Rouge and his work, though he still keeps up with music. In a recent *New Yorker* a review occurs of two new Davis songs, "Bang Bang" and "I'm Gonna Write Myself a Letter"; to date, his recordings have sold about a million copies. Jimmie was one of eleven children of a poor white cotton farmer. He worked his way through school, partly by teaching yodeling.

Governors in Louisiana serve a four-year term and cannot be re-elected except after an interval, in the familiar southern pattern. Davis's predecessor, Sam Houston Jones, is also an important presumptive candidate to succeed him. It was Jones who, most people agree, was largely responsible for breaking up the post-Huey Long dictatorship: he did this mostly by forcing through a civil service law. He is a lawyer and an anti-New Deal conservative. When Jones ran in 1940, his opponent was Earl K. Long, Huey's brother; Earl had the support of Maestri and the machine, but Jones beat him. Earl Long ran again—for lieutenant governor in 1944—and was beaten again. This is a personage almost as stormy as Huey. Once he bit a political opponent in the throat.[20]

Louisiana has an aggressive Department of Commerce and Industry, and points proudly to its progress in these fields.[21] It is one of the few southern states to have pushed hybrid corn development, as in Iowa, and by use of a mechanical cane cutter, roughly comparable to the mechanical cotton picker, its cane sugar industry has been largely renovated. It works hard on dehydrated sweet potatoes, on new feeds for livestock, and on the use of rice hulls for insulating material. Louisiana is the first American state in fur pelts (it has 16 million acres of forests), the second in sulphur, the third in natural gas, either the third or fourth in petroleum, and the fourth in salt.

All this dovetails into a highly fluid labor situation. In the summer of 1946 the legislature passed a law like those in Arkansas and Florida outlawing the closed shop. Governor Davis vetoed it. Then the legislature passed two measures which he did sign, locally called "Louisiana's Little Case Bill." One makes unions equally responsible with employees

[20] Cf. *Louisiana Hayride*, by Harnett T. Kane, p. 75, the best guide to the whole Long period.
[21] But its public debt remains more than twice the total budget.

for fulfillment of labor contracts; the other outlaws "violence or threats" in disputes and forbids payment of unemployment benefits to strikers.

Why is industry in the South in general, and in Louisiana in particular, so hostile to organized labor? I have given several reasons in Chapter 40. Another is of course of the simplest, that unionization makes labor costs high, which in turn puts the southern manufacturer at a disadvantage compared to his competitor in the North.

George W. Healy Jr., editor of the most famous of New Orleans newspapers, the *Times-Picayune*, drove me to Baton Rouge,[22] and here we saw the great Standard Oil (of New Jersey) refinery. The tall skinny smokestacks belch orange flame, like tapers; the gases produced are contained in enormous bulbous spheres, like retorts. Step by step, walking down the assembly line, we saw butyl rubber made. First it is a mass of hot white pebbles, then a yellowish gum, then long stringy strips, then a neat stack of thin gray sheets, and finally a bundle marked THIS SIDE UP.

The black crude comes into the refineries from Texas, Mississippi, and Arkansas as well as Louisiana itself; the fuel is natural gas from the fields near Monroe. Almost all the great companies have a heavy stake in Louisiana oil—Standard of New Jersey (its producing affiliate is the Carter Oil Company), Standard of California, Gulf (Mellon interests), Texas, Sun (Pew interests), and Humble. The plant I saw, aside from making rubber, processes 135,000 barrels of crude a day, and produces everything from high octane gas, light naphtha (=gasoline), light and heavy kerosene both, paraffin, and lubricating oil.

I spent one crowded morning in New Orleans as the guest of that well-known tycoon, Andrew Jackson Higgins, and visited several of his plants. Higgins, as everybody knows, builds boats. He is an extremely vocal and picturesque man with a marked instinct for controversy. There came a vivid episode recently when, after visiting Argentina, he not only had good words for Dictator Juan D. Perón; he wrote letters attacking Assistant Secretary of State Spruille Braden for his anti-Perón views. At the City Park plant I saw PT boats being made, these are built upside down, and the prefabricated ribs and keels are put into place on a long assembly line. Mass production here is like none other I ever saw, because most of the work is done in wood; there is little clang of metal, and the whole massive plant is strangely silent, with a wood-and-shavings odor. Higgins and Kaiser are often compared; they differ radically. Higgins has had a colorful lot of labor trouble; Kaiser almost none. Kaiser, as we know, was mostly government financed; Higgins not so much. Kaiser specialized in big ships, and Higgins in small ones. But Higgins, like Kaiser, is a self-made man. Thirty years ago he lost every-

[22] This is still another American city where there is a monopoly in journalism. Charles P. Manship is editor and publisher of both the Baton Rouge papers, and also owns the local radio station, WJBO.

thing in the lumber business; he started all over again as a hand in a sawmill, with nothing in the world, he told me, "except 35¢, a wife, two pistols, and a mandolin with a broken neck."

Finally, another word about New Orleans. Pre-eminently it is a river city. Here, at long last, the Ohio, the Arkansas, the Red, the Missouri, the Des Moines, the Illinois—to say nothing of the Mississippi that contains them all—reach the sea. Pre-eminently, too, its port (which is outside politics incidentally) makes it "the Hub of the Americas"; lately an organization known as International House has been established, to attract the Latin American export trade. Much is written about the famous and indeed unique charm of New Orleans; it is not so commonly realized that, in actual essence, it is a tough dockyard city. Also one should at least mention the two universities cheek by jowl, Tulane (Protestant) and Loyola (Catholic): Loyola has among other things its own 50,000-watt radio station, WWL, which brings it a handsome revenue. New Orleans is also a community where there is a pronounced Jewish influence; the late Lyle Saxon, the city's most eminent biographer, told me once, "The Jews have all the money here, and the Catholics have all the votes, so everybody gets along fine." The most distinguished living citizen of New Orleans is, however, of another category—Mrs. Elizabeth Meriwether Gilmer, now aged seventy-six, and known to millions under the name Dorothy Dix.

Do not think I am neglecting the Vieux Carré. Perhaps I am wrong but in a way this "French Quarter" seemed to me more Italian than French. But nowhere else in America is there such a concentration of good food. There are wonderfully good restaurants in New York, like the Colony, and in San Francisco, Beverly Hills, and Milwaukee; the point to make about New Orleans, it would seem, is that practically *all* restaurants are good. You can drop in anywhere and have a first-class meal; this may seem minor, but try to think of any other community in the United States of which it can be said; the general level of American restaurant cuisine, especially in the South and Middle West, is appalling. Then of course four of the top New Orleans restaurants— Antoine's, Galatoire's, Broussard's, and the Arnaud's of Count Casenave —are of an excellence unique in the world outside prewar France.

Heritage of Huey

The more one looks back to it, the more noteworthy it all seems. It is easy to be wise after the event; it is also (as somebody once said) wise. In almost every respect the career of Huey Long parallels that of the modern European dictator-tyrant, the Hitler or Mussolini. Huey Long, had he lived, might very well have brought Fascism to America.

The story is so well known that I will only fill in a detail or two and point to a contemporary moral. Huey was an engaging monster. He was infinitely more "human" than, say, Pilsudski or Kemal Atatürk; compared to Franco for instance he was the quintessence of warmth and charm. He was first and last a man of the people, and his appeal to the man in the street was intimate. Any dictator needs, above all, a powerful personality; Huey certainly had one. From the very beginning he had tremendous oratorical power (like Mussolini); he was (like Goering) often self-indulgent and lazy, and (like Hitler) something of a coward physically. He gave his movement religious overtones (like Salazar, Franco, Dollfuss); it was Gerald L. K. Smith, no less, who preached the funeral sermon at his grave. He was flashy (like Goebbels), bawdy (like Kemal), a sentimentalist (like Hitler), a braggart (like Metaxas), and a man with an extremely concrete intelligence (like Alexander of Jugoslavia). In one respect Huey differed from his European prototypes: he had a glistening sense of humor. Also he was a master of political abuse. Once he eliminated an enemy, who had a small beard, simply by calling him "trashy mouth." Huey could, however, write very effective English. He said on one occasion, "I was born into politics, a wedded man, with a storm for my bride."

Not everybody liked him of course. The anecdote about the man about to be hanged is famous:

Sheriff: Any last word?
Condemned man: No.
Huey: May I then use the condemned man's time to make a speech?
Condemned man: Hang me first.

Long spent some months in his youth as a salesman for a kind of lard, just as Hitler peddled post cards. Finally, what beat him down in the end was what beat Mussolini down: corruption.

Always he had great capacity to project himself, whether by getting drunk on Long Island, holding his famous *levee* in green pajamas, wisecracking about how he would tear the White House down when he got there, grinning his way through the Senate, and saying to a respectful interviewer who was endeavoring to find out about his character, "Just say I'm *sui generis*, and let it go at that."[23]

Huey was born poor (again like Mussolini); he was the eighth of nine children. He called himself a sharecropper, and even claimed Cajun blood (as Pilsudski claimed Lithuanian blood). He was an inveterate bookworm (again like Mussolini). He had a well-knit capacity to draw thugs of undoubted loyalty to his side (like Goering say), and he began public life by attacking the "interests" and "corporations" (just as Hitler attacked the department stores); he was responsible (again like

[23] Several of these quotations from Long are from *Louisiana Hayride*, *op. cit.*

Hitler) for a considerable public works program. He was (like Franco) absolutely ruthless to his enemies; he called people "Shinola" or "Kinky," hinting that they had Negro blood, just as Hitler accused his enemies of having Jewish blood. And let it never be forgotten that this Louisiana Pied Piper achieved more power in an American state than any other man in our history.

As to the exact circumstances of Huey's death there is still some mystery (as with Hitler's death), but most well-informed people in Louisiana accept now the commonly told version. Huey had imputed a touch of the tarbrush to a distinguished judge; a sensitive young man, who had married into the judge's family, brooded over this until it drove him into a frenzy, and he killed the Kingfish. The Long dictatorship did not, incidentally, end with Long. A shaky triumvirate carried on for some years, until 1940; during this period some of the knavery that took place outdid anything under Huey. What broke up the gang was, of course, federal prosecution for income tax evasion and similar irregularities; eighteen men went to jail, including the president of the university[24] and the governor who succeeded Long. To catch crooks (as we know well from the example of Chicago) the United States government has to wait until they become too successful.

Long was a lying demagogue, a prodigious self-seeker, vulgar, loose, and criminal. His own brother once testified that he had received a $10,000 bribe from a utility subsidiary. But the overriding point is something beyond all this. It is that Huey, who certainly did harm to Louisiana, also did good. He built quite good roads and public buildings; he abolished the poll tax; he seldom did any Negro baiting; he opened up the possibility of education to thousands of youngsters by making textbooks free; he built "free bridges" where traffic had been impossible without a toll; his Share the Wealth program had, in part, a perfectly sound social and economic basis; he was a people's man—until ambition, utter lack of any philosophical values, and corruption combined to bear him under. Why is this point so important? Because, if I may paraphrase Raymond Swing who wrote a prescient article about him in the *Nation* many years ago, it was impossible to understand how dangerous he was without understanding what good he did too. He gave "good works in return for dictatorship," and without the good works he could hardly have been a menace at all. Any future demagogue who attempts to carve a road to power in the United States—for instance through the next depression if one comes—is almost certain to follow Huey's path. There is, indeed, no other. Fascism will come in disguised as socialism. A man will make every promise to the underpossessed, and undeniably improve their circumstances; he will appeal to almost every shade and variety of liberal;

[24] The first president of Louisiana State University, the largest in the South, was none other than General William Tecumseh Sherman.

on the horizon, emerging, he will seem to be a savior, a disinterested messiah. The awakening comes later—with abrogation of civil liberties, military rule, seizure of the electorate, building of a Hitler-like machine, selling out to the big interests who were originally the opposition, concentration camps for the first followers and all the dissidents, and in the end bilking the people of what they thought they had.

Carnival to Conclude

Nothing like the New Orleans Carnival exists in America, as a fascinating survival of *noblesse oblige*, a tightly articulated social ritual, and plain fun-making vivacity and hi-jinks.

Mardi Gras (Fat Tuesday) is of course the day before Lent. From the first week in January until Ash Wednesday, the Carnival advances; then almost all other activity in New Orleans stops, and Canal Street (the widest important street in the United States incidentally) is roped off for five solid days though it is the main thoroughfare of the town; crescendo comes on Tuesday night, with parades and masked dancing on the streets, and the community explodes like a balloon packed with firecrackers.

But actually Carnival is a somewhat closed affair; for instance, as far as inner participation goes, Jews are excluded. "The Jews simply pack up and leave town during Carnival," I heard it said. Of course this is an exaggeration. But Jews are not admitted to the clubs on which Carnival depends.

These clubs are a very curious and esoteric business; there are thirty-three big ones, and many small. Each gives a costume ball (at some it is the women who are masked, not the men), and several stage extravagant parades. Some of these take place at night, with Negroes bearing torches; the floats can be miracles of painstaking and expensive artifice; this is the part of Carnival that the populace and the tourists see and enjoy. The balls are something else again. The clubs were, originally, and some still are, the extreme inner citadel of New Orleans snobbishness, wealth, and social prestige; normally only a handful of invitations are available to outsiders, and these are fought for vividly. Each club has a king, queen, and court; people may spend thousands of dollars for a single costume. The king of Mardi Gras is always king of the club called Rex, and the queen is the debutante Rex, the Lord of Misrule, chooses. Mostly queens are picked for their wealth and hierarchical position in the community, rather than for good looks; some queens have been plain as pins.

The lines of cleavage among the various clubs are as closely stratified as are the families in the Almanach de Gotha. The leading club is Comus. Its membership merges and overlaps with that of the Boston Club, which is not a Carnival club. Puzzled by these recondite matters I asked a gentleman who told me with serious pride that he had been a duke five times, exactly how the rival statures were determined; he answered with airy tartness, "Comus doesn't come to Rex, but Rex does go to Comus, and there's your answer." The grand climax of Carnival occurs, indeed, at midnight on Mardi Gras, when the king of Rex, with queen, leaves his own ball, and proceeds to that of Comus at the Boston Club, where the four kings and queens first meet.

No club is more interesting than that of the Negroes, of whom there are 200,000 in New Orleans. This is called Zulu, and its good-humored parade is a *sine qua non* of the entire Carnival. King of Zulu in 1946 was an undertaker, Clem J. Vandage.

The 1946 Mardi Gras was one of the most expensive, crowded, lush, and sensational in history, and 750,000 people saw it. But—labor note!— some of the night parades were not as brilliant as in former years, because the Negro torch bearers asked for $5.00 instead of $1.25 for their two-hour march, and some clubs refused to pay it.

What lesson has Carnival? Only that Americans (like most other of the earth's human beings) like to have fun once in a while, to show off in fancy dress, to drink and meet pretty girls, to keep ceremonial secrets, to belong to things, and to keep a vested interest in privileges of the past.

So to conclude now with the ten great states of the South. Let us push on to Texas.

Chapter 47

The Giant World of Texas

∿∿∿

Does half my heart lie buried there,
In Texas, down by the Rio Grande?
—Frank Desprez

THAT Texas has a quality all its own—spacious, militant, hospitable, beaming with self-satisfaction—is known to everybody, and its splendidly large vitality can be expressed in any number of ways, historically, geographically, and in terms of politics, economics, raw materials, folklore, what not. Texas is, of course, the only American state that, after nine years and 301 days as an independent republic, entered the United States of its own free will, and on what were more or less its own terms. And it is the only state that, without consent of Congress, may split itself into five different states at any time. An old joke says that it would have performed this fission long ago, except that nobody could decide which of the new Texas states would get the Alamo. In actual fact, of course, no matter what accretion of power such a self-division might bring in Washington, ten senators for instance, nobody in the whole great lump of a state would ever dream of it. Because then Texas would no longer be Texas, enormous, overflowing with euphoria, and unique. Its most preciously guarded attribute is its bigness.

There are at least four main points to be made about the Lone Star State at once. It does not properly belong to the South, the West, or even the Southwest; it is an empire, an entity, totally its own. Also it is beginning to seep over the edges; Oklahoma, Arizona, New Mexico, even California, feel its mighty impact, and if we were writing about Europe instead of the United States, one might easily be tempted to a paragraph about Texas "imperialism." A related item: most Texans don't know it, and most dislike being told, but actually this colossus of the United States, with its tremendous chauvinism and flamboyant pride in every kind of statistical achievement, is apparently not gaining but is to a small degree losing population. The estimated population was 6,389,690 in 1940; 6,255,691 in 1943.[1]

Second, despite its fantastically great economic power, Texas represents the kind of "exploitative" or "colonial" economy typical of all western states; it lives, and lives well, basically by the multifarious

---

[1] This decline was, however, almost certainly a temporary wartime phenomenon.

production of raw materials—cattle, cotton, sulphur, petroleum, a hundred others—but most of this reservoir of production is owned outside the state, not in. Texas is probably the richest "colony" on earth, India excepted, and though all its citizens will band together to assassinate anybody who says so, it has been badly fleeced by outsiders in its time; even Pappy O'Daniel once agreed that it was "New York's most valuable foreign possession." The state possesses only one wool-scouring plant, though it is by far the greatest American wool producer; one Dallas firm owns 17 per cent of the cotton spindles in the state, but most other textile mills are controlled outside; one important company (though not the biggest) supplying oil-well machinery is a subsidiary of U.S. Steel; about two-thirds of electric power is controlled through subsidiaries by Electric Bond & Share; not a single Texan is on the board of directors of the two most important sulphur companies;[2] and the greatest single industrial enterprise in the state, Humble Oil, is 72 per cent owned by Standard of New Jersey.

Third, Texas has by all odds the most virile "nationalism" of any American state. All sorts of stories are apposite; for instance the sign I saw in Fort Worth in May, 1945: BUY BONDS AND HELP TEXAS WIN THE WAR. And it is notorious that outside the San Antonio post office are three chutes for mail, marked City, Texas, and Other States and Foreign Countries. Yet this extremely acute local patriotism has not precluded an intelligent preoccupation—of course preoccupation is too mild a word—with world affairs. Partly by reason of the cotton business, which naturally promoted close ties to Great Britain, Texas was probably the least isolationist state in the union, and certainly the most interventionist in the West. So many Texans went to Canada to enlist before Pearl Harbor that Montreal wags talked of "the Royal Canadian Texan Air Force." Sam Rayburn told me (it's just a joke, don't mind), "Of course the real reason Congress passed Selective Service was to get someone in the Army not a Texan." As to the actual fighting of the war, the contribution of the state to the Army, Navy, Marines, and Air Force was spectacular. I choose only one illustration out of hundreds. Nineteen out of the seventy-nine men who took part in the Doolittle raid on Tokyo were Texans.

My fourth point would have to do with a complexity of intellectual, cultural, and social values. To put it baldly, it is that Texas, an immensely stalwart adolescent, is in a number of fields growing up.

Everywhere in the state wonderfully and slightly self-conscious

[2] See *The Brimstone Game*, by Professor R. H. Montgomery, pp. 65-66. Sulphur in Texas, which is largely controlled by the Mellons, is one of the richest and most effective monopolies in the world; the state produces about 85 per cent of the world's supply. It was Professor Montgomery incidentally who first used the phrase, "Texas is a colony of Manhattan."

patriots would ask me what Texas reminded me of most. As a rule, I would answer "Vermont," because Vermont too was, as we know, an independent republic for some years, because it too has a very special individuality and character, and, most important, because—exactly like Texas—it is a one-party state where almost every election is decided by the primary, though of course in Vermont a different party wins. Then I would be likely to add that Texas reminded me a good deal of Argentina. Not all Texans liked this. But the similarities are, indeed, extraordinary: cattle culture, absentee ownership, vast land holdings by semifeudal barons, a great preoccupation with weather, an under-developed middle class, interminable flatness and open spaces, and fierce political partisanship and nationalism. And, it might be added, the Texas "Regulars" are—or were—representative of a kind of reaction closely paralleling that of Argentina.

When I say that Texas, growing up, has just discovered that it needs a lot of brains, as well as brawn, I mean simply that it is facing for the first time a resolution of various intellectual dilemmas. Texas is having to learn to think, after years when the forces of nature provided such largess that such a painful and disciplining matter as abstract thought was hardly necessary. The state has had to discover that to have plenty of muscle isn't quite enough. Several of the Texas dilemmas are, it would seem, elementary. For instance most people want badly to maintain intact the industrialization that came with the war. Yet at the same time powerful forces in the legislature are violently antilabor; there was an attempt last year to force through a bill outlawing the closed shop. Apparently it had never occurred to many Texans that, to fulfill an industrial program, you must have not merely machines but men to work them. And of course to think such a dilemma through to its logical conclusion means that you have to make a painful choice—you have to give something up (either your precious new aircraft industry or your antipathy to labor); you can no longer have your planes and eat them too. As another example take the great dispute over education. Texas wanted, and wants, the greatest and richest university in the world. Yet it did not quite grasp the point that no university can be worthy of the name without being anchored on something that many conservative Texans feared, academic freedom.

Perhaps one should add a word about the newness of Texas, its youth as what might be called "a great power," and the violent speed and fortuitousness with which wealth was created or accumulated; this has had innumerable social consequences. In 1884, the state possessed 84 million dollars in bank deposits; in 1914, 246 million dollars; in 1944, well over $2,500,000,000. A kind of *nouveau riche* psychology swept the citizenry; of the 254 counties about 200 produce (among many other things) oil; and vast and instantaneous wealth struck a great

TEXAS and OKLAHOMA

variety of people, from the poorest tenant farmers up and down. That there should be a cultural lag was inevitable; that plenty of the newly rich should have done crazy things was inevitable; that the wave of wealth should have produced some obscurantism was inevitable. Another item: not only did Texas become rich; it was, and is, the only confederate state that did so. Hence, one sees in Texas a remarkable fusion of old "southern" characteristics, *plus* big money; atop the cattle and cotton reactionaries was imposed a layer of corporation owners, reckless gamblers in bootleg "hot" oil, and neo-carpetbaggers from the North.

Another point, minor in itself, worth making now is that so many prominent Texans should have been born elsewhere. At times, traveling through the state, I wondered if I would ever meet a native Texan; at times, I wondered if all really conspicuous Texans were born in Tennessee. Of course I am exaggerating. But for the record, Jesse Jones was born in Tennessee, and so were Sam Rayburn and Hatton Sumners; Will Clayton was born in Mississippi, and Lee O'Daniel in Ohio.

Still another preliminary point is the power of Texas in the national capital. At one time no fewer than eleven chairmen of Senate and House committees were Texans; today, though somewhat less, the figure still exceeds that of any other state. Tom Connally, former chairman of the Foreign Relations Committee, is a Texan, and so is Tom Clark, the attorney general; so is that useful citizen Maury Maverick, formerly of the Smaller War Plants Corporation, and so are Eisenhower, Nimitz, and a phenomenal number of military chieftains.

But all this is so far the merest scooping off of top cream. It is only the beginning of a beginning of the Texas story. Let us proceed.

Some Texas Jokes

A young lady, daughter of a great Texas rancher, arrived at an eastern finishing school, and was asked where she came from.

"Nueces County, Texas," she replied.

"And where may that be?"

"It's the northwest corner of my grandpappy's cow pasture."

Another little story has to do with Admiral Nimitz. The Texas theory of his success is that he was operating in the one thing in the world bigger than his home state, namely the Pacific Ocean.

And of course there is the anecdote of the New Englander who, visiting Texas, finds a lobster in his bed. Tactfully, and fully aware of Texan propensities to the grandiose, he tells his host, "Look at this Texas bedbug." The host shakes his head doubtfully and answers, "Must be a young one." This story belongs to the same genre as that of the Texan, visiting a fruit stand in California, who sees a watermelon. He rubs it, inquiring skeptically, "Is this the best avocado you have?" Answer (because chauvinism exists in California too as we know): "You son of a gun from Texas, keep your hands off that grape."

I like the story, doubtless antique, that I heard near San Antonio. A child asks a stranger where he comes from, whereupon his father rebukes him gently, "Never do that, son. If a man's from Texas, he'll tell you. If he's not, why embarrass him by asking?"

Once a Brooklyn GI was shipped to a Texas camp. It didn't take him long to get the feel of things. One evening, after wandering alone in the mesquite, he returned with seven rattles; these he showed proudly to his comrades, explaining, "I just killed a big Texas woim."

Recently in the Houston *Chronicle* appeared this small advertisement:

> MOVING FROM THE
> UNITED STATES
> TO TEXAS
>
> *Will be Permanent Resident*
> Need 2-bedroom house, apt. or
> duplex, preferably unfurnished
> or what have you for wife, 14-
> year-old boy and self?

Of Texas jokes there is no end, and most of them have to do with the state's monstrous girth, bulk, and heft. They become transmuted into that characteristic phenomenon of the United States, the tall tale; dozens of collectors seize upon these avidly, and improvise upon them day by day. At least two anthologies of Texas jokes exist, and have had a wide sale among the local patriots.[3] Serious experts in Texas tales, like that grand and salty scholar J. Frank Dobie (who is my candidate for being the most distinguished living Texan) are walking anthologies of contemporary folklore.

The Texas *Almanac*, an invaluable compendium, prints as of unknown origin the following "speech" by a visitor to the state, which has become a minor classic:

> Texas occupies all the Continent of North America except the small part set aside for the United States, Mexico, and Canada . . . and is bounded on the north by 25 or 30 states, on the east by all the oceans in the world except the Pacific . . . and on the west by the Pacific Ocean, the Milky Way, and the Sidereal Universe.
> Texas is so big that people in Brownsville call the Dallas people

[3] See *I Give You Texas* and *Tall Talk from Texas*, both by Boyce House and published by the Naylor Company, San Antonio. Some of the stories below are taken from these volumes, by permission. See also a lively book *Texas, A World in Itself*, by George Sessions Perry, which contains many admirable jokes and tall tales as well as much serious material.

Yankees, and the citizens of El Paso sneer at the citizens of Texarkana as being snobs of the effete east.[4]

It is 150 miles farther from El Paso to Texarkana than it is from Chicago to New York. Fort Worth is nearer St. Paul, Minnesota, than to Brownsville. . . . The United States with Texas off would look like a three-legged Boston terrier.

The chief occupation of the people of Texas is trying to keep from making all the money in the world. . . . Texans are so proud of Texas that they cannot sleep at night . . .

Unless your front gate is 18 miles from your front door you do not belong to society as constituted in Texas. . . . One Texan has forty miles of navigable river on his farm. If the proportion of cultivated land in Texas were the same as in Illinois, the value of Texas crops would equal those of all 47 other states. . . . Texas has enough land to supply every man, woman and child in the world with a tract five feet by twenty.

If all the hogs in Texas were one big hog, he would be able to dig the Panama Canal in three roots. If all the steers in Texas were one big steer, he could stand with his front feet in the Gulf of Mexico, one hind foot in Hudson Bay and the other in the Arctic Ocean, and with a sweep of his tail brush the mist from the Aurora Borealis. Some state![5]

One cycle of Texas stories has to do with the weather; Mr. House records some beauties:

The vagaries of Texas weather are illustrated by the experience of a hunter who told of seeing thousands of ducks on a lake. As he raised his gun to fire, a norther struck, freezing the water. At the roar of the gun, the ducks flew away, carrying the lake with them.

"Do you ever have cyclones up here?" a visitor in West Texas asked. "No, sir-e-e," he was informed. "We did have one once but it ran into a sandstorm about three miles out of town and was ripped to pieces."

When a man's hat blows off, he telegraphs to the station ahead. Or (another version) he just reaches up and pulls down another hat.

Such tales do, it is important to mention, derive with direct logic from everyday occurrences. While in Dallas I saw a small Associated Press dispatch describing how eight people were killed, twenty-eight injured, and ten small ranching communities wiped out, by a sudden freak windstorm that arrived and left again in a matter of minutes.

[4] A friend in Amarillo told me, "People in Houston think we're foreigners. And when I go to Houston, I think so too!"

[5] The remarkable thing about this Homeric catalogue is that some of the details are factually quite correct.

Then there is the historic-geographic cycle. I found maps of the United States as a Texan sees it, with marvelously distorted state frontiers, so that the Lone Star State stretches up to the Canadian border, and the Great Lakes are called "A Few Lakes Near Unexplored Territory"; I picked up postcards containing a history of the United States, "Texas Style," with items like "1620—First Texan sets foot on Plymouth Rock," "1778—Valley Forge—one of the darkest moments in history, next to the Alamo," "1845—the Union joins Texas," and "1945—Texans get Hitler's goat at Berchtesgaden—Germany collapses."

The stories about Texas prowess in World War II are literally without number. Someone asked a Texan early in 1944 how much longer the war would last. He replied, "One year to beat the Germans, one to beat the Japs, and one to get the damn Yankees out of Texas." Now this kind of story also derives from specific local phenomena. Texans on Okinawa asked to fight under a Texan flag, and—of course not quite seriously—former Governor Coke Stevenson issued a statement in August, 1945, to the effect that Texas would accept the Japanese surrender without demanding "a separate peace."

As to the Texas quality of gay belligerency a typical anecdote is this from *I Give You Texas*.

> "Tell us about the fight," a lawyer asked an elderly East Texas woman.
>
> "I didn't see no fight," she replied.
>
> "Well, tell us what you did see," said the attorney, leaning back lazily.
>
> "I went to a dance over at the Turners' house," the woman said, "and as the men swung around and changed partners, they would slap each other and one fellow hit another one harder than the other one liked and so he hit back and somebody out with a knife and somebody else drew a six shooter and another fellow out with a rifle that was under the bed and the air was full of yelling and smoke and bullets, and I saw there was going to be a fight, so I left."

But sooner or later we always get back to the recurrent theme of size, the concept of the grandiose. Texas is the place where you need a mousetrap to catch mosquitoes, where a man is so hardboiled that he sleeps in sandpaper sheets, where the grapefruit are so enormous that nine make a dozen, where Davy Crockett fanned himself with a hurricane, where a flock of sheep can get lost in the threads of a pipeline, where canaries sing bass, where if you spill some nails you will harvest a crop of crowbars, where houseflies carry dog tags for identification, where if you shoot at a javelina (peccary) it will spit your first bullet back, then race it toward you, and where that legendary creature Pecos Bill, the Texas equivalent of Paul Bunyan, could rope a streak of lightning.

A Bouquet of Superlatives

The Lone Star State is, in all conscience, big enough. I don't know any remark more relevant than one attributed to Pat Neff, a former governor who is now president of Baylor University, that Texas could wear Rhode Island as a watch fob. Its largest county, Brewster, is, quite seriously, six times bigger than Rhode Island; the second largest, Pecos, is more than twice the size of Delaware and is within a shade of being as big as Connecticut; of the total of 254 counties, actually 59 are as big as Rhode Island or bigger. Roughly, Texas is one-twelfth the size of the entire United States; one out of every twelve American square miles is Texan. It is calculated that if the state had the density of population of Massachusetts, its population would be 145,000,000 (instead of 6,255,691); one provincial town, Dalhart, is nearer to five other state capitals (those of New Mexico, Kansas, Colorado, Oklahoma, Nebraska) than to Austin. As an indication of the enormous spread of the state, one Texas football team once played in the Rose Bowl in California and another in the Sugar Bowl in New Orleans in the same year—as representatives of East and North![6]

Then consider some Texas firsts. The state wears the biggest hats in the world, and it has more pretty girls per square inch than any known segment of the earth's surface. It has produced more top-rank movie stars (Ginger Rogers, Joan Crawford) than any other state except possibly California, and Texas A&M is by far the largest military school in the nation. The assessed value of its public school system is five *billion* dollars, and it has sixty radio stations. The third biggest bookstore in the United States is in Dallas; the state capitol is the eighth biggest building in the world; and the deepest hole in the world (an oil well reaching 15,279 feet) is in Pecos County. Texas is the second state in the union in garlic production, third in asphalt, third in fuller's earth, third in sodium salts, and fourth in gypsum, cement, and rice. The world's largest vegetable farm is in Texas (at Edinburg), the world's greatest tomato center (at Jacksonville), and the world's largest spinach center (at Eagle Pass).[7] Uvalde, Texas, is the honey capital of the world, and Tyler is the rose capital of the world; Port Aransas is the world's biggest crude oil shipping port, and the Beaumont–Port Arthur region is the world's biggest oil-refining center. The state contains 410 different telephone companies, 4,000 different varieties of wild flowers, 95,200 oil wells, 7,090,000 cows, and 36,103,000 chickens. And it is the first state in the union in petroleum, natural gas, beef

---

[6] *Life*, April 10, 1939. Another source for Texas facts and figures is a superb article in *Fortune*, December, 1939. See also *Time*, June 8, 1936.

[7] But another great spinach center, Crystal City, has gone to the length of erecting a statue to Popeye on its main street.

cattle, helium, sulphur, cotton, sheep and goats, mohair and wool, hides, pipeline mileage, pecans, mules, carbon black, cotton gin machinery, and polo ponies.[8]

All this being said, one should perhaps add a note of another color. Texas, the old story says, is the state with more cattle and less milk, more rivers and less water, more schools and less education, more miles of view and less to see—than any place on earth!

And I cannot resist mentioning that when I told Texas friends that I was writing a book on the United States many immediately suggested that there should be two volumes, one on Texas, the other on the other forty-seven.

A Word on Sensitiveness

Like most things big, Texas is very sensitive; its *amour propre* may be easily damaged, its frontal defenses pierced. A year or so ago, Stanley Walker, stanch Texan that he is, wrote an editorial in the New York *Herald Tribune* mildly twitting his home state; the consequent eruption was enormous. The Fort Worth *Star-Telegram*, choking with rage, delivered itself of not less than 2,500 words of foaming counterattack,[9] and one reader wrote in: "I have never seen a copy of the *Herald Tribune*, but . . . it symbolizes much that is repulsive in American journalism. . . . The editorial was probably meant to be funny, but it looked vicious to me and uncalled-for. . . . The editorial, probably aware that Texas leads the United States in railway mileage, ignores that fact but makes the astounding misstatement that Texas does not have the best or fastest trains . . . The *Trib* says that one may catch better fish off Long Island than off the whole Texas coast. That's a bald-faced lie!"

Early in 1945 the Baltimore *Sun* ran a somewhat more severe editorial, entitled "Pious but Hopeless Request for Humility in Texas," and expressing the hope that in time it might become a bit self-critical. "Most of the states have produced over the years an occasional student. . . . Most have been called upon to examine, in the scientific spirit, the bases of their local pride and patriotism. . . . Texas, so far as we have heard, has never gone through this wholesome experience. In all history, no Texan has ever challenged the utter perfection of the Lone Star State, its climate, its geography, its history, its civilization. The only statement ever approaching such objective appraisal we have ever heard of was that of the man who confessed, in his cups, that there is

[8] Most of these and other similar facts and figures are neatly summarized in a gay pamphlet called *Texas Brags* by John Randolph, Houston, 1944.

[9] A major point in the reply was that Texas had contributed 172 "native" generals and 11 admirals to World War II; among the generals were Kreuger, Simpson, Chennault, Truscott, Eaker.

no spring in Big Spring. There is no record of what happened to that bibulant and perhaps it would be better not to inquire. But it would be pleasant, nevertheless, to learn from authoritative sources that Texas was populated by human beings and not by supermen."

No Texas reply to this churlish attack from Maryland has been recorded.

History: Two-Minute Glimpse

But we must retrace our steps briefly and see, as the phrase is, how Texas got that way; no state has a more fascinating history. It has existed under six different flags,[10] Spanish, French, Mexican, its own, Confederate, and American. The name "Texas" derives according to one theory from a mongrel Indo-Spanish word, *tejas,* which was an early salutation meaning "friendship"; and "Friendship" is still the motto of the state. The modern creators of Texas are, as everyone knows, Stephen F. Austin and Sam Houston. Austin, the son of a Missouri trader named Moses Austin, and a man who sat for a time in the Mexican parliament as a deputy for "Coahuila e Tejas," founded in 1821 the first American settlement in what is now Texas, at a town called San Felipe. Within a dozen years this colony grew to number two thousand Americans (and some British); that these stout pioneers should sooner or later revolt and declare their independence from Mexico was inevitable. The undisputed boss of the Texas revolution, when it came, was Sam Houston, a hard-living, hard-drinking, hard-eating chieftain, who was so tough that, as a contemporary said, "one drop of his blood would freeze a frog." The revolution became a war and in 1836 a group of 188 Texans under Colonel William Barrett Travis, trapped in the Alamo in San Antonio, refused to retreat or surrender and were massacred to a man, by the Mexicans, after making a suicidally heroic fight. Then six weeks later came the Battle of San Jacinto, in which Houston beat that preposterous creature Antonio Lopez de Santa Anna, killing some six hundred Mexicans with a loss of only eight of his own men. Thus Texas became an independent nation (March 2, 1836), and Houston was its first president. He was president twice, and—after statehood in 1846—governor. Then he was "deposed" when he supported the union as against the confederacy, and he died in 1863. There is no character in American history that quite rivals him. The Indians called him "Big Drunk."

The decade of independence cost the state dearly in some respects, but Texans still taste memories of that period with the warmest relish; I have heard people today assert that they'd like to be independent now.

[10] Call it seven if you include the green flag of that romantic insurrectionary Augustus Magee and his "Republican Army of the North" which invaded Texas in 1813.

Texas was duly recognized as an independent republic by the United States, Great Britain, France, Holland, and several German states; the building that housed the French Embassy at Austin still exists; Texas had its own army, navy (six small sailing vessels), postal services, currency, and the like. But of course merger into the union was inescapable. What held it up was the dispute over slavery; the South wanted Texas in; the North did not. All this happened when Houston was at the height of his powers, and he took advantage of it to do some of the brightest bargaining ever known. For one thing—though as a finesse rather than as a threat—he calmly suggested that Texas become a Crown Colony of Great Britain! The British, interested in cotton, might well have agreed and so Washington, nervous, accepted Houston's fancy terms. Texas entered the union by authority of a joint congressional resolution, something unique, and the state was given—among much else—the title to all its own public land, a right that no other state has. A convention met at Austin to ratify the agreement, and the last president, Anson Jones (who incidentally came from Massachusetts) lowered the Lone Star flag and told the legislature (February 19, 1846), "Gentlemen, the Republic of Texas is no more."[11]

I noted above that Texas, by terms of its special arrangement, may at any time subdivide itself. The actual text is: "New states of convenient size, not exceeding four in number, in addition to said state of Texas, may hereafter, by the consent of the state, be formed out of the territory thereof, which shall be entitled to admission under the provisions of the Federal Constitution." But Texas was too busy pushing itself around to think much of self-division. There was a Texas "war" with Mexico, and even an expedition against Santa Fe, in New Mexico. Once an invading Mexican army took San Antonio.

Where did the Texans come from, after statehood? A flip answer might be (a) Virginia and Tennessee; (b) Scotland. The state was settled crosswise. Most of the earlier settlers, of good old southern stock, simply moved in from across the Mississippi; the only important foreign group today, aside from the Mexicans, is the nucleus near San Antonio of folk of German extraction. As to the Scots, they came in early, bought enormous quantities of real estate, opened up the Panhandle, and are still of cogent importance to the State's economy. Also, as we have seen in Wyoming and other western states, Scottish and English financial power was considerable, if only because London banks were willing to lend Texans money cheap.

Texas history after the Civil War falls into several phases; first, that of dominance by the cattlemen; second, the growth of the great towns and a consequent dilution of ranch influence; third, the modern era

[11] See *Texas, A Guide to the Lone Star State*, in the American Guide Series.

which began with discovery of oil. The Spindletop gusher came in near Beaumont in 1901, and spilled out nine hundred thousand barrels of oil before it could even be capped. As to the cattlemen they are a tremendous story in themselves, and I will have a word for them in a chapter following; one signal factor was the invention of barbed wire, which made possible the fencing of land. During most of the modern period the chief political problem of Texas was prohibition. The first prohibition referendum was filed in 1881, and for years the state see-sawed for and against liquor, with the churches and the rural areas (which grew in importance all the time, as the great ranches were broken up for farms) supporting the drys, and the towns and politicians mostly wet. Nowadays this issue has diminished in importance—though local option movements are strong in many counties—and has been super-seded by others which we will soon explore.

Seeing It in Profile

I climbed the university tower at Austin, and Professor Clarence E. Ayres, who was once a teacher of mine at Chicago, showed me the view. A low black-green line to the west is the Balcones Escarpment, a geo-logical fault that all but splits the state; on the east a river valley leads placidly through black soil to brush country and then the sea.

Roughly—very roughly—one may from this vantage point divide the state in two; the imaginary demarcation would stretch from the south-eastern corner of the Panhandle to a point midway up the Rio Grande. And between these two Texases—east and west—the differences are profound. The east is, by and large, cotton country, with tenant farming, a Mississippi Delta culture, mushrooming industries, big towns, poor whites, most of the state's Negroes, and, of course, oil. The west (and part of the south) is the Texas of what used to be the open range, Mexicans, drugstore and other cowboys, great Hereford herds, dust, the high plains, mechanized agriculture, windmills, sheep, mountains (Texas is supposed to be "flat," but it has plenty of mountainous country and not less than eighty peaks over 5,000 feet high) and of mesquite and desert. There is, today, a very considerable intrastate migration; east Texas is losing population to the west, partly on account of erosion; much soil in east Texas has worn out. Also the west has fewer Negroes, and many Texans move out there for this reason. Much of the eastern portion of the state appears to be draining slowly toward the less thickly populated west.

Cotton cultivation, which is of transcendent importance, is another index of the differences between east and west. In the east, where Texas is most "southern," cotton is still farmed largely by tenants, working by hand on small tracts. But in the west it is produced for the most part by fairly big owner operators on fairly big plots of land who use machines. And let it always be remembered that Texas produces one-quarter of the total American cotton crop, which means about one-seventh of that of the entire world.

Each of the great divisions of Texas, east and west, may of course be further subdivided. In the east, back of the coastal plain, is both the "piney belt" centering on Tyler and the black soil region that sweeps like a scythe and contains Dallas, Austin, Waco. The piney belt is almost indistinguishable from Arkansas or North Carolina; it has huge timber deposits and red clayey soil. Here are the most backward Texans; here are oil, roses, rain, and the hinterland of Martin Dies. To the south are still other subdivisions, first the great expanse of brush and cattle country, second the irrigation-made garden known simply as "the Valley," i.e. the valley of the Rio Grande. This is a Texas still heavily underlaid with Spanish culture, and of wonderful fruit and vegetable farms, politics at their most corrupt, and a lively frontier spirit. Here too the state meets Mexico, and it should not be forgotten that Texas fronts on more of Latin America than any other state.

West Texas we may in turn subdivide—again very roughly—into the marvelous upland known as the Edwards Plateau, of deeply eroded limestone and possessed of what is called the finest climate in the world; the "Central Plains" and the "High Plains," which nowadays tend to grow sheep and wheat as well as cattle; the Panhandle which merges into Oklahoma; and, to the southwest, two tawny "provinces" of almost uninhabited semidesert, known as "Trans-Pecos" and the "Big Bend," which latter is the seat of the country's newest national park.

The Lone Star State is so copious and varied, in fact, that although all Texans consider themselves Texan, a sharp and growing sectionalism exists. This may express itself on all sorts of levels. For instance west Texas (132 counties) has its own chamber of commerce, and boasts of its own specialized statistics. The masthead of the Dallas *Times Herald* carries the slogan, "The Times Herald stands for Dallas *as a whole*" (italics mine); this in a city the population of which is three hundred thousand.

A word on place names. The author of *Texas Brags* has found eleven towns or villages named for minerals and the like (Mercury, Radium, Carbon, Gasoline, Earth, Mud); six for colors (Blue, Green, Magenta); more than thirty for trees (Ebony, Cypress, Mulberry, Peach); a dozen for fish and game (Sturgeon, Quail, Peacock, Turkey); and a hundred or so for Christian names (Jean, Lizzie, Agnes, Leo, Otto, Gus). Among miscellaneously named towns Texas has Climax, Lovelady, Pointblank, Lariat, Cistern, Dime, Box, Echo, Bronco, Gunsight, Sublime, Teacup, Pep, Cash, Nix, Cost, Grit, and Ace.

Snapshots of Six Texas Cities

HOUSTON, the biggest city in the state (population 384,514), is, with the possible exception of Tulsa, Oklahoma, the most reactionary community in the United States. It is the home, spiritual or temporal, of the Texas Regulars, of the ponderous oil tycoons, of attorneys like Judge T. A. Elkins, head of one of the biggest legal firms in the world, of distinguished women like Mrs. Oveta Culp Hobby, who is executive vice president of the Houston *Post* and who ran the Wacs, and of Jesse Jones. It is a city where few people think of anything but money, where the symphony orchestra is of the feeblest, and where the only tolerable bookshop was boycotted by many patrons because the proprietor announced in 1944 that he would vote for FDR. It is also the noisiest city I have ever visited, with a residential section mostly ugly and barren, a city without a single good restaurant, and of hotels with cockroaches. But it is also the city of a splendid university—Rice Institute—and of people like Colonel J. W. Evans, the president of the Cotton Exchange and one of the creators of the port of Houston, who has held practically every job the community can bestow that calls for genuine civic spirit and bears no salary.

Fifty years ago Houston was a village; today it is reliably predicted that it will have a million people in fifty years. The great geographer J. Russell Smith once said that it will be the New York of the late twentieth century, and I have heard serious-minded Texans, not Houstonians, aver that it will be the capital of the world a hundred years from now.[12]

What built Houston with such prodigious speed was a combination of the ship canal, oil, and cotton. Consider the canal. Houston is fifty miles from the sea; after a disastrous tidal wave killed six hundred people in Galveston and made that city temporarily derelict in 1900, the Houstonians decided to make a deep water port of their own. The canal, fifty miles long, stretches from Buffalo Bayou to the Gulf. And today, though the fact is hard to believe, Houston is the fourth ocean port in the United States, exceeding every rival except New York, Philadelphia, and Baltimore.[13]

There are more than one hundred great oil fields in the Houston area,

[12] People told me that Houston "is the only town in the West that is still a southern town," but I saw rather little evidence of this. Except for its frontier *élan* it might well be in Illinois.

[13] It is equally hard for non-Texans to realize that Beaumont, near Houston, is the seventh American port, outranking Boston, Los Angeles and San Francisco. And both Port Arthur and Texas City are bigger ports (eighth and eleventh in the country respectively) than Newport News, Portland, or Seattle. The town of Corpus Christi (seventeenth) is a kind of small and growing Houston. This has to do with ocean ports. The biggest Great Lakes port (and second only to New York in overall rank) is as we know Duluth, Minnesota.

and nine refineries are adjacent to the canal. The entire region between Houston and Beaumont seems, in fact, to be a single throbbing factory; it contains the biggest tin smelter in the world, and heavy chemicals, synthetics, plastics, are moving in. So the prophecies that Houston will some day be a kind of Pittsburgh are probably not far off the mark. It has, it would seem, everything: basic natural resources, climate, geography, and a healthy labor supply made available in part through the mechanization of agriculture.

The man who "owns" Houston is of course Jesse Jones (though its richest citizen, and reputedly the wealthiest man in Texas, is an oil operator named Roy Cullen). And Jones is to a considerable degree responsible for Houston's giddy industrial growth, because—I mean no criticism—as head of the RFC during the war he was in a position to locate new industry in the area. As to his personal holdings, they are immense. He owns the Houston *Chronicle* and its radio station KTRH; he owns or operates the three leading Houston hotels; he is the chief stockholder in the National Bank of Commerce, the city's richest bank, which in turn owns the Gulf building, its tallest skyscraper; he has very large real estate holdings, which include most of downtown Houston; his family owns the controlling share in the powerful Bankers Mortgage Company. Oddly enough Jones, a builder, has never paid much attention to oil. Many people, Texans as well as non-Texans, hate Jesse Jones; and hatred often snaps out of his own cold eyes. Meeting him I thought that he carried a stronger note of the implacable than anybody else I have ever talked to in American public life. As far as politics are concerned Jones cuts little ice in Texas, even in the Houston area; his political interests lie outside.

Houston is, of course, almost exclusively populated by people, like Jones, who were not born in Houston. The day I arrived I had a splendid lunch with a group of leading citizens; not one was Houston born. The host, Colonel Evans, was a Kentuckian; Lamar Fleming Jr., another guest (and one of the great cotton men of the world as well as a founder of the Texas Regulars) was born in Georgia. Later I talked to the leading newspaperman of the community and he said that half his staff were non-Texan as well as non-Houstonian.

Twenty-three miles east of Houston is the San Jacinto monument, which, taller than the Washington monument, is in fact the tallest stone structure in the world; perhaps irreverently I thought it looked like an oil derrick enormously magnified. Jesse Jones was largely responsible for building this formidable monstrosity, because—so he told me—the only two monuments in the country that he never tired of looking at were those to Washington and Lincoln in Washington, D.C., and he "drew a sketch" to combine them both, with San Jacinto as the result. Driving back to Houston with two friends I got a savory glimpse of the bigness of Texas in another field. We had lunch at a famous roadhouse, where I found that each of the three main courses was double: first came shrimps *and* crab, then shrimps *and* crab again (differently prepared), then fish *and* chicken.

DALLAS, a highly sophisticated little city (population 294,734), urbane as well as urban, quite chic, with a nice gloss and sheen, differs enor-' mously from Houston. It has (or had) a Little Theater and its cultural and professional life is vivid; it is the seat of an excellent university, Southern Methodist, of admirable hotels and restaurants and bookshops, and of what is probably the finest specialty store in the United States, Neiman-Marcus.

"Dallas is rich and beautiful," a Texan friend told me, "but it isn't Texas." What he meant is that it is not "west" Texas. For Dallas, though Fort Worth is only a metaphorical stone's throw away, no more connotes longhorns and coyotes than do Columbus, Ohio, or Charleston, West Virginia. Its wealth came originally from cotton, and until recently it was the largest internal cotton market in the country; but primarily it is a banking and jobbing and distributing center, the headquarters of railways and utilities; it is the second city in the United States in Rail-way Express business, the fourth in insurance, the fifth in number of telegrams.

"What did God give Dallas?" another Texan put it to me. "A group of men who had the will and enterprise to build a city where nobody thought a city could be built! Chicago had the geographical advantage of the Great Lakes; San Francisco had its bay and St. Louis its con-fluence of rivers. But Dallas had absolutely nothing." Of course this neglects the not inconsiderable factor that Dallas was the pivot of the richest region in America in regard to four prime commodities—wheat, cotton, cattle, oil. Then I heard the complaint, "Houston was just lucky, with Jesse Jones giving it all that money. If we had had a Jones, our population would be a million!" But most residents of Dallas would not move to Houston for anything on earth, not even money, because Hous-ton is somehow just a city whereas Dallas, though smaller, is a genuine metropolis and packed with charm.

Dallas was named, incidentally, for a Philadelphian who was probably the most obscure of all obscure American vice presidents (under Polk). It is conservatively minded on the whole, with a strong Baptist and Methodist tinge; I met one banker, sometimes considered its leading (conservative) citizen, who exploded, "This country's downfall into socialism began with the Federal Reserve Act in 1913!" For a long time Dallas was the most conspicuous open-shop city in the United States; it was dominated by the utilities and had the usual traction scandals; it was a seat of early Ku-Klux Klan power, though not so much so as Fort Worth. Its leading newspaper, the Dallas *News,* is probably the most "professional" paper in the state; Pappy O'Daniel once called it the "Kingpin of the Corporation Press." But under the late George Dealey, who died in 1946 at the age of eighty-six, it fought the Ku-Klux, and was one of the few Texas papers courageous enough to refuse wild-cat oil advertising while the oil boom raged.

Between Dallas and FORT WORTH (population 177,662), only thirty-three miles apart, is a chasm practically as definitive as the continental divide, and the two cities are, as everybody knows, famous rivals. But—I may be mistaken about this—I got the impression that the rivalry held more humor than bitterness, that it was all on the level of good clean Texas fun. Basically the cleavage between the two cities is of the simplest; Dallas is where the east ends, and Fort Worth is notoriously "where the west begins." Dallas is a baby Manhattan; Fort Worth is a cattle annex. Dallas has the suave and glittering clothes of Neiman-Marcus; Fort Worth has dust and stockyards.

For this a perfectly good historical reason exists. The Texas and Pacific Railway, reaching Dallas from the east in 1872, stopped there; the line was not pushed the few miles westward to Fort Worth till 1876. And in the four intervening years dozens of big eastern firms—mercantile establishments, distributors, and the like—got nicely settled in Dallas, and have stayed there ever since. Dallas was the end of the line. Another point is that William Gibbs McAdoo, after a bitter tussle, decided in the administration of Woodrow Wilson that the headquarters of the 11th Federal Reserve district should be Dallas, not Fort Worth. My banker friend may deplore the working of the Federal Reserve system—though he could not operate a day without it—but the fact that the Federal Reserve came to Dallas instead of Fort Worth is one of the reasons why his own bank, his own city, are so rich.

Because Fort Worth is smaller, it is apt to be more aggressive than its rival, and also more sensitive; it calls Dallas *nouveau riche,* and whispers that it is "Jewish dominated." The rivalry is a spur. Dallas had the Texas Centennial in 1936; so Fort Worth hired Billy Rose to put on a competing show and plastered Dallas with signs, 45 MINUTES WEST FOR WHOOPEE! DALLAS FOR EDUCATION, FORT WORTH FOR ENTERTAINMENT! But today the good citizens of Fort Worth, confronted with some civic problem, are apt to say, "Dallas will be doing this, so we'd better do it too." Sometimes the two towns have to cooperate, as in control of pollution of the Trinity River, on which both lie.

Fort Worth is not only one of the great cattle towns of the nation— delivered to its stockyards last year were almost nine hundred thousand head of cattle, more than a million hogs, more than two million sheep—

but also it is the biggest grain terminal west of Kansas City. Texas harvested 78 million bushels of wheat in 1944, an all-time record, and half this crop was marketed in Fort Worth; this is important in indicating the gradual swing from ranching to agriculture all over Texas; the ranches are breaking up. On the other hand, as anyone will remember who has seen Pare Lorentz's movie "The Plow That Broke the Plains," and as we know from previous chapters in this book, the conversion of grassland to wheat can kill the soil and make catastrophe. But to return to Fort Worth. Perhaps, in time, it will become more an agricultural than a cattle town. Yet, walking down its windy streets today, it is hard to accept this; half the men wear big pearl-gray Stetsons and fancy tall-heeled boots; the atmosphere is almost that of Cheyenne during the rodeo.

Much of the rivalry between Fort Worth and Dallas rose from the antics of an exuberant hell raiser and professional Texan named Amon G. Carter, the publisher of the Fort Worth *Star-Telegram*, and the town's most vociferous citizen. It is said that when Carter has to go to Dallas he takes a sandwich along, rather than begrime his spirit or stomach with food cooked in the rival city. It is difficult visiting Fort Worth, even when Mr. Carter is not there, to think that it contains anything else; but it does. In three widely varying fields, one may mention that (*a*) it is the international headquarters of the Oil Workers Union and its able president, O. A. Knight; (*b*) it is the home of one of the best trade papers in the country, the *Cattleman*; (*c*) it has Texas Christian University, a fierce competitor to Southern Methodist in Dallas.

AUSTIN, the capital of Texas (population 87,930), is one of the pleasantest small cities I've ever seen. The street signs are colored orange, and the lamps, uniquely in the world I imagine, shine from towers 165 feet high, thus softly floodlighting the whole town. And Austin is fantastically full of fantastically pretty girls. Texas had several capitals before Austin; in the old days, as in most western states, the capital was where the land office happened to be, and where the greatest number of folk could grab off land titles by fair means or foul. Indeed the two most conspicuous things in Austin today owe their existence to land values. One is the capitol building; the state swapped three million acres of ranch land in the Panhandle for the money (three million dollars) with which to build it. The other is the university, of which more anon.

Austin was called the "City of the Violet Crown" by O. Henry when he worked there; it contains a public monument, consisting mostly of bronze horses, which is the ugliest thing of its kind I have ever seen in the entire world; and its restaurants sold more and better beefsteaks,

even in the days of meat rationing, than any place I visited in America
except Butte, Montana.

I know nothing more beautiful in the United States—except perhaps
the wheat fields near Spokane—than the approach by airplane to certain
cities like SAN ANTONIO. They rise from the ocher plains like amber
cloud shapes; their skyscrapers, seemingly so incongruous, take on
the protective coloration that surrounds them; in a vast area of flatness,
they rise like vertical projections of the earth they rest on; they look
like huge Dutch ovens. Around them is illimitable horizontal space;
above, the high sky of the West. These sentinels and towers and stalagmites almost seem to have the quality of motion; one can almost imagine
them taking on a life of their own, and strutting proudly westward.

San Antonio (population 253,854) is, next to San Francisco, New
Orleans, and possibly Boston, the most colorful, the most "romantic"
city in America.[14] It is also a businesslike metropolis. Winding through
its heart is a stream, terraced and banked with green, seemingly below
the level of the city proper, like an iridescent trench; you slip along in
a Venetian gondola that brushes gently against the roots of concrete
skyscrapers. The gulf wind makes the nights cool, even in midsummer,
and flickering behind a web of branches are a thousand fireflies. But
look above; there you will see a red beacon shining like a giant's eye
from a roof thirty stories high. Atop another building, that of Standard
Oil, a monstrous globe rotates. But along the river banks Mexican girls
(in American slacks) flirt vividly, and boys wade in the waterfall for
pennies, and underneath every culvert, at each stage and boat stand,
are the lovemakers. Look above again. The windows shine and men are
still working. All the skyscrapers were products of the 20's; not one
today is owned by the men who built it.

Also San Antonio is a slum. The west side has a Mexican population
of around sixty thousand, which—some Negro communities in the
South aside—is the largest solid bloc of underpossessed in the United
States. These "Mexicans" (who are almost all American citizens) have
a life uniquely their own, and there is no doubt that they are severely
discriminated against, socially and economically. They go to their own
theaters,[15] eat their own food, and speak a patois called Tex-Mex in

---

[14] But when part of this chapter appeared in magazine form I got indignant
letters—chiefly from GI's—protesting bitterly that San Antonio, far from being
"romantic", was a "steaming, stinking, dirty hole" and worse. Also I had several
letters asking why I had not mentioned that it contains a superlative hotel; I take
pleasure in agreeing that the Hotel Saint Anthony is indeed one of the most
delightful in the United States.

[15] Mexican theaters as a rule run one Mexican or Spanish feature, one American
film with Spanish titles, and two complete sets of newsreels. Most have double-
size "love seats," which are explained away to northern tourists as places for a
plump lady and her children. Of course such theaters exist elsewhere than in San
Antonio; the most conspicuous movie in downtown Houston runs Mexican films.

which a word like dime is pronounced "dimey," a market is "marketa," and matches are "metchas." Also the community is self-divided; there are the "Inditos," of Indian stock and more Mexican than American, and the "Tejanos," who are more American than Mexican. For a Mexican to become fully absorbed into the white community is very rare; a few may own shops, drive-ins, and the like, but if they want to get along they adopt "American-sounding" names. There is no Jim Crow statute against Mexicans on the books, but most "good" restaurants and hotels won't admit them; for instance a scheme to train Mexican cadets at a primary flying school near Uvalde fell through because the local hotels and restaurants refused to serve them, though they had "accepted" detachments of officers from Turkey and Brazil.[16] Mexicans working for "white" Texans can, as a rule, only rise to certain minor posts; officially there is no segregation in the schools, but since most of the Mexican population lives in one district, segregation does exist in fact. A minor point is that many Mexicans—especially those from excellent old-Mexican families or youngsters who have served honorably in the American Army in World War II—resent so acutely the way they are generally treated that they pretend to be "Spanish," not Mexican at all, though they hate the Spaniards too. All this in a free democracy! Of course the basic fault is economic. The Mexicans are miserably underpaid; hence, they don't get enough to eat, their homes lack sanitation, and their health deteriorates. So the white entrepreneur, having shoved the Mexican into the gutter by paying what are probably the lowest wages in the United States, asserts that the Mexican is too poor or too dirty to be reclaimed, and thus keeps him down in a permanently vicious circle.

San Antonio is also a German town; one out of every six citizens is of German birth or descent. The chief street in the German section, once called Kaiserwilhelm Strasse, is now King William Street; but it is still nicknamed Sauerkraut Bend, and still maintains a good Kaffee Klatch atmosphere. The Germans came for the most part after the revolution of 1848. Nevertheless, there is always a big German vote for such Americans as Pappy O'Daniel, whom the German forefathers, if they were like Carl Schurz, would scarcely consider a fellow spirit. There are towns and villages in the San Antonio hinterland—Nimitz came from one of them—almost as German as towns and villages in Bavaria. And each has its own special quality; some are Lutheran, some are Catholic, one is Alsatian. The German newspaper in San Antonio is one of the most competently edited foreign language papers in the United States. (Also there is an excellent Spanish daily.)

San Antonio is also an Army town, with both Kelly and Randolph

[16] In April, 1945, the president of the Permanent Commission of the Mexican Congress and another deputy were refused luncheon at a restaurant in Pecos, Texas.

fields, and of course "Fort Sam" (Fort Sam Houston), the biggest
Army post in the country, and as everyone knows, it contains the Alamo,
which gives it a military symbolic character quite unique. Also San
Antonio is a Negro town; 9 per cent of its population is colored, and
it has one of the most picturesque Negro bosses in the United States.
Finally San Antonio is the "pecan capital of the world." Most of the
pickers are Mexican; there have been times when their wages were five
cents a day.

Politically San Antonio is run by the ranchmen plus the gambling
interests plus two men, P. L. Anderson who is the police and fire chief
(and who wears a diamond in his necktie that looks almost as big as a
peanut), and Owen Kilday, the sheriff of Bexar County. Kilday (one
of his brothers is a congressman, another is a priest) was in part
responsible for beating Maury Maverick, when Maury—incontestably
the best mayor San Antonio ever had—ran for re-election in 1941. The
way to play politics in San Antonio is to buy, or try to buy, the Mexican
vote, which is decisive; there is a cruel little joke, "An honest Mexican
is one who *stays* bought." Maury Maverick won when he carried the
west side, and lost when he didn't carry the west side. The Mexicans
voted for him because they liked and admired him and knew that he
would do for them what he could, not because they were bribed or
purchased.

The most interesting and courageous personality in San Antonio at
present is Archbishop Robert E. Lucey of the Roman Catholic church.
Lucey, a hard-fighting liberal, has ideas, vision, and ideals. He has
fought for equal rights for Mexicans and Negroes; he is the implacable
enemy of bad politics, nepotism, corruption. As a result he has some
choice enemies and the local bourgeoisie denounces him as a "red."
Another splendid priest is Father Tranchese of Guadaloupe Parish.
The kind of atmosphere in which men like these work may be illustrated
by the fact that the Hearst paper is the most liberal in the town! I met
one publisher who, talking of national affairs, said in all seriousness that
the entire bureaucracy in Washington should be scrapped—"except
the FBI!"

South of San Antonio are the most formidable of the great ranches,
like the King Ranch which, owned by the Kleberg family, covers more
than 1,250,000 acres in five different counties and is a feudal domain
like no other in the United States. It has a fascinating history, dating
back to a lucky landfall by a British sea captain; it is shaped roughly
like Connecticut, and you could put all of Connecticut in it without
hitting a wire fence. One of the Kleberg brothers served in Congress
for a time; a large factor in his recent defeat for re-election was that
part of his constituency, despite the Brobdingnagian proportions of the

ranch itself, became industrialized by war developments; this brought labor in, and labor is very anti-Kleberg.

West of San Antonio—to conclude this section—is the pleasant town of Uvalde, the home of "Cactus Jack" Garner, who was FDR's first vice president and who is today an embittered relic of the past.

EL PASO (population 96,810), in the west corner of the state, is the city of the Four C's—Climate, Cotton, Cattle, Copper. In a way it is run (like communities in New Mexico and Arizona) by "ex-lungers," folk who came out to get cured of tuberculosis. It is a friendly, vivid, animated town, the largest border town in the United States, and well governed. In a sense El Paso doesn't belong to Texas at all, but to New Mexico (for instance it gets its electric light from a company actually in New Mexican territory); nothing leads to it except five hundred miles of semidesert; and other Texans say that El Paso never goes to Austin at all, except to ask for money. In contrast to San Antonio it has pretty well solved the political aspects of its Mexican problem; it has more Mexicans proportionately to population (70 per cent) than San Antonio, but nobody "votes" them nowadays; there is no machine, and the mayor, J. E. Anderson, is an honest man. The El Pasoans like to say they are more independent politically than any other community in Texas; O'Daniel for instance ran at the bottom of the ticket in El Paso in both his last elections. El Paso, like San Antonio, is a good deal of an Army town; its great post is Fort Bliss. The dominant economic interest is the Phelps Dodge Corporation, about which we will hear more before this book is done.

El Paso is, incidentally, the seat of the only frontier dispute between the United States and a foreign nation. Some six hundred acres called the Chamizal Zone, including some valuable urban real estate, have been claimed by Mexico since 1894; what happened was that the course of the Rio Grande shifted, making property rights uncertain. Late in 1945, President Truman announced that he was giving his attention to this dispute.

Amarillo and the Dust Bowl

Grass was the mother and father of it all.
—Archibald MacLeish

Finally, AMARILLO. This fascinating place (population 51,686) is in a way the purest Texan city of them all. I do not mean, needless to say, pure in the moral sense. Amarillo is raw, violent, and the most open open-town in the country except possibly Las Vegas in Nevada. I mean pure in that it contains a distillation of some of the sharpest qualities of old Texas, and that it lies open and exposed to some of the mightiest forces ever let loose by nature.

Amarillo is the heart of the Panhandle, the "High Plains," and the short grass country. Look at any detailed map; the counties, row by row and tier on tier, are absolutely identical in size, mathematically square, and as artificially made as building blocks. The town is the natural capital of a region as big as New York and Pennsylvania together; and in this whole immense area, it is the *only* town of consequence; thus its hinterland includes half of Oklahoma and parts of Kansas and Nebraska (the celebrated Dust Bowl); and people drive some 350 miles to Dallas to shop. Like El Paso, it has little connection except by formality with Austin, which is twenty-four hours away by the fastest train; its citizens think of themselves as belonging to a separate Texan state. And since Amarillo is the center of the largest expanse of open prairie in the United States, at an altitude of 3,700 feet, its weather is notorious. There is a famous anecdote to the point; a German settler said, "De vedder out here I do not like. De rain vas all vind, and de vind vas all sand." It is brilliantly suggestive that Gene Howe usually starts his column in the Amarillo *Globe* with some such remark as "The weather—beastly!" Yet it may be a gloriously sunny day. What Mr. Howe means is that Amarillo needs moisture, and from the local point of view the weather is terrible unless it rains.

The region around Amarillo produces several natural wonders. In Deaf Smith County the water, heavily loaded with lime and phosphate, is supposed to cure bad teeth, and the tale goes that if you "drink a little, the lime will first build up under your fillings, then pinch them out."

The economy of Amarillo and the Panhandle is built on oil and natural gas, cattle, and wheat. Here was the country of Colonel Charles Goodnight, who built the first wire fences and who gave his name to one of the most famous of the longhorn trails, and of ranches like the XIT, which is, or was, Scottish owned and which once comprised not less than 3,050,000 acres, and was the largest property of its kind in North America, and the Matador, another monster owned by Scots. The cattlemen gave Amarillo much of the quality for which it is still famous; they would come to town after six months on a ranch, loaded with money and empty of everything else, and a lot of fireworks would result. I heard one story of a lady, the mother of three children, who alternated with her husband on these six-month visits, since someone had to stay home and watch the children; the lady's exploits with alcohol and otherwise far outshone anything a mere man ever did. Sometimes an oil gusher would be discovered right in the middle of a ranch; so, overnight, the rancher would become fantastically, inordinately rich. The complex phenomenon known as Amarillo society carries traces of this to this day. Multimillionaires learned table manners first, how to read second.

The story of natural gas is a story in itself; one of the standard Texas boasts is that it wastes more natural gas per day than the whole rest of the world produces. The Panhandle field is the world's largest, with reserves estimated at 25 *trillion* cubic feet; the annual production is almost two trillion cubic feet (of which about half is wasted); kitchen ranges burn it in a thousand towns all over the country. Natural gas has produced its own mythology, its own techniques, its own greatest expert, Professor Eugene P. Schoch of the University of Texas; some of it in the Panhandle is so rich that "you can squeeze the gasoline out of it." There are hundreds of individual owners and operators; the biggest is the Phillips Petroleum Company of Bartlesville, Oklahoma, the head of which was once a barber in Iowa.

Near Amarillo is the only important helium deposit in the United States; this is a government monopoly, and plays no role in the life of the town. Amarillo is also a great center for carbon black; this, the soot from burning gas, is used in processing rubber, and is "foreign" owned, in large part by Boston interests.

Amarillo's most conspicuous citizen is probably Gene Howe ("Panhandle Puck"), a conservative and individualistic editor whose column, "The Tactless Texan," is widely read in the area. Also he is a considerable factor in the political life of the town, though his policy is to play down local politics.[17] He was a leading Texas Regular. Howe is the son of the Kansas philosopher E. W. Howe, famous for his "Ventures in Common Sense." Another local worthy is Cal Farley, a professional wrestler and baseball player from Minnesota, who became one of the biggest tire distributors in the country, and who founded as a hobby the Boys' Ranch at Tascosa, a home for urban incorrigibles.

Beyond all this is the factor of the Dust Bowl that was, and that may someday be again. Everybody knows the legendary anecdote of the farmer who, arranging with a banker to inspect his farm and thus get a loan, saw the farm blow past the bank. And Gene Howe told me that in April, 1935, there were twenty-seven days out of thirty when, at noon, he could not see across the street.

Amarillo is, however, not the actual center of the Dust Bowl; that lies about fifty miles north, beginning at Dumas and stretching up into the Oklahoma strip. But Amarillo suffered too. The great drought began in 1935, which was the worst year, and lasted for seven years. Normally the rainfall is about twenty-one inches; from 1935 to 1942, it averaged less than ten, and moreover when the rain did come, it came too heavily,

[17] As a matter of fact Amarillo is not much interested in politics per se. The town is well run by a city manager, and it is quite a job to persuade anybody to be a candidate for mayor.

in drenching spurts, and washed away what little soil had not already been destroyed. On roads north of Amarillo you may still see drifts of dust along the highways, covering the fences; there are still houses totally dusted under. The region has always had sand storms but this was something else; it was *black* dust, the top soil of whole farms. The earth was exposed down to the hardpan, and in some cases no soil was left at all; the farms in the worst-hit areas have long since been abandoned. The soil that blew away fell, as we know, on Tennessee, on Vermont, on North Carolina, and even far out into the Atlantic.

The question naturally arises what Texas—and the nation as a whole —is doing to forefend repetition of this disaster. The Department of Agriculture and its soil conservation experts have set to work with the co-operation of Texas authorities; they have done well—so well that part of the area has been literally reconstructed. The great fundamental reasons behind the Dust Bowl were first that the land had been overgrazed, second that too much prairie had been plowed up for wheat. So, in general, restorative and preventive measures took three forms:

(1) Shelter belts, that is, trees like apricot, Russian olive, Chinese elm, that can survive the rigorous local conditions, have been planted by the hundred thousand since 1937-38. The United States government furnishes the trees free, and pays part of the labor costs. (2) Such cover crops as maize, soy beans, and sweet clover were planted, to hold the earth down, and get some root and fiber back into the soil. Also contour farming and terracing are being taught, and every effort made to persuade stockmen to pasture their herds lightly. (3) A series of "water controls" and "damming draws" is being built up.

Finally, a word on agriculture in general in this part of Texas. There is no tenant farming as in the South, no sharecropping; around Amarillo everybody owns either his ranch or his equipment, though plenty of big ranchers hire labor; normally a hand will get $125 per month plus a house, a cow, and chickens. To support a family in the Panhandle, a man needs three-quarters of a section, i.e. 480 acres. Most farms are much bigger, running from 640 up. And the "mechanized migrants" play more and more of a role, the tractor teams and fleets of itinerant combines, which we have already noted in Montana and the Northwest, and which move with the harvest across the country month by month.

So much by way of introduction. Let us turn now to the world of Texas politics.

Chapter 48

Who and Why in Texas Politics

The state of Texas is part of Mexico and is on the frontier
between that country and the United States. In the course of
the last few years the Anglo-Americans have penetrated into
this province, which is still thinly peopled; they purchase land,
they produce the commodities of the country, and supplant the
original population. It may easily be foreseen that if Mexico
takes no steps to check this change, the province of Texas will
very shortly cease to belong to that government.

—Alexis de Tocqueville in 1835

THERE is no single boss, no over-all machine, in Texas; the state is too
big for that, too various as we should realize by now. So the question
"Who runs Texas?" necessarily demands a composite answer.

Lots of people run for governor; there may be as many as twelve
candidates or more in an election. No governor in the history of the
state, though in theory he may be re-elected indefinitely, has ever served
more than two terms; the partisanship is too spirited, the competition
too acerb. But, be it noted, the Ferguson *family*, Pa and Ma between
them, served four terms. Most governors, as in many American states,
step up to the post; Stevenson and Hobby were lieutenant governors
and Hogg, Allred, Moody, Culbertson, were all attorneys general. Texas,
along with Wyoming, was the first state to elect a woman governor.
The chief power of a Texas governor lies in his capacity to make
appointments; no other state, except perhaps Oklahoma, permits such
concentration of authority.

The political history of modern Texas begins with the governorship
of a great man, Jim Hogg, who served from 1891 to 1895. All over the
state I heard it said not merely that Hogg was the best governor Texas
ever had, but that it has never had a really good one since. Hogg, whose
daughter (named Ima) is still a considerable influence in Houston, was
a people's man, who set out to break the stranglehold of the great corporations; he was a kind of Texas equivalent of Hiram Johnson. Also
he reflected the ascending influence of the rural communities, the small
farmers as against the ranchmen. In 1915 what might be called the
Ferguson.era began. James E. Ferguson was a kind of peasant demagogue who did some things well (for instance in rural education) and
who got constantly entangled in his own folksy ego; he was impeached
in 1917 when it became known that the brewery interests (prohibition

was a raging issue) had "lent" him $156,000. The impeachment verdict included a proviso that Ferguson could never again hold public office "in Texas." So, when things quieted down a bit, he ran his wife for governor instead—and got her elected—while he himself was content merely to be a candidate for the presidency of the United States! "Ma" (Miriam) Ferguson served from 1925 to 1927; of course her husband was to all intents and purposes the actual governor. In one period of twenty months, the Fergusons issued more than two thousand pardons; which was one way to build up popularity. "Ma" got in partly because she and Pa had courage enough to fight the Ku-Klux Klan, which is to their credit side. From 1927 to 1931 a useful governor named Dan Moody held the office; he had been a "boy-wonder" attorney general. Ma ran for governor four times more (and Pa once ran for the Senate but got beaten), and made it once, in 1933. The governor from 1935 to 1939 was another useful man, James V. Allred, who had formerly been both a Baptist minister and a professional baseball player; he was in turn succeeded by the incredible W. Lee O'Daniel, who was in turn succeeded by Coke R. Stevenson. That the Fergusons had a good deal to do with O'Daniel's first victory and with Stevenson's is usually accepted. In other words, from the time of Jim Hogg fifty years ago to the present, the most conspicuous public figures in the biggest state in the union were a pair of self-seeking old buffoons.

Coke Stevenson, governor from 1943 to 1947, is a different matter. No one ever accused him of being an intellectual giant, but he is not a buffoon. He is a cool customer if ever there was one, with curiously opaque eyes, a good infighter politically, someone who never rocks the boat, a compromiser about whom it was said that no hole was too small for him to get through. It is a familiar cliché that you have to be a Baptist to rise high politically in the Lone Star State, but Coke is a Methodist; he was named for a former governor (and senator), Richard Coke. Some people think he is far too friendly to big money; some deny this by asserting that he has never taken a stand for or against anything. But in his last years of office, practically every appointee to whom he gave an important job was a Texas Regular, i.e. someone who bolted the party against Roosevelt. Once, when Stevenson was asked to intervene in the university dispute which was then fiercely raging, he replied that he was too experienced a rancher to burn his lips on a hot coffeepot. Professor J. Frank Dobie, just back from England during the Blitz, replied that he had seen plenty of folks get burned by something much worse, people who were fighting for the same thing as the university—liberty to think as they please.

Coke was born in central-west (not "west-central") Texas,[1] and he

---

[1] He was the first governor in the history of the state born west of the Colorado River (not to be confused with the Colorado River of Colorado).

lives today near the town of Junction, in rugged and beautiful hill country. He owns a "small" ranch; that is, it runs to fourteen thousand acres. He worked hard as a boy, punching cattle by day and studying law at night; he was variously janitor, bookkeeper, and cashier in a bank; he is a solid, healthy man, six feet two and with a tidy waistline; personally, nobody could be friendlier, a better host, or more likable. He wears a small diamond stickpin shaped like a stirrup, and when I asked him who ran Texas he grinned and replied, "You tell me." He believes that what the state should be proudest of is its "spirit," and when I asked him what was the greatest decision he ever had to make, he answered amiably, "Never had any!"

The secret of Stevenson probably resides in the frontier from which he came. In Jeffersonian times he would have been a real Democrat; that is, he is opposed to government per se. But today this is only too apt to mean that, by pretending to ignore government, a man plays into the hands of special interests that may destroy it.

Stevenson decided not to risk running for re-election in 1946, and his successor is a man named Beauford H. Jester, formerly railroad commissioner. Jester is Texan bred and born, a middle-road lawyer who never held public office till 1942. His chief opponent was Dr. Homer P. Rainey, the ousted president of the university. All liberals in the state backed Rainey; the campaign was vigorous in the extreme; Jester won easily. One thing that embarrassed Rainey was a standing (and of course very unfair) challenge to read aloud before a mixed audience several passages from John Dos Passos' *USA*, which book had played a prickly role in the university wrangle. Rainey did not accept the challenge. When he accused Jester of a Ku-Klux past, Jester replied, "Rainey has lost his fast ball and curve ball; all he's got left is a mud ball." (*Time*, September 2, 1946.) Seriously what beat Rainey—and he did get a quarter of a million votes—were several familiar factors, such as money from the corporations, a vicious attempt to smear him as a "red," splitting of the vote among minor candidates, and fierce attack by all reactionary elements.

Turn now to the legislature, with 150 members in the house and 31 senators; all but one (an independent) are Democrats. Legislators get a wage of ten dollars per day for 120 days every other year; if the session lasts longer the pay drops to five dollars, and since most members are eager anyway to get back home, sessions tend to end quickly as the 120th day approaches. The hall of representatives, big and flat with large windows, looks exactly like a schoolroom. I know, because the friendly Texans asked me to talk to them there.

One important issue—as in so many states—is redistricting which by terms of the constitution is supposed to occur every ten years. But it hasn't been done since 1920, though as we know there have been considerable shifts of population, mostly to the south and west. Some thirty or forty legislators might lose their jobs if redistricting took place, and so they kill each new attempt to put it through. Another issue—permanent and apparently insoluble—is a modification of the basic tax structure, which the state needs badly.

As to political techniques and procedures behind the legislature, Texas is unusual in that it may have two primaries; there is a runoff if no one in the first wins a majority. This example of democracy at its purest sometimes defeats itself. Because, obviously, a candidate (in Primary No. 1) may be well in the lead while failing to get 50 per cent of the total vote; then, as has often happened, he will be beaten in Primary No. 2, if his nearest rivals combine against him. As to the final or general elections, they are of course of only academic interest, since under normal circumstances the Republican can never win. Nevertheless, we shall have a word to say about the Republican party later. Another point worth mention is the comparative meagerness of the total vote. Ohio and California, with only slightly larger populations, have three times as many voters; this is for the most part on account of the poll tax, which Texas still maintains. About 50 per cent of the total adult citizenry voted in California in 1944; the figure for Texas was only sixteen.[2]

Turn now to the lobbies. One eminent Texan told me, "The politics of this state is perfectly simple—it is run by about twenty corporations." I am inclined to think that this is an exaggeration, but from a negative point of view a case may be made for it; certainly it is difficult to think of any legislation that the big corporations do *not* want that gets through. The biggest single factor is petroleum; this is easy to explain in that the oil industry contributes about 60 per cent of the total state income, direct and indirect. And oil has been busy in politics since the days of the late Senator Joe Bailey whose career was wrecked when it was discovered that he had accepted a loan from an oil executive. The oil lobbyists work in any of a dozen ways. A simple method, perfectly legal, might be to pay a prominent politician a sound fee for "drilling rights" on his ranch, even though there was no probability of oil being found there. Associated with oil are the railways, the utilities, lumber, natural gas, and the sulphur interests.

The churches are very powerful in Texas; so, on the other side, are the liquor interests; so is the Texas Manufacturers Association; so, as everywhere in the South, is the *county* (as distinguished from the big city) vote. Newspapers play less of a political role, I should think, than in any important state; labor is a slowly rising element. There are other factors too. In Austin I heard that three B's control the legislature— Bourbon, Beefsteak, Blondes.

[2] Cf. *State Observer* (Austin), December 18, 1944.

After the great corporations the biggest and most potent lobby is that of education. Texas has, and has had since its day of independence, a real fetish for public education; $20,000,000 a year was spent on the schools (not including state universities) in 1920, and not less than $68,500,000 in 1944. Consider this latter figure. It is a whale of a lot of money. It is as much as the entire national budget of a country like Cuba. It has to be found somewhere. And Texas has no income tax. The schools get along mostly through the occupations tax, of which 25 per cent—by terms of the constitution—is set aside for school use. This can lead to intricate political maneuvering. Similarly one quarter of the gasoline tax (four cents) goes to the schools, and part of the poll tax. There was considerable commotion in the 1945 session of the legislature, when the ad valorem tax was raised in a jump from eighteen cents to the constitutional limit of thirty-five cents; the whole raise, which added about $6,500,000 per year to the tax bill, went to education. But do not be misled by the Texas inclination to boast in this regard. It expends a lot on schools, but a great many states expend more proportionately. For instance it spent, in 1944, $94.63 per pupil; New York spent $190.53. Texas, in fact, is actually the thirty-first American state—seventeenth from the bottom—in amount of expenditure on schools per student per year.

A derivative factor has to do with textbooks. Students get these free, of course. The state pays for them, and the Texas schoolbook order is the largest and most lucrative in the United States; the same arithmetic text will for instance be used in every school in the state, and choice of a book may mean a fortune to the publisher; hence it well behooves the big textbook companies (which are headquartered on the Atlantic seaboard) to maintain men in Dallas or Austin with close contacts with local politicians and the legislature. Two other points are relevant. First, most publishers hope naturally to sell the same text not merely in Texas but everywhere in the country; as a result they are inclined to look for authors who aim at a somewhat low common denominator. Second, the State Textbook Commission (in Texas as in other states) that names books for adoption has obviously the gravest kind of responsibility for selecting them well, but it does not always live up to this, and one may easily imagine the eagerness with which textbook salesmen seek to maintain cordial relations with the officials who decide what to buy, when for instance a certain text is on the point of becoming obsolete.[3] Another item is a covert and entirely unofficial semicensorship. That is, zealots who hold no position on the Textbook Com-

---

[3] "Pa" Ferguson once got involved in a nasty small scandal when he appointed himself as clerk of the Textbook Commission, whereupon it became revealed that the state was "paying more for spellers in enormous quantities than the same book can be bought at retail." Cf. Perry, *op. cit.*, p. 152.

mission or even on the State Board of Education attempt to influence a choice of texts as "conservative" as possible.

I have said that there are no statewide political machines in Texas; this is correct except for the fact that each new governor attempts to build his own. But few of these survive. It is personal loyalties, such as that to old Jim Ferguson, which count; such loyalties to a large extent run Texas. But the recipients of these loyalties cannot easily throw votes to another man, or to their successors. Each campaign starts newborn. All this being true, there should be a line for the exception— the strictly local machines in several southern counties, which are picturesque in the extreme. One, that which ran Hidalgo (near Browns- ville) for many years, was broken up by the death of the sheriff, A. Y. Baker. This Baker was a murderer. The story is well told by a journalist of grit and resource, who was in part responsible for unmasking him— Owen P. White, formerly of *Collier's*.[4] In Duval County near by the czar and dictator for years was a man named Archie Parr, whose "monarchy" was broken up by a revolution after, I heard it said, he had "served as state senator since God was a boy." But his son still carries on to an extent. Consider the Duval County vote in the Democratic primary in 1940. O'Daniel got 3,728 votes. Seven other candidates got 181 among them. That's really turning out the vote! Or consider another border county, Starr, which is pretty substantially run by the Guerra family. In the 1944 primaries Coke Stevenson got 1,396 votes; eight other candidates got exactly two!

Finally, since Texas is to all intents and purposes a one-party state, we must turn to what is behind the entire political picture, the Democratic party itself. And this leads us to the story of the Texas Regulars.

The Texas Regulars

> Four more years of those crack-pots and we are done—all finished—Eleanor and Sidney will take over and may the good Lord help us!
>
> —from Texas Regular Campaign Literature, 1944

Nowhere in the United States, not even on Wall Street or the Re- publican epicenters in Michigan and Pennsylvania, did I find such a perfervid hatred for Mr. Roosevelt as in Texas. I met lifelong Democrats who had hoped strenuously for a coalition Byrd-Bricker ticket in 1944; I met men who had been unfalteringly convinced that if FDR won again, "it would mean that the Mexicans and niggers will take us over." This kind of passion makes for ruthlessness. Another reason for ruth-

---

[4] In *The Autobiography of a Durable Sinner* and *Texas, An Informal Biography*, both of which contain some wonderful reading matter.

lessness is of course that the stakes are so large. Also this emotion included more than Roosevelt himself; it included all he stood for and all those that stood with him. For instance when Mr. Truman, campaigning for vice president, visited San Antonio in November, 1944, the mayor (Gus B. Mauermann) and the town boss P. L. Anderson (who incidentally is a former champion linotypist of the world) refused to go to the station to meet his train.

Here is a bit of campaign literature, distributed by the so-called Regulars. It came originally from the Almina (Kansas) *Plaindealer*, and as an example of intellectual deformity it has interest:

Gallivantin' Gal

Strike up the Band!
    Here's our Globe Trotter!

Call off the bombing for today
    Wheel out the Army ship
Hold up the war so Eleanor
    Can take another trip.

For 20,000 miles she goes
    To have her weekly fling,
And rub her nose against the nose
    Of some wild Zulu king!

'Twas by design and not by luck
    She chose this distant shore;
The only place she hasn't stuck
    Her nosey nose before.

Now, having rubbed the royal nose
    She crossed another sea,
To scare the natives I suppose
    And watch them plant a tree.

The happy thought occurred to me
    As homeward bound she sped;
Why couldn't they have shipped the tree
    And planted her instead?

To understand phenomena as wantonly distorted as this we must remember that since Texas *is* a one-party state, a lot of dissidence is inevitable within the party; there is no other place to go. The Democrats fight like bloody murder; then they find themselves still in the same ring when the fight is over. And this makes for nerves frayed and notched. There were "constitutional" versus "harmony" Democrats as far back as

1928. But for a Democrat to turn Republican would (*a*) be nauseous; (*b*) mean surrender of political power and privilege. All this is, however, more or less true everywhere in the South; why is the fissure so much more pronounced in Texas, the intensity so much more acute? I daresay one reason is that Texas is so much richer; the vested interests have more to win and lose. Another is the independent tradition and spirit of the Texan frontier. Then there are purely local sidelights. The Ku-Klux hangovers played a role. So did the fact that many people, loyal to Jack Garner, were apt to say, "If FDR couldn't get along with as good a Texan as Cactus Jack, there must be something wrong." And Elliott Roosevelt's business activities in Texas didn't help to make the family popular.

All this came to a head in 1944; in a presidential year Texas (again so grandiose!) has two conventions, not merely one. The first, which is usually held in Austin, roundabout May, selects delegates to the national convention. The second, held in September in a different city each presidential year (in 1944 it happened to be Dallas), selects the state chairman and state committee and adopts the platform. In 1944 all sorts of complications came. First, a group of fiercely anti-FDR Democrats led by George Butler (who is Jesse Jones's attorney and nephew-in-law incidentally) organized a definite bolt away from the party, calling themselves the Regulars though of course it was they who were irregular. They captured the Austin convention and named their own electors; this of course meant, if they got away with it, that pro-FDR voters would be disfranchised. And the resultant fight aroused national excitement, because Texas has twenty-three delegates, and it seemed conceivable at the time that the Regular insurrection could throw the national election (Roosevelt versus Dewey) to the House of Representatives. The Regulars intended to vote for Byrd, or some similar conservative candidate; they would ostensibly "represent" Texas at the national convention in Chicago, and the Texas voters who were *for* Roosevelt would have no votes at all. So a lot of folks, including the CIO, got busy. There was an appeal to the courts. Then came the Dallas convention and a critical roll call on seating a group of FDR electors. It won by just 29 votes out of 1,600. But it took almost two hours to tabulate the vote, and the Regulars, procrastinating, put up Martin Dies to speak, hoping to kill time until proxies and so on could be frantically rounded up. But Dies was booed to such an extent that he could not make the speech. The Roosevelt forces won. Then the Texas Supreme Court unanimously ruled that the FDR electors chosen at Dallas, superseding the Regulars named at Austin, should duly represent the state. But the Regulars, still fighting bitterly, refused to concede defeat; they split the party, and ran on their own third ticket. When election day came around, the Regulars were overwhelmingly squashed. Roosevelt got more than 800,000 votes to their 135,439; they even ran behind Dewey, who got 191,000. What other candidates received is an incidental sidelight—Norman Thomas got 594 votes in the entire state, and Gerald L. K. Smith 251.

After Roosevelt's death the Regulars formally dissolved themselves as a party, but they still exist in spirit. They control big elements of the Democratic organization, and probably could carry the senate though not the house. One way to put it would be to say that the Regulars have been pushed back on their haunches; another, that they have been driven underground.

A footnote to this tale. Jesse Jones, though his right-hand man Butler was a leading Regular, supported Roosevelt; so did Will Clayton, who like Jones was a powerful member of the FDR administration. But the offices of Anderson, Clayton, & Co. in Houston (the largest cotton brokers in the world) were the spiritual headquarters of the rebellion. Also they were something else—all three treasurers of the three rival parties worked in Anderson, Clayton. Yet, despite the fiercest political passion, they did their jobs amicably side by side, which is something typical of the United States, and something the man from Mars may not easily under-stand. Lamar Fleming Jr. was treasurer for the Regulars, Harmon Whit-tington for the Republicans, and a lady named Miss Cline for FDR. And Mrs. Clayton—who at the time was national chairman of the Women's Democratic League—is one of the stanchest liberals in the land.

Republicans in the Lone Star State

Texas as we know has plenty of Republicans; the state went for Hoover against Al Smith in 1928, though this was a special case; most Texans were not voting for a person at all, but against Catholicism and the wets.[5] Who are the Republicans in Texas? First, the "carpetbaggers" from the North, representatives of the big corporations, especially oil-men and their retinues. Second, many west Texans. Third, office seekers as described below. Fourth, practically all the Germans around San Antonio. Bexar County itself went for Roosevelt, but six of the seven counties adjoining were solidly pro-Dewey.

The Republican boss in Texas is a phenomenal old man named R. B. Creager, of Brownsville. He is a senior member of the Republican National Committee, and for years he controlled as much patronage as any *Democrat* in the state. The reason for this anomaly is that there have been only four Democratic administrations in the country since the Civil War (Cleveland, Wilson, FDR, Truman), which means that a very large backlog of Republican appointments (federal) existed in Texas, and many of these still survive. Texas has, for instance, more

[5] Lincoln, incidentally, only just beat McClellan in Texas, and Grant barely nosed out Greeley.

postmasterships by far than any other state. When Roosevelt entered office in 1932, practically all federal judges and almost all United States marshals in Texas were Republican. In other words, while the Republican party was in power in Washington, the dominant Republican in the state—though he did not hold elective office—was in a position to control an enormous number of appointments. This is what Mr. Creager did. I even heard it said, by the irreverent, that people around Creager today do not want their own party, the Republican, to win because then the patronage field would be immensely broadened, and they would lose part of their old power.

Pappy

Many eminent Texans serve the nation in Washington as we know, from Tom Connally to able representatives like Wright Patman and Lyndon B. Johnson, but these belong, it would seem, to the national rather than the peculiarly Texan scene. There is however another Texan, even though he lives in Washington nowadays instead of Austin, whom it is impossible to pass over. I mean Pappy.

Pappy (Wilbert Lee) O'Daniel, author of the song "Beautiful Texas" and former flour salesman, is a kind of American marcher-on-Rome who never marched. His career is an illuminating example of the way a man can rise from nothingness to the Senate, by weapons that include demagoguery, the credulity of people, and their fedupness with the ordinary run of politicians.

O'Daniel is in his middle fifties; he was born in Ohio, and moved to Kansas at an early age, where he built up a milling business. There is good reason to think that he was a Republican in those days—one more example of the artificiality of American party lines—and indeed when he became a senator his opponents liked to say that Kansas had, as a result, three senators, Texas only one. During his latter years he made a good deal of claim to religious inspiration (though he was never an overt evangelist like Billy Sunday or Aimee Semple McPherson) but apparently he never belonged to any church until 1938, when he joined the Christian (Disciples of Christ) church in Fort Worth, twelve days after he announced his candidacy for governor. And though Pappy has always claimed to represent the masses, through the democratic process, there seems to be evidence that he never bothered to register— for anybody or any party—until he was forty; one story is that he had not paid his poll tax, and so could not vote although he could be elected governor. Finally, to complete this record of dubious allegiances, his campaigns were largely based on cowboy songs, and of course O'Daniel, who is in reality a city-slicker type, has never punched cattle in his life.

Pappy moved from Kansas to Texas in 1925,[6] and presently learned the technique of selling flour by radio; for a time he worked as a radio announcer too. He organized a hillbilly band, with his children in the ensemble, wrote songs and ditties, and sold his own brand of Hillbilly flour, with "Pappy, Pass the Biscuits" as his motto. One belief is that he went into politics purely to get a bigger audience and hence a bigger market for his flour; his own explanation is that thousands of listeners urged him to run for governor; anyway the hillbilly band grew into quite a thing. By the time O'Daniel was running for senator a crooner named Texas Rose was part of the group; he toured the state in a sound truck (cost $15,000) with a replica of the Texas capitol on top; a flour barrel was passed around for contributions.

I cannot describe in detail—the most elementary considerations of space preclude it—the various O'Daniel campaigns. This Texas kingfish became the greatest vote getter in the history of the state. One Houston friend, when I asked him to explain this, replied "because Pappy is a carpetbagger, and so are we all." But this is surely only a fraction of the truth. O'Daniel appealed mostly to the farmers, who have so often taken a beating in Texas, and to the old folks who in every western state are a capacious reservoir of votes. At the beginning his entire campaign platform was the Ten Commandments! Nothing else. And he got part of the Baptist vote, the Methodist vote, the Christian vote. He attacked the corporations (who however contributed heavily to his later campaigns); he promised thirty dollars per month in state relief to everybody over sixty-five; he said that he would drive the old-style politicians out of Austin—all this makes a familiar pattern. Of course if we examine his record in the light of his various promises, it becomes laughable. After attacking the corporations he managed to get along with them; the aged and indigent are not getting anything like thirty dollars a month; and Austin is still full of politicians. His technique with the legislature, as described by McKay, was in general to submit legislation that he knew could not possibly pass, and then blame the legislature for not passing it. One of his sharpest tergiversations had to do with the sales tax. He came into office on the flatly repeated promise that he would fight a sales tax to the finish; immediately on being elected governor, he tried to push a sales tax through under a different name. During one angry session he is quoted as having said that "no power on earth" could make him tell "what tax he was for." Occasionally opponents would submit to him long lists of questions, ranging from "What was your war record during 1917 and 1918?" to "Why didn't you ask the legislature to repeal the poll tax law as you said you would?" His

---

[6] My sources for this section are many, but chiefly the scholarly and massive *W. Lee O'Daniel and Texas Politics*, by Seth S. McKay, published by the Texas Technological College, Lubbock, 1944.

rule was never to bother to answer. Of course he believed in "economy." But the 1941 legislature broke every record for appropriations.

Pappy first ran for governor in 1938; he got 50.9 per cent of the votes in the primary, and went on to beat a Republican opponent by 473,526 to 10,940. In the runoff, moreover, he threw his support to Coke Stevenson for lieutenant governor, and Stevenson's vote rose from 258,625 to 446,441—a striking example of Pappy's power. Running for re-election in 1940, O'Daniel won triumphantly again. Next came the Senate. It makes a flavorsome little episode. The veteran Texas Senator Morris Sheppard died in April, 1941. Pappy didn't know quite what to do. He could at once resign the governorship, on the understanding that Coke Stevenson, succeeding as governor, would then appoint him senator. But he might just possibly lose the special election that would have to be held within ninety days—in which case he would have lost the governorship too. So what he did was something else; even his admirers were stunned by skulduggery of such proportions. He appointed as Senator the eighty-seven-year-old son of General Sam Houston, also a general (in the National Guard). To say that Houston was senile is to put it mildly. The Lone Star State was to be represented in Washington by a scarcely-alive octogenarian. Pappy's plan was simple as well as grandiose. The special Senate election would be duly held, and Pappy would then run against the antique general and beat him, even granted that he was in shape to run; Pappy could thus both hold onto the governorship for a time and become a senator. (Houston, incidentally, had once run for governor back in 1892, as the *Republican* candidate; he got 1,332 votes out of 600,000 cast.) It took some time for General Houston to pull himself together and get to Washington. He arrived at the capitol on June 2, and duly took the oath of office, the oldest man ever to become a senator. Then on June 26 he died—of old age!

So Pappy had to begin all over again. This time he simply ran for the job himself. And it became clear why he had done so much maneuvering. He had begun to slip. The record had begun to show. He just squeezed in.[7] He got 175,590 votes; Lyndon Johnson, the runner-up, got 174,279. Pappy, who had boasted of the greatest majorities in the history of the state, found himself with one of 1,211, and an excessively dubious one at that. In 1942 he had to run for senator again, for the regular six-year term. He didn't get a clear majority in the first primary (in fact he would

[7] There were a lot of other candidates in this election, and a list of their occupations, as tabulated by McKay, is an interesting example of the way politics in Texas can hit almost anybody. The list is governor, attorney general, congressman, physician, minister, military expert, merchant, lawyer, teacher, former legislator, laundryman, farmer, communist leader, tax league official, insurance agent, chiropractor, salesman, plumber, radio commentator, and "kinsman of early Texas hero!"

have been beaten except that two candidates split the opposition vote) ; in the run-off he barely won.

When Pappy arrived in Washington he made his maiden speech on the second day, thus outraging convention, and announced that he would outlaw strikes, "purge Congress if his anti-strike bill was not passed. rescue Roosevelt from the professional politicians . . . and take care of the federal debt." (McKay, p. 469.) He voted against extension of the draft, and said (in a speech in Texas), "I don't think we are near war. We hear a lot of howling in Europe, but they aren't going to do us any harm over there." Meantime, although he had sworn that his campaign expenses in 1940 were only $4,031, an investigating committee of the Senate indicated that he had spent $56,000. Incidentally at about this time he made one speech—later it was explained that someone else had written it for him—in which he confused the Battle of San Jacinto with the Alamo!

O'Daniel may have contemplated "rescuing" FDR, but when 1944 came around he stumped Texas for the Regulars, and attacked the president with the most ferocious vigor. One instrument of this campaign (which was purely to try to beat Roosevelt in Texas—Pappy was not running for anything himself) was the newspaper published by his wife and sons, the *W. Lee O'Daniel News*. Federal authorities decided to have a look at this peculiar property, since there was some mystery as to where it got its newsprint in a time of acute paper shortage. Then the Senate Campaign Expenditures Committee investigated the paper's financial backing. One contributor of $25,000 was H. R. Cullen, the Houston oil man; another was E. H. Moore, Republican senator from Oklahoma (New York *Times*, October 19, 1944) of whom we shall say a word anon.

When O'Daniel—following the complete failure of his 1944 campaign —speaks in the Senate now, it is as if chalk were scraped on a blackboard. Sample of his prose style, from the *Congressional Record* of February 1, 1946: "We are simply debating the merits of this nefarious, communistic brain abscess No. 101, known as the FEPC bill."

In June, 1946, he filibustered for eight hours and twenty minutes in an attempt to kill OPA, thus ending all price controls. But, compared to some historic filibusters of the past, Pappy's had elements of the bogus; he spent half the time at least in reading telegrams from his constituents, and friendly senators interrupted him on many occasions, to give him a breathing spell, notably Bridges of New Hampshire. As for instance:

Mr. Bridges: Mr. President, will the Senator yield for a question?
Mr. O'Daniel: I yield for a question.
Mr. Bridges: Can the Senator think of anything more difficult than getting a bureaucrat to yield up control?

Mr. O'Daniel: I have never seen it done.

Mr. Bridges: That would be pretty nearly the $64 question, would it not?

Mr. O'Daniel: It is worth more than that.

Hammering away at OPA a little later, Pappy let this small remark slide out:

We would be in a terrible fix if we would get things in such bad shape that the American citizen could not make enough money to pay our salaries.

In July, 1946, O'Daniel had this colloquy with Shipstead of Minnesota, in discussion of currency inflation:

Mr. Shipstead: Does not the Senator realize that there will never be a shortage of money so long as the poplar and the spruce lasts in northern Minnesota, Wisconsin, and Canada? They make good paper.

Mr. O'Daniel: I recognize that, but I am not going to let the Senator from Minnesota get away with the suggestion that pulp from Minnesota provides all the paper that is used, because we produce wood pulp in Texas.

One of Pappy's sons is named Pat. According to Drew Pearson (New York *Daily Mirror*, April 15, 1946), this young man was given three chances to graduate from Officers Training School during the war, though less favored soldiers, once they failed, very seldom indeed got another try. The other son is named Mike. In July, 1946, Mike threatened to evict from an apartment house in Dallas a young war veteran who protested when he was told that his rent would be raised from $67.50 per month to $100. Pappy incidentally voted against the Veterans' Housing Bill.

A sub-O'Daniel exists in Texas, by name Vance Muse; he is the moving spirit of something called the Christian American Association, largely devoted to Jew-baiting, red-baiting, Negro-baiting and the like. Muse lives in Houston, and storms up and down the countryside; in the words of *Collier's*, "he has mined the sucker lists thirteen times for funds with which 'to save America' from assorted isms." Few people take him seriously any more. Frederick Woltman of Scripps-Howard went to Houston early in 1945 and wrote a series about Muse called "Menace or Myth?" with the conclusion that "he carries no weight in local civic, political, or labor-industry affairs." There was, it happened, a bill before the legislature at that time, forbidding the closed shop; this was what Muse wanted too, but proponents of the bill kept severely clear of him; his name, they said, would be the kiss of death.

Muse has pretensions to be a poet, as witness this composition which was used in an O'Daniel campaign:

BURDENSOME TAXES

. . . We have builded our beautiful highways
With taxes from city and farm,
But you can't pyramid those taxes,
Without doing our Texas great harm.

What Beat Martin Dies

The answer to this is a single word—industrialization. Texas, it isn't always realized, is the eleventh manufacturing state in the union, and this has of course served to produce a strong, still limited, but growing labor movement. The great airplane factories between Dallas and Fort Worth, the explosive boom in east Texas oil and the expansion of the whole Houston area naturally brought a labor influx. For the first time in Texas history this in turn brought in a lot of labor votes.[8]

Martin Dies represented from 1931 to 1945 the Second Congressional District centering on Beaumont, with Jefferson his home county. This had for years been an extremely apathetic region politically. It was like parts of Arkansas. Dies, literally, had gone to Congress (like his father before him) on about 5 per cent of the total potential vote. In 1944 the anti-Dies forces decided that he could be beaten. The CIO in particular went out to "get" him, and Carl A. McPeak, the regional director of the Political Action Committee, traveled to Beaumont in April, 1944, and organized the Citizens Protective League. Dies later charged that the CIO spent $250,000 in Jefferson County; actually McPeak's total expense account on his organizing mission was $7.20. What the PAC did first was to get out the vote, and as a result 25 per cent more people in Jefferson County voted in 1944 than had ever voted before. Also the labor people were shrewd enough to pick a good candidate; they chose a man who was *not* a laborite or a newcomer but a county judge, J. M. Combs, greatly respected in the community. Combs did not stand merely for labor; he stood for everybody who was mortally sick of Martin Dies,

---

[8] One should say in parentheses that in the nonindustrial areas labor is still very weak; the single illustration that only five newspapers in the entire state have Guild organizations—the Houston *Post*, El Paso *Herald*, San Antonio *Light*, Fort Worth *Record*, and Beaumont *Enterprise*—will suffice. In the state as a whole the CIO and AF of L are nip and tuck; the strongest CIO unions are in oil, steel and the aircraft division of the UAW concentrated in the Convair and North American plants near Dallas. The National Maritime Union in Houston has great possibilities of growth, and agricultural workers are beginning to organize in the valley. The reactionaries in Texas fight all these developments bitterly. Something in Houston called Fight for Free Enterprise Inc. adopted the artifice last summer of chartering a local organization called "Congress of Industrial Organizations" which was not the CIO, in order to confuse the issue.

which meant the reputable citizenry as a whole. Dies explored the situation, knew that he would be beaten, and simply withdrew from the race. Nevertheless a few people voted for him in the primary. Judge Combs got 34,916 votes; Dies got exactly five.

Dies then stumped the state for the "Regulars" in 1944 but he made only two speeches out of ten scheduled, because audiences simply refused to listen. It is perhaps relevant that I never once heard his name mentioned in all the time I was in the state, except when I specifically asked about him.

Recapitulation

To conclude this attempt to give a broad general picture of Texas and all its spectacular qualities, we must return—if only for a sentence—to the permanent realities. It must never be forgotten that Texas is, above all, three things: the greatest repository of petroleum wealth in the United States, the heart of cattle culture, and the most successful cotton-producing area in the world.

As to trends the whole enormous state is in a kind of ferment. The center of political gravity is shifting, albeit slowly, and the issue that cuts through all other issues can be expressed in one word, liberalism. Behind Texas is the frontier, all the Gasconade, the cattle rustlers, the romance, the swaddling clothes. Ahead is something more prosaic perhaps—the education of the propertied class to social responsibility, the shift in politics caused by labor, the breakup of feudal privilege, and the development of what the state needs above all, small, home-owned, decentralized industry. Texas is tossing and stirring like a mighty giant; the picture is almost classically that of early manhood struggling with itself. It has outgrown the solid South; it is outgrowing the old colonial economy; it is becoming thoroughly weary of people like Dies and O'Daniel; it looks brightly and with stalwart hope to a better world tomorrow.

Chapter 49

University, God, and Beef

vvvvvvvvvvvvvvvvvvvvvvvvvvvvvvvvvvvvvvvvvvvvvvvvvvvvvvvvvvvvvvvvvvvvvvvvvvvvvvvvvvvvvvvv

> The sun done riz, the sun done set
> An' we ain't outa Texas yet.
>
> —Cowboy Song

OF ALL the fabulous things in the Lone Star State, the most fabulous is quite possibly the university at Austin, and of all the issues that confront and perplex Texas, that of academic freedom at the university is probably the most peculiarly Texan. Practically all the conflicts, juxtapositions, and cleavages within cleavages that we have explored to this point find their best summary and expression in the dispute over the university.

Texas does things with a sweep. That we know well. The university was founded in 1881, and the state constitution specifically requires it to be an institution "of the first class." There was a reason for this. A prime cause of the Texas revolution against Mexico was dissatisfaction with the Mexican educational system; Texas wanted better schools. The university was endowed with two million acres of land, in perpetuity, the income from which was to be used for buildings, permanent equipment, and the like. But this block of land, out in central-west Texas, was not considered particularly valuable at the time; some of it sold for five cents an acre, and the regents leased it out for grazing. Then in 1923 came the discovery of oil, and the university became enormously rich overnight.

As a result its permanent fund today amounts to some fifty million dollars—and this despite an expenditure of almost eighteen million dollars on plant alone in the past few years. What is more, its holdings contain veins of potash, 750 feet thick, that may in time turn out to be even more valuable than the petroleum. Since 1923 the university and the oil interests have had a series of angry disputes. Dan Moody, when attorney general, brought one famous suit charging that the companies had maneuvered to draw millions of dollars worth of oil out of its properties; the suit was compromised. Meantime the university itself continued to expand. It did things in the biggest kind of way. It was willing to spend $4,500,000 on a library. In 1931 the Soviet government put up for sale a collection of incunabula valued at about three million

855

dollars, including two of the three pre-Gutenberg Bibles known to exist in the world; the Library of Congress in Washington was unable to afford this purchase, but the University of Texas bought the whole collection at once.[1] Then consider the way less valuable books were acquired. When a professor inaugurated a new course in public utilities law he was instructed to buy every book on the subject published in the English language. An allied point—though on a different level—is that, through the Caroline Margaret Campbell collection, the University of Texas possesses the biggest collection of mystery stories in existence.

Professor Homer P. Rainey, a substantial youngish educator with a good record, born in Texas and then successively president of Franklin College (in Indiana) and Bucknell University, became president of the university in 1939. The regents thought so highly of him that he got a salary actually higher than that of the football coach. Rainey was not a "pink" by any normal definition. He was a Rotarian, a Mason, and an ordained Baptist minister. The university had always had a fine liberal tradition, and he set out to maintain it; also he had very definite ideas about its responsibilities to the community as a whole.

By terms of the state constitution, the University of Texas has nine regents. These are appointed by the governor, three at a time for six-year terms, every two years. Jimmy Allred was governor when Rainey became president, and the regents were fairly liberal. Then came the governorships of O'Daniel and Coke Stevenson. Steadily the complexion of the board of regents changed. Among them were and are (at the moment of writing) D. F. Strickland, a "legislative counselor" (= lobbyist) for the biggest chain of movie theaters in the state, a man named W. Scott Schreiner whose family for a generation has maintained a kind of feudal barony near Kerrville, and above all Orville Bullington, a Wichita Falls millionaire, violently conservative and a key Republican. One illustration will suffice to show Mr. Bullington's type of mentality. In the senate investigation of the great quarrel that developed over Rainey he submitted a written statement which includes the sentence, "Let them [the Austin newspapers] say whether we did right in refusing to spend the money of the people to glorify the two anarchist or Communist murderers Socco and Vansetti [sic]."[2]

Political fights involving the university were no new thing. As far

[1] But later it was resold—without profit—to the Library of Congress, following a special congressional appropriation.

[2] Sacco and Vanzetti became an issue when the regents refused to authorize an appropriation (of $150!) for a study of the literary effects of the case. A remark credited to Regent Bullington, as quoted in *PM* (March 22, 1945) is that the Texas motto, "Discipline is the foundation of the state," should replace that of the university, "Ye shall know the truth and the truth shall set you free."

back as 1915, Pa Ferguson had a long drawn out struggle with it over control of its appropriations, and this led indirectly to his downfall and impeachment; Pa got beaten. But thirty years later the cards were stacked a different way, and Rainey had regent trouble almost from the beginning of his administration. Or, if you prefer, the regents had Rainey trouble. The resulting conflict was of the simplest. Not merely was it a question of who was to run the university, the president or the regents (and behind the regents the governor); it was a question, in concrete form, of academic freedom, of what *kind* of school the University of Texas was going to be, whether an adult and emancipated institution of learning in which teachers were permitted to acquire and transmit ideas, or a kind of intellectual greenhouse kept by a clique of millionaires. Perhaps this language is too strong, but passions rose very high over the issue. It cut through and across everything in the state. Not all the tycoon-regents agreed with their brethren. For instance the president of the board at the time, John H. Bickett, the general counsel of Southwestern Bell Telephone (a great power in the state), promptly resigned when Rainey was discharged; so did a Houston millionaire, Dan H. Harrison. Even so—and this is an illustration of what Texas itself thought of the fracas—the Austin *American* simply used the headline MULTIMILLIONAIRE REGENTS FIRE RAINEY when the story broke. A few days later came another headline, BIG BUSINESS PLOT TO RULE SCHOOLS TOLD.

Documentation on the case already fills a long shelf, and readers who would like more background might well read a brisk exchange of views in *Harper's Magazine* (August, November, and December, 1945) in which Bernard DeVoto, attacking the university, plays a lot of hell with a professor who defends it. Suffice it here to outline a few points and dates. One important item was Rainey's proposal to consolidate the medical school (which is at Galveston) into the university proper; the Galveston reactionaries fought this venomously and Houston gave them powerful support. In 1942 came an episode at Dallas; three instructors in economics protested at the conduct of an antilabor mass meeting (held under the auspices of a movie magnate, Karl Hoblitzelle, whose interests were—incidentally—represented by Regent Strickland at the legislature); the three instructors were discharged. Then during 1943 the more reactionary regents sought to change the tenure rules which safeguard professorial jobs, to make it easier to get rid of "undesirables." During 1944 there were all manner of incidents; the university had to call off some social science research, Rainey was badgered at every turn, the regents made use of an extraneous scandal about homosexuality, a red hunt began in which practically anybody who voted for FDR was called a "radical"; and an attempt was made to discharge a teacher who recommended to his students John Dos Passos' *USA*.[3] On October 1, 1944, pressure was put on Rainey to stop making any more speeches "in church"; because he had been defending himself and his administration before some Baptist audiences. On October 12 he counterattacked with a sixteen-point "indictment" outlining his case against the regents, whereupon—on November 1—he was fired.

All kinds of fireworks then broke loose; students demonstrated in mass, laid a coffin marked Academic Freedom at Governor Stevenson's door, and lowered the university flag to half-mast. Rainey, by terms of the tenure rule, could not be discharged in his capacity of professor, but his chair was abolished and he was deprived of salary. A noisy investigation began in the state senate; its results were not conclusive, and as of today no new president has ever been appointed. The student body backed Rainey practically to a man; so did the young alumni; the faculty was split. But, of 368 professors entitled to vote, only 115 were willing to sign a statement that they considered "academic freedom and tenure" safe at the University of Texas, and only 18 refused to sign a petition for Rainey's reinstatement. In other words, 253 professors at what was once one of the great universities in the land thought that academic freedom *was* endangered, that their jobs were *not* secure. Then the American Association of University Professors undertook an investigation; this is a very substantial body, with something of the same prestige as, say, the Federal Council of the Churches of Christ or the American Medical Association. Its interim report, issued in February, 1945, sharply criticized the regents and said that Rainey's dismissal "was a serious disregard of good academic practice generally observed by the governing boards of accredited institutions." Later—a heavy blow to Texans who thought that the South would stand by safely—the Southern Association of Colleges and Secondary Schools similarly expressed disapproval. Finally in June, 1946, the American Association formally placed the university on its list of "censured administrations" because of "attempts by a politically dominant group to impose its social and educational views" (New York *Times*, June 10, 1946).

Rainey, as we know, went into politics very much in the role of martyr, and was beaten for governor in 1946. The forces that ousted him from the university were identical with those that kept him from the governor's chair.

[3] One regent, Strickland, called this novel "the dirtiest, most obscene, most perverted book ever written in the English language."

Beef on the Range

> There were three waves of migration on this continent and the
> second was always the cattlemen. Ahead went the trappers and
> the Indian traders. . . . Behind the cattle came the farmers. . . .
> There were always cattle out ahead of the plows. And for a
> simplest reason. Beef and pork and mutton were the only crops
> in that land without roads which could take themselves to
> market . . . Cattle made the first frontier where white men
> lived. And grass made cattle.
>
> —Archibald MacLeish, *Green River*

> Other states were carved or born,
> Texas grew from hide and horn.
>
> —Berta Hart Nance

My host, Colonel Robert W. Briggs, said first, "All you have to
know is that a ranch is a beef factory. A successful rancher is simply
the one who grows most meat per acre."

We drove out of San Antonio on broad, smoothly straight roads and
then cut into the country to visit the Briggs ranch, not a big one (a
mere six thousand acres), perhaps not one very "typical," but interesting
in that it expertly makes the best of every inch of soil, in that it is run
by science as well as cowboys, with the most modern techniques. And
we talked of everything from the history of the cattle business to the
way the Klebergs run the King Ranch to the possibility that the world
may be presented some day with synthetic beef.

Why not? Synthetic shoe soles, which wear better than some leather,
exist right now, and there is nothing inherently impossible in the idea
of making meat from plastics. But if this should ever happen, it would
hit Texas, to say nothing of Iowa and Nebraska, a sledge-hammer blow.

Colonel Briggs drove me from one end of his ranch to the other;
we saw his sleek, placid Hereford cows and the humped, slate-colored
Brahma bulls; we watched his cowboys at work and I saw an example
of the astonishing fertility of this part of Texas: on one side of a
brook, wheat was growing; on the other red-top cane. Colonel Briggs
looked at the very grass—coarse native stuff—with pride and affection,
saying, "All this comes from mother earth; when we eat beef, it's
simply grass." And he pointed out that ranching in this part of the
world is more than just a business; it's a way of life.

We called for an hour at the ranch of a neighbor, W. T. Montgomery,
who for many years has been breeding prize bulls. One we saw is quite
an historic character, Monty Rupert, aged six, weighing 1,800 pounds
and worth twenty-five thousand dollars; out of him have come one
hundred thousand dollars worth of calves. He has won innumerable

prizes, and he still sires forty or fifty calves a year. Bulls like these are taken care of like babies, and when young are actually fed special Jersey milk; their mothers' isn't good enough.

Later in the afternoon I heard a small joke: "What is a Texan rancher?—A retired oil man!" During the 20's and 30's about one hundred thousand people moved into south and west Texas. The land, which had never been cleared, cost very little; even today you can buy it for a pittance. These migrants were not cattlemen. They hoped to strike oil. Then, if they didn't find oil, they made the property a ranch instead; this movement still goes on and some owners, even though no oil is produced, make more money on oil than from their herds, through royalties on future drilling. Also many rich oilmen put their profits into real estate.

The cow country of the United States, the largest beef-producing region in the world, which we alluded to so often in early chapters of this book, stretches upward from Texas like a broadening funnel. Texas is its root and heart, and it swells up to take in most of Montana, Wyoming, Colorado, and New Mexico; its eastern boundary is as we know the 98th meridian, cutting sharp and smooth through the Dakotas, Nebraska, Kansas, and Oklahoma. In this whole immense region, from Brownsville to the Canadian border, any cattleman is at home anywhere. The mores are the same; the vernacular and manner of speech are the same; the habit of mind is the same—love of open spaces, independent skepticism, a hatred of being pushed around by government, a dislike of small men in big cities.

There have, Colonel Briggs told me, been five great phases of cattle development. First was the Spanish period. The conquistadores brought in the longhorns—fierce and sturdy animals, all hide, hoof, and horns with little meat on them. The modern phrase that a steer is simply "a frame for beef" would not apply; in fact the longhorns were killed largely for hide and tallow; the meat was often left to rot. The great virtue of the longhorns was that they could stand drought—the major preoccupation of every early cattleman was water—and the arduous long drives. Today longhorns are virtually extinct. They have played a greater role in American folklore and history than any other animal, except possibly the bison, but as Dobie points out they have been very much neglected scientifically. Few museums have longhorn displays; few longhorn "reservations" exist; the San Antonio zoo has exactly one specimen. Most Texans under the age of fifty, say, have never seen a longhorn.

Second came the trail-driving era and there are plenty of men living who remember this—like one friend who grew up in a region where there wasn't a fence for 450 miles, and another who has lived in cattle country "since they put the grass out." The longhorns, herd after herd, were driven up to the Kansas railheads, like Abilene and Dodge City;

the most famous trails were the Goodnight-Loving and the Chisholm. Why did the cattle business grow? Because it was so inordinately lucrative. The great world of the East wanted meat, especially beef; and Texas had the beef to provide. Enormous fortunes were made hand over fist. A steer cost three dollars or so in Texas, and sold in Kansas for thirty dollars and up. And there was practically no overhead, since the land was free and all the cattle ate was grass, which was free too.

The third period began with the extension of the railways into Texas itself. The last drive afoot to Kansas came in 1887, and the transition to mechanical transport produced profound changes on the frontier. Fencing killed the open range, and made homesteading possible. Formerly the cattle business had been simply a matter of roaming through fenceless country, finding water, and shooting any interloper who tried to steal your herd. Now it became a strictly regulated industry, though not without excitements. The open rangers didn't like the way things were going; there were bitter fence-cutting wars. Intertangled with this development were two inventions. One was barbed wire, as mentioned in a preceding chapter; the other was the Colt revolver. Rifles cannot be easily loaded on horseback; when they were replaced by the much quicker and handier six-shooters, an epoch came to an end; violence was the more easily defended against and punished.

Overlapping this period came a fourth, that of improvement in the quality of stock. It was difficult to ship longhorns by rail; their horns were too big. And everybody wanted a heavier, more docile animal that would produce more beef. So the Hereford era began, and Herefords, with their straight-line backs, short legs, and straight bellies, still overwhelmingly dominate the beef-cattle world. This is because they are heaviest in the right place for the best meat, the loins. You judge cattle by their heads; but it's the other end that counts for beef. Of course there are other cattle than Herefords in Texas, for instance Durhams (shorthorns) and the black hornless Angus, which "finish high" and make good eating. But you have to "farm" Anguses; you cannot turn them loose. The Herefords themselves are crossbred with Brahmas which came originally from India, because Brahma blood resists better a bothersome fever tick. But the Brahma by itself is not a "finished beef animal."

We paused at one end of my host's ranch, in a flowering oval gully, and there I saw a "new" animal, the Santa Gertrudis. This bull, an "invention" of the Klebergs, is the only major animal ever created in the United States. He is very large and cherry colored; he was named for the main King Ranch headquarters; most important, he breeds true. The Santa Gertrudis is a "prepotent" bull, which means that he will reproduce his own kind; he does not "throw back." And the prettiest bull in the world is just a hunk of beef, if he cannot duplicate himself. The Klebergs made the Santa Gertrudis out of shorthorns crossed with

Brahma; the idea was to find an animal of a perfect beef type with Brahma stamina and capacity to survive drought in a rigorous habitat. Bob Kleberg, unable to change the character of the country, changed the character of the beef instead.

Fifth and finally, there is what might be called the modern period, the phase of scientific ranching. Colonel Briggs showed me proudly the new types of drought-resisting grass he was planting, while correcting mineral deficiencies in the soil with superphosphate from TVA. Beyond this there may be another phase. Texas "finishes" very little of its cattle; most is sent up to Iowa or Nebraska, as we know, and there fattened before being slaughtered. Texas would like to provide its own feeder lots in the future, if possible, and fatten its own beef within the state.

The natural history of a steer goes something like this. Most ranches have a breeding herd; the ambition is to have a 100 per cent calf crop, with each cow bringing in a calf a year. If a ranch needs mothers, it may buy eighteen-month or two-year-old heifers from a neighbor; the price will be between fifty and seventy-five dollars a head. Every self-respecting ranch has its own bulls, but as a rule the sire is brought in from outside, so as to avoid interbreeding; when the calf is a few months old it is "worked," i.e. vaccinated against blackleg, castrated, branded, and sometimes dehorned,[4] all in one operation. Then the calves go back to their mothers on the range. At weaning time they are taken away again; the ranch as a rule keeps the heifers for breeding, and packs the steers off to sale, when they weigh roughly four to five hundred pounds. Some steers remain in Texas, however, until maturity, which is from two years up; there is no point in keeping a steer older than four years, because after that he won't fatten. What happens to the old cows? They become canned luncheon meat. Old bulls are sold for sausage. I asked what kind of beef Texans themselves liked most. Answer: "Fresh-killed mature steers."

What Texas ranchmen thought of the national beef shortage crisis in October, 1946, cannot be written down for fear that the words will burn through the paper. In any lunatic disaster of such proportions, responsibility must be mixed; but certainly the cattlemen themselves, not only in Texas but elsewhere, have to assume a healthy share of it. There was a stupendous plenitude of beef both on the range and in the feeder lots. But the growers held on grimly to their stock, hoping for the better prices that would presumably come with de-control; the feeders simply wouldn't sell, and nobody gained but the black market. What this added up to in short was that the beef industry went on strike, as men like the Klebergs admitted frankly. Rather than sell at

---

[4] If cattle are without horns more can be squeezed together at the trough and in shipment.

the price set by the government—even if the country should go hungry—
they refused to sell at all.

A Line About Religion

God, as everybody knows, is a serious matter to most Texans, and
religion is militant and emphatic. The religious advertisements in the
Texas newspapers are not so crackpottish as those in California nor
quite so eccentric as in some northern cities, but choice examples may
be found. Some—for instance this about the egregious J. Frank Norris of
Fort Worth, editor of *The Fundamentalist*—are much more frankly
political than religious:

> Are we coming to the time when the whole of Asia will be under
> Slavonic domination? It is prophesied that there will be an army of
> two hundred million marching from the East to the West. Dr.
> Norris will discuss these matters of world-wide, vital interest . . .
> next Sunday night.

President Truman, in the autumn of 1945, intended to visit Waco and
accept a degree there from Baylor University, the chief Baptist institution
in the state. Mr. Truman did not get there. One reason was that the
Texas Baptist Convention adopted unanimously a resolution to the
effect that no college of theirs should confer honorary degrees on anybody, even the president of the United States, who had been known
to take a drink and play poker.[5]

Of course the fundamentalist motif goes far back. I find in H. L.
Mencken's *Americana* (1925) the following note:

> Troubles of the learned in the Bible Belt, as reported in a dispatch
> from Waco: Because he did not believe that Noah's Ark, with the
> dimensions mentioned in the Bible, was capable of accommodating
> a pair of all the animals extant in the world at Noah's time and
> because he had been criticized for expressing that belief, C. S.
> Fothergill, instructor in history at Baylor University, resigned
> today.

In former days evangelism and violence were often intertwined. For
instance an old-style thunderer who called himself "Brann the Iconoclast"
was shot in Waco by a Baptist enemy; before he died he managed to
draw his own gun and kill his adversary.

There are 15,062 churches in Texas, representing not less than 45
"major" and 87 "minor" denominations. The preponderant sect is of
course Baptist, since the Lone Star State is the "Baptist Empire."
There are several reasons for this; for one thing the Baptists got in on

[5] Yet Texas is probably the greatest draw-poker-playing state in the union.

the ground floor, along with the earliest pioneers and settlers; for another they were not content merely to be pastors, but went all over the state to build a serious institutional life, planting colleges and seminaries in strategic areas. They concentrated their financial power shrewdly, with the Baptist Foundation in Dallas as a repository for all endowment funds; purely for its own Texas schools and hospitals, its budget in 1945 was more than three million dollars.

It would be difficult to estimate exactly the extent of Baptist political interest. In a way the sect dominates Texas; yet there is no formal Baptist lobby. The church has no single outstanding leader, though men like Pat Neff and a prominent rancher named Kokernot certainly have wide influence; but no personage survives like the late George W. Truett of Dallas, whose smallest whisper could reverberate through the entire community. Essentially, though the rank and file of the congregation is distinctly on the lower economic level, Baptist power resides in a kind of tie-up between church, schools, and industry. Make a list of the fifty leading directors of various Baptist institutions, like Baylor or the hospital in Dallas; many of the fifty will turn out to be directors of big Texas corporations, and they constitute a kind of fluid ecclesiastical-big-business machine.

The Baptists are the most numerous denomination in Texas; Roman Catholics come next, and then the Methodists. The Methodists differ from the Baptists—from the local Texas point of view as well as in general—quite sharply; the statement is loose of course but they are more progressive, richer on the average, more tolerant about alcohol, and less fundamentalist. The old joke is that a Methodist is a Baptist who has learned to read and write. There are comparatively few Baptists at the University of Texas; the student body is in fact 30.2 per cent Methodist. But this is caused not only by the circumstance that many Baptists are less rich and thus cannot afford to send a boy or girl to Austin for four years, but also because they have so many denominational schools of their own. The Methodists are, on the whole, more liberal on labor than the Baptists, and they are certainly more liberal on the Negro question, though there are no mixed white-black congregations yet. Finally, it would seem that the Methodists are less politically minded than the Baptists. A good many Methodists voted for Coke Stevenson for governor, but not simply because he was a Methodist.

Again to qualify—there are some splendidly liberal Baptist pastors, young men like Dr. Blake Smith of Austin. Dr. Smith recently invited both a Negro and a Jew to address his Sunday evening congregation. Outraged, the secretary of the board of deacons resigned. But other elders supported Smith. One said, "I didn't like it, but I think Jesus Christ would have."

The Catholics, who number about 550,000 in the state and whose property is valued at eleven million dollars, are a vigorous force, and adroit and lively proselytizing goes on all the time. The Baptists are (by and large) more anti-Catholic than the Methodists; this is in part because most Catholics are wet. The Methodists try on the whole to get along;[6] as I heard it put in Austin, "We fight like the dickens against the Catholics, but also we fight for their right to do as they please." One Austin pastor told his flock that Roosevelt should withdraw Myron Taylor as ambassador to the Vatican; as a result he was called "anti-Catholic" by his own people, disapprovingly. Another Methodist told me with justifiable pride that "we can't criticize the Catholics any more without being criticized by our own people for criticizing." The Catholic attitude toward all this is that "the Methodists don't think that we have horns any longer, but the Baptists still know we have tails."

Finally there are the Christian Church (Disciples of Christ) with 74,990 members, with most of its influence centered on Texas Christian University at Fort Worth (with a famous football team) and, quite different, the Church of Christ with 84,672. This latter steadily eats into the lower ranks of Baptists. The Disciples of Christ, who believe in total immersion, are a Baptist offshoot.

Texas, we said in the preceding chapter, is growing up; this observation is also relevant in the religious field; an uneasy fermentation is proceeding in the churches. Plenty of hell-and-brimstone evangelism still exists and there are plenty of surviving fundamentalists; but the tone and temper of religious thought appears slowly to be changing. "People, once they are educated, won't stand for crudely outmoded damnation tactics in the pulpit any more," one university professor told me; "they are coming to ask for a twentieth-century attitude toward religion as toward much else."

Negro Problem and White Primary

Early in 1945 Professor J. Frank Dobie wrote an article in the Dallas *News* on "Modern Negro Citizenship," arguing moderately enough the Negro case for equal rights in voting, education, and the like. A minor monsoon swept the state. Dobie got hundreds of letters; most were favorable. But let me quote from one of the others:

SIR!!!
The very idea! Why, you nigger lovin son-of-a-gun. If you love them so much, why dont you go to a nigger school to teach?
Representing the very backbone of America, I say you cant do it! I wonted to go to college, but I'll just remain ignorant and all my

[6] But not so many years ago friction was so sharp vis-à-vis the Catholics that some Methodists were reluctant to observe Easter! This may sound incredible, but I heard it on excellent authority.

classmates and all *my* children will too, if there's going to be an ole sweating, dirty, *stinkin* nigger sitting up there by them.

Mr. High & Mighty, you see I happen to have something behind me that is more powerful than riches, or power. Yes—its bobby sox! *I'm the future of America!* At least, I have MY youth. Do YOU, MR. DOBIE?? How much longer WILL YOU LAST? I'll guarantee you wont last long if you love niggers so much. I'd just as soon take a shot at you as I would a nigger. (Which I would do, and *quickly!*) Mr. Dobie, I PROTEST. You may want to be ruled by niggers, but *I'm* not. I mean it, too. No NIGGERS!!!! Texas hates them! We'd just as soon have them back in slavery, if they DONT STAY IN THEIR PLACE! Their place IS TO STAY OUT OF OUR WAY!!

Some years ago a colored physician, named Smith, in the town of Bishop "was burned to death *after his hands and feet had been cut off. It was alleged that Dr. Smith, while riding in an automobile, collided with a car occupied by whites.*"[7] In 1945, a young Negro in Dallas named Akins was sentenced to death following a scuffle in which, after being shot himself, he grabbed a gun from a white man and inadvertently killed him. After prolonged litigation Akins' sentence was commuted to life imprisonment; but he might well have been executed had not protests come from all over the United States. And there is a town in west Texas today with signs on the roads, NIGGER! DON'T LET THE SUN SET ON YOU HERE!

All this being said, let us at once point out—though as always with proper qualification—that in the field of Negro relations too, Texas appears to be growing up. It will be a long, slow fight. But no town in Texas is as hysterically intolerant as Natchez, few communities are so dominated by fear, hatred, and bigotry as any of a hundred in Louisiana. Slowly, very slowly, people in Texas (where, in any case, Negroes were never quite the life-and-death problem of the South proper) are becoming more sophisticated, more cosmopolitan. Once Negroes, male and female alike, old and young, were sold in the Galveston market *by the pound*. They are by no means free citizens yet, in the full sense of citizenship. But the state has come a considerable way toward facing out the whole issue honestly.

So for the last time in this book we confront the most pressing and controversially acute of all domestic problems in the United States, that of the Negro. There are about 925,000 Negroes in the state, or 14.4 per cent of the population; this is of course a lower figure than in most southern states. Moreover there are large areas in west Texas in which there are scarcely any Negroes at all, as we know. There have been no lynchings in Texas for some years, and only one bad racial outbreak. This was in Beaumont in June, 1943; its root cause was white resentment at the Negro's growing economic power.

[7] *Americana*, 1925, *op. cit.*

Politically there are several hot and basic Negro issues. One—exactly as in the South itself—is of course the poll tax. This is either $1.50 or $1.75 per year, depending on locality; and there is a catch in that the tax must be paid before January 31, although the general election does not come till November, and many people, not accustomed to thinking about politics so far ahead, simply forget to pay. The potential Negro vote is over 300,000; in 1944 about 200,000 Negroes paid their poll tax, and about 75,000 actually voted in 1946. If the tax were abolished (there is small chance of this at present though various white-black organizations are hard at work on it), the Negro vote would jump considerably. Almost all Negroes vote Democratic, which goes without saying; equally without saying, it is the Regulars and other die-hards who most fear a rise in Negro voting strength, and hence keep the poll tax on the books.

Second, the "white primary" issue, which we have mentioned many times in other chapters. Negroes, poll tax or no poll tax, have always been forbidden by various rules of the Democratic party to vote in the Texas primaries. In 1944 came a test case before the United States Supreme Court, which ruled that, under the existing laws, Negroes could no longer be thus excluded. So in 1944 some fifty thousand Negroes voted in the primaries, for the first time in Texas history; in some districts Negro committeemen were elected. This produced the most acrimonious kind of fight; the reactionaries screamed that the Negroes "were going to take Texas over," and in 1945 a Houston legislator named Weaver Moore introduced a bill in the senate whereby the Supreme Court ruling could be evaded. That is, he proposed that the state election laws having to do with primaries should be rescinded; if this were done, there could be no issue of constitutionality, and the Democratic party could make or interpret its own rules from scratch, as it liked, without regard to federal rulings. As we know, exactly similar maneuvers have been made in other states. But in Texas the Moore bill failed. There will be other attempts to keep the white primary "pure." But—and again I must make the generalization as cautiously as possible—it seems that as time goes on it will become increasingly difficult to prevent Texas Negroes from voting.

Third, our friend the university again. No Negro may be admitted to the university; Negroes are even excluded from the correspondence courses! But several test cases are in progress, aiming to force a change. This became possible in 1945 following another Supreme Court decision; the Court held that the state of Missouri must either admit Negroes to its university, or build them another; and presumably what holds good for Missouri must hold for Texas too. White Texans tried to circumvent the Missouri decision by a neat little artifice, that of simply changing the name of a colored teachers' institution that already existed (but with extremely limited facilities) from "College" to "University." At the moment of writing, this university versus Negro issue is still unsettled.

The most interesting Negro in Texas, Boss Bellinger of San Antonio aside, is probably a moderate named Carter Wesley, the publisher of a string of newspapers including the Houston *Defender* and *Informer*, the Fort Worth *Mind*, and the Dallas *Express*, the oldest Negro paper in the state. All told, Wesley's papers have a circulation of about sixty thousand; they are intelligently edited and vigorously outspoken on most issues. Wesley is now fifty-three. He led his class at Fisk, went to Northwestern for a law degree, and practiced law in Oklahoma; for a time his partner was J. Austin Atkins, who also led a class at Fisk and who was a classmate of Charlie Taft's at Yale. Wesley built up a considerable fortune in Oklahoma, and was then wiped out by the depression; he returned to Houston, his birthplace, and started a new career in journalism.

In San Antonio I asked friends how the Negroes, submerged, got along with the Mexicans, also submerged. I was told that, by and large, Negroes were liked better by whites than Mexicans, and that on the whole Negroes were better paid and despite Jim Crowism had a better chance for education. There is comparatively little contact between the Mexican and Negro communities; each is tempted to play the other off against the whites.

Texas Miscellany

Texas is the state where failure to stop and render aid to an automobilist in trouble is a felony, and where something known as the Fruit of the Month Club prospers. It is a state where you may eat rattlesnake sandwiches and "Texas strawberries" (which come from a part of a bull) and where robbery with firearms is a capital offense but where murder may not be. Texas has the largest collection of Browningana in the world (at Baylor) and the largest women's college in the world (at Denton, near Dallas). It is the state where camels were once used for transport, where a university once gave the degree Mistress of Polite Literature, where a friend pointed out to me what he called very seriously "the second most beautiful" cemetery in the world, and where, eating rare beef, you can hear locutions like "I've bulldogged steers that wasn't hurt no worse than this!"

Chapter 50

Oklahoma and the Indians

〜〜

> Oklahoma has scarcely any history beyond the memory of living
> man . . . yet Coronado left his trail across Oklahoma before
> the Pilgrim Fathers were so much as conceived. . . . A hundred
> years ago Oklahoma was turned into a vast concentration camp
> for Red Indians, because it was such worthless land. Fifty years
> ago, white people from every state swarmed in to dispossess
> the banished Indians, because it was such valuable land.
>
> —George Milburn

THE story of Oklahoma is the story of Indians; the state is almost as
singular and distinctive as Utah and for much the same reason, that
it contains a unique minority. So far in this book we have scarcely mentioned Indians except in passing, because they are outside the main stream
of contemporary political considerations. But now—and in the chapter
to follow—the Indians, who were after all the original possessors of
this large and handsome continent, deserve a friendly word.

The Indians are so extremely numerous and conspicuous in Oklahoma
that their importance is, in fact, sometimes exaggerated. For instance
the legend is that, to get anywhere at all in the state, you have to have
some Indian blood. This isn't quite true. One commonly hears that every
Oklahoma governor has had a touch of Indian, but this isn't true at all;
no governors since statehood have had any Indian blood, though two—
among them Alfalfa Bill Murray—married women who were part Indian.
Oklahomans with Indian blood have indeed reached important positions
in public and private life. Charlie Carter (one-half Choctaw) and W. W.
Hastings (one-eighth Cherokee) were members of Congress for many
years, and William G. Stigler (half Choctaw) is a valuable member of
Congress now. The first American general to be killed after Pearl
Harbor, Clarence E. Tinker, was an Osage, and a distinguished former
senator, Robert L. Owen (though born in Virginia) is part Cherokee.
Will Rogers, as everyone knows, was a Cherokee, and Charlie Curtis,
vice president under Hoover, was a Kaw. Curtis, however, was not
Oklahoma born. At least 20 per cent of the Oklahoma legislature today
is Indian, and in some counties Indians hold at least half the elective
offices.

When I arrived in Oklahoma City I wasn't so naïve as to expect to meet feathered chieftains with names like Chief Bacon Rind, muttering war cries and wielding tomahawks, or squaws carrying crimson papooses. But I didn't quite anticipate what I did find. Perhaps I had been in the South too long. I was thinking in terms of an Indian "problem," and I had the uncomfortable premonition that I would now have to confront another race almost totally excluded from social affairs, as well as politically downtrodden and economically submerged. Judge R. M. Rainey, one of the leading lawyers of the town, asked me to lunch to meet some Indians. After ten minutes the notion that there could be any discrimination against *these* Indians was laughable. The guests were all men of distinction who had risen high. Ben Dwight (three-fourths Choctaw), a former principal chief of the Choctaw nation, is ex-Governor Kerr's principal secretary. Judge Reford Bond (one-eighth Chickasaw) is chairman of the Corporation Commission, state of Oklahoma, which has the important job of regulating all the oil companies, utilities, and the like. Earl Welch (one-sixteenth Chickasaw) is a supreme court justice and a former chief justice. Floyd Maytubby (three-eighths Chickasaw), a prominent insurance man, is governor of the Chickasaw nation.

Someone said at lunch, "My folks started marrying white people, until they damn well married all the Indian blood out!"

Indians vote in Oklahoma. They are citizens with theoretically full and equal rights. If there is any social disparagement, it is of the kind that would equally be exerted against whites on grounds of poverty or uncleanliness. They have been mercilessly exploited in land grabs, as we shall see, but there is no "minority" problem as such. The university has a large percentage of students with Indian blood, and there is no discernible trace of Indian "nationalism," though most Indians are proud of being Indian.

There are two major classifications of Indians in Oklahoma. First, members of the Five Civilized Tribes—Choctaw, Chickasaw, Cherokee, Seminole, and Creek. These are descendants of those who first settled "Indian Territory"; by and large they supply the leaders of the community. Second, the "blanket" Indians. These—like the Comanches, Pawnees, Pottawatomies, Apaches, Arapahoes—were nomads, not town dwellers, and they never reached anything like the development of the Five Civilized Tribes. The "blanket" Indians are so-called for the obvious reason that many still wear blankets. Most of what I discuss in this chapter has to do, not with the blanket Indians who are still a definitely inferior class though not officially discriminated against, but with the "civilized."

The "blanket" Indians live mostly on reservations, and a "reservation" Indian—like those we have briefly alluded to in Florida, Wyoming, and the Dakotas—is simply one who occupies land held in trust for him by the federal government. Such Indians are, as semiwards of the people as a whole, not subject to taxation; this is the chief difference between "reservation" and "nonreservation" Indians in practice. The idea is prevalent that a reservation is a kind of barbed wire enclosure, and that Indians are incarcerated there against their will. This is of course not true. Any Indian on any reservation may move in and out as he chooses; any Indian may, by simply asking to be removed from the rolls, change his status and leave for good. Thousands of Indian boys have done so. They have moved into the towns all over the West and have become drug clerks and mechanics and filling station helpers, indistinguishable from other citizens except for their darker skin. Many volunteered or were drafted and served honorably in World War II. Those Indians who still remain on reservations are, it is important to note, still hedged in and perplexed with some bothersome restrictions. For instance no one may legally sell liquor to an Indian nor can liquor be made on a reservation. Also property rights are restricted.

Approximately a third—128,000 out of 342,000—of all Indians in the United States live in Oklahoma. No fewer than thirty-five tribes are represented, and the gamut runs from men like those I met at lunch, for whom there is no Indian "problem" at all, to lazy old full-bloods (many full-bloods, I heard it said, are not an "extry-industrious people"), to the Osage oil millionaires, to tribesmen in miserable huts who have changed little since their horses were taken from them in the 1870's, which meant that they could no longer raid.

The Five Civilized Tribes got to Oklahoma in this manner: It is not a story of which Americans should be proud. In fact it is a disgraceful story. The tribes lived originally in southeastern United States—Georgia, Tennessee, Mississippi, Alabama—and the Cherokees in particular, under their great leader Sequoyah, built flourishing communities. They were literate for the most part and Christianized. But greedy whites, in the expanding economy of Andrew Jackson's day, usurped their land. The whites—assisted by the U. S. Army—simply grabbed it off. The Indians were expropriated and dispossessed without a shadow of legal right. A "treaty" was signed, known as the Treaty of Dancing Rabbit Creek, in 1832, whereby those expelled from their homes were in return promised land in what is now Oklahoma for "as long as the grass grows and the water runs." Four thousand tribesmen out of sixteen thousand died in the Trail of Tears that followed, as the Army forcibly marched them west; even the twentieth century, which has known some ugly forced marches, has produced few episodes worse than this. Eventually the Five Tribes were "settled" in what came to be known as "Indian Territory," that is, the eastern section of the Oklahoma of today. Here they set about patiently rebuilding their lost towns; the Choctaw "capital" was set up at Tuskahoma, the Chickasaw at

INSIDE U. S. A.

Tishimingo, the Cherokee at Tahlequah. About a century after it was founded, Tuskahoma got into the news again. An Oklahoma congressman suggested in 1946 that, of all things, it should be the United Nations capital.

The Five Tribes were allowed to be called "nations," and they did indeed retain a tribal autonomy, with their own written constitutions and courts of law. The Chickasaws called their chief a "governor," and the other four had, and have, a "principal chief"; before statehood these were elected by the tribal councils, but now they are appointed by the president of the United States. All Five Tribes reached a fairly high level of development in Oklahoma; Alexis de Tocqueville remarks with wonder that the Cherokees had their own newspaper. They ran their ranches well and brought in white teachers; most of their children could read and write, while grownups in Arkansas, say, next door, hardly knew the English alphabet.

Meantime something known as Oklahoma Territory, in the western part of what is now the state, was similarly organized for the blanket and other tribes. And whereas whites were allowed to enter Indian Territory, but not to settle there, they were forbidden any entrance at all to Oklahoma Territory till 1889. What this meant of course was that whisky traders, gunmen and the like came in illegally and made mincemeat of the Indians; missionaries also entered—legally—and a few stray travelers got in, like Washington Irving. Then Oklahoma as a whole "was turned loose on 'em," as I heard it put, after the great "run" of 1889. At the firing of a gun at noon on April 22, some twenty thousand white settlers were allowed to rush and stream over the frontier and stake out claims in what had been the Indian land. Indian Territory and Oklahoma Territory remained quite different entities until 1907. The Five Civilized Tribes in Indian Territory had their own tribal government, as noted above; Oklahoma Territory was, on the other hand, organized by Congress in the regular manner. There was a strong movement to make Indian Territory a separate state, with the name Sequoyah, but it withered away, and the two segments coalesced to make the present state of Oklahoma in 1907, when it was admitted to the union.

If you talk to such an enlightened and provocative citizen as John Collier, for more than a decade the U. S. commissioner of Indian Affairs, you will hear details of what happened to the Indians during this time— not merely in Oklahoma, but elsewhere in the West. For instance the Indian population of California fell from roughly 120,000 in 1850 to 20,000 in 1880; a great many died, like the Polynesians, of simple heartbreak. In Oklahoma the territory "reserved" to the Five Tribes was progressively cut down, and the Indians were exploited with mercilessness and savor. This book is not the place to sketch the intricate story of tribal rolls, "severalty," depredations upon land, cheap trickeries by white real estate men and lawyers. Nothing quite rivals it in American history except perhaps the marauding of the lumber interests in the Northwest—and trees are not, after all, human beings. The Indians were looted, ravished, and left to rot. The Indian Bureau became to all intents and purposes an anti-Indian Bureau. In the beginning the reason for this was mainly military. The Indians were considered to be a pest, and the sooner exterminated the better. This military policy, to destroy the Indian tribes as such, was passed over by the Army to the Department of the Interior, and became rationalized into a long-range attempt to "save" the Indians from their own "dark ways"; hence, anything that broke down Indian culture, that pulverized and atomized the structure of Indian life, was encouraged. Next, there came what Mr. Collier calls a "doctrinal curse," namely that Indian affairs should be considered not on the national level, but locally, so that every congress-man in an Indian area was free to play with what Indian booty he could acquire, if so inclined. The Indian Bureau, in order to get any appro-priations at all, had to sell out the Indians. Also, since it was policy to liquidate the Indians, the bureau made no effort to save their agriculture; countless millions of tons of topsoil were washed into rivers like the Rio Grande.

All this changed after 1932. Mr. Ickes became secretary of the interior, John Collier became commissioner of Indian affairs, Mr. Roosevelt encouraged their ideas, the Soil Conservation Service lent a hand, and in 1934 Congress passed a law, the Indian Reorganization Act, that instituted new procedures and a new policy. This included assistance to Indian social and economic progress, protection of Indian culture, and in general an effort to give the Indians a kind of tribal autonomy and self-government.

The chief Indian grievances at present seem to be the following: In the Southwest, where the Indian has overgrazed his land, he may find it impossible to buy more; many Navajos for instance would like to leave their reservations and would be willing to pay taxes as landowners, but are not allowed to do so. Also reservation Indians cannot, by law, go to court to settle claims against the government; a special act of Congress is necessary—and of course practically impossible to put through—before an Indian can sue. Above these are political con-siderations. Many reservation Indians are dissatisfied with their equivocal status that makes them both "citizens" and wards. In five states at least—Colorado, Washington, Utah, and New Mexico and Arizona as we shall see—Indians are forbidden to vote, though such an interdict is said by most lawyers to be clearly unconstitutional.

I have said that there is no Indian "nationalism." But a considerable self-consciousness and effervescence has come recently. For instance a Pueblo Council exists in New Mexico in which twenty-two tribes co-operate, and in 1944 a Council of American Indians was organized in Denver, representing a substantial number of tribes all over the country. Another point is that the Indians are no longer dying off. The trend toward extinction has been checked, and as of the moment at least the Indian birthrate—especially among Hopis, Apaches, Navajos, and Pueblos—is three or four times that of the white.

"Columbus, I am Here!"

But to return to Oklahoma and the Five Civilized Tribes. There are about 40,000 Cherokees today, 21,000 Choctaws, 12,000 Creeks, 6,000 Chickasaws, and 3,000 Seminoles. They resemble one another fairly closely, and get on well together. The Cherokees consider themselves the elite of the lot, and the Chickasaws and Choctaws are the richest; something like a billion and a half tons of coal is, for instance, believed to underlie their land and the potential income from this is, in theory, reserved to the tribe as a whole. Choctaws and Chickasaws were once the same tribe, and speak nearly an identical language, but Creek is quite different, and so is Cherokee. Creeks and Cherokees cannot understand Choctaw-Chickasaw. But Creeks and Seminoles can, as a rule, understand one another. There are also some religious differences. Seminoles, having been in Spanish- and French-occupied regions originally, were heavily proselytized by Roman Catholics, as were the Osages, but the others have tended to be Protestant. Most Creeks and Cherokees are Baptists or Methodists, most Chickasaws and Choctaws Presbyterian.

The name "Oklahoma" comes, incidentally, from two Choctaw words, *Okla* (= people) and *homma* (= red); it was first used in the Choctaw-Chickasaw Treaty of 1866.[1] One town in the state has the engaging name of Chickiechockie, after two children of a Choctaw-Chickasaw marriage who were named Chickie and Chockie.

I asked if Indians and Negroes ever married; the subject is complex. Both Choctaws and Chickasaws owned slaves, and even brought some slaves with them on the Trail of Tears; they looked on Negroes—and some still do—almost exactly as a southern planter did. After emancipation the Choctaws "adopted" Negroes as "Choctaw freedmen," and, in a separate classification, let them share in communal property. But to marry them was punishable by death under tribal law. This was true of the Cherokees also. Creeks, however, did intermarry, as did Seminoles. In this regard Oklahoma strikingly resembles the continent of South America. Just so did various Latin American countries acquire their distinctive characteristics by the degree of intermarriage between

---

[1] *Oklahoma Place Names*, by Charles N. Gould. University of Oklahoma Press, p. 106.

white, black, and Indian. The greater the admixture, the lower the standards of civilization is the rule. Look at Honduras, say, compared to Uruguay. In precise microcosm, the same differences exist today in parts of Oklahoma.

The problem of Indian landholding is inordinately technical. What remained of the Indian lands after a generation of looting was allocated to bona fide members of the tribe according to "head rights"; each Indian, regardless of age or sex, was given an "allotment," depending on tribal membership. To receive an allotment an Indian had to be registered on the tribal rolls which, a kind of census, were finally closed in 1906; since that time, nobody has gotten in. I heard one Indian say, "I have two younger sisters who are not on the rolls," i.e., who never got their allotment. Plenty of non-Indians around the turn of the century claimed Indian blood in order to get free land, and many whites married squaws to acquire their property.

A special case—very special—is that of the Osages, who are the richest community per capita on earth. These, members of a primitive blanket tribe, got the last and least desirable allotments of rocky non-fertile soil in the north of the state. Then oil, oil in unimaginable quantities, was discovered there. The total value of the Osage leases is estimated today at 280 million dollars. Long before this a perspicacious Indian agent had written subsurface rights into the tribal treaty, reserving all revenue to the tribe itself, *en bloc*, and so when oil was struck the returns were apportioned in more or less equal shares and practically all Osages got rich—at least on paper. But a great many were bilked and cheated out of what should have been their part of a common return by white lawyers and land agents who took advantage of their lack of education and business experience. They were played one against another, forced into expensive litigation, and hijacked to a turn.

The Indians in Oklahoma do not vote as a unit. But every white politician seeks to cater, naturally, to this considerable wedge of voters. One legend is that all members of the Five Civilized Tribes used to vote Republican, because they still resented having been squeezed out of their southern homes by Andy Jackson. But since the New Deal the Indian vote has been predominantly Democratic as a natural consequence of the Indian Reorganization Act.

I heard two Indian anecodotes in Oklahoma. One recounts that the first Indian GI to land in Italy in 1943 shouted to the beachhead, "Columbus, I am here!" The other records a brief colloquy between a stuffy New England lady and Will Rogers. She asked him if his people had come over on the Mayflower and he replied, "No, ma'am, but we met the boat."

Facts, Figures, and Impressions

> Oklahoma has always been wayward. . . . The regional tag to
> fit Oklahoma has not been made. Oklahoma is to sociology what
> Australia is to zoology. It is the place where the trials and errors
> of men, instead of nature, have been made only yesterday, and
> the results are as egregious as a duckbill or kangaroo. Okla-
> homa is full of manmade contradictions, perversities, and mon-
> strosities.
>
> —George Milburn

Oklahoma looks like a thickly hilted pistol pointing west, and it
contains two invisible dividing lines; the first follows the old demarcation
between Oklahoma Territory and Indian Territory. What was once
the former, the area to the west, is wheat and farming country, rolling
plains, with very little industrialization, few Negroes, few towns. What
was once Indian Territory, with Tulsa as its focus, is watered, with
mountains and streams, cattle, oil (which is also found in the west) and
cotton. Oklahoma is thus a state containing one of the most remarkable
of all American frontiers, the line where wheat and cotton meet.

Also you can divide Oklahoma north and south; the Rock Island
Railroad cuts it in two. The extreme north—including the old Cherokee
strip—is Kansan in flavor, and was mostly settled from the north; the
south is a cross between deep South and Texas. The north is by and
large Republican, the south Democratic. The state that Oklahoma most
resembles is of course Texas, if only because it too does everything with
color and individuality, but tell an Oklahoman that his state is a
"dependency" of Texas and he will bite your eyes out.

Packed with brawn and muscle, Oklahoma is the first state in production of broom corn and grain sorghums, the second in winter
wheat, and first or possibly second (depending on where you get your
statistics) in zinc. It runs neck and neck with Louisiana for third place
in petroleum, and it registers more than 10 per cent of all the Herefords
in the country. It is full of pecans, carbon black, glass for milk bottles,
and alabaster. It produces notable players of baseball (Carl Hubbell,
Pepper Martin), and its basketball team (Oklahoma A & M) was the
best in the nation in 1944. Also it produces brains, though—as in the
South—most of the bright youngsters are sucked out by better opportunities, better jobs and money, into the East and elsewhere. It has
developed some admirable politicians, like Mike Monroney, and a good
many writers of talent like Marquis James, Lynn Riggs, George
Milburn, and Stanley Vestal. Incidentally Oklahomans are still pretty
sensitive about Steinbeck's *Grapes of Wrath*, and they are not too
impressed by the unprecedented Broadway success *Oklahoma!*—maybe
because, until it becomes a movie, a musical comedy in New York is not

very tangible. Finally, in this cultural realm, the state's university press is, along with Chapel Hill and Yale, one of the most enterprising and distinguished in the country.[2]

Tall tales come out of Oklahoma just as out of Texas; one favorite describes the "crowbar hole." This is a hole through the wall that many houses have, designed to check the weather. You shove a crowbar through the hole; if it bends, the wind velocity outside is normal; if the bar breaks off, "it is better to stay in the house."

Tulsa, Oklahoma City, Oil

Between the two chief cities, Oklahoma City and Tulsa, there are interesting differences, and the two are rivals in the pattern sketched in this book so often—like Minneapolis and St. Paul, San Francisco and Los Angeles, Dallas and Fort Worth. Oklahoma City is bigger (population 204,424 as against Tulsa's 142,157), more sophisticated, more tranquil—though it has its own type of gustiness. Both cities rise sharp from the tawny plain, with a portcullis of skyscrapers, and seen from the air they are like checkerboards with brilliant alternating squares of green; Tulsa is more dramatic, more pictorial. Oklahoma City is not particularly jealous of Tulsa, regarding it somewhat as a great Dane may regard a noisy poodle, but Tulsa is apt to be jealous of Oklahoma City. Oklahoma City is one of the youngest in the country; it was created in a day—literally—on April 22, 1889, the day of the first great "run"; it has no Indian background. Tulsa, "oil capital of the world" as it calls itself, is a tough, get-rich-quick, heady town about as sensitive as corduroy. It was founded by the Creeks who named it for their former Alabama capital, Tallasi; its great boom began on June 25, 1901, when oil was struck. Yankee oilmen—mostly from Pennsylvania—poured in as the oil poured out. Most oil towns are likely to be reactionary, Houston for example; Tulsa is one of the most reactionary cities in the whole United States.

Also it is one of the most isolationist. In March, 1945, Lord Halifax, then the British ambassador, visited Oklahoma to take part in a coyote hunt. These are some of the words with which the Tulsa *Tribune* greeted him:

> Your advance man, Lord, tells us you will condescend to dine with a selected 200 of us. Nice of you. . . . You stipulate that you want at least 20 percent to be laboring men. Doggone it, Lord, if you aren't democratic. Twenty percent democratic.

[2] Oklahoma was incidentally the first state to develop aviation among farmers on a serious scale through the Flying Farmers organization, and it is the only one to have a kind of equivalent of the Passion Play at Oberammergau; this is the Good Friday pageant held every year at Lawton.

When a good neighbor borrows a cup of sugar, he returns a cup of sugar. That is a little matter of nice behavior you British do not know. England never returned anything. A gentleman, sir, pays his debts. John Bull is not a gentleman. Can you teach him to be one? Your debt on this World War, sir, is beyond your own arithmetic comprehension . . . And you never expect to pay a dime of it . . .

You expect us Americans to go on and pay your bills. It is time your leisure class went to work and paid your honest debts. . . . We gave you farm implements that we needed for our own soil. You gave those implements to other peoples as your benevolent gift. You sold them and put the cash in your pocket. That, sir, was just plain treachery and DISHONESTY.

Tulsa is a great oil town, but nowhere in the United States, not even Los Angeles, does petroleum make such an impact on the visitor as in Oklahoma City. The derricks rise actually on the governor's very lawn, and the wells slant under the basement of the capitol itself. The *Encyclopaedia Britannica* said of Oklahoma City in an edition printed not so long ago that the nearest oil field was thirty miles away; today, the town does its business directly on top of one. This field came in in 1928. It produced mad and fantastic scenes, as black oil gushed down the streets; previously the geologists had pronounced this to be a "red bed" area, in which oil was either absent or very difficult to reach. Another great field just twelve miles outside the city limits was discovered by a freak after the regular oil people had given it up. The steel derricks rise right out of the wheat and alfalfa now.

Oil leases are a tremendous business in Oklahoma. If the geologists think the prospects are good the oil companies will lease land long before any thought of actual drilling. The race for new properties is incessant. Once drilling begins and oil is produced the farmer who sold the lease gets one-eighth the proceeds as a royalty. Oil is, as we well know, fugacious; it is not like a lump of coal that will stay sitting; so if your neighbor drills, you have to drill too, or lose your oil. Except for this, the state would never have started drilling in the governor's front yard; private owners near by were draining oil away. In an effort to reduce the fantastic evils implicit in this system, Oklahoma limits the production of wells to two hundred barrels each per day. It well remembers the terrible experiences of 1932 when the price of crude dropped to ten cents a barrel.[3]

Oklahoma City has two more distinctions of which it speaks proudly. It has the largest percentage of American-born white population of any city in the union; the foreign born scarcely exist. The other is that it is the first American city of consequence to ask every citizen, even

[3] A splendid account of the Oklahoma City field is "Oil in the Back Yard," by Lillian Fryer Rainey, *Atlantic Monthly*, April, 1938.

proud ladies of southern descent, to submit to a test for venereal disease.

A potential danger in Oklahoma is that a prolonged drought might make another Dust Bowl. Wheat is way up, which means that more and more farmers are in 1946 being tempted to repeat the grisly mistake that followed World War I when, like their fellows in Texas, Montana, and elsewhere, they started plowing up range land for crops. Only three Oklahoma counties suffered in the great disaster of 1935, but these three were devastated. On a single day, I heard, fifty million *tons* of soil were blown away. People sat in Oklahoma City, with the sky invisible for three days in a row, holding dust masks over their faces and wet towels to protect their mouths at night, while the farms blew by.

Once More: Who Runs It?

> In God we trusted,
> In Kansas we busted;
> Now let 'er rip
> For the Cherokee strip.

No state has more explosive politics than Oklahoma, and its political behavior can be positively Balkanesque. Knock 'em, sock 'em, rock 'em is the rule. "In most places," a friend told me, "you clean a dirty blanket with a vacuum cleaner; here we hang it on a line and beat it with a rock." Not so long ago a celebrated outlaw and train robber, Al Jennings, got more than twenty thousand votes for governor. Out of a total of thirteen governors impeached in all American states since the foundation of the republic, two were Oklahoman, and Oklahoma has been a state for only forty years. Another governor was tried on criminal charges during his term of office, but acquitted. The state runs to the picturesque as well as the outrageous. Alfalfa Bill Murray, who was chairman of the constitutional convention that preceded statehood in 1907 and governor from 1931 to 1935, had some detonating mannerisms. For instance an unsuspecting visitor to the gubernatorial offices, sitting down in a chair carefully placed three feet from Murray's desk, might try to hitch himself closer, whereupon he would discover that the chair was nailed to the floor, and Murray would shout, "What the hell do you want?" Often the governor was barefoot, with his socks on the desk. When Murray was sworn in, his father, aged ninety-one, administered the oath. With his huge hawk nose, his neck shriveled into tendons around a protruding Adam's apple, with dripping white mustaches over a mouth perpetually chewing tobacco, Murray looked—and for that matter still looks, since the old boy is still alive, aged seventy-six—like a cantankerous hick in a burlesque show. In 1932 he bolted the ticket to run for president against FDR. He is a brilliant student of Thucydides, Adam Smith, and Huey Long, and has just published his memoirs in a book 1,683 pages long that costs twenty-one dollars.

In 1942, Senator Josh Lee, a New Deal Democrat, was beaten for re-election. One of the complications attending the campaign was that two other Josh Lees, one a furniture dealer and the other a farmer, ran against him in the primary. We have noted similar tricks in Nevada. But Oklahoma outdoes all other states. One game is to liven up elections by persuading folk whose names are identical with those of celebrities, living or dead, to run. The state has had Daniel Boone, Oliver Cromwell, Mae West, Joe E. Brown, Brigham Young, and William Cullen Bryant on its ballots.[4]

Speaking generally the following groups all have something to do with running Oklahoma. I have not attempted to enumerate them in order of importance.

First, the Baptist church. A prominent labor man told me that never in his experience has he known a nonpolitical organization to wield such covert political power. Parts of Oklahoma are still deep in the Bible belt. Take the matter of prohibition. It is indeed the strangest of paradoxes that Oklahoma is, with Mississippi and Kansas, one of the three dry states in the union, considering its robust and bawdy character otherwise.

Second, the oil interests. Their influence is, as in Texas, mostly negative; they do not so much do things as keep things from being done. One Oklahoma congressman told me, "They can certainly raise a terrible lot of money to try and beat you." The oil companies are divided between "majors" and independents, and sometimes they fight civil wars; for instance big-money oil vigorously opposed two recent men known as "oil governors"—Kerr and Marland—because neither would promise subservience to oil though they were oil men themselves. Most of the big companies operating in Oklahoma are absentee owned; this is a familiar pattern. Standard of New Jersey owns the Carter Oil Company and the Carter Pipe Line; Standard of Indiana owns the Stanolind Oil and Gas Company, the Stanolind Pipeline Co., and the Stanolind Crude Oil Purchasing Company; Standard of New York owns the Magnolia Oil Company, and Standard of Ohio, a more recent arrival, owns Sohio. Pure Oil is also important in the state, as are Sun Oil (Pew interests, Pennsylvania), and Gulf (Mellon). The chief independent is Phillips. Some oil companies are, it is interesting to note, retreating out of Oklahoma into Texas, because the Texas laws are more liberal. Also some rich Oklahomans moved south to Dallas, say, to take advantage of the Texas community property law.

Interestingly enough Oklahoma, on achieving statehood, warily sought

[4] *Oklahoma*, in the American Guide Series, p. 35.

to avoid dominance by the big corporations. For instance a clause in the actual constitution forbids legislators to ride on free passes. So far as I know this is the only case in the country where such a measure was taken to discourage the railway lobbies.

Third, as in California, the old folks. Oklahoma has a quite liberal Old Age Assistance Law, and some eighty thousand people are on the rolls, getting an average of thirty-four dollars per month each. Of every thousand Oklahomans of sixty-five or older, 496 are eligible to assistance benefits, as against a national ratio of 210. This means, among other things, that the state pays steep taxes, for instance 5½¢ per gallon on gasoline, and 5¢ per package of cigarettes.

Fourth—as in all western states—the education lobby. Oklahoma is very proud of its school record, and it operates more institutions of learning in proportion to population than any other state. Since the state contributes about half the total school budget, every local school district is up to its eyes in politics. The teachers, too, are sophisticated politically and highly vocal.[5]

Fifth—as in all southern states—the "County Rings." These are built around the seventy-seven county commissioners who have substantial public sums to administer since revenues from automobile licenses and the gasoline tax are divided equally between state and counties.

Other factors in Oklahoma are, on the whole, minor. Take the newspapers. The Chicago *Tribune*-like papers in Tulsa were venomously anti-Roosevelt but FDR carried the state every time he ran. The Oklahoma City papers are more respectable, and E. K. Gaylord, editor of both the *Times* and the *Daily Oklahoman*, is the nearest thing to a boss the city has. Another point is that the small county papers, as apart from big urban organs, have a considerable influence; this is a spreading out of a characteristic very common in the Middle West. What the county press represents is of course the voice of the farmer and, despite petroleum, agriculture is still Oklahoma's biggest industry.

As to labor, it was very weak until 1944, when the AF of L Teamsters, the Farmers Union, the Railway Brotherhoods, the General Welfare Association (representing the old age pensionnaires) and the CIO worked together—more or less—under a Unity Council. In 1945, after three tries, the CIO won an election at the Douglas plant which was making C-47's for the army, twelve miles out of Oklahoma City, and the CIO has organized one of the two big packing plants in the city. As to Negroes, the most interesting personality is Roscoe Dungee, editor of

[5] Oklahoma has had some choice textbook scandals, incidentally. Two officials were recently sent to the penitentiary for accepting bribes of sixty thousand dollars "for influencing textbook adoptions." Cf. *Public Men In and Out of Office*, ed. by J. L. Salter, p. 424.

the *Black Dispatch*; he is one of the outstanding Negro journalists in the country. There is no poll tax in the state, but Jim Crowism and segregation are the rule. A Presbyterian preacher in the university town of Norman recently invited Negroes into his church—and the community did not split asunder as predicted.

Oklahoma votes Democratic in a ratio of about three to one, and so the primaries are usually decisive; every governor since statehood has been a Democrat. But twice (Harding, 1920; Hoover, 1928) it voted for a Republican president. To conclude, what really runs Oklahoma is what runs so many other states, the ordinary middle-class voter with all his lamentable defects and limitations on the one side, and on the other his positive qualities like good will and down-to-the-ground common sense.

Bob Kerr and Others

The governor of Oklahoma from 1943 to 1947, Robert S. Kerr, is a large and lively man six feet four in height and weighing about 275 pounds, yet full of agility and bounce. Kerr was the keynoter at the Democratic convention in Chicago in 1944; until then he was little known outside Oklahoma. His career is archetypically "American," in its emphasis on the frontier virtues of diligence and enterprise, its promise of utterly boundless opportunity to the young and bright in heart, and its rewards both in material wealth and a maturing sense of social responsibility.

Kerr is a rich man; he is also, though a politician, an honest liberal. He was president for many years of the Midcontinent Oil and Gas Association, and had never run for office until he became governor. He writes a weekly column—still—for a group of country newspapers and without fail each Sunday morning teaches Sunday school to a large and enthusiastic class. He is a devout Baptist, but his wife—this is a mildly nontypical touch—is a Christian Scientist. Their churches face one another across the street.[6]

Kerr is the first Oklahoma-born governor. His father was a pioneer farmer who told him as a boy that he could be governor some day, if only he worked hard enough. This, a stock story related of almost all American governors, is in Kerr's case quite true. Father Kerr became a county clerk, and then went broke. Young Bob decided then and there never to let such a catastrophe happen to him, and he began making money at all sorts of jobs.

[6] In one room of the gubernatorial mansion incidentally a complete collection of the books published by the University of Oklahoma Press is nicely displayed. In another a measuring device is set against the wall, whereby the advancing height of the four strapping Kerr children can be taped.

Kerr was one of the few governors who did real homework on the questionnaire I sent him; he sent copies to six or seven officials and friends in various fields, and carefully worked over documents they each prepared. What he probably believes in most is the political infallibility of the common man; at the same time he hopes of course that the common man will be sensible enough to vote right, viz., for him.

His style can be somewhat orotund. Here is the peroration of his message to the legislature in 1943:

> The signal fires of the Plains Indians and the campfires of our forebears have long since ceased to send their flashing messages across the plain or mark the spot of the evening bivouac, but in the hearts of their sons and daughters there burns a brighter glow and a fiercer flame. It is our determination to climb ever upward along the pathway of human progress that leads to the stars. . . . We shall not now, in the midst of the storm whose thunders roll around this world, be unworthy of their courage. . . . They had the faith to go up and possess the land. With the mantle of their spirit upon our shoulders, let us march on into a brighter and more glorious dawn!

One of Oklahoma's senators is a tory Republican, E. H. (Ed) Moore of Tulsa, the other is a tory Democrat, Elmer Thomas. Moore, an extremely wealthy oil man, was once a Democrat himself; in fact he was a delegate to the Democratic National Convention in 1940. Then he flirted with the Willkieites, deserted Willkie because he was too liberal, and joined the Republican party. He is fanatically reactionary. In the *New Republic* charts issued in September, 1946, he, Hawkes of New Jersey, and Bushfield of South Dakota are the only three senators out of 96 with 100 percent negative voting records. (In the previous chart eight senators, as we noted in connection with Utah above, had this distinction.) Elmer Thomas is not quite so virulent a New Deal hater. On May 6, 1946, Drew Pearson charged him—also Bankhead of Alabama —with trading surreptitiously on the cotton market while publicly attacking the OPA price ceilings on cotton.

Politics takes, as we know, some strange twists and turnings in the United States. Consider the case of Jedediah Johnson, Democratic congressman from Oklahoma for twenty years. A persistent thorn in the flesh of the Department of the Interior, he tore away endlessly at Ickes and his appropriations. The Democratic high command offered him a life job as a judge in the customs court in New York. But Johnson himself, it seems, never knew of the offer until his name went to the Senate for confirmation. This was in March, 1945, but he was still sitting in the House in August. Finally he declined the judgeship. He told his constituents that he had given up this splendid offer in order to be able to continue serving them. The judgeship then went to a Negro, Irvin C. Mollison. Anti-Negro folk in Oklahoma decided that if the job was something a colored man could fill it couldn't be much of a job, and in the Congressional primaries of 1946 Johnson was soundly beaten—of course for other reasons too—and now has no public post at all. The implications of this story are various in the extreme; the United States can be a crazy country, and often is.

Mr. Ickes doughtily paid his respects to Mr. Johnson in several columns in the New York *Post* in September, 1946, after some mixed sniping:

On one occasion, Congressman Johnson solicited a job in Interior for James V. McClintic of Oklahoma, who had been defeated for re-election to Congress. Mr. McClintic, upon being interviewed, said that he had been a lawyer but that he did not feel able to work at a law job. He had no civil service status and, in any event, could not qualify for a job higher than that of clerk. So the great "economizer," Congressman Johnson, obligingly made provision in the Interior budget for a position paying $6,000, and exempt from the classified service. Thus I found myself with an employee on my personal staff of whose services I could really make no use. . . .

When I was Public Works Administrator Congressman Jed Johnson wished upon me his brother, Joshua W. Johnson, as manager of a housing project at Enid, Oklahoma. In October of 1942 he asked me to give a job to another brother, Carroll, and he also sought a place for Eva L. Johnson, the wife of Carroll. The Congressman wrote to the Indian Office about both his brother and sister-in-law, suggesting that they "might possibly be interested in a combination job for a while if you have something that would pay around $3,000 for him and a teaching job or matron of a dormitory for her."

We were not able to place Brother Carroll or his wife in either agency. We found that his experience had been in grocery stores as an inspector of fruits and vegetables. The influential Jed Johnson had previously gotten him a job to direct landscape work in the Soil Conservation Service, he having passed the civil service test for Rural Letter Carrier in 1941.

This could all be written off as trivial, except that it points a lesson sometimes forgotten or ignored—that a great many Congressmen indeed go in for nepotism, and that a professional political career depends very often on the patronage—jobs—it can bestow.

By all odds the best and most useful man-of-politics Oklahoma has is A. S. Mike Monroney, who in 1946 won the first *Collier's* award for distinguished public service in Congress, along with Vandenberg of Michigan. Monroney is an original. In one of his campaigns he sent picket lines to football games, with placards announcing MIKE MONRONEY —UNFAIR TO ORGANIZED POLITICIANS. But I am breaking my rule about keeping Congressmen out of this volume and I must save consideration of Monroney for another place.

Our long march through the United States is nearly done. Let us look now at the two states remaining, the desert states of the great Southwest.

Chapter 51

Last Stop: The New States of
the Southwest

~~~~~~

> O that the desert were my dwelling place!
> —Byron, *Childe Harold*

WE ENTER now still another new and altogether distinctive American world, that of New Mexico, Arizona, and the purple desert flowing endlessly under lonely stars, and once more we can note the illimitable opulence of the United States, its fabulous variety and range. This book is now something like four hundred thousand words long. It might easily have been much longer. And yet, nearing the end, we still find ourselves confronting new and singular phenomena, we still have to trace the outlines of another new, fresh, and vital American region.

Perhaps it is fitting to conclude this tour with New Mexico and Arizona because they are at once the oldest American states and the newest. Santa Fe has been a capital for three solid centuries, and Arizona has known white men since 1539. The village of Oraibi, in the Hopi country, is believed to be "the oldest continuously inhabited community in the U.S." But New Mexico was only admitted to the union on January 6, 1912, and Arizona on February 14, 1912; Arizona is thus the youngest American state by 39 days. For a time the two wanted to come in together as a single state.

Now having completed a full circle, we are back in the West again. This means, as we know, open spaces, friendliness, a lively tincture of political radicalism, sagebrush and cattle culture and the most lordly scenery known to man, colonial economy, dry farming, Indians, absentee capital, and, above all, the politics of water.

New Mexico and Santa Fe

> New Mexico has an austere and planetary look that daunts and
> challenges the soul.
> —Elizabeth Shepley Sergeant

It looks rather like Nevada, but is higher, ruggeder, more dramatic. Half the mountains seem to have their tops blown off. The state is the fourth biggest in the union—it is almost three times the size of New York—and the fifth most thinly settled. It has only 531,818 people, less than single cities like Buffalo or Pittsburgh, and the density of population is one of the lowest in the country, 4.4 to the square mile.

The foundation of New Mexican life and economy is, in a word, sunshine. True, there are mineral deposits (though nothing comparable to those of Arizona) and the livestock industry is important, but basically the state lives on its high, dry, sunny climate. The crisp exhilarating sunshine brings tourists in. Also this has contributed considerably to political leadership, in that so many New Mexicans who have risen high came out originally for their health. The state is more or less run by "lungers." For instance the late Bronson Cutting, one of the ablest senators the country has had this century, arrived in New Mexico on a stretcher. A great many doctors, dentists and so on in the state are, incidentally, patients who have recovered from tuberculosis. Cured by New Mexico, they now cure others.

The other signal uniqueness of New Mexico is racial background. There are three cultures here—Anglo-American, Spanish, Indian—and it is the only bilingual state in the union. English and Spanish are official languages, the constitution was ratified in both, and until recently there had to be interpreters in the legislature; to this day the courts and county offices in the "native" districts have interpreters, and legal notices must be posted everywhere in both tongues. The white population is roughly 63 per cent Anglo, 37 per cent Spanish; in addition there are about 50,000 Indians. This word "Anglo" is not used, so far as I know, anywhere else in the United States; it means people of North American stock in contradistinction to the Spanish and/or Mexicans, who are commonly called "natives."

I looked at a plaque on the low adobe wall:

EL PALACIO REAL
FORTRESS AND CASTLE BUILT BY ORDER OF THE
SPANISH CROWN, 1610-1612
SEAT OF GOVERNMENT UNDER THREE FLAGS
SPANISH, MEXICAN, AND AMERICAN
FROM 1610 TO 1910
THE RESIDENCE OF OVER 100 GOVERNORS AND CAPTAINS GENERAL
THE OLDEST PUBLIC BUILDING IN THE UNITED STATES

Also this dusty venerable building in Santa Fe with its squarely arched colonnades was for twelve years (1680-1692) the seat of government of the Pueblo Indians, and for a few days in 1862 a headquarters of the American Army of the Confederacy.

Indeed no city in the country is more heavily suffused, more choked with historical association, from the days of Francisco Vásquez de

Coronado to the days of Billy the Kid, "who was captured by killing,"
than Santa Fe. It was founded in 1609, and its first name was La Villa
Real de la Santa Fe de San Francisco; it is "the oldest capital within
the boundaries of the United States."[1] Even if Santa Fe, the town, had
no great interest in itself, it would be unmatched in flavor if only because
it was the western terminus of one of the most remarkable of all American highways—the Santa Fe Trail that stretched across the continent
from Independence, Missouri, with almost arrogant romanticism.[2]

A famous anecdote is told of William Butler Yeats. Asked to define
a literary movement he replied, "A literary movement consists of two
writers in the same city who hate each other."

The analogy does not apply to New Mexico strictly speaking, but
both Santa Fe and Taos to the north are famous for their literary and
artistic colonies. John Sloan, Victor Higgins, Oscar Berninghaus,
Robert Henri, George Bellows, Randall Davy, Gina Knee, have all lived
or live in the vicinity. The Harwood Foundation in Taos makes a colorful focus for the work of many others. As to writers the Santa Fe region
has produced a literature which few areas in the country can match—
with works by Mary Austin, D. H. Lawrence, Willa Cather, Witter
Bynner, Arthur Davison Ficke, John Gould Fletcher, Mabel Dodge
Luhan, Haniel Long, Harvey Fergusson, Paul Horgan, Eugene Manlove Rhodes, Oliver La Farge.

That New Mexico, which has given life to art from ancient Indian
rain dances to a story like Lawrence's "The Woman Who Rode Away,"
should also have given birth to the atomic bomb, is perhaps an irony that
measures the gamut of our civilization. As everybody knows the first
explosion of the bomb took place south of Albuquerque on the remote
and inaccessible Alamogordo military reservation; previously it had
been put together at the secret workshop made out of a boys' school at
Los Alamos, near Santa Fe. This is where Dr. Oppenheimer had his
tremendous laboratory. When I visited Santa Fe a few months before
the first test of the bomb the town was well aware that something strange
was going on, but nobody knew quite what. But I heard—even then—
about mysterious explosions in the near-by hills, about an inner cadre
of officers who were never permitted to leave their quarters even for
matters of life and death, about the incessant road traffic up the mountains under cover of night, about workers who went into those desolate
hills by the thousand, and for months were not seen again.

New Mexico, like Texas, has its boosters. The following ardent paean

---

[1] From *New Mexico* in the American Guide Series. Incidentally Santa Fe, one
of the smallest American capitals (population 20,325), is the only one not on the
main line of a railroad.

[2] This trail ended at La Fonda, one of the pleasantest hotels in the United States,
and still the nerve center of the town. An odd point is that the chef of this admirable
establishment should, of all things, have once been chef to Kaiser Wilhelm.

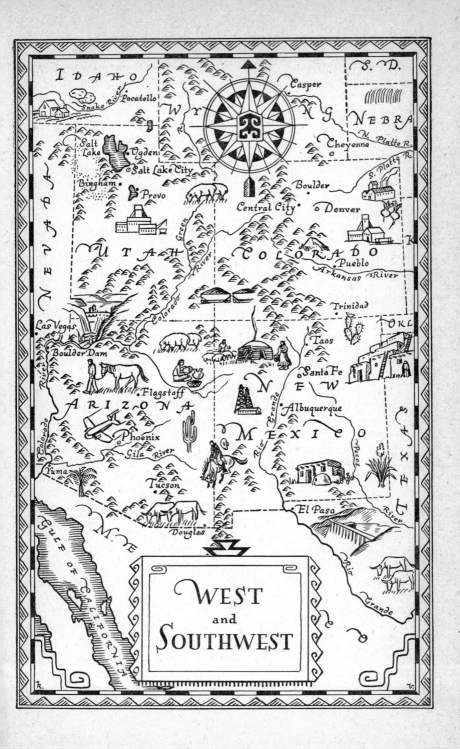

WEST
and
SOUTHWEST

was written by S. Omar (The Tentmaker) Barker of Tecolotenos, New Mexico, and was printed among other places in the El Paso *Herald-Post*:

> Actually, of course, Texas is no bigger than New Mexico. It only appears bigger because it is spread out so much thinner. The mean average thickness of New Mexico from sunshine to sea level is 5600 feet. The higher you go into the mountains the meaner it gets. . . . Mashed down and rolled out to the same thinness as Texas, New Mexico would reach all the way from Yalta to the Atlantic Charter with enough lapover to flap in the Texas wind. On the other hand, at the thickest point in Texas, an average New Mexico screwbilled angleworm could bore through to the bottom in one wiggle . . .
> Fourscore years before the first Texas cowboy scuffed a high-heeled boot on Plymouth Rock, a Mr. Coronado of Spain was eating corn off the cob in New Mexico and mailing home post-cards of five-storied Pueblo tourist courts marked "Come on over, the climb is fine." . . .
> New Mexico has plains so flat that the State Highway Department has to put up signs to show the water which way to run when it rains; yet the mountains are so steep that the bears which inhabit them have all developed corkscrew tails so they can sit down once in a while without sliding off into Texas. . . .
> Snow falls so deep in New Mexico's mountains that it takes 40,000 automobile loads of Texas hot air each summer to melt it. . . .
> New Mexico is game country too. If all the deer horns in the state were clustered together into one giant hatrack, it would make a good place for Texans to hang their hats when not talking through them . . .
> The charge that half the voters in New Mexico are sheep is erroneous. Buy and large, votes are no sheeper here than they are in Jersey City. But the sunshine is, 365 days of the year, and twice on Sundays.

Politics—it's a shame to have to get serious again—used to be pretty much of a closed business in New Mexico, and the state was run by what was called "the Third House," a group of lobbyists who met in the old De Vargas hotel. But the old gangs have been broken up. Politics is still so much of a business, however, that all officeholders must turn in 2 per cent of their earnings to the party headquarters.[3] Till recently New Mexico was one of the three American states in which candidates were chosen by convention instead of primaries (the others are Connecticut and Rhode Island), and the primaries are still, in contrast to the habit in several western states, "closed," that is restricted to registered members of each party. The chief pressure groups are the associations repre-

[3] Cf. *Rocky Mountain Politics*, op. cit., p. 240.

senting cattle and wool, the railways, and whatever group dominates the governor, or is dominated by him. A governor has great power in New Mexico.

The state has been Democratic since 1932, with the chief struggle a complex three-way feud within the Democratic party. The Republicans were so weak until 1946 that they didn't even maintain organizations in more than half the counties; eastern New Mexico, which has been heavily settled by Texans and Oklahomans—one must never forget the expanding power of Texas—is an important Democratic stronghold, and so is the cotton-growing south. The principal issue, as the liberal Democrats see it, is to preserve and maintain the social gains of the New Deal.

One detail which will puzzle those who cut their politics into neatly preconceived categories is that the Republicans did carry the state—in 1928. This was when Al Smith ran. Yet New Mexico, with its great "native" vote, is overwhelmingly Roman Catholic. The eleven "native" counties are Catholic almost to a man, but Smith did not carry one of them. In fact the only county he did carry was a non-Catholic county—a nice example of the unpredictableness of American political behavior.

Governor of the state from 1943 to 1947 was John J. Dempsey, a bluff, amiable, and able man. He was once a subway brakeman in New York, and rose to be vice president of the Brooklyn Rapid Transit Company. He moved west to go into the oil business in Oklahoma, and in 1928 progressed to New Mexico; he was a congressman for a time, and under secretary of the interior under Ickes. Dempsey ran for the Senate against Dennis Chavez, also an able man, in the 1946 primary, and was beaten. This was the culmination of a long intraparty quarrel. Dempsey was called a carpetbagger by the old-line Democrats, and was accused of rule by patronage; he played a lone hand, refused to kowtow, and gave the state an excellent administration. Chavez is a "native," and got the solid native vote. Both Chavez and Dempsey are Catholics, incidentally. Chavez led the Senate fight for the FEPC in the spring of 1946, which naturally helped his campaign. He comes of a Spanish family that has lived in New Mexico for three hundred years; he learned Spanish before English, and for a time worked as an interpreter.

Opposing Chavez for senator in the November runoff was no less a personage than the highly extroverted and inflammable Major General Patrick J. ("Pat") Hurley, who was Oklahoma born as everybody knows, but who lately became a New Mexican. Chavez beat him in a tight dramatic race. Hurley was the American ambassador to China who, early in 1946, blew off his top about so-called Communists in the State Department and their influence on Chinese policy. Hurley is of course a legendary character. He was a Tulsa lawyer; national attorney for the Choctaw nation; a private who rose to captain of cavalry in the Indian Territory Volunteer Militia; secretary of war (under Hoover) from

1929 to 1933; personal representative of Roosevelt in the Soviet Union and Near East in 1942-43; negotiator with countries as various as Mexico and Luxembourg; long-time boss of the Republican party in Oklahoma; soldier in the Far East after Pearl Harbor; and bristly Russia hater.

The other New Mexico senator is one of the best men in Washington, Carl A. Hatch; it was he who was largely responsible for Truman's appointment of Clinton P. Anderson, another New Mexican, as secretary of agriculture. A bluntly picturesque old wheel horse is Clyde Tingley, a former governor and the mayor of Albuquerque, a strong Chavez man. Tingley was born in Ohio, and has been Albuquerque's mayor and boss for year after year. This is a politician's politician. Once a friend advised him to stop murdering the King's English. Tingley replied, "I ain't goin' to stop saying ain't in any public speech, I ain't!"

More About Indians

Governor Dempsey took me first to Tesuque, not far from Santa Fe. The Pueblo Indians who live here are as different from the Indians I met in Oklahoma as—in another India—are the peasants in Mr. Gandhi's native village from the sophisticates of New Delhi and Allahabad. The compound is a big dirt yard, surrounded by one-story adobe huts which run into one another. The old squaws sit rocking in shady corners; children play with chili beans. These Indians are full-bloods; they are wards of the federal government; the braves wear long hair and blue marks on their foreheads; they grow corn, wheat, and alfalfa; they go to the movies in town once a week. The Pueblo is community property and its members are very poor, yes; but they have great stolidity and self-respect. Times have changed. The Indians were exempt from the draft in World War I, but not in World War II; and this tiny community contributed 10 per cent of its population to the service. Will the young men, having seen whatever was attractive or unattractive in the world outside, return to Tesuque, toss off their uniforms, go back to blankets? Or will they stay in the towns seeking jobs like whites? While I was in New Mexico, the answer to this question was not yet known; that it should have been asked with such curiosity is tribute enough to the hold the Indian way of life has on most Indians. It is a vegetarian kind of life, perhaps, but it gives a tribesman two things that are not often found together—as we well know—freedom *and* security. Any Tesuquan can leave this Pueblo, for a day or forever, if the governor, a member of the tribe named Martin Vigil, consents. But few ever do, Mr. Vigil told us. Incidentally the New Mexico police have no authority or jurisdiction within a reservation like this. A man may commit murder; no state official can touch him unless Mr. Vigil gives permission.

Next I went to a much larger and more celebrated Pueblo, that at

Taos, two miles outside the town of Don Fernando de Taos, with its valley view which D. H. Lawrence called the most beautiful in the world, and where his ghost still hangs close. This Pueblo is of course one. of the most famous "sights" in the United States. The five-story adobe dwellings, rising windowless mound on mound, date from the golden age of Pueblo culture (A.D. 900-1150); the soft-cornered church is gravely placid with its ocher roof cut in steps; old men doze in pink blankets; lizards crawl. Near by is the cemetery. This, actually, is Spanish rather than Indian, because the Indians bury their dead any which way; being Spanish it is gay with ribbons and artificial flowers and lines of bunting, with red-purple-green-orange streamers and pennants on stockades surrounding each wooden cross.

The Indians of Taos are very wise and superior, and their culture is more intact and survives more purely than any other Indian culture in the United States. They are what might be called anti-assimilationists; their idea is to avoid, rather than seek, the "fate" of Indians in Oklahoma. They hold their land not merely as government "wards," but by virtue of actual titles granted them by Spain, which precede by a century any North American penetration. These Indians want vigorously to stay unchanged, and they are extremely secretive and tenacious about their tribal ways. Intermarriage is very rare, and most tribesmen—except for children in the federally run schools—never speak a word of English if they can help it. Many as a matter of fact try to forget what English they do learn. They do, however, speak Spanish as a rule, so as to be able to communicate with the other Pueblos; because among Pueblos alone there are twenty-two different tongues. The Taos language is impossibly difficult, and has never been written down; the Indians do their best not to give it away, and even try to conceal their own names. One visiting scholar gave up after three months' work when he found that there are fifty-eight different ways of saying "I."

Of course, little by little, the purity of Indian exclusiveness has become dimmed. For instance Mrs. Luhan told me that the Pueblos not so long ago ground their own flour, and their bread was something to marvel at. But now they slip into town and shop at the A&P. The government does its best to help the Indians retain their seclusion. For instance nobody may take photographs in the Pueblo without authorization from the tribe.

There is no water or light inside the Taos dwellings, and very little money; not much is needed. The residents live on wild plums, rice, mutton, chili. The Pueblos have always been farmers, never nomads; their life is mostly pastoral, and their government a kind of communalism. A governor is elected every year, alternating between groups known as the Winter and Summer People, or the Squash and Turquoise People. Over this governor, however, is the *cacique* or high priest whose position is hereditary. Almost all the Indians are Roman Catholic; they cling at the same time to esoteric tribal ceremonies. Marriages take place by rotation, among seven clans, in order to avoid inbreeding; the generations are rotated like the crops. When a boy reaches puberty he leaves his mother, and goes out into the hills with the old men of the tribe for as long as a year and a half, living on corn meal and wild game, learning woodcraft, and undergoing tests for endurance. When a boy is returned to his family, he is considered to be a man. This kind of discipline is necessary if the tribe is to survive, and is of course encouraged by the old men who want above everything to keep the Pueblo continuous and viable. The adult Indian, on account of the elaborate nature of his ceremonial life, cannot in theory remain outside the Pueblo long, for fear of missing rituals at stated intervals; if he does miss these, he loses rank and advantage, and must atone. Hence, the inclusion of Indians in Selective Service was a severe blow to the Pueblo system. Those who fought made splendid soldiers, excellent at out-of-door life, good at machinery because of their delicate hands, and able to go without food or sleep for long periods. They were popular in the Army too. Almost every American child has been to the circus once or twice, and the idea of having a genuine Red Indian fighting next to him was a treat.

One of the six heroic marines who, by raising the Stars and Stripes on Iwo Jima, became immortalized, was a full-blooded Pima Indian, Pfc. Ira H. Hayes, of Bapchule, Arizona. It is a striking irony that though Private Hayes was capable of partaking in this feat, about which the entire country throbbed with pride, he is not allowed to vote.

The question of the vote for reservation Indians in New Mexico and Arizona is embarrassing. The Indians, if they got the franchise, would make the balance of power in New Mexico as of today, and in Arizona soon. They might be able to swing both states in the near future. This possibility keeps politicians of all camps awake. That the Indians, who as we know are in theory American citizens with full and equal rights, are so far deprived of the vote in New Mexico and Arizona is a glaring outrage in the eyes of most believers in democracy. New Mexico operates the technique of disfranchisement by denying the vote to "Indians not taxed," Arizona by a clause in the constitution meant originally for the feeble-minded to the effect that "people under guardianship" may not vote. The Indian Bureau has not, however, pressed a judicial decision on the constitutionality of these strictures out of fear that the Indians might be corrupted wholesale by white politicians, if they were allowed to vote while their standard of education and judgment remain inferior. But this is not the view of most officials on the spot, like John G. Evans, the general superintendent of the United Pueblos Agency, who thinks that the Indians will be quite competent politically.

As to the Indians themselves a good many—especially the oldsters—don't want the vote. The old men of the tribe fear that they might lose their influence and grip on the younger. Another reason is the apprehension that, if enfranchised, the Pueblos will be subject to property taxes but this would not necessarily turn out to be the case. The Indians, who have been misled a good deal, confuse the franchise and taxation issues; they do not understand that they might well be permitted to vote and still remain tax free. Also of course most Indians are so poor that their taxes would be negligible, and in any case would be offset by the benefits they would gain from social security, old age pensions, and the like, from which they are at present excluded.[4] Another fear is that, if enfranchised, the state governments would interfere with their way of life. But this trepidation is also said to be groundless, since Indian matters are exclusively a matter for federal authority. Finally, some Indians agree with those whites who assume that they could not stand up against political pressure; they say in all modesty, "Do we know enough to vote?" To which the answer is that, after all, they know who their own friends are, and could greatly improve their own condition by voting for candidates pledged to a reformist program in Indian affairs. All these phobias are, in a sense, theoretical. One much more concrete and drastic hits closer home. It is that the whites, somehow, sooner or later, will contrive to take their land away.

A point in this connection has to do with the watershed of that noble but muddy river, the Rio Grande. Like most American rivers, it has been allowed to run wild so that whereas the valley between Santa Fe and Albuquerque once contained 125,000 acres of good agricultural land, it now has less than half this amount. Various programs for the damming and control of the Rio Grande, to prevent silting and erosion, have been planned, but Congress has held up the appropriation. One project was given up because it would have flooded and made uninhabitable Pueblo territory. Here is a case where the federal government had to balance the merits of a much-needed reclamation scheme, on the one hand, with its responsibilities to the Indians on the other. The battle was fought mostly within the Department of the Interior, and the Indians won.

Altogether different from the Pueblos, who number about sixteen thousand in New Mexico, are the Apaches and especially the Navajos, who stretch over into vast tracts of Arizona and of whom there are perhaps fifty thousand in both states. The Navajos are nomads; their lands cover sixteen million acres and they live by grazing and raising wool; they are probably the most picturesque of all the Indians in

---

[4] Of course one reason why whites, on their side, oppose enfranchisement is that this would make state and local contributions to social security and the like cost more.

America. Their chief, a remarkable old warrior named Henry Chee
Dodge, is now eighty-five and has held the post for sixty-one uninterrupted years, though he was not a Navajo by birth. His father was killed
by raiders as far back as 1862, and he does not know who his mother
was.[5] But his own son went to Harvard, married a white girl, and is now
an Indian Bureau official. I know no more stimulating example in
America of the variety of experience possible to a man in a lifetime.

Politically the Indian problem is not so acute an issue in Arizona as
in New Mexico; economically it is more acute. For though Mr. Dodge
himself may be very rich, the Navajos and similar tribes—for instance
the Papagos who have a reservation as big as Connecticut—are very
poor and are progressively becoming poorer. Of the area of Arizona not
less than 20 million acres, about a third of the total, is Indian land.
But this has been so overgrazed that it is worn out. It will no longer
support the tribes and their sheep. The Navajos are, however, increasing
heavily in population. The tribes must find something else to do or some
other place to go, or starve. But there isn't any other job or place. Another acute Indian issue in Arizona is education, and here the record is
appalling. The illiteracy rate of the tribe is 80 per cent. The Navajos
have only fifty schools, and most of these were closed down during the
war; fourteen thousand boys and girls of school age, out of twenty
thousand, have no schools at all.

Finally, as to Indians, two words on the Apaches. One is that the
great outlaw chief Geronimo only gave up to the U.S. Army in 1886—
so recently has the American frontier been forced shut. The other is
that the Apaches still maintain one of the most curious of all anthropolog-
ical taboos; no married male may ever speak to or even look at his
mother-in-law!

"Outside" U. S. A.

The first thing I thought was, "Can this possibly be North America?
Can we really be in the United States?" Governor Dempsey had told
me that there are villages in New Mexico still 98 per cent "native,"
where Spanish-Mexican families have lived for generations, where no
word of English might be heard from one year to the next. So, by way
of finding evidence, we dropped in at the village of Chimayó, and visited
its famous church. I could not believe that I was not in Ecuador, Paraguay, or some remote oasis in Castille.

Two massive cottonwood trees provide a natural gate to the *san-
tuario*, and a walled garden imposes on the scene a sad tranquillity.
Women kneel; children pray. The church, made of both wood and adobe
and grained with age, looks like a series of soap boxes loosely piled

---

[5] Except that she was a member of what is called the Ma'iidesgizhni of Coyote
Pass Clan. See *New Mexico Magazine*, June, 1945, article by J. Wesley Huff.

atop one another. The floor is of clay, and in one corner stands—of all things—an oil stove. The religious ornaments are both fantastically primitive and fantastically ornate; along the walls stand the crutches of the maimed. These have been cured by Chimayó's healing sands, which the devout dig with their hands from a hole in the ground that is supposed never to fill up. On one side is a Mexican flag, behind lace curtains; on the other, heavy pearls loop around the neck of Christ.

The Spanish community in New Mexico is, like Spanish communities almost everywhere, cohesive, proud, and wary. There is very little assimilation between Anglos and "natives" as a rule, though young "native" girls may consider an Anglo to be a handsome catch. The great majority of "natives" are citizens who vote and political discrimination cannot be said to exist; social and economic discrimination may, however, be severe. For instance if a "native" in Anglo employ loses his job, he is apt—often with good reason—to call this the result of prejudice. The war broke down barriers to some extent. New Mexico had more American soldiers who were prisoners of the Japanese than any other state, because its national guard, full of boys who spoke Spanish, had been sent to the Philippines. Use of the term "Spanish-American" instead of "Mexican" was, incidentally, first pushed by the late Senator Cutting, who—like Chavez later—kept an appreciative eye on "native" voters. Some "natives," of authentic Spanish stock, are wealthy landowners; they are as supercilious on their side, and maybe with better reason, than even the most snobbish Anglos. The Spaniards have, as part of an effort to protect their culture, an organization with the curious name Sociedad Folklorica. The Spanish and Indians get along very well as a rule; the Indians find them more sympathetic, all in all, than they do the Anglos.

One unique Spanish survival is the secret religious society known as the Penitentes. These are Flagellants who have been outlawed both by the Roman Catholic church and the state but who nevertheless persist. In remote snowy hills men may, I heard, be actually crucified; the authorities may never even know about such crimes. But extremes like this are rare. What happens as a rule is that a Penitente is "chosen" —shoes left on his doorstep are the sign—and on Good Friday he is driven up into the hills, scourged, and chained for an interval to a cross made of telephone poles. The "Christ" wears a black mask—to be chosen is an enormous honor—and a "death cart" follows him, as members of the sect wave their knotted whips and sound discordant music on reed pipes. The ceremony ends with fireworks. The police, if any happen to be near by, may find bloody footprints in the snow on Easter Monday, and cases have been certified of Penitentes who died, not of crucifixion, but of exposure.

The "native" problem in Arizona is not so intimate and pressing as in New Mexico. Whereas intermarriage, though uncommon, does occur in and around Sante Fe, it is considerably more rare in Phoenix. There is a sizable Mexican vote, but it isn't closely organized. The Spanish-speaking folk in Arizona are, man for man, much like those in San Antonio or Los Angeles, and the issues they bring up are mostly local and in the realm of education and public health—issues arising out of deplorable slum conditions and no different basically from those attending the Irish in Boston, the Poles in Detroit, or the Italians in New York.

Negroes are not conspicuous in the Southwest, though the war brought a good many to Arizona. They fall between two stools—in that they are not given as much economic opportunity as the North provides, nor are they treated quite like livestock as in the South.

Osborn of Arizona

Here is one of the best of all American governors, and one of the most interesting men in the entire country. Sidney P. Osborn is an original, and only a frontier civilization could have produced him. He is an individualist almost to the point of idiosyncrasy, and some of his mannerisms reminded me of Harold Ickes. Osborn plays a lone hand. For instance he is the only American governor out of forty-eight who has never attended a governors' conference. His excuse for this is that the people elected him to stay in Phoenix and get some work done, and he sees no reason to be gallivanting around to Mackinac Island or Hershey, Pennsylvania. He is the first man in the capitol to get to his desk every morning, and as a rule the last to leave at night. The door to his private office has never been closed since his election in 1940. He sits in full view of the anteroom and sees all comers. He answers the telephone himself, and any secretary gets fired if she asks "Who's calling?" or inquires of a visitor what his business is.

His chief assistant for some years was William B. Chamberlain, formerly a newspaperman abroad. I asked Chamberlain how he had come to meet him. It appears that Chamberlain was visiting a rodeo at Sonoita, and saw a tall gaunt man sitting alone on the corral fence, next to the bucking chutes. "That's Sid," someone pointed out. It was the governor, amusing himself far from the crowd and hoping that no one would notice him or make a fuss.

This is not to say, however, that Osborn is not a good mixer politically and a stubborn and lively campaigner. During one primary he wrote a personal letter to every one of the six thousand men and women who signed his nominating petition. After election he actually made up a list of all the registered voters in the state, about 155,000, and sent a signed letter to every one; *each* voter in the state got a letter. They were mimeographed, but skillfully, and every salutation was carefully filled in—Osborn drew on his excellent memory for hundreds of first names and nicknames. People still come to Phoenix, bearing these letters, and asking to see him. Also Osborn checks every day every newspaper in the state. Anybody who is mentioned—even in a routine birth or marriage notice—gets a personal letter, signed. This was particularly appreciated during the war, when the governor wrote a note of condolence to the nearest of kin of every Arizona casualty.

Osborn was born in 1884 in Phoenix within walking distance of the capitol where he now works, and he is the state's second native-son governor. He comes of a remarkable family; all over Arizona the name "Osborn" is one to be reckoned with. His grandfather, John P. Osborn, a Scots-Irishman from Iowa and Kentucky, arrived in Arizona in 1864, long before the railways, and helped found Phoenix. This Osborn died in 1900, aged eighty-seven. The governor's father, Neri F. Osborn, was a ranchman who lived to be eighty-eight. He died in 1943, and thus the family spans the whole history of the state.

Young Osborn went to the public schools, and got interested in travel, journalism, and politics. Though an Arizonan of Arizonans, he saw Niagara Falls—a typical enough American happenstance—before he saw the Grand Canyon. At twenty-four he became a member of the constitutional convention that preceded statehood, and in 1912, while still in his early twenties, he was elected the new commonwealth's first secretary of state. He held this office for three terms, and was the youngest secretary of state in the country. He ran for governor in 1918 and again in 1924, but each time was beaten. What prompted him to run was mostly the Ku-Klux Klan. "It's never appealed to me to find fault with a man on account of his religion," he told me, and he campaigned right under the smoke of fiery crosses to force into the open what he thought, and still thinks, is an issue above all other issues, the right of people to think and worship as they please. Then he retired from active politics for fourteen years, until 1938. During this time he published and edited a journal of opinion called *Dunbar's Weekly*. Years before he had been a newsboy when Dunbar, an old-school personal journalist with a pungent wit, was on the staff of that newspaper which has as remarkable a name as any in the country, the *Tombstone Epitaph*. Osborn maintained Dunbar's caustic tradition, and had a lot of fun. Meantime he became an ardent FDR supporter. He ran for governor in 1938 and was beaten once more; this was his third defeat. Finally he won in 1940, and has been governor ever since. In the 1942 campaign he carried every county in the state, which had never been done before, and in 1944 he carried every precinct but twelve out of 432, something equally unprecedented. In this campaign he made only one speech. He led the ticket over Roosevelt by three to one, the first time a governor had ever run ahead of a presidential candidate, and he was the first man in Arizona ever to get more than one hundred thousand votes. Yet, when he was first sworn in, the policeman at the state house wouldn't let him enter, because he didn't recognize him and refused to believe that the new governor could be sauntering in alone.

Osborn has steel-colored hair, parted severely in the middle, and wears steel-rimmed glasses; his face shows self-effacement, homeliness, and a crotchety stubborn streak. It is a Grant Wood kind of face; the old Iowa strain shows through. His sense of humor is hardly acute and, when he gets angry, which is not too often, his thin lips pucker and quiver like those of a child who wants to cry.

The governor, when riding with the state highway patrol, never under any circumstances permits the siren to be sounded. "Folks don't like it," he explains. He has no hobbies, except reading history—when I saw him he was attacking a new biography of Martin Van Buren—and watching football. He has missed only four Rose Bowl games in twenty-three years; he thinks the greatest game he ever saw was Stanford vs. Nebraska in 1941. He hasn't seen a movie since 1940, except "This Is the Army." He never pushes out cigarette butts. He tosses the stub at an 18-inch ash tray about six feet away from his desk, and never misses; this procedure is fascinating to observe.

One small item is the matter of "Osborn time." This man is, as I say, an individualist. He had a fanatic admiration for Roosevelt, but he fanatically hates daylight-saving time. When, early in the war, FDR put the whole country on daylight time, Osborn didn't like the idea. The war plants in Arizona were working twenty-four hours a day anyway, and there was no question of electricity being saved. So he reversed the federal edict on his own authority and turned back to solar time. Air lines and railways passing through the state had to make note in their schedules that Arizona, on "Osborn time," was an hour behind. All this was of dubious legality, but the legislature made a compromise and let it stand.

The Osborn philosophy is pithy and of-the-earth. Like so many characters we have met in this book, he stands for the small man, the underdog. I asked him what he wanted most out of life and he replied "To do something for the every-day fella, the little guy who runs a little ranch, or has a small store somewheres." He added, "Give the every-day fella a chance, and the country will be safe. If *they* get along all right, other folks don't need to worry." He mentioned the terror so many people have of growing old. "Gol darn it, we must look after 'em decently. I want to help look after 'em." I asked him what his ambition was and he replied, "None. All I ever wanted to be was governor." He went on meditatively, "There's nothing anybody can do to me. What more can I ask for, except that sometime I should return something for all the good things done for me." Then: "I don't find fault so much with folks who try to rob the people, but with the people who stand for it and are helpless or dumb enough to get robbed." Finally: "Give me the vote of the man in the flivver, and you can have all the limousine vote there is."

Osborn's sources of power and the basis of his support are thus obvious. First, he has matched the modern mood and given effective leadership to a great mass of people who had none until he came along. Second, his intimate knowledge of the state and deep love for it command admiration. Once he lived in Washington for two years, as secretary to the Arizona delegation; he ticked off each day on a calendar, waiting for the time when he could get back. Another point is that everyone knows that he is absolutely honest. Never having had any money, so he told me, he has no interest in it. Finally, Osborn is an extremely determined and decisive personality. His mind is fixed.

One other unusual trait distinguishes the governor. All his official speeches, even those highly detailed and technical, are extemporaneous. They are taken down by a stenographer as he talks, and then printed without change under such a title as "The Governor's Extemporaneous Message to the Legislature."

Problems and Issues in the Valentine State

The desert shall rejoice, and blossom as the rose.

—*Isaiah*, xxxv, 1

Arizona, the fifth biggest state and the youngest, has a splendid, healthy, upswinging spirit; this is above all youthful country. For instance the first white child born in Tucson still lives there, aged seventy-seven.[6] Frontier days are still a living memory; people can recall fights with Apaches right around the corner. This is one reason why the U.S. Army is, incidentally, so popular in Arizona and indeed everywhere in the Southwest. To people in Ohio, say, the Army is pretty much of a myth except in wartime; to Arizona the "feds" were liberators and are still a very definite reality. The youthfulness of the state is also reflected by its social stratifications. In the center and north—for instance in towns like Prescott which was partly settled from New England—ranches have been in a single family ever since their foundation. In Tucson and Phoenix with their wonderful resort hotels, people claim seniority over others if they arrived at the railway station twenty minutes earlier. If you've been in Phoenix for a year, you're an old-timer. Then consider transportation. The railways came in in 1888, but they only tapped a small portion of the state. Arizona really began to grow and

---

[6] His name is Harry Arizona Drachman and he is custodian of the local Masonic lodge.

flourish when highway building began. The highways were ferociously opposed at first by the upper citizenry, because they meant more taxes. For instance James S. Douglas, a copper magnate and the father of Lewis W. Douglas, shouted out when the legislature passed a new road-building law in 1921, "If I had my way, I'd take a scarifier, and rip up every foot of paved road in Arizona!⁷ Now of course airplanes as well as automobiles ceaselessly span the state. I met one newspaperman who, as a growing boy, saw his first airplane—at a town called Willcox— before he had ever seen an automobile. An old Mexican looked at it too and thought it was an angel.

About 80 per cent of Arizona is still public land, and the federal government owns a greater proportion of it, some 69 per cent, than of any other state. It meets three other states at its northeast corner, incidentally the only point in the union where this phenomenon takes place. The population is still scanty, only 499,261 in 1940, but this is believed to have increased by 40 per cent in the past five years, because of war industry. Arizona is the biggest copper-producing state by far, and has been since 1907; it mines about one-third of all the copper in the country, as well as quantities great or small of every mineral known to the United States except tin. It has the largest stand of yellow-leaf pine in America, and it is the first state in long-staple cotton, the third in citrus fruit.

The two great forces pulling on Arizona are California and Texas; California still regards Arizona, like Nevada, as its own private hinterland, which the state acrimoniously resents. Texas, however, it considers to be a friend; Arizona was settled, except in the north, mostly by Texans, and Texas influence shows itself in the trends toward industrial farming and cattle as a big industry. California has a higher wage scale, and hence labor in Arizona welcomes what influence California has in this direction, while the employing class opposes it; the big citrus growers have mimicked California in forming semipolitcal pressure groups like Associated Farmers, which we dealt with at the very beginning of this book so many pages ago. For instance the Salt River Valley Growers-Shippers Organization in the Phoenix area, is supposed to be a "front" for California and reactionary interests generally. This has tied in with groups like the Democrats for Dewey organization and also Arizonans United which was formed to oppose relocation in Arizona of Japanese driven out of California.

Arizona has some odd distinctions. Only 329 square miles out of its 113,909 are water, which means that water is by far its greatest problem. It has scenic wonders unrivaled, like the Painted Desert and the Grand Canyon, and its history, though not so rowdy as that of Oklahoma, is

⁷ This was a somewhat violent old man. Later he was so outraged by the New Deal that he renounced American citizenship and became a Canadian.

nuggety and full of bounce. For instance Congress (or rather President Taft) refused its first plea for admission to the union, because the projected constitution was too radical—among other provisions it provided for the recall of judges; so the Arizonans simply rewrote the document as ordered, and then, when safely in, proceeded to pass exactly the same legislation that Washington had objected to. "Radical?" In the mid-twenties an Arizonan was sentenced to two hundred days in jail for saying "to hell with Coolidge."

Arizona differs from New Mexico in that Spanish and Indian culture never bit so deep; it has more diversification, much more industry. Above all, it has water, which New Mexico has not; that is to say it has irrigation. The country around Santa Fe is high ranch country; around Phoenix it is a blooming orange grove. The Salt River Irrigation project, on which Phoenix rises from the desert that would otherwise be its ashes, is the most spectacular thing of its kind I have ever seen. Pass over in an airplane; the burgeoning green of the irrigated valley overlays the desert as if painted there with shiny lacquer. This development derives from Roosevelt Dam,[8] which was one of the earliest federal reclamation projects. The total irrigated area is 750,000 acres, and Maricopa County, which was once as arid as flint, is now actually the seventh county in the country in value of agriculture produced.

Now for the last time we mention a great river, and practically all the recent history and politics of Arizona depend on it. The Colorado, as we know, rises near Wyoming, then flows crosswise through Colorado and Utah, and is successively the border between Arizona and Nevada, Arizona and California, and Arizona and Mexico itself. For more than twenty years an abstruse struggle over allocation of Colorado water has been going on. A doctrine known as "prior appropriation," well established in river law, provides that water belongs to whoever first uses it; California, at the bottom, was using most and grabbing all it could. "They are an ingenious lot in California," said Governor Osborn in a recent speech. "They have built a great state by their avariciousness." In 1922 the Upper Basin states—Wyoming, Colorado, Utah, and New Mexico—got permission from Congress to form a "compact" to divide the Colorado's flow; they wanted to tap it, by canals and so on, as it shot downstream. Roughly half of this flow, some 7½ million acre-feet per year, was assigned to the Upper Basin, the other half to the three Lower Basin states, California, Nevada, and Arizona. But for 22 years Arizona refused to join or accept this compact. The Arizonans thought that by the law of prior appropriation they should have full use of all Colorado water that flowed through their state. Came the 1930's, and the building of one of the supreme works of modern man in America, Boulder Dam. Arizona sent out the state guard, and by force of arms

---

[8] Named for Theodore, not FDR.

attempted to halt erection of this dam, out of fear that it would deflect its precious water to California and elsewhere; interminable legal quarrels and appeals to the Supreme Court took place. But Boulder Dam was built, Arizona or no Arizona. Not till 1944 did the state finally enter the compact; the situation today is that California gets 4,400,000 acre-feet of water, Nevada 300,000, and Arizona 2,800,000 acre-feet plus part of a surplus. Arizona was pulled into the compact mostly by Osborn. His line was that during wartime, co-operation between all states was essential, and that anyway Arizona could not afford to stay out longer. For an Arizona governor to approve the compact was as sensational, from a local point of view, as if Franklin D. Roosevelt had endorsed the Nazi party and German war aims during the war. Water is a fighting word in Arizona.

The Colorado's water became, in 1945, an international as well as a national issue during negotiations for the Mexican Water Treaty. For its last seventy miles the Colorado flows through Mexico, which also wanted a fair share of the water that makes the desert flower. California fought the treaty to the last inch, but lost. Some recondite and ugly intrigues attend this story. A good deal of the Mexican land which may become open to irrigation is owned, not by Mexican citizens, but by Californians. This land, dry, is worth twenty-five cents an acre; irrigated, it may be worth a hundred dollars. So absentee California landlords struggled against any treaty that would limit the flow until it suited their convenience. Now Mexico has agreed to use no more than 1,500,000 acre-feet per year.

With the harnessing of water comes, as we know, power. Boulder Dam has a potential capacity of ten billion kilowatt hours, which should make cheap power available to Arizona in unprecedented quantities; heretofore power has been scarce and dear. Arizona, by terms of the Boulder Canyon Project Act, is now entitled to 18 per cent of what the dam generates, and a State Power Authority has begun to function. Power in Arizona can air-condition houses, irrigate land, mechanize farming, attract new industry, terminate the present "stoop and bend" economy. But—it's an old, old story—the private power interests have fought public power development with acrid tenacity. Nevertheless a basic fact remains: give Arizona another million acres of irrigated land plus cheap power, and the state can go anywhere.

Politics and Such in Arizona

Arizona is overwhelmingly Democratic from a local point of view, though it sometimes votes Republican for president; fifty-seven out of the fifty-eight members of the legislature are Democrats,[9] and the senate,

[9] The lone Republican, named Jim Ewing, runs the Tucson "Town Cats" and is a great football booster.

numbering nineteen, is solidly Democratic. The governor, both senators, and both representatives are Democratic, and so are all state office-holders at the moment of writing without exception. Politics goes by patronage. When a new governor comes in, everybody loses his job, even members of the state highway patrol. That this is an unhealthiness goes without saying—unfortunately one only too common in the United States.

Since ten men make a majority in the senate, efforts to control Arizona center on this small group. It is easily influenced, and the legislators are, as in so many American states, of indifferent quality. They get eight dollars per day for a sixty-day session every two years; hence only men who can afford it—or who have a special economic interest in being a legislator—ever run. The legislature spends most of its time squabbling with the governor. This is a familiar American paradox, that the same people elect at the same time an executive and a legislature standing for different things. The chief reason for this, it would seem, is that the voters, desiring leadership, can see it personified in one man but cannot so easily choose among a group.

"The winter people," those who come down from the East and the Great Lakes states and elsewhere to partake of Arizona's mellifluous sunshine, are another conservative force. If they become permanent residents many turn Democratic (as with the similar community in Florida), since most elections are decided in the primaries and there is no political future to remaining a Republican. Then, within the Democratic party, they operate exactly like Republicans.

Arizona has a strong Catholic vote, particularly in the south, but it is not so predominantly Catholic as New Mexico. Nor, even though the state derives mostly from Texas, are Baptists the dominant sect; the Methodists outnumber them, with Presbyterians following close. One Catholic priest, Father Emmett McLaughlin, a Franciscan, has a considerable local reputation for his work "south of the tracks" in Phoenix among the Negroes, encouraging Negro education and welfare and proselyting them. Once a year he superintends a mixed black-white barbecue, and if it's near election time even the politicians come. A powerful and cohesive community is that of the Mormons; the Latter Day Saints are more conspicuous in Arizona than in any other state except Utah and possibly Idaho. As far back as 1885 a law forbidding polygamy had to be passed. The present-day junior congressman, Richard F. Harless, is a Mormon, and the community is, as always, a solid entity strongly conservative in politics, very well off—nobody ever meets a poor Mormon—and deeply social minded. The Mormons are the fathers of irrigation in Arizona as they were in Utah.

Among political forces are the utility companies, like Central Arizona Light and Power, the cattle and sheep growers and feeders' associations, the big-business citrus farmers, the insurance companies which like the utilities are mostly absentee owned, and, above all, copper. The big copper companies are Nevada Consolidated (subsidiary of Kennecott and the Guggenheim interests), with its great mines at Ray; Inspiration (subsidiary of Anaconda; mines at Miami); Miami (Lewisohn interests); Magma at Superior; American Smelting & Refining; and in particular the Phelps Dodge Corporation, which operates massive mines at Morenci, Bisbee, Ajo, and Jerome. It has reserves of 300 million tons of ore, and is far and away the biggest enterprise in the state.

Phelps Dodge has a long quasi-political history, and its influence in Arizona was once as pervasive as that of Anaconda in Montana. For at least thirty years—in fifteen consecutive legislatures—copper was the absolute boss, and I heard Arizona called "the most corporation-ruled state in the union." The companies, chiefly Phelps Dodge, not only maintained a lobby (they still do but not so conspicuously as before); they "did favors" in the pattern adumbrated in this book so often, by giving insurance contracts to "friends," promoting entrance into exclusive clubs, keeping their eye on judges. There were towns in Arizona— Clarkdale, Bisbee, Hayden—as completely "company towns" as any in the United States, where not so much as a loaf of bread could be baked without company permission, where the company appointed its own sheriffs, where an outsider might not even enter without consent. The companies used cheap Mexican labor in the old days, and belabored it unmercifully. They bribed anybody who got in their way, even governors, and the Corporation Commission of the state, designed to control such enterprises, became a commission actually of corporations; copper had such a grip on the whole community, in fact, that the Arizona term for conservative is still "copper collar."

But things aren't quite that way now. The same kind of change that is taking place in Montana came to Arizona. Democracy is expanding. Economic power gets spread out. Phelps Dodge is still a force certainly, but nothing like the force it was. Arizona is still partly in fief to absentee capital, but towns like Clarkdale are no longer hermetically sealed pools of private interest; they have become part of the United States.

Finally, consider the virile rise of agriculture. Mining, at best a wasting industry, is going down; agriculture is going up. For instance in 1944, Arizona mineral production had a value of 112 million dollars; agriculture passed it for the first time with 124 million dollars. Irrigation has made possible a lively and energetic variety of crops: lettuce, cantaloupe, pecans, carrots, above all citrus. The orange groves near Phoenix are a revelation of what science, man, and nature can produce working together. Incidentally the leaping growth of citrus still shocks and disconcerts some old Arizona hands. The cattlemen like to say, "That citrus stuff—almost as bad as a sheep herder!"

A last item worth mention is federal credit. So again we come full circle; this book first mentioned federal credit in California. A tremendous war industry, mostly in airplanes, sprang up in Arizona overnight; Alcoa built near Phoenix the largest aluminum extrusion plant in the world; of Arizona's total income of 565 million dollars, federal credit provided 165 million dollars in 1944. Among other things this brought skilled labor into the state in great numbers, something almost unknown before, and this in turn may bring new trends in politics. Once again we are confronted with the fermentations that the enormous fluidity of America makes possible, that continually give new yeast and flavor to social-minded democracy and its procedures.

Chapter 52

Finale

∿∿

BUT I have had to leave out so much!

What other country could have headlines like WAR WITH JAPAN PERILS WORLD SERIES, or speed "limits" of sixty miles an hour on the endless undulant roads of Utah, or the sign on the Success Cafe in Butte in 1932, EAT HERE OR I'LL VOTE FOR HOOVER, or another headline, one from a New York tabloid about a woman soon to be electrocuted, SHE'LL BURN, SIZZLE, FRY! or about the way salesmanship is the greatest profession in the land.

There is nothing in this book, and now it's too late to put it in, about how airplanes spray trees with DDT in Oregon or why Pullman washbowls have the water tap set in so close, or how Count Hermann Keyserling once said truly that the greatest American superstition was belief in facts, or how a canny Englishman pointed out that you can write a barometer of American ups and downs from the titles of popular songs, "Brother Can You Spare a Dime" to "Yes We Have No Bananas" to "Oh What a Beautiful Mornin'" to "Accentuate the Positive."

There is nothing in this book about the fact that Truman met Roosevelt only once between the time of his nomination as vice president and his accession to the presidency, and that Willkie and McNary had never met when in 1940 they were nominated for president and vice president respectively; nothing about the grave elk eating up the golf links near Salt Lake City, or how fifty years ago twenty-four American states forbade minors to smoke or chew tobacco in public; no mention of the sign in front of the Presbyterian Hospital, *For the Poor of New York without Regard to Race Creed or Color,* or of the contemptible filth-mongering of the Hearst press during a recent antifilth campaign; nothing of ear-shattering neologisms like Ripco, Kantwet, Trimz, Chix, Mor, Flexees, and Linit, or lunatic gibberish like L.S./M.F.T.

I haven't even mentioned that there were seventy-two thousand G.I.'s named Smith; or the sagging lines of men with brief cases in the big hotel lobbies and the crisp snapping bark of the clerks, "Sold Out!" or whaling towns like New Bedford in Massachusetts and a civilization as unique as that of Nantucket; or the way International Business Machines runs its company town and never sells, but only leases, certain of its machines; or children in scarlet mufflers patting their scarlet mittens together and listening to Santa Claus out in the snow in a Vermont public square; or college fraternities and sororities and their adolescent hocus-pocus; or the lonely red railway stations and their water towers and greased switches in northern Minnesota; or people as authentically part of the American scene as Little Orphan Annie, Terry and the Pirates, Blondie, and Superman.

Nothing about such forms of American music as police sirens and boogie woogie! Not even one word for name bands! Nothing about Joe Louis, the Stork Club, Leo Durocher, *Information Please*, or why Walter Winchell has to call Orson Welles "George O." Welles! Nothing about Dixie cups, the three Compton brothers who are all presidents of universities, the smooth elegant butcher shops of New York City, the hotel elevator lined with tile in Bismarck, North Dakota, the "junior sidewalk superintendents" outside Best's on Fifth Avenue, hoods on milk bottles, the silver fields acre-solid with discarded B-17's at Lubbock, Texas, such utterly key figures in politics as Bernard M. Baruch and Leslie Biffle, the wind slicing hot through the streets in Oklahoma City, the red-painted propeller tips of Continental Airlines, the shops for artificial limbs opening up in the western cities, the drunks propped on chairs on steaming nights along Sixth Avenue, the yellow egg-sized Castilian roses in New Mexico and the laurel in the valley of the Tennessee. Nothing—not a word!—about the railway brakeman with a ten thousand dollar collection of postage stamps in Montgomery, Alabama, about Hungry Sam Miller of Pennsylvania who once ate 144 fried eggs, 48 pies, and 200 oysters, about characters in contemporary American folklore like Clark Gable, Damon Runyan, Lana Turner, Billy Rose. Not a word about advertisements for "supertomatoes" or why all American radio stations begin with the letters K or W or the American general who once killed an Alaskan bear by yelling at it—the bear died of fright. Man from Mars, you don't know anything! You can't have the foggiest idea of what America is like if you don't know of Paul Bunyan's Babe, the weight of metal a lamp post can carry in New York City, Lunt and Fontanne, the songs of Hildegarde, Nicholas Murray Butler, and the policeman in Kansas City who once smoked 500 packages of Kools in a year to get a $9.50 inlaid bridge table, free.

There is nothing in this book about public libraries in America, which are incontestably the finest in the world, nothing about the retired broker aged sixty-nine whom I found working in the Kaiser shipyards, nothing of the way the sunset bends down the hills cupping Augusta in Maine and very little of what Will White saw across the Kansas plains. Nothing about the beautiful kids around the Beverly Wilshire pool in Los Angeles and the jalopies bumping along the high taut Dakota roads and the earth smoking and spitting hell near Harrisburg and the deep gray quiet lanes in upper New York state and the slow crunching wagons, drawn by ancient horses, packed full of golden-golden corn on hot Ohio afternoons.

And surely the man from Mars, our friend by now, should know that the microfilm edition of the New York *Times* costs $175.00 per year; that in some Atlanta bars you can check your bottle; that Calvin Coolidge once translated Dante—oh yes, this is a country crammed with the unexpected!—that radio helps to solve one of the supreme American problems which is loneliness, that the chamber of commerce in middle-sized cities must of necessity be its lowest common denominator, since it has to oppose anything likely to hurt anybody at all, and that you have to enter almost all state capitols by the side or back door, because the front steps are too long a climb.

Nothing in this book about how American children are so often ashamed of their parents, and vice versa! Nothing about how Postal Telegraph disappeared overnight without trace, or why ducks prefer muddy water to fresh in Wisconsin! Nothing about Cardinal Spellman, J. Edgar Hoover, Juan Trippe, Francis Biddle, Harold Ross, Beardsley Ruml, Marriner Eccles, the Dulles brothers, Nicky Arnstein, or Bishop Manning. Nothing about how a B.A. degree even from a good university means less today than a high school education did forty years ago, about how people at hotel conventions are tagged and ticketed like animals in a zoo, about the remarkable careers subsequently enjoyed by most heads of the Securities Exchange Commission and all the bright young lawyers who were once secretaries to Mr. Justice Holmes, or about bits of conversation overheard in night clubs, like "Say, I hear minks are going to take a hell of a drop, a really precipitous drop, but after all they had the greatest rise in the mercantile market."

There is very little in this book about the supreme inventiveness of Americans, their boastfulness, their practical aptitude for making things work, their sentimentality, or the crazy drugstore food they eat. Very little or nothing about the diocesan press, or the spectacular variety of technical and professional magazines. Nothing about the queues of sweating men in shirt sleeves, waiting for busses at Greyhound depots, or the wonderful mechanical ingenuity of American industrial fabricators—consider the newer kitchen gadgets—or the equally wonderful imitativeness of American industrial fabricators—consider how a dozen followers of Spam are packed in a can the identical shape and size. Nothing at all about the Big Inch Pipe Line, or even Little Inch, or the Canol project, or modern plastics, or even bobby socks and bubble gum. Nothing about the masterful way that Eastman Kodak packages and labels its goods, or how trains of both Northern Pacific and Great Northern pant together on adjoining tracks at Garrison, Montana, rivals worn out by the climb across the mountains. Or about the shop on Madison Avenue that sells "genuine diamond-back rattlesnake meat at $1.59 per five-ounce can," the magazine publisher who called the German labor leader, Dr. Ley, "one of the greatest geniuses who ever lived in this or any other age," about Lafayette Park in Washington where the four statues facing the White House are of four non-Americans, and of millions of people in New York who spend I don't know how many thousand man-hours per year waiting for red lights to turn green.

Nonserious Moment before Serious Matters

The cleanest city I saw in America was Phoenix, Arizona; the dirtiest, Indianapolis, Indiana; the ugliest—with an intense, concentrated, degrading ugliness—Knoxville, Tennessee. The most beautiful house I saw was in Princeton, New Jersey; the ugliest building was a brewery in Spokane, Washington. The most crowded town I visited was San Diego, with Columbus, Ohio, as a close second choice; the least crowded was St. Louis. The most unexpectedly good hotels were in Denver, Salt Lake City, San Antonio, Kansas City, and Spokane; the worst was in Charleston, South Carolina. The best beef I ever ate was in Montana, and the best ice cream in Richmond, Virginia; the best single meal I had in America was in Milwaukee, and the worst—but I give up!

The ugliest state capitol I saw was in Concord, New Hampshire, the most charming, that in Montpelier, Vermont; the most dramatic that of Nebraska, with Louisiana and North Dakota runners-up; the biggest, that of Rhode Island; the most unusual, because filled with showcases like a museum, that in Utah. The state with the dirtiest politics is probably Pennsylvania; the cleanest, a tossup between Wisconsin and Vermont. The worst-bossed state is Tennessee or New Jersey; the least-bossed, Washington or Arizona. The best-governed state is probably New York, and for the worst just blindfold yourself and stick a finger anywhere below the Mason and Dixon's line.

The most sensational view I ever saw in America is that from the Top of the Mark in the Hotel Mark Hopkins, in San Francisco, and the most spectacular road I have ever driven on is the Merritt Parkway in Connecticut. The most satisfying flight I ever took was from San Francisco up the coast past Mount Shasta; the most trying, from Jackson, Mississippi, to New Orleans. The smoothest roadbed I have ever known on an American railroad is the velvet line of the Milwaukee into Chicago; the worst trip I ever took on a railroad was from Salt Lake City to Cheyenne.

The city in America with the least visible street signs is Butte, Montana, and the town best policed is Pittsfield, Massachusetts. The most turbulent city is Chicago or Kansas City, and the quietest, Madison, Wisconsin or Santa Fe. The crudest newspaper in the United

States is (or was) the Denver *Post*; the most enterprising and courageous is the St. Louis *Post-Dispatch*. The best conversation I heard
was in Boston, Nashville, and Seattle; the best draft beer was in Baltimore or Denver; the rowdiest atmosphere was in Omaha or Memphis;
the funniest thing I saw was a Thurber drawing owned by the late
Bob Benchley, with the caption, "So you think you're going to leave
me, do you!"

Adding It Up: Tendencies and Questions

So now, at last, we come to the end of this long, detail-choked and
multicolored journey. Our procession through forty-eight states is
finally done. Without regard to any sectional or regional conclusions,
let us try now to sum it all up—to weave out and twist together some
of the variegated strands of this book, and hemstitch the whole job.

Everybody knows the celebrated epigram that all generalizations are
untrue including this one. However, sticking the neck out is good exercise for the head:

First, no one can fail to recognize the immense and superexcessive
physical vitality of the United States, a vitality often perverse and ill-
directed, but a vitality just the same—massive, overriding, and of incomparable scope. This is probably a contributing factor to two extremely notable American characteristics, competition for competition's
sake and worship of success.

Second, diversity within unity. Whoever invented the motto *E. Pluri-
bus Unum* has given the best three-word description of the United
States ever written. The triumph of America is the triumph of a coa-
lescing federal system. Complex as the nation is almost to the point
of insufferability, it interlocks. Homogeneity and diversity—these are
the stupendous rival magnets. Time and time again I felt, almost physically, the forces tending to pull a given community down to conformity,
no matter how it struggled. I felt that the nation was like some huge
monster bound down with an iron net, so that cushions in the flesh
bulged out—but the net holds, the iron brace tingles with strain but
contains its prisoner. Change the metaphor and think of the United States
as an immense blanket or patchwork quilt solid with different designs
and highlights. But, no matter what colors burn and flash in what
corners, the warp and woof, the basic texture and fabric is the same
from corner to corner, from end to end.

We could at considerable length sketch the main forces making for
disunity—extremist politicians, pleaders for special privilege, each-for-
himself-ism, and lack of discipline. Similarly the compounding unifying
forces are easily open to inspection—everything from Abraham Lincoln
to the advertising business, from abstractions in democratic theory to

the Five and Ten and the corner movie. America is the country that is at home no matter where it goes.

Third—the point is a convenient one to make sequentially but its importance is not too great—the United States is, despite unparalleled development of all the known means of communication, despite unity and diversity both (each of which should contribute to knowledge of the nation as a whole), still an enormously provincial nation. I do not know any country that is so ignorant about itself. Sociologists have collected appalling statistics to show how little of American history American school children know, and although many good citizens can tell a visitor glibly and with authority what is going on in Uruguay or the Ukraine they know astonishingly little about affairs in the next county or who owns the local gasworks. The New York newspapers are the best in the nation. But try finding out from them what is really going on in New Orleans or St. Paul.

Fourth, I have sought to avoid mentioning in this list so far the well-known fact that the United States is "big." Actually, though it is quite big, there are several other nations bigger—Russia, Canada, Brazil. Moreover physical bulk and size, or even physical incongruity, should not preclude self-knowledge and intercommunication.

I have also sought to avoid saying that the United States is "young" and "new." As a matter of fact it is not so very young or new; it has an older record than any other important country except England of history under one form of government; what people usually mean when they say "new" is merely that our pace is so fast and headlong. To use "newness" as an excuse for American rawness, crudity, lack of coherence, administrative futilities, and much infantilism and slipshodness in social behavior, is surely a too facile begging of the question.

The very powerful and deep-seated American tendency to lawlessness and love of violence, a factor in the national scene never to be discounted, cannot altogether be explained on the ground that we are children growing up. Plenty of children are not criminals. Actually American lawlessness has roots very deep in the past.

Perhaps a *fifth* general point might have to do with the frontier. I have several times mentioned that, in the 1890's, the American frontier in the traditional sense was considered closed. Of course a new "frontier" evolved promptly in the shape of high industrial wages, mass production, and the automobile industry in particular. But as a matter of fact there is plenty of frontier left in America; late in 1946 some western lands (except those that might contain ores of fissionable metals) were thrown open once more to homesteading. Cross the United States in an airplane; you cannot fail to note the huge and spectacular amount of emptiness; even in parts of the East and Middle West, to say nothing of the Great Plains and mountain states, you can fly for miles without seeing a house or a human being. The United States government still owns 455,183,251 acres of public domain, and almost anybody who wants to be a farmer can go out and get some, a fact unique in the panorama of the contemporary world. The generally prevalent idea that America is a "crowded" country is nonsensical. Don't remind me of this sentence while waiting for a hotel room in New York City. But keep in mind that, even with homesteading latterly discouraged for various reasons and then cut off by the war, about a million American acres of farm land are open for homestead entry every year.

Sixth, a major American problem, discanted upon so often in this book, is the accelerated speed and magnitude of consumption of our natural resources, the reckless and inordinate waste of timber, petroleum, and above all soil. Against this, as the most potentially hopeful corrective, stands the work of TVA and the development of the valley authority idea in general.

Seventh, the American nation is by no means so materialistic as is often thought, but the fact remains that what it seems to be most married to is money. The United States was built on industrial expansion under capitalism; the risks were great, the rewards were greater. And what should be more natural than that the giant bulk of the population, whether rich or poor, should be money conscious, inasmuch as millions upon millions of people came here during the past hundred years precisely in order to find the pot of gold shining just beyond Ellis Island.

Eighth, pressure groups. Who runs the United States? We have named so far an infinity of lobbies and special interests, from Coca-Cola to the Masonic orders, from the American Legion to the embattled schoolteachers, from the agricultural co-operatives in California to the dairymen in Vermont. Everybody, it seems, runs this country; a jovial answer to the question might well be, "Too many people!" If one should try to draw up a list of members of some mythical "inner circle," it could run to ten thousand names. And this—the intensely variegated and extraordinarily broad spread of public and private interest—is, as we stated in this book's Foreword, basically a factor making for health and strength. At the same time, it is only too painfully obvious that any organized pressure group devoted to special privilege is dangerous and evil if it militates against the needs and interests of the nation as a whole—and many do. Despite the proliferating variety of special interests and power factors, it is not too difficult to find a common denominator. The common denominator is of course the propertied class. I do not mean "big" property necessarily though that certainly counts. I mean property in the sense of a banker's loan large or small, a widow's trust fund, a professor's house, a student's jalopy, a workman's tools. That the United States of America is in final distillation and essence still run by the propertied class in the broadest sense of that term, is, it seems, the biggest single factor making for national unity. Also the fact that this class has failed in many of its duties, responsibilities, and obligations is the greatest single impediment to unity and the chief force making for discontent.

Now, *ninth,* we have also to consider men, that is leadership. There are cheap shysters in American public life, poltroons, chiselers, *parvenus,* and an infinitude of politicians bloated with intellectual edema. There are also wonderful old men like Stimson, and wonderful young men like Lilienthal. There is a splendid but disconcertingly small procession of able and useful citizens whether holding or aspiring to office or not—Stassen, La Guardia, Eisenhower, Bowles, Frank Graham, governors like Goodland, ex-governors like Arnall, Henry Wallace and Averell Harriman both, Krug and Ickes both, John G. Winant, General Marshall, General Bradley, Sumner Welles, Vannevar Bush, Milo Perkins, Aiken and Flanders of Vermont, Archibald MacLeish, David Sarnoff, Philip Murray, Dean Acheson (a conservative liberal), Will Clayton (a liberal conservative), Robert M. Hutchins, senators like O'Mahoney, Robert Moses, and Messrs. Justice Douglas, Jackson, *and* Hugo Black. The common denominator here is brains, integrity of conviction, good will, and social energy. That several folk on this list are Jews, that several are Catholics, that at least one is (or was) a violent isolationist, that one was born in Minsk, that both extreme conservatives and red-hot liberals are represented, and also that two or three of those named have violent hatreds for two or three others on the same list, makes no difference. They are all Americans who not only believe in America but in an America that could be better. What this country needs above all is effective national unity. Men like these can help provide it.

A familiar question is why so few United States citizens of the first category go into public life. The best answer in older days was double; men of the highest echelon in ability, imagination, brains, either devoted themselves to carving out the frontier or to making money, or both. Neither of these avenues for enterprise is, it would seem, quite what it used to be. A few folk, at least, seeing that payment must come nowadays in a different kind of coin are still entering into public careers at great personal sacrifice. But the number remains grotesquely small. Perhaps if the country itself had more confidence in its own institutions, a better sense of unity and direction and national will, more good people would be tempted to the enterprise of running it; yet it is only people themselves who can give will and direction, and so we have a vicious circle. An auxiliary point is that the United States has evolved no successful means of getting rid of a public servant once he has outlived his usefulness. It is after all an unkindness to our neighbors to make senescent party hacks our ambassadors abroad. As I heard it put in Washington, it would be God's mercy if we had a House of Lords.

That this country needs more and better disinterested (in the sense of unselfish) leadership goes without saying; *interested* leadership from the point of view of clarity of purpose, singleness of mind, stability of plan and aspiration. This brings us, *tenth,* to considerations of politics, since one reason why many good men do not adopt public careers is that the professional politicians squeeze them out. About politics in the large there are a good many things to be said, and on each a whole chapter might well be written.

(1) Politicians in America rise predominantly from what used to be called "the lower middle class"; most are self-made men—as we know from dozens of examples—with careers behind them in everything from dentistry to butter-and-eggs; most depend on their political jobs for a livelihood and most have little time, inclination, or opportunity for adult education; hence the dominating qualities of so many are greed, vulgarity, attention to special interest, avarice, and selfishness.

(2) The greatest danger to American democracy may well reside in that group most particularly pledged to espouse it, the professional politicians, since it is their own incompetence and ineptitude—if coupled with financial depression—that is most likely to cause a breakdown.

(3) All this is in part the fault and responsibility of the people themselves since it is the people who elect the politicians, and is a result of inadequate education. But political apathy, except at election time, is a famous American characteristic; that bad politics should be taken for granted by so many good citizens is a long-standing paradox. Of course this strikes at the very root of democratic theory and procedure; a dichotomy has existed since this republic was born and it is still a potent element, the instinct of Americans generally to distrust and hold in contempt government as such, while at the same time professing loyalty to the democratic principles without which government could not exist.

(4) The legend that this country operates under a two-party system is to a certain extent an illusion. The South, Texas, Vermont, parts of the Southwest, are so much dominated by one party that, as we well know, the general election is only a formality; and in many other sections of the country the real struggle is in the primaries. That the major parties overlap and have little inner cohesion, except once every four years, is a point too obvious to be stressed. The two-party system, such as it is, has its usefulness however; it has tended to prevent growth of the kind of splinter politics that temporarily destroyed democracy in France, say; also, since each party is big and diffuse enough to include both left and right wings in a sloppy embrace, it has tended to inhibit in America the development of politics based on class.

(5) Politically speaking the most important issue in the United States today is the persistent tendency toward conflict between the executive and legislative branches of the government; but this is outside the province of this book.

(6) The veterans. The phenomenon may be temporary: but it is the veterans who hold the edge in almost all political contests nowadays, as was clearly indicated in 1946. But since veterans themselves are widely separated into various camps and groups, their impact is not felt singly. Related to this is, in a way, the development—also probably temporary—whereby many military people are holding critically important jobs at home and abroad that would normally go to civilians. Almost beyond doubt the most important governmental agency this country has ever created will be the five-man Atomic Energy Commission set up last year. Attending this was a battle between civilians and the military. The civilians won, but it was not an altogether clear-cut victory.

(7) The rise of labor as a distinct and self-conscious political force for the first time in American history on a national level, in part through the agency of the PAC.

(8) A great capacity to dig deep and pull out unknowns. Somebody unheard of now may very well be president of the United States in 1952.

Eleventh, the most gravid, cancerous, and pressing of all American problems is that of the Negro, insoluble under present political and social conditions though capable of great amelioration.

Now, *twelfth,* I should like to make a special small category of the fact, so often indicated in this book, that most American men and issues resist being put in categories. American mixedupness, which was caused by the extreme fluidity of industrial and social development during the last century and by the melting pot, which really does melt, and also by the institution of universal free primary education, is a standing puzzle to observers. I have noted that party lines are not clear. Neither are many other lines. The CIO is supposed by some to be "Communistic." But Philip Murray and James B. Carey, two of its most distinguished leaders, are ardent Roman Catholics, and it is well known that Roman Catholics are never Communists. Labor leaders by general convention are often labeled "radical"; but John L. Lewis sometimes takes a line conservative in the extreme. The great metropolitan dailies live by advertising and might be presumed to be exclusively the mouthpieces of the commercial class; but in presentation of news the New York *Times* is much less the organ of a special interest than is the *Daily Worker.* High functionaries of the Catholic church are almost always assumed to be extreme conservatives; but two of the most outspoken liberals in the United States, except on matters involving Russia, are archbishops Lucey of San Antonio and Shiel of Chicago. Of course some leading Catholics *are* reactionary. There is a widespread belief that most Jews are liberal;

but of five leading political columnists of Jewish faith or origin (Lipp-mann, Sokolsky, Lawrence, Grafton, Krock), one is as reactionary as Metternich plus Sewell Avery, and two are very definite conservatives. But of course many leading Jews *are* liberal. One could go on almost indefinitely with such contradictions. There are two Democrats and one Republican on the Civil Service Commission; the Republican is the only liberal. Or take journalism again. The best-known liberal weekly in the country is in part financed by a fortune made by association with the Morgans, and its competitor for many years was similarly in part dependent on a great railway fortune. Or look at *PM* which is, or was, supported largely by Marshall Field.

Thirteenth, no conspectus even as brief as this could possibly be complete without mention of the role played by women in American life. Consider simply their stupendous purchasing power. Not only is American civilization more matriarchal and dominated by women than any other; women voters outnumber men and actually hold the balance at the polls.

Fourteenth, the future of this country depends more on foreign policy than on any other factor, but I do not deal with it in this book. Foreign policy is, of course, nothing more or less than a reflection of domestic policy, and a glance immediately above will show why it is so confused— as well as a multitude of previous passages. It isn't very easy for a country to have world sense when it hardly knows its own.

Occasionally somebody uses a phrase like "America believes" or "the United States thinks." The subliminal absurdity of this should be clear by now. "America" never thinks. What does think is a whole great lot of people in America who most of the time are thinking very different things.

. . . And to Conclude

The United States became great largely because it was founded on a deliberate idea—a complex and enveloping idea including equality of opportunity for all, government only by the consent of the governed, and the Bill of Rights; the form and spirit and texture of American society is based on individualism, civil liberties, and the democratic process. What will happen to it in a world that, even Mr. Churchill admits, has veered into a "permanent swing" toward totalitarianism and the left?

Two things are worth stating flatly. The long-run mood of this country is progressive. Never mind the 1946 off-year elections. Let no one think that the broad social gains that have come to the American people in the last generation can be easily dismissed; let no one think that Americans will ever again permit other Americans to starve without a struggle. There were, in this richest nation on earth,

22 million people on relief in 1935. On the other hand let nobody so delude himself as to think that the system of free enterprise (using that cliché in its broadest sense, and forgetting that it was often "free" only for the privileged, that it was often licensed enterprise) is dead in this country. The United States is still above all the land of the self-made man, where opportunities, though by no means "equal," are incontestably open to more citizens than anywhere else on earth.

In blunt, naked fact the paradox just expressed—more than a mere paradox, in fact, the most blatant and insulting kind of contradiction —lies deep in the glossy roots of the earliest American history and tradition. It goes straight back to the first expanding-muscle days; it was a focus of the controversy between Jefferson and Hamilton. The problem of how to reconcile economic libertarianism with political democracy: or, to put it in slightly different terms, how to insure that, if the economic system breaks down, the political system can still carry on, is certainly no new thing. Democracy and capitalism have often been intertwined; when one goes down, so may the other. But it has never been very easy to make the accumulation of private property and vested interests go to bed with such paraphernalia of democracy as free compulsory education, social service, and universal suffrage—and enjoy it.

Actually the age of the Pleistocene marauders and despoilers has passed. People in this country who think that 1929 can ever come again are very rare. If I were asked to prophesy I should say—though reiterating a conviction that the permanent durable ground swell in this country is progressive—that the United States may well have a temporary period of very definite conservatism or even of reaction. But the era of unmitigated monopolistic control of the means of production, of unlimited accumulation of property by economic anarchists, is as dead as Tutankhamen. This is a country the heart fabric of which is puritan and radical, in the old frontier sense of the word "radical," and it believes in two things above all else—no matter with what temporary divagations— progress and reform.

Not merely since the New Deal but since the turn of the century a tremendous transfer of power, political and economic power, from big holders of property to little has been going on. The stake of the nation in itself has been multifariously spread out. For a considerable time the propertied magnates were much stronger than the government, either the national government or the state legislatures. This produced in the end a variety of catastrophes, and the subsequent reaction brought about a condition wherein the government became stronger than the magnates. This is, very roughly, the situation that obtains today. But the essential self-perpetuating bone marrow of the capitalist system was, though deeply bitten into, not destroyed. The best definition of the New Deal

I ever heard was that it was an attempt by a lot of milksop liberals to save capitalism for the "dumb" capitalists themselves.

Further progress and reform is certainly going to be inevitable and necessary. The next New Deal will make the last New Deal look mild. Because, in plain fact, no matter how buttressed up and artificially stimulated and massaged, the free enterprise philosophy is not working well enough; it is not sufficient. *Fortune* estimated in 1940 that 23 per cent of the American people had perforce to live "outside" the American system, and stated flatly that there are faults in the system "that will prove to be fatal if not corrected." The lesson of much in Europe is that, if people have to choose between security and liberty, they will choose security. So at all costs the United States should avoid having to make this deplorable choice. Why not have both? What frightens so many people is "fear of government interference," "regimentation," and similar hobgoblins. These same hobgoblins have been wandering at large since the Interstate Commerce Commission was established in 1887; the great, indispensable, and altogether salutary institution of Rural Free Delivery was bitterly attacked as "socialism" when it was inaugurated in 1896; the United States did not even have an effective income tax until 1912. That so many Americans should fear government to the extent they do is an interesting phenomenon, since it means in a way that they fear themselves.

That some degree of government intervention and control in economic life—under the bright observing eyes of an absolutely free press and always under the stout guardianship of an absolute political democracy—has become a necessity, if only because of the enormously increased complexity and interdependence of the modern world, goes without saying. There is no group in this country that does not benefit from some sort of government enterprise. The most reactionary manufacturer wants the tariff. The most revolutionary plebeian wants public schools. Perhaps landlords don't like rent control. But they don't object to roads. Farmers don't like a lot that goes on in Washington. But what a mighty explosion there would be if the government stopped supporting the price of cotton or wheat!

The splitting asunder of the world between left and right, which is the result both of revolutionary forces and of complacency and greed, has not—we should now point out with emphasis—produced in the United States anything like the gap that divides much of Asia and Europe. For this we have, strange as it may seem, the free enterprise system itself to thank in that equality of opportunity is still, despite everything, a pivotal keystone of American life and thought. There is much dissatisfaction with the system; but, by and large, even the have nots believe in it. It is still another great American paradox that many underpossessed citizens are among the most conservative the country has. Yet one should sound a

note of warning here. Let the free enterprise system collapse, as a result
of mismanagement or inflation, and the mood of this nation could dangerously change. Let there be fifteen million unemployed again, and blood
can smear and spot the streets. Yet the folk who fear revolution most
are at one and the same time those who oppose most bitterly the government planning and controls that seek to fend off disaster.

Two more pervasive generalizations are possible about the United
States. One is that, more than any other, it is a lucky country with an
almost obsessive belief in the happy ending. Read the Declaration of
Independence, a remarkably pungent document; the phrase "pursuit of
happiness" comes very near the top. The other is that, more than any
country except England perhaps, it believes in compromise. The Constitution is fixed and absolute on its essential principles, freedom and the
rights of man. But underneath is a veritable mélange of compromises—
over states' rights, over slavery—and our whole history has been healthily
relaxed by compromise, which means the rational approach, reason, the
meeting of minds in honorable agreement after open argument. In these
two considerations there lies great hope. An instinct for happiness often
produces happiness; and nothing can be more valuable than reason, in an
age shaken and made miserable by lack of faith, with a disintegration of so
many values and with people pallid through fear and confusion and moral
crisis.

American scientists are ceaselessly attacking in every sphere the
frontiers of the unknown; American economists and social engineers have
at hand techniques that can forestall a new depression; there is no valid
reason why the American people cannot work out an evolution in which
freedom and security are combined. Creative good will, coherent large-
minded planning, clarity of vision, a grasp of the realities of the nation
as a whole, spring-mindedness, education and more education, a fixed
national purpose to make out of contemporary civilization weapons that
will cure, not kill—all this is possible. In a curious way it is earlier, not
later, than we think. The fact that a third of the nation is ill-housed and
ill-fed is, in simple fact, not so much a dishonor as a challenge. What
Americans have to do is enlarge the dimensions of the democratic process.
This country is, I once heard it put, absolutely "lousy with greatness"—
with not only the greatest responsibilities but with the greatest opportunities ever known to man.

Acknowledgments

Nine-tenths of this book is the result of direct evidence picked up by my own eyes and ears; overwhelmingly my sources are primary and personal, i.e., word-of-mouth. This is a proper and indeed unavoidable technique in journalism, and I make no pretense of being a historian. Yet certain historical passages were necessary, if only because that which precedes an event is often as interesting as the event itself, and because much in the contemporary American scene simply cannot be understood without some embryonic knowledge of the background. So I had to read a good deal of history and commentary. I like the direct eyes-and-ears approach; but after all you cannot "look" at the Dred Scott decision or "listen" to the Hartford Convention. Always I wanted to tell the whole story if I could. Some source material I have acknowledged in footnotes or the text itself as I went along. For other general sources the reader is referred to the bibliography and to a special list of material that follows.

The preparation of this book has, from first to last and from top to bottom, been a one-man job. I employed no professional researchers whatever. I tried to see what I could for myself. But a great number of friends and acquaintances helped me with the utmost benevolence and robust zeal, and I want to thank them all stoutly, at the same time issuing a disclaimer that nobody but me is to be held accountable for lopsided opinions, mistakes in judgment, or plain factual errors. A thousand generous people helped me. My real bibliography is the names that follow. But the final responsibility must be mine.

I prepared an early outline of this book and the book to ensue as long ago as September, 1944, and then followed it a few months later with a more concrete and ample syllabus. I sent this out to a variety of folk asking for their comments, if any; dozens responded and some went to the trouble of sending me long, well-considered memoranda, from which I derived great and chastening profit. Let me list some of their names, with thanks: Hamilton Fish Armstrong, editor of *Foreign Affairs*; Hamish Hamilton, my London publisher; the late Wendell L. Willkie; Professor Raymond Walsh of the CIO; Thomas W. Lamont of J. P. Morgan & Co.; Stuart Chase; colleagues like Dorothy Thompson, Jay Allen, Vincent Sheean, William L. Shirer, Walter Duranty, Edgar Ansel Mowrer, Junius B. Wood, Louis Fischer, and the late John T. Whitaker; Arthur H. Sulzberger of the New York *Times* and Helen R. Reid of the New York *Herald Tribune*; Thomas K. Finletter; James A. Farley; Archibald MacLeish; Frank Darvell of the British Ministry of Information and later British consul in Denver; Robert Moses of New York City; Howard Vincent O'Brien of Chicago; Norman Corwin and Edward R. Murrow in the world of radio; Herbert Nicholas of Exeter College, Oxford; Jonathan Daniels; Anne O'Hare McCormick; Nicholas Roosevelt; George S. Messersmith, American ambassador to Mexico, and John C. Wiley, American ambassador to Colombia; Robert Riskin of the world of the movies; Harry Sherman of the Book-of-the-Month Club; Mark Van Doren; Clifton Fadiman; Robin Cruikshank of the London *News Chronicle*; and the Schoeninger family of Carmel-by-the-Sea, California. Many of these helped me too by stimulating and corrective conversation.

Next I have to thank cordially those who read the entire book in manuscript—Cass Canfield of Harper and Brothers, my publisher; Carl Brandt, my agent; Tyler Kepner, of Brookline, Massachusetts, co-author of *America, Its History and People*; Marguerite Hoyle of Harper and Brothers; and John Fischer, of the editorial staff of *Harper's Magazine*, to all of whom my debt is inestimable. Also several folk read and criticized the MS in part, among them Lewis Gannett, literary editor of the New York *Herald Tribune*; Amy Loveman of the Book-of-the-Month Club; and Alexander Lindey, attorney at law. Hearty thanks are additionally due to Nancy Barnett, my secretary, who struggled ably and with patience over the whole manuscript, typing it in many drafts; Bernice Baumgarten of Brandt & Brandt; and to Kathleen Voute, who did the maps. And I have my son, John Jr., to thank for reading much of the script, especially in its early forms, and for working out the route on the front end paper. The back end paper is the work of the National Opinion Research Center of the University of Denver.

I sent various chapters and sections of the manuscript, though not the whole book, for criticism, correction, and amendment, to various friends in watch towers all over the country whom I had previously talked to. Among these, to whom my deep thanks are hereby rendered, are Professor J. Frank Dobie and Professor Robert H. Montgomery, both of the University of Texas; Chester H. Rowell and Ruth Newhall of the San Francisco *Chronicle*; Joseph Kinsey Howard, Montana newspaperman and author; Professor Morris E. Garnsey, chairman of the department of economics at the University of Colorado; John E. Lokar, secretary to ex-Governor Lausche of Ohio; Jennings Phillips Jr. of Salt Lake City, to whom my debt is indeed immense; James Pope, Don McWain, and Allan Trout of the Louisville *Courier-Journal*; James D. Blake of Harper and Brothers; Aubrey Drury, author of *California, an Intimate Guide*; George Springmeyer, attorney at law, Reno, Nevada; Richard L. Neuberger, member of the Oregon legislature, journalist, and author of *Our Promised Land*; Nelson C. Hazeltine and several of his associates on the Bonneville Power Administration; Judge and Mrs. R. M. Rainey of Oklahoma City; Harnett T. Kane, author of *New Orleans Woman*; Annette H. Peyser of the National Association for the Advancement of Colored People; John M. Henry of the Des Moines *Register* and *Tribune*; Charles Krutch, Chief of Graphic Services, TVA; William B. Chamberlain, secretary of the Sunshine Climate Club of Tucson, Arizona; Mrs. R. F. Love of the Wyoming *State Tribune and Leader*; and Virginius Dabney, distinguished editor of the Richmond *Times-Dispatch*. But again I want to emphasize that, just as I did every inch of the original research myself, so did I do all the irrevocable last-ditch checking myself, and if malproportions and blunders remain, the fault is mine alone, not that of these authorities I have named.

This book, and in particular the final detailed work thereon, was done under massive pressure of time and painful circumstance, and in its last stages it was written so quickly that there was no time for serialization. But some chapters did appear in various magazines, in abbreviated form thoroughly reworked and rewritten later, and for permission to reprint, I have the editors of *Harper's Magazine, Reader's Digest, Pageant, Liberty,* and *Holiday* to thank. Also the *Reader's Digest* helped substantially to make my long trip possible. I should mention too that I used a few passages that originally appeared in that splendid newspaper, the Chicago *Daily News,* for which I was a reporter and foreign correspondent for many years.

Finally I want to express with grateful emphasis my special thanks to a special few, for the pleasure and profit I derived from their encouragement, hospitality, and illuminating talk: Douglas Southall Freeman, historian, editor of the Richmond *News Leader,* and biographer of General Lee; Archibald MacLeish; Senator Ralph Flanders of Vermont; George W. Healy Jr., editor of the New Orleans *Times-Picayune;* Attorney General Robert W. Kenny of the State of California; David E. Lilienthal of TVA; Morris Ernst of New York City; Frederick L. Allen, editor of *Harper's Magazine,* and John Fischer whom I have named above; Leon Henderson; Walter White of the National Association for the Advancement of Colored People; Ralph Coghlan of the St. Louis *Post-Dispatch;* Estes Kefauver, congressman from Tennessee; Brooks Emeny of Cleveland and Waldo Pierson of Cincinnati; Clarence A. Dykstra, provost of the University of California, Los Angeles; Eleanor Roosevelt; H. L. Mencken; Countess Eleanor Palffy; James Kerney Jr., editor of the Trenton *Times,* and Manchester Boddy, editor of the Los Angeles *News;* Colonel Joseph W. Evans, president of the Houston Cotton Exchange; Roy A. Roberts of the Kansas City *Star;* Bartley C. Crum of San Francisco; Robert E. Sherwood; Roderick Peattie, professor of geography, Ohio State University; Raymond Swing; Carl Friedrich, professor of government at Harvard; Clare Boothe Luce; Sinclair Lewis; J. David Stern of Philadelphia; Gideon Seymour, executive editor of the Minneapolis *Star-Journal;* Silliman Evans, publisher of the Nashville *Tennessean;* Lillian Smith, author of *Strange Fruit;* E. D. Nicholson of United Airlines, Denver; Charles P. Curtis Jr., of Boston, co-editor of the *Practical Cogitator;* B. L. Anderson of Forth Worth, Texas, and David Caughren of Sauk Centre, Minnesota; former Chief Justice Howard A. Johnson of the supreme court of Montana; Mr. and Mrs. Albert D. Lasker; Dr. Cornelius Horace Traeger of New York; Barnet Nover, foreign affairs columnist of the Washington *Post,* and Thomas K. Finletter, attorney and former special assistant to the secretary of state.

List of Names

Without duplicating any mentioned in the various categories above, I wish here to list the names of all those who, in one way or other, helped me, and to whom I talked in the course of my long trip:*

---

* I have always wanted to print a similar list in the other *Inside* books, but I did not do so for fear of getting people into trouble. But the United States is, at the moment at least, still a democracy and I daresay I can mention any and all names without risk to anyone.

ACHESON, DEAN *Under Secretary of State,* Washington, D. C.

ACHESON, EDWARD *Prof.,* George Washington University, Washington, D. C.

ADAMS, CHARLES FRANCIS *Trustee,* Boston, Mass.

ADAMS, ESTHER Bayley Island, Maine

ADAMS, FREDERIC *Dean,* Trinity Cathedral, Trenton, N. J.

ADAMS, NATHAN *President,* First National Bank, Dallas, Tex.

AGER, PAUL *Chief Budget Officer,* Tennessee Valley Authority, Knoxville, Tenn.

AIKMAN, DUNCAN *Writer,* San Francisco, Calif.

ALCIATORE, ROY *Restaurateur,* New Orleans, La.

ALDERMAN, HENRY Bonneville Power Administration, Portland, Ore.

ALLEN, J. W. *Commanding Officer,* U. S. Naval Hospital, San Diego, Calif.

ALLIS, BARNEY Hotel Muehlbach, Kansas City, Mo.

ALSTON, CHARLES *Painter,* New York City

ANDERSON, P. L. *Police & Fire Commissioner,* San Antonio, Tex.

ANDERSON, CLINTON P. *Secretary of Agriculture,* Washington, D. C.

ANHOLT, HARRY M. Brown Palace Hotel, Denver, Colo.

ANIOL, CLAUDE *Photographer,* San Antonio, Tex.

APPLEBY, A. J. *Shipyard Worker,* Portland, Ore.

ARNALL, ELLIS G. *Former Governor* of Georgia, Atlanta, Ga.

ARONSON, A. Y. *Managing Editor,* Louisville *Times,* Louisville, Ky.

ATKINSON, ROY W. *Regional Director,* Political Action Committee, CIO, Seattle, Wash.

AUBURN, N. P. *Vice Pres. & Dean of Administration,* Univ. of Cincinnati, Cincinnati, Ohio

AUSTIN, C. M. *Director of Hospitals,* State of South Dakota, Sioux Falls, S. D.

AUSTIN, EDWARD T. *Editor-in-Chief, Tribune-Sun & Union,* San Diego, Calif.

AVERY, BEN Arizona *Republic,* Phoenix, Ariz.

AYERS, EBEN *Assistant Press Secretary,* White House, Washington, D. C.

AYRES, CLARENCE E. *Professor of Economics,* University of Texas, Austin, Tex.

BABCOCK, STANLEY *Past President,* Butte Miners' Union, CIO, Butte, Mont.

BACH, ROY N. *Federal Aid Division,* State Game & Fish Dept., Bismarck, N. D.

BACON, WILLIAM C. *President,* Bohemian Club, San Francisco, Calif.

BAILEY, CARL E. *Former Governor* of Arkansas, Little Rock, Ark.

BAILEY, THOMAS L. *Late Governor* of Mississippi, Jackson, Miss.

BAKER, LISLE JR. *Vice Pres. & Treasurer,* Louisville *Courier-Journal,* Louisville, Ky.

BALDERSTON, JOHN L. *Writer,* Beverly Hills, Calif.

BALDWIN, C. B. *Exec. Chairman,* National Citizens Political Action Committee, New York City

BALDWIN, RAYMOND E. *Senator from* Connecticut, Hartford, Conn.

BALL, JOSEPH H. *Senator* from Minnesota, Washington, D. C.

BALL, W. W. *Editor, News & Courier,* Charleston, S. C.

BANE, FRANK *Exec. Director,* Council of State Governments, Chicago, Ill.

BANKHEAD, JOHN H. *Late Senator* from Alabama, Washington, D. C.

BANKS, FRANK E. *Supervising Engineer,* Bureau of Reclamation, Coulee Dam, Wash.

BANNING, MARGARET CULKIN *Novelist,* Duluth, Minn.

BARDWELL, MALCOLM G. *Asst. Gen. Mgr.* Smaller War Plants Corp., Washington, D. C.

BARNES, DR. ALBERT *Art Collector, Writer & Critic,* Philadelphia, Pa.

BARNES, JOSEPH *Foreign Editor,* N. Y. Herald Tribune, New York City

BARNET, CLAUD Associated Negro Press, Chicago, Ill.

BARROWS, WILFRED M. *Statistician,* New England Council, Boston, Mass.

BARTH, ALAN *Writer,* Washington *Post,* Washington, D. C.

BAUGHMAN, HOWARD Hotel Hermitage, Nashville, Tenn.

BEALL, WELLWOOD *Vice Pres.* Boeing Aircraft Co., Seattle, Wash.

BEARDSLEY, C. R. Commerce Department, New York City

BECK, DAVE *President,* Joint Council of Teamsters, AF of L, Seattle, Wash.

BECKER, JOHN H. JR. Regional Committee for MVA, Omaha, Neb.

BEDFORD, CLAY Kaiser Industries, Richmond, Calif.

BEDICHEK, ROY Interscholastic League, Austin Tex.

BEHRENS, EARL C. *Political Editor,* San Francisco *Chronicle,* San Francisco, Calif.

BENEDITTO, ANGELO DE *Lt.* Airborne Photographic Division, U. S. Army, Denver, Colo.

BENNION, ADAM S. Utah Power & Light Co., Salt Lake City, Utah

BENNION, FRED *Exec. Sec'y,* Montana Taxpayers' Assn., Helena, Mont.

BENSON, ELMER A. *Chairman,* National Citizens Political Action Committee. *Former Governor* of Minnesota, Minneapolis, Minn.

BERGSON, PETER *Chairman,* Hebrew Committee for National Liberation in America, Washington, D. C.

BERNHARD, ANDREW *Managing Editor,* Pittsburgh *Post-Gazette,* Pittsburgh, Pa.

BERRY, DON *Editor, Record Herald & Tribune,* Indianola, Iowa

BESSE, RALPH *Attorney,* Squire, Sanders & Dempsey, Cleveland, Ohio.

BEZOFF, BEN *Radio Commentator,* KMYR, Denver, Colo.

BIBLE, ALAN *Attorney General,* State of Nevada, Carson City, Nev.

BIDDLE, MONCURE *Clubman,* Philadelphia, Pa.

BIGGERS, GEORGE C. *Vice Pres. & Gen. Manager,* Atlanta *Journal,* Atlanta, Ga.

BIMSON, WALTER *President,* Valley National Bank, Phoenix, Ariz.

BINGAY, MALCOLM W. *Editorial Director, Free Press,* Detroit, Mich.

BIRD, FRANCIS H. *Prof. of Commerce,* Univ. of Cincinnati. *Chairman of Board,* Federal Reserve Bank, Cincinnati, Ohio

BITTER, FRANCIS T. R. *Prof. & Physicist,* Cambridge, Mass.

BLACK, ROBERT *President,* White Motor Co., Cleveland, Ohio

LAKE, HENRY *Gen. Mgr.* Capper Publications, Topeka, Kan.

LANKE, HENRY *Producer,* Warner Bros., Hollywood, Calif.

LEGEN, G. C. *Superintendent,* Power House, Bonneville Dam, Ore.

LOCH, IVAN Bonneville Power Administration, Portland, Ore.

BLOOD, ROBERT O. *Former Governor* of New Hampshire. *Farmer & Surgeon,* Concord, N. H.

BLUE, ROBERT D. *Governor* of Iowa, Des Moines, Iowa.

BLUFORD, LUCILE Kansas City *Call,* Kansas City, Mo.

BOETTCHER, CLAUDE K. *Industrialist. Sugar Magnate,* Denver, Colo.

BOETTIGER, MRS. ANNA Hyde Park, N. Y.

BOHLEN, CHARLES *State Department Liaison Officer,* White House, Washington, D. C.

BOJENS, KEN *Lt. Public Relations Officer,* U. S. Navy, San Diego, Calif.

BOND, REFORD *Judge. Chairman,* Corporation Commission, Oklahoma City, Okla.

BOULTER, THORNTON *Editor,* San Diego *Tribune-Sun,* San Diego, Calif.

BOYETT, ERNEST *Executive Secretary to the Governor,* Austin, Tex.

BRAYMAN, HAROLD *Director,* Public Relations, E. I. Du Pont de Nemours Co., Wilmington, Del.

BRICE, JOHN A. *President, Atlanta Journal,* Atlanta, Ga.

BRIDGES, HARRY Congress of Industrial Organizations, San Francisco, Calif.

BRIER, ROYCE *Editorial Writer,* San Francisco *Chronicle,* San Francisco, Calif.

BRIGGS, COL. ROBERT W. *Rancher & Contractor,* San Antonio, Tex.

BRINEY, RUSSELL *Chief Editorial Writer,* Louisville *Courier-Journal,* Louisville, Ky.

BROMFIELD, LOUIS *Novelist & Farmer,* Mansfield, Ohio

BROUSSARD, JOSEPH C. *Restaurateur,* New Orleans, La.

BROWN, HARRY C. *Legislative Director* for Southern California, CIO, Los Angeles, Calif.

BROWN, J. DOUGLAS *Prof. of Economics,* Princeton University, Princeton, N. J.

BROWN, SEVELLON *Publisher,* Providence *Journal,* Providence, R. I.

BROWNING, CHARLES P. *National Representative,* Chicago *Defender,* Chicago, Ill.

BRUNDAGE, HENRY M. *Commissioner of Markets,* New York City

BRYAN, MALCOLM *Vice President,* Federal Reserve Bank, Atlanta, Ga.

BRYSON, CONRAD Station KTSM, El Paso, Tex.

BUCKWALTER, I. Z. *General Manager,* Lancaster Newspapers, Inc., Lancaster, Pa.

BUFFUM, FRANCIS *Secretary to Governor,* Concord, N. H.

BULLER, MRS. B. FRANK Lancaster Newspapers, Inc., Lancaster, Pa.

BULLITT, ORVILLE H. *Civic Leader,* Philadelphia, Pa.

BULLITT, WILLIAM C. *Former Ambassador* to France and U.S.S.R. *Author,* Washington, D. C.

BURNETT, WHIT *Author, Anthologist, Editor,* New York City

BURTON, HAROLD H. *Supreme Court Justice,* Washington, D. C.

BYFIELD, ERNEST L. Hotel Ambassador, Chicago, Ill.

BYRNE, JOHN B. *President,* Hartford Connecticut Trust Co., Hartford, Conn.

BYRNE, MARTIN *Director of Organization,* Farmers Union, Jamestown, N. D.

CABELL, MRS. HENRY F. Portland, Ore.

CAMERON, GEORGE T. *Publisher,* San Francisco *Chronicle,* San Francisco, Calif.

CAMPBELL, D. D. Braun & Co., Denver, Colo.

CAMPBELL, COL. THOMAS D. *Wheat Farmer,* Hardin, Mont.

CANBY, DR. HENRY SEIDEL *Author, Editor,* New York City

CANHAM, ERWIN D. *Executive Editor, Christian Science Monitor,* Boston, Mass.

CANNON, JOSEPH J. *Late Publicity Commissioner,* State of Utah, Salt Lake City, Utah

CAPRA, FRANK *Motion Picture Director and Producer,* Beverly Hills, Calif.

CARLL, CHARLES E. *Director,* Ford News Bureau, Ford Motor Co., Dearborn, Mich.

CARPENTER, W. S. *President,* E. I. Du Pont de Nemours & Co., Wilmington, Del.

CARROLL, JAMES J. Hotel Roney Plaza, Miami Beach, Fla.

CARROLL, MRS. MAURICE Natchez, Miss.

CARTER, ROBERT L. *Asst. Special Counsel,* Natl. Asso. Advancement of Colored People, New York City

CARTER, WILLIAM H. *Textile Manufacturer,* Needham Heights, Mass.

CASE, MARGARET *Society Editor, Vogue,* New York City.

CASE, ROBERT ORMOND *Writer, The Oregonian,* Portland, Ore.

CASENAVE, COUNT *Restaurateur,* New Orleans, La.

CASEY, LEE *Columnist, Rocky Mountain Daily News,* Denver, Colo.

CASSELL, L. J. Atchison, Topeka & Santa Fe R. R., Amarillo, Tex.

CAULEY, JOHN *Asst. City Editor,* Kansas City *Star,* Kansas City, Mo.

CHANDLER, ALBERT B. *Former Senator* from Kentucky, Washington, D. C.

CHAPMAN, ROY Station KTSM, El Paso, Tex.

CHASEN, DAVE *Restaurateur,* Beverly Hills, Calif.

CHERRINGTON, BEN M. *Chancellor,* University of Denver, Denver, Colo.

CHILDS, MARQUIS *Columnist,* Washington, D. C.

CHOATE, ROBERT B. *Publisher,* Boston *Herald,* Boston, Mass.

CHRISTENSON, S. A. *Bookseller,* Sioux Falls, S. D.

CHRISTENSON, WALTER E. *Editor, World Herald,* Omaha, Neb.

CHRISTOPHERSON, FRED C. *Exec. Editor, Daily Argus-Leader,* Sioux Falls, S. D.

CHUNG, DR. MARGARET *Physician & Civic Leader,* San Francisco, Calif.

CHURCH, FREDERICK C. *Insurance Exec.,* Boston, Mass.

CLARK, LT. CHARLES *Former Assistant Counsel,* Truman Committee, Washington, D. C.

CLARK, JOHN L. *Political Analyst,* Pittsburgh *Courier,* Pittsburgh, Pa.

CLARK, TOM *Attorney General,* Washington, D. C.

CLAYMAN, JACOB Congress of Industrial Organizations, Columbus, Ohio

CLAYTON, WILL *Under Secretary of State,* Washington, D. C.

CLEMENT, RUFUS E. *President,* Atlanta University, Atlanta, Ga.

CLEVELAND, CARL *Advertising Mgr.,* Boeing Aircraft Co., Seattle, Wash.

CLUGSTON, W. G. *Writer,* Topeka, Kan.

COCHRAN, MRS. CLAIRE *Sec'y to Senator Magnuson,* Washington, D. C.

COCHRANE, R. B. *Capt.* U. S. Army Engineers, Bonneville Dam, Ore.

COHEN, BETTY *Sec'y to Former Mayor F. H. La Guardia,* New York City.

COHN, DAVID L. *Writer,* New York City

COLLIER, TARLTON *Associate Editor, Courier-Journal,* Louisville, Ky.

COLLIER, JOHN *Former Commissioner of Indian Affairs,* Department of Interior. *President,* Institute of Ethnic Affairs, Washington, D. C.

COLLINS, BERTRAND *Merchant Marine,* Seattle, Wash.

COMBS, JUDGE J. M. *Congressman,* Beaumont, Tex.

COMPTON, KARL T. *President,* Massachusetts Institute of Technology, Cambridge, Mass.

CONANT, JAMES BRYANT *President,* Harvard University, Cambridge, Mass.

CONN, JERRY *Newspaperman,* Lancaster, Pa.

CONNALLY, TOM *Senator* from Texas, Washington, D. C.

CONNELLY, MATTHEW C. *Secretary to the President,* Washington, D. C.

CONNERY, DAVID *Director of Publicity,* United Automobile Workers, CIO, Detroit, Mich.

CONRAD, E. J. *President,* Bismarck *Capital,* Bismarck, N. D.

CONRAD, GAYLORD E. *Editor,* Bismarck *Capital,* Bismarck, N. D.

COREY, GEORGE *Attorney,* Utah Power & Light Co., Salt Lake City, Utah

CORNWALL, J. H. *Warehouseman,* Salt Lake City, Utah

COSTIGAN, HOWARD G. *Director,* Division of Progress & Development, State of Washington. *Radio Commentator,* Seattle, Wash.

COTTEN, W. B. Baton Rouge Refinery, Standard Oil of New Jersey, Baton Rouge, La.

COTTINGHAM, GEORGE W. *Editor,* Houston *Chronicle,* Houston, Tex.

COUSENS, FOSTER Department of Public Utilities, Commonwealth of Massachusetts, Boston, Mass.

COWLES, GARDNER JR. *Publisher,* Des Moines, Iowa.

COWLES, JOHN *Publisher,* Minneapolis, Minn.

COX, OSCAR *Attorney. Former General Counsel* FEA, OEM, and Lend Lease, Washington, D. C.

CRAUS, HENRY T. *Pres. News-Journal Co.,* Wilmington, Del.

CRIM, H. G. *White House Usher,* Washington, D. C.

CRITCHLOW, HORACE *Executive Secretary,* MVA Association, Denver, Colo.

CRONE, B. W. Kansas City *Times,* Kansas City, Mo.

CROUCH, COURTNEY Braun & Co., Kansas City, Mo.

CROUSE, RUSSEL *Playwright,* New York City

CROZIER, HARRY B. Unemployment Compensation Commission, Austin, Tex.

CRUMP, E. H. *Politician,* Memphis, Tenn.

CUKOR, GEORGE *Film Producer & Director,* Beverly Hills, Calif.

CUNEO, ERNEST *Attorney at law,* New York City

CURRENT, GLOSTER *Director of Branches,* Natl. Asso. Advancement of Colored People, New York City

CURREY, BROWNLEE *President,* Equitable Securities Corp. *Publisher, Southern Agriculturist,* Nashville, Tenn.

CURTIN, ROBERT E. E. I. Du Pont de Nemours Co., Wilmington, Del.

CUSHING, RICHARD J. *The Most Rev. Archbishop* of Boston, Boston, Mass.

DALE, EDGAR *Prof. of Educational Research,* Ohio State Univ., Columbus, Ohio

DANIELS, JOSEPHUS *Editor & Publisher, News and Observer,* Raleigh, N. C.

DARDEN, COLGATE W. JR. *Former Governor* of Virginia, Richmond, Va.

DAVENPORT, MRS. DORA *Chief County Probation Officer,* San Antonio, Tex.

DAVENPORT, RUSSELL W. *Writer, Poet & Editor,* New York City

DAVIDSON, JO *Sculptor. Chairman of* Independent Citizens Committee of the Arts, Sciences, and Professions, New York City

DAVIES, JOSEPH E. *Former Ambassador to* U.S.S.R. and Belgium, Washington, D. C.

DAVIS, CHESTER C. *President,* Federal Reserve Bank. *Former War Foods Administrator,* St. Louis, Mo.

DAVIS, DOWDAL H. *Advertising Mgr.,* Kansas City *Call,* Kansas City, Mo.

DAVIS, ELMER *Radio Commentator. Former Director* OWI, Washington, D. C.

DAVIS, HARVEY *Vice President,* Ohio State University, Columbus, Ohio

DAVIS, LEE New Orleans *Item,* New Orleans, La.

DAVIS, PAUL *President,* American National Bank, Nashville, Tenn.

DAWSON, MARTHA Rich's, Inc., Atlanta, Ga.

DEAN, W. L. *Banker & Director,* Santa Fe R. R., Topeka, Kan.

DELANEY, JOHN *Chairman,* Board of Transportation, New York City

de LUE, WILLARD *Newspaperman,* Boston, Mass.

DEMPSEY, JOHN J. *Former Governor* of New Mexico, Santa Fe, N. M.

DERNONCOURT, JOE CIO, Oklahoma City, Okla.

DEWEY, THOMAS E. *Governor* of New York, Albany, N. Y.

DICKINSON, HENRY F. *Attorney,* Carmel-by-the-Sea, Calif.

DICKINSON, J. M. *Breeder of Arabian Horses,* Nashville, Tenn.

DIERDORF, JOHN Pacific Power & Light Co., Portland, Ore.

DILLON, JAMES D. *Assistant Superintendent Industrial Relations,* Geneva Steel Co., Provo, Utah

DILLON, MARY *Former President,* Board of Education, New York City

DODDS, HAROLD W. *President,* Princeton University, Princeton, N. J.

DONOGHUE, JOSEPH A. *Regional Director,* Political Action Committee, CIO, Philadelphia, Pa.

DONOVAN, MAJ. GEN. WM. J. *Former Commanding Officer,* OSS. *Attorney,* New York City

DOUGHERTY, M. G. *Attorney. Member of* Arizona Power Authority, Phoenix, Ariz.

DOUGLAS, EMILY TAFT *Former Congresswoman* from Illinois, Washington, D. C.

DOUGLAS, HELEN GAHAGAN *Congresswoman* from Calif., Washington, D. C.

DOUGLAS, WILLIAM O. *Supreme Court Justice,* Washington, D. C.

DOWNEY, SHERIDAN *Senator* from California, Washington, D. C.

DRAPER, DOROTHY *Decorator,* New York City

DU BOIS, BEN F. *Banker,* Sauk Centre, Minn.

DUNN, BRIAN BORU *Writer,* Santa Fe, N. M.

DUNN, JAMES *Director of Finance,* State of California, Sacramento, Calif.

DUNN, ROY E. *Republican National Committeeman,* Minneapolis, Minn.

DU PONT, MR. & MRS. ALFRED V. Greenville, Del.

DUPUIS, CHARLES W. *President,* Central Trust Co., Cincinnati, Ohio

DUTTON, WILLIAM S. *Writer,* E. I. Du Pont de Nemours Co., Wilmington, Del.

DWIGHT, BEN *Former Governor* of the Choctaw Nation, Oklahoma City, Okla.

EARLE, GEORGE H. III *Former Governor* of Pennsylvania, Philadelphia, Pa.

EBY, HAROLD *Prof.* University of Washington, Seattle, Wash.

EDEN, WILLIAM J. *Member* of Corporation Commission, Phoenix, Ariz.

EDGE, WALTER E. *Former Ambassador* to France. *Governor* of New Jersey, Trenton, N. J.

EISENHOWER, GEN. DWIGHT D. *Chief of Staff,* U. S. Army, Washington, D. C.

ELLIOTT, JOHN B. Jameson Petroleum Company, Los Angeles, Calif.

ELLIS, JOHN B. *City Solicitor,* Cincinnati, Ohio

ELLIS, SCOTT *Farmer,* Dallas Center, Iowa

ELLISTON, HERBERT *Asso. Editor,* Washington *Post,* Washington, D. C.

ELSTAD, R. T. *General Mgr.,* Oliver Iron Mining Co., Hibbing, Minn.

EMERSON, HOWARD P. *Assistant Director,* Commerce Department, TVA, Knoxville, Tenn.

EPSTEIN, MAX *Industrialist. Connoisseur,* Chicago, Ill.

EVANS, ERNESTINE *Writer,* New York City

EVANS, JOHN G. *General Superintendent,* United Pueblos Agency, Albuquerque, N. M.

EVERETT, ROLLIN H. *Member City Council. Editor, The Sun,* Cincinnati, Ohio

EVJUE, WILLIAM T. *Editor, Capital Times,* Madison, Wis.

EWING, A. BRUCE Public Relations, Ford Motor Co., Dearborn, Mich.

EWING, ROBERT J. Station KWKA, Shreveport, La.

EZEKIEL, MORDECAI *Economic Adviser,* Dept. of Agriculture, Washington, D. C.

FABER, E. C. *Sgt.* State Highway Patrol, Des Moines, Iowa

FAGER, MAURICE E. Kansas Industrial Development Commission, Topeka, Kan.

FARLEY, CAL Boys' Ranch, Old Tascosa, Tex.

FARNSLEY, CHARLES P. *Attorney,* Louisville, Ky.

FAWCETT, VANCE Kaiser Industries, Oakland, Calif.

FENTON, DR. R. A. *Physician & Surgeon.* Portland, Ore.

FERGER, ROGER H. *Publisher,* Cincinnati *Inquirer,* Cincinnati, Ohio

FIELD, HARRY H. *Late Director,* National Opinion Research Center, Denver, Colo.

FILES, MISS RAE *Legislator,* Waxahachie, Tex.

FINLETTER, T. D. *Judge,* Municipal Court, Philadelphia, Pa.

FINNEGAN, RICHARD T. *Editor,* Chicago *Times,* Chicago, Ill.

FISCHER, BEN United Steel Workers of America, New Kensington, Pa.

FISHER, MARGARET Committee of Editors & Writers of the South, Atlanta, Ga.

FISHER, VORIES *Photographer,* Chicago, Ill.

FLEMING, LAMAR JR. *Cotton Broker,* Houston, Tex.

FLEMING, ROSCOE B. *Writer,* Denver, Colo.

FLETCHER, ROBERT H. *Author,* Montana Power Co., Butte, Mont.

FLIPPEN, ROBERT B. *Racial & Religious Adviser,* Booker T. Washington Community Center, San Francisco, Calif.

FLOYD, C. B. Santa Fe *New Mexican,* Santa Fe, N. M.

FLYNN, FRANK Station KFBC, Cheyenne, Wyo.

FORD, HENRY Ford Motor Co., Dearborn, Mich.

FORD, JEREMIAH D. *Prof. of Romance Languages,* Harvard University, Cambridge, Mass.

FORD, O'NEIL *Project Architect,* La Villita, San Antonio, Tex.

FORMAN, PHILIP *Judge,* Federal Court, Trenton, N. J.

FORTE, RALPH *Foreign Correspondent,* United Press, New York City

FOWLER, RICHARD B. Kansas City *Star,* Kansas City, Mo.

FRANK, JEROME N. *Former Chairman* SEC. *Judge* U. S. Circuit Court of Appeals, New York City

FRANKENSTEEN, RICHARD T. *Former Vice Pres.* United Automobile Workers, CIO, Detroit, Mich.

FRANKFURTER, FELIX *Supreme Court Justice,* Washington, D. C.

FULBRIGHT, J. WILLIAM *Senator* from Arkansas, Washington, D. C.

FULLER, W. PARMER *Manufacturer,* San Francisco, Calif.

FURLONG, WILLIAM HARRISON Inter-American Highway Association, San Antonio, Tex.

GAETH, ARTHUR *Radio Commentator. Vice Pres.* Intermountain Network, Salt Lake City, Utah

GALE, RICHARD *Former Congressman. Farmer,* Minneapolis, Minn.

GALLICO, PAUL *Writer,* New York City

GANTT, DR. W. HORSLEY *Director,* Pavlov Laboratory, Johns Hopkins Univ., Baltimore, Md.

GARDNER, GEORGE PEABODY *Trustee,* Boston, Mass.

GEORGE, HAROLD L., *Lt. Gen.* Air Transport Command, Army Air Forces, Washington, D. C.

GEROULD, RUSSELL *Secretary to Former Governor Saltonstall,* Boston, Mass.

GERVASI, FRANK *Writer,* Washington, D. C.

GIESEL, FRED *Business Manager,* Cincinnati *Post,* Cincinnati, Ohio

GILES, GROVER *Attorney General,* State of Utah, Salt Lake City, Utah

GILROY, EDWARD M. *Secretary to Governor Edge,* Trenton, N. J.

GLASSCOFF, DONALD G. *National Adjutant,* American Legion, Indianapolis, Ind.

GLENN, GEORGE E. JR. *President,* Exposition Cotton Mills, Atlanta, Ga.

GODFREY, ART *Music Dealer,* Sioux Falls, S. D.

GOLDWYN, SAM *Motion Picture Producer,* Hollywood, Calif.

GOOCH, J. A. *Attorney,* Fort Worth, Tex.

GOODELL, JULIAN *Judge,* Superior Court, San Francisco, Calif.

GORMLEY, ARTHUR T. *Business Mgr., Register & Tribune,* Des Moines, Iowa.

GRAHAM, CHARLES A. *Attorney. Chairman* MVA Association, Denver, Colo.

GRAHAM, FRANK *President,* University of North Carolina, Chapel Hill, N. C.

GRAHAM, JAMES D. *President,* State Federation of Labor (AF of L), Helena, Mont.

GORHAM, R. W. *Superintendent,* Rolling Mill, Geneva Steel Co., Provo, Utah

GRAFTON, SAMUEL *Columnist,* New York *Post,* New York City

GRAVES, ROSALIND *Newspaperwoman,* Fort Worth, Tex.

GREATON, EVERETT Maine Development Commission, Augusta, Me.

GRIFFITH, HERMAN *Decorator,* Duluth, Minn.

GRISWOLD, DWIGHT P. *Former Governor* of Nebraska, Lincoln, Neb.

GROVE, WILLIAM C. *Manager,* Station KFBC, Cheyenne, Wyo.

GRUENING, DR. ERNEST *Governor* of Alaska, New York City

GUFFEY, JOSEPH F. *Former Senator* from Pennsylvania, Washington, D. C.

GUND, GEORGE *President,* Cleveland Trust Co., Cleveland, Ohio

GUNTHER, JOHN JR. *Student,* Deerfield, Mass.

GURNEY, CHAN *Senator* from South Dakota, Sioux Falls, S. D.

GUYTON, PEARL VIVIAN *Writer,* Natchez, Miss.

HACKETT, C. M. E. I. Du Pont de Nemours & Co., Wilmington, Del.

HAGERTY, JAMES C. *Exec. Asst. to Governor,* Albany, N. Y.

HAGGART, R. S. *Commanding Officer,* U. S. Naval Training Center, San Diego, Calif.

HAGGERTY, C. J. *Sec'y-Treas.* Calif. State Federation of Labor, AF of L, San Francisco, Calif.

HALL, G. L. Transcontinental & Western Airlines, Amarillo, Tex.

HALLAM, CLEMENT B. *Exec. Editor, News Journal,* Wilmington, Del.

HALLORAN, M. W. *Political Writer, Star-Journal & Tribune,* Minneapolis, Minn.

HAMILTON, J. D. M. *Attorney. Former Chairman,* Republican National Committee, Philadelphia, Pa.

HANDLAN, WILLIAM *Director,* West Virginia Industrial & Publicity Commission, Charleston, W. Va.

HARDESTY, A. R. *North Texas Sub-Regional Director,* CIO, Dallas, Tex.

HARDING, ELLISON *President,* Fort Worth National Bank, Fort Worth, Tex.

HARPER, LUCIUS C. *Executive Editor,* Chicago *Defender,* Chicago, Ill.

HARRINGTON, OLIVER W. *Public Relations Director,* Natl. Asso. Advancement of Colored People, New York City

HARRIS, HEBERT Station WAGA, Atlanta, Ga.

HARRISON, JOSEPH *Professor* University of Washington, Seattle, Wash.

HARTEN, JAMES *Inspector. Police Aide to ex-Mayor La Guardia,* New York City

HARVEY, S. A. *Works Manager,* TVA, Muscle Shoals, Ala.

HARWELL, COLEMAN *Merchant. Former Exec. Editor,* Nashville *Tennessean,* Nashville, Tenn.

HASKELL, H. J. *Editor,* Kansas City *Star,* Kansas City, Mo.

HATCH, CARL A. *Senator* from New Mexico, Washington, D. C.

HAWKINS, FRANK *Editorial Writer,* Atlanta *Journal,* Atlanta, Ga.

HAWKINS, GEORGE *Connoisseur,* Mansfield, Ohio

HAYES, GORDON *Professor of Economics,* Ohio State University, Columbus, Ohio

HAYS, REUBEN B. *Vice Pres.* Federal Reserve Bank, Cleveland, Ohio

HEINSOHN, DR. EDMUND *Pastor,* University Methodist Church, Austin, Tex.

HELLEBUST, A. L. *Secretary,* North Dakota Farmers Union, Jamestown, N. D.

HEMENWAY, C. C. *Editor,* Hartford *Times,* Hartford, Conn.

HENRY, MRS. CHARLTON Philadelphia, Pa.

HERON, COL. ALEXANDER R. *Director,* Reconstruction & Re-employment, State of Calif., San Francisco, Calif.

HERRING, CLYDE *Late Governor* of Iowa, Washington, D. C.

HEWITT, DR. EDGAR L. *Director,* Museum of New Mexico, Santa Fe, N. M.

HIGGINS, ANDREW J. *Industrialist,* New Orleans La.

HIGGINS, MISS JOY M. Higgins Industries, New Orleans, La.

NBOTHAM, w. a. Federation of Atomic
entists, Washington, D. C.

RETH, HORACE A. *Governor* of Maine, Port-
l, Me.

, GEORGE R. *Former Director of Education
Research,* CIO, Denver, Colo.

, LISTER *Senator* from Alabama, Washington,
C.

BY, w. P. *Former Governor* of Texas. *Pres-
t, Houston Post,* Houston, Tex.

GES, MRS. ABNER Natchez, Miss.

GES, CHARLES E. *Mng. Dir.* Chamber of
mmerce, Charleston, W. Va.

FMAN, FERLE National Association Advance-
t of Colored People, New York City

BROOK, STEWART H. *Writer,* Portland, Ore.

COMB, PAUL B. *Editor, State Observer,*
stin, Tex.

LOWAY, w. A. *Former Regional Director,*
itical Action Committee, CIO, Kansas City,

LOWAY, w. J. *Former Governor,* Member
erstate Oil Compact Committee, Oklahoma
y, Okla.

SIE, ALVIN *Secretary,* Board of Trustees,
skegee Institute, Tuskegee, Ala.

TER, NORMAN *President,* Montana Trailways
ociation, Helena, Mont.

ANS, MRS. ROBERT Boston, Mass.

EYMAN, MRS. NANNIE WOOD *Collector of
toms,* Portland, Ore.

KINS, HARRY L., *the late.* Washington, D. C.

NBLOW, ARTHUR JR. *Motion Picture Pro-
er,* Beverly Hills, Calif.

TON, JOHN *Director,* U. S. Forest Service,
tland, Ore.

CHKISS, STUART *Rubber Executive,* Madison,
an.

GHLAND, MASON *Master of Hounds,* Hills-
o Hounds, Nashville, Tenn.

ARD, NATHANIEL R. *Editor,* Cleveland *News,*
veland, Ohio

ARD, w. K. *Bookseller,* Louisville, Ky.

E, GENE A. *President & Publisher,* Amarillo
ly *News,* Amarillo, Tex.

E, QUINCY *Radio Commentator,* New York
y

SE, CECIL Kansas City *Star,* Topeka, Kan.

T, E. PALMER *Former Publisher, The Ore-
ian. Editor & Publisher,* Denver *Post,* Denver,
o.

HES, CHARLES EVANS JR. *Chairman,* Mayor's
mittee on Race & Religion, New York City

L, CORDELL *Former Secretary of State,* Washton, D. C.

PHREY, H. J. *Mayor,* Minneapolis, Minn.

T, LESTER C. *Governor of Wyoming,* Chey-
e, Wyo.

TER, CROIL *Pres.* Northwest Airlines, St.
l, Minn.

TRESS, FRANK San Antonio *Express,* San
onio, Tex.

CHINS, ROBERT M. *Chancellor,* Univ. of
cago, Chicago, Ill.

TON, MAJOR S. E. *Director of Information,*
reau of Reclamation, Coulee Dam, Wash.

S, HAROLD L. *Former Secretary of Interior,*
shington, D. C.

RSOLL, RALPH MC A. *Journalist,* New York
y

AND, RAY W. *Col. Asst. Chief of Staff,* Air
nsport Command, U. S. Army Air Forces,
shington, D. C.

ISE, JOHN *Prof. of Economics,* Univ. of Kansas,
Lawrence, Kan.

IVINS, H. GRANT *Prof. of Animal Husbandry,*
Brigham Young University. *State Director,* OPA,
Provo, Utah

IZZARD, WESLEY S. *Editor-in-chief,* Amarillo
Daily News, Amarillo, Tex.

JACK, WILLIAM *Secretary of State,* Wyoming,
Cheyenne, Wyo.

JACKSON, H. W. JR. Universal Leaf Tobacco Co.,
Richmond, Va.

JACKSON, JOSEPH HENRY *Literary Editor,* San
Francisco *Chronicle,* San Francisco, Calif.

JACKSON, ROBERT H. *Supreme Court Justice,*
Washington, D. C.

JACKSON, THOMAS E. *Capt.* State Police, Santa
Fe, N. M.

JACOBSEN, JOHN M. *Regional Director,* Political
Action Committee, CIO, Minneapolis, Minn.

JANEWAY, ELIOT *Writer,* New York City

JENSEN, VERNON *Prof.* Univ. of Colorado, Boulder, Colo.

JOHNSON, DR. GUY B. *Exec. Director,* Southern
Regional Council, Atlanta, Ga.

JOHNSON, KENNETH F. *State Senator,* Carson
City, Nev.

JOHNSON, SPUD *Custodian,* Harwood Gallery,
Taos, N. M.

JOHNSTON, ERIC *President,* Motion Picture
Producers & Distributors Asso. *Ex-President,* U. S.
Chamber of Commerce, Washington, D. C.

JONES, ALTON *Director,* Correspondence Division,
Univ. of Idaho, Moscow, Idaho

JONES, BOB Sioux Falls *Argus-Leader,* Sioux
Falls, S. D.

JONES, GEORGE *Republican State Chairman,* Minneapolis, Minn.

JONES, HARRISON *Chairman of the Board,* Coca
Cola Co., Atlanta, Ga.

JONES, JESSE *Politician,* Washington, D. C.

JONES, MADISON S. JR. *Administrative Assistant,*
Natl. Asso. Advancement of Colored People, New
York City

JONES, RONALD E. *Vegetable Shipper. State Secretary,* Farmers' Union, Brooks, Ore.

JORDAN, JOSEPH Oliver Iron Mining Co., Hibbing, Minn.

JUDD, WALTER H. *Congressman* from Minnesota,
Washington, D. C.

KAISER, HENRY J. *Industrialist,* Oakland, Calif.

KALTENBORN, H. V. *Radio Commentator,* New
York City

KAPLAN, RABBI HARRY Ohio State University,
Columbus, Ohio

KEANE, GERTRUDE *Sec'y to ex-Mayor La Guardia,*
New York City

KELLER, KEN R. *Secretary to Governor,* Lincoln, Neb.

KELLS, L. L. *City Solicitor,* Sauk Centre, Minn.

KELLY, MRS. GEORGE M. D. Melrose, Natchez,
Miss.

KENDALL, WILLIAM Coca-Cola Company, Natchez,
Miss.

KENNAN, GEORGE F. Department of State, Washington, D. C.

KENNEDY, ROBERT E. Chicago *Times,* Chicago, Ill.

KENNIN, HARRY *Former State Senator. Exec.
Sec'y,* Bonneville Power Administration, Portland, Ore.

KERR, ROBERT S. *Ex-Governor* of Oklahoma, Oklahoma City, Okla.

KERR, T. S. *Dean,* College of Letters & Sciences,
Univ. of Idaho, Moscow, Idaho

KESTERSON, capt. tom *Pilot,* TVA, Knoxville, Tenn.
KILGORE, harley m. *Senator* from West Virginia, Washington, D. C.
KILGUSS, frederick c. *Exec. Sec'y to Governor,* Providence, R. I.
KING, burt Hotel Last Frontier, Las Vegas, Nev.
KING, john *Director of Radio & Research,* State Grange, Seattle, Wash.
KINGDON, frank *Chairman,* National Citizens Political Action Committee, New York City
KINTNER, robert *Vice-Pres.* American Broadcasting Company, New York City
KLINE, allan b. *Pres.* Iowa Farm Bureau Fed., Des Moines, Iowa
KNICKERBOCKER, fred h. *Executive Assistant,* Union Pacific Railroad, Salt Lake City, Utah
KNOX, harley e. *Mayor,* San Diego, Calif.
KORDA, hal *Asst. to Publisher,* San Diego *Journal,* San Diego, Calif.
KRAUS, gilbert t. *Attorney. Vice Pres.* Philadelphia *Record,* Philadelphia, Pa.
KREILSHEIMER, mr. & mrs. leo Seattle, Wash.
KROCK, arthur *Chief of Washington Bureau,* New York *Times,* Washington, D. C.
KROLL, jack *Director,* Political Action Committee, CIO, Cincinnati, Ohio
KUHNS, john c. *Asst. Regional Forester,* Portland, Ore.
KUNZ, ernst Hotel St. Anthony, San Antonio, Tex.
LA FOLLETTE, charles m. *Ex-Congressman* from Indiana, Washington, D. C.
LA FOLLETTE, isabel bacon *Asso. Editor, The Progressive,* Madison, Wis.
LA FOLLETTE, philip f. *Former Governor,* Madison, Wis.
LA FOLLETTE, robert m. jr. *Ex-Senator* from Wisconsin, Washington, D. C.
LA GUARDIA, fiorello h. *Former Mayor,* New York City
LAIRD, landon Kansas City *Star,* Kansas City, Mo.
LAMONT, robert p. jr. *Industrialist & Farmer,* Waukesha, Wis.
LANDESS, w. m. Program Exposition Unit, TVA, Knoxville, Tenn.
LANDON, alfred m. Republican Candidate for President, 1936, Topeka, Kan.
LANGLEY, james m. *Editor & Publisher,* Concord *Daily Monitor,* Concord, N. H.
LAPHAM, roger d. *Mayor,* San Francisco, Calif.
LARSEN, karley *President,* Northwestern District Council, International Woodworkers of America, CIO, Seattle, Wash.
LARSON, dorothy jane. *Writer,* Santa Fe, N. M.
LAUSCHE, frank j. *Former Governor* of Ohio, Columbus, Ohio
LAW, charles Congress of Industrial Organizations, Phoenix, Ariz.
LAW, f. m. *Chairman of the Board,* First National Bank, Houston, Tex.
LAW, f. m. jr. *Bookseller,* Houston, Tex.
LAWRENCE, david l. *Mayor* of Pittsburgh and *Democratic State Chairman,* Pittsburgh, Pa.
LAWRENCE, j. e. *Editor,* Lincoln *Star,* Lincoln, Neb.
LAZARUS, reuben a. *Asst. to Former Mayor La Guardia,* New York City
LECKRONE, walter *Editor,* Indianapolis *Times,* Indianapolis, Ind.
LEECH, margaret *Author,* New York City

LEFFLER, ross l. Carnegie-Illinois Steel Corp, Pittsburgh, Pa.
LEWIS, f. m. *Chief Electrical Engineer,* Bonneville Dam, Ore.
LEWIS, lloyd *Historian, Newspaperman,* Chicago, Ill.
LINDLEY, ernest *Columnist,* Washington, D. C.
LINDSAY, howard *Playwright. Actor,* New York City
LINN, harry d. *Sec'y of Agriculture,* State of Iowa, Des Moines, Iowa
LITTLE, walter Southern Pacific Railroad, Sacramento, Calif.
LITVAK, anatol *Motion Picture Director,* Pacific Palisades, Calif.
LIVINGSTON, goodhue jr. *Exec. Sec'y to Ex Mayor La Guardia,* New York City
LIVODA, michael *Sub-Regional Dir.* CIO, Denver, Colo.
LOBLE, lester h. *Democratic State Chairman* Helena, Mont.
LOCHARD, metz *Editor,* Chicago *Defender,* Chicago, Ill.
LOCKWOOD, paul *Secretary to the Governor* Albany, N. Y.
LONGWORTH, mrs. alice roosevelt Washington, D. C.
LONG, thomas a. *State Sec'y* CIO Council Denver, Colo.
LONG, william e. Kansas Industrial Development Commission, Topeka, Kan.
LORING, judge augustus peabody *Trustee an Agent,* North Plymouth, Mass.
LOTTINVILLE, savoie Univ. of Oklahoma Press Norman, Okla.
LOVETT, mrs. robert w. Boston, Mass.
LUBITSCH, ernst *Film Producer & Director* Beverly Hills, Calif.
LUCE, henry r. *Editor & Publisher,* New York City
LUCEY, the most rev. robert e. *Archbishop o* San Antonio, San Antonio, Tex.
LUHAN, mable dodge *Writer,* Taos, N. M.
LYNCH, julia *Writer,* San Francisco, Calif.
LYONS, leonard *Columnist,* New York *Post* New York City
McAFEE, william *Attorney,* McAfee & Gross man, Cleveland, Ohio
McCAREY, leo *Motion Picture Director,* Hollywood, Calif.
McCARRAN, patrick *Senator* from Nevada Washington, D. C.
McCARTHY, raymond f. *Special Agent,* Dept. o Justice, State of California, Sacramento, Calif
McCLASKEY, henry *Asst. Gen. Mgr.* Louisvill *Courier-Journal,* Louisville, Ky.
McCLENDON, james t. *Physician & Surgeon* National Association for Advancement of Colore People, Detroit, Mich.
McCLOY, john j. *Former Asst. Sec'y of War* Washington, D. C.
McCLUSKY, h. s. *Attorney. Referee* Industria Commission, Phoenix, Ariz.
McCRAKEN, tracy s. *Newspaper Publisher Democratic National Committeeman,* Cheyenne Wyo.
McCREEDY, h. t. *Asst. Regional Director,* Political Action Committee, CIO, Detroit, Mich.
McDERMOTT, michael j. *Special Asst. to th Secretary of State,* Washington, D. C.
MacGOWAN, howard Smaller War Plants Corp. Seattle, Wash.
McGRAW, don Row River Lumber Co., Portland Ore.

McGRAW, MRS. DON *Former President,* League of Women Voters, Portland, Ore.

MacGREGOR, ALEXANDER CAMPBELL *Wheat Farmer,* Hooper, Wash.

MacGREGOR, JOHN M. *General Manager,* MacGregor Land & Livestock Co., Hooper, Wash.

McGRATH, J. HOWARD *Senator* from Rhode Island. *Ex-U. S. Solicitor General,* Providence, R. I.

McGUIRE, DAVID R. *Director of Public Relations,* Higgins Industries, New Orleans, La.

McKAY, WALLACE City Light Co., Seattle, Wash.

McKEE, PAUL B. *President,* Portland Gas & Electric Co., Portland, Ore.

McKELLAR, KENNETH *Senator* from Tennessee, Washington, D. C.

McKEOUGH, RAYMOND S. Political Action Committee, CIO, Chicago, Ill.

McKINNON, CLINTON D. *Editor & Publisher,* San Diego *Daily Journal,* San Diego, Calif.

McKITRICK, DAVID Elmscourt, Natchez, Miss.

McLAUGHLIN, JOSEPH Democratic City Committee, Philadelphia, Pa.

McLEAN, EVALYN WALSH Washington, D. C.

McLEAN, ROBERT *President,* Phila. *Bulletin,* Philadelphia, Pa.

McMURRAY, ELIZABETH ANN *Bookseller,* Dallas, Tex.

McNEILL, J. S. JR. San Antonio *Light,* San Antonio, Tex.

McNEILL, WARREN Associated Press, Nashville, Tenn.

McNICHOLAS, THOMAS M. *Sec'y-Treas.* Tennessean Newspapers, Inc., Nashville, Tenn.

McNUTT, PAUL V. *High Commissioner to Philippines. Chairman,* War Manpower Commission, Washington, D. C.

McPEAK, CARL A. *Regional Director,* Political Action Committee, CIO, Dallas, Tex.

MADRY, ROBERT W. *Director of Publicity,* Univ. of North Carolina, Chapel Hill, N. C.

MAGNUSON, WARREN G. *Senator* from Washington, Washington, D. C.

MAHONEY, DANIEL J. *General Manager,* Miami *Daily News,* Miami, Fla.

MAHONEY, EUGENE C. *Democratic National Committeeman,* Sioux Falls, S. D.

MALLON, H. N. *President,* Dresser Industries, Cleveland, Ohio

MALONE, DUDLEY FIELD *Attorney,* Beverly Hills, Calif.

MALONE, GEORGE W. *Senator* from Nevada, Reno, Nev.

MANKIEWICZ, HERMAN *Dramatist & Motion Picture Writer,* Beverly Hills, Calif.

MANN, DAVID H. *Asst. Dir. of Publicity,* State of Utah, Salt Lake City, Utah

MANSFIELD, HAROLD *Director of Public Relations,* Boeing Aircraft Co., Seattle, Wash.

MANSHIP, CHARLES P. *Publisher,* Baton Rouge *State-Times-Morning Advocate,* Baton Rouge, La.

MARCANTONIO, VITO *Congressman* from New York, Washington, D. C.

MARDIKIAN, GEORGE *Restaurateur,* San Francisco, Calif.

MARKHAM, R. H. *Christian Science Monitor,* Boston, Mass.

MARSH, JUDGE ROBERT MC CURDY *Member Board of Health,* New York City

MARTIN, EDWARD *Senator* from Pennsylvania, Harrisburg, Pa.

MARTIN, JOSEPH W., JR. *Speaker,* House of Representatives & *Congressman* from Mass., Washington, D. C.

MASSEY, W. M. *Vice Pres.* Fort Worth National Bank, Fort Worth, Tex.

MATSON, CARLTON *Asso. Editor,* Cleveland *Press,* Cleveland, Ohio

MATTHEWS, ROBERT *Prof. of Law,* Ohio State Univ. Pres. League for Constitutional Rights, Columbus, Ohio

MAYTUBBY, FLOYD *Governor* of the Chickasaw Nation, Oklahoma City, Okla.

MATZKE, STANLEY A. *Former Chairman* Legislative Council, *Director* of Insurance, State of Nebraska, Lincoln, Neb.

MAURY, H. LOWNDES *Attorney,* Butte, Mont.

MAW, HERBERT B. *Governor* of Utah, Salt Lake City, Utah

MAXWELL, ELSA *Columnist,* New York City

MAYER, MILTON *Writer,* University of Chicago, Chicago, Ill.

MAYFIELD, FRANK M. Department Store Pres., St. Louis, Mo.

MAYS, BENJAMIN E. *President,* Morehouse College, Atlanta, Ga.

MAYS, T. H. American Air Lines, El Paso, Tex.

MEADOWS, C. W. *Governor* of W. Virginia, Charleston, W. Va.

MEALAND, RICHARD *Story Editor,* Paramount Pictures, Hollywood, Calif.

MEEMAN, EDWARD J. *Editor, Press-Scimitar,* Memphis, Tenn.

MENNINGER, DR. KARL A. *Psychiatrist,* Menninger Clinic, Topeka, Kan.

METCALFE, ORRICK *Automobile Dealer,* Natchez, Miss.

MILLS, CLARENCE *Judge,* District Court, Oklahoma City, Okla.

MILLS, WILLIAM W. *President,* Tax Commission, New York City

MITCHELL, GEORGE S. *Regional Dir.,* Political Action Committee, CIO, Atlanta, Ga.

MOHLER, J. C. State Board of Agriculture, Topeka, Kan.

MONRONEY, A. S. MIKE *Congressman* from Oklahoma, Washington, D. C.

MONTGOMERY, W. T. *Rancher & Cattleman,* San Antonio, Tex.

MOORE, M. L. *Shop Steward,* Boilermakers Union, TVA, Wilson Dam, Ala.

MOORMAN, DR. L. J. *Former Dean,* Univ. of Oklahoma, Norman, Okla.

MORANO, ALBERT P. *Sec'y to Former Congresswoman* Clare Boothe Luce, Washington, D. C.

MORGAN, DR. HARCOURT *Tennessee Valley Authority,* Knoxville, Tenn.

MORGENTHAU, HENRY JR. *Former Secretary of the Treasury,* Washington, D. C.

MORONY, JANET *Sec'y to Attorney General,* Sacramento, Calif.

MORRIS, NEWBOLD *Ex-President of Council,* New York City

MORROW, MARCO *Former Gen. Mgr.* Capper Publications, Topeka, Kan.

MORSE, WAYNE *Senator* from Oregon, Washington, D. C.

MOSER, LT. RICHARD G., USNR Bureau of Aeronautics, Navy Department, Summit, N. J.

MULLINS, W. E. Boston *Herald,* Boston, Mass.

MULROY, JAMES W. *Asst. Mgn. Editor,* Chicago *Sun,* Chicago, Ill.

MURDOCK, KENNETH B. *Prof. of English,* Harvard Univ., Cambridge, Mass.

MURPHY, CHARLES F. *City Magistrate,* New York City

MURPHY, DONALD R. *Editor, Wallace's Farmer,* Des Moines, Iowa

MURPHY, FRANCIS S. *General Manager,* Hartford *Times,* Hartford, Conn.

MURPHY, JOHN *Attorney,* Sioux Falls, S. D.

MURRAY, JAMES E. *Senator* from Montana, Washington, D. C.

MYERS, CAPT. HENRY *Pilot,* Presidential Plane, Air Transport Command, U. S. Army Air Forces, Washington, D. C.

NAFTALIN, ARTHUR *Sec'y to Mayor Humphrey,* Minneapolis, Minn.

NELSON, ROBERT W. *Vice Pres.* 1st National Bank, Cincinnati, Ohio

NEWBRANCH, H. E. *Editor-in-chief, World-Herald,* Omaha, Neb.

NEWCOMB, ROBERT *Co-editor, Copper Commando,* Butte, Mont.

NIBLEY, JOEL State Liquor Commission, Salt Lake City, Utah

NICHOLS, DUDLEY *Motion Picture Writer & Producer,* Hollywood, Calif.

NIGGLI, JOSEPHINA *Writer,* San Antonio, Tex.

NOLAN, JUDGE MARK District Court, Duluth, Minn.

NORDYKE, LEWIS *Writer,* Amarillo *Daily News,* Amarillo, Tex.

NORTH, JAMES M. *Editor,* Fort Worth *Star-Telegram,* Fort Worth, Tex.

NUNN, WILLIAM G. *Mgn. Editor,* Pittsburgh *Courier,* Pittsburgh, Pa.

NYE, JOHN H. *Exec. Ed. The Tennessean,* Nashville, Tenn.

O'CONNELL, JERRY, Democratic State Central Committee, Seattle, Wash.

ODUM, PROF. HOWARD W. Univ. of North Carolina, Chapel Hill, N. C.

O'DWYER, WILLIAM *Mayor,* New York City

O'FLAHERTY, HAL *Foreign Editor,* Chicago *Daily News,* Chicago, Ill.

O'GARA, GEORGE *Hardware Store Proprietor,* Sauk Centre, Minn.

O'LEARY, WILFRID *Attorney,* Cheyenne, Wyo.

OLSON, ORVILLE National Citizens Political Action Committee, Minneapolis, Minn.

O'MAHONEY, JOSEPH C. *Senator* from Wyoming, Washington, D. C.

O'NEAL, SAM A. *Director of Publicity,* Democratic National Committee, Washington, D. C.

ORECK, MARVIN *Merchant,* Duluth, Minn.

ORLICH, MARY *Vice Pres.* National CIO Women's Auxiliary. *Pres.* of International Mines, Mill, & Smeltermans Women's Auxiliary, Butte, Mont.

ORMEROD, MAJOR C. B. British Information Services, New York City

ORRELL, JESSE C. Steamfitters Union, TVA, Wilson Dam, Ala.

OSBORN, SIDNEY P. *Governor* of Arizona, Phoenix, Ariz.

OUTMAN, W. D. *Legislative Representative,* State of Florida, Washington, D. C.

OVERTURE, FRANK *Gen. Sec'y,* National Farmers Union, Amarillo, Tex.

OWENS, HAMILTON *Editor in Chief,* Baltimore *Sun,* Baltimore, Md.

OWTHWAITE, R. M. *Vice Pres.* John Morrell & Co., Packers, Topeka, Kan.

PANASKY, SAM *Theatre Owner,* Boston, Mass.

PAPPAS, THOMAS *Importer,* Boston, Mass.

PARKER, WILLIAM *Former Republican State Chairman,* Sauk Centre, Minn.

PARRAN, DR. THOMAS *Surgeon General of the U. S.,* Washington, D. C.

PARRISH, PHILIP *Editor, The Oregonian,* Portland, Ore.

PARSONS, GEOFFREY *Editor,* N. Y. *Herald Tribune,* New York City

PASCHALL, JOHN *Editor,* Atlanta *Journal,* Atlanta, Ga.

PATT, JOHN *Gen. Mgr.* WGAR, Cleveland, Ohio

PATTERSON, DR. FREDERICK B. *Pres.* Tuskegee Institute, Tuskegee, Ala.

PATTERSON, PAUL *Publisher,* Baltimore *Sun,* Baltimore, Md.

PATTERSON, JUDGE ROBERT *Secretary of War,* Washington, D. C.

PATTERSON, W. A. *President,* United Airlines, Chicago, Ill.

PAULL, HENRY *Attorney,* Duluth, Minn.

PEARSON, DREW *Columnist and Radio Commentator,* Washington, D. C.

PEARCE, BERNARD L. *Secretary,* Public Utility Districts, Seattle, Wash.

PECK, SAM J. *Hotel Proprietor,* Little Rock, Ark.

PEPPER, CLAUDE *Senator* from Florida, Washington, D. C.

PEPPER, GEORGE *Exec. Sec'y,* Hollywood Independent Citizens Committee of Arts, Sciences & Professions, Hollywood, Calif.

PEPPER, GEORGE WHARTON *Attorney.* Former *Senator,* Philadelphia, Pa.

PERRY, GLEN E. I. Du Pont de Nemours Co., Wilmington, Del.

PERRY, GEORGE SESSIONS *Newspaperman and Author,* Madison, Conn.

PERRY, JENNINGS *Author. Assoc. Editor,* Nashville *Tennessean,* Nashville, Tenn.

PETERS, EVAN J. Walter Thompson Co., Seattle, Wash.

PETERS, FERDINAND J. Kansas City, Mo.

PETERSEN, MARK E. *Member of Council of 12,* Church of Jesus Christ of Latter Day Saints, Salt Lake City, Utah

PETTIBONE, WALTER *Bookseller,* Scruggs, Vandervoort & Barney, St. Louis, Mo.

PHILIPP, CYRUS L. *Republican National Committeeman,* Milwaukee, Wis.

PIEL, DR. GERALD *Special Asst. to Henry Kaiser,* Kaiser Industries, New York City.

PINCKNEY, JOSEPHINE *Novelist,* Charleston, S. C.

POMEROY, DR. VIVIAN *Minister First Parish,* Milton, Mass.

POOLEY, EDWARD M. *Editor, Herald-Post,* El Paso, Tex.

POPE, JAMES P. *Former Senator* from Idaho, *Director* TVA, Knoxville, Tenn.

POTTER, GEORGE W. *Chief Editorial Writer, Journal-Bulletin,* Providence, R. I.

POYNTER, MR. & MRS. NELSON P. St. Petersburg *Times,* St. Petersburg, Fla.

PRENDERGAST, WALTER T. Washington, D. C.

PRICE, LUCIEN *Newspaperman. Writer,* Boston, Mass.

PRICHARD, EDWARD F. *Attorney. Politician,* Paris, Ky.

PROCTOR, MORTIMER R. *Former Governor* of Vermont, Montpelier, Vt.

PULITZER, JOSEPH *Editor & Publisher,* St. Louis *Post-Dispatch,* St. Louis, Mo.

PURINGTON, FRANCIS *Newspaperman. Exec. Sec'y to Governor,* Portland, Me.

PUSEY, MERLO J. *Writer,* Washington *Post,* Washington, D. C.

PYLE, HAROLD Houston *Chronicle,* Houston, Tex

RABBIT, THOMAS R. *State Senator. Editor, New World,* Seattle, Wash.

RAND, FRANK Sante Fe *New Mexican,* Santa Fe N. M.

RAVER, PAUL J. *Administrator,* Bonneville Power Administration, Portland, Ore.

RAYBURN, SAM *Congressman* from Texas. *Minority Leader,* House of Representatives, Washington, D. C.

READY, MICHAEL J. *Rev. Bishop* of Columbus, Columbus, Ohio

REDDING, WILLIAM *Literary Editor,* Kansas City *Star,* Kansas City, Mo.

REESE, BENJAMIN H. *Managing Editor, Post-Dispatch,* St. Louis, Mo.

REID, JAMES M. *News Editor,* Pittsburgh *Courier,* Pittsburgh, Pa.

REID, DR. ORA DE A. *Professor,* Atlanta University, Atlanta, Ga.

REMARQUE, ERICH MARIA *Novelist,* New York City

RESNICK, BEATRICE *Sec'y to ex-Mayor La Guardia,* New York City

REUTHER, VICTOR United Automobile Workers, CIO, Detroit, Mich.

REUTHER, WALTER P. *President,* United Auto Workers CIO, Detroit, Mich.

REYNOLDS, QUENTIN *Writer & War Correspondent,* New York City

RICH, DICK *Vice Pres.* Rich's, Inc., Atlanta, Ga.

RICH, JOHN F. American Friends Service Committee, Philadelphia, Pa.

RICHTER, KARL *Rabbi,* Mount Zion Congregation, Sioux Falls, S. D.

RIDLEY, CLARENCE E. *Director,* International City Managers Association, Chicago, Ill.

ROACH, T. E. *Vice Pres. & Gen. Mgr.* Northwestern Electric Co., Portland, Ore.

ROBBINS, STANTON *Former Director,* International House, New Orleans, La.

ROBERTS, GEORGE B. *Regional Dir.* Political Action Committee, CIO, Los Angeles, Calif.

ROBERTS, KENNETH *Novelist,* Kennebunkport, Me.

ROBERTS, PAUL *Dean,* St. John's Cathedral, Denver, Colo.

ROBERTSON, HARRISON M. *Gen. Counsel,* Brown & Williamson Tobacco Corp., Louisville, Ky.

ROCKEFELLER, NELSON A. *Former Co-ordinator Inter-American Affairs & Assistant Secretary of State,* Washington, D. C.

RODRIGUEZ, ERNEST State Police, Santa Fe, N. M.

ROESSER, CHARLES *Oilman,* Fort Worth, Tex.

ROMANOFF, PRINCE MIKE *Restaurateur,* Beverly Hills, Calif.

ROOSEVELT, FRANKLIN D. *Late President of the United States,* Washington, D. C.

ROPER, ELMO *Director, Fortune* Survey, New York City

ROSE, ROBERT H. *Supervisor,* National Park Service, Boulder City, Nev.

ROSENGREN, MR. & MRS. FRANK *Booksellers,* San Antonio, Tex.

ROTHSCHILD, JEROME *Attorney,* Philadelphia, Pa.

ROWE, JOHN J. *Bank President,* Cincinnati, Ohio

RUBEN, ARTHUR *Safety Inspector,* Utah Copper Co., Bingham, Utah

RUBIN, MORRIS H. *Editor, The Progressive,* Madison, Wis.

RUSSELL, HOLLIS *Bookseller,* Oklahoma City, Okla.

RUSSELL, J. S. *Acting Managing Editor, Register & Tribune,* Des Moines, Iowa

RUSSELL, MRS. JAMES H. Santa Fe, N. M.

RUTCHICK, ROGER *Sec'y to ex-Gov. Benson. Former Ass't State's Atty.,* Minneapolis, Minn.

RUTTENBERG, HAROLD J. *Research Director,* United Steel Workers of America, Pittsburgh, Pa.

RYAN, JOHN J. Transport Workers Union, CIO, Columbus, Ohio

RYAN, THOMAS H. *Attorney,* Denver, Colo.

SACHS, ALEXANDER *Economist,* New York City

ST. JOHN, ROBERT *War Correspondent,* Radio Commentator, New York City

SALMON, EDWIN A. *Chairman,* City Planning Commission, New York City

SALSITCH, LEROY *President,* Oliver Iron Mining Co., Duluth, Minn.

SALTONSTALL, LEVERETT *Senator* from Massachusetts, Washington, D. C.

SAMMONS, E. C. *President,* U. S. National Bank, Portland, Ore.

SAMMONS, MARJORIE *Co-editor, Copper Commando,* Butte, Mont.

SARNOFF, DAVID *President,* Radio Corp. of America, New York City

SAXON, LYLE, the late *Writer,* New Orleans, La.

SAYLOR, HARRY T. *Editor,* Philadelphia *Record,* Philadelphia, Pa.

SAYRE, HARRISON M. *President,* American Educational Press. *Chairman,* Ohio Commission for Democracy, Columbus, Ohio

SCHACTER, HARRY W. *President,* Kaufman Straus Co. *President,* Committee for Kentucky, Louisville, Ky.

SCHECHTER, A. A. *Vice President,* Mutual Broadcasting System, N.Y.C.

SCHLEE, GEORGE New York City

SCHLEMMER, F. C. *Project Manager,* Fontana Dam, TVA, Fontana, N. C.

SCHOENINGER, MR. & MRS. JOSEPH Carmel-by-the-Sea, Calif.

SCHOEPPEL, ANDREW F. *Governor* of Kansas, Topeka, Kan.

SCHUYLER, GEORGE S. *Author. Columnist. Manager,* Seaboard Edition, Pittsburgh *Courier,* New York City

SCOTT, EDGAR Montgomery, Scott & Co., Philadelphia, Pa.

SEARLES, R. D. Transcontinental & Western Airlines, Phoenix, Ariz.

SELTZER, LOUIS B. *Editor,* Cleveland *Press,* Cleveland, Ohio

SELZNICK, DAVID O. *Motion Picture Producer,* Hollywood, Calif.

SEWELL, SUMNER *Ex-Gov.* of Maine. *Ex-President,* American Export Airlines. Director Military Government, Baden, Germany, Augusta, Me.

SEYMOUR, CHARLES *President,* Yale University, New Haven, Conn.

SEYMOUR, FORREST W. *Asso. Editor, Register & Tribune,* Des Moines, Iowa

SHAW, SETH *Prof. of Horticulture,* Univ. of Utah, Salt Lake City, Utah

SHEARER, LT. DON State Highway Patrol, Omaha, Neb.

SHERMAN, HARRY S. *Gen. Superintendent,* Chisholm District, Oliver Iron Mining Co., Hibbing, Minn.

SHERMAN, M. S. *Editor & Publisher,* Hartford *Courant,* Hartford, Conn.

SHOUSE, JAMES D. *Vice Pres.* The Crosley Corp. *Gen. Manager,* Station WLW, Cincinnati, Ohio

SIDLO, THOMAS *Chairman,* United China Relief, Cleveland, Ohio

SIMMONS, ROBERT G. *Chief Justice Supreme Court,* Lincoln, Neb.

SIMMS, WILLIAM C. *Asst. to Mayor Humphrey,* Minneapolis, Minn.

SIMS, CECIL *Attorney,* Bass, Berry & Sims, Nashville, Tenn.

SIMS, MARIAN *Novelist,* Atlanta, Ga.

SMITH, DR. BLAKE *Pastor,* University Baptist Church, Austin, Tex.

SMITH, CHARLES L. *Chairman,* Utah War Finance Committee, Salt Lake City, Utah

SMITH, MAJ. GEN. C. R. *ex-Deputy Commander,* Air Transport Command, Army Air Forces, Washington, D. C.

SMITH, FRANKLIN G. *President,* Osborn Manufacturing Co., Cleveland, Ohio

SMITH, GEORGE ALBERT *President,* Church of Jesus Christ of Latter Day Saints, Salt Lake City, Utah

SMITH, PROF. HENRY NASH University of Texas, Austin, Tex.

SMITH, JOHN LEE *Lieut.-Gov.* of Texas, Austin, Tex.

SMITH, PAUL C. *Editor and Gen. Manager,* San Francisco *Chronicle,* San Francisco, Calif.

SMITH, REX American Air Lines, New York City

SMITH, VAN ZANDT *Attorney,* Fort Worth, Tex.

SMITH, JUDGE WILLIAM A. Supreme Court, State of Kansas, Topeka, Kan.

SMOOT, I. A. *Postmaster,* Salt Lake City, Utah

SNELLING, PAULA *Editor, South Today,* Clayton. Ga.

SPANG, JOSEPH *President,* Gillette Safety Razor Co., Boston, Mass.

SPARKS, CHAUNCEY M. *Ex-Governor* of Alabama, Montgomery, Ala.

STAPLETON, BENJAMIN F. *Mayor,* Denver, Colo.

STASSEN, HAROLD *Former Governor* of Minnesota, St. Paul, Minn.

STEARNS, ROBERT L. *Pres.* Univ. of Colorado, Boulder, Colo.

STEBBINS, DR. ERNEST L. *Former Commissioner of Health,* New York City

STEEL, JOHANNES *Radio Commentator,* New York City

STEINBECK, JOHN *Novelist,* New York City

STEPHENS, ROBERT W. *Vice President,* Guaranty Trust Co., New York City

STERN, WILLIAM *Republican Nat. Committeeman. Banker & Director,* Northwest Airlines, Fargo, N. D.

STETTINIUS, EDW. R. JR. *Former Secretary of State,* Washington, D. C.

STEUDEL, ARTHUR *President,* Sherwin Williams Co., Cleveland, Ohio

STEVENS, JAMES *Lumberman. Author,* Seattle, Wash.

STEVENSON, ALEXANDER *President* Foreign Affairs Committee of Nashville, Nashville, Tenn.

STEVENSON, COKE R. *Ex-Governor* of Texas, Austin, Tex.

STILWELL, GEN. JOSEPH, the late *Commanding Officer,* Army Ground Forces, Washington, D. C.

STIX, ERNEST W. Rice-Stix Co., St. Louis, Mo.

STOLTZ, MILDRED K. *State Director of Education,* Montana Farmers Union, Great Falls, Mont.

STONE, B. B. *Attorney,* Fort Worth, Tex.

STONG, BENTON J. *Editor, National Union Farmer,* Denver, Colo.

STOWE, LELAND *Writer & War Correspondent,* New York City

STRADLING, JAMES G. JR. John C. Winston Co., Atlanta, Ga.

STRODE, J. WILLIAM *Secretary to the Governor,* Phoenix, Ariz.

STRONG, HENRY B. *Exec. Sec'y to the Governor,* Hartford, Conn.

STURDEVANT, W. L. *Director of Information,* TVA, Knoxville, Tenn.

SULLENS, FREDERICK *Editor,* Jackson *Daily News,* Jackson, Miss.

SULZBERGER, CYRUS *Foreign Corresp.* N. Y. *Times,* New York City

SURLES, MAJ. GEN. ALEXANDER D. *Director of Public Relations,* War Department, Washington, D. C.

SWEETSER, ARTHUR *Former Deputy Director,* OWI, Washington, D. C.

SWOPE, HERBERT BAYARD. *Publicist. Former Editor, World,* New York City

TAFT, HULBERT *Editor,* Cincinnati *Times-Star,* Cincinnati, Ohio

TALBOT, GLENN *President,* N. D. Farmers Union, Jamestown, N. D.

TARVER, JACK *Columnist,* Atlanta *Constitution,* Atlanta, Ga.

TAYLOR, GLEN H. *Senator* from Idaho, Washington, D. C.

TAYLOR, ROBERT R. *Chairman,* Chicago Housing Authority, Chicago, Ill.

THACKREY, MR. & MRS. T. O. *Publishers,* New York *Post,* New York City

THOMAS, ELBERT D. *Senator* from Utah, Washington, D. C.

THOMAS, R. J. *Ex-President,* United Automobile Workers, Detroit, Mich.

THOMPSON, C. H. Kansas City *Star,* Kansas City, Mo.

THOMPSON, GEORGE *Banker,* Fort Worth, Tex.

THOMPSON, M. E. *Secretary to Former Gov. Arnall* and *Lt. Governor,* Atlanta, Ga.

THOMPSON, VIRGIL *Composer, Music Critic,* New York City

THYE, EDWARD J. *Senator* from Minnesota, St. Paul, Minn.

TINGLEY, CLYDE *Mayor,* Albuquerque, N. M.

TOBIN, MAURICE J. *Former Mayor* of Boston & *Governor* of Mass., Boston, Mass.

TOOMBES, GUY Hotel Utah, Salt Lake City, Utah

TRAPARISH, GABRIEL *Restaurateur,* Meaderville, Mont.

TRAUERMAN, CARL J. *Mining Engineer,* Butte, Mont.

TRUMAN, HARRY S. *President of the United States,* Washington, D. C.

TUCKER, HOMER S. *Division Manager,* Safeway Stores, Salt Lake City, Utah

TUCKER, MRS. NION San Francisco, Calif.

TUCKER, RAYMOND R. *Prof. of Chemical Engineering,* Washington Univ., St. Louis, Mo.

TURNER, HENRY C. *Chairman,* State Commission on Anti-Discrimination, Albany, N. Y.

TURNER, LILLIAN *Journalist,* Phoenix, Ariz.

TUTTLE, DONALD D. New Hampshire State Planning & Development Comm., Concord, N. H.

UREY, PROF. HAROLD C. *Chemist. Professor* University of Chicago, Chicago, Ill.

VANDENBERG, ARTHUR H. *Senator* from Michigan, Washington, D. C.

VANDENBERG, WILLIS G. Triple Ink Publications, Sheldon, Iowa

VANDERCOOK, JOHN W. *Radio Commentator,* New York City

VILLARD, OSWALD GARRISON *Publicist. Former Editor, Nation,* New York City

VINSON, FRED M. *Chief Justice,* Supreme Court, Washington, D. C.

VIVIAN, JOHN C. *Ex-Governor* of Colorado, Denver, Colo.

VOGEL, FRANK A. Non-Partisan League. *Former Mgr.* Bank of N. D., Bismarck, N. Dak.

von MEYSENBUG, HEDA New Orleans, La.

VOORHIS, JERRY *Former Congressman* from Calif., Washington, D. C.

WADE, CHARLES *Biologist. Supt. of Fishways,* Bonneville Dam, Ore.

WADSWORTH, JAMES W. *Congressman* from New York, Washington, D. C.

WAGNER, ROBERT F. *Senator* from New York, Washington, D. C.

WALDECK, COUNTESS *Writer,* New York City

WALL, SGT. JOHN L. Bonneville Dam, Ore.

WALL, JUDGE LUCIUS U. S. Circuit Court of Appeals, Sioux Falls, S. D.

WALLACE, HENRY A. *Former Secretary of Commerce. Former Vice President of the United States. Editor, New Republic,* New York City

WALLACE, TOM *Editor,* Louisville *Times,* Louisville, Ky.

WALLACE, WILLIAM R. *Attorney. Former Member,* Dem. Natl. Committee, Salt Lake City, Utah

WALNE, WALTER *Attorney at law,* Houston, Tex.

WALSH, H. A. *President,* Rotary Club, El Paso, Tex.

WALSH, PATRICK *Late Fire Commissioner,* New York City

WALTHALL, DR. J. H. *Asst. Chief Research & Development,* TVA, Wilson Dam, Ala.

WANGER, WALTER *Motion Picture Producer,* Hollywood, Calif.

WARDEN, O. S. *Publisher,* Great Falls *Tribune,* Great Falls, Mont.

WARING, THOMAS R. *Managing Editor, News & Courier,* Charleston, S. C.

WARNER, JACK *Motion Picture Producer,* Hollywood, Calif.

WARREN, ROBERT E. *State Publicity Director,* Denver, Colo.

WATSON, KENT Miami *Daily News,* Miami, Fla.

WATTS, RICHARD JR. *Author. Dramatic Critic,* New York City

WAYLAND, ROY Valley National Bank, Phoenix, Ariz.

WAYNE, FRANCES *Writer,* Denver *Post,* Denver, Colo.

WEAVER, DON E. *Ed. & Pub.* Fort Worth *Press,* Fort Worth, Tex.

WEBSTER, R. L. *Asst. Dir. of Information,* Dept. of Agriculture, Washington, D. C.

WEEKS, EDWARD JR. *Editor, Atlantic Monthly,* Boston, Mass.

WEIL, LEONARD D. Hackensack, N. J.

WEIL, TRUDA T. *Educational Aide to ex-Mayor La Guardia,* New York City

WEISS, SEYMOUR Hotel Roosevelt, New Orleans, La.

WELCH, EARL *Supreme Court Justice,* Oklahoma City, Okla.

WELLES, ORSON *Actor,* Beverly Hills, Calif.

WELLES, SUMNER *Former Under Secretary of State,* Washington, D. C.

WELLS, BETTY *Commentator,* Station KRNT, Des Moines, Iowa

WELLS, WILLIAM L. *Superintendent,* Gold Mine, Helena, Mont.

WELTZIN, J. F. *Dean,* School of Education, University of Idaho, Moscow, Idaho

WESLEY, CARTER *Publisher,* Houston *Informer,* Houston, Tex.

WEST, OLIVER *Exec. Vice Pres.,* Boeing Aircraft Co., Seattle, Wash.

WESTLEY, MARGARET Foreign Economic Administration, Washington, D. C.

WHEELER, AL State Highway Patrol, Cheyenne, Wyo.

WHEELER, BURTON K. *Ex-Senator* from Montana, Washington, D. C.

WHERRY, KENNETH S. *Senator* from Nebraska, Washington, D. C.

WHITTENBURG, S. B. *Editor,* Amarillo *Times,* Amarillo, Tex.

WIGGINS, D. M. *President,* Texas College of Mines & Metallurgy, El Paso, Tex.

WIGGINS, J. RUSSELL *Former Editor,* St. Paul *Pioneer Press. Asst. to Publisher,* N. Y. *Times,* New York City

WILKINS, JOSEPHINE Citizens' Fact-Finding Committee, Atlanta, Ga.

WILLIAMS, ALBERT *Attorney. Historian,* Nashville, Tenn.

WILLIAMS, ALFRED JR. *Pres.* A. Williams & Co., Booksellers, Raleigh, N. C.

WILLIAMS, PHILLIP H. Boston Club, New Orleans, La.

WILLIAMS, SID *Dir.* Young Peoples' Division, Democratic National Committee, Atlanta, Ga.

WILLS, WILLIAM H. *Late Gov.* of Vermont, Montpelier, Vt.

WILSON, ELEANOR *Newspaperwoman,* Fort Worth, Tex.

WILSON, M. L. *Former Under-Sec'y of Agriculture. Dir. of Extension Services,* Dept. of Agriculture, Washington, D. C.

WILSON, WILLIAM *Commissioner of Housing & Buildings,* New York City

WINCHELL, WALTER *Columnist and Radio Commentator,* New York City

WINN, FRANK United Automobile Workers (CIO), Detroit, Mich.

WINSHIP, LAURENCE L. *Managing Editor,* Boston *Globe,* Boston, Mass.

WISHART, ROBERT *Pres.* Hennepin County Council of CIO, Minneapolis, Minn.

WITMAN, SHEPHERD Council on World Affairs, Cleveland, Ohio

WOODS, MARK *Pres.* American Broadcasting Co., New York City

WORTHAM, GUS. *Pres.* American General Insurance Co., Houston, Tex.

WYATT, WILSON W. *Former U. S. Housing Expediter.* Louisville, Ky.

WYLER, KARL O. *Gen. Manager,* Station KTSM, El Paso, Tex.

YOUNG, CHARLES H. *Acting Director,* Dept. of Chemical Engineering, TVA, Wilson Dam, Ala.

ZANUCK, DARRYL F. 20th Century-Fox Film Corp., Santa Monica, Calif.

To which, finally, let me add assorted anonymous sharecroppers, railway conductors, waiters in hamburger stands, airplane pilots and stewardesses, newspaper reporters, school children white and Negro, taxi drivers, tenant farmers, traffic cops, soil experts, aircraft engineers, housewives, department store clerks, shipyard workers, shoeshine boys, and directors of publicity.

Bibliography

〜〜〜

Actually I used very little from these books, with certain positive exceptions. I read in them for background, saturation, mood. Every writer evolves, eventually, his own technique; he has to solve his own problems in his own peculiar way. I cannot learn much from reading except to fill gaps. I have to feel, hear, see. I read about a state or section of the country or a problem after, not before, I wrote my own text, as a general rule. Thus I had the sometimes pleasant and sometimes disconcerting experience of learning what I myself had missed.

Among works of reference I must mention first the long series of volumes in the American Guide Series, which, though of unequal merit, are all of substantial value if only because nothing exists like them. To save space, I do not include the separate state titles below. I read in or glanced at all forty-eight volumes on the states except those on Utah, the Dakotas, Georgia, Idaho, and Virginia, which were unobtainable when I wanted them. Also let me give especial credit to the *Home Book of Quotations*, edited by Burton Stevenson, and Bartlett's *Familiar Quotations* as revised by Christopher Morley and Louella D. Everett; many of the quotations I used as chapter or section heads came from these elephantine and invaluable tomes. I used the *Encyclopaedia Britannica* steadily, the *Dictionary of American Biography*, the *World Almanac* of course, the *Statistical Abstract of the United States*, various other almanacs and handbooks, and a useful volume published in Chicago by the Council of State Governments, called *The Book of the States, 1945-1946.*

ADAMIC, LOUIS. *Dynamite.* New York, 1934.

ADAMS, JAMES TRUSLOW. *Atlas of American History.* New York, 1943.

———. *The Epic of America.* New York, 1941.

ADAMS, RAMON F. *Western Words.* Norman, 1944.

AGELASTO, A. M. & OTHERS. *The Cotton Situation.* Washington, 1922.

AIKEN, GEORGE D. *Speaking from Vermont.* New York, 1938.

ALEXANDER, DE ALVA S. *Four Famous New Yorkers.* New York, 1923.

ALLEN, FREDERICK LEWIS. *Only Yesterday.* New York, 1931.

AMERICAN GUIDE SERIES. *Louisville.* New York, 1940.

———. *New Orleans City Guide.* Boston, 1938.

———. *New York City Guide.* New York, 1939.

———. *Provo, Pioneer Mormon City.* Portland, 1942.

ANDREWS, WAYNE. *Battle for Chicago.* New York, 1946.

ANIOL, CLAUDE B. *San Antonio.* New York, 1942.

ANONYMOUS. *The Mirrors of Wall Street.* New York, 1933.

ARNALL, ELLIS GIBBS. *The Shore Dimly Seen.* Philadelphia, 1946.

ASBURY, HERBERT. *Chicago, Gem of the Prairie.* Garden City, 1942.

SHENHURST, JOHN & RUTH L. *All About Chicago.* Boston, 1933.

THERTON, GERTRUDE. *California, an Intimate History.* New York, 1914.

BAEDEKER, KARL. *The United States.* London, 1893.

BALDWIN, HANSON & STONE, SHEPARD, eds. *We Saw It Happen.* New York, 1938.

BARTON, BRUCE. *A Parade of the States.* Garden City, 1932.

BASSO, HAMILTON. *Mainstream.* New York, 1943.

BEARD, CHARLES A. *American Government and Politics.* New York, 1941.

BEARD, CHARLES A. & MARY R. *A Basic History of the U.S.* New York, 1944.

BENÉT, STEPHEN VINCENT. *America.* New York, 1944.

BENNETT, ARNOLD. *Those United States.* London, 1926.

BERGE, WENDELL. *Economic Freedom for the West.* Lincoln, 1946.

BERLE, A. A. JR. & MEANS, G. C. *The Modern Corporation and Private Property.* New York, 1932.

BINGAY, MALCOLM W. *Detroit Is My Own Home Town.* Indianapolis, 1946.

BINNS, ARCHIE. *The Roaring Land.* New York, 1942.

BLIVEN, BRUCE, & MEZERIK, A. G. *What the Informed Citizen Needs to Know.* New York, 1945.

BOATRIGHT, MODY C. & DONALD DAY, eds. *From Hell to Breakfast.* Austin, 1944.

BOTKIN, B. A., ed. *A Treasury of American Folklore.* New York, 1944.

BRADFORD, SAMUEL. *History of Plimouth Plantation.* Boston, 1899.

BRODIE, FAWN M. *No Man Knows My History.* New York, 1945.

BROGAN, D. W. *Politics and Law in the U.S.* Cambridge, England, 1941.

———. *The American Character.* New York, 1944.

———. *U.S.A.* London, 1943.

BROMFIELD, LOUIS. *Pleasant Valley.* New York, 1943.

BROOKE, RUPERT. *Letters from America.* New York, 1916.

BROOKS, VAN WYCK. *The Flowering of New England.* New York, 1936.

———. *New England: Indian Summer.* New York, 1940.

———. *The World of Washington Irving.* Philadelphia, 1944.

BRYCE, JAMES. *The American Commonwealth.* New York, 1901.

BURT, STRUTHERS. *Philadelphia, Holy Experiment.* Garden City, 1945.

CARMER, CARL. *The Hudson.* New York, 1939.

———. *Stars Fell on Alabama.* New York, 1934.

CASH, W. J. *The Mind of the South.* New York, 1941.

CASS, FRANK HADLEY, ed. *Looking Northwest.* Portland, 1938.

CHASE, STUART. *Democracy under Pressure.* New York, 1945.

———. *Rich Land, Poor Land.* New York, 1936.

———. *For This We Fought.* New York, 1946.

CHRISTENSEN, A. N. & KIRKPATRICK, E. M., eds. *Running the Country.* New York, 1946.

935

Civic Assn. of Northeastern Minnesota. *Minnesota, a Duped State.* Hibbing, 1942.

CLARK, THOMAS D. *The Kentucky.* New York, 1942.

CLELAND, ROBERT GLASS. *From Wilderness to Empire.* New York, 1944.

CLUGSTON, W. G. *Facts You Should Know about Kansas.* Girard, 1945.

———. *Rascals in Democracy.* New York, 1940.

CLYMER, FLOYD. *Motor Scrapbook.* Los Angeles, 1944.

COHN, DAVID L. *Combustion on Wheels.* Boston, 1944.

COLBOURNE, MAURICE. *America and Britain.* London, 1943.

COLLINS, V. LANSING. *Princeton, Past and Present.* Princeton, 1945.

COMFORT, WILLIAM WISTAR. *Just Among Friends: The Quaker Way of Life.* Philadelphia, 1945.

COMMAGER, HENRY STEELE & NEVINS, ALLAN. *The Heritage of America.* Boston, 1945.

Commission on Interracial Cooperation. *America's Tenth Man.* Atlanta, 1944.

CORLE, EDWIN. *Desert Country.* New York, 1941.

CROSS, WILBUR L. *Connecticut Yankee.* New Haven, 1943.

CURTI, MERLE. *The Growth of American Thought.* New York, 1943.

CURTIS, CHARLES P., JR. '& GREENSLET, FERRIS, eds. *The Practical Cogitator.* Boston, 1945.

DABNEY, VIRGINIUS. *Below the Potomac.* New York, 1942.

DALE, EDWARD EVERETT. *Cow Country.* Norman, 1943.

DANIELS, JONATHAN. *A Southerner Discovers New England.* New York, 1940.

———. *A Southerner Discovers the South.* New York, 1943.

DAVENPORT, RUSSELL. *My Country.* New York, 1944.

DAVIS, CLYDE BRION. *The Arkansas.* New York, 1940.

DAVIS, M. E. M. *Under Six Flags.* Dallas, 1897.

DEBO, ANGIE. *Prairie City.* New York, 1944.

DICKENS, CHARLES. *American Notes.* London, 1842.

DOBIE, J. FRANK, ed. *Coffee in the Gourd.* Austin, 1935.

———. *Coronado's Children.* New York, 1930.

———. *The Longhorns.* Boston, 1941.

———. *A Texan in England.* Boston, 1945.

DONNELLY, THOMAS C., ed. *Rocky Mountain Politics.* Albuquerque, 1940.

DOS PASSOS, JOHN. *State of the Nation.* Boston, 1944.

———. *U.S.A.* New York, 1938.

DOUGLAS, C. L. *Cattle Kings of Texas.* Dallas, 1939.

DRAKE, ST. CLAIR & CAYTON, HORACE R. *Black Metropolis.* New York, 1945.

DRESSLER, ALBERT. *Emperor Norton.* San Francisco, 1927.

DUFFUS, R. L. & KRUTCH, CHARLES. *The Valley and Its People.* New York, 1944.

DUGGAN, I. W. & CHAPMAN, P. W. *Round the World With Cotton.* Washington, 1941.

DUTTON, WILLIAM S. *Du Pont: One Hundred and Forty Years.* New York, 1942.

EMBREE, EDWIN R. *American Negroes: A Handbook.* New York, 1942.

———. *Thirteen against the Odds.* New York, 1945.

ERNST, MORRIS L. *The Ultimate Power.* Garden City, 1937.

EVERETT, MARSHALL. *The Great Chicago Theater Disaster.* Chicago, 1904.

FARIS, JOHN T. *Seeing the Middle West.* Philadelphia, 1923.

Farm Tenancy Committee. *Farm Tenancy in Alabama.* Wetumpka, 1944.

FARROW, M. H. *The Texas Democrats.* San Antonio, 1944.

FAULKNER, H. U. & KEPNER, TYLER. *America: Its History and People.* New York, 1942.

Federal Trade Commission. *Report on Motor Vehicle Industry.* Washington, 1940.

FERGUSSON, ERNA. *Our Southwest.* New York, 1940.

Fifty-Fifth California Legislature Report. *Un-American Activities in California.* Sacramento, 1943.

FINLETTER, THOMAS K. *Can Representative Government Do the Job?* New York, 1945.

FISHER, ANNE B. *The Salinas.* New York, 1945.

FITZPATRICK, EDWARD A. *McCarthy of Wisconsin.* New York, 1944.

FOWLER, GENE. *Timber Line.* New York, 1933.

FOX, CHARLES DONALD. *The Truth about Florida.* New York, 1925.

FRANKLIN, JAY. *LaGuardia.* New York, 1937.

FULLER, GEORGE W. *A History of the Pacific Northwest.* New York, 1945.

GARRETTE, EVE. *A Political Handbook for Women.* Garden City, 1944.

GEFFS, MARY L. *Under Ten Flags.* Greeley, 1938.

GELLERMANN, WILLIAM. *Martin Dies.* New York, 1944.

GEORGE, W. L. *Hail Columbia!* New York, 1921.

GILFILLAN, ARCHER B. *Sheep.* Boston, 1936.

GLASSCOCK, C. B. *The Big Bonanza.* Portland, 1931.

GLAZIER, WILLARD. *Peculiarities of American Cities.* Philadelphia, 1885.

GLOVER, J. G. & CORNELL, W. B. *The Development of American Industries.* New York, 1936.

GODDARD, PLINY EARLE. *Indians of the Northwest Coast.* New York, 1934.

GOODMAN, JACK, ed. *While You Were Gone.* New York, 1946.

GOULD, CHARLES N. *Oklahoma Place Names.* Norman, 1933.

GRAVES, JOHN TEMPLE. *The Fighting South.* New York, 1943.

GRAY, JAMES. *The Illinois.* New York, 1940.

———. *Pine, Stream and Prairie.* New York, 1945.

GRUENING, ERNEST, ed. *These United States: A Symposium.* New York, 1923.

GUYTON, PEARL VIVIAN. *The Story of Connelly's Tavern.* Jackson, 1942.

HAFEN, LEROY R. & ANN W. *Colorado.* Denver, 1944.

HALEY, J. EVETTS. *Charles Schreiner, General Merchandise.* Austin, 1944.

HAMMER, LAURA V. *Short Grass and Longhorns.* Norman, 1945.

HANDLIN, OSCAR. *Boston's Immigrants 1790-1865.* Cambridge, 1941.

HANNA, PHIL TOWNSEND. *California through Four Centuries.* New York, 1935.

HANSEN, HARRY. *Midwest Portraits.* New York, 1923.

———. *The Chicago.* New York, 1942.

HARPER, ALLAN G., CORDOVA, ANDREW R., OBERO KALERNO. *Man & Resources in the Middle Rı Grande Valley.* Albuquerque, 1943.

HASKIN, FREDERIC J. *The American Governmen* New York, 1941.

HATCHER, HARLAN. *The Great Lakes.* New York, 1944.

——. *Lake Erie.* Indianapolis, 1945.

HAVIGHURST, WALTER. *Land of Promise: The Story of the Northwest Territory.* New York, 1946.

HAYSEED, LADY. *If the Prospect Pleases.* Norman, 1945.

HEBARD, GRACE RAYMOND. *The Pathbreakers from River to Ocean.* Glendale, 1940.

HERMAN, CHARLES H. *Recollections of Life and Doings in Chicago.* Chicago, 1945.

HINES, GORDON. *Alfalfa Bill, an Intimate Biography.* Oklahoma City, 1932.

HITCH, C. J. *America's Economic Strength.* London, 1941.

HOLBROOK, DONALD. *The Boston Trustee.* Boston, 1937.

HOLBROOK, STEWART H. *Iron Brew.* New York, 1939.

HOLZWORTH, JOHN M. *The Fighting Governor: The Story of William Langer.* Chicago, 1938.

HORN, STANLEY F. *This Fascinating Lumber Business.* Indianapolis, 1943.

HOUSE, BOYCE. *I Give You Texas.* San Antonio, 1943.

——. *Oil Boom.* Caldwell, 1941.

——. *Tall Tales from Texas.* San Antonio, 1944.

HOWARD, JOSEPH KINSEY. *Montana, High, Wide and Handsome.* New Haven, 1943.

HUBERMAN, LEO. *We, the People.* New York, 1932.

HUETTIG, MAE D. *Economic Control of the Motion Picture Industry.* Philadelphia, 1944.

HUMBLE, EMMA. *The Jayhawker Book.* Chicago, 1935.

HUNTER, MILTON R. *Brigham Young, the Colonizer.* Salt Lake City, 1941.

HUTTON, GRAHAM. *Midwest at Noon.* Chicago, 1946.

HUXLEY, ALDOUS. *Jesting Pilate.* London, 1930.

HYND, ALAN. *The Giant Killers.* New York, 1945.

JACKSON, JOSEPH HENRY, ed. *Continent's End.* New York, 1944.

JACKSON, JOSEPH H. & SUYDAM, E. G. *Anybody's Gold.* New York, 1941.

JAEGER, EDMUND C. *The California Deserts.* Stanford University, 1938.

JAMES, HENRY. *The American Scene.* New York, 1946.

JAMES, MARQUIS. *The Raven.* Garden City, 1929.

JAMES, WILL.* *Cowboys, North and South.* New York, 1923.

JOHNSON, GERALD W. *American Heroes and Hero-Worship.* New York, 1943.

JOHNSON, GERALD W., KENT, FRANK R., MENCKEN, H. L., OWENS, HAMILTON. *The Sun-Papers of Baltimore.* New York, 1937.

JOHNSON, ROBERT C. *John McLoughlin, Patriarch of the Northwest.* Portland, 1935.

JOSEPHSON, MATTHEW. *The Robber Barons.* New York, 1934.

KANE, HARNETT T. *Louisiana Hayride.* New York, 1941.

KARSNER, DAVID. *Silver Dollar: The Story of the Tabors.* New York, 1932.

KENNY, ROBERT W. *History and Proposed Settlement, Claims of California Indians.* Sacramento, 1944.

KIPLING, RUDYARD. *From Sea to Sea.* Garden City, 1923.

KUPPER, WINIFRED. *The Golden Hoof.* New York, 1945.

LAHNE, HERBERT J. *The Cotton Mill Worker.* New York, 1944.

LANE, ALLEN STANLEY. *Emperor Norton.* Caldwell, 1939.

LAUGHLIN, CLARA E. *So You're Seeing New England.* Boston, 1940.

LEADER, JOHN. *Oregon through Alien Eyes.* Portland, 1932.

LEIGHTON, GEORGE R. *Five Cities.* New York, 1939.

LEWIS, LLOYD & SMITH, HENRY JUSTIN. *Chicago, a History of Its Reputation.* New York, 1944.

LEWIS, OSCAR & HALL, CARROLL D. *Bonanza Inn.* New York, 1939.

LILIENTHAL, DAVID E. *TVA: Democracy on the March.* New York, 1944.

LINDBERG, J. C. & GUNDERSON, GERTRUDE B. *An Anthology of South Dakota Poetry.* Mitchell, 1935.

LOGAN, RAYFORD W., ed. *What the Negro Wants.* Chapel Hill, 1944.

LONG, HANIEL. *Piñon Country.* New York, 1941

——. *Pittsburgh Memoranda.* Santa Fé, 1935.

LONG, HUEY PIERCE. *My First Days in the White House.* Harrisburg, 1935.

LORD, CLIFFORD L. *Historical Atlas of the U.S.* New York, 1944.

LUNDBERG, FERDINAND. *America's Sixty Families.* New York, 1940.

——. *Imperial Hearst.* New York, 1936.

LYDGATE, WILLIAM A. *What America Thinks.* New York, 1944.

McGRAW, WILLIAM. *Professional Politicians.* Washington, 1940.

McKAY, S. S. *W. Lee O'Daniel and Texas Politics, 1938-42.* Lubbock, 1944.

McKELLAR, KENNETH. *Tennessee Senators.* Kingsport, 1942.

MacLEISH, ARCHIBALD. *American Opinion and the War.* New York, 1942.

——. *America Was Promises.* New York, 1939.

——. *The American Story.* New York, 1944.

——. *Land of the Free.* New York, 1938.

——. *A Time to Act.* Boston, 1943.

——. *A Time to Speak.* Boston, 1941.

McWILLIAMS, CAREY. *Brothers under the Skin.* Boston, 1945.

——. *Factories in the Field.* Boston, 1944.

——. *Ill Fares the Land.* Boston, 1944.

——. *Southern California Country.* New York, 1946.

MARKEY, MORRIS. *This Country of Yours.* Boston, 1932.

MARQUIS, SAMUEL S. *Henry Ford.* Boston, 1923.

MEARNS, JOHN S. ed. *The New York Red Book, 1945.* Albany, 1945.

MECHEM, KIRKE. *The Mythical Jayhawk.* Topeka, 1944.

MENCKEN, H. L. *The American Language.* New York, 1937.

——. *Americana, 1925.* London, 1925.

——. *Making a President.* New York, 1932.

——. *Prejudices, 2nd Series.* New York, 1920.

——. *Supplement One: The American Language.* New York, 1945.

MENEFEE, SELDEN. *Assignment: U.S.A.* New York, 1943.

MEYER, AGNES E. *Journey through Chaos.* New York, 1943.

MEZERIK, A. G. *Revolt of the South and West.* New York, 1946.

MILLER, JAMES MARTIN. *The Amazing Story of Henry Ford.* 1922.

MOLEY, RAYMOND. *The Hays Office.* Indianapolis, 1945.

MONTGOMERY, R. H. *The Brimstone Game: Monopoly in Action.* New York, 1940.

MOON, BUCKLIN, ed. *Primer for White Folks.* New York, 1945.

MORGAN, DALE L. *The Humboldt.* New York, 1943.

MOWAT, R. B. *The United States of America.* London, 1938.

MÜNSTERBERG, HUGO. *The Americans.* Garden City, 1914.

MURRAY, WILLIAM H. *Uncle Sam Needs a Doctor.* Boston, 1940.

MYERS, GUSTAVUS. *History of the Great American Fortunes.* New York, 1936.

MYRDAL, GUNNAR. *An American Dilemma.* New York, 1944.

NEUBERGER, RICHARD L. *Our Promised Land.* New York, 1939.

NEVINS, ALLAN & COMMAGER, HENRY STEELE. *The Pocket History of the United States.* New York, 1943.

NORRIS, GEORGE W. *Fighting Liberal.* New York, 1945.

ODUM, HOWARD W. *Race and Rumors of Race.* Chapel Hill, 1943.

——. *Southern Regions.* Chapel Hill, 1936.

Office of War Information. *A Handbook of the U.S.A.* Washington, 1944.

OGDEN, AUGUST RAYMOND. *The Dies Committee.* Washington, 1945.

OGG, F. A. & RAY, P. O. *Essentials of American Government.* New York, 1932.

OLDER, FREMONT. *My Own Story.* New York, 1926.

OTTLEY, ROI. *New World A-Coming.* Cleveland, 1945.

PARKES, H. B. *Recent America.* New York, 1941.

PARRINGTON, VERNON LOUIS. *Main Currents in American Thought.* New York, 1930.

PATTON, JACK & ROSENFELD, JOHN JR. *Texas History Movies.* Dallas, 1943.

PEATTIE, DONALD CULROSS. *Journey into America.* Boston, 1943.

PEATTIE, RODERICK, ed. *The Great Smokies and the Blue Ridge.* New York, 1943.

PEPPER, GEORGE WHARTON. *Philadelphia Lawyer.* Philadelphia, 1944.

PERCY, WILLIAM ALEXANDER. *Lanterns on the Levee.* New York, 1945.

PERRY, GEORGE SESSIONS. *Texas, a World In Itself.* New York, 1942.

PERRY, JENNINGS. *Democracy Begins at Home.* Philadelphia, 1944.

PETERSON, FLORENCE. *American Labor Unions.* New York, 1945.

POE, JOHN W. *The Death of Billy the Kid.* Boston, 1933.

POLLARD, LANCASTER. *A History of the State of Washington.* Portland, 1941.

PRATT, WALLACE E. *Oil in the Earth.* Lawrence, 1943.

PRINGLE, HENRY F. *Theodore Roosevelt.* New York, 1931.

QUINTANILLA, LUIS. *A Latin American Speaks.* New York, 1943.

RANDOLPH, JOHN. *Texas Brags.* Houston, 1945.

RANKIN, REBECCA. *Guide to the Municipal Government, City of New York.* New York, 1939.

RICHARDSON, BEN. *Great American Negroes.* New York, 1945.

RICHARDSON, RUPERT NORVAL. *Texas, the Lone Star State.* New York, 1943.

RINGEL, FRED J., ed. *America As Americans See It.* New York, 1932.

ROBERTSON, BEN. *Red Hills and Cotton.* New York, 1942.

ROSS, NANCY WILSON. *Farthest Reach.* New York, 1944.

ROSTEN, LEO C. *Hollywood.* New York, 1941.

RUSSELL, ELBERT. *The History of Quakerism.* New York, 1942.

SALTER, J. T., ed. *Public Men In and Out of Office.* Chapel Hill, 1946.

SANCHEZ, NELLIE V. *Stories of the States.* New York, 1941.

SAUNDERS, HILARY ST. GEORGE. *Pioneers! O Pioneers!* New York, 1944.

SAWYER, EUGENE T. *Tiburcio Vasquez.* Oakland, 1944.

SAXON, LYLE. *Fabulous New Orleans.* New York, 1928.

SCHAFER, JOSEPH. *History of the Pacific Northwest.* New York, 1942.

SCHOENBERNER, FRANZ (Simplicissimus). *Confessions of a European Intellectual.* New York, 1946.

SHERMAN, GEN. WILLIAM TECUMSEH. *Recollections of California, 1846-61,* Oakland, 1945.

SIEGFRIED, ANDRÉ. *America Comes of Age.* London, 1927.

SINCLAIR, UPTON. *I, Governor of California.* Los Angeles, 1933.

SMITH, HENRY JUSTIN. *Chicago, a Portrait.* New York, 1931.

SMITH, J. RUSSELL. *North America.* New York, 1925.

SMITH, LUCY MACK. *History of Joseph Smith.* Salt Lake City, 1945.

STEARNS, HAROLD E., ed. *America Now.* New York, 1938.

——. *Civilization in the United States.* New York, 1922.

STEED, HAL. *Georgia: Unfinished State.* New York, 1942.

STEGNER, WALLACE. *Mormon Country.* New York, 1942.

——. *One Nation.* Boston, 1945.

STEWART, GEORGE R. *Names on the Land.* New York, 1945.

STREET, JULIAN. *Abroad at Home.* New York, 1914.

STRUNSKY, SIMEON. *No Mean City.* New York, 1944.

SWING, RAYMOND. *Forerunners of American Fascism.* New York, 1935.

TAIT, SAMUEL W., JR. *The Wildcatters.* Princeton, 1946.

Texas Almanac, 1945-46. Dallas. 1945.

THOMAS, LOWELL. *Tall Stories.* New York, 1945.

THOMPSON, CHARLES MINER. *Independent Vermont.* Boston, 1942.

THOMPSON, DOROTHY. *In Support of the President.* Stamford, 1945.

THRALL, HOMER S. *History of Methodism in Texas.* Houston, 1872.

TOCQUEVILLE, ALEXIS DE. *Democracy in America.* New York, 1945.

TOWNE, C. W. *Her Majesty Montana.* Butte, 1939.

TRENT, LUCY C. *John Neely Bryan, Founder of Dallas.* Dallas, 1936.

TWAIN, MARK. *Life on the Mississippi.* New York, 1946.

TYLER, J. E. *A Short History of America.* London, 1940.

ULMANN, ALBERT. *New Yorkers: Stuyvesant to Roosevelt.* New York, 1928.

U. S. Department of Agriculture. *Facts About Cotton.* Washington, 1940.

U. S. Government. *Congressional Directory.* Washington, 1945.

U. S. Government. *U. S. Government Manual, 1945.* Washington, 1945.

U. S. House of Representatives. *Cotton: Hearings before the Subcommittee of the Committee on Agriculture.* Washington, 1944.

VANCE, RUPERT B. *The South's Place in the Nation.* Public Affairs Pamphlet, New York, 1944.

VAN DEVANDER, CHARLES. *The Big Bosses.* New York, 1944.

VESTAL, STANLEY. *Short Grass Country.* New York, 1941.

VIERTEL, WILLIAM. *City of New York Official Directory.* New York, 1944.

WARING, P. ALSTON & TELLER, W. M. *Roots in the Earth.* New York, 1943.

WARNER, C. A. *Texas Oil and Gas Since 1543.* Houston, 1939.

WATT, ROBERTA FRYE. *Four Wagons West.* Portland, 1941.

WEBB, WALTER PRESCOTT. *Divided We Stand.* Austin, 1944.

——. *The Great Plains.* Boston, 1936.

WELLS, H. G. *The Future in America.* New York, 1906.

WHITE, OWEN P. *The Autobiography of a Durable Sinner.* New York, 1942.

——. *Texas, an Informal Biography.* New York, 1945.

WHITE, WILLIAM ALLEN. *Autobiography.* New York, 1946.

WHITEMAN, LUTHER H. & LEWIS, SAMUEL L. *Glory Roads.* New York, 1936.

WHITNEY, WILLIAM DWIGHT. *Who Are the Americans?* London, 1941.

WIDTSOE, JOHN A. *Program of the Church of Jesus Christ of Latter-Day Saints.* Salt Lake City, 1937.

WISH, HARVEY. *Contemporary America.* New York, 1945.

WISSLER, CLARK. *Indians of the U.S.* Garden City, 1944.

Works Projects Administration. *Copper Camp.* New York, 1943.

WRIGHT, SEWELL PEASLEE, ed. *Chicago Murders.* New York, 1945.

YOUNG, LEVI EDGAR. *The Founding of Utah.* New York, 1923.

As to periodicals my debt is manifest, and is duly acknowledged at various points in the text. In particular I read the *Congressional Record, Fortune,* the *New Republic, Harper's Magazine,* the *New York Times,* the *New York Herald Tribune,* which I think is the best newspaper in the United States, *Time, Life, PM,* and the *New York Post.*

Sources

Let me specifically acknowledge finally some special sources of information which, for fear of cluttering the text too much, I did not identify by footnotes. They are tabulated by chapter, and not by page as would have been more proper and convenient, because of last-minute exigencies in going to press.

Foreword. The quotation from F. Scott Fitzgerald is from *The Crackup,* edited by Edmund Wilson, New Directions, New York, p. 197; that from Malcolm Cowley is from his beautiful poem "The Long Voyage," originally published in *Poetry, a Magazine of Verse.* Some of the statistical material on American superlatives and the like comes from *A Handbook of the United States of America,* listed in the Bibliography above. As to the Declaration of Independence, the Constitution, and the words "democracy," "republic," etc., cf. Beard, *Basic History,* pp. 121, 210, 223. The detail about artificial limbs is from *PM,* May 7, 1946. Source for the GI poll on the Germans is *Time,* February 4, 1946; the figures about women's shoes are from *Life,* April 8, 1946 and about jewels, horse racing, and national income from the New York *Times,* December 10, 1945 and July 23 and August 8, 1946. Details about vegetarians and gamblers are from Lydgate, *What America Thinks,* p. 79. Figures on pulp magazines are from *Time,* August 6, 1946, and about doughnuts and ice cream from *Look,* April 4, 1944. The venereal disease rate is from *PM,* August 5, 1946. Basic sources for my chart are the *World Almanac, The Book of the States,* the *Statistical Abstract of the United States,* and the New York *Times.*

Chapter 1. The quotation from John Muir about the Upper Sonora is from *California* in the American Guide Series, p. 24. The possibility that Fascism or Communism might arrive in California before any other American state has been noted by R. L. Duffus in the New York *Times.* The phrase "the first great migration of the automobile age" is from Carey McWilliams. I am uncertain of the source of the phrase "Detroit of airplanes." For some background about early California I am indebted to *California, op. cit.,* including the phrase "the greatest mass movement of people since the Crusades" and the quotations from Dennis Kearney. The figure 130,000,000 acres—the amount of railway land grants—is from James Truslow Adams' *Epic of America,* p. 278. Among sources for material about the early railway days are Oscar Lewis's admirable *The Big Four* and Fremont Older's *Autobiography;* see Lewis in particular for details about Leland Stanford, including the item about Ambrose Bierce. The quotation from *Life* about free sunshine is from the issue of October 22, 1945. That from R. G. Cleland's *From Wilderness to Empire* is by permission of Alfred A. Knopf, Inc.

Chapter 2. The quotation from Rudyard Kipling is from *American Notes.* My description of the Point Lobos case follows that of *Time.* The detail about Mayor Lapham's manner of playing cards is from an article by Cuyler Greene in *Cosmopolitan,* January, 1945. The Bridges remark about the difference between the right to strike and its exercise is from Bartley C. Crum in the New York *Times,* June 3, 1945. The quotation describing how Bridges was hounded is from Max Lerner in *PM,* July 5, 1944. The detail that any person regularly employed may borrow from the Bank of America on his signature is from *Time,* April 15, 1946. The interviewer to whom Kenny mentioned California's "free-wheeling political setup" was Mary Morris of *PM.* Authority for the statement that 2 per cent of California landowners control one-fourth of the total state acreage is *California,* p. 68. The telegram to Hearst editors was published in *PM.*

Chapter 3. The phrase "imperial position" is from Bryce. Description of Los Angeles as "19 suburbs in search of a metropolis" is from H. L. Mencken; as a "circus without a tent" from McWilliams; and as "less a city than a perpetual convention" from George Sessions Perry, *Saturday*

Evening Post, December 15, 1945. The quotations from H. L. Mencken's *Americana*, in this chapter and elsewhere, are by his kind permission. Charles Van Devander estimates in *The Big Bosses* that Merriam interests spent $10,000,000 to beat Sinclair, and the *Time* quotation is from the issue of October 22, 1934. The phrase from Raymond Swing is in his *Forerunners of American Fascism*. For much about Central Valley see articles in the *Nation* by Carey McWilliams and Bruce Bliven in the *New Republic*. For tidewater oil in general see "Under Water Wealth" by Harold L. Ickes, *Collier's*, February 23, 1946. I have followed closely Alan Barth of the Washington *Post* (in the *Nation*, November 3, 1945) for details of what happened to the tidelands bill in Congress.

Chapter 4. The *Fortune* quotation is from "Adventures of Harry and Joe in Autoland," March, 1946. Much of the material in this chapter was supplied to me through the courtesy of Vance Fawcett of Kaiser Industries.

Chapter 5. The Phrase "easy-going, soft-shoe Pat" in description of Senator McCarran is from Harold Ickes. The item that the House of Representatives once had a "silver member" and that a "silver party" once existed is from *Nevada* in the American Guide Series, p. 49.

Chapter 6. The quotation from Daniel Webster is from *Farthest Reach*, by Nancy Wilson Ross, p. 19. Population figures for Portland are from *Fortune*, February, 1945. The slogans on Oregon ballots are from an article in the *Progressive*, March 4, 1946, by Richard L. Neuberger.

Chapter 7. Some details about Wayne Morse are from *This Man Morse*, a campaign biography.

Chapter 8. Some statistics about the Columbia River are from the *Encyclopaedia Britannica*. The anecdote about Rufus Wood is from *Time*, June 10, 1946. The quotation describing the PUD's is from an article by McAlister Coleman, "More Power for PUD's," in *Common Sense*, September, 1944.

Chapter 10. The quotation from Professor Turner is in *If the Prospect Pleases*, by Ladd Haystead, that from Daniel Webster is in *Rocky Mountain Politics*, and that from Professor Webb is from his magnificent *The Great Plains*, p. 17. Professor Brogan's point that Canada had no Indian wars is in *The American Character*, p. 22. Figures on the 100th meridian are from a pamphlet on reclamation published by the Department of the Interior, and some details on the voting strength of the mountain states are from the National Opinion Research Center, Denver. American words deriving from cattle culture may be found in *Arizona* in the WPA Series. Items about Montana weather are from *Copper Camp* (Hastings House, New York), pp. 296-300, and from J. Russell Smith's *North America*, p. 413. Statistics about both aluminum and copper are from Wendell Berge's *Economic Freedom for the West*, pp. 36-37. The quotation from C. Hartley Grattan is from his article, "The Future of the Pacific Coast," *Harper's Magazine*, March, 1945. Apparently the originator of the anecdote about the colonial citizen buried in "foreign" clothes, etc., was the eminent Georgia public servant Henry Grady. It appears in different form in Steed's *Georgia, an Unfinished State*, and *Fortune*.

Chapter 11. The quotation about graveyards is from *These United States*, edited by Ernest Gruening, Vol. II, p. 45. Among studies analyzing population decline in Montana is that of Professor O. E. Baker of the University of Maryland, address to Montana State College, July 5, 1945. The 45.2 per cent figure on foreign-born is from *Montana* in the WPA Series, p. 57. The quotation "Butte is the black heart of Montana" is from Joseph Kinsey Howard's *Montana, High, Wide and Handsome*, p. 85. *Fortune* printed two comprehensive articles on Anaconda, December, 1936, and January, 1937. Figures on rural electrification are from a speech by Congressman Wesley A. D'Ewart, *Congressional Record*, July 23, 1946, and the *Farmers Union News*, July 27, 1945. Details of the auction of the Milwaukee road are from the valuable chronology in *Copper Camp*, p. 297. The 18 per cent figure about ownership of land is from Howard, *op. cit.*, p. 5. It was the Miami (Florida) *News* that said of Wheeler, "Well, well, look who's talking!"

Chapter 12. The Platte River quotation is from *Life*, August 30, 1943, and details about the Missouri River are in *The Conquest of the Missouri*, by Joseph Miles Hanson. Tables of electric power rates are from a pamphlet, *MVA or Stagnation*, published in Denver by the National Farmers Union. Figures on electric light, bathtubs, and such are from an article in *Collier's*, December 9, 1944, "One More River to Boss," by Kyle Crichton. Some details of the Pick-Sloan plan are from Joseph Kinsey Howard's "Golden River" in *Harper's*, August, 1945; the quotation from Mr. Howard at the head of the chapter is from an article in *Common Sense*, "MVA, Valley of Hope," August, 1945.

Chapter 13. The quotation at the head of the chapter is from *These United States*, II, 73; that from Brigham Young is from Wallace Stegner's *Mormon Country*, p. 87. Details of the financial interests and directorships of President Smith are from *The Improvement Era*, July, 1945, p. 389. Figures on education in Utah as compared with other states were supplied to me by Burton K. Farnsworth, director of education, state of Utah. The quotation on tobacco is from *The Improvement Era*, June, 1945, p. 360. The quotation about Indians in frontier days is from *Provo* in the American Guide Series. Source for some material on the Utah Power Company is a memorandum by Bear, Stearns & Co., members of the New York Stock Exchange.

Chapter 14. Most statistics in this chapter are from *Colorado*, one of the two or three best of all the volumes in the American Guide Series. The item about Bonfils and the toilets is from "Revolution in Denver," by Roscoe Fleming, the *Nation*, June 29, 1946. For the Tabors see *Silver Dollar*, by David Karsner.

Chapter 15. The quotation "Stop Roaming, Try Wyoming" is from a state pamphlet. Some but not all the figures on the size of various Wyoming towns are from *Wyoming* in the American Guide Series. The quotation from the Beards is in their *Basic History*.

Chapter 16. Senator Langer's description of UN as a "production of pure bunk" is from the New York *Times*, December 23, 1945. Details of American use of the recall are from *Essentials of American Government*, by Ogg & Ray, p. 520. The phrases quoted in description of the prairie near Pierre are from *Life*, October 6, 1941; so is the detail that one-tenth of the land of South Dakota is Indian. The fact that South Dakota forbids its legislators to accept railroad passes is from Bryce, I, 462. Also for general observations on railroad passes see Leighton, *Five Cities*, p. 168. Some Nebraska statistics are from two pamphlets published by the state, *The Nebraska Story* by ex-Governor Griswold (which originally appeared in the *Saturday Evening Post*), and *Nebraska the Sower*.

Chapter 17. The quotation "Kansas is a child of Plymouth Rock" is from William Allen White. The phrase "tilted slab" is from Clugston, *Facts You Should Know About Kansas*, a pamphlet published by Haldemann-Julius. The Carl Becker quotation is in *If the Prospect Pleases*, and that from Julian Street in his *Abroad at Home*. The Kansas primer I mention is *The Jayhawker Book*, by Emma Humble; both the jayhawker jingles come from this. The jayhawker phrase "sure wants to know where he's been" is from a post card put out by John Morrell & Co., packers. That Kansas has a law forbidding the Russian flag to be flown is from *Newsweek*, August 6, 1945. The limestone cave details are from the Omaha *World-Herald*. Much statistical material in this chapter comes from the various enticing pamphlets of the Kansas Industrial Development Commission. Figures on salt production are from a publication of the University of Kansas, *Kansas Mineral Resources for Wartime Industries*. That 1,200 federal agents would be necessary to keep liquor out of the state is from an AP story, and that Kansas is a common denominator of the whole continent is alluded to by practically all writers on the state. A good general statement is in Clugston, *op. cit.*

Chapter 18. The quotation from Lincoln is from the first inaugural; it appears in *The Practical Cogitator*, p. 377. That from Leacock is from Ringel's *America as Americans See It*, p. 361. The Great Lakes are called "the Mediterranean of the Western Hemisphere" in *Life*, April 22, 1940. The quotation from Hatcher is from his *The Great Lakes*, p. 361; that from Mark Twain is from *Life on the Mississippi*, pp. 9-10. For the Mississippi as an industrial highway, see an article in *Collier's*, "There's Money in the River," by Harry Henderson and Sam Shaw, January 26, 1946. Graham Hutton, *op. cit.* is authority for the statement that the Midwest provides two-thirds of the retail market of the nation. The phrase "The United States is the greatest single achievement of European civilization" is from Mowat, *op. cit.*, p. 129. H. G. Wells has some cogent things to say about the relation between immigration and the standard of living in his *Future of America*. A breakdown of population figures of American cities much more scientific and detailed than mine is in Hutton. Figures for the distribution of mail order catalogs are from *Newsweek*. That the United States "faces west" is remarked upon by almost all historians, for instance James Truslow Adams, *op. cit.*, p. 327. Many students, for instance Adams and Siegfried, have pointed out the curious fact that the United States was an "associated," not an allied power, in World War I; see especially Siegfried, p. 321. The record of various senators on Lend Lease is from *PM*, August 20, 1946.

Chapter 20. The quotation from Sinclair Lewis about Duluth is from the foreword to *Cass Timber-lane*. See also "Bear Facts About Duluth" by Nathan Cohen, *Reader's Digest*, January, 1945. The Duluth Chamber of Commerce gave me the Knott speech; it also appears in *A Treasury of American Folklore*. Authority for the passages about iron ore is the *United States Steel News*, June, 1937, which also contains the episode about John Mitchell, Benjamin Franklin and the map. The quotation from McCarthy is from the chapter on Wisconsin by Zona Gale in *These United States*, II, p. 184. For the cabinet split in regard to the seizure of the Case Company, see *PM*, June 22, 1946. That Wisconsin produces 12.5 per cent of all American milk is from the *Congressional Record*, January 24, 1946. For Governor Goodland, see "Wisconsin's Tough Old Man," an article by Richard L. Neuberger, *Saturday Evening Post*, February 16, 1946.

Chapter 21. The quotation from Archibald MacLeish is from his superb "Colloquy for the States," the poem which opens *A Time to Act*; that from J. Russell Smith is from *North America*. The figures on hybrid corn are from an Associated Press dispatch in the New York *Herald Tribune*, August 10, 1946, and the Omaha *World-Herald*, August 12, 1945. The list of Iowa firsts is from a pamphlet published by the state department of agriculture called *Why Iowa Is Great*. The figure 99.3 per cent as the literacy rate is from *Life*, September 30, 1946.

Chapter 22. The quotation about Pendergast and the insurance companies is from the New York *Herald Tribune*. Details about the Negro vote and Congressman Slaughter are from Bert Andrews, New York *Herald Tribune*, September 8, 1946; those about the new Missouri constitution are mostly from the New York *Times*, February 28, 1945. The item about the "unhealthiness of St. Louis" is from a Paris dispatch to the New York *Herald Tribune*, May 24, 1946. The remark quoted from Westbrook Pegler is from the New York *Journal-American*. One line in this chapter derives from the amiable conversation of Robert W. Kenny and Carey McWilliams.

Chapter 23. The anecdote about Colonel McCormick and the Rhode Island star appears in the *Saturday Evening Post* article by Jack Alexander cited in the text. That Colonel McCormick thinks that Chicago should be pronounced as if spelled "Chisago" is from the *New Yorker*, quoting the *Tribune*, November 23, 1946. The quotation from the Tokyo radio about Colonel McCormick is from the *Atlantic Monthly*, as picked up by the *New Republic*, July 26, 1943. The quotations from Chicago *Tribune* editorials are from various issues from 1942 to late in 1946. The headline mentioned in the *Nation* is from the *Tribune* of March 17, 1945; the dispatch from Paris appeared on October 24, 1945. The book cited by Leo C. Rosten is *The Washington Correspondents*. Colonel McCormick's views about American victories in World War II are from *Time*, October 15, 1945; for the colonel's opinions on Republican candidates for the presidency, see *Time*, August 26, 1946, and a remarkably revealing interview by Felix Belair in the New York *Times*, September 21, 1946. See Hutton, *op. cit.*, p. 140, for various Chicago "firsts." The quotations at the head of the University of Chicago section are from a speech by Mr. Hutchins, April 18, 1935, and from *Life*, July 16, 1945. The phrase that every student should be permitted to obtain a liberal education, etc., is from Hutchins' "Address on the State of the University," 1945. The two *Harper's* articles by Milton Mayer about Hutchins cited in the text were an invaluable source for this section; I have drawn several details from them, including the anecdote about Robert Lovett and the line about Ph.D's really becoming doctors of philosophy. That Hutchins would vote for Norman Thomas if the regular parties did not produce satisfactory platforms is also from Mr. Mayer. Two early surveys of Chicago crime are "Chicago's Gunsmoke Lifts" by James Mulroy in *Plain Talk*, and "Chicago Hands Up" in the *Forum*, by Kate Sargent. Details about the Genna dinners are from these. The figures for Capone's income are from an editorial in *Life*, also other statistical matter about Chicago murders, executions, etc. In the passage about American Action, the sentence that this organization "planned to work through the veterans" is from James Reston, New York *Times*, October 10, 1946. The names of the sub-deb clubs in Indiana are from *Life*, and the *Harper's* article about Asher is by John B. Martin.

Chapter 24. The quotation from Vandenberg's book is from *Time*, October 2, 1939, as is the passage about isolationism.

Chapter 25. The quotation from Woodrow Wilson is from David Cohn, *Combustion on Wheels*, p. 58; several of those from Ford are from an article in *Time*, March 17, 1941. I am uncertain of the source of the Ford quotation about death. That Couzens was a ten-dollar-a-week car checker is from Bingay, *op. cit.* p. 118. Several details about Harry Bennett are drawn from the *American Mercury* article cited in the text. That T. E. Murray had sixty-three grandchildren, together with other details about the family, is from *Fortune*, June, 1944. The *Time* photograph of Monsignor Sheen at the Ford wedding party appeared in the issue of February 4, 1946. The eleven-year profit averages in the automobile industry are from the report of the Federal Trade Commission mentioned in the text. The list of corporations in which General Motors holds interlocking directorships is from *General Motors, an Industrial Empire*, put out by the UAW. That the recent General Motors stock offering was "the largest new issue of all time" is from *Time*, and the item about Charles E. Wilson of General Electric is in an article in *Collier's* by Lester Velie, October 19, 1946. See also *Life*, September 9, 1945, and November 26, 1945. That 35 per cent of the entire reconversion job of the nation is in the hands of General Motors is from *Time*, September 24, 1945.

Chapter 26. The headline Bob and Martha Win is from Alexander H. Uhl in *PM*, October 4, 1942. Details about Taft's mother are from *Life*, March 18, 1940, in an article by Joseph Alsop and Robert Kintner. Taft's question about his father is from Alice R. Longworth, "What's the Matter with Bob Taft?" *Saturday Evening Post*, May 4, 1940, as is the remark about milk and benzedrine. For Taft's record on domestic legislation and his vote against TVA see the article by Carroll Kilpatrick cited in the text and *Time*, January 29, 1940. That Taft voted against Stimson is from *PM*, October 4, 1942. Anecdotes about Martha Taft are from the issue of *Time* just mentioned. The item about the soldier vote law is from the New York *Herald Tribune* as is the quotation from Walter Lippmann, February 22, 1945. For biographical details about Bricker see Malcolm Logan in the New York *Post*, March 20, 1943. The description of Mr. Bricker as "an honest Harding" is credited to Alice Longworth in William Allen White's *Autobiography*, p. 645, and the reference to Dewey is from the *Saturday Evening Post* article just cited. Some details about Bricker's domestic record are from the *New Republic* article mentioned in the text. The quotation about Bricker and bureaucracy is in a biography in the New York *Herald Tribune*, June 29, 1944.

Chapter 27. Most statistics about Ohio are from a letter to me from former Governor Lausche and a mimeographed document issued by the state chamber of commerce, "Ohio and Her Resources," May, 1945. That Van Wert is the peony capital of the world comes from the conversation of my friend John Zur. That Cincinnati was one of three cities greater than 100,000 in population in 1860 is from Hutton, *op cit.*, p. 97, and that Charles P. Taft was an attorney for the Amalgamated Clothing Workers is from "The Taft Brothers" by Carlisle Bargeron, *Pageant*, November, 1945. For strip mining see Harold L. Ickes in the New York *Post*, December 2, 1946.

Chapter 28. The quotation "God hath sifted a whole nation," etc., is from Adams, *op. cit.*; that about "New England divided against itself" is from Howard Mumford Jones in the *Atlantic Monthly*, April, 1940, "New England Dilemma." That 93 per cent of New England towns have town meetings is from *Massachusetts* in the American Guide Series, and that Massachusetts voters had to be Congregationalists is from Beard, *op. cit.*, p. 20. The quotation from Henry James is from Van Wyck Brooks, *New England: Indian Summer*, p. 400, and that from Henry Adams from *The Practical Cogitator*, p. 443. The quotation by Henry Steele Commager is from a review by him of *Puritanism and Democracy*, by Ralph Barton Perry, New York *Herald Tribune*, January 7, 1945. The McCormack-McDonough Colloquy is from the *Congressional Record*, July 12, 1946. The listing of foreign-born in Massachusetts was given me by Russell Gerould, former secretary to ex-Governor Saltonstall. Some biographical details about Senator Bridges are from the New York *Sun*, August 2, 1946.

Chapter 30. That Emerson and S.F.B. Morse got married in the same house is from Clara Laughlin, *So You're Seeing New England*, p. 432. That Senator Aiken reported his expenses as exactly 30¢ in one campaign is from the New York *Post*. Items about the Vermont State House are from the Burlington *Free Press*, December 11, 1944, and a pamphlet published by the State Department of Education, *Vermont and Its Opportunities*.

Chapter 31. The item about the Charitable Irish Society is from the article by Howard Mumford Jones cited above; that about Frederick W. Mansfield is from "The Cardinal and Cold Roast Boston" by Jack Alexander, *Saturday Evening Post*, October 4, 1941. Wallace Stegner, mentioned in the body of the chapter, is my authority for the connection between Coughlin, Moran, etc., and the Boston riots. Also see *Assignment USA*, by Selden Menefee. The quotation "What killed Boston" is from W. L. George, *Hail Columbia*, p. 36. That Archbishop Cushing claims proud descent from the South Boston Cushings is from a letter to *Life*,

February 5, 1945, by Walter B. Keegan. For an account of the riots differing from mine consult *Hoodlumism in Boston*, a pamphlet published by the Boston *Herald*, and for a contrary view of Massachusetts trusteeship see a booklet *The Boston Trustee*, by Donald Holbrook.

Chapter 32. Basic sources for Dewey are articles in *Life* by Noel F. Busch and Roger Butterfield, several articles in *Time*, the Wolcott Gibbs-John Bainbridge profile in the *New Yorker* cited in the text, the *Harper's* article by Richard H. Rovere similarly cited, a *New Republic* Supplement, several biographical sketches published in the New York *Herald Tribune*, and an exhaustive campaign pamphlet put out by Press Research Inc., Washington. The picture of Dewey sitting on the telephone books is in *Life*, March 20, 1944. The item from Leonard Lyons is from the New York *Post*, July 22, 1946. Dewey's remarks to S. T. Woolf are from the New York *Times* of October 27, 1946. I am uncertain of the source of the paragraph about movie and lecture offers. Anecdotes about the way Dewey kills flies, the sore throat that turned him from a concert career, etc., are from *Time* and *Life*. That Niagara means "bisected bottom lands" is from the New York *Red Book* published by the state, and the detail about 5,000 historical markers comes from *New York* in the American Guide Series, p. 24. Also I have drawn on this for background on Syracuse, Ithaca, and Albany. Most of my general statistics are from the first-rate publications of the state Department of Commerce, made available through the courtesy of Herbert C. Campbell, director, Bureau of Information, Division of Publicity. For the conflict between state and city over taxation I have used the New York *Times*. Most of the quotations from the New York *Daily News* are from recent issues. For the St. Lawrence waterway see a *Collier's* article by Carey Longmire, "Showdown on the St. Lawrence," November 13, 1945. The quotation about rats in Buffalo is from the Seattle *Times*, July 2, 1945. Several details in this chapter were suggested by Morris Ernst, and for one passage I am indebted to the wisdom of Barnet Nover.

Chapter 33. I owe much in this chapter to the inner table conversation on several occasions of Cass Canfield, Thomas K. Finletter, Frederick Lewis Allen, and John Fischer. Description of New York as both a synthesis and a negation of America comes from Hamilton Fish Armstrong, who also suggested the phrase "go East, young man." The detail about the City Hall being finished only on three sides is from Ernest Gruening in *These United States*. Some historical details are from the New York *Legislative Manual* and from the annual green handbook that the city issues. Calculations about New York City's population in comparison with that of various nations is from *Time*, December 3, 1945. The phrase "head and shoulders" (of Long Island) is from one of the interesting pamphlet guides put out by the state Department of Commerce; for details about the Port of New York see another of these, and also *Life*, November 20, 1945. The site of the oldest building in the city is from *New York City* in the American Guide Series, as is the item about locating street numbers. That 450,000 families live in "subhuman" conditions is from recent campaign material of the Liberal party. For biographical details about Mayor O'Dwyer I have followed generally an account in the New York *Herald Tribune*, and also Mr. O'Dwyer's own conversation. The historical item about Wall Street and Peter Stuyvesant is from *New York City, op. cit.* Sources for Morgan are the article in *Life* mentioned in the text and *Time*, June 5, 1933, March 22, 1943, and February 26, 1940. The "Götterdämmerung" expression is from this last, and also the phrase "government supervision and growing accountability to the public." Most quotations in this chapter are from Stevenson, *op. cit.*; that from Otto Kahn is from *The Mirrors of Wall Street*. For much background material on *New York in General* I want to thank Reuben A. Lazarus. Some details in the *Miscellany* are from an advertisement by Macy's in the New York *Herald Tribune*, February 9, 1945, and from the New York *Times*, December 8 and 22, 1946.

Chapter 35. The quotation from Westbrook Pegler is from the *New Yorker* profile of Hague cited in the text; that from Van Devander is from his useful *The Big Bosses*. The New York *Herald Tribune*, April 10, 1945, is my source for the statement that Jersey City spends more per capita than any other American city. Details about Prudential's threat to leave New Jersey are in the New York *Herald Tribune*, February 16, 1945. See *Public Men In and Out of Office*, p. 447, for Hague as leader of every New Jersey delegation to the Democratic National Convention since 1920. A few details about New Jersey as a state are from *New Jersey* in the WPA Series.

Chapter 36. The line about Beethoven is from *Beethoven, the Man Who Freed Music*, by Robert Haven Schauffler, p. 163. A source for Philadelphia politics is a speech by Congressman Michael J. Bradley distributed by the Philadelphia City Commission. Details on water are from *The Philadelphia Story*, a brochure published by the Democratic Program for the Improvement and Rehabilitation of the City of Philadelphia. My background on the Earle period derives partly from conversation with Mr. Earle and others and partly from Van Devander and the WPA Guide. Grundy's role in the Smoot-Hawley tariff is mentioned in the *Encyclopaedia Britannica*. The Penrose-brothel tidbit is from *Time*, October 28, 1946, and how political contributions are disguised as "loans" is mentioned in *The Philadelphia Story*.

Chapter 37. The quotation from Haniel Long is from *Pittsburgh Memorandum*, published by Writers' Edition, Santa Fe, New Mexico. Statistics on steel production and U. S. Steel are in part from *Life*, November 11, 1946, and from Keith Hutchinson in the *Nation*, April 6, 1946. For further details of U.S. Steel organization and management see the article in *Life* mentioned in the text. The source of the remark about automobiles being nothing but a stove in a carriage is Malcolm Bingay. The anecdote about Frick and Carnegie is from a review by Benjamin Stolberg of John K. Winkler's *Incredible Carnegie*. Labor statistics are mostly from pamphlets published by the United Steelworkers, like *The Braddock Steelworkers*, *Five Years of War Profits*, and *Steel Fights for the Nation*. For industrial folklore see *Pennsylvania* in the American Guide Series. The Amish precept is from the Department of Agriculture publication cited in the text. "Schoenste Lengevitch" is from *Pennsylvania, op. cit.*, p. 4, which also has details on Hexerei.

Chapter 38. Most material about the earlier history of the Du Ponts comes from conversation with members of the family. For inland waterways see *Life*, January 28, 1946; for rivers see *Rivers of the Eastern Shore*, by Hulbert Footner, in the Rivers of America Series. Culinary details are from *Maryland* in the American Guide Series.

Chapter 39. The quotation about Happy Chandler is from Potomacus in the *New Republic*, October 11, 1943, and that Chandler was so surprised about the swimming pool that you could have knocked him over with the springboard is from an article in the *Saturday Evening Post*. Other sources for this chapter are Leighton's *Five Cities* (for the detail about Keats's brother), and *Life*, October 19, 1944.

Chapter 40. The edition I used of *America Comes of Age* by André Siegfried was published in London in 1927. Authority for the statement that one-half of the male white population of the South was killed in the War Between the States is R. B. Mowat's suggestive brief history, cited above. This is also my source for the footnote about the Lincoln family. Some items about reconstruction come from Beard, and for threats of secession by the New England states see Adams, *op. cit.*, pp. 141-143. The quotation from Jonathan Daniels is from *A Southerner Discovers the South*, p. 1; that from W. J. Cash is from his splendid *The Mind of the South*, p. viii. That Delaware, Maryland and Kentucky were all slave states but grew no cotton is from Leo Huberman, *op. cit.*, p. 277. The idea that it was the North that seceded rather than the South was a favorite fancy of the late Ben Robertson. See his *Red Hills and Cotton*, p. 29. The article cited by David Cohn is "How the South Feels," *Atlantic Monthly*, January, 1944. A source of figures on cattle and cotton is Governor Arnall's "The Southern Frontier," *Atlantic Monthly*, September, 1946. Also see Dabney, "The South Looks Ahead," in *Foreign Affairs*, October, 1940. The quotation from Booker T. Washington is from an article "A Southerner Looks at the South" by Hodding Carter, New York *Times*, July 7, 1946; the syphilis figures are from *Look*, November 13, 1945. That there are only sixteen major orchestras is from the OWI handbook already cited and one item in my discussion of religion is from Bryce, II, 696. The quotation from H. L. Mencken is from an early volume of the *Prejudices* series. That Coca-Cola was once forbidden Sunday sale in Richmond is from Dabney, *op. cit.*, p. 240.

Chapter 41. The Negro problem as a white man's problem is from *Confessions of a European Intellectual* by Franz Schoenberner. The same idea has been expressed by many other writers. See Myrdal, I, 43. The quotation from Du Bois about Atlanta University is from *What the Negro Wants*, p. 49. The phrase in connection with the Shull case, "criminal information," is from an AP dispatch; the quotation from Governor Cherry is from *Time*, January 7, 1946. That 235 Negroes were lynched in 1892 without a single instance of punishment is from *Thirteen Against the Odds*, p. 162. "Discrimination in the nation's capital must go," etc., is from *Time*, January 21, 1946. The Du Bois quotation in the middle of the chapter is from *The Souls of Black Folk* and is quoted by Myrdal, II, 1187. Figures on the percentage of the Negro population in southern states are from *Life*, May 3, 1943. For "revisionists" on reconstruction see Myrdal II, 1315. The definition of the Negro as a man partly white, though independently arrived at, closely parallels Myrdal, I, 113. The quotation from Du Bois about color is from *Thirteen Against the Odds*, p. 157; that from H. G. Wells is from *The Future of America*, p. 194. The remark of Langston Hughes is in *A Primer for Whites*, p. 455. For Negro compromises on segregation see Myrdal, I, 794 ff. Figures on Negro health, education, etc., as against those for whites are from *The Negro in America*, by Maxwell S. Stewart, Public Affairs Pamphlet #95. The phrase from Mary McLeod Bethune is from *What the Negro Wants*, p. 253. That the FEPC is the first presidential executive order since the Emancipation Proclamation that specifically deals with Negroes is from another Public Affairs Pamphlet, *The Negro at War*, p. 27 et seq. The quotation from Shaw is from *Man and Superman*, and that from Jennings Perry is from *Democracy Begins at Home*, p. 107. The paradox about education occurs in Myrdal (I, 657), expressed in somewhat different terms. For much in this chapter I am indebted to the stimulating conversation of Lillian Smith.

Chapter 42. Details of the torture of an escaped Virginia prisoner are from *PM*, January 15, 1946; those about conscientious objectors are from Dabney in the New York *Times*, February 23 and October 5, 1946. That only 20 per cent of eligible voters vote is from Lowell Mellett, New York *Post*, February 20, 1945, and other political statistics are in *PM*, June 23, 1946. The item about former Governor Darden and the Confederate widows is from Drew Pearson. For some details of comparison between Virginia and North Carolina in the light of the Byrd economies see G. W. Johnson's essay on Byrd in *Life*, August 7, 1944. The North Carolina cat-chewing story is from the Raleigh *News & Observer*, April 12, 1945, and the Raleigh *Times*, April 11, 1945. The phrase "most American of all states" applied to North Carolina is from Odum, *op. cit.*, p. 543; that describing "the quintessence of Virginia's discontent" is from the conversation of Frank Graham. Some statistical material about North Carolina, as well as details of the cigarette paper industry, are from the State News Bureau, Raleigh. That there are 38,931 homes without toilets or privies in South Carolina is from the *Statistical Abstract of the U.S.*, 1944-45, p. 923. The anecdote about Broad Street and the admiral was told me by W. W. Ball. I obtained the West Virginia toast through the courtesy of Charles E. Hodges of the Charleston, West Virginia Chamber of Commerce, and most of my West Virginia statistics are from chamber of commerce pamphlets. Some Florida figures are from a thumb-size booklet *Florida* published by the state Department of Agriculture. Also see a pictorial map in *Time*, February 19, 1940.

Chapter 43. The quotation at the head of the chapter is from a recent letter by Mr. Lilienthal to the author; that from Jonathan Daniels is from *A Southerner Discovers the South*, p. 97. The passages quoted from the *New Statesman* (October 10, 1936) are by Frank Darvell. The formula in regard to chlorophyll is from *Fortune*, November, 1938, p. 85, in an article on solar energy. Several of the TVA statistics, especially those on comparative power rates, are from letters to me by W. L. Sturdevant, director of information, TVA; others come from Duffus, *op. cit.*, and from an article by Lilienthal in the *Atlantic Monthly*, January, 1946. The discussion of soil problems closely follows talks with Director H. A. Morgan of TVA, and charts prepared by him.

Chapter 44. Much of the material about Boss Crump was gathered from Crump himself. But (*a*) the episode about the legislature passing a special law in regard to a businessman is from "Ed Crump, Portrait of a Boss," by Harold B. Hinton, New York *Times*, September 29, 1946; (*b*) that Crump once gave away 30,000 hot dogs and 1,600 gallons of lemonade is from *Life*, September 2, 1946; (*c*) the 60,000 figure by which former Governor Gordon Browning both won and lost is from *Time*, May 27, 1946. Details of election stealing in McMinn County are from a statement by Representative John Jennings Jr. in the *Congressional Record*. My source for an item about McKellar is Drew Pearson, New York *Mirror*, May 29, 1945. Details about the Murrell statue and the eulogy on Brownlow, as well as the stories about the fattest man and the fattest hog, were given me by Albert Williams, attorney-at-law, Nashville, Tennessee. That Tennessee "ruled the nation" from 1830 to 1850 is from a speech by Congressman Estes Kefauver, *Congressional Record*, May 25, 1946. The phrase "South of the Piazza," etc., came to me by word of mouth; I found later that it is the opening sentence in *Arkansas* in the American Guide Series. Details of possible thorium and uranium deposits in Arkansas are from the New York *Times*, October 27, 1946. For the National Farm Labor Union see Victor Riesel, New York *Post*, October 14, 1946. Another version of the speech "Change the name of Arkansas" is in *A Treasury of American Folklore.*

Chapter 45. The Clark Foreman quote is from the New York *Times*, July 31, 1946, and the jingle about Georgia governors comes from Josephine Wilkins of the Citizens Fact-Finding Committee of Atlanta. For invaluable material on Georgia I am indebted to Margaret Fisher, secretary-treasurer of the Committee for Georgia and member of the Committee of Editors & Writers of the South. The phrase "cold bread country" is from an article "Revolution Down South" by Governor Arnall as told to Walter Davenport, *Collier's*, July 28, 1945. Quotations about chain gangs are from the "Report to the Governor on Prison Conditions in Georgia and the Southern States" by Frank Gross, president of the state senate, and Roy Harris, speaker of the house. Details about the attempt of Mr. Scott to run for coroner in Atlanta are from the New York *Times*, October 14, 1946. The late Governor Talmadge's statement to WOR was printed in *PM*, June 29, 1942. Talmadge's remark "Let 'em starve" is from Benjamin Stolberg in the *Nation*, March 4, 1936, "Buzz Windrip—Governor of Georgia." That seventeen states and the District of Columbia have two complete sets of school systems is from Myrdal, *op. cit.* I, p. 632. For several details about the Ku-Klux Klan, for instance that ministers are admitted for half-price and that the Southern Baptist Convention recently took a strong line against the Klan, I am indebted to a recent article by Ralph McGill of the Atlanta *Constitution*. See also columns by Victor Riesel in the New York *Post* throughout 1946. The quotation from Siegfried, "an extreme form of Protestant nationalism," is from *America Comes of Age*, p. 130. The quotation from Walter Winchell is from the New York *Daily Mirror*, June 11, 1946. Some material about the Columbians Inc., is from the New York *Herald Tribune*, August 21, 1946.

Chapter 46. The first quotation at the head of the chapter is from an article in the *New Republic*, "Revolution in Cotton," August 19, 1946; the second is from a letter to me by W. M. Hutchinson, secretary of the Cottonseed & Peanut Crushers Association of Georgia. The figures in the second paragraph are from *Cotton* cited in the text. Percentage of farms devoted to cotton in various states is from a pamphlet published by the Department of Agriculture, "Round the World with Cotton," 1941; this is also my main source for the historical paragraph that follows. That cotton is the only crop producing "food, feed, and fibre" is from *Cotton*, *op. cit.* p. 350, as are other details. For the mechanical cotton picker and its presumptive effect see "Exit King Cotton" by Peter F. Drucker, *Harper's Magazine*, May, 1946, and "Revolution in Cotton" by J. D. Ratcliff, *Collier's*, July 21, 1945. Details about "ramie" are from Virginius Dabney in the New York *Times*, September 15, 1945. For Hudson Strode and the University of Alabama see *Time*, July 30, 1945; for the Alabama campaign on venereal disease see *Time*, July 16, 1945, and *Reader's Digest*, September, 1946. My sources for Governor Folsom are mainly "The Mystery of Big Jim" by William O. Davis, the *Nation*, August 31, 1946, an article in *Life*, June 3, 1946, an article in the New York *Herald Tribune*, October 27, 1946, and columns by Thomas L. Stokes (New York *World-Telegram*) and Charles Van Devander and William O. Player Jr. (New York *Post*). Some details about Sparkman are from an article in the New York *Post*, September 16, 1946, by Oliver Pilat. "Liberalism" in Alabama in contradiction to Georgia is ably discussed by Stewart Alsop in the New York *Herald Tribune*, August 20, 1946. The quotation from the Natchez *Democrat* is from the *New Republic* of April 2, 1945. The phrase about Mississippi being the "hottest oil spot in the nation" is from an article by Harnett T. Kane in the *American Mercury*, December, 1944. The remark about differences between North Carolina and Mississippi is from Odum, p. 543, and the paragraph about the Bible-reading society, Andy Gump, and the shooting of an eighteen-year-old girl is from H. L. Mencken, *Americana*, pp. 35-36. For some recent material on Louisiana politics I am indebted to Harnett T. Kane, as well as articles in the New York *Times* by George W. Healy Jr. Some biographical details about Jimmie Davis are from *Time*, March 13, 1944. Mayor Maestri's remark to Mr. Roosevelt is from Kane, *Louisiana Hayride*, as is the witticism about prostitution. The passage by Raymond Swing about Huey Long appeared originally in the *Nation.*

Chapter 47. The detail about wool scouring is from *Texas* in the WPA Series; so are some of the figures about textile mills. The quotation from Lee O'Daniel describing Texas as a colony of Manhattan is from McKay, *op. cit.*, as are the jokes about the Royal Canadian Air Force and the statistics of the Doolittle raid. My catalogue of Texas superlatives derives in part from the *Texas Almanac*, published by the Dallas *News*, 1945. Many tall tales come originally from Dobie. The allegation that a drop of Sam Houston's blood would kill a frog is from *Professional Politicians*, by William McCraw. Figures on natural gas are from the *State Observer*, Austin, February 19, 1945, and from *Fortune*, December, 1939. That Dallas is the largest open-shop town in the United States is from *Fortune*. The Amarillo weather story has been printed numerous times, as has the story about bad teeth in Deaf Smith County. Some details about Dallas and Fort Worth are from *Time*, June 8, 1936, as well as some general Texas statistics. The quotation by Archibald MacLeish is from a magnificent article which first appeared anonymously in *Fortune* and was then reprinted in Mr. MacLeish's collected prose. The advertisement about housing from the Houston *Chronicle* was sent to me by Ilse Lea Schaefer.

Chapter 48. The quotation from de Tocqueville is from Vol. I of *Democracy in America* by Alexis de Tocqueville, reprinted by permission of Alfred A. Knopf, Inc. Copyright 1945 by Alfred A. Knopf, Inc. The amount spent by O'Daniel in his Senate campaign is in McKay, *op. cit.* p. 587. The *Collier's* article about Vance Muse is by Walter Davenport. The first O'Daniel quotation (the colloquy with Bridges) is from the *Congressional Record* of June 27, 1946; the second from that of July 12; the third from that of July 24.

Chapter 49. The detail about Brann the iconoclast is from *These United States*, I, p. 311. The fact that Negroes were once sold by the pound is from *Under Six Flags*, p. 43. For details about Congressman Kleberg see Drew Pearson, New York *Daily Mirror*, October 12, 1946.

Chapter 50. The quotations from George Milburn are from an admirable article "Oklahoma" in the *Yale Review*, Spring, 1946, reprinted by kind permission of the Yale University Press. The poem "In God We Trusted" etc. is from *Tulsa*, by Angie Debo. Some of my material about Congressman Jed Johnson is from Drew Pearson, New York *Daily Mirror*, July 27, 1946. The item about Alfalfa Bill Murray's father is from *Alfalfa Bill*, p. 277.

Chapter 51. The quotation from Elizabeth Shepley Sergeant is from *These United States, op. cit.* II, p. 250; that about Indians is from *The Hopi Way*, by Laura Thompson and Alice Joseph, published in the Indian Education Research Series. The phrase "captured by killing" is from *New Mexico* in the American Guide Series, p. 104, as are some details about mining. Figures on irrigation in the Rio Grande Valley are from Stuart Chase's *Rich Land Poor Land*, p. 112, and the "to hell with Coolidge" item is from H. L. Mencken's *Americana 1925*. The tall story in this chapter was sent me by Edna C. Schierenberg of Glencoe, New Mexico.

Chapter 52. The newspaper with the World Series headline was the Detroit *News*. My authority for Calvin Coolidge as a translator of Dante is Van Wyck Brooks, *New England: Indian Summer*, p. 435, and that twenty-four states once forbade minors to smoke is from Bryce, II, 547. The doughty general who slew the bear by yelling was the late Simon Bolivar Buckner Jr., who was himself killed on Okinawa; this item is from the Washington *Star*, March 3, 1945. For the long record of the United States in consecutive government see the OWI handbook already cited, p. 1. The quotations from *Fortune* are from its splendid American number, February, 1940, pp. 94 and 154. The phrase "lousy with greatness" is from the table talk of Robert E. Sherwood.

So now *Inside U.S.A.* is done.

Index

Abilene, Kansas, 261, 860
Absentee ownership, 151, 153-154, 211, 234, 238, 244, 285, 384, 403, 575, 620, 646-647, 673, 766, 768, 784, 816, 880, 886, 905
Ace, Texas, 826
Acheson, Dean, 326, 914
Acheson-Lilienthal Report, 737
Adams, Charles Francis, 461, 520-521, 570-571, 605
Adams, Henry, 507
Adams, James Truslow, 145(fn.), 146, 216, 459, 656
Adams, John, 461
Adams family, 705
Addams, Jane, 370
Addes, George F., 411
Ade, George, 386
Africa Colonization Society, 691
Agar, Herbert, 287
Agnes, Texas, 826
Agricultural Lands, Ltd., 452
Agricultural machinery, 279, 319, 335, 672
Agriculture, see under names of States
Aiello, Joe, 381
Aiken, George D., 103, 471, 540, 914
Ailshie, Margaret Cobb, 116
Ajo, Arizona, 905
Akins, Mr., 866
Akron, Ohio, 270, 332, 373, 386, 442, 443, 454, 631, 725
Akron, University of, 454
Alabama, 194, 247, 489, 637, 653, 654, 655, 662, 667, 671, 672, 674, 675, 676, 688, 690, 700, 701, 732, 733, 744, 745, 756, 778, 790, 791, 794-799, 871; Limestone County, 743; University of, 794; Winston County, 797
Alameda County, California, 19
Alamo, 402, 834
Alamogordo military reservation, 888
Alaska, 92-93, 229, 264
Albany, New York, 28, 527, 530, 538, 541, 542, 543, 544, 559
Albany, Oregon, 95
Albuquerque, New Mexico, 888, 891
Alcoholic Board of Control, 721(fn.)
Aldrich, Nelson W., 500
Aldrich, Winthrop W., 559, 798(fn.)
Alexander (Jugoslavia), 810
Alexander, Jack, 361(fn.)
Alexander Hamilton, the Greatest American, 395

Alexandria, Virginia, 710, 715
Alfred I. Du Pont (James), 633(fn.)
Algonquin Indians, 535
Alien Property Custodian, 325, 326
All Year Club of Southern California, 33
Allegheny Corporation, 570
Allegheny mountains, 271
Allegheny River, 601, 615
Allen, Ethan, 493, 494
Allen, Fred, 657
Allen, Frederick L., 922
Allen, Jay, 346, 360, 921
Allen, Lawrence, 54
Allen, Leo E., 282
Allentown, Pennsylvania, 602
Allied Chemical and Dye Corp., 635
Allied Control Commission, 561
Allis Chalmers Manufacturing Company, 279, 319, 411, 631, 793
Alloy, West Virginia, 716
Allred, James V., 839, 840, 856
Almina (Kansas) *Plaindealer,* 845
Alsop, Joseph, 432(fn.)
Alsop, Stewart, 726(fn.)
Alsops, the, 225
Alton Railroad, 358
Altoona, Pennsylvania, 602
Aluminum Company of America, 97, 128, 170, 568, 736(fn.), 746, 766, 906
Amalgamated Association of Iron and Steel Workers, 621
Amalgamated Clothing Workers of America, 450, 553
Amana, Iowa, 334
Amarillo, Texas, 146, 163, 234, 819(fn.), 835
Amarillo *Globe,* 836
Amarillo society, 836
Amerada Petroleum Corporation, 290
America Comes of Age (Siegfried), 276(fn.), 653
America First, 175, 242, 278, 382, 383, 427, 435, 532
America, Its History and People (Kepner), 921
America Preferred, 390
American Action, Inc., 382, 383
American Airlines, Inc., 758
American Association of University Professors, 733, 858
American Bar Association, 105, 470
American Brass Company, 167
American Bridge Co., 617

American Broadcasting Company, 245
American Character, The (Brogan), 273(fn.), 631(fn.)
American Citizens Club, 291(fn.)
American Civil Liberties Union, 670
American College of Surgeons, 703
American Commonwealth, The (Bryce), 3, 166
American Council on Race Relations, 285(fn.)
American Dilemma, An (Myrdal), 284(fn.), 654, 683
American Farm Bureau Federation, see Farm Bureau
American Federation of Labor, 20, 25, 26, 39, 50-51, 54, 62, 95-96, 98, 99, 100, 101, 112, 143, 222, 292(fn.), 297, 371, 387, 427, 449, 556, 559, 584, 621, 626, 647, 674, 675, 788, 853(fn.), 881
American Guide Series, 4(fn.), 93, 227, 258(fn.), 262(fn.), 499(fn.), 555(fn.), 601(fn.), 628(fn.), 637(fn.), 640, 642 (fn.), 643, 824(fn.), 880(fn.), 888(fn.)
American-Hawaiian Steamship Company, 24
American Hellenic Educational and Progressive Association, 291(fn.)
American Heroes and Hero Worship (Johnson), 632(fn.)
American Iron & Steel Institute, 617, 624
American Iron Association, 617
American Labor Party, 529, 541, 552, 563, 564
American Legion, 39, 94, 95, 205, 221, 291(fn.), 338, 349, 382, 490, 706, 913
American Library Association, 371
American Locomotive Company, 538
American Medical Association, 371, 858
American Men of Science, 194
American Mercury, 221(fn.), 373(fn.), 405(fn.)
American Names, 144
American Nationalist party, 722
American Notes (Dickens), 273 (fn.), 684(fn.)
American Overseas Airlines Inc., 489
American Pioneer Trails Association, 173

American Radiator & Standard Sanitary Corp., 631
American Rolling Mill Company, 623-624
American Smelting and Refining Company, 211, 905
American Snuff Company, 631
American Speech, 696(fn.)
American Steel & Wire Company, 617, 618
American Telephone & Telegraph Company, 290, 418, 474, 559, 569, 572
American Tobacco Company, 418, 568, 713, 714
American Veterans' Committee, 559, 703
American Viscose Corp., 631, 635, 716
American Wildlife Institute, 249
Americana (Mencken), 44, 764, 863, 866(fn.)
America's Sixty Families, 634 (fn.)
Amherst College, 474
Amish Mennonites, *see* Mennonites
Amoskeag mill, 491
Amsterdam, New York, 538
Amsterdam News, 575
Anaconda, Montana, 160(fn.), 167
Anaconda Copper Mining Company, 115, 153, 155, 156, 158, 160, 163, 164, 165-174, 177, 185, 222, 247, 523, 570, 905
Anaconda Wire and Cable Company, 167, 171
Anderson, C. Elmer, 295
Anderson, Clayton, & Co., 847
Anderson, Clinton, 612, 891
Anderson, J. E., 835
Anderson, John Murray, 527
Anderson, Margaret, 374
Anderson, Marian, 387
Anderson, Maxwell, 248(fn.)
Anderson, P. L., 834, 845, 922
Anderson, Sherwood, 374, 439, 441
Andes Copper Mining Company, 167
Andover Boys' School, 474
Andrews, Wayne, 372(fn.)
Andrews, William T., 575
Anheuser, Lilly
Annapolis, Maryland, 638
Annemessex River, 637
Antioch College, 454
Antiquities Act of 1906, 233
Anti-Saloon League, 267, 440, 669
Anti-Semitism, *see* Jews
Antoine's restaurant, 809
Anzio, 689
Apache Indians, 870, 874, 894, 895, 900
Appalachians, 601
Apples, 707
Appleton, Wisconsin, 319
Appomattox, 655
Arapahoe Indians, 235, 870
Arends, Leslie C., 282
Argentina, 431, 808, 816
Arizona, 77, 144, 216, 438(fn.), 654, 661, 759, 814, 835, 873, 886, 897-906, 910; agriculture, 905; climate, 90; federal credit, 906; Indians, 893; irrigation, 6, 902, 904; labor in, 253(fn.); Maricopa County, 902; Mormons in, 193, 904; nicknames for, 258(fn.); politics, 897-900, 903-905; population, 901; power, 903; railroads in, 900; water, 6, 901
Arizona Oil Company, 167
Arizonans United, 901
Arkansas, xiii, 89, 195, 259, 271, 503, 653, 654, 655, 657, 658, 659, 660, 662, 667, 672, 678, 690, 700, 701, 724, 739, 753, 762-766, 782, 804, 807, 808, 826, 853, 872; divorce laws in, 77; labor, 765
Arkansas *Gazette*, 765
Arkansas Power & Light Company, 745, 766
Arkansas River, 748, 809
Arkies, 147, 659
Arlington, Oregon, 94
Arlington Club, 91
Armco Employees Independent Union, 291(fn.)
Armco Girls Association, 291(fn.)
Armour, Philip, 371
Armstrong, Hamilton Fish, 552, 559, 921
Arnall, Ellis, 153, 655, 662, 673, 680, 731, 767, 769-776, 778, 781, 789, 914
Arnaud's of Count Casenave, 809
Arnold, Benedict, 403
Arnold, Thurman, 230
Arnstein, Nicky, 909
Asher, Court, 390
Asheville, North Carolina, 719
Ashland, Wisconsin, 272
Ashtabula, Ohio, 272
Askov, Minnesota, 300
Aspen, Colorado, 559
Associated Farmers, 38, 39, 901
Associated Gas & Electric Co., 631
Associated Hospital Service of N. Y., 577
Associated Industries of Kentucky, 641
Associated Press, 365, 788(fn.)
Association of Southern Women for the Prevention of Lynching, 688
Astor, John Jacob, 85, 310
Astor Hotel, 383
Astoria, Oregon, 85
Atchison, Kansas, 263
Athens, Alabama, 685
Athens, Ohio, 454
Athens, Tennessee, 755
Atherton, Gertrude, 7, 10(fn.), 395
Atkins, J. Austin, 868
Atkinson, Roy, 98, 116
Atlanta, Georgia, xiii, 3, 128 (fn.), 246(fn.), 424, 574, 653, 655, 656, 659, 664, 669, 670, 673, 674(fn.), 676, 679, 680, 681, 682, 683, 686, 688, 689, 696, 725, 743, 767, 768, 770, 775-777, 780, 781, 783-784, 785, 785(fn.), 786, 786(fn.), 787, 788, 789
Atlanta, University of, 679, 680, 777, 798
Atlanta *Constitution*, 676, 768, 784, 787(fn.)
Atlanta *Daily World*, 777
Atlanta *Journal*, 667, 676, 682, 784
Atlanta *World*, 626
Atlantic Charter, 588
Atlantic City, New Jersey, 550 (fn.), 595
Atlantic City, Wyoming, 230
Atlantic Coast Line Railroad Co., 646
Atlantic Monthly, 125, 366, 460, 463, 466, 515, 662, 662(fn.), 746, 779(fn.), 879(fn.)
Atlas Lumnite Cement Co., 617
Atlas Powder Co., 631
Atomic bomb, xiii, 119-120, 149, 187, 291, 363, 378, 396, 469, 544, 636, 737, 888
Atomic energy, 631, 672, 737, 740, 766, 796
Atomic Energy Bill, 470
Atomic Energy Commission, 737, 916
Atterbury, W. W., 567
Attlee, Clement R., 363
Attu, 785
Auburn, New York, 537
Auctioneers, 759
Audubon, John James, 447
Augsman, Elmer, 385
Augusta, Maine, 458, 485, 488, 908
Aull, Arthur, 343
Austin, A. A., 575
Austin, Mary, 888
Austin, Minnesota, 318
Austin, Moses, 823
Austin, Stephen F., 823
Austin, Texas, 90, 821, 824, 825, 826, 831, 835, 836, 843, 846, 849, 855, 856, 864, 865
Austin, Warren R., 471, 472
Austin, *American*, 857
Australasia, 2
Autobiography (Steffens), 590
Autobiography (White), 257
The Autobiography of a Durable Sinner (White), 844(fn.)
Automobile Manufacturers Association, 400, 412(fn.)
Automobiles, 317, 398-419, 606, 616, 629, 631
Avery, Sewell L., 278, 618, 620, 917
Axtell, Enos A., 347
Aycock, Charles B., 721
Ayres, Professor Clarence E., 825
Babcock, H. E., 524
Back Bay, 461
Bad Lands, 157, 246
Baedeker, Karl, x, 369, 557
Bahamas, 798(fn.)
Bailey, Josiah W., 722
Bainbridge, John, 530(fn.)
Baker, A. Y., 844

Baker, George F., 567, 619
Baker, Newton, 429, 444, 571
Bakersfield, California, 3, 61
Baldwin, Matthias, 798
Baldwin, Raymond E., 503, 505
Baldwin, Stanley, 754
Baldwin Locomotive Works, 602
Balfour, Lord, 706
Ball, Joseph H., 294-295, 304
Ball, W. W., 726, 727, 800
Baltimore, Maryland, 128(fn.), 553, 558, 576, 630, 637-639, 784, 827, 911
Baltimore Afro-American, 627
Baltimore & Ohio Railroad, 358, 442, 568, 572, 714
Baltimore Sun, 612, 638, 822
Bamberger, Simon, 203-204, 210
BancOhio, 452
Bancroft, George, 22
Bangor, Maine, 486
Bank of America, 27, 28, 38, 46
Bank of Montreal, 419
Bankers Trust Company of New York, 419, 620(fn.)
Bankhead, John H., 796, 883
Banking Act of 1933, 569, 571
Banks, Frank E., 122
Bannack, Montana, 162
Bapchule, Arizona, 893
Baptist church, 284, 349, 376, 648, 668, 760, 766, 772, 788, 799, 874, 882
Bar Harbor, Maine, 485
Barbour, James, 705
Barker, S. Omar, 889
Barkley, Alben W., 648, 649, 676
Barnes, Albert, 601
Barnett, Nancy, 921
Barr, Stringfellow, 638
Barre, Vermont, 493, 495, 498
Barry, Philip, 605
Barry, Richard, 590(fn.)
Barth, Alan, 59
Bartlesville, Oklahoma, 837
Baruch, Bernard M., 570, 669, 737, 908
Baseball, 271(fn.), 351, 431, 437, 554, 648, 650, 703, 761, 876
Basic History, 236
Basin, Montana, 160
Basques, 116
Basso, Hamilton, 666
Baton Rouge, Louisiana, 250, 807, 808
Battle for Chicago (Andrews), 372(fn.)
Battle of San Jacinto, 823, 851
Battle of the Bear's Paw, 161
"Battle of the Overpass," 411
Baumgarten, Bernice, 921
Bauxite, 615, 672
Baxter, George W., 229
Baylor University, 821, 863, 864, 868
Bayonne, New Jersey, 597
Bayou Lafourche, 804
Beach, North Dakota, 240
Beach, Rex, 229
Beacon Hill, 516
Beard, Charles A., 236, 287
Beardsley, C. R., 588
Beatrice, Nebraska, 252

Beaumont, Texas, 821, 825, 827 (fn.), 828, 853, 866
Beaumont Enterprise, 853(fn.)
Beck, Dave, 85, 98, 100-101
Becker, Carl, 258, 264
Bedford, Clay P., 70
Beethoven, Ludwig van, 602
Behn, Sosthenes, 568
Belcastro, James, 381
Belin, Alice, 633
Bell, Arthur Lowler Osborn Fountaine, 52
Bell, Elliot V., 566, 566(fn.), 567
Bell Aircraft plant, 498, 659
Bell Telephone Company of Canada, 419
Bellett, Lowell, 225
Bellinger, Boss, 868
Bellows, George, 888
Belmont, Massachusetts, 520
Beloit, Wisconsin, 319
Below the Potomac (Dabney), 662(fn.), 670
Benchley, Bob, 911
Bendix, 385, 412
Beneficial Life Insurance Company, 191
Beneš, Eduard, 377
Benét, Stephen Vincent, 144, 271, 711, 767
Benjamin Franklin High School (NYC), 573
Bennett, Arnold, 369
Bennett, Harry, 399, 405, 406-408
Bennett, Marion T., 290
Benny, Jack, 49, 760
Benson, Elmer A., 296, 297, 298-299, 300-301, 306
Benson, Ezra T., 203
Benson, Simon, 91
Benton, Thomas Hart, 281
Berezney, Peter, 385
Berge, Wendell, 144, 148, 152
Berger, Victor L., 321(fn.)
Berkeley, California, 4, 19, 61
Berle, Adolf A., Jr., 563, 572, 619(fn.)
Berlin, New Hampshire, 464
Bernard, Charlie, 405
Berninghaus, Oscar, 888
Berryville, Virginia, 707
Berwind, Edward J., 568
Best & Co., 908
Bethlehem, Pennsylvania, 602
Bethlehem Steel Company, 312, 444, 567, 620, 623, 631
Bethune, Mary McLeod, 696
Beverly, Massachusetts, 517
Beverly Hills, California, 44, 48(fn.), 809
Bez, Nicholas, 98
Bickett, John H., 857
Biddeford, Maine, 487
Biddle, Francis, 25, 462(fn.), 648, 909
Bienville, Jean, 804
Bierce, Ambrose, 7, 12
Bierce, Sarah, 691
Biffle, Leslie, 908
The Big Bosses, 590(fn.), 609 (fn.)
Big Horn River, 183

Big Inch Pipe Line, 909
Big Sandy, 640
Big Spring, Texas, 823
Big Steel, see also United States Steel Corporation, 70, 73, 212, 617-621
Biggs, Burch C., 755
Bigler, Governor, (Cal.), 14(fn.)
Bilbo, Theodore G., 108, 547, 576, 655, 657, 677, 691, 696, 699, 745, 788, 786, 799, 801
Bill of Rights, 706
Billings, Montana, 162-163, 172
Billingsley, Sherman, 559
Billy the Kid, 761, 888
Binder, Carroll, 374
Bingay, Malcolm W., 404, 419 (fn.)
Bingham, Barry, 647
Bingham, Utah, 211
Binghamton, New York, 538
Bioff, Willie, 50
Bird-in-Hand, Pennsylvania, 628
Birmingham, Alabama, x, 615, 655, 660, 670, 672, 674, 736, 794
Bisbee, Arizona, 559, 905
Bishop, Texas, 866
Bismarck, North Dakota, 183, 237, 238, 243, 244, 250, 671, 908
Bismarck Capital, 238
Bittner, Van A., 621, 675
Black, Hugo, 676, 914
Black, James B., 620
Black, Robert, 445
Black Boy (Wright), 801(fn.)
Black Dispatch, 882
Black Dragon society, 787
Black Hills, 246
Black Metropolis, 385(fn.)
Blake, Doris, 368
Blake, James D., 921
Blake, William, 15, 120
Blanchard, Doc, 671
Blanchard, Lem, 262
Blease, Cole L., 675
Bliven, Bruce, 124, 559
Blood, Dr. Robert O., 490
"Bloody" Harlan, Kentucky, 643
Bloom, Sol, 541
Bloomington Pantagraph, 375
Blowdell-Donovan Lumber Company, 141
Bloy, Leon, 379
Blu, Elmer, 313
Blue, Robert D., 250(fn.), 334, 338, 339
Blue, Texas, 826
Blue Network, 360
Blue River, 215
Blue Sky law, 260
Bluefield, West Virginia, 715
Bluegrass, 642-643, 759
Bluford, Lucile, 356
Board of Economic Warfare, 325, 327
Bobbs-Merrill Company, 387
Boddy, Manchester, 40, 922
Boeing Aircraft Company, 98, 101, 119, 142-143, 263
Boettcher, Claude K., 214, 215, 220, 223
Boettiger, Anna Roosevelt, 99

Bogart, Humphrey, 49
Boise, Idaho, 108, 113, 114, 117
Boise *Statesman*, 113
Bolivia, 671
Bolté, Charles G., 559
Bolton, Frances, 798(fn.)
Bond, Reford, 870
Bone, Homer T., 99, 172
Bonfils, F. G., 225
Bonneville Dam, 66, 69, 118-123, 127-128, 132, 142, 187, 744, 745, 746
Bonneville Power Administration, 120-121, 127-128, 132, 921
The Book of the States, 1945-1946,
Bookmobiles, 739
Books, banning of, 517-518
Boone, Daniel, 603, 640, 880
Borah, Leo A., 252(fn.)
Borah, William Edgar, 110, 116-117, 175
Borden Company, 319
Borglum, Gutzon, 246
The Boss, 596
Boston, Massachusetts, 90, 128 (fn.), 224, 385, 387, 426, 456, 457, 458, 461, 462, 464, 467, 469, 472, 474, 476, 477(fn.), 510, 478, 479, 483(fn.), 486, 496, 498, 500, 507, 508, 509, 511, 512, 513, 515, 516, 517, 518-521, 525, 553, 584, 603, 605, 661, 705, 832, 897, 911; trustees in, 518-519
Boston & Maine Railway, 490
Boston Club, 805, 812-813
Boston *Globe*, 498, 512
Boston *Herald*, 459, 462, 509, 509(fn.), 510(fn.), 511
Boston Social Register, 462
Boston *Transcript*, 459
Boston Transit Commission, 483
Boston University, 520
Boston's Immigrants 1790-1865, a Study in Acculturation (Handlin), 513(fn.)
Boswell amendment, 796-797
Bosworth, Robert G., 222
Bottolfsen, Clarence A., 110, 115
Boulder, Colorado, 218
Boulder, Montana, 158, 160
Boulder Canyon Project Act, 903
Boulder Dam, 66, 68, 69, 124, 540, 736, 902-903
Bovard, Oliver K., 280
Bowdoin College, 474
Bowen, Albert E., 200, 203
Bowers, Lloyd, 432
Bowers, Martha, 432
Bowery(NYC), 574
Bowles, Chester, 103, 333, 471, 504, 581, 914
Bowling Green University, 454
Box, Texas, 826
Boyer, Charles, 49
Boys' Ranch, 837
Bozeman, John, 162, 163
Bozeman, Montana, 172, 177
Bozrah, Connecticut, 504
Braden, Spruille, 808
Braddock, Pennsylvania, 617
Bradford, Roark, 666

Bradford, Robert F., 462, 507, 508
Bradley, Albert, 418
Bradley, Fred, 290
Bradley, Phillips, 154(fn.)
Brahmins, 461, 470, 472, 507, 519
Brainerd, Minnesota, 295
Brandeis, George, 255
Brandeis, Louis D., xiii, 433, 516
Brandt, Carl, 921
Brandy Gulch, California, 10
Brandywine River, 632, 633
Brant, Irving, 531
Brazil, 400, 404, 615, 696, 783
Breckinridge, Desha, 644
Brennan, George, 373
Bretton Woods Agreements, 104, 250, 324, 435
Brewers, 319
Brewster, Owen, 470, 609
"Brewster's Millions," 760
Bricker, John, 30, 282, 428, 430-431, 436-439, 525, 532, 844
Bricker, Mrs. John, 437
Bridge Builders, Inc., 66
Bridgeport, Connecticut, 505, 506, 552
Bridgeport, Ohio, 441
Bridger, Jim, 162, 163
Bridges, Harry, 15, 21, 23, 24-27, 34, 39, 101, 103, 219, 609, 851
Bridges, Styles, 471
Briggs, Colonel Robert W., 859, 860, 862
Bright, Colonel William H., 228
The Brimstone Game (Montgomery), 815(fn.)
Brinkley, John R., 268
Brinsers, 628
Bristol, Pennsylvania, 69, 611
Bristol, Virginia, 758(fn.)
Bristol Myers Co., 514
British loan, 241, 250, 290-291, 324, 362, 434, 541
British Ministry of Information, 921
Broadway Association, 383
Brogan, Professor D. W., 15, 76, 147, 273, 631(fn.), 681(fn.)
Bromfield, Louis, 189, 441, 442
Bronco, Texas, 826
Bronx, New York, 541, 542, 543, 545, 546, 547, 549, 554, 565, 574, 597, 653
Brook Farm, 457
Brookline, Massachusetts, 215, 461, 520
Brooklyn, New York, 227, 541, 546, 553, 554, 559(fn.), 560, 563, 565, 574, 818
Brooklyn Bridge, 551
Brooklyn *Eagle*, 564(fn.)
Brooklyn Rapid Transit Company, 890
Brooks, C. Wayland, 362
Brooks, Van Wyck, 466
Brotherhood of Sleeping Car Porters, 699
Brothers Under the Skin (McWilliams), 2(fn.)
Broun, Heywood, 408

Broussard's restaurant, 809
Browder, Earl, 248(fn.)
Brown, Clarence J., 282
Brown, Earl, 286
Brown, Joe E., 880
Brown, John, 259, 260, 261
Brown, John Nicholas, 500
Brown, Melville C., 229
Brown & Sharpe, 499
Brown University, 474, 499
Browne, George E., 50
Browne, Lewis, 194
Browning, Gordon, 750
Brownlow, William G., 761
Brownsville, Pennsylvania, 617
Brownsville, Texas, 818, 819, 847, 860
Brubaker, Howard, 107, 511, 532-533
Brundage, Henry M., 584, 586
Brunswick, Maine, 485
Brush Creek, 346
Bryan, Clara, 402-403
Bryan, William Jennings, 53, 82, 253, 488, 667, 668
Bryant, William Cullen, 85, 880
Bryce, James, x, 3, 6(fn.), 12, 42, 146, 165, 232, 244(fn.), 345, 499, 552, 613, 667
Bryn Mawr College, 432, 601, 608
Buck, C. Douglass, 634
Buck, Dean Paul Herman, 466
Bucknell University, 856
Budd Company, 602
Buffalo, New York, 272, 446, 447, 536-537, 559, 659, 702, 887
Buffalo River, 537
Bugas, John S., 408, 413
Buick, 417
Building Together, 779(fn.)
Bullington, Orville, 856
Bullitt, William C., 403(fn.), 588, 609, 610
Bullock, Matthew W., 483
Bund, 95, 176, 382, 405, 789
Bunker Hill and Sullivan Mining Company, 115
Bunyan, Paul, 262, 272, 625, 820, 908
Burbank, Luther, 7, 402
Burke, Adrian, 586
Burlington, Vermont, 493, 497, 498
Burlington Railroad, 358, 474
Burr, Aaron, 564
Burton, Harold, 425, 440, 584
Burwell, Dean Charles Sidney, 466
Busch, Adolphus, 353
Busch, Noel, 527(fn.), 540(fn.)
Bush, Vannevar, 469, 914
Bush Terminal, 554
Bushfield, Harlan J., 103, 210 (fn.), 248, 369, 436, 634, 883
Bushwhackers, 341
Business and Professional Women's Club, 291(fn.)
Butler, Ellis Parker, 334
Butler, George, 846
Butler, Hugh, 250
Butler, Nicholas Murray, 908
Butte, Anaconda, and Pacific Railway Company, 167

Butte, Montana, 129(fn.), 145, 147, 157, 160, 163-172, 174, 176, 177, 178, 832, 907, 910
Butte *Miner*, 177
Butte Miners Union, 164, 165
Butte Water Company, 167
Butterfield's Overland Dispatch Line, 261
Buttram, Jim, 755
Buy Now for Security, 239
Byberry hospital, 606
Byers, W. N., 224
Byllesby, H. M., and Company, 326
Bynner, Witter, 888
Byrd, Harry Flood, 705, 706, 707-711, 726, 844, 846
Byrd, Richard, 706, 707(fn.)
Byrd, Tom, 707(fn.)
Byrd, William I, 707
Byrd, William II, 707
Byrnes, James F., 106, 396, 648, 686, 723, 727
Byron, George, 886

Cabell, James, 712
Cabot, Sebastian, 486
Cabot family, 705
Cabrillo, Juan Rodriguez, 8
Cadillac, 417
Cagney, James, 49
Cain, Harry B., 97(fn.)
Cairo, Illinois, 273
Cajuns, 804
Calais, Maine, 464
Caldwell, Erskine, 518, 666
Calhoun, Chad F., 70
Calhoun, John C., 675
California, ix, xv, 1-28, 33-75, 76, 77, 80, 144, 167, 182, 195, 214, 264(fn.), 343, 354, 418, 442 (fn.), 466, 491, 533, 535, 538, 543, 544, 572, 573, 662, 663, 728, 729, 788, 814, 818, 881, 901, 902, 903; admitted to Union, 9; agriculture, 2, 5, 16, 38, 56, 534; Alameda County, 19; area, 2; assemblymen, 31 (fn.); budget, 63; capitol, 4; Central Valley, 3, 5, 56-57; Chamber of Commerce, 33, 39; climate, 4, 7, 44-45, 90; comparison with Florida, 7; comparison with Texas, 6; cults in, 51; culture, 7; Death Valley, 3; education in, 40; electoral votes, 1; federal job holders, 41; highways, 3; history, 7, 85, 216; housing, 5; Imperial Valley, 56; income per capita, 2; independent republic, 6, 8, 9; Indians, 85, 872; industry, 2, 5, 6, 41, 64-75, 152, 743; irrigation, 4, 6, 44, 56; labor in, 24-27, 39-40, 50-51; lobbyists in, 32-33, 38-41; Los Angeles County, 3, 5, 6, 39; median age in, 5; miscellany, 63; Negroes in, 4, 45, 60-62; pensionnaires, 40, 51-52, 53, 54, 207; petroleum, 57-60; politics, 13-15, 18-24, 30, 32, 33-37, 49, 52-54, 254, 842; population, 2, 4-6, 45, 551; railroads, 3, 10,

11, 253; reconversion, 2, 5; San Bernardino County, 3, 72 (fn,); self-supporting attributes, 1; Siskiyou County, 62; topography, 2; University of, 4, 7, 28, 46, 63, 449, 922; water, 4, 6, 44, 55, 56-57, 215
California, an Intimate Guide (Drury), 921
California, an Intimate History (Atherton), 10(fn.)
California Authority for Production, 53
California Bankers Association, 27
California Fruit Growers Exchange, 38
California Tax Payers Association, 33
California Trail, 343
Californians, Inc., 33
Callaway, Cason J., 620, 779
Calumet, Illinois, 288
Calvert family, 638
Cambridge, Massachusetts, 467, 469, 469(fn.), 475, 515, 520, 603
Cambridge, Ohio, 441(fn.)
Camden, New Jersey, 606
Cameron, George T., 35, 36, 40
Camp, Walter, 256
Camp Gordon, Georgia, 424
Campbell, Caroline Margaret, 856
Campbell, Tom, 137, 179-181
Campbellites, 648, 760
Canada, 271, 272, 313, 362, 366, 404, 410, 544, 804
Candler, Asa G., 784, 785
Canfield, Cass, 921
Canham, Erwin D., 518
Canton, Ohio, 443
Canton *Daily News*, 443
Cantrell, Mr., 755, 756
Cape Cod, Massachusetts, 371, 465
Cape May, New Jersey, 597
Capital University, 454
Capone, Al, 10, 370, 379, 381, 728
Capper, Arthur, 265, 337
Capper's Farmer, 265
Capper's Weekly, 265
Carbon, Texas, 826
Cardston, Alberta, 194
Carey, James B., 916
Carey Coach Company, 585
Carlson, Anton J., 281
Carmack, Edward W., 750, 758
Carmel, California, 4
Carmel-by-the-Sea, California, 921
Carmichael, James V., 768, 769
Carnegie, Andrew, 617, 618
Carnegie Corporation of New York, 683(fn.)
Carnegie Exhibition, 625
Carnegie-Illinois Steel Corp., 617
Carnegie Natural Gas Co., 617
Carpenter, Jacob, 723
Carpenter, R. R. M., 636
Carpenter, Walter S., Jr., 636
Carr, Ralph L., 222
Carroll, John A., 223(fn.)
Carroll, Luke B., 282(fn.), 319 (fn.)

Carruth, Hayden, 245
Carson City, Nevada, 76
Cartensen, Henry, 98
Carter, Amon G., 831
Carter, Charlie, 869
Carter, Elmer, 576
Carter, Hodding, 676, 800
Carter Oil Company, 808, 880
Carter Pipe Line, 880
Carver, George Washington, xiii, 627, 798
Carville, E. P., 77
Cascades, 86-87
Case, Francis, 247
Case, J. I., Company, 319
Case bill, 241, 247, 436, 796
Casey, Mr., 10
Casey, Robert J., 374
Cash, Texas, 826
Cash, W., 658, 671
Casper, Wyoming, 227, 234, 236
Cather, Willa, 252, 888
Catholic church, xi, xiv, 77, 89, 150, 157, 193, 193(fn.), 210, 216(fn.), 222, 252, 279-280, 288, 325, 327, 334, 341, 349, 351, 352, 353, 372, 382, 389, 408, 411, 422, 427, 451, 465, 473, 500, 509, 513-514, 515, 516-517, 521, 541, 544(fn.), 553, 554, 577, 589, 603, 622, 625, 626, 648, 661, 668, 669, 786-787, 788, 794, 804, 805, 806, 809, 834, 847, 864, 865, 865(fn.), 874, 890, 893, 904, 914, 916
Catholic Telegraph-Register, 280
Cattle, *see also* Livestock, 138, 149, 157, 218, 228, 229, 230, 493, 629, 663, 728, 794, 815, 816, 817, 824, 826, 829, 830, 836, 848, 859, 861, 876
Cattleman, 831
Caucasian Problem, 688(fn.), 691(fn.)
Caughren, David, 922
Cedar Rapids, Iowa, 335
Celler, Emanuel, 541
Cellophane, 635
Central Arizona Light and Power Company, 904
Central City, Colorado, 218, 219
Central Cooperative Wholesale Association, 243
Central Maine Power Company, 487, 489, 490
Central Pacific Railroad, 11, 12, 64
Central Park (NYC), 554
Central Valley (California), 3, 5, 56-57, 663
Century Association, 577
Century of Progress World's Fair, 380
Cermak, Tony, 373
Cervi, Eugene, 223
Cézanne, Paul, 675
Chaliapin, Feodor Ivanovich, 271
Chamberlain, John, 531, 770(fn.)
Chamberlain, William B., 897, 921
Chandler, Albert Benjamin, 643, 648-649
Chandler, Harry, 35, 36

Chapel Hill, North Carolina, 218, 654, 718, 721, 722, 877
Chaplin, William E., 229
Chapman, Charles H., 95
Chapman, Virgil, 648
Chapultepec Conference, 471
Charitable Irish Society (Boston), 480, 513
Charles II, King, 501, 601
Charleston, South Carolina, 659, 675, 720, 724-725, 800, 802, 910
Charleston (S. C.) *News and Courier*, 726, 727
Charleston, West Virginia, 716, 829
Charlotte, North Carolina, 671, 719
Charlottesville, Virginia, 712(fn.)
Chase, Ray P., 301
Chase, Stuart, 109, 124, 125, 287, 921
Chase National Bank, 27, 566, 572
Chattanooga, Tennessee, 672, 738, 739, 740, 760, 785
Chattanooga Chamber of Commerce, 732
Chattanooga Electric Power Board, 732
Chautauqua, 535
Chavez, Dennis, 890, 896
Chemical Bank & Trust Company, 572
Chennault, Claire L., 822(fn.)
Cherokee Dam, 740
Cherokee Indians, 870, 871, 872, 874
Cherrington, Dr. Ben M., 219 (fn.)
Cherry, R. Gregg, 688
Chesapeake & Ohio Railway Company, 358, 717
Chesapeake Bay, 630, 637
Chester, Montana, 161
Chester, West Virginia, 715
Chestnut Hill, Pennsylvania, 604
Chevrolet, 404, 415, 417
Cheyenne, Wyoming, 152, 220, 227, 228, 229, 230, 234, 235, 337(fn.), 831, 910
Cheyenne *Eagle*, 231
Cheyenne Light Fuel and Power Company, 234
Cheyenne River, 183
Cheyenne *State-Tribune and Leader*, 231, 232, 921
Chicago, Burlington & Quincy Railroad, 253
Chicago, Illinois, 2, 3, 10, 29, 93, 100, 128, 142, 152, 220, 255, 271, 272, 274, 276, 278, 280, 281, 282, 291, 344, 348, 358, 359, 361, 362, 367, 368, 369-374, 375, 382, 410, 442, 446, 447, 460, 471, 476, 497, 528, 535, 537, 539, 555(fn.), 592, 620, 621, 629, 672, 708, 730, 737, 743, 783, 787, 792, 811, 819, 825, 882, 910; crime in, 379-381; Negroes in, 62, 283, 285, 360, 383-385, 626
Chicago, Milwaukee, St. Paul & Pacific Railroad Co., 168, 174, 910

Chicago, University of, 218, 365, 374, 375-379, 387, 636, 638, 747, 747(fn.)
Chicago Association of Commerce, 381
Chicago Council on Foreign Relations, 444
Chicago *Daily News*, 235, 280, 351, 373, 374, 381, 922
Chicago *Defender*, 383-384
Chicago *Evening Post*, 374
Chicago *Herald-American*, 373
Chicago Planning Commission, 372
Chicago *Sun*, 373, 378(fn.), 380, 381, 382
Chicago *Times*, 365, 373
Chicago *Tribune*, 22, 225, 237, 271, 280, 288, 289, 359-369, 374, 379, 384-385, 386(fn.), 403, 648, 881
Chichiechockie, Oklahoma, 874
Chickamauga Dam, 740
Chickasaw Indians, 870, 871, 872, 874
Child labor, 612
Childe Harold (Byron), 886
Children's Magazine, 501
Childs, Marquis W., 104, 710
Chile, 371
Chile Copper Company, 167
Chimayó, New Mexico, 895-896
China, 2, 83, 186, 558, 798(fn.)
Chinook, Montana, 161
Chippewa Indians, 310
Chisholm Trail, 861
Choctaw Club, 805
Choctaw Indians, 870, 871, 874
Chow, Albert, 46
Christenberry, Robert, 383
Christian American Association, 765, 852
Christian Front, 516, 543, 554, 563
Christian Science Monitor, 518
Christian Scientists, 553, 882
Christiana Securities Company, 634
Christopherson, F. C., 249
Chronology of Iron and Steel, 617(fn.)
Chrysler, Walter, 419
Chrysler Corporation, 290, 400, 411, 412, 418, 419
Chung, Dr. Margaret J., 46
Church of the Brethren, 628
Churchill, Randolph, 523
Churchill, Winston, 544, 917
Churchill Downs, 640, 646
Cicotte, Ed, 405
Cigarette paper industry, 719 (fn.)
Cigarettes, 672, 713
Cigars, 713
Cincinnati, New Orleans, and Texas Pacific Railroad, 447 (fn.)
Cincinnati, Ohio, 128(fn.), 280, 351, 357, 426, 431, 433, 438, 440, 441, 443, 446-450, 451, 454, 625, 671
Cincinnati, University of, 432, 454

Cincinnati *Enquirer*, 447
Cincinnati Milling Machine Company, 447
Cincinnati *Post*, 446
Cincinnati *Times-Star*, 432, 450
Cistern, Texas, 826
Cities Service Company, 220, 234
Citizens Fact-Finding Movement, 774
Citizens Protective League, 853
City College (NYC), 577
City Light (Seattle), 129-130
Civic Association of Northeastern Minnesota, 313(fn.)
Civil Aeronautics Board, 93
Civil Service Commission, 97, 917
Civil Service *Leader*, 557
Civil War, 80, 341, 353, 494, 615, 654, 655, 656, 677, 678, 714, 717, 721, 824
Claghorn, Senator, 657
Clapp, Gordon R., 738
Clapp, William, 125
Clapper, Raymond, 223, 302
Clark, Bennett Champ, 291
Clark, Clarence D., 229
Clark, D. Worth, 110, 291
Clark, J. Reuben Jr., 198-199, 202-203, 206
Clark, Thomas D., 643, 817
Clark, Tom C., 59, 686, 778
Clark, William, 85, 161, 173, 343
Clark, William A., 167-168, 177
Clark family (Idaho), 115
Clarkdale, Arizona, 905
Clarksdale, Mississippi, 793
Clarksville, Tennessee, 759
Clason's Point, 554
Clauson, Leon R., 319
Clay, Henry, 640
Clayton, Georgia, 664, 773
Clayton, William L., 471, 474, 817, 847, 914
Clayton, Mrs. William L., 847
Clayton Act, 191
Clearwater Timber Company, 115
Cleland, R. G., 11
Clement, M. W., 608
Clement, Rufus E., 680
Clements, J. Burke, 177
Clermont, 535
Cleveland, Grover, 30, 142, 476, 537, 540, 543, 706, 847
Cleveland, Ohio, 53, 142, 270, 272, 283, 410, 422, 423, 424, 425, 426(fn.), 428, 429, 440, 441, 443-447, 448, 450, 451, 466, 553, 584, 615, 715
Cleveland Council on World Affairs, 444
Cleveland *News*, 446
Cleveland *Plain Dealer*, 446, 450
Cleveland *Press*, 446
Cleveland Trust Company, 444
Clifford, Clark, 350
Climate, *see* under names of States
Climax, Texas, 86
Climax Molybdenum Company, 153, 222
Clinch River, 733
Cline, Miss., 847
Clinton, De Witt, 524

Clinton, Tennessee, 636
Clinton Laboratories, 378
Cloquet, Minnesota, 311
Clugston, W. G., 256, 258(fn.), 260(fn.), 268(fn.)
Coal, 601, 615, 616, 624, 674, 717
Cobb, Irvin S., 642
Coca-Cola Co., 166, 191, 631, 669, 670, 672, 732, 768, 783, 784-786, 803, 913
Cœur d'Alene, Idaho, 115
Coffee, John M., 100
Coghlan, Ralph, 590(fn.), 592 (fn.), 922
Cohen, Betty, 580, 581, 583, 584, 586, 587
Cohen, Joseph, 219
Cohn, David L., 404(fn.), 662, 779(fn.)
Coke, Richard, 840
Cole, Gordon H., 709(fn.)
Colella, Phil, 385
Coleman, Thomas E., 325
Colfax, Washington, 135
Collegiate Reformed Protestant Dutch church, 553
Collett, Judge, 350
Collier, John, 872, 873
Collier, Randolph, 34
Collier's Magazine, 188, 725 (fn.), 844, 852, 884
Collings, Ben, 649
Colombia, 371
Colonial Airlines Inc., 488
Colony restaurant, 809
Colorado, 55, 67, 115, 144, 146, 151, 152, 195, 213-226, 227-228, 258, 259, 572, 821, 860, 873, 902; agriculture, 216, 217; climate, 150; electric power, 185; history, 216; industry, 220; labor, 222; lumber, 218; mining, 216-217; politics, 148, 149, 220-223; railroads, 220; scenery, 213, 214; University, 218-219, 921; water, 214-216
Colorado Education Association, 221
Colorado Fuel and Iron Company, 153, 220
Colorado River, 3, 29, 56, 215, 840(fn.)
Colorado Springs, Colorado, 217, 223
Columbia, Missouri, 356
Columbia, South Carolina, 723
Columbia, Tennessee, 685, 759
Columbia Basin Inter-Agency Committee, 132
Columbia Construction Co., 66-67
Columbia Gas & Electric Corp., 568
Columbia River, 85, 118-123, 227, 732, 748
Columbia Steel & Brass Corp., 211
Columbia University, 105, 526, 554
Columbia Valley Authority, 97, 104, 132-133, 171
Columbians, Inc., 789
Columbus, Ohio, 152, 271(fn.),
423, 428, 430(fn.), 431, 438, 441, 442, 443, 448, 450-452, 454, 466, 829, 910
Columbus Citizen, 446
Columbus Dispatch, 451, 452
Comanche Indians, 870
Combs, J. M., 853
Combustion on Wheels (Cohn), 404(fn.)
Comer, Donald, 794
Commager, Henry Steele, 459
Commercial Club (Chicago), 372
Committee for Constitutional Government, 537
Committee for Economic Development, 472
Committee for Georgia, 771(fn.), 779(fn.)
Committee for Kentucky, 640
Commodity Credit Corporation, 138
Common Sense, 365
Commonwealth & Southern Corporation, 572, 631, 735, 745, 768
Communists, xiv, 2, 25, 26, 39, 49, 50-51, 54, 98, 99, 100, 133, 205, 206, 223, 277, 285, 287, 297, 301, 322, 325, 353, 360, 365, 371, 377, 381, 382, 389, 390, 409, 410, 411, 545, 547, 563, 576, 609, 622, 668, 676, 689, 706, 788, 803, 856, 890, 916
Compton, Arthur, 378
Compton, Karl T., 466, 467
Comstock Lode, 80, 81
Comus Club, 812-813
Conant, James Bryant, 378(fn.), 461, 466, 469
Concord, Massachusetts, 465
Concord, New Hampshire, 458, 490, 492
Concord (New Hampshire) Monitor, 492, 910
Coney Island, 554
Conference of Studio Unions, 50-51
Congress of Industrial Organizations, see also Political Action Committee, 22, 25, 26, 35, 39-40, 54, 62, 70, 74, 95-96, 98, 99, 100, 101, 107, 116, 164, 222, 234, 247, 292(fn.), 301, 306, 325, 349, 355, 371, 409, 411, 426, 430, 440, 443, 448, 449, 471, 472, 479, 488, 521, 575, 595, 621, 622, 626, 674, 675, 710, 782, 782(fn.), 788, 796, 846, 853, 853(fn.), 881, 916, 921
Congressional Record, 111, 112, 287(fn.), 290, 309, 503, 514, 572, 657, 699, 709, 755, 755 (fn.), 757(fn.), 851
Connally, Tom, 80, 763, 848
Connecticut, 167, 195, 251, 441, 457, 458, 459, 470, 471, 472 (fn.), 483, 485, 499, 501-506, 723, 821, 834, 895, 910; agriculture, 467; income per capita, 2(fn.); industry, 501, 502,
505; labor, 504; politics, 503, 890; Tolland County, 502
Connecticut Yankee (Cross), 502-503
Connelly, Marc, 49
The Conqueror, 395
Conrad, Gaylord, 238
Consolidated Builders, Inc., 67
Consolidated Edison Company of New York, Inc., 419, 553(fn.), 572
Consolidated Vultee Aircraft Corp., 55
Constable, John, 604
Continental Airlines, 908
Continental Oil Company, 234, 264
Conway, Massachusetts, 371
Cookingham, L. P., 345
Coolidge, Calvin, 14, 30, 175(fn.), 417, 439, 450, 482, 495, 539, 570, 734, 909
Cooper, Gary, 49, 159, 181
Cooper, Kent, 365, 386
Cooper Union, 577
Cooperative Grain Marketing in the United States, 243(fn.)
Co-operatives, 238, 242-244, 318, 336-337
Copper Camp (WPA), 163
Copperopolis, Montana, 158
Corcoran, John H., 475
Corcoran, Tommy, 110
Cordon, Guy, 148
Corey, William E., 619
Corn, 256, 262, 328-331, 335-336, 374, 385, 743, 780, 790, 807
Corn Exchange Bank Trust Co., 568, 608
Cornell University, 180, 524, 537, 541, 798
Corning, Mayor, 544
Corning, New York, 538
Coronado, Francisco Vásquez de, 887-888
Corporations, 569-573, 623, 631, 771
Corpus Christi, Texas, 827(fn.)
Corrupt Practices Act, 382
Cortes, Hernando, 8
Corvallis, Oregon, 95
Corwin, Norman, 49, 921
Cost, Texas, 826
Costello, Frank J., 564
Costello, John M., 35
Costelloe, Dr. Edward C., 585
Costigan, Howard G., 98, 99
Cotton, 268, 329(fn.), 341-342, 660, 664, 673, 724, 759, 760, 763, 780, 782, 790-794, 800, 802, 805, 815, 817, 824, 825-826, 827, 829, 847, 854, 876
Cotton Textile Institute of the United States, 670
Couch, Harvey, 766, 800
Coughlin, Bathhouse John, 372
Coughlin, Father Charles E., xv, 50, 53, 176, 280, 288, 363 (fn.), 382, 515, 516
Council Bluffs, Iowa, 335
Council of American Indians, 874
Council of State Governments, 371

Council on Foreign Relations, 577
Couzens, James, 403
Covington, Kentucky, 644(fn.), 652
Cow Shanty, Connecticut, 505
Cowles, Gardner, 337
Cowles, John, 302, 303, 337
Cowley, Malcolm, vii, 505(fn.)
Cox, James M., 440, 784
Craighead, Barclay, 177
Crane, Charles R., 370
Craney, Ed, 177
Crawford, G. G., 621
Crawford, Joan, 821
Creager, R. B., 847, 848
Creek Indians, 870, 874, 877
Creoles, 804, 804(fn.)
Cripple Creek, Colorado, 216
Crock of Gold, 562
Crocker, William H., 567
Crockett, Davy, 762, 820
Cromwell, Oliver, 880
Cronin, Dick, 385
Crosby, Bing, 49
Crosby, John, 362
Crosley Corporation, 447
Cross, Wilbur, 459, 502
Cross and Flag, 176
Crossroads Middletown, 291
Crowley, Leo T., 325-327, 595
Crown Point, Oregon, 120
Crown Zellerbach Pulp and Paper Company, 141
Cruikshank, Robin, 921
Crum, Bartley C., 922
Crump, E. H., 346, 589, 655, 746, 749-755, 760, 762, 762(fn.), 805
Crump, E. H. & Company, 752
Crump, E. H., Buggy and Harness Company, 752
The Crusader, 795
Crystal City, Texas, 821(fn.)
Cub Room, 558
Cuba, 69, 221, 545, 634
Culbertson, Charles A., 839
Cullen, H. R., 851
Cullen, Roy, 828
Cultural History of Japan (Sansom), 683
Culture of a Contemporary Rural Community, 629(fn.)
Cumberland Gap, Kentucky, 640
Cumberland Trail, 761
Cummings, Homer, 178, 470
Curley, James Michael, 456, 478, 482, 498, 508, 510
Curran, Edward L., 363(fn.)
Curran, Joe, 26
Curray, Kid, 161
Curry, John Steuart, 261, 281
Curtis, Charles, 869, 922
Curtis, Cyrus H., 568
Curzon, Marquess of, 370
Cushing, Richard James, 464, 480-481, 517
Custer, George, 145, 147, 158
Cutting, Bronson, 887, 896
Cyclone Fence Division—American Steel & Wire Co., 617
Cypress, Texas, 826
Czechoslovakia, 616

Dabney, Virginius, 657, 662, 662 (fn.), 670, 676, 684(fn.), 921
Daddario, Captain Emilio Quincy, 505
Daily Worker, 564(fn.), 576, 916
Dalhart, Texas, 821
Dallas, Texas, 90, 128(fn.), 224, 353, 538, 574, 783, 815, 818, 819, 821, 826, 829, 830, 831, 836, 843, 846, 852, 853, 857, 864, 866, 868, 877, 880
Dallas Express, 868
Dallas News, 830, 865
Dallas Times Herald, 826
Dalmas, Sophie, 632
Daly, Marcus, 167-168, 171
Daly's Theater, 557
Danaher, John A., 291, 471
Danbury, Ohio, 441
Dancewicz, Boly, 385
Daniels, Jonathan, 489(fn.), 658, 676, 720, 731, 786(fn.), 921
Daniels, Josephus, 659-660, 668, 720
Darden, Colgate W., Jr., 711
Darden, Mrs. Colgate W., Jr., 711
Darden, Miles, 762
Dark Entry, Connecticut, 505
Darrow, Clarence, xiii
Dartmouth College, 474, 483, 490, 491, 596
Darvell, Frank, 921
Daugherty, Harry M., 178
Daughters of the American Revolution, 513
Davenport, Iowa, 335
David, Donald K., 466, 467
Davis, Julius Richard, 543
Davis, Arthur V., 568
Davis, Benjamin J., Jr., 576
Davis, Elmer, 245, 326, 386
Davis, Glen, 671
Davis, James J., 291, 609, 611
Davis, Jefferson, 527, 640, 712, 803
Davis, Jimmie H., 806-807
Davis, John W., 178(fn.), 559
Davis, Norman H., 570
Davis, William H., 561
Davy, Randall, 888
Dawes, General Charles G., 372
Day, Harriet, 437
Daylight saving time, 438
Dayton, Ohio, 449(fn.)
Dayton, Tennessee, 667
DDT, 635, 907
De Gaulle, General Charles, 587
De Soto, Kansas, 263
De Valera, Mr., 513
De Voto, Bernard, 8, 196, 457, 857
De Witt Clinton, 535
Deadwood, South Dakota, 144, 246, 247
Deal, New Jersey, 596
Dealey, George, 830
Dearborn, Michigan, 398, 399, 412
Dearborn Independent, 403
Death Valley, 3, 546
Debs, Eugene, 91
Decatur, Alabama, 736
Declaration of Independence, xi, 600, 616-617, 630, 705, 920

Dedham, Massachusetts, 520
Deepwater, New Jersey, 636
Deere, John, 279, 335
Deere & Company, 793
Deerfield Boys' School, 474
Defender, 176
Defense Plant Corporation, 73, 211, 672
Del Norte County, California, 62
Del Rio, Texas, 268
DeLacy, Hugh, 99
Delaney, John, 587
Delaplane, Stanton, 63
Delaware, xiii, 140, 155, 235, 273, 466, 601, 607, 630-634, 638, 654, 785(fn.), 821; area, 630; counties, 630; history, 630; Kent County, 630(fn.); Newcastle County, 630(fn.); population, 630, 631; Sussex County, 630 (fn.)
Delaware, Ohio, 454
Delaware River, 597, 606, 607
Dell, Floyd, 374
Democracy Begins at Home: the Tennessee Fight on the Poll Tax, 754(fn.)
Democracy in America (Tocqueville), 154(fn.)
Dempsey, Jack, xiii, 110
Dempsey, John J., 250(fn.), 890, 891, 895
Denison University, 454
Dennis, Charles H., 280
Denton, Texas, 868
Denver, Colorado, xiii, 69, 94, 128(fn.), 145, 148, 151, 152, 153, 214, 215, 216, 217, 218, 220, 223, 228, 242, 256, 466, 760, 874, 910, 911
Denver, James W., 224
Denver, University of, 219(fn.), 226, 921
Denver Post, 106, 206, 214, 220, 225, 911
Denver Rocky Mountain News, 223, 224, 225
Depression, 108, 611, 621, 673, 734, 747, 778, 781, 811
Derby, 640
Dern, George, 203
Des Moines, Iowa, 3, 328, 332, 334, 335, 337, 754
Des Moines Register and Tribune, 280, 330, 337-338, 921
Des Moines River, 809
Deseret News, 190, 203, 205, 206, 207
Desnet, Idaho, 114
Desprez, Frank, 814
Detroit, Michigan, 74, 88, 128 (fn.), 142, 151, 272, 274, 276, 280, 285, 286, 355, 373, 382, 398, 405, 407, 408, 409, 410, 411, 412, 413, 414, 417, 444, 446, 448, 488, 536, 539, 552, 553, 555(fn.), 584, 603(fn.), 616, 618, 622, 626, 631, 743, 897
Detroit Free Press, 404
Detroit Is My Own Home Town (Bingay), 404(fn.)
Deuel, Wallace R., 374
Deutsch, Albert, 606

Dever, Paul A., 478
Dewey, George, 525
Dewey, George Martin, 525
Dewey, Thomas, 525
Dewey, Thomas E., 20, 36, 222, 233, 282, 302-303, 369, 392, 426, 430-431, 436, 439, 450, 479, 487, 489, 498, 500, 503, 505, 523-533, 537, 539, 540, 541, 542(fn.), 544, 544(fn.), 560, 561, 563, 564, 565(fn.), 588, 611, 627, 846, 847, 901
Dewey, Mrs. Thomas E., 527(fn.)
Diamond, "Legs," 530
Dickens, Charles, 273-274, 536, 684
Dickinson, Emily, 118, 457
Dictionary of American Biography, 644
Dies, Martin, 363(fn.), 826, 846, 853, 854
Dies Committee, 35, 39, 91, 789
DiGiovanni, Anthony J., 544
Dillinger gang, 471
Dillon, Mary, 583
Dillon, Montana, 172
Dime, Texas, 826
Disciples of Christ, 648
Disney, Walt, 49, 51
District of Columbia, see also Washington, D. C., 28, 781
Dix, Dorothy, 809
Dixon, Governor (Montana), 169
Dobie, J. Frank, 818, 840, 860, 865, 921
Dodd, Mr., 504
Dodge, Henry Chee, 895
Dodge brothers, 403, 404
Dodge City, Kansas, 261, 860
Dodgers, 554
Dodgingtown, Connecticut, 505
Doherty, Henry L., 234
Dollfuss, Engelbert, 810
Donahey, Alvin Victor, 452-453
Dondero, Mrs. Mary C., 489
Donnell, Forrest C., 349, 350
Donnelly, Antoinette, 368
Donnelly, Phil, 349(fn.)
Donnelly, Thomas C., 77(fn.)
Donner party, 8
Donovan, William J., 537, 544 (fn.)
Doolittle raid, 815
Dorais, Gus, 406
Dorchester, Massachusetts, 515, 516, 525
Dos Passos, John, 374, 841, 858
Douglas, Helen Gahagan, 37
Douglas, James S., 901
Douglas, Lewis W., 559, 563, 901
Douglas, William O., 29, 914
Douglass, Frederick, 691
Dover, Delaware, 29, 76(fn.), 630, 631
Dover, Massachusetts, 480
Downey, Sheridan, 37, 54, 229
Drachman, Harry Arizona, 900 (fn.)
Downie, Mildred, see Morse, Mrs. Wayne
Drainage Canal, 371
Drake, Sir Francis, 8
Dreher, Carl, 130(fn.)
Dreiser, Theodore, 385, 386

Drexel & Company, 419
Drew, Daniel, 535
Driscoll, Alfred E., 594
Drucci, "Schemer," 381
Drum, Hugh A., 544(fn.)
Drury, Aubrey, 921
Dryden, John, 199
Du Bois, W. E. B., 575, 679, 680, 681, 682, 688, 690, 691, 693, 695
Dubinsky, David, 553
Dublin, Ohio, 450
Ducktown, Georgia, 663
Duco, 635
Duffus, R. L., 734(fn.)
Duke, J. B., 713
Duke University, 671, 722, 784
Dulles brothers, 909
Duluth, Missabe. & Iron Range Railway, 311
Dumas, Texas, 837
Dumbarton Oaks Agreements, 32, 532, 779
Dunbar's Weekly, 898
Duncan, Isadora, 7
Dungee, Roscoe, 881
Dunn, James C., 471
Dunn, Roy E., 299, 302-303
Du Pont, Lammot, 369(fn.), 383, 419, 632, 633, 634
DuPont Belle Ammonia plant, 716
Du Pont de Nemours, E. I., & Co., 572, 631, 635-637
Du Pont family, 568, 573, 630, 631-636
Duluth, Minnesota, 272, 301, 309-310, 312, 424, 539, 754, 827(fn.)
Dunkards, 628
Duquesne Light Company, 625
Durant, William C., 419
Duranty, Walter, 52, 921
Durham, North Carolina, 284, 672, 713, 719, 722
Durocher, Leo, 908
Dust Bowl, 239, 683, 837-838, 879
Dutch Guiana, 615
Dwight, Ben, 870
Dwight, Timothy, 432, 494
Dykstra, Clarence, 449, 922

Eagle Mountain, 72(fn.)
Eagle Pass, Texas, 821
Eagles club, 611(fn.)
Eaker, General, 822(fn.)
Earle, George H., 610
Earth, Texas, 826
East Chicago, Indiana, 167, 234
East India Company, 616
East River, 555, 557
East St. Louis, Illinois, 357, 375
Eastern Air Lines, Inc., 729
Eastland, James O., 799
Eastman, E. V., 245
Eastman Kodak Company, 537, 909
Easton, Pennsylvania, 603
Ebony, Texas, 826
Eccles, Marriner, 909
Echo, Texas, 826
Economic Analysis of the State of Minnesota, 313(fn.)

Economic Freedom for the West (Berge), 144
Economic Stabilization Board, 472
Economists National Committee on Monetary Policy, 82
Edge, Walter Evans, 594
Edgemoor, Delaware, 636
Edinburg, Texas, 821
Edison, Charles, 593, 595
Edison, Thomas E., xiii, 81, 402
Edison Electric Institute, 409, 746
Edson, C. L., 343(fn.), 763
Edward VII, King, 706
Edwards, Jonathan, 494
Edwards, Mayor (Seattle), 130
Egan, Leo, 542
Eggers, Frank Hague, 596
Egtvedt, Claire, 98
Einstein, Albert, 599, 681, 740
Eisenhower, Dwight, xiv, 147, 264, 661(fn.), 817, 914
Eisenhower, Milton S., 264, 419
El Centro, California, 61
El Paso, Texas, 819, 835, 836
El Paso Herald, 853(fn.)
El Paso Herald-Post, 890
"Eleanor Clubs," 697
Electric Bond and Share Company, 115, 126, 127, 208, 254, 568, 766, 815
Electric power, see Power; and under names of States
Elgin, Illinois, 375
Elisha, James, 794
Elizabeth, Queen, 705
Elkins, T. A., 827
Elks club, 277, 611(fn.)
Ellender, Allen J., 436, 700
Ellis, Scott, 330-332
Ellis Island, 555
Elmira, New York, 538
Ely, Joseph B., 509
Emancipation Proclamation, 699
Emanuel, Victor, 326
Emeny, Brooks, 922
Emerson, Ralph Waldo, 460, 491, 518, 714
Emeryville, California, 74
Emigrant Industrial Savings Bank, 419
Emmet, Daniel D., 705
Emory University, 784
Emporia Gazette, 257
Encyclopaedia Britannica, 58(fn.), 166, 167, 200(fn.), 371, 376, 781, 878
End Poverty in California, 53
Endicott, New York, 538
England, see Great Britain
Enid, Oklahoma, 884
Ephraim, Wisconsin, 318
Ephrata, Washington, 125
The Epic of America (Adams), 145(fn.), 656(fn.)
Erickson, Leif, 169, 171, 174, 178, 179(fn.)
Erie, Lake, 272, 311, 445, 602
Erie, Pennsylvania, 272
Erie Railroad, 442
Ernst, Morris, 922
Escanaba, Michigan, 272
Essex, Connecticut, 501

Ethridge, Mark, 647, 660, 672, 673, 676
Ethyl Corporation, 419
Eugene, Oregon, 105
Eureka Springs, Arkansas, 766
Evans, H. W., 389(fn.)
Evans, J. W., 827, 828, 922
Evans, John G., 893
Evans, Silliman, 753, 922
Evans, Stewart, 405
Evans, Warden, 764
Evanston, Illinois, 370
Evansville, Indiana, 231, 385, 386(fn.)
Eveleth, Minnesota, 311
Everett, Rollin H., 449
Everett, Washington, 97
Everett House (NYC), 557
Everglades, 728
Everleigh sisters, 370
Evjue, William T., 280
Exploits of Elaine (film), 537
Export-Import Bank, 325

Facts About Maine, 486
Facts You Should Know About Kansas (Clugston), 258(fn.)
Fadiman, Clifton, 556(fn.), 772, 921
Fair, Jim, 81
Fair Employment Practice Commission, 104, 241, 355, 435, 677, 696, 699, 700, 776, 801, 890
Fairbanks, Douglas, 220
Fairbanks Morse & Company, 319
Fairless, Benjamin, S., 619, 620, 623
Fall River, Massachusetts, 464
Farben, I. G., 327, 636
Fargo, North Dakota, 215
Farley, Cal, 837
Farley, James, 53, 87, 558, 921
Farm Bureau, 32, 39, 336-337, 339
Farm Credit Administration, 243 (fn.)
Farm Journal, 611
Farm Security Administration, 674(fn.)
Farmers Education Union, 241
Farmers Independence Council, 612
Farmers Union, 32, 95, 99, 178, 181, 226, 242-243, 336, 881
Farmers Union Central Exchange, 243
Farmers Union Grain Terminal Association, 243-244
Farmers Union Oil Company, 243
Farragut, David, 762
Farrell, James A., 567, 619
Farrell, James T., 374
Farson, Negley, 374
Fascists, xiv-xv, 2, 52, 176, 306, 364, 377, 382, 390, 809, 811
Fatt, Frank, 46
Faulkner, William, 664, 667
Fayetteville, North Carolina, 719
Federal Bureau of Investigation, 88, 281, 367, 408, 581, 671, 686, 774, 778, 788, 789, 834

Federal Communications Commission, 231(fn.), 497, 514, 644
Federal Council of the Churches of Christ in America, 450, 668, 858
Federal Crop Insurance Law, 240
Federal Deposit Insurance Corporation, 240, 325-327, 392
Federal Housing Authority, 88, 240, 304
Federal Oil Compact, 58
Federal Power Commission, 128, 132, 185, 209, 327(fn.), 766
Federal Reserve System, 76(fn.), 472, 501, 571, 829, 830
Federal Trade Commission, 403 (fn.), 404, 417, 714
Federation of Women's Clubs, 95, 292(fn.)
Felse family, 605(fn.)
Ferber, Edna, 321
Ferguson, James E., 839-840, 843(fn.), 857
Ferguson, "Ma" (Miriam), 840
Ferguson, Harvey, 888
Fermi, Professor, 378
Ferris, Woodbridge N., 394
Fertility, Pennsylvania, 628
Fessenden, Mrs. Henry, 477
Ficke, Arthur Davison, 888
Field, Marshall, 178, 281, 371, 372, 373(fn.), 425, 917
Field, Marshall, III, 373
Fight for Free Enterprise Inc., 853(fn.)
The Fighting South (Graves), 660
Fillmore, Millard, 537, 540(fn.)
Fine, Benjamin, 377(fn.)
Finger Lakes, 537
Finletter, Thomas K., 326, 921, 922
Finnegan, Richard J., 373
Fire Island, 536
First Bank Stock, Inc., 244
First Boston Corporation, 624
First National Bank of Boston, 474
Fischer, John, 921, 922
Fischer, Louis, 921
Fish, 121-122, 126, 141
Fish, Hamilton, 291, 532
Fisher, Arthur, 155
Fisher, Dorothy Canfield, 264
Fisher, Frank of J., 639
Fisher, Vardis, 117
Fisher Bodies, 417, 419, 448
Fisher brothers, 568, 713
Fisher's Island, New York, 505
Fisk, Jim, 535
Fisk University, 760, 798
Fitchburg, Massachusetts, 152, 464
Fitzgerald, F. Scott, vii
Fitzpatrick, Daniel R., 352, 357
Fitzpatrick, John F., 210
Five Cities (Leighton), 255(fn.), 650(fn.)
Five Civilized Tribes, 870, 871, 872, 874, 875
Five Nations Confederacy, 535
Flanders, Ralph E., 472, 492, 496, 914, 922
Fleeson, Doris, 267(fn.)

Flegenheimer, Arthur, 530
Fleisher family, 605
Fleming, Lamar, Jr., 828, 847
Fleming, Roscoe, 216(fn.), 225
Flemington, New Jersey, 598
Fletcher, Henry P., 302
Fletcher, John Gould, 888
Fletcher, Robert H., 160, 161, 172
Flint, Edith Foster, 281
Flint, Michigan, 412, 416, 417
Florence, South Carolina, 725
Florida, 7, 28, 239, 491, 572, 589, 593, 627, 633, 637, 653, 654, 655, 656, 658, 659, 661, 662, 663, 666, 676, 690, 701, 727-729, 807, 870, 904; climate, 730; Dade County, 728; divorce laws in, 77; politics, 728
Florida East Coast Railway, 633
Florida Power Corporation, 729
Florida Times-Union, 668
Flying Farmers, 877(fn.)
Flynn, Edward J., 554, 563
Flynn, Elizabeth Gurley, 100
Foch, Marshal, 706
Fodor, M. W., 374
Folger, John H., 676
Folsom, "Big Bill," 794, 795-796
Fond du Lac, Wisconsin, 323
Fontana, California, 65, 69, 70, 72-73, 151, 623
Fontana Dam, 740, 742, 744
Fontanne, Lynn, 908
"For Whom the Bell Tolls," 49, 50
Forbes, J. A., 9
Ford, Edsel, 407
Ford, Mrs. Edsel, 407, 408
Ford, Henry, xiii, 131, 139, 274, 398-409, 411-412, 417, 567, 569, 745
Ford, Mrs. Henry, 402-403, 744
Ford, Henry II, 398, 399, 407, 408
Ford, Mrs. Henry II, 408
Ford, James L., Jr., 357
Ford, Sam C., 177, 231(fn.)
Ford, William, 402
Ford Foundation, 409
Ford Motor Company, 70, 74, 403-404, 411, 419, 572, 631, 786
Ford Peace Ship expedition, 403
Fordham University, 470, 559, 560
Foreign Affairs, 552, 921
Foreign Economic Administration, 327, 595
Foreign Policy Association, 444
Foreign Relations Committee, 80, 817
Foreman, Clark, 768
Forerunners of American Fascism (Swing), 745(fn.)
Forest Grove, Oregon, 95
Forest Hills, Long Island, 55
Forest Service, 139, 141, 142, 157
Foresters, 611(fn)
Forever Amber, 518
Forrest, Nathan B., 787
Fort Bliss, Texas, 835
Fort Collins, Colorado, 231

Fort Dodge, Iowa, 335
Fort Knox, Kentucky, 536, 640
Fort Laramie, Wyoming, 162
Fort Madison, Iowa, 335
Fort Necessity, Pennsylvania, 602
Fort Peck, Montana, 186
Fort Sam Houston, Texas, 834
Fort Vancouver, 86
Fort Wayne, Indiana, 385
Fort Worth, Texas, 353, 663, 815, 819, 829, 830, 831, 848, 853, 863, 865, 877
Fort Worth *Mind*, 868
Fort Worth *Record*, 853(fn)
Fort Worth *Star Telegram*, 822, 831
Fortune, 4(fn.), 25, 26, 56, 74, 76, 124, 136(fn.), 141(fn.), 401 (fn.), 406(fn.), 460(fn.), 469 (fn.), 529(fn.), 558, 637 (fn.), 662(fn.), 821(fn.), 919
Fosburgh, Mr. 65
Fosburgh, Bessie, *see* Kaiser, Mrs. Henry
Fosdick, Harry Emerson, 559
Foster, Stephen, 447
Fothergill, C. S., 863
Fowles, Frank H., 34
France, 286, 310, 346, 364, 532, 601, 615, 616, 632, 635, 638, 688, 696
Franco, Francisco, 280, 352, 382, 625, 810, 811
Frank, Aaron, 91
Frank, Charlie, 424
Frankensteen, Richard T., 410, 411-412
Frankfort, Kentucky, 29, 76(fn.)
Frankfurter, Frank, 648, 795
Franklin, Benjamin, 313, 602, 605
Franklin, Jay, 134
Franklin and Marshall College, 628
Franklin College, 856
Fraser, Joseph W., 74
Freeman, Douglas Southall, 660, 799, 922
Freeman, Frank, 49
Freight rates, 73, 151-153, 218, 264, 539, 672, 775
Frémont, John, 9
French Broad River, 733
French Canadians, 465, 487, 490, 493, 500, 804
Fresno, California, 3, 61
Fresno *Republican*, 15
Frew, Walter Edwin, 568
Frick, H. C., Coke Co., 617
Frick, Henry, 609, 617, 618
Friedrich, Carl, 521, 922
From Wilderness to Empire (Cleland), 11
Fulbright, James William, 97, 676, 763
Full Employment bill, 436
Fuller, Henry B., 374
The Fundamentalist, 863

Gable, Clark, 908
Gaeth, Arthur, 205-206
Gaines, Lloyd, 356
Galatoire's restaurant, 809
Gale, Zona, 321
Galli Curci, Amelita, 271

Gallup poll, 226, 598, 660
Galveston, Texas, 827, 857, 866
Gambling, 78-79, 165-166, 260, 282, 346, 379(fn.), 426, 543, 560, 582, 584, 647, 663, 729, 751, 763, 766, 806, 834
Gandhi, 807
Gangsterism, 380-381, 787
Gannett, Frank, 537
Gannett, Lewis, 921
Gannon, Robert I., 559
Gap, Pennsylvania, 628
Garbo, Greta, 301
Garden, Mary, 370
Gardner, Ed, 514
Gardner, O. Max, 670, 721
Garfield, James, 439(fn.)
Garner, Cactus Jack, 678, 835, 846
Garnsey, Morris E., 921
Garrison, Lloyd K., 321, 419
Garrison, Montana, 909
Garsson investigation, 100, 648
Garvey, Marcus, 691
Gary, Elbert H., 619, 620
Gary, Indiana, 272, 312, 385, 618
Gas House District (NYC), 554
Gasoline, Texas, 826
Gastonia, North Carolina, 719, 723
Gates, Ralph F., 389
Gates, Thomas S., 605
Gaylord, E. K., 881
Gaynor, Mayor (New York City), 500
Geddes, Norman Bel, 443
Geier family, 447
General Education in a Free Society, 469
General Electric Company, 419, 474, 537, 568, 571, 783
General Mills, Inc., 318
General Motors Corporation, 70, 104, 290, 310-311, 400, 404, 410, 412, 415, 416, 417-419, 572, 618, 619, 634, 636, 786
Generation of Vipers (Wylie), 437
Genesee Valley, 537
Geneva Steel Company, 211, 212
Gennas gang, 380
George III, King, 495
George V, King, 370
George, Henry, 7, 53
George, W. L., 359, 518, 549
George, Walter F., 678, 700
George School, 608
George Washington bridge, 551
George White's Scandals, 527
Georgia, 151, 153, 195, 343, 572, 575, 620, 653, 654, 655, 656, 660, 662, 663, 666, 667, 669, 671, 672, 673, 675, 678, 690, 700, 701, 706, 733, 744, 745, 767-789, 790, 791, 794, 796, 828, 871; Fulton County, 768; legislature, 254(fn.); tobacco in, 712; University of, 671, 770, 773-774, 778
Georgia Academy of Political and Social Science, 672(fn.)
Georgia Power Company, 768
Georgia School of Technology, 671, 739

Gerard, James W., 567, 568(fn.)
Gerard, Kansas, 264
German Turnverein, 253
Germantown, Pennsylvania, 604
Germantown Friends School, 608
Germany, 274, 289, 364, 396, 404, 434, 545, 615
Gerry, Peter G., 470
Gettysburg, Pennsylvania, 602
Giannini, Amadeo P., 27-28, 38, 74, 80, 565, 568
Gibbs, Wolcott, 530(fn.), 536
Gibson, Colonel Ernest W., 496
Gifford, Walter S., 559, 568
Gilbert, Cass, 718
Gillette, Guy, 291
Gilmer, Mrs. Elizabeth Meriwether, 809
Gimbel Brothers, Inc., 597
Gimbel family, 605
Girard Trust, 608
Girdler, Tom, 621, 623
Glacier National Park, 181
Glasgow, Ellen, 666, 712
Glass, Carter, 570, 709, 711, 757
Glastonbury, Vermont, 497(fn.)
Glen Cove, Long Island, 538
Glendale, California, 44
Glewwe, Esther, see Stassen, Mrs. Harold
Gloucester, Massachusetts, 508
Gloversville, New York, 538
Goddard, Paulette, 49
Goebbels, Paul, 676, 810
Goebel, William, 644
Goering, Hermann, 545, 810
Goff, Frederick C., 444
Going My Way, 418(fn.)
Gold Coast, 691
Gold Rush of 1849, 8, 10, 16, 89, 216
Golden Gate, 4
Goldman, Emma, 91
Goldstein, Jonah J., 563
Goldstein, Nathaniel L., 544, 563 (fn.), 564, 564(fn.)
Goldwyn, Sam, 49, 51
"Gone With the Wind," 783
Good Neighbor policy, 615
Goodale, Stephen L., 617(fn.)
Goodland, Walter S., 318, 325, 914
Goodnight, Charles, 836
Goodnight-Loving Trail, 861
Goodyear Tire & Rubber Company, 418
Goose River, 637
Gordon, Frank L., 34
Gordon, Nebraska, 250
Gordon, Ruth, 219
Gordon, Walter, 61
Gordon, "Waxey," 530
Gordon *Journal*, 250
Gorki, 405, 414
Gossett, Charles C., 115
Gossler, P. M., 568
Gouge Eye, California, 10
Gould, Charles N., 874(fn.)
Gould, Jay, 535
Governors, 30-31
Governors' Conference, 371
Governors' Conference (Mackinac), 305

Governor's Island, 555
Grace, Eugene G., 567, 620, 621, 624
Grady, Henry W., 783(fn.), 790
Grafton, Samuel, 206, 225, 917
Graham, Charles A., 225
Graham, Frank, 676, 722, 914
Grand Canyon, 118, 235, 901
Grand Central Station, 523
Grand Coulee Dam, 66, 67, 69, 85, 118-121, 123-126, 130, 132, 142, 186, 187, 540, 736, 737, 742
Grand Forks, North Dakota, 180, 238
Grand Rapids, Michigan, 393
Grand Rapids *Herald*, 393, 394
Grand Teton National Park, 233
Grange, 95, 98, 127, 292(fn.), 266, 336, 496
Grant, Heber J., 191, 202, 210
Grant, Ulysses Simpson, 81, 265, 439(fn.), 803, 847(fn.)
Granville, Ohio, 454
Grapes of Wrath (Steinbeck), 876
Grassy Point, New York, 558
Grattan, C. Hartley, 151-152, 734(fn.)
Graves, John Temple, 660, 661 (fn.)
Gray's Harbor, Washington, 66, 99
Greasy Ridge, Ohio, 442
Great Britain, 9, 16, 86, 89, 193, 216(fn.), 228, 229, 286, 287, 289, 290, 296, 353(fn.), 365, 404, 431, 491, 494, 532, 534, 541, 544, 545, 566, 597, 601, 615, 616, 632, 638, 691, 779, 790, 815, 824
Great Falls, Montana, 145, 159-160, 167, 173, 183
Great Falls *Leader*, 160
Great Falls *Tribune*, 160, 171,
Great Lakes, 271-272, 535, 539, 540, 601, 820
Great Lakes, The (Hatcher), 272 (fn.)
Great Northern Railway Co., 93, 156, 161, 174, 244, 909
Great Plains, 239
The Great Plains (Webb), 145, 146
The Great Salmon Experiment (Neuberger), 126(fn.)
Great Smokies, 719, 743
The Great Smokies and the Blue Ridge, 722
Great Western Sugar Company, 220
Greater North Dakota Association, 244
Greeley, Horace, 847(fn.)
Greeley, W. B., 98
Green, Avantus, 763, 764
Green, Dwight H., 362
Green, Samuel, 788, 789
Green, Texas, 826
Green, Theodore Francis, 210, 470
Green, William, 568
Green Bay, Wisconsin, 277, 280, 318

Green Meadows, Maryland, 102
Green Mountains, 497
Green River, 227
Greenberg, Hank, 405(fn.)
Greenfield Village, 401-402, 409
Greensboro, Alabama, 795
Greensboro, North Carolina, 719
Greensboro, Vermont, 494
Greenville, Mississippi, 673
Greenville, South Carolina, 723, 788
Greenville (Miss.) *Delta Democrat Times*, 676
Greenwich, Connecticut, 501, 506, 590
Greenwich, Ohio, 441
Greenwich Village (NYC), 554, 574
Greenwood *Star*, 676
Grew, Joseph C., 471, 491
Grey, Mrs. Reginald, 477
Greyhound Bus Lines, 318
Greysolon Sieur du Lhut, Daniel de, 310
Gridiron Club, 430, 436
Griswold, Dwight, 250
Grit, Texas, 826
Groton Boys' School, 474
Grotto, 611(fn.)
Groves, Leslie R., 636
Gruening, Ernest, 342
Grundy, Joseph, 609, 611
Guaranty Trust Co. of N. Y., 419, 565
Guerra family, 844
Guffey, Joseph, 609, 610, 611
Guggenheim, Daniel, 568, 905
Gulf of Mexico, 273, 804
Gulf Oil Corporation, 264, 624, 808, 880
Gumbo, 246
Gunsight, Texas, 826
Gunther, John, Jr., 921
Gupton-Jones College of Mortuary Science, 760
Gus, Texas, 826
Gustavson, R. G., 218
Gustavus Adolphus, 630
Gypsy Moon (Frankensteen), 411

Hackett, Francis, 374
Hackley, S. D., 70
Habsburg, Otto, 552
Hagerty, James C., 523
Haggin, Mr., 643
Hague, Frank, 346, 348, 487, 589-596, 749
Hague, Frank Joseph, Jr., 595-596
Hahn, Emily, 321
Haiti, 573, 688, 798(fn.)
Hale, Robert, 473
Halifax, Lord, 602, 877
Hall, Leonard, 343
Hall of Fame (NYU), 554
Halleck, Charles A., 282
Halsey, Stuart & Co., 566
Halsey, William F., 303
Ham & Eggs, 16, 22, 37, 53-54
Hamburg Heaven, 557
Hamilton, Alexander, 391
Hamilton, Hamish, 921
Hamilton, John D. M., 248(fn.)
Hamilton, Montana, 172

Hampton Institute, 797, 798
Hamtramck, Michigan, 276, 552
Hand, Learned, 559
The Handbook of the United States (OWI), 76
Handlin, Oscar, 513(fn.)
Handy, W. C., 752
Hanes, Leigh B., 227
Hanford, Alfred Chester, 466
Hanford, Washington, 119, 636, 737
Hangtown, California, 10
Hanna, Marcus A., 440
Hannegan, Robert, 36, 350, 563
Hannum, Alberta Pierson, 722
Hansen, Alvin H., 248(fn.)
Hansen, Harry, 374
Hapeville (Ga.) *Statesman*, 779
Hardin, Montana, 179, 180, 181
Harding, Warren, 14, 436, 439 (fn.), 759, 882
Hardwick, Vermont, 495
Harlem, 61, 384, 573-576, 626, 691
Harless, Richard, 904
Harper, William Rainey, 376
Harper's Ferry, West Virginia, 714
Harper's Magazine, 47(fn.), 130 (fn.), 153(fn.), 168(fn.), 173, 329(fn.), 367(fn.), 377(fn.), 379, 389(fn.), 390, 399, 453 (fn.), 530(fn.), 734(fn.), 746, 763, 857, 921, 922
Harriman, Averell, 914
Harris, Albert S. M., Jr., 684-685
Harris, Edward A., 59, 60
Harris, John, 257
Harrisburg, Pennsylvania, 602, 613, 626, 716, 908
Harrison, Benjamin, 28, 160, 439 (fn.), 705
Harrison, Carter, 370
Harrison, Dan H., 857
Harrison, Pat, 799
Harrison, William Henry, 705
Harriss, Robert, 383
Harte, Bret, 7, 43, 460
Harten, James, 581
Hartford, Connecticut, 151, 463, 474, 503, 504, 505, 545
Hartford *Courant*, 505
Hartz, W. Homer, 382, 383
Harvard University, 24, 29, 433, 466, 468-469, 476, 483, 504, 508, 514, 515, 516, 576, 599, 681, 747, 895, 922
Harwood Foundation, 888
Hastings, W. W., 869
Hatch, Carl A., 891
Hatcher, Harlan, 272(fn.), 44 (fn.)
Hatcher, Joe, 753
Haverford College, 608
Havilland, Olivia de, 49
Havre, Montana, 172
Havre de Grace, Maryland, 63
Hawaii, 62, 193, 221
Hawkes, Albert W., 210(fn.) 883
Hawkins, Augustus F., 61
Hay, John, 46
Hayden, Arizona, 905
Hayden, Charles, 568

Hayes, Edward A., 382
Hayes, Ira H., 893
Hayes, Rutherford, 28, 439(fn.), 706
Haynes, Lacy, 267
Hays office, 51
Haywood, Big Bill, 100, 164
Hazeltine, Nelson, 134, 921
Healy, George W., Jr., 808, 922
Hearst, William Randolph, 40-41, 168, 246, 287, 363(fn.), 365, 401, 568
Hearst newspapers, 40, 64, 92, 373, 377
Heavenly Days (film), 436
Hecht, Ben, 374
Heffelfinger family, 318
Heflin, Tom, 675
Heidelberg College, 454
Heifetz, Jascha, 7, 579
Heintz, Ralph M., 445
Heinze, F. Augustus, 168
Helena, Montana, 152, 156, 158-159, 160, 169, 172, 177
Helena *Independent-Record*, 171
Helium, 837
Hell's Delight, California, 10
Hell's Half Acre, Wyoming, 230
Hell's Kitchen (NYC), 554
Hemingway, Ernest, xiii, 49, 374 (fn.), 460, 728
Henderson, Bruce, 795
Henderson, Leon, 922
Henderson, North Carolina, 673
Heney, Francis J., 13
Henri, Robert, 888
Henry, John M., 337, 921
Henry Knox, 755
Henry, O., 42, 831
Henry, Patrick, 275, 705
Henry, William, *see* O'Connell, Cardinal
Henry Ford (Marquis), 404
Hercules Powder Co., 631
Herrick, Robert, 374, 491
Herron, Nellie, 432
Hershey, Pennsylvania, 602, 897
Hertze family, 371
Hibbing, Minnesota, 310, 311, 312-313, 314
Hibernians, Ancient Order of, 291(fn.)
Hickenlooper, Bourke B., 210 (fn.), 338
Hicks, Elias, 608
Hidalgo, Texas, 844
Higgins, Andrew Jackson, 804, 805, 808
Higgins, Victor, 888
Hildegarde, 908
Hildreth, Horace A., 486, 509
Hill, George Washington, 568, 714
Hill, Jim, 93, 174, 244
Hill, Lister, 436, 676, 794
Hillman, Sidney, 448, 553, 612
Hilo, Hawaii, 194
Hines, Jimmy, 529, 543, 561
Hinton, Harold B., 766(fn.)
The History of Rome Hanks, 518
Hitler, Adolf, xii, 252, 287, 414, 541, 546, 605, 683, 752, 803, 809, 810-811, 812
Hiwassee River, 733, 740

Hoan, Daniel W., 321
Hobby, Mrs. Oveta Culp, 827
Hobby, William P., 839
Hoblitzelle, Karl, 857
Hoboken, New Jersey, 598
Hoey, Clyde, R., 721
Hofer Company, 745
Hoffman, Clare E., 283
Hoffman, Paul, 385
Hogg, Ima, 839
Hogg, Jim, 839, 840
Hogs, 328-329
Holbrook, Stewart, 310(fn.)
Holding Company Act, 178
Holiday, 922
Holladay's Overland Line, 261
Holland, Michigan, 334(fn.)
Holland, Spessard, 676
Hollywood, California, 28, 39, 40, 43, 44, 47-51, 474, 549, 555, 574, 807
Hollywood Free World Association, 49
Hollywood Independent Citizens' Committee for the Arts, Sciences and Professions, 36, 49-50
Holman, Rufus C., 106, 107, 291, 294(fn.)
Holmes, John Haynes, 559
Holmes, Julius C., 471
Holmes, Oliver W., xiii, 507, 909
Holmes, R. C., 568
Holston River, 733, 740
Homans, Mrs. 461
"Home on the Range" (song), 261
"Home Sweet Home," 536
Homestake Mining Company, 246-247
Homestead Act of 1862, 145, 332
Homestead Massacre, 602
Honduras, 875
Hooper, Washington, 134, 137, 138
Hoover, Herbert, 36, 148, 148 (fn.), 202, 237, 433, 288, 367, 430, 439, 452, 489, 503, 539, 567, 568, 610, 658, 734, 847, 882, 890
Hoover, John Edgar, 408, 909
Hope, Arkansas, 763, 765
Hope Club, 91
Hopi Indians, 874
Hopkins, Ernest M., 491
Hopkins, Harry, 323, 327
Hoppe, Willie, 97
Hopper, Hedda, 48
Horgan, Paul, 888
Hormel, Geo. A., & Company, 318
Hornblow, Arthur, 49
Horne, Lena, 761
Horstman, Al, 427
Hostetter Connelsville Coke Co., 617
Hot Springs, Arkansas, 763
Hotchkiss, Connecticut, 403
The Hounds, 10
Housatonic River, 456
House, Boyce, 818(fn.)
Household, 265
Housing, 241, 283, 285, 392, 430

(fn.), 436, 448, 524, 558, 560, 696, 743
Houston, Sam, 823, 850
Houston, Texas, 474, 670, 676, 819(fn.), 827, 829, 832(fn.), 839, 847, 852, 853, 853(fn.), 857, 868, 877
Houston *Chronicle*, 818, 828
Houston Cotton Exchange, 922
Houston *Defender and Informer*. 868
Houston *Post*, 827, 853(fn.)
Howard, Joseph Kinsey, 165, 168(fn.), 183, 185, 921
Howard, Perry H., 799
Howard, Roy, 386, 568
Howard University, 798
Howe, E. W., 837
Howe, Ed, 264
Howe, Gene, 836, 837
Howell, Varina, 803
Howells, William Dean, 457
Hoyle, Marguerite, 921
Hoyt, E. Palmer, 106, 225
Hubbell, Carl, 876
Hudson, Henry, 551
Hudson Bay, 311
Hudson Falls, New York, 538
Hudson River, 534, 535, 538, 555, 597, 598
Hudson's Bay Company, 9, 86, 89
Huff, J. Wesley, 895(fn.)
Huffman, James W., 429, 440
Hughes, Charles Evans, 15(fn.), 540, 543
Hughes, Charles Evans, Jr., 528, 587
Hughes, Langston, 264, 627, 694 (fn.)
Hughes, Rupert, 49
Hull, Cordell, 149, 754
Hull House. 370
Hull-Rust-Mahoning Open Pit Iron Ore Mine, 312-313
Humble Oil & Refining Company, 264, 808, 815
Humphrey, H. J., Jr., 318
Hungary, 431
Hunt, Duane G., 210
Hunt, Lester C., 229, 230-231, 232
Hunt, Ormond E., 418
Hunter College, 554
Huntington, Collis P., 64
Hurley, Patrick J., 890
Hurst, John of W., 639
Huston, Walter, 219
Hutcheson, "Big Bill," 387
Hutchins, Robert M., 375-379, 914
Hutchinson, Jesse, Jr., 7
Hutchinson, Martin A., 710
Hutchinson *News-Herald*, 257
Hutchison, Keith, 418(fn.)
Hutt, Frances Eileen, 527
Hutton, Graham, 275, 276, 287, 368, 374(fn.)
Hutton, S. E., 123-124, 125, 742
Huxley, Aldous, 7, 42, 52
Hybrid Corn, *see* Corn
Hyde Park, New York, 546

I Am organization, 52
I Give You Texas (House), 818 (fn.), 820

Ickes, Harold, 36, 58, 59, 60, 105, 106, 121, 233, 436, 453, 527, 581, 873, 883, 884, 890, 897, 914

Idaho, xv, 76, 85, 86, 94, 144, 158, 161, 195, 234, 273, 348, 558, 641, 904; agriculture, 114; area, 113; divorce laws in, 77; electric power in, 114, 208(fn.); irrigation, 114; labor in, 116; lobbies, 115, 116; Mormons in, 193; natural resources, 113; Negroes in, 151; politics, 107-113, 114, 115-116; railways, 113; religion in, 114, 115; Sun Valley, 117, 214; University of, 114

Idaho Falls, Idaho, 194

Idaho Power Company, 115

Idaho Statesman, 116

Idlewild airport, 558

If Hamilton Were Here Today, 395

Igo, California, 63

Ill Fares the Land (McWilliams), 38, 137

Illinois, 155, 167, 230, 259, 270, 271, 275, 328, 343, 357, 386 (fn.), 390, 418, 453, 497, 559, 626, 737, 739, 819, 827(fn.); agriculture, 328, 330, 334, 374, 385; Cook County, 375; electoral votes, 1; politics, 33, 248, 369; state employees per capita, 710

Illinois, University of, 375

Illinois Central Railroad, 358, 370, 800

Illinois Commerce Commission, 121

Illinois Farmers Association, 242

Illinois Manufacturers Association, 382

Illinois River, 374, 809

Illinois State Rural Electrification Committee, 121

Illwaco, Washington, 66

Impelliteri, Vincent R., 544

Imperial Chemicals, Ltd., 419

Imperial Valley, 56

Imperialism, 364, 615

The Improvement Era, 191

In His Steps (Sheldon), 264

Inca, North Carolina, 673

Independence, Missouri, 197, 343, 888

Independence Hall, 402, 600

Independent Voters Association, 240

India, 2, 83, 681, 780, 790

Indian Reorganization Act, 873, 875

Indian Wars, 147

Indiana, 155, 259, 260, 270, 275, 280, 282, 343, 370, 385, 441, 453, 559, 607, 739, 745, 789, 856; agriculture in, 330, 385; industry, 385; Ku-Klux Klan in, 221, 433; Lake County, 385; lobbies, 388

Indianapolis, Indiana, 152, 217 (fn.), 276, 281, 382, 385, 386-388, 910

Indianapolis Times, 386, 389, 390

Indianola, Iowa, 337(fn.)

Indianola Record Herald, 337 (fn.)

Indianola Tribune, 337(fn.)

Indians, 85, 161, 216, 235, 239, 247, 310, 534-535, 551, 601, 604, 728, 869-875, 888, 891-895; Five Civilized Tribes, 870, 871, 872, 874, 875

Indo-China, 364

Industrial Association of San Francisco, 33

Industry, see under names of States

"Information Please," 772, 908

Ingersoll, Ralph McAllister, 178

Inland Steel Co., 620

Inland Waterway, 637

Innes, George, 278

Inside Asia, ix, 553

Inside Europe, ix, 280

Inside Latin America, ix

Inspiration Consolidated Copper Co., 905

Institute, West Virginia, 716

Institute for Advanced Study, 599

Insull, Samuel, 126, 370, 568

Insurance, 266, 337, 347, 388-389, 568(fn.), 572, 575, 624

Insurance Underwriters Association, 292(fn.)

Intercourse, Pennsylvania, 628

International Alliance of Theatrical and Stage Employees, 50-51

International Business Machines Co., Inc., 907

International Correspondence Schools, 602

International Harvester Company, 258, 279, 418, 793

International House, 809

International Ladies Garment Workers Union, 553

International Latex Corp., 631

International Longshoremen's and Warehousemen's Union, 25, 27

International News Service, 431

International Nickel Company, 419, 620(fn.)

International Rapids, 539

International Smelting and Refining Company, 167

International Telephone & Telegraph Corp., 568

International Union of Mine, Mill, and Smelter Workers, 164, 222

International Woodworkers of America, 98

Interstate Commerce Commission, 12, 152, 153, 919

Interstate Commerce Committee (Senate), 33

Investment Trust Act, 569

Iowa, 144, 237, 251(fn.), 253, 259, 260, 270, 271, 280, 282, 286, 318(fn.), 328-340, 559, 662, 743, 807, 837, 859, 862; agriculture, 328-335, 385; cooperatives in, 243, 336-337; education, 339; electric power, 185; industry in, 335; livestock in, 328-329; politics, 336-339; refugees from, 4, 42, 51-52, 334; roads, 339-340

Iowa Light & Power Company, 331

Iowa Manufacturers Association, 338

Iron, 601, 672, 794

Iron Brew (Holbrook), 310(fn.)

Iroquois Indians, 535

Irrigation, see under names of States

Irvin, Pennsylvania, 625

Irvin, William A., 619, 620(fn.)

Irving, Washington, 872

Isaacs, Stanley M., 576

Isaiah, 900

Iselin, New Jersey, 546

Isherwood, Christopher, 7

Isolationism, 174-175, 178, 246, 250, 252, 286-292, 305, 320, 324, 361, 377, 378, 382, 386 (fn.), 434, 435, 471, 531, 532, 541

Issei, 46

Istanbul, 549

Italy, 155, 561, 573, 754

Itasca, Lake, 318

Ithaca, New York, 537

Ives, Irving M., 541, 544, 544 (fn.)

Ives Bill, 576

Ivins, Anthony W., 202

Iwo Jima, 689

Jack, William S., 445

Jack, William "Scotty," 228, 235

Jack-Mormons, 192(fn.)

Jackling, Daniel O., 568

Jackson, Andrew, 660, 677, 762, 871, 875

Jackson, Michigan, 277, 525

Jackson, Mississippi, 799, 800, 801, 910

Jackson, Robert H., 914

Jackson, Thomas (Stonewall), 660, 712, 760

Jackson Hole National Monument, 233-234

Jackson (Miss.) News, 800

Jacksonville, Florida, 353(fn.), 728, 729

Jacksonville, Texas, 821

Jaeckle, Edwin F., 537, 543

Jamaica, 691

James, Arthur Curtiss, 568

James, Henry, 461, 637

James, Jesse, 761

James, Marquis, 633(fn.), 876

James brothers, 342, 457

Jamestown, North Dakota, 242

Jamestown, Virginia, 616, 681, 705

Janesville, Wisconsin, 319

Janeway, Eliot, 437(fn.)

Jangling Plains, Connecticut, 50

Japan, 2, 155, 209, 274, 289, 364, 367, 404, 414, 431, 434, 440, 531, 532, 544, 545, 615, 683, 787

Japanese Exclusion League, 47

Jay Em, Wyoming, 230

Jean, Texas, 826

Jeffers, Robinson, 7, 276

Jeffers, William M., 153, 255

Jefferson, proposed state of, 62

Jefferson, Thomas, xvi, 246, 275, 631, 691, 705, 706, 712(fn.)
Jefferson City, Missouri, 183, 356
Jehovah's Witnesses, 515
Jennings, Al, 879
Jennings, John, Jr., 755
Jerome, Arizona, 905
Jersey City, New Jersey, 348, 487, 552, 589-596, 749
Jester, Beauford H., 841
Jews, xii, 35, 210, 244, 252, 287, 301, 389, 390, 403, 404, 411, 505, 515, 516, 544, 552, 553, 554, 563, 567, 575, 577, 605 (fn.), 627, 669, 728, 786-787, 789, 798, 803, 809, 811, 812, 914, 916, 917
"Jews Hill," 605(fn.)
Jockey Club, 646-647
John Brown's Body (Benet), 711
John Marshall School of Law, 424
Johns Hopkins University, 638, 639
Johnson, Alvin, 158
Johnson, Andrew, 754, 763
Johnson, Carroll, 884
Johnson, Edwin C., 222-223
Johnson, Enoch L., 595
Johnson, Eva L., 884
Johnson, Gerald W., 632(fn.), 707(fn.)
Johnson, Grove L., 13, 15
Johnson, Guy B., 676
Johnson, Hiram, 13-15, 16, 18, 36, 175, 391, 839
Johnson, Howard A., 158(fn.), 160, 922
Johnson, Jack, 691
Johnson, Jedediah, 883-884
Johnson, Joshua W., 884
Johnson, Kenneth, 78, 79
Johnson, Lyndon B., 848, 850
Johnson, Nunnally, 48
Johnson, Olin D., 726
Johnson, S. C. & Son, Inc., 319
Johnson, Tom, 429
Johnson Act, 569
Johnson City, Tennessee, 758(fn.)
Johnston, Eric, 51, 94, 223
Jones, Anson, 824
Jones, Harrison, 785
Jones, Howard Mumford, 456
Jones, Jesse, 73, 327, 484, 588, 672, 798(fn.), 817, 827, 828, 829, 846, 847
Jones, John C., 684
Jones, Rufus M., 608
Jones, Sam Houston, 807
Jones, Tom, 801
Jones & Laughlin Steel Corp., 621
Jones Beach, 536
Jordon, David Starr, 7
Joseph, Chief, 161
Joseph, Lazarus, 544
Jugoslavia, 400
Junction, Texas, 841
Juneau, Alaska, 92

Kahn, Albert, 405
Kaiser, Edgar, 65, 66, 69
Kaiser, Henry, 28, 64-75, 119,

151, 212, 223, 569, 623, 808, 908
Kaiser, Mrs. Henry, 65
Kaiser, Henry, Jr., 65, 69
Kaltenborn, H. V., 559
Kanawha Valley, West Virginia, 716
Kane, Harnett T., 666, 807(fn.), 921
Kansas, 258(fn.), 262(fn.)
Kansas, 144, 146, 149, 216, 224, 243, 248(fn.), 251, 252, 256-269, 270, 271, 288, 333, 337, 351, 356, 386, 466, 729, 789, 821, 836, 849, 860, 880, 908; agriculture, 251(fn.), 263, 268-269; co-operatives in, 243; electric power, 185; history of, 259; industry in, 263-264, 335; Johnson County, 354; mineral resources, 263-264; nicknames for, 258(fn.); politics, 260-261; prohibition and, 254, 267; schools in, 339; university of, 259, 356, 777
Kansas Buyers Guide, 263
Kansas City, Kansas, 259, 264 (fn.), 354, 355
Kansas City, Missouri, 183, 197, 218, 255, 256, 259, 260(fn.), 267, 271(fn.), 343, 344-356, 372, 449(fn.), 460, 538, 590, 592(fn.), 708, 749, 751, 831, 908, 910
Kansas City, University of, 356
Kansas City Call, 356
Kansas City Star, 266-267, 268 (fn.), 341, 349, 351, 922
Kansas Farmer, 265
Karsner, David, 223(fn.)
Katchaloff, 271
Keane, Gertrude, 581
Kearney, Dennis, 10-11
Kearns estate, 210
Keats, John, 652, 653
Keefe, Frank B., 324
Kefauver, Estes, 676, 922
Keller, K. T., 419
Kelley, Cornelius F., 168, 171, 173, 174, 570
Kellogg, Idaho, 115
Kellogg, Wilbur M., 449
Kelly, Edward J., 362, 368, 372, 373
Kelly, Frank V., 554, 563
Kelly field, 833-834
Kelly-Nash political machine, 348, 373, 708, 749
Kelsey-Hayes, 412, 415
Kemal Atatürk, 810
Kenna, Hinky Dink, 372
Kennecott Copper Corporation, 153, 211, 419, 905
Kennedy, Joseph P., 456, 513
Kenny, Hubert A., 221
Kenny, Robert W., 18-19, 21-23, 30, 34, 36, 39, 59, 80, 922
Kenosha, Wisconsin, 277, 319
Kenova, West Virginia, 715
Kent, Ohio, 454
Kentucky, 640, 642(fn.), 643
The Kentucky (Clark), 643, 644 (fn.)
Kentucky, xiii, 85, 341(fn.), 342,

572, 639, 640-652, 653, 654, 659, 660, 667, 671, 676, 733, 744, 746, 750(fn.), 759, 784, 786; agriculture, 640-641; education in, 641; Harlan County, 471, 670; lobbies in, 646; miscellany, 652; politics, 643-652; tobacco in, 713
Kentucky Bankers Association, 641
Kentucky Derby, 640, 646
Kentucky Education Association, 647
Kentucky Merchants Association, 640
Kentucky Utilities Company, 647, 746
Kepner, Professor Tyler, 921
Kern County Land Company, 57
Kearney, James, Jr., 592, 922
Kerr, Robert S., 250, 870, 880, 882-883
Kerrville, Texas, 856
Ketchell, Stanley, 181
Kettering, Charles F., 418, 419
Key West, Florida, 728
Keyserling, Count Herman, 907
Kiernan, John, 772
Kilday, Owen, 834
Kilgore, Harley M., 717
Kilpatrick, Carroll, 434(fn.)
Kimball, Edward A., 338
Kimmell, Admiral, 405
King, James, 10
King Ranch, 834, 859, 861
Kingsport, Tennessee, 758(fn.)
Kintner, Robert, 432(fn.)
Kipke, Harry, 405
Kipling, Rudyard, 18, 369, 513, 537, 679
Kips Bay, New York, 554
Kirkpatrick, Helen, 374
Kitty Foyle (Morley), 512, 603
Kiwanis Club, 266, 292(fn.)
Kleberg, Bob, 861
Kleberg family, 834, 835, 859, 861, 862-863
Kleenex Company, 319
Kline, Allan B., 336
Knapp, George L., 714
Knee, Gina, 888
Knight, John S., 373
Knight, O. A., 831
Knights of Columbus, 280, 515
Knights of Pythias, 611(fn.)
Knights of the Golden Eagle, 611(fn.)
Knott, Proctor, 309
Knowland, Joseph R., 35, 36
Knowland, William F., 36, 37
Knox, Frank, 303, 373
Knox, Hartley, 55-56, 650
Knoxville, Tennessee, 668, 733, 737(fn.), 738, 758, 760, 761, 910
Knudsen, William S., 404, 406
Knuth, Edna, 69
Knutson, Harold, 283
Kohler, Wisconsin, 319
Kohler Company, 319
Kokernot, Rancher, 864
Kollmorgen, Walter M., 629(fn.)
Kooksia, Idaho, 108
Koppers Company, Inc., 624, 717

Koppers Gas & Coke Company, 624
Kotex Company, 319
Kraft Foods Company, 319
Krazy Kat Supermarket, 770
Kreuger, Walter, 822(fn.)
Kreymborg, Alfred, 573
Krock, Arthur, 433(fn.), 531 (fn.), 917
Kroll, Jack, 448
Krug, Julius A., 321, 914
Krutch, Charles, 734(fn.), 921
Krutch, Joseph Wood, 369
Kuhn, Fritz, 405
Kuhn Loeb & Co., 565, 567
Ku-Klux Klan, 88, 95, 221, 286, 320, 382, 387, 389, 390, 409, 433, 468, 567, 669, 686, 768, 775, 778, 786-789, 799, 805, 829, 830, 839, 841, 846, 898

Labor, see under names of States; names of Unions
La Farge, Oliver, 888
Lafayette, Marie Joseph, 706, 803
Laffoon, Ruby, 643, 649
La Follette, Bronson Cutting 322
La Follette, Charles M., 388
La Follette, Jo Davidson, 322
La Follette, Philip F., 322-324, 433
La Follette, Robert Marion, 321
La Follette, Robert Marion, Jr., 16, 178, 209, 242, 257, 287, 291, 300, 322-324, 433, 738
La Follette, Robert Marion III, 322
La Follette Civil Liberties Committe, 410
La Follette Committee, 38
La Guardia, Fiorello, 245, 364, 500, 530, 560, 561, 564, 565, 778, 806, 914
La Guardia Field, 536, 555
Lake Erie (Hatcher), 272(fn.), 441(fn.)
Lake of the Woods, 313
Lake Okeechobee, 728
Lake Pend Oreille, 114
Lake Placid, New York, 65, 66, 538
Lake Tahoe, 4, 68, 354
Lake Washington, 92, 139, 142
Lamar Democrat, 343
Lamont, Thomas W., 568, 570, 620, 921
Lancaster, Pennsylvania, 231, 627-629
Lancaster Intelligence Journal, 629
Lancaster New Era, 629
Lancaster News, 629
Land grant colleges, 454, 599
Land o' Lakes Creameries, Inc., 318
Land Title Bank and Trust Co., 600
Lander, Wyoming, 230, 231, 234
Landess, W. M., 742
Landis, Gerard W., 290
Landis, James M., 25
Landis, Kenesaw M., 648
Landon, Alf M., 256-257, 265, 332, 352(fn.), 450, 452, 612

Lane, Frank K., 179
Lane, Thomas T., 468
Langer, William, 103, 238, 240-.242
Langley, James M., 492
Lapham, Roger D., 23-25, 55
La Porte, Indiana, 370
Laramie, Wyoming, 145, 234
Laramie Boomerang, 231
Laramie Bulletin, 231
Lardner, Ring, 374
Lariat, Texas, 826
Larkin, Thomas O., 9
Larrivee, Allan, 481
Larsen, Karly, 98, 100
Las Vegas, Nevada, 77-78, 79, 165, 835
Lasher, Mr. and Mrs. Albert D., 922
Latin America, 806, 874
Latter Day Saints, see Mormons
Lausche, Charles, 423
Lausche, Frank J., 422-430, 431, 437(fn.), 440, 718, 921
Lausche, Mrs. Frank J., 423, 437
Lausche, Harold, 423
Lausche, William J., 423
Lausier, Mayor (Biddeford, Me.), 487
Lavoisier, Antoine, 632
Lawrence, D. H., 888, 892
Lawrence, David L., 610, 917
Lawrence, James E., 252
Lawrence, Kansas, 256, 356
Lawrence, Massachusetts, 424, 468, 501
Lawrenceville, Tennessee, 685
Laws, Arthur H., 222
Lawton, Oklahoma, 877(fn.)
Lawyers Trust Company, 419
Lazarus, Reuben A., 578, 586
Leacock, Stephen, 270
Lead, South Dakota, 246, 247
Leader, John, 85
Leader (N. D.), 245
Leaders in Education, 194
Leadville, Colorado, 216
League of Nations, 202, 324, 779
League of Women Voters, 95, 349
Lease, Mary Elizabeth, 256
Leaves of Grass (Whitman), 518
Leckrone, Walter, 386
Ledo Road, 186
Lee, Bob, 365
Lee, Harold B., 203
Lee, Henry, 705
Lee, Higginson, & Company, 520
Lee, J. Bracken, 204-205
Lee, Josh, 880
Lee, Robert E., 660, 705, 712, 714, 922
Lee family, 705
Leguenecahe, Pete, 116
Lehman, Herbert H., 528, 530, 539, 544, 560, 627
Leighton, George R., 255(fn.), 650(fn.)
Leiter, Levi Z., 370
LeMay, Curtis, 440
Lemke, William, 53, 240, 242
Lend lease, 91, 175, 250, 291, 320, 327, 361, 366, 391, 435, 472, 532
Leo, Texas, 826

Leon & Eddie's, 571
Leonard, Richard T., 410-411, 413
Leopold-Loeb case, 379(fn.)
Lepke, Louis, 560
Lerner, Max, 552
Leslie's Weekly, 399
Let's Look Into Kansas, 263
Lavin, Meyer, 374
Levinson, Edward, 412(fn.)
Lewis, E. C., 761
Lewis, John L., xiv, 105-106, 386, 453, 621, 622, 717, 916
Lewis, Lloyd, 278, 374
Lewis, Meriwether, 85, 173, 343
Lewis, Sinclair, 194, 306, 309, 314-317, 922
Lewis, Zan, 231
Lewisburg, Tennessee, 759
Lewisohn interests, 905
Lewisohn Stadium (NYC), 686
Lewiston, Maine, 487
Lewistown Democrat-News, 160
Lexington, Kentucky, 642
Lexington, Mississippi, 685
Lexington, Tennessee, 762
Lexington, Virginia, 660, 712 (fn.)
Lexington Herald, 644
Ley, Dr., 910
Libbey Investment Company, 191
Libby-Owens Glass Company, 716
Liberia, 691, 798(fn.)
Liberty, 922
Liberty Bell, 402, 603
Liberty League, 382, 612
Libraries, 908
Library of Congress, 856
Lieutenant Governors, 31
Life, 4, 58, 188, 239(fn.), 246, 272(fn.), 286, 342(fn.), 343, 344(fn.), 376(fn.), 412(fn.), 432(fn.), 433(fn.), 437(fn.), 480, 515, 526, 527, 531, 540 (fn.), 560(fn.), 567, 569, 618, 619, 623, 707(fn.), 725, 729, 770(fn.), 821(fn.)
Life With Father (play), 518
Liggett, Walter W., 373(fn.)
Liggett and Myers Tobacco Co., 713, 714
Light, H. N., 387
Lilienthal, David E., 321, 676, 731, 732, 733, 734(fn.), 735, 736-738, 739, 742, 746, 757, 757(fn.), 914, 922
Lily Dale spiritualists, 535
Lincoln, Abraham, 77, 86, 246, 270, 375, 402, 436, 640, 655, 656(fn.), 684, 691, 793, 828, 847 (fn.), 911
Lincoln, James R., 445
Lincoln, Nebraska, 250
Lincoln, proposed state of, 94
Lincoln Electric Company, 445
"Lincoln-Roosevelt League," 15
Lincoln Star, 252
Lincoln University, 356
Lindbergh, Charles A., 175, 274 289, 314, 463(fn.), 405, 450 529, 531, 570, 598, 706
Lindbergh Kidnapping Law, 200
Lindey, Alexander, 921
Lindsay, Ben, 217

Lindsay, Vachel, 374
Linn, Harry D., 330
Linn, James Weber, 281, 377
Lions Club, 266, 292(fn.)
Lippmann, Walter, 53, 54, 206, 225, 435, 591, 917
Little, Walter, 32
Little Big Horn, 147
Little Falls, Minnesota, 314, 315
Little Inch Pipe Line, 909
Little Review, 374
Little Rock, Arkansas, 672, 763, 765
Little Steel, 620, 621(fn.)
Little Tennessee River, 733
Livermore, California, 68
Liverpool, England, 539, 650
Livestock, see also Cattle, 137-138, 149, 228, 229-230, 232, 233, 251, 269, 663, 887
Livingston, Goodhue, Jr., 581
Lizzie, Texas, 826
Lloyd, Harold, 220
Lloyd, William Bross, 361(fn.)
Lloyd's, 624
Lobbies, see also Pressure Groups, 32-33, 38-41, 49-50, 59, 115, 116, 129, 188, 209, 232, 247, 248, 348-349, 388, 440, 540, 543, 613, 646, 745, 746, 771, 786, 842-843, 913
Lochard, Metz, 383, 384
Locke, Alonzo, 760
Lockwood, Paul E., 523
Lodge, Henry Cabot, 391, 396
Lodge, Henry Cabot, Jr., 472, 478, 510
Lodge, John Davis, 472(fn.)
Loeb, William, 568
Loesch, Frank J., 372
Logan, M. M., 649
Logan, Malcolm, 437(fn.)
Logan, Rayford W., 688(fn.)
Logan, Utah, 194
Lokar, John E., 428, 921
London, England, 538, 625
London, Jack, 7
London Daily Express, 368(fn.)
London Daily Mail, 368(fn.)
London News Chronicle, 368(fn.), 921
London News of the World, 368 (fn.)
London Times, 732
Long, Earl K., 807
Long, Haniel, 615, 888
Long, Huey, 54, 666, 675, 705, 745, 779, 804, 805, 806, 807, 809-811, 880
Long, William E., 256
Long Beach, California, 57, 63, 67
Long-Bell Lumber Company, 141
Long Island, 505, 534, 536, 538, 554, 604, 810
Longfellow, Henry Wadsworth, 68, 446
Longo case, 592
Longworth, Alice, 433, 433(fn.), 434
Look, 337
Lorentz, Pare, 831
Lorillard, P., Co., 713

Los Alamos, New Mexico, 119, 888
Los Angeles, California, 3, 4, 5, 6, 7, 8, 9, 12, 19, 22, 26, 31, 35, 39(fn.), 41, 42-45, 54, 56, 67, 72, 128(fn.), 157, 210, 212, 224, 277, 520, 555(fn.), 584, 603(fn.), 827(fn.), 877, 878, 897, 908; Chamber of Commerce, 32, 39, 44; courts, 63; negroes in, 60-62
Los Angeles Aqueduct, 4
Los Angeles Church Federation, 39
Los Angeles News, 40, 922
Los Angeles Times, 14, 35, 40
Los Angeles Turf Club, 418(fn.)
Lost Mule Flat, 144
Lost Weekend (movie), 647(fn.)
Louis, Joe, 908
Louis XVI, King, 571
Louisiana, 195, 230, 653, 654, 655, 656, 659, 666, 672, 675, 690, 700, 701, 727, 804-813, 866, 876, 910
Louisiana Hayride (Kane), 807 (fn.), 810(fn.)
Louisiana Purchase, 252
Louisiana State University, 811 (fn.)
Louisville, Kentucky, 29, 91, 271 (fn.), 446, 454, 644, 645, 646, 647, 648, 649, 650, 651, 653, 654, 668, 760, 761
Louisville and Nashville Railroad, 644, 646
Louisville Courier-Journal, 287, 642, 646, 647, 648, 660, 921
Louisville Gas and Electric Company, 651
l'Ouverture, Toussaint, 688
Love, Mrs. R. F., 921
Love of the Three Kings (Opera), 581
Lovejoy, Amos L., 90
Lovelady, Texas, 826
Lovett, Robert A., 326
Lovett, Robert Morss, 281, 377
Loveman, Amy, 921
Low, Charlie, 46
Lowell, A. Lawrence, 460, 461, 516
Lowell, Massachusetts, 501
Lowell family, 705
Loy, Myrna, 181
Loyola University, 353, 809
Lubbock, Texas, 849(fn.), 908
Lubin, Isador, 627
Luce, Clare Boothe, 145, 408, 473, 503, 922
Luce, Henry, 104, 558
Lucey, Robert E., 834, 916
Luciano, Lucky, 529
Lucite, 635
"Luck of Roaring Camp" (Harte), 460
Ludington, Wisconsin, 272
Ludlow Massacre, 222
Ludwig, Emil, 7
Luhan, Mabel Dodge, 888, 892
Lumber industry, 139-142, 157, 311, 321, 672, 800(fn.), 809
Lundberg, Ferdinand, 634(fn.)

Lundeberg, Harry, 26
Lundeen, Ernest, 294
Lundley, Ernest, 225
Lunt, Alfred, 321, 908
Lutheran Church, 244, 252
Lyautey, Louis, 196
Lydgate, W. A., 287(fn.)
Lynching, 684-688, 694, 699, 700, 778, 789, 801
Lyons, Leonard, 48, 111(fn.), 527-528

McAdoo, William Gibbs, 36, 830
McAttee, Leon, 685
McCarey, Leo, 418(fn.)
McCarran, Pat, 6, 59(fn.), 77, 80, 84, 392
McCarten, John, 405(fn.), 406 (fn.), 589(fn.)
McCarthy, Charles, 318, 324 (fn.), 325
McCarthy, Joseph R., 324
McClanahan, Councilman, 45
McClellan, George, 487(fn.)
McClintic, James V., 884
McCloy, John J., 326, 558
McConaughty, Dr. James L., 505 (fn.)
McCord, Jim, 760
McCormack, John W., 473
McCormack, Thomas, 34
McCormick, Anne O'Hare, 921
McCormick, Medill, 361
McCormick, Robert Rutherford, 287, 359, 360-367, 383, 568
McCormick, Robert Sanderson, 361
McCormick, Mrs. Rockefeller, 371
McCoy, Kid, 181, 405
McCracken, Tracy S., 231-232, 234
McCutcheon, John, 280
McDonnel, Anne, 408
McDonnell, James Francis, 408
McDonough, Gordon L., 473-474
McGee, Fibber, 436
McGill, Ralph, 676, 787(fn.)
McGoldrick, Joseph D., 559
McGrath, J. Howard, 499
McGuffey, W. H., 402
McGuinness, Peter, J., 554
McGuire, Molly, 602
McGurn, "Machine Gun" Jack, 381
McHugh, Vincent, 556(fn.)
McKaine, Osceola, 701
McKay, Claude, 264
McKay, David O., 194, 203, 205, 207
McKay, Seth S., 849, 849(fn.), 850(fn.), 851
McKean, Dayton David, 589 (fn.), 596
McKellar, Kenneth M., 388, 609, 731, 732, 750, 752, 756-758, 762
McKelway, St. Clair, 342(fn.)
McKenzie, John, 586
McKinley, William, 439(fn.), 440, 537, 706
McLaughlin, Emmett, 904
McLaughlin, John, 86
McLevy, Jasper, 505

McMahon, Brien, 470
McMinnville, Oregon, 95
McNamaras trial, 40
McNary, Charles L., 94, 96, 121, 907
McNutt, Paul, 302, 387
McPeak, Carl A., 853
McPherson, Aimee Semple, 16, 52, 848
McWain, Don, 921
McWilliams, Carey, 2(fn.), 8, 14, 38, 52, 137, 272(fn.)

Mabey, Charles R., 203(fn.)
MacArthur, General Douglas, 289, 321, 323, 324, 362, 395, 649, 660
Maccabees, 611(fn.)
MacGregor, Alexander Campbell, 137
MacGregor, John M., 137
MacGregor Land & Livestock Company, 134, 137
Mackay, Clarence H., 570
Mackinac, Michigan, 305, 420, 897
MacLeish, Archibald, 328, 371 (fn.), 471, 835, 859, 914, 921, 922
MacNaughton, E. B., 91
Macon, Georgia, 152, 672, 689
Macy, R. H. & Co., Inc., 278, 577, 597
Madison, Dolly, 427(fn.)
Madison, Wisconsin, 102, 105, 321, 323, 326, 910
Madison Capital Times, 280, 327
Madison family, 705
Madison-Kipp Company, 325
Madras, 785
Maestri, Robert S., 805-806
Magarac, Joe, 625
Magee, Augustus, 823(fn.)
Magenta, Texas, 826
Magma Copper Sales Corp., 905
Magnolia Oil Company, 264, 880
Magnuson, Warren G., 89, 97, 99
Main Line (Pennsylvania), 602, 604, 605, 606, 610
Main Street (Lewis), 314-317
Maine, 151, 247, 250, 341, 458, 465, 471, 491, 493, 510; agriculture, 467, 486, 496; area, 485; Aroostook County, 485, 486, 488; French Canadians in, 465; history, 486; industry, 487; politics, 486-487
Maine, Minnesota, 29
Makanda, Illinois, 466
Malcomson, Alex Y., 403
Malick, Clay, 219
Maloney, George W., 77(fn.)
Mammoth Cave, 640
Manchester, New Hampshire, 464, 489, 490, 491
Manhattan, see New York City, New York
Manhattan Project, 378, 636
Manila, Philippine Islands, 431
Manitowac, Wisconsin, 318
Mankin, Helen Douglas, 768
Mankind United, 52, 54
Mann, Thomas, 7, 49

Mann Act, 200
Manning, Bishop, 909
Manning, Helen Taft, 432
Mansfield, Frederick, W., 517
Mansfield, Mike, 175
Mansfield, Ohio, 442
Mansfield, Sheriff, 756
Manship, Charles P., 808(fn.)
Manti, Utah, 194
Manton, Martin, 530
Marcantonio, Vito, 541, 545, 563, 573
March, Fredric, 220
Mardi Gras, 804, 812-813
Mare, Walter de la, 142
Mare Island, California, 67
Marianna, Arkansas, 745
Marietta, Georgia, 659
Marietta, Ohio, 442
Marion, Indiana, 171
Mark Hopkins Hotel, 6, 61, 910
Markham, R. H., 518
Marks, Bill, 81
Marland, Ernest W., 880
Marquette, Michigan, 272
Marquand, John P., 466
Marquis, Samuel S., 401, 404 (fn.)
Marsh, Robert McCurdy, 582, 583, 585
Marshall, George C., xiv, 531, 660, 661(fn.), 914
Marshall, John, 705, 712
Marshall, Thurgood, 575
Martha's Vineyard, 538
Martin, Edward, 602, 609
Martin, Joseph W., Jr., 435, 473
Martin, John Bartlow, 367(fn.), 389(fn.)
Martin, Pepper, 876
Martinsburg, West Virginia, 711
Marx, Karl, 550
Maryland, 637(fn.)
Maryland, 607, 630, 637-639, 653, 654; history, 637-638
Maryland Hunt Club, 638
Masbaum family, 605
Mason, Lucy Randolph, 782(fn.)
Mason City, Iowa, 335
Masons, 193, 266, 338, 408-409, 611(fn.), 756, 765
Massachusetts, 195, 456, 457, 458, 466, 486, 490, 498, 500, 501, 507-522, 559, 572, 638, 699, 821, 824; agriculture, 467; Berkshire County, 508; foreign born in, 464; legislature, 31; Middlesex County, 509; politics, 37, 282, 475-484, 507-517; state employees per capita, 710
Massachusetts Institute of Technology, 466, 637
Masters, Edgar Lee, 374
Mastrangelo, John, 385
Maternal and Child Welfare Act, 631
Mather, Samuel W., 444
Mauermann, Gus B., 845
Maury, H. Lowndes, 156, 164, 169
Maury, Reuben, 157(fn.)
Maverick, Maury, 157(fn.), 817, 834

Maw, Herbert B., 190, 204, 207-209
Maxwell, Elsa, 559
May, Andrew J., 648
Mayer, Louis B., 48, 112, 418
Mayer, Milton, 365, 377(fn.), 391
Mayflower, 461, 692
Maynor, Dorothy, 387
Mayo Brothers, xiii
Mayo Clinic, 318
Mays, Benjamin E., 680
Maytag Company, 335
Maytubby, Floyd, 870
Mead, James, 544
Meaderville, Montana, 165
Meadows, Clarence W., 717, 718
Means, Gardiner C., 619(fn.)
Mechem, Kirke, 262
Medalie, George Z., 528
Medford, Oregon, 89
Medicine Hat, Alberta, 144
Medill, Joseph, 361
Meeman, Edward J., 751, 751 (fn.)
Meharry medical school, 760
Melby, Dr. E. O., 172
Melbank Corporation, 624
Mellbank Surety Corporation, 624
Mellett, Don, 443
Mellett, Lowell, 668(fn.), 709
Mellon, Andrew William, 567
Mellon, Richard K., 624
Mellon, T., & Sons, 624
Mellon, W. L., 625
Mellon family, 369(fn.), 445, 573, 624, 625, 808
Mellon National Bank, 624
Mellon Securities Corporation, 624
Melrose, Massachusetts, 520
Melungeons, 759
Memphis, Tennessee, xiii, 128 (fn.), 474, 655, 663, 670, 693, 745, 746, 749, 751, 753, 754, 755, 757, 758, 759, 760, 805, 911
"Memphis Blues," 752
Memphis Commercial Appeal, 751 (fn.)
Memphis Press-Scimitar, 751
Mencken, H. L., 42, 44, 638-639, 666, 696(fn.), 863, 922
Menninger, Dr. Karl A., 256
Mennonites, 259-260, 334, 342, 627-629
Menominee, Michigan, 272
Mercer, Asa, 93-94
Merchants and Manufacturers Association, 38, 39
Mercury, Texas, 826
Meredith Publishing Company, 337
Merriam, Charles E., 281
Merriam, Governor (Cal.), 53
Merrimac, 660
Merrimac Valley Authority, 468
Merritt Parkway (Conn.), 910
Merrow, Chester E., 473
Mesa, Arizona, 194
Mesabi Range, 310, 616
Messersmith, George S., 921
Mestrovic, Steve, 625
Metallurgical Laboratory, 378
Metaxas, John, 810

Metcalf family, 500
Methodist church, 266, 338, 451, 648, 668, 760, 787, 865(fn.), 874
Metro-Goldwyn Mayer, 49, 112
Metropolitan Life Insurance Company, 572
Metzman, Gustav, 558
Mexican Water Treaty, 903
Mexicans, 511, 573, 832, 833, 835
Mexico, 8, 9, 83, 216, 227, 228, 371, 806, 823, 835, 839, 855, 891, 902
Mexico, Gulf of, *see* Gulf of Mexico
Meyers, Victor Aloysius, 92
Mezerik, A. G., 794(fn.)
Miami, Arizona, 167, 905
Miami, Florida, 7(fn.), 239, 373, 550(fn.), 653, 671, 728, 729, 730, 788, 805
Miami Beach, Florida, 727, 730
Miami Copper Co., 905
Miami *Daily News*, 730, 784
Miami University, 454
Michie, Charles A., 367(fn.)
Michigan, 151, 155, 167, 270, 276, 281, 282, 311, 370, 390, 438, 572, 589, 641, 789, 800 (fn.), 844; labor, 504; politics, 391; University of, 176, 526
Michigan, Lake, 271, 288, 311, 318, 371, 420
Michigan Central Railroad, 403
Michigan Farmer, 265
Midcontinent Oil and Gas Association, 882
Middlesex, Connecticut, 506
Middle West, 251, 261, 270-455, 476, 539, 602, 672
Middletown, Ohio, 291, 441(fn.)
Midland Steel, 412
Midwest at Noon (Hutton), 275 (fn.), 368
Mieszkowski, Ed, 385
Milburn, George, 869, 876
Miles, Colonel Nelson A., 161
Milestone, Lewis, 49
Millay, Edna St. Vincent, vii, xiii
Mille, Cecil B. de, 49
Miller, Gilbert, 559
Miller, Hungry Sam, 908
Miller, Nathan L., 620
Millerites, 535
Millikin, Eugene, 148, 210(fn.), 223
Millikin, Mrs. Eugene, 223
Mills, William W., 586
Milltown, New Jersey, 546
Milton Junction, Wisconsin, 326
Milwaukee, Wisconsin, 142, 271 (fn.), 272, 283, 288, 318, 319, 320, 321, 325, 446, 536, 572, 809, 910
Milwaukee *Journal*, 289(fn.)
Mind of the South (Cash), 671
Minden, Louisiana, 684
Mineral Ridge, Ohio, 466
Ministerial Association, 292(fn.)
Minneapolis, Minnesota, 93, 155, 271(fn.), 296, 300, 303, 304, 306, 309, 318, 337, 409, 516, 536, 725, 736, 877

Minneapolis *Star-Journal*, 302, 922
Minnesota, 144, 157, 174, 237, 238, 239, 260, 270, 320, 321, 327, 420, 615-616, 618, 639, 837; agriculture in, 330; Dakota County, 298, 299; history, 296; iron ore in, 310-314; Mesabi pits, 717; politics, 293-308; railroads in, 908; University of, 104, 293, 297
Minnesota, A Duped State, 313 (fn.)
Minnesota Point, Minnesota, 309
Minnesota Resources Commission, 313(fn.)
Minor, Don Estevan, 803
Minot, Henry J., 481
Minot, North Dakota, 240
Minsk, White Russia, 552
Mission to Moscow (film), 451
Mississippi, xiii, 195, 489, 640, 653, 654, 655, 658, 662, 666, 667, 672, 675, 678, 681, 690, 700, 701, 729, 733, 744, 745, 752, 762(fn.), 790, 796, 799-803, 808, 817, 871, 880; nicknames for, 258(fn.); University of, 745
Mississippi Daughters of the American Revolution, 803
Mississippi Delta, 683, 763
Mississippi Power & Light Company, 745, 800
Mississippi River, 183, 187, 270, 271, 272-274, 311, 358, 650, 654, 663, 733, 760, 765, 802, 809
Missoula, Montana, 172
The Missouri (Vestal), 183 (fn.)
Missouri, 147, 196, 230, 258, 259, 262, 270, 275, 282, 334, 341-358, 386, 453, 524, 642, 653, 654, 659, 739, 765, 867; education in, 356; electric power, 185; Jackson County, 346, 347; labor in, 349; lobbies in, 348-349; Negroes in, 343, 352-356; Pike County, 343; politics, 341, 344-350; self-supporting attributes, 1; University of, 356
Missouri Pacific Railroad Company, 358, 765
Missouri River, 144, 159-160, 183-189, 239, 246, 258, 273, 342, 358, 748, 760, 809
Missouri Valley Authority, 169, 173, 178, 183-189, 215, 219, 234, 242, 245, 358
Mitchell, Charles E., 530, 568, 570
Mitchell, George S., 674(fn.), 791(fn.)
Mitchell, Harry B., 97
Mitchell, Hugh, 97, 133, 210
Mitchell, John, 313
Mitchell, Margaret, 666
Mitchell, Sidney Z., 568
Mitchell, William D., 367
Mitscher, Admiral Marc A., 321
Mitsui family, 632
Miyama, Mr., 24
Mobile, Alabama, 550, 659, 689, 794, 795

Mobile & Ohio Railroad, 358
The Modern Corporation and Private Property, 619
Mohawk Valley, 535
Moline, Illinois, 335(fn.)
Mollison, Irvin C., 884
Monmouth, Oregon, 95
Monroe, Georgia, 778
Monroe, Harriet, 374
Monroe, James, 557, 579
Monroe, Louisiana, 808
Monroe family, 705
Monroney, Mike, 324, 876, 884-885
Monsanto Chemical Company, 348
Mont Blanc, 91
Montana, xiii, xv, 86, 109, 115, 144, 148, 149, 150, 155-182, 244, 247, 259, 453, 523, 534, 662, 671, 683, 860, 910; agriculture, 157, 179-181, 838; area, 155; climate, 150; electric power, 185; indians, 235; industry, 165-174, 185; miscellany, 181-182; newspapers in, 160, 171, 181-182; politics, 169, 174; population, 155-156, 157; railroads, 179; Silver Bow County, 164; University of, 172
Montana Builder, 174
Montana Farming Corporation, 179
Montana, High, Wide and Handsome (Howard), 165, 185(fn.)
Montana Highway Historical Markers (Fletcher), 161(fn.)
Montana Labor News, 172
Montana Power Company, 160, 168, 169, 172-174, 209
Montana Standard, 171
"Montana Twins in Trouble" (Howard), 168(fn.), 173
Montemezzi, Italy, 7, 581
Monterey, California, 4, 9, 425
Montgomery, Alabama, 663, 671, 794, 797, 908
Montgomery, R. H., 815(fn.), 921
Montgomery, W. T., 859
Montgomery Ward & Company, 278
Montpelier, Ohio, 441(fn.)
Montpelier, Vermont, 76(fn.), 493, 495, 497, 910
Montreal, Canada, 539
Moody, Dan, 839, 840, 856
Moody, William Vaughan, 374
Mooney, Thomas, 40
Moore, A. Harry, 590, 593, 595
Moore, E. H., 210(fn.), 851, 883
Moore, Weaver, 867
Moose, fraternal order of, 277, 609, 611(fn.)
Moran, "Bugs," 381
Moran, Francis P., 516
Moravians, 628
More, Louis, 432
More, Paul Elmer, 432
Morehouse College, 680, 777
Morenci, Arizona, 905
Morgan, Arthur E., 735
Morgan, Edmund Morris, 466
Morgan, Harcourt A., 738, 740

Morgan, Henry, 571
Morgan, Irene, 703
Morgan, J. P., 16, 179, 287, 419, 505, 538, 539, 565, 566, 567, 569, 570, 570(fn.), 571, 618, 618(fn.)
Morgan, J. P., Jr., 619
Morgan, J. P., & Company, Inc., 311, 570, 571, 620, 921
Morgan Stanley & Company, Inc., 566, 571
Morgenthau, Henry, Jr., 627
Morley, Christopher, 512
Mormons, 77, 113, 115-116, 190-212, 232, 343, 535, 607(fn.), 608, 904
Moroni, 197
Morris, Esther, 228
Morris, Nelson, 371
Morris, Newbold, 563, 564, 564 (fn.), 581
Morisania, 554
Morrison, de Lesseps S., 676, 806
Morse, J. Mitchell, 790
Morse, Samuel F. B., 102, 491
Morse, Wayne, 85, 88, 96, 102-107, 108, 148
Morton, Ferdinand Q., 575
Moscow, Idaho, x, 113, 114, 466
Moscow Art Theater, 271
Moscow Idahoan, 114
Moses, C. Hamilton, 766
Moses, Robert, 536, 561, 563, 578, 579, 914, 921
Moskvin, Ivan, 271
Mote, Carl H., 390
Motherwell, Hiram, 374
Motion Picture Alliance for the Preservation of American Ideals, 49-50
Motion Picture Producers and Distributors Association, 51
Mott Haven, 554
Mound Bayou, Mississippi, 684 (fn.)
Mount Holyoke College, 474
Mount Hood, 91
Mount Lassen, 4
Mount Rainier, 92
Mount Shasta, 3, 4, 910
Mount Sterling, Ohio, 437
Mount Vernon, Ohio, 442
Mount Vernon, Virginia, 402
Mount Whitney, 2
Mountain Whippoorwill (Benét), 767
Movie industry, 47-51
Mowat, R. B., 656(fn.)
Mowrer, Edgar A., 225, 921
Mowrer brothers, 374
Mud, Texas, 826
Muir, John, 4, 139
Mulberry, Texas, 826
Mulligan, James H., 644
Mullins, W. E., 509
Mulroy, James W., 379(fn.)
Multnomah Falls, 120
Mumford, Mrs. George S., 477
Muncie, Indiana, 291, 385, 390, 521
Mundelein, Cardinal, 370
Murder Incorporated, 560, 561
Murdock, Abe, 210

Murdock, Kenneth B., 29, 458
Murphy, Boss, 590(fn.)
Murphy, Charles F., 581
Murphy, Frank, 300
Murphy, Mark, 225(fn.)
Murphy, Mary Ellen, 225(fn.)
Murray, Alfalfa Bill, 869, 879
Murray, James E., 148, 174, 187, 188
Murray, Philip, 26, 621, 622-623, 914, 916
Murray, Thomas E., 408
Murray Bay, Canada, 433
Murrell, John A., 761
Murrow, Edward R., 921
Muscle Shoals, Alabama, 733, 734, 740, 743
Muse, Vance, 765, 852
Museum of Modern Art, 247, 577
Music, 907, 908
Muskegon, Michigan, 277
Mussolini, Benito, 364, 605, 752, 754, 809, 810
Mustard, 137
Mutual Broadcasting System, 366 (fn.)
"My Old Kentucky Home," 640
Myrdal, Gunnar, 284(fn.), 286, 383, 627(fn.), 654, 682, 683, 691, 694, 696(fn.), 697, 702 (fn.), 704, 776, 777(fn.), 802 (fn.)
Mystic Shrine, 611(fn.)
The Mythical Jayhawk (Mechem), 262

Nance, Berta Hart, 859
Nantucket, Massachusetts, 907
Napoleon, Ohio, 442
Narragansett race track, 499
Nash, Ogden, 564
Nash, Pat, 372
Nash Motors, 319
Nashville, Tennessee, 676, 750 (fn.), 751, 758, 759, 760, 761, 802, 911
Nashville American, 761
Nashville Banner, 668
Nashville Tennessean, 753, 754, 922
Natchez, Mississippi, 802-803
Natchez, Texas, 866
Natchez Democrat, 801
Nathan, George Jean, 559
Nation, 59, 257(fn.), 327(fn.), 369, 391, 418(fn.), 434(fn.), 592(fn.), 763, 811
Nation, Carry, 260, 571
National Association for the Advancement of Colored People, 575, 685, 688, 689, 921, 922
National Association of Manufacturers, 32, 38, 74, 101, 338, 405, 641
National Bank of Detroit, 419
National Broadcasting Company, 360
National Cash Register Company, 449(fn.)
National Citizens Political Action Committee, see Political Action Committee
National City Bank of New York, 530, 563, 566, 568

National Committee to Uphold Constitutional Government, 612
National Copperheads, 54
National Dollar Stores, 46
National Economic Council of New York, 382
National Farm Labor Union, 765
National Farmers Union, see Farmers Union
National Geographic, 252(fn.)
National Housing Agency, 650
National Labor Relations Board, 319, 365, 622
National Maritime Union, 26, 853(fn.)
National Mining Co., 617
National Opinion Research Center, 226, 921
National Progressives of America, 30, 323
National Recovery Administration, 377, 612
National Resources Committee, 571
National Tube Co., 617
National War Labor Board, 24, 105, 106, 649, 722, 782
Natural gas, 837
Nauvoo, Illinois, 196
Navajo Indians, 873, 874, 894, 895
Nazis, 88
Nebraska, 55, 124, 144, 146, 149, 215, 216, 237, 238, 248(fn.), 250-255, 258, 259, 270, 288, 296, 320, 799, 821, 836, 859, 860, 862, 910; agriculture, 251, 328, 330, 334; capitol, 250; climate, 251; electric power, 185, 254-255; labor in, 253; legislature, 31, 253-254; livestock, 251(fn.); politics, 250-255, 306, 308; population, 185, 251; prohibition and, 254; railroads in, 253; University of, 218
Nebraska Power Company, 255
Needham, Massachusetts, 475
Neenah, Wisconsin, 319
Neff, Pat, 821, 864
Negroes, 4, 45, 60-62, 88, 150-151, 283-286, 343, 352-356, 383-385, 387, 389, 405, 449, 451, 454, 483, 547, 573-576, 626-627, 653, 654, 655, 659, 661, 663, 664, 669, 673, 674, 679-704, 706, 708, 720-721, 722, 726, 749, 753, 754, 760, 765, 766, 768, 773, 776-778, 780, 781, 783, 786-787, 788, 789, 794, 795, 796, 798-799, 800-801, 803, 811, 812, 834, 865-868, 874, 876, 881-882, 897, 904, 916
Nelson, Battling, 181
Nelson, Donald, 51
Nelson, Martin A., 299
Nelson, William Rockhill, 351
Neosho, Missouri, 342
Neuberger, Richard L., 92(fn.), 96, 126(fn.), 921
Neutrality Act, 175, 391, 435
Nevada, 6, 76-84, 144, 204, 228, 354, 662, 703(fn.), 719, 76

(fn.), 887, 901, 902, 903; area, 76; divorces and, 77-78, 631 (fn.); gambling in, 78-79; metal in, 80, 81-83; politics, 77, 79, 82; population, 76; public finance, 78-79
Nevada Consolidated Copper Company, 905
New Bedford, Massachusetts, 907
New Caledonia, 785
New Deal, 19, 29, 37, 41, 48, 64, 82, 101, 102, 106, 121, 133, 138, 148, 149, 181, 189, 204, 207, 240, 241, 253, 323, 355, 361, 367, 382, 385, 390, 392, 430, 450, 470, 524, 532, 533, 565, 569, 606, 609, 627, 678, 707, 757, 778, 791, 807, 875, 880, 883, 901, 918, 919
New England, ix, 151, 216, 259, 260, 270, 274, 336, 344, 441, 446, 456-522, 535, 539, 540, 637, 653, 656, 658, 665, 671, 683, 705, 761, 804, 900; agriculture, 467; foreign born, 464; industry, 468, 672; senators, 469-474; town meetings, 460
New England Council, 472, 512
New England Society of Cleveland, 29(fn.)
New England Watch and Ward Society, 517-518
New Hampshire, 87, 194, 195, 458, 465, 489-495, 510, 522, 779; agriculture, 467; comparison with Vermont, 492; French Canadians in, 465; industry, 491, 492; labor, 490; legislature, 489
New Hampshire Public Service Company, 490
New Harmony, Indiana, 388(fn.)
New Haven, Connecticut, 464, 469, 502, 506
New Helvetia, 9
New Jersey, xv, 151, 174, 402, 466, 539, 589-599, 607, 638, 645, 749, 910; education, 599; governors term, 30; Hudson County, 592, 593, 595; industry, 598; legislature, 31, 594; politics, 34, 282, 589-596, 613; railroads, 211; roads, 597, 598; state employees per capita, 710
New Mexico, 888(fn.)
New Mexico, 144, 149, 151, 194, 220, 654, 661, 666, 814, 821, 835, 860, 873, 886, 904, 908; area, 887; Indians, 891-895; median age in, 5; politics, 890; population, 887
New Mexico Magazine, 895(fn.)
New Orleans, Louisiana, xiii, 155, 223, 249, 353, 353(fn.), 409, 446, 539, 558, 637, 648, 650, 659, 668, 670, 675, 676, 786, 792, 801, 802, 804, 804 (fn.), 805, 806, 808-809, 812-813, 832, 910, 912
New Orleans Times-Picayune, 805(fn.), 808, 922
New Orleans Woman (Kane), 921

New Republic, 11, 48, 54(fn.), 124, 178(fn.), 210, 287(fn.), 330, 369(fn.), 434, 438(fn.), 470, 504, 559, 573, 591, 612 (fn.), 621(fn.), 634, 677, 714, 794(fn.), 801, 883
New Rochelle, New York, 575
New School for Social Research, 577
New Statesman, 735
New World A-Coming, 574(fn.)
New York, 534(fn.)
New York, ix, 1, 7, 49, 151, 155, 167, 192, 194, 195, 251, 260, 271, 286, 418, 485, 491, 493, 523-577, 620, 641, 699, 762, 788, 815, 836, 843, 908, 910; agriculture in, 523-524, 534; budget, 63; Chautauqua County, 371; Dutchess County, 523; electoral votes, 1; federal job holders, 41; income per capita, 2(fn.); industry, 536-538; legislature, 31, 543; Nassau County, 538; politics, 282; 440, 523-533, 540, 602; population, 5; Queens County, 553, 555, 574; state employees per capita, 710
New York Central System, 358, 419, 442, 537, 558, 572, 577
New York City, 555(fn.)
New York City, New York, 2, 28, 42, 68, 124, 128, 155, 271, 278, 288, 348, 355, 364, 370, 410, 417, 431, 442, 442(fn.), 443, 448, 496, 499, 500, 501, 518, 523, 524, 529, 534, 535, 536, 539, 540(fn.), 541, 542, 543(fn.), 544-547, 549-588, 589, 590(fn.), 591, 593, 597, 598, 603, 620, 630, 637, 681, 686, 728, 729, 786, 792, 809, 819, 827, 827(fn.), 897, 907, 908, 910, 912, 913; area, 551; divorces in, 576; finance, 542, 543(fn.); foreign born in, 552; industry in, 553; population, 551; religion in, 552-553; skyscrapers in, 556
New York Daily Mirror, 29, 542, 564(fn.), 683(fn.), 852
New York Daily News, 97, 157 (fn.), 188, 361, 362, 367, 368, 368(fn.), 454, 544-547, 564 (fn.), 623, 732
New York Herald Tribune, 72, 171, 233, 282(fn.), 319(fn.), 347, 347(fn.), 362, 368(fn.), 435(fn.), 509, 553(fn.), 559, 564, 564(fn.), 649, 686, 706, 714, 726(fn.), 795(fn.), 822, 921
New York Journal-American, 564(fn.)
New York Post, 26(fn.), 111 (fn.), 113(fn.), 267(fn.), 293(fn.), 383, 390(fn.), 437 (fn.), 527, 564(fn.), 668(fn.), 709, 710, 793(fn.), 884
New York Stock Exchange, 377, 419, 566, 568
New York Sun, 564(fn.), 732
New York Times, 73, 82, 212,

242(fn.), 304(fn.), 333, 334 (fn.), 346(fn.), 377(fn.), 381 (fn.), 382, 404, 411(fn.), 433 (fn.), 452(fn.), 459, 498, 528, 531(fn.), 542, 555, 556(fn.), 559, 564(fn.), 566(fn.), 570 (fn.), 571, 590(fn.), 625(fn.), 633(fn.), 657, 668, 685(fn.), 687, 732, 746, 760, 766(fn.), 768, 788(fn.), 851, 909, 916, 921
New York Tribune, 550
New York University, 172, 554, 577
New York World-Telegram, 44, 97(fn.), 386, 564(fn.), 795 (fn.)
New York Young Republican Club, 528
New Yorker, 107, 230, 511, 530 (fn.), 533, 553(fn.), 559, 589 (fn.), 593(fn.), 596(fn.), 807
New Zealand, 364, 732
Newark, New Jersey, 545, 552, 593, 597
Newberg, Oregon, 95
Newbern, North Carolina, 719
Newberry, Truman, 403
Newbranch, H. E., 280
Newhall, Ruth, 921
Newnan, Georgia, 770, 771
Newman, Harry, 405(fn.)
Newport, Delaware, 636
Newport, Rhode Island, 499, 500, 538, 568
Newport News, Virginia, 827(fn.)
News-Week, 320(fn.)
Newton, Byron R., 523, 555
Newton, Iowa, 335
Newton, Louie D., 668
Newton, Massachusetts, 476, 520
Nez Perce Indians, 161
Niagara Falls, New York, 272, 534, 539, 724, 744
Niagara Falls Power Company, 536
Nicaragua, 798(fn.)
Nichols, Dudley, 49, 50
Nicholas, Herbert, 921
Nicholson, E. D., 922
Nicholson, Meredith, 386
Nickerson, H. C., 228
Nieman-Marcus, 829, 830
Nimitz, Chester, 817, 833
98th meridian, 239
Nisei, 24, 46-47, 88, 222, 573, 789
Nitti the Enforcer, 379
Nix, Texas, 826
No Mean City (Strunsky), 550 (fn.)
Nobel prize, 420
Noble, Robert, 54
Non-Partisan League, 239-241, 247
Norbeck, Peter, 247, 249
Norfolk, Virginia, 449(fn.), 721
Norfolk & Western Railway Co., 717
Norfolk Journal and Guide, 627
Norman, Oklahoma, 881
Norris, Frank, 7
Norris, George, 16, 121, 253, 254, 306, 471, 733, 740, 758

Norris, J. Frank, 863
North, 772, 788, 794
North, Sterling, 374
North America (Smith), 463
North Brother Island, 555
North Carolina, 607, 616, 653, 654, 658, 659, 660, 662, 665, 667, 671, 672, 675, 687, 690, 701, 708, 718-723, 733, 740, 744, 749, 759, 800, 826, 838; "autonomous" status, 6(fn.); Cleveland County, 721; divorces in, 719; liberalism of, 719; politics, 678; population, 718; Randolph County, 718; "State of Franklin," 63; tobacco in, 712; Univeristy of, 654, 703, 721, 722
North Dakota, 136, 144, 146, 149, 156(fn.), 174, 237-255, 260, 270, 320, 321, 336, 662, 860, 870, 910; agriculture, 238-239; co-operatives in, 242-244, 337; electric power, 185; newspapers, 237; pheasants in, 248 (fn.); politics, 239-242, 296; population, 185, 244; railroads, 237, 244; University of, 180
North Platte River, 215, 216
Northern Pacific Railway Co., 93, 162, 174, 312, 909
Northwest, ix, 85-143, 616, 732, 745, 873
Northwest Airlines, Inc., 318
Northwest Bancorporation, 244
Northwest Ordinance of 1787, 145
Northwest Territory, 446
Northwestern Electric Co., 127
Northwestern Mutual Life Insurance Company, 572
Northwestern University, 121, 868
Norwalk, Connecticut, 505
Norwalk, Ohio, 442
Notre Dame University, 385, 406, 626
Nover, Barnet, 922
Nunn, Colorado, 217
Nunn, H. L., 319
Nunn, William G., 626
Nuremberg trials, 22, 363, 435
Nye, Gerald P., 16, 175, 178, 240, 242, 242(fn.), 291
Nylon, 635

Oak Park, Illinois, 374(fn.)
Oak Ridge, Tennessee, 378, 636, 672, 737, 746 737(fn.)
Oakland, California, 19, 68, 449 (fn.)
Oakland *Tribune*, 35
O'Banion, Dean, 370, 380
Oberlin College, 454
O'Brian, John Lord, 537
O'Brien, Howard Vincent, 374, 921
Ochs, Adolph S., 568
O'Connell, Cardinal, 512, 516-517
O'Connell, Jerry, 176
O'Connor, Basil, 798(fn.)
O'Daniel, Mike, 852
O'Daniel, Pappy (Wilbert Lee), 109, 112, 815, 817, 830, 833,

835, 840, 844, 848, 852, 854, 856
O'Daniel, Pat, 852
Odd Fellows, 611(fn.), 756
Odum, Howard W., 258(fn.), 654, 660, 661, 661(fn.), 662, 665, 666, 667, 676, 799(fn.)
O'Dwyer, James, 559(fn.)
O'Dwyer, John, 559(fn.)
O'Dwyer, William, 498, 542, 542(fn.), 544, 558, 559-564, 564(fn.)
Odyssey, 213
Office of Defense Transportation, 584
Office of Emergency Management, 106
Office of Price Administration, 97, 103, 333, 348, 436, 504, 584, 624, 644, 851, 852, 883
Office of Strategic Services, 537
Office of War Information, 76, 209
O'Flaherty, Hal, 374
Ogburn, Professor, 379
Ogden, Utah, 152, 203, 210
Ogdensburg, New York, 539
O'Hara, Maureen, 48
Ohio, 196, 239, 270, 271, 275, 280, 282, 422-455, 457, 485, 572, 624, 659, 707, 715, 745, 762, 800, 829, 891; agriculture in, 330, 442; education in, 454-455; industry, 442, 534; lobbies, 440; politics, 422-440; presidents from, 439; University of, 285-286, 437, 454, 777, 922
Ohio City, Ohio, 231
Ohio Farmer, 265
Ohio River, 446, 448, 453-454, 615, 650, 715, 733, 764, 809
Ohio State Journal, 452
Ohio Valley Authority, 453
Ohio Wesleyan University, 454
Oil *see also* Petroleum, 36(fn.), 57-60, 266, 713, 800, 805, 808, 816, 825, 826, 827, 829, 830, 836, 853, 855, 875, 876, 877, 878
Oil Well Supply Co., 617
Oil Workers Union, 831
Okies, 4, 8, 147, 659
Okinawa, 687
Oklahoma, 880(fn.)
Oklahoma (play), 876
Oklahoma, xiii, 146, 152, 216, 238, 258, 259, 353, 527, 559, 653, 654, 661, 814, 821, 826, 836, 837, 839, 860, 868, 869-885, 890, 891; politics, 879-885
Oklahoma A & M College, 876
Oklahoma City, Oklahoma, 869, 877, 878, 908
Oklahoma City *Daily Oklahoman*, 881
Oklahoma City *Times*, 881
Oklahoma Place Names (Gould), 874(fn.)
Oklahoma Territory, 872
O'Konski, Alvin E., 320, 324
Old Age Pension Union, 98

Older, Fremont, 13
Olds, Irving S., 620
Oliver Corporation, 279
Oliver Cromwell (warship), 501
Oliver Iron Mining Company, 310-314
Olson, Culbert Levy, 20, 36, 54
Olson, Floyd, 296-297, 299
Olympia, Washington, 29, 99
Omaha, Nebraska, 152, 183, 211, 250, 251, 255, 259, 332, 342, 537, 911
Omaha *World Herald*, 237, 251, 255, 280
O'Mahoney, Joseph C., 149, 235, 572, 914
One World (Willkie), 303
Oneida Community, 535
Ono, California, 63
Ontario, Canada, 540
Ontario, Lake, 537
Oppenheimer, Dr. J. Robert, xiii, 888
Oraibi, Arizona, 886
Orange, New Jersey, 545
Ordway, A. B., 69
Oregon, 3, 9, 76, 85-92, 113, 116 (fn.), 144, 145, 194, 213, 221, 249, 286, 745, 762(fn.), 907; Curry County, 62; electric power, 89, 127-133, 185, 255; labor in, 87, 90, 95-96; land tenure in, 90; liquor regulation in, 90; lumber, 139-142, 218; Peoples' Utility Districts, 131-132, 254; politics, 87, 88, 94-96, 102-107; railways, 89, 94; religious factor in, 89; settlement, 87, 89; University of, 105
Oregon Territory, 86
Oregon Through Alien Eyes (Leader), 85
Oregon Trail, 261, 343
Osage Indians, 874, 875
Osage Trail, 261
Osawatomie, Kansas, 259
Osborn, John P., 898
Osborn, Neri F., 898
Osborn, Sidney P., 251, 897, 902, 903
Osborn Manufacturing Company, 445
Oshkosh, Wisconsin, 319
Oshkosh Trunks, Inc., 319
O'Sullivan, James, 125
Oswego, New York, 728
Otis, Harrison Grey, 14
Otoe Indians, 252
Ottley, Roi, 574(fn.)
Otto, Texas, 826
Ottumwa, Iowa, 335
Our Promised Land (Neuberger) 92(fn.), 921
Outland, George, 37
Overton, John H., 188
Owen, Robert, 388(fn.), 869
Owens, Hamilton, 638
Owens, John W., 612
Owosso, Michigan, 525
Oxford, Ohio, 454
Oxnam, Dr. G. Bromley, 668
Oyster Bay, Long Island, 538
Ozarks, 342-343, 348, 351, 765

Pacific Gas and Electric Company, 38, 620
Pacific Northwest, 85-143
Pacific Power and Light Co., 127
Packard, James, 445
Paducah, Kentucky, 733
Pageant, 922
Palffy, Countess Eleanor, 922
Palisades, 598
Palm Beach, Florida, 728
Palmer, Perrine, Jr., 806
Palmer, Potter, 371
Panama Canal, 272, 371, 625
Pan-American Highway, 227
Pan American World Airways System, 729
Paoli, Pennsylvania, 604
Papago Indians, 895
Paradise, Pennsylvania, 628
Paraguay, 780
Paramount Pictures Corp., 49, 51
Parent Teachers Association, (Oregon), 95
Paris, France, 785
Paris, Maine, 464
Parker Pen Company, 319
Parkman, Francis, 462
Parkman, Henry, Jr., 462
Parma, Italy, 559
Parr, Archie, 844
Pasadena, California, 4, 44
Passos, John Dos, 841
Pastore, John, 500
Patman, Wright, 848
Pathfinder, 611, 612
Patterson, Eleanor (Cissy), 361, 363(fn.)
Patterson, Ellis, 19, 39
Patterson, Frederick D., 798-799
Patterson, Joseph Medill, 361, 362, 363(fn.), 368, 568
Patterson, Robert P., 326
Patterson, Robert W., 361, 362
Patton, George S., 289
Patton, James G., 187, 226
Pauley, Edwin W., 60, 471
Pawling, New York, 523, 527
Pawnee Indians, 870
Pawtucket, Rhode Island, 171
Peabody, Endicott, 462
Peach, Texas, 826
Peacock, Texas, 826
Pearl Harbor, 274, 286, 320, 323, 364, 367, 382, 405, 470, 546, 561, 628, 757
Pearson, Drew, 225, 245, 756-757, 789(fn.), 852, 883
Peattie, Donald Culross, 7, 722
Peattie, Roderick, 722, 922
Peck, Gregory, 49
Pecora hearings, 569-570
Pecos, Texas, 833(fn.)
Pecos Bill, 820
Peculiar, Missouri, 281
Pegler, Westbrook, 43, 206, 222, 225, 232, 346, 591, 676
Pekiomenville, Pennsylvania, 628
Pella, Iowa, 334
Pelley, William D., 176
Pemberton, J. S., 784
Pendennis Club, 91, 652
Pendergast, James M., 347
Pendergast, Jim, 345
Pendergast, Thomas J., 344-348,

352, 355, 590, 590(fn.), 592, 708, 749
Pendleton, Oregon, 89, 102
Penn, William, 600, 601, 605, 607
Pennsylvania, 601(fn.), 628 (fn.)
Pennsylvania, ix, 271, 334, 442, 446, 454, 458, 538, 572, 600-629, 715, 723, 728, 789, 836, 844, 908, 910; agriculture, 601, 627; Bucks County, 601; Chester County, 610; electoral votes, 1; history, 601; industry, 534, 601, 615; legislature, 613; oil in, 58; politics, 34, 248, 254(fn.), 440, 609-614, 626; population, 5, 551; University of, 665
"Pennsylvania Company for Insurances on Lives and Granting Annuities," 608
Pennsylvania Farmer, 265
Pennsylvania Game News, 601 (fn.)
Pennsylvania Manufacturers Association, 611
Pennsylvania Railroad, 210, 358, 381, 419, 442, 567, 572, 602, 604, 608
Pennsylvania Steel Works, 616
Pennyrile, 642
Penrose, Boies, 609, 613
Pensacola, Florida, 728
People's Utility Districts, 131-132, 254
People's Voice, 172, 575
Peoria, Illinois, 374
Pep, Texas, 826
Pepper, Claude, 676
Pepper, Wharton, 605
Perkins, Frances, 24, 105
Perkins, Milo, 914
Permanente Cement Company, 67
Permanente Metals Corporation, 67, 71
Perón, Juan D., 808
Perry, George Sessions, 448, 606, 818(fn.)
Perry, Jennings, 676, 701, 753, 754(fn.)
Pershing, John J., 247, 570, 706
Perth Amboy, New Jersey, 167
Peru, Maine, 464
Petain, Henri, 706
Peterkin, Julia, 666
Petersen, Hjalmar, 300, 306
Petersen, Mark E., 203, 206
Petrillo, James, 111
Petrol Corporation of California, 60
Petroleum, see also Oil, 234, 264, 672, 815, 842, 854
Pettycoat Slide, California, 10
Pettygrove, Francis W., 90
Pew, Joseph Newton, Jr., 609, 610, 611-613, 808, 880
Peyser, Annette H., 921
Pheasants, 237, 248-249
Phelan, James D., 13
Phelps Dodge Corporation, 153, 835, 905
Phi Beta Kappa, 796
Philadelphia, Pennsylvania, 89, 152, 233, 426, 462(fn.), 519, 555(fn.), 558, 559, 597, 598,

602, 603, 609, 613, 630, 672, 827
Philadelphia Assembly, 725
Philadelphia Club, 604-605
Philadelphia Record, 603, 606 (fn.), 612
Philippine Islands, 431
Phillips, Cabell, 687(fn.)
Phillips, Jennings, Jr., 921
Phillips, Wendell, 462
Phillips, William, 462
Phillips Exeter Boys' School, 474
Phillips Petroleum Company, 837, 880
Phoenix, Arizona, 55, 231, 897, 898, 900, 901, 902, 904, 905, 906, 910
Phylon, 679
Pick, Colonel Lewis A., 186-189
Pidgeon, Walter, 49
Pierce, S. S., 457
Pigeon River, 313
Pierre, South Dakota, 76(fn.), 183, 237, 245
Pierson, Waldo, 922
Piety Hill, California, 10
Pike, Dora, see Taylor, Mrs. Glen H.
Pike's Peak, 214
Pike's Route to Pawnee Village, 261
Pilgrim's Progress, 213
Pillsbury Flour Mills Company, 318
Pilot, 514
Pilsudski, Joseph, 810
Pimlico race track, 638
Pinchot, Gifford, 605
Pinckney, Josephine, 666, 724
Pins and Needles, 553
Pioneering with Fruits and Berries (Aiken), 472
Pioneering with Wild Flowers (Aiken), 472
Pioneers! O Pioneers!, 359-360
Pitchfork, Wyoming, 230
Pittman, Key, 80, 762(fn.)
Pittsburgh, Pennsylvania, 143, 151, 181, 233, 285, 357, 385, 445, 446, 455, 553, 601, 602-607, 610, 615-627, 628, 637, 702, 715, 828, 887; Negroes in, 626-627
Pittsburgh Courier, 626, 627
Pittsburgh Limestone Corp., 617
Pittsburgh Memoranda, 615
Pittsburgh Point, Pennsylvania, 602
Pittsburgh Steamship Company, 311
Pittsburgh Steel Casting Company, 616
Pittsburgh University, 625, 626
Pittsfield, Massachusetts, 465, 910
Plaindealing River, 637
Plasterers Helpers Union (AFL), 559
Platt, Thomas C., 537
Platte River, 183, 234, 252
Plaza Hotel (NYC), 559, 589
Pleasant Valley, Ohio, 442
Pleasantville, New York, 538
"The Plow that Broke the Plains" (movie), 831

Plumley, Charles A., 473
Plummer, Henry, 162
Plymouth Rock, 256, 457, 782
PM, 27, 33(fn.), 128(fn.), 178, 289(fn.), 327(fn.), 367(fn.), 432(fn.), 515, 515(fn.), 531 (fn.), 552, 564(fn.), 606, 611 (fn.), 621(fn.), 700(fn.), 708 (fn.), 709(fn.), 732, 770 (fn.), 856(fn.), 917
Pocatello, Idaho, 108, 109, 110, 114
Poe, Edgar Allan, 712
Poetry, 374
Poindexter, Senator, 762(fn.)
Point Lobos, 20
Pointblank, Texas, 826
Poker Flat, California, 10
Poland, 175, 431
Poletti, Charles, 559
Political Action Committee, 32, 37, 40, 116, 178, 297, 353, 382, 383, 426, 448, 471, 479, 611, 674(fn.), 853, 916
Politics, see under names of States
Polk, James K., 8, 86, 685, 763, 829
Poll tax, 241, 675, 696, 699-701, 709, 710, 750, 753, 754, 755, 756, 766, 774, 784, 796, 811, 842, 848, 867, 882
Polygamy, 28(fn.), 116, 195, 199-201, 904
Pony Express, 227, 261
Pope, James P., 736, 738, 921
Popper, Arthur, 586
Populism, 260, 265
Port Angeles, Washington, 85
Port Aransas, Texas, 821
Port Arthur, Texas, 821, 827 (fn.)
Port of New York Authority, 555, 597
Portage, Wisconsin, 324
Porter, Paul, 644
Portland, Maine, xiii, 87, 90, 487
Portland, Oregon, xiii, 29, 86, 87, 88, 89, 90-92, 96-100, 108, 127, 128, 144, 152, 210, 466, 516, 574, 681, 738, 805, 827(fn.)
Portland General Electric Co., 127
Portland Oregonian, 94, 106, 225
Portsmouth, New Hampshire, 489
Portsmouth Steel Corporation, 615
Postal Telegraph, 80, 909
Potomac River, 710
Potomacus, 438(fn.), 612(fn.)
Pottawatamie Indians, 870
Pottstown, Pennsylvania, 616
Poughkeepsie, New York, 231, 538
Powell, Adam Clayton, Jr., 576
Powell, Chester,
Powell, Clilan B., 575
Powell River, 733
Power, public vs. private, 126-133, 183-189, 651, 744
Practical Cogitator, 922
Pratt estate, 539
Preakness, 638
Prentice, George D., 761

Presbyterian church, 648, 760, 874
Prescott, Arizona, 900
Pressman, Lee, 621
Pressure groups, see also Lobbies, 2, 32-33, 38-41, 49-50, 98, 207, 220, 228, 490, 502, 717, 746, 880-881, 901, 904-905, 913
Preston, Keith, 374
Price, Byron, 326, 386
Price, Utah, 204-205
Prichard, Edward F., Jr., 648
Priest, J. Percy, 676
Primer for White Folks, A (Brown), 286
Princeton, New Jersey, 596, 910
Princeton University, 599, 722
Procter &* Gamble Manufacturing Company, 447
Proctor, M. R., 494(fn.), 496
Proctor, Vermont, 497
Proctorsville, Vermont, 497
The Progressive, 96
Progressive Opinion, 197
Prohibition, 147, 150, 204, 254, 267, 334, 380-381, 388, 406, 647, 669, 721(fn.), 801, 825, 839, 880
Protected Home Circle, 611(fn.)
Proust, Marcel, 369, 420
Providence, Rhode Island, 91, 464, 498, 805
Providence Journal, 500
Provident Trust Company, 608
Provincetown, Massachusetts, 508
Provo, Utah, 211
Prudential Insurance Company of America, 572, 593
Pryor, Sam, 302
Public Men, 532(fn.), 589(fn.), 590(fn.), 593(fn.), 595(fn.)
Public Men In and Out of Office, 726(fn.), 881(fn.)
Public Service Company of Colorado, 220, 234
Public Utility Districts, 131-132, 173, 254
Public Utility Holding Company Act, 126
Public Works Administration, 606
Puccini, Giacomo, 579
Pueblo, Colorado, 145, 220, 222
Pueblo Indians, 874, 888, 891, 894
Puerto Rico, 221, 573
Puget Sound, 92, 550
Puget Sound Power and Light Co., 127, 130, 132
Puke Ravine, California, 10
Pulaski Skyway (N.J.), 597
Pulitzer, Joseph, 351-352
Pulitzer prizes, 59, 63, 352, 645
Pullman, George M., 371
Pullman Company, 419, 631, 907
Pure Food and Drug Act, 569
Putnam, Roger Lowell, 462, 478
Pure Oil Co., 880
Putney Boys' School, 474
Pyle, Ernie, 223, 385, 388

Quail, Texas, 826
Quaker Oats Company, 335
Quakers, 598, 603, 607-609, 628

Quay, Matthew S., 609
Quebec, Canada, 465
Queen Mab, 126
Queen Mary, 58, 125
Quill, Michael J., 554-555

Racine, Wisconsin, 272, 319, 320, 370
Rackets, 379-381, 426, 528, 529, 530, 560, 591, 622, 787
Racquet Club, 604
Radcliffe College, 474
Radebaugh, Dr., 304
Radio Corporation of America 290, 552(fn.)
Radio stations, 908; KDKA, 602; KFPY, 177; KRNT, 337; KSL, 191, 205, 206; KTRH 828; WBNS, 452; WGN, 366 (fn.); WJBO, 808(fn.); WLW, 448; WNAX, 337 WOR, 778; WWL, 809
Radium, Texas, 826
Radum, California, 67
Railroads, see also names of Railroads; and under names of States, 11-12, 38, 145, 153 174, 179, 211, 220, 321, 358 447(fn.), 476, 567, 577, 646 736, 761, 773, 775, 800, 861 900, 907
Rainey, Homer P., 841, 856, 857 858
Rainey, Lillian Fryer, 878(fn.)
Rainey, R. M., 870, 921
Raleigh, North Carolina, 713 719
Raleigh, Walter, 616
Raleigh (N.C.) News and Observer, 462(fn.), 668, 719, 72●
Rand McNally Co., 759
Randall's Island, 555
Randolph, John, 822(fn.)
Randolph, Philip, 699
Randolph field, 833-834
Random House, Inc., 555(fn.)
Rankin, Jeannette, 150
Rankin, John E., 189, 540, 655 789, 799
Rascals in Democracy (Clugston), 256, 268(fn.)
Rascoe, Burton, 374
Raskob, John J., 568, 570, 634
Rates, freight, see Freight rate
Raver, Paul J., 121, 132, 133
Rawlings, Marjorie Kinnan, 66●
Rawlins Daily News, 231
Ray, Arizona, 905
Rayburn, Sam, 815, 817
Reader's Digest, 188, 453(fn.)● 538, 725(fn.), 763, 922
Reading I've Liked (Fadiman), 556(fn.)
Reams, Frazer, 429
Reciprocal Trade Treaties, 149
Reconstruction Finance Corpora tion, 65, 72, 73, 392, 568, 82
Reconversion, 2
Red Cross, 292(fn.), 522
Red Oak, Iowa, 335
Red River, 809
Redding, California, 67
Redistricting, 375, 751
Reece, B. Carroll, 103

Reed, Clyde M., 210(fn.)
Reed, Jack, 88
Reed, James A., 346
Reed College, 89
Reese, Carroll, 525(fn.)
Rehan, Ada, 557
Reid, Helen R., 921
Reid, Ira de Augustine, 679
Reid, Mrs. Ogden, 559
Reidsville, North Carolina, 713
Reles, Abe "Kid Twist," 560
Remarque, Erich, 7
Reno, Nevada, 3, 63, 77-78, 79, 147, 165, 231
Renoir, Pierre Auguste, 271
Renton, Washington, 119, 142
Rentschler, Gordon S., 563
Report on the Motor Vehicle Industry, 403(fn.)
Republic Steel Corp., 620, 621-622, 623
Resnick, Beatrice, 581, 584, 587
Reston, James, 333, 382(fn.)
Retail Merchants Association, 292(fn.)
Reuter's news agency, 363, 446
Reuther, Roy, 414
Reuther, Victor, 413-414, 416
Reuther, Walter P., 410-411, 412, 412(fn.), 413-418, 622
Revercomb, Chapman, 718
Revere, Paul, 457
Revolutionary War, 441, 534, 603, 607
Rex Club, 812-813
Reynolds, R. J., Company, 713, 714
Reynolds, Robert R., 722
Reynolds Metals Co., Inc., 766
Rheims, New York, 538
Rhinelander, Wisconsin, 141(fn.)
Rhoades, D. A., 69
Rhode Island (American Guide Series), 499(fn.)
Rhode Island, 167, 362, 457, 458, 461, 465, 485, 498-500, 559, 607, 660, 721, 821, 910; area, 499; "autonomous" status, 6 (fn.); French Canadians in, 465; history, 498-499; industry, 498; legislature, 31; politics, 499, 890
Rhodes, Cecil, 196, 366
Rhodes, Eugene Manlove, 888
Rice, Grantland, 671
Rice Institute, 827
Richards, George, 202, 207
Richmond, California, 39, 65, 69, 70-72
Richmond, New York, 555
Richmond, University of, 712
Richmond, Virginia, 654, 655, 669, 672, 705, 710, 711-712, 713, 715, 716, 910
Richmond News Leader, 922
Richmond Times Dispatch, 657, 758, 921
Ridgefield, Ohio, 441
Riesel, Victor, 26(fn.), 793(fn.)
Riggs, Lynn, 876
Riker's Island, 555
Riley, James Whitcomb, 386
Rio Grande River, 825, 826, 894
Riskin, Robert, 921

Ritzville, Washington, 135
River Rouge, 401, 405(fn.), 411
Rivera, Diego, 261(fn.)
Rivers, E. D., 768, 771
Roberts, Elizabeth Madox, 374
Roberts, Kenneth, 486
Roberts, Owen J., 605
Roberts, Roy A., 351, 922
Robertson, A. Willis, 711
Robertson, Edward V., 210(fn.), 235
Robeson, Paul, 387, 627, 681
Robinson, Edward G., 220
Robinson, Frank B., 114-115
Robinson, Jackie, 703
Robinson, Joe, 678, 766
Robinson, S. M., 784
Robsion, John, 648
"Rochester," 760
Rochester, Minnesota, 318
Rochester, New York, xiii, 449 (fn.), 537, 715, 783
Rock Island, Illinois, 335(fn.)
Rock Island Railroad, 220, 876
Rock Springs, Wyoming, 230, 234
Rock Springs Miner, 231
Rock Springs Rocket, 231
Rockawalkin River, 637
Rockefeller, John D., xiii, 230, 376, 444, 713
Rockefeller, John D., Jr., 233, 561, 567
Rockefeller, Nelson A., 471
Rockefeller Center, 68, 261(fn.), 557
Rockefeller family, 220, 573, 618, 624
Rockefeller Foundation, 57
Rockford, Illinois, 375
Rockingham Park, 490
Rocky Mountain Politics (Donnelly), 77(fn.), 890(fn.)
Rocky Mountains, 145, 271, 342
Rogell, Billy, 406
Rogers, Edith Nourse, 473
Rogers, Ginger, 49, 821
Rogers, Will, 802, 869, 875
Rogers, Will, Jr., 19, 36, 37
Rollins College, 728
Roman Catholic church, see Catholic church
Rome, New York, 537
Roosevelt, Eleanor, 225, 481, 488, 586, 697, 777, 845, 922
Roosevelt, Elliott, 846
Roosevelt, Franklin Delano, xiii, 2, 19, 20, 24, 30, 36, 48, 49, 53, 58, 61, 71, 79, 84, 91, 94, 96, 97(fn.), 99, 100, 101, 105, 106, 107, 121, 125, 148, 175, 178, 187, 204, 206, 208, 220, 222, 233, 241, 242, 247, 251, 253, 256, 289, 294, 296, 297, 300, 307, 308, 320, 323, 326, 327, 332, 339, 348, 352, 355, 361, 364, 365, 367, 377, 390, 396, 426, 427, 434, 439(fn.), 440, 447, 459, 471, 472, 479, 481, 489, 492, 497, 503, 512 (fn.), 516, 523, 530, 531, 532, 534, 539, 540, 544, 545, 546, 554, 561, 563, 565, 588, 595, 596, 604, 605, 609, 611, 627, 634, 645, 677, 678, 699, 703,

707, 708, 717, 720, 726, 733, 734, 754, 757, 757(fn.), 758, 766, 777, 778, 806, 827, 835, 840, 844, 845, 846, 847, 848, 851, 857, 865, 873, 879, 891, 898, 899, 903, 907; death of, 19, 348, 732, 847
Roosevelt, Franklin D., Jr., 634
Roosevelt, James, 36-37, 99
Roosevelt, Nicholas, 921
Roosevelt, Theodore, xiii, 14, 30, 142, 233, 246, 393, 431, 439, 470, 482, 491-492, 535, 537, 538, 540, 543, 557, 564, 703, 706, 798
Roosevelt Dam, 902
Roosevelt Lake, 124
Roper poll, 226
Roraback, Boss, 502
Rose, Arnold, 683(fn.)
Rose, Billy, 830, 908
Rosenberg, Anna, 581
Rosenman, Sam, 558
Rosenwald, Julius, 278, 568, 798
Rosenwald family, 605(fn.)
Ross, Harold, 559, 909
Ross, J. D., 130
Ross, Mrs. Nellie Tayloe, 229
Rosten, Leo C., 365
Rostow, Eugene V., 47(fn.)
Rotary Club, 266, 292(fn.), 315, 371, 771
Rothschild family, 632
Rouzeau, Edgar T., 795(fn.)
Rovai, Fred, 385
Rovere, Richard H., 530(fn.)
Rowell, Chester H., 15, 921
Rubenstein, Artur, 7, 49
Ruef, Abraham, 13-14
Ruggerio, Frank, 385
Rukeyser, M. S., 206
Ruml, Beardsley, 909
Runyon, Damon, 908
Running the Country, 590(fn.)
Rural Electrification Administration, 131, 173, 331-332, 738, 791
Rural Free Delivery, 919
Rushville, Indiana, 390
Russell, J. S., 330
Russia, see Soviet Union
Rust, John D., 793
Rutgers University, 599
Rutland, Vermont, 493
Ruttenberg, Harold J., 615
Ryan, Elmer J., 298
Ryan, John D., 168, 171, 172, 567
Rye, New York, 501

Sacco, Nicola, 40, 456, 460, 856
Sacramento, California, 3, 4, 9, 19, 32, 39, 49, 450(fn.)
Sacramento River, 56, 57
"Sahara of the Bozart" (Mencken), 666
Sailors' Union of the Pacific, 26
St. Andrew Society, 725
St. Augustine, Florida, 727
St. Cecilia Society, 604, 725
St. George, Utah, 194
St. John, Robert, 360
St. Johns College, 638
St. Joseph, Missouri, 345

St. Lawrence waterway, 539-540
St. Louis, Missouri, 12, 62, 152, 158, 183, 233, 280, 343, 344, 348, 349, 350-353, 356, 357-358, 386(fn.), 446, 474, 558, 625, 653, 671, 784, 910
St. Louis Chamber of Commerce, 358
St. Louis *Globe-Democrat*, 353
St. Louis *Post-Dispatch*, 59, 60, 187, 188, 280, 287, 343, 344, 349, 351-353, 357, 358, 590 (fn.), 731, 911, 922
St. Louis River, 310, 313
St. Louis *Star-Times*, 353
St. Louis University, 353, 356
St. Mary's College, 345
St. Paul, Minnesota, 128(fn.), 141, 242, 244, 271(fn.), 296, 302, 304, 450(fn.), 819, 877, 912
Saks, 597
Salamanca, University of, 559
Salazar, Antonio, 810
Salem, Massachusetts, 457, 476
Salem, Ohio, 441(fn.)
Salem, Oregon, 29, 89, 95
Salem *Statesman*, 95
Salerno, Joseph, 521
Salinas, California, 4, 38, 231
Salisbury, Connecticut, 467(fn.)
Salmon, Edwin A., 585
Salt Lake City, Utah, xiii, 148, 190, 193-194, 196, 197, 198, 199, 201, 210, 211, 214, 907
Salt Lake City *Telegram*, 210
Salt Lake City *Tribune*, 210
Salt River Valley Growers-Shippers Organization, 901
Salter, J. L., 881(fn.)
Saltonstall, Alice, 476, 480
Saltonstall, Emily, 477, 483
Saltonstall, Endicott Peabody, 478
Saltonstall, Leverett, 294, 431, 456, 464, 469, 474-484, 507, 509, 510, 515(fn.)
Saltonstall, Leverett, Jr., 477
Saltonstall, Peter, 477
Saltonstall, Richard, 476
Saltonstall, Mrs. Richard, 477
Salvation Army, 258
Samson, Sir George, 683
San Antonio, Texas, 511, 538, 558, 800, 815, 818, 824, 832, 834, 835, 845, 847, 859, 860, 868, 897, 910
San Antonio *Light*, 853(fn.)
San Diego, California, 3, 5, 34, 38, 39, 54-56, 61, 210, 449 (fn.), 650, 910
San Felipe, Texas, 823
San Francisco, California, 2, 4, 5, 6, 7(fn.), 10, 14, 22, 26, 27, 31, 40, 42-46, 56, 92, 128 (fn.), 210, 255, 288, 552, 687, 809, 827(fn.), 829, 832, 877, 910; Chamber of Commerce, 33, 39; Chinatown, 45-56; mayor, 23-24, 25; Negroes in, 60-62
San Francisco Charter, 32, 176, 241, 305, 394, 435
San Francisco *Chronicle*, 15, 28, 35, 40, 62-63, 921

San Francisco Conference, 293, 305, 307, 391, 396
San Francisco *Examiner*, 40
San Jacinto, Battle of, 823, 851
San Jacinto monument, 828
San Joaquin River, 56
San Jose, California, 27, 425
San Juan Hill (NYC), 574
San Pedro, California, 63
Sand Lotters, 10, 11
Sandburg, Carl, 369, 374
Sanders, Dave, 245
Sandusky, Ohio, 272
Sandy Hook, New Jersey, 597
Sandy River, 120
Santa Anita, California, 63
Santa Barbara, California, 4, 146
Santa Fe, New Mexico, 145, 824, 886, 887, 888, 897, 902, 910
Santa Fe Cutoff, 261
Santa Fe Railroad, 12, 38, 220, 260, 572
Santa Fe Trail, 261, 343, 888
Santa Monica, California, 7
Saranac, New York, 538
Saratoga, New York, 536, 538
Sarnoff, David, 552(fn.), 914
Saroyan, William, 7, 464
Saturday Evening Post, 188, 225, 361(fn.), 433(fn.), 448, 602, 606(fn.), 649
Sauk Centre, 314-317
Sault Ste. Marie, Michigan, 272, 625
Saunders, Hilary St. George, 359
Savannah, Georgia, 353(fn.), 725
Saxon, Lyle, 809
Scalise, John, 381
Scandinavian Total Abstinence League, 241
Scanlon, Patrick J., 514
Scarborough, William, 691
Schacter, Harry W., 640
Schenectady, New York, 537-538
Scherman, Harry, 921
Schevill, Ferdinand, 281
Schlemmer, F. C., 743
Schlesinger, Arthur, Jr., 457
Schmedeman, Albert G., 326
Schoch, Professor Eugene P., 837
Schoellkopf family, 536
Schoenberner, Franz, 679
Schoeninger family, 921
Schoeppel, Andrew, 256
Scholz, Dr. Herbert, 477(fn.)
Schreiner, W. Scott, 856
Schultz, "Dutch," 530
Schumach, Murray, 555(fn.)
Schurz, Carl, 833
Schuyler, Delia, 223
Schuyler, George S., 627, 688, 690, 691, 691(fn.)
Schuylkill River, 604, 607
Schwab, Charles M., 567, 619, 620, 621
Schwellenbach, Lewis, 94, 99
Schwenkfelders, 628
Scopes, schoolmaster, 667
Scott, C. E., 777
Scott, Hazel, 576
Scott, Leslie, 95
Scott, Lizabeth, 48
Scottoriggio, Joseph, 573
Scranton, Pennsylvania, 552

Scratch Gravel Mountains, 158
Screen Playwrights, 50
Screen Writers Guild, 50
Scripps-Howard newspapers, 386, 446, 645, 750(fn.), 751(fn.), 852
Seabury investigation, 565
Seaford, Delaware, 636
Seagram Distillers Corp., 647
Seamen's International Union, 26
Sears Roebuck and Company, 278
The Seasons, 168
Seattle, Washington, 29, 86, 90, 92-94, 100, 116, 119, 127, 128, 129-131, 134, 139, 142, 143, 152, 156, 165, 176, 210, 584, 603, 738, 827(fn.), 911
Seattle *Post-Intelligencer*, 99
"Secret Six," 381
Securities Act of 1934, 569
Securities and Exchange Commission, 126, 128, 130, 173, 220, 254, 326, 392, 418, 538, 567, 569, 729, 909
Seldes, George, 360
Selective Service Act, 209, 250, 320, 434, 628, 660, 778
Selznick, David, 49, 51
Seminole Indians, 728, 870, 874
Seneca Falls, North Dakota, 245
Senate Campaign Expenditures Committee, 851
Senate Military Affairs Committee, 649
Senate Naval Affairs Committee, 36(fn.), 59, 60
Sensenbrenner family, 319
Sentinels of the Republic, 612
Sequoia National Park, 3
Sergeant, Elizabeth Shepley, 886
Seven Stars, Pennsylvania, 602
Seventh-Day Adventists, 628
Sewall, Sumner, 250, 487-488
Sewall, Mrs. Sumner, 488
Sewanee, Tennessee, 770
Seymour, Charles, 469
Seymour, Forrest, 330
Seymour, Gideon, 304, 922
Shakers, 491, 535
Shakespeare, William, 385
Shankle, George E., 258(fn.)
Sharecroppers, 663-665, 670
Sharp, Ivor, 206
Shasta Dam, 57
Shaw, Bernard, 681, 703
Shaw, "Totem" James A., 70
Sheaffer, W. A., Pen Company, 335
Sheal, Jane, *see* Lausche, Mrs. Frank J.
Sheboygan, Wisconsin, 318
Sheean, Vincent, 360, 686, 733, 921
Sheen, Monsignor Fulton J., 408, 563
Sheep, 137-138, 149, 207, 218, 228, 229, 826
Sheet Metal Workers International Association, 112
Shelby, North Carolina, 721
Sheldon, Charles M., 264
Shell Oil Co., Inc., 264
Shelly, Percy, 126
Shenandoah, Pennsylvania, 602

Shenandoah Valley, 631
Sheppard, Morris, 850
Sherman, William, 783, 811 (fn.)
Sherman Antitrust Act, 714
Sherrill, Colonel C. O., 449
Sherwin-Williams Co., 635
Sherwood, Robert E., 922
Shiel, Archbishop, 916
Shinnecock Indian Reservation, 535
Shipstead, Henrik, 178, 178(fn.), 241(fn.), 242, 291, 295, 308, 324, 852
Shirer, William L., 360, 733, 921
Shoong, Joe, 46
Shore Dimly Seen, 776
Short, Dewey, 287
Short, General, 405
Shoshone Indians, 235
Shriners, 756
Shull, Lynwood E., 686
Sky Farm, 433
Siegel, Eli, 155
Siegfried, André, 275-276, 654, 787
Sierra Nevada Mountains, 3, 4
Sikeston, Missouri, 342
Silver, Abba Hillel, 446
Silver Dollar (Karsner), 223 (fn.)
Silver King mine, 210
Silver Purchase Act, 82
Simkhovitch, Mary, 559
Simmons, William Joseph, 787
Simms, Mrs. Ruth Hanna McCormick, 361, 375
Simpson, William Sowden, 822 (fn.)
Sinatra, Frank, 281
Sinclair, Harry F., 236
Sinclair, Upton, 7, 36, 39(fn.), 44(fn.), 49, 53
Sinclair Oil Corp., 234, 264
Sing Sing, 529, 536
Sinks, Alfred H., 453(fn.)
Sinnett, Bert, 485
Sinton, Annie, 432
Sioux City, Iowa, 183, 187, 335
Sioux Falls, South Dakota, 237, 247, 249
Sioux Falls Argus-Leader, 248, 249
Sioux Indians, 247, 310
Siskiyou County, California, 62
Sitting Bull, 145, 147, 163
Six Companies, 46
Six Co's. Inc., 66, 69
Skagit, Washington, 130
Skoglund, Robert, 385
Slaughter, Roger C., 347, 355
Slemons, Mildred DeLaney, 773
Sloan, Alfred, 369(fn.), 570
Sloan, George A., 620(fn.)
Sloan, John, 888
Sloan, W. G., 186, 187-189
Smaller War Plants Corporation, 817
Smart Set, 376
Smith, Dr., 866
Smith, A. O., Company, 319
Smith, Adam, 880
Smith, Al, 498, 524, 540, 543, 543(fn.), 564, 595, 634, 658, 667, 678, 847, 890

Smith, Blake, 864
Smith, "Cotton Ed", 675, 726
Smith, Edgar, 106
Smith, Franklin G., 445
Smith, George Albert, 191, 201-202, 205, 206
Smith, Gerald L. K., xv, 45, 50, 176, 224, 280, 353, 362, 382, 439, 532, 810
Smith, Henry Justin, 280, 374
Smith, Howard W., 711
Smith, J. Russell, 328, 463, 827
Smith, Joseph, 192, 196, 197, 201, 202, 494
Smith, L. C., 537
Smith, Lillian, 664, 666, 669, 682(fn.), 689, 692, 697, 773, 922
Smith, Margaret Chase, 473
Smith, Paul C., 28, 40, 43
Smith, William Alden, 393
Smith College, 474
Smoke abatement, 357
Smoot, Reed, 202, 207
Smoot-Hawley tariff bill, 611
Snake River, 114, 118, 123, 227
Snell, Earl, 94, 96
Snelling, Paula, 692
Snow, Wilbert, 504-505, 505(fn.)
Snyder, John W., 350
Social Justice, 176
Social Register (NYC), 558
Social Security, 599, 612
Society for the Prevention of Cruelty to Animals, 432
Society of Friends, see Quakers
Society of Independent Producers, 51
Socony Vacuum Oil Company, Inc., 290
Sohio, 880
Soil Conservation Service, 873, 884
Sokolsky, George, 206, 225, 917
Solvay chemicals, 537
Somerset, Vermont, 497(fn.)
Somerset Club, 426, 476, 500, 516
Somervell, Brehon, 563
Sons of the American Revolution, 102
Soo Canal, 272
Sorensen, Charles E., 404
Sorrell, Herbert, 50
Souls of Black Folk (Du Bois), 682(fn.)
South, 516, 653-813, 915
South America, 545
South Bend, Indiana, 385, 387, 412
South Boston, Massachusetts, 467, 482, 512, 513
South Brother Island, 555
South Carolina, 485, 653, 654-655, 656, 660, 662, 665, 666, 667, 669, 671, 675, 678, 686, 690, 700, 701, 702, 719, 720, 723-724, 775(fn.), 786, 801; divorces in, 719; legislature, 31; Negroes in, 726; politics, 348, 726
South Charleston, West Virginia, 716
South Chicago, Illinois, 312

South Dakota, 144, 146, 149, 174, 194, 230, 237, 245-249, 251, 270, 320, 641, 662, 860, 870; electric power, 185; labor in, 253(fn.); livestock, 237; newspapers, 237, 248; pheasants in, 237, 248-249; politics, 247-248, 369, 613; population, 185, 247; railroads, 237, 253
South Pass City, Wyoming, 228
South St. Paul, Minnesota, 243, 298, 304
South Today, 692(fn.), 697(fn.)
Southern Association of Colleges and Secondary Schools, 858
Southern Baptist Convention, 788
Southern California Country (McWilliams), 2(fn.), 14
Southern Colorado Power Company, 220
Southern Conference for Human Welfare, 676, 768, 779(fn.)
Southern Frontier, 700(fn.)
Southern Methodist University, 831
Southern Pacific Railroad, 11, 32, 39, 45, 94
The Southern Patriot, 666
Southern Regional Council, 676, 682
Southern Regions (Odum), 258 fn.), 667(fn.)
Southern Regions of the United States (Odum), 661
Southern Watchman, 795
A Southerner Discovers New England (Daniels), 489(fn.)
Southerner Discovers the South (Daniels), 786(fn.)
Southwestern Bell Telephone Company, 857
Southwestern Gas & Electric Company, 745
Soviet Purchasing Commission, 538
Soviet Union, 2, 9, 91, 175, 179-180, 205, 289, 311, 325, 359, 360, 364, 382, 396, 405, 414, 471, 515, 541, 544, 545, 548, 588, 597, 615, 661, 891
Spain, 280, 306, 325, 352, 382, 559
Spanel, Abraham N., 631
Spangler, Harrison E., 338
Spanish American War Veterans, 292(fn.)
Sparkman, John J., 676, 794, 796
Sparks, Chauncey M., 731, 797, 798
Spartanburg, South Carolina, 723
Speer, J. Ramsey, 617(fn.)
Speer, Robert W., 224
Speidel, Merritt C., 231
Spellman, Cardinal, 909
Spelman College, 781
Spencer, Charles E., Jr., 466, 467
Spindletop gusher, 825
The Spoilers (Beach), 229
Spokane, Washington, 65, 89, 94, 113, 125, 127, 134, 177, 832, 910
Spokane Spokesman Review, 113
Sprague, Charles, 95

Sprague, J. Russell, 538
Springfield, Illinois, 29, 375
Springfield, Massachusetts, 462
Springfield, Ohio, 441(fn.)
Springfield, Vermont, 495, 496
Springmeyer, George, 921
Sprout Brook, New York, 65
Spruce mine, 311
Stacy, Judge, 419
Stagg, A. A., 502
Stalin, Joseph, 179, 181, 289, 364, 546
Stamford, Connecticut, 506
Standard Brands, Inc., 570
Standard Gas & Electric Company, 326-327, 651
Standard Oil Company, 38, 168, 832
Standard Oil Company (California), 808
Standard Oil Company (Indiana), 234, 290, 880
Standard Oil Company (New Jersey), 290, 418, 567, 572, 593, 598, 636, 808, 815, 880
Standard Oil Company (New York), 234, 880
Standard Oil Company (Ohio), 880
Stanford, Leland, 12, 13, 64
Stanley, Robert C., 620(fn.)
Stanolind Crude Oil Purchasing Company, 880
Stanolind Oil and Gas Company, 880
Stanolind Pipeline Co., 880
Stapleton, Benjamin Franklin, 224
Starr, Frederick, 281
Starrett, Vincent, 374
Stassen, Arthur, 297
Stassen, Elmer, 297
Stassen, Glen, 304
Stassen, Harold Edward, 104, 207, 250, 282, 286, 293-308, 309, 369, 430, 431, 525, 773, 914
Stassen, Mrs. Harold Edward, 304
Stassen, Kathleen, 304
Stassen, William, 297
Stassen, William, Jr., 297
State Names, Flags, Seals, Songs, Birds, Flowers, and Other Symbols (Shankle), 258(fn.)
State Observer (Texas), 842 (fn.)
State Temperance Society (Kansas), 267
Staten Island, 555, 559, 597
States, geographical classifications, 76, 144, 653; rights, 28-30, 186, 686
Statistical Abstract of the United States, 76
Statue of Liberty, 551, 556
Stavredes, Ted, 481
Stearns, Robert L., 218, 219
Stebbins, Dr. Ernest L., 582, 583
Steel, 601, 615-625, 672, 794
Steel, Kurt, 329(fn.)
Steele, A. T., 374
Steelton, Pennsylvania, 616

Stefan, Karl, 290
Steffens, Lincoln, 7, 590
Stegner, Wallace, 515, 516
Steinbeck, John, 7, 876
Steinman family, 629
Steinmetz, Charles, 402
Stephens, Percy Rector, 526, 527
Stephenson, David C., 389
Stern, J. David, 603, 605, 610, 922
Stern, William, 244(fn.)
Sterner, Richard, 683(fn.)
Stettinius, Edward R., Jr., 471, 472, 619, 712(fn.)
Steubenville, Ohio, 442
Stevenson, Adlai, 326
Stevenson, Coke R., 820, 839, 840, 844, 850, 856, 858
Stewart, James G., 426
Stewart, Kenneth, 770(fn.)
Stewart, Tom, 667
Stewart, William M., 80
Stigler, William, 869
Still, William Grant, 691
Stimson, Henry L., 367, 435, 914
Stine, Charles M. A., 635
Stockton, California, 3, 100
Stokes, Thomas L., 97(fn.), 225, 645, 750(fn.)
Stokowski, Leopold, 605
Stoltz, Leon, 359-360
Stone, Fred, 220
Stone, Harlan, 491
Stone, I. F., 327(fn.)
Stone, M. R., 113
Stone Mountain, 246(fn.), 787, 788
Stoneman, William H., 374
Stony Creek, Connecticut, 522
Stork Club, 279, 558, 908
Stoughton, William, 456
Stowe, Harriet Beecher, 447
Strange Fruit, 518, 664, 689, 922
Stratton, Mr., 223
Stratton, Vermont, 497
Stravinsky, Igor, 7, 47
Strawbridge & Clothier (Dep't store), 608
Strawn, Silas H., 362
Street, Julian, 359, 445
Strickland, D. F., 856, 857, 858 (fn.)
Strickland, Robert, 768
Strikes, 319, 388, 390, 411, 412, 413-416, 419, 545, 563, 621, 623, 624, 625, 782
Strip mining, 453
Strode, Hudson, 794
Strunsky, Simeon, 550(fn.), 557 (fn.)
Studebaker, 385
Sturgeon, Texas, 826
Stuyvesant, Peter, 538, 566
Sublime, Texas, 826
Successful Farming, 337
Suez Canal, 272
Sufi, Abdul Hamid, 575
Sugar, 220-221
Sugar Hill (NYC), 574-575, 576
Sukui No Michi, 209
Sullens, Frederick, 800
Sullivan, J. J., 445
Sullivan, Louis, 370
Sullivan, Mark, 225

Sullivan, Roger, 373
Sullivan, Thomas F., 48
Sulzberger, Arthur H., 559, 921
Sumners, Hatton, 817
Sun Oil Company, 808, 880
Sun Valley, Idaho, 117, 214
Sunday, Billy, 848
Sunday Breakfast Club, 604
Sunshine Climate Club, 922
Sunflower Ordnance Works, 263
Sunshine Mining Company, 115
Superior, Arizona, 905
Superior, Lake, 272, 309, 311, 313
Superior, Wisconsin, 272, 309, 320
Susquehanna River, 601
Sutter, John Augustus, 9, 10
Swanson, Claude A., 707
Swarthmore College, 608
Swarthout, Gladys, 219
Swell-Head Diggings, California, 10
Swift, Gustavus, 371
Swift, Harold H., 377
Swift, John E., 515
Swift & Company, 315
Swing, Raymond, 52, 245, 256, 257(fn.), 374, 745(fn.), 811, 922
Switzerland, 400
Swope, Gerard, 568
Swope, Herbert Bayard, 558
Symington, W. Stuart, 350
Syracuse, New York, 537, 541

Tablet, 554
Tabor, H. A. W., 223
Tabor, Moxcy, 223
Tacoma, Washington, 89, 92, 93, 97(fn.), 100, 127, 141
Taft, Alphonso, 432
Taft, Charles Phelps, 432, 868
Taft, Charles Phelps II, 449, 450
Taft, Horace, 432
Taft, Hulbert, 432, 450
Taft, Martha, 432, 433
Taft, Robert A., 103, 282, 302, 333, 369, 391, 392, 430-436, 437(fn.), 438, 439, 449, 470, 525, 525(fn.), 531, 609, 612, 707
Taft, Mrs. Robert A., 437
Taft, William Howard, 204, 431, 439(fn.), 706
Tahlequah, Oklahoma, 872
Talbot, Glenn, 242
Tall Talk from Texas (House), 818(fn.)
Tallasi, Alabama, 877
Talmadge, Eugene, 696, 705, 767-769, 771, 773, 774, 777-779, 789, 796
Talmadge, Herman, 769-770
Tammany Hall, 529, 561-562, 563, 564-565, 805
Tammen, Harry, 225
Tampa, Florida, 670, 672, 728
Tampa Morning Tribune, 668
Taos, New Mexico, 556, 724, 888, 892
Tariff, 609, 611
Tarkington, Booth, 386, 485, 486
Tascosa, Texas, 837

Tate, Allen, 666
Tattnell penitentiary, 774
Taylor, Arod, 113
Taylor, Edmond, 360
Taylor, Glen H., 107-112, 115, 116, 148
Taylor, Mrs. Glen H., 108-109, 112
Taylor, Myron C., 567, 619, 620 (fn.), 621, 865
Taylor, P. J., 113
Taylor Grazing Act of 1934, 145, 229
Teacup, Texas, 826
Teagle, Walter C., 567
Teamsters Union, 100
Teapot Dome scandals, 178, 235-236, 352
Tecolotenos, New Mexico, 890
Tedious River, 637
Tehachapi, 4
Television, 598
Temporary National Economic Committee, 572
Tenerowicz, Representative, 627
Tennessee, 147, 255, 342, 642, 653, 654, 655, 658, 659, 663, 667, 672, 685, 690, 700, 701, 721, 727, 731-762, 764, 766, 778, 787, 804, 817, 824, 838, 871, 908, 910; Davidson County, 759; McMinn County, 755; Meigs County, 739, 759; politics, 678, 749; railroads, 646; Sevier County, 759(fn.); Shelby County, 749, 750; University of, 738, 739
Tennessee Coal Iron & Railroad Co., 617, 673
Tennessee Manufacturers Association, 732
Tennessee River, 454, 733-734, 739, 740
Tennessee Valley Authority, ix, 29, 56, 122, 124, 130, 133, 173, 184, 185, 186, 398, 420, 435, 453, 468, 540, 655, 683, 731-748, 752, 753, 756, 757, 757(fn.), 758, 766, 796, 862, 913, 921, 922
Tenney, Jack B., 54
Tennyson, Alfred Lord, 653
Tensed, Idaho, 114
Terminiello, Arthur W., 795
Teschemacher, H. E., 229
Tesuque, New Mexico, 891
Texarkana, Texas, 819
Texas, ix, 146, 216, 228, 230, 232, 332, 353, 386, 442(fn.), 495, 499, 527, 629, 653, 654, 658, 660, 661, 663, 665, 667, 671, 678, 700, 701, 702, 723, 724, 758, 763, 764, 765, 768, 775(fn.), 784, 790, 805, 808, 814-868, 876, 890, 901, 904; A. & M. College of, 821; academic freedom, 816; agriculture, 838, 854; Bexar County, 847; Brewster County, 821; cattle in, 149, 158, 816, 817, 824, 826, 829, 830, 836, 854, 859, 861; comparison with California, 6; culture in, 7;

Deaf Smith County, 836; Duval County, 844; education in, 843; girls in, 90, 821, 831; Great Britain and, 9; history, 823-825; imperialism, 814; independent republic, 6, 494(fn.), 814, 823-824; industry, 672, 816; Jefferson County, 853; lobbies, 842; miscellany, 821, 868; "nationalism," 6; Negroes in, 726, 865-868; oil in, 59, 816, 825, 826, 827, 829, 830, 836, 853, 854, 855; Pecos County, 821; politics, 837, 839-854, 915; population, 814; railroads in, 12(fn.), 861; religious factors in, 863-865; Starr County, 844; University of, 7, 218, 773, 855, 857, 858, 864, 921; weather, 819
Texas, A Guide to the Lone Star State (American Guide Series), 824(fn.)
Texas, A World in Itself (Perry), 818(fn.)
Texas, An Informal Biography (White), 844(fn.)
Texas Almanac, 818
Texas and Pacific Railway, 830
Texas Brags, 763, 822(fn.), 826
Texas Christian University, 831, 865
Texas City, Texas, 827(fn.)
The Texas Company, 234, 264, 568, 808
Texas Manufacturers Association, 842
Texas Regulars, 827, 828, 837, 840, 844-847
Texas Rose, 849
Texas Technological College, 849 (fn.)
Thacher, Thomas, 528
Thatcher, M. W., 244
These Are the Things to Do (Smith), 682(fn.)
These United States, 95(fn.), 217(fn.), 245(fn.), 342, 385 (fn.), 639(fn.)
Thirteen Against the Odds (White), 694(fn.)
Thomas, Elbert, 204, 209, 436
Thomas, Elmer, 883
Thomas, Lowell, 527
Thomas, Norman, 287, 378, 495, 847
Thomas, R. J., 74, 410-411
Thompson, Big Bill, 370
Thompson, Dorothy, 206, 245, 532, 732, 921
Thompson, James, 166
Thompson, Maurice, 422
Thompson, Melvin E., 769-770
Thoreau, Henry, 460
Thorkelson, Congressman, 176
Thorndike, Dr. E. L., 194
Three O'Clock Dinner (Pinckney) 724
Throg's Neck, 554
Thurber, James, 911
Thurmond, J. Strom, 726
Thye, Edward J., 295, 308
Tidewater, Virginia, 659

Tiffin, Ohio, 454
Tilden, Samuel J., 540
Timber, see Lumber industry
Time, 22, 52, 53, 83(fn.), 326 (fn.), 365(fn.), 383, 408, 432 (fn.), 445(fn.), 472, 480, 510, 511, 527(fn.), 563(fn.), 571, 571(fn.), 622(fn.), 624(fn.), 685(fn.), 796(fn.), 821(fn.), 841
Times Square (NYC), 597
Tingley, Clyde, 891
Tinker, Clarence E., 869
Tishimingo, Oklahoma, 872
Tobacco, 660, 664, 712-714, 719
Tobacco Road, 767
Tobey, Charles W., 471
Tobin, Dan, 100, 387, 456
Tobin, Maurice J., 479, 507-509, 510, 511, 514, 515, 584
Tocqueville, Alexis de, x, 154, 272, 419, 501, 839, 872
Tokyo War College, 209
Toledo, Ohio, 270, 271(fn.), 272, 442, 447, 454
Toledo, University of, 454
Toluca, Mexico, 247
Tom Thumb, 505
Tombstone Epitaph, 898
Toney, Charles E., 575
Tong, Tommy, 45
Tooele, Utah, 167
Toolen, Rt. Rev. T. J., 795
Topeka, Kansas, 256, 257, 258, 259, 261, 263, 264(fn.), 265, 267, 268
Topeka Daily Capital, 257, 265
Torre, Haya de la, 552
Toscanini, Arturo, 550
Towne, Charles, 172
Townley, A. C., 239-240
Townsend, Dr. Francis E., 52, 53, 54
Townsend plan, 44(fn.), 53, 89, 94, 95, 241, 729
Tracy, Spencer, 49
Traeger, Dr. Cornelius Horace, 922
Tragic Ground (Caldwell), 518
The Trail of a Tradition, 395
Trail of Tears, 871, 874
Trail of the Hawk (Lewis), 314
Trail of the Lonesome Pine, 640
Tranchese, Father, 834
Transport Workers Union, 555
Transquaking River, 637
Traparish, Teddy, 165
Travis, Colonel William Barrett, 823
Treaty of Dancing Rabbit Creek, 871
Treaty of Paris, 313
Tred Avon River, 637
Trefethen, E. E., Jr., 69
Trenton, New Jersey, 546, 552, 592
Trenton Times, 922
Tresca, Carlo, 577
Tri-City Airport, Tennessee, 758
Trigg, Harold, 676
Trinity River, 830
Trippe, Juan, 909
Trotsky, Leon, 552

Trout, Allan, 921
Troy, New York, 538
Truett, George W., 864
Truex, Ernest, 220
Trukee, California, 3
Truman, President Harry S.,
  xiii, xiv, 21, 22, 59(fn.), 61,
  87, 96, 103-104, 105, 148(fn.),
  179, 187, 197, 319, 341, 342,
  343, 345, 347, 350, 355, 396,
  418, 439(fn.), 471, 539, 543,
  546, 596, 605, 623, 650, 727,
  732, 737, 758, 773, 835, 845,
  847, 863, 891, 907
Truman Committee, 470, 649
Truscott, Lucian, 822(fn.)
Trust Company of Georgia, 768,
  784
Truth, 201
Tuck, William M., 711
Tucker, Raymond R., 357
Tucson, Arizona, 144, 900
Tujunga, California, 44
Tulane University, 353, 809
Tule Lake Relocation Center, 24
Tulsa, Oklahoma, 152, 224, 800,
  827, 876, 877-878, 881, 883,
  890
Tulsa Tribune, 877
Tunnell, James M., 210, 635
Turkey, Texas, 826
Turner, Frederick Jackson, 2,
  144, 321
Turner, Lana, 908
Tuscaloosa, Alabama, 794
Tuskahoma, Oklahoma, 871
Tuskegee Institute, 689, 739, 797-
  798
Tuttle, Charles H., 528
Tuxedo, New York, 527
TVA—Democracy on the March
  (Lilienthal), 734(fn.)
Twain, Mark, 81, 195, 272-273,
  505
Tweed, Boss, 535
Twentieth Century Fox Film
  Corp., 49, 51
Twenty-One Club, 558
Tyler, John, 706
Tyler, Texas, 821, 826

Uhl, Alexander H., 432
Uihleins, 319
Uinta mountain range, 4(fn.)
Un-American Activities, 789
Uncle Tom's Cabin (play), 506,
  765
Unemployed Citizens League, 99
Union Carbide and Carbon Corp.,
  716
Union League, 426, 604
Union Pacific Railroad, 11, 153,
  191, 210, 220, 227, 228, 232,
  253, 255, 260, 474, 572
Union Supply Co., 617
Union Trust bank, 624
United Airlines, 227, 922
United Automobile Workers, 74,
  319, 403, 407, 409-416, 417
  (fn.), 418, 618, 622, 634
United Fruit Company, 474
United Mine Workers, 621, 674,
  717
United Nations, 104, 241, 246,

292, 307, 364, 396, 506, 515,
  546, 550, 554, 561, 607, 872;
  Security Council, 471
United Nations Relief and Rehabilitation Administration, 287,
  391
United Office and Professional
  Workers, 575
United Press, 22, 431
United Pueblos Agency, 893
United States (Baedeker), 557
United States, ix-xvi, 28, 32,
  911-920; Agriculture Department, 132, 243(fn.), 328, 332,
  336, 628, 629(fn.), 838; Army,
  59, 72, 132, 133, 602, 655, 684,
  757; Bureau of Labor Statistics, 714; Constitution, xi,
  600, 630, 797, 920; Congress,
  xiv, 28(fn.), 31, 82, 83, 206,
  676, 677; House of Representatives, 59, 59(fn.); Indian
  Bureau, 873, 893, 895; Interior Department, 59, 132,
  133, 873, 883, 894; Justice
  Department, 51, 105, 367, 686,
  687, 714, 778, 789; Maritime
  Commission, 71-72; Navy, 59,
  236, 303, 367, 546, 602; Senate, 59(fn.); State Department,
  9, 32, 615, 890; Supreme
  Court, 25, 59, 153, 178, 200
  (fn.), 412, 431, 633, 683, 702,
  702(fn.), 703, 766, 773, 775,
  775(fn.), 796; Treasury Department, 82, 83; War Department, 378, 636
United States Employment Service, 29
The United States of America
  (Mowat), 656(fn.)
United States Potash Co., Inc.,
  153
United States Shoe Corporation,
  447
United States Steel Corporation,
  73, 211, 290, 311, 314, 417,
  418, 419, 444, 567, 572, 615,
  617, 619, 621, 623, 673, 747,
  815
United Steel Workers of America,
  222, 409, 615, 618, 620, 621-
  624
United Supply Co., 617
Universal Atlas Cement Co., 617
University of Oklahoma Press,
  882(fn.)
University of the South, 770
U'Ren, William S., 88
Urey, Professor, 378
Uruguay, 875
U. S. A. (Brogan), 76, 681(fn.)
USA (Passos), 841, 858
U. S. Coal & Coke Co., 617
U. S. Electric Power Corpora-
  tion, 326
U. S. Steel Supply Co., 617
Utah, xv, 11, 76-77, 113, 114,
  144, 149, 151, 190-212, 228,
  534, 719, 869, 873, 883, 902,
  904, 907, 910; admitted to
  Union, 28(fn.); agriculture,
  210; industry, 211; Mormons
  and, 116, 190-212; politics,

207-210; population, 211; pres-
  sure groups, 207; railways,
  210; Uinta mountain range,
  4(fn.); University of, 207
Utah Central Railroad, 211
Utah Copper Company, 211, 568
Utah-Idaho Sugar Company, 191
Utah Liquor Control Commission,
  208
Utah Power & Light Company,
  207, 208
Utah Savings & Trust Company,
  191
Utah State National Bank, 191
Utes, 216
Utica, New York, 65, 66, 537
Uvalde, Texas, 821, 833, 835

Vallejo, California, 67
Valley and Its People, 734(fn.)
Van Buren, Martin, 540
Van Cise, Philip, 225
Van Devander, Charles, 293(fn.),
  590(fn.), 591, 609(fn.), 611
  (fn.)
Van Doren, Mark, 921
Van Doren family, 559
Van Merritt beer, 318
Van Nuys, California, 229
Van Sweringer, Mantis J., 445,
  567
Van Sweringer, Oris P., 445,
  567
Van Wert, Ohio, 442
Vancouver, Washington, 65, 67,
  71, 119, 128, 142
Vandage, Clem J., 813
Vandenberg, Arthur, 282, 302,
  369, 391, 397, 470, 707, 884
Vanderbilt, Cornelius, 535, 568
  (fn.)
Vanderbilt, Mrs., 558
Vanderbilt, William, 308, 499
Vanderbilt Hotel (NYC), 561
Vanderbilt University, 655, 760
Vandercook, John W., 245
Vanport, Oregon, 90
Vanzetti, Bartolomeo, 40, 456,
  460, 465, 856
Vardeman, James K., 350
Vare, William S., 609, 613
Vassar College, 522, 536, 781
Vaughan, Harry H., 350
Veblen, Thorstein, xiii, 321
Ventura, California, 51
Vergennes, Vermont, 497
Vermont, 87, 173, 195, 250 (fn.),
  432, 458, 465, 467, 471, 485,
  489, 491, 559, 759(fn.), 838,
  908, 910, 913; agriculture, 467,
  492, 493, 496; comparison with
  New Hampshire, 492; compari-
  son with Rhode Island, 498;
  Franklin County, 498; inde-
  pendent republic, 6, 493, 816;
  industry, 467, 495, 498; poli-
  tics, 204, 247, 497, 522, 609,
  613, 915; University of, 494
Verne, Jules, 314
Vestal, Stanley, 183(fn.), 876
Veterans, 916
Veterans Industrial Association,
  765

Veterans of Foreign Wars, 292 (fn.), 706
Vicksburg, Mississippi, 663
Viereck, George Sylvester, 176
Vieux Carré, 809
Vigil, Martin, 891
Vigilantes, 10, 182, 381
Villard, Oswald Garrison, 287
Vinson, Fred, 644
Virginia, 342, 439, 446, 572, 630, 653, 654, 657, 659, 667, 671, 672, 690, 692, 700, 705, 706-708, 711, 719, 720, 721, 723, 733, 739, 744, 752, 759, 762, 788, 797, 824; state employees per capita, 710; tobacco in, 712; University of, 706
Virginia, Minnesota, 311
Virginia City, Montana, 158, 162
Virginia City, Nevada, 80-81, 82, 158, 219
Virginia Company, 616
Virginia Electric and Power Company, 711
Virginia Historical Society, 712
Virginia Military Institute, 660
Vivian, John C., 215
Volga Germans, 259-260
Volpe, Anthony (Mops), 381
Voorhees, Enders M., 619, 620
Voorhis, Jerry, 37
Voute, Kathleen, 921

W. Lee O'Daniel and Texas Politics (McKay), 849(fn.)
W. Lee O'Daniel News, 851
Waco, Texas, 826, 863
Wacs, 827
Wadsworth, James W., 350, 541, 543
Wagner, Robert F., 107-108, 436, 540-541, 564, 627
Wagner Act, 50, 533, 540
Waldorf-Astoria Towers, 556
Walker, Edwin, 219
Walker, James J., 24, 564, 565
Walker, Stanley, 822
Wall Street, 253, 403, 530, 538, 565, 567-573
Walla Walla, Washington, 29, 89
Wallace, Henry, xiv, 22, 50, 103, 104, 111, 241, 286, 297, 327, 330, 337, 435, 470, 484, 772, 914
Wallace, Judge, 580, 581
Wallace's Farmer, 337
Wallender, Arthur W., 560
Wallgren, Mon C., 89, 96-97, 98, 99, 101
Walsh, David I., 291, 472, 509, 532
Walsh, Patrick, 585
Walsh, Raymond, 921
Walsh, Thomas J., 174, 176
Walsh, William, 385
Walters, "Stuffy," 386
Waltham, Massachusetts, 464
Wanamaker, John, 597
Wanger, Walter, 49, 51
War Assets Administration, 212
War Between the States, *see* Civil War

War Mediation Board, 24
War Production Board, 80, 219, 417, 472, 586
War Refugee Board, 561
Warden, O. S., 160, 171
Warner, Harry M., 567
Warner Bros. Pictures Inc., 49, 51
Warren, Earl, 14, 18-22, 30, 34, 36, 37, 40, 61, 282
Warren, Francis E., 229
Warsaw, Poland, 680
Wartime Economic Affairs, 450
Washington, 93
Washington, 66, 85-90, 92-94, 96-101, 113, 134, 144, 145, 148, 157, 214, 229, 533, 572, 641, 701, 762(fn.), 873, 910; agriculture, 134-138; electric power, 89, 101, 127-133, 185, 255; industry, 139-143; Kings County, 99; labor in, 87, 90, 95, 98; liquor regulation in, 90; lumber, 139-142; pension plan, 87, 98; politics, 87; pressure groups, 98; Public Utility Districts, 131, 173, 254; railways, 89, 98; religious factor in, 89, 98; settlement, 87, 89; University of, 101; Whitman County, 135
Washington, Booker T., xiii, 664, 703, 798
Washington, D. C., *see also* District of Columbia, xiv, 41, 128 (fn.), 143, 550, 553, 567, 568, 630, 653, 654, 671, 683, 689, 714, 758, 784, 791, 798, 828, 910; water supply, 710
Washington, George, 246, 600, 602, 705, 712, 764
Washington and Lee University, 712(fn.)
Washington Commonwealth Federation, 98-99
Washington monument, 828
Washington *Post,* 922
Washington State Taxpayers League, 88(fn.)
Washington *Times-Herald,* 361, 367
Washington University, 353, 356, 357
Washington Water Power Co., 127
Water, *see* under names of States
Waterbury, Connecticut, 502, 504
Waterloo, Iowa, 335
Watertown, Connecticut, 432
Watertown, Massachusetts, 476
Waterville, Maine, 487
Watoga State Park, West Virginia, 717
Watson, Tom, 675, 768
Watterson, "Marse Henry," 647
Waymack, W. W., 280, 330
Wayne University, 413
We Saw It Happen, 566(fn.)
Webb, Walter Prescott, 145, 146
Webster, Daniel, 86, 146, 459
Webster, Noah, 505
Weekly Roll Call, 176
Weeks, Edward A., Jr., 463, 466

Weeks, Sinclair, 479
Weil, Truda T., 582, 583, 585
Weinbrennarians, 628
Weir, Ernest T., 383, 623, 718
Weirgate, Texas, 141(fn.)
Weirton, West Virginia, 718
Weirton Steel Co., 620, 623
Weiss, Hymie, 381
Welch, Earl, 870
Welf, Mrs. Josephine, 423
Welfare Island, 555
Welland Canal, 539
Welles, Orson, 49, 908
Welles, Sumner, 914
Wellesley College, 474
Wells, H. G., 270, 277, 314, 379, 694
Welty, Eudora, 666
Wenatchee *World,* 125
Werfel, Franz, 7
Wescott, Glenway, 374
Wesley, Carter, 676, 868
Wesselhoeft, Alice, *see* Saltonstall, Alice
West, 144-236, 251, 270, 275, 447, 534, 535, 595, 653, 662, 672, 673, 886
West, George, 477
West, Mae, 880
West, Rebecca, 48
West Indies, 486, 723
West Point, New York, 83, 91, 536, 660
West St. Paul, Minnesota, 297
West Virginia, xv, 453, 559, 623, 654, 662, 667, 671, 714-718, 829; history, 715-716; industry, 716; Kanawha Valley, 716; politics, 717; Watoga State Park, 717
West Virginia Manufacturers Association, 717
Westchester, New York, 277, 536, 542, 553, 554
Western Air Lines, Inc., 191
Western Colorado Power Company, 208(fn.)
Western Federation of Miners, 164
Western News, 172
Western Reserve Historical Society, 444
Western Reserve University, 29 (fn.), 454
Western Voice, 224
Westinghouse Electric Corporation, 624
Westman, C. F., 245
Westminister Hotel (NYC), 557
Westover, Virginia, 706
Westport, Connecticut, 465, 501, 505
Weyerhaeuser, Frederick E., 567
Weyerhaeuser family, 115, 141
Whalen, Grover, 587
What America Thinks (Lydgate), 287(fn.)
What Cheer, Iowa, 281
What the Negro Wants, 688 (fn.), 691(fn.), 701(fn.)
Wheat, 94, 134-138, 149, 157, 160, 179-181, 217, 237, 239, 268-269, 272, 329(fn.), 333-

334, 550, 616, 785, 790, 794, 836, 876, 879
Wheaton, Illinois, 360
Wheeler, Burton K., 16, 155, 169, 174-179, 241, 242, 257, 291, 324, 435
Wheeling, West Virginia, 413, 714, 715
Whiskey Rebellion, 602
Whitaker, John T., 374, 921
White, Compton, 117
White, Owen P., 844
White, Stanford, 499
White, Wallace A., 470
White, Walter, 574, 693, 694 (fn.), 702, 702(fn.), 922
White, William Allen, 256, 257, 258(fn.), 267, 287, 908
White Motor Company, 445
White primary, 675, 701, 749, 766, 775(fn.), 796, 865-868
White supremacy, 659, 670, 675, 701, 800-801, 803
Whiting, Indiana, 385
Whitman, Walt, vii, 518, 549, 598
Whitney, Eli, 501, 723, 793
Whitney, George, 570
Whitney, Richard, 377, 530, 568
Whitney, W. D., 271(fn.), 631 (fn.)
Whittington, Harmon, 847
Who Are the Americans (Whitney), 271(fn.), 631(fn.)
Who's Who, 194, 209, 509, 589
Wichita, Kansas, 259, 263
Wichita Falls, Texas, 856
Wickard, Claude R., 791
Widtsoe, John A., 200, 203
Wiggin, Albert H., 568
Wiggins, J. Russell, 304
Wilberforce University, 454, 691
Wild Bill Hickok, 246
Wild Ducks, 249
Wilder, Thornton, 321
Wilderness to Empire (Cleland), 11
Wiley, Alexander, 320
Wiley, John C., 921
Wilhelm, Kaiser, 888(fn.)
Wilhelmina, Queen, 168
Wilkes-Barre, Pennsylvania, 602
Wilkins, Roy, 575
Willard, Daniel, 568
Willcox, Arizona, 901
William and Mary College, 706
William Penn Charter School, 608
Williams, Albert, 761
Williams, Aubrey, 103, 241
Williams, John Sharp, 675, 799
Williams, Sid, 781
Williams College, 474
Williamsburg, Virginia, 706
Willis, Raymond E., 210(fn.)
Willis, Simeon, 645
Willkie, H. Fred, 640
Willkie, Wendell, xiii, 20, 36, 37, 49, 94, 191, 222, 247, 286, 288, 302-303, 332, 390, 395, 431, 450, 472, 479, 487, 504, 530, 609, 613, 640, 703, 731, 735, 772, 883, 907, 921

Willow Run, 69, 70, 74, 401, 405, 659
Wills, William H., 497
Wilmington, Delaware, 29, 215, 630, 633, 634, 636, 637, 638
Wilmington Journal, 634
Wilmington News, 634
Wilmington Trust Company, 636
Wilson (film), 436
Wilson, Arkansas, 765
Wilson, Charles E. (GE), 417
Wilson, Charles E. (GM), 417 (fn.), 418, 418(fn.)
Wilson, Edmund, 597
Wilson, North Carolina, 660
Wilson, William, 585-586
Wilson, Woodrow, xiii, 15, 30, 252, 398, 440, 470, 489, 537, 599, 678, 830, 847
Wilson-Hughes election (1916), 1
Wilson-Snyder Mfg. Corp., 617
Winant, John G., 491, 914
Winchell, Walter, 29, 225, 232, 245, 683(fn.), 786, 908
Winchester, Virginia, 707
The Winds of Fear (Carter), 676
Windsor Hotel (NYC), 557
Wingfield, George, 79
Winn, Matt, 646
Winnetka, Illinois, 370
Winrod, Gerald B., 176, 363(fn.)
Winston-Salem, North Carolina, 713, 719
Winter Park, Florida, 728
Wisconsin, xv, 195, 238, 242, 243, 251, 252, 270, 271, 280, 311, 318-327, 370, 386 (fn.), 420, 559, 701, 909, 910; Green County, 321; politics, 303, 321-327; University of, 105, 321
Wisconsin Bank Shares Company, 326
Wisconsin Public Service Commission, 737
With This We Challenge, an Epitome of Arkansas, 763
Wolf family, 605(fn.)
Wolfe, Harry Preston, 451-452
Wolfe, Robert F., 451-452
Wolfe, Thomas, 666
Wolfe Farms, 452
Wolfe Wear-U-Well Shoe Corporation, 452
Woll, Matthew, 568
Woltman, Frederick, 852
"The Woman Who Rode Away" (Lawrence), 888
Woman's Christian Temperance Union, 241-267, 535, 652, 669
Women's Democratic League, 847
Wood, Charles Erskine Scott, 91
Wood, Grant, 281, 330
Wood, Junius B., 374, 921
Wood, Robert E., 278, 383
Wood, Sam, 49, 50
Woodard, Isaac, 686
Woodmen of the World, 611(fn.)
Woodring, Harry H., 265, 267
Woodruff, Ernest, 784
Woodruff, Robert W., 784-785
Woods, Rufus, 125
Woodville, Mississippi, 801

Woolf, S. J., 528
Woolsey, Timothy, 494
Woonsocket, Rhode Island, 465, 499
Wooster College, 454
Works Projects Administration, 163, 204, 565, 780, 781
Worland News, 231
World Almanac, 115
World War I, 244, 252, 286, 324, 403, 691
World War II, 252-253, 287, 364, 366-367, 405, 534, 546, 602, 628, 687, 689, 706
Worthington, Ohio, 450
Wright, Frank Lloyd, xiii, 43, 321
Wright, Richard, 666, 691, 801 (fn.)
Wrigley, William, 371
Wrigley, William, Jr., Co., 631
Wyatt, Wilson, 645, 650, 621-652
Wylie, Philip, 437
Wyoming, 86, 144, 150, 215, 216, 227-236, 261, 536, 839, 860, 870, 902; area, 227; cars per capita, 147; electric power, 185, 208(fn.), 234; history, 228; Indians, 235; industry 228; Johnson County War, 230; labor in, 234; livestock, 228, 229-230, 232, 233; miscellany, 230; Mormons in, 193, 232; Negroes in, 151; newspapers, 231-232; petroleum, 234; politics, 148, 149, 230-235; population, 227; University of, 234
Wyoming State Tribune and Leader, 231, 232, 921

X-Ray, 390
Xenia, Ohio, 454

Yakima, Washington, 29, 89, 134
Yakima (Wash.) Chamber of Commerce, 138
Yale Review, 158
Yale University, 47, 433, 468-469, 470, 494, 497, 502, 599, 868, 877
Yale University Press, 469, 877
Yalta conference, 546
Yankee Stadium, 554
"Yarb Folk," 598
The Year of Decision (De Voto), 8
Yeats, William Butler, 888
Yellow Springs, Ohio, 454
Yellow Truck and Coach Company, 419
Yellowstone, 172
Yellowstone River, 183, 227
York, Maine, 486
York, Pennsylvania, 603
Yorktown, Pennsylvania, 600
Yorkville (NYC), 574
Yosemite National Park, 3, 233
Young, Brigham, 190, 196, 200, 202, 204, 494, 880
Young, Owen D., 568, 571
Young, Robert R., 358
Young Men's Christian Association, 437, 450

Young Women's Christian Association, 285, 437
Youngstown, Ohio, 442
Youngstown Sheet & Tube Co., 620
Your Part in Georgia's Politics, 771 (fn.)

Zanuck, Darryl, 49
Zemurray, Sam, 474
"Ziegfeld Follies of 1946," 761
Zion Savings Bank & Trust Company, 191
Zionchek, Marion A., 99

Zion's Co-operative Mercantile Institution, 190, 191
Zitlitz, Dr., 249
Zukor, Adolph, 567
Zulu Club, 813
Zuta, Jack, 381